Edited By: John Purcell jvpurcel@oakland.edu
Printed in Canada
1995

Contents

I   User Commands   7

II System Calls   509

III Library Functions   677

IV Special files   895

V   File Formats   921

VI Games   995

VII Miscellaneous   999

VIII Administration and Privileged Commands   1035

IX Kernel Reference Guide   1187

Copyright

_exit(2), access(2), alarm(2), close(2), dup(2), fcntl(2), link(2), mkdir(2), mknod(2), open(2), read(2), rename(2), rmdir(2), symlink(2), write(2)
Copyright (C) 1992 Drew Eckhardt; 1993 Michael Haardt, Ian Jackson.

unlink(2), remove(3)
Copyright (C) 1992 Drew Eckhardt; 1993 Ian Jackson.

chdir(2), chmod(2), chown(2), chroot(2), clone(2), execve(2), fork(2), getrlimit(2), gettimeofday(2), kill(2), nice(2), pause(2),pipe(2), reboot(2), setup(2), stime(2), swapon(2), sync(2), time(2), times(2), umask(2), uname(2), uselib(2), utime(2),
Copyright (c) 1992 Drew Eckhardt (drew@cs.colorado.edu), March 28, 1992

mprotect(2)
Copyright (C) 1995 Michael Shields <shields@tembel.org>.

select(2)
copyright (C) 1992 Drew Eckhardt, copyright (C) 1995 Michael Shields.

acct(2), brk(2), intro(2), ioperm(2), phys(2), ptrace(2), setsid(2), termios(2), ascii(7), crypt(3), environ(5), ftime(3), ftw(3), group(5), hd(4), intro(1), intro(3), intro(4), intro(5), intro(6), intro(7), intro(8), isatty(3), issue(5), longjmp(3), mem(3), motd(5), nologin(5), null(4), passwd(5), ram(4), securetty(5), setjmp(3), shells(5), termcap(7), tty(4), ttys(4), ttytype(5), utmp(5), lp(4), perror(3)
Copyright (c) 1993, 1994, 1995 Michael Haardt

bind(2), connect(2), flock(2), fsync(2), getdomainname(2), getdtablesize(2), getgid(2), getgroups(2), gethostid(2), gethostname(2), getpagesize(2), getpid(2), getuid(2), idle(2), iopl(2), profil(2), recv(2), sigvec(2), undocumented(2), vhangup(2), vm86(2), acosh(3), getdirentries(3), ctrlaltdel(8), dmesg(8), fdformat(8), fdisk(8), fsck.minix(8), ipcrm(8), ipcs(8), sync(8), sd(4), clear(1), clock(8), domainname(1), mkfs.minix(8), mkswap(8), passwd(1), rdev(8), reset(1), setfdprm(8), setserial(8), shutdown(8), kbdrate(8), update_state(8), chkdupexe(1), cytune(8)
Copyright 1992, 1993, 1994, 1995 Rickard E. Faith (faith@cs.unc.edu)

getdents(2), llseek(2), readdir(2), syslog(2), console.4
Copyright 1994, 1995 Andries Brouwer (aeb@cwi.nl)

mount(2)
Copyright 1993 Rickard E. Faith (faith@cs.unc.edu) Copyright 1994 Andries E. Brouwer (aeb@cwi.nl)

adjtimex(2), bdflush(2), ipc(2), modify_ldt(2), obsolete(2), socketcall(2), unimplemented(2)
Copyright (c) 1995 Michael Chastain (mec@shell.portal.com)

accept(2), getpeername(2), listen(2), lseek(2), getpriority(2), getsockname(2), getsockopt(2), ioctl(2), killpg(2), mmap(2), readlink(2), send(2), setpgid(2), setregid(2), setreuid(2), shutdown(2), sigblock(2), sigpause(2), socket(2), socketpair(2), statfs(2),truncate(2), alloca(3), fclose(3), ferror(3), fflush(3), fread(3), fseek(3), getpass(3), mailaddr(7), popen(3), printf(3), scanf(3), setbuf(3), stdarg(3), stdio(3), banner(6), cal(1), col(1), colcrt(1), colrm(1), column(1), fstab(5), getoptprog(1), logger(1), look(1), lpc(8), lpd(8), lpq(1), lpr(1), lprm(1), lptest(1), mesg(1), mount(8), pac(8), ping(8), syslog.conf(5), syslogd(8), tsort(8), vipw(1), write(1), vi(1), rev(1), biff(1), tset(1), w(1), aliases(5), ftp(1), ftpd(8), inetd(8), newaliases(1), rcp(1), resolver(5), rexecd(8), rlogin(1), routed(8), rpc.rusersd(8), rpc.rwalld(8), rsh(1), rshd(8), rup(1), rusers(1), rwall(1), rwho(1), rwhod(8), sendmail(8), sliplogin(8), talk(1), talkd(8), telnet(1), telnetd(8), tftp(1), tftpd(8), timed(8), timedc(8), traceroute(8)
Copyright (c) 1980, 1983, 1985, 1989, 1990, 1991, 1992 The Regents of the University of

California. All rights reserved.

getitimer(2)
Copyright 1993 by Darren Senn (sinster@scintilla.santa-clara.ca.us)

modules(2), ksyms(1), insmod(1), lsmod(1), rmmod(1)
Copyright (c) 1994, 1995 Bjorn Ekwall <bj0rn@blox.se>

msgctl(2), msgget(2), msgop(2), semctl(2), semget(2), semop(2), ftok(3), ipc(5)
Copyright 1993 Giorgio Ciucci (giorgio@crcc.it)

setgid(2), setuid(2), realpath(3)
Copyright (C), 1994, Graeme W. Wilford. (Wilf.)

shmctl(2), shmget(2), shmop(2)
Copyright (c) 1993 Luigi P. Bai (lpb@softint.com) July 28, 1993

sigaction(2), signal(2), sigsetops(3)
Copyright (c) 1994 Mike Battersby <mike@starbug.apana.org.au>

stat(2)
Copyright (c) 1992 Drew Eckhardt (drew@cs.colorado.edu), March 28, 1992 Parts Copyright (c) 1995 Nicolai Langfeldt (janl@ifi.uio.no), 1/1/95

sysinfo(2), adjustclock(9), ctrl-alt-del(9), filesystems(9), file_table(9), file_table_init(9), get_empty_filp(9), grow_files(9), in_group_p(9), insert_file_free(9), kernel_mktime(9), proc_sel(9), put_file_last(9), remove_file_free(9)
(C)opyright 1993 by Dan Miner (dminer@nyx.cs.du.edu)

wait(2), wait4(2), confstr(3), ctermid(3), fnmatch(3), fpathconf(3), getcwd(3), getopt(3), gets(3), isalpha(3), malloc(3), signal(7), sleep(3), suffixes(7), sysconf(3), system(3), hier(7), assert(3), glob(3), killpg(3),locale(7), localeconv(3), puts(3), raise(3), readv(3), setlocale(3)
(c) 1993 by Thomas Koenig (ig25@rz.uni-karlsruhe.de)

abort(3), abs(3), acos(3),asin(3), asinh(3),atan(3), atan2(3), atanh(3), atexit(3), atof(3), atoi(3), atol(3), bcmp(3), bcopy(3), bstring(3), byteorder(3), bzero(3), ceil(3), closedir(3), confstr(3), copysign(3), cos(3), cosh(3), ctime(3), difftime(3), div(3), drand48(3), drem(3), ecvt(3), erf(3), exec(3), exit(3), exp(3), fabs(3), ffs(3), fgetgrent(3), fgetpwent(3), fmod(3), fopen(3), frexp(3), gcvt(3), getenv(3), getgrent(3), getgrnam(3), gethostbyname(3), getmntent(3), getnetent(3), getprotoent(3), getpw(3), getpwent(3), getpwnam(3), getservent(3), getusershell(3), hypot(3), index(3), inet(3), infnan(3), initgroups(3), isinf(3), j0(3), labs(3), ldexp(3), ldiv(3), lgamma(3), mblen(3), mbstowcs(3), mbtowc(3), memccpy(3), memchr(3), memcmp(3), memcpy(3), memfrob(3), memmem(3), memmove(3), memset(3), mkstemp(3), mktemp(3), modf(3), on_exit(3), opendir(3), psignal(3), putenv(3), putpwent(3), qsort(3), rand(3), random(3), readdir(3), resolver(3), rewinddir(3), rint(3), scandir(3), seekdir(3), setenv(3), siginterrupt(3), sin(3), sinh(3), sqrt(3), strcmp(3), strcat(3), strchr(3), strcmp(3), strcoll(3), strcpy(3), strdup(3), strerror(3), strfry(3), strftime(3), string(3), strlen(3), strpbreak(3), strptime(3), strsep(3), strsignal(3), strspn(3), strstr(3), strtod(3), strtok(3), strtol(3), strtoul(3), strxfrm(3), swab(3), tan(3), tanh(3), telldir(3), tempnam(3), tmpfile(3), tmpnam(3), toupper(3), tzset(3), usleep(3), wcstombs(3), wctomb(3)
Copyright 1993 David Metcalfe (david@prism.demon.co.uk)

add_timer(9), console_ioctl(4), ttyname(3), vcs(4)
Copyright (c) 1995 Jim Van Zandt <jrv@vanzandt.mv.com>

catgets(3), catopen(3), hostid(1)
Copyright 1993 Mitchum DSouza <m.dsouza@mrc-applied-psychology.cambridge.ac.uk>

fd(4)
Copyright (c) 1993 Michael Haardt (michael@cantor.informatik.rwth-aachen.de) and 1994,1995 Alain Knaff (Alain.Knaff@imag.fr)

getutent(3)
Copyright 1995 Mark D. Roth (roth@uiuc.edu)

hsearch(3)
Copyright 1993 Ulrich Drepper (drepper@karlsruhe.gmd.de)

iso88591(7), proc(5), sed(1)
Copyright 1993-1995 Daniel Quinlan (quinlan@yggdrasil.com)

st(4)
Copyright 1995 Robert K. Nichols (Robert.K.Nichols@att.com)

agetty(8)
W.Z. Venema <wietse@wzv.win.tue.nl>
Peter Orbaek <poe@daimi.aau.dk>

cfdisk(8)
Copyright 1994 Kevin E. Martin (martin@cs.unc.edu)

chfn(1), chsh.1
(c) 1994 by salvatore valente <svalente@athena.mit.edu>

crond(8), crontab(1)
Copyright 1994 Matthew Dillon (dillon@apollo.west.oic.com)

kill(1)
Copyright 1994 Salvatore Valente (svalente@mit.edu)
Copyright 1992 Rickard E. Faith (faith@cs.unc.edu)

klogd(8), sysklogd(8)
Copyright 1994 Dr. Greg Wettstein, Enjellic Systems Development.

setterm(1)
Copyright 1990 Gordon Irlam (gordoni@cs.ua.oz.au)
Copyright 1992 Rickard E. Faith (faith@cs.unc.edu)

tunelp(8), ps(1), psupdate(8)
Copyright 1992 Michael K. Johnson (johnsonm@nigel.vnet.net)

xinetd(1)
(c) Copyright 1992 by Panagiotis Tsirigotis

bash(1)
Copyright 1995 Chet Ramey chet@ins.CWRU.Edu

adduser(8)
Copyright 1995 by Ted Hajek, 1994 by Ian Murdock.

e2fsck(8)
Copyright 1993, 1994 by Theodore Ts'o.

free(1), tload(1)

This page Copyright (C) 1993 Matt Welsh, mdw@sunsite.unc.edu.

top(1)
This file Copyright 1992 Robert J. Nation

vmstat(8)
This page Copyright (C) 1994 Henry Ware <al172@yfn.ysu.edu>

bdftopcf(1x), beforelight(1x), bitmap(1x), editres(1x), fsinfo(1x), flsfonts(1x),fstobdf(1x), iceauth(1x), imake(1x), lbxproxy(1x), lndir(1x), makedepend(1x), makestrs(1x), mkdirhier(1x), mkfontdir(1x), oclock(1x), resize(1x), sessreg(1x), showrgb(1x), smproxy(1x), startx(1x), x11perf(1x), x11perfcomp(1x), xauth(1x), xclipboard(1x), xclock(1x), xcmsdb(1x), xconsole(1x), xcutsel(1x), xdm(1x), xdpyinfo(1x), xf86config(1x), xfd(1x), xfs(1x), xhost(1x), xinit(1x), xkill(1x), xlogo(1x), xlsatoms(1x), xlsclients(1x), xlsfonts(1x), xmag(1x), xmkmf(1x), xmodmap(1x), xon(1x), xprop(1x), xrdb(1x), xrefresh(1x), xset(1x), xsetroot(1x), xsm(1x), xsmclient(1x), xstdcmap(1x), xterm(1x), xwd(1x), xwininfo(1x), xwud(1x)
Copyright (c) 1993, 1994 X Consortium

portmap(8)
Copyright (c) 1987 Sun Microsystems
Copyright (c) 1990, 1991 The Regents of the University of California.

rpcgen.new(1)
Copyright (c) 1988,1990 Sun Microsystems, Inc.

rstart(1x), rstartd(1x)
Copyright (c) 1993 Quarterdeck Office Systems

showmount(8)
Copyright 1993 Rick Sladkey <jrs@world.std.com>

twm(1x)
Copyright (c) 1993, 1994 X Consortium
Portions copyright 1988 Evans & Sutherland Computer Corporation.
Portions copyright 1989 Hewlett-Packard Company

xieperf.1x
Copyright 1993, 1994 by AGE Logic, Inc.

Many thanks to the above contributors for providing excellent quality man pages and also to the Free Software Foundation for providing the rest.

Section I

User Commands

INTRO(1)

NAME
intro – Introduction to user commands

DESCRIPTION
This chapter describes user commands.

AUTHORS
Look at the header of the manual page for the author(s) and copyright conditions. Note that these can be different from page to page!

NAME

addftinfo – add information to troff font files for use with groff

SYNOPSIS

addftinfo [*–param***value**...] *res unitwidth font*

DESCRIPTION

addftinfo reads a troff font file and adds some additional font-metric information that is used by the groff system. The font file with the information added is written on the standard output. The information added is guessed using some parametric information about the font and assumptions about the traditional troff names for characters. The main information added is the heights and depths of characters. The *res* and *unitwidth* arguments should be the same as the corresponding parameters in the DESC file; *font* is the name of the file describing the font; if *font* ends with **I** the font will be assumed to be italic.

OPTIONS

Each of the options changes one of the parameters that is used to derive the heights and depths. Like the existing quantities in the font file, each *value* is in inches/*res* for a font whose point size is *unitwidth*. *param* must be one of:

    x-height   The height of lowercase letters without ascenders such as x.
    fig-height   The height of figures (digits).
    asc-height   The height of characters with ascenders, such as b, d or l.
    body-height   The height of characters such as parentheses.
    cap-height   The height of uppercase letters such as A.
    comma-depth   The depth of a comma.
    desc-depth   The depth of characters with descenders, such as p,q, or y.
    body-depth   The depth of characters such as parentheses.

addftinfo makes no attempt to use the specified parameters to guess the unspecified parameters. If a parameter is not specified the default will be used. The defaults are chosen to have the reasonable values for a Times font.

SEE ALSO

font(5) **groff_font**(5), **groff**(1), **groff_char**(7)

AFMTODIT(1)   AFMTODIT(1)

NAME
afmtodit – create font files for use with groff –Tps

SYNOPSIS
afmtodit [**–ns**] [**–d**desc_file] [**–e**enc_file] [**–i**n] [**–a**n] afm_file map_file font

DESCRIPTION
afmtodit creates a font file for use with groff and **grops**. **afmtodit** is written in perl; you must have perl version 3 installed in order to run **afmtodit**. afm_file is the AFM (Adobe Font Metric) file for the font. map_file is a file that says which groff character names map onto each PostScript character name; this file should contain a sequence of lines of the form

    ps_char groff_char

where ps_char is the PostScript name of the character and groff_char is the groff name of the character (as used in the groff font file.) The same ps_char can occur multiple times in the file; each groff_char must occur at most once. font is the groff name of the font. If a PostScript character is in the encoding to be used for the font but is not mentioned in map_file then **afmtodit** will put it in the groff font file as an unnamed character, which can be accessed by the \N escape sequence in **troff**. The groff font file will be output to a file called font.

If there is a downloadable font file for the font, it may be listed in the file **/usr/lib/groff/font/devps/download**; see **grops**(1).

If the –i option is used, **afmtodit** will automatically generate an italic correction, a left italic correction and a subscript correction for each character (the significance of these parameters is explained in **groff_font**(5)); these parameters may be specified for individual characters by adding to the afm_file lines of the form:

    italicCorrectionps_char n
    leftItalicCorrectionps_char n
    subscriptCorrectionps_char n

where ps_char is the PostScript name of the character, and n is the desired value of the corresponding parameter in thousandths of an em. These parameters are normally needed only for italic (or oblique) fonts.

OPTIONS

    –n   Don't output a **ligatures** command for this font. Use this with constant-width fonts.

    –s   The font is special. The effect of this option is to add the **special** command to the font file.

    –ddesc_file   The device description file is desc_file rather than the default **DESC**.

    –eenc_file   The PostScript font should be reencoded to use the encoding described in enc_file. The format of enc_file is described in **grops**(1).

    –an   Use n as the slant parameter in the font file; this is used by groff in the positioning of accents. By default **afmtodit** uses the negative of the ItalicAngle specified in the afm file; with true italic fonts it is sometimes desirable to use a slant that is less than this. If you find that characters from an italic font have accents placed too far to the right over them, then use the **–a** option to give the font a smaller slant.

    –in   Generate an italic correction for each character so that the character's width plus the character's italic correction is equal to n thousandths of an em plus the amount by which the right edge of the character's bounding is to the right of the character's origin. If this would result in a negative italic correction, use a zero italic correction instead.

            Also generate a subscript correction equal to the product of the tangent of the slant of the font and four fifths of the x-height of the font.

If this would result in a subscript correction greater than the italic correction, use a subscript correction equal to the italic correction instead.

Also generate a left italic correction for each character equal to *n* thousandths of an em plus the amount by which the left edge of the character's bounding box is to the left of the character's origin. The left italic correction may be negative.

This option is normally needed only with italic (or oblique) fonts. The font files distributed with groff were created using an option of −**i**50 for italic fonts.

FILES

'/usr/lib/groff/font/devps/download'u+2n /usr/lib/groff/font/devps/DESC Device description file.

/usr/lib/groff/font/devps/*F*   Font description file for font *F*.

/usr/lib/groff/font/devps/download   List of downloadable fonts.

/usr/lib/groff/font/devps/text.enc   Encoding used for text fonts.

/usr/lib/groff/font/devps/generate/textmap   Standard mapping.

SEE ALSO

groff(1), grops(1), groff_font(5), perl(1)

NAME

appres – list X application resource database

SYNOPSIS

appres [[class [instance]] [–1] [toolkitoptions]

DESCRIPTION

The *appres* program prints the resources seen by an application (or subhierarchy of an application) with the specified *class* and *instance* names. It can be used to determine which resources a particular program will load. For example,

%   appres XTerm

will list the resources that any *xterm* program will load. If no application class is specified, the class *-AppResTest-* is used.

To match a particular instance name, specify an instance name explicitly after the class name, or use the normal Xt toolkit option. For example,

%   appres XTerm myxterm

or

%   appres XTerm –name myxterm

To list resources that match a subhierarchy of an application, specify hierarchical class and instance names. The number of class and instance components must be equal, and the instance name should not be specified with a toolkit option. For example,

%   appres Xman.TopLevelShell.Form xman.topBox.form

will list the resources of widgets of *xman* topBox hierarchy. To list just the resources matching a specific level in the hierarcy, use the –1 option. For example,

%   appres XTerm.VT100 xterm.vt100 –1

will list the resources matching the *xterm* vt100 widget.

SEE ALSO

X(1), xrdb(1), listres(1)

AUTHOR

Jim Fulton, MIT X Consortium

NAME

ar – create, modify, and extract from archives.

SYNOPSIS

ar [**-**] *dmpqrtx*[abcilosuvV] [*membername*] *archive files* ...

DESCRIPTION

The GNU **ar** program creates, modifies, and extracts from archives. An *archive* is a single file holding a collection of other files in a structure that makes it possible to retrieve the original individual files (called *members* of the archive).

The original files' contents, mode (permissions), timestamp, owner, and group are preserved in the archive, and may be reconstituted on extraction.

GNU **ar** can maintain archives whose members have names of any length; however, depending on how **ar** is configured on your system, a limit on member-name length may be imposed (for compatibility with archive formats maintained with other tools). If it exists, the limit is often 15 characters (typical of formats related to a.out) or 16 characters (typical of formats related to coff).

ar is considered a binary utility because archives of this sort are most often used as *libraries* holding commonly needed subroutines.

ar will create an index to the symbols defined in relocatable object modules in the archive when you specify the modifier ' **s** '. Once created, this index is updated in the archive whenever **ar** makes a change to its contents (save for the ' **q** ' update operation). An archive with such an index speeds up linking to the library, and allows routines in the library to call each other without regard to their placement in the archive.

You may use ' **nm** –s ' or ' **nm** ––print–armap ' to list this index table. If an archive lacks the table, another form of **ar** called

ranlib can be used to add just the table.

ar insists on at least two arguments to execute: one keyletter specifying the *operation* (optionally accompanied by other keyletters specifying *modifiers*), and the archive name to act on.

Most operations can also accept further *files* arguments, specifying particular files to operate on.

OPTIONS

GNU **ar** allows you to mix the operation code *p* and modifier flags *mod* in any order, within the first command-line argument.

If you wish, you may begin the first command-line argument with a dash.

The *p* keyletter specifies what operation to execute; it may be any of the following, but you must specify only one of them:

d *Delete* modules from the archive. Specify the names of modules to be deleted as *files* ; the archive is untouched if you specify no files to delete.

If you specify the ' **v** ' modifier, **ar** will list each module as it is deleted.

m Use this operation to *move* members in an archive.

The ordering of members in an archive can make a difference in how programs are linked using the library, if a symbol is defined in more than one member.

If no modifiers are used with **m** , any members you name in the *files* arguments are moved to the *end* of the archive; you can use the ' **a** ', ' **b** ', or ' **i** ' modifiers to move them to a specified place instead.

p   *Print* the specified members of the archive, to the standard output file. If the ' **v** ' modifier is specified, show the member name before copying its contents to standard output.

If you specify no *files* , all the files in the archive are printed.

q   *Quick* append ; add *files* to the end of *archive* , without checking for replacement.

The modifiers ' **a** ', ' **b** ', and ' **i** ' do *not* affect this operation; new members are always placed at the end of the archive.

The modifier ' **v** ' makes **ar** list each file as it is appended.

Since the point of this operation is speed, the archive's symbol table index is not updated, even if it already existed; you can use ' **ar** s ' or **ranlib** explicitly to update the symbol table index.

r   Insert *files* into *archive* (with *replacement*). This operation differs from ' **q** ' in that any previously existing members are deleted if their names match those being added.

If one of the files named in *files* doesn't exist, **ar** displays an error message, and leaves undisturbed any existing members of the archive matching that name.

By default, new members are added at the end of the file; but you may use one of the modifiers ' **a** ', ' **b** ', or ' **i** ' to request placement relative to some existing member.

The modifier ' **v** ' used with this operation elicits a line of output for each file inserted, along with one of the letters ' **a** ' or ' **r** ' to indicate whether the file was appended (no old member deleted) or replaced.

t   Display a *table* listing the contents of *archive* , or those of the files listed in *files* that are present in the archive. Normally only the member name is shown; if you also want to see the modes (permissions), timestamp, owner, group, and size, you can request that by also specifying the ' **v** ' modifier.

If you do not specify any *files* , all files in the archive are listed.

If there is more than one file with the same name (say, ' **fie** ') in an archive (say ' **b.a** '), ' **ar** t b.a fie ' will list only the first instance; to see them all, you must ask for a complete listing—in our example, ' **ar** t b.a '.

x   *Extract* members (named *files*) from the archive. You can use the ' **v** ' modifier with this operation, to request that

ar list each name as it extracts it.

If you do not specify any *files* , all files in the archive are extracted.

A number of modifiers (*mod*) may immediately follow the *p*

keyletter, to specify variations on an operation's behavior:

a   Add new files *after* an existing member of the archive. If you use the modifier **a** , the name of an existing archive member must be present as the *membername* argument, before the

archive specification.

b   Add new files *before* an existing member of the archive. If you use the modifier **b** , the name of an existing archive member must be present as the *membername* argument, before the

archive specification. (same as ' **i** ').

c   *Create* the archive. The specified *archive* is always created if it didn't exist, when you request an update. But a warning is issued unless you specify in advance that you expect to create it, by using this modifier.

i   Insert new files *before* an existing member of the archive. If you use the modifier **i** , the name of an existing archive member must be present as the *membername* argument, before the

archive specification. (same as ' **b** ').

l	This modifier is accepted but not used.
o	Preserve the *original* dates of members when extracting them. If you do not specify this modifier, files extracted from the archive will be stamped with the time of extraction.
s	Write an object-file index into the archive, or update an existing one, even if no other change is made to the archive. You may use this modifier flag either with any operation, or alone. Running ' **ar** s ' on an archive is equivalent to running ' **ranlib** ' on it.
u	Normally, **ar** r ... inserts all files listed into the archive. If you would like to insert *only* those of the files you list that are newer than existing members of the same names, use this modifier. The ' **u** ' modifier is allowed only for the operation ' **r** ' (replace). In particular, the combination ' **qu** ' is not allowed, since checking the timestamps would lose any speed advantage from the operation ' **q** '.
v	This modifier requests the *verbose* version of an operation. Many operations display additional information, such as filenames processed, when the modifier ' **v** ' is appended.
V	This modifier shows the version number of **ar**.

SEE ALSO

' **binutils** ' entry in info ; The GNU Binary Utilities , Roland H. Pesch (October 1991). **nm(1)** , **ranlib(1)** .

COPYING

Copyright (c) 1991 Free Software Foundation, Inc.

Permission is granted to make and distribute verbatim copies of this manual provided the copyright notice and this permission notice are preserved on all copies.

Permission is granted to copy and distribute modified versions of this manual under the conditions for verbatim copying, provided that the entire resulting derived work is distributed under the terms of a permission notice identical to this one.

Permission is granted to copy and distribute translations of this manual into another language, under the above conditions for modified versions, except that this permission notice may be included in translations approved by the Free Software Foundation instead of in the original English.

ARCH(1)

NAME

arch – print architecture

SYNOPSIS

arch

DESCRIPTION

arch displays machine architecture type.

SEE ALSO

uname(1), uname(2)

NAME

GNU as—the portable GNU assembler.

SYNOPSIS

as [-a | -al | -as] [-D] [-f] [-I *path*] [-K] [-L] [-o *objfile*] [-R] [-v] [-w] [—\|\ *files* ...]

i960-only options:
[-ACA | -ACA_A | -ACB | -ACC | -AKA | -AKB | -AKC | -AMC] [-b] [-no-relax]

m680x0-only options:
[-l] [-mc68000 | -mc68010 | -mc68020]

DESCRIPTION

GNU **as** is really a family of assemblers. If you use (or have used) the GNU assembler on one architecture, you should find a fairly similar environment when you use it on another architecture. Each version has much in common with the others, including object file formats, most assembler directives (often called *pseudo-ops*) and assembler syntax.

For information on the syntax and pseudo-ops used by GNU **as**, see ' **as** ' entry in **info** (or the manual Using as: The GNU Assembler).

as is primarily intended to assemble the output of the GNU C compiler **gcc** for use by the linker **ld**. Nevertheless, we've tried to make **as** assemble correctly everything that the native assembler would. This doesn't mean **as** always uses the same syntax as another assembler for the same architecture; for example, we know of several incompatible versions of 680x0 assembly language syntax.

Each time you run **as** it assembles exactly one source program. The source program is made up of one or more files. (The standard input is also a file.)

If **as** is given no file names it attempts to read one input file from the **as** standard input, which is normally your terminal. You may have to type **ctl-D** to tell **as** there is no more program to assemble. Use ' — ' if you need to explicitly name the standard input file in your command line.

as may write warnings and error messages to the standard error file (usually your terminal). This should not happen when **as** is run automatically by a compiler. Warnings report an assumption made so that **as** could keep assembling a flawed program; errors report a grave problem that stops the assembly.

OPTIONS

-a | -al | -as	Turn on assembly listings; ' -al ', listing only, ' -as ', symbols only, ' -a ', everything.
-D	This option is accepted only for script compatibility with calls to other assemblers; it has no effect on **as** .
-f	"fast"-skip preprocessing (assume source is compiler output).
-I*path*	Add *path* to the search list for **.include** directives.
-K	Issue warnings when difference tables altered for long displacements.
-L	Keep (in symbol table) local symbols, starting with ' **L** '
-o*objfile*	Name the object-file output from **as**
-R	Fold data section into text section
-v	Announce **as** version
-W	Suppress warning messages
—|*files*...	Source files to assemble, or standard input (—)
-A*var*	(When configured for Intel 960.) Specify which variant of the 960 architecture is the target.

cygnus support   21 January 1992

-b   (When configured for Intel 960.) Add code to collect statistics about branches taken.

-no-relax   (When configured for Intel 960.) Do not alter compare-and-branch instructions for long displacements; error if necessary.

-l   (When configured for Motorola 68000.) Shorten references to undefined symbols, to one word instead of two.

-mc68000 | -mc68010 | -mc68020   (When configured for Motorola 68000.) Specify what processor in the 68000 family is the target (default 68020)

Options may be in any order, and may be before, after, or between file names. The order of file names is significant.

' — ' (two hyphens) by itself names the standard input file explicitly, as one of the files for **as** to assemble.

Except for ' — ' any command line argument that begins with a hyphen (' – ') is an option. Each option changes the behavior of **as** . No option changes the way another option works. An option is a ' – ' followed by one or more letters; the case of the letter is important. All options are optional.

The ' **-o** ' option expects exactly one file name to follow. The file name may either immediately follow the option's letter (compatible with older assemblers) or it may be the next command argument (GNU standard).

These two command lines are equivalent:
as –o my–object–file.o mumble.s
as –omy–object–file.o mumble.s

SEE ALSO

' **as** ' entry in info ; Using as: The GNU Assembler ; **gcc**(1), **ld**(1).

COPYING

Copyright (c) 1991, 1992 Free Software Foundation, Inc.

Permission is granted to make and distribute verbatim copies of this manual provided the copyright notice and this permission notice are preserved on all copies.

Permission is granted to copy and distribute modified versions of this manual under the conditions for verbatim copying, provided that the entire resulting derived work is distributed under the terms of a permission notice identical to this one.

Permission is granted to copy and distribute translations of this manual into another language, under the above conditions for modified versions, except that this permission notice may be included in translations approved by the Free Software Foundation instead of in the original English.

BASH(1)

NAME

bash – GNU Bourne–Again SHell

SYNOPSIS

bash [options] [file]

COPYRIGHT

DESCRIPTION

Bash is an **sh**–compatible command language interpreter that executes commands read from the standard input or from a file. **Bash** also incorporates useful features from the *Korn* and *C* shells (**ksh** and **csh**).

Bash is ultimately intended to be a conformant implementation of the IEEE Posix Shell and Tools specification (IEEE Working Group 10032).

OPTIONS

In addition to the single–character shell options documented in the description of the **set** builtin command, **bash** interprets the following flags when it is invoked:

- **–c** *string* If the **–c** flag is present, then commands are read from *string*. If there are arguments after the *string*, they are assigned to the positional parameters, starting with $0.

- **–i** If the **–i** flag is present, the shell is *interactive*.

- **–s** If the **–s** flag is present, or if no arguments remain after option processing, then commands are read from the standard input. This option allows the positional parameters to be set when invoking an interactive shell.

- **–** A single – signals the end of options and disables further option processing. Any arguments after the – are treated as filenames and arguments. An argument of —— is equivalent to an argument of –.

Bash also interprets a number of multi–character options. These options must appear on the command line before the single–character options to be recognized.

- **–norc** Do not read and execute the personal initialization file *˜/.bashrc* if the shell is interactive. This option is on by default if the shell is invoked as **sh**.

- **–noprofile** Do not read either the system–wide startup file */etc/profile* or any of the personal initialization files *˜/.bash_profile*, *˜/.bash_login*, or *˜/.profile*. By default, **bash** normally reads these files when it is invoked as a login shell (see **INVOCATION** below).

- **–rcfile** *file* Execute commands from *file* instead of the standard personal initialization file *˜/.bashrc*, if the shell is interactive (see **INVOCATION** below).

- **–version** Show the version number of this instance of **bash** when starting.

- **–quiet** Do not be verbose when starting up (do not show the shell version or any other information). This is the default.

- **–login** Make **bash** act as if it had been invoked as a login shell.

- **–nobraceexpansion** Do not perform curly brace expansion (see **Brace** Expansion below).

- **–nolineediting** Do not use the GNU *readline* library to read command lines if interactive.

- **–posix** Change the behavior of bash where the default operation differs from the Posix 1003.2 standard to match the standard

ARGUMENTS

If arguments remain after option processing, and neither the −c nor the −s option has been supplied, the first argument is assumed to be the name of a file containing shell commands. If **bash** is invoked in this fashion, is set to the name of the file, and the positional parameters are set to the remaining arguments. **Bash** reads and executes commands from this file, then exits. **Bash's** exit status is the exit status of the last command executed in the script.

DEFINITIONS

 blank A space or tab.

 word A sequence of characters considered as a single unit by the shell. Also known as a **token**.

 name A *word* consisting only of alphanumeric characters and underscores, and beginning with an alphabetic character or an underscore. Also referred to as an **identifier**.

 metacharacter A character that, when unquoted, separates words. One of the following:

  control operator A *token* that performs a control function. It is one of the following symbols:

RESERVED WORDS

Reserved words are words that have a special meaning to the shell. The following words are recognized as reserved when unquoted and either the first word of a simple command (see **SHELL GRAMMAR** below) or the third word of a **case** or **for** command:

SHELL GRAMMAR

Simple Commands

A *simple command* is a sequence of optional variable assignments followed by *blank*-separated words and redirections, and terminated by a *control operator*. The first word specifies the command to be executed. The remaining words are passed as arguments to the invoked command.

The return value of a *simple command* is its exit status, or 128+*n* if the command is terminated by signal *n*.

Pipelines

A *pipeline* is a sequence of one or more commands separated by the character |. The format for a pipeline is:

[!] *command* [| *command2* ...]

The standard output of *command* is connected to the standard input of *command2*. This connection is performed before any redirections specified by the command (see **REDIRECTION** below).

If the reserved word ! precedes a pipeline, the exit status of that pipeline is the logical NOT of the exit status of the last command. Otherwise, the status of the pipeline is the exit status of the last command. The shell waits for all commands in the pipeline to terminate before returning a value.

Each command in a pipeline is executed as a separate process (i.e., in a subshell).

Lists

A *list* is a sequence of one or more pipelines separated by one of the operators **;**, **&**, **&&**, or , and terminated by one of **;**, **&**, or <**newline**>.

Of these list operators, **&&** and have equal precedence, followed by **;** and **&,** which have equal precedence.

BASH(1)   BASH(1)

If a command is terminated by the control operator **&**, the shell executes the command in the *background* in a subshell. The shell does not wait for the command to finish, and the return status is 0. Commands separated by a **;** are executed sequentially; the shell waits for each command to terminate in turn. The return status is the exit status of the last command executed.

The control operators **&&** and denote AND lists and OR lists, respectively. An AND list has the form

command **&&** *command2*

command2 is executed if, and only if, *command* returns an exit status of zero.

An OR list has the form

command *command2*

command2 is executed if and only if *command* returns a non–zero exit status. The return status of AND and OR lists is the exit status of the last command executed in the list.

Compound Commands

A *compound command* is one of the following:

- (*list*)   *list* is executed in a subshell. Variable assignments and builtin commands that affect the shell's environment do not remain in effect after the command completes. The return status is the exit status of *list*.

- { *list*; }   *list* is simply executed in the current shell environment. This is known as a *group command*. The return status is the exit status of *list*.

- **for** *name* [**in** *word*;] **do** *list* ; **done**   The list of words following **in** is expanded, generating a list of items. The variable *name* is set to each element of this list in turn, and *list* is executed each time. If the **in** *word* is omitted, the **for** command executes *list* once for each positional parameter that is set (see **PARAMETERS** below).

- **select** *name* [**in** *word*;] **do** *list* ; **done**   The list of words following **in** is expanded, generating a list of items. The set of expanded words is printed on the standard error, each preceded by a number. If the **in** *word* is omitted, the positional parameters are printed (see **PARAMETERS** below). The **PS3** prompt is then displayed and a line read from the standard input. If the line consists of the number corresponding to one of the displayed words, then the value of *name* is set to that word. If the line is empty, the words and prompt are displayed again. If EOF is read, the command completes. Any other value read causes *name* to be set to null. The line read is saved in the variable **REPLY**. The *list* is executed after each selection until a **break** or **return** command is executed. The exit status of **select** is the exit status of the last command executed in *list*, or zero if no commands were executed.

- **case** *word* **in** [*pattern* [| *pattern*]]   A **case** command first expands *word*, and tries to match it against each *pattern* in turn, using the same matching rules as for pathname expansion (see **Pathname** Expansion below). When a match is found, the corresponding *list* is executed. After the first match, no subsequent matches are attempted. The exit status is zero if no patterns are matches. Otherwise, it is the exit status of the last command executed in *list*.

- **if** *list* **then** *list*   [**elif** *list* **then** *list*] ...   [**else** *list*] **fi**   The **if** *list* is executed. If its exit status is zero, the **then** *list* is executed. Otherwise, each **elif** *list* is executed in turn, and if its exit status is zero, the corresponding **then** *list* is executed and the command completes. Otherwise, the **else** *list* is executed, if present. The exit status is the exit status of the last command executed, or zero if no condition tested true.

- **while** *list* **do** *list* **done**

until *list* **do** *list* **done**   The **while** command continuously executes the **do** *list* as long as the last command in *list* returns an exit status of zero. The **until** command is identical to the **while** command, except that the test is negated; the **do** *list* is executed as long as the last command in *list* returns a non-zero exit status. The exit status of the **while** and **until** commands is the exit status of the last **do** *list* command executed, or zero if none was executed.

[**function**] *name* () { *list*; }   This defines a function named *name*. The *body* of the function is the *list* of commands between { and }. This list is executed whenever *name* is specified as the name of a simple command. The exit status of a function is the exit status of the last command executed in the body. (See **FUNCTIONS** below.)

COMMENTS

In a non–interactive shell, or an interactive shell in which the **-o** interactive–comments option to the **set** builtin is enabled, a word beginning with **#** causes that word and all remaining characters on that line to be ignored. An interactive shell without the **-o** interactive–comments option enabled does not allow comments.

QUOTING

Quoting is used to remove the special meaning of certain characters or words to the shell. Quoting can be used to disable special treatment for special characters, to prevent reserved words from being recognized as such, and to prevent parameter expansion.

Each of the *metacharacters* listed above under **DEFINITIONS** has special meaning to the shell and must be quoted if they are to represent themselves. There are three quoting mechanisms: the *escape character*, single quotes, and double quotes.

A non-quoted backslash (\) is the *escape character*. It preserves the literal value of the next character that follows, with the exception of <newline>. If a \<newline> pair appears, and the backslash is not quoted, the \<newline> is treated as a line continuation (that is, it is effectively ignored).

Enclosing characters in single quotes preserves the literal value of each character within the quotes. A single quote may not occur between single quotes, even when preceded by a backslash.

Enclosing characters in double quotes preserves the literal value of all characters within the quotes, with the exception of $, ', and \. The characters $ and ' retain their special meaning within double quotes. The backslash retains its special meaning only when followed by one of the following characters: $, ', ", \, or <**newline**>. A double quote may be quoted within double quotes by preceding it with a backslash.

The special parameters * and @ have special meaning when in double quotes (see **PARAMETERS** below).

PARAMETERS

A *parameter* is an entity that stores values, somewhat like a variable in a conventional programming language. It can be a *name*, a number, or one of the special characters listed below under **Special Parameters**. For the shell's purposes, a *variable* is a parameter denoted by a *name*.

A parameter is set if it has been assigned a value. The null string is a valid value. Once a variable is set, it may be unset only by using the **unset** builtin command (see **SHELL BUILTIN COMMANDS** below).

A *variable* may be assigned to by a statement of the form

name=[*value*]

If *value* is not given, the variable is assigned the null string. All *values* undergo tilde expansion, parameter and variable expansion, command substitution, arithmetic expansion, and quote removal. If the variable has its **−i** attribute set (see **declare** below in **SHELL BUILTIN COMMANDS**) then *value* is subject to arithmetic expansion even if the $[...]

syntax does not appear. Word splitting is not performed, with the exception of "$@" as explained below under **Special Parameters**. Pathname expansion is not performed.

Positional Parameters

A *positional* parameter is a parameter denoted by one or more digits, other than the single digit 0. Positional parameters are assigned from the shell's arguments when it is invoked, and may be reassigned using the **set** builtin command. Positional parameters may not be assigned to with assignment statements. The positional parameters are temporarily replaced when a shell function is executed (see **FUNCTIONS** below).

When a positional parameter consisting of more than a single digit is expanded, it must be enclosed in braces (see **EXPANSION** below).

Special Parameters

The shell treats several parameters specially. These parameters may only be referenced; assignment to them is not allowed.

* *   Expands to the positional parameters, starting from one. When the expansion occurs within double quotes, it expands to a single word with the value of each parameter separated by the first character of the **IFS** special variable. That is, "$*" is equivalent to "$1c$2c...", where c is the first character of the value of the **IFS** variable. If **IFS** is null or unset, the parameters are separated by spaces.

* @   Expands to the positional parameters, starting from one. When the expansion occurs within double quotes, each parameter expands as a separate word. That is, " $@ " is equivalent to "$1" "$2" ... When there are no positional parameters, "$@" and expand to nothing (i.e., they are removed).

* #   Expands to the number of positional parameters in decimal.

* ?   Expands to the status of the most recently executed foreground pipeline.

* –   Expands to the current option flags as specified upon invocation, by the **set** builtin command, or those set by the shell itself (such as the **–i** flag).

* $ Expands to the process ID of the shell. In a () subshell, it expands to the process ID of the current shell, not the subshell.

* !   Expands to the process ID of the most recently executed background (asynchronous) command.

* 0   Expands to the name of the shell or shell script. This is set at shell initialization. If **bash** is invoked with a file of commands, is set to the name of that file. If **bash** is started with the **–c** option, then is set to the first argument after the string to be executed, if one is present. Otherwise, it is set to the pathname used to invoke **bash**, as given by argument zero.

* _   Expands to the last argument to the previous command, after expansion. Also set to the full pathname of each command executed and placed in the environment exported to that command.

Shell Variables

The following variables are set by the shell:

    PPID   The process ID of the shell's parent.

    PWD   The current working directory as set by the **cd** command.

    OLDPWD   The previous working directory as set by the **cd** command.

    REPLY   Set to the line of input read by the **read** builtin command when no arguments are supplied.

    UID   Expands to the user ID of the current user, initialized at shell startup.

    EUID   Expands to the effective user ID of the current user, initialized at shell startup.

BASH Expands to the full pathname used to invoke this instance of **bash**.

BASH_VERSION Expands to the version number of this instance of **bash**.

SHLVL Incremented by one each time an instance of **bash** is started.

RANDOM Each time this parameter is referenced, a random integer is generated. The sequence of random numbers may be initialized by assigning a value to **RANDOM**. If **RANDOM** is unset, it loses its special properties, even if it is subsequently reset.

SECONDS Each time this parameter is referenced, the number of seconds since shell invocation is returned. If a value is assigned to **SECONDS**, the value returned upon subsequent references is the number of seconds since the assignment plus the value assigned. If **SECONDS** is unset, it loses its special properties, even if it is subsequently reset.

LINENO Each time this parameter is referenced, the shell substitutes a decimal number representing the current sequential line number (starting with 1) within a script or function. When not in a script or function, the value substituted is not guaranteed to be meaningful. When in a function, the value is not the number of the source line that the command appears on (that information has been lost by the time the function is executed), but is an approximation of the number of *simple* commands executed in the current function. If **LINENO** is unset, it loses its special properties, even if it is subsequently reset.

HISTCMD The history number, or index in the history list, of the current command. If **HISTCMD** is unset, it loses its special properties, even if it is subsequently reset.

OPTARG The value of the last option argument processed by the **getopts** builtin command (see **SHELL BUILTIN COMMANDS** below).

OPTIND The index of the next argument to be processed by the **getopts** builtin command (see **SHELL BUILTIN COMMANDS** below).

HOSTTYPE Automatically set to a string that uniquely describes the type of machine on which **bash** is executing. The default is system-dependent.

OSTYPE Automatically set to a string that describes the operating system on which **bash** is executing. The default is system-dependent.

The following variables are used by the shell. In some cases, **bash** assigns a default value to a variable; these cases are noted below.

IFS The *Internal* Field Separator that is used for word splitting after expansion and to split lines into words with the **read** builtin command. The default value is "<space><tab><newline>".

PATH The search path for commands. It is a colon-separated list of directories in which the shell looks for commands (see **COMMAND** EXECUTION below). The default path is system-dependent, and is set by the administrator who installs **bash**. A common value is "/usr/gnu/bin:/usr/local/bin:/usr/ucb:/bin:/usr/bin:.".

HOME The home directory of the current user; the default argument for the **cd** builtin command.

CDPATH The search path for the **cd** command. This is a colon-separated list of directories in which the shell looks for destination directories specified by the **cd** command. A sample value is ".:~:/usr".

ENV If this parameter is set when **bash** is executing a shell script, its value is interpreted as a filename containing commands to initialize the shell, as in *.bashrc*. The value of **ENV** is subjected to parameter expansion, command substitution, and arithmetic expansion before being interpreted as a pathname. **PATH** is not used to search for the resultant pathname.

MAIL If this parameter is set to a filename and the **MAILPATH** variable is not set, **bash** informs the user of the arrival of mail in the specified file.

MAILCHECK Specifies how often (in seconds) **bash** checks for mail. The default is 60 seconds. When it is time to check for mail, the shell does so before prompting. If this variable is unset, the shell disables mail checking.

MAILPATH A colon-separated list of pathnames to be checked for mail. The message to be printed may be specified by separating the pathname from the message with a '?'. $_ stands for the name of the current mailfile. Example:

   MAILPATH='/usr/spool/mail/bfox?"You have mail":~/shell-mail?"$_ has mail!"'

Bash supplies a default value for this variable, but the location of the user mail files that it uses is system dependent (e.g., /usr/spool/mail/**$USER**).

MAIL_WARNING If set, and a file that **bash** is checking for mail has been accessed since the last time it was checked, the message "The mail in *mailfile* has been read" is printed.

PS1 The value of this parameter is expanded (see **PROMPTING** below) and used as the primary prompt string. The default value is "**bash\\$** ".

PS2 The value of this parameter is expanded and used as the secondary prompt string. The default is "**>** ".

PS3 The value of this parameter is used as the prompt for the *select* command (see **SHELL GRAMMAR** above).

PS4 The value of this parameter is expanded and the value is printed before each command **bash** displays during an execution trace. The first character of **PS4** is replicated multiple times, as necessary, to indicate multiple levels of indirection. The default is "**+** ".

HISTSIZE The number of commands to remember in the command history (see **HISTORY** below). The default value is 500.

HISTFILE The name of the file in which command history is saved. (See **HISTORY** below.) The default value is *~/.bash_history*. If unset, the command history is not saved when an interactive shell exits.

HISTFILESIZE The maximum number of lines contained in the history file. When this variable is assigned a value, the history file is truncated, if necessary, to contain no more than that number of lines. The default value is 500.

OPTERR If set to the value 1, **bash** displays error messages generated by the **getopts** builtin command (see **SHELL BUILTIN COMMANDS** below). **OPTERR** is initialized to 1 each time the shell is invoked or a shell script is executed.

PROMPT_COMMAND If set, the value is executed as a command prior to issuing each primary prompt.

IGNOREEOF Controls the action of the shell on receipt of an **EOF** character as the sole input. If set, the value is the number of consecutive **EOF** characters typed as the first characters on an input line before **bash** exits. If the variable exists but does not have a numeric value, or has no value, the default value is 10. If it does not exist, **EOF** signifies the end of input to the shell. This is only in effect for interactive shells.

TMOUT If set to a value greater than zero, the value is interpreted as the number of seconds to wait for input after issuing the primary prompt. **Bash** terminates after waiting for that number of seconds if input does not arrive.

FCEDIT The default editor for the **fc** builtin command.

FIGNORE A colon-separated list of suffixes to ignore when performing filename completion (see **READLINE** below). A filename whose suffix matches one of the entries in **FIGNORE** is excluded from the list of matched filenames. A sample value is ".o:~".

INPUTRC The filename for the readline startup file, overriding the default of *~/.inputrc* (see **READLINE** below).

notify If set, **bash** reports terminated background jobs immediately, rather than waiting until before printing the next primary prompt (see also the **−b** option to the **set** builtin command).

history_control

HISTCONTROL If set to a value of *ignorespace*, lines which begin with a **space** character are not entered on the history list. If set to a value of *ignoredups*, lines matching the last history line are not entered. A value of *ignoreboth* combines the two options. If unset, or if set to any other value than those above, all lines read by the parser are saved on the history list.

command_oriented_history If set, **bash** attempts to save all lines of a multiple-line command in the same history entry. This allows easy re-editing of multi-line commands.

glob_dot_filenames If set, **bash** includes filenames beginning with a '.' in the results of pathname expansion.

allow_null_glob_expansion If set, **bash** allows pathname patterns which match no files (see **Pathname** Expansion below) to expand to a null string, rather than themselves.

histchars The two or three characters which control history expansion and tokenization (see **HISTORY** EXPANSION below). The first character is the *history expansion character*, that is, the character which signals the start of a history expansion, normally '!'. The second character is the *quick substitution* character, which is used as shorthand for re-running the previous command entered, substituting one string for another in the command. The default is '^'. The optional third character is the character which signifies that the remainder of the line is a comment, when found as the first character of a word, normally '#'. The history comment character causes history substitution to be skipped for the remaining words on the line. It does not necessarily cause the shell parser to treat the rest of the line as a comment.

nolinks If set, the shell does not follow symbolic links when executing commands that change the current working directory. It uses the physical directory structure instead. By default, **bash** follows the logical chain of directories when performing commands which change the current directory, such as **cd**. See also the description of the **−P** option to the **set** builtin (**SHELL BUILTIN COMMANDS** below).

hostname_completion_file

HOSTFILE Contains the name of a file in the same format as */etc/hosts* that should be read when the shell needs to complete a hostname. The file may be changed interactively; the next time hostname completion is attempted **bash** adds the contents of the new file to the already existing database.

noclobber If set, **bash** does not overwrite an existing file with the >, >&, and <> redirection operators. This variable may be overridden when creating output files by using the redirection operator >| instead of > (see also the **−C** option to the **set** builtin command).

auto_resume This variable controls how the shell interacts with the user and job control. If this variable is set, single word simple commands without redirections are treated as candidates for resumption of an existing stopped job. There is no ambiguity allowed; if there is more than one job beginning with the string typed, the job most recently accessed is selected. The *name* of a stopped job, in this context, is the command line used to start it. If set to the value *exact*, the string supplied must match the name of a stopped job exactly; if set to *substring*, the string supplied needs to match a substring of the name of a stopped job. The *substring* value provides functionality analogous to the %? job id (see **JOB** CONTROL below). If set to any other value, the supplied string must be a prefix of a stopped job's name; this provides functionality analogous to the % job id.

no_exit_on_failed_exec If this variable exists, a non-interactive shell will not exit if it cannot execute the file specified in the **exec** builtin command. An interactive shell does not exit if **exec** fails.

cdable_vars If this is set, an argument to the **cd** builtin command that is not a directory is assumed to be the name of a variable whose value is the directory to change to.

EXPANSION

Expansion is performed on the command line after it has been split into words. There are seven kinds of expansion performed: *brace expansion, tilde expansion, parameter and variable expansion, command substitution, arithmetic expansion, word splitting,* and *pathname expansion*.

The order of expansions is: brace expansion, tilde expansion, parameter, variable, command, and arithmetic substitution (done in a left–to–right fashion), word splitting, and pathname expansion.

On systems that can support it, there is an additional expansion available: *process substitution*.

Only brace expansion, word splitting, and pathname expansion can change the number of words of the expansion; other expansions expand a single word to a single word. The single exception to this is the expansion of "$@" as explained above (see **PARAMETERS**).

Brace Expansion

Brace expansion is a mechanism by which arbitrary strings may be generated. This mechanism is similar to *pathname expansion*, but the filenames generated need not exist. Patterns to be brace expanded take the form of an optional *preamble*, followed by a series of comma-separated strings between a pair of braces, followed by an optional *postamble*. The preamble is prepended to each string contained within the braces, and the postamble is then appended to each resulting string, expanding left to right.

Brace expansions may be nested. The results of each expanded string are not sorted; left to right order is preserved. For example, a{d,c,b}e expands into 'ade ace abe'.

Brace expansion is performed before any other expansions, and any characters special to other expansions are preserved in the result. It is strictly textual. **Bash** does not apply any syntactic interpretation to the context of the expansion or the text between the braces.

A correctly-formed brace expansion must contain unquoted opening and closing braces, and at least one unquoted comma. Any incorrectly formed brace expansion is left unchanged.

This construct is typically used as shorthand when the common prefix of the strings to be generated is longer than in the above example:

mkdir /usr/local/src/bash/{old,new,dist,bugs}

or

chown root /usr/{ucb/{ex,edit},lib/{ex?.?*,how_ex}}

Brace expansion introduces a slight incompatibility with traditional versions of **sh**, the Bourne shell. **sh** does not treat opening or closing braces specially when they appear as part of a word, and preserves them in the output. **Bash** removes braces from words as a consequence of brace expansion. For example, a word entered to **sh** as *file{1,2}* appears identically in the output. The same word is output as *file1* file2 after expansion by **bash**. If strict compatibility with **sh** is desired, start **bash** with the **–nobraceexpansion** flag (see **OPTIONS** above) or disable brace expansion with the **+o** braceexpand option to the **set** command (see **SHELL** BUILTIN COMMANDS below).

Tilde Expansion

If a word begins with a tilde character ('~'), all of the characters preceding the first slash (or all characters, if there is no slash) are treated as a possible *login name*. If this *login name* is the null string, the tilde is replaced with the value of the parameter **HOME**. If **HOME** is unset, the home directory of the user executing the shell is substituted instead.

If a '+' follows the tilde, the value of **PWD** replaces the tilde and '+'. If a '–' follows, the value of **OLDPWD** is substituted. If the value following the tilde is a valid *login name*, the tilde and *login name* are replaced with the home directory associated with that name. If the name is invalid, or the tilde expansion fails, the word is unchanged.

Each variable assignment is checked for unquoted instances of tildes following a : or =. In these cases, tilde substitution is also performed. Consequently, one may use pathnames with tildes in assignments to **PATH**, **MAILPATH**, and **CDPATH**, and the shell assigns the expanded value.

Parameter Expansion

The '$' character introduces parameter expansion, command substitution, or arithmetic expansion. The parameter name or symbol to be expanded may be enclosed in braces, which are optional but serve to protect the variable to be expanded from characters immediately following it which could be interpreted as part of the name.

> ${*parameter*}   The value of *parameter* is substituted. The braces are required when *parameter* is a positional parameter with more than one digit, or when *parameter* is followed by a character which is not to be interpreted as part of its name.

In each of the cases below, *word* is subject to tilde expansion, parameter expansion, command substitution, and arithmetic expansion. **Bash** tests for a parameter that is unset or null; omitting the colon results in a test only for a parameter that is unset.

> ${*parameter*:–*word*}   **Use Default Values**. If *parameter* is unset or null, the expansion of *word* is substituted. Otherwise, the value of *parameter* is substituted.

> ${*parameter*:=*word*}   **Assign Default Values**. If *parameter* is unset or null, the expansion of *word* is assigned to *parameter*. The value of *parameter* is then substituted. Positional parameters and special parameters may not be assigned to in this way.

> ${*parameter*:?*word*}   **Display Error if Null or Unset**. If *parameter* is null or unset, the expansion of *word* (or a message to that effect if *word* is not present) is written to the standard error and the shell, if it is not interactive, exits. Otherwise, the value of *parameter* is substituted.

> ${*parameter*:+*word*}   **Use Alternate Value**. If *parameter* is null or unset, nothing is substituted, otherwise the expansion of *word* is substituted.

> ${#*parameter*}   The length in characters of the value of *parameter* is substituted. If *parameter* is * or @, the length substituted is the length of * expanded within double quotes.

> ${*parameter*#*word*}
> ${*parameter*##*word*}   The *word* is expanded to produce a pattern just as in pathname expansion. If the pattern matches the beginning of the value of *parameter*, then the expansion is the value of *parameter* with the shortest matching pattern deleted (the "#" case) or the longest matching pattern deleted (the "##" case).

> ${*parameter*%*word*}
> ${*parameter*%%*word*}   The *word* is expanded to produce a pattern just as in pathname expansion. If the pattern matches a trailing portion of the value of *parameter*, then the expansion is the value of *parameter* with the shortest matching pattern deleted (the "%" case) or the longest matching pattern deleted (the "%%" case).

Command Substitution

Command substitution allows the output of a command to replace the command name. There are two forms:

$(*command***)**

or

`***command***`

performs the expansion by executing *command* and replacing the command substitution with the standard output of the command, with any trailing newlines deleted.

When the old-style backquote form of substitution is used, backslash retains its literal meaning except when followed by $, ` , or \. When using the $(*command*) form, all characters between the parentheses make up the command; none are treated specially.

Command substitutions may be nested. To nest when using the old form, escape the inner backquotes with backslashes.

If the substitution appears within double quotes, word splitting and pathname expansion are not performed on the results.

Arithmetic Expansion

Arithmetic expansion allows the evaluation of an arithmetic expression and the substitution of the result. There are two formats for arithmetic expansion:

$[*expression***]**

$((*expression***))**

The *expression* is treated as if it were within double quotes, but a double quote inside the braces or parentheses is not treated specially. All tokens in the expression undergo parameter expansion, command substitution, and quote removal. Arithmetic substitutions may be nested.

The evaluation is performed according to the rules listed below under **ARITHMETIC EVALUATION**. If *expression* is invalid, **bash** prints a message indicating failure and no substitution occurs.

Process Substitution

Process substitution is supported on systems that support named pipes (*FIFOs*) or the **/dev/fd** method of naming open files. It takes the form of <(*list*) or >(*list*). The process *list* is run with its input or output connected to a *FIFO* or some file in **/dev/fd**. The name of this file is passed as an argument to the current command as the result of the expansion. If the >(*list*) form is used, writing to the file will provide input for *list*. If the <(*list*) form is used, the file passed as an argument should be read to obtain the output of *list*.

On systems that support it, *process substitution* is performed simultaneously with *parameter and variable expansion*, *command substitution*, and *arithmetic expansion*.

Word Splitting

The shell scans the results of parameter expansion, command substitution, and arithmetic expansion that did not occur within double quotes for *word splitting*.

The shell treats each character of **IFS** as a delimiter, and splits the results of the other expansions into words on these characters. If the value of **IFS** is exactly <**space**><**tab**><**newline**>, the default, then any sequence of **IFS** characters serves to delimit words. If **IFS** has a value other than the default, then sequences of the whitespace characters **space** and **tab** are ignored at the beginning and end of the word, as long as the whitespace character is in the value of **IFS** (an **IFS** whitespace character). Any character in **IFS** that is not **IFS** whitespace, along with any adjacent **IFS** whitespace characters, delimits a field. A sequence of **IFS** whitespace characters is also treated as a delimiter. If the value of **IFS** is null, no word splitting occurs. **IFS** cannot be unset.

Explicit null arguments ("" or '') are retained. Implicit null arguments, resulting from the expansion of *parameters* that have no values, are removed.

Note that if no expansion occurs, no splitting is performed.

Pathname Expansion

After word splitting, unless the **-f** option has been set, **bash** scans each *word* for the characters *****, **?**, and **[**. If one of these characters appears, then the word is regarded as a *pattern*, and replaced with an alphabetically sorted list of pathnames matching the pattern. If no matching pathnames are found, and the shell variable **allow_null_glob_expansion** is unset, the word is left unchanged. If the variable is set, and no matches are found, the word is removed. When a pattern is used for pathname generation, the character "**.**" at the start of a name or immediately following a slash must be matched explicitly, unless the shell variable **glob_dot_filenames** is set. The slash character must always be matched explicitly. In other cases, the "**.**" character is not treated specially.

The special pattern characters have the following meanings:

*****	Matches any string, including the null string.
?	Matches any single character.
[...]	Matches any one of the enclosed characters. A pair of characters separated by a minus sign denotes a *range*; any character lexically between those two characters, inclusive, is matched. If the first character following the [is a **!** or a **^** then any character not enclosed is matched. A **-** or **]** may be matched by including it as the first or last character in the set.

Quote Removal

After the preceding expansions, all unquoted occurrences of the characters ****, **'**, and **"** are removed.

REDIRECTION

Before a command is executed, its input and output may be *redirected* using a special notation interpreted by the shell. Redirection may also be used to open and close files for the current shell execution environment. The following redirection operators may precede or appear anywhere within a *simple* command or may follow a *command*. Redirections are processed in the order they appear, from left to right.

In the following descriptions, if the file descriptor number is omitted, and the first character of the redirection operator is <, the redirection refers to the standard input (file descriptor 0). If the first character of the redirection operator is >, the redirection refers to the standard output (file descriptor 1).

The word that follows the redirection operator in the following descriptions is subjected to brace expansion, tilde expansion, parameter expansion, command substitution, arithmetic expansion, quote removal, and pathname expansion. If it expands to more than one word, **bash** reports an error.

Note that the order of redirections is significant. For example, the command

ls > dirlist 2>&1

directs both standard output and standard error to the file *dirlist*, while the command

ls 2>&1 > dirlist

directs only the standard output to file *dirlist*, because the standard error was duplicated as standard output before the standard output was redirected to *dirlist*.

Redirecting Input

Redirection of input causes the file whose name results from the expansion of *word* to be opened for reading on file descriptor *n*, or the standard input (file descriptor 0) if *n* is not specified.

The general format for redirecting input is:

[*n*]<*word*

Redirecting Output

Redirection of output causes the file whose name results from the expansion of *word* to be opened for writing on file descriptor *n*, or the standard output (file descriptor 1) if *n* is not specified. If the file does not exist it is created; if it does exist it is truncated to zero size.

The general format for redirecting output is:

[*n*]>*word*

If the redirection operator is >|, then the value of the **-C** option to the **set** builtin command is not tested, and file creation is attempted. (See also the description of **noclobber** under **Shell Variables** above.)

Appending Redirected Output

Redirection of output in this fashion causes the file whose name results from the expansion of *word* to be opened for appending on file descriptor *n*, or the standard output (file descriptor 1) if *n* is not specified. If the file does not exist it is created.

The general format for appending output is:

[*n*]>>*word*

Redirecting Standard Output and Standard Error

Bash allows both the standard output (file descriptor 1) and the standard error output (file descriptor 2) to be redirected to the file whose name is the expansion of *word* with this construct.

There are two formats for redirecting standard output and standard error:

&>*word*

and

>&*word*

Of the two forms, the first is preferred. This is semantically equivalent to

>*word* 2>&1

Here Documents

This type of redirection instructs the shell to read input from the current source until a line containing only *word* (with no trailing blanks) is seen. All of the lines read up to that point are then used as the standard input for a command.

The format of here-documents is as follows:

<<[−]*word here-document delimiter*

No parameter expansion, command substitution, pathname expansion, or arithmetic expansion is performed on *word*. If any characters in *word* are quoted, the *delimiter* is the result of quote removal on *word*, and the lines in the here-document are not expanded. Otherwise, all lines of the here-document are subjected to parameter expansion, command substitution, and arithmetic expansion. In the latter case, the pair \<**newline**> is ignored, and \ must be used to quote the characters \, $, and '.

If the redirection operator is <<−, then all leading tab characters are stripped from input lines and the line containing *delimiter*. This allows here-documents within shell scripts to be indented in a natural fashion.

Duplicating File Descriptors

The redirection operator

[*n*]<&*word*

is used to duplicate input file descriptors. If *word* expands to one or more digits, the file descriptor denoted by *n* is made to be a copy of that file descriptor. If *word* evaluates to −, file descriptor *n* is closed. If *n* is not specified, the standard input (file descriptor 0) is used.

The operator

[n]>&word

is used similarly to duplicate output file descriptors. If *n* is not specified, the standard output (file descriptor 1) is used. As a special case, if *n* is omitted, and *word* does not expand to one or more digits, the standard output and standard error are redirected as described previously.

Opening File Descriptors for Reading and Writing

The redirection operator

[n]<>word

causes the file whose name is the expansion of *word* to be opened for both reading and writing on file descriptor *n*, or as the standard input and standard output if *n* is not specified. If the file does not exist, it is created.

FUNCTIONS

A shell function, defined as described above under **SHELL GRAMMAR**, stores a series of commands for later execution. Functions are executed in the context of the current shell; no new process is created to interpret them (contrast this with the execution of a shell script). When a function is executed, the arguments to the function become the positional parameters during its execution. The special parameter # is updated to reflect the change. Positional parameter 0 is unchanged.

Variables local to the function may be declared with the **local** builtin command. Ordinarily, variables and their values are shared between the function and its caller.

If the builtin command **return** is executed in a function, the function completes and execution resumes with the next command after the function call. When a function completes, the values of the positional parameters and the special parameter # are restored to the values they had prior to function execution.

Function names may be listed with the **−f** option to the **declare** or **typeset** builtin commands. Functions may be exported so that subshells automatically have them defined with the **−f** option to the **export** builtin.

Functions may be recursive. No limit is imposed on the number of recursive calls.

ALIASES

The shell maintains a list of *aliases* that may be set and unset with the **alias** and **unalias** builtin commands (see **SHELL BUILTIN COMMANDS** below). The first word of each command, if unquoted, is checked to see if it has an alias. If so, that word is replaced by the text of the alias. The alias name and the replacement text may contain any valid shell input, including the *metacharacters* listed above, with the exception that the alias name may not contain =. The first word of the replacement text is tested for aliases, but a word that is identical to an alias being expanded is not expanded a second time. This means that one may alias **ls** to **ls −F**, for instance, and **bash** does not try to recursively expand the replacement text. If the last character of the alias value is a *blank*, then the next command word following the alias is also checked for alias expansion.

Aliases are created and listed with the **alias** command, and removed with the **unalias** command.

There is no mechanism for using arguments in the replacement text, as in **csh**. If arguments are needed, a shell function should be used.

Aliases are not expanded when the shell is not interactive.

The rules concerning the definition and use of aliases are somewhat confusing. **Bash** always reads at least one complete line of input before executing any of the commands on that line. Aliases are expanded when a command is read, not when it is executed. Therefore, an alias definition appearing on the same line as another command does not take effect until the next line of input is read. This means that the commands following the alias definition on that line are not affected by the new alias. This behavior is also an issue when functions are executed. Aliases are expanded when the function definition is read, not when the function is executed, because a function definition is itself a compound command. As a consequence, aliases defined in a function are not available until after that function is executed. To be safe, always put alias definitions on a separate line, and do not use **alias** in compound commands.

Note that for almost every purpose, aliases are superseded by shell functions.

JOB CONTROL

Job control refers to the ability to selectively stop (*suspend*) the execution of processes and continue (*resume*) their execution at a later point. A user typically employs this facility via an interactive interface supplied jointly by the system's terminal driver and **bash**.

The shell associates a *job* with each pipeline. It keeps a table of currently executing jobs, which may be listed with the **jobs** command. When **bash** starts a job asynchronously (in the *background*), it prints a line that looks like:

[1] 25647

indicating that this job is job number 1 and that the process ID of the last process in the pipeline associated with this job is 25647. All of the processes in a single pipeline are members of the same job. **Bash** uses the *job* abstraction as the basis for job control.

To facilitate the implementation of the user interface to job control, the system maintains the notion of a *current terminal process group ID*. Members of this process group (processes whose process group ID is equal to the current terminal process group ID) receive keyboard-generated signals such as **SIGINT**. These processes are said to be in the *foreground*. Background processes are those whose process group ID differs from the terminal's; such processes are immune to keyboard-generated signals. Only foreground processes are allowed to read from or write to the terminal. Background processes which attempt to read from (write to) the terminal are sent a **SIGTTIN** (SIGTTOU) signal by the terminal driver, which, unless caught, suspends the process.

If the operating system on which **bash** is running supports job control, **bash** allows you to use it. Typing the *suspend* character (typically ^Z, Control-Z) while a process is running causes that process to be stopped and returns you to **bash**. Typing the *delayed suspend* character (typically ^Y, Control-Y) causes the process to be stopped when it attempts to read input from the terminal, and control to be returned to **bash**. You may then manipulate the state of this job, using the **bg** command to continue it in the background, the **fg** command to continue it in the foreground, or the **kill** command to kill it. A ^Z takes effect immediately, and has the additional side effect of causing pending output and typeahead to be discarded.

There are a number of ways to refer to a job in the shell. The character % introduces a job name. Job number *n* may be referred to as **%n**. A job may also be referred to using a prefix of the name used to start it, or using a substring that appears in its command line. For example, **%ce** refers to a stopped **ce** job. If a prefix matches more than one job, **bash** reports an error. Using **%?ce**, on the other hand, refers to any job containing the string **ce** in its command line. If the substring matches more than one job, **bash** reports an error. The symbols **%%** and **%+** refer to the shell's notion of the *current job*, which is the last job stopped while it was in the foreground. The *previous job* may be referenced using **%−**. In output pertaining to jobs (e.g., the output of the **jobs** command), the current job is always flagged with a +, and the previous job with a −.

Simply naming a job can be used to bring it into the foreground: **%1** is a synonym for **"fg %1"**, bringing job 1 from the background into the foreground. Similarly, **"%1 &"** resumes job 1 in the background, equivalent to **"bg %1"**.

The shell learns immediately whenever a job changes state. Normally, **bash** waits until it is about to print a prompt before reporting changes in a job's status so as to not interrupt any other output. If the **-b** option to the **set** builtin command is set, **bash** reports such changes immediately. (See also the description of **notify** variable under **Shell Variables** above.)

If you attempt to exit **bash** while jobs are stopped, the shell prints a message warning you. You may then use the **jobs** command to inspect their status. If you do this, or try to exit again immediately, you are not warned again, and the stopped jobs are terminated.

SIGNALS

When **bash** is interactive, it ignores SIGTERM (so that **kill 0** does not kill an interactive shell), and SIGINT is caught and handled (so that the **wait** builtin is interruptible). In all cases, **bash** ignores SIGQUIT. If job control is in effect, **bash** ignores SIGTTIN, SIGTTOU, and SIGTSTP.

Synchronous jobs started by **bash** have signals set to the values inherited by the shell from its parent. When job control is not in effect, background jobs (jobs started with **&**) ignore SIGINT and SIGQUIT. Commands run as a result of command substitution ignore the keyboard-generated job control signals SIGTTIN, SIGTTOU, and SIGTSTP.

COMMAND EXECUTION

After a command has been split into words, if it results in a simple command and an optional list of arguments, the following actions are taken.

If the command name contains no slashes, the shell attempts to locate it. If there exists a shell function by that name, that function is invoked as described above in **FUNCTIONS**. If the name does not match a function, the shell searches for it in the list of shell builtins. If a match is found, that builtin is invoked.

If the name is neither a shell function nor a builtin, and contains no slashes, **bash** searches each element of the **PATH** for a directory containing an executable file by that name. If the search is unsuccessful, the shell prints an error message and returns a nonzero exit status.

If the search is successful, or if the command name contains one or more slashes, the shell executes the named program. Argument 0 is set to the name given, and the remaining arguments to the command are set to the arguments given, if any.

If this execution fails because the file is not in executable format, and the file is not a directory, it is assumed to be a *shell script*, a file containing shell commands. A subshell is spawned to execute it. This subshell reinitializes itself, so that the effect is as if a new shell had been invoked to handle the script, with the exception that the locations of commands remembered by the parent (see **hash** below under **SHELL BUILTIN COMMANDS**) are retained by the child.

If the program is a file beginning with **#!**, the remainder of the first line specifies an interpreter for the program. The shell executes the specified interpreter on operating systems that do not handle this executable format themselves. The arguments to the interpreter consist of a single optional argument following the interpreter name on the first line of the program, followed by the name of the program, followed by the command arguments, if any.

ENVIRONMENT

When a program is invoked it is given an array of strings called the *environment*. This is a list of *name–value* pairs, of the form *name*=value.

The shell allows you to manipulate the environment in several ways. On invocation, the shell scans its own environment and creates a parameter for each name found, automatically marking it for *export* to child processes. Executed commands inherit the environment. The **export** and **declare** –x commands allow parameters and functions to be added to and deleted from the environment. If the value of a parameter in the environment is modified, the new value becomes part of the environment, replacing the old. The environment inherited by any executed command consists of the shell's initial environment, whose values may be modified in the shell, less any pairs removed by the **unset** command, plus any additions via the **export** and **declare** –x commands.

The environment for any *simple* command or function may be augmented temporarily by prefixing it with parameter assignments, as described above in **PARAMETERS**. These assignment statements affect only the environment seen by that command.

If the **–k** flag is set (see the **set** builtin command below), then *all* parameter assignments are placed in the environment for a command, not just those that precede the command name.

When **bash** invokes an external command, the variable _ is set to the full path name of the command and passed to that command in its environment.

EXIT STATUS

For the purposes of the shell, a command which exits with a zero exit status has succeeded. An exit status of zero indicates success. A non–zero exit status indicates failure. When a command terminates on a fatal signal, **bash** uses the value of 128+**signal** as the exit status.

If a command is not found, the child process created to execute it returns a status of 127. If a command is found but is not executable, the return status is 126.

Bash itself returns the exit status of the last command executed, unless a syntax error occurs, in which case it exits with a non–zero value. See also the **exit** builtin command below.

PROMPTING

When executing interactively, **bash** displays the primary prompt **PS1** when it is ready to read a command, and the secondary prompt **PS2** when it needs more input to complete a command. **Bash** allows these prompt strings to be customized by inserting a number of backslash-escaped special characters that are decoded as follows:

\t	the current time in HH:MM:SS format
\d	the date in "Weekday Month Date" format (e.g., "Tue May 26")
\n	newline
\s	the name of the shell, the basename of (the portion following the final slash)
\w	the current working directory
\W	the basename of the current working directory
\u	the username of the current user
\h	the hostname
\#	the command number of this command
\!	the history number of this command
\$	if the effective UID is 0, a #, otherwise a $
\nnn	the character corresponding to the octal number **nnn**
\\	a backslash
\[	begin a sequence of non-printing characters, which could be used to embed a terminal control sequence into the prompt
\]	end a sequence of non-printing characters

The command number and the history number are usually different: the history number of a command is its position in the history list, which may include commands restored from the history file (see **HISTORY** below), while the command number is the position in the sequence of commands executed during the current shell session. After the string is decoded, it is expanded via parameter expansion, command substitution, arithmetic expansion, and word splitting.

READLINE

This is the library that handles reading input when using an interactive shell, unless the –**nolineediting** option is given. By default, the line editing commands are similar to those of emacs. A vi-style line editing interface is also available.

In this section, the emacs-style notation is used to denote keystrokes. Control keys are denoted by C–*key*, e.g., C–n means Control-N. Similarly, *meta* keys are denoted by M–*key*, so M–x means Meta-X. (On keyboards without a *meta* key, M–*x* means ESC *x*, i.e., press the Escape key then the *x* key. This makes ESC the *meta prefix*. The combination M–C–*x* means ESC–Control–*x*, or press the Escape key then hold the Control key while pressing the *x* key.)

The default key-bindings may be changed with an /.inputrc file. The value of the shell variable **INPUTRC**, if set, is used instead of ˜/.inputrc. Other programs that use this library may add their own commands and bindings.

For example, placing

M–Control–u: universal–argument

or

C–Meta–u: universal–argument

into the /.inputrc would make M–C–u execute the readline command *universal–argument*.

The following symbolic character names are recognized: *RUBOUT, DEL, ESC, LFD, NEWLINE, RET, RETURN, SPC, SPACE,* and *TAB*. In addition to command names, readline allows keys to be bound to a string that is inserted when the key is pressed (a *macro*).

Readline is customized by putting commands in an initialization file. The name of this file is taken from the value of the **INPUTRC** variable. If that variable is unset, the default is ˜/.inputrc. When a program which uses the readline library starts up, the init file is read, and the key bindings and variables are set. There are only a few basic constructs allowed in the readline init file. Blank lines are ignored. Lines beginning with a **#** are comments. Lines beginning with a **$** indicate conditional constructs. Other lines denote key bindings and variable settings.

The syntax for controlling key bindings in the ˜/.inputrc file is simple. All that is required is the name of the command or the text of a macro and a key sequence to which it should be bound. The name may be specified in one of two ways: as a symbolic key name, possibly with *Meta-* or *Control-* prefixes, or as a key sequence. When using the form **keyname**:*function-name* or *macro*, **keyname** is the name of a key spelled out in English. For example:

Control-u: universal–argument
Meta-Rubout: backward-kill-word
Control-o: ">&output"

In the above example, *C-u* is bound to the function **universal–argument**, *M-DEL* is bound to the function **backward–kill–word**, and *C-o* is bound to run the macro expressed on the right hand side (that is, to insert the text >&*output* into the line).

In the second form, **"keyseq"**:*function-name* or *macro*, **keyseq** differs from **keyname** above in that strings denoting an entire key sequence may be specified by placing the sequence within double quotes. Some GNU Emacs style key escapes can be used, as in the following example:

"\C-u": universal–argument
"\C-x\C-r": re–read–init–file
"\e[11˜": "Function Key 1"

In this example, *C-u* is again bound to the function **universal–argument**. *C-x C-r* is bound to the function **re–read–init–file**, and *ESC [1 1 ˜* is bound to insert the text **Function Key 1**. The full set of escape sequences is

\C-	control prefix	
\M-	meta prefix	
\e	an escape character	
****	backslash	
\"	literal "	
\'	literal '	

When entering the text of a macro, single or double quotes should be used to indicate a macro definition. Unquoted text is assumed to be a function name. Backslash will quote any character in the macro text, including " and '.

Bash allows the current readline key bindings to be displayed or modified with the **bind** builtin command. The editing mode may be switched during interactive use by using the **–o** option to the **set** builtin command (see **SHELL** BUILTIN COMMANDS below).

Readline has variables that can be used to further customize its behavior. A variable may be set in the *inputrc* file with a statement of the form

set *variable–name value*

Except where noted, readline variables can take the values **On** or **Off**. The variables and their default values are:

horizontal–scroll–mode (Off)   When set to **On**, makes readline use a single line for display, scrolling the input horizontally on a single screen line when it becomes longer than the screen width rather than wrapping to a new line.

editing–mode (emacs)   Controls whether readline begins with a set of key bindings similar to *emacs* or *vi*. **editing–mode** can be set to either **emacs** or **vi**.

mark–modified–lines (Off)   If set to **On**, history lines that have been modified are displayed with a preceding asterisk (*).

bell–style (audible)   Controls what happens when readline wants to ring the terminal bell. If set to **none**, readline never rings the bell. If set to **visible**, readline uses a visible bell if one is available. If set to **audible**, readline attempts to ring the terminal's bell.

comment–begin ("#")   The string that is inserted in **vi** mode when the **vi–comment** command is executed.

meta–flag (Off)   If set to **On**, readline will enable eight-bit input (that is, it will not strip the high bit from the characters it reads), regardless of what the terminal claims it can support.

convert–meta (On)   If set to **On**, readline will convert characters with the eighth bit set to an ASCII key sequence by stripping the eighth bit and prepending an escape character (in effect, using escape as the *meta prefix*).

output–meta (Off)   If set to **On**, readline will display characters with the eighth bit set directly rather than as a meta-prefixed escape sequence.

completion–query–items (100)   This determines when the user is queried about viewing the number of possible completions generated by the **possible–completions** command. It may be set to any integer value greater than or equal to zero. If the number of possible completions is greater than or equal to the value of this variable, the user is asked whether or not he wishes to view them; otherwise they are simply listed on the terminal.

keymap (emacs)   Set the current readline keymap. The set of legal keymap names is *emacs, emacs-standard, emacs-meta, emacs-ctlx, vi, vi-move, vi-command*, and *vi-insert*. *vi* is equivalent to *vi-command*; *emacs* is equivalent to *emacs-standard*. The default value is *emacs*; the value of **editing–mode** also affects the default keymap.

show–all–if–ambiguous (Off)   This alters the default behavior of the completion functions. If set to **on**, words which have more than one possible completion cause the matches to be listed immediately instead of ringing the bell.

expand–tilde (Off)   If set to **on**, tilde expansion is performed when readline attempts word completion.

Readline implements a facility similar in spirit to the conditional compilation features of the C preprocessor which allows key bindings and variable settings to be performed as the result of tests. There are three parser directives used.

The construct allows bindings to be made based on the editing mode, the terminal being used, or the application using readline. The text of the test extends to the end of the line; no characters are required to isolate it.

mode The **mode=** form of the **$if** directive is used to test whether readline is in emacs or vi mode. This may be used in conjunction with the **set keymap** command, for instance, to set bindings in the *emacs-standard* and *emacs-ctlx* keymaps only if readline is starting out in emacs mode.

term The **term=** form may be used to include terminal-specific key bindings, perhaps to bind the key sequences output by the terminal's function keys. The word on the right side of the = is tested against the full name of the terminal and the portion of the terminal name before the first −. This allows *sun* to match both *sun* and *sun−cmd*, for instance.

application The **application** construct is used to include application−specific settings. Each program using the readline library sets the *application name*, and an initialization file can test for a particular value. This could be used to bind key sequences to functions useful for a specific program. For instance, the following command adds a key sequence that quotes the current or previous word in Bash:
$if Bash
Quote the current or previous word
"\C-xq": "\eb\"\ef\""
$endif

[$ endif] This command, as you saw in the previous example, terminates an $if command.

$ else Commands in this branch of the **$if** directive are executed if the test fails.

Readline commands may be given numeric *arguments*, which normally act as a repeat count. Sometimes, however, it is the sign of the argument that is significant. Passing a negative argument to a command that acts in the forward direction (e.g., **kill−line**) causes that command to act in a backward direction. Commands whose behavior with arguments deviates from this are noted.

When a command is described as *killing* text, the text deleted is saved for possible future retrieval (*yanking*). The killed text is saved in a *kill−ring*. Consecutive kills cause the text to be accumulated into one unit, which can be yanked all at once. Commands which do not kill text separate the chunks of text on the kill−ring.

The following is a list of the names of the commands and the default key sequences to which they are bound.

Commands for Moving

beginning−of−line (C−a)	Move to the start of the current line.
end−of−line (C−e)	Move to the end of the line.
forward−char (C−f)	Move forward a character.
backward−char (C−b)	Move back a character.
forward−word (M−f)	Move forward to the end of the next word. Words are composed of alphanumeric characters (letters and digits).
backward−word (M−b)	Move back to the start of this, or the previous, word. Words are composed of alphanumeric characters (letters and digits).
clear−screen (C−l)	Clear the screen leaving the current line at the top of the screen. With an argument, refresh the current line without clearing the screen.
redraw−current−line	Refresh the current line. By default, this is unbound.

Commands for Manipulating the History

accept–line (Newline, Return)
Accept the line regardless of where the cursor is. If this line is non–empty, add it to the history list according to the state of the **HISTCONTROL** variable. If the line is a modified history line, then restore the history line to its original state.

previous–history (C–p)
Fetch the previous command from the history list, moving back in the list.

next–history (C–n)
Fetch the next command from the history list, moving forward in the list.

beginning–of–history (M–<)
Move to the first line in the history.

end–of–history (M–>)
Move to the end of the input history, i.e., the line currently being entered.

reverse–search–history (C–r)
Search backward starting at the current line and moving 'up' through the history as necessary. This is an incremental search.

forward–search–history (C–s)
Search forward starting at the current line and moving 'down' through the history as necessary. This is an incremental search.

non–incremental–reverse–search–history (M–p)   Search backward through the history starting at the current line using a non–incremental search for a string supplied by the user.

non–incremental–forward–search–history (M–n)   Search forward through the history using a non–incremental search for a string supplied by the user.

history–search–forward
Search forward through the history for the string of characters between the start of the current line and the current point. This is a non-incremental search. By default, this command is unbound.

history–search–backward
Search backward through the history for the string of characters between the start of the current line and the current point. This is a non-incremental search. By default, this command is unbound.

yank–nth–arg (M–C–y)
Insert the first argument to the previous command (usually the second word on the previous line) at point (the current cursor position). With an argument *n*, insert the *n*th word from the previous command (the words in the previous command begin with word 0). A negative argument inserts the *n*th word from the end of the previous command.

yank–last–arg (M–., M–_)
Insert the last argument to the previous command (the last word on the previous line). With an argument, behave exactly like @code{yank-nth-arg}.

shell–expand–line (M–C–e)
Expand the line the way the shell does when it reads it. This performs alias and history expansion as well as all of the shell word expansions. See **HISTORY** EXPANSION below for a description of history expansion.

history–expand–line (M–^)
Perform history expansion on the current line. See **HISTORY** EXPANSION below for a description of history expansion.

insert-last-argument (M-., M-_) A synonym for **yank-last-arg**.

operate-and-get-next (C-o) Accept the current line for execution and fetch the next line relative to the current line from the history for editing. Any argument is ignored.

Commands for Changing Text

delete-char (C-d) Delete the character under the cursor. If point is at the beginning of the line, there are no characters in the line, and the last character typed was not **C-d**, then return **EOF**.

backward-delete-char (Rubout) Delete the character behind the cursor. When given a numeric argument, save the deleted text on the kill-ring.

quoted-insert (C-q, C-v) Add the next character that you type to the line verbatim. This is how to insert characters like **C-q**, for example.

tab-insert (C-v TAB) Insert a tab character.

self-insert (a, b, A, 1, !, ...) Insert the character typed.

transpose-chars (C-t) Drag the character before point forward over the character at point. Point moves forward as well. If point is at the end of the line, then transpose the two characters before point. Negative arguments don't work.

transpose-words (M-t) Drag the word behind the cursor past the word in front of the cursor moving the cursor over that word as well.

upcase-word (M-u) Uppercase the current (or following) word. With a negative argument, do the previous word, but do not move point.

downcase-word (M-l) Lowercase the current (or following) word. With a negative argument, do the previous word, but do not move point.

capitalize-word (M-c) Capitalize the current (or following) word. With a negative argument, do the previous word, but do not move point.

Killing and Yanking

kill-line (C-k) Kill the text from the current cursor position to the end of the line.

backward-kill-line (C-x C-Rubout) Kill backward to the beginning of the line.

unix-line-discard (C-u) Kill backward from point to the beginning of the line.

kill-whole-line Kill all characters on the current line, no matter where the cursor is. By default, this is unbound.

kill-word (M-d) Kill from the cursor to the end of the current word, or if between words, to the end of the next word. Word boundaries are the same as those used by **forward-word**.

backward-kill-word (M-Rubout) Kill the word behind the cursor. Word boundaries are the same as those used by **backward-word**.

unix-word-rubout (C-w) Kill the word behind the cursor, using white space as a word boundary. The word boundaries are different from backward-kill-word.

delete-horizontal-space Delete all spaces and tabs around point. By default, this is unbound.

yank (C-y) Yank the top of the kill ring into the buffer at the cursor.

yank-pop (M-y) Rotate the kill-ring, and yank the new top. Only works following **yank** or **yank-pop**.

Numeric Arguments

digit-argument (M-0, M-1, ..., M--)   Add this digit to the argument already accumulating, or start a new argument. M-- starts a negative argument.

universal-argument   Each time this is executed, the argument count is multiplied by four. The argument count is initially one, so executing this function the first time makes the argument count four. By default, this is not bound to a key.

Completing

complete (TAB)   Attempt to perform completion on the text before point. **Bash** attempts completion treating the text as a variable (if the text begins with **$**), username (if the text begins with ˜), hostname (if the text begins with @), or command (including aliases and functions) in turn. If none of these produces a match, filename completion is attempted.

possible-completions (M-?)   List the possible completions of the text before point.

insert-completions   Insert all completions of the text before point that would have been generated by **possible-completions**. By default, this is not bound to a key.

complete-filename (M-/)   Attempt filename completion on the text before point.

possible-filename-completions (C-x /)   List the possible completions of the text before point, treating it as a filename.

complete-username (M-˜)   Attempt completion on the text before point, treating it as a username.

possible-username-completions (C-x ˜)   List the possible completions of the text before point, treating it as a username.

complete-variable (M-$)   Attempt completion on the text before point, treating it as a shell variable.

possible-variable-completions (C-x $)   List the possible completions of the text before point, treating it as a shell variable.

complete-hostname (M-@)   Attempt completion on the text before point, treating it as a hostname.

possible-hostname-completions (C-x @)   List the possible completions of the text before point, treating it as a hostname.

complete-command (M-!)   Attempt completion on the text before point, treating it as a command name. Command completion attempts to match the text against aliases, reserved words, shell functions, builtins, and finally executable filenames, in that order.

possible-command-completions (C-x !)   List the possible completions of the text before point, treating it as a command name.

dynamic-complete-history (M-TAB)   Attempt completion on the text before point, comparing the text against lines from the history list for possible completion matches.

complete-into-braces (M-{)   Perform filename completion and return the list of possible completions enclosed within braces so the list is available to the shell (see **Brace** Expansion above).

Keyboard Macros

start-kbd-macro (C-x ()   Begin saving the characters typed into the current keyboard macro.

	end–kbd–macro (C-x))	Stop saving the characters typed into the current keyboard macro and save the definition.
	call–last–kbd–macro (C-x e)	Re-execute the last keyboard macro defined, by making the characters in the macro appear as if typed at the keyboard.

Miscellaneous

	re–read–init–file (C–x C–r)	Read in the contents of your init file, and incorporate any bindings or variable assignments found there.
	abort (C–g)	Abort the current editing command and ring the terminal's bell (subject to the setting of **bell–style**).
	do–uppercase–version (M–a, M–b, ...)	Run the command that is bound to the corresponding uppercase character.
	prefix–meta (ESC)	Metafy the next character typed. **ESC f** is equivalent to **Meta–f**.
	undo (C–_, C–x C–u)	Incremental undo, separately remembered for each line.
	revert–line (M–r)	Undo all changes made to this line. This is like typing the **undo** command enough times to return the line to its initial state.
	tilde–expand (M–~)	Perform tilde expansion on the current word.
	dump–functions	Print all of the functions and their key bindings to the readline output stream. If a numeric argument is supplied, the output is formatted in such a way that it can be made part of an *inputrc* file.
	display–shell–version (C–x C–v)	Display version information about the current instance of **bash**.
	emacs–editing–mode (C–e)	When in **vi** editing mode, this causes a switch to **emacs** editing mode.

HISTORY

When interactive, the shell provides access to the *command history*, the list of commands previously typed. The text of the last **HISTSIZE** commands (default 500) is saved in a history list. The shell stores each command in the history list prior to parameter and variable expansion (see **EXPANSION** above) but after history expansion is performed, subject to the values of the shell variables **command_oriented_history** and **HISTCONTROL**. On startup, the history is initialized from the file named by the variable **HISTFILE** (default *~/.bash_history*). **HISTFILE** is truncated, if necessary, to contain no more than **HISTFILESIZE** lines. The builtin command **fc** (see **SHELL BUILTIN COMMANDS** below) may be used to list or edit and re-execute a portion of the history list. The **history** builtin can be used to display the history list and manipulate the history file. When using the command-line editing, search commands are available in each editing mode that provide access to the history list. When an interactive shell exits, the last **HISTSIZE** lines are copied from the history list to **HISTFILE**. If **HISTFILE** is unset, or if the history file is unwritable, the history is not saved.

HISTORY EXPANSION

The shell supports a history expansion feature that is similar to the history expansion in **csh**. This section describes what syntax features are available. This feature is enabled by default for interactive shells, and can be disabled using the **H** option to the **set** builtin command (see **SHELL** BUILTIN COMMANDS below). Non-interactive shells do not perform history expansion.

History expansion is performed immediately after a complete line is read, before the shell breaks it into words. It takes place in two parts. The first is to determine which line from the previous history to use during substitution. The second is to select portions of that line for inclusion into the current one. The line selected from the previous history is the *event*, and the portions of that line that are acted upon are *words*. The line is broken into words in the same fashion as when reading input, so that several *metacharacter*–separated words surrounded by quotes are considered as one word. Only backslash (\) and single quotes can quote the history escape character, which is ! by default.

The shell allows control of the various characters used by the history expansion mechanism (see the description of **histchars** above under **Shell Variables**).

Event Designators

An event designator is a reference to a command line entry in the history list.

> ! Start a history substitution, except when followed by a **blank**, newline, = or (.
>
> !! Refer to the previous command. This is a synonym for '!–1'.
>
> !*n* Refer to command line *n*.
>
> !–*n* Refer to the current command line minus *n*.
>
> !*string* Refer to the most recent command starting with *string*.
>
> !?*string*[?] Refer to the most recent command containing *string*.
>
> ^*string1*^*string2*^ Quick substitution. Repeat the last command, replacing *string1* with *string2*. Equivalent to "!!:s/*string1*/*string2*/" (see **Modifiers** below).
>
> !# The entire command line typed so far.

Word Designators

A **:** separates the event specification from the word designator. It can be omitted if the word designator begins with a ^, $, *, or %. Words are numbered from the beginning of the line, with the first word being denoted by a 0 (zero).

> **0** (zero) The zeroth word. For the shell, this is the command word.
>
> *n* The *n*th word.
>
> ^ The first argument. That is, word 1.
>
> $ The last argument.
>
> % The word matched by the most recent '?*string*?' search.
>
> *x*–*y* A range of words; '–*y*' abbreviates '0–*y*'.
>
> * All of the words but the zeroth. This is a synonym for '*1–£*'. It is not an error to use * if there is just one word in the event; the empty string is returned in that case.
>
> **x*** Abbreviates *x*–£.
>
> **x**– Abbreviates *x*–£ like **x***, but omits the last word.

Modifiers

After the optional word designator, you can add a sequence of one or more of the following modifiers, each preceded by a ':'.

> h Remove a trailing pathname component, leaving only the head.
>
> r Remove a trailing suffix of the form *.xxx*, leaving the basename.
>
> e Remove all but the trailing suffix.
>
> t Remove all leading pathname components, leaving the tail.
>
> p Print the new command but do not execute it.
>
> q Quote the substituted words, escaping further substitutions.

BASH(1)   BASH(1)

      x   Quote the substituted words as with **q**, but break into words at **blanks** and newlines.

     s/old**/**new**/**   Substitute *new* for the first occurrence of *old* in the event line. Any delimiter can be used in place of **/**. The final delimiter is optional if it is the last character of the event line. The delimiter may be quoted in *old* and *new* with a single backslash. If & appears in *new*, it is replaced by *old*. A single backslash will quote the &.

     &   Repeat the previous substitution.

     g   Cause changes to be applied over the entire event line. This is used in conjunction with ':s' (e.g., ':gs*/old/new/*') or ':&'. If used with ':s', any delimiter can be used in place of /, and the final delimiter is optional if it is the last character of the event line.

ARITHMETIC EVALUATION

The shell allows arithmetic expressions to be evaluated, under certain circumstances (see the **let** builtin command and **Arithmetic Expansion**). Evaluation is done in long integers with no check for overflow, though division by 0 is trapped and flagged as an error. The following list of operators is grouped into levels of equal-precedence operators. The levels are listed in order of decreasing precedence.

      − +   unary minus and plus

      ! ˜   logical and bitwise negation

      * / %   multiplication, division, remainder

      + −   addition, subtraction

      << >>   left and right bitwise shifts

      <= >= < > comparison

      == !=   equality and inequality

      &   bitwise AND

      ^   bitwise exclusive OR

      | bitwise OR

      &&   logical AND

      || logical OR

      = *= /= %= += −= <<= >>= &= ^= |=   assignment

Shell variables are allowed as operands; parameter expansion is performed before the expression is evaluated. The value of a parameter is coerced to a long integer within an expression. A shell variable need not have its integer attribute turned on to be used in an expression.

Constants with a leading 0 are interpreted as octal numbers. A leading *0x* or *0X* denotes hexadecimal. Otherwise, numbers take the form [*base#*]n, where *base* is a decimal number between 2 and 36 representing the arithmetic base, and *n* is a number in that base. If *base* is omitted, then base 10 is used.

Operators are evaluated in order of precedence. Sub-expressions in parentheses are evaluated first and may override the precedence rules above.

SHELL BUILTIN COMMANDS

    : [*arguments*]   No effect; the command does nothing beyond expanding *arguments* and performing any specified redirections. A zero exit code is returned.

    . *filename* [*arguments*]

    source *filename* [*arguments*]   Read and execute commands from *filename* in the current shell environment and return the exit status of the last command executed from *filename*. If *filename* does not contain a slash, pathnames in **PATH** are used to find the directory containing *filename*. The file searched for in **PATH** need not be executable. The current directory is searched if no file is found in **PATH**. If any *arguments* are supplied, they become the positional parameters when *file* is executed. Otherwise the positional parameters are unchanged. The return status is the status of the last command exited within the script (0 if no commands are executed), and false if *filename* is not found.

alias [*name*[=*value*] ...]   **Alias** with no arguments prints the list of aliases in the form *name*=*value* on standard output. When arguments are supplied, an alias is defined for each *name* whose *value* is given. A trailing space in *value* causes the next word to be checked for alias substitution when the alias is expanded. For each *name* in the argument list for which no *value* is supplied, the name and value of the alias is printed. **Alias** returns true unless a *name* is given for which no alias has been defined.

bg [*jobspec*]   Place *jobspec* in the background, as if it had been started with **&**. If *jobspec* is not present, the shell's notion of the *current job* is used. **bg** *jobspec* returns 0 unless run when job control is disabled or, when run with job control enabled, if *jobspec* was not found or started without job control.

bind [−m *keymap*] [−lvd] [-q *name*]

bind [−m *keymap*] **-f** *filename*

bind [−m *keymap*] *keyseq*:*function-name*   Display current **readline** key and function bindings, or bind a key sequence to a **readline** function or macro. The binding syntax accepted is identical to that of *.inputrc*, but each binding must be passed as a separate argument; e.g., '"\C-x\C-r": re−read−init−file'. Options, if supplied, have the following meanings:

−m *keymap*   Use *keymap* as the keymap to be affected by the subsequent bindings. Acceptable *keymap* names are *emacs, emacs-standard, emacs-meta, emacs-ctlx, vi, vi-move, vi-command*, and *vi-insert*. *vi* is equivalent to *vi-command*; *emacs* is equivalent to *emacs-standard*.

−l   List the names of all **readline** functions

−v   List current function names and bindings

−d   Dump function names and bindings in such a way that they can be re-read

−f *filename*   Read key bindings from *filename*

−q *function*   Query about which keys invoke the named *function*

The return value is 0 unless an unrecognized option is given or an error occurred.

break [*n*]   Exit from within a **for**, **while**, or **until** loop. If *n* is specified, break *n* levels. *n* must be 1. If *n* is greater than the number of enclosing loops, all enclosing loops are exited. The return value is 0 unless the shell is not executing a loop when **break** is executed.

builtin *shell−builtin* [*arguments*]   Execute the specified shell builtin, passing it *arguments*, and return its exit status. This is useful when you wish to define a function whose name is the same as a shell builtin, but need the functionality of the builtin within the function itself. The **cd** builtin is commonly redefined this way. The return status is false if *shell−builtin* is not a shell builtin command.

cd [*dir*]   Change the current directory to *dir*. The variable **HOME** is the default *dir*. The variable **CDPATH** defines the search path for the directory containing *dir*. Alternative directory names are separated by a colon (:). A null directory name in **CDPATH** is the same as the current directory, i.e., ".". If *dir* begins with a slash (/), then **CD-PATH** is not used. An argument of – is equivalent to $OLDPWD . The return value is true if the directory was successfully changed; false otherwise.

command [-p**Vv**] *command* [*arg* ...] Run *command* with *args* suppressing the normal shell function lookup. Only builtin commands or commands found in the **PATH** are executed. If the **–p** option is given, the search for *command* is performed using a default value for **PATH** that is guaranteed to find all of the standard utilities. If either the **–V** or **–v** option is supplied, a description of *command* is printed. The **–v** option causes a single word indicating the command or pathname used to invoke *command* to be printed; the **–V** option produces a more verbose description. An argument of –– disables option checking for the rest of the arguments. If the **–V** or **–v** option is supplied, the exit status is 0 if *command* was found, and 1 if not. If neither option is supplied and an error occurred or *command* cannot be found, the exit status is 127. Otherwise, the exit status of the **command** builtin is the exit status of *command*.

continue [*n*] Resume the next iteration of the enclosing **for**, **while**, or **until** loop. If *n* is specified, resume at the *n*th enclosing loop. *n* must be 1. If *n* is greater than the number of enclosing loops, the last enclosing loop (the 'top–level' loop) is resumed. The return value is 0 unless the shell is not executing a loop when **continue** is executed.

declare [–**frxi**] [*name*[=*value*]]

typeset [–**frxi**] [*name*[=*value*]] Declare variables and/or give them attributes. If no *name*s are given, then display the values of variables instead. The options can be used to restrict output to variables with the specified attribute.

–f   Use function names only

–r   Make *name*s readonly. These names cannot then be assigned values by subsequent assignment statements.

–x   Mark *name*s for export to subsequent commands via the environment.

–i   The variable is treated as an integer; arithmetic evaluation (see **ARITHMETIC EVALUATION** '') '' is performed when the variable is assigned a value.

Using '+' instead of '–' turns off the attribute instead. When used in a function, makes *name*s local, as with the **local** command. The return value is 0 unless an illegal option is encountered, an attempt is made to define a function using "-f foo=bar", one of the *name*s is not a legal shell variable name, an attempt is made to turn off readonly status for a readonly variable, or an attempt is made to display a non-existant function with -f.

dirs [-l] [+/–n]   Display the list of currently remembered directories. Directories are added to the list with the **pushd** command; the **popd** command moves back up through the list.

+n   displays the *n*th entry counting from the left of the list shown by **dirs** when invoked without options, starting with zero.

–n   displays the *n*th entry counting from the right of the list shown by **dirs** when invoked without options, starting with zero.

–l   produces a longer listing; the default listing format uses a tilde to denote the home directory.

The return value is 0 unless an illegal option is supplied or *n* indexes beyond the end of the directory stack.

echo [**–neE**] [*arg* ...]   Output the *arg*s, separated by spaces. The return status is always 0. If **–n** is specified, the trailing newline is suppressed. If the **–e** option is given, interpretation of the following backslash-escaped characters is enabled. The **–E** option disables the interpretation of these escape characters, even on systems where they are interpreted by default.

\a	alert (bell)
\b	backspace
\c	suppress trailing newline
\f	form feed
\n	new line
\r	carriage return
\t	horizontal tab
\v	vertical tab
\\	backslash
\nnn	the character whose ASCII code is *nnn* (octal)

enable [**–n**] [**–all**] [*name* ...]   Enable and disable builtin shell commands. This allows the execution of a disk command which has the same name as a shell builtin without specifying a full pathname. If **–n** is used, each *name* is disabled; otherwise, *names* are enabled. For example, to use the **test** binary found via the **PATH** instead of the shell builtin version, type "enable -n test". If no arguments are given, a list of all enabled shell builtins is printed. If only **–n** is supplied, a list of all disabled builtins is printed. If only **–all** is supplied, the list printed includes all builtins, with an indication of whether or not each is enabled. **enable** accepts **–a** as a synonym for **–all**. The return value is 0 unless a *name* is not a shell builtin.

eval [*arg* ...]   The *args* are read and concatenated together into a single command. This command is then read and executed by the shell, and its exit status is returned as the value of the **eval** command. If there are no *args*, or only null arguments, **eval** returns true.

exec [[**–**] *command* [*arguments*]]   If *command* is specified, it replaces the shell. No new process is created. The *arguments* become the arguments to *command*. If the first argument is **–**, the shell places a dash in the zeroth arg passed to *command*. This is what login does. If the file cannot be executed for some reason, a non-interactive shell exits, unless the shell variable **no_exit_on_failed_exec** exists, in which case it returns failure. An interactive shell returns failure if the file cannot be executed. If *command* is not specified, any redirections take effect in the current shell, and the return status is 0.

exit [*n*]   Cause the shell to exit with a status of *n*. If *n* is omitted, the exit status is that of the last command executed. A trap on **EXIT** is executed before the shell terminates.

export [**–nf**] [*name*[=*word*]] ...

export –p   The supplied *names* are marked for automatic export to the environment of subsequently executed commands. If the **–f** option is given, the *names* refer to functions. If no *names* are given, or if the **–p** option is supplied, a list of all names that are exported in this shell is printed. The **-n** option causes the export property to be removed from the named variables. An argument of **--** disables option checking for the rest of the arguments. **export** returns an exit status of 0 unless an illegal option is encountered, one of the *names* is not a legal shell variable name, or **-f** is supplied with a *name* that is not a function.

fc [**-e** *ename*] [**-nlr**] [*first*] [*last*]
fc -s [*pat=rep*] [*cmd*]

Fix Command. In the first form, a range of commands from *first* to *last* is selected from the history list. *First* and *last* may be specified as a string (to locate the last command beginning with that string) or as a number (an index into the history list, where a negative number is used as an offset from the current command number). If *last* is not specified it is set to the current command for listing (so that **fc** -1 -10 prints the last 10 commands) and to *first* otherwise. If *first* is not specified it is set to the previous command for editing and -16 for listing.

The **-n** flag suppresses the command numbers when listing. The **-r** flag reverses the order of the commands. If the **-l** flag is given, the commands are listed on standard output. Otherwise, the editor given by *ename* is invoked on a file containing those commands. If *ename* is not given, the value of the **FCEDIT** variable is used, and the value of **EDITOR** if **FCEDIT** is not set. If neither variable is set, vi is used. When editing is complete, the edited commands are echoed and executed.

In the second form, *command* is re-executed after each instance of *pat* is replaced by *rep*. A useful alias to use with this is "r=fc -s", so that typing "r cc" runs the last command beginning with "cc" and typing "r" re-executes the last command.

If the first form is used, the return value is 0 unless an illegal option is encountered or *first* or *last* specify history lines out of range. If the **-e** option is supplied, the return value is the value of the last command executed or failure if an error occurs with the temporary file of commands. If the second form is used, the return status is that of the command re-executed, unless *cmd* does not specify a valid history line, in which case **fc** returns failure.

fg [*jobspec*]

Place *jobspec* in the foreground, and make it the current job. If *jobspec* is not present, the shell's notion of the *current job* is used. The return value is that of the command placed into the foreground, or failure if run when job control is disabled or, when run with job control enabled, if *jobspec* does not specify a valid job or *jobspec* specifies a job that was started without job control.

getopts *optstring name* [*args*]   **getopts** is used by shell procedures to parse positional parameters. *optstring* contains the option letters to be recognized; if a letter is followed by a colon, the option is expected to have an argument, which should be separated from it by white space. Each time it is invoked, **getopts** places the next option in the shell variable *name*, initializing *name* if it does not exist, and the index of the next argument to be processed into the variable **OPTIND**. **OPTIND** is initialized to 1 each time the shell or a shell script is invoked. When an option requires an argument, **getopts** places that argument into the variable **OPTARG**. The shell does not reset **OPTIND** automatically; it must be manually reset between multiple calls to **getopts** within the same shell invocation if a new set of parameters is to be used.

getopts can report errors in two ways. If the first character of *optstring* is a colon, *silent* error reporting is used. In normal operation diagnostic messages are printed when illegal options or missing option arguments are encountered. If the variable **OPTERR** is set to 0, no error message will be displayed, even if the first character of *optstring* is not a colon.

If an illegal option is seen, **getopts** places ? into *name* and, if not silent, prints an error message and unsets **OPTARG**. If **getopts** is silent, the option character found is placed in **OPTARG** and no diagnostic message is printed.

If a required argument is not found, and **getopts** is not silent, a question mark (**?**) is placed in *name*, **OPTARG** is unset, and a diagnostic message is printed. If **getopts** is silent, then a colon (**:**) is placed in *name* and **OPTARG** is set to the option character found.

getopts normally parses the positional parameters, but if more arguments are given in *args*, **getopts** parses those instead. **getopts** returns true if an option, specified or unspecified, is found. It returns false if the end of options is encountered or an error occurs.

hash [–r] [*name*] For each *name*, the full pathname of the command is determined and remembered. The –r option causes the shell to forget all remembered locations. If no arguments are given, information about remembered commands is printed. An argument of –– disables option checking for the rest of the arguments. The return status is true unless a *name* is not found or an illegal option is supplied.

help [*pattern*] Display helpful information about builtin commands. If *pattern* is specified, **help** gives detailed help on all commands matching *pattern*; otherwise a list of the builtins is printed. The return status is 0 unless no command matches *pattern*.

history [*n*]
history –rwan [*filename*] With no options, display the command history list with line numbers. Lines listed with a * have been modified. An argument of *n* lists only the last *n* lines. If a non-option argument is supplied, it is used as the name of the history file; if not, the value of **HISTFILE** is used. Options, if supplied, have the following meanings:

–a Append the "new" history lines (history lines entered since the beginning of the current **bash** session) to the history file

–n Read the history lines not already read from the history file into the current history list. These are lines appended to the history file since the beginning of the current **bash** session.

–r Read the contents of the history file and use them as the current history

–w Write the current history to the history file, overwriting the history file's contents.

The return value is 0 unless an illegal option is encountered or an error occurs while reading or writing the history file.

jobs [–lnp] [*jobspec* ...]

jobs –**x** *command* [*args* ...]   The first form lists the active jobs. The –**l** option lists process IDs in addition to the normal information; the –**p** option lists only the process ID of the job's process group leader. The –**n** option displays only jobs that have changed status since last notified. If *jobspec* is given, output is restricted to information about that job. The return status is 0 unless an illegal option is encountered or an illegal *jobspec* is supplied.

If the –**x** option is supplied, **jobs** replaces any *jobspec* found in *command* or *args* with the corresponding process group ID, and executes *command* passing it *args*, returning its exit status.

kill [-s *sigspec* | –*sigspec*] [*pid* | *jobspec*] ...

kill –**l** [*signum*]   Send the signal named by *sigspec* to the processes named by *pid* or *jobspec*. *sigspec* is either a signal name such as **SIGKILL** or a signal number. If *sigspec* is a signal name, the name is case insensitive and may be given with or without the **SIG** prefix. If *sigspec* is not present, then **SIGTERM** is assumed. An argument of –**l** lists the signal names. If any arguments are supplied when –**l** is given, the names of the specified signals are listed, and the return status is 0. An argument of —— disables option checking for the rest of the arguments. **kill** returns true if at least one signal was successfully sent, or false if an error occurs or an illegal option is encountered.

let *arg* [*arg* ...]   Each *arg* is an arithmetic expression to be evaluated (see **ARITHMETIC EVALUATION**). If the last *arg* evaluates to 0, **let** returns 1; 0 is returned otherwise.

local [*name*[=*value*] ...]   For each argument, create a local variable named *name*, and assign it *value*. When **local** is used within a function, it causes the variable *name* to have a visible scope restricted to that function and its children. With no operands, **local** writes a list of local variables to the standard output. It is an error to use **local** when not within a function. The return status is 0 unless **local** is used outside a function, or an illegal *name* is supplied.

logout   Exit a login shell.

popd [+/–n]   Removes entries from the directory stack. With no arguments, removes the top directory from the stack, and performs a **cd** to the new top directory.

+n   removes the *n*th entry counting from the left of the list shown by **dirs**, starting with zero. For example: "popd +0" removes the first directory, "popd +1" the second.

–n   removes the *n*th entry counting from the right of the list shown by **dirs**, starting with zero. For example: "popd -0" removes the last directory, "popd -1" the next to last.

BASH(1)   BASH(1)

If the **popd** command is successful, a **dirs** is performed as well, and the return status is 0. **popd** returns false if an illegal option is encountered, the directory stack is empty, a non-existent directory stack entry is specified, or the directory change fails.

    pushd [*dir*]

    pushd +/–n   Adds a directory to the top of the directory stack, or rotates the stack, making the new top of the stack the current working directory. With no arguments, exchanges the top two directories and returns 0, unless the directory stack is empty.

        +n   Rotates the stack so that the *n*th directory (counting from the left of the list shown by **dirs**) is at the top.

        –n   Rotates the stack so that the *n*th directory (counting from the right) is at the top.

        dir   adds *dir* to the directory stack at the top, making it the new current working directory.

If the **pushd** command is successful, a **dirs** is performed as well. If the first form is used, **pushd** returns 0 unless the cd to *dir* fails. With the second form, **pushd** returns 0 unless the directory stack is empty, a non-existant directory stack element is specified, or the directory change to the specified new current directory fails.

    pwd   Print the absolute pathname of the current working directory. The path printed contains no symbolic links if the **–P** option to the **set** builtin command is set. See also the description of **nolinks** under **Shell** Variables above). The return status is 0 unless an error occurs while reading the pathname of the current directory.

    read [**–r**] [*name* ...]   One line is read from the standard input, and the first word is assigned to the first *name*, the second word to the second *name*, and so on, with leftover words assigned to the last *name*. Only the characters in **IFS** are recognized as word delimiters. If no *names* are supplied, the line read is assigned to the variable **REPLY**. The return code is zero, unless end-of-file is encountered. If the **–r** option is given, a backslash-newline pair is not ignored, and the backslash is considered to be part of the line.

    readonly [**–f**] [*name* ...]

    readonly -p   The given *names* are marked readonly and the values of these *names* may not be changed by subsequent assignment. If the **–f** option is supplied, the functions corresponding to the *names* are so marked. If no arguments are given, or if the **–p** option is supplied, a list of all readonly names is printed. An argument of —— disables option checking for the rest of the arguments. The return status is 0 unless an illegal option is encountered, one of the *names* is not a legal shell variable name, or **–f** is supplied with a *name* that is not a function.

    return [*n*]   Causes a function to exit with the return value specified by *n*. If *n* is omitted, the return status is that of the last command executed in the function body. If used outside a function, but during execution of a script by the **.** (**source**) command, it causes the shell to stop executing that script and return either *n* or the exit status of the last command executed within the script as the exit status of the script. If used outside a function and not during execution of a script by **.**, the return status is false.

    set [——**abefhkmnptuvxldCHP**] [**-o** *option*] [*arg* ...]   Automatically mark variables which are modified or created for export to the environment of subsequent commands.

        –b   Cause the status of terminated background jobs to be reported immediately, rather than before the next primary prompt. (Also see **notify** under **Shell** Variables above).

	−e	Exit immediately if a *simple-command* (see **SHELL GRAMMAR** above) exits with a non−zero status. The shell does not exit if the command that fails is part of an *until* or *while* loop, part of an *if* statement, part of a **&&** or list, or if the command's return value is being inverted via **!**.
	−f	Disable pathname expansion.
	−h	Locate and remember function commands as functions are defined. Function commands are normally looked up when the function is executed.
	−k	All keyword arguments are placed in the environment for a command, not just those that precede the command name.
	−m	Monitor mode. Job control is enabled. This flag is on by default for interactive shells on systems that support it (see **JOB** CONTROL above). Background processes run in a separate process group and a line containing their exit status is printed upon their completion.
	−n	Read commands but do not execute them. This may be used to check a shell script for syntax errors. This is ignored for interactive shells.

−o *option-name*   The *option-name* can be one of the following:

allexport   Same as **−a**.

braceexpand   The shell performs brace expansion (see **Brace** Expansion above). This is on by default.

emacs   Use an emacs-style command line editing interface. This is enabled by default when the shell is interactive, unless the shell is started with the **−nolineediting** option.

errexit   Same as **−e**.

histexpand   Same as **−H**.

ignoreeof   The effect is as if the shell command 'IGNOREEOF=10' had been executed (see **Shell** Variables above).

interactive−comments   Allow a word beginning with **#** to cause that word and all remaining characters on that line to be ignored in an interactive shell (see **COMMENTS** above).

monitor   Same as **−m**.

noclobber   Same as **−C**.

noexec   Same as **−n**.

noglob   Same as **−f**.

nohash   Same as **−d**.

notify   Same as **−b**.

nounset   Same as **−u**.

physical   Same as **−P**.

posix   Change the behavior of bash where the default operation differs from the Posix 1003.2 standard to match the standard.

privileged   Same as **−p**.

verbose   Same as **−v**.

vi   Use a vi-style command line editing interface.

xtrace   Same as **−x**.

If no *option-name* is supplied, the values of the current options are printed.

	−p	Turn on *privileged* mode. In this mode, the file is not processed, and shell functions are not inherited from the environment. This is enabled automatically on startup if the effective user (group) id is not equal to the real user (group) id. Turning this option off causes the effective user and group ids to be set to the real user and group ids.

−t		Exit after reading and executing one command.
−u		Treat unset variables as an error when performing parameter expansion. If expansion is attempted on an unset variable, the shell prints an error message, and, if not interactive, exits with a non-zero status.
−v		Print shell input lines as they are read.
−x		After expanding each *simple-command*, **bash** displays the expanded value of **PS4**, followed by the command and its expanded arguments.
−l		Save and restore the binding of *name* in a **for** *name* [in **word**] command (see **SHELL** GRAMMAR above).
−d		Disable the hashing of commands that are looked up for execution. Normally, commands are remembered in a hash table, and once found, do not have to be looked up again.
−C		The effect is as if the shell command 'noclobber=' had been executed (see **Shell** Variables above).
−H		Enable **!** style history substitution. This flag is on by default when the shell is interactive.
−P		If set, do not follow symbolic links when performing commands such as **cd** which change the current directory. The physical directory is used instead.
−−		If no arguments follow this flag, then the positional parameters are unset. Otherwise, the positional parameters are set to the *args*, even if some of them begin with a −.
−		Signal the end of options, cause all remaining *args* to be assigned to the positional parameters. The −**x** and −**v** options are turned off. If there are no *args*, the positional parameters remain unchanged.

The flags are off by default unless otherwise noted. Using + rather than − causes these flags to be turned off. The flags can also be specified as options to an invocation of the shell. The current set of flags may be found in $− . After the option arguments are processed, the remaining *n args* are treated as values for the positional parameters and are assigned, in order, to $1 , $2 , ... $*n* . If no options or *args* are supplied, all shell variables are printed. The return status is always true unless an illegal option is encountered.

shift [*n*]		The positional parameters from *n*+1 ... are renamed to **....** Parameters represented by the numbers **$#** down to **$#**−*n*+1 are unset. If *n* is 0, no parameters are changed. If *n* is not given, it is assumed to be 1. *n* must be a non-negative number less than or equal to **$#**. If *n* is greater than **$#**, the positional parameters are not changed. The return status is greater than 0 if *n* is greater than or less than 0; otherwise 0.
suspend [−**f**]		Suspend the execution of this shell until it receives a **SIGCONT** signal. The −**f** option says not to complain if this is a login shell; just suspend anyway. The return status is 0 unless the shell is a login shell and −**f** is not supplied, or if job control is not enabled.
test *expr*		
[*expr*]		Return a status of 0 (true) or 1 (false) depending on the evaluation of the conditional expression *expr*. Expressions may be unary or binary. Unary expressions are often used to examine the status of a file. There are string operators and numeric comparison operators as well. Each operator and operand must be a separate argument. If *file* is of the form /dev/fd/*n*, then file descriptor *n* is checked.
−**b** *file*		True if *file* exists and is block special.
−**c** *file*		True if *file* exists and is character special.
−**d** *file*		True if *file* exists and is a directory.
−**e** *file*		True if *file* exists.
−**f** *file*		True if *file* exists and is a regular file.

BASH(1)   BASH(1)

-g *file*   True if *file* exists and is set-group-id.

-k *file*   True if *file* has its "sticky" bit set.

-L *file*   True if *file* exists and is a symbolic link.

-p *file*   True if *file* exists and is a named pipe.

-r *file*   True if *file* exists and is readable.

-s *file*   True if *file* exists and has a size greater than zero.

-S *file*   True if *file* exists and is a socket.

-t *fd*   True if *fd* is opened on a terminal.

-u *file*   True if *file* exists and its set-user-id bit is set.

-w *file*   True if *file* exists and is writable.

-x *file*   True if *file* exists and is executable.

-O *file*   True if *file* exists and is owned by the effective user id.

-G *file*   True if *file* exists and is owned by the effective group id.

file1 -nt *file2*   True if *file1* is newer (according to modification date) than *file2*.

file1 -ot *file2*   True if *file1* is older than file2.

file1 -ef *file*   True if *file1* and *file2* have the same device and inode numbers.

-z *string*   True if the length of *string* is zero.

-n *string*

string   True if the length of *string* is non–zero.

string1 = *string2*   True if the strings are equal.

string1 != *string2* True if the strings are not equal.

! *expr*   True if *expr* is false.

expr1 -a *expr2*   True if both *expr1* AND *expr2* are true.

expr1 -o *expr2*   True if either *expr1* OR *expr2* is true.

arg1 **OP** arg2   OP is one of -eq, -ne, -lt, -le, -gt, or -ge. These arithmetic binary operators return true if *arg1* is equal, not-equal, less-than, less-than-or-equal, greater-than, or greater-than-or-equal than *arg2*, respectively. *Arg1* and *arg2* may be positive integers, negative integers, or the special expression -l *string*, which evaluates to the length of *string*.

times   Print the accumulated user and system times for the shell and for processes run from the shell. The return status is 0.

trap [–l] [*arg*] [*sigspec*]   The command *arg* is to be read and executed when the shell receives signal(s) *sigspec*. If *arg* is absent or –, all specified signals are reset to their original values (the values they had upon entrance to the shell). If *arg* is the null string this signal is ignored by the shell and by the commands it invokes. *sigspec* is either a signal name defined in <*signal.h*>, or a signal number. If *sigspec* is **EXIT** (0) the command *arg* is executed on exit from the shell. With no arguments, **trap** prints the list of commands associated with each signal number. The –l option causes the shell to print a list of signal names and their corresponding numbers. An argument of — disables option checking for the rest of the arguments. Signals ignored upon entry to the shell cannot be trapped or reset. Trapped signals are reset to their original values in a child process when it is created. The return status is false if either the trap name or number is invalid; otherwise **trap** returns true.

type [–all] [–type | –path] *name* [*name* ...]   With no options, indicate how each *name* would be interpreted if used as a command name. If the –type flag is used, **type** prints a phrase which is one of *alias*, *keyword*, *function*, *builtin*, or *file* if *name* is an alias, shell reserved word, function, builtin, or disk file, respectively. If the name is not found, then nothing is printed, and an exit status of false is returned. If the **–path** flag is used, **type** either returns the name of the disk file that would be executed if *name* were specified as a command name, or nothing if **–type** would not return *file*. If a command is hashed, **–path** prints the hashed value, not necessarily the file that appears first in **PATH**. If the **–all** flag is used, **type** prints all of the places that contain an executable named *name*. This includes aliases and functions, if and only if the **–path** flag is not also used. The table of hashed commands is not consulted when using **–all**. **type** accepts **–a**, **–t**, and **–p** in place of **–all**, **–type**, and **–path**, respectively. An argument of —— disables option checking for the rest of the arguments. **type** returns true if any of the arguments are found, false if none are found.

ulimit [–SHacdfmstpnuv [*limit*]]   **Ulimit** provides control over the resources available to the shell and to processes started by it, on systems that allow such control. The value of *limit* can be a number in the unit specified for the resource, or the value **unlimited**. The **H** and **S** options specify that the hard or soft limit is set for the given resource. A hard limit cannot be increased once it is set; a soft limit may be increased up to the value of the hard limit. If neither **H** nor **S** is specified, the command applies to the soft limit. If *limit* is omitted, the current value of the soft limit of the resource is printed, unless the **H** option is given. When more than one resource is specified, the limit name and unit is printed before the value. Other options are interpreted as follows:

–a	all current limits are reported
–c	the maximum size of core files created
–d	the maximum size of a process's data segment
–f	the maximum size of files created by the shell
–m	the maximum resident set size
–s	the maximum stack size
–t	the maximum amount of cpu time in seconds
–p	the pipe size in 512-byte blocks (this may not be set)
–n	the maximum number of open file descriptors (most systems do not allow this value to be set, only displayed)
–u	the maximum number of processes available to a single user
–v	The maximum amount of virtual memory available to the shell

An argument of —— disables option checking for the rest of the arguments. If *limit* is given, it is the new value of the specified resource (the **–a** option is display only). If no option is given, then **–f** is assumed. Values are in 1024-byte increments, except for **–t**, which is in seconds, **–p**, which is in units of 512-byte blocks, and **–n** and **–u**, which are unscaled values. The return status is 0 unless an illegal option is encountered, a non-numeric argument other than **unlimited** is supplied as *limit*, or an error occurs while setting a new limit.

umask [–S] [*mode*]   The user file-creation mask is set to *mode*. If *mode* begins with a digit, it is interpreted as an octal number; otherwise it is interpreted as a symbolic mode mask similar to that accepted by *chmod*(1). If *mode* is omitted, or if the **–S** option is supplied, the current value of the mask is printed. The **–S** option causes the mask to be printed in symbolic form; the default output is an octal number. An argument of —— disables option checking for the rest of the arguments. The return status is 0 if the mode was successfully changed or if no *mode* argument was supplied, and false otherwise.

unalias [–a] [*name* ...] Remove *name*s from the list of defined aliases. If **–a** is supplied, all alias definitions are removed. The return value is true unless a supplied *name* is not a defined alias.

unset [–fv] [*name* ...] For each *name*, remove the corresponding variable or, given the **–f** option, function. An argument of —— disables option checking for the rest of the arguments. Note that **PATH**, **IFS**, **PPID**, **PS1**, **PS2**, **UID**, and **EUID** cannot be unset. If any of **RANDOM**, **SECONDS**, **LINENO**, or **HISTCMD** are unset, they lose their special properties, even if they are subsequently reset. The exit status is true unless a *name* does not exist or is non-unsettable.

wait [*n*] Wait for the specified process and return its termination status. *n* may be a process ID or a job specification; if a job spec is given, all processes in that job's pipeline are waited for. If *n* is not given, all currently active child processes are waited for, and the return status is zero. If *n* specifies a non-existant process or job, the return status is 127. Otherwise, the return status is the exit status of the last process or job waited for.

INVOCATION

A *login shell* is one whose first character of argument zero is a –, or one started with the **–login** flag.

An *interactive* shell is one whose standard input and output are both connected to terminals (as determined by *isatty*(3)), or one started with the **–i** option. **PS1** is set and includes **i** if **bash** is interactive, allowing a shell script or a startup file to test this state.

Login shells:
On login (subject to the **–noprofile** option):
if */etc/profile* exists, source it.

if ˜/.bash_profile exists, source it,
else if ˜/.bash_login exists, source it,
else if ˜/.profile exists, source it.

On exit:
if ˜/.bash_logout exists, source it.

Non-login interactive shells:
On startup (subject to the **–norc** and **–rcfile** options):
if ˜/.bashrc exists, source it.

Non-interactive shells:
On startup:
if the environment variable **ENV** is non-null, expand
it and source the file it names, as if the command
if ["$ENV"]; then . $ENV; fi
had been executed, but do not use **PATH** to search
for the pathname. When not started in Posix mode, bash
looks for **BASH_ENV** before **ENV**.

If Bash is invoked as **sh**, it tries to mimic the behavior of **sh** as closely as possible. For a login shell, it attempts to source only */etc/profile* and ˜/.profile, in that order. The **–noprofile** option may still be used to disable this behavior. A shell invoked as **sh** does not attempt to source any other startup files.

When **bash** is started in *posix* mode, as with the **–posix** command line option, it follows the Posix standard for startup files. In this mode, the **ENV** variable is expanded and that file sourced; no other startup files are read.

SEE ALSO

    Bash Features, Brian Fox and Chet Ramey

    The Gnu Readline Library, Brian Fox and Chet Ramey

    The Gnu History Library, Brian Fox and Chet Ramey

    A System V Compatible Implementation of 4.2BSD Job Control, David Lennert

    Portable Operating System Interface (POSIX) Part 2: Shell and Utilities, IEEE

    sh(1), *ksh*(1), *csh*(1)

    emacs(1), *vi*(1)

    readline(3)

FILES

/bin/bash	The **bash** executable
/etc/profile	The systemwide initialization file, executed for login shells
/.bash_profile	The personal initialization file, executed for login shells
/.bashrc	The individual per-interactive-shell startup file
/.inputrc	Individual *readline* initialization file

AUTHORS

Brian Fox, Free Software Foundation (primary author)
bfox@ai.MIT.Edu

Chet Ramey, Case Western Reserve University
chet@ins.CWRU.Edu

BUG REPORTS

If you find a bug in **bash,** you should report it. But first, you should make sure that it really is a bug, and that it appears in the latest version of **bash** that you have.

Once you have determined that a bug actually exists, mail a bug report to *bash–maintainers@prep.ai.MIT.Edu*. If you have a fix, you are welcome to mail that as well! Suggestions and 'philosophical' bug reports may be mailed to bug-bash@*prep.ai.MIT.Edu* or posted to the Usenet newsgroup **gnu.bash.bug**.

ALL bug reports should include:

    The version number of **bash**

    The hardware and operating system

    The compiler used to compile

    A description of the bug behaviour

    A short script or 'recipe' which exercises the bug

Comments and bug reports concerning this manual page should be directed to *chet@ins.CWRU.Edu*.

BUGS

It's too big and too slow.

There are some subtle differences between **bash** and traditional versions of **sh**, mostly because of the **POSIX** specification.

Aliases are confusing in some uses.

BIFF(1)

NAME
biff – be notified if mail arrives and who it is from

SYNOPSIS
biff [ny]

DESCRIPTION
Biff informs the system whether you want to be notified when mail arrives during the current terminal session.

Options supported by biff :

    n Disables notification.

    y Enables notification.

When mail notification is enabled, the header and first few lines of the message will be printed on your screen whenever mail arrives. A

    biff y

command is often included in the file .login or .profile to be executed at each login.

Biff operates asynchronously. For synchronous notification use the MAIL variable of sh(1) or the mail variable of csh(1).

SEE ALSO
csh(1), mail(1), sh(1), comsat(8)

HISTORY
The biff command appeared in BSD 4.0.

BSD 4   March 14, 1991   58

CAL(1)   CAL(1)

NAME

cal – displays a calendar

SYNOPSIS

cal [-jy] [month [year]]

DESCRIPTION

Cal displays a simple calendar. If arguments are not specified, the current month is displayed. The options are as follows:

- -j Display julian dates (days one-based, numbered from January 1).
- -y Display a calendar for the current year.

A single parameter specifies the year (1 - 9999) to be displayed; note the year must be fully specified:

> cal 89

will *not* display a calendar for 1989. Two parameters denote the month (1 - 12) and year. If no parameters are specified, the current month's calendar is displayed.

A year starts on Jan 1.

The Gregorian Reformation is assumed to have occurred in 1752 on the 3rd of September. By this time, most countries had recognized the reformation (although a few did not recognize it until the early 1900's.) Ten days following that date were eliminated by the reformation, so the calendar for that month is a bit unusual.

HISTORY

A cal command appeared in Version 6 AT&T UNIX.

CAT(1L)

NAME

cat – concatenate files and print on the standard output

SYNOPSIS

cat [–benstuvAET] [—-number] [—-number-nonblank] [—-squeeze-blank] [—-show-nonprinting] [—-show-ends] [—-show-tabs] [—-show-all] [—-help] [—-version] [file...]

DESCRIPTION

This manual page documents the GNU version of **cat**. **cat** writes the contents of each given file, or the standard input if none are given or when a file named '–' is given, to the standard output.

OPTIONS

–b, —-number-nonblank	Number all nonblank output lines, starting with 1.
–e	Equivalent to *–vE*.
–n, —-number	Number all output lines, starting with 1.
–s, —-squeeze-blank	Replace multiple adjacent blank lines with a single blank line.
–t	Equivalent to *–vT*.
–u	Ignored; for Unix compatibility.
–v, —-show-nonprinting	Display control characters except for LFD and TAB using '^' notation and precede characters that have the high bit set with 'M-'.
–A, —-show-all	Equivalent to *–vET*.
–E, —-show-ends	Display a '$' after the end of each line.
–T, —-show-tabs	Display TAB characters as '^I'.
—-help	Print a usage message and exit with a non-zero status.
—-version	Print version information on standard output then exit.

CHATTR(1)

NAME

chattr – change file attributes on a Linux second extended file system

SYNOPSIS

chattr [**–RV**] [**-v** version] [mode] *files*...

DESCRIPTION

chattr changes the files attributes on an second extended file system.

The format of a symbolic mode is +-=[Sacdisu].

The operator '+' causes the selected attributes to be added to the existing attributes of the files; '-' causes them to be removed; and '=' causes them to be the only attributes that the files have.

The letters 'Sacdisu' select the new attributes for the files: synchronous updates (S), append only (a), compressed (c), immutable (i), no dump (d), secure deletion (s), and undeletable (u).

OPTIONS

- *-R*   Recursively change attributes of directories and their contents.
- *-V*   Verbosely describe changed attributes.
- *-v* version   Set the files version.

ATTRIBUTES

A file with the 'a' attribute set can only be open in append mode for writing.

A file with the 'c' attribute set is automatically compressed on the disk by the kernel. A read from this file returns uncompressed data. A write to this file compresses data before storing them on the disk.

A file with the 'd' attribute set is not candidate for backup when the **dump**(8) program is run.

A file with the 'i' attribute cannot be modified: it cannot be deleted or renamed, no link can be created to this file and no data can be written to the file. Only the superuser can set or clear this attribute.

When a file with the 's' attribute set is deleted, its blocks are zeroed and written back to the disk.

When a file with the 'S' attribute set is modified, the changes are written synchronously on the disk; this is equivalent to the 'sync' mount option applied to a subset of the files.

When a file with the 'u' attribute set is deleted, its contents is saved. This allows the user to ask for its undeletion.

AUTHOR

chattr has been written by Remy Card <card@masi.ibp.fr>, the developer and maintainer of the ext2 fs.

BUGS AND LIMITATIONS

As of ext2 fs 0.5a, the 'c' and 'u' attribute are not honoured by the kernel code.

These attributes will be implemented in a future ext2 fs version.

AVAILABILITY

chattr is available for anonymous ftp from ftp.ibp.fr and tsx-11.mit.edu in /pub/linux/packages/ext2fs.

SEE ALSO

lsattr(1)

CHFN(1)

Linux Reference Manual

CHFN(1)

NAME

chfn – change your finger information

SYNOPSIS

chfn [–f full-name] [–o office] [–p office-phone] [–h home-phone] [–u] [–v] [username]

DESCRIPTION

chfn is used to change your finger information. This information is stored in the */etc/passwd* file, and is displayed by the **finger** program. The Linux **finger** command will display four pieces of information that can be changed by **chfn** : your real name, your work room and phone, and your home phone.

COMMAND LINE

Any of the four pieces of information can be specified on the command line. If no information is given on the command line, **chfn** enters interactive mode.

INTERACTIVE MODE

In interactive mode, **chfn** will prompt for each field. At a prompt, you can enter the new information, or just press return to leave the field unchanged. Enter the keyword "none" to make the field blank.

OPTIONS

–f, —-full-name	Specify your real name.
–o, —-office	Specify your office room number.
–p, —-office-phone	Specify your office phone number.
–h, —-home-phone	Specify your home phone number.
–u, —-help	Print a usage message and exit.
-v, —-version	Print version information and exit.

SEE ALSO

finger(1), **passwd**(5)

AUTHOR

Salvatore Valente <svalente@mit.edu>

CHGRP(1L) FSF CHGRP(1L)

NAME

chgrp – change the group ownership of files

SYNOPSIS

chgrp [–Rcfv] [—-recursive] [—-changes] [—-silent] [—-quiet] [—-verbose] [—-help] [—-version] group file...

DESCRIPTION

This manual page documents the GNU version of **chgrp**. **chgrp** changes the group ownership of each given file to the named group, which can be either a group name or a numeric group ID.

OPTIONS

    –c, —-changes   Verbosely describe only files whose ownership actually changes.

    –f, —-silent, —-quiet   Do not print error messages about files whose ownership cannot be changed.

    –v, —-verbose   Verbosely describe ownership changes.

    –R, —-recursive   Recursively change ownership of directories and their contents.

    —-help   Print a usage message on standard output and exit successfully.

    —-version   Print version information on standard output then exit successfully.

NAME

chkdupexe – find duplicate executables

SYNOPSIS

chkdupexe

DESCRIPTION

chkdupexe will scan many standard directories that hold executable, and report duplicates.

AUTHOR

Nicolai Langfeldt

BUGS

Requires GNU **ls**(1).

Search paths that point to the same directory will cause many bogus duplicates to be found. You might want to edit the script to eliminate some paths that are equivalent on your machine.

NAME

chmod – change the access permissions of files

SYNOPSIS

chmod [–Rcfv] [—recursive] [—changes] [—silent] [—quiet] [—verbose] [—help] [—version] mode file...

DESCRIPTION

This manual page documents the GNU version of **chmod**. **chmod** changes the permissions of each given file according to *mode*, which can be either a symbolic representation of changes to make, or an octal number representing the bit pattern for the new permissions.

The format of a symbolic mode is '[ugoa...][[+-=][rwxXstugo...]...][,...]'. Multiple symbolic operations can be given, separated by commas.

A combination of the letters 'ugoa' controls which users' access to the file will be changed: the user who owns it (u), other users in the file's group (g), other users not in the file's group (o), or all users (a). If none of these are given, the effect is as if 'a' were given, but bits that are set in the umask are not affected.

The operator '+' causes the permissions selected to be added to the existing permissions of each file; '-' causes them to be removed; and '=' causes them to be the only permissions that the file has.

The letters 'rwxXstugo' select the new permissions for the affected users: read (r), write (w), execute (or access for directories) (x), execute only if the file is a directory or already has execute permission for some user (X), set user or group ID on execution (s), save program text on swap device (t), the permissions that the user who owns the file currently has for it (u), the permissions that other users in the file's group have for it (g), and the permissions that other users not in the file's group have for it (o).

A numeric mode is from one to four octal digits (0-7), derived by adding up the bits with values 4, 2, and 1. Any omitted digits are assumed to be leading zeros. The first digit selects the set user ID (4) and set group ID (2) and save text image (1) attributes. The second digit selects permissions for the user who owns the file: read (4), write (2), and execute (1); the third selects permissions for other users in the file's group, with the same values; and the fourth for other users not in the file's group, with the same values.

chmod never changes the permissions of symbolic links; the **chmod** system call cannot change their permissions. This is not a problem since the permissions of symbolic links are never used. However, for each symbolic link listed on the command line, **chmod** changes the permissions of the pointed-to file. In contrast, **chmod** ignores symbolic links encountered during recursive directory traversals.

OPTIONS

–c, —changes Verbosely describe only files whose permissions actually change.

–f, —silent, —quiet Do not print error messages about files whose permissions cannot be changed.

–v, —verbose Verbosely describe changed permissions.

–R, —recursive Recursively change permissions of directories and their contents.

—help Print a usage message on standard output and exit successfully.

—version Print version information on standard output then exit successfully.

GNU File Utilities

CHOWN(1L)

NAME

chown – change the user and group ownership of files

SYNOPSIS

chown [–Rcfv] [—-recursive] [—-changes] [—-help] [—-version] [—-silent] [—-quiet] [—-verbose] [user][:.][group] file...

DESCRIPTION

This manual page documents the GNU version of **chown**. **chown** changes the user and/or group ownership of each given file, according to its first non-option argument, which is interpreted as follows. If only a user name (or numeric user ID) is given, that user is made the owner of each given file, and the files' group is not changed. If the user name is followed by a colon or dot and a group name (or numeric group ID), with no spaces between them, the group ownership of the files is changed as well. If a colon or dot but no group name follows the user name, that user is made the owner of the files and the group of the files is changed to that user's login group. If the colon or dot and group are given, but the user name is omitted, only the group of the files is changed; in this case, **chown** performs the same function as **chgrp**.

OPTIONS

–c, —-changes	Verbosely describe only files whose ownership actually changes.
–f, —-silent, —-quiet	Do not print error messages about files whose ownership cannot be changed.
–v, —-verbose	Verbosely describe ownership changes.
–R, —-recursive	Recursively change ownership of directories and their contents.
—-help	Print a usage message on standard output and exit successfully.
—-version	Print version information on standard output then exit successfully.

CHSH(1)

NAME

chsh – change your login shell

SYNOPSIS

chsh [–s shell] [–l] [–u] [–v] [username]

DESCRIPTION

chsh is used to change your login shell. If a shell is not given on the command line, **chsh** prompts for one.

VALID SHELLS

chsh will accept the full pathname of any executable file on the system. However, it will issue a warning if the shell is not listed in the */etc/shells* file.

OPTIONS

    –s, —-shell   Specify your login shell.

    –l, —-list-shells   Print the list of shells listed in */etc/shells* and exit.

    –u, —-help   Print a usage message and exit.

    -v, —-version   Print version information and exit.

SEE ALSO

login(1), **passwd**(5), **shells**(5)

AUTHOR

Salvatore Valente <svalente@mit.edu>

CTAGS(1) CTAGS(1)

NAME

ctags - Generates "tags" and (optionally) "refs" files

SYNOPSIS

ctags [-**BSstvraT**] *filesnames*...

DESCRIPTION

ctags generates the "tags" and "refs" files from a group of C source files. The "tags" file is used by Elvis' ":tag" command, control-] command, and -t option. The "refs" file is sometimes used by the *ref(1)* program.

Each C source file is scanned for #define statements and global function definitions. The name of the macro or function becomes the name of a tag. For each tag, a line is added to the "tags" file which contains:

- the name of the tag
- a tab character
- the name of the file containing the tag
- a tab character
- a way to find the particular line within the file.

The filenames list will typically be the names of all C source files in the current directory, like this:

$ ctags -stv *.[ch]

OPTIONS

-**B** Normally, ctags encloses regular expressions in slashes (/regexp/) which causes *elvis* to search from the top of the file. The -**B** flag causes ctags to enclose the regular expressions in question marks (?regexp?) so *elvis* will search backward from the bottom of the file. This rarely matters.

-**t** Include typedefs. A tag will be generated for each user-defined type. Also tags will be generated for struct and enum names. Types are considered to be global if they are defined in a header file, and static if they are defined in a C source file.

-**v** Include variable declarations. A tag will be generated for each variable, except for those that are declared inside the body of a function.

-**s** Include static tags. *Ctags* will normally put global tags in the "tags" file, and silently ignore the static tags. This flag causes both global and static tags to be added. The name of a static tag is generated by prefixing the name of the declared item with the name of the file where it is defined, with a colon in between. For example, "static foo(){}" in "bar.c" results in a tag named "bar.c:foo".

-**S** Include static tags, but make them look like global tags. Most tags-aware programs don't like the "filename:tagname" tags produced by the -s flag, so -S was added as an alternative. If *elvis* and *ref* are the only programs that read the tags file, then you don't need -S; otherwise you do.

-**r** This causes *ctags* to generate both "tags" and "refs". Without -**r**, it would only generate "tags".

-**a** Append to "tags", and maybe "refs". Normally, *ctags* overwrites these files each time it is invoked. This flag is useful when you have to many files in the current directory for you to list them on a single command-line; it allows you to split the arguments among several invocations.

-**T** This flag isn't available on all systems. UNIX has it, but most others don't. The -**T** flag prevents ctags from generating a "tags" file. This is useful when you want to generate a "refs" without changing "tags".

FILES

tags   A cross-reference that lists each tag name, the name of the source file that contains it, and a way to locate a particular line in the source file.

refs   The "refs" file contains the definitions for each tag in the "tags" file, and very little else. This file can be useful, for example, when licensing restrictions prevent you from making the source code to the standard C library readable by everybody, but you still everybody to know what arguments the library functions need.

BUGS

ctags is sensitive to indenting and line breaks. Consequently, it might not discover all of the tags in a file that is formatted in an unusual way.

SEE ALSO

elvis(1), refs(1)

AUTHOR

Steve Kirkendall
kirkenda@cs.pdx.edu

NAME

cksum – checksum and count the bytes in a file

SYNOPSIS

cksum [—help] [—version] [file...]

DESCRIPTION

This manual page documents the GNU version of **cksum**. **cksum** computes a cyclic redundancy check (CRC) for each named file, or the standard input if none are given or when a file named '–' is given. It prints the CRC for each file along with the number of bytes in the file, and the file name unless no arguments were given.

cksum is typically used to make sure that files have been transferred by unreliable means (such as netnews) have not been corrupted, by comparing the **cksum** output for the received files with the **cksum** output for the original files. The CRC algorithm is specified by the POSIX.2 standard. It is not compatible with the BSD or System V **sum** programs; it is more robust.

    —help   Print a usage message and exit with a non-zero status.

    —version   Print version information on standard output then exit.

CLEAR(1)

NAME
clear – clear terminal screen

SYNOPSIS
clear

DESCRIPTION
clear calls **tput**(1) with the *clear* argument. This causes **tput** to attempt to clear the screen checking the data in */etc/termcap* (for the GNU or BSD **tput**) or in the terminfo database (for the **ncurses tput**) and sending the appropriate sequence to the terminal. This command can be redirected to clear the screen of some other terminal.

SEE ALSO
reset(1), **stty**(1), **tput**(1)

AUTHOR
Rik Faith (faith@cs.unc.edu)

NAME

col – filter reverse line feeds from input

SYNOPSIS

col [-bfx] [-l num]

DESCRIPTION

Col filters out reverse (and half reverse) line feeds so the output is in the correct order with only forward and half forward line feeds, and replaces white-space characters with tabs where possible. This can be useful in processing the output of nroff(1) and tbl(1).

Col reads from standard input and writes to standard output.

The options are as follows:

- -b Do not output any backspaces, printing only the last character written to each column position.
- -f Forward half line feeds are permitted ("fine" mode). Normally characters printed on a half line boundary are printed on the following line.
- -x Output multiple spaces instead of tabs.
- -lnum Buffer at least num lines in memory. By default, 128 lines are buffered.

The control sequences for carriage motion that col understands and their decimal values are listed in the following table:

ESC7	reverse line feed (escape then 7)
ESC8	half reverse line feed (escape then 8)
ESC9	half forward line feed (escape then 9)
backspace	moves back one column (8); ignored in the first column
carriage return	(13)
newline	forward line feed (10); also does carriage return
shift in	shift to normal character set (15)
shift out	shift to alternate character set (14)
space	moves forward one column (32)
tab	moves forward to next tab stop (9)
vertical tab	reverse line feed (11)

All unrecognized control characters and escape sequences are discarded.

Col keeps track of the character set as characters are read and makes sure the character set is correct when they are output.

If the input attempts to back up to the last flushed line, col will display a warning message.

SEE ALSO

expand(1), nroff(1), tbl(1).

HISTORY

A col command appeared in Version 6 AT&T UNIX.

COLCRT(1)

NAME

colcrt – filter nroff output for CRT previewing

SYNOPSIS

colcrt [-] [-2] [file ...]

DESCRIPTION

Colcrt provides virtual half-line and reverse line feed sequences for terminals without such capability, and on which overstriking is destructive. Half-line characters and underlining (changed to dashing '–') are placed on new lines in between the normal output lines.

Available options:

- - Suppress all underlining. This option is especially useful for previewing *allboxed* tables from tbl(1).
- -2 Causes all half-lines to be printed, effectively double spacing the output. Normally, a minimal space output format is used which will suppress empty lines. The program never suppresses two consecutive empty lines, however. The -2 option is useful for sending output to the line printer when the output contains superscripts and subscripts which would otherwise be invisible.

EXAMPLES

A typical use of colcrt would be

```
tbl exum2.n | nroff --ms | colcrt -- | more
```

SEE ALSO

nroff(1), troff(1), col(1), more(1), ul(1)

BUGS

Should fold underlines onto blanks even with the - option so that a true underline character would show.

Can't back up more than 102 lines.

General overstriking is lost; as a special case '|' overstruck with '' or underline becomes '+.'

Lines are trimmed to 132 characters.

Some provision should be made for processing superscripts and subscripts in documents which are already double-spaced.

HISTORY

The colcrt command appeared in BSD 3.0.

COLRM(1)

NAME

colrm – remove columns from a file

SYNOPSIS

colrm [startcol [endcol]]

DESCRIPTION

Colrm removes selected columns from a file. Input is taken from standard input. Output is sent to standard output.

If called with one parameter the columns of each line will be removed starting with the specified column. If called with two parameters the columns from the first column to the last column will be removed.

Column numbering starts with column 1.

SEE ALSO

awk(1), column(1), expand(1), paste(1)

HISTORY

The colrm command appeared in BSD 3.0 .

COLUMN(1)

NAME
column - columnate lists

SYNOPSIS
column [-tx] [-ccolumns] [-ssep] [...file]

DESCRIPTION
The column utility formats its input into multiple columns. Rows are filled before columns. Input is taken from file operands, or, by default, from the standard input. Empty lines are ignored.

The options are as follows:

- -c Output is formatted for a display columns wide.
- -s Specify a set of characters to be used to delimit columns for the -t option.
- -t Determine the number of columns the input contains and create a table. Columns are delimited with whitespace, by default, or with the characters supplied using the -s option. Useful for pretty-printing displays.
- -x Fill columns before filling rows.

Column exits 0 on success, >0 if an error occurred.

ENVIRONMENT
- COLUMNS The environment variable COLUMNS is used to determine the size of the screen if no other information is available.

EXAMPLES
(printf "PERM LINKS OWNER SIZE MONTH DAY HH:MM/YEAR NAME"; ls -l | sed 1d) | column -t

SEE ALSO
colrm(1), ls(1), paste(1), sort(1)

HISTORY
The column command appeared in BSD 4.3 Reno.

NAME

comm – compare two sorted files line by line

SYNOPSIS

comm [–123] [—help] [—version] file1 file2

DESCRIPTION

This manual page documents the GNU version of **comm**. **comm** prints lines that are common, and lines that are unique, to two input files. The two files must be sorted before **comm** can be used. The file name '–' means the standard input.

With no options, **comm** produces three column output. Column one contains lines unique to *file1*, column two contains lines unique to *file2*, and column three contains lines common to both files.

OPTIONS

The options *–1*, *–2*, and *–3* suppress printing of the corresponding columns.

    —-help   Print a usage message and exit with a non-zero status.

    —-version   Print version information on standard output then exit.

NAME

cp – copy files

SYNOPSIS

cp [options] source dest
cp [options] source... directory
Options:
[–abdfilprsuvxPR] [–S backup-suffix] [–V {numbered,existing,simple}] [—backup] [—no-dereference] [—force] [—interactive] [—one-file-system] [—preserve] [—recursive] [—update] [—verbose] [—suffix=backup-suffix]

[—version-control={numbered,existing,simple}] [—archive] [—parents] [—link] [—symbolic-link] [—help] [—version]

DESCRIPTION

This manual page documents the GNU version of **cp**. If the last argument names an existing directory, **cp** copies each other given file into a file with the same name in that directory. Otherwise, if only two files are given, it copies the first onto the second. It is an error if the last argument is not a directory and more than two files are given. By default, it does not copy directories.

OPTIONS

–a, —-archive Preserve as much as possible of the structure and attributes of the original files in the copy. The same as *–dpR*.

–b, —-backup Make backups of files that are about to be overwritten or removed.

–d, —-no-dereference Copy symbolic links as symbolic links rather than copying the files that they point to, and preserve hard link relationships between source files in the copies.

–f, —-force Remove existing destination files.

–i, —-interactive Prompt whether to overwrite existing regular destination files.

–l, —-link Make hard links instead of copies of non-directories.

–P, —-parents Form the name of each destination file by appending to the target directory a slash and the specified name of the source file. The last argument given to **cp** must be the name of an existing directory. For example, the command 'cp —parents a/b/c existing_dir' copies the file *a/b/c* to *existing_dir/a/b/c,* creating any missing intermediate directories.

–p, —-preserve Preserve the original files' owner, group, permissions, and timestamps.

–r Copy directories recursively, copying all non-directories as if they were regular files.

–s, —-symbolic-link Make symbolic links instead of copies of non-directories. All source filenames must be absolute (starting with '/') unless the destination files are in the current directory. This option produces an error message on systems that do not support symbolic links.

–u, —-update Do not copy a nondirectory that has an existing destination with the same or newer modification time.

–v, —-verbose Print the name of each file before copying it.

–x, —-one-file-system Skip subdirectories that are on different filesystems from the one that the copy started on.

–R, —-recursive Copy directories recursively.

—-help Print a usage message on standard output and exit successfully.

—-version Print version information on standard output then exit successfully.

-S, —suffix backup-suffix   The suffix used for making simple backup files can be set with the **SIMPLE_BACKUP_SUFFIX** environment variable, which can be overridden by this option. If neither of those is given, the default is '~', as it is in Emacs.

-V, —version-control {numbered,existing,simple}   The type of backups made can be set with the **VERSION_CONTROL** environment variable, which can be overridden by this option. If **VERSION_CONTROL** is not set and this option is not given, the default backup type is 'existing'. The value of the **VERSION_CONTROL** environment variable and the argument to this option are like the GNU Emacs 'version-control' variable; they also recognize synonyms that are more descriptive. The valid values are (unique abbreviations are accepted):

't' or 'numbered'   Always make numbered backups.

'nil' or 'existing'   Make numbered backups of files that already have them, simple backups of the others.

'never' or 'simple'   Always make simple backups.

CRONTAB(1)

NAME

crontab – manipulate per-user crontabs (Dillon's Cron)

SYNOPSIS

crontab file [-u user] – replace crontab from file

crontab - [-u user] – replace crontab from stdin

crontab -l [user] – list crontab for user

crontab -e [user] – edit crontab for user

crontab -d [user] – delete crontab for user

crontab -c dir – specify crontab directory

DESCRIPTION

crontab manipulates the crontab for a particular user. Only the superuser may specify a different user and/or crontab directory. Generally the -e option is used to edit your crontab. crontab will use /usr/bin/vi or the editor specified by your VISUAL environment variable to edit the crontab.

Unlike other crond/crontabs, this crontab does not try to do everything under the sun. Frankly, a shell script is much more able to manipulate the environment then cron and I see no particular reason to use the user's shell (from his password entry) to run cron commands when this requires special casing of non-user crontabs, such as those for UUCP. When a crontab command is run, this crontab runs it with /bin/sh and sets up only three environment variables: USER, HOME, and SHELL.

crond automatically detects changes in the time. Reverse-indexed time changes less then an hour old will NOT re-run crontab commands already issued in the recovered period. Forward-indexed changes less then an hour into the future will issue missed commands exactly once. Changes greater then an hour into the past or future cause crond to resynchronize and not issue missed commands. No attempt will be made to issue commands lost due to a reboot, and commands are not reissued if the previously issued command is still running. For example, if you have a crontab command 'sleep 70' that you wish to run once a minute, cron will only be able to issue the command once every two minutes. If you do not like this feature, you can run your commands in the background with an '&'.

The crontab format is roughly similar to that used by vixiecron, but without complex features. Individual fields may contain a time, a time range, a time range with a skip factor, a symbolic range for the day of week and month in year, and additional subranges delimited with commas. Blank lines in the crontab or lines that begin with a hash (#) are ignored. If you specify both a day in the month and a day of week, the result is effectively ORd... the crontab entry will be run on the specified day of week and on the specified day in the month.

```
# MIN HOUR DAY MONTH DAYOFWEEK COMMAND
# at 6:10 a.m. every day
10 6 * * * date

# every two hours at the top of the hour
0 */2 * * * date

# every two hours from 11p.m. to 7a.m., and at 8a.m.
0 23-7/2,8 * * * date

# at 11:00 a.m. on the 4th and on every mon, tue, wed
0 11 4 * mon-wed date

# 4:00 a.m. on january 1st
0 4 1 jan * date
```

once an hour, all output appended to log file
0 4 1 jan * date >>/var/log/messages 2>&1

The command portion of the line is run with **/bin/sh** −c <command> and may therefore contain any valid bourne shell command. A common practice is to run your command with **exec** to keep the process table uncluttered. It is also common to redirect output to a log file. If you do not, and the command generates output on stdout or stderr, the result will be mailed to the user in question. If you use this mechanism for special users, such as UUCP, you may want to create an alias for the user to direct the mail to someone else, such as root or postmaster.

Internally, this cron uses a quick indexing system to reduce CPU overhead when looking for commands to execute. Several hundred crontabs with several thousand entries can be handled without using noticable CPU resources.

BUGS

Ought to be able to have several crontab files for any given user, as an organizational tool.

AUTHOR

Matthew Dillon (dillon@apollo.west.oic.com)

CSPLIT(1L)

NAME

csplit – split a file into sections determined by context lines

SYNOPSIS

csplit [–sqkz] [–f prefix] [–b suffix] [–n digits] [—-prefix=prefix] [—-suffix–format=suffix] [—-digits=digits] [—-quiet] [—-silent] [—-keep-files] [—-elide–empty–files] [—-help] [—-version] file pattern...

DESCRIPTION

This manual page documents the GNU version of **csplit**. **csplit** creates zero or more output files containing sections of the given input *file*, or the standard input if the name '–' is given. By default, **csplit** prints the number of bytes written to each output file after it has been created.

The contents of the output files are determined by the *pattern* arguments. An error occurs if a pattern argument refers to a nonexistent line of the input file, such as if no remaining line matches a given regular expression. After all the given patterns have been matched, any remaining output is copied into one last output file. The types of pattern arguments are:

> *line*
>> Create an output file containing the current line up to (but not including) line *line* (a positive integer) of the input file. If followed by a repeat count, also create an output file containing the next *line* lines of the input file once for each repeat.

> */regexp/[offset]*
>> Create an output file containing the current line up to (but not including) the next line of the input file that contains a match for *regexp*. The optional *offset* is a '+' or '–' followed by a positive integer. If it is given, the input up to the matching line plus or minus *offset* is put into the output file, and the line after that begins the next section of input.

> *%regexp%[offset]*
>> Like the previous type, except that it does not create an output file, so that section of the input file is effectively ignored.

> *{repeat-count}*
>> Repeat the previous pattern *repeat-count* (a positive integer) additional times. An asterisk may be given in place of the (integer) repeat count, in which case the preceeding pattern is repeated as many times as necessary until the input is exausted.

The output file names consist of a prefix followed by a suffix. By default, the suffix is merely an ascending linear sequence of two-digit decimal numbers starting with 00 and ranging up to 99, however this default may be overridden by either the —-*digits* option or by the —-*suffix–format* option. (See below.) In any case, concatenating the output files in sorted order by file name produces the original input file, in order. The default output file name prefix is 'xx'.

By default, if **csplit** encounters an error or receives a hangup, interrupt, quit, or terminate signal, it removes any output files that it has created so far before it exits.

OPTIONS

> *–f, —-prefix=prefix*   Use *prefix* as the output file name prefix string.

> *–b, —-suffix–format=suffix*   Use *suffix* as the output file name suffix string. When this option is specified, the suffix string must include exactly one printf(3) style conversion specification (such as %d, possibly including format specification flags, a field width, a precision specifications, or all of these kinds of modifiers). The conversion specification must be suitable for converting a binary integer argument to readable form. Thus, only 'd', 'i', 'u', 'o', 'x', and 'X' format specifiers

CSPLIT(1L)　　　　　　　　　　FSF　　　　　　　　　　CSPLIT(1L)

are allowed. The entire suffix string is given (with the current output file number) to sprintf(3) to form the file name suffixes for each of the individual output files in turn. Note that when this option is used, the —-*digits* option is ignored.

–n, —-digits=digits　　　Use output file names containing numbers that are *digits* digits long instead of the default 2.

–k, —-keep-files　　　Do not remove output files when errors are encountered.

–z, —-elide–empty–files　　　Suppress the generation of zero-length output files. (In cases where the section delimiters of the input file are supposed to mark the first lines of each of the sections, the first output file will generally be a zero-length file unless you use this option.) Note that the output file sequence numbers will always run consecutively, starting from 0, even in cases where zero-length output sections are suppressed due to the use of this option.

–s, –q, —-silent, —-quiet　　Do not print counts of output file sizes.

—-help　　　Print a usage message and exit with a non-zero status.

—-version　　　Print version information on standard output then exit.

cu(1)   cu(1)

NAME

cu – Call up another system

SYNOPSIS

cu [options] [system | phone | "dir"]

DESCRIPTION

The *cu* command is used to call up another system and act as a dial in terminal. It can also do simple file transfers with no error checking.

cu takes a single argument, besides the options. If the argument is the string "dir" cu will make a direct connection to the port. This may only be used by users with write access to the port, as it permits reprogramming the modem.

Otherwise, if the argument begins with a digit, it is taken to be a phone number to call. Otherwise, it is taken to be the name of a system to call. The **–z** or **––system** option may be used to name a system beginning with a digit, and the **–c** or **––phone** option may be used to name a phone number that does not begin with a digit.

cu locates a port to use in the UUCP configuration files. If a simple system name is given, it will select a port appropriate for that system. The **–p**, **––port**, **–l**, **––line**, **–s** and **––speed** options may be used to control the port selection.

When a connection is made to the remote system, *cu* forks into two processes. One reads from the port and writes to the terminal, while the other reads from the terminal and writes to the port.

cu provides several commands that may be used during the conversation. The commands all begin with an escape character, initially ~ (tilde). The escape character is only recognized at the beginning of a line. To send an escape character to the remote system at the start of a line, it must be entered twice. All commands are either a single character or a word beginning with % (percent sign).

cu recognizes the following commands:

~. Terminate the conversation.

~! command   Run command in a shell. If command is empty, starts up a shell.

~$ command   Run command, sending the standard output to the remote system.

~| command   Run command, taking the standard input from the remote system.

~+ command   Run command, taking the standard input from the remote system and sending the standard output to the remote system.

~#, ~%break   Send a break signal, if possible.

~c directory, ~%cd directory   Change the local directory.

~> file   Send a file to the remote system. This just dumps the file over the communication line. It is assumed that the remote system is expecting it.

~<   Receive a file from the remote system. This prompts for the local file name and for the remote command to execute to begin the file transfer. It continues accepting data until the contents of the **eofread** variable are seen.

~p from to, ~%put from to   Send a file to a remote Unix system. This runs the appropriate commands on the remote system.

~t from to, ~%take from to   Retrieve a file from a remote Unix system. This runs the appropriate commands on the remote system.

~s variable value   Set a *cu* variable to the given value. If value is not given, the variable is set to **true**.

~! variable   Set a *cu* variable to **false**.

~z   Suspend the cu session. This is only supported on some systems. On systems for which ^Z may be used to suspend a job, ~^Z will also suspend the session.

Taylor UUCP 1.05   83

~%nostop   Turn off XON/XOFF handling.

~%stop   Turn on XON/XOFF handling.

~v   List all the variables and their values.

~?   List all commands.

cu also supports several variables. They may be listed with the ~v command, and set with the ~s or ~! commands.

escape   The escape character. Initially ~ (tilde).

delay   If this variable is true, *cu* will delay for a second after recognizing the escape character before printing the name of the local system. The default is true.

eol   The list of characters which are considered to finish a line. The escape character is only recognized after one of these is seen. The default is carriage return, ^U, ^C, ^O, ^D, ^S, ^Q, ^R.

binary   Whether to transfer binary data when sending a file. If this is false, then newlines in the file being sent are converted to carriage returns. The default is false.

binary-prefix   A string used before sending a binary character in a file transfer, if the **binary** variable is true. The default is ^Z.

echo-check   Whether to check file transfers by examining what the remote system echoes back. This probably doesn't work very well. The default is false.

echonl   The character to look for after sending each line in a file. The default is carriage return.

timeout   The timeout to use, in seconds, when looking for a character, either when doing echo checking or when looking for the **echonl** character. The default is 30.

kill   The character to use delete a line if the echo check fails. The default is ^U.

resend   The number of times to resend a line if the echo check continues to fail. The default is 10.

eofwrite   The string to write after sending a file with the ~> command. The default is ^D.

eofread   The string to look for when receiving a file with the ~< command. The default is $, which is intended to be a typical shell prompt.

verbose   Whether to print accumulated information during a file transfer. The default is true.

OPTIONS

The following options may be given to *cu*.

-e, ---parity=even	Use even parity.
-o, ---parity=odd	Use odd parity.
---**parity=none**	Use no parity. No parity is also used if both **-e** and **-o** are given.
-h, ---halfduplex	Echo characters locally (half-duplex mode).
-z system, ---system system	The system to call.
-c phone-number, ---phone phone-number	The phone number to call.
-p port, ---port port	Name the port to use.
-a port	Equivalent to ---**port** port.
-l line, ---line line	Name the line to use by giving a device name. This may be used to dial out on ports that are not listed in the UUCP configuration files. Write access to the device is required.
-s speed, ---speed speed	The speed (baud rate) to use.

–*#*		Where *#* is a number, equivalent to ––**speed** *#*.
–**n**, ––prompt		Prompt for the phone number to use.
–**d**		Enter debugging mode. Equivalent to –**debug** all.
–**x** type, ––debug type		Turn on particular debugging types. The following types are recognized: abnormal, chat, handshake, uucp-proto, proto, port, config, spooldir, execute, incoming, outgoing. Only abnormal, chat, handshake, port, config, incoming and outgoing are meaningful for *cu*.
		Multiple types may be given, separated by commas, and the ––**debug** option may appear multiple times. A number may also be given, which will turn on that many types from the foregoing list; for example, ––**debug** 2 is equivalent to ––**debug** abnormal,chat. ––**debug** all may be used to turn on all debugging options.
–**I** file, ––config file		Set configuration file to use. This option may not be available, depending upon how *cu* was compiled.
–**v**, ––version		Report version information and exit.
––**help**		Print a help message and exit.

BUGS

This program does not work very well.

FILES

The file name may be changed at compilation time, so this is only an approximation.

/usr/lib/uucp/config - Configuration file.

AUTHOR

Ian Lance Taylor <ian@airs.com>

NAME

cut – remove sections from each line of files

SYNOPSIS

cut {–b byte-list, —bytes=byte-list} [–n] [—help] [—version] [file...]

cut {–c character-list, —characters=character-list} [—help] [—version] [file...]

cut {–f field-list, —fields=field-list} [–d delim] [–s] [—delimiter=delim] [—only-delimited] [—help] [—version] [file...]

DESCRIPTION

This manual page documents the GNU version of **cut**. **cut** prints sections of each line of each input file, or the standard input if no files are given. A file name of '-' means standard input. Which sections are printed is selected by the options.

OPTIONS

The *byte-list*, *character-list*, and *field-list* are one or more numbers or ranges (two numbers separated by a dash) separated by commas. The first byte, character, and field are numbered 1. Incomplete ranges may be given: '–m' means '1–m'; 'n–' means 'n' through end of line or last field.

–b, —bytes byte-list	Print only the bytes in positions listed in *byte-list*. Tabs and backspaces are treated like any other character; they take up 1 byte.
–c, —characters character-list	Print only characters in positions listed in *character-list*. The same as –b for now, but internationalization will change that. Tabs and backspaces are treated like any other character; they take up 1 character.
–f, —fields field-list	Print only the fields listed in *field-list*. Fields are separated by a TAB by default.
–d, —delimiter delim	For –f, fields are separated by the first character in *delim* instead of by TAB.
–n	Do not split multibyte characters (no-op for now).
–s, —only-delimited	For –f, do not print lines that do not contain the field separator character.
—help	Print a usage message and exit with a non-zero status.
—version	Print version information on standard output then exit.

DATE(1)　　　　　　　　　　　　　　　　　　　　　　　　　　　　DATE(1)

NAME
date – show and set date and time

SYNOPSIS
date [**–u**] [**–c**] [**–n**] [**–d** dsttype] [**–t** minutes-west] [**–a** [+|-]*sss.fff*] [+*format*] [[*yyyy*]*mmddhhmm*[*yy*][.*ss*]]

DESCRIPTION
Date without arguments writes the date and time to the standard output in the form

　　　　　　　　　　　　　Wed Mar 8 14:54:40 EST 1989

with **EST** replaced by the local time zone's abbreviation (or by the abbreviation for the time zone specified in the **TZ** environment variable if set). The exact output format depends on the locale.

If a command-line argument starts with a plus sign ('+'), the rest of the argument is used as a *format* that controls what appears in the output. In the format, when a percent sign ('%') appears, it and the character after it are not output, but rather identify part of the date or time to be output in a particular way (or identify a special character to output):

	Sample output	Explanation
%a	Wed	Abbreviated weekday name*
%A	Wednesday	Full weekday name*
%b	Mar	Abbreviated month name*
%B	March	Full month name*
%c	Wed Mar 08 14:54:40 1989	Date and time*
%C	19	Century
%d	08	Day of month (always two digits)
%D	03/08/89	Month/day/year (eight characters)
%e	8	Day of month (leading zero blanked)
%h	Mar	Abbreviated month name*
%H	14	24-hour-clock hour (two digits)
%I	02	12-hour-clock hour (two digits)
%j	067	Julian day number (three digits)
%k	2	12-hour-clock hour (leading zero blanked)
%l	14	24-hour-clock hour (leading zero blanked)
%m	03	Month number (two digits)
%M	54	Minute (two digits)
	Sample output	Explanation
%n	\n	newline character
%p	PM	AM/PM designation
%r	02:54:40 PM	Hour:minute:second AM/PM designation
%R	14:54	Hour:minute
%S	40	Second (two digits)
%t	\t	tab character
%T	14:54:40	Hour:minute:second
%U	10	Sunday-based week number (two digits)　　* The
%w	3	Day number (one digit, Sunday is 0)
%W	10	Monday-based week number (two digits)
%x	03/08/89	Date*
%X	14:54:40	Time*
%y	89	Last two digits of year
%Y	1989	Year in full
%Z	EST	Time zone abbreviation
%+	Wed Mar 8 14:54:40 EST 1989	Default output format*

exact output depends on the locale.

If a character other than one of those shown above appears after a percent sign in the format, that following character is output. All other characters in the format are copied unchanged

DATE(1)   DATE(1)

to the output; a newline character is always added at the end of the output.

In Sunday-based week numbering, the first Sunday of the year begins week 1; days preceding it are part of "week 0." In Monday-based week numbering, the first Monday of the year begins week 1.

To set the date, use a command line argument with one of the following forms:

1454	24-hour-clock hours (first two digits) and minutes	
081454	Month day (first two digits), hours, and minutes	
03081454	Month (two digits, January is 01), month day, hours, minutes	
8903081454	Year, month, month day, hours, minutes	
0308145489	Month, month day, hours, minutes, year	If the cen-
	(on System V-compatible systems)	
030814541989	Month, month day, hours, minutes, four-digit year	
198903081454	Four-digit year, month, month day, hours, minutes	

tury, year, month, or month day is not given, the current value is used. Any of the above forms may be followed by a period and two digits that give the seconds part of the new time; if no seconds are given, zero is assumed.

These options are available:

–u or **–c**   Use GMT when setting and showing the date and time.

–n   Do not notify other networked systems of the time change.

–d *dsttype*   Set the kernel-stored Daylight Saving Time type to the given value. (The kernel-stored DST type is used mostly by "old" binaries.)

–t *minutes-west*   Set the kernel-stored "minutes west of GMT" value to the one given on the command line. (The kernel-stored DST type is used mostly by "old" binaries.)

–a *adjustment*   Change the time forward (or backward) by the number of seconds (and fractions thereof) specified in the *adjustment* argument. Either the seconds part or the fractions part of the argument (but not both) may be omitted. On BSD-based systems, the adjustment is made by changing the rate at which time advances; on System-V-based systems, the adjustment is made by changing the time.

FILES

/usr/lib/locale/*L*/LC_TIME description of time locale *L*
/usr/local/etc/zoneinfo time zone information directory
/usr/local/etc/zoneinfo/localtime local time zone file
/usr/local/etc/zoneinfo/posixrules used with POSIX-style TZ's
/usr/local/etc/zoneinfo/GMT for UTC leap seconds

If **/usr/local/etc/zoneinfo/GMT** is absent, UTC leap seconds are loaded from **/usr/local/etc/zoneinfo/posixrules**.

DD(1L)   FSF   DD(1L)

NAME

dd – convert a file while copying it data dumper

SYNOPSIS

dd [——help] [——version] [if=file] [of=file] [ibs=bytes] [obs=bytes] [bs=bytes] [cbs=bytes] [skip=blocks] [seek=blocks] [count=blocks] [conv={ascii, ebcdic, ibm, block, unblock, lcase, ucase, swab, noerror, notrunc, sync}]

DESCRIPTION

This manual page documents the GNU version of **dd**. **dd** copies a file (from the standard input to the standard output, by default) with a user-selectable blocksize, while optionally performing conversions on it.

OPTIONS

Numbers can be followed by a multiplier:
b=512, c=1, k=1024, w=2, xm=number m

——*help*	Print a usage message on standard output and exit successfully.
——*version*	Print version information on standard output then exit successfully.
if=file	Read from *file* instead of the standard input.
of=file	Write to *file* instead of the standard output. Unless *conv=notrunc* is given, truncate *file* to the size specified by *seek=* (0 bytes if *seek=* is not given).
ibs=bytes	Read *bytes* bytes at a time.
obs=bytes	Write *bytes* bytes at a time.
bs=bytes	Read and write *bytes* bytes at atime. Override ibs and obs.
cbs=bytes	Convert *bytes* bytes at a time.
skip=blocks	Skip *blocks* ibs-sized blocks at start of input.
seek=blocks	Skip *blocks* obs-sized blocks at start of output.
count=blocks	Copy only *blocks* ibs-sized input blocks.
conv=conversion[,conversion...]	Convert the file as specified by the *conversion* arguments.

Conversions:

ascii	Convert EBCDIC to ASCII.
ebcdic	Convert ASCII to EBCDIC.
ibm	Convert ASCII to alternate EBCDIC.
block	Pad newline-terminated records to size of cbs, replacing newline with trailing spaces.
unblock	Replace trailing spaces in cbs-sized block with newline.
lcase	Change uppercase characters to lowercase.
ucase	Change lowercase characters to uppercase.
swab	Swap every pair of input bytes. Unlike the Unix dd, this works when an odd number of bytes are read. If the input file contains an odd number of bytes, the last byte is simply copied (since there is nothing to swap it with).
noerror	Continue after read errors.
notrunc	Do not truncate the output file.
sync	Pad every input block to size of ibs with trailing NULs.

DEPMOD(1) — Linux Module Support

NAME

depmod, modprobe – handle loadable modules automatically

SYNOPSIS

depmod [–a]
depmod module1.o module2.o ...

modprobe module.o [symbol=value ...]
modprobe –t tag pattern
modprobe –a –t tag pattern **modprobe** –l [–t tag] pattern
modprobe –r module
modprobe –c

DESCRIPTION

These utilities are intended to make a Linux modular kernel manageable for all users, administrators and distribution maintainers.

Depmod creates a "Makefile"-like dependency file, based on the symbols it finds in the set of modules mentioned on the command line (or in a default place). This dependency file can later be used by **modprobe** to automatically load the relevant module(s).

Modprobe is used to load a set of modules, either a single module, a stack of dependant modules, or all modules that are marked with a specified tag.

Modprobe will automatically load all base modules needed in a module stack, as described by the dependency file modules.dep. If the loading of one of these modules fails, the whole current stack of modules will be unloaded (by rmmod) automatically.

Modprobe has two ways of loading modules. One way (the probe mode) will try to load a module out of a list (defined by **pattern**). It stops loading as soon as one module load successfully. This can be used to autoload one ethernet driver out of a list for example. The other way, is to load all modules from a list. This can be used to load some modules at boot time.

With the option **-r**, modprobe will automatically unload a stack of modules, similar to the way **rmmod** -r does.

Option -l combined with option -t list all available modules of a certain type. An enhanced **mount** command could use the command

modprobe -l -t fs

to get the list of all file system drivers available and on request load the proper one. So, the mount command could become more generic as well... (The kerneld solve this without changing the mount utility)

Option -c will print all configuration (default + configuration file).

The normal use of **depmod** is to include the line "/sbin/depmod -a" in one of the rc-files in /etc/rc.d, so that the correct module dependencies will be available immediately after booting the system.

Option **-d** put depmod in debug mode. It outputs all command it is issuing.

Option **-e** output the list of unresolved symbol for each module, Normally depmod only output the list of unloadable modules.

Option **-v** output the list of all processed modules.

Modules may be located at different place in the filesystem, but there will always be some need to override this, especially for module developers. We expect some official standard will emerge, defined by the FSSTND. Until that time you might as well use this suggested directory structure.

DEPMOD(1) — Linux Module Support

CONFIGURATION

The behaviour of **depmod** and **modprobe** can be adjusted by the (optional) configuration file **/etc/conf.modules**

The configuration file consists of a set of lines.
All empty lines, and all text on a line after a '#', will be ignored.
Lines may be continued by ending the line with a '\'.
The remaining lines should all conform to one of the following formats:

parameter=value options module symbol=value ... alias module real_name

All values in the "parameter" lines will be processed by a shell, which means that "shell tricks" like wild-cards and commands enclosed in back-quotes can be used:

path[misc]=/lib/modules/1.1.5?/misc path[net]=/lib/modules/`uname -r`/net

Parameters may be repeated multiple times.

These are the legal parameters:

    depfile=DEPFILE_PATH   This is the path to the dependency file that will be created by **depmod** and used by **modprobe**.

    path=SOME_PATH   The **path** parameter specifies a directory to search for the modules.

    path[tag]=SOME_PATH   The path parameter can carry an optional tag. This tells us a little more about the purpose of the modules in this directory and allows some automated operations by **modprobe**. The tag is appended to the "path" keyword enclose in square brackets. If the tag is missing, the tag "misc" is assumed.
One very useful tag is **boot,** which can be used to mark all modules that should be loaded at boot-time.

If the configuration file '/etc/conf.modules' is missing, or if any parameter is not overridden, the following defaults are assumed:

depfile=/lib/modules/`uname -r`/modules.dep
path[boot]=/lib/modules/boot

path[fs]=/lib/modules/`uname -r`/fs
path[misc]=/lib/modules/`uname -r`/misc
path[net]=/lib/modules/`uname -r`/net
path[scsi]=/lib/modules/`uname -r`/scsi

path[fs]=/lib/modules/default/fs
path[misc]=/lib/modules/default/misc
path[net]=/lib/modules/default/net
path[scsi]=/lib/modules/default/scsi

path[fs]=/lib/modules/fs
path[misc]=/lib/modules/misc
path[net]=/lib/modules/net
path[scsi]=/lib/modules/scsi

All "option" lines specify the default options that are needed for a module, as in:

    modprobe de620 bnc=1

These options will be overridden by any options given on the **modprobe** command line.

The "alias" lines can be used to give alias names to modules. A line in /etc/conf.modules that looks like this:

alias iso9660 isofs

makes it possible to write **modprobe iso9660** although there is no such module available.

STRATEGY

The idea is that **modprobe** will look first at the directory containing modules compiled for the current release of the kernel. If the module is not found there, **modprobe** will look in the directory containing modules for a default release.

When you install a new linux, the modules should be moved to a directory related to the release (and version) of the kernel you are installing. Then you should do a symlink from this directory to the "default" directory.

Each time you compile a new kernel, the command **make modules_install** will create a new directory, but won't change the default.

When you get a module unrelated to the kernel distribution you should place it in one of the version-independent directories under /lib/modules.

This is the default strategy, which can be overridden in /etc/conf.modules.

EXAMPLES

modprobe -t net	Load one of the modules that are stored in the directory tagged "net". Each module are tried until one succeed (default: /lib/modules/net).
modprobe -a -t boot	All modules that are stored in the directory tagged "boot" will be loaded (default: /lib/modules/boot).
modprobe slip.o	This will attempt to load the module slhc.o if it was not previously loaded, since the slip module needs the functionality in the slhc module. This dependency will be described in the file "modules.dep" that was created automatically by **depmod**
modprobe -r slip.o	will unload slip.o. It will also unload slhc.o automatically, unless it is used by some other module as well (like e.g. ppp.o).

FILES

/etc/conf.modules,
/lib/modules/*/modules.dep,
/lib/modules/*

SEE ALSO

lsmod(1), kerneld(8), ksyms(1), modules(2),

REQUIERED UTILITIES

insmod(1), nm(1) rmmod(1),

NOTES

The pattern supplied to modprobe will often be escaped to ensure that it is evaluated in the proper context

AUTHOR

Jacques Gelinas (jack@solucorp.qc.ca)
Bjorn Ekwall (bj0rn@blox.se)

BUGS

Naah...

NAME

df – summarize free disk space

SYNOPSIS

df [–aikPv] [–t fstype] [–x fstype] [—all] [—inodes] [—type=fstype] [—exclude–type=fstype] [—kilobytes] [—portability] [—print–type] [—help] [—version] [filename...]

DESCRIPTION

This manual page documents the GNU version of **df**. **df** displays the amount of disk space available on the filesystem containing each file name argument. If no file name is given, the space available on all currently mounted filesystems is shown. Disk space is shown in 1K blocks by default, unless the environment variable POSIXLY_CORRECT is set, in which case 512-byte blocks are used.

If an argument is the absolute file name of a disk device node containing a mounted filesystem, **df** shows the space available on that filesystem rather than on the filesystem containing the device node (which is always the root filesystem). This version of **df** cannot show the space available on unmounted filesystems, because on most kinds of systems doing so requires very nonportable intimate knowledge of filesystem structures.

OPTIONS

–a, —all Include in the listing filesystems that have 0 blocks, which are omitted by default. Such filesystems are typically special-purpose pseudo-filesystems, such as automounter entries. On some systems, filesystems of type "ignore" or "auto" are also omitted by default and included in the listing by this option.

–i, —inodes List inode usage information instead of block usage. An inode (short for "index node") is a special kind of disk block that contains information about a file, such as its owner, permissions, timestamps, and location on the disk.

–k, —kilobytes Print sizes in 1K blocks instead of 512-byte blocks. This overrides the environment variable POSIXLY_CORRECT.

–P, —portability Use the POSIX output format. This is like the default format except that the information about each filesystem is always printed on exactly one line; a mount device is never put on a line by itself. This means that if the mount device name is more than 20 characters long (as for some network mounts), the columns are misaligned.

–T, —print–type Print a type string for each filesystem. Any such printed filesystem type name may be used as an argument to either of the —type= or —exclude–type= options.

–t, —type=fstype Limit the listing to filesystems of type *fstype*. Multiple filesystem types can be shown by giving multiple *–t* options. By default, all filesystem types are listed.

–x, —exclude–type=fstype Limit the listing to filesystems not of type *fstype*. Multiple filesystem types can be eliminated by giving multiple *–x* options. By default, all filesystem types are listed.

–v Ignored; for compatibility with System V versions of **df**.

—help Print a usage message on standard output and exit successfully.

—version Print version information on standard output then exit successfully.

DOMAINNAME(1) Linux Programmer's Manual DOMAINNAME(1)

NAME

domainname – set or print domain of current host

SYNOPSIS

domainname [name]

DESCRIPTION

domainname prints the domainname of the current host, from the **getdomainname**(3) library call. If an argument is present and the effective UID is 0, **domainname** changes the name of the host, with the **setdomainname**(2) system call. This is usually done at boot time in the */etc/rc.local* script.

FILES

/etc/rc.local

SEE ALSO

getdomainname(3), **setdomainname**(2), **uname**(1), **uname**(2)

AUTHOR

Lars Wirzenius by substituting in hostname.c

DSPLIT(1)

NAME

dsplit – split a large file into pieces

SYNOPSIS

dsplit [**–size** *nnn*] [*input_file* [*output_base*]]

DESCRIPTION

dsplit splits binary files into smaller chunks so that they may be placed on floppy disks.

OPTIONS

–size nnn   Specifies the size of each output file, in bytes. The default is 1457000, which is enough to will a 1.44 MB floppy disk.

input_file   Specifies the name of the file to split up. A – indicates standard input. The default is standard input.

output_base   Specifies the name of the output files to be written. **dsplit** will append 000, 001, ..., to the *output_base*. The default is "dsplit".

AUTHOR'S NOTES

Submitted-by: arnstein@netcom.com (David Arnstein)
Posting-number: Volume 40, Issue 51
Archive-name: dsplit/part01
Environment: MS-DOS, UNIX

Here is a portable binary file splitting program. It reads a binary file and splits it into pieces. I use this program to put large binary files on floppy disks. For this reason, the default size of the output files is 1,457,000 bytes, which just about fills up a 1.44 MB floppy disk.

Unlike other binary split programs I have seen, dsplit does not malloc a huge block of memory. Dsplit is suitable for use under MSDOS and other primitive operating systems.

(The program came from gatekeeper.dec.com:/pub/usenet/comp.sources.misc/volume40/dsplit).

DU(1L) FSF DU(1L)

NAME
du – summarize disk usage

SYNOPSIS
du [–abcklsxDLS] [—all] [—total] [—count-links] [—summarize] [—bytes] [—kilobytes] [—-one-file-system] [—-separate-dirs] [—-dereference] [—-dereference-args] [—help] [—-version] [filename...]

DESCRIPTION
This manual page documents the GNU version of **du**. **du** displays the amount of disk space used by each argument and for each subdirectory of directory arguments. The space is measured in 1K blocks by default, unless the environment variable POSIXLY_CORRECT is set, in which case 512-byte blocks are used.

OPTIONS

–*a*, —*all* Display counts for all files, not just directories.

–*b*, —*bytes* Print sizes in bytes.

–*c*, —*total* Write a grand total of all of the arguments after all arguments have been processed. This can be used to find out the disk usage of a directory, with some files excluded.

–*k*, —*kilobytes* Print sizes in kilobytes. This overrides the environment variable POSIXLY_CORRECT.

–*l*, —*count-links* Count the size of all files, even if they have appeared already in another hard link.

–*s*, —*summarize* Display only a total for each argument.

–*x*, —*one-file-system* Skip directories that are on different filesystems from the one that the argument being processed is on.

–*D*, —*dereference-args* Dereference symbolic links that are command line arguments. Does not affect other symbolic links. This is helpful for finding out the disk usage of directories like /usr/tmp where they are symbolic links.

–*L*, —*dereference* Dereference symbolic links (show the disk space used by the file or directory that the link points to instead of the space used by the link).

–*S*, —*separate-dirs* Count the size of each directory separately, not including the sizes of subdirectories.

—*help* Print a usage message on standard output and exit successfully.

—*version* Print version information on standard output then exit successfully.

BUGS
On BSD systems, **du** reports sizes that are half the correct values for files that are NFS-mounted from HP-UX systems. On HP-UX systems, it reports sizes that are twice the correct values for files that are NFS-mounted from BSD systems. This is due to a flaw in HP-UX; it also affects the HP-UX **du** program.

EDITRES(1)

NAME

editres – a dynamic resource editor for X Toolkit applications

SYNTAX

editres [*–toolkitoption* ...]

OPTIONS

Editres accepts all of the standard X Toolkit command line options (see *X(1)*). The order of the command line options is not important.

DESCRIPTION

Editres is a tool that allows users and application developers to view the full widget hierarchy of any X Toolkit application that speaks the Editres protocol. In addition, editres will help the user construct resource specifications, allow the user to apply the resource to the application and view the results dynamically. Once the user is happy with a resource specification editres will append the resource string to the user's X Resources file.

USING EDITRES

Editres provides a window consisting of the following four areas:

> Menu Bar   A set of popup menus that allow you full access to editres's features.
>
> Panner   The panner allows a more intuitive way to scroll the application tree display.
>
> Message Area   Displays information to the user about the action that editres expects of her.
>
> Application Widget Tree   This area will be used to display the selected application's widget tree.

To begin an editres session select the **Get Widget Tree** menu item from the command menu. This will change the pointer cursor to cross hair. You should now select the application you wish look at by clicking on any of its windows. If this application understands the editres protocol then editres will display the application's widget tree in its tree window. If the application does not understand the editres protocol editres will inform you of this fact in the message area after a few seconds delay.

Once you have a widget tree you may now select any of the other menu options. The effect of each of these is described below.

COMMANDS

> Get Widget Tree   Allows the user to click on any application that speaks the editres protocol and receive its widget tree.
>
> Refresh Current Widget Tree   Editres only knows about the widgets that exist at the present time. Many applications create and destroy widgets on the fly. Selecting this menu item will cause editres to ask the application to resend its widget tree, thus updating its information to the new state of the application.
>
> For example, xman only creates the widgets for its *topbox* when it starts up. None of the widgets for the manual page window are created until the user actually clicks on the *Manual Page* button. If you retrieved xman's widget tree before the the manual page is active, you may wish to refresh the widget tree after the manual page has been displayed. This will allow you to also edit the manual page's resources.
>
> Dump Widget Tree to a File   For documenting applications it is often useful to be able to dump the entire application widget tree to an ASCII file. This file can then be included in the manual page. When this menu item is selected a popup dialog is activated. Type the name of the file in

EDITRES(1)   EDITRES(1)

this dialog, and either select *okay*, or type a carriage-return. Editres will now dump the widget tree to this file. To cancel the file dialog, select the *cancel* button.

Show Resource Box   This command will popup a resource box for the current application. This resource box (described in detail below) will allow the user to see exactly which resources can be set for the widget that is currently selected in the widget tree display. Only one widget may be currently selected; if greater or fewer are selected editres will refuse to pop up the resource box and put an error message in the **Message Area**.

Set Resource   This command will popup a simple dialog box for setting an arbitrary resource on all selected widgets. You must type in the resource name, as well as the value. You can use the Tab key to switch between the resource name field the resource value field.

Quit   Exits editres.

TREE COMMANDS

The **Tree** menu contains several commands that allow operations to be performed on the widget tree.

Select Widget in Client   This menu item allows you to select any widget in the application; editres will then highlight the corresponding element the widget tree display. Once this menu item is selected the pointer cursor will again turn to a crosshair, and you must click any pointer button in the widget you wish to have displayed. Since some widgets are fully obscured by their children, it is not possible to get to every widget this way, but this mechanism does give very useful feedback between the elements in the widget tree and those in the actual application.

Select All

Unselect All

Invert All   These functions allow the user to select, unselect, or invert all widgets in the widget tree.

Select Children

Select Parents   These functions select the immediate parent or children of each of the currently selected widgets.

Select Descendants

Select Ancestors   These functions select all parents or children of each of the currently selected widgets. This is a recursive search.

Show Widget Names

Show Class Names

Show Widget Windows   When the tree widget is initially displayed the labels of each widget in the tree correspond to the widget names. These functions will cause the label of **all** widgets in the tree to be changed to show the class name, IDs, or window associated with each widget in the application. The widget IDs, and windows are shown as hex numbers.

In addition there are keyboard accelerators for each of the Tree operations. If the input focus is over an individual widget in the tree, then that operation will only effect that widget. If the input focus is in the Tree background it will have exactly the same effect as the corresponding menu item.

The translation entries shown may be applied to any widget in the application. If that widget is a child of the Tree widget, then it will only affect that widget, otherwise it will have the same effect as the commands in the tree menu.

Flash Active Widgets This command is the inverse of the **Select Widget in Client** command, it will show the user each widget that is currently selected in the widget tree, by flashing the corresponding widget in the application *numFlashes* (three by default) times in the *flashColor*.

Key	Option	Translation Entry
space	Unselect	Select(nothing)
w	Select	Select(widget)
s	Select	Select(all)
i	Invert	Select(invert)
c	Select	Children Select(children)
d	Select Descendants	Select(descendants)
p	Select Parent	Select(parent)
a	Select Ancestors	Select(ancestors)
N	Show Widget Names	Relabel(name)
C	Show Class Names	Relabel(class)
I	Show Widget IDs	Relabel(id)
W	Show Widget Windows	Relabel(window)
T	Toggle Widget/Class Name	Relabel(toggle)

Clicking button 1 on a widget adds it to the set of selected widgets. Clicking button 2 on a widget deselects all other widgets and then selects just that widget. Clicking button 3 on a widget toggles its label between the widget's instance name the widget's class name.

USING THE RESOURCE BOX

The resource box contains five different areas. Each of the areas, as they appear on the screen, from top to bottom will be discussed.

> The Resource Line This area at the top of the resource box shows the current resource name exactly as it would appear if you were to save it to a file or apply it.
>
> The Widget Names and Classes This area allows you to select exactly which widgets this resource will apply to. The area contains four lines, the first contains the name of the selected widget and all its ancestors, and the more restrictive dot (.) separator. The second line contains less specific the Class names of each widget, and well as the less restrictive star (*) separator. The third line contains a set of special buttons called **Any Widget** which will generalize this level to match any widget. The last line contains a set of special buttons called **Any Widget Chain** which will turn the single level into something that matches zero or more levels.
>
> The initial state of this area is the most restrictive, using the resource names and the dot separator. By selecting the other buttons in this area you can ease the restrictions to allow more and more widgets to match the specification. The extreme case is to select all the **Any Widget Chain** buttons, which will match every widget in the application. As you select different buttons the tree display will update to show you exactly which widgets will be effected by the current resource specification.
>
> Normal and Constraint Resources The next area allows you to select the name of the normal or constraint resources you wish to set. Some widgets may not have constraint resources, so that area will not appear.
>
> Resource Value This next area allows you to enter the resource value. This value should be entered exactly as you would type a line into your resource file. Thus it should contain no unescaped new-lines. There are a few special character sequences for this file:
>
> \n - This will be replaced with a newline.
>
> \### - Where # is any octal digit. This will be replaced with a single byte that contains this sequence interpreted as an octal number. For

example, a value containing a NULL byte can be stored by specifying \000.
\<new-line> - This will compress to nothing.
\\ - This will compress to a single backslash.

Command Area This area contains several command buttons, described in this section.

Set Save File This button allows the user to modify file that the resources will be saved to. This button will bring up a dialog box that will ask you for a filename; once the filename has been entered, either hit carriage-return or click on the *okay* button. To pop down the dialog box without changing the save file, click the *cancel* button.

Save This button will append the **resource line** described above to the end of the current save file. If no save file has been set the **Set Save File** dialog box will be popped up to prompt the user for a filename.

Apply This button attempts to perform a XtSetValues call on all widgets that match the **resource line** described above. The value specified is applied directly to all matching widgets. This behavior is an attempt to give a dynamic feel to the resource editor. Since this feature allows users to put an application in states it may not be willing to handle, a hook has been provided to allow specific applications to block these SetValues requests (see **Blocking Editres Requests** below).

Unfortunately due to design constraints imposed on the widgets by the X Toolkit and the Resource Manager, trying to coerce an inherently static system into dynamic behavior can cause strange results. There is no guarantee that the results of an apply will be the same as what will happen when you save the value and restart the application. This functionality is provided to try to give you a rough feel for what your changes will accomplish, and the results obtained should be considered suspect at best. Having said that, this is one of the neatest features of editres, and I strongly suggest that you play with it, and see what it can do.

Save and Apply This button combines the Save and Apply actions described above into one button.

Popdown Resource Box This button will remove the resource box from the display.

BLOCKING EDITRES REQUESTS

The editres protocol has been built into the Athena Widget set. This allows all applications that are linked against Xaw to be able to speak to the resource editor. While this provides great flexibility, and is a useful tool, it can quite easily be abused. It is therefore possible for any Xaw application to specify a value for the editresBlock resource described below, to keep editres from divulging information about its internals, or to disable the SetValues part of the protocol.

editresBlock (Class **EditresBlock**) Specifies which type of blocking this application wishes to impose on the editres protocol.

The accepted values are:

  all Block all requests.

  setValues Block all SetValues requests. As this is the only editres request that actually modifies the application, this is in effect stating that the application is read-only.

  none Allow all editres requests.

EDITRES(1)   EDITRES(1)

Remember that these resources are set on any Xaw application, **not editres**. They allow individual applications to keep all or some of the requests editres makes from ever succeeding. Of course, editres is also an Xaw application, so it may also be viewed and modified by editres (rather recursive, I know), these commands can be blocked by setting the **editresBlock** resource on editres itself.

RESOURCES

For *editres* the available application resources are:

    numFlashes (Class **NumFlashes**)   Specifies the number of times the widgets in the application will be flashed when the **Show Active Widgets** command in invoked.

    flashTime (Class **FlashTime**)   Amount of time between the flashes described above.

    flashColor (Class **flashColor**)   Specifies the color used to flash application widgets. A bright color should be used that will immediately draw your attention to the area being flashed, such as red or yellow.

    saveResourcesFile (Class **SaveResourcesFile**)   This is the file the resource line will be append to when the **Save** button activated in the resource box.

WIDGETS

In order to specify resources, it is useful to know the hierarchy of the widgets which compose *editres*. In the notation below, indentation indicates hierarchical structure. The widget class name is given first, followed by the widget instance name.

```
Editres editres
     Paned paned
          Box box
               MenuButton commands
                    SimpleMenu menu
                         SmeBSB sendTree
                         SmeBSB refreshTree
                         SmeBSB dumpTreeToFile
                         SmeLine line
                         SmeBSB getResourceList
                         SmeLine line
                         SmeBSB quit
               MenuButton treeCommands
                    SimpleMenu menu
                         SmeBSB showClientWidget
                         SmeBSB selectAll
                         SmeBSB unselectAll
                         SmeBSB invertAll
                         SmeLine line
                         SmeBSB selectChildren
                         SmeBSB selectParent
                         SmeBSB selectDescendants
                         SmeBSB selectAncestors
                         SmeLine line
                         SmeBSB showWidgetNames
                         SmeBSB showClassNames
                         SmeBSB showWidgetIDs
                         SmeBSB showWidgetWindows
                         SmeLine line
                         SmeBSB flashActiveWidgets
          Paned hPane
               Panner panner
               Label userMessage
               Grip grip
          Porthole porthole
```

Tree tree
 Toggle <name of widget in application>

  TransientShell resourceBox
  Paned pane
  Label resourceLabel
  Form namesAndClasses
  Toggle dot
  Toggle star
  Toggle any
  Toggle name
  Toggle class

  Label namesLabel
  List namesList
  Label constraintLabel
  List constraintList
  Form valueForm
  Label valueLabel
  Text valueText
  Box commandBox
  Command setFile
  Command save
  Command apply
  Command saveAndApply
  Command cancel
  Grip grip
 Grip grip

ENVIRONMENT

 DISPLAY to get the default host and display number.

 XENVIRONMENT to get the name of a resource file that overrides the global resources stored in the RESOURCE_MANAGER property.

FILES

<XRoot>/lib/X11/app-defaults/Editres - specifies required resources

SEE ALSO

X(1), xrdb(1), Athena Widget Set

RESTRICTIONS

This is a prototype, there are lots of nifty features I would love to add, but I hope this will give you some ideas about what a resource editor can do.

AUTHOR

Chris D. Peterson, formerly MIT X Consortium

ELVIS(1)

NAME

elvis, ex, vi, view, input - The editor

SYNOPSIS

elvis [*flags*] [**+***cmd*] [*files*...]

DESCRIPTION

Elvis is a text editor which emulates *vi/ex*.

On systems which pass the program name as an argument, such as Unix and Minix, you may also install *elvis* under the names "ex", "vi", "view", and "input". These extra names would normally be links to elvis; see the "ln" shell command.

When *elvis* is invoked as "vi", it behaves exactly as though it was invoked as "elvis". However, if you invoke *elvis* as "view", then the readonly option is set as though you had given it the "-R" flag. If you invoke *elvis* as "ex", then *elvis* will start up in the colon command mode instead of the visual command mode, as though you had given it the "-e" flag. If you invoke *elvis* as "input" or "edit", then *elvis* will start up in input mode, as though the "-i" flag was given.

OPTIONS

- **-r**   To the real vi, this flag means that a previous edit should be recovered. *Elvis*, though, has a separate program, called *elvrec(1)*, for recovering files. When you invoke *elvis* with -r, *elvis* will tell you to run *elvrec*.
- **-R**   This sets the "readonly" option, so you won't accidentally overwrite a file.
- **-s**   This set the "safer" option, which disables many potentially harmful commands. It has not been rigorously proven to be absolutely secure, however.
- **-t** *tag*   This causes *elvis* to start editing at the given tag.
- **-m** [*file*]   *Elvis* will search through *file* for something that looks like an error message from a compiler. It will then begin editing the source file that caused the error, with the cursor sitting on the line where the error was detected. If you don't explicitly name a *file*, then "errlist" is assumed.
- **-e**   *Elvis* will start up in colon command mode.
- **-v**   *Elvis* will start up in visual command mode.
- **-i**   *Elvis* will start up in input mode.
- **-w** *winsize*   Sets the "window" option's value to *winsize*.
- **+***command* or **-c** *command*   If you use the **+***command* parameter, then after the first file is loaded *command* is executed as an EX command. A typical example would be "elvis +237 foo", which would cause *elvis* to start editing foo and then move directly to line 237. The "-c *command*" variant was added for UNIX SysV compatibility.

FILES

- /tmp/elv*   During editing, *elvis* stores text in a temporary file. For UNIX, this file will usually be stored in the /tmp directory, and the first three characters will be "elv". For other systems, the temporary files may be stored someplace else; see the version-specific section of the documentation.
- tags   This is the database used by the *:tags* command and the **-t** option. It is usually created by the *ctags(1)* program.
- .exrc or elvis.rc   On UNIX-like systems, a file called ".exrc" in your home directory is executed as a series of *ex* commands. A file by the same name may be executed in the current directory, too. On non-UNIX systems, ".exrc" is usually an invalid file name; there, the initialization file is called "elvis.rc" instead.

ENVIRONMENT

TERM This is the name of your terminal's entry in the termcap or terminfo database. The list of legal values varies from one system to another.

TERMCAP Optional. If your system uses termcap, and the TERMCAP variable is unset, then elvis will read your terminal's definition from **/etc/termcap**. If TERMCAP is set to the full pathname of a file (starting with a '/') then elvis will look in the named file instead of **/etc/termcap**. If TERMCAP is set to a value which doesn't start with a '/', then its value is assumed to be the full termcap entry for your terminal.

TERMINFO Optional. If your system uses terminfo, and the TERMINFO variable is unset, then elvis will read your terminal's definition from the database in the **/usr/lib/terminfo** database. If TERMINFO is set, then its value is used as the database name to use instead of **/usr/lib/terminfo**.

LINES, COLUMNS Optional. These variables, if set, will override the screen size values given in the termcap/terminfo for your terminal. On windowing systems such as X, elvis has other ways of determining the screen size, so you should probably leave these variables unset.

EXINIT Optional. This variable can hold EX commands which will be executed instead of the .exrc file in your home directory.

SHELL Optional. The SHELL variable sets the default value for the "shell" option, which determines which shell program is used to perform wild-card expansion in file names, and also which is used to execute filters or external programs. The default value on UNIX systems is "/bin/sh".

Note: Under MS-DOS, this variable is called COMSPEC instead of SHELL.

HOME This variable should be set to the name of your home directory. elvis looks for its initialization file there; if HOME is unset then the initialization file will not be executed.

TAGPATH Optional. This variable is used by the "ref" program, which is invoked by the shift-K, control-], and :tag commands. See "ref" for more information.

TMP, TEMP These optional environment variables are only used in non-UNIX versions of elvis. They allow you to supply a directory name to be used for storing temporary files.

SEE ALSO

ctags(1), ref(1), elvprsv(1), elvrec(1)

Elvis - A Clone of Vi/Ex, the complete *elvis* documentation.

BUGS

There is no LISP support. Certain other features are missing, too.

Auto-indent mode is not quite compatible with the real vi. Among other things, 0^D and ^^D don't do what you might expect.

Long lines are displayed differently. The real vi wraps long lines onto multiple rows of the screen, but *elvis* scrolls sideways.

AUTHOR

Steve Kirkendall
kirkenda@cs.pdx.edu

Many other people have worked to port *elvis* to various operating systems. To see who deserves credit, run the *:version* command from within *elvis*, or look in the system-specific section of the complete documentation.

ELVPRSV(1)

NAME

elvprsv - Preserve the the modified version of a file after a crash.

SYNOPSIS

elvprsv ["-*why elvis died*"] /**tmp**/*filename*...
elvprsv -**R** /**tmp**/*filename*...

DESCRIPTION

elvprsv preserves your edited text after *elvis* dies. The text can be recovered later, via the *elvprsv* program.

For UNIX-like systems, you should never need to run this program from the command line. It is run automatically when *elvis* is about to die, and it should be run (via /etc/rc) when the computer is booted. THAT'S ALL!

For non-UNIX systems such as MS-DOS or VMS, you can either use *elvprsv* the same way as under UNIX systems (by running it from your AUTOEXEC.BAT file), or you can run it separately with the "-R" flag to recover the files in one step.

If you're editing a file when *elvis* dies (due to a bug, system crash, power failure, etc.) then *elvprsv* will preserve the most recent version of your text. The preserved text is stored in a special directory; it does NOT overwrite your text file automatically. (If the preservation directory hasn't been set up correctly, then elvprsv will simply send you a mail message describing how to manually run elvprsv.)

elvprsv will send mail to any user whose work it preserves, if your operating system normally supports mail.

FILES

/tmp/elv*   The temporary file that *elvis* was using when it died.

/usr/preserve/p*   The text that is preserved by *elvprsv*.

/usr/preserve/Index   A text file which lists the names of all preserved files, and the names of the /usr/preserve/p* files which contain their preserved text.

BUGS

Due to the permissions on the /usr/preserve directory, on UNIX systems *elvprsv* must be run as superuser. This is accomplished by making the *elvprsv* executable be owned by "root" and turning on its "set user id" bit.

If you're editing a nameless buffer when *elvis* dies, then *elvprsv* will pretend that the file was named "foo".

AUTHOR

Steve Kirkendall
kirkenda@cs.pdx.edu

ELVREC(1)

NAME

elvrec - Recover the modified version of a file after a crash

SYNOPSIS

elvrec [*preservedfile* [*newfile*]]

DESCRIPTION

If you're editing a file when *elvis* dies, the system crashes, or power fails, the most recent version of your text will be preserved. The preserved text is stored in a special directory; it does NOT overwrite your text file automatically.

The *elvrec* program locates the preserved version of a given file, and writes it over the top of your text file – or to a new file, if you prefer. The recovered file will have nearly all of your changes.

To see a list of all recoverable files, run *elvrec* with no arguments.

(Note: if you haven't set up a directory for file preservation, then *elvis*' you'll have to manually run the *elvprsv* program instead of *elvrec*.)

FILES

/usr/preserve/p*	The text that was preserved when *elvis* died.
/usr/preserve/Index	A text file which lists the names of all preserved files, and the names of the /usr/preserve/p* files which contain their preserved text.

BUGS

elvrec is very picky about filenames. You must tell it to recover the file using exactly the same pathname as when you were editing it. The simplest way to do this is to go into the same directory that you were editing, and invoke *elvrec* with the same filename as *elvis*. If that doesn't work, then try running *elvrec* with no arguments, to see exactly which pathname it is using for the desired file.

Due to the permissions on the /usr/preserve directory, on UNIX systems *elvrec* must be run as superuser. This is accomplished by making the *elvrec* executable be owned by "root" and setting its "set user id" bit.

If you're editing a nameless buffer when *elvis* dies, then *elvrec* will pretend that the file was named "foo".

AUTHOR

Steve Kirkendall
kirkenda@cs.pdx.edu

EXPAND(1L) FSF EXPAND(1L)

NAME

expand – convert tabs to spaces

SYNOPSIS

expand [–tab1[,tab2[,...]]] [–t tab1[,tab2[,...]]] [–i] [––tabs=tab1[,tab2[,...]]] [––initial] [––help] [––version] [file...]

DESCRIPTION

This manual page documents the GNU version of **expand**. **expand** writes the contents of each given file, or the standard input if none are given or when a file named '–' is given, to the standard output, with tab characters converted to the appropriate number of spaces. By default, **expand** converts all tabs to spaces. It preserves backspace characters in the output; they decrement the column count for tab calculations. The default action is equivalent to –8 (set tabs every 8 columns).

OPTIONS

–, –t, ––tabs tab1[,tab2[,...]]	If only one tab stop is given, set the tabs *tab1* spaces apart instead of the default 8. Otherwise, set the tabs at columns *tab1*, *tab2*, etc. (numbered from 0) and replace any tabs beyond the tabstops given with single spaces. If the tabstops are specified with the *–t* or ––*tabs* option, they can be separated by blanks as well as by commas.
–i, ––*initial*	Only convert initial tabs (those that precede all non space or tab characters) on each line to spaces.
––*help*	Print a usage message and exit with a non-zero status.
––*version*	Print version information on standard output then exit.

FIND(1L)

NAME

find – search for files in a directory hierarchy

SYNOPSIS

find [path...] [expression]

DESCRIPTION

This manual page documents the GNU version of **find**. **find** searches the directory tree rooted at each given file name by evaluating the given expression from left to right, according to the rules of precedence (see section OPERATORS), until the outcome is known (the left hand side is false for *and* operations, true for *or*), at which point **find** moves on to the next file name.

The first argument that begins with '–', '(', ')', ',', or '!' is taken to be the beginning of the expression; any arguments before it are paths to search, and any arguments after it are the rest of the expression. If no paths are given, the current directory is used. If no expression is given, the expression '–print' is used.

find exits with status 0 if all files are processed successfully, greater than 0 if errors occur.

EXPRESSIONS

The expression is made up of options (which affect overall operation rather than the processing of a specific file, and always return true), tests (which return a true or false value), and actions (which have side effects and return a true or false value), all separated by operators. –and is assumed where the operator is omitted. If the expression contains no actions other than –prune, –print is performed on all files for which the expression is true.

OPTIONS

All options always return true. They always take effect, rather than being processed only when their place in the expression is reached. Therefore, for clarity, it is best to place them at the beginning of the expression.

- –daystart Measure times (for –amin, –atime, –cmin, –ctime, –mmin, and –mtime) from the beginning of today rather than from 24 hours ago.
- –depth Process each directory's contents before the directory itself.
- –follow Dereference symbolic links. Implies –noleaf.
- –help, —help Print a summary of the command-line usage of **find** and exit.
- –maxdepth *levels* Descend at most *levels* (a non-negative integer) levels of directories below the command line arguments. '–maxdepth 0' means only apply the tests and actions to the command line arguments.
- –mindepth *levels* Do not apply any tests or actions at levels less than *levels* (a non-negative integer). '–mindepth 1' means process all files except the command line arguments.
- –mount Don't descend directories on other filesystems. An alternate name for –xdev, for compatibility with some other versions of **find**.
- –noleaf Do not optimize by assuming that directories contain 2 fewer subdirectories than their hard link count. This option is needed when searching filesystems that do not follow the Unix directory-link convention, such as CD-ROM or MS-DOS filesystems or AFS volume mount points. Each directory on a normal Unix filesystem has at least 2 hard links: its name and its '.' entry. Additionally, its subdirectories (if any) each have a '..' entry linked to that directory. When **find** is examining a directory, after it has statted 2 fewer subdirectories than the directory's link count, it knows that the rest of the entries in the directory are non-directories ('leaf' files in the directory tree). If only the files' names need to be examined, there is no need to stat them; this gives a significant increase in search speed.

GNU File Utilities

FIND(1L)　　　　　　　　　　　　　　　　　　　　　　　　　FIND(1L)

　　　　−−version, −−−version　　Print the **find** version number and exit.
　　　　−xdev　　　　Don't descend directories on other filesystems.

TESTS

Numeric arguments can be specified as

+*n*	for greater than *n*,
−*n*	for less than *n*,
n	for exactly *n*.
−amin *n*	File was last accessed *n* minutes ago.
−anewer *file*	File was last accessed more recently than *file* was modified. − anewer is affected by −follow only if −follow comes before − anewer on the command line.
−atime *n*	File was last accessed *n**24 hours ago.
−cmin *n*	File's status was last changed *n* minutes ago.
−cnewer *file*	File's status was last changed more recently than *file* was modified. −cnewer is affected by −follow only if −follow comes before −cnewer on the command line.
−ctime *n*	File's status was last changed *n**24 hours ago.
−empty	File is empty and is either a regular file or a directory.
−false	Always false.
−fstype *type*	File is on a filesystem of type *type*. The valid filesystem types vary among different versions of Unix; an incomplete list of filesystem types that are accepted on some version of Unix or another is: ufs, 4.2, 4.3, nfs, tmp, mfs, S51K, S52K. You can use −printf with the %F directive to see the types of your filesystems.
−gid *n*	File's numeric group ID is *n*.
−group *gname*	File belongs to group *gname* (numeric group ID allowed).
−ilname *pattern*	Like −lname, but the match is case insensitive.
−iname *pattern*	Like −name, but the match is case insensitive. For example, the patterns 'fo*' and 'F??' match the file names 'Foo', 'FOO', 'foo', 'fOo', etc.
−inum *n*	File has inode number *n*.
−ipath *pattern*	Like −path, but the match is case insensitive.
−iregex *pattern*	Like −regex, but the match is case insensitive.
−links *n*	File has *n* links.
−lname *pattern*	File is a symbolic link whose contents match shell pattern *pattern*. The metacharacters do not treat '/' or '.' specially.
−mmin *n*	File's data was last modified *n* minutes ago.
−mtime *n*	File's data was last modified *n**24 hours ago.
−name *pattern*	Base of file name (the path with the leading directories removed) matches shell pattern *pattern*. The metacharacters ('*', '?', and '[]') do not match a '.' at the start of the base name. To ignore a directory and the files under it, use −prune; see an example in the description of −path.
−newer *file*	File was modified more recently than *file*. −newer is affected by −follow only if −follow comes before −newer on the command line.
−nouser	No user corresponds to file's numeric user ID.
−nogroup	No group corresponds to file's numeric group ID.

FIND(1L)   FIND(1L)

      –path *pattern*   File name matches shell pattern *pattern*. The metacharacters do not treat '/' or '.' specially; so, for example,

                                find . –path './sr*sc'

                              will print an entry for a directory called './src/misc' (if one exists). To ignore a whole directory tree, use –prune rather than checking every file in the tree. For example, to skip the directory 'src/emacs' and all files and directories under it, and print the names of the other files found, do something like this:

                                find . –path './src/emacs' -prune -o -print

      –perm *mode*   File's permission bits are exactly *mode* (octal or symbolic). Symbolic modes use mode 0 as a point of departure.

      –perm *–mode*   All of the permission bits *mode* are set for the file.

      –perm +*mode*   Any of the permission bits *mode* are set for the file.

      –regex *pattern*   File name matches regular expression *pattern*. This is a match on the whole path, not a search. For example, to match a file named './fubar3', you can use the regular expression '.*bar.' or '.*b.*3', but not 'b.*r3'.

      –size *n*[bckw]   File uses *n* units of space. The units are 512-byte blocks by default or if 'b' follows *n*, bytes if 'c' follows *n*, kilobytes if 'k' follows *n*, or 2-byte words if 'w' follows *n*. The size does not count indirect blocks, but it does count blocks in sparse files that are not actually allocated.

      –true   Always true.

      –type *c*   File is of type *c*:

                            b   block (buffered) special

                            c   character (unbuffered) special

                            d   directory

                            p   named pipe (FIFO)

                            f   regular file

                            l   symbolic link

                            s   socket

      –uid *n*   File's numeric user ID is *n*.

      –used *n*   File was last accessed *n* days after its status was last changed.

      –user *uname*   File is owned by user *uname* (numeric user ID allowed).

      –xtype *c*   The same as –type unless the file is a symbolic link. For symbolic links: if –follow has not been given, true if the file is a link to a file of type *c*; if –follow has been given, true if *c* is 'l'. In other words, for symbolic links, -xtype checks the type of the file that –type does not check.

ACTIONS

      –exec *command* ;   Execute *command*; true if 0 status is returned. All following arguments to **find** are taken to be arguments to the command until an argument consisting of ';' is encountered. The string '{}' is replaced by the current file name being processed everywhere it occurs in the arguments to the command, not just in arguments where it is alone, as in some versions of **find**. Both of these constructions might need to be escaped (with a '\') or quoted to protect them from expansion by the shell. The command is executed in the starting directory.

GNU File Utilities

FIND(1L)   FIND(1L)

-fls *file*   True; like -ls but write to *file* like -fprint.

-fprint *file*   True; print the full file name into file *file*. If *file* does not exist when **find** is run, it is created; if it does exist, it is truncated. The file names "/dev/stdout" and "/dev/stderr" are handled specially; they refer to the standard output and standard error output, respectively.

-fprint0 *file*   True; like -print0 but write to *file* like -fprint.

-fprintf *file format*   True; like -printf but write to *file* like -fprint.

-ok *command* ;   Like -exec but ask the user first (on the standard input); if the response does not start with 'y' or 'Y', do not run the command, and return false.

-print   True; print the full file name on the standard output, followed by a newline.

-print0   True; print the full file name on the standard output, followed by a null character. This allows file names that contain newlines to be correctly interpreted by programs that process the **find** output.

-printf *format*   True; print *format* on the standard output, interpreting '\' escapes and '%' directives. Field widths and precisions can be specified as with the 'printf' C function. Unlike -print, -printf does not add a newline at the end of the string. The escapes and directives are:

   \a   Alarm bell.
   \b   Backspace.
   \c   Stop printing from this format immediately and flush the output.
   \f   Form feed.
   \n   Newline.
   \r   Carriage return.
   \t   Horizontal tab.
   \v   Vertical tab.
   \\   A literal backslash ('\').

   A '\' character followed by any other character is treated as an ordinary character, so they both are printed.

   %%   A literal percent sign.
   %a   File's last access time in the format returned by the C 'ctime' function.
   %A*k*   File's last access time in the format specified by *k*, which is either '@' or a directive for the C 'strftime' function. The possible values for *k* are listed below; some of them might not be available on all systems, due to differences in 'strftime' between systems.

      @   seconds since Jan. 1, 1970, 00:00 GMT.

      Time fields:

      H   hour (00..23)
      I   hour (01..12)
      k   hour (0..23)
      l   hour (1..12)
      M   minute (00..59)
      p   locale's AM or PM

GNU File Utilities

FIND(1L) FIND(1L)

        r time, 12-hour (hh:mm:ss [AP]M)
        S second (00..61)
        T time, 24-hour (hh:mm:ss)
        X locale's time representation (H:M:S)
        Z time zone (e.g., EDT), or nothing if no time zone is determinable

Date fields:

        a locale's abbreviated weekday name (Sun..Sat)
        A locale's full weekday name, variable length (Sunday..Saturday)
        b locale's abbreviated month name (Jan..Dec)
        B locale's full month name, variable length (January..December)
        c locale's date and time (Sat Nov 04 12:02:33 EST 1989)
        d day of month (01..31)
        D date (mm/dd/yy)
        h same as b
        j day of year (001..366)
        m month (01..12)
        U week number of year with Sunday as first day of week (00..53)
        w day of week (0..6)
        W week number of year with Monday as first day of week (00..53)
        x locale's date representation (mm/dd/yy)
        y last two digits of year (00..99)
        Y year (1970...)

%b File's size in 512-byte blocks (rounded up).

%c File's last status change time in the format returned by the C 'ctime' function.

%Ck File's last status change time in the format specified by k, which is the same as for %A.

%d File's depth in the directory tree; 0 means the file is a command line argument.

%f File's name with any leading directories removed (only the last element).

%F Type of the filesystem the file is on; this value can be used for −fstype.

%g File's group name, or numeric group ID if the group has no name.

%G File's numeric group ID.

%h Leading directories of file's name (all but the last element).

%H Command line argument under which file was found.

%i File's inode number (in decimal).

%k File's size in 1K blocks (rounded up).

%l Object of symbolic link (empty string if file is not a symbolic link).

%m File's permission bits (in octal).

%n Number of hard links to file.

FIND(1L)   FIND(1L)

%p File's name.

%P File's name with the name of the command line argument under which it was found removed.

%s File's size in bytes.

%t File's last modification time in the format returned by the C 'ctime' function.

%T*k* File's last modification time in the format specified by *k*, which is the same as for %A.

%u File's user name, or numeric user ID if the user has no name.

%U File's numeric user ID.

A '%' character followed by any other character is discarded (but the other character is printed).

  –prune   If –depth is not given, true; do not descend the current directory.
               If –depth is given, false; no effect.

  –ls   True; list current file in 'ls –dils' format on standard output. The block counts are of 1K blocks, unless the environment variable POSIXLY_CORRECT is set, in which case 512-byte blocks are used.

OPERATORS

Listed in order of decreasing precedence:

  (*expr*)   Force precedence.

  ! *expr*   True if *expr* is false.

  –not *expr*   Same as ! *expr*.

  expr1 expr2   And (implied); *expr2* is not evaluated if *expr1* is false.

  expr1 –a *expr2*   Same as *expr1 expr2*.

  expr1 –and *expr2*   Same as *expr1 expr2*.

  expr1 –o *expr2*   Or; *expr2* is not evaluated if *expr1* is true.

  expr1 –or *expr2*   Same as *expr1* –o *expr2*.

  expr1 , *expr2*   List; both *expr1* and *expr2* are always evaluated. The value of *expr1* is discarded; the value of the list is the value of *expr2*.

SEE ALSO

locate(1L), **locatedb**(5L), **updatedb**(1L), **xargs**(1L) **Finding Files** (on-line in Info, or printed)

FMT(1L)

NAME
fmt – simple optimal text formatter

SYNOPSIS
fmt [–cstu] [–width] [–w width] [–p prefix] [––crown-margin] [––split-only] [––tagged-paragraph] [––uniform-spacing] [––width=width] [––prefix=prefix] [––help] [––version] [file ...]

DESCRIPTION
This manual page documents the GNU version of **fmt**. **fmt** is a simple text formatter that fills and joins lines to produce output lines of (up to) the specified *width* (default 75). However **fmt** uses a **best-fit** line breaking algorithm, by a simple version of Breaking Paragraphs into Lines, Donald E. Knuth and Michael F. Plass, *Software—Practice and Experience* **11** (1981) 1119–1184.

fmt concatenates the *files* listed as arguments. If none are given, **fmt** formats text from the standard input.

Blank lines are preserved in the output, as is the spacing between words (unless *–u* is used). In contrast to BSD **fmt**, tabs are expanded on input and re-introduced on output.

Indentation is preserved in the output, and input lines with differing indentation are not joined (unless *–c* or *–t* is used). Note that although the BSD **fmt** manual also states this, the BSD version does in fact join following lines with less indentation.

fmt prefers breaking lines at the end of a sentence, and tries to avoid line breaks after the first word of a sentence or before the last word of a sentence. A sentence break is defined as either the end of a paragraph or a word ending in [.?!], followed by two spaces or end of line, ignoring any intervening parentheses or quotes.

OPTIONS

-c, –crown-margin
: Crown margin mode. Preserve the indentation of the first two lines within a paragraph, and align the left margin of each subsequent line with that of the second line.

-t, –tagged-paragraph
: Tagged paragraph mode: just like crown mode, except that the indentation of the first line of a paragraph must be different from the indentation of the second. Otherwise the first line is treated as a one-line paragraph.

-s, –split-only
: Split lines only. Do not join short lines to form longer ones. This prevents sample lines of code, and other such formatted text, from being unduly combined.

-u, –uniform-spacing
: Uniform spacing. Reduce spacing between words to one space, except at the end of a sentence (two spaces).

-width, -w width, –width=width
: Fill output lines to up to *width* columns (default 75). **fmt** prefers to make lines about 7% shorter, to give it room to balance line lengths.

-p, –prefix=prefix
: Only lines beginning with the prefix (possibly preceded by white space) are re-arranged; the prefix (with any preceding white space) is stripped for the formatting and re-attached to each formatted output line. One use is to format certain kinds of program comments, while leaving the code unchanged.

––help
: Print a usage message and exit with a non-zero status.

––version
: Print version information on standard output then exit.

NAME

fmt - adjust line-length for paragraphs of text

SYNOPSIS

fmt [*–width*] [*files*]...

DESCRIPTION

fmt is a simple text formatter. It inserts or deletes newlines, as necessary, to make all lines in a paragraph be approximately the same width. It preserves indentation and word spacing.

The default line width is 72 characters. You can override this with the *–width* flag. If you don't name any files on the command line, then *fmt* will read from stdin.

It is typically used from within *vi* to adjust the line breaks in a single paragraph. To do this, move the cursor to the top of the paragraph, type "!}fmt", and hit <Return>.

AUTHOR

Steve Kirkendall
kirkenda@cs.pdx.edu

FOLD(1L)

NAME

fold – wrap each input line to fit in specified width

SYNOPSIS

fold [–bs] [–w width] [—-bytes] [—-spaces] [—-width=width] [—-help] [—-version] [file...]

DESCRIPTION

This manual page documents the GNU version of **fold**. **fold** prints the specified files, or the standard input when no files are given or the filename '–' is encountered, on the standard output. It breaks long lines into multiple shorter lines by inserting a newline at column 80. It counts screen columns, so tab characters usually take more than one column, backspace characters decrease the column count, and carriage return characters set the column count back to zero.

OPTIONS

–b, —-bytes Count bytes rather than columns, so that tabs, backspaces, and carriage returns are each counted as taking up one column, just like other characters.

–s, —-spaces Break at word boundaries. If the line contains any blanks, the line is broken after the last blank that falls within the maximum line length. If there are no blanks, the line is broken at the maximum line length, as usual.

–w, —-width width Use a maximum line length of *width* columns instead of 80.

—-help Print a usage message and exit with a non-zero status.

—-version Print version information on standard output then exit.

NAME

free – Display amount of free and used memory in the system

SYNOPSIS

free [-b | -k | -m] [-o] [-s delay] [-t]

DESCRIPTION

free displays the total amount of free and used physical and swap memory in the system, as well as the shared memory and buffers used by the kernel.

Options

The -b switch displays the amount of memory in bytes; the -k switch (set by default) displays it in kilobytes; the -m switch displays it in megabytes.

The -t switch displays a line containing the totals.

The -o switch disables the display of a "buffer adjusted" line. Unless specified free subtracts/adds buffer memory from/to the used/free memory reports (respectively!).

The -s switch activates continuous polling *delay* seconds apart. You may actually specify any floating point number for *delay*, usleep(3) is used for microsecond resolution delay times.

FILES

/proc/meminfo – memory informati

SEE ALSO

ps(1), top(1)

AUTHORS

Written by Brian Edmonds.

NAME

ftp – ARPANET file transfer program

SYNOPSIS

ftp [-v] [-d] [-i] [-n] [-g] [host]

DESCRIPTION

Ftp is the user interface to the ARPANET standard File Transfer Protocol. The program allows a user to transfer files to and from a remote network site.

Options may be specified at the command line, or to the command interpreter.

-v Verbose option forces ftp to show all responses from the remote server, as well as report on data transfer statistics.

-n Restrains ftp from attempting auto-login upon initial connection. If auto-login is enabled, ftp will check the (see below) file in the user's home directory for an entry describing an account on the remote machine. If no entry exists, ftp will prompt for the remote machine login name (default is the user identity on the local machine), and, if necessary, prompt for a password and an account with which to login.

-i Turns off interactive prompting during multiple file transfers.

-d Enables debugging.

-g Disables file name globbing.

The client host with which ftp is to communicate may be specified on the command line. If this is done, ftp will immediately attempt to establish a connection to an FTP server on that host; otherwise, ftp will enter its command interpreter and await instructions from the user. When ftp is awaiting commands from the user the prompt

ftp>

is provided to the user. The following commands are recognized by ftp :

    ! [command] [args]   Invoke an interactive shell on the local machine. If there are arguments, the first is taken to be a command to execute directly, with the rest of the arguments as its arguments.

    $ macro-name [args]   Execute the macro macro-name that was defined with the macdef command. Arguments are passed to the macro unglobbed.

    account [passwd]   Supply a supplemental password required by a remote system for access to resources once a login has been successfully completed. If no argument is included, the user will be prompted for an account password in a non-echoing input mode.

    append local-file [remote-file]   Append a local file to a file on the remote machine. If remote-file is left unspecified, the local file name is used in naming the remote file after being altered by any ntrans or nmap setting. File transfer uses the current settings for type, format, mode, and structure.

    ascii   Set the file transfer type to network ASCII. This is the default type.

    bell   Arrange that a bell be sounded after each file transfer command is completed.

    binary   Set the file transfer type to support binary image transfer.

    bye   Terminate the FTP session with the remote server and exit ftp. An end of file will also terminate the session and exit.

    case   Toggle remote computer file name case mapping during mget commands. When case is on (default is off), remote computer file names with all letters in upper case are written in the local directory with the letters mapped to lower case.

cd remote-directory   Change the working directory on the remote machine to remote-directory.

cdup   Change the remote machine working directory to the parent of the current remote machine working directory.

chmod mode file-name   Change the permission modes of the file file-name on the remote sytem to mode.

close   Terminate the FTP session with the remote server, and return to the command interpreter. Any defined macros are erased.

cr   Toggle carriage return stripping during ascii type file retrieval. Records are denoted by a carriage return/linefeed sequence during ascii type file transfer. When cr is on (the default), carriage returns are stripped from this sequence to conform with the unix single linefeed record delimiter. Records on nonunix remote systems may contain single linefeeds; when an ascii type transfer is made, these linefeeds may be distinguished from a record delimiter only when cr is off.

delete remote-file   Delete the file remote-file on the remote machine.

debug [debug-value]   Toggle debugging mode. If an optional debug-value is specified it is used to set the debugging level. When debugging is on, ftp prints each command sent to the remote machine, preceded by the string ¿

dir [remote-directory] [local-file]   Print a listing of the directory contents in the directory, remote-directory, and, optionally, placing the output in local-file. If interactive prompting is on, ftp will prompt the user to verify that the last argument is indeed the target local file for receiving dir output. If no directory is specified, the current working directory on the remote machine is used. If no local file is specified, or local-file is -, output comes to the terminal.

disconnect   A synonym for close.

form format   Set the file transfer form to format. The default format is file.

get remote-file [local-file]   Retrieve the remote-file and store it on the local machine. If the local file name is not specified, it is given the same name it has on the remote machine, subject to alteration by the current case, ntrans, and nmap settings. The current settings for type, form, mode, and structure are used while transferring the file.

glob   Toggle filename expansion for mdelete, mget and mput. If globbing is turned off with glob, the file name arguments are taken literally and not expanded. Globbing for mput is done as in csh 1. For mdelete and mget, each remote file name is expanded separately on the remote machine and the lists are not merged. Expansion of a directory name is likely to be different from expansion of the name of an ordinary file: the exact result depends on the foreign operating system and ftp server, and can be previewed by doing mls remote-files Note: mget and mput are not meant to transfer entire directory subtrees of files. That can be done by transferring a tar 1 archive of the subtree (in binary mode).

hash   Toggle hash-sign ("#") printing for each data block transferred. The size of a data block is 1024 bytes.

help [command]   Print an informative message about the meaning of command. If no argument is given, ftp prints a list of the known commands.

idle [seconds]   Set the inactivity timer on the remote server to seconds seconds. If seconds is ommitted, the current inactivity timer is printed.

lcd [directory]   Change the working directory on the local machine. If no directory is specified, the user's home directory is used.

FTP(1)   FTP(1)

ls [remote-directory] [local-file]   Print a listing of the contents of a directory on the remote machine. The listing includes any system-dependent information that the server chooses to include; for example, most systems will produce output from the command ls l. (See also nlist.) If remote-directory is left unspecified, the current working directory is used. If interactive prompting is on, ftp will prompt the user to verify that the last argument is indeed the target local file for receiving ls output. If no local file is specified, or if local-file is -, the output is sent to the terminal.

macdef macro-name   Define a macro. Subsequent lines are stored as the macro macro-name; a null line (consecutive newline characters in a file or carriage returns from the terminal) terminates macro input mode. There is a limit of 16 macros and 4096 total characters in all defined macros. Macros remain defined until a close command is executed. The macro processor interprets '$' and '\' as special characters. A '$' followed by a number (or numbers) is replaced by the corresponding argument on the macro invocation command line. A '$' followed by an 'i' signals that macro processor that the executing macro is to be looped. On the first pass '$i' is replaced by the first argument on the macro invocation command line, on the second pass it is replaced by the second argument, and so on. A '\' followed by any character is replaced by that character. Use the '\' to prevent special treatment of the '$'.

mdelete [remote-files]   Delete the remote-files on the remote machine.

mdir remote-files local-file   Like dir, except multiple remote files may be specified. If interactive prompting is on, ftp will prompt the user to verify that the last argument is indeed the target local file for receiving mdir output.

mget remote-files   Expand the remote-files on the remote machine and do a get for each file name thus produced. See glob for details on the filename expansion. Resulting file names will then be processed according to case, ntrans, and nmap settings. Files are transferred into the local working directory, which can be changed with lcd directory; new local directories can be created with !mkdir directory.

mkdir directory-name   Make a directory on the remote machine.

mls remote-files local-file   Like nlist, except multiple remote files may be specified, and the local-file must be specified. If interactive prompting is on, ftp will prompt the user to verify that the last argument is indeed the target local file for receiving mls output.

mode [mode-name]   Set the file transfer mode to mode-name. The default mode is stream mode.

modtime file-name   Show the last modification time of the file on the remote machine.

mput local-files   Expand wild cards in the list of local files given as arguments and do a put for each file in the resulting list. See glob for details of filename expansion. Resulting file names will then be processed according to ntrans and nmap settings.

newer file-name   Get the file only if the modification time of the remote file is more recent that the file on the current system. If the file does not exist on the current system, the remote file is considered newer. Otherwise, this command is identical to get.

nlist [remote-directory] [local-file]   Print a list of the files in a directory on the remote machine. If remote-directory is left unspecified, the current working directory is used. If interactive prompting is on, ftp will prompt the user to verify that the last argument is indeed the target local file for receiving nlist output. If no local file is specified, or if local-file is -, the output is sent to the terminal.

FTP(1)   FTP(1)

nmap [inpattern] outpattern   Set or unset the filename mapping mechanism. If no arguments are specified, the filename mapping mechanism is unset. If arguments are specified, remote filenames are mapped during mput commands and put commands issued without a specified remote target filename. If arguments are specified, local filenames are mapped during mget commands and get commands issued without a specified local target filename. This command is useful when connecting to a nonunix remote computer with different file naming conventions or practices. The mapping follows the pattern set by inpattern and outpattern. Inpattern is a template for incoming filenames (which may have already been processed according to the ntrans and case settings). Variable templating is accomplished by including the sequences '$1', '$2',..., '$9' in inpattern. Use '\' to prevent this special treatment of the '$' character. All other characters are treated literally, and are used to determine the nmap inpattern variable values. For example, given inpattern $1.$2 and the remote file name "mydata.data", $1 would have the value "mydata", and $2 would have the value "data". The outpattern determines the resulting mapped filename. The sequences '$1', '$2',...., '$9' are replaced by any value resulting from the inpattern template. The sequence '$0' is replace by the original filename. Additionally, the sequence seq1, seq2 is replaced by seq1 if seq1 is not a null string; otherwise it is replaced by seq2. For example, the command

nmap $1.$2.$3 [$1,$2].[$2,file]

would yield the output filename "myfile.data" for input filenames "myfile.data" and "myfile.data.old", "myfile.file" for the input filename "myfile", and "myfile.myfile" for the input filename ".myfile". Spaces may be included in outpattern, as in the example: 'nmap $1 sed "s/ *$//" > $1'. Use the '\' character to prevent special treatment of the '$','[',']', and ',' characters.

ntrans [inchars] [outchars]   Set or unset the filename character translation mechanism. If no arguments are specified, the filename character translation mechanism is unset. If arguments are specified, characters in remote filenames are translated during mput commands and put commands issued without a specified remote target filename. If arguments are specified, characters in local filenames are translated during mget commands and get commands issued without a specified local target filename. This command is useful when connecting to a nonunix remote computer with different file naming conventions or practices. Characters in a filename matching a character in inchars are replaced with the corresponding character in outchars. If the character's position in inchars is longer than the length of outchars, the character is deleted from the file name.

open host [port]   Establish a connection to the specified host FTP server. An optional port number may be supplied, in which case, ftp will attempt to contact an FTP server at that port. If the auto-login option is on (default), ftp will also attempt to automatically log the user in to the FTP server (see below).

prompt   Toggle interactive prompting. Interactive prompting occurs during multiple file transfers to allow the user to selectively retrieve or store files. If prompting is turned off (default is on), any mget or mput will transfer all files, and any mdelete will delete all files.

proxy ftp-command   Execute an ftp command on a secondary control connection. This command allows simultaneous connection to two remote ftp servers for transferring files between the two servers. The first proxy command should be an open, to establish the secondary control connection. Enter the command "proxy ?" to see other ftp commands executable on the secondary connection. The following commands behave differently when prefaced by proxy : open will not define new macros during the auto-login process, close will not erase existing macro definitions, get and mget transfer files from the host on the primary control connection to the host on the secondary control connection, and put, mput, and append transfer files from the host on the secondary control connection to the host on the primary control connection. Third party file transfers depend upon support of the ftp protocol PASV command by the server on the secondary control connection.

put local-file [remote-file]   Store a local file on the remote machine. If remote-file is left unspecified, the local file name is used after processing according to any ntrans or nmap settings in naming the remote file. File transfer uses the current settings for type, format, mode, and structure.

pwd   Print the name of the current working directory on the remote machine.

quit   A synonym for bye.

quote arg1 arg2...   The arguments specified are sent, verbatim, to the remote FTP server.

recv remote-file [local-file]   A synonym for get.

reget remote-file [local-file]   Reget acts like get, except that if local-file exists and is smaller than remote-file, local-file is presumed to be a partially transferred copy of remote-file and the transfer is continued from the apparent point of failure. This command is useful when transferring very large files over networks that are prone to dropping connections.

remotehelp [command-name]   Request help from the remote FTP server. If a command-name is specified it is supplied to the server as well.

remotestatus [file-name]   With no arguments, show status of remote machine. If file-name is specified, show status of file-name on remote machine.

rename [from] [to]   Rename the file from on the remote machine, to the file to.

reset   Clear reply queue. This command re-synchronizes command/reply sequencing with the remote ftp server. Resynchronization may be necessary following a violation of the ftp protocol by the remote server.

restart marker   Restart the immediately following get or put at the indicated marker. On unix systems, marker is usually a byte offset into the file.

rmdir directory-name   Delete a directory on the remote machine.

runique   Toggle storing of files on the local system with unique filenames. If a file already exists with a name equal to the target local filename for a get or mget command, a ".1" is appended to the name. If the resulting name matches another existing file, a ".2" is appended to the original name. If this process continues up to ".99", an error message is printed, and the transfer does not take place. The generated unique filename will be reported. Note that runique will not affect local files generated from a shell command (see below). The default value is off.

send local-file [remote-file]   A synonym for put.

sendport   Toggle the use of PORT commands. By default, ftp will attempt to use a PORT command when establishing a connection for each data transfer. The use of PORT commands can prevent delays when performing multiple file transfers. If the PORT command fails, ftp will use the default data port. When the use of PORT commands is disabled, no attempt will be made to use PORT commands for each data transfer. This is useful for certain FTP implementations which

FTP(1)   FTP(1)

     do ignore PORT commands but, incorrectly, indicate they've been accepted.
  site arg1 arg2... The arguments specified are sent, verbatim, to the remote FTP server as a SITE command.
  size file-name Return size of file-name on remote machine.
  status Show the current status of ftp.
  struct [struct-name] Set the file transfer structure to struct-name. By default stream structure is used.
  sunique Toggle storing of files on remote machine under unique file names. Remote ftp server must support ftp protocol STOU command for successful completion. The remote server will report unique name. Default value is off.
  system Show the type of operating system running on the remote machine.
  tenex Set the file transfer type to that needed to talk to TENEX machines.
  trace Toggle packet tracing.
  type [type-name] Set the file transfer type to type-name. If no type is specified, the current type is printed. The default type is network ASCII.
  umask [newmask] Set the default umask on the remote server to newmask. If newmask is ommitted, the current umask is printed.
  user user-name [password] [account] Identify yourself to the remote FTP server. If the password is not specified and the server requires it, ftp will prompt the user for it (after disabling local echo). If an account field is not specified, and the FTP server requires it, the user will be prompted for it. If an account field is specified, an account command will be relayed to the remote server after the login sequence is completed if the remote server did not require it for logging in. Unless ftp is invoked with auto-login disabled, this process is done automatically on initial connection to the FTP server.
  verbose Toggle verbose mode. In verbose mode, all responses from the FTP server are displayed to the user. In addition, if verbose is on, when a file transfer completes, statistics regarding the efficiency of the transfer are reported. By default, verbose is on.
  ? [command] A synonym for help.

Command arguments which have embedded spaces may be quoted with quote '"' marks.

ABORTING A FILE TRANSFER

To abort a file transfer, use the terminal interrupt key (usually Ctrl-C). Sending transfers will be immediately halted. Receiving transfers will be halted by sending a ftp protocol ABOR command to the remote server, and discarding any further data received. The speed at which this is accomplished depends upon the remote server's support for ABOR processing. If the remote server does not support the ABOR command, an ftp> prompt will not appear until the remote server has completed sending the requested file.

The terminal interrupt key sequence will be ignored when ftp has completed any local processing and is awaiting a reply from the remote server. A long delay in this mode may result from the ABOR processing described above, or from unexpected behavior by the remote server, including violations of the ftp protocol. If the delay results from unexpected remote server behavior, the local ftp program must be killed by hand.

FILE NAMING CONVENTIONS

Files specified as arguments to ftp commands are processed according to the following rules.

If the file name - is specified, the stdin (for reading) or stdout (for writing) is used.

If the first character of the file name is |, the remainder of the argument is interpreted as a shell command. Ftp then forks a shell, using popen 3 with the argument supplied, and reads (writes) from the stdout (stdin). If the shell command includes spaces, the argument must be quoted; e.g. " ls -lt". A particularly useful example of this mechanism is: dir more.

Failing the above checks, if "globbing" is enabled, local file names are expanded according to the rules used in the csh 1 ; c.f. the glob command. If the ftp command expects a single local file (.e.g. put), only the first filename generated by the "globbing" operation is used.

For mget commands and get commands with unspecified local file names, the local filename is the remote filename, which may be altered by a case, ntrans, or nmap setting. The resulting filename may then be altered if runique is on.

For mput commands and put commands with unspecified remote file names, the remote filename is the local filename, which may be altered by a ntrans or nmap setting. The resulting filename may then be altered by the remote server if sunique is on.

FILE TRANSFER PARAMETERS

The FTP specification specifies many parameters which may affect a file transfer. The type may be one of ascii, image (binary), ebcdic, and local byte size (for PDP Ns -10's and PDP Ns -20's mostly). Ftp supports the ascii and image types of file transfer, plus local byte size 8 for tenex mode transfers.

Ftp supports only the default values for the remaining file transfer parameters: mode, form, and struct.

THE .netrc FILE

The file contains login and initialization information used by the auto-login process. It resides in the user's home directory. The following tokens are recognized; they may be separated by spaces, tabs, or new-lines:

    machine name   Identify a remote machine name. The auto-login process searches the file for a machine token that matches the remote machine specified on the ftp command line or as an open command argument. Once a match is made, the subsequent tokens are processed, stopping when the end of file is reached or another machine or a default token is encountered.

    default   This is the same as machine name except that default matches any name. There can be only one default token, and it must be after all machine tokens. This is normally used as:

    default login anonymous password user@site

thereby giving the user automatic anonymous ftp login to machines not specified in This can be overridden by using the -n flag to disable auto-login.

    login name   Identify a user on the remote machine. If this token is present, the auto-login process will initiate a login using the specified name.

    password string   Supply a password. If this token is present, the auto-login process will supply the specified string if the remote server requires a password as part of the login process. Note that if this token is present in the file for any user other than anonymous, ftp will abort the auto-login process if the is readable by anyone besides the user.

    account string   Supply an additional account password. If this token is present, the auto-login process will supply the specified string if the remote server requires an additional account password, or the auto-login process will initiate an ACCT command if it does not.

macdef name   Define a macro. This token functions like the ftp macdef command functions. A macro is defined with the specified name; its contents begin with the next line and continue until a null line (consecutive new-line characters) is encountered. If a macro named init is defined, it is automatically executed as the last step in the auto-login process.

ENVIRONMENT

Ftp utilizes the following environment variables.

HOME   For default location of a file, if one exists.

SHELL   For default shell.

SEE ALSO

ftpd 8

HISTORY

The ftp command appeared in BSD 4.2.

BUGS

Correct execution of many commands depends upon proper behavior by the remote server.

An error in the treatment of carriage returns in the BSD 4.2 ascii-mode transfer code has been corrected. This correction may result in incorrect transfers of binary files to and from BSD 4.2 servers using the ascii type. Avoid this problem by using the binary image type.

NAME

fuser – identify processes using files

SYNOPSIS

fuser [–a|–s] [–*signal*] [–**kmuv**] *filename* ... [–] [–*signal*] [–**kmuv**] *filename* ...
fuser [–l]

DESCRIPTION

fuser displays the PIDs of processes using the specified files or file systems. In the default display mode, each file name is followed by a letter denoting the type of access:

- **c** current directory.
- **e** executable being run.
- **f** open file. **f** is omitted in default display mode.
- **r** root directory.
- **m** mmap'ed file or shared library.

fuser returns a non-zero return code if none of the specified files is accessed or in case of a fatal error. If at least one access has been found, **fuser** returns zero.

OPTIONS

- **–a** show all files specified on the command line. By default, only files that are accessed by at least one process are shown.
- **–k** kill processes accessing the file. Unless changed with **-***signal*, SIGKILL is sent. An **fuser** process never kills itself, but may kill other **fuser** processes.
- **–l** list all known signal names.
- **–m** *filename* specifies a file on a mounted file system or a block device that is mounted. All processes accessing files on that file system are listed. If a directory file is specified, it is automatically changed to *filename/*. to use any file system that might be mounted on that directory.
- **–s** silent operation. **–a**, **–u** and **–v** are ignored in this mode.
- **–***signal* use the specified signal instead of SIGKILL when killing processes. Signals can be specified either by name (e.g. **–HUP**) or by number (e.g. **–1**).
- **–u** append the user name of the process owner to each PID.
- **–v** verbose mode. Processes are shown in a **ps**-like style. The fields PID, USER and COMMAND are similar to **ps**. ACCESS shows how the process accesses the file.
- **–** reset all options and set the signal back to SIGKILL.

FILES

/proc location of the proc file system

EXAMPLES

fuser -km /home kills all processes accessing the file system /home in any way.

if fuser -s /dev/ttyS1; then :; else *something*; **fi** invokes *something* if no other process is using /dev/ttyS1.

RESTRICTIONS

Processes accessing the same file or file system several times in the same way are only shown once.

AUTHOR

Werner Almesberger <almesber@di.epfl.ch>

SEE ALSO

kill(1), killall(1), ps(1), kill(2)

GAWK(1) Utility Commands GAWK(1)

NAME

gawk – pattern scanning and processing language

SYNOPSIS

gawk [POSIX or GNU style options] **–f** *program-file* [—] file ...
gawk [POSIX or GNU style options] [—] *program-text* file ...

DESCRIPTION

Gawk is the GNU Project's implementation of the AWK programming language. It conforms to the definition of the language in the 1003.2 Command Language And Utilities Standard. This version in turn is based on the description in *The AWK Programming Language*, by Aho, Kernighan, and Weinberger, with the additional features defined in the System V Release 4 version of *awk*. *Gawk* also provides some GNU-specific extensions.

The command line consists of options to *gawk* itself, the AWK program text (if not supplied via the **–f** or **—file** options), and values to be made available in the **ARGC** and **ARGV** predefined AWK variables.

OPTIONS

Gawk options may be either the traditional one letter options, or the GNU style long options. style options start with a single "–", while GNU long options start with "—". GNU style long options are provided for both GNU-specific features and for mandated features. Other implementations of the AWK language are likely to only accept the traditional one letter options.

Following the standard, *gawk*-specific options are supplied via arguments to the **–W** option. Multiple **–W** options may be supplied, or multiple arguments may be supplied together if they are separated by commas, or enclosed in quotes and separated by white space. Case is ignored in arguments to the **–W** option. Each **–W** option has a corresponding GNU style long option, as detailed below. Arguments to GNU style long options are either joined with the option by an = sign, with no intervening spaces, or they may be provided in the next command line argument.

Gawk accepts the following options.

–F *fs*
—field-separator=*fs*   Use *fs* for the input field separator (the value of the **FS** predefined variable).

–v *var=val*
—assign=*var=val*   Assign the value *val*, to the variable *var*, before execution of the program begins. Such variable values are available to the **BEGIN** block of an AWK program.

–f *program-file*
—file=*program-file*   Read the AWK program source from the file *program-file*, instead of from the first command line argument. Multiple **–f** (or **—file**) options may be used.

–mf=*NNN*
–mr=*NNN*   Set various memory limits to the value *NNN*. The **f** flag sets the maximum number of fields, and the **r** flag sets the maximum record size. These two flags and the **–m** option are from the AT&T Bell Labs research version of *awk*. They are ignored by *gawk*, since *gawk* has no pre-defined limits.

–W compat
—compat   Run in *compatibility* mode. In compatibility mode, *gawk* behaves identically to *awk*; none of the GNU-specific extensions are recognized. See **GNU EXTENSIONS**, below, for more information.

–W copyleft

Free Software Foundation   Nov 24 1994   127

-W copyright
—copyleft
—copyright Print the short version of the GNU copyright information message on the error output.

-W help
-W usage
—help
—usage Print a relatively short summary of the available options on the error output. Per the GNU Coding Standards, these options cause an immediate, successful exit.

-W lint
—lint Provide warnings about constructs that are dubious or non-portable to other AWK implementations.

-W posix
—posix This turns on *compatibility* mode, with the following additional restrictions:

\x escape sequences are not recognized.

The synonym **func** for the keyword **function** is not recognized.

The operators ** and **= cannot be used in place of ^ and ^=.

-W source=*program-text*
—source=*program-text* Use *program-text* as AWK program source code. This option allows the easy intermixing of library functions (used via the **-f** and **—file** options) with source code entered on the command line. It is intended primarily for medium to large size AWK programs used in shell scripts.

The **-W source=** form of this option uses the rest of the command line argument for *program-text*; no other options to **-W** will be recognized in the same argument.

-W version
—version Print version information for this particular copy of *gawk* on the error output. This is useful mainly for knowing if the current copy of *gawk* on your system is up to date with respect to whatever the Free Software Foundation is distributing. Per the GNU Coding Standards, these options cause an immediate, successful exit.

— Signal the end of options. This is useful to allow further arguments to the AWK program itself to start with a "–". This is mainly for consistency with the argument parsing convention used by most other programs.

In compatibility mode, any other options are flagged as illegal, but are otherwise ignored. In normal operation, as long as program text has been supplied, unknown options are passed on to the AWK program in the **ARGV** array for processing. This is particularly useful for running AWK programs via the "#!" executable interpreter mechanism.

AWK PROGRAM EXECUTION

An AWK program consists of a sequence of pattern-action statements and optional function definitions.

pattern { *action statements* }
function *name(parameter list)* { *statements* }

Gawk first reads the program source from the *program-file*(s) if specified, from arguments to **-W source=**, or from the first non-option argument on the command line. The **-f** and **-W source=** options may be used multiple times on the command line. *Gawk* will read the program text as if all the *program-files* and command line source texts had been concatenated together. This is useful for building libraries of AWK functions, without having to include them in each new AWK program that uses them. It also provides the ability to mix library functions with command line programs.

The environment variable **AWKPATH** specifies a search path to use when finding source files named with the **–f** option. If this variable does not exist, the default path is
"**.:/usr/lib/awk:/usr/local/lib/awk**".
If a file name given to the **–f** option contains a "/" character, no path search is performed.

Gawk executes AWK programs in the following order. First, all variable assignments specified via the **–v** option are performed. Next, *gawk* compiles the program into an internal form. Then, *gawk* executes the code in the **BEGIN** block(s) (if any), and then proceeds to read each file named in the **ARGV** array. If there are no files named on the command line, *gawk* reads the standard input.

If a filename on the command line has the form *var=val* it is treated as a variable assignment. The variable *var* will be assigned the value *val*. (This happens after any **BEGIN** block(s) have been run.) Command line variable assignment is most useful for dynamically assigning values to the variables AWK uses to control how input is broken into fields and records. It is also useful for controlling state if multiple passes are needed over a single data file.

If the value of a particular element of **ARGV** is empty (""), *gawk* skips over it.

For each line in the input, *gawk* tests to see if it matches any *pattern* in the AWK program. For each pattern that the line matches, the associated *action* is executed. The patterns are tested in the order they occur in the program.

Finally, after all the input is exhausted, *gawk* executes the code in the **END** block(s) (if any).

VARIABLES AND FIELDS

AWK variables are dynamic; they come into existence when they are first used. Their values are either floating-point numbers or strings, or both, depending upon how they are used. AWK also has one dimensional arrays; arrays with multiple dimensions may be simulated. Several pre-defined variables are set as a program runs; these will be described as needed and summarized below.

Fields

As each input line is read, *gawk* splits the line into *fields*, using the value of the **FS** variable as the field separator. If **FS** is a single character, fields are separated by that character. Otherwise, **FS** is expected to be a full regular expression. In the special case that **FS** is a single blank, fields are separated by runs of blanks and/or tabs. Note that the value of **IGNORECASE** (see below) will also affect how fields are split when **FS** is a regular expression.

If the **FIELDWIDTHS** variable is set to a space separated list of numbers, each field is expected to have fixed width, and *gawk* will split up the record using the specified widths. The value of **FS** is ignored. Assigning a new value to **FS** overrides the use of **FIELDWIDTHS**, and restores the default behavior.

Each field in the input line may be referenced by its position, $1 , $2 , and so on. $0 is the whole line. The value of a field may be assigned to as well. Fields need not be referenced by constants:

n = 5
print $n

prints the fifth field in the input line. The variable **NF** is set to the total number of fields in the input line.

References to non-existent fields (i.e. fields after $NF) produce the null-string. However, assigning to a non-existent field (e.g., $(NF+2) = 5) will increase the value of **NF**, create any intervening fields with the null string as their value, and cause the value of $0 to be recomputed, with the fields being separated by the value of **OFS**. References to negative numbered fields cause a fatal error.

Built-in Variables

AWK's built-in variables are:

ARGC The number of command line arguments (does not include options to *gawk*, or the program source).

ARGIND The index in **ARGV** of the current file being processed.

ARGV Array of command line arguments. The array is indexed from 0 to **ARGC** – 1. Dynamically changing the contents of **ARGV** can control the files used for data.

CONVFMT The conversion format for numbers, "%.6g", by default.

ENVIRON An array containing the values of the current environment. The array is indexed by the environment variables, each element being the value of that variable (e.g., **ENVIRON["HOME"]** might be **/u/arnold**). Changing this array does not affect the environment seen by programs which *gawk* spawns via redirection or the **system()** function. (This may change in a future version of *gawk*.)

ERRNO If a system error occurs either doing a redirection for **getline**, during a read for **getline**, or during a **close()**, then **ERRNO** will contain a string describing the error.

FIELDWIDTHS A white-space separated list of fieldwidths. When set, *gawk* parses the input into fields of fixed width, instead of using the value of the **FS** variable as the field separator. The fixed field width facility is still experimental; expect the semantics to change as *gawk* evolves over time.

FILENAME The name of the current input file. If no files are specified on the command line, the value of **FILENAME** is "–". However, **FILENAME** is undefined inside the **BEGIN** block.

FNR The input record number in the current input file.

FS The input field separator, a blank by default.

IGNORECASE Controls the case-sensitivity of all regular expression operations. If **IGNORECASE** has a non-zero value, then pattern matching in rules, field splitting with **FS**, regular expression matching with ˜ and !˜, and the **gsub()**, **index()**, **match()**, **split()**, and **sub()** pre-defined functions will all ignore case when doing regular expression operations. Thus, if **IGNORECASE** is not equal to zero, /aB/ matches all of the strings "ab", "aB", "Ab", and "AB". As with all AWK variables, the initial value of **IGNORECASE** is zero, so all regular expression operations are normally case-sensitive.

NF The number of fields in the current input record.

NR The total number of input records seen so far.

OFMT The output format for numbers, "%.6g", by default.

OFS The output field separator, a blank by default.

ORS The output record separator, by default a newline.

RS The input record separator, by default a newline. **RS** is exceptional in that only the first character of its string value is used for separating records. (This will probably change in a future release of *gawk*.) If **RS** is set to the null string, then records are separated by blank lines. When **RS** is set to the null string, then the newline character always acts as a field separator, in addition to whatever value **FS** may have.

RSTART The index of the first character matched by **match()**; 0 if no match.

RLENGTH The length of the string matched by **match()**; –1 if no match.

SUBSEP The character used to separate multiple subscripts in array elements, by default "\034".

Arrays

Arrays are subscripted with an expression between square brackets ([and]). If the expression is an expression list (*expr*, *expr* ...) then the array subscript is a string consisting of the concatenation of the (string) value of each expression, separated by the value of the **SUBSEP** variable. This facility is used to simulate multiply dimensioned arrays. For example:

i = "A" ; j = "B" ; k = "C"
x[i, j, k] = "hello, world\n"

assigns the string **"hello, world\n"** to the element of the array **x** which is indexed by the string **"A\034B\034C"**. All arrays in AWK are associative, i.e. indexed by string values.

The special operator **in** may be used in an **if** or **while** statement to see if an array has an index consisting of a particular value.

if (val in array)
print array[val]

If the array has multiple subscripts, use **(i, j) in array**.

The **in** construct may also be used in a **for** loop to iterate over all the elements of an array.

An element may be deleted from an array using the **delete** statement. The **delete** statement may also be used to delete the entire contents of an array.

Variable Typing And Conversion

Variables and fields may be (floating point) numbers, or strings, or both. How the value of a variable is interpreted depends upon its context. If used in a numeric expression, it will be treated as a number, if used as a string it will be treated as a string.

To force a variable to be treated as a number, add 0 to it; to force it to be treated as a string, concatenate it with the null string.

When a string must be converted to a number, the conversion is accomplished using *atof*(3). A number is converted to a string by using the value of **CONVFMT** as a format string for *sprintf*(3), with the numeric value of the variable as the argument. However, even though all numbers in AWK are floating-point, integral values are *always* converted as integers. Thus, given

CONVFMT = "%2.2f"
a = 12
b = a ""

the variable **b** has a string value of **"12"** and not **"12.00"**.

Gawk performs comparisons as follows: If two variables are numeric, they are compared numerically. If one value is numeric and the other has a string value that is a "numeric string," then comparisons are also done numerically. Otherwise, the numeric value is converted to a string and a string comparison is performed. Two strings are compared, of course, as strings. According to the standard, even if two strings are numeric strings, a numeric comparison is performed. However, this is clearly incorrect, and *gawk* does not do this.

Uninitialized variables have the numeric value 0 and the string value "" (the null, or empty, string).

PATTERNS AND ACTIONS

AWK is a line oriented language. The pattern comes first, and then the action. Action statements are enclosed in **and .BR** . Either the pattern may be missing, or the action may be missing, but, of course, not both. If the pattern is missing, the action will be executed for every single line of input. A missing action is equivalent to

{ **print** }

which prints the entire line.

Comments begin with the "**#**" character, and continue until the end of the line. Blank lines may be used to separate statements. Normally, a statement ends with a newline, however, this is not the case for lines ending in a ",", "{", "?", ":", "&&", or "||". Lines ending in **do** or **else** also have their statements automatically continued on the following line. In other cases, a line can be continued by ending it with a "\", in which case the newline will be ignored.

Multiple statements may be put on one line by separating them with a ";". This applies to both the statements within the action part of a pattern-action pair (the usual case), and to the pattern-action statements themselves.

Patterns

AWK patterns may be one of the following:

BEGIN
END
/*regular expression*/
relational expression
pattern **&&** *pattern*
pattern **||** *pattern*
pattern **?** *pattern* **:** *pattern*
(*pattern*)
! *pattern*
pattern1, *pattern2*

BEGIN and **END** are two special kinds of patterns which are not tested against the input. The action parts of all **BEGIN** patterns are merged as if all the statements had been written in a single **BEGIN** block. They are executed before any of the input is read. Similarly, all the **END** blocks are merged, and executed when all the input is exhausted (or when an **exit** statement is executed). **BEGIN** and **END** patterns cannot be combined with other patterns in pattern expressions. **BEGIN** and **END** patterns cannot have missing action parts.

For /*regular expression*/ patterns, the associated statement is executed for each input line that matches the regular expression. Regular expressions are the same as those in *egrep*(1), and are summarized below.

A *relational expression* may use any of the operators defined below in the section on actions. These generally test whether certain fields match certain regular expressions.

The **&&**, **||**, and **!** operators are logical AND, logical OR, and logical NOT, respectively, as in C. They do short-circuit evaluation, also as in C, and are used for combining more primitive pattern expressions. As in most languages, parentheses may be used to change the order of evaluation.

The **?:** operator is like the same operator in C. If the first pattern is true then the pattern used for testing is the second pattern, otherwise it is the third. Only one of the second and third patterns is evaluated.

The *pattern1*, *pattern2* form of an expression is called a *range pattern*. It matches all input records starting with a line that matches *pattern1*, and continuing until a record that matches *pattern2*, inclusive. It does not combine with any other sort of pattern expression.

Regular Expressions

Regular expressions are the extended kind found in *egrep*. They are composed of characters as follows:

- *c*   matches the non-metacharacter *c*.
- *c*   matches the literal character *c*.
- .   matches any character except newline.
- ^   matches the beginning of a line or a string.
- $ matches the end of a line or a string.
- [*abc*...]   character class, matches any of the characters *abc*....
- [^*abc*...] negated character class, matches any character except *abc*... and newline.
- *r1*|*r2*   alternation: matches either *r1* or *r2*.

r1r2	concatenation: matches *r1*, and then *r2*.	
r+	matches one or more *r*'s.	
r*	matches zero or more *r*'s.	
r?	matches zero or one *r*'s.	
(r)	grouping: matches *r*.	

The escape sequences that are valid in string constants (see below) are also legal in regular expressions.

Actions

Action statements are enclosed in braces, **and .BR** . Action statements consist of the usual assignment, conditional, and looping statements found in most languages. The operators, control statements, and input/output statements available are patterned after those in C.

Operators

The operators in AWK, in order of increasing precedence, are

= += −=	
*= /= %= ^=	Assignment. Both absolute assignment (*var* = *value*) and operator-assignment (the other forms) are supported.
?:	The C conditional expression. This has the form *expr1* **?** *expr2* **:** *expr3* . If *expr1* is true, the value of the expression is *expr2*, otherwise it is *expr3*. Only one of *expr2* and *expr3* is evaluated.
||	Logical OR.
&&	Logical AND.
~ !~	Regular expression match, negated match. **NOTE:** Do not use a constant regular expression (**/foo/**) on the left-hand side of a ~ or !~. Only use one on the right-hand side. The expression **/foo/** ~ *exp* has the same meaning as **(($0** ~ **/foo/)** ~ *exp*). This is usually *not* what was intended.
< >	
<= >=	
!= ==	The regular relational operators.
blank	String concatenation.
+ −	Addition and subtraction.
* / %	Multiplication, division, and modulus.
+ − !	Unary plus, unary minus, and logical negation.
^	Exponentiation (** may also be used, and **= for the assignment operator).
++ −−	Increment and decrement, both prefix and postfix.
$	Field reference.

Control Statements

The control statements are as follows:

if (*condition*) *statement* [**else** *statement*]
while (*condition*) *statement* **do** *statement* **while** (*condition*) **for** (*expr1*; *expr2*; *expr3*) *statement* **for** (*var* **in** *array*) *statement* **break continue delete** *array*[*index*] **delete** *array* **exit** [*expression*]
{ *statements* }

I/O Statements

The input/output statements are as follows:

close(*filename*)	Close file (or pipe, see below).
getline	Set $0 from next input record; set NF, NR, FNR.
getline <*file*	Set $0 from next record of *file*; set NF.
getline *var*	Set *var* from next input record; set NF, FNR.
getline *var* <*file*	Set *var* from next record of *file*.
next	Stop processing the current input record. The next input record is read and processing starts over with the first pattern in the AWK program. If the end of the input data is reached, the END block(s), if any, are executed.
next file	Stop processing the current input file. The next input record read comes from the next input file. FILENAME is updated, FNR is reset to 1, and processing starts over with the first pattern in the AWK program. If the end of the input data is reached, the END block(s), if any, are executed.
print	Prints the current record.
print *expr-list*	Prints expressions. Each expression is separated by the value of the OFS variable. The output record is terminated with the value of the ORS variable.
print *expr-list* >*file*	Prints expressions on *file*. Each expression is separated by the value of the OFS variable. The output record is terminated with the value of the ORS variable.
printf *fmt, expr-list*	Format and print.
printf *fmt, expr-list* >*file*	Format and print on *file*.
system(*cmd-line*)	Execute the command *cmd-line*, and return the exit status. (This may not be available on non- systems.)

Other input/output redirections are also allowed. For print and printf, >>*file* appends output to the *file*, while | *command* writes on a pipe. In a similar fashion, *command* | getline pipes into getline. The getline command will return 0 on end of file, and −1 on an error.

The *printf* Statement

The AWK versions of the printf statement and sprintf() function (see below) accept the following conversion specification formats:

%c	An ASCII character. If the argument used for %c is numeric, it is treated as a character and printed. Otherwise, the argument is assumed to be a string, and the only first character of that string is printed.
%d	A decimal number (the integer part).
%i	Just like %d.
%e	A floating point number of the form [−]d.ddddddE[+−]dd.
%f	A floating point number of the form [−]ddd.dddddd.
%g	Use e or f conversion, whichever is shorter, with nonsignificant zeros suppressed.
%o	An unsigned octal number (again, an integer).
%s	A character string.
%x	An unsigned hexadecimal number (an integer).

%X   Like %x, but using ABCDEF instead of abcdef.

%%   A single % character; no argument is converted.

There are optional, additional parameters that may lie between the % and the control letter:

- The expression should be left-justified within its field.

width The field should be padded to this width. If the number has a leading zero, then the field will be padded with zeros. Otherwise it is padded with blanks. This applies even to the non-numeric output formats.

.prec A number indicating the maximum width of strings or digits to the right of the decimal point.

The dynamic *width* and *prec* capabilities of the C printf() routines are supported. A * in place of either the width or prec specifications will cause their values to be taken from the argument list to printf or sprintf().

Special File Names

When doing I/O redirection from either print or printf into a file, or via getline from a file, *gawk* recognizes certain special filenames internally. These filenames allow access to open file descriptors inherited from *gawk*'s parent process (usually the shell). Other special filenames provide access information about the running gawk process. The filenames are:

/dev/pid   Reading this file returns the process ID of the current process, in decimal, terminated with a newline.

/dev/ppid   Reading this file returns the parent process ID of the current process, in decimal, terminated with a newline.

/dev/pgrpid   Reading this file returns the process group ID of the current process, in decimal, terminated with a newline.

/dev/user   Reading this file returns a single record terminated with a newline. The fields are separated with blanks. $1 is the value of the *getuid*(2) system call, $2 is the value of the *geteuid*(2) system call, $3 is the value of the *getgid*(2) system call, and $4 is the value of the *getegid*(2) system call. If there are any additional fields, they are the group IDs returned by *getgroups*(2). Multiple groups may not be supported on all systems.

/dev/stdin   The standard input.

/dev/stdout   The standard output.

/dev/stderr   The standard error output.

/dev/fd/*n*   The file associated with the open file descriptor *n*.

These are particularly useful for error messages. For example:

print "You blew it!" > "/dev/stderr"

whereas you would otherwise have to use

print "You blew it!" | "cat 1>&2"

These file names may also be used on the command line to name data files.

Numeric Functions

AWK has the following pre-defined arithmetic functions:

atan2(*y*, *x*)   returns the arctangent of *y/x* in radians.

cos(*expr*)   returns the cosine in radians.

exp(*expr*)   the exponential function.

int(*expr*)	truncates to integer.
log(*expr*)	the natural logarithm function.
rand()	returns a random number between 0 and 1.
sin(*expr*)	returns the sine in radians.
sqrt(*expr*)	the square root function.
srand(*expr*)	use *expr* as a new seed for the random number generator. If no *expr* is provided, the time of day will be used. The return value is the previous seed for the random number generator.

String Functions

AWK has the following pre-defined string functions:

gsub(*r*, *s*, *t*)	for each substring matching the regular expression *r* in the string *t*, substitute the string *s*, and return the number of substitutions. If *t* is not supplied, use $0 .
index(*s*, *t*)	returns the index of the string *t* in the string *s*, or 0 if *t* is not present.
length(*s*)	returns the length of the string *s*, or the length of $0 if *s* is not supplied.
match(*s*, *r*)	returns the position in *s* where the regular expression *r* occurs, or 0 if *r* is not present, and sets the values of RSTART and RLENGTH.
split(*s*, *a*, *r*)	splits the string *s* into the array *a* on the regular expression *r*, and returns the number of fields. If *r* is omitted, FS is used instead. The array *a* is cleared first.
sprintf(*fmt*, *expr-list*)	prints *expr-list* according to *fmt*, and returns the resulting string.
sub(*r*, *s*, *t*)	just like gsub(), but only the first matching substring is replaced.
substr(*s*, *i*, *n*)	returns the *n*-character substring of *s* starting at *i*. If *n* is omitted, the rest of *s* is used.
tolower(*str*)	returns a copy of the string *str*, with all the upper-case characters in *str* translated to their corresponding lower-case counterparts. Non-alphabetic characters are left unchanged.
toupper(*str*)	returns a copy of the string *str*, with all the lower-case characters in *str* translated to their corresponding upper-case counterparts. Non-alphabetic characters are left unchanged.

Time Functions

Since one of the primary uses of AWK programs is processing log files that contain time stamp information, *gawk* provides the following two functions for obtaining time stamps and formatting them.

systime()	returns the current time of day as the number of seconds since the Epoch (Midnight UTC, January 1, 1970 on systems).
strftime(*format*, *timestamp*)	formats *timestamp* according to the specification in *format*. The *timestamp* should be of the same form as returned by systime(). If *timestamp* is missing, the current time of day is used. See the specification for the strftime() function in C for the format conversions that are guaranteed to be available. A public-domain version of *strftime*(3) and a man page for it are shipped with *gawk*; if that version was used to build *gawk*, then all of the conversions described in that man page are available to *gawk*.

String Constants

String constants in AWK are sequences of characters enclosed between double quotes (""). Within strings, certain *escape sequences* are recognized, as in C. These are:

\\	A literal backslash.
\a	The "alert" character; usually the ASCII BEL character.
\b	backspace.
\f	form-feed.
\n	new line.
\r	carriage return.
\t	horizontal tab.
\v	vertical tab.
\x*hex digits*	The character represented by the string of hexadecimal digits following the \x. As in C, all following hexadecimal digits are considered part of the escape sequence. (This feature should tell us something about language design by committee.) E.g., "\x1B" is the ASCII ESC (escape) character.
ddd	The character represented by the 1-, 2-, or 3-digit sequence of octal digits. E.g. "\033" is the ASCII ESC (escape) character.
c	The literal character *c*.

The escape sequences may also be used inside constant regular expressions (e.g., /[\\\t\f\n\r\v]/ matches whitespace characters).

FUNCTIONS

Functions in AWK are defined as follows:

function *name(parameter list)* { *statements* }

Functions are executed when called from within the action parts of regular pattern-action statements. Actual parameters supplied in the function call are used to instantiate the formal parameters declared in the function. Arrays are passed by reference, other variables are passed by value.

Since functions were not originally part of the AWK language, the provision for local variables is rather clumsy: They are declared as extra parameters in the parameter list. The convention is to separate local variables from real parameters by extra spaces in the parameter list. For example:

function f(p, q, a, b) { # a & b are local
..... }

/abc/ { ... ; f(1, 2) ; ... }

The left parenthesis in a function call is required to immediately follow the function name, without any intervening white space. This is to avoid a syntactic ambiguity with the concatenation operator. This restriction does not apply to the built-in functions listed above.

Functions may call each other and may be recursive. Function parameters used as local variables are initialized to the null string and the number zero upon function invocation.

The word **func** may be used in place of **function**.

EXAMPLES

Print and sort the login names of all users:

BEGIN { FS = ":" }
{ print $1 | "sort" }

Count lines in a file:

```
{ nlines++ }
END { print nlines }
```

Precede each line by its number in the file:

```
{ print FNR, $0 }
```

Concatenate and line number (a variation on a theme):

```
{ print NR, $0 }
```

SEE ALSO

egrep(1), *getpid*(2), *getppid*(2), *getpgrp*(2), *getuid*(2), *geteuid*(2), *getgid*(2), *getegid*(2), *getgroups*(2)

The AWK Programming Language, Alfred V. Aho, Brian W. Kernighan, Peter J. Weinberger, Addison-Wesley, 1988. ISBN 0-201-07981-X.

The GAWK Manual, Edition 0.15, published by the Free Software Foundation, 1993.

POSIX COMPATIBILITY

A primary goal for *gawk* is compatibility with the standard, as well as with the latest version of *awk*. To this end, *gawk* incorporates the following user visible features which are not described in the AWK book, but are part of *awk* in System V Release 4, and are in the standard.

The **–v** option for assigning variables before program execution starts is new. The book indicates that command line variable assignment happens when *awk* would otherwise open the argument as a file, which is after the **BEGIN** block is executed. However, in earlier implementations, when such an assignment appeared before any file names, the assignment would happen *before* the **BEGIN** block was run. Applications came to depend on this "feature." When *awk* was changed to match its documentation, this option was added to accommodate applications that depended upon the old behavior. (This feature was agreed upon by both the AT&T and GNU developers.)

The **–W** option for implementation specific features is from the standard.

When processing arguments, *gawk* uses the special option "——" to signal the end of arguments. In compatibility mode, it will warn about, but otherwise ignore, undefined options. In normal operation, such arguments are passed on to the AWK program for it to process.

The AWK book does not define the return value of **srand**(). The System V Release 4 version of *awk* (and the standard) has it return the seed it was using, to allow keeping track of random number sequences. Therefore **srand**() in *gawk* also returns its current seed.

Other new features are: The use of multiple **–f** options (from MKS *awk*); the **ENVIRON** array; the **a**, and **v** escape sequences (done originally in *gawk* and fed back into AT&T's); the **tolower**() and **toupper**() built-in functions (from AT&T); and the C conversion specifications in **printf** (done first in AT&T's version).

GNU EXTENSIONS

Gawk has some extensions to *awk*. They are described in this section. All the extensions described here can be disabled by invoking *gawk* with the **–W compat** option.

The following features of *gawk* are not available in *awk*.

> The **x** escape sequence.
>
> The **systime**() and **strftime**() functions.
>
> The special file names available for I/O redirection are not recognized.
>
> The **ARGIND** and **ERRNO** variables are not special.

The **IGNORECASE** variable and its side-effects are not available.

The **FIELDWIDTHS** variable and fixed width field splitting.

No path search is performed for files named via the **–f** option. Therefore the **AWKPATH** environment variable is not special.

The use of **next file** to abandon processing of the current input file.

The use of **delete** *array* to delete the entire contents of an array.

The AWK book does not define the return value of the **close()** function. *Gawk's* **close()** returns the value from *fclose*(3), or *pclose*(3), when closing a file or pipe, respectively.

When *gawk* is invoked with the **–W compat** option, if the *fs* argument to the **–F** option is "t", then **FS** will be set to the tab character. Since this is a rather ugly special case, it is not the default behavior. This behavior also does not occur if **–W posix** has been specified.

HISTORICAL FEATURES

There are two features of historical AWK implementations that *gawk* supports. First, it is possible to call the **length()** built-in function not only with no argument, but even without parentheses! Thus,

a = length

is the same as either of

a = length()
a = length($0)

This feature is marked as "deprecated" in the standard, and *gawk* will issue a warning about its use if **–W lint** is specified on the command line.

The other feature is the use of either the **continue** or the **break** statements outside the body of a **while**, **for**, or **do** loop. Traditional AWK implementations have treated such usage as equivalent to the **next** statement. *Gawk* will support this usage if **–W compat** has been specified.

ENVIRONMENT VARIABLES

If **POSIXLY_CORRECT** exists in the environment, then *gawk* behaves exactly as if — **posix** had been specified on the command line. If —**lint** has been specified, *gawk* will issue a warning message to this effect.

BUGS

The **–F** option is not necessary given the command line variable assignment feature; it remains only for backwards compatibility.

If your system actually has support for **/dev/fd** and the associated **/dev/stdin**, **/dev/stdout**, and **/dev/stderr** files, you may get different output from *gawk* than you would get on a system without those files. When *gawk* interprets these files internally, it synchronizes output to the standard output with output to **/dev/stdout**, while on a system with those files, the output is actually to different open files. Caveat Emptor.

VERSION INFORMATION

This man page documents *gawk*, version 2.15.

Starting with the 2.15 version of *gawk*, the **–c**, **–V**, **–C**, **–D**, **–a**, and **–e** options of the 2.11 version are no longer recognized. This fact will not even be documented in the manual page for the next major version.

AUTHORS

The original version of *awk* was designed and implemented by Alfred Aho, Peter Weinberger, and Brian Kernighan of AT&T Bell Labs. Brian Kernighan continues to maintain and enhance it.

Paul Rubin and Jay Fenlason, of the Free Software Foundation, wrote *gawk*, to be compatible with the original version of *awk* distributed in Seventh Edition . John Woods contributed a number of bug fixes. David Trueman, with contributions from Arnold Robbins, made *gawk* compatible with the new version of *awk*. Arnold Robbins is the current maintainer.

The initial DOS port was done by Conrad Kwok and Scott Garfinkle. Scott Deifik is the current DOS maintainer. Pat Rankin did the port to VMS, and Michal Jaegermann did the port to the Atari ST. The port to OS/2 was done by Kai Uwe Rommel, with contributions and help from Darrel Hankerson.

BUG REPORTS

If you find a bug in *gawk*, please send electronic mail to **bug-gnu-utils@prep.ai.mit.edu**, *with* a carbon copy to **arnold@gnu.ai.mit.edu**. Please include your operating system and its revision, the version of *gawk*, what C compiler you used to compile it, and a test program and data that are as small as possible for reproducing the problem.

Before sending a bug report, please do two things. First, verify that you have the latest version of *gawk*. Many bugs (usually subtle ones) are fixed at each release, and if your's is out of date, the problem may already have been solved. Second, please read this man page and the reference manual carefully to be sure that what you think is a bug really is, instead of just a quirk in the language.

ACKNOWLEDGEMENTS

Brian Kernighan of Bell Labs provided valuable assistance during testing and debugging. We thank him.

GEQN(1)

NAME

geqn – format equations for troff

SYNOPSIS

geqn [**–rvCNR**] [**–d**cc] [**–T**$name$] [**–M**dir] [**–f**F] [**–s**n] [**–p**n] [**–m**n] [$files$ ...]

DESCRIPTION

This manual page describes the GNU version of **eqn**, which is part of the groff document formatting system. **eqn** compiles descriptions of equations embedded within **troff** input files into commands that are understood by **troff**. Normally, it should be invoked using the **–e** option of **groff**. The syntax is quite compatible with Unix eqn. The output of GNU eqn cannot be processed with Unix troff; it must be processed with GNU troff. If no files are given on the command line, the standard input will be read. A filename of – will cause the standard input to be read.

eqn searches for the file **eqnrc** using the path **.:/usr/lib/groff/tmac:/usr/lib/tmac**. If it exists, eqn will process it before the other input files. The **–R** option prevents this.

GNU eqn does not provide the functionality of neqn: it does not support low-resolution, typewriter-like devices (although it may work adequately for very simple input).

OPTIONS

- **–C**   Recognize **.EQ** and **.EN** even when followed by a character other than space or newline.
- **–N**   Don't allow newlines within delimiters. This option allows **eqn** to recover better from missing closing delimiters.
- **–v**   Print the version number.
- **–r**   Only one size reduction.
- **–m**n The minimum point-size is n. eqn will not reduce the size of subscripts or superscripts to a smaller size than n.
- **–T**$name$ The output is for device $name$. The only effect of this is to define a macro $name$ with a value of **1**. Typically **eqnrc** will use this to provide definitions appropriate for the output device. The default output device is **ps**.
- **–M**dir Search dir for **eqnrc** before the default directories.
- **–R**   Don't load **eqnrc**.
- **–f**F This is equivalent to a **gfont**F command.
- **–s**n This is equivalent to a **gsize**n command. This option is deprecated. eqn will normally set equations at whatever the current point size is when the equation is encountered.
- **–p**n This says that subscripts and superscripts should be n points smaller than the surrounding text. This option is deprecated. Normally eqn makes sets subscripts and superscripts at 70% of the size of the surrounding text.

USAGE

Only the differences between GNU eqn and Unix eqn are described here.

Most of the new features of GNU eqn are based on . There are some references to the differences between and GNU eqn below; these may safely be ignored if you do not know .

Automatic spacing

eqn gives each component of an equation a type, and adjusts the spacing between components using that type. Possible types are:

- ordinary   an ordinary character such as 1 or x;
- operator   a large operator such as ;

binary	a binary operator such as +;
relation	a relation such as =;
opening	a opening bracket such as (;
closing	a closing bracket such as);
punctuation	a punctuation character such as ,;
inner	a subformula contained within brackets;
suppress	spacing that suppresses automatic spacing adjustment.

Components of an equation get a type in one of two ways.

type *e*   This yields an equation component that contains *e* but that has type *t*, where *t* is one of the types mentioned above. For example, **times** is defined as

         type "binary" \(mu

The name of the type doesn't have to be quoted, but quoting protects from macro expansion.

chartype *text*   Unquoted groups of characters are split up into individual characters, and the type of each character is looked up; this changes the type that is stored for each character; it says that the characters in *text* from now on have type *t*. For example,

         chartype "punctuation" .,;:

would make the characters **.,;:** have type punctuation whenever they subsequently appeared in an equation. The type *t* can also be **letter** or **digit**; in these cases **chartype** changes the font type of the characters. See the Fonts subsection.

New primitives

e1 **smallover** *e2*   This is similar to **over**; **smallover** reduces the size of *e1* and *e2*; it also puts less vertical space between *e1* or *e2* and the fraction bar. The **over** primitive corresponds to the **over** primitive in display styles; **smallover** corresponds to **over** in non-display styles.

vcenter *e*   This vertically centers *e* about the math axis. The math axis is the vertical position about which characters such as + and - are centered; also it is the vertical position used for the bar of fractions. For example, **sum** is defined as

         { type "operator" vcenter size +5 \(*S }

e1 **accent** *e2*   This sets *e2* as an accent over *e1*. *e2* is assumed to be at the correct height for a lowercase letter; *e2* will be moved down according if *e1* is taller or shorter than a lowercase letter. For example, **hat** is defined as

         accent { "^" }

dotdot, **dot**, **tilde**, **vec** and **dyad** are also defined using the **accent** primitive.

e1 **uaccent** *e2*   This sets *e2* as an accent under *e1*. *e2* is assumed to be at the correct height for a character without a descender; *e2* will be moved down if *e1* has a descender. **utilde** is pre-defined using **uaccent** as a tilde accent below the baseline.

splittext   This has the same effect as simply

         text

but *text* is not subject to macro expansion because it is quoted; *text* will be split up and the spacing between individual characters will be adjusted.

nosplit*text*   This has the same effect as

text

but because *text* is not quoted it will be subject to macro expansion; *text* will not be split up and the spacing between individual characters will not be adjusted.

*e***opprime**   This is a variant of **prime** that acts as an operator on *e*. It produces a different result from **prime** in a case such as A**opprimesub**1: with **opprime** the **1** will be tucked under the prime as a subscript to the **A** (as is conventional in mathematical typesetting), whereas with **prime** the **1** will be a subscript to the prime character. The precedence of **opprime** is the same as that of **bar** and **under**, which is higher than that of everything except **accent** and **uaccent**. In unquoted text a ' that is not the first character will be treated like **opprime**.

special*text***e**   This constructs a new object from *e* using a **gtroff**(1) macro named *text*. When the macro is called, the string **0s** will contain the output for *e*, and the number registers **0w**, **0h**, **0d**, **0skern** and **0skew** will contain the width, height, depth, subscript kern, and skew of *e*. (The *subscript kern* of an object says how much a subscript on that object should be tucked in; the *skew* of an object says how far to the right of the center of the object an accent over the object should be placed.) The macro must modify **0s** so that it will output the desired result with its origin at the current point, and increase the current horizontal position by the width of the object. The number registers must also be modified so that they correspond to the result.

For example, suppose you wanted a construct that 'cancels' an expression by drawing a diagonal line through it.

```
.EQ
define cancel 'special Ca'
.EN
.de Ca
.ds 0s \Z'\\*(0s'\v'\\n(0du'\D'l \\n(0wu -\\n(0hu-\\n(0du'\v'\\n(0hu'
..
```

Then you could cancel an expression *e* with **cancel** *e*

Here's a more complicated construct that draws a box round an expression:

```
.EQ
define box 'special Bx'
.EN
.de Bx
.ds 0s \Z'\h'1n'\\*(0s'\
\Z'\v'\\n(0du+1n'\D'l \\n(0wu+2n 0'\D'l 0 -\\n(0hu-\\n(0du-2n'\
\D'l -\\n(0wu-2n 0'\D'l 0 \\n(0hu+\\n(0du+2n"\h'\\n(0wu+2n'
.nr 0w +2n
.nr 0d +1n
.nr 0h +1n
..
```

Customization

The appearance of equations is controlled by a large number of parameters. These can be set using the **set** command.

    set_p_**n**   This sets parameter _p_ to value _n_ ; _n_ is an integer. For example,

        set x_height 45

        says that **eqn** should assume an x height of 0.45 ems.

Possible parameters are as follows. Values are in units of hundredths of an em unless otherwise stated. These descriptions are intended to be expository rather than definitive.

minimum_size   eqn will not set anything at a smaller point-size than this. The value is in points.

fat_offset   The **fat** primitive emboldens an equation by overprinting two copies of the equation horizontally offset by this amount.

over_hang   A fraction bar will be longer by twice this amount than the maximum of the widths of the numerator and denominator; in other words, it will overhang the numerator and denominator by at least this amount.

accent_width   When **bar** or **under** is applied to a single character, the line will be this long. Normally, **bar** or **under** produces a line whose length is the width of the object to which it applies; in the case of a single character, this tends to produce a line that looks too long.

delimiter_factor   Extensible delimiters produced with the **left** and **right** primitives will have a combined height and depth of at least this many thousandths of twice the maximum amount by which the sub-equation that the delimiters enclose extends away from the axis.

delimiter_shortfall   Extensible delimiters produced with the **left** and **right** primitives will have a combined height and depth not less than the difference of twice the maximum amount by which the sub-equation that the delimiters enclose extends away from the axis and this amount.

null_delimiter_space   This much horizontal space is inserted on each side of a fraction.

script_space   The width of subscripts and superscripts is increased by this amount.

thin_space   This amount of space is automatically inserted after punctuation characters.

medium_space   This amount of space is automatically inserted on either side of binary operators.

thick_space   This amount of space is automatically inserted on either side of relations.

x_height   The height of lowercase letters without ascenders such as x.

axis_height   The height above the baseline of the center of characters such as and . It is important that this value is correct for the font you are using.

default_rule_thickness   This should set to the thickness of the \\(ru character, or the thickness of horizontal lines produced with the \\D escape sequence.

num1   The **over** command will shift up the numerator by at least this amount.

num2	The **smallover** command will shift up the numerator by at least this amount.
denom1	The **over** command will shift down the denominator by at least this amount.
denom2	The **smallover** command will shift down the denominator by at least this amount.
sup1	Normally superscripts will be shifted up by at least this amount.
sup2	Superscripts within superscripts or upper limits or numerators of **smallover** fractions will be shifted up by at least this amount. This is usually less than sup1.
sup3	Superscripts within denominators or square roots or subscripts or lower limits will be shifted up by at least this amount. This is usually less than sup2.
sub1	Subscripts will normally be shifted down by at least this amount.
sub2	When there is both a subscript and a superscript, the subscript will be shifted down by at least this amount.
sup_drop	The baseline of a superscript will be no more than this much amount below the top of the object on which the superscript is set.
sub_drop	The baseline of a subscript will be at least this much below the bottom of the object on which the subscript is set.
big_op_spacing1	The baseline of an upper limit will be at least this much above the top of the object on which the limit is set.
big_op_spacing2	The baseline of a lower limit will be at least this much below the bottom of the object on which the limit is set.
big_op_spacing3	The bottom of an upper limit will be at least this much above the top of the object on which the limit is set.
big_op_spacing4	The top of a lower limit will be at least this much below the bottom of the object on which the limit is set.
big_op_spacing5	This much vertical space will be added above and below limits.
baseline_sep	The baselines of the rows in a pile or matrix will normally be this far apart. In most cases this should be equal to the sum of **num1** and **denom1**.
shift_down	The midpoint between the top baseline and the bottom baseline in a matrix or pile will be shifted down by this much from the axis. In most cases this should be equal to **axis_height**.
column_sep	This much space will be added between columns in a matrix.
matrix_side_sep	This much space will be added at each side of a matrix.
draw_lines	If this is non-zero, lines will be drawn using the \D escape sequence, rather than with the \l escape sequence and the \(ru character.
body_height	The amount by which the height of the equation exceeds this will be added as extra space before the line containing the equation (using \x.) The default value is 85.
body_depth	The amount by which the depth of the equation exceeds this will be added as extra space after the line containing the equation (using \x.) The default value is 35.
nroff	If this is non-zero, then **ndefine** will behave like **define** and **tdefine** will be ignored, otherwise **tdefine** will behave like **define** and **ndefine** will be ignored. The default value is 0 (This is typically changed to 1 by the **eqnrc** file for the **ascii** and **latin1** devices.)

A more precise description of the role of many of these parameters can be found in Appendix H of *The book*.

Macros

Macros can take arguments. In a macro body, $ n where *n* is between 1 and 9, will be replaced by the *n-th* argument if the macro is called with arguments; if there are fewer than *n* arguments, it will be replaced by nothing. A word containing a left parenthesis where the part of the word before the left parenthesis has been defined using the **define** command will be recognized as a macro call with arguments; characters following the left parenthesis up to a matching right parenthesis will be treated as comma-separated arguments; commas inside nested parentheses do not terminate an argument.

sdefine*name*X*anything*X   This is like the **define** command, but *name* will not be recognized if called with arguments.

includefile   Include the contents of *file*. Lines of *file* beginning with **.EQ** or **.EN** will be ignored.

ifdef*name*X*anything*X   If *name* has been defined by **define** (or has been automatically defined because *name* is the output device) process *anything*; otherwise ignore *anything*. *X* can be any character not appearing in *anything*.

Fonts

eqn normally uses at least two fonts to set an equation: an italic font for letters, and a roman font for everything else. The existing **gfont** command changes the font that is used as the italic font. By default this is **I**. The font that is used as the roman font can be changed using the new **grfont** command.

grfont*f*   Set the roman font to *f*.

The **italic** primitive uses the current italic font set by **gfont**; the **roman** primitive uses the current roman font set by **grfont**. There is also a new **gbfont** command, which changes the font used by the **bold** primitive. If you only use the **roman**, **italic** and **bold** primitives to changes fonts within an equation, you can change all the fonts used by your equations just by using **gfont**, **grfont** and **gbfont** commands.

You can control which characters are treated as letters (and therefore set in italics) by using the **chartype** command described above. A type of **letter** will cause a character to be set in italic type. A type of **digit** will cause a character to be set in roman type.

FILES

/usr/lib/groff/tmac/eqnrc
Initialization file.

BUGS

Inline equations will be set at the point size that is current at the beginning of the input line.

SEE ALSO

groff(1), **gtroff**(1), **groff_font**(5), *The* book

GETOPT(1)

NAME
getopt – parse command options

SYNOPSIS
set – 'getopt optstring $*'

DESCRIPTION
Getopt is used to break up options in command lines for easy parsing by shell procedures, and to check for legal options. Optstring is a string of recognized option letters (see getopt(3)); if a letter is followed by a colon, the option is expected to have an argument which may or may not be separated from it by white space. The special option —— is used to delimit the end of the options. Getopt will place —— in the arguments at the end of the options, or recognize it if used explicitly. The shell arguments (**$1 $2** ...) are reset so that each option is preceded by a – and in its own shell argument; each option argument is also in its own shell argument.

EXAMPLE
The following code fragment shows how one might process the arguments for a command that can take the options a and b , and the option o , which requires an argument.

```
set ---- 'getopt abo: $*'
if test $? != 0
then
        echo 'Usage: ...'
        exit 2
fi
for i
do
        case "$i"
        in
                --a|--b)
                        flag=$i; shift;;
                --o)
                        oarg=$2; shift; shift;;
                ----)
                        shift; break;;
        esac
done
```

This code will accept any of the following as equivalent:

```
cmd --aoarg file file
cmd --a --o arg file file
cmd --oarg -a file file
cmd --a --oarg ---- file file
```

SEE ALSO
sh(1), getopt(3)

DIAGNOSTICS
Getopt prints an error message on the standard error output when it encounters an option letter not included in optstring .

HISTORY
Written by Henry Spencer, working from a Bell Labs manual page. Behavior believed identical to the Bell version.

GETOPT(1)

BUGS

Whatever getopt(3) has.

Arguments containing white space or imbedded shell metacharacters generally will not survive intact; this looks easy to fix but isn't.

The error message for an invalid option is identified as coming from getopt rather than from the shell procedure containing the invocation of getopt ; this again is hard to fix.

The precise best way to use the set command to set the arguments without disrupting the value(s) of shell options varies from one shell version to another. varies from one shell version to another.

GINDXBIB(1)

NAME
gindxbib – make inverted index for bibliographic databases

SYNOPSIS
gindxbib [–vw] [–c file] [–d dir] [–f file] [–h n] [–i string] [–k n] [–l n] [–n n] [–o file] [–t n] [*filename ...*]

DESCRIPTION

gindxbib makes an inverted index for the bibliographic databases in *filename ...* for use with **grefer**(1), **glookbib**(1), and **lkbib**(1). The index will be named *filename*.**i**; the index is written to a temporary file which is then renamed to this. If no filenames are given on the command line because the **–f** option has been used, and no **–o** option is given, the index will be named **Ind.i**.

Bibliographic databases are divided into records by blank lines. Within a record, each fields starts with a % character at the beginning of a line. Fields have a one letter name which follows the % character.

The values set by the **–c**, **–n**, **–l** and **–t** options are stored in the index; when the index is searched, keys will be discarded and truncated in a manner appropriate to these options; the original keys will be used for verifying that any record found using the index actually contains the keys. This means that a user of an index need not know whether these options were used in the creation of the index, provided that not all the keys to be searched for would have been discarded during indexing and that the user supplies at least the part of each key that would have remained after being truncated during indexing. The value set by the **–i** option is also stored in the index and will be used in verifying records found using the index.

OPTIONS

- **–v** Print the version number.
- **–w** Index whole files. Each file is a separate record.
- **–c***file* Read the list of common words from *file* instead of **/usr/lib/groff/eign**.
- **–d***dir* Use *dir* as the pathname of the current working directory to store in the index, instead of the path printed by **pwd**(1). Usually *dir* will be a symbolic link that points to the directory printed by **pwd**(1).
- **–f***file* Read the files to be indexed from *file*. If *file* is –, files will be read from the standard input. The **–f** option can be given at most once.
- **–i***string* Don't index the contents of fields whose names are in *string*. Initially *string* is **XYZ**.
- **–h***n* Use the first prime greater than or equal to *n* for the size of the hash table. Larger values of *n* will usually make searching faster, but will make the index larger and **gindxbib** use more memory. Initially *n* is 997.
- **–k***n* Use at most *n* keys per input record. Initially *n* is 100.
- **–l***n* Discard keys that are shorter than *n*. Initially *n* is 3.
- **–n***n* Discard the *n* most common words. Initially *n* is 100.
- **–o***basename* The index should be named *basename*.**i**.
- **–t***n* Truncate keys to *n*. Initially *n* is 6.

FILES

- *filename*.**i** Index.
- **Ind.i** Default index name.
- **/usr/lib/groff/eign** List of common words.
- **indxbib***XXXXXX* Temporary file.

SEE ALSO
grefer(1), **lkbib**(1), **glookbib**(1)

Groff Version 1.09 16 April 1993 149

GLOOKBIB(1)

NAME
glookbib – search bibliographic databases

SYNOPSIS
glookbib [**–v**] [**–i**_string_] [**–t**_n_] _filename_...

DESCRIPTION
glookbib prints a prompt on the standard error (unless the standard input is not a terminal), reads from the standard input a line containing a set of keywords, searches the bibliographic databases _filename_... for references containing those keywords, prints any references found on the standard output, and repeats this process until the end of input. For each database _filename_ to be searched, if an index _filename_**.i** created by **gindxbib**(1) exists, then it will be searched instead; each index can cover multiple databases.

OPTIONS
- **–v**   Print the version number.
- **–i**_string_   When searching files for which no index exists, ignore the contents of fields whose names are in _string_.
- **–t**_n_   Only require the first _n_ characters of keys to be given. Initially _n_ is 6.

FILES
filename**.i**   Index files.

SEE ALSO
grefer(1), **lkbib**(1), **gindxbib**(1)

GNROFF(1)

NAME

gnroff – emulate nroff command with groff

SYNOPSIS

gnroff [**–h**] [**–i**] [**–m**name] [**–n**num] [**–o**list] [**–r**cn] [**–T**name] [file ...]

DESCRIPTION

The **gnroff** script emulates the **nroff** command using groff. The **–T** option with an argument other than **ascii** and **latin1** will be ignored. The **–h** option is equivalent to the **grotty –h** option. The **–i**, **–n**, **–m**, **–o** and **–r** options have the effect described in **gtroff**(1). In addition **gnroff** silently ignores options of **–e**, **–q** or **–s**.

SEE ALSO

groff(1), **gtroff**(1), **grotty**(1)

GPIC(1) GPIC(1)

NAME

gpic – compile pictures for troff or TeX

SYNOPSIS

gpic [**–nvC**] [*filename* ...]
gpic –t [**–cvzC**] [*filename* ...]

DESCRIPTION

This manual page describes the GNU version of **pic**, which is part of the groff document formatting system. **pic** compiles descriptions of pictures embedded within **troff** or input files into commands that are understood by or **troff**. Each picture starts with a line beginning with **.PS** and ends with a line beginning with **.PE**. Anything outside of **.PS** and **.PE** is passed through without change.

It is the user's responsibility to provide appropriate definitions of the **PS** and **PE** macros. When the macro package being used does not supply such definitions (for example, old versions of –ms), appropriate definitions can be obtained with **–mpic**: these will center each picture.

OPTIONS

Options that do not take arguments may be grouped behind a single –. The special option — can be used to mark the end of the options. A filename of – refers to the standard input.

–C Recognize **.PS** and **.PE** even when followed by a character other than space or newline.

–n Don't use the groff extensions to the troff drawing commands. You should use this if you are using a postprocessor that doesn't support these extensions. The extensions are described in **groff_out**(5). The **–n** option also causes pic not to use zero-length lines to draw dots in troff mode.

–t mode.

–c Be more compatible with **tpic**. Implies **–t**. Lines beginning with \ are not passed through transparently. Lines beginning with . are passed through with the initial . changed to \. A line beginning with **.ps** is given special treatment: it takes an optional integer argument specifying the line thickness (pen size) in milliinches; a missing argument restores the previous line thickness; the default line thickness is 8 milliinches. The line thickness thus specified takes effect only when a non-negative line thickness has not been specified by use of the **thickness** attribute or by setting the **linethick** variable.

–v Print the version number.

–z In mode draw dots using zero-length lines.

The following options supported by other versions of **pic** are ignored:

–D Draw all lines using the \D escape sequence. **pic** always does this.

–T*dev* Generate output for the **troff** device *dev*. This is unnecessary because the **troff** output generated by **pic** is device-independent.

USAGE

This section describes only the differences between GNU pic and the original version of pic. Many of these differences also apply to newer versions of Unix pic.

mode

mode is enabled by the **–t** option. In mode, pic will define a vbox called **\graph** for each picture. You must yourself print that vbox using, for example, the command

\centerline{\box\graph}

Groff Version 1.09 14 February 1994 152

GPIC(1)

Actually, since the vbox has a height of zero this will produce slightly more vertical space above the picture than below it;

\centerline{\raise 1em\box\graph}

would avoid this.

You must use a driver that supports the **tpic** specials, version 2.

Lines beginning with \ are passed through transparently; a % is added to the end of the line to avoid unwanted spaces. You can safely use this feature to change fonts or to change the value of **baselineskip**. Anything else may well produce undesirable results; use at your own risk. Lines beginning with a period are not given any special treatment.

Commands

for *variable* = *expr1* **to** *expr2* [**by** [*]*expr3*] **do** *X body X* Set *variable* to *expr1*. While the value of *variable* is less than or equal to *expr2*, do *body* and increment *variable* by *expr3*; if **by** is not given, increment *variable* by 1. If *expr3* is prefixed by * then *variable* will instead be multiplied by *expr3*. *X* can be any character not occurring in *body*.

if *expr* **then** *X if-true X* [**else** *Y if-false Y*] Evaluate *expr*; if it is non-zero then do *if-true*, otherwise do *if-false*. *X* can be any character not occurring in *if-true*. *Y* can be any character not occurring in *if-false*.

print *arg*... Concatenate the arguments and print as a line on stderr. Each *arg* must be an expression, a position, or text. This is useful for debugging.

command *arg*... Concatenate the arguments and pass them through as a line to troff or. Each *arg* must be an expression, a position, or text. This has a similar effect to a line beginning with . or \, but allows the values of variables to be passed through.

sh *X command X* Pass *command* to a shell. *X* can be any character not occurring in *command*.

copy *"filename"* Include *filename* at this point in the file.

copy [*"filename"*] **thru** *X body X* [**until** *"word"*]

copy [*"filename"*] **thru** *macro* [**until** *"word"*] This construct does *body* once for each line of *filename*; the line is split into blank-delimited words, and occurrences of $ i in *body*, for *i* between 1 and 9, are replaced by the *i*-th word of the line. If *filename* is not given, lines are taken from the current input up to **.PE**. If an **until** clause is specified, lines will be read only until a line the first word of which is *word*; that line will then be discarded. *X* can be any character not occurring in *body*. For example,

```
.PS
copy thru % circle at ($1,$2) % until "END"
1 2
3 4
5 6
END
box
.PE
```

is equivalent to

Groff Version 1.09   14 February 1994   153

```
.PS
circle at (1,2)
circle at (3,4)
circle at (5,6)
box
.PE
```

The commands to be performed for each line can also be taken from a macro defined earlier by giving the name of the macro as the argument to **thru**.

reset

    reset *variable1*, *variable2* ... Reset pre-defined variables *variable1*, *variable2* ... to their default values. If no arguments are given, reset all pre-defined variables to their default values. Note that assigning a value to **scale** also causes all pre-defined variables that control dimensions to be reset to their default values times the new value of scale.

    plot *expr* [*"text"*] This is a text object which is constructed by using *text* as a format string for sprintf with an argument of *expr*. If *text* is omitted a format string of %**g** is used. Attributes can be specified in the same way as for a normal text object. Be very careful that you specify an appropriate format string; pic does only very limited checking of the string. This is deprecated in favour of **sprintf**.

    variable:=*expr* This is similar to = except *variable* must already be defined, and the value of *variable* will be changed only in the innermost block in which it is defined. (By contrast, = defines the variable in the current block if it is not already defined there, and then changes the value in the current block.)

Arguments of the form

    *X*anything*X*

are also allowed to be of the form

    anything

In this case *anything* can contain balanced occurrences of **and .BR** . Strings may contain *X* or imbalanced occurrences of **and .BR** .

Expressions

The syntax for expressions has been significantly extended:

$x\char`\^y$ (exponentiation)
sin(x)
cos(x)
atan2(y,x)
log(x) (base 10)
exp(x) (base 10, ie 10'-.4m'x'.4m')
sqrt(x)
int(x)
rand() (return a random number between 0 and 1)
rand(x) (return a random number between 1 and x; deprecated)

max(*e1*,*e2*)
min(*e1*,*e2*)
!*e*
e1 && *e2*
e1 || *e2*
e1 == *e2*
e1 != *e2*
e1 >= *e2*
e1 > *e2*
e1 <= *e2*
e1 < *e2*
"*str1*" == "*str2*"
"*str1*" != "*str2*"

String comparison expressions must be parenthesised in some contexts to avoid ambiguity.

Other Changes

A bare expression, *expr*, is acceptable as an attribute; it is equivalent to *dir*expr, where *dir* is the current direction. For example

    line 2i

means draw a line 2 inches long in the current direction.

The maximum width and height of the picture are taken from the variables **maxpswid** and **maxpsht**. Initially these have values 8.5 and 11.

Scientific notation is allowed for numbers. For example

x = 5e–2

Text attributes can be compounded. For example,

"foo" above ljust

is legal.

There is no limit to the depth to which blocks can be examined. For example,

[A: [B: [C: box]]] with .A.B.C.sw at 1,2
circle at last [].A.B.C

is acceptable.

Arcs now have compass points determined by the circle of which the arc is a part.

Circles and arcs can be dotted or dashed. In mode splines can be dotted or dashed.

Boxes can have rounded corners. The **rad** attribute specifies the radius of the quarter-circles at each corner. If no **rad** or **diam** attribute is given, a radius of **boxrad** is used. Initially, **boxrad** has a value of 0. A box with rounded corners can be dotted or dashed.

The **.PS** line can have a second argument specifying a maximum height for the picture. If the width of zero is specified the width will be ignored in computing the scaling factor for the picture. Note that GNU pic will always scale a picture by the same amount vertically as horizontally. This is different from the DWB 2.0 pic which may scale a picture by a different amount vertically than horizontally if a height is specified.

Each text object has an invisible box associated with it. The compass points of a text object are determined by this box. The implicit motion associated with the object is also determined by this box. The dimensions of this box are taken from the width and height attributes; if the width attribute is not supplied then the width will be taken to be **textwid**; if the height attribute is not supplied then the height will be taken to be the number of text strings associated with the object times **textht**. Initially **textwid** and **textht** have a value of 0.

In places where a quoted text string can be used, an expression of the form

    sprintf(*format*,*arg*,...)

can also be used; this will produce the arguments formatted according to *format*, which should be a string as described in **printf**(3) appropriate for the number of arguments supplied, using only the **e**, **f**, **g** or **%** format characters.

The thickness of the lines used to draw objects is controlled by the **linethick** variable. This gives the thickness of lines in points. A negative value means use the default thickness: in output mode, this means use a thickness of 8 milliinches; in output mode with the **-c** option, this means use the line thickness specified by **.ps** lines; in troff output mode, this means use a thickness proportional to the pointsize. A zero value means draw the thinnest possible line supported by the output device. Initially it has a value of -1. There is also a **thick[ness]** attribute. For example,

circle thickness 1.5

would draw a circle using a line with a thickness of 1.5 points. The thickness of lines is not affected by the value of the **scale** variable, nor by the width or height given in the **.PS** line.

Boxes (including boxes with rounded corners), circles and ellipses can be filled by giving then an attribute of **fill[ed]**. This takes an optional argument of an expression with a value between 0 and 1; 0 will fill it with white, 1 with black, values in between with a proportionally gray shade. A value greater than 1 can also be used: this means fill with the shade of gray that is currently being used for text and lines. Normally this will be black, but output devices may provide a mechanism for changing this. Without an argument, then the value of the variable **fillval** will be used. Initially this has a value of 0.5. The invisible attribute does not affect the filling of objects. Any text associated with a filled object will be added after the object has been filled, so that the text will not be obscured by the filling.

Arrow heads will be drawn as solid triangles if the variable **arrowhead** is non-zero and either mode is enabled or the **–x** option has been given. Initially **arrowhead** has a value of 1.

The troff output of pic is device-independent. The **–T** option is therefore redundant. All numbers are taken to be in inches; numbers are never interpreted to be in troff machine units.

Objects can have an **aligned** attribute. This will only work when the postprocessor is **grops**. Any text associated with an object having the **aligned** attribute will be rotated about the center of the object so that it is aligned in the direction from the start point to the end point of the object. Note that this attribute will have no effect for objects whose start and end points are coincident.

In places where *n***th** is allowed '*expr*'**th** is also allowed. Note that '**th** is a single token: no space is allowed between the ' and the **th**. For example,

    for i = 1 to 4 do {
    line from 'i'th box.nw to 'i+1'th box.se
    }

FILES
/usr/lib/groff/tmac/tmac.pic Example definitions of the **PS** and **PE** macros.

SEE ALSO
gtroff(1), **groff_out**(5), **tex**(1)
Tpic: Pic for
AT&T Bell Laboratories, Computing Science Technical Report No. 116, PIC — A Graphics Language for Typesetting. (This can be obtained by sending a mail message to netlib@research.att.com with a body of 'send 116 from research/cstr'.)

BUGS
Input characters that are illegal for **groff** (ie those with ASCII code 0 or between 013 and 037 octal or between 0200 and 0237 octal) are rejected even in mode.

The interpretation of **fillval** is incompatible with the pic in 10th edition Unix, which interprets 0 as black and 1 as white.

GPROF(1)   GPROF(1)

NAME

gprof – display call graph profile data

SYNOPSIS

gprof [–abcsz] [–e|–E *name*] [–f|–F *name*] [–k *fromname* toname] [*objfile* [*gmon.out*]]

DESCRIPTION

gprof produces an execution profile of C, Pascal, or Fortran77 programs. The effect of called routines is incorporated in the profile of each caller. The profile data is taken from the call graph profile file ('gmon.out' default) which is created by programs that are compiled with the **–pg** option of **cc(1)**, **pc(1)**, and **f77(1)**. The **–pg** option also links in versions of the library routines that are compiled for profiling. **Gprof** reads the given object file (the default is 'a.out') and establishes the relation between its symbol table and the call graph profile from 'gmon.out'. If more than one profile file is specified, the **gprof** output shows the sum of the profile information in the given profile files.

Gprof calculates the amount of time spent in each routine. Next, these times are propagated along the edges of the call graph. Cycles are discovered, and calls into a cycle are made to share the time of the cycle. The first listing shows the functions sorted according to the time they represent including the time of their call graph descendents. Below each function entry is shown its (direct) call graph children, and how their times are propagated to this function. A similar display above the function shows how this function's time and the time of its descendents is propagated to its (direct) call graph parents.

Cycles are also shown, with an entry for the cycle as a whole and a listing of the members of the cycle and their contributions to the time and call counts of the cycle.

Second, a flat profile is given, similar to that provided by **prof(1)**. This listing gives the total execution times, the call counts, the time in milliseconds the call spent in the routine itself, and the time in milliseconds the call spent in the routine itself including its descendents.

Finally, an index of the function names is provided.

OPTIONS

The following options are available:

   –a   suppresses the printing of statically declared functions. If this option is given, all relevant information about the static function (e.g., time samples, calls to other functions, calls from other functions) belongs to the function loaded just before the static function in the 'objfile' file.

   –b   suppresses the printing of a description of each field in the profile.

   –c   the static call graph of the program is discovered by a heuristic that examines the text space of the object file. Static-only parents or children are shown with call counts of 0.

   –e *name*   suppresses the printing of the graph profile entry for routine *name* and all its descendents (unless they have other ancestors that aren't suppressed). More than one **–e** option may be given. Only one *name* may be given with each **–e** option.

   –E *name*   suppresses the printing of the graph profile entry for routine *name* (and its descendents) as **–e** , above, and also excludes the time spent in *name* (and its descendents) from the total and percentage time computations. (For example, **–E** mcount **–E** mcleanup is the default.)

   –f *name*   prints the graph profile entry of only the specified routine *name* and its descendents. More than one **–f** option may be given. Only one *name* may be given with each **–f** option.

   –F *name*   prints the graph profile entry of only the routine *name* and its descendants (as **–f** , above) and also uses only the times of the printed routines in total time and percentage computations. More than one **–F** option may be given. Only one *name* may be given with each **−F** option. The **−F** option overrides the **−E** option.

−k *fromname toname* will delete any arcs from routine *fromname* to routine *toname*. This can be used to break undesired cycles. More than one **−k** option may be given. Only one pair of routine names may be given with each **−k** option.

−s a profile file 'gmon.sum' is produced that represents the sum of the profile information in all the specified profile files. This summary profile file may be given to later executions of gprof (probably also with a **−s**) to accumulate profile data across several runs of an 'objfile' file.

−v prints the version number for gprof, and then exits.

−z displays routines that have zero usage (as shown by call counts and accumulated time). This is useful with the **−c** option for discovering which routines were never called.

FILES

a.out the namelist and text space.
gmon.out dynamic call graph and profile.
gmon.sum summarized dynamic call graph and profile.

SEE ALSO

monitor(3), profil(2), cc(1), prof(1)

"An Execution Profiler for Modular Programs", by S. Graham, P. Kessler, M. McKusick; Software − Practice and Experience, Vol. 13, pp. 671-685, 1983.

"gprof: A Call Graph Execution Profiler", by S. Graham, P. Kessler, M. McKusick; Proceedings of the SIGPLAN '82 Symposium on Compiler Construction, SIGPLAN Notices, Vol. 17, No 6, pp. 120-126, June 1982.

HISTORY

Gprof appeared in 4.2 BSD.

BUGS

The granularity of the sampling is shown, but remains statistical at best. We assume that the time for each execution of a function can be expressed by the total time for the function divided by the number of times the function is called. Thus the time propagated along the call graph arcs to the function's parents is directly proportional to the number of times that arc is traversed.

Parents that are not themselves profiled will have the time of their profiled children propagated to them, but they will appear to be spontaneously invoked in the call graph listing, and will not have their time propagated further. Similarly, signal catchers, even though profiled, will appear to be spontaneous (although for more obscure reasons). Any profiled children of signal catchers should have their times propagated properly, unless the signal catcher was invoked during the execution of the profiling routine, in which case all is lost.

The profiled program must call **exit(2)** or return normally for the profiling information to be saved in the 'gmon.out' file.

GREFER(1)　　　　　　　　　　　　　　　　　　　　　　　　　GREFER(1)

NAME

grefer – preprocess bibliographic references for groff

SYNOPSIS

grefer [–benvCPRS] [–a n] [–c fields] [–f n] [–i fields] [–k field] [–l m,n] [–p filename] [–s fields] [–t n] [–B field.macro] [*filename...*]

DESCRIPTION

This file documents the GNU version of **refer**, which is part of the groff document formatting system. **refer** copies the contents of *filename*... to the standard output, except that lines between **.[** and **.]** are interpreted as citations, and lines between **.R1** and **.R2** are interpreted as commands about how citations are to be processed.

Each citation specifies a reference. The citation can specify a reference that is contained in a bibliographic database by giving a set of keywords that only that reference contains. Alternatively it can specify a reference by supplying a database record in the citation. A combination of these alternatives is also possible.

For each citation, **refer** can produce a mark in the text. This mark consists of some label which can be separated from the text and from other labels in various ways. For each reference it also outputs **groff** commands that can be used by a macro package to produce a formatted reference for each citation. The output of **refer** must therefore be processed using a suitable macro package. The **–ms** and **–me** macros are both suitable. The commands to format a citation's reference can be output immediately after the citation, or the references may be accumulated, and the commands output at some later point. If the references are accumulated, then multiple citations of the same reference will produce a single formatted reference.

The interpretation of lines between **.R1** and **.R2** as commands is a new feature of GNU refer. Documents making use of this feature can still be processed by Unix refer just by adding the lines

.de R1
.ig R2
..

to the beginning of the document. This will cause **troff** to ignore everything between **.R1** and **.R2**. The effect of some commands can also be achieved by options. These options are supported mainly for compatibility with Unix refer. It is usually more convenient to use commands.

refer generates **.lf** lines so that filenames and line numbers in messages produced by commands that read **refer** output will be correct; it also interprets lines beginning with **.lf** so that filenames and line numbers in the messages and **.lf** lines that it produces will be accurate even if the input has been preprocessed by a command such as **gsoelim**(1).

OPTIONS

Most options are equivalent to commands (for a description of these commands see the **Commands** subsection):

–b	no-label-in-text; no-label-in-reference
–e	**accumulate**
–n	**no-default-database**
–C	**compatible**
–P	**move-punctuation**
–S	label "(A.n|Q) ', ' (D.y|D)"; bracket-label " (") "; "
–a*n*	**reverse A***n*
–c*fields*	**capitalize** *fields*

Groff Version 1.09　　　　　　　　　14 February 1994　　　　　　　　　159

−f*n*	label %*n*
−i*fields*	search-ignore *fields*
−k	label L%a
−k*field*	label *field*%a
−l	label A.nD.y%a
−l*m*	label A.n+*m*D.y%a
−l,*n*	label A.nD.y−*n*%a
−l*m*,*n*	label A.n+*m*D.y−*n*%a
−p*filename*	database *filename*
−s*spec*	sort *spec*
−t*n*	search-truncate *n*

These options are equivalent to the following commands with the addition that the filenames specified on the command line are processed as if they were arguments to the **bibliography** command instead of in the normal way:

−B	annotate X AP; no-label-in-reference
−B*field.macro*	**annotate** *field macro*; **no-label-in-reference**

The following options have no equivalent commands:

−v	Print the version number.
−R	Don't recognize lines beginning with **.R1/.R2**.

USAGE
Bibliographic databases

The bibliographic database is a text file consisting of records separated by one or more blank lines. Within each record fields start with a % at the beginning of a line. Each field has a one character name that immediately follows the %. It is best to use only upper and lower case letters for the names of fields. The name of the field should be followed by exactly one space, and then by the contents of the field. Empty fields are ignored. The conventional meaning of each field is as follows:

A	The name of an author. If the name contains a title such as **Jr.** at the end, it should be separated from the last name by a comma. There can be multiple occurrences of the **A** field. The order is significant. It is a good idea always to supply an **A** field or a **Q** field.
B	For an article that is part of a book, the title of the book
C	The place (city) of publication.
D	The date of publication. The year should be specified in full. If the month is specified, the name rather than the number of the month should be used, but only the first three letters are required. It is a good idea always to supply a **D** field; if the date is unknown, a value such as **in** press or **unknown** can be used.
E	For an article that is part of a book, the name of an editor of the book. Where the work has editors and no authors, the names of the editors should be given as **A** fields and , (ed) or , (eds) should be appended to the last author.
G	US Government ordering number.
I	The publisher (issuer).
J	For an article in a journal, the name of the journal.
K	Keywords to be used for searching.
L	Label.

	N	Journal issue number.
	O	Other information. This is usually printed at the end of the reference.
	P	Page number. A range of pages can be specified as *m–n*.
	Q	The name of the author, if the author is not a person. This will only be used if there are no **A** fields. There can only be one **Q** field.
	R	Technical report number.
	S	Series name.
	T	Title. For an article in a book or journal, this should be the title of the article.
	V	Volume number of the journal or book.
	X	Annotation.

For all fields except **A** and **E**, if there is more than one occuremce of a particular field in a record, only the last such field will be used.

If accent strings are used, they should follow the character to be accented. This means that the **AM** macro must be used with the **–ms** macros. Accent strings should not be quoted: use one \ rather than two.

Citations

The format of a citation is

.[*opening-text*
flags keywords
fields
.]*closing-text*

The *opening-text*, *closing-text* and *flags* components are optional. Only one of the *keywords* and *fields* components need be specified.

The *keywords* component says to search the bibliographic databases for a reference that contains all the words in *keywords*. It is an error if more than one reference if found.

The *fields* components specifies additional fields to replace or supplement those specified in the reference. When references are being accumulated and the *keywords* component is non-empty, then additional fields should be specified only on the first occasion that a particular reference is cited, and will apply to all citations of that reference.

The *opening-text* and *closing-text* component specifies strings to be used to bracket the label instead of the strings specified in the **bracket-label** command. If either of these components is non-empty, the strings specified in the **bracket-label** command will not be used; this behaviour can be altered using the [and] flags. Note that leading and trailing spaces are significant for these components.

The *flags* component is a list of non-alphanumeric characters each of which modifies the treatment of this particular citation. Unix refer will treat these flags as part of the keywords and so will ignore them since they are non-alphanumeric. The following flags are currently recognized:

	#	This says to use the label specified by the **short-label** command, instead of that specified by the **label** command. If no short label has been specified, the normal label will be used. Typically the short label is used with author-date labels and consists of only the date and possibly a disambiguating letter; the # is supposed to be suggestive of a numeric type of label.
	[	Precede *opening-text* with the first string specified in the **bracket-label** command.
	]	Follow *closing-text* with the second string specified in the **bracket-label** command.

One advantages of using the [and] flags rather than including the brackets in *opening-text* and *closing-text* is that you can change the style of bracket used in the document just by changing the **bracket-label** command. Another advantage is that sorting and merging of citations will not necessarily be inhibited if the flags are used.

If a label is to be inserted into the text, it will be attached to the line preceding the .[line. If there is no such line, then an extra line will be inserted before the .[line and a warning will be given.

There is no special notation for making a citation to multiple references. Just use a sequence of citations, one for each reference. Don't put anything between the citations. The labels for all the citations will be attached to the line preceding the first citation. The labels may also be sorted or merged. See the description of the <> label expression, and of the **sort-adjacent-labels** and **abbreviate-label-ranges** command. A label will not be merged if its citation has a non-empty *opening-text* or *closing-text*. However, the labels for a citation using the] flag and without any *closing-text* immediately followed by a citation using the [flag and without any *opening-text* may be sorted and merged even though the first citation's *opening-text* or the second citation's *closing-text* is non-empty. (If you wish to prevent this just make the first citation's *closing-text* \ **&**.)

Commands

Commands are contained between lines starting with **.R1** and **.R2**. Recognition of these lines can be prevented by the –R option. When a .R1 line is recognized any accumulated references are flushed out. Neither **.R1** nor **.R2** lines, nor anything between them is output.

Commands are separated by newlines or ;s. # introduces a comment that extends to the end of the line (but does not conceal the newline). Each command is broken up into words. Words are separated by spaces or tabs. A word that begins with extends to the next that is not followed by another . If there is no such the word extends to the end of the line. Pairs of in a word beginning with collapse to a single . Neither # nor ; are recognized inside s. A line can be continued by ending it with \; this works everywhere except after a #.

* Each command *name* that is marked with * has an associated negative command **no-***name* that undoes the effect of *name*. For example, the **no-sort** command specifies that references should not be sorted. The negative commands take no arguments.

In the following description each argument must be a single word; *field* is used for a single upper or lower case letter naming a field; *fields* is used for a sequence of such letters; *m* and *n* are used for a non-negative numbers; *string* is used for an arbitrary string; *filename* is used for the name of a file.

    abbreviate**fields***string***1*string*2**string***3*string*4 Abbreviate the first names of *fields*. An initial letter will be separated from another initial letter by *string1*, from the last name by *string2*, and from anything else (such as a **von** or **de**) by *string3*. These default to a period followed by a space. In a hyphenated first name, the initial of the first part of the name will be separated from the hyphen by *string4*; this defaults to a period. No attempt is made to handle any ambiguities that might result from abbreviation. Names are abbreviated before sorting and before label construction.

    abbreviate-label-ranges*string Three or more adjacent labels that refer to consecutive references will be abbreviated to a label consisting of the first label, followed by *string* followed by the last label. This is mainly useful with numeric labels. If *string* is omitted it defaults to –.

    accumulate* Accumulate references instead of writing out each reference as it is encountered. Accumulated references will be written out whenever a reference of the form

        .[
        $LIST$
        .]

is encountered, after all input files hve been processed, and whenever **.R1** line is recognized.

annotate*field*string *field* is an annotation; print it at the end of the reference as a paragraph preceded by the line

.*string*

If *macro* is omitted it will default to **AP**; if *field* is also omitted it will default to **X**. Only one field can be an annotation.

articles*string*... *string*... are definite or indefinite articles, and should be ignored at the beginning of **T** fields when sorting. Initially, **the**, **a** and **an** are recognized as articles.

bibliography*filename*... Write out all the references contained in the bibliographic databases *filename*...

bracket-label*string1***string2***string3* In the text, bracket each label with *string1* and *string2*. An occurrence of *string2* immediately followed by *string1* will be turned into *string3*. The default behaviour is

bracket-label *([. *(.] ", "

capitalize*fields* Convert *fields* to caps and small caps.

compatible* Recognize **.R1** and **.R2** even when followed by a character other than space or newline.

database*filename*... Search the bibliographic databases *filename*... For each *filename* if an index *filename*.**i** created by **gindxbib**(1) exists, then it will be searched instead; each index can cover multiple databases.

date-as-label*string* *string* is a label expression that specifies a string with which to replace the **D** field after constructing the label. See the **Label expressions** subsection for a description of label expressions. This command is useful if you do not want explicit labels in the reference list, but instead want to handle any necessary disambiguation by qualifying the date in some way. The label used in the text would typically be some combination of the author and date. In most cases you should also use the **no-label-in-reference** command. For example,

date-as-label D.+yD.y%a*D.-y

would attach a disambiguating letter to the year part of the **D** field in the reference.

default-database* The default database should be searched. This is the default behaviour, so the negative version of this command is more useful. refer determines whether the default database should be searched on the first occasion that it needs to do a search. Thus a **no-default-database** command must be given before then, in order to be effective.

discard*fields* When the reference is read, *fields* should be discarded; no string definitions for *fields* will be output. Initially, *fields* are **XYZ**.

et-al*string*m*n* Control use of et al in the evaluation of @ expressions in label expressions. If the number of authors needed to make the author sequence unambiguous is *u* and the total number of authors is *t* then the last *t − u* authors will be replaced by *string* provided that *t − u* is not less than *m* and *t* is not less than *n*. The default behaviour is

et-al " et al" 2 3

include*filename* Include *filename* and interpret the contents as commands.

join-authors*string1***string2***string3* This says how authors should be joined together. When there are exactly two authors, they will be joined with *string1*. When there are more than two authors, all but the last two will be joined with *string2*, and the last two authors will be joined with *string3*. If *string3* is omitted, it will default to *string1*; if *string2* is also omitted it will also default to *string1*. For example,

join-authors " " ", " ", and "
will restore the default method for joining authors.

label-in-reference* When outputting the reference, define the string [F to be the reference's label. This is the default behaviour; so the negative version of this command is more useful.

label-in-text* For each reference output a label in the text. The label will be separated from the surrounding text as described in the **bracket-label** command. This is the default behaviour; so the negative version of this command is more useful.

label*string* *string* is a label expression describing how to label each reference.

separate-label-second-parts*string* When merging two-part labels, separate the second part of the second label from the first label with *string*. See the description of the <> label expression.

move-punctuation* In the text, move any punctuation at the end of line past the label. It is usually a good idea to give this command unless you are using superscripted numbers as labels.

reverse*string Reverse the fields whose names are in *string*. Each field name can be followed by a number which says how many such fields should be reversed. If no number is given for a field, all such fields will be reversed.

search-ignore*fields While searching for keys in databases for which no index exists, ignore the contents of *fields*. Initially, fields **XYZ** are ignored.

search-truncate*n Only require the first *n* characters of keys to be given. In effect when searching for a given key words in the database are truncated to the maximum of *n* and the length of the key. Initially *n* is 6.

short-label*string *string* is a label expression that specifies an alternative (usually shorter) style of label. This is used when the **#** flag is given in the citation. When using author-date style labels, the identity of the author or authors is sometimes clear from the context, and so it may be desirable to omit the author or authors from the label. The **short-label** command will typically be used to specify a label containing just a date and possibly a disambiguating letter.

sort*string Sort references according to **string**. References will automatically be accumulated. *string* should be a list of field names, each followed by a number, indicating how many fields with the name should be used for sorting. + can be used to indicate that all the fields with the name should be used. Also . can be used to indicate the references should be sorted using the (tentative) label. (The Label expressions subsection describes the concept of a tentative label.)

sort-adjacent-labels* Sort labels that are adjacent in the text according to their position in the reference list. This command should usually be given if the **abbreviate-label-ranges** command has been given, or if the label expression contains a <> expression. This will have no effect unless references are being accumulated.

Label expressions

Label expressions can be evaluated both normally and tentatively. The result of normal evaluation is used for output. The result of tentative evaluation, called the tentative label, is used to gather the information that normal evaluation needs to disambiguate the label. Label expressions specified by the **date-as-label** and **short-label** commands are not evaluated tentatively. Normal and tentative evaluation are the same for all types of expression other than @, *, and % expressions. The description below applies to normal evaluation, except where otherwise specified.

field	
field **n**	The *n*-th part of *field*. If *n* is omitted, it defaults to 1.
'string'	The characters in *string* literally.
@	All the authors joined as specified by the **join-authors** command. The whole of each author's name will be used. However, if the references are sorted by author (that is the sort specification starts with **A+**), then authors' last names will be used instead, provided that this does not introduce ambiguity, and also an initial subsequence of the authors may be used instead of all the authors, again provided that this does not introduce ambiguity. The use of only the last name for the *i*-th author of some reference is considered to be ambiguous if there is some other reference, such that the first *i* - 1 authors of the references are the same, the *i*-th authors are not the same, but the *i*-th authors' last names are the same. A proper initial subsequence of the sequence of authors for some reference is considered to be ambiguous if there is a reference with some other sequence of authors which also has that subsequence as a proper initial subsequence. When an initial subsequence of authors is used, the remaining authors are replaced by the string specified by the **et-al** command; this command may also specify additional requirements that must be met before an initial subsequence can be used. **@** tentatively evaluates to a canonical representation of the authors, such that authors that compare equally for sorting purpose will have the same representation.
%n	
%a	
%A	
%i	
%I	The serial number of the reference formatted according to the character following the **%**. The serial number of a reference is 1 plus the number of earlier references with same tentative label as this reference. These expressions tentatively evaluate to an empty string.
*expr******	If there is another reference with the same tentative label as this reference, then *expr*, otherwise an empty string. It tentatively evaluates to an empty string.
*expr***+n**	
*expr***–n**	The first (**+**) or last (**–**) *n* upper or lower case letters or digits of *expr*. Troff special characters (such as **\('a**) count as a single letter. Accent strings are retained but do not count towards the total.
*expr***.l**	*expr* converted to lowercase.
*expr***.u**	*expr* converted to uppercase.
*expr***.c**	*expr* converted to caps and small caps.
*expr***.r**	*expr* reversed so that the last name is first.
*expr***.a**	*expr* with first names abbreviated. Note that fields specified in the **abbreviate** command are abbreviated before any labels are evaluated. Thus **.a** is useful only when you want a field to be abbreviated in a label but not in a reference.
*expr***.y**	The year part of *expr*.
*expr***.+y**	The part of *expr* before the year, or the whole of *expr* if it does not contain a year.
*expr***.–y**	The part of *expr* after the year, or an empty string if *expr* does not contain a year.
*expr***.n**	The last name part of *expr*.
expr1expr2	*expr1* except that if the last character of *expr1* is **–** then it will be replaced by *expr2*.

expr1 expr2   The concatenation of *expr1* and *expr2*.

expr1|expr2   If *expr1* is non-empty then *expr1* otherwise *expr2*.

expr1&expr2   If *expr1* is non-empty then *expr2* otherwise an empty string.

expr1?expr2:expr3   If *expr1* is non-empty then *expr2* otherwise *expr3*.

<*expr*>   The label is in two parts, which are separated by *expr*. Two adjacent two-part labels which have the same first part will be merged by appending the second part of the second label onto the first label separated by the string specified in the **separate-label-second-parts** command (initially, a comma followed by a space); the resulting label will also be a two-part label with the same first part as before merging, and so additional labels can be merged into it. Note that it is permissible for the first part to be empty; this maybe desirable for expressions used in the **short-label** command.

(*expr*)   The same as *expr*. Used for grouping.

The above expressions are listed in order of precedence (highest first); **&** and **|** have the same precedence.

Macro interface

Each reference starts with a call to the macro]-. The string [F will be defined to be the label for this reference, unless the **no-label-in-reference** command has been given. There then follows a series of string definitions, one for each field: string [X corresponds to field X. The number register [P is set to 1 if the P field contains a range of pages. The [T, [A and [O number registers are set to 1 according as the T, A and O fields end with one of the characters .?!. The [E number register will be set to 1 if the [E string contains more than one name. The reference is followed by a call to the][macro. The first argument to this macro gives a number representing the type of the reference. If a reference contains a J field, it will be classified as type 1, otherwise if it contains a B field, it will type 3, otherwise if it contains a G or R field it will be type 4, otherwise if contains a I field it will be type 2, otherwise it will be type 0. The second argument is a symbolic name for the type: **other**, **journal-article**, **book**, **article-in-book** or **tech-report**. Groups of references that have been accumulated or are produced by the **bibliography** command are preceded by a call to the]< macro and followed by a call to the]> macro.

FILES

/usr/dict/papers/Ind'u+2n /usr/dict/papers/Ind Default database.

file.i   Index files.

SEE ALSO

gindxbib(1), **glookbib**(1), **lkbib**(1)

BUGS

In label expressions, <> expressions are ignored inside .*char* expressions.

GREP(1)

NAME

grep, egrep, fgrep – print lines matching a pattern

SYNOPSIS

grep [–[[AB]] *num*] [–[CEFGVBchilnsvwx]] [–e] *pattern* | –f*file*] [*files...*]

DESCRIPTION

Grep searches the named input *files* (or standard input if no files are named, or the file name – is given) for lines containing a match to the given *pattern*. By default, grep prints the matching lines.

There are three major variants of grep, controlled by the following options.

- **–G** Interpret *pattern* as a basic regular expression (see below). This is the default.
- **–E** Interpret *pattern* as an extended regular expression (see below).
- **–F** Interpret *pattern* as a list of fixed strings, separated by newlines, any of which is to be matched.

In addition, two variant programs egrep and fgrep are available. Egrep is similiar (but not identical) to grep\–E, and is compatible with the historical Unix egrep. Fgrep is the same as grep\–F.

All variants of grep understand the following options:

- **–***num* Matches will be printed with *num* lines of leading and trailing context. However, grep will never print any given line more than once.
- **–A** *num* Print *num* lines of trailing context after matching lines.
- **–B** *num* Print *num* lines of leading context before matching lines.
- **–C** Equivalent to –2.
- **–V** Print the version number of grep to standard error. This version number should be included in all bug reports (see below).
- **–b** Print the byte offset within the input file before each line of output.
- **–c** Suppress normal output; instead print a count of matching lines for each input file. With the –v option (see below), count non-matching lines.
- **–e** *pattern* Use *pattern* as the pattern; useful to protect patterns beginning with –.
- **–f** *file* Obtain the pattern from *file*.
- **–h** Suppress the prefixing of filenames on output when multiple files are searched.
- **–i** Ignore case distinctions in both the *pattern* and the input files.
- **–L** Suppress normal output; instead print the name of each input file from which no output would normally have been printed.
- **–l** Suppress normal output; instead print the name of each input file from which output would normally have been printed.
- **–n** Prefix each line of output with the line number within its input file.
- **–q** Quiet; suppress normal output.
- **–s** Suppress error messages about nonexistent or unreadable files.
- **–v** Invert the sense of matching, to select non-matching lines.
- **–w** Select only those lines containing matches that form whole words. The test is that the matching substring must either be at the beginning of the line, or preceded by a non-word constituent character.

GREP(1)   GREP(1)

                  Similarly, it must be either at the end of the line or followed by a non-word constituent character. Word-constituent characters are letters, digits, and the underscore.

    –x   Select only those matches that exactly match the whole line.

REGULAR EXPRESSIONS

A regular expression is a pattern that describes a set of strings. Regular expressions are constructed analagously to arithmetic expressions, by using various operators to combine smaller expressions.

Grep understands two different versions of regular expression syntax: "basic" and "extended." In GNU\grep, there is no difference in available functionality using either syntax. In other implementations, basic regular expressions are less powerful. The following description applies to extended regular expressions; differences for basic regular expressions are summarized afterwards.

The fundamental building blocks are the regular expressions that match a single character. Most characters, including all letters and digits, are regular expressions that match themselves. Any metacharacter with special meaning may be quoted by preceding it with a backslash.

A list of characters enclosed by [and] matches any single character in that list; if the first character of the list is the caret ^ then it matches any character *not* in the list. For example, the regular expression [0123456789] matches any single digit. A range of ASCII characters may be specified by giving the first and last characters, separated by a hyphen. Finally, certain named classes of characters are predefined. Their names are self explanatory, and they are [:alnum:], [:alpha:], [:cntrl:], [:digit:], [:graph:], [:lower:], [:print:], [:punct:], [:space:], [:upper:], and [:xdigit:]. For example, [[:alnum:]] means [0-9A-Za-z], except the latter form is dependent upon the ASCII character encoding, whereas the former is portable. (Note that the brackets in these class names are part of the symbolic names, and must be included in addition to the brackets delimiting the bracket list.) Most metacharacters lose their special meaning inside lists. To include a literal] place it first in the list. Similarly, to include a literal ^ place it anywhere but first. Finally, to include a literal – place it last.

The period . matches any single character. The symbol \w is a synonym for [[:alnum:]] and \W is a synonym for [^[:alnum]].

The caret ^ and the dollar sign are metacharacters that respectively match the empty string at the beginning and end of a line. The symbols \< and \> respectively match the empty string at the beginning and end of a word. The symbol \b matches the empty string at the edge of a word, and \B matches the empty string provided it's *not* at the edge of a word.

A regular expression matching a single character may be followed by one of several repetition operators:

    ?   The preceding item is optional and matched at most once.
    *   The preceding item will be matched zero or more times.
    +   The preceding item will be matched one or more times.
    n   The preceding item is matched exactly *n* times.
    n ,   The preceding item is matched *n* or more times.
    , m   The preceding item is optional and is matched at most *m* times.
    n , m   The preceding item is matched at least *n* times, but not more than *m* times.

Two regular expressions may be concatenated; the resulting regular expression matches any string formed by concatenating two substrings that respectively match the concatenated subexpressions.

Two regular expressions may be joined by the infix operator |; the resulting regular expression matches any string matching either subexpression.

Repetition takes precedence over concatenation, which in turn takes precedence over alternation. A whole subexpression may be enclosed in parentheses to override these precedence rules.

The backreference \n, where n is a single digit, matches the substring previously matched by the nth parenthesized subexpression of the regular expression.

In basic regular expressions the metacharacters |, (, and) lose their special meaning; instead use the backslashed versions \?, \+, \{, \|, \(, and \).

In egrep the metacharacter { loses its special meaning; instead use \{ .

DIAGNOSTICS

Normally, exit status is 0 if matches were found, and 1 if no matches were found. (The .B −v option inverts the sense of the exit status.) Exit status is 2 if there were syntax errors in the pattern, inaccessible input files, or other system errors.

BUGS

Email bug reports to bug-gnu-utils@prep.ai.mit.edu. Be sure to include the word "grep" somewhere in the "Subject:" field.

Large repetition counts in the m , n construct may cause grep to use lots of memory. In addition, certain other obscure regular expressions require exponential time and space, and may cause grep to run out of memory.

Backreferences are very slow, and may require exponential time.

NAME

grodvi – convert groff output to TeX dvi format

SYNOPSIS

grodvi [–d] [–w*n*] [–F*dir*] [*files*...]

DESCRIPTION

grodvi is a driver for groff that produces dvi format. Normally it should be run by groff–Tdvi. This will run gtroff–Tdvi; it will also input the macros /usr/lib/groff/tmac/tmac.dvi; if the input is being preprocessed with geqn it will also input /usr/lib/groff/font/devdvi/eqnchar.

The dvi file generated by grodvi can be printed by any correctly-written dvi driver. The troff drawing primitives are implemented using the tpic version 2 specials. If the driver does not support these, the \D commands will not produce any output.

There is an additional drawing command available:

\D'R*dh dv*'   Draw a rule (solid black rectangle), with one corner at the current position, and the diagonally opposite corner at the current position +(*dh,dv*). Afterwards the current position will be at the opposite corner. This produces a rule in the dvi file and so can be printed even with a driver that does not support the tpic specials unlike the other \D commands.

The groff command \X'*anything*' is translated into the same command in the dvi file as would be produced by \special{ *anything* } in TeX; *anything* may not contain a newline.

Font files for grodvi can be created from tfm files using tfmtodit(1). The font description file should contain the following additional commands: internalname name The name of the tfm file (without the .tfm extension) is *name*.

checksum*n*   The checksum in the tfm file is *n*.
designsize*n* The designsize in the tfm file is *n*.

These are automatically generated by tfmtodit.

In troff the \N escape sequence can be used to access characters by their position in the corresponding tfm file; all characters in the tfm file can be accessed this way.

OPTIONS

–d   Do not use tpic specials to implement drawing commands. Horizontal and vertical lines will be implemented by rules. Other drawing commands will be ignored.

–v   Print the version number.

–w*n* Set the default line thickness to *n* thousandths of an em.

–F*dir* Search directory *dir*/devdvi for font and device description files.

FILES

/usr/lib/groff/font/devdvi/DESC	Device description file.
/usr/lib/groff/font/devdvi/ F	Font description file for font *F*.
/usr/lib/groff/tmac/tmac.dvi	Macros for use with grodvi.

BUGS

Dvi files produced by grodvi use a different resolution (57816 units per inch) to those produced by TeX. Incorrectly written drivers which assume the resolution used by TeX, rather than using the resolution specified in the dvi file will not work with grodvi.

When using the –d option with boxed tables, vertical and horizontal lines can sometimes protrude by one pixel. This is a consequence of the way TeX requires that the heights and widths of rules be rounded.

GRODVI(1)

SEE ALSO
tfmtodit(1), groff(1), gtroff(1), geqn(1), groff_out(5), groff_font(5), groff_char(7)

GROFF(1)

NAME

groff – front end for the groff document formatting system

SYNOPSIS

groff [–tpeszaivhblCENRVXZ] [–w*name*] [–W*name*] [–m*name*] [–F*dir*] [–T*dev*]
[–f*fam*] [–M*dir*] [–d*cs*] [–r*cn*] [–n*num*] [–o*list*] [–P*arg*] [*files* ...]

DESCRIPTION

groff is a front-end to the groff document formatting system. Normally it runs the gtroff program and a postprocessor appropriate for the selected device. Available devices are:

ps	For PostScript printers and previewers
dvi	For TeX dvi format
X75	For a 75 dpi X11 previewer
X100	For a 100dpi X11 previewer
ascii	For typewriter-like devices
latin1	For typewriter-like devices using the ISO Latin-1 character set.

The postprocessor to be used for a device is specified by the postpro command in the device description file. This can be overridden with the –X option.

The default device is ps. It can optionally preprocess with any of gpic, geqn, gtbl, grefer, or gsoelim.

Options without an argument can be grouped behind a single –. A filename of – denotes the standard input.

The grog command can be used to guess the correct groff command to use to format a file.

OPTIONS

–h	Print a help message.
–e	Preprocess with geqn.
–t	Preprocess with gtbl.
–p	Preprocess with gpic.
–s	Preprocess with gsoelim.
–R	Preprocess with grefer. No mechanism is provided for passing arguments to grefer because most grefer options have equivalent commands which can be included in the file. See grefer(1) for more details.
–v	Make programs run by groff print out their version number.
–V	Print the pipeline on stdout instead of executing it.
–z	Suppress output from gtroff. Only error messages will be printed.
–Z	Do not postprocess the output of gtroff. Normally groff will automatically run the appropriate postprocessor.
–P*arg*	Pass *arg* to the postprocessor. Each argument should be passed with a separate –P option. Note that groff does not prepend – to *arg* before passing it to the postprocessor.
–l	Send the output to a printer. The command used for this is specified by the print command in the device description file.
–L*arg*	Pass *arg* to the spooler. Each argument should be passed with a separate –L option. Note that groff does not prepend – to *arg* before passing it to the postprocessor.
–T*dev*	Prepare output for device *dev*. The default device is ps.

GROFF(1)

-X   Preview with gxditview instead of using the usual postprocessor. This is unlikely to produce good results except with –Tps.

-N   Don't allow newlines with eqn delimiters. This is the same as the –N option in geqn.

-a

-b

-i

-C

-E

-wname

-Wname

-mname

-olist

-dcs

-rcn

-Fdir

Groff Version 1.09   29 October 1992   173

−M*dir*

−f*fam*

−n*num* These are as described in gtroff(1).

ENVIRONMENT

GROFF_COMMAND_PREFIX	If this is set *X*, then groff will run *X*troff instead of gtroff. This also applies to tbl, pic, eqn, refer and soelim. It does not apply to grops, grodvi, grotty and gxditview.
GROFF_TMAC_PATH	A colon separated list of directories in which to search for macro files.
GROFF_TYPESETTER	Default device.
GROFF_FONT_PATH	A colon separated list of directories in which to search for the dev*name* directory.
PATH	The search path for commands executed by groff.
GROFF_TMPDIR	The directory in which temporary files will be created. If this is not set and TMPDIR is set, temporary files will be created in that directory. Otherwise temporary files will be created in /tmp. The grops(1) and grefer(1) commands can create temporary files.

FILES

/usr/lib/groff/font/dev*name*/DESC Device description file for device *name*.

/usr/lib/groff/font/dev*name*/F   Font file for font *F* of device *name*.

AUTHOR

James Clark <jjc@jclark.com>

BUGS

Report bugs to bug-groff@prep.ai.mit.edu. Include a complete, self-contained example that will allow the bug to be reproduced, and say which version of groff you are using.

COPYRIGHT

Copyright 1989, 1990, 1991, 1992 Free Software Foundation, Inc.

groff is free software; you can redistribute it and/or modify it under the terms of the GNU General Public License as published by the Free Software Foundation; either version 2, or (at your option) any later version.

groff is distributed in the hope that it will be useful, but WITHOUT ANY WARRANTY; without even the implied warranty of MERCHANTABILITY or FITNESS FOR A PARTICULAR PURPOSE. See the GNU General Public License for more details.

You should have received a copy of the GNU General Public License along with groff; see the file COPYING. If not, write to the Free Software Foundation, 675 Mass Ave, Cambridge, MA 02139, USA.

GROFF(1)

AVAILABILITY

The most recent released version of groff is always available for anonymous ftp from prep.ai.mit.edu (18.71.0.38) in the directory pub/gnu.

SEE ALSO

grog(1), gtroff(1), gtbl(1), gpic(1), geqn(1), gsoelim(1), grefer(1), grops(1), grodvi(1), grotty(1), gxditview(1), groff_font(5), groff_out(5), groff_ms(7), groff_me(7), groff_char(7)

GROG(1)

NAME
grog – guess options for groff command

SYNOPSIS
grog [*–option* ...] [*files* ...]

DESCRIPTION
grog reads *files* and guesses which of the groff(1) options –e, –man, –me, –mm, –ms, –p, –s, and –t are required for printing *files*, and prints the groff command including those options on the standard output. A filename of – is taken to refer to the standard input. If no files are specified the standard input will be read. Any specified options will be included in the printed command. No space is allowed between options and their arguments. For example,

    'grog –Tdvi paper.ms'

will guess the appropriate command to print paper.ms and then run it after adding the –Tdvi option.

SEE ALSO
doctype(1), groff(1), gtroff(1), gtbl(1), gpic(1), geqn(1), gsoelim(1)

GROPS(1)

NAME

grops – PostScript driver for groff

SYNOPSIS

grops [–glv] [–b*n*] [–c*n*] [–w*n*] [–F*dir*] [*files*...]

DESCRIPTION

grops translates the output of GNU troff to PostScript. Normally grops should be invoked by using the groff command with a –Tps option. If no files are given, grops will read the standard input. A filename of – will also cause grops to read the standard input. PostScript output is written to the standard output. When grops is run by groff options can be passed to grops using the groff –P option.

OPTIONS

–b*n*   Workaround broken spoolers and previewers. Normally grops produces output that conforms the Document Structuring Conventions version 3.0. Unfortunately some spoolers and previewers can't handle such output. The value of *n* controls what grops does to its output acceptable to such programs. A value of 0 will cause grops not to employ any workarounds. Add 1 if no %%BeginDocumentSetup and %%EndDocumentSetup comments should be generated; this is needed for early versions of TranScript that get confused by anything between the %%EndProlog comment and the first %%Page comment. Add 2 if lines in included files beginning with %! should be stripped out; this is needed for Sun's pageview previewer. Add 4 if %%Page, %%Trailer and %%EndProlog comments should be stripped out of included files; this is needed for spoolers that don't understand the %%BeginDocument and %%EndDocument comments. Add 8 if the first line of the PostScript output should be %!PS-Adobe-2.0 rather than %!PS-Adobe-3.0; this is needed when using Sun's Newsprint with a printer that requires page reversal. The default value can be specified by a

broken*n*

command in the DESC file. Otherwise the default value is 0.

–c*n*   Print *n* copies of each page.

–g   Guess the page length. This generates PostScript code that guesses the page length. The guess will be correct only if the imageable area is vertically centered on the page. This option allows you to generate documents that can be printed both on letter (8.511) paper and on A4 paper without change.

–l   Print the document in landscape format.

–F*dir*   Search the directory *dir*/dev*name* for font and device description files; *name* is the name of the device, usually ps.

–w*n*   Lines should be drawn using a thickness of *n* thousandths of an em.

–v   Print the version number.

USAGE

There are styles called R, I, B, and BI mounted at font positions 1 to 4. The fonts are grouped into families A, BM, C, H, HN, N, P and T having members in each of these styles:

AR	AR AvantGarde-Book
AI	AI AvantGarde-BookOblique
AB	AB AvantGarde-Demi

ABI	ABI AvantGarde-DemiOblique	
BMR	BMR Bookman-Light	
BMI	BMI Bookman-LightItalic	
BMB	BMB Bookman-Demi	
BMBI	BMBI Bookman-DemiItalic	
CR	CR Courier	
CI	CI Courier-Oblique	
CB	CB Courier-Bold	
CBI	CBI Courier-BoldOblique	
HR	HR Helvetica	
HI	HI Helvetica-Oblique	
HB	HB Helvetica-Bold	
HBI	HBI Helvetica-BoldOblique	
HNR	HNR Helvetica-Narrow	
HNI	HNI Helvetica-Narrow-Oblique	
HNB	HNB Helvetica-Narrow-Bold	
HNBI	HNBI Helvetica-Narrow-BoldOblique	
NR	NR NewCenturySchlbk-Roman	
NI	NI NewCenturySchlbk-Italic	
NB	NB NewCenturySchlbk-Bold	
NBI	NBI NewCenturySchlbk-BoldItalic	
PR	PR Palatino-Roman	
PI	PI Palatino-Italic	
PB	PB Palatino-Bold	
PBI	PBI Palatino-BoldItalic	
TR	TR Times-Roman	
TI	TI Times-Italic	
TB	TB Times-Bold	
TBI	TBI Times-BoldItalic	

There is also the following font which is not a member of a family:

ZCMI   ZCMI ZapfChancery-MediumItalic

There are also some special fonts called SS and S. Zapf Dingbats is available as ZD and a reversed version of ZapfDingbats (with symbols pointing in the opposite direction) is available as ZDR; most characters in these fonts are unnamed and must be accessed using \N.

grops understands various X commands produced using the \X escape sequence; grops will only interpret commands that begin with a ps: tag.

\X'ps:*exec*code'   This executes the arbitrary PostScript commands in *code*. The PostScript currentpoint will be set to the position of the \X command before executing *code*. The origin will be at the top left corner of the page, and y coordinates will increase down the page. A procedure u will be defined that converts groff units to the coordinate system in effect. For example,

\X'ps: exec \nx u 0 rlineto stroke'

Groff Version 1.09   14 February 1994   178

will draw a horizontal line one inch long. *code* may
make changes to the graphics state, but any changes
will persist only to the end of the page. A dictionary containing the definitions specified by the def
and mdef will be on top of the dictionary stack. If
your code adds definitions to this dictionary, you
should allocate space for them using \X'ps*mdefn*'.
Any definitions will persist only until the end of
the page. If you use the \Y escape sequence with
an argument that names a macro, *code* can extend
over multiple lines. For example,

.nr x 1i
.de y
ps: exec
\nx u 0 rlineto
stroke
..
\Yy

is another way to draw a horizontal line one inch long.

\X'ps:*file*name'   This is the same as the exec command except that the
PostScript code is read from file *name*.

\X'ps:*def*code'   Place a PostScript definition contained in *code* in the pro-
logue. There should be at most one definition per \X
command. Long definitions can be split over several \X
commands; all the *code* arguments are simply joined together separated by newlines. The definitions are placed
in a dictionary which is automatically pushed on the dictionary stack when an exec command is executed. If you
use the \Y escape sequence with an argument that names
a macro, *code* can extend over multiple lines.

\X'ps:*mdefn*code'   Like def, except that *code* may contain up to *n* definitions. grops needs to know how many definitions *code*
contains so that it can create an appropriately sized Post-
Script dictionary to contain them.

\X'ps:*import*file*llxllyurxury*width[*height*]'   Import a PostScript graphic from
file. The arguments *llx, lly, urx*, and *ury* give the bound-
ing box of the graphic in the default PostScript coordinate system; they should all be integers; *llx* and *lly* are
the x and y coordinates of the lower left corner of the
graphic; *urx* and *ury* are the x and y coordinates of the
upper right corner of the graphic; *width* and *height* are
integers that give the desired width and height in groff
units of the graphic. The graphic will be scaled so that
it has this width and height and translated so that the
lower left corner of the graphic is located at the position associated with \X command. If the height argument is omitted it will be scaled uniformly in the x and
y directions so that it has the specified width. Note that
the contents of the \X command are not interpreted by
troff; so vertical space for the graphic is not automatically added, and the *width* and *height* arguments are not
allowed to have attached scaling indicators. If the Post-
Script file complies with the Adobe Document Structuring Conventions and contains a %%BoundingBox comment, then the bounding box can be automatically extracted from within groff by using the sy request to run
the psbb command.

The −mps macros (which are automatically loaded when grops is run by the groff command) include a PSPIC macro which allows a picture to be easily imported. This has the format

.PSPIC *file* [**−L** | **-R** | **−I** *n*] [*width* [*height*]]

file is the name of the file containing the illustration; *width* and *height* give the desired width and height of the graphic. The *width* and *height* arguments may have scaling indicators attached; the default scaling indicator is i. This macro will scale the graphic uniformly in the x and y directions so that it is no more than *width* wide and *height* high. By default, the graphic will be horizontally centered. The −L and −R cause the graphic to be left-aligned and right-aligned respectively. The −I option causes the graphic to be indented by *n*.

\X'ps: invis'

\X'ps: endinvis'   No output will be generated for text and drawing commands that are bracketed with these \X commands. These commands are intended for use when output from troff will be previewed before being processed with grops; if the previewer is unable to display certain characters or other constructs, then other substitute characters or constructs can be used for previewing by bracketing them with these \X commands.

For example, gxditview is not able to display a proper \(em character because the standard X11 fonts do not provide it; this problem can be overcome by executing the following request

.char \(em \X'ps: invis'\
\Z'\v'-.25m'\h'.05m'\D'l .9m 0'\h'.05m''\
\X'ps: endinvis'\(em

In this case, gxditview will be unable to display the \(em character and will draw the line, whereas grops will print the \(em character and ignore the line.

The input to grops must be in the format output by gtroff(1). This is described in groff_out(1). In addition the device and font description files for the device used must meet certain requirements. The device and font description files supplied for ps device meet all these requirements. afmtodit(1) can be used to create font files from AFM files. The resolution must be an integer multiple of 72 times the sizescale. The ps device uses a resolution of 72000 and a sizescale of 1000. The device description file should contain a command

paperlength*n*

which says that output should be generated which is suitable for printing on a page whose length is *n* machine units. Each font description file must contain a command

internalname*psname*

which says that the PostScript name of the font is *psname*. It may also contain a command

encoding*enc_file*

which says that the PostScript font should be reencoded using the encoding described in *enc_file*; this file should consist of a sequence of lines of the form:

pschar code

where *pschar* is the PostScript name of the character, and *code* is its position in the encoding expressed as a decimal integer. The code for each character given in the font file must correspond to the code for the character in encoding file, or to the code in the default encoding for the font if the PostScript font is not to be reencoded. This code can be used with the \N escape sequence in troff to select the character, even if the character does not have a groff name. Every character in the font file must exist in the PostScript font, and the widths given in the font file must match the widths used in the PostScript font. grops will assume that a character with a groff name of space is blank (makes no marks on the page); it can make use of such a character to generate more efficient and compact PostScript output.

grops can automatically include the downloadable fonts necessary to print the document. Any downloadable fonts which should, when required, be included by grops must be listed in the file /usr/lib/groff/font/devps/download; this should consist of lines of the form

    font filename

where *font* is the PostScript name of the font, and *filename* is the name of the file containing the font; lines beginning with # and blank lines are ignored; fields may be separated by tabs or spaces; *filename* will be searched for using the same mechanism that is used for groff font metric files. The download file itself will also be searched for using this mechanism.

If the file containing a downloadable font or imported document conforms to the Adobe Document Structuring Conventions, then grops will interpret any comments in the files sufficiently to ensure that its own output is conforming. It will also supply any needed font resources that are listed in the download file as well as any needed file resources. It is also able to handle inter-resource dependencies. For example, suppose that you have a downloadable font called Garamond, and also a downloadable font called Garamond-Outline which depends on Garamond (typically it would be defined to copy Garamond's font dictionary, and change the PaintType), then it is necessary for Garamond to be appear before Garamond-Outline in the PostScript document. grops will handle this automatically provided that the downloadable font file for Garamond-Outline indicates its dependence on Garamond by means of the Document Structuring Conventions, for example by beginning with the following lines

    %!PS-Adobe-3.0 Resource-Font
    %%DocumentNeededResources: font Garamond
    %%EndComments
    %%IncludeResource: font Garamond

In this case both Garamond and Garamond-Outline would need to be listed in the download file. A downloadable font should not include its own name in a %%DocumentSuppliedResources comment.

grops will not interpret %%DocumentFonts comments. The %%DocumentNeededResources, %%DocumentSuppliedResources, %%IncludeResource, %%BeginResource and %%EndResource comments (or possibly the old %%DocumentNeededFonts, %%DocumentSuppliedFonts, %%IncludeFont, %%BeginFont and %%EndFont comments) should be used.

FILES

/usr/lib/groff/font/devps/DESC Device description file.

    /usr/lib/groff/font/devps/*F*   Font description file for font *F*.

    /usr/lib/groff/font/devps/download   List of downloadable fonts.

    /usr/lib/groff/font/devps/text.enc   Encoding used for text fonts.

    /usr/lib/groff/tmac/tmac.ps   Macros for use with grops; automatically loaded by troffrc

    /usr/lib/groff/tmac/tmac.pspic   Definition of PSPIC macro, automatically loaded by tmac.ps.

GROPS(1)   GROPS(1)

/usr/lib/groff/tmac/tmac.psold   Macros to disable use of characters not present in older PostScript printers; automatically loaded by tmac.ps.

/usr/lib/groff/tmac/tmac.psnew   Macros to undo the effect of tmac.psold.

/tmp/grops*XXXXXX*   Temporary file.

SEE ALSO

afmtodit(1), groff(1), gtroff(1), psbb(1), groff_out(5), groff_font(5), groff_char(7)

GROTTY(1)

NAME
grotty – groff driver for typewriter-like devices

SYNOPSIS
grotty [–hfbuodBUv] [–F*dir*] [*files* ...]

DESCRIPTION
grotty translates the output of GNU troff into a form suitable for typewriter-like devices. Normally grotty should invoked by using the groff command with a –Tascii or –Tlatin1 option. If no files are given, grotty will read the standard input. A filename of – will also cause grotty to read the standard input. Output is written to the standard output.

Normally grotty prints a bold character *c* using the sequence '*c* BACKSPACE *c*' and a italic character *c* by the sequence '_ BACKSPACE *c*'. These sequences can be displayed on a terminal by piping through ul(1). Pagers such as more(1) or less(1) are also able to display these sequences. Use either –B or –U when piping into less(1); use –b when piping into more(1). There is no need to filter the output through col(1) since grotty never outputs reverse line feeds.

The font description file may contain a command

    internalname*n*

where *n* is a decimal integer. If the 01 bit in *n* is set, then the font will be treated as an italic font; if the 02 bit is set, then it will be treated as a bold font. The code field in the font description field gives the code which will be used to output the character. This code can also be used in the \N escape sequence in troff.

OPTIONS

–F*dir*	Search the directory *dir*/dev*name* for font and device description files; *name* is the name of the device, usually ascii or latin1.
–h	Use horizontal tabs in the output. Tabs are assumed to be set every 8 columns.
–f	Use form feeds in the output. A form feed will be output at the end of each page that has no output on its last line.
–b	Suppress the use of overstriking for bold characters.
–u	Suppress the use of underlining for italic characters.
–B	Use only overstriking for bold-italic characters.
–U	Use only underlining for bold-italic characters.
–o	Suppress overstriking (other than for bold or underlined characters).
–d	Ignore all \D commands. Without this grotty will render \D'l...' commands that have at least at least one zero argument (and so are either horizontal or vertical) using –, | and + characters.
–v	Print the version number.

FILES

/usr/lib/groff/font/devascii/DESC	Device description file for ascii device.
/usr/lib/groff/font/devascii/ F	Font description file for font *F* of ascii device.
/usr/lib/groff/font/devlatin1/DESC	Device description file for latin1 device.
/usr/lib/groff/font/devlatin1/ F	Font description file for font *F* of latin1 device.
/usr/lib/groff/tmac/tmac.tty	Macros for use with grotty.
/usr/lib/groff/tmac/tmac.tty-char	Additional klugey character definitions for use with grotty.

GROTTY(1) GROTTY(1)

BUGS

grotty is intended only for simple documents.

There is no support for fractional horizontal or vertical motions.

There is no support for \D commands other than horizontal and vertical lines.

Characters above the first line (ie with a vertical position of 0) cannot be printed.

SEE ALSO

groff(1), gtroff(1), groff_out(5), groff_font(5), groff_char(7), ul(1), more(1), less(1)

NAME

gsoelim – interpret .so requests in groff input

SYNOPSIS

gsoelim [–Cv] [*files* ...]

DESCRIPTION

gsoelim reads *files* and replaces lines of the form

.so*file*

by the contents of *file*. It is useful if files included with so need to be preprocessed. Normally, gsoelim should be invoked with the –s option of groff.

OPTIONS

–C   Recognize .so even when followed by a character other than space or newline.

–v   Print the version number.

SEE ALSO

groff(1)

GTBL(1)

NAME
gtbl – format tables for troff

SYNOPSIS
gtbl [–Cv] [*files...*]

DESCRIPTION
This manual page describes the GNU version of tbl, which is part of the groff document formatting system. tbl compiles descriptions of tables embedded within troff input files into commands that are understood by troff. Normally, it should be invoked using the –t option of groff. It is highly compatible with Unix tbl. The output generated by GNU tbl cannot be processed with Unix troff; it must be processed with GNU troff. If no files are given on the command line, the standard input will be read. A filename of – will cause the standard input to be read.

OPTIONS
- –C   Recognize .TS and .TE even when followed by a character other than space or newline.
- –v   Print the version number.

USAGE
Only the differences between GNU tbl and Unix tbl are described here.

Normally tbl attempts to prevent undesirable breaks in the table by using diversions. This can sometimes interact badly with macro packages' own use of diversions, when footnotes, for example, are used. The nokeep option tells tbl not to try and prevent breaks in this way.

The decimalpoint option specifies the character to be recognized as the decimal point character in place of the default period. It takes an argument in parentheses, which must be a single character, as for the tab option.

The f format modifier can be followed by an arbitrary length font name in parentheses.

There is a d format modifier which means that a vertically spanning entry should be aligned at the bottom of its range.

There is no limit on the number of columns in a table, nor any limit on the number of text blocks. All the lines of a table are considered in deciding column widths, not just the first 200. Table continuation (.T&) lines are not restricted to the first 200 lines.

Numeric and alphabetic items may appear in the same column.

Numeric and alphabetic items may span horizontally.

tbl uses register, string, macro and diversion names beginning with 3. When using tbl you should avoid using any names beginning with a 3.

BUGS
You should use .TSH/.TH in conjunction with a supporting macro package for *all* multi-page boxed tables. If there is no header that you wish to appear at the top of each page of the table, place the .TH line immediately after the format section. Do not enclose a multi-page table within keep/release macros, or divert it in any other way.

A text block within a table must be able to fit on one page.

The bp request cannot be used to force a page-break in a multi-page table. Instead, define BP as follows

```
.de BP
.ie '\\n(.z" .bp \\$1
.el \!.BP \\$1
..
```

Groff Version 1.09   1 April 1993

and use **BP** instead of **bp**.
SEE ALSO
groff(1), **gtroff**(1)

define -*-

NAME

gtroff – format documents

SYNOPSIS

gtroff [–abivzCER] [–w name] [–W name] [–d cs] [–f fam] [–m name] [–n num] [–o list] [–r cn] [–T name] [–F dir] [–M dir] [\files...\]

DESCRIPTION

This manual page describes the GNU version of troff, which is part of the groff document formatting system. It is highly compatible with Unix troff. Usually it should be invoked using the groff command, which will also run preprocessors and postprocessors in the appropriate order and with the appropriate options.

OPTIONS

- **–a** Generate an ASCII approximation of the typeset output.
- **–b** Print a backtrace with each warning or error message. This backtrace should help track down the cause of the error. The line numbers given in the backtrace may not always correct: troff's idea of line numbers gets confused by as or am requests.
- **–i** Read the standard input after all the named input files have been processed.
- **–v** Print the version number.
- **–w**name Enable warning *name*. Available warnings are described in the Warnings subsection below. Multiple –w options are allowed.
- **–W**name Inhibit warning *name*. Multiple –W options are allowed.
- **–E** Inhibit all error messages.
- **–z** Suppress formatted output.
- **–C** Enable compatibility mode.
- **–d**cs

- **–d**name=s Define *c* or *name* to be a string *s*; *c* must be a one letter name.
- **–f**fam Use *fam* as the default font family.
- **–m**name Read in the file tmac.*name*. Normally this will be searched for in /usr/lib/groff/tmac.
- **–R** Don't load troffrc.
- **–n**num Number the first page *num*.
- **–o**list, Output only pages in *list*, which is a comma-separated list of page ranges; *n* means print page *n*, *m–n* means print every page between *m* and *n*, *–n* means print every page up to *n*, *n–* means print every page from *n*. Troff will exit after printing the last page in the list.
- **–r**cn

- **–r**name=n Set number register *c* or *name* to *n*; *c* must be a one character name; *n* can be any troff numeric expression.
- **–T**name Prepare output for device *name*, rather than the default ps.

Groff Version 1.09   14 February 1994   188

GTROFF(1)   GTROFF(1)

    –F*dir*   Search *dir* for subdirectories dev*name* (*name* is the name of the device) for the DESC file and font files before the normal /usr/lib/groff/font.

    –M*dir*   Search directory *dir* for macro files before the normal /usr/lib/groff/tmac.

USAGE

Only the features not in Unix troff are described here.

Long names

The names of number registers, fonts, strings/macros/diversions, special characters can be of any length. In escape sequences, where you can use (*xx* for a two character name, you can use [*xxx*] for a name of arbitrary length:

    \[*xxx*]   Print the special character called *xxx*.

    \f[*xxx*]   Set font *xxx*.

    *[*xxx*]   Interpolate string *xxx*.

    \n[*xxx*]   Interpolate number register *xxx*.

Fractional pointsizes

A scaled point is equal to 1/sizescale points, where sizescale is specified in the DESC file (1 by default.) There is a new scale indicator z which has the effect of multiplying by sizescale. Requests and escape sequences in troff interpret arguments that represent a pointsize as being in units of scaled points, but they evaluate each such argument using a default scale indicator of z. Arguments treated in this way are the argument to the ps request, the third argument to the cs request, the second and fourth arguments to the tkf request, the argument to the \H escape sequence, and those variants of the \s escape sequence that take a numeric expression as their argument.

For example, suppose sizescale is 1000; then a scaled point will be equivalent to a millipoint; the request .ps 10.25 is equivalent to .ps 10.25z and so sets the pointsize to 10250 scaled points, which is equal to 10.25 points.

The number register \n(.s returns the pointsize in points as decimal fraction. There is also a new number register \n[.ps] that returns the pointsize in scaled points.

It would make no sense to use the z scale indicator in a numeric expression whose default scale indicator was neither u nor z, and so troff disallows this. Similarly it would make no sense to use a scaling indicator other than z or u in a numeric expression whose default scale indicator was z, and so troff disallows this as well.

There is also new scale indicator s which multiplies by the number of units in a scaled point. So, for example, \n[.ps]s is equal to 1m. Be sure not to confuse the s and z scale indicators.

Numeric expressions

Spaces are permitted in a number expression within parentheses.

M indicates a scale of 100ths of an em.

    e1>?*e2*   The maximum of *e1* and *e2*.

    e1<?*e2*   The minimum of *e1* and *e2*.

    (*c*;*e*)   Evaluate *e* using *c* as the default scaling indicator. If *c* is missing, ignore scaling indicators in the evaluation of *e*.

New escape sequences

    \A'*anything*'   This expands to 1 or 0 according as *anything* is or is not acceptable as the name of a string, macro, diversion, number register, environment or font. It will return 0 if *anything* is empty. This is useful if you want to lookup user input in some sort of associative table.

Groff Version 1.09   14 February 1994

\C'xxx'   Typeset character named xxx. Normally it is more convenient to use \[xxx]. But \C has the advantage that it is compatible with recent versions of UNIX and is available in compatibility mode.

\E   This is equivalent to an escape character, but it's not interpreted in copy-mode. For example, strings to start and end superscripting could be defined like this:

             .ds { \v'-.3m'\s'\En[.s]*6u/10u'
             .ds } \s0\v'.3m'

The use of \E ensures that these definitions will work even if *{ gets interpreted in copy-mode (for example, by being used in a macro argument.)

\N'n'   Typeset the character with code n in the current font. n can be any integer. Most devices only have characters with codes between 0 and 255. If the current font does not contain a character with that code, special fonts will *not* be searched. The \N escape sequence can be conveniently used on conjunction with the char request:

             .char \[phone] \f(ZD\N'37'

             The code of each character is given in the fourth column in the font description file after the charset command. It is possible to include unnamed characters in the font description file by using a name of ——; the \N escape sequence is the only way to use these.

\R'namen'   This has the same effect as

             .nrnamen

\s(nn

             \s(nn Set the point size to nn points; nn must be exactly two digits.

\s[n]

\s[n]

\s'n'

             \s'n' Set the point size to n scaled points; n is a numeric expression with a default scale indicator of z.

\Vx

             \V(xx

\V[xxx**]** Interpolate the contents of the environment variable xxx, as returned by getenv(3). \V is interpreted in copy-mode.

\Yx

\Y(xx

\Y[xxx**]** This is approximately equivalent to \X'*[xxx]'. However the contents of the string or macro xxx are not interpreted; also it is permitted for xxx to have been defined as a macro and thus contain newlines (it is not permitted for the argument to \X to contain newlines). The inclusion of newlines requires an extension to the Unix troff output format, and will confuse drivers that do not know about this extension.

\Z'anything**'** Print anything and then restore the horizontal and vertical position; anything may not contain tabs or leaders.

\$0 The name by which the current macro was invoked. The als request can make a macro have more than one name.

\$* In a macro, the concatenation of all the arguments separated by spaces.

\$@ In a macro, the concatenation of all the arguments with each surrounded by double quotes, and separated by spaces.

\$(nn

\$[nnn] In a macro, this gives the nn-th or nnn-th argument. Macros can have a unlimited number of arguments.

\?anything**\?** When used in a diversion, this will transparently embed anything in the diversion. anything is read in copy mode. When the diversion is reread, anything will be interpreted. anything may not contain newlines; use \! if you want to embed newlines in a diversion. The escape sequence \? is also recognised in copy mode and turned into a single internal code; it is this code that terminates anything. Thus

.nr x 1
.nf
.di d
\?\\?\\\\?\\\\\\\\nx\\\\?\\?\?
.di
.nr x 2
.di e
.d
.di
.nr x 3
.di f
.e
.di
.nr x 4
.f

will print 4.

\/ This increases the width of the preceding character so that the spacing between that character and the following character will be correct if the following character is a roman character. For example, if an italic f is immediately followed by a roman right parenthesis, then in many fonts the top right portion of the f will overlap the top left of the right parenthesis producing *f*), which is ugly. Inserting \/ produces and avoids this problem. It is a good idea to use this escape sequence whenever an italic character is immediately followed by a roman character without any intervening space.

\,   This modifies the spacing of the following character so that the spacing between that character and the preceding character will correct if the preceding character is a roman character. For example, inserting \, between the parenthesis and the f changes (*f* to It is a good idea to use this escape sequence whenever a roman character is immediately followed by an italic character without any intervening space.

\)   Like \& except that it behaves like a character declared with the **cflags** request to be transparent for the purposes of end of sentence recognition.

\~   This produces an unbreakable space that stretches like a normal inter-word space when a line is adjusted.

\#   Everything up to and including the next newline is ignored. This is interpreted in copy mode. This is like \% except that \% does not ignore the terminating newline.

New requests

.aln*xxyy*   Create an alias *xx* for number register object named *yy*. The new name and the old name will be exactly equivalent. If *yy* is undefined, a warning of type reg will be generated, and the request will be ignored.

.als*xxyy*   Create an alias *xx* for request, string, macro, or diversion object named *yy*. The new name and the old name will be exactly equivalent (it is similar to a hard rather than a soft link). If *yy* is undefined, a warning of type mac will be generated, and the request will be ignored. The de, am, di, da, ds, and as requests only create a new object if the name of the macro, diversion or string diversion is currently undefined or if it is defined to be a request; normally they modify the value of an existing object.

.asciify*xx*   This request only exists in order to make it possible to make certain gross hacks work with GNU troff. It 'unformats' the diversion *xx* in such a way that ASCII characters that were formatted and diverted into *xx* will be treated like ordinary input characters when *xx* is reread. For example, this

```
.tr @.
.di x
@nr\n\1
.br
.di
.tr @@
.asciify x
.x
```

will set register n to 1.

.backtrace   Print a backtrace of the input stack on stderr.

.break   Break out of a while loop. See also the while and continue requests. Be sure not to confuse this with the br request.

.cflags*n c1 c2...*   Characters *c1, c2,...* have properties determined by *n*, which is ORed from the following:

1   the character ends sentences (initially characters .?! have this property);

2   lines can be broken before the character (initially no characters have this property); a line will not be broken at a character with

	this property unless the characters on each side both have non-zero hyphenation codes.
4	lines can be broken after the character (initially characters − \(hy \(em have this property); a line will not be broken at a character with this property unless the characters on each side both have non-zero hyphenation codes.
8	the character overlaps horizontally (initially characters \(ul \(rn \(ru have this property);
16	the character overlaps vertically (initially character \(br has this property);
32	an end of sentence character followed by any number of characters with this property will be treated as the end of a sentence if followed by a newline or two spaces; in other words the character is transparent for the purposes of end of sentence recognition; this is the same as having a zero space factor in TeX (initially characters ')]*\(dg \(rq have this property).

.charc*string*   Define character *c* to be *string*. Every time character *c* needs to be printed, *string* will be processed in a temporary environment and the result will be wrapped up into a single object. Compatibility mode will be turned off and the escape character will be set to \ while *string* is being processed. Any emboldening, constant spacing or track kerning will be applied to this object rather than to individual characters in *string*. A character defined by this request can be used just like a normal character provided by the output device. In particular other characters can be translated to it with the tr request; it can be made the leader character by the lc request; repeated patterns can be drawn with the character using the \l and \L escape sequences; words containing the character can be hyphenated correctly, if the hcode request is used to give the character a hyphenation code. There is a special anti-recursion feature: use of character within the character's definition will be handled like normal characters not defined with char. A character definition can be removed with the rchar request.

.chopxx   Chop the last character off macro, string, or diversion *xx*. This is useful for removing the newline from the end of diversions that are to be interpolated as strings.

.closestream   Close the stream named *stream*; *stream* will no longer be an acceptable argument to the write request. See the open request.

.continue   Finish the current iteration of a while loop. See also the while and break requests.

.cp *n*   If *n* is non-zero or missing, enable compatibility mode, otherwise disable it. In compatibility mode, long names are not recognised, and the incompatibilities caused by long names do not arise.

.doxxx   Interpret *xxx* with compatibility mode disabled. For example,

    .do fam T

would have the same effect as

    .fam T

except that it would work even if compatibility mode had been enabled. Note that the previous compatibility mode is restored before any files sourced by *xxx* are interpreted.

.famxx   Set the current font family to *xx*. The current font family is part of the current environment. See the description of the sty request for more information on font families.

.fspecial*f*s1 s2...   When the current font is *f*, fonts *s1*, *s2*, ... will be special, that is, they will searched for characters not in the current font. Any fonts specified in the special request will be searched after fonts specified in the fspecial request.

.ftr*f*g   Translate font *f* to *g*. Whenever a font named *f* is referred to in \f escape sequence, or in the ft, ul, bd, cs, tkf, special, fspecial, fp, or sty requests, font *g* will be used. If *g* is missing, or equal to *f* then font *f* will not be translated.

.hcodec1*code1*c2*code2*...   Set the hyphenation code of character *c1* to *code1* and that of *c2* to *code2*. A hyphenation code must be a single input character (not a special character) other than a digit or a space. Initially each lower-case letter has a hyphenation code, which is itself, and each upper-case letter has a hyphenation code which is the lower case version of itself. See also the hpf request.

.hla*lang*   Set the current hyphenation language to *lang*. Hyphenation exceptions specified with the hw request and hyphenation patterns specified with the hpf request are both associated with the current hyphenation language. The hla request is usually invoked by the troffrc file.

.hlm*n*   Set the maximum number of consecutive hyphenated lines to *n*. If *n* is negative, there is no maximum. The default value is –1. This value is associated with the current environment. Only lines output from an environment count towards the maximum associated with that environment. Hyphens resulting from \% are counted; explicit hyphens are not.

.hpf*file*   Read hyphenation patterns from *file*; this will be searched for in the same way that tmac.*name* is searched for when the –m*name* option is specified. It should have the same format as the argument to the \patterns primitive in TeX; the letters appearing in this file are interpreted as hyphenation codes. A % character in the patterns file introduces a comment that continues to the end of the line. The set of hyphenation patterns is associated with the current language set by the hla request. The hpf request is usually invoked by the troffrc file.

.hym*n*   Set the *hyphenation* margin to *n*: when the current adjustment mode is not b, the line will not be hyphenated if the line is no more than *n* short. The default hyphenation margin is 0. The default scaling indicator for this request is *m*. The hyphenation margin is associated with the current environment. The current hyphenation margin is available in the \n[.hym] register.

.hys*n*   Set the *hyphenation* space to *n*: when the current adjustment mode is b don't hyphenate the line if the line can be justified by adding no more than *n* extra space to each word space. The default hyphenation space is 0. The default scaling indicator for this request is m. The hyphenation space is associated with the current environment. The current hyphenation space is available in the \n[.hys] register.

.kern*n*   If *n* is non-zero or missing, enable pairwise kerning, otherwise disable it.

.mso*file*   The same as the so request except that *file* is searched for in the same way that tmac.*name* is searched for when the –m*name* option is specified.

.nroff   Make the n built-in condition true and the t built-in condition false. This can be reversed using the troff request.

.open*stream*filename   Open *filename* for writing and associate the stream named *stream* with it. See also the close and write requests.

.open_stream_**filename** Like open, but if _filename_ exists, append to it instead of truncating it.

.pnr Print the names and contents of all currently defined number registers on stderr.

.psocommand This is behaves like the so request except that input comes from the standard output of _command_.

.ptr Print the names and positions of all traps (not including input line traps and diversion traps) on stderr. Empty slots in the page trap list are printed as well, because they can affect the priority of subsequently planted traps.

.rchar_c1_**c2**... Remove the definitions of characters _c1_, _c2_,... This undoes the effect of a char request.

.rj

.rj_n_ Right justify the next _n_ input lines. Without an argument right justify the next input line. The number of lines to be right justified is available in the \n[.rj] register. This implicitly does .ce0. The ce request implicitly does .rj0.

.rn_nnxxyy_ Rename number register _xx_ to _yy_.

.shc_c_ Set the soft hyphen character to _c_. If _c_ is omitted, the soft hyphen character will be set to the default \(hy. The soft hyphen character is the character which will be inserted when a word is hyphenated at a line break. If the soft hyphen character does not exist in the font of the character immediately preceding a potential break point, then the line will not be broken at that point. Neither definitions (specified with the char request) nor translations (specified with the tr request) are considered when finding the soft hyphen character.

.shift_n_ In a macro, shift the arguments by _n_ positions: argument _i_ becomes argument _i−n_; arguments 1 to _n_ will no longer be available. If _n_ is missing, arguments will be shifted by 1. Shifting by negative amounts is currently undefined.

.special_s1_**s2**... Fonts _s1_, _s2_, are special and will be searched for characters not in the current font.

.sty_nf_ Associate style _f_ with font position _n_. A font position can be associated either with a font or with a style. The current font is the index of a font position and so is also either a font or a style. When it is a style, the font that is actually used is the font the name of which is the concatenation of the name of the current family and the name of the current style. For example, if the current font is 1 and font position 1 is associated with style R and the current font family is T, then font TR will be used. If the current font is not a style, then the current family is ignored. When the requests cs, bd, tkf, uf, or fspecial are applied to a style, then they will instead be applied to the member of the current family corresponding to that style. The default family can be set with the −f option. The styles command in the DESC file controls which font positions (if any) are initially associated with styles rather than fonts.

.tkf_fs1n1s2n2_ Enable track kerning for font _f_. When the current font is _f_ the width of every character will be increased by an amount between _n1_ and _n2_; when the current point size is less than or equal to _s1_ the width will be increased by _n1_; when it is greater than or equal to _s2_ the width will be increased by _n2_; when the point size is greater than or equal to _s1_ and less than or equal to _s2_ the increase in width is a linear function of the point size.

.trf*filename* Transparently output the contents of file *filename*. Each line is output as it would be were it preceded by \!; however, the lines are not subject to copy-mode interpretation. If the file does not end with a newline, then a newline will be added. For example, you can define a macro *x* containing the contents of file *f*, using

    .di*x*
    .trf*f*
    .di

Unlike with the cf request, the file cannot contain characters such as NUL that are not legal troff input characters.

.trnt abcd   This is the same as the tr request except that the translations do not apply to text that is transparently throughput into a diversion with \!. For example,

.tr ab
.di x
\!.tm a
.di
.x

will print b; if trnt is used instead of tr it will print a.

.troff   Make the n built-in condition false, and the t built-in condition true. This undoes the effect of the nroff request.

.vpt*n*   Enable vertical position traps if *n* is non-zero, disable them otherwise. Vertical position traps are traps set by the wh or dt requests. Traps set by the it request are not vertical position traps. The parameter that controls whether vertical position traps are enabled is global. Initially vertical position traps are enabled.

.warn*n*   Control warnings. *n* is the sum of the numbers associated with each warning that is to be enabled; all other warnings will be disabled. The number associated with each warning is listed in the 'Warnings' section. For example, .warn 0 will disable all warnings, and .warn 1 will disable all warnings except that about missing characters. If *n* is not given, all warnings will be enabled.

.while*c anything*   While condition *c* is true, accept *anything* as input; *c* can be any condition acceptable to an if request; *anything* can comprise multiple lines if the first line starts with \{ and the last line ends with \} . See also the break and continue requests.

.write*stream anything*   Write *anything* to the stream named *stream*. *stream* must previously have been the subject of an open request. *anything* is read in copy mode; a leading will be stripped.

Extended requests

.cf*filename*   When used in a diversion, this will embed in the diversion an object which, when reread, will cause the contents of *filename* to be transparently copied through to the output. In Unix troff, the contents of *filename* is immediately copied through to the output regardless of whether there is a current diversion; this behaviour is so anomalous that it must be considered a bug.

.ev*xx*   If *xx* is not a number, this will switch to a named environment called *xx*. The environment should be popped with a matching ev request without any arguments, just as for numbered environments. There is no limit on the number of named environments; they will be created the first time that they are referenced.

.fp*n*f1*f2*   The fp request has an optional third argument. This argument gives the external name of the font, which is used for finding the font description file. The second argument gives the internal name of the font which is used to refer to the font in troff after it has been mounted. If there is no third argument then the internal name will be used as the external name. This feature allows you to use fonts with long names in compatibility mode.

.ss*m*n   When two arguments are given to the ss request, the second argument gives the *sentence space size*. If the second argument is not given, the sentence space size will be the same as the word space size. Like the word space size, the sentence space is in units of one twelfth of the spacewidth parameter for the current font. Initially both the word space size and the sentence space size are 12. The sentence space size is used in two circumstances: if the end of a sentence occurs at the end of a line in fill mode, then both an inter-word space and a sentence space will be added; if two spaces follow the end of a sentence in the middle of a line, then the second space will be a sentence space. Note that the behaviour of Unix troff will be exactly that exhibited by GNU troff if a second argument is never given to the ss request. In GNU troff, as in Unix troff, you should always follow a sentence with either a newline or two spaces.

.ta*n1*n2...nnT*r1*r2...rn   Set tabs at positions *n1*, *n2*,..., *nn* and then set tabs at *nn+r1*, *nn+r2*,..., *nn+rn* and then at *nn+rn+r1*, *nn+rn+r2*,..., *nn+rn+rn*, and so on. For example,

.ta T .5i

will set tabs every half an inch.

New number registers

The following read-only registers are available:

\n[.C]   1 if compatibility mode is in effect, 0 otherwise.

\n[.cdp]   The depth of the last character added to the current environment. It is positive if the character extends below the baseline.

\n[.ce]   The number of lines remaining to be centered, as set by the ce request.

\n[.cht]   The height of the last character added to the current environment. It is positive if the character extends above the baseline.

\n[.csk]   The skew of the last character added to the current environment. The *skew* of a character is how far to the right of the center of a character the center of an accent over that character should be placed.

\n[.ev]   The name or number of the current environment. This is a string-valued register.

\n[.fam]   The current font family. This is a string-valued register.

\n[.fp]   The number of the next free font position.

\n[.g]   Always 1. Macros should use this to determine whether they are running under GNU troff.

\n[.hla]   The current hyphenation language as set by the hla request.

\n[.hlc]   The number of immediately preceding consecutive hyphenated lines.

\n[.hlm]   The maximum allowed number of consecutive hyphenated lines, as set by the hlm request.

\n[.hy]	The current hyphenation flags (as set by the hy request.)	
\n[.hym]	The current hyphenation margin (as set by the hym request.)	
\n[.hys]	The current hyphenation space (as set by the hys request.)	
\n[.in]	The indent that applies to the current output line.	
\n[.kern]	1 if pairwise kerning is enabled, 0 otherwise.	
\n[.lg]	The current ligature mode (as set by the lg request.)	
\n[.ll]	The line length that applies to the current output line.	
\n[.lt]	The title length as set by the lt request.	
\n[.ne]	The amount of space that was needed in the last ne request that caused a trap to be sprung. Useful in conjunction with the \n[.trunc] register.	
\n[.pn]	The number of the next page: either the value set by a pn request, or the number of the current page plus 1.	
\n[.ps]	The current pointsize in scaled points.	
\n[.psr]	The last-requested pointsize in scaled points.	
\n[.rj]	The number of lines to be right-justified as set by the rj request.	
\n[.sr]	The last requested pointsize in points as a decimal fraction. This is a string-valued register.	
\n[.tabs]	A string representation of the current tab settings suitable for use as an argument to the ta request.	
\n[.trunc]	The amount of vertical space truncated by the most recently sprung vertical position trap, or, if the trap was sprung by a ne request, minus the amount of vertical motion produced by the ne request. In other words, at the point a trap is sprung, it represents the difference of what the vertical position would have been but for the trap, and what the vertical position actually is. Useful in conjunction with the \n[.ne] register.	
\n[.ss]		

\n[.sss] These give the values of the parameters set by the first and second arguments of the ss request.

\n[.vpt] 1 if vertical position traps are enabled, 0 otherwise.

\n[.warn] The sum of the numbers associated with each of the currently enabled warnings. The number associated with each warning is listed in the 'Warnings' subsection.

\n(.x The major version number. For example, if the version number is 1.03 then \n(.x will contain 1.

\n(.y The minor version number. For example, if the version number is 1.03 then \n(.y will contain 03.

The following registers are set by the \w escape sequence:

\n[rst]		
\n[rsb]	Like the st and sb registers, but takes account of the heights and depths of characters.	
\n[ssc]	The amount of horizontal space (possibly negative) that should be added to the last character before a subscript.	
\n[skw]	How far to right of the center of the last character in the \w argument, the center of an accent from a roman font should be placed over that character.	

The following read/write number registers are available:

\n[systat]   The return value of the system() function executed by the last sy request.

\n[slimit]   If greater than 0, the maximum number of objects on the input stack. If less than or equal to 0, there is no limit on the number of objects on the input stack. With no limit, recursion can continue until virtual memory is exhausted.

Miscellaneous

Fonts not listed in the DESC file are automatically mounted on the next available font position when they are referenced. If a font is to be mounted explicitly with the fp request on an unused font position, it should be mounted on the first unused font position, which can be found in the \n[.fp] register; although troff does not enforce this strictly, it will not allow a font to be mounted at a position whose number is much greater than that of any currently used position.

Interpolating a string does not hide existing macro arguments. Thus in a macro, a more efficient way of doing

. xx \\$@

is

*[xx]\\

If the font description file contains pairwise kerning information, characters from that font will be kerned. Kerning between two characters can be inhibited by placing a \& between them.

In a string comparison in a condition, characters that appear at different input levels to the first delimiter character will not be recognised as the second or third delimiters. This applies also to the tl request. In a \w escape sequence, a character that appears at a different input level to the starting delimiter character will not be recognised as the closing delimiter character. When decoding a macro argument that is delimited by double quotes, a character that appears at a different input level to the starting delimiter character will not be recognised as the closing delimiter character. The implementation of \$@ ensures that the double quotes surrounding an argument will appear the same input level, which will be different to the input level of the argument itself. In a long escape name] will not be recognized as a closing delimiter except when it occurs at the same input level as the opening]. In compatibility mode, no attention is paid to the input-level.

There are some new types of condition:

.if*r*xxx   True if there is a number register named *xxx*.

.if*d*xxx   True if there is a string, macro, diversion, or request named *xxx*.

.if*c*ch   True if there is a character *ch* available; *ch* is either an ASCII character or a special character \(*xx* or \[*xxx*]; the condition will also be true if *ch* has been defined by the char request.

Warnings

The warnings that can be given by troff are divided into the following categories. The name associated with each warning is used by the –w and –W options; the number is used by the warn request, and by the .warn register.

char 1   Non-existent characters. This is enabled by default.

number 2   Invalid numeric expressions. This is enabled by default.

break 4   In fill mode, lines which could not be broken so that their length was less than the line length. This is enabled by default.

delim 8   Missing or mismatched closing delimiters.

el 16   Use of the el request with no matching ie request.

scale 32   Meaningless scaling indicators.

range 64   Out of range arguments.

syntax 128   Dubious syntax in numeric expressions.

di 256   Use of di or da without an argument when there is no current diversion.

mac 512   Use of undefined strings, macros and diversions. When an undefined string, macro or diversion is used, that string is automatically defined as empty. So, in most cases, at most one warning will be given for each name.

reg 1024   Use of undefined number registers. When an undefined number register is used, that register is automatically defined to have a value of 0. a definition is automatically made with a value of 0. So, in most cases, at most one warning will be given for use of a particular name.

tab 2048   Inappropriate use of a tab character. Either use of a tab character where a number was expected, or use of tab character in an unquoted macro argument.

right-brace 4096   Use of \} where a number was expected.

missing 8192   Requests that are missing non-optional arguments.

input 16384   Illegal input characters.

escape 32768   Unrecognized escape sequences. When an unrecognized escape sequence is encountered, the escape character is ignored.

space 65536   Missing space between a request or macro and its argument. This warning will be given when an undefined name longer than two characters is encountered, and the first two characters of the name make a defined name. The request or macro will not be invoked. When this warning is given, no macro is automatically defined. This is enabled by default. This warning will never occur in compatibility mode.

font 131072   Non-existent fonts. This is enabled by default.

ig 262144   Illegal escapes in text ignored with the ig request. These are conditions that are errors when they do not occur in ignored text.

There are also names that can be used to refer to groups of warnings:

all   All warnings except di, mac and reg. It is intended that this covers all warnings that are useful with traditional macro packages.

w   All warnings.

Incompatibilities

Long names cause some incompatibilities. Unix troff will interpret

.dsabcd

as defining a string ab with contents cd. Normally, GNU troff will interpret this as a call of a macro named dsabcd. Also Unix troff will interpret *[or \n[as references to a string or number register called [. In GNU troff, however, this will normally be interpreted as the start of a long name. In *compatibility* mode GNU troff will interpret these things in the traditional way. In compatibility mode, however, long names are not recognised. Compatibility mode can be turned on with the –C command line option, and turned on or off with the cp request. The number register \n(.C is 1 if compatibility mode is on, 0 otherwise.

GNU troff does not allow the use of the escape sequences \e\|\^\&\}\{\(space) \'\'\-_\!\%\c in names of strings, macros, diversions, number registers, fonts or environments; Unix troff does. The \A escape sequence may be helpful in avoiding use of these escape sequences in names.

Fractional pointsizes cause one noteworthy incompatibility. In Unix troff the ps request ignores scale indicators and so

.ps 10u

will set the pointsize to 10 points, whereas in GNU troff it will set the pointsize to 10 scaled points.

In GNU troff there is a fundamental difference between unformatted, input characters, and formatted, output characters. Everything that affects how an output character will be output is stored with the character; once an output character has been constructed it is unaffected by any subsequent requests that are executed, including bd, cs, tkf, tr, or fp requests. Normally output characters are constructed from input characters at the moment immediately before the character is added to the current output line. Macros, diversions and strings are all, in fact, the same type of object; they contain lists of input characters and output characters in any combination. An output character does not behave like an input character for the purposes of macro processing; it does not inherit any of the special properties that the input character from which it was constructed might have had. For example,

.di x
\\\\
.br
.di
.x

will print \\ in GNU troff; each pair of input \s is turned into one output \ and the resulting output \s are not interpreted as escape characters when they are reread. Unix troff would interpret them as escape characters when they were reread and would end up printing one \. The correct way to obtain a printable \ is to use the \e escape sequence: this will always print a single instance of the current escape character, regardless of whether or not it is used in a diversion; it will also work in both GNU troff and Unix troff. If you wish for some reason to store in a diversion an escape sequence that will be interpreted when the diversion is reread, you can either use the traditional \! transparent output facility, or, if this is unsuitable, the new \? escape sequence.

ENVIRONMENT

GROFF_TMAC_PATH A colon separated list of directories in which to search for macro files.

GROFF_TYPESETTER Default device.

GROFF_FONT_PATH A colon separated list of directories in which to search for the dev*name* directory. troff will search in directories given in the –F option before these, and in standard directories (.:/usr/lib/groff/font:/usr/lib/font:/usr/lib/font) after these.

FILES

/usr/lib/groff/font/devname/DESC /usr/lib/groff/tmac/troffrc Initialization file

/usr/lib/groff/tmac/tmac.*name*	Macro files
/usr/lib/groff/font/dev*name*/DESC	Device description file for device *name*.
/usr/lib/groff/font/dev*name*/F	Font file for font *F* of device *name*.

SEE ALSO

groff(1) gtbl(1), gpic(1), geqn(1), grops(1), grodvi(1), grotty(1), groff_font(5), groff_out(5), groff_char(7)

GZIP(1)

NAME

gzip, gunzip, zcat – compress or expand files

SYNOPSIS

gzip [–acdfhlLnNrtvV19] [–Ssuffix] [*name* ...]
gunzip [–acfhlLnNrtvV] [–Ssuffix] [*name* ...]
zcat [–fhLV] [*name* ...]

DESCRIPTION

Gzip reduces the size of the named files using Lempel-Ziv coding (LZ77). Whenever possible, each file is replaced by one with the extension .gz, while keeping the same ownership modes, access and modification times. (The default extension is –gz for VMS, z for MSDOS, OS/2 FAT, Windows NT FAT and Atari.) If no files are specified, or if a file name is "-", the standard input is compressed to the standard output. *Gzip* will only attempt to compress regular files. In particular, it will ignore symbolic links.

If the compressed file name is too long for its file system, *gzip* truncates it. *Gzip* attempts to truncate only the parts of the file name longer than 3 characters. (A part is delimited by dots.) If the name consists of small parts only, the longest parts are truncated. For example, if file names are limited to 14 characters, gzip.msdos.exe is compressed to gzi.msd.exe.gz. Names are not truncated on systems which do not have a limit on file name length.

By default, *gzip* keeps the original file name and timestamp in the compressed file. These are used when decompressing the file with the –N option. This is useful when the compressed file name was truncated or when the time stamp was not preserved after a file transfer.

Compressed files can be restored to their original form using *gzip* -d or *gunzip* or *zcat*. If the original name saved in the compressed file is not suitable for its file system, a new name is constructed from the original one to make it legal.

gunzip takes a list of files on its command line and replaces each file whose name ends with .gz, -gz, .z, -z, _z or .Z and which begins with the correct magic number with an uncompressed file without the original extension. *gunzip* also recognizes the special extensions .tgz and .taz as shorthands for .tar.gz and .tar.Z respectively. When compressing, *gzip* uses the .tgz extension if necessary instead of truncating a file with a .tar extension.

gunzip can currently decompress files created by *gzip,* zip, compress, compress -H or *pack.* The detection of the input format is automatic. When using the first two formats, *gunzip* checks a 32 bit CRC. For *pack,* gunzip checks the uncompressed length. The standard *compress* format was not designed to allow consistency checks. However *gunzip* is sometimes able to detect a bad .Z file. If you get an error when uncompressing a .Z file, do not assume that the .Z file is correct simply because the standard *uncompress* does not complain. This generally means that the standard *uncompress* does not check its input, and happily generates garbage output. The SCO compress -H format (lzh compression method) does not include a CRC but also allows some consistency checks.

Files created by *zip* can be uncompressed by gzip only if they have a single member compressed with the 'deflation' method. This feature is only intended to help conversion of tar.zip files to the tar.gz format. To extract zip files with several members, use *unzip* instead of *gunzip.*

zcat is identical to *gunzip* –c. (On some systems, *zcat* may be installed as *gzcat* to preserve the original link to *compress.*) *zcat* uncompresses either a list of files on the command line or its standard input and writes the uncompressed data on standard output. *zcat* will uncompress files that have the correct magic number whether they have a .gz suffix or not.

Gzip uses the Lempel-Ziv algorithm used in *zip* and PKZIP. The amount of compression obtained depends on the size of the input and the distribution of common substrings. Typically, text such as source code or English is reduced by 60–70%. Compression is generally much better than that achieved by LZW (as used in *compress*),

Huffman coding (as used in *pack*), or adaptive Huffman coding (*compact*).

Compression is always performed, even if the compressed file is slightly larger than the original. The worst case expansion is a few bytes for the gzip file header, plus 5 bytes every 32K block, or an expansion ratio of 0.015% for large files. Note that the actual number of used disk blocks almost never increases. *gzip* preserves the mode, ownership and timestamps of files when compressing or decompressing.

OPTIONS

-a --ascii
: Ascii text mode: convert end-of-lines using local conventions. This option is supported only on some non-Unix systems. For MSDOS, CR LF is converted to LF when compressing, and LF is converted to CR LF when decompressing.

-c --stdout --to-stdout
: Write output on standard output; keep original files unchanged. If there are several input files, the output consists of a sequence of independently compressed members. To obtain better compression, concatenate all input files before compressing them.

-d --decompress --uncompress
: Decompress.

-f --force
: Force compression or decompression even if the file has multiple links or the corresponding file already exists, or if the compressed data is read from or written to a terminal. If the input data is not in a format recognized by *gzip*, and if the option --stdout is also given, copy the input data without change to the standard ouput: let *zcat* behave as *cat*. If -f is not given, and when not running in the background, *gzip* prompts to verify whether an existing file should be overwritten.

-h --help
: Display a help screen and quit.

-l --list
: For each compressed file, list the following fields:

  compressed size: size of the compressed file uncompressed size: size of the uncompressed file ratio: compression ratio (0.0% if unknown) uncompressed_name: name of the uncompressed file

  The uncompressed size is given as -1 for files not in gzip format, such as compressed .Z files. To get the uncompressed size for such a file, you can use:

  zcat file.Z | wc -c

  In combination with the --verbose option, the following fields are also displayed:

  method: compression method crc: the 32-bit CRC of the uncompressed data date & time: time stamp for the uncompressed file

  The compression methods currently supported are deflate, compress, lzh (SCO compress -H) and pack. The crc is given as ffffffff for a file not in gzip format.

  With --name, the uncompressed name, date and time are those stored within the compress file if present.

  With --verbose, the size totals and compression ratio for all files is also displayed, unless some sizes are unknown. With --quiet, the title and totals lines are not displayed.

-L --license
: Display the *gzip* license and quit.

-n --no-name
: When compressing, do not save the original file name and time stamp by default. (The original name is always saved if the name had to be truncated.) When decompressing, do not restore the original file name if present (remove only the *gzip* suffix from the compressed file name) and do not restore the original time stamp if present (copy it from the compressed file). This option is the default when decompressing.

local

-N –name   When compressing, always save the original file name and time stamp; this is the default. When decompressing, restore the original file name and time stamp if present. This option is useful on systems which have a limit on file name length or when the time stamp has been lost after a file transfer.

-q –quiet   Suppress all warnings.

-r –recursive   Travel the directory structure recursively. If any of the file names specified on the command line are directories, *gzip* will descend into the directory and compress all the files it finds there (or decompress them in the case of *gunzip*).

-S .suf –suffix .suf   Use suffix .suf instead of .gz. Any suffix can be given, but suffixes other than .z and .gz should be avoided to avoid confusion when files are transferred to other systems. A null suffix forces gunzip to try decompression on all given files regardless of suffix, as in:

gunzip -S "" * (*.* for MSDOS)

Previous versions of gzip used the .z suffix. This was changed to avoid a conflict with *pack*(1).

-t –test   Test. Check the compressed file integrity.

-v –verbose   Verbose. Display the name and percentage reduction for each file compressed or decompressed.

-V –version   Version. Display the version number and compilation options then quit.

-# –fast –best   Regulate the speed of compression using the specified digit #, where –1 or —fast indicates the fastest compression method (less compression) and –9 or —best indicates the slowest compression method (best compression). The default compression level is –6 (that is, biased towards high compression at expense of speed).

ADVANCED USAGE

Multiple compressed files can be concatenated. In this case, *gunzip* will extract all members at once. For example:

gzip -c file1 > foo.gz gzip -c file2 >> foo.gz

Then gunzip -c foo

is equivalent to

cat file1 file2

In case of damage to one member of a .gz file, other members can still be recovered (if the damaged member is removed). However, you can get better compression by compressing all members at once:

cat file1 file2 | gzip > foo.gz

compresses better than

gzip -c file1 file2 > foo.gz

If you want to recompress concatenated files to get better compression, do:

gzip -cd old.gz | gzip > new.gz

If a compressed file consists of several members, the uncompressed size and CRC reported by the –list option applies to the last member only. If you need the uncompressed size for all members, you can use:

gzip -cd file.gz | wc -c

If you wish to create a single archive file with multiple members so that members can later be extracted independently, use an archiver such as tar or zip. GNU tar supports

local

GZIP(1)   GZIP(1)

the -z option to invoke gzip transparently. gzip is designed as a complement to tar, not as a replacement.

ENVIRONMENT

The environment variable GZIP can hold a set of default options for *gzip*. These options are interpreted first and can be overwritten by explicit command line parameters. For example: for sh: GZIP="-8v –name"; export GZIP for csh: setenv GZIP "-8v –name" for MSDOS: set GZIP=-8v –name

On Vax/VMS, the name of the environment variable is GZIP_OPT, to avoid a conflict with the symbol set for invocation of the program.

SEE ALSO

znew(1), zcmp(1), zmore(1), zforce(1), gzexe(1), zip(1), unzip(1), compress(1), pack(1), compact(1)

DIAGNOSTICS

Exit status is normally 0; if an error occurs, exit status is 1. If a warning occurs, exit status is 2.

Usage: gzip [-cdfhlLnNrtvV19] [-S suffix] [file ...]
>   Invalid options were specified on the command line.

file: not in gzip format
>   The file specified to *gunzip* has not been compressed.

file: Corrupt input. Use zcat to recover some data.
>   The compressed file has been damaged. The data up to the point of failure can be recovered using
>
>   zcat file > recover

file: compressed with *xx* bits, can only handle *yy* bits

File was compressed (using LZW) by a program that could deal with more *bits* than the decompress code on this machine. Recompress the file with gzip, which compresses better and uses less memory.

file: already has .gz suffix – no change
>   The file is assumed to be already compressed. Rename the file and try again.

file already exists; do you wish to overwrite (y or n)?
>   Respond "y" if you want the output file to be replaced; "n" if not.

gunzip: corrupt input
>   A SIGSEGV violation was detected which usually means that the input file has been corrupted.

xx.x%
>   Percentage of the input saved by compression. (Relevant only for –v and –l)

– not a regular file or directory: ignored
>   When the input file is not a regular file or directory, (e.g. a symbolic link, socket, FIFO, device file), it is left unaltered.

– has *xx* other links: unchanged
>   The input file has links; it is left unchanged. See *ln*(1) for more information. Use the –f flag to force compression of multiply-linked files.

CAVEATS

When writing compressed data to a tape, it is generally necessary to pad the output with zeroes up to a block boundary. When the data is read and the whole block is passed to *gunzip* for decompression, *gunzip* detects that there is extra trailing garbage after the compressed data and emits a warning by default. You have to use the –quiet option to suppress the warning. This option can be set in the GZIP environment variable as in: for sh: GZIP="-q" tar -xfz –block-compress /dev/rst0 for csh: (setenv GZIP -q; tar -xfz –block-compr /dev/rst0

In the above example, gzip is invoked implicitly by the -z option of GNU tar. Make sure that the same block size (-b option of tar) is used for reading and writing compressed data on tapes. (This example assumes you are using the GNU version of tar.)

BUGS

The –list option reports incorrect sizes if they exceed 2 gigabytes. The –list option reports sizes as -1 and crc as ffffffff if the compressed file is on a non seekable media.

In some rare cases, the –best option gives worse compression than the default compression level (-6). On some highly redundant files, *compress* compresses better than *gzip*.

GZEXE(1)   GZEXE(1)

NAME

gzexe – compress executable files in place

SYNOPSIS

gzexe [name ...]

DESCRIPTION

The *gzexe* utility allows you to compress executables in place and have them automatically uncompress and execute when you run them (at a penalty in performance). For example if you execute "gzexe /bin/cat" it will create the following two files: -r-xr-xr-x 1 root bin 9644 Feb 11 11:16 /bin/cat
-r-xr-xr-x 1 bin bin 24576 Nov 23 13:21 /bin/cat˜ /bin/cat˜ is the original file and /bin/cat is the self-uncompressing executable file. You can remove /bin/cat˜ once you are sure that /bin/cat works properly.

This utility is most useful on systems with very small disks.

OPTIONS

    –d   Decompress the given executables instead of compressing them.

SEE ALSO

gzip(1), znew(1), zmore(1), zcmp(1), zforce(1)

CAVEATS

The compressed executable is a shell script. This may create some security holes. In particular, the compressed executable relies on the PATH environment variable to find *gzip* and some other utilities *(tail,* chmod, ln, sleep).

BUGS

gzexe attempts to retain the original file attributes on the compressed executable, but you may have to fix them manually in some cases, using *chmod* or *chown.*

HEAD(1L)

NAME

head – output the first part of files

SYNOPSIS

head [–c N[bkm]] [–n N] [–qv] [-—bytes=N[bkm]] [-—lines=N] [-—quiet] [-—silent] [-—verbose] [-—help] [-—version] [file...]

head [–Nbcklmqv] [file...]

DESCRIPTION

This manual page documents the GNU version of head. head prints the first part (10 lines by default) of each given file; it reads from standard input if no files are given or when a filename of '–' is encountered. If more than one file is given, it prints a header consisting of the file's name enclosed in '==>' and '<==' before the output for each file.

OPTIONS

head accepts two option formats: the new one, in which numbers are arguments to the option letters, and the old one, in which the number precedes any option letters.

–c N, -—bytes N
: Print first N bytes. N is a nonzero integer, optionally followed by one of the following characters to specify a different unit.

    b 512-byte blocks.
    k 1-kilobyte blocks.
    m 1-megabyte blocks.

–l, –n N, -—lines N
: Print first N lines.

–q, -—quiet, -—silent
: Never print filename headers.

–v, -—verbose
: Always print filename headers.

-—help
: Print a usage message and exit with a non-zero status.

-—version
: Print version information on standard output then exit.

HEXDUMP(1)

NAME

hexdump – ascii, decimal, hexadecimal, octal dump

SYNOPSIS

hexdump [-bcdovx] [-e format_string] [-f format_file] [-n length] [-s skip] [file ...]

DESCRIPTION

The hexdump utility is a filter which displays the specified files, or the standard input, if no files are specified, in a user specified format.

The options are as follows:

- -b *One-byte octal display*. Display the input offset in hexadecimal, followed by sixteen space-separated, three column, zero-filled, bytes of input data, in octal, per line.
- -c One-byte character display. Display the input offset in hexadecimal, followed by sixteen space-separated, three column, space-filled, characters of input data per line.
- -d Two-byte decimal display. Display the input offset in hexadecimal, followed by eight space-separated, five column, zero-filled, two-byte units of input data, in unsigned decimal, per line.
- -e format_string Specify a format string to be used for displaying data.
- -f format_file Specify a file that contains one or more newline separated format strings. Empty lines and lines whose first non-blank character is a hash mark (#) are ignored.
- -n length Interpret only length bytes of input.
- -o *Two-byte octal display*. Display the input offset in hexadecimal, followed by eight space-separated, six column, zero-filled, two byte quantities of input data, in octal, per line.
- -s offset Skip offset bytes from the beginning of the input. By default, offset is interpreted as a decimal number. With a leading 0x or 0X , offset is interpreted as a hexadecimal number, otherwise, with a leading 0 , offset is interpreted as an octal number. Appending the character b , k , or m to offset causes it to be interpreted as a multiple of 512 , 1024 , or 1048576 , respectively.
- -v The -v option causes hexdump to display all input data. Without the -v option, any number of groups of output lines, which would be identical to the immediately preceding group of output lines (except for the input offsets), are replaced with a line comprised of a single asterisk.
- -x *Two-byte hexadecimal display*. Display the input offset in hexadecimal, followed by eight, space separated, four column, zero-filled, two-byte quantities of input data, in hexadecimal, per line.

For each input file, hexdump sequentially copies the input to standard output, transforming the data according to the format strings specified by the -e and -f options, in the order that they were specified.

Formats

A format string contains any number of format units, separated by whitespace. A format unit contains up to three items: an iteration count, a byte count, and a format.

The iteration count is an optional positive integer, which defaults to one. Each format is applied iteration count times.

The byte count is an optional positive integer. If specified it defines the number of bytes to be interpreted by each iteration of the format.

If an iteration count and/or a byte count is specified, a single slash must be placed after the iteration count and/or before the byte count to disambiguate them. Any whitespace before or after the slash is ignored.

The format is required and must be surrounded by double quote (" ") marks. It is interpreted as a fprintf-style format string (see fprintf(3)), with the following exceptions:

- An asterisk (*) may not be used as a field width or precision.
- A byte count or field precision is required for each "s" conversion character (unlike the fprintf(3) default which prints the entire string if the precision is unspecified).
- The conversion characters "h", "l", "n", "p" and "q" are not supported.
- The single character escape sequences described in the C standard are supported:

NUL	\0
\<alert character\>	\a
\<backspace\>	\b
\<form-feed\>	\f
\<newline\>	\n
\<carriage return\>	\r
\<tab\>	\t
\<vertical tab\>	\v

Hexdump also supports the the following additional conversion strings:

- _a[dox] Display the input offset, cumulative across input files, of the next byte to be displayed. The appended characters d, o, and x specify the display base as decimal, octal or hexadecimal respectively.
- _A[dox] Identical to the _a conversion string except that it is only performed once, when all of the input data has been processed.
- _c Output characters in the default character set. Nonprinting characters are displayed in three character, zero-padded octal, except for those representable by standard escape notation (see above), which are displayed as two character strings.
- _p Output characters in the default character set. Nonprinting characters are displayed as a single ".".
- _u Output US ASCII characters, with the exception that control characters are displayed using the following, lower-case, names. Characters greater than 0xff, hexadecimal, are displayed as hexadecimal strings.

000 nul	001 soh	002 stx	003 etx	004 eot	005 enq
006 ack	007 bel	008 bs	009 ht	00A lf	00B vt
00C ff	00D cr	00E so	00F si	010 dle	011 dc1
012 dc2	013 dc3	014 dc4	015 nak	016 syn	017 etb
018 can	019 em	01A sub	01B esc	01C fs	01D gs
01E rs	01F us	0FF del			

The default and supported byte counts for the conversion characters are as follows:

- %_c, %_p, %_u, %c One byte counts only.
- %d, %i, %o, %u, %X, %x Four byte default, one, two and four byte counts supported.
- %E, %e, %f, %G, %g Eight byte default, four byte counts supported.

The amount of data interpreted by each format string is the sum of the data required by each format unit, which is the iteration count times the byte count, or the iteration count times the number of bytes required by the format if the byte count is not specified.

The input is manipulated in "blocks", where a block is defined as the largest amount of data specified by any format string. Format strings interpreting less than an input block's worth of data, whose last format unit both interprets some number of bytes and does not have a specified iteration count, have the iteration count incremented until the entire input block has been processed or there is not enough data remaining in the block to satisfy the format string.

If, either as a result of user specification or hexdump modifying the iteration count as described above, an iteration count is greater than one, no trailing whitespace characters are output during the last iteration.

It is an error to specify a byte count as well as multiple conversion characters or strings unless all but one of the conversion characters or strings is _a or _A. If, as a result of the specification of the -n option or end-of-file being reached, input data only partially satisfies a format string, the input block is zero-padded sufficiently to display all available data (i.e. any format units overlapping the end of data will display some number of the zero bytes).

Further output by such format strings is replaced by an equivalent number of spaces. An equivalent number of spaces is defined as the number of spaces output by an "s" conversion character with the same field width and precision as the original conversion character or conversion string but with any "+", " ", "#" conversion flag characters removed, and referencing a NULL string.

If no format strings are specified, the default display is equivalent to specifying the -x option.

hexdump exits 0 on success and >0 if an error occurred.

EXAMPLES

Display the input in perusal format: "%06.6_ao " 12/1 "%3_u "
"\t\t" "%_p "
"\n"

Implement the –x option: "%07.7_Ax\n"
"%07.7_ax " 8/2 "%04x " "\n"

SEE ALSO

adb(1)

HOSTID(1)

NAME
hostid – set or print system's host id.

SYNTAX
hostid [–v] [*decimal-id*]

DESCRIPTION
The **hostid** command prints the current host id number in hexadecimal and both decimal and hexadecimal in parenthesis if the –v option is given. This numeric value is expected to be unique across all hosts and is normally set to resemble the host's Internet address.

Only the super-user can set the hostid by giving an argument. This value is stored in the file /etc/hostid and need only be performed once.

AUTHOR
Hostid is written by Mitch DSouza – (m.dsouza@mrc-apu.cam.ac.uk)

SEE ALSO
gethostid(2), sethostid(2)

NAME

hostname – show or set the system's host name
dnsdomainname – show the system's domain name

SYNOPSIS

hostname [–d] [––**domain**] [–F**filename**] [––**filefilename**] [–f] [––**fqdn**] [–h] [––**help**]
[––**long**] [–s] [––**short**] [–v] [––**version**] [**name**]
dnsdomainname

DESCRIPTION

Hostname is the program that is used to either set the host name or display the current host or domain name of the system. This name is used by many of the networking programs to identify the machine.

When called without any arguments, the program displays the current name as set by the **hostname** command. You can change the output format to display always the short or the long host name (FQDN). When called with arguments, the program will set the value of the host name to the value specified. This usually is done only once, at system startup time, by the */etc/rc.d/rc.inet1* configuration script.

Note, that only the super-user can change the host name.

If the program was called as **dnsdomainname** it will show the DNS domain name. You can't change the DNS domain name with **dnsdomainname** (see below).

OPTIONS

–d, ––domain		Display the name of the DNS domain. Don't use the command **domainname** to get the DNS domain name because it will show the NIS domain name and not the DNS domain name.
–F, ––file filename		Read the host name from the specified file. Comments (lines starting with a '#') are ignored.
–f, ––fqdn, ––long		Display the FQDN (Fully Qualified Domain Name). A FQDN consists of a short host name and the DNS domain name. Unless you are using bind or NIS for host lookups you can change the FQDN and the DNS domain name (which is part of the FQDN) in the */etc/hosts* file.
–h, ––help		Print a usage message on standard output and exit successfully.
–s, ––short		Display the short host name.
–v, ––version		Print version information on standard output and exit successfully.

FILES

/etc/hosts

AUTHOR

Peter Tobias, <tobias@server.et-inf.fho-emden.de>

IMAKE(1)

NAME

imake – C preprocessor interface to the make utility

SYNOPSIS

imake [**–D**define] [**–I**dir] [**–T**template] [**–f** filename] [**–C** filename] [**–s** filename] [**–e**] [**–v**]

DESCRIPTION

Imake is used to generate *Makefiles* from a template, a set of *cpp* macro functions, and a per-directory input file called an *Imakefile*. This allows machine dependencies (such as compiler options, alternate command names, and special *make* rules) to be kept separate from the descriptions of the various items to be built.

OPTIONS

The following command line options may be passed to *imake*:

- **–D**define — This option is passed directly to *cpp*. It is typically used to set directory-specific variables. For example, the X Window System uses this flag to set *TOPDIR* to the name of the directory containing the top of the core distribution and *CURDIR* to the name of the current directory, relative to the top.

- **–I**directory — This option is passed directly to *cpp*. It is typically used to indicate the directory in which the *imake* template and configuration files may be found.

- **–T**template — This option specifies the name of the master template file (which is usually located in the directory specified with *–I*) used by *cpp*. The default is *Imake.tmpl*.

- **–f** filename — This option specifies the name of the per-directory input file. The default is *Imakefile*.

- **–C** filename — This option specifies the name of the .c file that is constructed in the current directory. The default is *Imakefile.c*.

- **–s** filename — This option specifies the name of the *make* description file to be generated but *make* should not be invoked. If the *filename* is a dash (–), the output is written to *stdout*. The default is to generate, but not execute, a *Makefile*.

- **–e** — This option indicates the *imake* should execute the generated *Makefile*. The default is to leave this to the user.

- **–v** — This option indicates that *imake* should print the *cpp* command line that it is using to generate the *Makefile*.

HOW IT WORKS

Imake invokes *cpp* with any *–I* or *–D* flags passed on the command line and passes the name of a file containing the following 3 lines:

#define IMAKE_TEMPLATE "Imake.tmpl"
#define INCLUDE_IMAKEFILE <Imakefile>
#include IMAKE_TEMPLATE

where *Imake.tmpl* and *Imakefile* may be overridden by the *–T* and *–f* command options, respectively.

The IMAKE_TEMPLATE typically reads in a file containing machine-dependent parameters (specified as *cpp* symbols), a site-specific parameters file, a file defining variables, a file containing *cpp* macro functions for generating *make* rules, and finally the *Imakefile* (specified by INCLUDE_IMAKEFILE) in the current directory. The *Imakefile* uses the macro functions to indicate what targets should be built; *imake* takes care of generating the appropriate rules.

Imake configuration files contain two types of variables, imake variables and make variables. The imake variables are interpreted by cpp when *imake* is run. By convention they are mixed case. The make variables are written into the *Makefile* for later interpretation by *make*. By convention make variables are upper case.

The rules file (usually named *Imake.rules* in the configuration directory) contains a variety of *cpp* macro functions that are configured according to the current platform. *Imake* replaces any occurrences of the string "@@" with a newline to allow macros that generate more than one line of *make* rules. For example, the macro

```
#define program_target(program, objlist) @@\
program: objlist @@\
$(CC) –o $@ objlist $(LDFLAGS)
```

when called with *program_target(foo, foo1.o foo2.o)* will expand to

```
foo: foo1.o foo2.o
$(CC) –o $@ foo1.o foo2.o $(LDFLAGS)
```

Imake also replaces any occurrences of the word "XCOMM" with the character "#" to permit placing comments in the Makefile without causing "invalid directive" errors from the preprocessor.

Some complex *imake* macros require generated *make* variables local to each invocation of the macro, often because their value depends on parameters passed to the macro. Such variables can be created by using an *imake* variable of the form **XVARdef***n*, where *n* is a single digit. A unique *make* variable will be substituted. Later occurrences of the variable **XVARuse***n* will be replaced by the variable created by the corresponding **XVARdef***n*.

On systems whose *cpp* reduces multiple tabs and spaces to a single space, *imake* attempts to put back any necessary tabs (*make* is very picky about the difference between tabs and spaces). For this reason, colons (:) in command lines must be preceded by a backslash (\).

USE WITH THE X WINDOW SYSTEM

The X Window System uses *imake* extensively, for both full builds within the source tree and external software. As mentioned above, two special variables, *TOPDIR* and *CURDIR*, are set to make referencing files using relative path names easier. For example, the following command is generated automatically to build the *Makefile* in the directory *lib/X/* (relative to the top of the sources):

```
% ../../config/imake –I../../config \
–DTOPDIR=../../. –DCURDIR=./lib/X
```

When building X programs outside the source tree, a special symbol *UseInstalled* is defined and *TOPDIR* and *CURDIR* are omitted. If the configuration files have been properly installed, the script *xmkmf*(1) may be used.

INPUT FILES

Here is a summary of the files read by *imake* as used by X. The indentation shows what files include what other files. Imake.tmpl generic variables
site.def site-specific, BeforeVendorCF defined
.cf machine-specific
Lib.rules shared library rules
site.def site-specific, AfterVendorCF defined
Imake.rules rules
Project.tmpl X-specific variables
Lib.tmpl shared library variables
Imakefile
Library.tmpl library rules
Server.tmpl server rules
Threads.tmpl multi-threaded rules

Note that *site.def* gets included twice, once before the *.cf* file and once after. Although

IMAKE(1) IMAKE(1)

most site customizations should be specified after the *.cf file, some, such as the choice of compiler, need to be specified before, because other variable settings may depend on them.

The first time *site.def* is included, the variable BeforeVendorCF is defined, and the second time, the variable AfterVendorCF is defined. All code in *site.def* should be inside an #ifdef for one of these symbols.

FILES

Imakefile.c temporary input file for cpp
/tmp/Imf.XXXXXX temporary Makefile for -s
/tmp/IIf.XXXXXX temporary Imakefile if specified Imakefile uses # comments
/lib/cpp default C preprocessor

SEE ALSO

make(1), xmkmf(1)
S. I. Feldman, Make — A Program for Maintaining Computer Programs

ENVIRONMENT VARIABLES

The following environment variables may be set, however their use is not recommended as they introduce dependencies that are not readily apparent when *imake* is run:

IMAKEINCLUDE If defined, this should be a valid include argument for the C preprocessor.
E.g., "–I/usr/include/local." Actually, any valid *cpp* argument will work here.

IMAKECPP If defined, this should be a valid path to a preprocessor program. E.g., "/usr/local/cpp". By default, *imake* will use /lib/cpp.

IMAKEMAKE If defined, this should be a valid path to a make program, such as "/usr/local/make". By default, *imake* will use whatever *make* program is found using *execvp(3)*. This variable is only used if the "–e" option is specified.

AUTHOR

Todd Brunhoff, Tektronix and MIT Project Athena; Jim Fulton, MIT X Consortium

INSMOD(1) — Linux Module Support

NAME

insmod – install loadable modules (aout and ELF format)

SYNOPSIS

insmod [–fkmsxv] [–o internal_name] object_file [symbol=value ...]

DESCRIPTION

Insmod installs a loadable module in the kernel.

Insmod tries to load a module into the kernel, and resolves all symbols from the exported kernel symbols, with version information, if available. The module will get its name by removing the '.o' extension from the basename of the object file.
If the '.o' extension is omitted, insmod will attempt to locate the module in some common default directories. If the environment contains the variable MODPATH, where all directories are separated with ':', insmod will look in these directories for the module, in the specified order.

It is possible to load unversioned modules in a versioned kernel, and all combinations of these.
It is also possible to load ELF modules into an a.out kernel, and all combinations of these.
It is possible to stack modules, i.e. let one module use a previously loaded module. All modules that are referenced are updated with this reference. This ensures that a module can't be unloaded if there is another module that refers to it.
It is possible to change integer values in the module when loading it. This makes it possible to "tune" the module.

The options are as follows:

- **–f** The –f option tries to load the module even if the kernel or symbol versions differs from the version expected by the module. A warning will be issued if the module is locked to a specific kernel version that differs from the current version.

- **–k** This option should really only be used by modprobe, to indicate that the module insertion was requested by kerneld. All modules inserted using this option will be subject to auto-removal by the kerneld utiliy if they have been unused for more that a minute. (I.e. the usage count is zero and no modules depend on this module.)
  If the kernel is not "kerneld-aware", the module will be rejected by the kernel. Just load it without the "-k" option, and all should be well.

- **–m** The –m option will make insmod ouput a load map, that will make it easier to debug your modules after a kernel panic...
  Thanks to Derek Atkins <warlord@MIT.EDU>.

- **–o** The –o option allows the module to be named to an explicit name instead of having a name derived from the name of the object file.
  Note that this option can also be placed _after_ the module name, so that the syntax of insmod looks more similar to ld.

- **symbol=value[,value] ...** The values of all integer or character pointer symbols in the module can be changed at load-time by naming a symbol and giving the new value(s).
  If the symbol is defined as an array of integers or character pointers, the elements in the array can be initialized by giving the values separated by commas (','). Specific array entries can be skipped by omitting the value, as in 'symbol=value1,,value2'.
  Each integer value can be given as a decimal, octal or hexadecimal value: 17, 021 or 0x11.
  If the first character in the given value is non-numeric, the value is interpreted as a string. The symbol is assumed to be a character pointer, which will be initialized to point to the string. Extra space in the module will be

| INSMOD(1) | Linux Module Support | INSMOD(1) |

allocated for the string itself.
Note the syntax: no spaces are allowed around the '=' or ','-signs!

- −s   With this option insmod will produce debugging information and error messages using the syslog facility. (Also used by "kerneld", if you have installed it.)
- −v   If you want verbose information from the loading, select this option.
- −x   is the no-export-flag, which will inhibit the default insmod behaviour: i.e. inserting all the module's external symbols into the kernel symbol table. Note that the kernel will still update the references that the module makes to previously loaded modules.

SEE ALSO

rmmod(1), modprobe(1), depmod(1), lsmod(1), ksyms(1), modules(2), genksyms(8)

HISTORY

The module support was first concieved by Anonymous (as far as I know...).
Linux version by Bas Laarhoven <bas@vimec.nl>,
0.99.14 version by Jon Tombs <jon@gtex02.us.es>,
extended by Bjorn Ekwall <bj0rn@blox.se>.
ELF help from Eric Youngdale <eric@aib.com>

BUGS

Insmod relies on the "fact" that symbols, for which one wants to change the value, are defined as integers or character pointers, and that sizeof(int) == sizeof(char *).

NAME

install – copy files and set their attributes GNU!file installer

SYNOPSIS

install [options] [–s] [––strip] source dest
install [options] [–s] [––strip] source... directory
install [options] [–d,––directory] directory...
Options:
[–c] [–g group] [–m mode] [–o owner] [––group=group] [––mode=mode] [––owner=owner]
[––help] [––version]

DESCRIPTION

This manual page documents the GNU version of **install**. **install** copies files and sets their permission modes and, if possible, their owner and group. Used similarly to **cp**; typically used in Makefiles to copy programs into their destination directories. It can also be used to create the destination directories and any leading directories, and to set the final directory's modes. It refuses to copy files onto themselves.

OPTIONS

- –c Ignored; for compatibility with old Unix versions of install.

- –d, ––directory Create each given directory and its leading directories, if they do not already exist. Set the owner, group and mode as given on the command line or to the defaults. Also gives any leading directories that are created those attributes. This is different from the SunOS 4.x *install*, which gives directories that it creates the default attributes.

- –g, ––group group Set the group ownership of the installed file or directory to the group ID of *group* (default is process's current group). *group* may also be a numeric group ID.

- –m, ––mode mode Set the permission mode for the installed file or directory to *mode*, which can be either an octal number, or a symbolic mode as in chmod, with 0 as the point of departure. The default mode is 0755.

- –o, ––owner owner If run as root, set the ownership of the installed file to the user ID of *owner* (default is root). *owner* may also be a numeric user ID.

- –s, ––strip Strip the symbol tables from installed programs.

- ––help Print a usage message on standard output and exit successfully.

- ––version Print version information on standard output then exit successfully.

NAME

join – join lines of two files on a common field

SYNOPSIS

join [–a 1|2] [–v 1|2] [–e empty-string] [–o field-list...] [–t char] [–j[1|2] field] [–1 field] [–2 field] file1 file2
join {––help,––version}

DESCRIPTION

This manual page documents the GNU version of **join**. **join** prints to the standard output a line for each pair of input lines, one each from *file1* and *file2*, that have identical join fields. Either filename (but not both) can be '–', meaning the standard input. *file1* and *file2* should be already sorted in increasing order (not numerically) on the join fields; unless the *–t* option is given, they should be sorted ignoring blanks at the start of the line, as **sort** does when given the *–b* option.

The defaults are: the join field is the first field in each line; fields in the input are separated by one or more blanks, with leading blanks on the line ignored; fields in the output are separated by a space; each output line consists of the join field, the remaining fields from *file1*, then the remaining fields from *file2*.

OPTIONS

–a file-number Print a line for each unpairable line in file *file-number* (either 1 or 2), in addition to the normal output.

–e string Replace empty output fields (those that are missing in the input) with *string*.

–1, –j1 field Join on field *field* (a positive integer) of file 1.

–2, –j2 field Join on field *field* (a positive integer) of file 2.

–j field Equivalent to *–1 field –2 field*.

–o field-list... Construct each output line according to the format in *field-list*. Each element in *field-list* consists of a file number (either 1 or 2), a period, and a field number (a positive integer). The elements in the list are separated by commas or blanks. Multiple *field-list* arguments can be given after a single *–o* option; the values of all lists given with *–o* are concatenated together.

–t char Use character *char* as the input and output field separator.

–v file-number Print a line for each unpairable line in file *file-number* (either 1 or 2), instead of the normal output.

In addition, when GNU **join** is invoked with exactly one argument, the following options are recognized:

––*help* Print a usage message on standard output and exit successfully.

––*version* Print version information on standard output then exit successfully.

KILL(1)

NAME

kill – terminate a process

SYNOPSIS

kill [–s signal | –p] [**-a**] pid ...
kill -l [**signal**]

DESCRIPTION

kill sends the specified signal to the specified process. If no signal is specified, the TERM signal is sent. The TERM signal will kill processes which do not catch this signal. For other processes, if may be necessary to use the KILL (9) signal, since this signal cannot be caught.

Most modern shells have a builtin kill function.

OPTIONS

pid ...	Specify the list of processes that **kill** should signal. Each *pid* can be a process id, or a process name.
–s	Specify the signal to send. The signal may be given as a signal name or number.
–p	Specify that **kill** should only print the process id *(pid)* of the named process, and should not send it a signal.
–l	Print a list of signal names. These are found in */usr/include/linux/signal.h*

SEE ALSO

bash(1), **tcsh**(1), **kill**(2), **sigvec**(2)

AUTHOR

Taken from BSD 4.4. The ability to translate process names to process ids was added by Salvatore Valente <svalente@mit.edu>.

KILLALL(1)

NAME

killall – kill processes by name

SYNOPSIS

killall [**–iv**] [*–signal*] *name* ...
killall [**–l**]

DESCRIPTION

killall sends a signal to all processes running any of the specified commands. If no signal name is specified, SIGTERM is sent.

Signals can be specified either by name (e.g. **–HUP**) or by number (e.g. **–1**). Signal 0 (check if a process exists) can only be specified by number.

If the command name contains a slash (/), processes executing that particular file will be selected for killing, independent of their name.

killall returns a non-zero return code if no process has been killed for any of the listed commands. If at least one process has been killed for each command, **killall** returns zero.

A **killall** process never kills itself (but may kill other **killall** processes).

OPTIONS

 –i Interactively ask for confirmation of killing.
 –l List all known signal names.
 –v Report if the signal was successfully sent.

FILES

/proc location of the proc file system

KNOWN BUGS

Killing by file only works for executables that are kept open during execution, i.e. impure executables can't be killed this way.

AUTHOR

Werner Almesberger <almesber@di.epfl.ch>

SEE ALSO

kill(1), fuser(1), ps(1), kill(2)

NAME

ksyms – shows the exported kernel symbols.

SYNOPSIS

ksyms [–a] [–h] [–m]

DESCRIPTION

Ksyms shows information about all all exported kernel symbols. The format is:

address name [defining module]

The describing header can be turned off with the option '-h'.

Normally, only the symbols defined by the loaded modules are show, but with the option '-a', all exported symbols can be seen.

The information can also be seen in /proc/ksyms. A shell-script version 'ksyms.sh' can be used to get the information from '/proc/ksyms' instead, but this program gets the symbol information directly from the kernel with a system call.

With the option '-m' (stands for memory map), you can also see the starting address and the size of the allocated memory for every loaded module.

SEE ALSO

insmod(1), modprobe(1), depmod(1), rmmod(1), lsmod(1), modules(2)

HISTORY

The **ksyms** command was first concieved by Bjorn Ekwall <bj0rn@blox.se>.
The '-m' option was inspired by David Hinds <dhinds@allegro.stanford.edu>

BUGS

Ksyms might have some, but they are well hidden...

LAST(1)   LAST(1)

NAME
last — indicate last logins by user or terminal

SYNOPSIS
last [*–number*] [*–f filename*] [*–t tty*] [*–h hostname*] [*–i address*] [*–l*] [*–y*] [*name*...]

DESCRIPTION
Last looks back in the **wtmp** file which records all logins and logouts for information about a user, a teletype or any group of users and teletypes. Arguments specify names of users or teletypes of interest. If multiple arguments are given, the information which applies to any of the arguments is printed. For example "**last root console**" would list all of root's sessions as well as all sessions on the console terminal. **Last** displays the sessions of the specified users and teletypes, most recent first, indicating the times at which the session began, the duration of the session, and the teletype which the session took place on. If the session is still continuing or was cut short by a reboot, **last** so indicates.

The pseudo-user **reboot** logs in at reboots of the system.

Last with no arguments displays a record of all logins and logouts, in reverse order.

If **last** is interrupted, it indicates how far the search has progressed in **wtmp**. If interrupted with a quit signal **last** indicates how far the search has progressed so far, and the search continues.

OPTIONS
–number   limit the number of entries displayed to that specified by *number*.

–f filename   Use *filename* as the name of the accounting file instead of **/var/log/wtmp**.

–h hostname   List only logins from *hostname*.

–i IP address List only logins from *IP address*.

–l   List IP addresses of remote hosts instead of truncated host names.

–t tty   List only logins on *tty*.

–y   Also report year of dates.

FILES
/var/log/wtmp — login data base

NAME

ld – the GNU linker

SYNOPSIS

ld   [–o.I output] .I objfile ... .br .RB ["–A *output*] *objfile* ...
[**–A** *architecture*] [**–b**\ *input-format*] [**–Bstatic**] [**–c**\ *commandfile*]
[**–d**|**–dc**|**–dp**]
[**–defsym**\ *symbol* = *expression*] [**–e**\ *entry*] [**–F**] [**–F**\ *format*] [**–format**\ *input-format*] [**–g**] [**–G** *size*] [**––help**] [**–i**] [**–l** *ar*] [**–L** *searchdir*] [**–M**] [**–Map** *mapfile*] [**–m** *emulation*] [**–n**|**–N**] [**–noinhibit-exec**]
[**–oformat**\ *output-format*] [**–R**\ *filename*] [**–relax**] [**–r**|**–Ur**] [**–S**] [**–s**] [**–sort–common**] [**–T**\ *commandfile*] [**–Ttext**\ *textorg*] [**–Tdata**\ *dataorg*] [**–Tbss**\ *bssorg*] [**–t**] [**–u**\ *sym*] [**–V**] [**–v**] [**––verbose**]
[**––version**] [**–warn–common**] [**–warn–once**] [**–X**] [**–x**]

DESCRIPTION

ld combines a number of object and archive files, relocates their data and ties up symbol references. Often the last step in building a new compiled program to run is a call to **ld** .

ld accepts Linker Command Language files to provide explicit and total control over the linking process. This man page does not describe the command language; see the ' **ld** ' entry in ' **info** ', or the manual ld: the GNU linker , for full details on the command language and on other aspects of the GNU linker.

This version of **ld** uses the general purpose BFD libraries to operate on object files. This allows **ld** to read, combine, and write object files in many different formats—for example, COFF or

a.out . Different formats may be linked together to produce any available kind of object file. You can use ' **objdump** –i ' to get a list of formats supported on various architectures; see **objdump(1)**.

Aside from its flexibility, the GNU linker is more helpful than other linkers in providing diagnostic information. Many linkers abandon execution immediately upon encountering an error; whenever possible,

ld continues executing, allowing you to identify other errors (or, in some cases, to get an output file in spite of the error).

The GNU linker **ld** is meant to cover a broad range of situations, and to be as compatible as possible with other linkers. As a result, you have many choices to control its behavior through the command line, and through environment variables.

OPTIONS

The plethora of command-line options may seem intimidating, but in actual practice few of them are used in any particular context. For instance, a frequent use of **ld** is to link standard Unix object files on a standard, supported Unix system. On such a system, to link a file **hello.o** :

$ ld –o output /lib/crt0.o hello.o –lc

This tells **ld** to produce a file called **output** as the result of linking the file **/lib/crt0.o** with **hello.o** and the library **libc.a** which will come from the standard search directories.

The command-line options to **ld** may be specified in any order, and may be repeated at will. For the most part, repeating an option with a different argument will either have no further effect, or override prior occurrences (those further to the left on the command line) of an option.

The exceptions—which may meaningfully be used more than once—are

–A , **–b** (or its synonym **–format**), **–defsym** ,

–L , –l , –R , and –u .

The list of object files to be linked together, shown as *objfile* , may follow, precede, or be mixed in with command-line options; save that an *objfile* argument may not be placed between an option flag and its argument.

Usually the linker is invoked with at least one object file, but other forms of binary input files can also be specified with **–l** ,

–R , and the script command language. If *no* binary input files at all are specified, the linker does not produce any output, and issues the message ' **No** input files '.

Option arguments must either follow the option letter without intervening whitespace, or be given as separate arguments immediately following the option that requires them.

    -A*architecture*   In the current release of **ld** , this option is useful only for the Intel 960 family of architectures. In that **ld** configuration, the *architecture* argument is one of the two-letter names identifying members of the 960 family; the option specifies the desired output target, and warns of any incompatible instructions in the input files. It also modifies the linker's search strategy for archive libraries, to support the use of libraries specific to each particular architecture, by including in the search loop names suffixed with the string identifying the architecture.

For example, if your **ld** command line included ' **–ACA** ' as well as ' **–ltry** ', the linker would look (in its built-in search paths, and in any paths you specify with **–L**) for a library with the names

try
libtry.a
tryca
libtryca.a

The first two possibilities would be considered in any event; the last two are due to the use of ' **–ACA** '.

Future releases of **ld** may support similar functionality for other architecture families.

You can meaningfully use **–A** more than once on a command line, if an architecture family allows combination of target architectures; each use will add another pair of name variants to search for when **–l** specifies a library.

    –b *input-format*   Specify the binary format for input object files that follow this option on the command line. You don't usually need to specify this, as

ld is configured to expect as a default input format the most usual format on each machine. *input-format* is a text string, the name of a particular format supported by the BFD libraries.

–format *input-format*
has the same effect, as does the script command **TARGET** .

You may want to use this option if you are linking files with an unusual binary format. You can also use **–b** to switch formats explicitly (when linking object files of different formats), by including

–b *input-format*

before each group of object files in a particular format.

The default format is taken from the environment variable **GNUTARGET** . You can also define the input format from a script, using the command **TARGET** .

ld(1)   GNU Development Tools   ld(1)

    –Bstatic   This flag is accepted for command-line compatibility with the SunOS linker, but has no effect on **ld** .

    –c *commandfile*   Directs **ld** to read link commands from the file *commandfile* . These commands will completely override **ld** 's default link format (rather than adding to it); *commandfile* must specify everything necessary to describe the target format. You may also include a script of link commands directly in the command line by bracketing it between ' ' **and** ' .B ' characters.

    –d
    –dc
    –dp   These three options are equivalent; multiple forms are supported for compatibility with other linkers. Use any of them to make **ld**

                                    assign space to common symbols even if a relocatable output file is specified (**–r**). The script command **FORCE_COMMON_ALLOCATION** has the same effect.

    -defsym *symbol*   = *expression*

                                    Create a global symbol in the output file, containing the absolute address given by *expression* . You may use this option as many times as necessary to define multiple symbols in the command line. A limited form of arithmetic is supported for the *expression* in this context: you may give a hexadecimal constant or the name of an existing symbol, or use + and – to add or subtract hexadecimal constants or symbols. If you need more elaborate expressions, consider using the linker command language from a script.

    -e *entry*   Use *entry* as the explicit symbol for beginning execution of your program, rather than the default entry point. for a discussion of defaults and other ways of specifying the entry point.

    –F
    -F*format*   Some older linkers used this option throughout a compilation toolchain for specifying object-file format for both input and output object files. **ld** 's mechanisms (the **–b** or **–format** options for input files, the **TARGET** command in linker scripts for output files, the **GNUTARGET** environment variable) are more flexible, but but it accepts (and ignores) the **–F** option flag for compatibility with scripts written to call the old linker.

    –format *input–format* Synonym for **–b** *input–format* .

    –g   Accepted, but ignored; provided for compatibility with other tools.

    –G *size*   Set the maximum size of objects to be optimized using the GP register to *size* under MIPS ECOFF. Ignored for other object file formats.

    —help   Print a summary of the command-line options on the standard output and exit. This option and **—version** begin with two dashes instead of one for compatibility with other GNU programs. The other options start with only one dash for compatibility with other linkers.

    –i   Perform an incremental link (same as option **–r**).

    –l*ar*   Add an archive file *ar* to the list of files to link. This option may be used any number of times. **ld** will search its path-list for occurrences of **lib** *ar* .a for every *ar* specified.

−L*searchdir* This command adds path *searchdir* to the list of paths that **ld** will search for archive libraries. You may use this option any number of times.

The default set of paths searched (without being specified with **−L**) depends on what emulation mode **ld** is using, and in some cases also on how it was configured. The paths can also be specified in a link script with the **SEARCH_DIR** command.

−M Print (to the standard output file) a link map—diagnostic information about where symbols are mapped by **ld** , and information on global common storage allocation.

−Map *mapfile* Print to the file *mapfile* a link map—diagnostic information about where symbols are mapped by **ld** , and information on global common storage allocation.

−m *emulation* Emulate the *emulation* linker. You can list the available emulations with the *—-verbose* option. This option overrides the compiled-in default, which is the system for which you configured **ld**.

−N specifies readable and writable **text** and **data** sections. If the output format supports Unix style magic numbers, the output is marked as **OMAGIC** .

When you use the ' **−N** ' option, the linker does not page-align the data segment.

−n sets the text segment to be read only, and **NMAGIC** is written if possible.

−noinhibit−exec Normally, the linker will not produce an output file if it encounters errors during the link process. With this flag, you can specify that you wish the output file retained even after non-fatal errors.

−o *output* output

output is a name for the program produced by **ld** ; if this option is not specified, the name ' **a.out** ' is used by default. The script command **OUTPUT** can also specify the output file name.

−oformat *output–format* Specify the binary format for the output object file. You don't usually need to specify this, as

ld is configured to produce as a default output format the most usual format on each machine. *output-format* is a text string, the name of a particular format supported by the BFD libraries. The script command **OUTPUT_FORMAT** can also specify the output format, but this option overrides it.

−R *filename* file

Read symbol names and their addresses from *filename* , but do not relocate it or include it in the output. This allows your output file to refer symbolically to absolute locations of memory defined in other programs.

−relax An option with machine dependent effects. Currently this option is only supported on the H8/300.

On some platforms, use this option to perform global optimizations that become possible when the linker resolves addressing in your program, such as relaxing address modes and synthesizing new instructions in the output object file.

On platforms where this is not supported, ' **−relax** ' is accepted, but has no effect.

−r	Generates relocatable output—i.e., generate an output file that can in turn serve as input to **ld** . This is often called *partial linking* . As a side effect, in environments that support standard Unix magic numbers, this option also sets the output file's magic number to **OMAGIC** . If this option is not specified, an absolute file is produced. When linking C++ programs, this option *will* not resolve references to constructors; **−Ur** is an alternative. This option does the same as **−i** .
−S	Omits debugger symbol information (but not all symbols) from the output file.
−s	Omits all symbol information from the output file.
−sort−common	Normally, when **ld** places the global common symbols in the appropriate output sections, it sorts them by size. First come all the one byte symbols, then all the two bytes, then all the four bytes, and then everything else. This is to prevent gaps between symbols due to alignment constraints. This option disables that sorting.
−Tbss *org*	
−Tdata *org*	
−Ttext *org*	Use *org* as the starting address for—respectively—the **bss** , **data** , or the **text** segment of the output file. *textorg* must be a hexadecimal integer.
−T *commandfile*	
−T*commandfile*	Equivalent to **−c** *commandfile* ; supported for compatibility with other tools.
−t	Prints names of input files as **ld** processes them.
−u *sym*	Forces *sym* to be entered in the output file as an undefined symbol. This may, for example, trigger linking of additional modules from standard libraries. **−u** may be repeated with different option arguments to enter additional undefined symbols.
−Ur	For anything other than C++ programs, this option is equivalent to **−r** : it generates relocatable output—i.e., an output file that can in turn serve as input to **ld** . When linking C++ programs, **−Ur** *will* resolve references to constructors, unlike **−r** .
−−verbose	Display the version number for **ld** and list the supported emulations. Display which input files can and can not be opened.
−v, −V	Display the version number for **ld** .
−−version	Display the version number for **ld** and exit.
−warn−common	Warn when a common symbol is combined with another common symbol or with a symbol definition. Unix linkers allow this somewhat sloppy practice, but linkers on some other operating systems do not. This option allows you to find potential problems from combining global symbols.
−warn−once	Only warn once for each undefined symbol, rather than once per module which refers to it.
−X	If **−s** or **−S** is also specified, delete only local symbols beginning with ' **L** '.
−x	If **−s** or **−S** is also specified, delete all local symbols, not just those beginning with ' **L** '.

ENVIRONMENT

You can change the behavior of **ld** with the environment variable **GNUTARGET**.

GNUTARGET determines the input-file object format if you don't use **–b** (or its synonym **–format**). Its value should be one of the BFD names for an input format. If there is no **GNUTARGET** in the environment, **ld** uses the natural format of the host. If **GNUTARGET** is set to **default** then BFD attempts to discover the input format by examining binary input files; this method often succeeds, but there are potential ambiguities, since there is no method of ensuring that the magic number used to flag object-file formats is unique. However, the configuration procedure for BFD on each system places the conventional format for that system first in the search-list, so ambiguities are resolved in favor of convention.

SEE ALSO

objdump(1)

'**ld**' and '**binutils**' entries in **info**

ld: the GNU linker, Steve Chamberlain and Roland Pesch; The GNU Binary Utilities, Roland H. Pesch.

COPYING

Copyright (c) 1991, 1992 Free Software Foundation, Inc.

Permission is granted to make and distribute verbatim copies of this manual provided the copyright notice and this permission notice are preserved on all copies.

Permission is granted to copy and distribute modified versions of this manual under the conditions for verbatim copying, provided that the entire resulting derived work is distributed under the terms of a permission notice identical to this one.

Permission is granted to copy and distribute translations of this manual into another language, under the above conditions for modified versions, except that this permission notice may be included in translations approved by the Free Software Foundation instead of in the original English.

LKBIB(1)

NAME

lkbib – search bibliographic databases

SYNOPSIS

lkbib [**–v**] [**–i***fields*] [**–p***filename*] [**–t***n*] *key*...

DESCRIPTION

lkbib searches bibliographic databases for references that contain the keys *key*... and prints any references found on the standard output. **lkbib** will search any databases given by **–p** options, and then a default database. The default database is taken from the REFER environment variable if it is set, otherwise it is **/usr/dict/papers/Ind**. For each database *filename* to be searched, if an index *filename*.**i** created by **gindxbib**(1) exists, then it will be searched instead; each index can cover multiple databases.

OPTIONS

    –v   Print the version number.

    –p*filename*   Search *filename*. Multiple **–p** options can be used.

    –i*string*   When searching files for which no index exists, ignore the contents of fields whose names are in *string*.

    –t*n*   Only require the first *n* characters of keys to be given. Initially *n* is 6.

ENVIRONMENT

    REFER   Default database.

FILES

/usr/dict/papers/Ind Default database to be used if the REFER environment variable is not set. *filename*.**i** Index files.

SEE ALSO

grefer(1), **glookbib**(1), **gindxbib**(1)

NAME

ln – make links between files

SYNOPSIS

ln [options] source [dest]
ln [options] source... directory
Options:
[–bdfinsvF] [–S backup-suffix] [–V {numbered,existing,simple}]

[––version-control={numbered,existing,simple}] [––backup] [––directory] [––force] [––interactive] [––no–dereference] [––symbolic] [––verbose] [––suffix=backup-suffix] [––help] [––version]

DESCRIPTION

This manual page documents the GNU version of **ln**. If the last argument names an existing directory, **ln** links each other given file into a file with the same name in that directory. If only one file is given, it links that file into the current directory. Otherwise, if only two files are given, it links the first onto the second. It is an error if the last argument is not a directory and more than two files are given. It makes hard links by default. By default, it does not remove existing files.

OPTIONS

- *–b, ––backup* Make backups of files that are about to be removed.
- *–d, –F, ––directory* Allow the super-user to make hard links to directories.
- *–f, ––force* Remove existing destination files.
- *–i, ––interactive* Prompt whether to remove existing destination files.
- *–n, ––no-dereference* When the specified destination is a symbolic link to a directory, attempt to replace the symbolic link rather than dereferencing it to create a link in the directory to which it points. This option is most useful in conjunction with ––force.
- *–s, ––symbolic* Make symbolic links instead of hard links. This option produces an error message on systems that do not support symbolic links.
- *–v, ––verbose* Print the name of each file before linking it.
- *––help* Print a usage message on standard output and exit successfully.
- *––version* Print version information on standard output then exit successfully.
- *–S, ––suffix backup-suffix* The suffix used for making simple backup files can be set with the **SIMPLE_BACKUP_SUFFIX** environment variable, which can be overridden by this option. If neither of those is given, the default is '~', as it is in Emacs.
- *–V, ––version-control {numbered,existing,simple}* The type of backups made can be set with the **VERSION_CONTROL** environment variable, which can be overridden by this option. If **VERSION_CONTROL** is not set and this option is not given, the default backup type is 'existing'. The value of the **VERSION_CONTROL** environment variable and the argument to this option are like the GNU Emacs 'version-control' variable; they also recognize synonyms that are more descriptive. The valid values are (unique abbreviations are accepted):
- 't' or 'numbered' Always make numbered backups.
- 'nil' or 'existing' Make numbered backups of files that already have them, simple backups of the others.
- 'never' or 'simple' Always make simple backups.

LNDIR(1)

NAME

lndir – create a shadow directory of symbolic links to another directory tree

SYNOPSIS

lndir fromdir [todir]

DESCRIPTION

Lndir makes a shadow copy *todir* of a directory tree *fromdir,* except that the shadow is not populated with real files but instead with symbolic links pointing at the real files in the *fromdir* directory tree. This is usually useful for maintaining source code for different machine architectures. You create a shadow directory containing links to the real source which you will have usually NFS mounted from a machine of a different architecture, and then recompile it. The object files will be in the shadow directory, while the source files in the shadow directory are just symlinks to the real files.

This has the advantage that if you update the source, you need not propagate the change to the other architectures by hand, since all source in shadow directories are symlinks to the real thing: just cd to the shadow directory and recompile away.

The *todir* argument is optional and defaults to the current directory. The *fromdir* argument may be relative (e.g., ../src) and is relative to *todir* (not the current directory).

Note that RCS, SCCS, and CVS.adm directories are not shadowed.

If you add files, simply run *lndir* again. Deleting files is a more painful problem; the symlinks will just point into never never land.

BUGS

Patch gets upset if it cannot change the files. You should never run *patch* from a shadow directory anyway.

You need to use something like

find todir –type l –print | xargs rm

to clear out all files before you can relink (if fromdir moved, for instance). Something like

find . \! –type d –print

will find all files that are not directories.

LOCATE(1L)

NAME

locate – list files in databases that match a pattern

SYNOPSIS

locate [–d path] [——database=path] [——version] [——help] pattern...

DESCRIPTION

This manual page documents the GNU version of **locate**. For each given pattern, **locate** searches one or more databases of file names and displays the file names that contain the pattern. Patterns can contain shell-style metacharacters: '*', '?', and '[]'. The metacharacters do not treat '/' or '.' specially. Therefore, a pattern 'foo*bar' can match a file name that contains 'foo3/bar', and a pattern '*duck*' can match a file name that contains 'lake/.ducky'. Patterns that contain metacharacters should be quoted to protect them from expansion by the shell. If a pattern is a plain string — it contains no metacharacters — **locate** displays all file names in the database that contain that string anywhere. If a pattern does contain metacharacters, **locate** only displays file names that match the pattern exactly. As a result, patterns that contain metacharacters should usually begin with a '*', and will most often end with one as well. The exceptions are patterns that are intended to explicitly match the beginning or end of a file name. The file name databases contain lists of files that were on the system when the databases were last updated. The system administrator can choose the file name of the default database, the frequency with which the databases are updated, and the directories for which they contain entries; see **updatedb**(1L).

OPTIONS

    –d path, ——database=*path*   Instead of searching the default file name database, search the file name databases in *path*, which is a colon-separated list of database file names. You can also use the environment variable **LOCATE_PATH** to set the list of database files to search. The option overrides the environment variable if both are used. The file name database format changed starting with GNU **find** and **locate** version 4.0 to allow machines with diffent byte orderings to share the databases. This version of **locate** can automatically recognize and read databases produced for older versions of GNU **locate** or Unix versions of **locate** or **find**.

    ——help   Print a summary of the options to **locate** and exit.

    ——version   Print the version number of **locate** and exit.

ENVIRONMENT

    LOCATE_PATH   Colon-separated list of databases to search.

SEE ALSO

find(1L), **locatedb**(5L), **updatedb**(1L), **xargs**(1L) **Finding Files** (on-line in Info, or printed)

LOGGER(1)

NAME

logger – make entries in the system log

SYNOPSIS

logger [-is] [-f file] [-p pri] [-t tag] [message ...]

DESCRIPTION

Logger provides a shell command interface to the syslog(3) system log module.

Options:

- -i Log the process id of the logger process with each line.
- -s Log the message to standard error, as well as the system log.
- -f file Log the specified file.
- -p pri Enter the message with the specified priority. The priority may be specified numerically or as a "facility.level" pair. For example, "–p local3.info" logs the message(s) as informational level in the local3 facility. The default is "user.notice."
- -t tag Mark every line in the log with the specified tag.
- message Write the message to log; if not specified, and the -f flag is not provided, standard input is logged.

The logger utility exits 0 on success, and >0 if an error occurs.

EXAMPLES

logger System rebooted

logger –p local0.notice –t HOSTIDM –f /dev/idmc

SEE ALSO

syslog(3), syslogd(8)

STANDARDS

The logger command is expected to be IEEE Std 1003.2 ("POSIX") compatible.

NAME

login – sign on

SYNOPSIS

login [name]
login –p
login –h hostname
login –f name

DESCRIPTION

login is used when signing onto a system. It can also be used to switch from one user to another at any time (most modern shells have support for this feature built into them, however).

If an argument is not given, **login** prompts for the username.

If the user is *not* root, and if */etc/nologin* exists, the contents of of this file are printed to the screen, and the login is terminated. This is typically used to prevent logins when the system is being taken down.

If the user is root, then the login must be occuring on a tty listed in */etc/securetty*. Failures will be logged with the **syslog** facility.

After these conditions are checked, the password will be requested and checks (if a password is required for this username). Ten attempts are allowed before **login** dies, but after the first three, the response starts to get very slow. Login failures are reported via the **syslog** facility. This facility is also used to report any successful root logins.

If the file *.hushlogin* exists, then a "quiet" login is performed (this disables the checking of the checking of mail and the printing of the last login time and message of the day). Otherwise, if */var/log/lastlog* exists, the last login time is printed (and the current login is recorded).

Random administrative things, such as setting the UID and GID of the tty are performed. The TERM environment variable is preserved, if it exists (other environment variables are preserved if the **–p** option is used). Then the HOME, PATH, SHELL, TERM, MAIL, and LOGNAME environment variables are set. PATH defaults to */usr/local/bin:/bin:/usr/bin:.* for normal users, and to */sbin:/bin:/usr/sbin:/usr/bin* for root. Last, if this is not a "quiet" login, the message of the day is printed and the file with the user's name in */usr/spool/mail* will be checked, and a message printed if it has non-zero length.

The user's shell is then started. If no shell is specified for the user in **/etc/passwd**, then **/bin/sh** is used. If there is no directory specified in */etc/passwd*, then / is used (the home directory is checked for the *.hushlogin* file described above).

OPTIONS

–p Used by **getty**(8) to tell **login** not to destroy the environment

–f Used to skip a second login authentication. This specifically does **not** work for root, and does not appear to work well under Linux.

–h Used by other servers (i.e., **telnetd**(8)) to pass the name of the remote host to **login** so that it may be placed in utmp and wtmp. Only the superuser may use this option.

FILES

/var/run/utmp
/var/log/wtmp
/var/log/lastlog
/usr/spool/mail/*
/etc/motd
/etc/passwd
/etc/nologin

/etc/usertty
.hushlogin

SEE ALSO
init(8), **getty**(8), **mail**(1), **passwd**(1), **passwd**(5), **environ**(7), **shutdown**(8)

BUGS
Linux, unlike other draconian operating systems, does not check quotas.

The undocumented BSD **–r** option is not supported. This may be required by some **rlogind**(8) programs.

AUTHOR
Derived from BSD login 5.40 (5/9/89) by Michael Glad (glad@daimi.dk) for HP-UX
Ported to Linux 0.12: Peter Orbaek (poe@daimi.aau.dk)

LOOK(1)

NAME

look – display lines beginning with a given string

SYNOPSIS

look [-dfa] [-t termchar] string [file]

DESCRIPTION

The look utility displays any lines in file which contain string as a prefix. As look performs a binary search, the lines in file must be sorted.

If file is not specified, the file /usr/dict/words is used, only alphanumeric characters are compared and the case of alphabetic characters is ignored.

Options:

- -d Dictionary character set and order, i.e. only alphanumeric characters are compared.
- -f Ignore the case of alphabetic characters.
- -a Use the alternate dictionary /usr/dict/web2
- -t Specify a string termination character, i.e. only the characters in string up to and including the first occurrence of termchar are compared.

The look utility exits 0 if one or more lines were found and displayed, 1 if no lines were found, and >1 if an error occurred.

FILES

- /usr/dict/words the dictionary
- /usr/dict/web2 the alternate dictionary

SEE ALSO

grep(1), sort(1)

COMPATIBILITY

The original manual page stated that tabs and blank characters participated in comparisons when the -d option was specified. This was incorrect and the current man page matches the historic implementation.

HISTORY

Look appeared in Version 7 AT&T Unix.

LPQ(1)

NAME
lpq – spool queue examination program

SYNOPSIS
lpq [-l] [-P printer] [job # ...] [user ...]

DESCRIPTION
Lpq examines the spooling area used by lpd(8) for printing files on the line printer, and reports the status of the specified jobs or all jobs associated with a user. Lpq invoked without any arguments reports on any jobs currently in the queue.

Options:

- -P Specify a particular printer, otherwise the default line printer is used (or the value of the PRINTER variable in the environment). All other arguments supplied are interpreted as user names or job numbers to filter out only those jobs of interest.
- -l Information about each of the files comprising the job entry is printed. Normally, only as much information as will fit on one line is displayed.

For each job submitted (i.e. invocation of lpr(1)) lpq reports the user's name, current rank in the queue, the names of files comprising the job, the job identifier (a number which may be supplied to lprm(1) for removing a specific job), and the total size in bytes. Job ordering is dependent on the algorithm used to scan the spooling directory and is supposed to be FIFO (First in First Out). File names comprising a job may be unavailable (when lpr(1) is used as a sink in a pipeline) in which case the file is indicated as "(standard input)".

If lpq warns that there is no daemon present (i.e. due to some malfunction), the lpc(8) command can be used to restart the printer daemon.

ENVIRONMENT
If the following environment variable exists, it is used by lpq:

- PRINTER Specifies an alternate default printer.

FILES
- /etc/printcap To determine printer characteristics.
- /var/spool/* The spooling directory, as determined from printcap. item /var/spool/*/cf* Control files specifying jobs.
- Pa /var/spool/*/lock The lock file to obtain the currently active job.
- /usr/share/misc/termcap For manipulating the screen for repeated display.

SEE ALSO
lpr(1), lprm(1), lpc(8), lpd(8)

HISTORY
Lpq appeared in BSD 3 .

BUGS
Due to the dynamic nature of the information in the spooling directory lpq may report unreliably. Output formatting is sensitive to the line length of the terminal; this can results in widely spaced columns.

DIAGNOSTICS
Unable to open various files. The lock file being malformed. Garbage files when there is no daemon active, but files in the spooling directory.

LPR(1)   LPR(1)

NAME

lpr – off line print

SYNOPSIS

lpr [-P printer] [-# num] [-C class] [-J job] [-T title] [-U user] [-i [numcols]] [-1234 font] [-w num] [-cdfghlnmprstv] [name ...]

DESCRIPTION

Lpr uses a spooling daemon to print the named files when facilities become available. If no names appear, the standard input is assumed.

The following single letter options are used to notify the line printer spooler that the files are not standard text files. The spooling daemon will use the appropriate filters to print the data accordingly.

- -c The files are assumed to contain data produced by cifplot(1)
- -d The files are assumed to contain data from TeX (DVI format from Stanford).
- -f Use a filter which interprets the first character of each line as a standard FORTRAN carriage control character.
- -g The files are assumed to contain standard plot data as produced by the plot routines (see also plot for the filters used by the printer spooler).
- -l Use a filter which allows control characters to be printed and suppresses page breaks.
- -n The files are assumed to contain data from ditroff (device independent troff).
- -p Use pr(1) to format the files (equivalent to print).
- -t The files are assumed to contain data from troff(1) (cat phototypesetter commands).
- -v The files are assumed to contain a raster image for devices like the Benson Varian.

These options apply to the handling of the print job:

- -P Force output to a specific printer. Normally, the default printer is used (site dependent), or the value of the environment variable PRINTER is used.
- -h Suppress the printing of the burst page.
- -m Send mail upon completion.
- -r Remove the file upon completion of spooling or upon completion of printing (with the -s option).
- -s Use symbolic links. Usually files are copied to the spool directory. The -s option will use symlink(2) to link data files rather than trying to copy them so large files can be printed. This means the files should not be modified or removed until they have been printed.

The remaining options apply to copies, the page display, and headers:

- -# num The quantity num is the number of copies desired of each file named. For example,

    lpr –#3 foo.c bar.c more.c

    would result in 3 copies of the file foo.c, followed by 3 copies of the file bar.c, etc. On the other hand,

    cat foo.c bar.c more.c | lpr –#3

    will give three copies of the concatenation of the files. Often a site will disable this feature to encourage use of a photocopier instead.

- 1234 font Specifies a font to be mounted on font position i. The daemon will construct a .railmag file referencing the font pathname.
- -C Ar class Job classification to use on the burst page. For example,

LPR(1) LPR(1)

   lpr –C EECS foo.c

   causes the system name (the name returned by hostname(1)) to be replaced on the burst page by EECS , and the file foo.c to be printed.

- -J Ar job Job name to print on the burst page. Normally, the first file's name is used.
- -T Ar title Title name for pr(1), instead of the file name.
- -U user User name to print on the burst page, also for accounting purposes. This option is only honored if the real user-id is daemon (or that specified in the printcap file instead of daemon), and is intended for those instances where print filters wish to requeue jobs.
- -i numcols The output is indented. If the next argument is numeric numcols , it is used as the number of blanks to be printed before each line; otherwise, 8 characters are printed.
- -w Ns Ar num Uses num as the page width for pr(1).

ENVIRONMENT

If the following environment variable exists, it is used by lpr :

- PRINTER Specifies an alternate default printer.

FILES

- /etc/passwd Personal identification.
- /etc/printcap Printer capabilities data base.
- /usr/sbin/lpd* Line printer daemons.
- /var/spool/output/* Directories used for spooling.
- /var/spool/output/*/cf* Daemon control files.
- /var/spool/output/*/df* Data files specified in "cf" files.
- /var/spool/output/*/tf* Temporary copies of "cf" files.

SEE ALSO

lpq(1), lprm(1), pr(1), symlink(2), printcap(5), lpc(8), lpd(8)

HISTORY

The lpr command appeared in BSD 3 .

DIAGNOSTICS

If you try to spool too large a file, it will be truncated. Lpr will object to printing binary files. If a user other than root prints a file and spooling is disabled, lpr will print a message saying so and will not put jobs in the queue. If a connection to lpd(1) on the local machine cannot be made, lpr will say that the daemon cannot be started. Diagnostics may be printed in the daemon's log file regarding missing spool files by lpd(1).

BUGS

Fonts for troff(1) and TeX reside on the host with the printer. It is currently not possible to use local font libraries.

LPRM(1)

NAME

lprm – remove jobs from the line printer spooling queue

SYNOPSIS

lprm [-P printer] [- job # ...] [user ...]

DESCRIPTION

Lprm will remove a job, or jobs, from a printer's spool queue. Since the spooling directory is protected from users, using lprm is normally the only method by which a user may remove a job. The owner of a job is determined by the user's login name and host name on the machine where the lpr(1) command was invoked.

Options and arguments:

- -P printer Specify the queue associated with a specific printer (otherwise the default printer is used).
- - If a single - is given, lprm will remove all jobs which a user owns. If the super-user employs this flag, the spool queue will be emptied entirely.
- user Causes lprm to attempt to remove any jobs queued belonging to that user (or users). This form of invoking lprm is useful only to the super-user.
- job # A user may dequeue an individual job by specifying its job number. This number may be obtained from the lpq(1) program, e.g.

```
lpq --l

1st:ken             [job #013ucbarpa]
     (standard input)    100 bytes
lprm 13
```

If neither arguments or options are given, Lprm will delete the currently active job if it is owned by the user who invoked lprm .

Lprm announces the names of any files it removes and is silent if there are no jobs in the queue which match the request list.

Lprm will kill off an active daemon, if necessary, before removing any spooling files. If a daemon is killed, a new one is automatically restarted upon completion of file removals.

ENVIRONMENT

If the following environment variable exists, it is utilized by lprm .

- PRINTER If the environment variable PRINTER exists, and a printer has not been specified with the -P option, the default printer is assumed from PRINTER .

FILES

- /etc/printcap Printer characteristics file.
- /var/spool/* Spooling directories.
- /var/spool/*/lock Lock file used to obtain the pid of the current daemon and the job number of the currently active job.

SEE ALSO

lpr(1), lpq(1), lpd(8)

DIAGNOSTICS

"Permission denied" if the user tries to remove files other than his own.

BUGS

Since there are race conditions possible in the update of the lock file, the currently active job may be incorrectly identified.

LPRM(1)
HISTORY
The lprm command appeared in BSD 3.0 .

LPTEST(1)

NAME

lptest – generate lineprinter ripple pattern

SYNOPSIS

lptest [length] [count]

DESCRIPTION

Lptest writes the traditional "ripple test" pattern on standard output. In 96 lines, this pattern will print all 96 printable ASCII characters in each position. While originally created to test printers, it is quite useful for testing terminals, driving terminal ports for debugging purposes, or any other task where a quick supply of random data is needed.

The length argument specifies the output line length if the the default length of 79 is inappropriate.

The count argument specifies the number of output lines to be generated if the default count of 200 is inappropriate. Note that if count is to be specified, length must be also be specified.

HISTORY

Lptest appeared in BSD 4.3.

NAME

ls, dir, vdir – list contents of directories

SYNOPSIS

ls [–abcdfgiklmnpqrstuxABCFGLNQRSUX1] [–w cols] [–T cols] [–I pattern] [—all] [—escape] [—directory] [—inode] [—kilobytes] [—numeric-uid-gid] [–no-group] [—hide-control-chars] [—reverse] [—size] [—width=cols] [—tabsize=cols] [—almost-all] [—-ignore-backups] [—classify] [—file-type] [—full-time]

[—ignore=pattern] [—dereference] [—literal] [—quote-name] [—recursive] [—sort={none, time, size, extension}] [—format={long, verbose, commas, across, vertical, single-column}] [—time={atime, access, use, ctime, status}] [—help] [—version] [name...]

DESCRIPTION

This manual page documents the GNU version of **ls**. **dir** and **vdir** are versions of **ls** with different default output formats. These programs list each given file or directory name. Directory contents are sorted alphabetically. For **ls**, files are by default listed in columns, sorted vertically, if the standard output is a terminal; otherwise they are listed one per line. For **dir**, files are by default listed in columns, sorted vertically. For **vdir**, files are by default listed in long format.

OPTIONS

–a, —all List all files in directories, including all files that start with '.'.

–b, —escape Quote nongraphic characters in file names using alphabetic and octal backslash sequences like those used in C.

–c, —time=ctime, —time=status Sort directory contents according to the files' status change time instead of the modification time. If the long listing format is being used, print the status change time instead of the modification time.

–d, —directory List directories like other files, rather than listing their contents.

–f Do not sort directory contents; list them in whatever order they are stored on the disk. The same as enabling –a and –U and disabling –l, –s, and –t.

—full-time List times in full, rather than using the standard abbreviation heuristics.

–g Ignored; for Unix compatibility.

–i, —inode Print the index number of each file to the left of the file name.

–k, —kilobytes If file sizes are being listed, print them in kilobytes. This overrides the environment variable POSIXLY_CORRECT.

–l, —format=long, —format=verbose In addition to the name of each file, print the file type, permissions, number of hard links, owner name, group name, size in bytes, and timestamp (the modification time unless other times are selected). For files with a time that is more than 6 months old or more than 1 hour into the future, the timestamp contains the year instead of the time of day.

–m, —format=commas List files horizontally, with as many as will fit on each line, separated by commas.

–n, —numeric-uid-gid List the numeric UID and GID instead of the names.

–p Append a character to each file name indicating the file type.

–q, —hide-control-chars Print question marks instead of nongraphic characters in file names.

–r, —reverse Sort directory contents in reverse order.

–s, —size Print the size of each file in 1K blocks to the left of the file name. If the environment variable POSIXLY_CORRECT is set, 512-byte blocks are used instead.

–t, —-sort=time   Sort directory contents by timestamp instead of alphabetically, with the newest files listed first.

–u, —-time=atime, —-time=access, —-time=use   Sort directory contents according to the files' last access time instead of the modification time. If the long listing format is being used, print the last access time instead of the modification time.

–x, —-format=across, —-format=horizontal   List the files in columns, sorted horizontally.

–A, —-almost-all   List all files in directories, except for '.' and '..'.

–B, —-ignore-backups   Do not list files that end with '~', unless they are given on the command line.

–C, —-format=vertical   List files in columns, sorted vertically.

–F, —-classify   Append a character to each file name indicating the file type. For regular files that are executable, append a '*'. The file type indicators are '/' for directories, '@' for symbolic links, '|' for FIFOs, '=' for sockets, and nothing for regular files.

–G, —-no–group   Inhibit display of group information in a long format directory listing.

–L, —-dereference   List the files linked to by symbolic links instead of listing the contents of the links.

–N, —-literal   Do not quote file names.

–Q, —-quote-name   Enclose file names in double quotes and quote nongraphic characters as in C.

–R, —-recursive   List the contents of all directories recursively.

–S, —-sort=size   Sort directory contents by file size instead of alphabetically, with the largest files listed first.

–U, —-sort=none   Do not sort directory contents; list them in whatever order they are stored on the disk. This option is not called *–f* because the Unix **ls** *–f* option also enables *–a* and disables *–l, –s,* and *–t*. It seems useless and ugly to group those unrelated things together in one option. Since this option doesn't do that, it has a different name.

–X, —-sort=extension   Sort directory contents alphabetically by file extension (characters after the last '.'); files with no extension are sorted first.

–1, —-format=single-column   List one file per line.

–w, —-width cols   Assume the screen is *cols* columns wide. The default is taken from the terminal driver if possible; otherwise the environment variable **COLUMNS** is used if it is set; otherwise the default is 80.

–T, —-tabsize cols   Assume that each tabstop is *cols* columns wide. The default is 8.

–I, —-ignore pattern   Do not list files whose names match the shell pattern *pattern* unless they are given on the command line. As in the shell, an initial '.' in a filename does not match a wildcard at the start of *pattern*.

—-help   Print a usage message on standard output and exit successfully.

—-version   Print version information on standard output then exit successfully.

BUGS

On BSD systems, the *–s* option reports sizes that are half the correct values for files that are NFS-mounted from HP-UX systems. On HP-UX systems, it reports sizes that are twice the correct values for files that are NFS-mounted from BSD systems. This is due to a flaw in HP-UX; it also affects the HP-UX **ls** program.

LSATTR(1)

NAME

lsattr – list file attributes on a Linux second extended file system

SYNOPSIS

lsattr [**–Radv**] [files...]

DESCRIPTION

lsattr lists the files attributes on an second extended file system.

OPTIONS

- *-R*   Recursively list attributes of directories and their contents.
- *-a*   List all files in directories, including files that start with '.'.
- *-d*   List directories like other files, rather than listing their contents.
- *-v*   List the files version.

AUTHOR

lsattr has been written by Remy Card <card@masi.ibp.fr>, the developer and maintainer of the ext2 fs.

BUGS

There are none :-).

AVAILABILITY

lsattr is available for anonymous ftp from ftp.ibp.fr and tsx-11.mit.edu in /pub/linux/packages/ext2fs.

SEE ALSO

chattr(1)

LSMOD(1) Linux Module Support LSMOD(1)

NAME
lsmod – shows the loaded modules.

SYNOPSIS
lsmod

DESCRIPTION
Lsmod shows information about all loaded modules. The format is:

name size (in 4k pages) [list of referring modules]

This information is a copy of the contents of /proc/modules.

SEE ALSO
insmod(1), modprobe(1), depmod(1), rmmod(1), ksyms(1), modules(2)

HISTORY
The module support was first concieved by Anonymous (as far as I know...). Linux version by Bas Laarhoven <bas@vimec.nl>, 0.99.14 version by Jon Tombs <jon@gtex02.us.es>, extended by Bjorn Ekwall <bj0rn@blox.se>.

BUGS
Lsmod might have some, but they are well hidden...

MAKE(1L)

NAME
make – GNU make utility to maintain groups of programs

SYNOPSIS
make [**–f** makefile] [option] ... target ...

WARNING
This man paage is an extract of the documentation of *GNU* make . It is updated only occasionally, because the GNU project does not use nroff. For complete, current documentation, refer to the Info file **make** or the DVI file **make.dvi** which are made from the Texinfo source file **make.texinfo**.

DESCRIPTION
The purpose of the *make* utility is to determine automatically which pieces of a large program need to be recompiled, and issue the commands to recompile them. This manual describes the GNU implementation of *make*, which was written by Richard Stallman and Roland McGrath. Our examples show C programs, since they are most common, but you can use *make* with any programming language whose compiler can be run with a shell command. In fact, *make* is not limited to programs. You can use it to describe any task where some files must be updated automatically from others whenever the others change.

To prepare to use *make*, you must write a file called the *makefile* that describes the relationships among files in your program, and the states the commands for updating each file. In a program, typically the executable file is updated from object files, which are in turn made by compiling source files.

Once a suitable makefile exists, each time you change some source files, this simple shell command:

make

suffices to perform all necessary recompilations. The *make* program uses the makefile data base and the last-modification times of the files to decide which of the files need to be updated. For each of those files, it issues the commands recorded in the data base.

make executes commands in the *makefile* to update one or more target *names*, where *name* is typically a program. If no **–f** option is present, *make* will look for the makefiles *GNUmakefile*, *makefile*, and *Makefile*, in that order.

Normally you should call your makefile either *makefile* or *Makefile*. (We recommend *Makefile* because it appears prominently near the beginning of a directory listing, right near other important files such as *README*.) The first name checked, *GNUmakefile*, is not recommended for most makefiles. You should use this name if you have a makefile that is specific to GNU *make*, and will not be understood by other versions of *make*. If *makefile* is '–', the standard input is read.

make updates a target if it depends on prerequisite files that have been modified since the target was last modified, or if the target does not exist.

OPTIONS
–b

–m These options are ignored for compatibility with other versions of *make*.

–C *dir* Change to directory *dir* before reading the makefiles or doing anything else. If multiple **–C** options are specified, each is interpreted relative to the previous one: **–C** / **–C** etc is equivalent to **–C** /etc. This is typically used with recursive invocations of *make*.

–d Print debugging information in addition to normal processing. The debugging information says which files are being considered for remaking, which file-times are being compared and with what results, which files actually need to be remade, which implicit rules are considered and which are applied— everything interesting about how *make* decides what to do.

-e   Give variables taken from the environment precedence over variables from makefiles.

-f *file*   Use *file* as a makefile.

-i   Ignore all errors in commands executed to remake files.

-I *dir*   Specifies a directory *dir* to search for included makefiles. If several –I options are used to specify several directories, the directories are searched in the order specified. Unlike the arguments to other flags of *make*, directories given with –I flags may come directly after the flag: –I*dir* is allowed, as well as –I *dir*. This syntax is allowed for compatibility with the C preprocessor's –I flag.

-j *jobs*   Specifies the number of jobs (commands) to run simultaneously. If there is more than one –j option, the last one is effective. If the –j option is given without an argument, *make* will not limit the number of jobs that can run simultaneously.

-k   Continue as much as possible after an error. While the target that failed, and those that depend on it, cannot be remade, the other dependencies of these targets can be processed all the same.

-l

-l *load*   Specifies that no new jobs (commands) should be started if there are others jobs running and the load average is at least *load* (a floating-point number). With no argument, removes a previous load limit.

-n   Print the commands that would be executed, but do not execute them.

-o *file*   Do not remake the file *file* even if it is older than its dependencies, and do not remake anything on account of changes in *file*. Essentially the file is treated as very old and its rules are ignored.

-p   Print the data base (rules and variable values) that results from reading the makefiles; then execute as usual or as otherwise specified. This also prints the version information given by the –v switch (see below). To print the data base without trying to remake any files, use **make –p –f**/*dev/null*.

-q   "Question mode". Do not run any commands, or print anything; just return an exit status that is zero if the specified targets are already up to date, nonzero otherwise.

-r   Eliminate use of the built-in implicit rules. Also clear out the default list of suffixes for suffix rules.

-s   Silent operation; do not print the commands as they are executed.

-S   Cancel the effect of the –k option. This is never necessary except in a recursive *make* where –k might be inherited from the top-level *make* via MAKEFLAGS or if you set –k in MAKEFLAGS in your environment.

-t   Touch files (mark them up to date without really changing them) instead of running their commands. This is used to pretend that the commands were done, in order to fool future invocations of *make*.

-v   Print the version of the *make* program plus a copyright, a list of authors and a notice that there is no warranty. After this information is printed, processing continues normally. To get this information without doing anything else, use **make –v –f**/*dev/null*.

-w   Print a message containing the working directory before and after other processing. This may be useful for tracking down errors from complicated nests of recursive *make* commands.

-W *file*   Pretend that the target *file* has just been modified. When used with the –n flag, this shows you what would happen if you were to modify that file. Without –n, it is almost the same as running a *touch* command on the given file before running *make*, except that the modification time is changed only in the imagination of *make*.

SEE ALSO

/usr/local/doc/gnumake.dvi   The GNU Make Manual

BUGS

See the chapter 'Problems and Bugs' in *The GNU Make Manual* .

AUTHOR

This manual page contributed by Dennis Morse of Stanford University. It has been reworked by Roland McGrath.

MAKEDEPEND(1)

NAME

makedepend – create dependencies in makefiles

SYNOPSIS

makedepend [–D*name*=*def*] [–D*name*] [–I*includedir*] [–Y*includedir*] [–a] [–f*makefile*] [–o*objsuffix*] [–p*objprefix*] [–s*string*] [–w*width*] [–v] [–m] [— *otheroptions* —] sourcefile ...

DESCRIPTION

Makedepend reads each *sourcefile* in sequence and parses it like a C-preprocessor, processing all *#include, #define, #undef, #ifdef, #ifndef, #endif, #if* and *#else* directives so that it can correctly tell which *#include,* directives would be used in a compilation. Any *#include,* directives can reference files having other *#include* directives, and parsing will occur in these files as well.

Every file that a *sourcefile* includes, directly or indirectly, is what **makedepend** calls a "dependency". These dependencies are then written to a *makefile* in such a way that **make(1)** will know which object files must be recompiled when a dependency has changed.

By default, **makedepend** places its output in the file named *makefile* if it exists, otherwise *Makefile*. An alternate makefile may be specified with the **–f** option. It first searches the makefile for the line

DO NOT DELETE THIS LINE — make depend depends on it.

or one provided with the **–s** option, as a delimiter for the dependency output. If it finds it, it will delete everything following this to the end of the makefile and put the output after this line. If it doesn't find it, the program will append the string to the end of the makefile and place the output following that. For each *sourcefile* appearing on the command line, **makedepend** puts lines in the makefile of the form

sourcefile.o: dfile ...

Where "sourcefile.o" is the name from the command line with its suffix replaced with ".o", and "dfile" is a dependency discovered in a *#include* directive while parsing *sourcefile* or one of the files it included.

EXAMPLE

Normally, **makedepend** will be used in a makefile target so that typing "make depend" will bring the dependencies up to date for the makefile. For example,

SRCS = file1.c file2.c ...
CFLAGS = –O –DHACK –I../foobar –xyz
depend:
makedepend — $(CFLAGS) — $(SRCS)

OPTIONS

Makedepend will ignore any option that it does not understand so that you may use the same arguments that you would for **cc(1)**.

–D*name*=*def* or **–D***name*	Define. This places a definition for *name* in **makedepend's** symbol table. Without =*def* the symbol becomes defined as "1".
–I*includedir*	Include directory. This option tells **makedepend** to prepend *includedir* to its list of directories to search when it encounters a *#include* directive. By default, **makedepend** only searches the standard include directories (usually /usr/include and possibly a compiler-dependent directory).
–Y*includedir*	Replace all of the standard include directories with the single specified include directory; you can omit

	the *includedir* to simply prevent searching the standard include directories.
−a	Append the dependencies to the end of the file instead of replacing them.
−fmakefile	Filename. This allows you to specify an alternate makefile in which **makedepend** can place its output.
−oobjsuffix	Object file suffix. Some systems may have object files whose suffix is something other than ".o". This option allows you to specify another suffix, such as ".b" with *-o.b* or ":obj" with *-o:obj* and so forth.
−pobjprefix	Object file prefix. The prefix is prepended to the name of the object file. This is usually used to designate a different directory for the object file. The default is the empty string.
−sstring	Starting string delimiter. This option permits you to specify a different string for **makedepend** to look for in the makefile.
−wwidth	Line width. Normally, **makedepend** will ensure that every output line that it writes will be no wider than 78 characters for the sake of readability. This option enables you to change this width.
−v	Verbose operation. This option causes **makedepend** to emit the list of files included by each input file on standard output.
−m	Warn about multiple inclusion. This option causes **makedepend** to produce a warning if any input file includes another file more than once. In previous versions of **makedepend** this was the default behavior; the default has been changed to better match the behavior of the C compiler, which does not consider multiple inclusion to be an error. This option is provided for backward compatibility, and to aid in debugging problems related to multiple inclusion.
— options —	If **makedepend** encounters a double hyphen (—) in the argument list, then any unrecognized argument following it will be silently ignored; a second double hyphen terminates this special treatment. In this way, **makedepend** can be made to safely ignore esoteric compiler arguments that might normally be found in a CFLAGS **make** macro (see the **EXAMPLE** section above). All options that **makedepend** recognizes and appear between the pair of double hyphens are processed normally.

ALGORITHM

The approach used in this program enables it to run an order of magnitude faster than any other "dependency generator" I have ever seen. Central to this performance are two assumptions: that all files compiled by a single makefile will be compiled with roughly the same *-I* and *-D* options; and that most files in a single directory will include largely the same files.

Given these assumptions, **makedepend** expects to be called once for each makefile, with all source files that are maintained by the makefile appearing on the command line. It parses each source and include file exactly once, maintaining an internal symbol table for each. Thus, the first file on the command line will take an amount of time proportional to the amount of time that a normal C preprocessor takes. But on subsequent files, if it encounter's an include file that it has already parsed, it does not parse it again.

For example, imagine you are compiling two files, *file1.c* and *file2.c*, they each include the header file *header.h*, and the file *header.h* in turn includes the files *def1.h* and *def2.h*. When you run the command

makedepend file1.c file2.c

makedepend will parse *file1.c* and consequently, *header.h* and then *def1.h* and *def2.h*. It then decides that the dependencies for this file are

file1.o: header.h def1.h def2.h

But when the program parses *file2.c* and discovers that it, too, includes *header.h*, it does not parse the file, but simply adds *header.h*, *def1.h* and *def2.h* to the list of dependencies for *file2.o*.

SEE ALSO

cc(1), make(1)

BUGS

makedepend parses, but does not currently evaluate, the SVR4 #predicate(token-list) pre-processor expression; such expressions are simply assumed to be true. This may cause the wrong *#include* directives to be evaluated.

Imagine you are parsing two files, say *file1.c* and *file2.c*, each includes the file *def.h*. The list of files that *def.h* includes might truly be different when *def.h* is included by *file1.c* than when it is included by *file2.c*. But once **makedepend** arrives at a list of dependencies for a file, it is cast in concrete.

AUTHOR

Todd Brunhoff, Tektronix, Inc. and MIT Project Athena

MCOOKIE(1) Linux Programmer's Manual MCOOKIE(1)

NAME

mcookie – generate magic cookies for xauth

SYNOPSIS

mcookie

DESCRIPTION

mcookie generates a 128-bit random hexadecimal number for use with the X authority system. Typical usage:

xauth add :0 . 'mcookie'

SEE ALSO

X(1), **xauth**(1)

NAME

md5sum – generate/check MD5 message digests

SYNOPSIS

md5sum [–bv] [–c [file]]
md5sum file ...

DESCRIPTION

md5sum generates and checks MD5 message digests, as described in RFC-1321. The "message digest" produced can be thought of as a 128-bit "signature" of the input file. Typically, **md5sum** is used to verify the integrity of files made available for distribution via anonymous ftp (for example, announcements for new versions of **irc(1)** usually contain MD5 signatures). Message digests for a tree of files can be generated with a command similar to the following:

find . -type f -print | xargs md5sum

The output of this command is suitable as input for the **–c** option.

OPTIONS

–c [*file*]   Check message digests. Input is taken from **stdin** or from the spcified *file*. The input should be in the same format as the output generated by **md5sum**.

–v   Verbose. Print file names when checking.

–b   Read files in binary mode (otherwise, end-of-file conventions will be ignored).

HISTOY

The **md5sum** program was written by Branko Lankester and may be freely distributed. The original source code is in the MIT PGP 2.6.2 distribution. Those concerned about the integrity of this version should obtain the original sources and compile their own version.

The underlying implementation of Ron Rivest's MD5 algorithm was written by Colin Plumb and is in the Public Domain. (Equivalent code is also available from RSA Data Security, Inc.)

SEE ALSO

sum(1), **cksum**(1), **pgp**(1)

MESG(1)

NAME
mesg – display (do not display) messages from other users

SYNOPSIS
mesg [n] [y]

DESCRIPTION
The **mesg** utility is invoked by a users to control write access others have to the terminal device associated with the standard error output. If write access is allowed, then programs such as **talk**(1) and **write**(1) may display messages on the terminal.

Traditionally, write access is allowed by default. However, as users become more conscious of various security risks, there is a trend to remove write access by default, at least for the primary login shell. To make sure your ttys are set the way you want them to be set, **mesg** should be executed in your login scripts.

Options available:

    n   Disallows messages.
    y   Permits messages to be displayed.

If no arguments are given, **mesg** displays the present message status to the standard error output.

The **mesg** utility exits with one of the following values:

    \0   Messages are allowed.
    \1   Messages are not allowed.
    1   An error has occurred.

FILES
/dev/[pt]ty[pq]?

SEE ALSO
biff(1), **talk**(1), **write**(1), **wall**(1), **login**(1), **xterm**(1)

HISTORY
A **mesg** command appeared in Version 6 AT&T UNIX.

MKDIR(1L)　　　　　　　　　　　　FSF　　　　　　　　　　　　MKDIR(1L)

NAME
mkdir – make directories

SYNOPSIS
mkdir [–p] [–m mode] [——parents] [——mode=mode] [——help] [——version] dir...

DESCRIPTION
This manual page documents the GNU version of **mkdir**. **mkdir** creates a directory with each given name. By default, the mode of created directories is 0777 minus the bits set in the umask.

OPTIONS

–m, ——mode mode   Set the mode of created directories to *mode*, which is symbolic as in chmod and uses the default mode as the point of departure.

–p, ——parents   Ensure that each given directory exists. Create any missing parent directories for each argument. Parent directories default to the umask modified by 'u+wx'. Do not consider an argument directory that already exists to be an error.

——help   Print a usage message on standard output and exit successfully.

——version   Print version information on standard output then exit successfully.

GNU File Utilities

MKDIRHIER(1)

NAME

mkdirhier – makes a directory hierarchy

SYNOPSIS

mkdirhier directory ...

DESCRIPTION

The *mkdirhier* command creates the specified directories. Unlike *mkdir* if any of the parent directories of the specified directory do not exist, it creates them as well.

SEE ALSO

mkdir(1)

MKFIFO(1L)

NAME

mkfifo – make FIFOs (named pipes)

SYNOPSIS

mkfifo [–m mode] [—-mode=mode] [—-help] [—-version] filename...

DESCRIPTION

This manual page documents the GNU version of **mkfifo**. **mkfifo** creates a FIFO with each given name. By default, the mode of created FIFOs is 0666 minus the bits set in the umask.

OPTIONS

    –m, —-mode mode   Set the mode of created FIFOs to *mode*, which is symbolic as in chmod and uses the default mode as the point of departure.

    —-help   Print a usage message on standard output and exit successfully.

    —-version   Print version information on standard output then exit successfully.

MKNOD(1L)

NAME

mknod – make special files

SYNOPSIS

mknod [options] filename {bcu} major minor
mknod [options] filename p
Options:
[–m mode] [—-mode=mode] [—-help] [—-version]

DESCRIPTION

This manual page documents the GNU version of **mknod**. **mknod** creates a FIFO, character special file, or block special file with the given file name. By default, the mode of created files is 0666 minus the bits set in the umask.

The argument after *filename* specifies the type of file to make: p for a FIFO
b for a block (buffered) special file
c or u for a character (unbuffered) special file

When making a block or character special file, the major and minor device numbers must be given after the file type.

OPTIONS

–m, —-mode mode Set the mode of created files to *mode*, which is symbolic as in chmod and uses the default mode as the point of departure.

—-help Print a usage message on standard output and exit successfully.

—-version Print version information on standard output then exit successfully.

NAME

more – file perusal filter for crt viewing

SYNOPSIS

more [-dlfpcsu] [-num] [+/ pattern] [+ linenum]

DESCRIPTION

More is a filter for paging through text one screenful at a time. This version is especially primitve. Users should realize that less(1) provides more(1) emulation and extensive enhancements.

OPTIONS

Command line options are described below. Options are also taken from the environment variable MORE (make sure to precede them with a dash ("-")) but command line options will override them.

- -num This option specifies an integer which is the screen size (in lines).
- -d more will prompt the user with the message "[Press space to continue, 'q' to quit.]" and will display "[Press 'h' for instructions.]" instead of ringing the bell when an illegal key is pressed.
- -l more usually treats (form feed) as a special character, and will pause after any line that contains a form feed. The -l option will prevent this behavior.
- -f Causes to count logical, rather than screen lines (i.e., long lines are not folded).
- -p Do not scroll. Instead, clear the whole screen and then display the text.
- -c Do not scroll. Instead, paint each screen from the top, clearing the remainder of each line as it is displayed.
- -s Squeeze multiple blank lines into one.
- -u Suppress underlining.
- +/ The +/ option specifies a string that will be searched for before each file is displayed.
- +num Start at line number

COMMANDS

Interactive commands for more are based on vi(1). Some commands may be preceded by a decimal number, called k in the descriptions below. In the following descriptions, ^X means control-X.

- h or ?
  Help: display a summary of these commands. If you forget all the other commands, remember this one.
- SPACE
  Display next k lines of text. Defaults to current screen size.
- z
  Display next k lines of text. Defaults to current screen size. Argument becomes new default.
- RETURN
  Display next k lines of text. Defaults to 1. Argument becomes new default.
- d or Ô
  Scroll k lines. Default is current scroll size, initially 11. Argument becomes new default.
- q or Q INTERRUPT
  Exit.

- s
  Skip forward k lines of text. Defaults to 1.
- f
  Skip forward k screenfuls of text. Defaults to 1.
- b or ^B
  Skip backwards k screenfuls of text. Defaults to 1.
- '
  Go to place where previous search started.
- =
  Display current line number.
- /pattern
  Search for kth occurrence of regular expression. Defaults to 1.
- n
  Search for kth occurrence of last r.e. Defaults to 1.
- !¡cmd¿ or :!¡cmd¿
  Execute <cmd> in a subshell
- v
  Start up /usr/bin/vi at current line
- ^L
  Redraw screen
- :n
  Go to kth next file. Defaults to 1.
- :p
  Go to kth previous file. Defaults to 1.
- lc :f
  Display current file name and line number
- .
  Repeat previous command

ENVIRONMENT

More utilizes the following environment variables, if they exist:

- MORE This variable may be set with favored options to more .
- SHELL Current shell in use (normally set by the shell at login time).
- TERM Specifies terminal type, used by more to get the terminal characteristics necessary to manipulate the screen.

SEE ALSO

vi(1), less(1)

AUTHORS

Eric Shienbrood, UC Berkeley
Modified by Geoff Peck, UCB to add underlining, single spacing
Modified by John Foderaro, UCB to add -c and MORE environment variable

HISTORY

The more command appeared in BSD 3.0 . This man page documents more version 5.19 (Berkeley 6/29/88), which is currently in use in the Linux community. Documentation was produced using several other versions of the man page, and extensive inspection of the source code.

MV(1L) FSF MV(1L)

NAME
mv – rename files

SYNOPSIS
mv [options] source dest
mv [options] source... directory
Options:
[–bfiuv] [–S backup-suffix] [–V {numbered,existing,simple}] [––backup] [––force] [––interactive] [––update] [––verbose] [––suffix=backup-suffix]

[––version-control={numbered,existing,simple}] [––help] [––version]

DESCRIPTION
This manual page documents the GNU version of **mv**. If the last argument names an existing directory, **mv** moves each other given file into a file with the same name in that directory. Otherwise, if only two files are given, it moves the first onto the second. It is an error if the last argument is not a directory and more than two files are given. It can move only regular files across filesystems. If a destination file is unwritable, the standard input is a tty, and the –*f* or ––*force* option is not given, **mv** prompts the user for whether to overwrite the file. If the response does not begin with 'y' or 'Y', the file is skipped.

OPTIONS

–b, ––*backup* Make backups of files that are about to be removed.

–f, ––*force* Remove existing destination files and never prompt the user.

–i, ––*interactive* Prompt whether to overwrite each destination file that already exists. If the response does not begin with 'y' or 'Y', the file is skipped.

–u, ––*update* Do not move a nondirectory that has an existing destination with the same or newer modification time.

–v, ––*verbose* Print the name of each file before moving it.

––*help* Print a usage message on standard output and exit successfully.

––*version* Print version information on standard output then exit successfully.

–S, ––*suffix backup-suffix* The suffix used for making simple backup files can be set with the **SIMPLE_BACKUP_SUFFIX** environment variable, which can be overridden by this option. If neither of those is given, the default is '~', as it is in Emacs.

–V, ––*version-control* {*numbered,existing,simple*} The type of backups made can be set with the **VERSION_CONTROL** environment variable, which can be overridden by this option. If **VERSION_CONTROL** is not set and this option is not given, the default backup type is 'existing'. The value of the **VERSION_CONTROL** environment variable and the argument to this option are like the GNU Emacs 'version-control' variable; they also recognize synonyms that are more descriptive. The valid values are (unique abbreviations are accepted):

't' or 'numbered' Always make numbered backups.

'nil' or 'existing' Make numbered backups of files that already have them, simple backups of the others.

'never' or 'simple' Always make simple backups.

NAMEI(1)

NAME

namei - follow a pathname until a terminal point is found

SYNOPSIS

namei *[-mx] pathname [pathname ...]*

DESCRIPTION

Namei uses its arguments as pathnames to any type of Unix file (symlinks, files, directories, and so forth). *Namei* then follows each pathname until a terminal point is found (a file, directory, char device, etc). If it finds a symbolic link, we show the link, and start following it, indenting the output to show the context.

This program is useful for finding a "too many levels of symbolic links" problems.

For each line output, *namei* outputs a the following characters to identify the file types found:

f: = the pathname we are currently trying to resolve
d = directory
l = symbolic link (both the link and it's contents are output)
s = socket
b = block device
c = character device
- = regular file
? = an error of some kind

Namei prints an informative message when the maximum number of symbolic links this system can have has been exceeded.

OPTIONS

    -x   Show mount point directories with a 'D', rather than a 'd'.

    -m   Show the mode bits of each file type in the style of ls(1), for example 'rwxr-xr-x'.

AUTHOR

Roger Southwick (rogers@amadeus.wr.tek.com)

BUGS

To be discovered.

CAVEATS

Namei will follow an infinite loop of symbolic links forever. To escape, use SIGINT (usually ^C).

SEE ALSO

ls(1), stat(1)

NEWALIASES(1)

NAME

newaliases – rebuild the data base for the mail aliases file

SYNOPSIS

newaliases

DESCRIPTION

Newaliases rebuilds the random access data base for the mail aliases file It must be run each time is changed in order for the change to take effect.

SEE ALSO

aliases 5 , sendmail 8

HISTORY

The newaliases command appeared in BSD 4.0 .

NEWGRP(1)

NAME

newgrp – log in to a new group

SYNOPSIS

newgrp [*group*]

DESCRIPTION

Newgrp changes the group identification of its caller, analogously to **login**(1). The same person remains logged in, and the current directory is unchanged, but calculations of access permissions to files are performed with respect to the new group ID.

If no group is specified, the GID is changed to the login GID.

FILES

/etc/group
/etc/passwd

SEE ALSO

login(1), **group**(5)

NAME

nl – number lines of files

SYNOPSIS

nl [–h header-style] [–b body-style] [–f footer-style] [–p] [–d cc] [–v start-number] [–i increment] [–l lines] [–s line-separator] [–w line-no-width] [–n {ln,rn,rz}] [——header-numbering=style] [——body-numbering=style] [——footer-numbering=style] [——first-page=number] [——page-increment=number] [——no-renumber] [——join-blank-lines=number] [——number-separator=string] [——number-width=number] [——number-format={ln,rn,rz}] [——section-delimiter=cc] [——help] [——version] [file...]

DESCRIPTION

This manual page documents the GNU version of **nl**. **nl** copies each given file, or the standard input if none are given or when a file named '–' is given, to the standard output, with line numbers added to some or all of the lines.

nl considers its input to be composed of logical pages; by default, the line number is reset to 1 at the top of each logical page. **nl** treats all of the input files as a single document; it does not reset line numbers or logical pages between files.

A logical page consists of three sections: header, body, and footer. Any of the sections can be empty. Each can be numbered in a different style from the others.

The beginnings of the sections of logical pages are indicated in the input file by a line containing nothing except one of the delimiter strings shown below:

\:\:\:   start of header
\:\:   start of body
\:   start of footer

The two characters from which these strings are made can be changed with an option (see below), but the pattern and length of each string cannot be changed.

The section delimiter strings are replaced by an empty line on output. Any text that comes before the first section delimiter string in the input file is considered to be part of a body section, so a file that does not contain any section delimiter strings is considered to consist of a single body section.

OPTIONS

–h, ——header-numbering=style	See ——footer-numbering.
–b, ——body-numbering=style	See ——footer-numbering.
–f, ——footer-numbering=style	Select the numbering style for lines in the footer section of each logical page. When a line is not numbered, the current line number is not incremented, but the line number separator character is still prepended to the line. The styles are:

    a   number all lines

    t   number only nonempty lines (default for body)

    n   number no lines (default for header and footer)

    p*regexp*   number only lines that contain a match for *regexp*

–p, ——no-renumber	Do not reset the line number at the start of a logical page.
–v, ——first-page=number	Set the initial line number on each logical page to *number* (default 1).

–i, —-page-increment=number		Increment line numbers by *number* (default 1).
–l, —-join-blank-lines=number		Consider *number* (default 1) consecutive empty lines to be one logical line for numbering, and only number the last one. Where fewer than *number* consecutive empty lines occur, do not number them. An empty line is one that contains no characters, not even spaces or tabs.
–s, —-number-separator=string		Separate the line number from the text line in the output with *string* (default is a TAB character).
–w, —-number-width=number		Use *number* characters for line numbers (default 6).
–n, —-number-format={ln,rn,rz}		Select the line numbering format:
	ln	left justified, no leading zeros
	rn	right justified, no leading zeros (default)
	rz	right justified, leading zeros
–d, —-section-delimiter=cc		Set the two delimiter characters that indicate the beginnings of logical page sections; if only one is given, the second remains ':'. To enter '\', use '\\'.
—-help		Print a usage message and exit with a non-zero status.
—-version		Print version information on standard output then exit.

nlmconv(1)

NAME

nlmconv—converts object code into an NLM

SYNOPSIS

nlmconv [**-I**bfdname|—input–target=bfdname] [**-O**bfdname|
—output–target=bfdname] [**-T**headerfile|—header–file=headerfile]
[**-V**|—**version**] [—**help**] **infile outfile**

DESCRIPTION

nlmconv converts the relocatable object file **infile** into the NetWare Loadable Module **outfile**, optionally reading *headerfile* for NLM header information. For instructions on writing the NLM command file language used in header files, see *The NetWare Tool Maker Specification Manual*, available from Novell, Inc. **nlmconv** currently works with i386 object files in **COFF**, **ELF**, or **a.out** format, and with SPARC object files in **ELF** or **a.out** format. **nlmconv** uses the GNU Binary File Descriptor library to read *infile*.

OPTIONS

–**I** *bfdname*, —**input–target**=*bfdname* Consider the source file's object format to be *bfdname*, rather than attempting to deduce it.

–**O** *bfdname*, —**output–target**=*bfdname* Write the output file using the object format *bfdname*. **nlmconv** infers the output format based on the input format, e.g. for an i386 input file the output format is *nlm32–i386*.

–**T** *headerfile*, —**header–file**=*headerfile* Reads *headerfile* for NLM header information. For instructions on writing the NLM command file language used in header files, see *The NetWare Tool Maker Specification Manual*, available from Novell, Inc.

–**V**, —**version** Show the version number of **nlmconv** and exit.

–**h**, —**help** Show a summary of the options to **nlmconv** and exit.

SEE ALSO

' **binutils** ' entry in info ; The GNU Binary Utilities , Roland H. Pesch (June 1993).

COPYING

Copyright (c) 1993 Free Software Foundation, Inc.

Permission is granted to make and distribute verbatim copies of this manual provided the copyright notice and this permission notice are preserved on all copies.

Permission is granted to copy and distribute modified versions of this manual under the conditions for verbatim copying, provided that the entire resulting derived work is distributed under the terms of a permission notice identical to this one.

Permission is granted to copy and distribute translations of this manual into another language, under the above conditions for modified versions, except that this permission notice may be included in translations approved by the Free Software Foundation instead of in the original English.

NAME

nm – list symbols from object files.

SYNOPSIS

nm [–a|—debug–syms] [–g|—extern–only] [–B] [–C|—demangle] [–D|—dynamic] [–s|—print–armap] [–o|—print–file–name] [–n|—-numeric–sort] [–p|—no–sort] [–r|—reverse–sort] [—size–sort] [–u|—undefined–only] [—help] [—version] [–t *radix*|—radix=*radix*] [–P|-portability] [–f *format*|—format=*format*] [—target=*bfdname*] [*objfile* ...]

DESCRIPTION

GNU **nm** lists the symbols from object files *objfile*. If no object files are given as arguments, **nm** assumes ' **a.out** '.

OPTIONS

The long and short forms of options, shown here as alternatives, are equivalent.

–A

–o

—print–file–name   Precede each symbol by the name of the input file where it was found, rather than identifying the input file once only before all of its symbols.

–a

—debug–syms   Display debugger-only symbols; normally these are not listed.

–B   The same as **—format=bsd** (for compatibility with the MIPS **nm**).

–C

—demangle   Decode (*demangle*) low-level symbol names into user-level names. Besides removing any initial underscore prepended by the system, this makes C++ function names readable.

–D

—dynamic   Display the dynamic symbols rather than the normal symbols. This is only meaningful for dynamic objects, such as certain types of shared libraries.

–f *format*   Use the output format *format*, which can be "bsd", "sysv", or "posix". The default is 'bsd". Only the first character of *format* is significant; it can be either upper or lower case.

–g

—extern–only   Display only external symbols.

–n

–v

—numeric–sort   Sort symbols numerically by their addresses, not alphabetically by their names.

–p

—no–sort   Don't bother to sort the symbols in any order; just print them in the order encountered.

–P

—portability   Use the POSIX.2 standard output format instead of the default format. Equivalent to "–f posix".

–s

—print–armap When listing symbols from archive members, include the index: a mapping (stored in the archive by **ar** or **ranlib**) of what modules contain definitions for what names.

–r

—reverse–sort Reverse the sense of the sort (whether numeric or alphabetic); let the last come first.

—size–sort Sort symbols by size. The size is computed as the difference between the value of the symbol and the value of the symbol with the next higher value. The size of the symbol is printed, rather than the value.

–t *radix*

—radix=*radix* Use *radix* as the radix for printing the symbol values. It must be "d" for decimal, "o" for octal, or "x" for hexadecimal.

—target=*bfdname* Specify an object code format other than your system's default format. See **objdump(1)**, for information on listing available formats.

–u

—undefined–only Display only undefined symbols (those external to each object file).

–V

—version Show the version number of **nm** and exit.

—help Show a summary of the options to **nm** and exit.

SEE ALSO

'**binutils**' entry in info ; The GNU Binary Utilities , Roland H. Pesch (October 1991); **ar(1)**, **objdump(1)**, **ranlib(1)**.

COPYING

Copyright (c) 1991 Free Software Foundation, Inc.

Permission is granted to make and distribute verbatim copies of this manual provided the copyright notice and this permission notice are preserved on all copies.

Permission is granted to copy and distribute modified versions of this manual under the conditions for verbatim copying, provided that the entire resulting derived work is distributed under the terms of a permission notice identical to this one.

Permission is granted to copy and distribute translations of this manual into another language, under the above conditions for modified versions, except that this permission notice may be included in translations approved by the Free Software Foundation instead of in the original English.

NAME

objcopy – copy and translate object files

SYNOPSIS

objcopy [**–F***bfdname*|—target=*bfdname*]
[**–I***bfdname*| —input–target=*bfdname*] [**–O***bfdname*|
—output–target=*bfdname*] [**–R***sectionname*|
—remove–section=*sectionname*] [**–S**| —**strip–all**] [**–g**|
—**strip–debug**] [**–x**|—**discard–all**] [**–X**|
—**discard–locals**] [**–b***byte*|—byte=*byte*] [**–i***interleave*|
—interleave=*interleave*] [**–v**|—**verbose**] [**–V**|
—**version**] [—**help**] infile [outfile]

DESCRIPTION

The GNU **objcopy** utility copies the contents of an object file to another. **objcopy** uses the GNU BFD Library to read and write the object files. It can write the destination object file in a format different from that of the source object file. The exact behavior of **objcopy** is controlled by command-line options.

objcopy creates temporary files to do its translations and deletes them afterward. **objcopy** uses BFD to do all its translation work; it knows about all the formats BFD knows about, and thus is able to recognize most formats without being told explicitly.

infile and *outfile* are the source and output files respectively. If you do not specify *outfile*, **objcopy** creates a temporary file and destructively renames the result with the name of the input file.

OPTIONS

–I *bfdname*, —**input–target=***bfdname*
: Consider the source file's object format to be *bfdname*, rather than attempting to deduce it.

–O *bfdname*, —**output–target=***bfdname*
: Write the output file using the object format *bfdname*.

–F *bfdname*, —**target=***bfdname*
: Use *bfdname* as the object format for both the input and the output file; i.e. simply transfer data from source to destination with no translation.

–R *sectionname*, —**remove-section=***sectionname*
: Remove the named section from the file. This option may be given more than once. Note that using this option inappropriately may make the output file unusable.

–S, —**strip–all**
: Do not copy relocation and symbol information from the source file.

–g, —**strip–debug**
: Do not copy debugging symbols from the source file.

–x, —**discard–all**
: Do not copy non-global symbols from the source file.

–X, —**discard–locals**
: Do not copy compiler-generated local symbols. (These usually start with "L" or ".".)

–b *byte*, —**byte=***byte*
: Keep only every *byte*th byte of the input file (header data is not affected). *byte* can be in the range from 0 to the interleave-1. This option is useful for creating files to program ROMs. It is typically used with an srec output target.

–i *interleave*, —**interleave**=*interleave*	Only copy one out of every *interleave* bytes. Which one to copy is selected by the **–b** or —**byte** option. The default is 4. The interleave is ignored if neither **–b** nor —**byte** is given.
–v, —verbose	Verbose output: list all object files modified. In the case of archives,"**objcopy –V**" lists all members of the archive.
–V, —version	Show the version number of **objcopy** and exit.
—help	Show a summary of the options to **objcopy** and exit.

SEE ALSO

' **binutils** ' entry in info ; The GNU Binary Utilities , Roland H. Pesch (June 1993).

COPYING

Copyright (c) 1993 Free Software Foundation, Inc.

Permission is granted to make and distribute verbatim copies of this manual provided the copyright notice and this permission notice are preserved on all copies.

Permission is granted to copy and distribute modified versions of this manual under the conditions for verbatim copying, provided that the entire resulting derived work is distributed under the terms of a permission notice identical to this one.

Permission is granted to copy and distribute translations of this manual into another language, under the above conditions for modified versions, except that this permission notice may be included in translations approved by the Free Software Foundation instead of in the original English.

NAME

objdump – display information from object files.

SYNOPSIS

objdump [–a|—archive–headers] [–b\ *bfdname* |—target= *bfdname*]
[–d|—disassemble] [–D|—disassemble-all] [–f|—file–headers]
[–h|—section–headers |—headers] [–i|—info] [–j\ *section* |
—section= *section*] [–l|—line–numbers] [–m\ *machine* |—
-architecture= *machine*] [–r|—reloc] [–R|—dynamic–reloc]
[–s|—full–contents] [—stabs] [–t|—syms] [–T|—dynamic–
syms] [–x|—all–headers] [—version] [—help] *objfile* ...

DESCRIPTION

objdump displays information about one or more object files. The options control what particular information to display. This information is mostly useful to programmers who are working on the compilation tools, as opposed to programmers who just want their program to compile and work.

objfile... are the object files to be examined. When you specify archives, **objdump** shows information on each of the member object files.

OPTIONS

Where long and short forms of an option are shown together, they are equivalent. At least one option besides –l (—**line–numbers**) must be given.

–a

—archive–headers   If any files from *objfile* are archives, display the archive header information (in a format similar to ' **ls** –l '). Besides the information you could list with ' **ar** tv ', ' **objdump** –a ' shows the object file format of each archive member.

–b *bfdname*

—target=*bfdname*   Specify the object-code format for the object files to be *bfdname* . This may not be necessary; *objdump* can automatically recognize many formats. For example,

   objdump –b oasys –m vax –h fu.o

display summary information from the section headers (' **–h** ') of ' **fu.o** ', which is explicitly identified (' **–m** ') as a Vax object file in the format produced by Oasys compilers. You can list the formats available with the ' **–i** ' option.

–d

—disassemble   Display the assembler mnemonics for the machine instructions from *objfile* . This option only disassembles those sections which are expected to contain instructions.

–D

—disassemble-all   Like **–d**, but disassemble the contents of all sections, not just those expected to contain instructions.

–f

—file–headers   Display summary information from the overall header of each file in *objfile* .

–h

—section–headers

objdump(1) GNU Development Tools objdump(1)

—headers Display summary information from the section headers of the object file.

—help Print a summary of the options to **objdump** and exit.

–i

—info Display a list showing all architectures and object formats available for specification with –b or –m.

–j *name*

—section=*name* Display information only for section *name*

–l

—line–numbers Label the display (using debugging information) with the filename and source line numbers corresponding to the object code shown. Only useful with –d or –D.

–m *machine*

—architecture=*machine* Specify the object files *objfile* are for architecture *machine*. You can list available architectures using the ' –i ' option.

–r

—reloc Print the relocation entries of the file. If used with –d or –d, the relocations are printed interspersed with the disassembly.

–R

—dynamic–reloc Print the dynamic relocation entries of the file. This is only meaningful for dynamic objects, such as certain types of shared libraries.

–s

—full–contents Display the full contents of any sections requested.

—stabs Display the contents of the .stab, .stab.index, and .stab.excl sections from an ELF file. This is only useful on systems (such as Solaris 2.0) in which .stab debugging symbol-table entries are carried in an ELF section. In most other file formats, debugging symbol-table entries are interleaved with linkage symbols, and are visible in the —syms output.

–t

—syms Symbol Table. Print the symbol table entries of the file. This is similar to the information provided by the ' **nm** ' program.

–T

—dynamic–syms Dynamic Symbol Table. Print the dynamic symbol table entries of the file. This is only meaningful for dynamic objects, such as certain types of shared libraries. This is similar to the information provided by the ' **nm** ' program when given the –D (—dynamic) option.

—version Print the version number of **objdump** and exit.

–x

—all–headers Display all available header information, including the symbol table and relocation entries. Using ' –x ' is equivalent to specifying all of ' –a –f –h –r –t '.

SEE ALSO

' **binutils** ' entry in info ; The GNU Binary Utilities , Roland H. Pesch (October 1991); nm(1).

COPYING

Copyright (c) 1991 Free Software Foundation, Inc.

Permission is granted to make and distribute verbatim copies of this manual provided the copyright notice and this permission notice are preserved on all copies.

objdump(1) GNU Development Tools objdump(1)

Permission is granted to copy and distribute modified versions of this manual under the conditions for verbatim copying, provided that the entire resulting derived work is distributed under the terms of a permission notice identical to this one.

Permission is granted to copy and distribute translations of this manual into another language, under the above conditions for modified versions, except that this permission notice may be included in translations approved by the Free Software Foundation instead of in the original English.

OD(1L)   FSF   OD(1L)

NAME

od – dump files in octal and other formats

SYNOPSIS

od [–abcdfhiloxv] [–s[bytes]] [–w[bytes]] [–A radix] [–j bytes] [–N bytes] [–t type] [—skip–bytes=bytes] [—address–radix=radix] [—read–bytes=bytes] [—format=type] [—output–duplicates] [—strings[=bytes]] [—width[=bytes]] [—traditional] [—help] [—version] [file...]

DESCRIPTION

This manual page documents the GNU version of **od**. **od** writes to the standard output the contents of the given files, or of the standard input if the name '–' is given. Each line of the output consists of the offset in the input file in the leftmost column of each line, followed by one or more columns of data from the file, in a format controlled by the options. By default, **od** prints the file offsets in octal and the file data as two-byte octal numbers.

OPTIONS

  –A, —address–radix=radix Select the base in which file offsets are printed. *radix* can be one of the following:

    d decimal

    o octal

    x hexadecimal

    n none (do not print offsets)

    The default is octal.

  –j, —skip–bytes=bytes Skip *bytes* input bytes before formatting and writing. If **bytes** begins with '0x' or '0X', it is interpreted in hexadecimal; otherwise, if it begins with '0', in octal; otherwise, in decimal. Appending 'b' multiplies it by 512, 'k' by 1024, and 'm' by 1048576.

  –N, —read–bytes=bytes Only output up to *bytes* bytes of each input file. Any prefixes and suffixes on **bytes** are interpreted as for the *–j* option.

  –t, —format=type Select the format in which to output the file data. *type* is a string of one or more of the below type indicator characters. If you include more than one type indicator character in a single *type* string or use this option more than once, **od** writes one copy of each output line using each of the data types that you specified, in the order that you specified.

    a named character

    c ASCII character or backslash escape

    d signed decimal

    f floating point

    o octal

    u unsigned decimal

    x hexadecimal

    Except for types 'a' and 'c', you can specify the number of bytes to use in interpreting each number in the given data type by following the type indicator character with a decimal integer. Alternately, you can specify the size of one of the C compiler's built-in data types by following the type indicator character with one of the following characters. For integers (d, o, u, x):

C char
S short
I int
L long

For floating point (f):

F float
D double
L long double

–v, —-output–duplicates Output consecutive lines that are identical. By default, when two or more consecutive output lines would be equal, **od** outputs only the first line, and puts just an asterisk on the following line to indicate that identical lines have been elided.

–s, —-strings[=bytes] Instead of the normal output, output only string constants in the input, which are a run of at least *bytes* ASCII graphic (or formatting) characters, terminated by a NUL. If *bytes* is omitted, it defaults to 3.

–w, —-width[=bytes] The number of input bytes to format per output line. It must be a multiple of the least common multiple of the sizes associated with the specified output types. If *bytes* is omitted, it defaults to 32. If this option is not given, it defaults to 16.

—-help Print a usage message and exit with a non-zero status.

—-version Print version information on standard output then exit.

The next several options map the old, pre-POSIX format specification options to the corresponding POSIX format specs. GNU **od** accepts any combination of old- and new-style options. Format specification options accumulate.

–a Output as named characters. Equivalent to *–t a*.

–b Output as octal bytes. Equivalent to *–t oC*.

–c Output as ASCII characters or backslash escapes. Equivalent to *–t c*.

–d Output as unsigned decimal shorts. Equivalent to *–t u2*.

–f Output as floats. Equivalent to *–t fF*.

–h Output as hexadecimal shorts. Equivalent to *–t x2*.

–i Output as decimal shorts. Equivalent to *–t d2*.

–l Output as decimal longs. Equivalent to *–t d4*.

–o Output as octal shorts. Equivalent to *–t o2*.

–x Output as hexadecimal shorts. Equivalent to *–t x2*.

—-traditional Recognize the pre-POSIX non-option arguments that some older versions of od accepted. The following syntax

  od —-traditional [file] [[+]offset[.][b] [[+]label[.][b]]]

can be used to specify at most one file and optional arguments specifying an offset and a pseudo-start address, *label*. By default, *offset* is interpreted as an octal number specifying how many input bytes to skip before formatting and writing. The optional trailing decimal point forces the interpretation of *offset* as a decimal number. If no decimal is specified and the offset begins with '0x' or '0X' it is interpreted as a hexadecimal number. If there is a trailing 'b', the number of bytes skipped will be *offset* multiplied by 512. The label argument is interpreted just like offset, but it specifies an initial pseudo-address. The pseudo addresses are displayed in parentheses following any normal address.

NAME

passwd – change password

SYNOPSIS

passwd [name]

DESCRIPTION

passwd will change the specified user's password. Only the superuser is allowed to change other user's passwords. If the user is not root, then the old password is prompted for and verified.

A new password is prompted for twice, to avoid typing mistakes. Unless the user is the superuser, the new password must have more than six characters, and must have either both upper and lower case letters, or non-letters. Some passwords which are similar to the user's name are not allowed.

FILES

/etc/passwd
/etc/shells

SEE ALSO

chsh(1), **chfn**(1)

BUGS

A password consisting of all digits is allowed.
No warnings are printed if the superuser chooses a poor password.
The **–f** and **–s** options are not supported.

AUTHOR

Peter Orbaek (poe@daimi.aau.dk)

PASTE(1L)

NAME

paste – merge lines of files

SYNOPSIS

paste [–s] [–d delim-list] [——serial] [——delimiters=delim-list] [——help] [——version] [file...]

DESCRIPTION

This manual page documents the GNU version of **paste**. **paste** prints lines consisting of sequentially corresponding lines of each given file, separated by TABs, terminated by a newline. If no files are given, the standard input is used. A file name of '-' means standard input.

OPTIONS

–s, ——serial Paste the lines of one file at a time rather than one line from each file.

–d, ——delimiters delim-list Consecutively use the characters in *delim-list* instead of TAB to separate merged lines. When *delim-list* is exhausted, start again at its beginning.

——help Print a usage message and exit with a non-zero status.

——version Print version information on standard output then exit.

PFBTOPS(1)   PFBTOPS(1)

NAME

pfbtops – translate a PostScript font in .pfb format to ASCII

SYNOPSIS

pfbtops [*pfb_file*]

DESCRIPTION

pfbtops translates a PostScript font in **.pfb** format to ASCII. If *pfb_file* is omitted the pfb file will be read from the standard input. The ASCII format PostScript font will be written on the standard output. PostScript fonts for MS-DOS are normally supplied in **.pfb** format.

The resulting ASCII format PostScript font can be used with groff. It must first be listed in **/usr/lib/groff/font/devps/download**.

SEE ALSO

grops(1)

NAME

pr – convert text files for printing

SYNOPSIS

pr [+PAGE] [–COLUMN] [–abcdfFmrtv] [–e[in-tab-char[in-tab-width]]] [–h header] [–i[out-tab-char[out-tab-width]]] [–l page-length] [–n[number-separator[digits]]] [–o left-margin] [–s[column-separator]] [–w page-width] [––help] [––version] [file...]

DESCRIPTION

This manual page documents the GNU version of **pr**. **pr** prints on the standard output a paginated and optionally multicolumn copy of the text files given on the command line, or of the standard input if no files are given or when the file name '–' is encountered. Form feeds in the input cause page breaks in the output.

OPTIONS

PAGE Begin printing with page *PAGE*.

–COLUMN Produce *COLUMN*-column output and print columns down. The column width is automatically decreased as *COLUMN* increases; unless you use the *–w* option to increase the page width as well, this option might cause some columns to be truncated.

–a Print columns across rather than down.

–b Balance columns on the last page.

–c Print control characters using hat notation (e.g., '^G'); print other unprintable characters in octal backslash notation.

–d Double space the output.

–e[in-tab-char[in-tab-width]] Expand tabs to spaces on input. Optional argument *in-tab-char* is the input tab character, default tab. Optional argument *in-tab-width* is the input tab character's width, default 8.

–F, –f Use a formfeed instead of newlines to separate output pages.

–h header Replace the filename in the header with the string *header*.

––help Print a usage message and exit with a non-zero status.

–i[out-tab-char[out-tab-width]] Replace spaces with tabs on output. Optional argument *out-tab-char* is the output tab character, default tab. Optional argument *out-tab-width* is the output tab character's width, default 8.

–l page-length Set the page length to *page-length* lines. The default is 66. If *page-length* is less than 10, the headers and footers are omitted, as if the *–t* option had been given.

–m Print all files in parallel, one in each column.

–n[number-separator[digits]] Precede each column with a line number; with parallel files, precede each line with a line number. Optional argument *number-separator* is the character to print after each number, default tab. Optional argument *digits* is the number of digits per line number, default 5.

–o left-margin Offset each line with a margin *left-margin* spaces wide. The total page width is this offset plus the width set with the *–w* option.

–r Do not print a warning message when an argument file cannot be opened. Failure to open a file still makes the exit status nonzero, however.

–s[column-separator] Separate columns by the single character *column-separator*, default tab, instead of spaces.

–t Do not print the 5-line header and the 5-line trailer that are normally on each page, and do not fill out the bottoms of pages (with blank lines or formfeeds).

−*v* Print unprintable characters in octal backslash notation.

—*-version* Print version information on standard output then exit.

−*w page-width* Set the page width to *page-width* columns. The default is 72.

NAME

ps – report process status

SYNOPSIS

ps [–][**lujsvmaxScewhrnu**][t*xx*] [**O**[+|-]*k1*[[+|-]*k2*...]] [*pids*]

there are also two long options:

—**sort***X*[+|-]*key*[,[+|-]*key*[,...]]

—**help**

More long options are on the way...

DESCRIPTION

ps gives a snapshot of the current processes. If you want a repetitive update of this status, use **top**. This man page documents the **/proc**-based version of **ps**, or tries to.

COMMAND–LINE OPTIONS

Command line arguments may optionally be preceeded by a '–', but there is no need for it. There are also some "long options" in GNU style; see below for those.

l	long format
u	user format: gives user name and start time
j	jobs format: pgid sid
s	signal format
v	vm format
m	displays memory info (combine with **p** flag to get number of pages).
f	"forest" family tree format for command line
a	show processes of other users too
x	show processes without controlling terminal
S	add child cpu time and page faults
c	command name from task_struct
e	show environment after command line and ' + '
w	wide output: don't truncate command lines to fit on one line.
h	no header
r	running procs only
n	numeric output for **USER** and **WCHAN**.
t*xx*	only procs with controlling tty *xx*; use for *xx* the same letters as shown in the **TT** field. The tty name must be given immediately after the option, with no intervening space, e.g. **ps -tv1**.
O[+|-]*k1*[,[+|-]*k2*[,...]]	Order the process listing according to the multi-level sort specified by the sequence of *short* keys from **SORT KEYS**, *k1*, *k2*, ... Default order specifications exist for each of the various formats of **ps**. These are over-ridden by a user specified ordering. The '+' is quite optional, merely re-iterating the default direction on a key. '-' reverses direction only on the key it precedes. As with **t** and *pids*, the O option must be the last option in a single command argument, but specifications in successive arguments are catenated.
pids	List only the specified processes; they are comma-delimited. The list must be given immediately after the last option in a single command-line argument, with no intervening space, e.g. **ps -j1,4,5**. Lists specified in subsequent arguments are catenated, e.g. **ps** -l 1,2 3,4 5 6 will list all of the processes 1-6 in long format.

LONG COMMAND–LINE OPTIONS

These options are preceeded by a double–hyphen.

    —sortX[+|-]key[,[+|-]key[,...]] Choose a *multi-letter key* from the **SORT KEYS** section. X may be any convenient separator character. To be GNU-ish use '='. The '+' is really optional since default direction is increasing numerical or lexicographic order. E.g.: **ps** -jax –sort=uid,-ppid,+pid

    —help Get a help message that summarizes the usage and gives a list of supported sort keys. This list may be more up to date than this man page.

SORT KEYS

Note that the values used in sorting are the internal values **ps** uses and *not* the 'cooked' values used in some of the output format fields. If someone wants to volunteer to write special comparison functions for the cooked values, ... ;-)

SHORT LONG DESCRIPTION

c cmd simple name of executable

C cmdline full command line

f flags flags as in long format F field

g pgrp process group ID

G tpgid controlling tty process group ID

j cutime cumulative user time

J cstime cumulative system time

k utime user time

K stime system time

m min_flt number of minor page faults

M maj_flt number of major page faults

n cmin_flt cumulative minor page faults

N cmaj_flt cumulative major page faults

o session session ID

p pid process ID

P ppid parent process ID

r rss resident set size

R resident resident pages

s size memory size in kilobytes

S share amount of shared pages

t tty the minor device number of tty

T start_time time process was started

U uid user ID number

u user user name

v vsize total VM size in bytes

y priority kernel scheduling priority

FIELD DESCRIPTIONS

PRI   This is the counter field in the task struct. It is the time in **HZ** of the process's possible timeslice.

NI   Standard unix nice value; a positive value means less cpu time.

SIZE   Virtual image size; size of text+data+stack.

RSS   Resident set size; kilobytes of program in memory.

WCHAN   Name of the kernel function where the process is sleeping, with the '**sys_**' stripped from the function name. If **/boot/psdatabase** does not exist, it is just a hex number instead.

STAT   Information about the status of the process. The first field is **R** for runnable, **S** for sleeping, **D** for uninterruptible sleep, **T** for stopped or traced, or **Z** for a zombie process. The second field contains **W** if the process has no resident pages. The third field is **N** if the process has a positive nice value (**NI** field).

TT   Controlling tty.

PAGEIN   Number of major page faults (page faults that cause pages to be read from disk, including pages read from the buffer cache).

TRS   Text resident size.

SWAP   Kilobytes (or pages if **–p** is used) on swap device.

SHARE   Shared memory.

UPDATING

This **proc**-based **ps** works by reading the files in the **proc** filesystem, mounted on **/proc**. This **ps** does not need to be suid **kmem** or have any privileges to run. *Do not give this ps any special permissions.*

You will need to update the **/boot/psdatabase** file by running **/usr/sbin/psupdate** to get meaningful information from the **WCHAN** field. This should be done every time you compile a new kernel.

NOTES

The member **used_math** of **task_struct** is not shown, since **crt0.s** checks to see if math is present. This causes the math flag to be set for all processes, and so it is worthless.

Programs swapped out to disk will be shown without command line arguments, and unless the **c** option is given, in parentheses.

%CPU shows the cputime/realtime percentage. It will not add up to 100% unless you are lucky. It is time used divided by the time the process has been running.

The **SIZE** and **RSS** fields don't count the page tables and the **task_struct** of a proc; this is at least 12k of memory that is always resident. **SIZE** is the virtual size of the proc (code+data+stack).

BUGS

Tty names are hard coded: virtual consoles are v1, v2, ... serial lines are s0 and s1, pty's are pp0, pp1 ..., pq0, pq1, ...

AUTHOR

ps was originally written by Branko Lankester (lankeste@fwi.uva.nl) Michael K. Johnson (johnsonm@sunsite.unc.edu) re-wrote it significantly to use the proc filesystem, changing a few things in the process. Michael Shields (mjshield@nyx.cs.du.edu) added the multiple-pids feature. Charles Blake(cblake@ucsd.edu) added multi-level sorting and is the current maintainer of the proc-ps suite.

PSBB(1)

NAME
psbb – extract bounding box from PostScript document

SYNOPSIS
psbb *file*

DESCRIPTION
psbb reads *file* which should be a PostScript document conforming to the Document Structuring conventions and looks for a **%%BoundingBox** comment. If it finds one, it prints a line

    llx lly urx ury

on the standard output and exits with zero status. If it doesn't find such a line or if the line is invalid it prints a message and exits with non-zero status.

SEE ALSO
grops(1)

PSTREE(1)

NAME

pstree – display a tree of processes

SYNOPSIS

pstree [–a] [–c] [–h] [–l] [–p] [–u] [*pid*|*user*]

DESCRIPTION

pstree shows running processes as a tree. The tree is rooted at either *pid* or **init** if *pid* is omitted. If a user name is specified, all process trees rooted at processes owned by that user are shown.

pstree visually merges identical branches by putting them in square brackets and prefixing them with the repetition count, e.g.

```
init─┬─getty
     |─getty
     |─getty
     '─getty
becomes

init────4*[getty]
```

OPTIONS

- **–a** Show command line arguments. If the command line of a process is swapped out, that process is shown in parentheses. **–a** implicitly disables compaction.
- **–c** Disable compaction of identical subtrees. By default, subtrees are compacted whenever possible.
- **–h** Highlight the current process and its ancestors. This is a no-op if the terminal doesn't support highlighting or if neither the current process nor any of its ancestors are in the subtree being shown.
- **–l** Display long lines. By default, lines are truncated to the display width or 132 if output is sent to a non-tty or if the display width is unknown.
- **–p** Show PIDs. PIDs are shown as decimal numbers in parentheses after each process name. **–p** implicitly disables compaction.
- **–u** Show uid transitions. Whenever the uid of a process differs from the uid of its parent, the new uid is shown in parentheses after the process name.

FILES

/proc location of the proc file system

AUTHOR

Werner Almesberger <almesber@di.epfl.ch>

SEE ALSO

ps(1), top(1)

NAME

psupdate – update the ps database of kernel offsets

SYNOPSIS

psupdate [system path]

DESCRIPTION

psupdate updates the /boot/psdatabase file to correspond to the current kernel image system map file, /usr/src/linux/vmlinux by default.

Options

If your system map file is not /usr/src/linux/vmlinux, you may give the name of an alternate map file on the command line.

FILES

/boot/psdatabase
/usr/src/linux/vmlin

SEE ALSO

ps(1), top(1), utmp(5)

AUTHORS

Original code written by Branko Lankaster, horribly munged by Michael K. Johnson in a desperate effort to add /etc/psdatabase support to procps. Someday, it should be re-written, and the support in ps for alternate namelists added. Anyone want to volunteer to be added to the **AUTHORS** section?

NAME

ranlib – generate index to archive.

SYNOPSIS

ranlib [**–v**|**–V**] *archive*

DESCRIPTION

ranlib generates an index to the contents of an archive, and stores it in the archive. The index lists each symbol defined by a member of an archive that is a relocatable object file.

You may use '**nm –s**' or '**nm ––print-armap**' to list this index.

An archive with such an index speeds up linking to the library, and allows routines in the library to call each other without regard to their placement in the archive.

The GNU **ranlib** program is another form of GNU **ar**; running **ranlib** is completely equivalent to executing '**ar –s**'.

OPTIONS

    –v   Print the version number of **ranlib** and exit.

SEE ALSO

'**binutils**' entry in info ; The GNU Binary Utilities , Roland H. Pesch (October 1991); **ar**(1), **nm**(1).

COPYING

Copyright (c) 1991 Free Software Foundation, Inc.

Permission is granted to make and distribute verbatim copies of this manual provided the copyright notice and this permission notice are preserved on all copies.

Permission is granted to copy and distribute modified versions of this manual under the conditions for verbatim copying, provided that the entire resulting derived work is distributed under the terms of a permission notice identical to this one.

Permission is granted to copy and distribute translations of this manual into another language, under the above conditions for modified versions, except that this permission notice may be included in translations approved by the Free Software Foundation instead of in the original English.

RCP(1)

NAME

rcp – remote file copy

SYNOPSIS

rcp [-px] [-k realm] file1 file2
rcp [-px] [-r] [-k Ar realm] file ... directory

DESCRIPTION

Rcp copies files between machines. Each file or directory argument is either a remote file name of the form "rname@rhost:path", or a local file name (containing no ':' characters, or a '/' before any ':'s).

> -r If any of the source files are directories, rcp copies each subtree rooted at that name; in this case the destination must be a directory.
>
> -p The -p option causes rcp to attempt to preserve (duplicate) in its copies the modification times and modes of the source files, ignoring the umask . By default, the mode and owner of file2 are preserved if it already existed; otherwise the mode of the source file modified by the umask 2 on the destination host is used.
>
> -k The -k option requests rcp to obtain tickets for the remote host in realm realm instead of the remote host's realm as determined by krb_realmofhost 3 .
>
> -x The -x option turns on DES encryption for all data passed by rcp . This may impact response time and CPU utilization, but provides increased security.

If path is not a full path name, it is interpreted relative to the login directory of the specified user ruser on rhost , or your current user name if no other remote user name is specified. A path on a remote host may be quoted (using \, ", or) so that the metacharacters are interpreted remotely.

Rcp does not prompt for passwords; it performs remote execution via rsh 1 , and requires the same authorization.

Rcp handles third party copies, where neither source nor target files are on the current machine.

SEE ALSO

cp 1 , ftp 1 , rsh 1 , rlogin 1

HISTORY

The rcp command appeared in BSD 4.2 . The version of rcp described here has been reimplemented with Kerberos in BSD 4.3 Reno .

BUGS

Doesn't detect all cases where the target of a copy might be a file in cases where only a directory should be legal.

Is confused by any output generated by commands in a or file on the remote host.

The destination user and hostname may have to be specified as "rhost.rname" when the destination machine is running the BSD 4.2 version of rcp .

RDIST(1)

NAME

rdist – remote file distribution program

SYNOPSIS

rdist [-nqbRhivwy] [-f distfile] [-d var=value] [-m host] [name ...]
rdist [-nqbRhivwy] -c name ... [login@host:dest]

DESCRIPTION

Rdist is a program to maintain identical copies of files over multiple hosts. It preserves the owner, group, mode, and mtime of files if possible and can update programs that are executing. Rdist reads commands from distfile to direct the updating of files and/or directories.

Options specific to the first SYNOPSIS form:

    - If distfile is - , the standard input is used.

    -f distfile Use the specified distfile.

If either the -f or - option is not specified, the program looks first for distfile , then Distfile to use as the input. If no names are specified on the command line, rdist will update all of the files and directories listed in distfile . Otherwise, the argument is taken to be the name of a file to be updated or the label of a command to execute. If label and file names conflict, it is assumed to be a label. These may be used together to update specific files using specific commands.

Options specific to the second SYNOPSIS form:

    -c Forces rdist to interpret the remaining arguments as a small distfile .

    The equivalent distfile is as follows.

    name ... -¿ login@ host install dest ;

Options common to both forms:

    -b Binary comparison. Perform a binary comparison and update files if they differ rather than comparing dates and sizes.

    -d var=value Define var to have value . The -d option is used to define or override variable definitions in the distfile . Value can be the empty string, one name, or a list of names surrounded by parentheses and separated by tabs and/or spaces.

    -h Follow symbolic links. Copy the file that the link points to rather than the link itself.

    -i Ignore unresolved links. Rdist will normally try to maintain the link structure of files being transferred and warn the user if all the links cannot be found.

    -m host Limit which machines are to be updated. Multiple -m arguments can be given to limit updates to a subset of the hosts listed in the distfile .

    -n Print the commands without executing them. This option is useful for debugging distfile .

    -q Quiet mode. Files that are being modified are normally printed on standard output. The -q option suppresses this.

    -R Remove extraneous files. If a directory is being updated, any files that exist on the remote host that do not exist in the master directory are removed. This is useful for maintaining truly identical copies of directories.

    -v Verify that the files are up to date on all the hosts. Any files that are out of date will be displayed but no files will be changed nor any mail sent.

    -w Whole mode. The whole file name is appended to the destination directory name. Normally, only the last component of a name is used when renaming files. This will preserve the directory structure of the files being copied instead of flattening the directory structure. For example, renaming a list of files such as (dir1/f1 dir2/f2) to dir3 would create files dir3/dir1/f1 and dir3/dir2/f2 instead of dir3/f1 and dir3/f2.

-y Younger mode. Files are normally updated if their mtime and size (see stat 2) disagree. The -y option causes rdist not to update files that are younger than the master copy. This can be used to prevent newer copies on other hosts from being replaced. A warning message is printed for files which are newer than the master copy.

Distfile contains a sequence of entries that specify the files to be copied, the destination hosts, and what operations to perform to do the updating. Each entry has one of the following formats.

<variable name> '=' <name list> [label:]<source list> '->' <destination list> <command list> [label:]<source list> '::' <time_stamp file> <command list>

The first format is used for defining variables. The second format is used for distributing files to other hosts. The third format is used for making lists of files that have been changed since some given date. The source list specifies a list of files and/or directories on the local host which are to be used as the master copy for distribution. The destination list is the list of hosts to which these files are to be copied. Each file in the source list is added to a list of changes if the file is out of date on the host which is being updated (second format) or the file is newer than the time stamp file (third format).

Labels are optional. They are used to identify a command for partial updates.

Newlines, tabs, and blanks are only used as separators and are otherwise ignored. Comments begin with '#' and end with a newline.

Variables to be expanded begin with '$' followed by one character or a name enclosed in curly braces (see the examples at the end).

The source and destination lists have the following format: <name> or '(' <zero or more names separated by white-space> ')'

The shell meta-characters '[', ']', '{', '}', '*', and '?' are recognized and expanded (on the local host only) in the same way as csh 1 . They can be escaped with a backslash. The '~' character is also expanded in the same way as csh 1 but is expanded separately on the local and destination hosts. When the -w option is used with a file name that begins with '~', everything except the home directory is appended to the destination name. File names which do not begin with '/' or '~' use the destination user's home directory as the root directory for the rest of the file name.

The command list consists of zero or more commands of the following format.

    'install' <options> opt_dest_name ';'

    'notify' <name list> ';'

    'except' <name list> ';'

    'except_pat' <pattern list> ';'

    'special' <name list> string ';'

The install command is used to copy out of date files and/or directories. Each source file is copied to each host in the destination list. Directories are recursively copied in the same way. Opt_dest_name is an optional parameter to rename files. If no install command appears in the command list or the destination name is not specified, the source file name is used. Directories in the path name will be created if they do not exist on the remote host. To help prevent disasters, a non-empty directory on a target host will never be replaced with a regular file or a symbolic link. However, under the '-R' option a non-empty directory will be removed if the corresponding filename is completely absent on the master host. The options are '-R', '-h', '-i', '-v', '-w', '-y', and '-b' and have the same semantics as options on the command line except they only apply to the files in the source list. The login name used on the destination host is the same as the local host unless the destination name is of the format "login@host".

The notify command is used to mail the list of files updated (and any errors that may have occurred) to the listed names. If no '@' appears in the name, the destination host is appended to the name (e.g., name1@host, name2@host, ...).

The except command is used to update all of the files in the source list except for the files listed in name list . This is usually used to copy everything in a directory except certain files.

The except_pat command is like the except command except that pattern list is a list of regular expressions (see ed 1 for details). If one of the patterns matches some string within a file name, that file will be ignored. Note that since '\' is a quote character, it must be doubled to become part of the regular expression. Variables are expanded in pattern list but not shell file pattern matching characters. To include a '$', it must be escaped with '\'.

The special command is used to specify sh 1 commands that are to be executed on the remote host after the file in name list is updated or installed. If the name list is omitted then the shell commands will be executed for every file updated or installed. The shell variable 'FILE' is set to the current filename before executing the commands in string . String starts and ends with '"' and can cross multiple lines in distfile . Multiple commands to the shell should be separated by ';'. Commands are executed in the user's home directory on the host being updated. The special command can be used to rebuild private databases, etc. after a program has been updated.

The following is a small example: HOSTS = (matisse root@arpa)

FILES = (/bin /lib /usr/bin /usr/games /usr/include/{*.h,{stand,sys,vax*,pascal,machine}/*.h} /usr/lib /usr/man/man? /usr/ucb /usr/local/rdist)

EXLIB = (Mail.rc aliases aliases.dir aliases.pag crontab dshrc sendmail.cf sendmail.fc sendmail.hf sendmail.st uucp vfont)

${FILES} -> ${HOSTS} install -R ; except /usr/lib/${EXLIB} ; except /usr/games/lib ; special /usr/lib/sendmail "/usr/lib/sendmail -bz" ;

srcs: /usr/src/bin -> arpa except_pat (\\.o\$ /SCCS\$) ;

IMAGEN = (ips dviimp catdvi)

imagen: /usr/local/${IMAGEN} -> arpa install /usr/local/lib ; notify ralph ;

${FILES} :: stamp.cory notify root@cory ;

FILES

    distfile input command file

    /tmp/rdist* temporary file for update lists

SEE ALSO

sh 1 , csh 1 , stat 2

HISTORY

The rdist command appeared in BSD 4.3 .

DIAGNOSTICS

A complaint about mismatch of rdist version numbers may really stem from some problem with starting your shell, e.g., you are in too many groups.

BUGS

Source files must reside on the local host where rdist is executed.

There is no easy way to have a special command executed after all files in a directory have been updated.

Variable expansion only works for name lists; there should be a general macro facility.

Rdist aborts on files which have a negative mtime (before Jan 1, 1970).

There should be a 'force' option to allow replacement of non-empty directories by regular files or symlinks. A means of updating file modes and owners of otherwise identical files is also needed.

NAME

reconfig – convert old Xconfig to new XF86Config

SYNOPSIS

reconfig < *Xconfig* > *XF86Config*

DESCRIPTION

The *reconfig* program converts the Xconfig file format used in XFree86 versions prior to 3.1 into the XF86Config format currently used. The XF86Config format contains more information than the Xconfig format, so manual editing is required after converting.

SEE ALSO

XFree86(1), XF86Config(4/5), xf86config(1)

AUTHOR

Gertjan Akkerman.

BUGS

Comment lines are stripped out when converting.

REF(1)

NAME

ref - Display a C function header

SYNOPSIS

ref [-t] [-x] [-c *class*]... [-f *file*]... *tag*

DESCRIPTION

ref quickly locates and displays the header of a function. To do this, *ref* looks in the "tags" file for the line that describes the function, and then scans the source file for the function. When it locates the function, it displays an introductory comment (if there is one), the function's declaration, and the declarations of all arguments.

SEARCH METHOD

ref uses a fairly sophisticated tag look-up algorithm. If you supply a filename via **-f** *file*, then elvis first scans the tags file for a static tag from that file. This search is limited to the tags file in the current directory.

If you supply a classname via **-c** *class*, then elvis searches for a tag from that class. This search is not limited to the current directory; You can supply a list of directories in the environment variable *TAGPATH*, and *ref* will search through the "tags" file in each directory until it finds a tag in the desired class.

If that fails, *ref* will then try to look up an ordinary global tag. This search checks all of the directories listed in *TAGPATH*, too. If the tag being sought doesn't contain any colons, and you haven't given a -x flag, then any static tags in a tags file will be treated as global tags.

If you've given the **-t** flag, then *ref* will simply output the tag line that it found, and then exit. Without **-t**, though, *ref* will search for the tag line. It will try to open the source file, which should be in the same directory as the tags file where the tag was discovered. If the source file doesn't exist, or is unreadable, then *ref* will try to open a file called "refs" in that directory. Either way, *ref* will try to locate the tag, and display whatever it finds.

INTERACTION WITH ELVIS

ref is used by *elvis*' shift-K command. If the cursor is located on a word such as "splat", in the file "foo.c", then *elvis* will invoke *ref* with the command "ref -f foo.c splat".

If *elvis* has been compiled with the -DEXTERNAL_TAGS flag, then *elvis* will use *ref* to scan the tags files. This is slower than the built-in tag searching, but it allows *elvis* to access the more sophisticated tag lookup provided by *ref*. Other than that, external tags should act exactly like internal tags.

OPTIONS

-t Output tag info, instead of the function header.

-f *file* The tag might be a static function in *file*. You can use several -f flags to have *ref* consider static tags from more than one file.

-c *class* The tag might be a member of class *class*. You can use several -c flags to have *ref* consider tags from more than one class.

FILES

tags List of function names and their locations, generated by *ctags*.

refs Function headers extracted from source files (optional).

ENVIRONMENT

TAGPATH List of directories to be searched. The elements in the list are separated by either semicolons (for MS-DOS, Atari TOS, and AmigaDos), or by colons (every other operating system). For each operating system, *ref* has a built-in default which is probably adequate.

NOTES

You might want to generate a "tags" file the directory that contains the source code for standard C library on your system. If licensing restrictions prevent you from making the library source readable by everybody, then you can have *ctags* generate a "refs" file, and make "refs" readable by everybody.

If your system doesn't come with the library source code, then perhaps you can produce something workable from the *lint* libraries.

SEE ALSO

elvis(1), ctags(1)

AUTHOR

Steve Kirkendall
kirkenda@cs.pdx.edu

NAME

reset – reset the terminal

SYNOPSIS

clear

DESCRIPTION

reset calls **tput**(1) with the *clear*, *rmacs*, *rmm*, *rmul*, *rs1*, *rs2*, and *rs3* arguments. This causes **tput** to send appropriate reset strings to the terminal based on information in */etc/termcap* (for the GNU or BSD **tput**) or in the terminfo database (for the **ncurses tput**). This sequence seems to be sufficient to reset the Linux VC's when they start printing "funny-looking" characters. For good measure, **stty**(1) is called with the *sane* argument in an attempt to get cooked mode back.

SEE ALSO

reset(1), **stty**(1), **tput**(1)

AUTHOR

Rik Faith (faith@cs.unc.edu)

REV(1)　　　　　　　　　　　　　　　　　　　　REV(1)

NAME
rev – reverse lines of a file

SYNOPSIS
rev [file]

DESCRIPTION
The rev utility copies the specified files to the standard output, reversing the order of characters in every line. If no files are specified, the standard input is read.

RLOGIN(1)

NAME

rlogin – remote login

SYNOPSIS

rlogin [-8EKLdx] [-e char] [-k realm] [-l username] host

DESCRIPTION

Rlogin starts a terminal session on a remote host host.

Rlogin first attempts to use the Kerberos authorization mechanism, described below. If the remote host does not supporting Kerberos the standard Berkeley authorization mechanism is used. The options are as follows:

-8 The -8 option allows an eight-bit input data path at all times; otherwise parity bits are stripped except when the remote side's stop and start characters are other than ^S/^Q.

-E The -E option stops any character from being recognized as an escape character. When used with the -8 option, this provides a completely transparent connection.

-K The -K option turns off all Kerberos authentication.

-L The -L option allows the rlogin session to be run in "litout" (see tty 4) mode.

-d The -d option turns on socket debugging (see setsockopt 2) on the TCP sockets used for communication with the remote host.

-e The -e option allows user specification of the escape character, which is "~" by default. This specification may be as a literal character, or as an octal value in the form \nnn.

-k The -k option requests rlogin to obtain tickets for the remote host in realm realm instead of the remote host's realm as determined by krb_realmofhost 3 .

-x The -x option turns on DES encryption for all data passed via the rlogin session. This may impact response time and CPU utilization, but provides increased security.

A line of the form "<escape char>." disconnects from the remote host. Similarly, the line "<escape char>^Z" will suspend the rlogin session, and "<escape char><delayed-suspend char>" suspends the send portion of the rlogin, but allows output from the remote system. By default, the tilde ("~") character is the escape character, and normally control-Y ("^Y") is the delayed-suspend character.

All echoing takes place at the remote site, so that (except for delays) the rlogin is transparent. Flow control via ^S/^Q and flushing of input and output on interrupts are handled properly.

KERBEROS AUTHENTICATION

Each user may have a private authorization list in the file in their home directory. Each line in this file should contain a Kerberos principal name of the form principal.instance@realm . If the originating user is authenticated to one of the principals named in access is granted to the account. The principal accountname.@localrealm is granted access if there is no file. Otherwise a login and password will be prompted for on the remote machine as in login 1 . To avoid certain security problems, the file must be owned by the remote user.

If Kerberos authentication fails, a warning message is printed and the standard Berkeley rlogin is used instead.

ENVIRONMENT

The following environment variable is utilized by rlogin :

TERM Determines the user's terminal type.

SEE ALSO

rsh 1 , kerberos 3 , krb_sendauth 3 , krb_realmofhost 3

RLOGIN(1)

HISTORY

The rlogin command appeared in BSD 4.2 .

BUGS

Rlogin will be replaced by telnet 1 in the near future.

More of the environment should be propagated.

RM(1L) FSF RM(1L)

NAME

rm – remove files

SYNOPSIS

rm [–dfirvR] [—directory] [—force] [—interactive] [—recursive] [—help] [—version] [—verbose] name...

DESCRIPTION

This manual page documents the GNU version of **rm**. **rm** removes each specified file. By default, it does not remove directories. If a file is unwritable, the standard input is a tty, and the *–f* or *—force* option is not given, **rm** prompts the user for whether to remove the file. If the response does not begin with 'y' or 'Y', the file is skipped.

GNU **rm**, like every program that uses the getopt function to parse its arguments, lets you use the — option to indicate that all following arguments are non-options. To remove a file called '–f' in the current directory, you could type either

rm — –f

or

rm ./–f

The Unix **rm** program's use of a single '–' for this purpose predates the development of the getopt standard syntax.

OPTIONS

–d, —directory Remove directories with 'unlink' instead of 'rmdir', and don't require a directory to be empty before trying to unlink it. Only works for the super-user. Because unlinking a directory causes any files in the deleted directory to become unreferenced, it is wise to **fsck** the filesystem after doing this.

–f, —force Ignore nonexistent files and never prompt the user.

–i, —interactive Prompt whether to remove each file. If the response does not begin with 'y' or 'Y', the file is skipped.

–r, –R, —recursive Remove the contents of directories recursively.

–v, —verbose Print the name of each file before removing it.

—help Print a usage message on standard output and exit successfully.

—version Print version information on standard output then exit successfully.

NAME

rmdir – remove empty directories

SYNOPSIS

rmdir [–p] [—parents] [—help] [—version] dir...

DESCRIPTION

This manual page documents the GNU version of **rmdir**. **rmdir** removes each given empty directory. If any non-option argument does not refer to an existing empty directory, it is an error.

OPTIONS

–p, —parents Remove any parent directories that are explicitly mentioned in an argument, if they become empty after the argument file is removed.

—help Print a usage message on standard output and exit successfully.

—version Print version information on standard output then exit successfully.

NAME

rmmod – unload loadable modules

SYNOPSIS

rmmod [–r] module ...

DESCRIPTION

Rmmod unloads loadable modules from the kernel.

Rmmod tries to unload a set of modules from the kernel, with the restriction that they are not in use and that they are not referred to by other modules.

If more than one module is named on the command line, the modules will be removed in the given order. This supports unloading of stacked modules.

With the option '-r' a recursive removal of modules will be attempted. This means that if a top module in a stack is named on the command line, all modules that are used by this module will be removed as well, if possible.

SEE ALSO

insmod(1), lsmod(1), ksyms(1), modules(2)

HISTORY

The module support was first concieved by Anonymous (as far as I know...). Linux version by Bas Laarhoven <bas@vimec.nl>, 0.99.14 version by Jon Tombs <jon@gtex02.us.es>, extended by Bjorn Ekwall <bj0rn@blox.se>.

BUGS

Rmmod might have some, but they are well hidden...

RPCGEN(1)

NAME

rpcgen – an RPC protocol compiler

SYNOPSIS

rpcgen infile
rpcgen [–D name[= value]] [–T] [–K secs] infile
rpcgen –c|–h|–l|–m|–t [–o outfile] infile
rpcgen [–I] –s nettype [–o outfile] infile
rpcgen –n netid [–o outfile] infile

DESCRIPTION

rpcgen is a tool that generates C code to implement an RPC protocol. The input to rpcgen is a language similar to C known as RPC Language (Remote Procedure Call Language). rpcgen is normally used as in the first synopsis where it takes an input file and generates up to four output files. If the *infile* is named proto.x, then rpcgen will generate a header file in proto.h, XDR routines in proto_xdr.c, server-side stubs in proto_svc.c, and client-side stubs in proto_clnt.c. With the –T option, it will also generate the RPC dispatch table in proto_tbl.i. With the –Sc option, it will also generate sample code which would illustrate how to use the remote procedures on the client side. This code would be created in proto_client.c. With the –Ss option, it will also generate a sample server code which would illustrate how to write the remote procedures. This code would be created in proto_server.c. The server created can be started both by the port monitors (for example, inetd or listen) or by itself. When it is started by a port monitor, it creates servers only for the transport for which the file descriptor 0 was passed. The name of the transport must be specified by setting up the environmental variable PM_TRANSPORT. When the server generated by rpcgen is executed, it creates server handles for all the transports specified in NETPATH environment variable, or if it is unset, it creates server handles for all the visible transports from /etc/netconfig file. Note: the transports are chosen at run time and not at compile time. When the server is self-started, it backgrounds itself by default. A special define symbol RPC_SVC_FG can be used to run the server process in foreground. The second synopsis provides special features which allow for the creation of more sophisticated RPC servers. These features include support for user provided #defines and RPC dispatch tables. The entries in the RPC dispatch table contain:

> pointers to the service routine corresponding to that procedure,
>
> a pointer to the input and output arguments
>
> the size of these routines A server can use the dispatch table to check authorization and then to execute the service routine; a client library may use it to deal with the details of storage management and XDR data conversion. The other three synopses shown above are used when one does not want to generate all the output files, but only a particular one. Some examples of their usage is described in the EXAMPLE section below. When rpcgen is executed with the –s option, it creates servers for that particular class of transports. When executed with the –n option, it creates a server for the transport specified by *netid*. If *infile* is not specified, rpcgen accepts the standard input. The C preprocessor, cc –E [see cc(1)], is run on the input file before it is actually interpreted by rpcgen. For each type of output file, rpcgen defines a special preprocessor symbol for use by the rpcgen programmer:

RPC_HDR   defined when compiling into header files

RPC_XDR   defined when compiling into XDR routines

RPC_SVC   defined when compiling into server-side stubs

RPC_CLNT defined when compiling into client-side stubs

RPC_TBL   defined when compiling into RPC dispatch tables Any line beginning with '%' is passed directly into the output file, uninterpreted by rpcgen. For every data type referred to in *infile*, rpcgen assumes that there exists a routine with the string xdr_ prepended to the name of the data type. If this routine does not exist in the RPC/XDR library, it must be provided. Providing an undefined

RPCGEN(1)   RPCGEN(1)

data type allows customization of XDR routines. The following options are available:

- −a   Generate all the files including sample code for client and server side.
- −b   This generates code for the SunOS4.1 style of rpc. It is for backward compatibilty. This is the default.
- −5   This generates code for the SysVr4 style of rpc. It is used by the Transport Independent RPC that is in Svr4 systems. By default rpcgen generates code for SunOS4.1 stype of rpc.
- −c   Compile into XDR routines.
- −C   Generate code in ANSI C. This option also generates code that could be compiled with the C++ compiler. This is the default.
- −k   Generate code in K&R C. The default is ANSI C.
- −D*name[=value]*   Define a symbol *name*. Equivalent to the #define directive in the source. If no *value* is given, *value* is defined as 1. This option may be specified more than once.
- −h   Compile into C data-definitions (a header file). −T option can be used in conjunction to produce a header file which supports RPC dispatch tables.
- −I   Generate a service that can be started from inetd. The default is to generate a static service that handles transports selected with −s. Using −I allows starting a service by either method.
- -K *secs*   By default, services created using rpcgen wait 120 seconds after servicing a request before exiting. That interval can be changed using the -K flag. To create a server that exits immediately upon servicing a request, -K 0 can be used. To create a server that never exits, the appropriate argument is -K -1.

  When monitoring for a server, some portmonitors, like listen(1M), *always* spawn a new process in response to a service request. If it is known that a server will be used with such a monitor, the server should exit immediately on completion. For such servers, rpcgen should be used with -K -1.

- −l   Compile into client-side stubs.
- −m   Compile into server-side stubs, but do not generate a main routine. This option is useful for doing callback-routines and for users who need to write their own main routine to do initialization.
- −n *netid*   Compile into server-side stubs for the transport specified by *netid*. There should be an entry for *netid* in the netconfig database. This option may be specified more than once, so as to compile a server that serves multiple transports.
- −N   Use the newstyle of rpcgen. This allows procedures to have multiple arguments. It also uses the style of parameter passing that closely resembles C. So, when passing an argument to a remote procedure you do not have to pass a pointer to the argument but the argument itself. This behaviour is different from the oldstyle of rpcgen generated code. The newstyle is not the default case because of backward compatibility.
- −o *outfile*   Specify the name of the output file. If none is specified, standard output is used (−c, −h, −l, −m, −n, −s, −sc, −ss and −t modes only).
- −s *nettype*   Compile into server-side stubs for all the transports belonging to the class *nettype*. The supported classes are netpath, visible, circuit_n, circuit_v, datagram_n, datagram_v, tcp, and udp [see rpc(3N) for the meanings associated with these classes]. This option may be specified more than once. Note: the transports are chosen at run time and not at compile time.
- −Sc   Generate sample code to show the use of remote procedure and how to bind to the server before calling the client side stubs generated by rpcgen.
- −Ss   Generate skeleton code for the remote procedures on the server side. You would need to fill in the actual code for the remote procedures.

RPCGEN(1)

    –t   Compile into RPC dispatch table.

    –T   Generate the code to support RPC dispatch tables. The options –c, –h, –l, –m, –s and –t are used exclusively to generate a particular type of file, while the options –D and –T are global and can be used with the other options.

NOTES

The RPC Language does not support nesting of structures. As a work-around, structures can be declared at the top-level, and their name used inside other structures in order to achieve the same effect. Name clashes can occur when using program definitions, since the apparent scoping does not really apply. Most of these can be avoided by giving unique names for programs, versions, procedures and types. The server code generated with –n option refers to the transport indicated by *netid* and hence is very site specific.

EXAMPLE

The following example:

    $ rpcgen –T prot.x generates the five files: prot.h, prot_clnt.c, prot_svc.c, prot_xdr.c and prot_tbl.i. The following example sends the C data-definitions (header file) to the standard output.

    $ rpcgen –h prot.x To send the test version of the -DTEST, server side stubs for all the transport belonging to the class datagram_n to standard output, use:

    $ rpcgen –s datagram_n –DTEST prot.x To create the server side stubs for the transport indicated by *netid* tcp, use:

    $ rpcgen –n tcp –o prot_svc.c prot.x

SEE ALSO

cc(1).

RSH(1)

NAME

rsh – remote shell

SYNOPSIS

rsh [-Kdnx] [-k realm] [-l username] host command

DESCRIPTION

Rsh executes command on host.

Rsh copies its standard input to the remote command, the standard output of the remote command to its standard output, and the standard error of the remote command to its standard error. Interrupt, quit and terminate signals are propagated to the remote command; rsh normally terminates when the remote command does. The options are as follows:

-K The -K option turns off all Kerberos authentication.

-d The -d option turns on socket debugging (using setsockopt 2) on the TCP sockets used for communication with the remote host.

-k The -k option causes rsh to obtain tickets for the remote host in realm instead of the remote host's realm as determined by krb_realmofhost 3 .

-l By default, the remote username is the same as the local username. The -l option allows the remote name to be specified. Kerberos authentication is used, and authorization is determined as in rlogin 1 .

-n The -n option redirects input from the special device (see the BUGS section of this manual page).

-x The -x option turns on DES encryption for all data exchange. This may introduce a significant delay in response time.

If no command is specified, you will be logged in on the remote host using rlogin 1 .

Shell metacharacters which are not quoted are interpreted on local machine, while quoted metacharacters are interpreted on the remote machine. For example, the command

rsh otherhost cat remotefile >> localfile

appends the remote file remotefile to the local file localfile , while

rsh otherhost cat remotefile >> other_remotefile

appends remotefile to other_remotefile .

FILES

/etc/hosts

SEE ALSO

rlogin 1 , kerberos 3 , krb_sendauth 3 , krb_realmofhost 3

HISTORY

The rsh command appeared in BSD 4.2 .

BUGS

If you are using csh 1 and put a rsh in the background without redirecting its input away from the terminal, it will block even if no reads are posted by the remote command. If no input is desired you should redirect the input of rsh to using the -n option.

You cannot run an interactive command (like rogue 6 or vi 1) using rsh ; use rlogin 1 instead.

Stop signals stop the local rsh process only; this is arguably wrong, but currently hard to fix for reasons too complicated to explain here.

RSTART(1)

NAME
rstart - a sample implementation of a Remote Start client

SYNOPSIS
rstart [–c *context*] [–g] [–l *username*] [–v] *hostname command args* ...

DESCRIPTION
Rstart is a simple implementation of a Remote Start client as defined in "A Flexible Remote Execution Protocol Based on **rsh**". It uses *rsh* as its underlying remote execution mechanism.

OPTIONS

–c *context* This option specifies the *context* in which the command is to be run. A *context* specifies a general environment the program is to be run in. The details of this environment are host-specific; the intent is that the client need not know how the environment must be configured. If omitted, the context defaults to **X**. This should be suitable for running X programs from the host's "usual" X installation.

–g Interprets *command* as a *generic command*, as discussed in the protocol document. This is intended to allow common applications to be invoked without knowing what they are called on the remote system. Currently, the only generic commands defined are **Terminal**, **LoadMonitor**, **ListContexts**, and **ListGenericCommands**.

–l *username* This option is passed to the underlying *rsh*; it requests that the command be run as the specified user.

–v This option requests that *rstart* be verbose in its operation. Without this option, *rstart* discards output from the remote's *rstart* helper, and directs the *rstart* helper to detach the program from the *rsh* connection used to start it. With this option, responses from the helper are displayed and the resulting program is not detached from the connection.

NOTES
This is a trivial implementation. Far more sophisticated implementations are possible and should be developed.

Error handling is nonexistant. Without **–v**, error reports from the remote are discarded silently. With **–v**, error reports are displayed.

The $DISPLAY environment variable is passed. If it starts with a colon, the local hostname is prepended. The local domain name should be appended to unqualified host names, but isn't.

The $SESSION_MANAGER environment variable should be passed, but isn't.

X11 authority information is passed for the current display.

ICE authority information should be passed, but isn't. It isn't completely clear how *rstart* should select what ICE authority information to pass.

Even without **–v**, the sample *rstart* helper will leave a shell waiting for the program to complete. This causes no real harm and consumes relatively few resources, but if it is undesirable it can be avoided by explicitly specifying the "exec" command to the shell, e.g. 0 rstart somehost exec xterm

This is obviously dependent on the command interpreter being used on the remote system; the example given will work for the Bourne and C shells.

SEE ALSO
rstartd(1), rsh(1), A Flexible Remote Execution Protocol Based on **rsh**

AUTHOR

Jordan Brown, Quarterdeck Office Systems

RSTARTD(1)

NAME

rstartd - a sample implementation of a Remote Start rsh helper

SYNOPSIS

rstartd

rstartd.real [–c *configfilename*]

DESCRIPTION

Rstartd is an implementation of a Remote Start "helper" as defined in "A Flexible Remote Execution Protocol Based on **rsh**".

This document describes the peculiarities of *rstartd* and how it is configured.

OPTIONS

–c *configfilename* This option specifies the "global" configuration file that *rstartd* is to read. Normally, *rstartd* is a shell script that invokes *rstartd.real* with the **-c** switch, allowing local configuration of the location of the configuration file. If *rstartd.real* is started without the -c option, it reads <XRoot>/lib/X11/rstart/config, where <XRoot> refers to the root of the X11 install tree.

INSTALLATION

It is critical to successful interoperation of the Remote Start protocol that *rstartd* be installed in a directory which is in the "default" search path, so that default rsh requests and the ilk will be able to find it.

CONFIGURATION AND OPERATION

Rstartd is by design highly configurable. One would like things like configuration file locations to be fixed, so that users and administrators can find them without searching, but reality is that no two vendors will agree on where things should go, and nobody thinks the original location is "right". Thus, *rstartd* allows one to relocate **all** of its files and directories.

Rstartd has a hierarchy of configuration files which are executed in order when a request is made. They are: 0 global config per-user ("local") config global per-context config per-user ("local") per-context config config from request

As you might guess from the presence of "config from request", all of the config files are in the format of an *rstart* request. *Rstartd* defines a few additional keywords with the INTERNAL- prefix for specifying its configuration.

Rstartd starts by reading and executing the global config file. This file will normally specify the locations of the other configuration files and any systemwide defaults.

Rstartd will then read the user's local config file, default name $HOME/.rstart.

Rstartd will then start interpreting the request.

Presumably one of the first lines in the request will be a CONTEXT line. The context name is converted to lower case.

Rstartd will read the global config file for that context, default name <XRoot>/lib/X11/rstart/contexts/<name>, if any.

It will then read the user's config file for that context, default name $HOME/.rstart.contexts/<name>, if any.

(If neither of these exists, *rstartd* aborts with a Failure message.)

Rstartd will finish interpreting the request, and execute the program specified.

This allows the system administrator and the user a large degree of control over the operation of *rstartd*. The administrator has final say, because the global config file doesn't need to specify a per-user config file. If it does, however, the user can override anything from the global file, and can even completely replace the global context config files.

The config files have a somewhat more flexible format than requests do; they are allowed to contain blank lines and lines beginning with "#" are comments and ignored. (#s in the middle of lines are data, not comment markers.)

Any commands run are provided a few useful pieces of information in environment variables. The exact names are configurable, but the supplied defaults are:

$RSTART_CONTEXT the name of the context
$RSTART_GLOBAL_CONTEXTS the global contexts directory
$RSTART_LOCAL_CONTEXTS the local contexts directory
$RSTART_GLOBAL_COMMANDS the global generic commands directory
$RSTART_LOCAL_COMMANDS the local generic commands directory

$RSTART_{GLOBAL,LOCAL}_CONTEXTS should contain one special file, @List, which contains a list of the contexts in that directory in the format specified for ListContexts. The supplied version of ListContexts will cat both the global and local copies of @List.

Generic commands are searched for in several places: (defaults)

per-user per-context directory ($HOME/.rstart.commands/<context>)
global per-context directory (<XRoot>/lib/X11/rstart/commands/<context>)

per-user all-contexts directory ($HOME/.rstart.commands)
global all-contexts directory (<XRoot>/lib/X11/rstart/commands)

(Yes, this means you can't have an all-contexts generic command with the same name as a context. It didn't seem like a big deal.)

Each of these directories should have a file called @List that gives the names and descriptions of the commands in that directory in the format specified for ListGenericCommands.

CONFIGURATION KEYWORDS

There are several "special" *rstart* keywords defined for *rstartd* configuration. Unless otherwise specified, there are no defaults; related features are disabled in this case.

      INTERNAL-REGISTRIES name ...   Gives a space-separated list of "MISC" registries that this system understands. (Registries other than this are accepted but generate a Warning.)

      INTERNAL-LOCAL-DEFAULT relative_filename   Gives the name ($HOME relative) of the per-user config file.

      INTERNAL-GLOBAL-CONTEXTS absolute_directory_name   Gives the name of the system-wide contexts directory.

      INTERNAL-LOCAL-CONTEXTS relative_directory_name   Gives the name ($HOME relative) of the per-user contexts directory.

      INTERNAL-GLOBAL-COMMANDS absolute_directory_name   Gives the name of the system-wide generic commands directory.

      INTERNAL-LOCAL-COMMANDS relative_directory_name   Gives the name ($HOME relative) of the per-user generic commands directory.

      INTERNAL-VARIABLE-PREFIX prefix   Gives the prefix for the configuration environment variables *rstartd* passes to its kids.

      INTERNAL-AUTH-PROGRAM authscheme program argv[0] argv[1] ...   Specifies the program to run to set up authentication for the specified authentication scheme. "program argv[0] ..." gives the program to run and its arguments, in the same form as the EXEC keyword.

RSTARTD(1)   RSTARTD(1)

INTERNAL-AUTH-INPUT authscheme   Specifies the data to be given to the authorization program as its standard input. Each argument is passed as a single line. $n, where n is a number, is replaced by the n'th argument to the "AUTH authscheme arg1 arg2 ..." line.

INTERNAL-PRINT arbitrary text   Prints its arguments as a Debug message. Mostly for *rstartd* debugging, but could be used to debug config files.

NOTES

When using the C shell, or any other shell which runs a script every time the shell is started, the script may get run several times. In the worst case, the script may get run **three** times: By rsh, to run *rstartd*. By *rstartd*, to run the specified command. By the command, e.g. *xterm*.

rstartd currently limits lines, both from config files and requests, to BUFSIZ bytes.

DETACH is implemented by redirecting file descriptors 0,1, and 2 to /dev/null and forking before executing the program.

CMD is implemented by invoking $SHELL (default /bin/sh) with "-c" and the specified command as arguments.

POSIX-UMASK is implemented in the obvious way.

The authorization programs are run in the same context as the target program - same environment variables, path, etc. Long term this might be a problem.

In the X context, GENERIC-CMD Terminal runs xterm. In the OpenWindows context, GENERIC-CMD Terminal runs cmdtool.

In the X context, GENERIC-CMD LoadMonitor runs xload. In the OpenWindows context, GENERIC-CMD LoadMonitor runs perfmeter.

GENERIC-CMD ListContexts lists the contents of @List in both the system-wide and per-user contexts directories. It is available in all contexts.

GENERIC-CMD ListGenericCommands lists the contents of @List in the system-wide and per-user commands directories, including the per-context subdirectories for the current context. It is available in all contexts.

CONTEXT None is not implemented.

CONTEXT Default is really dull.

For installation ease, the "contexts" directory in the distribution contains a file "@Aliases" which lists a context name and aliases for that context. This file is used to make symlinks in the contexts and commands directories.

All **MISC** values are passed unmodified as environment variables.

One can mistreat *rstartd* in any number of ways, resulting in anything from stupid behavior to core dumps. Other than by explicitly running programs I don't think it can write or delete any files, but there's no guarantee of that. The important thing is that (a) it probably won't do anything REALLY stupid and (b) it runs with the user's permissions, so it can't do anything catastrophic.

@List files need not be complete; contexts or commands which are dull or which need not or should not be advertised need not be listed. In particular, per-user @List files should not list things which are in the system-wide @List files. In the future, perhaps ListContexts and ListGenericCommands will automatically suppress lines from the system-wide files when there are per-user replacements for those lines.

Error handling is OK to weak. In particular, no attempt is made to properly report errors on the exec itself. (Perversely, exec errors could be reliably reported when detaching, but not when passing the stdin/out socket to the app.)

RSTARTD(1)   RSTARTD(1)

If compiled with -DODT1_DISPLAY_HACK, *rstartd* will work around a bug in SCO ODT version 1. (1.1?) (The bug is that the X clients are all compiled with a bad library that doesn't know how to look host names up using DNS. The fix is to look up a host name in $DISPLAY and substitute an IP address.) This is a trivial example of an incompatibility that *rstart* can hide.

SEE ALSO

rstart(1), rsh(1), A Flexible Remote Execution Protocol Based on **rsh**

AUTHOR

Jordan Brown, Quarterdeck Office Systems

RUP(1)

NAME

rup – remote status display

SYNOPSIS

rup [-dhlt] [host ...]

DESCRIPTION

rup displays a summary of the current system status of a particular host or all hosts on the local network. The output shows the current time of day, how long the system has been up, and the load averages. The load average numbers give the number of jobs in the run queue averaged over 1, 5 and 15 minutes.

The following options are available:

-d For each host, report what it's local time is. This is useful for checking time syncronization on a network.

-h Sort the display alphabetically by host name.

-l Sort the display by load average.

-t Sort the display by up time.

The rpc.rstatd 8 daemon must be running on the remote host for this command to work. rup uses an RPC protocol defined in /usr/include/rpcsvc/rstat.x.

EXAMPLE

example% rup otherhost
otherhost up 6 days, 16:45, load average: 0.20, 0.23, 0.18
example%

DIAGNOSTICS

rup: RPC: Program not registered The rpc.rstatd 8 daemon has not been started on the remote host.

rup: RPC: Timed out A communication error occurred. Either the network is excessively congested, or the rpc.rstatd 8 daemon has terminated on the remote host.

rup: RPC: Port mapper failure - RPC: Timed out The remote host is not running the portmapper (see portmap 8), and cannot accomodate any RPC-based services. The host may be down.

SEE ALSO

ruptime 1 , portmap 8 , rpc.rstatd 8

HISTORY

The rup command appeared in SunOS .

RUSERS(1)

NAME

rusers – who is logged in to machines on local network

SYNOPSIS

rusers [-al] [host ...]

DESCRIPTION

The rusers command produces output similar to who, but for the list of hosts or all machines on the local network. For each host responding to the rusers query, the hostname with the names of the users currently logged on is printed on each line. The rusers command will wait for one minute to catch late responders.

The following options are available:

-a Print all machines responding even if no one is currently logged in.

-l Print a long format listing. This includes the user name, host name, tty that the user is logged in to, the date and time the user logged in, the amount of time since the user typed on the keyboard, and the remote host they logged in from (if applicable).

DIAGNOSTICS

rusers: RPC: Program not registered The rpc.rusersd 8 daemon has not been started on the remote host.

rusers: RPC: Timed out A communication error occurred. Either the network is excessively congested, or the rpc.rusersd 8 daemon has terminated on the remote host.

rusers: RPC: Port mapper failure - RPC: Timed out The remote host is not running the portmapper (see portmap 8), and cannot accomodate any RPC-based services. The host may be down.

SEE ALSO

rwho 1 users 1 , who 1 , portmap 8 , rpc.rusersd 8

HISTORY

The rusers command appeared in SunOS .

BUGS

The sorting options are not implemented.

RWALL(1)

NAME
rwall – send a message to users logged on a host

SYNOPSIS
rwall host

DESCRIPTION
The rwall command sends a message to the users logged into the specified host. The message to be sent can be typed in and terminated with EOF or it can be in a file .

DIAGNOSTICS
> rwall: RPC: Program not registered The rpc.rwalld 8 daemon has not been started on the remote host.
>
> rwall: RPC: Timed out A communication error occurred. Either the network is excessively congested, or the rpc.rwalld 8 daemon has terminated on the remote host.
>
> rwall: RPC: Port mapper failure - RPC: Timed out The remote host is not running the portmapper (see portmap 8), and cannot accomodate any RPC-based services. The host may be down.

SEE ALSO
wall 1 , portmap 8 , rpc.rwalld 8

HISTORY
The rwall command appeared in SunOS .

RWHO(1)

NAME

rwho – who is logged in on local machines

SYNOPSIS

rwho -a

DESCRIPTION

The rwho command produces output similar to who, but for all machines on the local network. If no report has been received from a machine for 11 minutes then rwho assumes the machine is down, and does not report users last known to be logged into that machine.

If a user hasn't typed to the system for a minute or more, then rwho reports this idle time. If a user hasn't typed to the system for an hour or more, then the user will be omitted from the output of rwho unless the -a flag is given.

FILES

Pa /var/rwho/whod.* information about other machines

SEE ALSO

finger 1, rup 1, ruptime 1, rusers 1, who 1, rwhod 8

HISTORY

The rwho command appeared in BSD 4.3.

BUGS

This is unwieldy when the number of machines on the local net is large.

SCRIPT(1)

NAME

script – make typescript of terminal session

SYNOPSIS

script [-a] [file]

DESCRIPTION

Script makes a typescript of everything printed on your terminal. It is useful for students who need a hardcopy record of an interactive session as proof of an assignment, as the typescript file can be printed out later with lpr(1).

If the argument file is given, script saves all dialogue in file . If no file name is given, the typescript is saved in the file typescript .

Option:

- -a Append the output to file or typescript , retaining the prior contents.

The script ends when the forked shell exits (a control-D to exit the Bourne shell, sh(1), and exit, logout or control-d (if ignoreeof is not set) for the C-shell, csh(1)) .

Certain interactive commands, such as vi(1), create garbage in the typescript file. Script works best with commands that do not manipulate the screen, the results are meant to emulate a hardcopy terminal.

ENVIRONMENT

The following environment variable is utilized by script :

- SHELL If the variable SHELL exists, the shell forked by script will be that shell. If SHELL is not set, the Bourne shell is assumed. (Most shells set this variable automatically).

SEE ALSO

csh(1) (for the history mechanism).

HISTORY

The script command appeared in BSD 3.0 .

BUGS

Script places everything in the log file, including linefeeds and backspaces. This is not what the naive user expects.

SED(1)

NAME

sed – stream-oriented editor

SYNOPSIS

sed [–hnV] [–e script] [–f script-file] [––help] [––quiet] [––silent] [––version] [––expression=script] [––file=script-file] [file ...]

DESCRIPTION

sed reads the specified files or the standard input if no files are specified, makes editing changes according to a list of commands, and writes the results to the standard output.

OPTIONS

–h, ––help   Print a usage message on standard output and exit successfully.

–n, ––quiet, ––silent   Suppress the default output. **sed** only displays lines explicitly specified for output with the *p* command or the *p* flag of the *s* command. The default behavior is to echo each line of input, after edits, to the standard output.

–V, ––version   Print the version number on the standard output and exit successfully.

–e script, ––expression=script   Append one or more commands specified in the string *script* to the list of commands. If there is just one **–e** option and no **–f** options, the **–e** flag may be omitted.

–f script-file, ––file=script-file   Append the editing commands from *script-file* to the list of commands.

Multiple **–e** and **–f** commands may be specified. Scripts are added to the list of commands to execute in the order specified, regardless of their origin.

USAGE

Operation

sed operates as follows:

Each line of input, not including its terminating newline character, is successively copied into a **pattern space** (a temporary buffer).

All editing commands whose **addresses** match that pattern space are sequentially applied to the pattern space.

When reaching the end of the command list, the pattern space is written to the standard output (except under **-n**) with an appended newline.

The pattern space is cleared and the process is repeated for each line in the input.

With **sed**, original input files remain unchanged since editing commands only modify a copy of the input.

Some **sed** commands use a **hold space** to save all or part of the pattern space for later retrieval.

Command Syntax

A **sed** script consists of commands with the general form:

    [*address*[*,address*]][!]*command*[*arguments*]

Typically, there is only one command per line, but commands may also be concatenated on a single line by semicolons.

Whitespace characters may be inserted before the first address and the command portions of the script command.

Addresses

A **sed** command, as indicated above, can specify zero, one, or two addresses. An address can be:

> A **line number**, represented in decimal. The internal line number count maintained by **sed** is cumulative across input files and is not reset for each input file.
>
> A **pattern** which is a regular expression, represented by \cpatternc, where c is any character except backslash ('\') or newline. In the address '\xabc\xdefx', the second 'x' stands for itself, so the regular expression is 'abcxdef'. However, the preferred (and equivalent) method to construct a regular expression is to enclose the pattern in slashes — '/pattern/'. Additionally, \n can be used to match any newline in the pattern space, except for the final newline character.
>
> A $ character which addresses the last line of input.
>
> GNU **sed** also implements a new type of address. The address has form $n\tilde{\ }m$, which matches any line where the line number modulo m is equal to n modulo m. If m is 0 or missing, then 1 is used in its place. This feature is not specified by POSIX.

The following rules apply to addressed commands:

> A command line with **no address** selects each input line.
>
> A command line with **one address** selects any line matching the address. Several commands accept only one address: =, a, i, r, and q.
>
> A command line with **two comma-separated addresses** selects the first matching line and all following lines up to and including the line matching the second address. If the second address starts before or is the same line as the first address, then only the first line is selected.
>
> An **address followed by '!'** selects all lines that do not match the address.

Regular Expressions

Regular expressions are patterns used in selecting text. For example, the **sed** command

/*string*/p

prints all lines containing *string*.

In addition to a specifying string literals, regular expressions can represent classes of strings. Strings thus represented are said to be matched by the corresponding regular expression. If it is possible for a regular expression to match several strings in a line, then the left-most longest match is the one selected.

The following symbols are used in constructing **search** patterns:

> The null regular expression is equivalent to the last regular expression used.
>
> *c*   Any character *c* not listed below, including '{', '}', '(', ')', '<', '>', '|', and '+' matches itself.
>
> \c   Any backslash-escaped character *c*, except for '{', '}', '(', ')', '<', '>', '|', and '+' matches itself.
>
> '-1n'.   Matches any single character except newline.
>
> [*char-class*]   Matches any single character, other than newline, in *char-class*. To include a ']' in *char-class*, it must be the first character. A range of characters may be specified by separating the end characters of the range with a '-', e.g., 'a-z' specifies the lower case characters. The following literal expressions can also be used in *char-class* to specify sets of characters:
>
>> [:alnum:]   [:cntrl:]   [:lower:]   [:space:]
>> [:alpha:]   [:digit:]   [:print:]   [:upper:]
>> [:blank:]   [:graph:]   [:punct:]   [:xdigit:]
>
> If '-' appears as the first or last character of *char-class*, then it matches itself. All other characters in *char-class* match themselves.

[^char-class] Matches any single character, other than newline, not in char-class. char-class is defined as above.

^ If '^' is the first character of a regular expression, then it anchors the regular expression to the beginning of a line. Otherwise, it matches itself.

$ If '$' is the last character of a regular expression, it anchors the regular expression to the end of a line. Otherwise, it matches itself.

\<
\> Anchors the single character regular expression or subexpression immediately following it to the beginning (\<) or ending (\>) of a *word*, i.e., in ASCII, a maximal string of alphanumeric characters, including the underscore (_).

\(re\) Defines a (possibly null) subexpression *re*. Subexpressions may be nested. A subsequent backreference of the form '\n', where *n* is a number in the range [1,9], expands to the text matched by the *n*th subexpression. For example, the regular expression '\(a.c\)\1' matches the string 'abcabc', but not 'abcadc'. Subexpressions are ordered relative to their left delimiter.

* Matches the single character regular expression or subexpression immediately preceding it zero or more times. If '*' is the first character of a regular expression or subexpression, then it matches itself. The '*' operator sometimes yields unexpected results. For example, the regular expression 'b*' matches the beginning of the string 'abbb' (as opposed to the substring 'bbb'), since a null match is the only left-most match.

\+ Matches the single character regular expression or subexpression immediately preceding it one or more times.

\| Match the regular expression or subexpression specified before or after it.

\{n,m\} or \{n,\} or \{n\} Matches the single character regular expression or subexpression immediately preceding it at least *n* and at most *m* times. If *m* is omitted, then it matches at least *n* times. If the comma is also omitted, then it matches exactly *n* times.

(\group\) Match the enclosed *group* of regular expressions.

The following characters only have special meaning when used in **replacement** patterns:

\ Escape the following character.

\n Matches the *n*th pattern previously saved by '\(' and '\)', where *n* is a number from 0 to 9. Previously saved patterns are counted from the left-most position on the line.

& Prints the entire search pattern when used in a replacement string.

Comments

If the first nonwhite character in a line is a **#** (pound sign), **sed** treats that line as a comment, and ignores it. If, however, the first such line is of the form:

#n

sed runs as if the **–n** flag were specified.

Grouping Commands

Braces ('{', '}') can be used to nest one address within another or to apply multiple commands to the same address. [*address*][,*address*]{
command 1 command 2 ...
}

The opening '{' must end a line and the closing '}' must be on a line by itself.

Commands

The maximum number of permissible addresses for each command is indicated in parentheses in the list below.

An argument denoted *text* consists of one or more lines of text. If *text* is longer than one line in length, then any newline characters must be hidden by preceding them with a backslash ('\').

An argument denoted *read-filename* or *write-filename* must terminate the command line and must be preceded by exactly one space. Each *write-filename* is created before processing begins.

    (0)   An empty command is ignored.

    (0) *#comment*   The line is a comment and is ignored by **sed**. If, however, the first such line in a script is of the form '#n', then **sed** behaves as if the **–n** flag had been specified.

    (0) **:** *label*   Affix *label* to a line in the script for a transfer of control by *b* or *t* commands.

    (1) **=**   Write the current line number on the standard output as a line.

    (1) **a**\

    text   Append *text* following each line matched by the address on the standard output before reading the next input line.

    (2) **b** *label*   Unconditionally transfer control to the ':' command bearing the *label*. If no *label* is specified, then branch to the end of the script; no more commands are executed on the current pattern space.

    (2) **c**\

    text   Change the pattern space by replacing the selected pattern with *text*. When multiple lines are specified, all lines in the pattern space are replaced with a single copy of *text*. The end result is that the pattern space is deleted and no further editing commands can be applied to it.

    (2) **d**   Delete the pattern space, preventing the line from being passed to the standard output, and start the next cycle.

    (2) **D**   Delete the initial segment of the pattern space through the first newline and start the next cycle.

    (2) **g**   Replace the contents of the pattern space by the contents of the hold space.

    (2) **G**   Append a newline character followed by the contents of the hold space to the pattern space.

    (2) **h**   Replace the contents of the hold space by the contents of the pattern space.

    (2) **H**   Append a newline character followed by the contents of the pattern space to the hold space.

    (1) **i**\

    text   Insert *text* by writing it to the standard output.

    (2) **l**   Write the pattern space to standard output in a visually unambiguous form. Non-printing characters are displayed as either 3-digit octal values, preceded by a '\', or as one of the following character constant escape sequences:

        \\ backslash
        \a alert
        \b backspace
        \f form-feed
        \n newline
        \r carriage-return
        \t tab
        \v vertical tab

Long lines are folded, with the point of folding indicated by a backslash ('\') and a newline character. The end of every line is marked with a '$'.

(2) **n** Copy the pattern space to the standard output. Replace the pattern space with the next line of input.

(2) **N** Append the next line of input to the pattern space with an embedded newline. (The current line number changes.)

(2) **p** Print the pattern space to the standard output.

(2) **P** Copy the initial segment of the pattern space through the first newline to the standard output.

(1) **q** Quit by transferring control to the end of the script and do not start a new cycle. The pattern space is still written to the standard output.

(2) **r** *read-filename*   Read the contents of *read-filename*. Place them on the output before reading the next input line.

(2) **s**/*regular*expression/replacement/flags   Substitute the *replacement* string for instances of the *regular expression* in the pattern space. Any character may be used instead of '/'. For a fuller description, see the above section on replacement patterns. *flags* is zero or more of:

n   Substitute for just the *n*th occurrence of the *regular expression*.

g   Globally substitute for all non-overlapping instances of the *regular expression* rather than just the first one.

p   Print the pattern space if a replacement was made.

w *write-filename*   Append the pattern space to *write-filename* if a replacement was made.

(2) **t** *label*   Branch to the ':' command bearing the *label* if any substitutions have been made since the most recent reading of an input line or execution of a **t**. If *label* is empty, branch to the end of the script.

(2) **w** *write-filename*   Append the pattern space to *write-filename*.

(2) **x**   Exchange the contents of the pattern and hold spaces.

(2) **y**/*string1*/*string2*/   Replace all occurrences of characters in *string1* with the corresponding character in *string2*. The lengths of *string1* and *string2* must be equal. Any character other than '' or newline can be used instead of slash to delimit the strings. Within *string1* and *string2*, the delimiter itself can be used as a literal character if it is preceded by a backslash.

DIAGNOSTICS

Command only uses one address	A command that takes one address had two addresses specified.
Command doesn't take any addresses	A command that takes no addresses had an address specified.
Extra characters after command	A command had extra text after the end.
Unexpected End-of-file	The end of a script was reached before it should have been. This usually occurs when a command is started, but not finished.
No previous regular expression	A meta-character calling for a previous regular expression before any regular expressions were used.
Missing command	An address was not followed by a command.
Unknown command	A command was not one of the ones recognized by **sed**.

Unexpected ','		A command had a spurious comma after an address.
Multiple '!'s		More than one '!' (exclamation point) was used in a command.
Unexpected '}'		A '}' character was given in a command without a preceding '{'.
Unexpected '{'		A '{' character was given in a command without a following '}'.
} doesn't want any addresses		'}' should be alone on a line.
: doesn't want any addresses		The ':' command should not be preceded by an address.
Unterminated 's' command		The replacement field of the 's' command should be completed with a '/' character.
multiple 'p' options to 's' command		The 'p' option was given more than once in an 's' command.
multiple 'g' options to 's' command		The 'g' option was given more than once in an 's' command.
multiple number options to 's' command		More than one number option was given to an 's' command.
Unknown option to 's'		An unknown option was used for the 's' command. Maybe you shouldn't do that.
strings for y command are different lengths		There should be a one-to-one mapping between strings for the 'y' command.
missing ' ' before filename		There was no space between a 'r', 'w', or 's///w' command, and the filename specified for that command.
Hopelessly evil compiled in limit on number of open files.		**re-compile sed**. An attempt was made to open too many files, no matter how you look at it.

SEE ALSO

awk(1), **ed**(1), **grep**(1), **perl**(1), **regex**(3)

HISTORY

A **sed** command appeared in Version 7 AT&T UNIX.

STANDARDS

GNU **sed** is expected to be a superset of the IEEE Std1003.2 (POSIX) specification.

CAVEATS

GNU **sed** uses the POSIX basic regular expression syntax. According to the standard, the meaning of some escape sequences is undefined in this syntax; notably '\|' and '\+'.

As in all GNU programs that use POSIX basic regular expressions, **sed** interprets these escape sequences as meta-characters. So, 'x\+' matches one or more occurrences of 'x'. 'abc\|def' matches either 'abc' or 'def'.

This syntax may cause problems when running scripts written for other versions of **sed**. Some **sed** programs have been written with the assumption that '\|' and '\+' match the literal characters '|' and '+'. Such scripts must be modified by removing the spurious backslashes if they are to be used with GNU **sed**.

BUGS

It has long been noted that GNU **sed** is much slower than other implementations. The current bottleneck is the way **sed** reads and writes data files. It should read large blocks at a

SED(1)

time (or even map files, where that is supported). When possible, it should avoid copying it's input from one place in memory to another. Patches to make it do those things are welcome!

SETTERM(1)   Linux Programmer's Manual   SETTERM(1)

NAME

setterm – set terminal attributes

SYNOPSIS

setterm [–term terminal_name]
setterm [–reset]
setterm [–initialize]
setterm [–cursor [on|off]]
setterm [–keyboard pc|olivetti|dutch|extended]
setterm [–repeat [on|off]]
setterm [–appcursorkeys [on|off]]
setterm [–linewrap [on|off]]
setterm [–snow [on|off]]
setterm [–softscroll [on|off]]
setterm [–defaults]
setterm [–foreground black|red|green|yellow|blue|magenta|cyan|white|default]
setterm [–background black|red|green|yellow|blue|magenta|cyan|white|default]
setterm [–ulcolor black|grey|red|green|yellow|blue|magenta|cyan|white]
setterm [–ulcolor bright red|green|yellow|blue|magenta|cyan|white]
setterm [–hbcolor black|grey|red|green|yellow|blue|magenta|cyan|white]
setterm [–hbcolor bright red|green|yellow|blue|magenta|cyan|white]
setterm [–inversescreen [on|off]]
setterm [–bold [on|off]]
setterm [–half-bright [on|off]]
setterm [–blink [on|off]]
setterm [–reverse [on|off]]
setterm [–underline [on|off]]
setterm [–store]
setterm [–clear [all|rest]]
setterm [–tabs [tab1 tab2 tab3 ...]] where (tabn = 1-160)
setterm [–clrtabs [tab1 tab2 tab3 ...] where (tabn = 1-160)
setterm [–regtabs [1-160]]
setterm [–blank [0-60]]
setterm [–dump [1-NR_CONS]]
setterm [–append [1-NR_CONS]]
setterm [–file dumpfilename]
setterm [–standout [attr]]

DESCRIPTION

setterm writes to standard output a character string that will invoke the specified terminal capabilities. Where possibile */etc/termcap* is consulted to find the string to use. Some options however do not correspond to a **termcap**(5) capability. In this case, if the terminal type is "minix-vc", or "minix-vcam" the string that invokes the specified capabilities on the PC Minix virtual console driver is output. Options that are not implemented by the terminal are ignored.

OPTIONS

Most options are self explanatory. The less obvious options are as follows:

    –term   can be used to override the TERM environment variable.

    –reset   displays the terminal reset string, which typically resets the terminal to its power on state.

    –initialize   displays the terminal initialization string, which typically sets the terminal's rendering options, and other attributes to the default values.

    –default   sets the terminal's rendering options to the default values.

    –store   stores the terminal's current rendering options as the default values.

SEE ALSO

tput(1), **stty**(1), **termcap**(5), **tty**(4)

BUGS

Differences between the Minux and Linux versions are not documented.

AUTHORS

Gordon Irlam (gordoni@cs.ua.oz.au)
Adaption to Linux by Peter MacDonald
Enhancements by Mika Liljeberg (liljeber@cs.Helsinki.FI)

SHOWRGB(1)

NAME

showrgb – uncompile an rgb color-name database

SYNOPSIS

showrgb [*database*]

DESCRIPTION

The *showrgb* program reads an rgb color-name database compiled for use with the dbm database routines and converts it back to source form, printing the result to standard output. The default database is the one that X was built with, and may be overridden on the command line. Specify the database name without the *.pag* or *.dir* suffix.

FILES

    <XRoot>/lib/X11/rgb   default database.

SIZE(1) GNU Development Tools

NAME

size – list section sizes and total size.

SYNOPSIS

size   [–A | –B | —format=*compatibility*] [—help] [–d | –o | –x | —radix=*number*] [—target=*bfdname*] [–V | —version] *objfile* ...

DESCRIPTION

The GNU **size** utility lists the section sizes—and the total size—for each of the object files *objfile* in its argument list. By default, one line of output is generated for each object file or each module in an archive.

OPTIONS

–A

–B

—format *compatibility*   Using one of these options, you can choose whether the output from GNU **size** resembles output from System V **size** (using ' –A ', or ' —**format=sysv** '), or Berkeley **size** (using ' –B ', or ' —**format=berkeley** '). The default is the one-line format similar to Berkeley's.

—help   Show a summary of acceptable arguments and options.

–d

–o

–x

—radix *number*   Using one of these options, you can control whether the size of each section is given in decimal (' –d ', or ' —**radix** 10 '); octal (' –o ', or ' —**radix** 8 '); or hexadecimal (' –x ', or ' —**radix** 16 '). In ' —**radix** *number*

', only the three values (8, 10, 16) are supported. The total size is always given in two radices; decimal and hexadecimal for ' –d ' or ' –x ' output, or octal and hexadecimal if you're using ' –o '.

—target *bfdname*   You can specify a particular object-code format for *objfile* as *bfdname* . This may not be necessary; *size* can automatically recognize many formats. See **objdump(1)** for information on listing available formats.

–V

—version   Display version number information on **size** itself.

SEE ALSO

' **binutils** ' entry in **info**; *The*GNU*Binary*Utilities, Roland H. Pesch (October 1991); **ar(1), objdump(1)**.

COPYING

Copyright (c) 1991 Free Software Foundation, Inc.

Permission is granted to make and distribute verbatim copies of this manual provided the copyright notice and this permission notice are preserved on all copies.

Permission is granted to copy and distribute modified versions of this manual under the conditions for verbatim copying, provided that the entire resulting derived work is distributed under the terms of a permission notice identical to this one.

Permission is granted to copy and distribute translations of this manual into another language, under the above conditions for modified versions, except that this permission notice may be included in translations approved by the Free Software Foundation instead of in the original English.

NAME

sort – sort lines of text files

SYNOPSIS

sort [–cmus] [–t separator] [–o output-file] [–T tempdir] [–bdfiMnr] [+POS1 [–POS2]] [–k POS1[,POS2]] [file...]
sort {—-help,—-version}

DESCRIPTION

This manual page documents the GNU version of **sort**. **sort** sorts, merges, or compares all the lines from the given files, or the standard input if no files are given. A file name of '-' means standard input. By default, **sort** writes the results to the standard output.

sort has three modes of operation: sort (the default), merge, and check for sortedness. The following options change the operation mode:

    –c   Check whether the given files are already sorted: if they are not all sorted, print an error message and exit with a status of 1.

    –m   Merge the given files by sorting them as a group. Each input file should already be individually sorted. It always works to sort instead of merge; merging is provided because it is faster, in the case where it works.

A pair of lines is compared as follows: if any key fields have been specified, **sort** compares each pair of fields, in the order specified on the command line, according to the associated ordering options, until a difference is found or no fields are left.

If any of the global options *Mbdfinr* are given but no key fields are specified, **sort** compares the entire lines according to the global options.

Finally, as a last resort when all keys compare equal (or if no ordering options were specified at all), **sort** compares the lines byte by byte in machine collating sequence. The last resort comparison honors the *-r* global option. The *–s* (stable) option disables this last-resort comparison so that lines in which all fields compare equal are left in their original relative order. If no fields or global options are specified, *–s* has no effect.

GNU **sort** has no limits on input line length or restrictions on bytes allowed within lines. In addition, if the final byte of an input file is not a newline, GNU **sort** silently supplies one.

If the environment variable **TMPDIR** is set, **sort** uses it as the directory in which to put temporary files instead of the default, /tmp. The *–T tempdir* option is another way to select the directory for temporary files; it overrides the environment variable.

The following options affect the ordering of output lines. They may be specified globally or as part of a specific key field. If no key fields are specified, global options apply to comparison of entire lines; otherwise the global options are inherited by key fields that do not specify any special options of their own.

    –b   Ignore leading blanks when finding sort keys in each line.

    –d   Sort in 'phone directory' order: ignore all characters except letters, digits and blanks when sorting.

    –f   Fold lower case characters into the equivalent upper case characters when sorting so that, for example, 'b' is sorted the same way 'B' is.

    –i   Ignore characters outside the ASCII range 040-0176 octal (inclusive) when sorting.

    –M   An initial string, consisting of any amount of white space, followed by three letters abbreviating a month name, is folded to UPPER case and compared in the order 'JAN' < 'FEB' < ... < 'DEC.' Invalid names compare low to valid names.

    –n   Compare according to arithmetic value an initial numeric string consisting of optional white space, an optional – sign, and zero or more digits, optionally followed by a decimal point and zero or more digits.

SORT(1L)   FSF   SORT(1L)

    –r   Reverse the result of comparison, so that lines with greater key values appear earlier in the output instead of later.

Other options are:

    –o output-file   Write output to *output-file* instead of to the standard output. If *output-file* is one of the input files, **sort** copies it to a temporary file before sorting and writing the output to *output-file*.

    –t separator   Use character *separator* as the field separator when finding the sort keys in each line. By default, fields are separated by the empty string between a non-whitespace character and a whitespace character. That is to say, given the input line ' foo bar', **sort** breaks it into fields ' foo' and ' bar'. The field separator is not considered to be part of either the field preceding or the field following it.

    –u   For the default case or the *–m* option, only output the first of a sequence of lines that compare equal. For the *–c* option, check that no pair of consecutive lines compares equal.

    +POS1 [–POS2]   Specify a field within each line to use as a sorting key. The field consists of the portion of the line starting at POS1 and up to (but not including) POS2 (or to the end of the line if POS2 is not given). The fields and character positions are numbered starting with 0.

    –k POS1[,POS2]   An alternate syntax for specifying sorting keys. The fields and character positions are numbered starting with 1.

A position has the form *f.c*, where *f* is the number of the field to use and *c* is the number of the first character from the beginning of the field (for *+pos*) or from the end of the previous field (for *–pos*). The *.c* part of a position may be omitted in which case it is taken to be the first character in the field. If the *–b* option has been given, the *.c* part of a field specification is counted from the first nonblank character of the field (for *+pos*) or from the first nonblank character following the previous field (for *–pos*).

A *+pos* or *-pos* argument may also have any of the option letters *Mbdfinr* appended to it, in which case the global ordering options are not used for that particular field. The *–b* option may be independently attached to either or both of the *+pos* and *–pos* parts of a field specification, and if it is inherited from the global options it will be attached to both. If a *–n* or *–M* option is used, thus implying a *–b* option, the *–b* option is taken to apply to both the *+pos* and the *–pos* parts of a key specification. Keys may span multiple fields.

In addition, when GNU **join** is invoked with exactly one argument, the following options are recognized:

    —help   Print a usage message on standard output and exit successfully.

    —version   Print version information on standard output then exit successfully.

COMPATIBILITY

Historical (BSD and System V) implementations of **sort** have differed in their interpretation of some options, particularly *–b*, *–f*, and *–n*. GNU sort follows the POSIX behavior, which is usually (but not always!) like the System V behavior. According to POSIX *–n* no longer implies *–b*. For consistency, *–M* has been changed in the same way. This may affect the meaning of character positions in field specifications in obscure cases. If this bites you the fix is to add an explicit *–b*.

BUGS

The different meaning of field numbers depending on whether *-k* is used is confusing. It's all POSIX's fault!

SPLIT(1L)

NAME

split – split a file into pieces

SYNOPSIS

split [–lines] [–l lines] [–b bytes[bkm]] [–C bytes[bkm]] [––lines=lines]
[––bytes=bytes[bkm]] [––line-bytes=bytes[bkm]] [––help] [––version] [infile [outfile-prefix]]

DESCRIPTION

This manual page documents the GNU version of **split**. **split** creates one or more output files (as many as necessary) containing consecutive sections of the *infile*, or the standard input if none is given or the name '–' is given. By default, **split** puts 1000 lines of the input file, or whatever is left if it is less than that, into each output file.

The output file names consist of a prefix followed by a group of letters, chosen so that concatenating the output files in sorted order by file name produces the original input file, in order. The default output file name prefix is 'x'. If the *outfile-prefix* argument is given, it is used as the output file name prefix instead.

OPTIONS

–lines, –l lines, ––lines=lines   Put *lines* lines of the input file into each output file.

–b bytes[bkm], ––bytes=bytes[bkm]   Put *bytes* bytes of the input file into each output file. *bytes* is a nonzero integer, optionally followed by one of the following characters to specify a different unit.

    b   512-byte blocks.

    k   1-kilobyte blocks.

    m   1-megabyte blocks.

–C bytes[bkm], ––line-bytes=bytes[bkm]   Put into each output file as many complete lines of the input file as is possible without exceeding *bytes* bytes. If a line that is longer than *bytes* bytes occurs, put *bytes* bytes of it into each output file until less than *bytes* bytes of the line are left, then continue normally. *bytes* has the same format as for the ––*bytes* option.

––help   Print a usage message and exit with a non-zero status.

––version   Print version information on standard output then exit.

STARTX(1)

NAME
startx – initialize an X session

SYNOPSIS
startx [[*client*] options ..] [— [*server*] options ...]

DESCRIPTION
NOTE: The *startx* script supplied with the X11 distribution is a sample designed more as a base for customization than as a finished product. Site administrators are urged to customize it for their site. And to update this manual page when they do!

The *startx* script is a front end to *xinit* that provides a somewhat nicer user interface for running a single session of the X Window System. It is typically run with no arguments.

To determine the client to run, *startx* first looks for a file called *.xinitrc* in the user's home directory. If that is not found, it uses the file *xinitrc* in the *xinit* library directory. If command line client options are given, they override this behavior. To determine the server to run, *startx* first looks for a file called *.xserverrc* in the user's home directory. If that is not found, it uses the file *xserverrc* in the *xinit* library directory. If command line server options are given, they override this behavior. Users rarely need to provide a *.xserverrc* file. See the *xinit*(1) manual page for more details on the arguments.

The *.xinitrc* is typically a shell script which starts many clients according to the user's preference. When this shell script exits, *startx* kills the server and performs any other session shutdown needed. Most of the clients started by *.xinitrc* should be run in the background. The last client should run in the foreground; when it exits, the session will exit. People often choose a session manager, window manager, or *xterm* as the "magic" client.

EXAMPLE
Below is a sample *xinitrc* that starts several applications and leaves the window manager running as the "last" application. Assuming that the window manager has been configured properly, the user then chooses the "Exit" menu item to shut down X.

    xrdb –load $HOME/.Xresources
    xsetroot –solid gray &
    xbiff –geometry –430+5 &
    oclock –geometry 75x75–0–0 &
    xload –geometry –80–0 &
    xterm –geometry +0+60 –ls &
    xterm –geometry +0–100 &
    xconsole –geometry –0+0 –fn 5x7 &
    exec twm

ENVIRONMENT VARIABLES
    DISPLAY   This variable gets set to the name of the display to which clients should connect. Note that this gets *set*, not read.

FILES
    $(HOME)/.xinitrc   Client to run. Typically a shell script which runs many programs in the background.

    $(HOME)/.xserverrc   Server to run. The default is X.

    <XRoot>/lib/X11/xinit/xinitrc   Client to run if the user has no *.xinitrc* file. <XRoot> refers to the root of the X11 install tree.

    <XRoot>/lib/X11/xinit/xserverrc   Client to run if the user has no *.xserverrc* file. This is only needed if the server needs special arguments or is not named. <XRoot> refers to the root of the X11 install tree.

SEE ALSO
xinit(1)

strings(1)   GNU Development Tools   strings(1)

NAME

strings – print the strings of printable characters in files

SYNOPSIS

strings   [–a | – | —all] [–f | —print–file–name] [–o] [—help] [–v | —version]
[–n *min–len* | –*min–len* | —**bytes**= *min–len*] [–**t** *o,x,d* [—**target**=*bfdname*]
| —**radix**= *o,x,d*] *file*

DESCRIPTION

For each *file* given, GNU **strings** prints the printable character sequences that are at least 4 characters long (or the number given with the options below) and are followed by a NUL or newline character. By default, it only prints the strings from the initialized data sections of object files; for other types of files, it prints the strings from the whole file.

strings is mainly useful for determining the contents of non-text files.

OPTIONS

The long and short forms of options, shown here as alternatives, are equivalent.

    –a
    —all
    –   Do not scan only the initialized data section of object files; scan the whole files.

    –f
    —print–file–name   Print the name of the file before each string.

    —help   Print a summary of the options to **strings** on the standard output and exit.

    –v
    —version   Print the version number of **strings** on the standard output and exit.

    –n *min–len*   *–min–len*

    –bytes=*min–len*   Print sequences of characters that are at least *min–len* characters long, instead of the default 4.

    –t o,x,d

    —radix=o,x,d   Print the offset within the file before each string. The single character argument specifies the radix of the offset—octal, hexadecimal, or decimal.

    —target=*bfdname*   Specify an object code format other than your system's default format. See **objdump(1)**, for information on listing available formats.

    –o   Like **–t o**.

SEE ALSO

'**binutils**' entry in info ; The GNU Binary Utilities , Roland H. Pesch (October 1991); **ar(1)**, **nm(1)**, **objdump(1)**, **ranlib(1)**.

COPYING

Copyright (c) 1993 Free Software Foundation, Inc.

Permission is granted to make and distribute verbatim copies of this manual provided the copyright notice and this permission notice are preserved on all copies.

Permission is granted to copy and distribute modified versions of this manual under the conditions for verbatim copying, provided that the entire resulting derived work is distributed under the terms of a permission notice identical to this one.

Permission is granted to copy and distribute translations of this manual into another language, under the above conditions for modified versions, except that this permission notice may be included in translations approved by the Free Software Foundation instead of in the original English.

strip(1) GNU Development Tools strip(1)

NAME
strip – Discard symbols from object files.

SYNOPSIS
strip [–F*bfdname*|—target=*bfdname*] [–I*bfdname*|
—input–target=*bfdname*] [–O*bfdname*|—output–target=*bfdname*] [–
R*sectionname*|—remove–section=*sectionname*] [-s|—**strip–all**] [–S|-
g|—**strip–debug**] [–x|—**discard–all**] [–X|—**discard–locals**] [–v|—
-**verbose**] [–V|—**version**] [–V|—**help**] *objfile* ...

DESCRIPTION
GNU **strip** discards all symbols from the object files *objfile*. The list of object files may include archives. At least one object file must be given.

strip modifies the files named in its argument, rather than writing modified copies under different names.

OPTIONS

–F *bfdname*

—**target**=*bfdname*   Treat the original *objfile* as a file with the object code format *bfdname*, and rewrite it in the same format.

—**help**   Show a summary of the options to **strip** and exit.

–I *bfdname*fdname"

—**input–target**=*bfdname*   Treat the original *objfile* as a file with the object code format *bfdname*.

–O *bfdname*

—**output–target**=*bfdname*   Replace *objfile* with a file in the output format *bfd-name*.

–R *sectionname*

—**remove–section**=*sectionname*   Remove the named section from the file. This option may be given more than once. Note that using this option inappropriately may make the object file unusable.

–s

—**strip–all**   Remove all symbols.

–S

-g

—**strip–debug**   Remove debugging symbols only.

–x

—**discard–all**   Remove non-global symbols.

–X —**discard–locals**   Remove compiler-generated local symbols. (These usually start with "L" or ".".)

–v

—**verbose**   Verbose output: list all object files modified. In the case of archives, **strip –V** lists all members of the archive.

–V

—**version**   Show the version number for **strip** and exit.

SEE ALSO
' **binutils** ' entry in **info**; *The GNU Binary Utilities*, Roland H. Pesch (October 1991).

COPYING

Copyright (c) 1991 Free Software Foundation, Inc.

Permission is granted to make and distribute verbatim copies of this manual provided the copyright notice and this permission notice are preserved on all copies.

Permission is granted to copy and distribute modified versions of this manual under the conditions for verbatim copying, provided that the entire resulting derived work is distributed under the terms of a permission notice identical to this one.

Permission is granted to copy and distribute translations of this manual into another language, under the above conditions for modified versions, except that this permission notice may be included in translations approved by the Free Software Foundation instead of in the original English.

SUM(1L)

NAME

sum – checksum and count the blocks in a file

SYNOPSIS

sum [–rs] [—sysv] [—help] [—version] [file...]

DESCRIPTION

This manual page documents the GNU version of **sum**. **sum** computes a 16-bit checksum for each named file, or the standard input if none are given or when a file named '–' is given. It prints the checksum for each file along with the number of blocks in the file (rounded up). By default each corresponding file name is also printed if at least two arguments are specified. With the —-*sysv* option, corresponding file name are printed when there is at least one file argument. By default, the GNU **sum** computes checksums using an algorithm that is compatible with the BSD **sum** and prints file sizes in units of 1K blocks.

OPTIONS

–*r* Use the default (BSD compatible) algorithm. This option is included for compatibility with the System V **sum**. Unless the –*s* option was also given, it has no effect.

–*s*, —-*sysv* Compute checksums using an algorithm that is compatible with the one the System V **sum** uses by default and print file sizes in units of 512-byte blocks instead of 1K.

—-*help* Print a usage message and exit with a non-zero status.

—-*version* Print version information on standard output then exit.

SuperProbe(1)

NAME

SuperProbe - probe for and identify installed video hardware.

SYNOPSIS

SuperProbe [-verbose] [-no16] [-excl *list*] [-mask10] [-order *list*] [-noprobe *list*] [-bios *base*]

[-no_bios] [-no_dac] [-no_mem] [-info]

DESCRIPTION

SuperProbe is a a program that will attempt to determine the type of video hardware installed in an EISA/ISA/VLB-bus system by checking for known registers in various combinations at various locations (MicroChannel and PCI machines may not be fully supported; many work with the use of the **-no_bios** option). This is an error-prone process, especially on Unix (which usually has a lot more esoteric hardware installed than MS-DOS system do), so SuperProbe may likely need help from the user.

SuperProbe runs on SVR3, SVR4, Linux, 386BSD/FreeBSD/NetBSD, Minix-386, and Mach. It should be trivial to extend it to work on any other Unix-like operating system, and even non-Unix operating systems. All of the OS dependencies are isolated to a single file for each OS.

At this time, *SuperProbe* can identify MDA, Hercules, CGA, MCGA, EGA, VGA, and an entire horde of SVGA chipsets (see the *-info* option, below). It can also identify several HiColor/True-color RAMDACs in use on SVGA boards, and the amount of video memory installed (for many chipsets). It can identify 8514/A and some derivatives, but not XGA, or PGC (although the author intends to add those capabilities). Nor can it identify other esoteric video hardware (like Targa, TIGA, or Microfield boards).

OPTIONS

- **-verbose**   *SuperProbe* will be verbose and provide lots of information as it does its work.

- **-no16**   *SuperProbe* will not attempt to use any ports that require 16-bit I/O address decoding. The original ISA bus only specified that I/O ports be decoded to 10 bits. Therefore some old cards (including many 8-bit cards) will mis-decode references to ports that use the upper 6 bits, and may get into funny states because they think that they are being addressed when they are not. It is recommended that this option be used initially if any 8-bit cards are present in the system.

- **-excl**\ *list* *SuperProbe* will not attempt to access any I/O ports on the specified exclusion list. Some video cards use rather non-standard I/O ports that may conflict with other cards installed in your system. By specifying to *SuperProbe* a list of ports already in use, it will know that there cannot be any video cards that use those ports, and hence will not probe them (which could otherwise confuse your hardware). The exclusion list is specified as a comma-separated list of I/O ports or port ranges. A range is specified as "low-high", and is inclusive. The ports can be specified in decimal, in octal (numbers begin with '0'), or hexadecimal (numbers begin with '0x').

- **-mask10**   This option is used in combination with *-excl*. It tells *SuperProbe* that when comparing an I/O port under test against the exclusion list, the port address should be masked to 10 bits. This is important with older 8-bit cards that only do 10 bit decoding, and for some cheap 16-bit cards as well. This option is simply a less-drastic form of the *-no16* option.

- **-order**\ *list* This option specifies which chipsets *SuperProbe* should test, and in which order. The *list* parameter is a comma-separated list of chipset names. This list overrides the built-in default testing order. To find the list of acceptable names, use the *-info* option described below. Note that items displayed as "Standard video hardware" are not usable with the *-order* option.

-noprobe*list*   This options specifies which chipsets *SuperProbe* should **not** test. The order of testing will either be the default order, or that specified with the *-order* option described above. The *list* parameter is a comma-separated list of chipset names. To find the list of acceptable names, use the *-info* option described below. Note that items displayed as "Standard video hardware" are not usable with the *-noprobe* option.

-bios*base*   This option specifies the base address for the graphics-hardware BIOS. By default, *SuperProbe* will attempt to locate the BIOS base on its own (the normal address is 0xC0000). If it fails to correctly locate the BIOS (an error message will be printed if this occurs), the *-bios* option can be used to specify the base.

-no_bios   Disallow reading of the video BIOS and assume that an EGA or later (VGA, SVGA) board is present as the primary video hardware.

-no_dac   Skip probing for the RAMDAC type when an (S)VGA is identified.

-no_mem   Skip probing for the amount of installed video memory.

-info   *SuperProbe* will print out a listing of all the video hardware that it knows how to identify.

EXAMPLES

To run *SuperProbe* in its most basic and automated form, simply enter:

        SuperProbe

Note - you may want to redirect *stdout* to a file when you run *SuperProbe* (especially if your OS does not support Virtual Terminals on the console).

However, if you have any 8-bit cards installed, you should initially run *SuperProbe* as:

        SuperProbe -verbose -no16

(the *-verbose* option is included so you can see what *SuperProbe* is skipping).

Finer granularity can be obtained with an exclusion list, for example:

        SuperProbe -verbose -excl 0x200,0x220-0x230,0x250

which will not test for any device that use port 0x200, ports 0x220 through 0x230, inclusive, or port 0x250. If you have any 8-bit cards installed, you should add *-mask10* to the list of options.

To restrict the search to Western Digital, Tseng, and Cirrus chipset, run *SuperProbe* as follows:

        SuperProbe -order WD,Tseng,Cirrus

BUGS

Probably a lot at this point. Please report any bugs or incorrect identifications to the author.

It is possible that SuperProbe can lock up your machine. Be sure to narrow the search by using the *-no16*, *-excl*, and *-mask10* options provided to keep SuperProbe from conflicting with other installed hardware.

SEE ALSO

The *vgadoc3.zip* documentation package by Finn Thoegersen, available in the MS-DOS archives of many FTP repositories.

Programmer's Guide to the EGA and VGA Cards, 2nd Ed, by Richard Ferraro.

AUTHOR

David E. Wexelblat <dwex@xfree86.org>
with help from David Dawes <dawes@xfree86.org> and the XFree86 development team.

TAC(1L)

NAME

tac – concatenate and print files in reverse

SYNOPSIS

tac [–br] [–s separator] [—before] [—regex] [—separator=separator] [—help] [—version] [file...]

DESCRIPTION

This manual page documents the GNU version of **tac**. **tac** copies each given file, or the standard input if none are given or when a file name of '-' is encountered, to the standard output with the order of the records reversed. The records are separated by instances of a string, or a newline if none is given. By default, the separator string is attached to the end of the record that it follows in the file.

OPTIONS

–b, —before   The separator is attached to the beginning of the record that it precedes in the file.

–r, —regex   The separator is a regular expression.

–s string, —-separator=string   Use *string* as the record separator.

—help   Print a usage message and exit with a non-zero status.

—version   Print version information on standard output then exit.

TAIL(1L)   FSF   TAIL(1L)

NAME
tail – output the last part of files

SYNOPSIS
tail [–c [+]N[bkm]] [–n [+]N] [–fqv] [——bytes=[+]N[bkm]] [——lines=[+]N] [——follow] [——quiet] [——silent] [——verbose] [——help] [——version] [file...]

tail [{–,+}Nbcfklmqv] [file...]

DESCRIPTION
This manual page documents the GNU version of **tail**. **tail** prints the last part (10 lines by default) of each given file; it reads from standard input if no files are given or when a filename of '–' is encountered. If more than one file is given, it prints a header consisting of the file's name enclosed in '==>' and '<==' before the output for each file.

The GNU **tail** can output any amount of data, unlike the Unix version, which uses a fixed size buffer. It has no –r option (print in reverse). Reversing a file is really a different job from printing the end of a file; the BSD **tail** can only reverse files that are at most as large as its buffer, which is typically 32k. A reliable and more versatile way to reverse files is the GNU **tac** command.

OPTIONS
tail accepts two option formats: the new one, in which numbers are arguments to the option letters, and the old one, in which a '+' or '–' and optional number precede any option letters.

If a number ('N') starts with a '+', **tail** begins printing with the Nth item from the start of each file, instead of from the end.

<table>
<tr><td>–c N, ——bytes N</td><td>Tail by N bytes. N is a nonzero integer, optionally followed by one of the following characters to specify a different unit.
b 512-byte blocks.
k 1-kilobyte blocks.
m 1-megabyte blocks.</td></tr>
<tr><td>–f, ——follow</td><td>Loop forever trying to read more characters at the end of the file, on the assumption that the file is growing. Ignored if reading from a pipe. If more than one file is given, **tail** prints a header whenever it gets output from a different file, to indicate which file that output is from.</td></tr>
<tr><td>–l, –n N, ——lines N</td><td>Tail by N lines. –l is only recognized using the old option format.</td></tr>
<tr><td>–q, ——quiet, ——silent</td><td>Never print filename headers.</td></tr>
<tr><td>–v, ——verbose</td><td>Always print filename headers.</td></tr>
<tr><td>——help</td><td>Print a usage message and exit with a non-zero status.</td></tr>
<tr><td>——version</td><td>Print version information on standard output then exit.</td></tr>
</table>

TALK(1)

NAME
talk – talk to another user

SYNOPSIS
talk person [ttyname]

DESCRIPTION
Talk is a visual communication program which copies lines from your terminal to that of another user.

Options available:

> person If you wish to talk to someone on your own machine, then person is just the person's login name. If you wish to talk to a user on another host, then person is of the form user@host.
>
> ttyname If you wish to talk to a user who is logged in more than once, the ttyname argument may be used to indicate the appropriate terminal name, where ttyname is of the form

When first called, talk sends the message Message from TalkDaemon@his_machine...
talk: connection requested by your_name@your_machine.
talk: respond with: talk your_name@your_machine

to the user you wish to talk to. At this point, the recipient of the message should reply by typing

talk your_name@your_machine

It doesn't matter from which machine the recipient replies, as long as his login-name is the same. Once communication is established, the two parties may type simultaneously, with their output appearing in separate windows. Typing control-L L̂ will cause the screen to be reprinted, while your erase, kill, and word kill characters will behave normally. To exit, just type your interrupt character; talk then moves the cursor to the bottom of the screen and restores the terminal to its previous state.

Permission to talk may be denied or granted by use of the mesg 1 command. At the outset talking is allowed. Certain commands, in particular nroff 1 and pr 1, disallow messages in order to prevent messy output.

FILES
> /etc/hosts to find the recipient's machine
>
> /var/run/utmp to find the recipient's tty

SEE ALSO
mail 1, mesg 1, who 1, write 1

BUGS
The version of talk 1 released with BSD 4.3 uses a protocol that is incompatible with the protocol used in the version released with BSD 4.2.

HISTORY
The talk command appeared in BSD 4.2.

TELNET(1)   TELNET(1)

NAME

telnet – User interface to the TELNET protocol

SYNOPSIS

telnet [-d] [-a] [-n tracefile] [-e escapechar] [[-l user] host [port]]

DESCRIPTION

The telnet command is used to communicate with another host using the TELNET protocol. If telnet is invoked without the host argument, it enters command mode, indicated by its prompt telnet>. In this mode, it accepts and executes the commands listed below. If it is invoked with arguments, it performs an open command with those arguments.

Options:

-d Sets the initial value of the debug toggle to TRUE

-a Attempt automatic login. Currently, this sends the user name via the USER variable of the ENVIRON option if supported by the remote system. The name used is that of the current user as returned by getlogin 2 if it agrees with the current user ID, otherwise it is the name associated with the user ID.

-n tracefile Opens tracefile for recording trace information. See the set tracefile command below.

-l user When connecting to the remote system, if the remote system understands the ENVIRON option, then user will be sent to the remote system as the value for the variable USER. This option implies the -a option. This option may also be used with the open command.

-e escape char Sets the initial

telnet escape character to escape char. If escape char is omitted, then there will be no escape character.

host Indicates the official name, an alias, or the Internet address of a remote host.

port Indicates a port number (address of an application). If a number is not specified, the default telnet port is used.

Once a connection has been opened, telnet will attempt to enable the TELNET LINEMODE option. If this fails, then telnet will revert to one of two input modes: either character at a time or old line by line depending on what the remote system supports.

When LINEMODE is enabled, character processing is done on the local system, under the control of the remote system. When input editing or character echoing is to be disabled, the remote system will relay that information. The remote system will also relay changes to any special characters that happen on the remote system, so that they can take effect on the local system.

In character at a time mode, most text typed is immediately sent to the remote host for processing.

In old line by line mode, all text is echoed locally, and (normally) only completed lines are sent to the remote host. The local echo character (initially ^E) may be used to turn off and on the local echo (this would mostly be used to enter passwords without the password being echoed).

If the LINEMODE option is enabled, or if the localchars toggle is TRUE (the default for old line by line; see below), the user's quit, intr, and flush characters are trapped locally, and sent as TELNET protocol sequences to the remote side. If LINEMODE has ever been enabled, then the user's susp and eof are also sent as TELNET protocol sequences, and quit is sent as a TELNET ABORT instead of BREAK There are options (see toggle autoflush and toggle autosynch below) which cause this action to flush subsequent output to the terminal (until the remote host acknowledges the TELNET sequence) and flush previous terminal input (in the case of quit and intr).

BSD 4.2 July 27, 1991 347

TELNET(1) TELNET(1)

While connected to a remote host, telnet command mode may be entered by typing the telnet escape character (initially ^]). When in command mode, the normal terminal editing conventions are available.

The following telnet commands are available. Only enough of each command to uniquely identify it need be typed (this is also true for arguments to the mode, set, toggle, unset, slc, environ, and display commands).

- close   Close a TELNET session and return to command mode.
- display argument...   Displays all, or some, of the set and toggle values (see below).
- mode type   Type is one of several options, depending on the state of the TELNET session. The remote host is asked for permission to go into the requested mode. If the remote host is capable of entering that mode, the requested mode will be entered.

  - character   Disable the TELNET LINEMODE option, or, if the remote side does not understand the LINEMODE option, then enter character at a time mode.
  - line   Enable the TELNET LINEMODE option, or, if the remote side does not understand the LINEMODE option, then attempt to enter old-line-by-line mode.
  - isig Pq –isig   Attempt to enable (disable) the TRAPSIG mode of the LINEMODE option. This requires that the LINEMODE option be enabled.
  - edit Pq –edit   Attempt to enable (disable) the EDIT mode of the LINEMODE option. This requires that the LINEMODE option be enabled.
  - softtabs Pq –softtabs   Attempt to enable (disable) the SOFT_TAB mode of the LINEMODE option. This requires that the LINEMODE option be enabled.
  - litecho Pq –litecho   Attempt to enable (disable) the LIT_ECHO mode of the LINEMODE option. This requires that the LINEMODE option be enabled.
  - ?   Prints out help information for the mode command.

- open host [-l user] [-port]   Open a connection to the named host. If no port number is specified, telnet will attempt to contact a TELNET server at the default port. The host specification may be either a host name (see hosts 5) or an Internet address specified in the dot notation (see inet 3). The -l option may be used to specify the user name to be passed to the remote system via the ENVIRON option. When connecting to a non-standard port, telnet omits any automatic initiation of TELNET options. When the port number is preceeded by a minus sign, the inital option negotiation is done. After establishing a connection, the file in the users home directory is opened. Lines beginning with a # are comment lines. Blank lines are ignored. Lines that begin without whitespace are the start of a machine entry. The first thing on the line is the name of the machine that is being connected to. The rest of the line, and successive lines that begin with whitespace are assumed to be telnet commands and are processed as if they had been typed in manually to the telnet command prompt.

- quit   Close any open TELNET session and exit telnet. An end of file (in command mode) will also close a session and exit.

- send arguments   Sends one or more special character sequences to the remote host. The following are the arguments which may be specified (more than one argument may be specified at a time):

  - abort   Sends the TELNET ABORT (Abort processes) sequence.

TELNET(1) TELNET(1)

ao   Sends the TELNET AO (Abort Output) sequence, which should cause the remote system to flush all output from the remote system to the user's terminal.

ayt Sends the TELNET AYT (Are You There) sequence, to which the remote system may or may not choose to respond.

brk Sends the TELNET BRK (Break) sequence, which may have significance to the remote system.

ec   Sends the TELNET EC (Erase Character) sequence, which should cause the remote system to erase the last character entered.

el   Sends the TELNET EL (Erase Line) sequence, which should cause the remote system to erase the line currently being entered.

eof Sends the TELNET EOF (End Of File) sequence.

eor Sends the TELNET EOR (End of Record) sequence.

escape Sends the current telnet escape character (initially ^]).

ga   Sends the TELNET GA (Go Ahead) sequence, which likely has no significance to the remote system.

getstatus If the remote side supports the TELNET STATUS command, getstatus will send the subnegotiation to request that the server send its current option status.

ip   Sends the TELNET IP (Interrupt Process) sequence, which should cause the remote system to abort the currently running process.

nop Sends the TELNET NOP (No OPeration) sequence.

susp Sends the TELNET SUSP (SUSPend process) sequence.

synch Sends the TELNET SYNCH sequence. This sequence causes the remote system to discard all previously typed (but not yet read) input. This sequence is sent as TCP urgent data (and may not work if the remote system is a BSD 4.2 system – if it doesn't work, a lower case r may be echoed on the terminal).

?   Prints out help information for the send command.

set argument value

unset argument value   The set command will set any one of a number of telnet variables to a specific value or to TRUE. The special value off turns off the function associated with the variable, this is equivalent to using the unset command. The unset command will disable or set to FALSE any of the specified functions. The values of variables may be interrogated with the display command. The variables which may be set or unset, but not toggled, are listed here. In addition, any of the variables for the toggle command may be explicitly set or unset using the set and unset commands.

echo   This is the value (initially ^E) which, when in line by line mode, toggles between doing local echoing of entered characters (for normal processing), and suppressing echoing of entered characters (for entering, say, a password).

eof   If telnet is operating in LINEMODE or old line by line mode, entering this character as the first character on a line will cause this character to be sent to the remote system. The initial value of the eof character is taken to be the terminal's eof character.

erase If telnet is in localchars mode (see toggle localchars below), and if telnet is operating in character at a time mode, then when this character is typed, a TELNET EC sequence (see send ec above) is sent to the remote system. The initial value for the erase character is taken to be the terminal's erase character.

TELNET(1)   TELNET(1)

escape This is the telnet escape character (initially ^[) which causes entry into telnet command mode (when connected to a remote system).

flushoutput If telnet is in localchars mode (see toggle localchars below) and the flushoutput character is typed, a TELNET AO sequence (see send ao above) is sent to the remote host. The initial value for the flush character is taken to be the terminal's flush character.

interrupt If telnet is in localchars mode (see toggle localchars below) and the interrupt character is typed, a TELNET IP sequence (see send ip above) is sent to the remote host. The initial value for the interrupt character is taken to be the terminal's intr character.

kill If telnet is in localchars mode (see toggle localchars below), and if telnet is operating in character at a time mode, then when this character is typed, a TELNET EL sequence (see send el above) is sent to the remote system. The initial value for the kill character is taken to be the terminal's kill character.

lnext If telnet is operating in LINEMODE or old line by line mode, then this character is taken to be the terminal's lnext character. The initial value for the lnext character is taken to be the terminal's lnext character.

quit If telnet is in localchars mode (see toggle localchars below) and the quit character is typed, a TELNET BRK sequence (see send brk above) is sent to the remote host. The initial value for the quit character is taken to be the terminal's quit character.

reprint If telnet is operating in LINEMODE or old line by line mode, then this character is taken to be the terminal's reprint character. The initial value for the reprint character is taken to be the terminal's reprint character.

start If the TELNET TOGGLE-FLOW-CONTROL option has been enabled, then this character is taken to be the terminal's start character. The initial value for the kill character is taken to be the terminal's start character.

stop If the TELNET TOGGLE-FLOW-CONTROL option has been enabled, then this character is taken to be the terminal's stop character. The initial value for the kill character is taken to be the terminal's stop character.

susp If telnet is in localchars mode, or LINEMODE is enabled, and the suspend character is typed, a TELNET SUSP sequence (see send susp above) is sent to the remote host. The initial value for the suspend character is taken to be the terminal's suspend character.

tracefile Thi is the file to which the output, caused by netdata or option tracing being TRUE, will be written. If it is set to -, then tracing information will be written to standard output (the default).

worderase If telnet is operating in LINEMODE or old line by line mode, then this character is taken to be the terminal's worderase character. The initial value for the worderase character is taken to be the terminal's worderase character.

? Displays the legal set unset commands.

slc state The slc command (Set Local Characters) is used to set or change the state of the the special characters when the TELNET LINEMODE option has been enabled. Special characters are characters that get mapped to TELNET commands sequences (like ip or quit) or line editing characters (like erase and kill). By default, the local special characters are exported.

export Switch to the local defaults for the special characters. The local default characters are those of the local terminal at the time when telnet was started.

TELNET(1) TELNET(1)

       import   Switch to the remote defaults for the special characters. The remote default characters are those of the remote system at the time when the TELNET connection was established.

       check   Verify the current settings for the current special characters. The remote side is requested to send all the current special character settings, and if there are any discrepencies with the local side, the local side will switch to the remote value.

       ?   Prints out help information for the slc command.

environ arguments...   The environ command is used to manipulate the the variables that my be sent through the TELNET ENVIRON option. The initial set of variables is taken from the users environment, with only the DISPLAY and PRINTER variables being exported by default. The USER variable is also exported if the -a or -l options are used.

Valid arguments for the environ command are:

define variable value   Define the variable variable to have a value of value. Any variables defined by this command are automatically exported. The value may be enclosed in single or double quotes so that tabs and spaces may be included.

   undefine variable   Remove variable from the list of environment variables.

   export variable   Mark the variable variable to be exported to the remote side.

   unexport variable   Mark the variable variable to not be exported unless explicitly asked for by the remote side.

   list   List the current set of environment variables. Those marked with a * will be sent automatically, other variables will only be sent if explicitly requested.

   ?   Prints out help information for the environ command.

toggle arguments...   Toggle (between TRUE and FALSE) various flags that control how telnet responds to events. These flags may be set explicitly to TRUE or FALSE using the set and unset commands listed above. More than one argument may be specified. The state of these flags may be interrogated with the display command. Valid arguments are:

   autoflush   If autoflush and localchars are both TRUE, then when the ao, or quit characters are recognized (and transformed into TELNET sequences; see set above for details), telnet refuses to display any data on the user's terminal until the remote system acknowledges (via a TELNET TIMING MARK option) that it has processed those TELNET sequences. The initial value for this toggle is TRUE if the terminal user had not done an "stty noflsh", otherwise FALSE (see stty 1).

   autosynch   If autosynch and localchars are both TRUE, then when either the intr or quit characters is typed (see set above for descriptions of the intr and quit characters), the resulting TELNET sequence sent is followed by the TELNET SYNCH sequence. This procedure should cause the remote system to begin throwing away all previously typed input until both of the TELNET sequences have been read and acted upon. The initial value of this toggle is FALSE.

   binary   Enable or disable the TELNET BINARY option on both input and output.

   inbinary   Enable or disable the TELNET BINARY option on input.

   outbinary   Enable or disable the TELNET BINARY option on output.

   crlf   If this is TRUE, then carriage returns will be sent as ¡CR¿¡LF¿. If this is FALSE, then carriage returns will be send as ¡CR¿¡NUL¿. The initial value for this toggle is FALSE.

TELNET(1) TELNET(1)

crmod
: Toggle carriage return mode. When this mode is enabled, most carriage return characters received from the remote host will be mapped into a carriage return followed by a line feed. This mode does not affect those characters typed by the user, only those received from the remote host. This mode is not very useful unless the remote host only sends carriage return, but never line feed. The initial value for this toggle is FALSE.

debug
: Toggles socket level debugging (useful only to the super user). The initial value for this toggle is FALSE.

localchars
: If this is TRUE, then the flush, interrupt, quit, erase, and kill characters (see set above) are recognized locally, and transformed into (hopefully) appropriate TELNET control sequences (respectively ao, ip, brk, ec, and el ; see send above). The initial value for this toggle is TRUE in old line by line mode, and FALSE in character at a time mode. When the LINEMODE option is enabled, the value of localchars is ignored, and assumed to always be TRUE. If LINEMODE has ever been enabled, then quit is sent as abort, and eof and **suspend** are sent as eof and susp, see send above).

netdata
: Toggles the display of all network data (in hexadecimal format). The initial value for this toggle is FALSE.

options
: Toggles the display of some internal telnet protocol processing (having to do with TELNET options). The initial value for this toggle is FALSE.

prettydump
: When the netdata toggle is enabled, if prettydump is enabled the output from the netdata command will be formated in a more user readable format. Spaces are put between each character in the output, and the begining of any TELNET escape sequence is preceeded by a '*' to aid in locating them.

?
: Displays the legal toggle commands.

z
: Suspend telnet. This command only works when the user is using the csh 1.

! command
: Execute a single command in a subshell on the local system. If command is ommitted, then an interactive subshell is invoked.

status
: Show the current status of telnet. This includes the peer one is connected to, as well as the current mode.

? command
: Get help. With no arguments, telnet prints a help summary. If a command is specified, telnet will print the help information for just that command.

ENVIRONMENT

Telnet uses at least the HOME, SHELL, DISPLAY, and TERM envirnonent variables. Other envirnoment variables may be propogated to the other side via the TELNET ENVIRON option.

FILES

~/.telnetrc user customized telnet startup values

HISTORY

The Telnet command appeared in BSD 4.2.

NOTES

On some remote systems, echo has to be turned off manually when in old line by line mode.

In old line by line mode or LINEMODE the terminal's eof character is only recognized (and sent to the remote system) when it is the first character on a line.

TFMTODIT(1)

NAME
tfmtodit – create font files for use with groff –Tdvi

SYNOPSIS
tfmtodit [**–sv**] [**–g***gf_file*] [**–k***skewchar*] *tfm_file map_file font*

DESCRIPTION
tfmtodit creates a font file for use with groff –Tdvi. *tfm_file* is the name of the font metric file for the font. *map_file* is a file giving the groff names for characters in the font; this file should consist of a sequence of lines of the form:

    n c1 c2 ...

where *n* is a decimal integer giving the position of the character in the font, and $c_1, c_2,...$ are the groff names of the character. If a character has no groff names but exists in the tfm file, then it will be put in the groff font file as an unnamed character. *font* is the name of the groff font file. The groff font file is written to *font*.

The **–s** option should be given if the font is special (a font is *special* if **troff** should search it whenever a character is not found in the current font.) If the font is special, it should be listed in the **fonts** command in the DESC file; if it is not special, there is no need to list it, since **troff** can automatically mount it when it's first used.

To do a good job of math typesetting, groff requires font metric information not present in the tfm file. The reason for this is that has separate math italic fonts whereas groff uses normal italic fonts for math. The additional information required by groff is given by the two arguments to the **math_fit** macro in the Metafont programs for the Computer Modern fonts. In a text font (a font for which **math_fitting** is false), Metafont normally ignores these two arguments. Metafont can be made to put this information in the gf file by loading the following definition after **cmbase** when creating **cm.base**:

    def ignore_math_fit(expr left_adjustment,right_adjustment) =
    special "adjustment";
    numspecial left_adjustment*16/designsize;
    numspecial right_adjustment*16/designsize;
    enddef;

The gf file created using this modified **cm.base** should be specified with the **–g** option. The **–g** option should not be given for a font for which **math_fitting** is true.

OPTIONS

    –v   Print the version number.

    –s   The font is special. The effect of this option is to add the **special** command to the font file.

    –k*n*   The skewchar of this font is at position *n*. *n* should be an integer; it may be given in decimal, or with a leading **0** in octal, or with a leading **0x** in hexadecimal. The effect of this option is to ignore any kerns whose second component is the specified character.

    –g*gf_file*   *gf_file* is a gf file produced by Metafont containing special and numspecial commands giving additional font metric information.

FILES
/usr/lib/groff/font/devdvi/DESC   Device description file.

    /usr/lib/groff/font/devdvi/*F*   Font description file for font *F*.

SEE ALSO
groff(1), **grodvi**(1), **groff_font**(5)

TFTP(1) TFTP(1)

NAME
tftp – trivial file transfer program

SYNOPSIS
tftp [host]

DESCRIPTION
Tftp is the user interface to the Internet TFTP (Trivial File Transfer Protocol), which allows users to transfer files to and from a remote machine. The remote host may be specified on the command line, in which case tftp uses host as the default host for future transfers (see the connect command below).

COMMANDS
Once tftp is running, it issues the prompt

tftp¿

and recognizes the following commands:

> ? command-name ... Print help information.
>
> ascii Shorthand for "mode ascii"
>
> binary Shorthand for "mode binary"
>
> connect host-name port Set the host (and optionally port) for transfers. Note that the TFTP protocol, unlike the FTP protocol, does not maintain connections betweeen transfers; thus, the connect command does not actually create a connection, but merely remembers what host is to be used for transfers. You do not have to use the connect command; the remote host can be specified as part of the get or put commands.
>
> get filename
>
> get remotename localname
>
> get file1 file2 ... fileN Get a file or set of files from the specified sources . Source can be in one of two forms: a filename on the remote host, if the host has already been specified, or a string of the form hosts:filename to specify both a host and filename at the same time. If the latter form is used, the last hostname specified becomes the default for future transfers.
>
> mode transfer-mode Set the mode for transfers; transfer-mode may be one of ascii or binary . The default is ascii .
>
> put file
>
> put localfile remotefile
>
> put file1 file2 ... fileN remote-directory Put a file or set of files to the specified remote file or directory. The destination can be in one of two forms: a filename on the remote host, if the host has already been specified, or a string of the form hosts:filename to specify both a host and filename at the same time. If the latter form is used, the hostname specified becomes the default for future transfers. If the remote-directory form is used, the remote host is assumed to be a UNIX machine.
>
> quit Exit tftp . An end of file also exits.
>
> rexmt retransmission-timeout Set the per-packet retransmission timeout, in seconds.
>
> status Show current status.
>
> timeout total-transmission-timeout Set the total transmission timeout, in seconds.
>
> trace Toggle packet tracing.
>
> verbose Toggle verbose mode.

BUGS
Because there is no user-login or validation within the TFTP protocol, the remote site will probably have some sort of file-access restrictions in place. The exact methods are specific to each site and therefore difficult to document here.

BSD 4.3 April 22, 1991

TFTP(1)

HISTORY

The tftp command appeared in BSD 4.3 .

NAME

tload – graphic representation of system load average

SYNOPSIS

tload [-s scale] [-d delay] [tty]

DESCRIPTION

tload prints a graph of the current system load average to the specified *tty* (or the tty of the tload process if none is specified).

Options

The *-s scale* option allows a vertical scale to be specified for the display (in characters between graph ticks); thus, a smaller value represents a larger scale, and vice versa.

The *-d delay* sets the delay between graph updates in seconds.

FILES

/proc/loadavg – load average informati

SEE ALSO

ps(1), top(1), uptime(1), w(1)

BUGS

The *-d delay* option sets the time argument for an alarm(2); if -d 0 is specified, the alarm is set to 0, which will never send the SIGALRM and update the display.

AUTHORS

Branko Lankester, David Engel (david@ods.com), and
Michael K. Johnson (johnsonm@sunsite.unc.edu).

TOP(1) Linux Programmer's Manual TOP(1)

NAME

top – display top CPU processes

SYNOPSIS

top [–] [**d** *delay*] [**q**] [**S**] [**s**] [**i**]

DESCRIPTION

top provides an ongoing look at processor activity in real time. It displays a listing of the most CPU-intensive tasks on the system, and can provide an interactive interface for manipulating processes.

COMMAND-LINE OPTIONS

- d Specifies the delay between screen updates. You can change this with the **s** interactive command.
- q This causes **top** to refresh without any delay. If the caller has superuser priviledges, top runs with the highest possible priority.
- S Specifies cumulative mode, where each process is listed with the CPU time that it *as* well as its dead children has spent. This is like the **-S** flag to **ps**(1). See the discussion below of the **S** interactive command.
- s Tells **top** to run in secure mode. This disables the potentially dangerous of the interactive commands (see below). A secure **top** is a nifty thing to leave running on a spare terminal.
- i Start **top** ignoring any idle or zombie processes. See the interactive command **i** below.

FIELD DESCRIPTIONS

top displays a variety of information about the processor state. The display is updated every 5 seconds by default, but you can change that with the **d** command-line option or the **s** interactive command.

uptime	This line displays the time the system has been up, and the three load averages for the system. The load averages are the average number of process ready to run during the last 1, 5 and 15 minutes. This line is just like the output of **uptime**(1).
processes	The total number of processes running at the time of the last update. This is also broken down into the number of tasks which are running, sleeping, stopped, or undead.
CPU states	Shows the percentage of CPU time in user mode, system mode, niced tasks, and idle. (Niced tasks are only those whose nice value is negative.) Time spent in niced tasks will also be counted in system and user time, so the total will be more than 100%.
Mem	Statistics on memory usage, including total available memory, free memory, used memory, shared memory, and memory used for buffers.
Swap	Statistics on swap space, including total swap space, available swap space, and used swap space. This and **Mem** are just like the output of **free**(1).
PID	The process ID of each task.
USER	The user name of the task's owner.
PRI	The priority of the task.
NI	The nice value of the task. Negative nice values are lower priority.
SIZE	The size of the task's code plus data plus stack space, in kilobytes, is shown here.

Linux Feb 1 1993 357

	RSS	The total amount of physical memory used by the task, in kilobytes, is shown here.
	SHRD	The amount of shared memory used by the task is shown in this column.
	ST	The state of the task is shown here. The state is either **S** for sleeping, **D** for uninterruptible sleep, **R** for running, **Z** for zombies, or **T** for stopped or traced.
	TIME	Total CPU time the task has used since it started. If cumulative mode is on, this also includes the CPU time used by the process's children which have died. You can set cumulative mode with the **S** command line option or toggle it with the interactive command **S**.
	%CPU	The task's share of the CPU time since the last screen update, expressed as a percentage of total CPU time.
	%MEM	The task's share of the physical memory.
	COMMAND	The task's command name, which will be truncated if it is too long to be displayed on one line. Tasks in memory will have a full command line, but swapped-out tasks will only have the name of the program in parentheses (for example, "(getty)").

INTERACTIVE COMMANDS

Several single-key commands are recognized while **top** is running. Some are disabled if the
s option has been given on the command line.

- L̂ Erases and redraws the screen.

h or ? Displays a help screen giving a brief summary of commands, and the status of secure and cumulative modes.

- k Kill a process. You will be prompted for the PID of the task, and the signal to send to it. For a normal kill, send signal 15. For a sure, but rather abrupt, kill, send signal 9. The default signal, as with **kill**(1), is 15, SIGTERM. This command is not available in secure mode.

- i Ignore idle and zombie processes. This is a toggle switch.

n or # Change the number of processes to show. You will be prompted to enter the number. This overrides automatic determination of the number of processes to show, which is based on window size measurement. If 0 is specified, then top will show as many processes as will fit on the screen; this is the default.

- q Quit.

- r Re-nice a process. You will be prompted for the PID of the task, and the value to nice it to. Entering a positve value will cause a process to be niced to negative values, and lose priority. If root is running **top**, a negative value can be entered, causing a process to get a higher than normal priority. The default renice value is 10. This command is not available in secure mode.

- S This toggles cumulative mode, the equivalent of **ps -S**, i.e., that CPU times will include a process's defunct children. For some programs, such as compilers, which work by forking into many seperate tasks, normal mode will make them appear less demanding than they actually are. For others, however, such as shells and **init**, this behavior is correct. In any case, try cumulative mode for an alternative view of CPU use.

- s Change the delay between updates. You will be prompted to enter the delay time, in seconds, between updates. Fractional values are recognized down to microseconds. Entering 0 causes continuous updates. The default value is 5 seconds. Note that low values cause nearly unreadably fast displays, and greatly raise the load. This command is not available in secure mode.

NOTES

This **proc**-based **top** works by reading the files in the **proc** filesystem, mounted on **/proc**. If **/proc** is not mounted, **top** will not work.

%CPU shows the cputime/realtime percentage in the period of time between updates. For the first update, a short delay is used, and **top** itself dominates the CPU usage. After that, **top** will drop back, and a more reliable estimate of CPU usage is available.

The **SIZE** and **RSS** fields don't count the page tables and the **task_struct** of a process; this is at least 12K of memory that is always resident. **SIZE** is the virtual size of the process (code+data+stack).

Keep in mind that a process must die for its time to be recorded on its parent by cumulative mode. Perhaps more useful behavior would be to follow each process upwards, adding time, but that would be more expensive, possibly prohibitively so. In any case, that would make **top**'s behavior incompatible with **ps**.

SEE ALSO

ps(1), **free**(1), **uptime**(1), **kill**(1), **renice**(1).

BUGS

If the window is less than about 70x7, **top** will not format information correctly.

AUTHOR

top was originally written by Roger Binns, based on Branko Lankester's (lankeste@fwi.uva.nl) ps program. Robert Nation (nation@rocket.sanders.lockheed.com) re-wrote it significantly to use the proc filesystem, based on Michael K Johnson's (johnsonm@sunsite.unc.edu) proc-based ps program. Many changes were made, including secure and cumulative modes and a general cleanup, by Michael Shields (mjshield@nyx.cs.du.edu).

TOUCH(1L)

NAME

touch – change file timestamps

SYNOPSIS

touch [–acfm] [–r reference-file] [–t MMDDhhmm[[CC]YY][.ss]] [–d time] [—time={atime, access, use, mtime, modify}] [—date=time] [—file=reference-file] [—no-create] [—help] [—version] file...

DESCRIPTION

This manual page documents the GNU version of **touch**. **touch** changes the access and modification times of each given file to the current time. Files that do not exist are created empty. If the first file name given would be a valid argument to the *–t* option and no timestamp is given with any of the *–d*, *–r*, or *–t* options and the — argument is not given, that argument is interpreted as the time for the other files instead of as a filename.

If changing both the access and modification times to the current time, **touch** can change the timestamps for files that the user running it does not own but has write permission for. Otherwise, the user must own the files.

OPTIONS

–a, —-*time=atime*, —-*time=access*, —-*time=use*	Change the access time only.
–c, —-*no-create*	Do not create files that do not exist.
–d, —-*date time*	Use *time* (which can be in various common formats) instead of the current time. It can contain month names, timezones, 'am' and 'pm', etc.
–f	Ignored; for compatibility with BSD versions of **touch**.
–m, —-*time=mtime*, —-*time=modify*	Change the modification time only.
–r, —-*file reference-file*	Use the times of *reference-file* instead of the current time.
–t MMDDhhmm[[CC]YY][.ss]	Use the argument (months, days, hours, minutes, optional century and years, optional seconds) instead of the current time.
—-*help*	Print a usage message on standard output and exit successfully.
—-*version*	Print version information on standard output then exit successfully.

TR(1L)   FSF   TR(1L)

NAME

tr – translate or delete characters

SYNOPSIS

tr [–cst] [—-complement] [—-squeeze–repeats] [—-truncate–set1] string1 string2
tr {–s,—-squeeze–repeats} [–c] [—-complement] string1
tr {–d,—-delete} [–c] string1
tr {–d,—-delete} {–s,—-squeeze–repeats} [–c] [—-complement] string1 string2

GNU **tr** also accepts the —-help and —-version options.

DESCRIPTION

This manual page documents the GNU version of **tr**. **tr** copies the standard input to the standard output, performing one of the following operations:

>   translate, and optionally squeeze repeated characters in the result
>   squeeze repeated characters
>   delete characters
>   delete characters, then squeeze repeated characters from the result

The *string1* and (if given) *string2* arguments define ordered sets of characters, referred to below as set1 and set2. These sets are the characters of the input that **tr** operates on. The —-*complement* (*–c*) option replaces set1 with its complement (all of the characters that are not in set1).

SPECIFYING SETS OF CHARACTERS

The format of the *string1* and *string2* arguments resembles the format of regular expressions; however, they are not regular expressions, only lists of characters. Most characters simply represent themselves in these strings, but the strings can contain the shorthands listed below, for convenience. Some of them can be used only in *string1* or *string2*, as noted below.

Backslash escapes. A backslash followed by a character not listed below causes an error message.

>   \a   Control-G.
>   \b   Control-H.
>   \f   Control-L.
>   \n   Control-J.
>   \r   Control-M.
>   \t   Control-I.
>   \v   Control-K.
> \ooo   The character with the value given by *ooo*, which is 1 to 3 octal digits.
>   \\   A backslash.

Ranges. The notation '*m–n*' expands to all of the characters from *m* through *n*, in ascending order. *m* should collate before *n*; if it doesn't, an error results. As an example, '0–9' is the same as '0123456789'. Although GNU **tr** does not support the System V syntax that uses square brackets to enclose ranges, translations specified in that format will still work as long as the brackets in string1 correspond to identical brackets in string2.

Repeated characters. The notation '[*c*n*]' in *string2* expands to *n* copies of character *c*. Thus, '[y*6]' is the same as 'yyyyyy'. The notation '[*c**]' in *string2* expands to as many copies of *c* as are needed to make set2 as long as set1. If *n* begins with a 0, it is interpreted in octal, otherwise in decimal.

Character classes. The notation '[:*class-name*:]' expands to all of the characters in the (predefined) class named *class-name*. The characters expand in no particular order, except for the 'upper' and 'lower' classes, which expand in ascending order. When the ---*delete* (–d) and ---*squeeze–repeats* (–s) options are both given, any character class can be used in *string2*. Otherwise, only the character classes 'lower' and 'upper' are accepted in *string2*, and then only if the corresponding character class ('upper' and 'lower', respectively) is specified in the same relative position in *string1*. Doing this specifies case conversion. The class names are given below; an error results when an invalid class name is given.

alnum Letters and digits.
alpha Letters.
blank Horizontal whitespace.
cntrl Control characters.
digit Digits.
graph Printable characters, not including space.
lower Lowercase letters.
print Printable characters, including space.
punct Punctuation characters.
space Horizontal or vertical whitespace.
upper Uppercase letters.
xdigit Hexadecimal digits.

Equivalence classes. The syntax '[=*c*=]' expands to all of the characters that are equivalent to *c*, in no particular order. Equivalence classes are a recent invention intended to support non-English alphabets. But there seems to be no standard way to define them or determine their contents. Therefore, they are not fully implemented in GNU **tr**; each character's equivalence class consists only of that character, which makes this a useless construction currently.

TRANSLATING

tr performs translation when *string1* and *string2* are both given and the ---delete (–*d*) option is not given. **tr** translates each character of its input that is in set1 to the corresponding character in set2. Characters not in set1 are passed through unchanged. When a character appears more than once in set1 and the corresponding characters in set2 are not all the same, only the final one is used. For example, these two commands are equivalent:

tr aaa xyz
tr a z

A common use of **tr** is to convert lowercase characters to uppercase. This can be done in many ways. Here are three of them:

tr abcdefghijklmnopqrstuvwxyz ABCDEFGHIJKLMNOPQRSTUVWXYZ
tr a-z A-Z
tr '[:lower:]' '[:upper:]'

When **tr** is performing translation, set1 and set2 should normally have the same length. If set1 is shorter than set2, the extra characters at the end of set2 are ignored.

On the other hand, making set1 longer than set2 is not portable; POSIX.2 says that the result is undefined. In this situation, the BSD **tr** pads set2 to the length of set1 by repeating the last character of set2 as many times as necessary. The System V **tr** truncates set1 to the length of set2.

By default, GNU **tr** handles this case like the BSD **tr** does. When the ---truncate–set1 (–*t*) option is given, GNU **tr** handles this case like the System V **tr** instead. This option is ignored for operations other than translation.

Acting like the System V **tr** in this case breaks the relatively common BSD idiom:

tr -cs A-Za-z0-9 '\012'

because it converts only zero bytes (the first element in the complement of set1), rather than all non-alphanumerics, to newlines.

SQUEEZING REPEATS AND DELETING

When given just the —delete (–d) option, **tr** removes any input characters that are in set1.

When given just the —squeeze–repeats (–s) option, **tr** replaces each input sequence of a repeated character that is in set1 with a single occurrence of that character.

When given both the —delete and the —squeeze–repeats options, **tr** first performs any deletions using set1, then squeezes repeats from any remaining characters using set2.

The —squeeze–repeats option may also be used when translating, in which case **tr** first performs translation, then squeezes repeats from any remaining characters using set2.

Here are some examples to illustrate various combinations of options:

Remove all zero bytes:

tr -d '\000'

Put all words on lines by themselves. This converts all non-alphanumeric characters to newlines, then squeezes each string of repeated newlines into a single newline:

tr -cs '[a-zA-Z0-9]' '[\n*]'

Convert each sequence of repeated newlines to a single newline:

tr -s '\n'

GNU **tr** also accepts the following options in any combination with the others.

    —*help*   Print a usage message and exit with a non-zero status.

    —*version*   Print version information on standard output then exit.

WARNING MESSAGES

Setting the environment variable POSIXLY_CORRECT turns off several warning and error messages, for strict compliance with POSIX.2. The messages normally occur in the following circumstances:

1. When the —*delete* option is given but —*squeeze–repeats* is not, and *string2* is given, GNU **tr** by default prints a usage message and exits, because *string2* would not be used. The POSIX specification says that *string2* must be ignored in this case. Silently ignoring arguments is a bad idea.

2. When an ambiguous octal escape is given. For example, \400 is actually \40 followed by the digit 0, because the value 400 octal does not fit into a single byte.

Note that GNU **tr** does not provide complete BSD or System V compatibility. For example, there is no option to disable interpretation of the POSIX constructs [:alpha:], [=c=], and [c*10]. Also, GNU **tr** does not delete zero bytes automatically, unlike traditional UNIX versions, which provide no way to preserve zero bytes.

TSET(1)　　　　　　　　　　　　　　　　　　　　　　　　　　　　　TSET(1)

NAME

tset, reset – terminal initialization

SYNOPSIS

tset [-IQrs] [-t] [-e ch] [-i ch] [-k ch] [-m mapping] [terminal]
tset -h
tset -V
reset [-IQrs] [-t] [-e ch] [-i ch] [-k ch] [-m mapping] [terminal]
reset -h
reset -V

DESCRIPTION

Tset initializes terminals. Tset first determines the type of terminal that you are using. This determination is done as follows, using the first terminal type found.

　　　The terminal argument specified on the command line.

　　　The value of the TERM environmental variable.

　　　The terminal type associated with the standard error output device in the /etc/ttytype file.

　　　The default terminal type, "unknown".

If the terminal type was not specified on the command-line, the -m option mappings are then applied (see below for more information). Then, if the terminal type begins with a question mark ("?"), the user is prompted for confirmation of the terminal type. An empty response confirms the type, or, another type can be entered to specify a new type. Once the terminal type has been determined, the termcap entry for the terminal is retrieved. If no termcap entry is found for the type, the user is prompted for another terminal type.

Once the termcap entry is retrieved, the window size, backspace, interrupt and line kill characters (among many other things) are set and the terminal and tab initialization strings are sent to the standard error output. Finally, if the erase, interrupt and line kill characters have changed, or are not set to their default values, their values are displayed to the standard error output.

When invoked as reset, tset sets cooked and echo modes, turns off cbreak and raw modes, turns on newline translation and resets any unset special characters to their default values before doing the terminal initialization described above. This is useful after a program dies leaving a terminal in a abnormal state. Note, you may have to type <LF>reset<LF> (the line-feed character is normally control-J) to get the terminal to work, as carriage-return may no longer work in the abnormal state. Also, the terminal will often not echo the command.

OPTIONS

The options are as follows:

　　-t　The terminal type is displayed to the standard output, and the terminal is not initialized in any way.

　　-e　Set the erase character to ch.

　　-I　Do not send the terminal or tab initialization strings to the terminal.

　　-i　Set the interrupt character to ch.

　　-k　Set the line kill character to ch.

　　-m　Specify a mapping from a port type to a terminal. See below for more information.

　　-r　Print the terminal type to the standard error output.

　　-s　Print the sequence of shell commands to initialize the environment variables COLUMNS, LINES, TERM and TERMCAP to the standard output.

　　Q　Don't display any values for the erase, interrupt and line kill characters.

TSET(1)

-w   Force setting of display size as defined in /etc/termcap file.

-h   Print short usage message.

-V   Print version number.

The arguments for the -e , -i and -k options may either be entered as actual characters or by using the hat notation, i.e. control-h may be specified as Ĥ or ĥ .

SETTING THE ENVIRONMENT

It is often desirable to set the terminal type and information about the terminal's capabilities and display size in the shell's environment. This is done with the -s option; when this option is specified, the commands to enter the information into the shell's environment are output to the standard output. If the SHELL environmental variable ends in "csh", the output commands are for the csh 1 , otherwise, they are for sh 1 . Note, the output commands for the csh set and unset the shell variable noglob . The following line in the .login or .profile files will initialize the environment correctly:

   eval 'tset -s options ... '

TERMINAL TYPE MAPPING

When the terminal is not hardwired into the system (or the current system information is incorrect) the terminal type derived from the /etc/ttytype file or the TERM environmental variable is often something generic like network , dialup , or unknown . When tset is used in a startup script .profile for sh 1 users or .login for csh 1 users) it is often desirable to provide information about the type of terminal used on such ports. The purpose of the -m option is to map from some set of conditions to a terminal type, that is, to tell tset "If I'm on this port at a particular speed, guess that I'm on that kind of terminal".

The argument to the -m option consists of an optional port type, an optional operator, an optional baud rate specification, an optional colon (":") character and a terminal type. The port type is a string (delimited by either the operator or the colon character). The operator may be any combination of: &>, &<, &@ , and &! ; &> means greater than, &< means less than, &@ means equal to and &! inverts the sense of the test. The baud rate is specified as a number and is compared with the speed of the standard error output (which should be the control terminal). The terminal type is a string.

If the terminal type is not specified on the command line, the -m mappings are applied to the terminal type. If the port type and baud rate match the mapping, the terminal type specified in the mapping replaces the current type. If more than one mapping is specified, the first applicable mapping is used.

For example, consider the following:

   dialup>9600:vt100 .

The port type is dialup , the operator is > , the baud rate specification is 9600 , and the terminal type is vt100 . The result of this mapping is to specify that if the terminal type is dialup , and the baud rate is greater than 9600 baud, a terminal type of vt100 will be used.

If no port type is specified, the terminal type will match any port type, for example,

   -m dialup:vt100 -m :?xterm

will cause any dialup port, regardless of baud rate, to match the terminal type

   vt100 ,

and any non-dialup port type to match the terminal type

   ?xterm .

Note, because of the leading question mark, the user will be queried on a default port as to whether they are actually using an xterm terminal.

TSET(1)   TSET(1)

No whitespace characters are permitted in the -m option argument. Also, to avoid problems with metacharacters, it is suggested that the entire -m option argument be placed within single quote characters, and that csh users insert a backslash character ("\") before any exclamation marks ("!").

ENVIRONMENT

The tset command utilizes the SHELL, and TERM environment variables.

Tset can set COLUMNS, LINES, TERM and TERMCAP environmental variables.

FILES

/etc/ttytype   system port name to terminal type mapping database

/etc/termcap   terminal capability database

SEE ALSO

csh 1 , tcsh 1 , sh 1 , bash 1 , stty 1 , tty 4 , termcap 5 , ttytype 5 , environ 7

HISTORY

The tset command appeared in BSD 3.0 .

COMPATIBILITY

The -A , -E , -h , -S , -u and -v options have been deleted from the tset utility. None of them were documented in 4.3BSD and all are of limited utility at best. The -a , -d and -p options are similarly not documented or useful, but were retained as they appear to be in widespread use. It is strongly recommended that any usage of these three options be changed to use the -m option instead. The -n option remains, but has no effect. It is still permissible to specify the -e , -i and -k options without arguments, although it is strongly recommended that such usage be fixed to explicitly specify the character.

Executing tset as reset no longer implies the -Q option. Also, the interaction between the -option and the terminal argument in some historic implementations of tset has been removed and has been replaced with -t option.

Finally, the tset implementation has been completely redone (as part of the addition to the system of a IEEE Std1003.1-1988 ("POSIX") compliant terminal interface) and will no longer compile on systems with older terminal interfaces.

TSORT(1)

NAME

tsort – topological sort of a directed graph

SYNOPSIS

tsort [file]

DESCRIPTION

Tsort takes a list of pairs of node names representing directed arcs in a graph and prints the nodes in topological order on standard output. Input is taken from the named file, or from standard input if no file is given.

Node names in the input are separated by white space and there must be an even number of nodes.

Presence of a node in a graph can be represented by an arc from the node to itself. This is useful when a node is not connected to any other nodes.

If the graph contains a cycle (and therefore cannot be properly sorted), one of the arcs in the cycle is ignored and the sort continues. Cycles are reported on standard error.

SEE ALSO

ar(1)

HISTORY

A tsort command appeared in AT&T v7. This tsort command and manual page are derived from sources contributed to Berkeley by Michael Rendell of Memorial University of Newfoundland.

TWM(1)

NAME

twm – Tab Window Manager for the X Window System

SYNTAX

twm [**–display** *dpy*] [**–s**] [**–f** *initfile*] [**–v**]

DESCRIPTION

Twm is a window manager for the X Window System. It provides titlebars, shaped windows, several forms of icon management, user-defined macro functions, click-to-type and pointer-driven keyboard focus, and user-specified key and pointer button bindings.

This program is usually started by the user's session manager or startup script. When used from *xdm(1)* or *xinit(1)* without a session manager, *twm* is frequently executed in the foreground as the last client. When run this way, exiting *twm* causes the session to be terminated (i.e., logged out).

By default, application windows are surrounded by a "frame" with a titlebar at the top and a special border around the window. The titlebar contains the window's name, a rectangle that is lit when the window is receiving keyboard input, and function boxes known as "titlebuttons" at the left and right edges of the titlebar.

Pressing pointer Button1 (usually the left-most button unless it has been changed with *xmodmap*) on a titlebutton will invoke the function associated with the button. In the default interface, windows are iconified by clicking (pressing and then immediately releasing) the left titlebutton (which looks like a Dot). Conversely, windows are deiconified by clicking in the associated icon or entry in the icon manager (see description of the variable **ShowIconManager** and of the function **f.showiconmgr**).

Windows are resized by pressing the right titlebutton (which resembles a group of nested squares), dragging the pointer over edge that is to be moved, and releasing the pointer when the outline of the window is the desired size. Similarly, windows are moved by pressing in the title or highlight region, dragging a window outline to the new location, and then releasing when the outline is in the desired position. Just clicking in the title or highlight region raises the window without moving it.

When new windows are created, *twm* will honor any size and location information requested by the user (usually through *-geometry* command line argument or resources for the individual applications). Otherwise, an outline of the window's default size, its titlebar, and lines dividing the window into a 3x3 grid that track the pointer are displayed. Clicking pointer Button1 will position the window at the current position and give it the default size. Pressing pointer Button2 (usually the middle pointer button) and dragging the outline will give the window its current position but allow the sides to be resized as described above. Clicking pointer Button3 (usually the right pointer button) will give the window its current position but attempt to make it long enough to touch the bottom the screen.

OPTIONS

Twm accepts the following command line options:

–display *dpy*   This option specifies the X server to use.

–s   This option indicates that only the default screen (as specified by **–display** or by the **DISPLAY** environment variable) should be managed. By default, *twm* will attempt to manage all screens on the display.

–f *filename*   This option specifies the name of the startup file to use. By default, *twm* will look in the user's home directory for files named *.twmrc.num* (where *num* is a screen number) or *.twmrc*.

–v   This option indicates that *twm* should print error messages whenever an unexpected X Error event is received. This can be useful when debugging applications but can be distracting in regular use.

TWM(1)   TWM(1)

CUSTOMIZATION

Much of *twm*'s appearance and behavior can be controlled by providing a startup file in one of the following locations (searched in order for each screen being managed when *twm* begins):

> **$HOME/.twmrc.***screennumber*   The *screennumber* is a small positive number (e.g. 0, 1, etc.) representing the screen number (e.g. the last number in the DISPLAY environment variable *host:displaynum.screennum*) that would be used to contact that screen of the display. This is intended for displays with multiple screens of differing visual types.
>
> **$HOME/.twmrc**   This is the usual name for an individual user's startup file.
>
> **<XRoot>/lib/X11/twm/system.twmrc**   If neither of the preceding files are found, *twm* will look in this file for a default configuration. This is often tailored by the site administrator to provide convenient menus or familiar bindings for novice users. <XRoot> refers to the root of the X11 install tree.

If no startup files are found, *twm* will use the built-in defaults described above. The only resource used by *twm* is *bitmapFilePath* for a colon-separated list of directories to search when looking for bitmap files (for more information, see the *Athena Widgets* manual and *xrdb(1)*).

Twm startup files are logically broken up into three types of specifications: *Variables*, *Bindings*, *Menus*. The *Variables* section must come first and is used to describe the fonts, colors, cursors, border widths, icon and window placement, highlighting, autoraising, layout of titles, warping, use of the icon manager. The *Bindings* section usually comes second and is used to specify the functions that should be to be invoked when keyboard and pointer buttons are pressed in windows, icons, titles, and frames. The *Menus* section gives any user-defined menus (containing functions to be invoked or commands to be executed).

Variable names and keywords are case-insensitive. Strings must be surrounded by double quote characters (e.g. "blue") and are case-sensitive. A pound sign (#) outside of a string causes the remainder of the line in which the character appears to be treated as a comment.

VARIABLES

Many of the aspects of *twm*'s user interface are controlled by variables that may be set in the user's startup file. Some of the options are enabled or disabled simply by the presence of a particular keyword. Other options require keywords, numbers, strings, or lists of all of these.

Lists are surrounded by braces and are usually separated by whitespace or a newline. For example:

AutoRaise { "emacs" "XTerm" "Xmh" } or **AutoRaise**
{
"emacs"
"XTerm"
"Xmh"
}

When a variable containing a list of strings representing windows is searched (e.g. to determine whether or not to enable autoraise as shown above), a string must be an exact, case-sensitive match to the window's name (given by the WM_NAME window property), resource name or class name (both given by the WM_CLASS window property). The preceding example would enable autoraise on windows named "emacs" as well as any *xterm* (since they are of class "XTerm") or xmh windows (which are of class "Xmh").

String arguments that are interpreted as filenames (see the **Pixmaps**, **Cursors**, and **Icon-**

Directory below) will prepend the user's directory (specified by the **HOME** environment variable) if the first character is a tilde (~). If, instead, the first character is a colon (:), the name is assumed to refer to one of the internal bitmaps that are used to create the default titlebars symbols: **:xlogo**

or **:delete** (both refer to the X logo), **:dot** or **:iconify** (both refer to the dot), **:resize** (the nested squares used by the resize button), **:menu** (a page with lines), and **:question** (the question mark used for non-existent bitmap files).

The following variables may be specified at the top of a *twm* startup file. Lists of Window name prefix strings are indicated by *win-list*. Optional arguments are shown in square brackets:

AutoRaise { *win-list* } This variable specifies a list of windows that should automatically be raised whenever the pointer enters the window. This action can be interactively enabled or disabled on individual windows using the function **f.autoraise**.

AutoRelativeResize This variable indicates that dragging out a window size (either when initially sizing the window with pointer Button2 or when resizing it) should not wait until the pointer has crossed the window edges. Instead, moving the pointer automatically causes the nearest edge or edges to move by the same amount. This allows the resizing of windows that extend off the edge of the screen. If the pointer is in the center of the window, or if the resize is begun by pressing a titlebutton, *twm* will still wait for the pointer to cross a window edge (to prevent accidents). This option is particularly useful for people who like the press-drag-release method of sweeping out window sizes.

BorderColor *string* [{ *wincolorlist* }] This variable specifies the default color of the border to be placed around all non-iconified windows, and may only be given within a **Color**, **Grayscale** or **Monochrome** list. The optional *wincolorlist* specifies a list of window and color name pairs for specifying particular border colors for different types of windows. For example:
BorderColor
"gray50"
{
"XTerm" "red"
"xmh" "green"
}
The default is "black".

BorderTileBackground *string* [{ *wincolorlist* }] This variable specifies the default background color in the gray pattern used in unhighlighted borders (only if **NoHighlight** hasn't been set), and may only be given within a **Color**, **Grayscale** or **Monochrome** list. The optional *wincolorlist* allows per-window colors to be specified. The default is "white".

BorderTileForeground *string* [{ *wincolorlist* }] This variable specifies the default foreground color in the gray pattern used in unhighlighted borders (only if **NoHighlight** hasn't been set), and may only be given within a **Color**, **Grayscale** or **Monochrome** list. The optional *wincolorlist* allows per-window colors to be specified. The default is "black".

BorderWidth *pixels* This variable specifies the width in pixels of the border surrounding all client window frames if **ClientBorderWidth** has not been specified. This value is also used to set the border size of windows created by *twm* (such as the icon manager). The default is 2.

ButtonIndent *pixels* This variable specifies the amount by which titlebuttons should be indented on all sides. Positive values cause the buttons to be smaller than the window text and highlight area so that they stand out. Setting this and the **TitleButtonBorderWidth** variables to 0 makes titlebuttons be as tall and wide as possible. The default is 1.

ClientBorderWidth   This variable indicates that border width of a window's frame should be set to the initial border width of the window, rather than to the value of **BorderWidth**.

Color { *colors-list* }   This variable specifies a list of color assignments to be made if the default display is capable of displaying more than simple black and white. The *colors-list* is made up of the following color variables and their values: **DefaultBackground, DefaultForeground, MenuBackground, MenuForeground, MenuTitleBackground, MenuTitleForeground, MenuShadowColor, PointerForeground,** and **PointerBackground**. The following color variables may also be given a list of window and color name pairs to allow per-window colors to be specified (see **BorderColor** for details): **BorderColor, IconManagerHighlight, BorderTitleBackground, BorderTitleForeground, TitleBackground, TitleForeground, IconBackground, IconForeground, IconBorderColor, IconManagerBackground,** and **IconManagerForeground**. For example:
Color
{
MenuBackground "gray50"
MenuForeground "blue"
BorderColor "red" { "XTerm" "yellow" }
TitleForeground "yellow"
TitleBackground "blue"
}
All of these color variables may also be specified for the **Monochrome** variable, allowing the same initialization file to be used on both color and monochrome displays.

ConstrainedMoveTime *milliseconds*   This variable specifies the length of time between button clicks needed to begin a constrained move operation. Double clicking within this amount of time when invoking **f.move** will cause the window to be moved only in a horizontal or vertical direction. Setting this value to 0 will disable constrained moves. The default is 400 milliseconds.

Cursors { *cursor-list* }   This variable specifies the glyphs that *twm* should use for various pointer cursors. Each cursor may be defined either from the **cursor** font or from two bitmap files. Shapes from the **cursor** font may be specified directly as: 0 *cursorname* "*string*"

where *cursorname* is one of the cursor names listed below, and *string* is the name of a glyph as found in the file <XRoot>/include/X11/cursorfont.h (without the "XC_" prefix). If the cursor is to be defined from bitmap files, the following syntax is used instead: 0 *cursorname* "*image*" "*mask*"
The *image* and *mask* strings specify the names of files containing the glyph image and mask in *bitmap(1)* form. The bitmap files are located in the same manner as icon bitmap files. The following example shows the default cursor definitions:

```
Cursors
{
        Frame           "top_left_arrow"
        Title           "top_left_arrow"
        Icon            "top_left_arrow"
        IconMgr  "top_left_arrow"
        Move            "fleur"
        Resize          "fleur"
        Menu            "sb_left_arrow"
        Button          "hand2"
        Wait            "watch"
        Select          "dot"
        Destroy "pirate"
}
```

DecorateTransients   This variable indicates that transient windows (those containing a WM_TRANSIENT_FOR property) should have titlebars. By default, transients are not reparented.

DefaultBackground *string*   This variable specifies the background color to be used for sizing and information windows. The default is "white".

DefaultForeground *string*   This variable specifies the foreground color to be used for sizing and information windows. The default is "black".

DontIconifyByUnmapping { *win-list* }   This variable specifies a list of windows that should not be iconified by simply unmapping the window (as would be the case if **IconifyByUnmapping** had been set). This is frequently used to force some windows to be treated as icons while other windows are handled by the icon manager.

DontMoveOff   This variable indicates that windows should not be allowed to be moved off the screen. It can be overridden by the **f.forcemove** function.

DontSqueezeTitle [{ *win-list* }]   This variable indicates that titlebars should not be squeezed to their minimum size as described under **SqueezeTitle** below. If the optional window list is supplied, only those windows will be prevented from being squeezed.

ForceIcons   This variable indicates that icon pixmaps specified in the **Icons** variable should override any client-supplied pixmaps.

FramePadding *pixels*   This variable specifies the distance between the titlebar decorations (the button and text) and the window frame. The default is 2 pixels.

Grayscale { *colors* }   This variable specifies a list of color assignments that should be made if the screen has a GrayScale default visual. See the description of **Colors**.

IconBackground *string* [{ *win-list* }]   This variable specifies the background color of icons, and may only be specified inside of a **Color**, **Grayscale** or **Monochrome** list. The optional *win-list* is a list of window names and colors so that per-window colors may be specified. See the **BorderColor** variable for a complete description of the *win-list*. The default is "white".

IconBorderColor *string* [{ *win-list* }]   This variable specifies the color of the border used for icon windows, and may only be specified inside of a **Color**, **Grayscale** or **Monochrome** list. The optional *win-list* is a list of window names and colors so that per-window colors may be specified. See the **BorderColor** variable for a complete description of the *win-list*. The default is "black".

IconBorderWidth *pixels*   This variable specifies the width in pixels of the border surrounding icon windows. The default is 2.

IconDirectory *string*   This variable specifies the directory that should be searched if if a bitmap file cannot be found in any of the directories in the **bitmapFilePath** resource.

IconFont *string*   This variable specifies the font to be used to display icon names within icons. The default is "variable".

IconForeground *string* [{ *win-list* }]   This variable specifies the foreground color to be used when displaying icons, and may only be specified inside of a **Color**, **Grayscale** or **Monochrome** list. The optional *win-list* is a list of window names and colors so that per-window colors may be specified. See the **BorderColor** variable for a complete description of the *win-list*. The default is "black".

IconifyByUnmapping [{ *win-list* }]   This variable indicates that windows should be iconified by being unmapped without trying to map any icons. This assumes that the user will remap the window through the icon manager, the **f.warpto** function, or the *TwmWindows* menu. If the optional *win-list* is provided, only those windows will be iconified by simply unmapping. Windows that have both this and the **IconManagerDontShow** options set may not be accessible if no binding to the *TwmWindows* menu is set in the user's startup file.

IconManagerBackground *string* [{ *win-list* }]   This variable specifies the background color to use for icon manager entries, and may only be specified inside of a **Color**, **Grayscale** or **Monochrome** list. The optional *win-list* is a list of window names and colors so that per-window colors may be specified. See the **BorderColor** variable for a complete description of the *win-list*. The default is "white".

IconManagerDontShow [{ *win-list* }]   This variable indicates that the icon manager should not display any windows. If the optional *win-list* is given, only those windows will not be displayed. This variable is used to prevent windows that are rarely iconified (such as *xclock* or *xload*) from taking up space in the icon manager.

IconManagerFont *string*   This variable specifies the font to be used when displaying icon manager entries. The default is "variable".

IconManagerForeground *string* [{ *win-list* }]   This variable specifies the foreground color to be used when displaying icon manager entries, and may only be specified inside of a **Color**, **Grayscale** or **Monochrome** list. The optional *win-list* is a list of window names and colors so that per-window colors may be specified. See the **BorderColor** variable for a complete description of the *win-list*. The default is "black".

IconManagerGeometry *string* [*columns*]   This variable specifies the geometry of the icon manager window. The *string* argument is standard geometry specification that indicates the initial full size of the icon manager. The icon manager window is then broken into *columns* pieces and scaled according to the number of entries in the icon manager. Extra entries are wrapped to form additional rows. The default number of columns is 1.

IconManagerHighlight *string* [{ *win-list* }]   This variable specifies the border color to be used when highlighting the icon manager entry that currently has the focus, and can only be specified inside of a **Color**, **Grayscale** or **Monochrome** list. The optional *win-list* is a list of window names and colors so that per-window colors may be specified. See the **BorderColor** variable for a complete description of the *win-list*. The default is "black".

IconManagers { *iconmgr-list* }   This variable specifies a list of icon managers to create. Each item in the *iconmgr-list* has the following format: 0 *"winname"* [*"iconname"*] *"geometry" columns*

where *winname* is the name of the windows that should be put into this icon manager, *iconname* is the name of that icon manager window's icon, *geometry* is a standard geometry specification, and *columns* is the number of columns in this icon manager as described in **IconManagerGeometry**. For example:
IconManagers
{
"XTerm" "=300x5+800+5" 5
"myhost" "=400x5+100+5" 2
}
Clients whose name or class is "XTerm" will have an entry created in the "XTerm" icon manager. Clients whose name was "myhost" would be put into the "myhost" icon manager.

IconManagerShow { *win-list* }   This variable specifies a list of windows that should appear in the icon manager. When used in conjunction with the **Icon-**

ManagerDontShow variable, only the windows in this list will be shown in the icon manager.

IconRegion *geomstring vgrav hgrav gridwidth gridheight*   This variable specifies an area on the root window in which icons are placed if no specific icon location is provided by the client. The *geomstring* is a quoted string containing a standard geometry specification. If more than one **Icon-Region** lines are given, icons will be put into the succeeding icon regions when the first is full. The *vgrav* argument should be either **North** or **South** and control and is used to control whether icons are first filled in from the top or bottom of the icon region. Similarly, the *hgrav* argument should be either **East** or **West** and is used to control whether icons should be filled in from left from the right. Icons are laid out within the region in a grid with cells *gridwidth* pixels wide and *gridheight* pixels high.

Icons { *win-list* }   This variable specifies a list of window names and the bitmap filenames that should be used as their icons. For example:
Icons
{
"XTerm" "xterm.icon"
"xfd" "xfd_icon"
}
Windows that match "XTerm" and would not be iconified by unmapping, and would try to use the icon bitmap in the file "xterm.icon". If **ForceIcons** is specified, this bitmap will be used even if the client has requested its own icon pixmap.

InterpolateMenuColors   This variable indicates that menu entry colors should be interpolated between entry specified colors. In the example below:
Menu "mymenu"
{
"Title" ("black":"red") f.title
"entry1" f.nop
"entry2" f.nop
"entry3" ("white":"green") f.nop
"entry4" f.nop
"entry5" ("red":"white") f.nop
}
the foreground colors for "entry1" and "entry2" will be interpolated between black and white, and the background colors between red and green. Similarly, the foreground for "entry4" will be half-way between white and red, and the background will be half-way between green and white.

MakeTitle { *win-list* }   This variable specifies a list of windows on which a titlebar should be placed and is used to request titles on specific windows when **NoTitle** has been set.

MaxWindowSize *string*   This variable specifies a geometry in which the width and height give the maximum size for a given window. This is typically used to restrict windows to the size of the screen. The default width is 32767 - screen width. The default height is 32767 - screen height.

MenuBackground *string*   This variable specifies the background color used for menus, and can only be specified inside of a **Color** or **Monochrome** list. The default is "white".

MenuFont *string*   This variable specifies the font to use when displaying menus. The default is "variable".

MenuForeground *string*   This variable specifies the foreground color used for menus, and can only be specified inside of a **Color**, **Grayscale** or **Monochrome** list. The default is "black".

MenuShadowColor *string*   This variable specifies the color of the shadow behind pull-down menus and can only be specified inside of a **Color**, **Grayscale** or **Monochrome** list. The default is "black".

MenuTitleBackground *string*   This variable specifies the background color for **f.title** entries in menus, and can only be specified inside of a **Color**, **Grayscale** or **Monochrome** list. The default is "white".

MenuTitleForeground *string*   This variable specifies the foreground color for **f.title** entries in menus and can only be specified inside of a **Color** or **Monochrome** list. The default is "black".

Monochrome { *colors* }   This variable specifies a list of color assignments that should be made if the screen has a depth of 1. See the description of **Colors**.

MoveDelta *pixels*   This variable specifies the number of pixels the pointer must move before the **f.move** function starts working. Also see the **f.deltastop** function. The default is zero pixels.

NoBackingStore   This variable indicates that *twm*'s menus should not request backing store to minimize repainting of menus. This is typically used with servers that can repaint faster than they can handle backing store.

NoCaseSensitive   This variable indicates that case should be ignored when sorting icon names in an icon manager. This option is typically used with applications that capitalize the first letter of their icon name.

NoDefaults   This variable indicates that *twm* should not supply the default titlebuttons and bindings. This option should only be used if the startup file contains a completely new set of bindings and definitions.

NoGrabServer   This variable indicates that *twm* should not grab the server when popping up menus and moving opaque windows.

NoHighlight [{ *win-list* }]   This variable indicates that borders should not be highlighted to track the location of the pointer. If the optional *win-list* is given, highlighting will only be disabled for those windows. When the border is highlighted, it will be drawn in the current **BorderColor**. When the border is not highlighted, it will be stippled with a gray pattern using the current **BorderTileForeground** and **BorderTileBackground** colors.

NoIconManagers   This variable indicates that no icon manager should be created.

NoMenuShadows   This variable indicates that menus should not have drop shadows drawn behind them. This is typically used with slower servers since it speeds up menu drawing at the expense of making the menu slightly harder to read.

NoRaiseOnDeiconify   This variable indicates that windows that are deiconified should not be raised.

NoRaiseOnMove   This variable indicates that windows should not be raised when moved. This is typically used to allow windows to slide underneath each other.

NoRaiseOnResize   This variable indicates that windows should not be raised when resized. This is typically used to allow windows to be resized underneath each other.

NoRaiseOnWarp   This variable indicates that windows should not be raised when the pointer is warped into them with the **f.warpto** function. If this option is set, warping to an occluded window may result in the pointer ending up in the occluding window instead the desired window (which causes unexpected behavior with **f.warpring**).

NoSaveUnders   This variable indicates that menus should not request save-unders to minimize window repainting following menu selection. It is typically used with displays that can repaint faster than they can handle save-unders.

NoStackMode [{ *win-list* }]   This variable indicates that client window requests to change stacking order should be ignored. If the optional *win-list* is given, only requests on those windows will be ignored. This is typically used to prevent applications from relentlessly popping themselves to the front of the window stack.

NoTitle [{ *win-list* }]   This variable indicates that windows should not have titlebars. If the optional *win-list* is given, only those windows will not have titlebars. **MakeTitle** may be used with this option to force titlebars to be put on specific windows.

NoTitleFocus   This variable indicates that *twm* should not set keyboard input focus to each window as it is entered. Normally, *twm* sets the focus so that focus and key events from the titlebar and icon managers are delivered to the application. If the pointer is moved quickly and *twm* is slow to respond, input can be directed to the old window instead of the new. This option is typically used to prevent this "input lag" and to work around bugs in older applications that have problems with focus events.

NoTitleHighlight [{ *win-list* }]   This variable indicates that the highlight area of the titlebar, which is used to indicate the window that currently has the input focus, should not be displayed. If the optional *win-list* is given, only those windows will not have highlight areas. This and the **SqueezeTitle** options can be set to substantially reduce the amount of screen space required by titlebars.

OpaqueMove   This variable indicates that the **f.move** function should actually move the window instead of just an outline so that the user can immediately see what the window will look like in the new position. This option is typically used on fast displays (particularly if **NoGrabServer** is set).

Pixmaps { *pixmaps* }   This variable specifies a list of pixmaps that define the appearance of various images. Each entry is a keyword indicating the pixmap to set, followed by a string giving the name of the bitmap file. The following pixmaps may be specified: 0 **Pixmaps** { TitleHighlight "gray1" }

The default for *TitleHighlight* is to use an even stipple pattern.

Priority *priority*   This variable sets *twm*'s priority. *priority* should be an unquoted, signed number (e.g. 999). This variable has an effect only if the server supports the SYNC extension.

RandomPlacement   This variable indicates that windows with no specified geometry should be placed in a pseudo-random location instead of having the user drag out an outline.

ResizeFont *string*   This variable specifies the font to be used for in the dimensions window when resizing windows. The default is "fixed".

RestartPreviousState   This variable indicates that *twm* should attempt to use the WM_STATE property on client windows to tell which windows should be iconified and which should be left visible. This is typically used to try to regenerate the state that the screen was in before the previous window manager was shutdown.

SaveColor { *colors-list* }   This variable indicates a list of color assignments to be stored as pixel values in the root window property _MIT_PRIORITY_COLORS. Clients may elect to preserve these values when installing their own colormap. Note that use of this mechanism is a way an for application to avoid the "technicolor" problem, whereby useful screen objects such as window borders and titlebars disappear when a programs custom colors are installed by the window manager. For example:
SaveColor
{
BorderColor
TitleBackground

```
TitleForeground
"red"
"green"
"blue"
}
```
This would place on the root window 3 pixel values for borders and titlebars, as well as the three color strings, all taken from the default colormap.

ShowIconManager This variable indicates that the icon manager window should be displayed when *twm* is started. It can always be brought up using the **f.showiconmgr** function.

SortIconManager This variable indicates that entries in the icon manager should be sorted alphabetically rather than by simply appending new windows to the end.

SqueezeTitle [{ *squeeze-list* }] This variable indicates that *twm* should attempt to use the SHAPE extension to make titlebars occupy only as much screen space as they need, rather than extending all the way across the top of the window. The optional *squeeze-list* may be used to control the location of the squeezed titlebar along the top of the window. It contains entries of the form: 0 *"name" justification num denom*

where *name* is a window name, *justification* is either **left**, **center**, or **right**, and *num* and *denom* are numbers specifying a ratio giving the relative position about which the titlebar is justified. The ratio is measured from left to right if the numerator is positive, and right to left if negative. A denominator of 0 indicates that the numerator should be measured in pixels. For convenience, the ratio 0/0 is the same as 1/2 for **center** and -1/1 for **right**. For example:
SqueezeTitle { "XTerm" left 0 0 "xterm1" left 1 3 "xterm2" left 2 3 "oclock" center 0 0 "emacs" right 0 0 }

The **DontSqueezeTitle** list can be used to turn off squeezing on certain titles.

StartIconified [{ *win-list* }] This variable indicates that client windows should initially be left as icons until explicitly deiconified by the user. If the optional *win-list* is given, only those windows will be started iconic. This is useful for programs that do not support an *-iconic* command line option or resource.

TitleBackground *string* [{ *win-list* }] This variable specifies the background color used in titlebars, and may only be specified inside of a **Color**, **Grayscale** or **Monochrome** list. The optional *win-list* is a list of window names and colors so that per-window colors may be specified. The default is "white".

TitleButtonBorderWidth *pixels* This variable specifies the width in pixels of the border surrounding titlebuttons. This is typically set to 0 to allow titlebuttons to take up as much space as possible and to not have a border. The default is 1.

TitleFont *string* This variable specifies the font to be used for displaying window names in titlebars. The default is "variable".

TitleForeground *string* [{ *win-list* }] This variable specifies the foreground color used in titlebars, and may only be specified inside of a **Color**, **Grayscale** or **Monochrome** list. The optional *win-list* is a list of window names and colors so that per-window colors may be specified. The default is "black".

TitlePadding *pixels* This variable specifies the distance between the various buttons, text, and highlight areas in the titlebar. The default is 8 pixels.

UnknownIcon *string* This variable specifies the filename of a bitmap file to be used as the default icon. This bitmap will be used as the icon of all

TWM(1)   TWM(1)

clients which do not provide an icon bitmap and are not listed in the **Icons** list.

UsePPosition *string*   This variable specifies whether or not *twm* should honor program-requested locations (given by the **PPosition** flag in the WM_NORMAL_HINTS property) in the absence of a user-specified position. The argument *string* may have one of three values: **"off"** (the default) indicating that *twm* should ignore the program-supplied position, **"on"** indicating that the position should be used, and **"non-zero"** indicating that the position should used if it is other than (0,0). The latter option is for working around a bug in older toolkits.

WarpCursor [{ *win-list* }]   This variable indicates that the pointer should be warped into windows when they are deiconified. If the optional *win-list* is given, the pointer will only be warped when those windows are deiconified.

WindowRing { *win-list* }   This variable specifies a list of windows along which the **f.warpring** function cycles.

WarpUnmapped   This variable indicates that the **f.warpto** function should deiconify any iconified windows it encounters. This is typically used to make a key binding that will pop a particular window (such as *xmh*), no matter where it is. The default is for **f.warpto** to ignore iconified windows.

XorValue *number*   This variable specifies the value to use when drawing window outlines for moving and resizing. This should be set to a value that will result in a variety of of distinguishable colors when exclusive-or'ed with the contents of the user's typical screen. Setting this variable to 1 often gives nice results if adjacent colors in the default colormap are distinct. By default, *twm* will attempt to cause temporary lines to appear at the opposite end of the colormap from the graphics.

Zoom [*count*]   This variable indicates that outlines suggesting movement of a window to and from its iconified state should be displayed whenever a window is iconified or deiconified. The optional *count* argument specifies the number of outlines to be drawn. The default count is 8.

The following variables must be set after the fonts have been assigned, so it is usually best to put them at the end of the variables or beginning of the bindings sections:

DefaultFunction *function*   This variable specifies the function to be executed when a key or button event is received for which no binding is provided. This is typically bound to **f.nop**, **f.beep**, or a menu containing window operations.

WindowFunction *function*   This variable specifies the function to execute when a window is selected from the **TwmWindows** menu. If this variable is not set, the window will be deiconified and raised.

BINDINGS

After the desired variables have been set, functions may be attached titlebuttons and key and pointer buttons. Titlebuttons may be added from the left or right side and appear in the titlebar from left-to-right according to the order in which they are specified. Key and pointer button bindings may be given in any order.

Titlebuttons specifications must include the name of the pixmap to use in the button box and the function to be invoked when a pointer button is pressed within them: 0 **LeftTitleButton** *"bitmapname"* = *function*

or 0 **RightTitleButton** *"bitmapname"* = *function*

The *bitmapname* may refer to one of the built-in bitmaps (which are scaled to match **Title-Font**) by using the appropriate colon-prefixed name described above.

Key and pointer button specifications must give the modifiers that must be pressed, over which parts of the screen the pointer must be, and what function is to be invoked. Keys are

TWM(1)　　　　　　　　　　　　　　　　　　　　　　　　　　　　　TWM(1)

given as strings containing the appropriate keysym name; buttons are given as the keywords
Button1-**Button5**: 0 "FP1" = *modlist* : *context* : *function* **Button1** = *modlist* : *context* : *function*

The *modlist* is any combination of the modifier names **shift**, **control**, **lock**, **meta**, **mod1**, **mod2**, **mod3**, **mod4**, or **mod5** (which may be abbreviated as **s**, **c**, **l**, **m**, **m1**, **m2**, **m3**, **m4**, **m5**, respectively) separated by a vertical bar (). Similarly, the *context* is any combination of **window**, **title**, **icon**, **root**, **frame**, **iconmgr**, their first letters (**iconmgr** abbreviation is **m**), or **all**, separated by a vertical bar. The *function* is any of the **f.** keywords described below. For example, the default startup file contains the following bindings:

Button1 = : root : f.menu "TwmWindows"
Button1 = m : window | icon : f.function "move-or-lower"
Button2 = m : window | icon : f.iconify
Button3 = m : window | icon : f.function "move-or-raise"
Button1 = : title : f.function "move-or-raise"
Button2 = : title : f.raiselower
Button1 = : icon : f.function "move-or-iconify"
Button2 = : icon : f.iconify
Button1 = : iconmgr : f.iconify
Button2 = : iconmgr : f.iconify

A user who wanted to be able to manipulate windows from the keyboard could use the following bindings:

"F1" = : all : f.iconify
"F2" = : all : f.raiselower
"F3" = : all : f.warpring "next"
"F4" = : all : f.warpto "xmh"
"F5" = : all : f.warpto "emacs"
"F6" = : all : f.colormap "next"
"F7" = : all : f.colormap "default"
"F20" = : all : f.warptoscreen "next"
"Left" = m : all : f.backiconmgr
"Right" = m | s : all : f.forwiconmgr
"Up" = m : all : f.upiconmgr
"Down" = m | s : all : f.downiconmgr

Twm provides many more window manipulation primitives than can be conveniently stored in a titlebar, menu, or set of key bindings. Although a small set of defaults are supplied (unless the **NoDefaults** is specified), most users will want to have their most common operations bound to key and button strokes. To do this, *twm* associates names with each of the primitives and provides *user-defined functions* for building higher level primitives and *menus* for interactively selecting among groups of functions.

User-defined functions contain the name by which they are referenced in calls to **f.function** and a list of other functions to execute. For example:

Function "move-or-lower" { f.move f.deltastop f.lower }
Function "move-or-raise" { f.move f.deltastop f.raise }
Function "move-or-iconify" { f.move f.deltastop f.iconify }
Function "restore-colormap" { f.colormap "default" f.lower }

The function name must be used in **f.function** exactly as it appears in the function specification.

In the descriptions below, if the function is said to operate on the selected window, but is invoked from a root menu, the cursor will be changed to the **Select** cursor and the next window to receive a button press will be chosen:

　　　　! *string*　　This is an abbreviation for **f.exec** *string*.

　　　　f.autoraise　This function toggles whether or not the selected window is raised whenever entered by the pointer. See the description of the variable **AutoRaise**.

f.backiconmgr This function warps the pointer to the previous column in the current icon manager, wrapping back to the previous row if necessary.

f.beep This function sounds the keyboard bell.

f.bottomzoom This function is similar to the **f.fullzoom** function, but resizes the window to fill only the bottom half of the screen.

f.circledown This function lowers the top-most window that occludes another window.

f.circleup This function raises the bottom-most window that is occluded by another window.

f.colormap *string* This function rotates the colormaps (obtained from the WM_COLORMAP_WINDOWS property on the window) that *twm* will display when the pointer is in this window. The argument *string* may have one of the following values: **"next"**, **"prev"**, and **"default"**. It should be noted here that in general, the installed colormap is determined by keyboard focus. A pointer driven keyboard focus will install a private colormap upon entry of the window owning the colormap. Using the click to type model, private colormaps will not be installed until the user presses a mouse button on the target window.

f.deiconify This function deiconifies the selected window. If the window is not an icon, this function does nothing.

f.delete This function sends the WM_DELETE_WINDOW message to the selected window if the client application has requested it through the WM_PROTOCOLS window property. The application is supposed to respond to the message by removing the indicated window. If the window has not requested WM_DELETE_WINDOW messages, the keyboard bell will be rung indicating that the user should choose an alternative method. Note this is very different from f.destroy. The intent here is to delete a single window, not necessarily the entire application.

f.deltastop This function allows a user-defined function to be aborted if the pointer has been moved more than *MoveDelta* pixels. See the example definition given for **Function "move-or-raise"** at the beginning of the section.

f.destroy This function instructs the X server to close the display connection of the client that created the selected window. This should only be used as a last resort for shutting down runaway clients. See also f.delete.

f.downiconmgr This function warps the pointer to the next row in the current icon manager, wrapping to the beginning of the next column if necessary.

f.exec *string* This function passes the argument *string* to /bin/sh for execution. In multiscreen mode, if *string* starts a new X client without giving a display argument, the client will appear on the screen from which this function was invoked.

f.focus This function toggles the keyboard focus of the server to the selected window, changing the focus rule from pointer-driven if necessary. If the selected window already was focused, this function executes an **f.unfocus**.

f.forcemove This function is like **f.move** except that it ignores the **DontMoveOff** variable.

f.forwiconmgr This function warps the pointer to the next column in the current icon manager, wrapping to the beginning of the next row if necessary.

f.fullzoom This function resizes the selected window to the full size of the display or else restores the original size if the window was already zoomed.

f.function *string* This function executes the user-defined function whose name is specified by the argument *string*.

f.hbzoom This function is a synonym for **f.bottomzoom**.

f.hideiconmgr This function unmaps the current icon manager.

f.horizoom This variable is similar to the **f.zoom** function except that the selected window is resized to the full width of the display.

f.htzoom This function is a synonym for **f.topzoom**.

f.hzoom This function is a synonym for **f.horizoom**.

f.iconify This function iconifies or deiconifies the selected window or icon, respectively.

f.identify This function displays a summary of the name and geometry of the selected window. If the server supports the SYNC extension, the priority of the client owning the window is also displayed. Clicking the pointer or pressing a key in the window will dismiss it.

f.lefticonmgr This function similar to **f.backiconmgr** except that wrapping does not change rows.

f.leftzoom This variable is similar to the **f.bottomzoom** function but causes the selected window is only resized to the left half of the display.

f.lower This function lowers the selected window.

f.menu *string* This function invokes the menu specified by the argument *string*. Cascaded menus may be built by nesting calls to **f.menu**.

f.move This function drags an outline of the selected window (or the window itself if the **OpaqueMove** variable is set) until the invoking pointer button is released. Double clicking within the number of milliseconds given by **ConstrainedMoveTime** warps the pointer to the center of the window and constrains the move to be either horizontal or vertical depending on which grid line is crossed. To abort a move, press another button before releasing the first button.

f.nexticonmgr This function warps the pointer to the next icon manager containing any windows on the current or any succeeding screen.

f.nop This function does nothing and is typically used with the **DefaultFunction** or **WindowFunction** variables or to introduce blank lines in menus.

f.previconmgr This function warps the pointer to the previous icon manager containing any windows on the current or preceding screens.

f.priority *string* This function sets the priority of the client owning the selected window to the numeric value of the argument *string*, which should be a signed integer in double quotes (e.g. "999"). This function has an effect only if the server supports the SYNC extension.

f.quit This function causes *twm* to restore the window's borders and exit. If *twm* is the first client invoked from *xdm*, this will result in a server reset.

f.raise This function raises the selected window.

f.raiselower This function raises the selected window to the top of the stacking order if it is occluded by any windows, otherwise the window will be lowered.

f.refresh This function causes all windows to be refreshed.

f.resize This function displays an outline of the selected window. Crossing a border (or setting **AutoRelativeResize**) will cause the outline to begin to rubber band until the invoking button is released. To abort a resize, press another button before releasing the first button.

f.restart This function kills and restarts *twm*.

f.righticonmgr This function is similar to **f.nexticonmgr** except that wrapping does not change rows.

f.rightzoom This variable is similar to the **f.bottomzoom** function except that the selected window is only resized to the right half of the display.

f.saveyourself This function sends a WM_SAVEYOURSELF message to the selected window if it has requested the message in its WM_PROTOCOLS window property. Clients that accept this message are supposed to checkpoint all state associated with the window and update the WM_COMMAND property as specified in the ICCCM. If the selected window has not selected for this message, the keyboard bell will be rung.

f.showiconmgr This function maps the current icon manager.

f.sorticonmgr This function sorts the entries in the current icon manager alphabetically. See the variable **SortIconManager**.

f.title This function provides a centered, unselectable item in a menu definition. It should not be used in any other context.

f.topzoom This variable is similar to the **f.bottomzoom** function except that the selected window is only resized to the top half of the display.

f.unfocus This function resets the focus back to pointer-driven. This should be used when a focused window is no longer desired.

f.upiconmgr This function warps the pointer to the previous row in the current icon manager, wrapping to the last row in the same column if necessary.

f.vlzoom This function is a synonym for **f.leftzoom**.

f.vrzoom This function is a synonym for **f.rightzoom**.

f.warpring *string* This function warps the pointer to the next or previous window (as indicated by the argument *string*, which may be **"next"** or **"prev"**) specified in the **WindowRing** variable.

f.warpto *string* This function warps the pointer to the window which has a name or class that matches *string*. If the window is iconified, it will be deiconified if the variable **WarpUnmapped** is set or else ignored.

f.warptoiconmgr *string* This function warps the pointer to the icon manager entry associated with the window containing the pointer in the icon manager specified by the argument *string*. If *string* is empty (i.e. ""), the current icon manager is chosen.

f.warptoscreen *string* This function warps the pointer to the screen specified by the argument *string*. *String* may be a number (e.g. **"0"** or **"1"**), the word **"next"** (indicating the current screen plus 1, skipping over any unmanaged screens), the word **"back"** (indicating the current screen minus 1, skipping over any unmanaged screens), or the word **"prev"** (indicating the last screen visited.

f.winrefresh This function is similar to the **f.refresh** function except that only the selected window is refreshed.

f.zoom This function is similar to the **f.fullzoom** function, except that the only the height of the selected window is changed.

MENUS

Functions may be grouped and interactively selected using pop-up (when bound to a pointer button) or pull-down (when associated with a titlebutton) menus. Each menu specification contains the name of the menu as it will be referred to by **f.menu**, optional default foreground and background colors, the list of item names and the functions they should invoke, and optional foreground and background colors for individual items:

Menu *"menuname"* [*("deffore":"defback")*] { *string1* [*("fore1":"backn")*] *function1 string2* [*("fore2":"backn")*] *function2* . . . *stringN* [*("foreN":"backN")*] *functionN* }

The *menuname* is case-sensitive. The optional *deffore* and *defback* arguments specify the foreground and background colors used on a color display to highlight menu entries. The *string* portion of each menu entry will be the text which will appear in the menu. The optional *fore* and *back* arguments specify the foreground and background colors of the menu entry when the pointer is not in the entry. These colors will only be used on a color display. The default is to use the colors specified by the **MenuForeground** and **MenuBackground** variables. The *function* portion of the menu entry is one of the functions, including any user-defined functions, or additional menus.

There is a special menu named **TwmWindows** which contains the names of all of the client and *twm*-supplied windows. Selecting an entry will cause the **WindowFunction** to be executed on that window. If **WindowFunction** hasn't been set, the window will be deiconified and raised.

ICONS

Twm supports several different ways of manipulating iconified windows. The common pixmap-and-text style may be laid out by hand or automatically arranged as described by the **IconRegion** variable. In addition, a terse grid of icon names, called an icon manager, provides a more efficient use of screen space as well as the ability to navigate among windows from the keyboard.

An icon manager is a window that contains names of selected or all windows currently on the display. In addition to the window name, a small button using the default iconify symbol will be displayed to the left of the name when the window is iconified. By default, clicking on an entry in the icon manager performs **f.iconify**. To change the actions taken in the icon manager, use the the **iconmgr** context when specifying button and keyboard bindings.

Moving the pointer into the icon manager also directs keyboard focus to the indicated window (setting the focus explicitly or else sending synthetic events **NoTitleFocus** is set). Using the **f.upiconmgr**, **f.downiconmgr f.lefticonmgr**, and **f.righticonmgr** functions, the input focus can be changed between windows directly from the keyboard.

BUGS

The resource manager should have been used instead of all of the window lists.

The **IconRegion** variable should take a list.

Double clicking very fast to get the constrained move function will sometimes cause the window to move, even though the pointer is not moved.

If **IconifyByUnmapping** is on and windows are listed in **IconManagerDontShow** but not in **DontIconifyByUnmapping**, they may be lost if they are iconified and no bindings to **f.menu "TwmWindows"** or **f.warpto** are setup.

FILES

$HOME/.twmrc.<screen number>
$HOME/.twmrc
<XRoot>/lib/X11/twm/system.twmrc

ENVIRONMENT VARIABLES

    DISPLAY   This variable is used to determine which X server to use. It is also set during **f.exec** so that programs come up on the proper screen.

    HOME   This variable is used as the prefix for files that begin with a tilde and for locating the *twm* startup file.

SEE ALSO

X(1), Xserver(1), xdm(1), xrdb(1)

AUTHORS

Tom LaStrange, Solbourne Computer; Jim Fulton, MIT X Consortium; Steve Pitschke, Stardent Computer; Keith Packard, MIT X Consortium; Dp file.

SEE ALSO

X(1), Xserver(1), x

UL(1)

NAME

ul – do underlining

SYNOPSIS

ul [-i] [-t terminal] [name ...]

DESCRIPTION

Ul reads the named files (or standard input if none are given) and translates occurrences of underscores to the sequence which indicates underlining for the terminal in use, as specified by the environment variable TERM. The file /etc/termcap is read to determine the appropriate sequences for underlining. If the terminal is incapable of underlining, but is capable of a standout mode then that is used instead. If the terminal can overstrike, or handles underlining automatically, ul degenerates to cat(1). If the terminal cannot underline, underlining is ignored.

The following options are available:

- -i Underlining is indicated by a separate line containing appropriate dashes '–'; this is useful when you want to look at the underlining which is present in an nroff output stream on a crt-terminal.
- -t terminal Overrides the terminal type specified in the environment with terminal.

ENVIRONMENT

The following environment variable is used:

- TERM The TERM variable is used to relate a tty device with its device capability description (see termcap(5)). TERM is set at login time, either by the default terminal type specified in /etc/ttys or as set during the login process by the user in their login file (see setenv(1)).

SEE ALSO

man(1), nroff(1), colcrt(1)

BUGS

Nroff usually outputs a series of backspaces and underlines intermixed with the text to indicate underlining. No attempt is made to optimize the backward motion.

HISTORY

The ul command appeared in BSD 3.0.

UNEXPAND(1L)

NAME

unexpand – convert spaces to tabs

SYNOPSIS

unexpand [–tab1[,tab2[,...]]] [–t tab1[,tab2[,...]]] [–a] [––tabs=tab1[,tab2[,...]]] [––all] [––help] [––version] [file...]

DESCRIPTION

This manual page documents the GNU version of **unexpand**. **unexpand** writes the contents of each given file, or the standard input if none are given or when a file named '–' is given, to the standard output, with strings of two or more space or tab characters converted to as many tabs as possible followed by as many spaces as are needed. By default, **unexpand** converts only initial spaces and tabs (those that precede all non space or tab characters) on each line. It preserves backspace characters in the output; they decrement the column count for tab calculations. By default, tabs are set at every 8th column.

OPTIONS

–, –t, ––tabs tab1[,tab2[,...]]   If only one tab stop is given, set the tabs *tab1* spaces apart instead of the default 8. Otherwise, set the tabs at columns *tab1*, *tab2*, etc. (numbered from 0) and leave spaces and tabs beyond the tabstops given unchanged. If the tabstops are specified with the *–t* or ––*tabs* option, they can be separated by blanks as well as by commas. This option implies the *–a* option.

–a, ––all   Convert all strings of two or more spaces or tabs, not just initial ones, to tabs.

––help   Print a usage message and exit with a non-zero status.

––version   Print version information on standard output then exit.

UNIQ(1L)

NAME

uniq – remove duplicate lines from a sorted file

SYNOPSIS

uniq [–cdu] [–f skip-fields] [–s skip-chars] [–w check-chars] [–#skip-fields] [+#skip-chars] [——count] [——repeated] [——unique] [——skip-fields=skip-fields] [——skip-chars=skip-chars] [——check-chars=check-chars] [——help] [——version] [infile] [outfile]

DESCRIPTION

This manual page documents the GNU version of **uniq**. **uniq** prints the unique lines in a sorted file, discarding all but one of a run of matching lines. It can optionally show only lines that appear exactly once, or lines that appear more than once. **uniq** requires sorted input because it compares only consecutive lines.

If the output file is not specified, **uniq** writes to the standard output. If the input file is not specified, it reads from the standard input.

OPTIONS

- *–u, ——unique* Only print unique lines.
- *–d, ——repeated* Only print duplicate lines.
- *–c, ——count* Print the number of times each line occurred along with the line.
- *–number, –f, ——skip-fields=number* In this option, *number* is an integer representing the number of fields to skip over before checking for uniqueness. The first *number* fields, along with any blanks found before *number* fields is reached, are skipped over and not counted. Fields are defined as a strings of non-space, non-tab characters, that are separated from each other by spaces and tabs.
- *+number, –s, ——skip-chars=number* In this option, *number* is an integer representing the number of characters to skip over before checking for uniqueness. The first *number* characters, along with any blanks found before *number* characters is reached, are skipped over and not counted. If you use both the field and character skipping options, fields are skipped over first.
- *–w, ——check-chars=number* Specify the number of characters to compare in the lines, after skipping any specified fields and characters. Normally the entire rest of the lines are compared.
- *——help* Print a usage message and exit with a non-zero status.
- *——version* Print version information on standard output then exit.

UPDATEDB(1L)

NAME

updatedb – update a file name database

SYNOPSIS

updatedb [*options*]

DESCRIPTION

This manual page documents the GNU version of **updatedb**, which updates file name databases used by GNU **locate**. The file name databases contain lists of files that were in particular directory trees when the databases were last updated. The file name of the default database is determined when **locate** and **updatedb** are configured and installed. The frequency with which the databases are updated and the directories for which they contain entries depend on how often **updatedb** is run, and with which arguments. In networked environments, it often makes sense to build a database at the root of each filesystem, containing the entries for that filesystem. **updatedb** is then run for each filesystem on the fileserver where that filesystem is on a local disk, to prevent thrashing the network. Users can select which databases **locate** searches using an environment variable or command line option; see **locate**(1L). Databases can not be concatenated together. The file name database format changed starting with GNU **find** and **locate** version 4.0 to allow machines with diffent byte orderings to share the databases. The new GNU **locate** can read both the old and new database formats. However, old versions of **locate** and **find** produce incorrect results if given a new-format database.

OPTIONS

——localpaths='*path1* path2...' Non-network directories to put in the database. Default is /.

——netpaths='*path1* path2...' Network (NFS, AFS, RFS, etc.) directories to put in the database. Default is none.

——prunepaths='*path1* path2...' Directories to not put in the database, which would otherwise be. Default is /tmp /usr/tmp /var/tmp /afs.

——output=*dbfile* The database file to build. Default is system-dependent, but typically /usr/local/var/locatedb.

——netuser=*user* The user to search network directories as, using **su**(1). Default is **daemon**.

——old–format Create the database in the old format instead of the new one.

——version Print the version number of **updatedb** and exit.

——help Print a summary of the options to **updatedb** and exit.

SEE ALSO

find(1L), **locate**(1L), **locatedb**(5L), **xargs**(1L) **Finding Files** (on-line in Info, or printed)

UPTIME(1) Linux Programmer's Manual UPTIME(1)

NAME

uptime – Tell how long the system has been running.

SYNOPSIS

uptime

DESCRIPTION

uptime gives a one line display of the following information. The current time, how long the system has been running, how many users are currently logged on, and the system load averages for the past 1, 5, and 15 minutes.

This is the same information contained in the header line displayed by *w*(1).

FILES

/var/run/utmp information about who is currently logged on
/proc process information

AUTHORS

uptime was written by Larry Greenfield (greenfie@gauss.rutgers.edu) and Michael K. Johnson (johnsonm@sunsite.unc.edu).

SEE ALSO

ps(1), top(1), utmp(5), w(1)

uucp(1)

NAME

uucp – Unix to Unix copy

SYNOPSIS

uucp [options] source-file destination-file

uucp [options] source-file... destination-directory

DESCRIPTION

The *uucp* command copies files between systems. Each *file* argument is either a pathname on the local machine or is of the form

    system!path

which is interpreted as being on a remote system. In the first form, the contents of the first file are copied to the second. In the second form, each source file is copied into the destination directory.

A file be transferred to or from *system2* via *system1* by using

    system1!system2!path.

Any pathname that does not begin with / or ~ will be appended to the current directory (unless the **–W** or **—noexpand** option is used); this resulting path will not necessarily exist on a remote system. A pathname beginning with a simple ~ starts at the UUCP public directory; a pathname beginning with ~name starts at the home directory of the named user. The ~ is interpreted on the appropriate system. Note that some shells will interpret a simple ~ to the local home directory before *uucp* sees it; to avoid this the ~ must be quoted.

Shell metacharacters ? * [ ] are interpreted on the appropriate system, assuming they are quoted to prevent the shell from interpreting them first.

The copy does not take place immediately, but is queued up for the *uucico* (8) daemon; the daemon is started immediately unless the **–r** or **—nouucico** switch is given. In any case, the next time the remote system is called the file(s) will be copied.

OPTIONS

The following options may be given to *uucp*.

    –c, —nocopy   Do not copy local source files to the spool directory. If they are removed before being processed by the *uucico* (8) daemon, the copy will fail. The files must be readable by the *uucico* (8) daemon, and by the invoking user.

    –C, —copy   Copy local source files to the spool directory. This is the default.

    –d, —directories   Create all necessary directories when doing the copy. This is the default.

    –f, —nodirectories   If any necessary directories do not exist for the destination path, abort the copy.

    –g grade, **—grade** grade   Set the grade of the file transfer command. Jobs of a higher grade are executed first. Grades run 0 ... 9 A ... Z a ... z from high to low.

    –m, —mail   Report completion or failure of the file transfer by *mail* (1).

    –n user, **—notify** user   Report completion or failure of the file transfer by *mail* (1) to the named user on the remote system.

    –r, —nouucico   Do not start *uucico* (8) daemon immediately; merely queue up the file transfer for later execution.

uucp(1)   uucp(1)

  -j, —jobid   Print jobid on standard output. The job may be later cancelled
                       by passing the jobid to the –k switch of *uustat* (1). It is possible
                       for some complex operations to produce more than one jobid,
                       in which case each will be printed on a separate line. For ex-
                       ample

                       uucp sys1!˜user1/file1 sys2!˜user2/file2 ˜user3
                       will generate two separate jobs, one for the system *sys1* and one
                       for the system *sys2*.

  –W, —noexpand   Do not prepend remote relative path names with the current dir-
                       ectory.

  –x type, —debug type Turn on particular debugging types. The following types
                       are recognized: abnormal, chat, handshake, uucp-proto, proto,
                       port, config, spooldir, execute, incoming, outgoing. Only ab-
                       normal, config, spooldir and execute are meaningful for *uucp*.

                       Multiple types may be given, separated by commas, and the —
                       -**debug** option may appear multiple times. A number may also
                       be given, which will turn on that many types from the foregoing
                       list; for example, —**debug** 2 is equivalent to —**debug** abnor-
                       mal,chat.

  –I file, —config file Set configuration file to use. This option may not be avail-
                       able, depending upon how *uucp* was compiled.

  –v, —version   Report version information and exit.

  —**help**   Print a help message and exit.

FILES

The file names may be changed at compilation time or by the configuration file, so these are
only approximations.

/usr/lib/uucp/config - Configuration file.
/usr/spool/uucp - UUCP spool directory.
/usr/spool/uucp/Log - UUCP log file.
/usr/spool/uucppublic - Default UUCP public directory.

SEE ALSO

mail(1), uux(1), uustat(1), uucico(8)

BUGS

Some of the options are dependent on the capabilities of the *uucico* (8) daemon on the remote
system.

The –n and –m switches do not work when transferring a file from one remote system to
another.

File modes are not preserved, except for the execute bit. The resulting file is owned by the
uucp user.

AUTHOR

Ian Lance Taylor <ian@airs.com>

NAME

uustat – UUCP status inquiry and control

SYNOPSIS

uustat –a

uustat —all

uustat [–eKRiMNQ] [–sS system] [–uU user] [–cC command] [–oy hours] [–B lines] [—executions] [—kill-all] [—rejuvenate-all] [—prompt] [—mail] [—notify] [—no-list] [—system system] [—not-system system] [—user user] [—not-user user] [—command command] [—not-command command] [—older-than hours] [—younger-than hours] [—mail-lines lines]

uustat [**–kr** jobid] [**—kill** jobid] [**—rejuvenate** jobid]

uustat –q [**–sS** system] [**–oy** hours] [**—system** system] [**—not-system** system] [**—older-than** hours] [**—younger-than** hours]

uustat —list [**–sS** system] [**–oy** hours] [**—system** system] [**—not-system** system] [**—older-than** hours] [**—younger-than** hours]

uustat –m

uustat —status

uustat –p

uustat —ps

DESCRIPTION

The *uustat* command can display various types of status information about the UUCP system. It can also be used to cancel or rejuvenate requests made by *uucp* (1) or *uux* (1).

By default *uustat* displays all jobs queued up for the invoking user, as if given the —**user** option with the appropriate argument.

If any of the **–a**, —**all**, **–e**, —**executions**, **–s**, —**system**, **–S**, —**not-system**, **–u**, —**user**, –U, —**not-user**, **–c**, —**command**, **–C**, —**not-command**, **–o**, —**older-than**, **–y**, —**younger-than** options are given, then all jobs which match the combined specifications are displayed.

The **–K** or —**kill-all** option may be used to kill off a selected group of jobs, such as all jobs more than 7 days old.

OPTIONS

The following options may be given to *uustat*.

   –a, —all   List all queued file transfer requests.

   –e, —executions   List queued execution requests rather than queued file transfer requests. Queued execution requests are processed by *uuxqt* (8) rather than *uucico* (8). Queued execution requests may be waiting for some file to be transferred from a remote system. They are created by an invocation of *uux* (1).

   –s system, —system system   List all jobs queued up for the named system. These options may be specified multiple times, in which case all jobs for all the systems will be listed. If used with —**list** only the systems named will be listed.

   –S system, —not-system system   List all jobs queued for systems other than the one named. These options may be specified multiple times, in which case no jobs from any of the specified systems will be listed. If used with —**list** only the systems not named will be listed. These options may not be used with **–s** or —**system**.

   –u user, —user user   List all jobs queued up for the named user. These options may be specified multiple times, in which case all jobs for all the users will be listed.

–U user, **––not-user** user   List all jobs queued up for users other than the one named. These options may be specified multiple times, in which case no jobs from any of the specified users will be listed. These options may not be used with **–u** or **––user**.

–c command, **––command** command   List all jobs requesting the execution of the named command. If **command** is *ALL* this will list all jobs requesting the execution of some command (as opposed to simply requesting a file transfer). These options may be specified multiple times, in which case all jobs requesting any of the commands will be listed.

–C command, **––not-command** command   List all jobs requesting execution of some command other than the named command, or, if **command** is *ALL,* list all jobs that simply request a file transfer (as opposed to requesting the execution of some command). These options may be specified multiple times, in which case no job requesting one of the specified commands will be listed. These options may not be used with **–c** or **––command**.

–o hours, **––older-than** hours   List all queued jobs older than the given number of hours. If used with **––list** only systems whose oldest job is older than the given number of hours will be listed.

–y hours, **––younger-than** hours   List all queued jobs younger than the given number of hours. If used with **––list** only systems whose oldest job is younger than the given number of hours will be listed.

–k jobid, **––kill** jobid   Kill the named job. The job id is shown by the default output format, as well as by the **–j** or **––jobid** option to *uucp* (1) or *uux* (1). A job may only be killed by the user who created the job, or by the UUCP administrator or the superuser. The **–k** or **––kill** options may be used multiple times on the command line to kill several jobs.

–r jobid, **––rejuvenate** jobid   Rejuvenate the named job. This will mark it as having been invoked at the current time, affecting the output of the **–o, ––older-than, –y,** or **––younger-than** options and preserving it from any automated cleanup daemon. The job id is shown by the default output format, as well as by the **–j** or **––jobid** options to *uucp* (1) or *uux* (1). A job may only be rejuvenated by the user who created the job, or by the UUCP administrator or the superuser. The **–r** or **––rejuvenate** options may be used multiple times on the command line to rejuvenate several jobs.

–q, ––list   Display the status of commands, executions and conversations for all remote systems for which commands or executions are queued. The **–s, ––system, –S, ––not-system, –o, ––older-than, –y,** and **––younger-than** options may be used to restrict the systems which are listed. Systems for which no commands or executions are queued will never be listed.

–m, ––status   Display the status of conversations for all remote systems.

–p, ––ps   Display the status of all processes holding UUCP locks on systems or ports.

–i, ––prompt   For each listed job, prompt whether to kill the job or not. If the first character of the input line is *y* or *Y* the job will be killed.

–K, ––kill-all   Automatically kill each listed job. This can be useful for automatic cleanup scripts, in conjunction with the **––mail** and **––notify** options.

–R, ––rejuvenate-all   Automatically rejuvenate each listed job. This may not be used with **––kill-all.**

–M, ––mail   For each listed job, send mail to the UUCP administrator. If the job is killed (due to **––kill-all** or **––prompt** with an affirmative response) the mail will indicate that. A comment specified by the ——**comment** option may be included. If the job is an execution, the initial portion of its standard input will be included in the mail message; the number of lines to include may be set with the ——**mail-lines** option (the default is 100). If the standard input contains null characters, it is assumed to be a binary file and is not included.

–N, ——**notify** For each listed job, send mail to the user who requested the job. The mail is identical to that sent by the **–M** or ——**mail** options.

–W, ——**comment** Specify a comment to be included in mail sent with the **–M,** ——**-mail, –N,** or ——**notify** options.

–Q, ——**no-list** Do not actually list the job, but only take any actions indicated by the **–i,** ——**prompt, –K,** ——**kill-all, –M,** ——**mail, –N** or ——**notify** options.

–x type, ——**debug** type Turn on particular debugging types. The following types are recognized: abnormal, chat, handshake, uucp-proto, proto, port, config, spooldir, execute, incoming, outgoing. Only abnormal, config, spooldir and execute are meaningful for *uustat*.

Multiple types may be given, separated by commas, and the ——**debug** option may appear multiple times. A number may also be given, which will turn on that many types from the foregoing list; for example, ——**debug** 2 is equivalent to ——**debug** abnormal,chat.

–I file, ——**config** file Set configuration file to use. This option may not be available, depending upon how *uustat* was compiled.

–v, ——**version** Report version information and exit.

——**help** Print a help message and exit.

EXAMPLES

uustat –all Display status of all jobs. A sample output line is as follows:

> bugsA027h bugs ian 04-01 13:50 Executing rmail ian@airs.com (sending 1283 bytes)

The format is

> jobid system user queue-date command (size)

The jobid may be passed to the ——**kill** or ——**rejuvenate** options. The size indicates how much data is to be transferred to the remote system, and is absent for a file receive request. The ——**system,** ——**not-system,** ——**user,** ——**not-user,** ——**command,** ——**not-command,** ——**older-than,** and ——**younger-than** options may be used to control which jobs are listed.

uustat –executions Display status of queued up execution requests. A sample output line is as follows:

> bugs bugs!ian 05-20 12:51 rmail ian

The format is

> system requestor queue-date command

The ——**system,** ——**not-system,** ——**user,** ——**not-user,** ——**command,** ——**not-command,** ——**older-than,** and ——**younger-than** options may be used to control which requests are listed.

uustat –list Display status for all systems with queued up commands. A sample output line is as follows:

> bugs 4C (1 hour) 0X (0 secs) 04-01 14:45 Dial failed

This indicates the system, the number of queued commands, the age of the oldest queued command, the number of queued local executions, the age of the oldest queued execution, the date of the last conversation, and the status of that conversation.

uustat –status Display conversation status for all remote systems. A sample output line is as follows:

> bugs 04-01 15:51 Conversation complete

This indicates the system, the date of the last conversation, and the status of that conversation. If the last conversation failed, *uustat* will indicate how many attempts have been made to call the system. If the retry period is currently preventing calls to that system, *uustat* also displays the time when the next call will be permitted.

uustat –ps Display the status of all processes holding UUCP locks. The output format is system dependent, as *uustat* simply invokes *ps* (1) on each process holding a lock.

> uustat –command rmail –older-than 168 –kill-all –no-list –mail –notify –comment "Queued for over 1 week"

This will kill all *rmail* commands that have been queued up waiting for delivery for over 1 week (168 hours). For each such command, mail will be sent both to the UUCP administrator and to the user who requested the rmail execution. The mail message sent will include the string given by the —**comment** option. The —**no-list** option prevents any of the jobs from being listed on the terminal, so any output from the program will be error messages.

FILES

The file names may be changed at compilation time or by the configuration file, so these are only approximations.

/usr/lib/uucp/config - Configuration file.

/usr/spool/uucp - UUCP spool directory.

SEE ALSO

ps(1), rmail(1), uucp(1), uux(1), uucico(8), uuxqt(8).

AUTHOR

Ian Lance Taylor (ian@airs.com)

NAME

uux – Remote command execution over UUCP

SYNOPSIS

uux [options] command

DESCRIPTION

The *uux* command is used to execute a command on a remote system, or to execute a command on the local system using files from remote systems. The command is not executed immediately; the request is queued until the *uucico* (8) daemon calls the system and executes it. The daemon is started automatically unless one of the **–r** or **––nouucico** options is given.

The actual command execution is done by the *uuxqt* (8) daemon.

File arguments can be gathered from remote systems to the execution system, as can standard input. Standard output may be directed to a file on a remote system.

The command name may be preceded by a system name followed by an exclamation point if it is to be executed on a remote system. An empty system name is taken as the local system.

Each argument that contains an exclamation point is treated as naming a file. The system which the file is on is before the exclamation point, and the pathname on that system follows it. An empty system name is taken as the local system; this must be used to transfer a file to a command being executed on a remote system. If the path is not absolute, it will be appended to the current working directory on the local system; the result may not be meaningful on the remote system. A pathname may begin with ~/, in which case it is relative to the UUCP public directory (usually /usr/spool/uucppublic) on the appropriate system. A pathname may begin with ~name/, in which case it is relative to the home directory of the named user on the appropriate system.

Standard input and output may be redirected as usual; the pathnames used may contain exclamation points to indicate that they are on remote systems. Note that the redirection characters must be quoted so that they are passed to *uux* rather than interpreted by the shell. Append redirection (>>) does not work.

All specified files are gathered together into a single directory before execution of the command begins. This means that each file must have a distinct base name. For example,

    uux 'sys1!diff sys2!~user1/foo sys3!~user2/foo >!foo.diff'

will fail because both files will be copied to sys1 and stored under the name foo.

Arguments may be quoted by parentheses to avoid interpretation of exclamation points. This is useful when executing the *uucp* command on a remote system.

OPTIONS

The following options may be given to *uux*.

–, –p, ––stdin	Read standard input and use it as the standard input for the command to be executed.
–c, ––nocopy	Do not copy local files to the spool directory. This is the default. If they are removed before being processed by the *uucico* (8) daemon, the copy will fail. The files must be readable by the *uucico* (8) daemon, as well as the by the invoker of *uux*.
–C, ––copy	Copy local files to the spool directory.
–l, ––link	Link local files into the spool directory. If a file can not be linked because it is on a different device, it will be copied unless one of the **–c** or **––nocopy** options also appears (in other words, use of **––link** switches the default from **––nocopy** to **––copy**). If the files are changed before being processed by the *uucico* (8) daemon, the changed versions will be used. The files must be

readable by the *uucico* (8) daemon, as well as by the invoker of *uux*.

–g grade, ––grade grade Set the grade of the file transfer command. Jobs of a higher grade are executed first. Grades run 0 ... 9 A ... Z a ... z from high to low.

–n, ––notification=no Do not send mail about the status of the job, even if it fails.

–z, ––notification=error Send mail about the status of the job if an error occurs. For many *uuxqt* daemons, including the Taylor UUCP *uuxqt*, this is the default action; for those, **––notification=error** will have no effect. However, some *uuxqt* daemons will send mail if the job succeeds unless the **––notification=error** option is used, and some other *uuxqt* daemons will not send mail if the job fails unless the **––notification=error** option is used.

–r, ––nouucico Do not start the *uucico* (8) daemon immediately; merely queue up the execution request for later processing.

–j, ––jobid Print jobids on standard output. A jobid will be generated for each file copy operation required to perform the operation. These file copies may be cancelled by passing the jobid to the ––**kill** switch of *uustat* (1), which will make the execution impossible to complete.

–a address, ––requestor address Report job status to the specified e-mail address.

–x type, ––debug type Turn on particular debugging types. The following types are recognized: abnormal, chat, handshake, uucp-proto, proto, port, config, spooldir, execute, incoming, outgoing. Only abnormal, config, spooldir and execute are meaningful for *uux*.

Multiple types may be given, separated by commas, and the –––debug option may appear multiple times. A number may also be given, which will turn on that many types from the foregoing list; for example, ––**debug** 2 is equivalent to ––**debug** abnormal,chat.

–I file, ––config file Set configuration file to use. This option may not be available, depending upon how *uux* was compiled.

–v, ––version Report version information and exit.

––**help** Print a help message and exit.

EXAMPLES

uux -z - sys1!rmail user1 Execute the command "rmail user1" on the system sys1, giving it as standard input whatever is given to *uux* as standard input. If a failure occurs, send a message using *mail* (1).

uux 'diff -c sys1!~user1/file1 sys2!~user2/file2 >!file.diff' Fetch the two named files from system sys1 and system sys2 and execute *diff* putting the result in file.diff in the current directory. The current directory must be writable by the *uuxqt* (8) daemon for this to work.

uux 'sys1!uucp ~user1/file1 (sys2!~user2/file2)' Execute *uucp* on the system sys1 copying file1 (on system sys1) to sys2. This illustrates the use of parentheses for quoting.

RESTRICTIONS

The remote system may not permit you to execute certain commands. Many remote systems only permit the execution of *rmail* and *rnews*.

Some of the options are dependent on the capabilities of the *uuxqt* (8) daemon on the remote system.

uux(1)   uux(1)

FILES

The file names may be changed at compilation time or by the configuration file, so these are only approximations.

/usr/lib/uucp/config - Configuration file.
/usr/spool/uucp - UUCP spool directory.
/usr/spool/uucp/Log - UUCP log file.
/usr/spool/uucppublic - Default UUCP public directory.

SEE ALSO

mail(1), uustat(1), uucp(1), uucico(8), uuxqt(8)

BUGS

Files can not be referenced across multiple systems.

Too many jobids are output by ―**jobid,** and there is no good way to cancel a local execution requiring remote files.

AUTHOR

Ian Lance Taylor (ian@airs.com)

uuxqt(8)

NAME

uuxqt – UUCP execution daemon

SYNOPSIS

uuxqt [options]

DESCRIPTION

The *uuxqt* daemon executes commands requested by *uux* (1) from either the local system or from remote systems. It is started automatically by the *uucico* (8) daemon (unless *uucico* (8) is given the **–q** or **––nouuxqt** option).

There is normally no need to run this command, since it will be invoked by *uucico* (8). However, it can be used to provide greater control over the processing of the work queue.

Multiple invocations of *uuxqt* may be run at once, as controlled by the *max-uuxqts* configuration command.

OPTIONS

The following options may be given to *uuxqt*.

> **–c** command, **––command** command   Only execute requests for the specified command. For example:
>
>> uuxqt –command rmail
>
> **–s** system, **––system** system   Only execute requests originating from the specified system.
>
> **–x** type, **––debug** type   Turn on particular debugging types. The following types are recognized: abnormal, chat, handshake, uucp-proto, proto, port, config, spooldir, execute, incoming, outgoing. Only abnormal, config, spooldir and execute are meaningful for *uuxqt*.
>
>> Multiple types may be given, separated by commas, and the ––**debug** option may appear multiple times. A number may also be given, which will turn on that many types from the foregoing list; for example, ––**debug** 2 is equivalent to ––**debug** abnormal,chat.
>>
>> The debugging output is sent to the debugging file, usually one of /usr/spool/uucp/Debug, /usr/spool/uucp/DEBUG, or /usr/spool/uucp/.Admin/audit.local.
>
> **–I** file, ––**config**   Set configuration file to use. This option may not be available, depending upon how *uuxqt* was compiled.
>
> **–v**, ––**version**   Report version information and exit.
>
> ––**help**   Print a help message and exit.

FILES

The file names may be changed at compilation time or by the configuration file, so these are only approximations.

/usr/lib/uucp/config - Configuration file.
/usr/spool/uucp - UUCP spool directory.
/usr/spool/uucp/Log - UUCP log file.
/usr/spool/uucppublic - Default UUCP public directory.
/usr/spool/uucp/Debug - Debugging file.

SEE ALSO

uucp(1), uux(1), uucico(8)

AUTHOR

Ian Lance Taylor (ian@airs.com)

NAME

w – who present users are and what they are doing

SYNOPSIS

w [-hin] [-user]

DESCRIPTION

The w utility prints a summary of the current activity on the system, including what each user is doing. The first line displays the current time of day, how long the system has been running, the number of users logged into the system, and the load averages. The load average numbers give the number of jobs in the run queue averaged over 1, 5 and 15 minutes.

The fields output are the user's login name, the name of the terminal the user is on, the host from which the user is logged in, the time the user logged on, the time since the user last typed anything, and the name and arguments of the current process.

The options are as follows:

- -h Suppress the heading.
- -i Output is sorted by idle time.
- -n Show network addresses as numbers (normally
- -w interprets addresses and attempts to display them symbolically).

If a user name is specified, the output is restricted to that user.

FILES

/var/run/utmp   list of users on the system

SEE ALSO

who 1 , finger 1 , ps 1 , uptime 1 ,

BUGS

The notion of the current process is muddy. The current algorithm is "the highest numbered process on the terminal that is not ignoring interrupts, or, if there is none, the highest numbered process on the terminal". This fails, for example, in critical sections of programs like the shell and editor, or when faulty programs running in the background fork and fail to ignore interrupts. (In cases where no process can be found, w prints .)

The CPU time is only an estimate, in particular, if someone leaves a background process running after logging out, the person currently on that terminal is charged with the time.

Background processes are not shown, even though they account for much of the load on the system.

Sometimes processes, typically those in the background, are printed with null or garbaged arguments. In these cases, the name of the command is printed in parentheses.

The w utility does not know about the new conventions for detection of background jobs. It will sometimes find a background job instead of the right one.

COMPATIBILITY

The -f , -l , -s , and -w flags are no longer supported.

HISTORY

The w command appeared in BSD 3.0 .

WALL(1)

NAME
wall – write a message to users

SYNOPSIS
wall [file]

DESCRIPTION
Wall displays the contents of file or, by default, its standard input, on the terminals of all currently logged in users.

Only the super-user can write on the terminals of users who have chosen to deny messages or are using a program which automatically denies messages.

SEE ALSO
mesg(1), talk(1), write(1), shutdown(8)

HISTORY
A wall command appeared in AT&T v7.

NAME

wc – print the number of bytes, words, and lines in files

SYNOPSIS

wc [–clw] [—bytes] [—chars] [—lines] [—words] [—help] [—version] [file...]

DESCRIPTION

This manual page documents the GNU version of **wc**. **wc** counts the number of bytes, whitespace-separated words, and newlines in each given file, or the standard input if none are given or when a file named '–' is given. It prints one line of counts for each file, and if the file was given as an argument, it prints the filename following the counts. If more than one filename is given, **wc** prints a final line containing the cumulative counts, with the filename 'total'. The counts are printed in the order: lines, words, bytes.

By default, **wc** prints all three counts. Options can specify that only certain counts be printed. Options do not undo others previously given, so **wc** —*bytes* —*words* prints both the byte counts and the word counts.

OPTIONS

–*c*, —*bytes*, —*chars*	Print only the byte counts.
–*w*, —*words*	Print only the word counts.
–*l*, —*lines*	Print only the newline counts.
—*help*	Print a usage message and exit with a non-zero status.
—*version*	Print version information on standard output then exit.

WHEREIS(1)

NAME

whereis – locate the binary, source, and manual page files for a command

SYNOPSIS

whereis [**–bmsu**] [**–BMS** *directory*... **–f**] *filename* ...

DESCRIPTION

whereis locates source/binary and manuals sections for specified files. The supplied names are first stripped of leading pathname components and any (single) trailing extension of the form *.ext,* for example, *.c*. Prefixes of **s.** resulting from use of source code control are also dealt with. **whereis** then attempts to locate the desired program in a list of standard Linux places:

/bin
/usr/bin
/etc
/usr/etc
/sbin
/usr/sbin
/usr/games
/usr/games/bin
/usr/emacs/etc
/usr/lib/emacs/19.22/etc
/usr/lib/emacs/19.23/etc
/usr/lib/emacs/19.24/etc
/usr/lib/emacs/19.25/etc
/usr/lib/emacs/19.26/etc
/usr/lib/emacs/19.27/etc
/usr/lib/emacs/19.28/etc
/usr/lib/emacs/19.29/etc
/usr/lib/emacs/19.30/etc
/usr/TeX/bin
/usr/tex/bin
/usr/interviews/bin/LINUX
/usr/bin/X11
/usr/X11/bin
/usr/X11R5/bin
/usr/X11R6/bin
/usr/X386/bin
/usr/local/bin
/usr/local/etc
/usr/local/sbin
/usr/local/games
/usr/local/games/bin
/usr/local/emacs/etc
/usr/local/TeX/bin
/usr/local/tex/bin
/usr/local/bin/X11
/usr/contrib,
/usr/hosts,
/usr/include,
/usr/g++-include,

OPTIONS

–b Search only for binaries.

–m Search only for manual sections.

–s Search only for sources.

	−u	Search for unusual entries. A file is said to be unusual if it does not have one entry of each requested type. Thus 'whereis\\-m\\-u*' asks for those files in the current directory which have no documentation.
	−B	Change or otherwise limit the places where **whereis** searches for binaries.
	−M	Change or otherwise limit the places where **whereis** searches for manual sections.
	−S	Change or otherwise limit the places where **whereis** searches for sources.
	−f	Terminate the last directory list and signals the start of file names, and *must* be used when any of the −B, −M, or −S options are used.

EXAMPLE

Find all files in **/usr/bin** which are not documented in **/usr/man/man1** with source in **/usr/src**:

example% cd /usr/bin
example% whereis −u −M /usr/man/man1 −S /usr/src −f *

FILES

/{bin,sbin,etc}

/usr/{lib,bin,old,new,local,games,include,etc,src,man,sbin, X386, TeX, g++-include}

/usr/local/{X386,TeX,X11,include,lib,man,etc,bin,games, emacs}

SEE ALSO

chdir(2V)

BUGS

Since **whereis** uses **chdir**(2V) to run faster, pathnames given with the −M, −S, or −B must be full; that is, they must begin with a '/'.

NAME

write – send a message to another user

SYNOPSIS

write *user* [*ttyname*]

DESCRIPTION

Write allows you to communicate with other users, by copying lines from your terminal to theirs.

When you run the **write** command, the user you are writing to gets a message of the form:

Message from yourname@yourhost on yourtty at hh:mm ...

Any further lines you enter will be copied to the specified user's terminal. If the other user wants to reply, they must run **write** as well.

When you are done, type an end-of-file or interrupt character. The other user will see the message **EOF** indicating that the conversation is over.

You can prevent people (other than the super-user) from writing to you with the **mesg**(1) command. Some commands, for example **nroff**(1) and **pr**(1), may disallow writing automatically, so that your output isn't overwritten.

If the user you want to write to is logged in on more than one terminal, you can specify which terminal to write to by specifying the terminal name as the second operand to the **write** command. Alternatively, you can let **write** select one of the terminals – it will pick the one with the shortest idle time. This is so that if the user is logged in at work and also dialed up from home, the message will go to the right place.

The traditional protocol for writing to someone is that the string '–o', either at the end of a line or on a line by itself, means that it's the other person's turn to talk. The string 'oo' means that the person believes the conversation to be over.

SEE ALSO

mesg(1), **talk**(1), **who**(1)

HISTORY

A **write** command appeared in Version 6 AT&T UNIX.

XARGS(1L)

NAME

xargs – build and execute command lines from standard input

SYNOPSIS

xargs [–0prtx] [–e[eof-str]] [–i[replace-str]] [–l[max-lines]] [–n max-args] [–s max-chars] [–P max-procs] [––null] [––eof[=eof-str]] [––replace[=replace-str]] [––max-lines[=max-lines]] [––interactive] [––max-chars=max-chars] [––verbose] [––exit] [––max-procs=max-procs] [––max-args=max-args] [––no-run-if-empty] [––version] [––help] [command [initial-arguments]]

DESCRIPTION

This manual page documents the GNU version of **xargs**. **xargs** reads arguments from the standard input, delimited by blanks (which can be protected with double or single quotes or a backslash) or newlines, and executes the *command* (default is /bin/echo) one or more times with any *initial-arguments* followed by arguments read from standard input. Blank lines on the standard input are ignored. **xargs** exits with the following status: 0 if it succeeds
123 if any invocation of the command exited with status 1-125
124 if the command exited with status 255
125 if the command is killed by a signal
126 if the command cannot be run
127 if the command is not found
1 if some other error occurred.

OPTIONS

––null, –0 Input filenames are terminated by a null character instead of by whitespace, and the quotes and backslash are not special (every character is taken literally). Disables the end of file string, which is treated like any other argument. Useful when arguments might contain white space, quote marks, or backslashes. The GNU find –print0 option produces input suitable for this mode.

––eof[=eof-str], –e[eof-str] Set the end of file string to *eof-str*. If the end of file string occurs as a line of input, the rest of the input is ignored. If *eof-str* is omitted, there is no end of file string. If this option is not given, the end of file string defaults to "_".

––help Print a summary of the options to **xargs** and exit.

––replace[=replace-str], –i[replace-str] Replace occurences of *replace-str* in the initial arguments with names read from standard input. Also, un-quoted blanks do not terminate arguments. If *replace-str* is omitted, it defaults to "{}" (like for 'find –exec'). Implies *–x* and *–l 1*.

––max-lines[=max-lines], -l[max-lines] Use at most *max-lines* nonblank input lines per command line; *max-lines* defaults to 1 if omitted. Trailing blanks cause an input line to be logically continued on the next input line. Implies *–x*.

––max-args=max-args, –n max-args Use at most *max-args* arguments per command line. Fewer than *max-args* arguments will be used if the size (see the –s option) is exceeded, unless the –x option is given, in which case **xargs** will exit.

––interactive, –p Prompt the user about whether to run each command line and read a line from the terminal. Only run the command line if the response starts with 'y' or 'Y'. Implies *–t*.

––no-run-if-empty, –r If the standard input does not contain any nonblanks, do not run the command. Normally, the command is run once even if there is no input.

––max-chars=max-chars, –s max-chars Use at most *max-chars* characters per command line, including the command and initial arguments and the terminating nulls at the ends of the argument strings. The default is as large as possible, up to 20k characters.

XARGS(1L) XARGS(1L)

    —*verbose, –t*   Print the command line on the standard error output before executing it.
    —*version*   Print the version number of **xargs** and exit.
    —*exit, –x*   Exit if the size (see the *–s* option) is exceeded.
    —*max-procs=max-procs, –P max-procs*   Run up to *max-procs* processes at a time; the default is 1. If *max-procs* is 0, **xargs** will run as many processes as possible at a time. Use the *–n* option with *–P*; otherwise chances are that only one exec will be done.

SEE ALSO

find(1L), **locate**(1L), **locatedb**(5L), **updatedb**(1) **Finding Files** (on-line in Info, or printed)

XAUTH(1)

NAME
xauth – X authority file utility

SYNOPSIS
xauth [**–f** *authfile*] [**–vqib**] [*command arg ...*]

DESCRIPTION
The *xauth* program is used to edit and display the authorization information used in connecting to the X server. This program is usually used to extract authorization records from one machine and merge them in on another (as is the case when using remote logins or granting access to other users). Commands (described below) may be entered interactively, on the *xauth* command line, or in scripts. Note that this program does **not** contact the X server. Normally *xauth* is not used to create the authority file entry in the first place; *xdm* does that.

OPTIONS
The following options may be used with *xauth*. They may be given individually (e.g., –q –i) or may combined (e.g., –qi).

–f *authfile* This option specifies the name of the authority file to use. By default, *xauth* will use the file specified by the XAUTHORITY environment variable or *Xauthority* in the user's home directory.

–q This option indicates that *xauth* should operate quietly and not print unsolicited status messages. This is the default if an *xauth* command is is given on the command line or if the standard output is not directed to a terminal.

–v This option indicates that *xauth* should operate verbosely and print status messages indicating the results of various operations (e.g., how many records have been read in or written out). This is the default if *xauth* is reading commands from its standard input and its standard output is directed to a terminal.

–i This option indicates that *xauth* should ignore any authority file locks. Normally, *xauth* will refuse to read or edit any authority files that have been locked by other programs (usually *xdm* or another *xauth*).

–b This option indicates that *xauth* should attempt to break any authority file locks before proceeding. Use this option only to clean up stale locks.

COMMANDS
The following commands may be used to manipulate authority files:

add *displayname protocolname hexkey* An authorization entry for the indicated display using the given protocol and key data is added to the authorization file. The data is specified as an even-lengthed string of hexadecimal digits, each pair representing one octet. The first digit of each pair gives the most significant 4 bits of the octet, and the second digit of the pair gives the least significant 4 bits. For example, a 32 character hexkey would represent a 128-bit value. A protocol name consisting of just a single period is treated as an abbreviation for *MIT-MAGIC-COOKIE-1*.

[n]extract *filename displayname...* Authorization entries for each of the specified displays are written to the indicated file. If the *nextract* command is used, the entries are written in a numeric format suitable for non-binary transmission (such as secure electronic mail). The extracted entries can be read back in using the *merge* and *nmerge* commands. If the filename consists of just a single dash, the entries will be written to the standard output.

[n]list [*displayname*...]   Authorization entries for each of the specified displays (or all if no displays are named) are printed on the standard output. If the *nlist* command is used, entries will be shown in the numeric format used by the *nextract* command; otherwise, they are shown in a textual format. Key data is always displayed in the hexadecimal format given in the description of the *add* command.

[n]merge [*filename*...]   Authorization entries are read from the specified files and are merged into the authorization database, superceding any matching existing entries. If the *nmerge* command is used, the numeric format given in the description of the *extract* command is used. If a filename consists of just a single dash, the standard input will be read if it hasn't been read before.

remove *displayname*...   Authorization entries matching the specified displays are removed from the authority file.

source *filename*   The specified file is treated as a script containing *xauth* commands to execute. Blank lines and lines beginning with a sharp sign (#) are ignored. A single dash may be used to indicate the standard input, if it hasn't already been read.

info   Information describing the authorization file, whether or not any changes have been made, and from where *xauth* commands are being read is printed on the standard output.

exit   If any modifications have been made, the authority file is written out (if allowed), and the program exits. An end of file is treated as an implicit *exit* command.

quit   The program exits, ignoring any modifications. This may also be accomplished by pressing the interrupt character.

help [*string*]   A description of all commands that begin with the given string (or all commands if no string is given) is printed on the standard output.

?   A short list of the valid commands is printed on the standard output.

DISPLAY NAMES

Display names for the *add*, *[n]extract*, *[n]list*, *[n]merge*, and *remove* commands use the same format as the DISPLAY environment variable and the common *–display* command line argument. Display-specific information (such as the screen number) is unnecessary and will be ignored. Same-machine connections (such as local-host sockets, shared memory, and the Internet Protocol hostname *localhost*) are referred to as *hostname*/unix:*displaynumber* so that local entries for different machines may be stored in one authority file.

EXAMPLE

The most common use for *xauth* is to extract the entry for the current display, copy it to another machine, and merge it into the user's authority file on the remote machine:

% xauth extract – $DISPLAY | rsh otherhost xauth merge –

ENVIRONMENT

This *xauth* program uses the following environment variables:

XAUTHORITY   to get the name of the authority file to use if the *–f* option isn't used.

HOME   to get the user's home directory if XAUTHORITY isn't defined.

FILES

$HOME/.Xauthority   default authority file if XAUTHORITY isn't defined.

BUGS

Users that have unsecure networks should take care to use encrypted file transfer mechanisms to copy authorization entries between machines. Similarly, the *MIT-MAGIC-COOKIE-1* protocol is not very useful in unsecure environments. Sites that are interested in additional security may need to use encrypted authorization mechanisms such as Kerberos.

Spaces are currently not allowed in the protocol name. Quoting could be added for the truly perverse.

AUTHOR

Jim Fulton, MIT X Consortium

XCMSDB(1)

NAME

xcmsdb – Device Color Characterization utility for X Color Management System

SYNOPSIS

xcmsdb [**–query**] [**–remove**] [**–format 32|16|8**] [*filename*]

DESCRIPTION

xcmsdb is used to load, query, or remove Device Color Characterization data stored in properties on the root window of the screen as specified in section 7, Device Color Characterization, of the ICCCM. Device Color Characterization data (also called the Device Profile) is an integral part of Xlib's X Color Management System (Xcms), necessary for proper conversion of color specification between device-independent and device-dependent forms. Xcms uses 3x3 matrices stored in the XDCCC_LINEAR_RGB_MATRICES property to convert color specifications between CIEXYZ and RGB Intensity (XcmsRGBi, also referred to as linear RGB). Xcms then uses display gamma information stored in the XDCCC_LINEAR_RGB_CORRECTION property to convert color specifications between RGBi and RGB device (XcmsRGB, also referred to as device RGB).

Note that Xcms allows clients to register *function sets* in addition to its built-in function set for CRT color monitors. Additional function sets may store their device profile information in other properties in function set specific format. This utility is unaware of these non-standard properties.

The ASCII readable contents of *filename* (or the standard input if no input file is given) are appropriately transformed for storage in properties, provided the **–query** or **–remove** options are not specified.

OPTIONS

xcmsdb program accepts the following options:

–query   This option attempts to read the XDCCC properties off the screen's root window. If successful, it transforms the data into a more readable format, then sends the data to standard out.

–remove   This option attempts to remove the XDCCC properties on the screen's root window.

–format 32|16|8   Specifies the property format (32, 16, or 8 bits per entry) for the XDCCC_LINEAR_RGB_CORRECTION property. Precision of encoded floating point values increases with the increase in bits per entry. The default is 32 bits per entry.

SEE ALSO

xprop(1), Xlib documentation

ENVIRONMENT

DISPLAY   to figure out which display and screen to use.

AUTHOR

Chuck Adams, Tektronix Inc. Al Tabayoyon, SynChromatics Inc. (added multi-visual support)

XCONSOLE(1)

NAME

xconsole – monitor system console messages with X

SYNOPSIS

xconsole [-*toolkitoption* ...] [-file *file-name*] [-notify] [-stripNonprint] [-daemon] [-verbose] [-exitOnFail]

DESCRIPTION

The *xconsole* program displays messages which are usually sent to /dev/console.

OPTIONS

Xconsole accepts all of the standard X Toolkit command line options along with the additional options listed below:

> **–file** *file-name*   To monitor some other device, use this option to specify the device name. This does not work on regular files as they are always ready to be read from.
>
> **–notify** –nonotify   When new data are received from the console and the notify option is set, the icon name of the application has " *" appended, so that it is evident even when the application is iconified. –notify is the default.
>
> **–daemon**   This option causes *xconsole* to place itself in the background, using fork/exit.
>
> **–verbose**   When set, this option directs *xconsole* to display an informative message in the first line of the text buffer.
>
> **–exitOnFail**   When set, this option directs *xconsole* to exit when it is unable to redirect the console output.

X DEFAULTS

This program uses the *Athena* Text widget, look in the *Athena* Widget Set documentation for controlling it.

WIDGETS

In order to specify resources, it is useful to know the hierarchy of the widgets which compose *xconsole*. In the notation below, indentation indicates hierarchical structure. The widget class name is given first, followed by the widget instance name.

XConsole xconsole
    XConsole text

ENVIRONMENT

> **DISPLAY**   to get the default host and display number.
>
> **XENVIRONMENT**   to get the name of a resource file that overrides the global resources stored in the RESOURCE_MANAGER property.

FILES

<XRoot>/lib/X11/app-defaults/XConsole - specifies required resources

SEE ALSO

X(1), xrdb(1), Athena Text widget

AUTHOR

Keith Packard (MIT X Consortium)

XDM(1)

NAME

xdm – X Display Manager with support for XDMCP, host chooser

SYNOPSIS

xdm [**–config** *configuration_file*] [**–nodaemon**] [**–debug** *debug_level*] [**–error** *error_log_file*] [**–resources** *resource_file*] [**–server** *server_entry*] [**–session** *session_program*]

DESCRIPTION

Xdm manages a collection of X displays, which may be on the local host or remote servers. The design of *xdm* was guided by the needs of X terminals as well as the X Consortium standard XDMCP, the *X Display Manager Control Protocol*. *Xdm* provides services similar to those provided by *init*, *getty* and *login* on character terminals: prompting for login name and password, authenticating the user, and running a "session."

A "session" is defined by the lifetime of a particular process; in the traditional character-based terminal world, it is the user's login shell. In the *xdm* context, it is an arbitrary session manager. This is because in a windowing environment, a user's login shell process does not necessarily have any terminal-like interface with which to connect. When a real session manager is not available, a window manager or terminal emulator is typically used as the "session manager," meaning that termination of this process terminates the user's session.

When the session is terminated, *xdm* resets the X server and (optionally) restarts the whole process.

When *xdm* receives an Indirect query via XDMCP, it can run a *chooser* process to perform an XDMCP BroadcastQuery (or an XDMCP Query to specified hosts) on behalf of the display and offer a menu of possible hosts that offer XDMCP display management. This feature is useful with X terminals that do not offer a host menu themselves.

Because *xdm* provides the first interface that users will see, it is designed to be simple to use and easy to customize to the needs of a particular site. *Xdm* has many options, most of which have reasonable defaults. Browse through the various sections of this manual, picking and choosing the things you want to change. Pay particular attention to the **Session Program** section, which will describe how to set up the style of session desired.

OVERVIEW

xdm is highly configurable, and most of its behavior can be controlled by resource files and shell scripts. The names of these files themselves are resources read from the file *xdm-config* or the file named by the **–config** option.

xdm offers display management two different ways. It can manage X servers running on the local machine and specified in *Xservers*, and it can manage remote X servers (typically X terminals) using XDMCP (the XDM Control Protocol) as specified in the *Xaccess* file.

The resources of the X clients run by *xdm* outside the user's session, including *xdm*'s own login window, can be affected by setting resources in the *Xresources* file.

For X terminals that do not offer a menu of hosts to get display management from, *xdm* can collect willing hosts and run the *chooser* program to offer the user a menu. For X displays attached to a host, this step is typically not used, as the local host does the display management.

After resetting the X server, *xdm* runs the *Xsetup* script to assist in setting up the screen the user sees along with the *xlogin* widget.

When the user logs in, *xdm* runs the *Xstartup* script as root.

Then *xdm* runs the *Xsession* script as the user. This system session file may do some additional startup and typically runs a script in the user's home directory. When the *Xsession* script exits, the session is over.

At the end of the session, the *Xreset* script is run to clean up, the X server is reset, and the cycle starts over.

The file */usr/X11R6/lib/X11/xdm/xdm-errors* will contain error messages from *xdm* and anything output to stderr by *Xsetup, Xstartup, Xsession* or *Xreset*. When you have trouble getting *xdm* working, check this file to see if *xdm* has any clues to the trouble.

OPTIONS

All of these options, except **–config** itself, specify values that can also be specified in the configuration file as resources.

–config *configuration_file*   Names the configuration file, which specifies resources to control the behavior of *xdm*. *<XRoot>/lib/X11/xdm/xdm-config* is the default. See the section **Configuration File**.

–nodaemon   Specifies "false" as the value for the **DisplayManager.daemonMode** resource. This suppresses the normal daemon behavior, which is for *xdm* to close all file descriptors, disassociate itself from the controlling terminal, and put itself in the background when it first starts up.

–debug *debug_level*   Specifies the numeric value for the **DisplayManager.debugLevel** resource. A non-zero value causes *xdm* to print lots of debugging statements to the terminal; it also disables the **DisplayManager.daemonMode** resource, forcing *xdm* to run synchronously. To interpret these debugging messages, a copy of the source code for *xdm* is almost a necessity. No attempt has been made to rationalize or standardize the output.

–error *error_log_file*   Specifies the value for the **DisplayManager.errorLogFile** resource. This file contains errors from *xdm* as well as anything written to stderr by the various scripts and programs run during the progress of the session.

–resources *resource_file*   Specifies the value for the **DisplayManager*resources** resource. This file is loaded using *xrdb* to specify configuration parameters for the authentication widget.

–server *server_entry*   Specifies the value for the **DisplayManager.servers** resource. See the section **Local Server Specification** for a description of this resource.

–udpPort *port_number*   Specifies the value for the **DisplayManager.requestPort** resource. This sets the port-number which *xdm* will monitor for XDMCP requests. As XDMCP uses the registered well-known UDP port 177, this resource should not be changed except for debugging.

–session *session_program*   Specifies the value for the **DisplayManager*session** resource. This indicates the program to run as the session after the user has logged in.

–xrm *resource_specification*   Allows an arbitrary resource to be specified, as in most X Toolkit applications.

RESOURCES

At many stages the actions of *xdm* can be controlled through the use of its configuration file, which is in the X resource format. Some resources modify the behavior of *xdm* on all displays, while others modify its behavior on a single display. Where actions relate to a specific display, the display name is inserted into the resource name between "DisplayManager" and the final resource name segment.

For local displays, the resource name and class are as read from the *Xservers* file.

For remote displays, the resource name is what the network address of the display resolves to. See the **removeDomain** resource. The name must match exactly; *xdm* is not aware of all the network aliases that might reach a given display. If the name resolve fails, the address is used. The resource class is as sent by the display in the XDMCP Manage request.

Because the resource manager uses colons to separate the name of the resource from its value and dots to separate resource name parts, *xdm* substitutes underscores for both dots and colons when generating the resource name. For example,
DisplayManager.expo_x_org_0.startup is the name of the resource which defines the startup shell file for the "expo.x.org:0" display.

DisplayManager.servers This resource either specifies a file name full of server entries, one per line (if the value starts with a slash), or a single server entry. See the section **Local Server Specification** for the details.

DisplayManager.requestPort This indicates the UDP port number which *xdm* uses to listen for incoming XDMCP requests. Unless you need to debug the system, leave this with its default value of 177.

DisplayManager.errorLogFile Error output is normally directed at the system console. To redirect it, set this resource to a file name. A method to send these messages to *syslog* should be developed for systems which support it; however, the wide variety of interfaces precludes any system-independent implementation. This file also contains any output directed to stderr by the *Xsetup, Xstartup, Xsession* and *Xreset* files, so it will contain descriptions of problems in those scripts as well.

DisplayManager.debugLevel If the integer value of this resource is greater than zero, reams of debugging information will be printed. It also disables daemon mode, which would redirect the information into the bit-bucket, and allows non-root users to run *xdm,* which would normally not be useful.

DisplayManager.daemonMode Normally, *xdm* attempts to make itself into a daemon process unassociated with any terminal. This is accomplished by forking and leaving the parent process to exit, then closing file descriptors and releasing the controlling terminal. In some environments this is not desired (in particular, when debugging). Setting this resource to "false" will disable this feature.

DisplayManager.pidFile The filename specified will be created to contain an ASCII representation of the process-id of the main *xdm* process. *Xdm* also uses file locking on this file to attempt to eliminate multiple daemons running on the same machine, which would cause quite a bit of havoc.

DisplayManager.lockPidFile This is the resource which controls whether *xdm* uses file locking to keep multiple display managers from running amok. On System V, this uses the *lockf* library call, while on BSD it uses *flock*.

DisplayManager.authDir This names a directory in which *xdm* stores authorization files while initializing the session. The default value is *<XRoot>/lib/X11/xdm*.

DisplayManager.autoRescan This boolean controls whether *xdm* rescans the configuration, servers, access control and authentication keys files after a session terminates and the files have changed. By default it is "true." You can force *xdm* to reread these files by sending a SIGHUP to the main process.

DisplayManager.removeDomainname When computing the display name for XDMCP clients, the name resolver will typically create a fully qualified host name for the terminal. As this is sometimes confusing, *xdm* will remove the domain name portion of the host name if it is the same as the domain name of the local host when this variable is set. By default the value is "true."

DisplayManager.keyFile XDM-AUTHENTICATION-1 style XDMCP authentication requires that a private key be shared between *xdm* and the terminal. This resource specifies the file containing those values. Each entry in the file consists of a display name and the shared key. By default, *xdm* does not include support for XDM-AUTHENTICATION-1, as it requires DES which is not generally distributable because of United States export restrictions.

DisplayManager.accessFile To prevent unauthorized XDMCP service and to allow forwarding of XDMCP IndirectQuery requests, this file contains a database of hostnames which are either allowed direct access to this

XDM(1)   XDM(1)

machine, or have a list of hosts to which queries should be forwarded to. The format of this file is described in the section **XDMCP Access Control.**

DisplayManager.exportList   A list of additional environment variables, separated by white space, to pass on to the *Xsetup*, *Xstartup*, *Xsession*, and *Xreset* programs.

DisplayManager.randomFile   A file to checksum to generate the seed of authorization keys. This should be a file that changes frequently. The default is */dev/mem*.

DisplayManager.greeterLib   On systems that support a dynamically-loadable greeter library, the name of the library. Default is *<XRoot>/lib/X11/xdm/libXdmGreet.so*.

DisplayManager.choiceTimeout   Number of seconds to wait for display to respond after user has selected a host from the chooser. If the display sends an XDMCP IndirectQuery within this time, the request is forwarded to the chosen host. Otherwise, it is assumed to be from a new session and the chooser is offered again. Default is 15.

DisplayManager.*DISPLAY*.resources   This resource specifies the name of the file to be loaded by *xrdb* as the resource database onto the root window of screen 0 of the display. The *Xsetup* program, the Login widget, and *chooser* will use the resources set in this file. This resource data base is loaded just before the authentication procedure is started, so it can control the appearance of the login window. See the section **Authentication Widget,** which describes the various resources that are appropriate to place in this file. There is no default value for this resource, but *<XRoot>/lib/X11/xdm/Xresources* is the conventional name.

DisplayManager.*DISPLAY*.chooser   Specifies the program run to offer a host menu for Indirect queries redirected to the special host name CHOOSER. *<XRoot>/lib/X11/xdm/chooser* is the default. See the sections **XDMCP Access Control** and **Chooser.**

DisplayManager.*DISPLAY*.xrdb   Specifies the program used to load the resources. By default, *xdm* uses *<XRoot>/bin/xrdb*.

DisplayManager.*DISPLAY*.cpp   This specifies the name of the C preprocessor which is used by *xrdb*.

DisplayManager.*DISPLAY*.setup   This specifies a program which is run (as root) before offering the Login window. This may be used to change the appearance of the screen around the Login window or to put up other windows (e.g., you may want to run *xconsole* here). By default, no program is run. The conventional name for a file used here is *Xsetup*. See the section **Setup Program.**

DisplayManager.*DISPLAY*.startup   This specifies a program which is run (as root) after the authentication process succeeds. By default, no program is run. The conventional name for a file used here is *Xstartup*. See the section **Startup Program.**

DisplayManager.*DISPLAY*.session   This specifies the session to be executed (not running as root). By default, *<XRoot>/bin/xterm* is run. The conventional name is *Xsession*. See the section **Session Program.**

DisplayManager.*DISPLAY*.reset   This specifies a program which is run (as root) after the session terminates. Again, by default no program is run. The conventional name is *Xreset*. See the section **Reset Program.**

DisplayManager.*DISPLAY*.openDelay

DisplayManager.*DISPLAY*.openRepeat

DisplayManager.*DISPLAY***.openTimeout**

DisplayManager.*DISPLAY***.startAttempts** These numeric resources control the behavior of *xdm* when attempting to open intransigent servers. **openDelay** is the length of the pause (in seconds) between successive attempts, **openRepeat** is the number of attempts to make, **openTimeout** is the amount of time to wait while actually attempting the open (i.e., the maximum time spent in the *connect*(2) system call) and **startAttempts** is the number of times this entire process is done before giving up on the server. After **openRepeat** attempts have been made, or if **openTimeout** seconds elapse in any particular attempt, *xdm* terminates and restarts the server, attempting to connect again. This process is repeated **startAttempts** times, at which point the display is declared dead and disabled. Although this behavior may seem arbitrary, it has been empirically developed and works quite well on most systems. The default values are 5 for **openDelay**, 5 for **openRepeat**, 30 for **openTimeout** and 4 for **startAttempts**.

DisplayManager.*DISPLAY***.pingInterval**

DisplayManager.*DISPLAY***.pingTimeout** To discover when remote displays disappear, *xdm* occasionally pings them, using an X connection and *XSync* calls. **pingInterval** specifies the time (in minutes) between each ping attempt, **pingTimeout** specifies the maximum amount of time (in minutes) to wait for the terminal to respond to the request. If the terminal does not respond, the session is declared dead and terminated. By default, both are set to 5 minutes. If you frequently use X terminals which can become isolated from the managing host, you may wish to increase this value. The only worry is that sessions will continue to exist after the terminal has been accidentally disabled. *xdm* will not ping local displays. Although it would seem harmless, it is unpleasant when the workstation session is terminated as a result of the server hanging for NFS service and not responding to the ping.

DisplayManager.*DISPLAY***.terminateServer** This boolean resource specifies whether the X server should be terminated when a session terminates (instead of resetting it). This option can be used when the server tends to grow without bound over time, in order to limit the amount of time the server is run. The default value is "false."

DisplayManager.*DISPLAY***.userPath** *Xdm* sets the PATH environment variable for the session to this value. It should be a colon separated list of directories; see *sh*(1) for a full description. ":/bin:/usr/bin:/usr/X11R6/bin:/usr/ucb" is a common setting. The default value can be specified at build time in the X system configuration file with DefaultUserPath.

DisplayManager.*DISPLAY***.systemPath** *Xdm* sets the PATH environment variable for the startup and reset scripts to the value of this resource. The default for this resource is specified at build time by the DefaultSystemPath entry in the system configuration file; "/etc:/bin:/usr/bin:/usr/X11R6/bin:/usr/ucb" is a common choice. Note the absence of "." from this entry. This is a good practice to follow for root; it avoids many common Trojan Horse system penetration schemes.

DisplayManager.*DISPLAY***.systemShell** *Xdm* sets the SHELL environment variable for the startup and reset scripts to the value of this resource. It is */bin/sh* by default.

DisplayManager.*DISPLAY***.failsafeClient** If the default session fails to execute, *xdm* will fall back to this program. This program is executed with no arguments, but executes using the same environment variables as the session would have had (see the section **Session Program**). By default, <*XRoot*>*/bin/xterm* is used.

DisplayManager.*DISPLAY***.grabServer**

DisplayManager.*DISPLAY***.grabTimeout**   To improve security, *xdm* grabs the server and keyboard while reading the login name and password. The **grabServer** resource specifies if the server should be held for the duration of the name/password reading. When "false," the server is ungrabbed after the keyboard grab succeeds, otherwise the server is grabbed until just before the session begins. The default is "false." The **grabTimeout** resource specifies the maximum time *xdm* will wait for the grab to succeed. The grab may fail if some other client has the server grabbed, or possibly if the network latencies are very high. This resource has a default value of 3 seconds; you should be cautious when raising it, as a user can be spoofed by a look-alike window on the display. If the grab fails, *xdm* kills and restarts the server (if possible) and the session.

DisplayManager.*DISPLAY***.authorize**

DisplayManager.*DISPLAY***.authName**   **authorize** is a boolean resource which controls whether *xdm* generates and uses authorization for the local server connections. If authorization is used, **authName** is a list of authorization mechanisms to use, separated by white space. XDMCP connections dynamically specify which authorization mechanisms are supported, so **authName** is ignored in this case. When **authorize** is set for a display and authorization is not available, the user is informed by having a different message displayed in the login widget. By default, **authorize** is "true." **authName** is "MIT-MAGIC-COOKIE-1," or, if XDM-AUTHORIZATION-1 is available, "XDM-AUTHORIZATION-1 MIT-MAGIC-COOKIE-1."

DisplayManager.*DISPLAY***.authFile**   This file is used to communicate the authorization data from *xdm* to the server, using the **–auth** server command line option. It should be kept in a directory which is not world-writable as it could easily be removed, disabling the authorization mechanism in the server.

DisplayManager.*DISPLAY***.authComplain**   If set to "false," disables the use of the **unsecureGreeting** in the login window. See the section **Authentication Widget.** The default is "true."

DisplayManager.*DISPLAY***.resetSignal**   The number of the signal *xdm* sends to reset the server. See the section **Controlling the Server.** The default is 1 (SIGHUP).

DisplayManager.*DISPLAY***.termSignal**   The number of the signal *xdm* sends to terminate the server. See the section **Controlling the Server.** The default is 15 (SIGTERM).

DisplayManager.*DISPLAY***.resetForAuth**   The original implementation of authorization in the sample server reread the authorization file at server reset time, instead of when checking the initial connection. As *xdm* generates the authorization information just before connecting to the display, an old server would not get up-to-date authorization information. This resource causes *xdm* to send SIGHUP to the server after setting up the file, causing an additional server reset to occur, during which time the new authorization information will be read. The default is "false," which will work for all MIT servers.

DisplayManager.*DISPLAY***.userAuthDir**   When *xdm* is unable to write to the usual user authorization file ($HOME/.Xauthority), it creates a unique file name in this directory and points the environment variable XAUTHORITY at the created file. It uses */tmp* by default.

CONFIGURATION FILE

First, the *xdm* configuration file should be set up. Make a directory (usually <XRoot>/lib/X11/xdm, where <XRoot> refers to the root of the X11 install tree) to contain all of the relevant files. In the examples that follow, we use /usr/X11R6 as the value of <XRoot>.

XDM(1)   XDM(1)

Here is a reasonable configuration file, which could be named *xdm-config*:

DisplayManager.servers: /usr/X11R6/lib/X11/xdm/Xservers
DisplayManager.errorLogFile: /usr/X11R6/lib/X11/xdm/xdm-errors
DisplayManager*resources: /usr/X11R6/lib/X11/xdm/Xresources
DisplayManager*startup: /usr/X11R6/lib/X11/xdm/Xstartup
DisplayManager*session: /usr/X11R6/lib/X11/xdm/Xsession
DisplayManager.pidFile: /usr/X11R6/lib/X11/xdm/xdm-pid
DisplayManager._0.authorize: true
DisplayManager*authorize: false

Note that this file mostly contains references to other files. Note also that some of the resources are specified with "*" separating the components. These resources can be made unique for each different display, by replacing the "*" with the display-name, but normally this is not very useful. See the **Resources** section for a complete discussion.

XDMCP ACCESS CONTROL

The database file specified by the **DisplayManager.accessFile** provides information which *xdm* uses to control access from displays requesting XDMCP service. This file contains three types of entries: entries which control the response to Direct and Broadcast queries, entries which control the response to Indirect queries, and macro definitions.

The format of the Direct entries is simple, either a host name or a pattern, which is distinguished from a host name by the inclusion of one or more meta characters ('*' matches any sequence of 0 or more characters, and '?' matches any single character) which are compared against the host name of the display device. If the entry is a host name, all comparisons are done using network addresses, so any name which converts to the correct network address may be used. For patterns, only canonical host names are used in the comparison, so ensure that you do not attempt to match aliases. Preceding either a host name or a pattern with a '!' character causes hosts which match that entry to be excluded.

An Indirect entry also contains a host name or pattern, but follows it with a list of host names or macros to which indirect queries should be sent.

A macro definition contains a macro name and a list of host names and other macros that the macro expands to. To distinguish macros from hostnames, macro names start with a '%' character. Macros may be nested.

Indirect entries may also specify to have *xdm* run *chooser* to offer a menu of hosts to connect to. See the section **Chooser**.

When checking access for a particular display host, each entry is scanned in turn and the first matching entry determines the response. Direct and Broadcast entries are ignored when scanning for an Indirect entry and vice-versa.

Blank lines are ignored, '#' is treated as a comment delimiter causing the rest of that line to be ignored, and '*newline*' causes the newline to be ignored, allowing indirect host lists to span multiple lines. Here is an example Xaccess file:

```
#
# Xaccess - XDMCP access control file
#


#
# Direct/Broadcast query entries
#

!xtra.lcs.mit.edu # disallow direct/broadcast service for xtra
bambi.ogi.edu # allow access from this particular display
.lcs.mit.edu # allow access from any display in LCS


#
# Indirect query entries
```

```
#
%HOSTS expo.lcs.mit.edu xenon.lcs.mit.edu \
excess.lcs.mit.edu kanga.lcs.mit.edu

extract.lcs.mit.edu xenon.lcs.mit.edu #force extract to contact xenon
!xtra.lcs.mit.edu dummy #disallow indirect access
.lcs.mit.edu %HOSTS #all others get to choose
```

CHOOSER

For X terminals that do not offer a host menu for use with Broadcast or Indirect queries, the *chooser* program can do this for them. In the *Xaccess* file, specify "CHOOSER" as the first entry in the Indirect host list. *Chooser* will send a Query request to each of the remaining host names in the list and offer a menu of all the hosts that respond.

The list may consist of the word "BROADCAST," in which case *chooser* will send a Broadcast instead, again offering a menu of all hosts that respond. Note that on some operating systems, UDP packets cannot be broadcast, so this feature will not work.

Example *Xaccess* file using *chooser*:

```
extract.lcs.mit.edu CHOOSER %HOSTS #offer a menu of these hosts
xtra.lcs.mit.edu CHOOSER BROADCAST #offer a menu of all hosts
```

The program to use for *chooser* is specified by the **DisplayManager.***DISPLAY***.chooser** resource. For more flexibility at this step, the chooser could be a shell script. *Chooser* is the session manager here; it is run instead of a child *xdm* to manage the display.

Resources for this program can be put into the file named by **DisplayManager.***DISPLAY***.resources**.

When the user selects a host, *chooser* prints the host chosen, which is read by the parent *xdm*, and exits. *xdm* closes its connection to the X server, and the server resets and sends another **Indirect** XDMCP request. *xdm* remembers the user's choice (for **DisplayManager.choiceTimeout** seconds) and forwards the request to the chosen host, which starts a session on that display.

LOCAL SERVER SPECIFICATION

The resource **DisplayManager.servers** gives a server specification or, if the values starts with a slash (/), the name of a file containing server specifications, one per line.

Each specification indicates a display which should constantly be managed and which is not using XDMCP. This method is used typically for local servers only. If the resource or the file named by the resource is empty, *xdm* will offer XDMCP service only.

Each specification consists of at least three parts: a display name, a display class, a display type, and (for local servers) a command line to start the server. A typical entry for local display number 0 would be:
:0 Digital-QV local /usr/X11R6/bin/X :0

The display types are:
local local display: *xdm* must run the server
foreign remote display: *xdm* opens an X connection to a running server

The display name must be something that can be passed in the **–display** option to an X program. This string is used to generate the display-specific resource names, so be careful to match the names (e.g., use ":0 Sun-CG3 local /usr/X11R6/bin/X :0" instead of "localhost:0 Sun-CG3 local /usr/X11R6/bin/X :0" if your other resources are specified as "DisplayManager._0.session"). The display class portion is also used in the display-specific resources, as the class of the resource. This is useful if you have a large collection of similar displays (such as a corral of X terminals) and would like to set resources for groups of them. When using XDMCP, the display is required to specify the display class, so the manual for your particular X terminal should document the display class string for your device. If it doesn't,

XDM(1)   XDM(1)

you can run *xdm* in debug mode and look at the resource strings which it generates for that device, which will include the class string.

When *xdm* starts a session, it sets up authorization data for the server. For local servers, *xdm* passes "**–auth** *filename*" on the server's command line to point it at its authorization data. For XDMCP servers, *xdm* passes the authorization data to the server via the Accept XDMCP request.

RESOURCES FILE

The *Xresources* file is loaded onto the display as a resource database using *xrdb*. As the authentication widget reads this database before starting up, it usually contains parameters for that widget:
xlogin*login.translations: #override\
Ctrl<Key>R: abort-display()\n\
<Key>F1: set-session-argument(failsafe) finish-field()\n\
<Key>Return: set-session-argument() finish-field()
xlogin*borderWidth: 3
xlogin*greeting: CLIENTHOST
#ifdef COLOR
xlogin*greetColor: CadetBlue
xlogin*failColor: red
#endif

Please note the translations entry; it specifies a few new translations for the widget which allow users to escape from the default session (and avoid troubles that may occur in it). Note that if #override is not specified, the default translations are removed and replaced by the new value, not a very useful result as some of the default translations are quite useful (such as "<Key>: insert-char ()" which responds to normal typing).

This file may also contain resources for the setup program and *chooser*.

SETUP PROGRAM

The *Xsetup* file is run after the server is reset, but before the Login window is offered. The file is typically a shell script. It is run as root, so should be careful about security. This is the place to change the root background or bring up other windows that should appear on the screen along with the Login widget.

In addition to any specified by **DisplayManager.exportList**, the following environment variables are passed:
DISPLAY the associated display name
PATH the value of **DisplayManager.***DISPLAY***.systemPath** SHELL the value of **DisplayManager.***DISPLAY***.systemShell** XAUTHORITY may be set to an authority file

Note that since *xdm* grabs the keyboard, any other windows will not be able to receive keyboard input. They will be able to interact with the mouse, however; beware of potential security holes here. If **DisplayManager.***DISPLAY***.grabServer** is set, *Xsetup* will not be able to connect to the display at all. Resources for this program can be put into the file named by **DisplayManager.***DISPLAY***.resources**.

Here is a sample *Xsetup* script:
#!/bin/sh
Xsetup_0 – setup script for one workstation
xcmsdb < /usr/X11R6/lib/monitors/alex.0
xconsole –geometry 480x130–0–0 –notify –verbose –exitOnFail &

AUTHENTICATION WIDGET

The authentication widget reads a name/password pair from the keyboard. Nearly every imaginable parameter can be controlled with a resource. Resources for this widget should be put into the file named by **DisplayManager.***DISPLAY***.resources**. All of these have reasonable default values, so it is not necessary to specify any of them.

xlogin.Login.width, xlogin.Login.height, xlogin.Login.x, xlogin.Login.y The geometry of the Login widget is normally computed automatically. If you wish to position it elsewhere, specify each of these resources.

xlogin.Login.foreground The color used to display the typed-in user name.

xlogin.Login.font The font used to display the typed-in user name.

xlogin.Login.greeting A string which identifies this window. The default is "X Window System."

xlogin.Login.unsecureGreeting When X authorization is requested in the configuration file for this display and none is in use, this greeting replaces the standard greeting. The default is "This is an unsecure session"

xlogin.Login.greetFont The font used to display the greeting.

xlogin.Login.greetColor The color used to display the greeting.

xlogin.Login.namePrompt The string displayed to prompt for a user name. *Xrdb* strips trailing white space from resource values, so to add spaces at the end of the prompt (usually a nice thing), add spaces escaped with backslashes. The default is "Login: "

xlogin.Login.passwdPrompt The string displayed to prompt for a password. The default is "Password: "

xlogin.Login.promptFont The font used to display both prompts.

xlogin.Login.promptColor The color used to display both prompts.

xlogin.Login.fail A message which is displayed when the authentication fails. The default is "Login incorrect"

xlogin.Login.failFont The font used to display the failure message.

xlogin.Login.failColor The color used to display the failure message.

xlogin.Login.failTimeout The number of seconds that the failure message is displayed. The default is 30.

xlogin.Login.translations This specifies the translations used for the login widget. Refer to the X Toolkit documentation for a complete discussion on translations. The default translation table is:
Ctrl<Key>H: delete-previous-character() \n\
Ctrl<Key>D: delete-character() \n\
Ctrl<Key>B: move-backward-character() \n\
Ctrl<Key>F: move-forward-character() \n\
Ctrl<Key>A: move-to-begining() \n\
Ctrl<Key>E: move-to-end() \n\
Ctrl<Key>K: erase-to-end-of-line() \n\
Ctrl<Key>U: erase-line() \n\
Ctrl<Key>X: erase-line() \n\
Ctrl<Key>C: restart-session() \n\
Ctrl<Key>\\: abort-session() \n\
<Key>BackSpace: delete-previous-character() \n\
<Key>Delete: delete-previous-character() \n\
<Key>Return: finish-field() \n\
<Key>: insert-char() \

The actions which are supported by the widget are:

   delete-previous-character   Erases the character before the cursor.

   delete-character   Erases the character after the cursor.

   move-backward-character   Moves the cursor backward.

   move-forward-character   Moves the cursor forward.

   move-to-begining   (Apologies about the spelling error.) Moves the cursor to the beginning of the editable text.

XDM(1)   XDM(1)

    move-to-end   Moves the cursor to the end of the editable text.

    erase-to-end-of-line   Erases all text after the cursor.

    erase-line   Erases the entire text.

    finish-field   If the cursor is in the name field, proceeds to the password field; if the cursor is in the password field, checks the current name/password pair. If the name/password pair is valid, *xdm* starts the session. Otherwise the failure message is displayed and the user is prompted again.

    abort-session   Terminates and restarts the server.

    abort-display   Terminates the server, disabling it. This action is not accessible in the default configuration. There are various reasons to stop *xdm* on a system console, such as when shutting the system down, when using *xdmshell*, to start another type of server, or to generally access the console. Sending *xdm* a SIGHUP will restart the display. See the section **Controlling XDM**.

    restart-session   Resets the X server and starts a new session. This can be used when the resources have been changed and you want to test them or when the screen has been overwritten with system messages.

    insert-char   Inserts the character typed.

    set-session-argument   Specifies a single word argument which is passed to the session at startup. See the section **Session Program**.

    allow-all-access   Disables access control in the server. This can be used when the .Xauthority file cannot be created by *xdm*. Be very careful using this; it might be better to disconnect the machine from the network before doing this.

STARTUP PROGRAM

The *Xstartup* file is typically a shell script. It is run as root and should be very careful about security. This is the place to put commands which add entries to */etc/utmp* (the *sessreg* program may be useful here), mount users' home directories from file servers, display the message of the day, or abort the session if logins are not allowed.

In addition to any specified by **DisplayManager.exportList**, the following environment variables are passed:
DISPLAY the associated display name
HOME the initial working directory of the user
USER the user name
PATH the value of **DisplayManager.***DISPLAY***.systemPath** SHELL the value of **DisplayManager.***DISPLAY***.systemShell** XAUTHORITY may be set to an authority file

No arguments are passed to the script. *Xdm* waits until this script exits before starting the user session. If the exit value of this script is non-zero, *xdm* discontinues the session and starts another authentication cycle.

The sample *Xstartup* file shown here prevents login while the file */etc/nologin* exists. Thus this is not a complete example, but simply a demonstration of the available functionality.

Here is a sample *Xstartup* script:
```
#!/bin/sh
#
# Xstartup
#
# This program is run as root after the user is verified
#
if [ -f /etc/nologin ]; then
xmessage -file /etc/nologin
exit 1
fi
```

```
sessreg -a -l $DISPLAY -x /usr/X11R6/lib/xdm/Xservers $USER
/usr/X11R6/lib/xdm/GiveConsole
exit 0
```

SESSION PROGRAM

The *Xsession* program is the command which is run as the user's session. It is run with the permissions of the authorized user.

In addition to any specified by **DisplayManager.exportList**, the following environment variables are passed:
DISPLAY the associated display name
HOME the initial working directory of the user
USER the user name
PATH the value of **DisplayManager.**/*DISPLAY*.**userPath** SHELL the user's default shell (from *getpwnam*)
XAUTHORITY may be set to a non-standard authority file
KRB5CCNAME may be set to a Kerberos credentials cache file

At most installations, *Xsession* should look in $HOME for a file *xsession,* which contains commands that each user would like to use as a session. *Xsession* should also implement a system default session if no user-specified session exists. See the section **Typical Usage**.

An argument may be passed to this program from the authentication widget using the 'set-session-argument' action. This can be used to select different styles of session. One good use of this feature is to allow the user to escape from the ordinary session when it fails. This allows users to repair their own *.xsession* if it fails, without requiring administrative intervention. The example following demonstrates this feature.

This example recognizes the special "failsafe" mode, specified in the translations in the *Xresources* file, to provide an escape from the ordinary session. It also requires that the .xsession file be executable so we don't have to guess what shell it wants to use.

```
#!/bin/sh
#
# Xsession
#
# This is the program that is run as the client
# for the display manager.

case $# in
1)
    case $1 in
    failsafe)
        exec xterm -geometry 80x24-0-0
        ;;
    esac
esac

startup=$HOME/.xsession
resources=$HOME/.Xresources

if [ -f "$startup" ]; then
    exec "$startup"
else
    if [ -f "$resources" ]; then
        xrdb -load "$resources"
    fi
    twm &
    xman -geometry +10-10 &
    exec xterm -geometry 80x24+10+10 -ls
fi
```

The user's *.xsession* file might look something like this example. Don't forget that the file must have execute permission. #! /bin/csh
no –f in the previous line so .cshrc gets run to set $PATH
twm &
xrdb –merge "$HOME/.Xresources"
emacs –geometry +0+50 &
xbiff –geometry –430+5 &
xterm –geometry –0+50 -ls

RESET PROGRAM

Symmetrical with *Xstartup*, the *Xreset* script is run after the user session has terminated. Run as root, it should contain commands that undo the effects of commands in *Xstartup*, removing entries from */etc/utmp* or unmounting directories from file servers. The environment variables that were passed to *Xstartup* are also passed to *Xreset*.

A sample *Xreset* script: #!/bin/sh
#
Xreset
#
This program is run as root after the session ends
#
sessreg –d –l $DISPLAY –x /usr/X11R6/lib/xdm/Xservers $USER
/usr/X11R6/lib/xdm/TakeConsole
exit 0

CONTROLLING THE SERVER

Xdm controls local servers using POSIX signals. SIGHUP is expected to reset the server, closing all client connections and performing other cleanup duties. SIGTERM is expected to terminate the server. If these signals do not perform the expected actions, the resources **DisplayManager.***DISPLAY***.resetSignal** and **DisplayManager.***DISPLAY***.termSignal** can specify alternate signals.

To control remote terminals not using XDMCP, *xdm* searches the window hierarchy on the display and uses the protocol request KillClient in an attempt to clean up the terminal for the next session. This may not actually kill all of the clients, as only those which have created windows will be noticed. XDMCP provides a more sure mechanism; when *xdm* closes its initial connection, the session is over and the terminal is required to close all other connections.

CONTROLLING XDM

Xdm responds to two signals: SIGHUP and SIGTERM. When sent a SIGHUP, *xdm* rereads the configuration file, the access control file, and the servers file. For the servers file, it notices if entries have been added or removed. If a new entry has been added, *xdm* starts a session on the associated display. Entries which have been removed are disabled immediately, meaning that any session in progress will be terminated without notice and no new session will be started.

When sent a SIGTERM, *xdm* terminates all sessions in progress and exits. This can be used when shutting down the system.

Xdm attempts to mark its various sub-processes for *ps*(1) by editing the command line argument list in place. Because *xdm* can't allocate additional space for this task, it is useful to start *xdm* with a reasonably long command line (using the full path name should be enough). Each process which is servicing a display is marked *–display*.

OTHER POSSIBILITIES

You can use *xdm* to run a single session at a time, using the 4.3 *init* options or other suitable daemon by specifying the server on the command line:
xdm –server ":0 SUN-3/60CG4 local /usr/X11R6/bin/X :0"

Or, you might have a file server and a collection of X terminals. The configuration for this

is identical to the sample above, except the *Xservers* file would look like
extol:0 VISUAL-19 foreign
exalt:0 NCD-19 foreign
explode:0 NCR-TOWERVIEW3000 foreign

This directs *xdm* to manage sessions on all three of these terminals. See the section **Controlling Xdm** for a description of using signals to enable and disable these terminals in a manner reminiscent of *init*(8).

LIMITATIONS

One thing that *xdm* isn't very good at doing is coexisting with other window systems. To use multiple window systems on the same hardware, you'll probably be more interested in *xinit*.

FILES

    <XRoot>/lib/X11/xdm/xdm-config   the default configuration file

    $HOME/.Xauthority   user authorization file where *xdm* stores keys for clients to read

    <XRoot>/lib/X11/xdm/chooser   the default chooser

    <XRoot>/bin/X11/xrdb   the default resource database loader

    <XRoot>/bin/X11/X   the default server

    <XRoot>/bin/X11/xterm   the default session program and failsafe client

    <XRoot>/lib/X11/xdm/A<display>-<suffix>   the default place for authorization files

    /tmp/K5C<display>   Kerberos credentials cache

Note: <XRoot> refers to the root of the X11 install tree.

SEE ALSO

X(1), *xinit*(1), *xauth*(1), *Xsecurity*(1), *sessreg*(1), *Xserver*(1),
X Display Manager Control Protocol

AUTHOR

Keith Packard, MIT X Consortium

NAME

xdpyinfo – display information utility for X

SYNOPSIS

xdpyinfo [–display *displayname*] [–queryExtensions] [–ext *extension-name*]

DESCRIPTION

Xdpyinfo is a utility for displaying information about an X server. It is used to examine the capabilities of a server, the predefined values for various parameters used in communicating between clients and the server, and the different types of screens and visuals that are available.

By default, numeric information (opcode, base event, base error) about protocol extensions is not displayed. This information can be obtained with the **–queryExtensions** option. Use of this option on servers that dynamically load extensions will likely cause all possible extensions to be loaded, which can be slow and can consume significant server resources.

Detailed information about a particular extension is displayed with the **–ext** *extensionName* option. If *extensionName* is **all**, information about all extensions supported by both *xdpyinfo* and the server is displayed.

ENVIRONMENT

DISPLAY   To get the default host, display number, and screen.

SEE ALSO

X(1), xwininfo(1), xprop(1), xrdb(1)

AUTHOR

Jim Fulton, MIT X Consortium

xf86config(1)   xf86config(1)

NAME
xf86config – generate an XF86Config file

SYNOPSIS
xf86config

DESCRIPTION
xf86config is an interactive program for generating an XF86Config file for use with XFree86 X servers.

FILES
<xroot>/lib/X11/Cards Video cards database

SEE ALSO
XFree86(1), XF86Config(4/5), reconfig(1)

AUTHOR
Harm Hanemaayer.

XFD(1)

NAME

xfd – display all the characters in an X font

SYNOPSIS

xfd [–options ...] **–fn** *fontname*

DESCRIPTION

The *xfd* utility creates a window containing the name of the font being displayed, a row of command buttons, several lines of text for displaying character metrics, and a grid containing one glyph per cell. The characters are shown in increasing order from left to right, top to bottom. The first character displayed at the top left will be character number 0 unless the **–start** option has been supplied in which case the character with the number given in the **–start** option will be used.

The characters are displayed in a grid of boxes, each large enough to hold any single character in the font. Each character glyph is drawn using the PolyText16 request (used by the *Xlib* routine **XDrawString16**). If the **–box** option is given, a rectangle will be drawn around each character, showing where an ImageText16 request (used by the *Xlib* routine **XDrawImageString16**) would cause background color to be displayed.

The origin of each glyph is normally set so that the character is drawn in the upper left hand corner of the grid cell. However, if a glyph has a negative left bearing or an unusually large ascent, descent, or right bearing (as is the case with *cursor* font), some character may not appear in their own grid cells. The **–center** option may be used to force all glyphs to be centered in their respective cells.

All the characters in the font may not fit in the window at once. To see the next page of glyphs, press the *Next* button at the top of the window. To see the previous page, press *Prev*. To exit *xfd*, press *Quit*.

Individual character metrics (index, width, bearings, ascent and descent) can be displayed at the top of the window by clicking on the desired character.

The font name displayed at the top of the window is the full name of the font, as determined by the server. See *xlsfonts* for ways to generate lists of fonts, as well as more detailed summaries of their metrics and properties.

OPTIONS

xfd accepts all of the standard toolkit command line options along with the additional options listed below:

–fn *font* This option specifies the font to be displayed. This can also be set with the FontGrid **font** resource. A font must be specified.

–box This option indicates that a box should be displayed outlining the area that would be filled with background color by an ImageText request. This can also be set with the FontGrid **boxChars** resource. The default is False.

–center This option indicates that each glyph should be centered in its grid. This can also be set with the FontGrid **centerChars** resource. The default is False.

–start *number* This option specifies the glyph index of the upper left hand corner of the grid. This is used to view characters at arbitrary locations in the font. This can also be set with the FontGrid **startChar** resource. The default is 0.

–bc *color* This option specifies the color to be used if ImageText boxes are drawn. This can also be set with the FontGrid **boxColor** resource.

–rows *numrows* This option specifies the number of rows in the grid. This can also be set with the FontGrid **cellRows** resource.

–columns *numcols* This option specifies the number of columns in the grid. This can also be set with the FontGrid **cellColumns** resource.

WIDGETS

In order to specify resources, it is useful to know the widgets which compose *xfd*. In the notation below, indentation indicates hierarchical structure. The widget class name is given first, followed by the widget instance name. The application class name is Xfd.

```
Xfd xfd
    Paned pane
        Label fontname
        Box box
            Command quit
            Command prev
            Command next
        Label select
        Label metrics
        Label range
        Label start
        Form form
        FontGrid grid
```

FONTGRID RESOURCES

The FontGrid widget is an application-specific widget, and a subclass of the Simple widget in the Athena widget set. The effects and instance names of this widget's resources are given in the **OPTIONS** section. Capitalize the first letter of the resource instance name to get the corresponding class name.

APPLICATION SPECIFIC RESOURCES

The instance names of the application specific resources are given below. Capitalize the first letter of the resource instance name to get the corresponding class name. These resources are unlikely to be interesting unless you are localizing xfd for a different language.

selectFormat Specifies a printf-style format string used to display information about the selected character. The default is "character 0x%02x%02x (%u,%u) (%#o,%#o)". The arguments that will come after the format string are char.byte1, char.byte2, char.byte1, char.byte2, char.byte1, char.byte2. char.byte1 is byte 1 of the selected character. char.byte2 is byte 2 of the selected character.

metricsFormat Specifies a printf-style format string used to display character metrics. The default is "width %d; left %d, right %d; ascent %d, descent %d (font %d, %d)". The arguments that will come after the format string are the character metrics width, lbearing, rbearing, character ascent, character descent, font ascent, and font descent.

rangeFormat Specifies a printf-style format string used to display the range of characters currently being displayed. The default is "range: 0x%02x%02x (%u,%u) thru 0x%02x%02x (%u,%u)". The arguments that will come after the format string are the following fields from the XFontStruct that is returned from opening the font: min_byte1, min_char_or_byte2, min_byte1, min_char_or_byte2, max_byte1, max_char_or_byte2, max_byte1, max_char_or_byte2.

startFormat Specifies a printf-style format string used to display information about the character at the upper left corner of the font grid. The default is "upper left: 0x%04x (%d,%d)". The arguments that will come after the format string are the new character, the high byte of the new character, and the low byte of the new character.

nocharFormat Specifies a printf-style format string to display when the selected character does not exist. The default is "no such character 0x%02x%02x (%u,%u) (%#o,%#o)". The arguments that will come after the format string are the same as for the **selectFormat** resource.

XFD(1) XFD(1)

SEE ALSO
X(1), xlsfonts(1), xrdb(1), xfontsel(1), *X Logical Font Description Conventions*

BUGS
The program should skip over pages full of non-existent characters.

AUTHOR
Jim Fulton, MIT X Consortium; previous program of the same name by Mark Lillibridge, MIT Project Athena.

XFree86(1)

NAME

XFree86 - X11R6 for UNIX on x86 platforms

DESCRIPTION

XFree86 is a collection of X servers for UNIX-like OSs on Intel x86 platforms. This work is derived from *X386\1.2* which was contributed to X11R5 by Snitily Graphics Consulting Service.

CONFIGURATIONS

XFree86 operates under the following operating systems:

.5i

- SVR3.2: SCO 3.2.2, 3.2.4, ISC 3.x, 4.x
- SVR4.0: ESIX, Microport, Dell, UHC, Consensys, MST, ISC, AT&T, NCR
- SVR4.2: Consensys, Univel (UnixWare)
- Solaris (x86) 2.1, 2.4
- FreeBSD 1.1.5, 2.0, 2.0.5, NetBSD 1.0 (i386 port only)
- BSD/386 version 1.1 and BSD/OS 2.0
- Mach (from CMU)
- Linux
- Amoeba version 5.1
- Minix-386vm version 1.6.25.1
- LynxOS AT versions 2.2.1 and 2.3

NETWORK CONNECTIONS

XFree86 supports connections made using the following reliable byte-streams:

    Local   *XFree86* supports local connections via Streams pipe via various mechanisms, using the following paths (*n* represents the display number):

/dev/X/server.**n** (SVR3 and SVR4)
/dev/X/Nserver.**n** (SVR4)
/dev/X**n**S and /dev/X**n**R (SCO SVR3)

On SVR4.0.4, if the *Advanced Compatibility Package* is installed, and in SVR4.2, *XFree86* supports local connections from clients for SCO XSight/ODT, and (with modifications to the binary) clients for ISC SVR3.

    Unix Domain   *XFree86* uses */tmp/.X11-unix/X***n** as the filename for the socket, where *n* is the display number.

    TCPIP   *XFree86* listens on port htons(6000+*n*), where *n* is the display number.

    Amoeba RPC   This is the default communication medium used under native Amoeba. Note that under Amoeba, the server should be started with a "*hostname:displaynumber*" argument.

ENVIRONMENT VARIABLES

For operating systems that support local connections other than Unix Domain sockets (SVR3 and SVR4), there is a compiled-in list specifying the order in which local connections should be attempted. This list can be overridden by the *XLOCAL* environment variable described below. If the display name indicates a best-choice connection should be made (e.g. *:0.0*), each connection mechanism is tried until a connection succeeds or no more mechanisms are available. Note: for these OSs, the Unix Domain socket connection is treated differently from the other local connection types. To use it the connection must be made to *unix:0.0*.

The *XLOCAL* environment variable should contain a list of one more more of the following:

        NAMED
        PTS
        SCO
        ISC

which represent SVR4 Named Streams pipe, Old-style USL Streams pipe, SCO XSight Streams pipe, and ISC Streams pipe, respectively. You can select a single mechanism (e.g. *XLOCAL=NAMED*), or an ordered list

(e.g. *XLOCAL="NAMED:PTS:SCO"*).

This variable overrides the compiled-in defaults. For SVR4 it is recommended that *NAMED* be the first preference connection. The default setting is *PTS:NAMED:ISC:SCO*.

To globally override the compiled-in defaults, you should define (and export if using *sh* or *ksh*) *XLOCAL* globally. If you use *startx/xinit*, the definition should be at the top of your *.xinitrc* file. If you use *xdm*, the definitions should be early on in the *<XRoot>/lib/X11/xdm/Xsession* script.

OPTIONS

In addition to the normal server options described in the *Xserver(1)* manual page, *XFree86* accepts the following command line switches:

- **vt***XX*   *XX* specifies the Virtual Terminal device number which *XFree86* will use. Without this option, *XFree86* will pick the first available Virtual Terminal that it can locate. This option applies only to SVR3, SVR4, Linux, and BSD OSs with the 'syscons' or 'pcvt' driver.
- **–probeonly**   Causes the server to exit after the device probing stage. The XF86Config file is still used when this option is given, so information that can be auto-detected should be commented out.
- **–quiet**   Suppress most informational messages at startup.
- **–bpp** *n*   Set number of bits per pixel. The default is 8. Legal values are 8, 15, 16, 24, 32. Not all servers support all values.
- **–weight** *nnn*   Set RGB weighting at 16 bpp. The default is 565. This applies only to those servers which support 16 bpp.
- **–gamma** *value*   Set the gamma correction. *value* must be between 0.1 and 10. The default is 1.0 This value is applied equally to the R, G and B values. Not all servers support this.
- **–rgamma** *value*   Set the red gamma correction. *value* must be between 0.1 and 10. The default is 1.0 Not all servers support this.
- **–ggamma** *value*   Set the green gamma correction. *value* must be between 0.1 and 10. The default is 1.0 Not all servers support this.
- **–bgamma** *value*   Set the blue gamma correction. *value* must be between 0.1 and 10. The default is 1.0 Not all servers support this.
- **–showconfig**   Print out a list of screen drivers configured in the server.
- **–verbose**   Maximise information printed at startup (more than the default).
- **–xf86config** *file*   Read the server configuration from *file*. This option is only available when the server is run as root (i.e, with real-uid 0).
- **–keeptty**   Prevent the server from detaching its initial controlling terminal. This option is only useful when debugging the server.

KEYBOARD

Multiple key presses recognized directly by *XFree86* are:

- **Ctrl+Alt+Backspace**   Immediately kills the server – no questions asked. (Can be disabled by specifying "DontZap" in the **ServerFlags** section of the XF86Config file.)
- **Ctrl+Alt+Keypad-Plus**   Change video mode to next one specified in the configuration file, (increasing video resolution order).
- **Ctrl+Alt+Keypad-Minus**   Change video mode to previous one specified in the configuration file, (decreasing video resolution order).

Ctrl+Alt+F1...F12	For BSD systems using the syscons driver and Linux, these keystroke combinations are used to switch to Virtual Console 1 through 12.

SETUP

XFree86 uses a configuration file called **XF86Config** for its initial setup. Refer to the *XF86Config(4/5)* manual page for more information.

FILES

<XRoot>/bin/XF86_SVGA	The color SVGA X server
<XRoot>/bin/XF86_Mono	The monochrome X server for VGA and other mono cards
<XRoot>/bin/XF86_S3	The accelerated S3 X server
<XRoot>/bin/XF86_Mach8	The accelerated Mach8 X server
<XRoot>/bin/XF86_Mach32	The accelerated Mach32 X server
<XRoot>/bin/XF86_Mach64	The accelerated Mach64 X server
<XRoot>/bin/XF86_P9000	The accelerated P9000 X server
<XRoot>/bin/XF86_AGX	The accelerated AGX X server
<XRoot>/bin/XF86_W32	The accelerated ET4000/W32 X server
<XRoot>/bin/XF86_8514	The accelerated 8514/A X server
/etc/XF86Config	Server configuration file
<XRoot>/lib/X11/XF86Config.*hostname*	Server configuration file
<XRoot>/lib/X11/XF86Config	Server configuration file
<XRoot>/bin/	Client binaries
<XRoot>/include/	Header files
<XRoot>/lib/	Libraries
<XRoot>/lib/X11/fonts/	Fonts
<XRoot>/lib/X11/rgb.txt	Color names to RGB mapping
<XRoot>/lib/X11/XErrorDB	Client error message database
<XRoot>/lib/X11/app-defaults/	Client resource specifications
<XRoot>/man/man?/	Manual pages
/etc/X*n*.hosts	Initial access control list for display *n*

Note: <XRoot> refers to the root of the X11 install tree.

SEE ALSO

X(1), Xserver(1), xdm(1), xinit(1), XF86Config(4/5), xf86config(1), XF86_SVGA(1), XF86_VGA16(1), XF86_Mono(1), XF86_Accel(1), xvidtune(1)

AUTHORS

For X11R5, *XF86 1.2* was provided by:

Thomas Roell, *roell@informatik.tu-muenchen.de* TU-Muenchen: Server and SVR4 stuff

Mark W. Snitily, *mark@sgcs.com* SGCS: SVR3 support, X Consortium Sponsor

... and many more people out there on the net who helped with ideas and bug-fixes.

XFree86 was integrated into X11R6 by the following team:

Stuart Anderson *anderson@metrolink.com* , Doug Anson *danson@lgc.com* ,
Gertjan Akkerman *akkerman@dutiba.twi.tudelft.nl* ,
Mike Bernson *mike@mbsun.mlb.org* ,

Robin Cutshaw *robin@XFree86.org*, David Dawes *dawes@XFree86.org*,
Marc Evans *marc@XFree86.org*, Pascal Haible *haible@izfm.uni-stuttgart.de*,
Matthieu Herrb *Matthieu.Herrb@laas.fr*, Dirk Hohndel *hohndel@XFree86.org*,
David Holland *davidh@use.com*, Alan Hourihane *alanh@fairlite.demon.co.uk*,
Jeffrey Hsu *hsu@soda.berkeley.edu*, Glenn Lai *glenn@cs.utexas.edu*,
Ted Lemon *mellon@ncd.com*, Rich Murphey *rich@XFree86.org*,
Hans Nasten *nasten@everyware.se*, Mark Snitily *mark@sgcs.com*,
Randy Terbush *randyt@cse.unl.edu*, Jon Tombs *tombs@XFree86.org*,
Kees Verstoep *versto@cs.vu.nl*, Paul Vixie *paul@vix.com*,
Mark Weaver *Mark_Weaver@brown.edu*, David Wexelblat *dwex@XFree86.org*,
Philip Wheatley *Philip.Wheatley@ColumbiaSC.NCR.COM*,
Thomas Wolfram *wolf@prz.tu-berlin.de*,
Orest Zborowski *orestz@eskimo.com*

The XFree86 enhancement package was provided by:

    David Dawes, *dawes@XFree86.org* Release coordination, administration of FTP repository and mailing lists. Source tree management and integration, accelerated server integration, fixing, and coding.

    Glenn Lai, *glenn@cs.utexas.edu* The SpeedUp code for ET4000 based SVGA cards, and ET4000/W32 accelerated server.

    Jim Tsillas, *jtsilla@ccs.neu.edu* Many server speedups from the fX386 series of enhancements.

    David Wexelblat, *dwex@XFree86.org* Integration of the fX386 code into the default server, many driver fixes, and driver documentation, assembly of the VGA card/monitor database, development of the generic video mode listing. Accelerated server integration, fixing, and coding.

    Dirk Hohndel, *hohndel@XFree86.org* Linux shared libraries and release coordination. Accelerated server integration and fixing. Generic administrivia and documentation.

Amancio Hasty Jr., *hasty@netcom.com*	Porting to **386BSD** version 0.1 and XS3 development.
Rich Murphey, *rich@XFree86.org*	Ported to **386BSD** version 0.1 based on the original port by Pace Willison. Support for **386BSD**, **FreeBSD**, and **NetBSD**.
Robert Baron, *Robert.Baron@ernst.mach.cs.cmu.edu*	Ported to **Mach**.
Orest Zborowski, *orestz@eskimo.com*	Ported to **Linux**.
Doug Anson, *danson@lgc.com*	Ported to **Solaris x86**.
David Holland, *davidh@use.com*	Ported to **Solaris x86**.
David McCullough, *davidm@stallion.oz.au*	Ported to **SCO SVR3**.
Michael Rohleder, *michael.rohleder@stadt-frankfurt.de*	Ported to **ISC SVR3**.
Kees Verstoep, *versto@cs.vu.nl*	Ported to **Amoeba** based on Leendert van Doorn's original Amoeba port of X11R5.
Marc Evans, *Marc@XFree86.org*	Ported to **OSF/1**.
Philip Homburg, *philip@cs.vu.nl*	Ported to **Minix-386vm**.
Thomas Mueller, *tm@systrix.de*	Ported to **LynxOS**.
Jon Tombs, *tombs@XFree86.org*	S3 server and accelerated server coordination.
Harald Koenig, *koenig@tat.physik.uni-tuebingen.de*	S3 server development.
Bernhard Bender, *br@elsa.mhs.compuserve.com*	S3 server development.

Kevin Martin, *martin@cs.unc.edu*	Overall work on the base accelerated servers (ATI and 8514/A), and Mach64 server.
Rik Faith, *faith@cs.unc.edu*	Overall work on the base accelerated servers (ATI and 8514/A).
Tiago Gons, *tiago@comosjn.hobby.nl*	Mach8 and 8514/A server development
Hans Nasten, *nasten@everyware.se*	Mach8, 8514/A, and S3 server development and BSD/386 support
Mike Bernson, *mike@mbsun.mlb.org*	Mach32 server development.
Mark Weaver, *Mark_Weaver@brown.edu*	Mach32 server development.
Craig Groeschel, *craig@metrolink.com*	Mach32 server development.
Henry Worth, *Henry.Worth@amail.amdahl.com*	AGX server.
Erik Nygren, *nygren@mit.edu*	P9000 server.
Harry Langenbacher *harry@brain.jpl.nasa.gov*	P9000 server.
Chris Mason, *mason@mail.csh.rit.edu*	P9000 server.
Henrik Harmsen *harmsen@eritel.se*	P9000 server.
Simon Cooper, *scooper@vizlab.rutgers.edu*	Cirrus accelerated code (based on work by Bill Reynolds).
Harm Hanemaayer, *hhanemaa@cs.ruu.nl*	Cirrus accelerated code, and ARK driver.
Mike Tierney, *floyd@eng.umd.edu*	WD accelerated code.
Bill Conn, *conn@bnr.ca*	WD accelerated code.
Brad Bosch, *brad@lachman.com*	WD 90C24A support.
Alan Hourihane, *alanh@fairlite.demon.co.uk*	Trident SVGA driver
Marc La France, *Marc.La-France@ualberta.ca*	ATI vgawonder SVGA driver
Steve Goldman, *sgoldman@encore.com*	Oak 067/077 SVGA driver.
Jorge Delgado, *ernar@dit.upm.es*	Oak SVGA driver, and 087 accelerated code.
Bill Conn, *conn@bnr.ca*	WD accelerated code.
Paolo Severini, *lendl@dist.dist.unige.it*	AL2101 SVGA driver
Ching-Tai Chiu, *cchiu@netcom.com*	Avance Logic ALI SVGA driver
Manfred Brands, *mb@oceonics.nl*	Cirrus 64xx SVGA driver
Randy Hendry, *randy@sgi.com*	Cirrus 6440 support in the cl64xx SVGA driver
Frank Dikker, *dikker@cs.utwente.nl*	MX SVGA driver
Regis Cridlig, *cridlig@dmi.ens.fr*	Chips & Technology driver
Jon Block, *block@frc.com*	Chips & Technology driver
Mike Hollick, *hollick@graphics.cis.upenn.edu*	Chips & Technology driver
Peter Trattler, *peter@sbox.tu-graz.ac.at*	RealTek SVGA driver
Craig Struble, *cstruble@acm.vt.edu*	Video7 SVGA driver
Gertjan Akkerman, *akkerman@dutiba.twi.tudelft.nl*	16 colour VGA server, and XF86Config parser.
Davor Matic, *dmatic@Athena.MIT.EDU*	Hercules driver.
Pascal Haible, *haible@izfm.uni-stuttgart.de*	Banked monochrome VGA support, Hercules support, and mono frame buffer support for dumb monochrome devices

... and many more people out there on the net who helped with beta-testing this enhancement.

XFree86 source is available from the FTP server *ftp.XFree86.org*, among others. Send email to *XFree86@XFree86.org* for details.

XHOST(1)

NAME

xhost – server access control program for X

SYNOPSIS

xhost [[+−]name ...]

DESCRIPTION

The *xhost* program is used to add and delete host names or user names to the list allowed to make connections to the X server. In the case of hosts, this provides a rudimentary form of privacy control and security. It is only sufficient for a workstation (single user) environment, although it does limit the worst abuses. Environments which require more sophisticated measures should implement the user-based mechanism or use the hooks in the protocol for passing other authentication data to the server.

OPTIONS

Xhost accepts the following command line options described below. For security, the options that effect access control may only be run from the "controlling host". For workstations, this is the same machine as the server. For X terminals, it is the login host.

- **−help** Prints a usage message.
- **[+]***name* The given *name* (the plus sign is optional) is added to the list allowed to connect to the X server. The name can be a host name or a user name.
- **−***name* The given *name* is removed from the list of allowed to connect to the server. The name can be a host name or a user name. Existing connections are not broken, but new connection attempts will be denied. Note that the current machine is allowed to be removed; however, further connections (including attempts to add it back) will not be permitted. Resetting the server (thereby breaking all connections) is the only way to allow local connections again.
- **+** Access is granted to everyone, even if they aren't on the list (i.e., access control is turned off).
- **−** Access is restricted to only those on the list (i.e., access control is turned on).
- *nothing* If no command line arguments are given, a message indicating whether or not access control is currently enabled is printed, followed by the list of those allowed to connect. This is the only option that may be used from machines other than the controlling host.

NAMES

A complete name has the syntax "family:name" where the families are as follows:

inet Internet host
dnet DECnet host
nis Secure RPC network name
krb Kerberos V5 principal
local contains only one name, the empty string

The family is case insensitive. The format of the name varies with the family.

When Secure RPC is being used, the network independent netname (e.g., "nis:unix.*uid@domainname*") can be specified, or a local user can be specified with just the username and a trailing at-sign (e.g., "nis:pat@").

For backward compatibility with pre-R6 *xhost*, names that contain an at-sign (@) are assumed to be in the nis family. Otherwise the inet family is assumed.

DIAGNOSTICS

For each name added to the access control list, a line of the form "*name* being added to access control list" is printed. For each name removed from the access control list, a line of

XHOST(1)

the form *"name* being removed from access control list" is printed.

FILES

/etc/X*.hosts

SEE ALSO

X(1), Xsecurity(1), Xserver(1), xdm(1)

ENVIRONMENT

DISPLAY to get the default host and display to use.

BUGS

You can't specify a display on the command line because **–display** is a valid command line argument (indicating that you want to remove the machine named *"display"* from the access list).

The X server stores network addresses, not host names. This is not really a bug. If somehow you change a host's network address while the server is still running, *xhost* must be used to add the new address and/or remove the old address.

AUTHORS

Bob Scheifler, MIT Laboratory for Computer Science,
Jim Gettys, MIT Project Athena (DEC).

NAME

xinetd – the extended Internet services daemon

SYNOPSIS

xinetd [*options*]

DESCRIPTION

xinetd performs the same function as **inetd**: it starts programs that provide Internet services. Instead of having such servers started at system initialization time, and be dormant until a connection request arrives, **xinetd** is the only daemon process started and it listens on all service ports for the services listed in its configuration file. When a request comes in, **xinetd** starts the appropriate server. Because of the way it operates, **xinetd** (as well as **inetd**) is also referred to as a super-server.

The services listed in **xinetd**'s configuration file can be separated into two groups. Services in the first group are called *multi-threaded* and they require the forking of a new server process for each new connection request. The new server then handles that connection. For such services, **xinetd** keeps listening for new requests so that it can spawn new servers. On the other hand, the second group includes services for which the service daemon is responsible for handling all new connection requests. Such services are called *single-threaded* and **xinetd** will stop handling new requests for them until the server dies. Services in this group are usually datagram-based.

So far, the only reason for the existence of a super-server was to conserve system resources by avoiding to fork a lot of processes who might be dormant for most of their lifetime. While fulfilling this function, **xinetd** takes advantage of the idea of a super-server to provide features such as access control and logging. Furthermore, **xinetd** is not limited to services listed in /etc/services. Therefore, anybody can use of **xinetd** to start special-purpose servers.

OPTIONS

- **–d** Enables debug mode. This produces a lot of debugging output, and it makes it possible to use a debugger on **xinetd**.

- **–syslog** *syslog_facility* This option enables syslog logging of **xinetd**-produced messages using the specified syslog facility. The following facility names are supported: *daemon, auth, user, local[0-7]* (check *syslog.conf*(5) for their meanings). This option is ineffective in debug mode since all relevant messages are sent to the terminal.

- **–filelog** *logfile* **xinetd**-produced messages will be placed in the specified file. Messages are always appended to the file. If the file does not exist, it will be created. This option is ineffective in debug mode since all relevant messages are sent to the terminal.

- **–f** *config_file* Determines the file that **xinetd** uses for configuration. The default is /etc/xinetd.conf.

- **–pid** The process pid is written to standard error. This option is ineffective in debug mode.

- **–loop** *rate* This option sets the loop rate beyond which a service is considered in error and is deactivated. The loop rate is specified in terms of the number of servers per second that can be forked for a process. The speed of your machine determines the correct value for this option. The default rate is 10.

- **–reuse** If this option is used, **xinetd** will set the socket option *SO_REUSEADDR* before binding the service socket to an Internet address. This allows binding of the address even if there are programs that use it, which happens when a previous instance of **xinetd** has started some servers that are still running. This option has no effect on RPC services.

- **–limit** *proc_limit* This option places a limit on the number of concurrently running processes that can be started by **xinetd**. Its purpose is to prevent process table overflows.

XINETD(1L)   XINETD(1L)

> **–logprocs** *limit*   This option places a limit on the number of concurrently running servers for remote userid acquisition.
>
> **–shutdownprocs** *limit*   This option places a limit on the number of concurrently running servers for service shutdown (forked when the RECORD option is used).

The *syslog* and *filelog* options are mutually exclusive. If none is specified, the default is syslog using the *daemon* facility. You should not confuse **xinetd** messages with messages related to service logging. The latter are logged only if this is specified via the configuration file.

CONFIGURATION FILE

The configuration file determines the services provided by **xinetd**. Any line whose first non-white-space character is a '#' is considered a comment line. Empty lines are ignored.

The file contains entries of the form:

service <service_name>
{
<attribute> <assign_op> <value> <value> ...
...
}

The assignment operator, *assign_op,* can be one of '=', '+=', '-='. The majority of attributes support only the simple assignment operator, '='. Attributes whose value is a set of values support all assignment operators. For such attributes, '+=' means adding a value to the set and '-=' means removing a value from the set. A list of these attributes will be given after all the attributes are described.

Each entry defines a service identified by the *service_name*. The following is a list of available attributes:

> id   This attribute is used to uniquely identify a service. This is useful because there exist services that can use different protocols and need to be described with different entries in the configuration file. By default, the service id is the same as the service name.
>
> type   Possible values are:
>
> RPC   if this is an RPC service
>
> INTERNAL   if this is a service provided by **xinetd**.
>
> UNLISTED   if this is a service not listed in */etc/services*.
>
> flags   Possible flag values are:
>
> REUSE   Set the *SO_REUSEADDR* flag on the service socket.
>
> INTERCEPT   intercept packets or accepted connections in order to verify that they are coming from acceptable locations (internal or multi-threaded services cannot be intercepted).
>
> NORETRY   avoid retry attempts in case of fork failure.
>
> socket_type   Possible values are:
>
> *stream*   stream-based service
>
> *dgram*   datagram-based service
>
> *raw*   service that requires direct access to IP
>
> *seqpacket*   service that requires reliable sequential datagram transmission
>
> protocol   determines the protocol that is employed by the service. The protocol must exist in */etc/protocols*. If this attribute is not defined, the default protocol employed by the service will be used.

XINETD(1L)

wait
: This attribute determines if the service is single-threaded or multi-threaded. If its value is *yes* the service is single-threaded; this means that **xinetd** will start the server and then it will stop handling requests for the service until the server dies. If the attribute value is *no*, the service is multi-threaded and **xinetd** will keep handling new service requests.

user
: determines the uid for the server process. The user name must exist in */etc/passwd*. This attribute is ineffective if the effective user ID of **xinetd** is not super-user.

group
: determines the gid for the server process. The group name must exist in */etc/group*. If a group is not specified, the group of *user* will be used (from */etc/passwd*). This attribute is ineffective if the effective user ID of **xinetd** is not super-user.

instances
: determines the number of servers that can be simultaneously active for a service. By default, there is no limit. The value of this attribute can be either a number or UNLIMITED which means that there is no limit.

server
: determines the program to execute for this service.

server_args
: determines the arguments passed to the server. In contrast to **inetd**, the server name should *not* be included in *server_args*.

only_from
: determines the remote hosts to which the particular service is available. Its value is a list of IP addresses which can be specified in any combination of the following ways:

a) a numeric address in the form of %d.%d.%d.%d. If the rightmost components are 0, they are treated as wildcards (for example, 128.138.12.0 matches all hosts on the 128.138.12 subnet). 0.0.0.0 matches all Internet addresses.

b) a factorized address in the form of %d.%d.%d.{%d,%d,...}. There is no need for all 4 components (i.e. %d.%d.{%d,%d,...%d} is also ok). However, the factorized part must be at the end of the address.

c) a network name (from */etc/networks*)

d) a host name. All IP addresses of the specified host name will be used.

""
: Specifying this attribute without a value makes the service available to nobody.

no_access
: determines the remote hosts to which the particular service is unavailable. Its value can be specified in the same way as the value of the **only_from** attribute. These two attributes determine the location access control enforced by **xinetd**. If none of the two is specified for a service, the service is available to anyone. If both are specified for a service, the one that is the better match for the address of the remote host determines if the service is available to that host (for example, if the **only_from** list contains 128.138.209.0 and the **no_access** list contains 128.138.209.10 then the host with the address 128.138.209.10 can not access the service).

access_times
: determines the time intervals when the service is available. An interval has the form *hour:min-hour:min* (connections *will* be accepted at the bounds of an interval). Hours can range from 0 to 23 and minutes from 0 to 59.

log_type
: determines where the service log output is sent. There are two formats:

SYSLOG syslog_facility [syslog_level]
: The log output is sent to syslog at the specified facility. If a level is present, the messages will be recorded at that level instead of LOG_INFO (which is the default level).

FILE file [soft_limit [hard_limit]]
: The log output is appended to *file* which will be created if it does not exist. Two limits on the size of the log file can be optionally specified. The first limit is a soft one; **xinetd** will log a message the first time this limit is exceeded (if **xinetd** logs to syslog, the message will be sent at the LOG_ALERT priority level). The second limit is a hard limit; **xinetd** will stop logging for the affected service (if the log file is a

10 May 1992   441

common log file, then more than one service may be affected) and will log a message about this (if **xinetd** logs to syslog, the message will be sent at the LOG_ALERT priority level). If a hard limit is not specified, it defaults to the soft limit increased by 1% but the extra size must be within the parameters LOG_EXTRA_MIN and LOG_EXTRA_MAX (defined in *config.h*).

log_on_success determines what information is logged when a server is started and when that server exits (the service id is always included in the log entry). Any combination of the following values may be specified:

PID   logs the server process id (if the service is implemented by **xinetd** without forking another process the logged process id will be 0)

HOST   logs the remote host address

TIME   logs the time when the server was started

USERID logs the user id of the remote user using the RFC 931 identification protocol. This option is available only for multi-threaded stream services.

EXIT   logs the fact that a server exited along with the exit status or the termination signal (the process id is also logged if the PID option is used)

DURATION   logs the duration of a service session

log_on_failure determines what information is logged when a server cannot be started (either because of a lack of resources or because of access control restrictions). The service id is always included in the log entry along with the reason for failure. Any combination of the following values may be specified:

HOST   logs the remote host address

TIME   logs the time when the server was started

USERID logs the user id of the remote user using the RFC 931 identification protocol. This option is available only for multi-threaded stream services.

ATTEMPT logs the fact that a failed attempt was made

RECORD records information from the remote end in case the server could not be started. This allows monitoring of attempts to use the service. For example, the login service logs the local user, remote user and terminal type. Currently, the services that support this option are: *login, shell, exec, finger*.

rpc_version   determines the RPC version for a RPC service. The version can be a single number or a range in the form *number-number*.

env   The value of this attribute is a list of strings of the form 'name=value'. These strings will be added to the environment before starting a server (therefore the server's environment will include **xinetd**'s environment plus the specified strings).

passenv The value of this attribute is a list of environment variables from **xinetd**'s environment that will be passed to the server.

port   determines the service port. If this attribute is specified for a service listed in */etc/services*, it must be equal to the port number listed in that file.

You don't need to specify all of the above attributes for each service. The necessary attributes for a service are:

socket_type

user   (non-*unlisted* services only)

server   (non-*internal* services only)

wait

protocol   (*RPC* and *unlisted* services only)

10 May 1992

```
          rpc_version       (RPC services only)
          port              (unlisted services only)
```

The following attributes support all assignment operators:

```
          only_from
          no_access
          log_on_success
          log_on_failure
          passenv
          env               (does not support the '-=' operator)
```

These attributes can also appear more than once in a service entry. The remaining attributes support only the '=' operator and can appear at most once in a service entry.

The configuration file may also contain a single defaults entry that has the form

```
defaults
{
<attribute> = <value> <value> ...
...
}
```

This entry provides default attribute values for service entries that don't specify those attributes. Possible default attributes:

```
          log_type
          log_on_success    (cumulative effect)
          log_on_failure    (cumulative effect)
          only_from         (cumulative effect)
          no_access         (cumulative effect)
          passenv           (cumulative effect)
          instances
          disabled          (cumulative effect)
```

Attributes with a cumulative effect can be specified multiple times with the values specified each time accumulating (i.e. '=' does the same thing as '+='). With the exception of *disabled* they all have the same meaning as if they were specified in a service entry. *disabled* determines services that are disabled even if they have entries in the configuration file. This allows for quick reconfiguration by specifying disabled services with the *disabled* attribute instead of commenting them out. The value of this attribute is a list of space separated service ids.

INTERNAL SERVICES

xinetd provides the following services internally (both stream and datagram based): *echo, time, daytime, chargen,* and *discard.* These services are under the same access restrictions as all other services except for the ones that don't require **xinetd** to fork another process for them. Those ones (*time, daytime,* and the datagram-based *echo, chargen,* and *discard*) have no limitation in the number of **instances**.

CONTROLLING XINETD

xinetd performs certain actions when it receives certain signals. The actions associated with the specific signals can be redefined by editing *config.h* and recompiling.

          SIGUSR1   causes a soft reconfiguration, which means that **xinetd** rereads the
                            configuration file and adjusts accordingly.

10 May 1992   443

SIGUSR2   causes a hard reconfiguration, which is the same as a soft reconfiguration except that servers for services that are no longer available are terminated. Access control is performed again on running servers by checking the remote location, access times and server instances. If the number of server instances is lowered, some arbitrarily picked servers will be killed to satisfy the limit; this will happen *after* any servers are terminated because of failing the remote location or access time checks. Also, if the INTERCEPT flag was clear and is set, any running servers for that service will be terminated; *the purpose of this is to ensure that after a hard reconfiguration there will be no running servers that can accept packets from addresses that do not meet the access control criteria.*

SIGQUIT   causes program termination.

SIGTERM   terminates all running servers before terminating **xinetd**.

SIGHUP   causes an internal state dump (the default dump file is */tmp/xinetd.dump*; to change the filename, edit *config.h* and recompile).

SIGIOT   causes an internal consistency check to verify that the data structures used by the program have not been corrupted. When the check is completed **xinetd** will generate a message that says if the check was successful or not.

On reconfiguration the log files are closed and reopened. This allows removal of old log files. Also, the following attributes *cannot* be changed on reconfiguration: **socket_type, wait, protocol, type.**

XINETD LOG FORMAT

Log entries are lines with the following format:

entry: *service-id data*

The *data* depends on the *entry*. Possible *entry* types:

START   generated when a server is started
EXIT   generated when a server exits
FAIL   generated when it is not possible to start a server
DATA   generated when an attempt to start a server fails and the service supports the *RECORD* log option.
USERID   generated if the *USERID* log option is used.

In the following, the information enclosed in brackets appears if the appropriate log option is used.

A *START* entry has the format:

START: *service-id* [pid=%d] [from=%d.%d.%d.%d] [time=*time*]

Time is given as *year/month/day@hour:minutes:seconds*.

An *EXIT* entry has the format:

EXIT: *service-id* [type=%d] [pid=%d] [duration=%d(sec)]

type can be either status or signal. The number is either the exit status or the signal that caused process termination.

A *FAIL* entry has the format:

FAIL: *service-id reason* [from=%d.%d.%d.%d] [time=*time*]

Possible *reasons* are:

fork   a certain number of consecutive fork attempts failed (this number is a configurable parameter)

XINETD(1L) XINETD(1L)

    time   the time check failed
    address   the address check failed
    service_limit   the allowed number of server instances for this service would be exceeded
    process_limit   a limit on the number of forked processes was specified and it would be exceeded

A *DATA* entry has the format:

DATA: *service-id data*

The *data* logged depends on the service.

    login   remote_user=%s local_user=%s tty=%s
    exec   remote_user=%s verify=*status* command=%s
                 Possible *status* values:
    ok   the password was correct
    failed   the password was incorrect
    baduser   no such user
    shell   remote_user=%s local_user=%s command=%s
    finger   *received string* or *EMPTY-LINE*

A *USERID* entry has the format:

USERID: *text*

The *text* is the response of the RFC 931 daemon at the remote end excluding the port numbers (which are included in the response).

EXAMPLE

```
#
# Sample configuration file for xinetd
#
defaults
{
        log_type        = FILE /var/log/servicelog
        log_on_success  = PID
        log_on_failure  = HOST TIME RECORD
        only_from       = 128.138.193.0 128.138.204.0 128.138.209.0
        only_from       = 128.138.252.1
        instances       = 10
        disabled        = rstatd
}
#
# Note 1: the protocol attribute is not required
# Note 2: the instances attribute overrides the default
#
service login
{
        socket_type     = stream
        protocol        = tcp
        wait            = no
```

```
            user            = root
            server          = /usr/etc/in.rlogind
            instances       = UNLIMITED
}
#
# Note 1: the instances attribute overrides the default
# Note 2: the log_on_success flags are augmented
#
service shell
{
            socket_type     = stream
            wait            = no
            user            = root
            instances       = UNLIMITED
            server          = /usr/etc/in.rshd
            log_on_success  += HOST TIME RECORD
}

service ftp
{
            socket_type     = stream
            wait            = no
            user            = root
            server          = /usr/etc/in.ftpd
            server_args     = -l
            instances       = 4
            log_on_success  += DURATION HOST USERID
            access_times    = 2:00-9:00 12:00-24:00
}
#
# This entry and the next one specify internal services. Since this
# is the same service using a different socket type, the id attribute
# is used to uniquely identify each entry
#
service echo
{
            id          = echo-stream
            type        = INTERNAL
            socket_type = stream
            user        = root
            wait        = no
}
service echo
{
            id          = echo-dgram
```

```
        type        = INTERNAL
        socket_type = dgram
        user        = root
        wait        = no
}
#
# Sample RPC service
#
service rstatd
{
        type         = RPC
        socket_type  = dgram
        protocol     = udp
        server       = /usr/etc/rpc.rstatd
        wait         = yes
        user         = root
        rpc_version  = 2-4
        env          = LD_LIBRARY_PATH=/etc/securelib
}
#
# Sample unlisted service
#
service unlisted
{
        type        = UNLISTED
        socket_type = stream
        protocol    = tcp
        wait        = no
        server      = /home/user/some_server
        port        = 20020
}
```

FILES

/etc/xinetd.conf   default configuration file

/tmp/xinetd.dump   default dump file

SEE ALSO

inetd(8),

Postel J., *Echo Protocol*, RFC 862, May 1983

Postel J., *Discard Protocol*, RFC 863, May 1983

Postel J., *Character Generator Protocol*, RFC 864, May 1983

Postel J., *Daytime Protocol*, RFC 867, May 1983

Postel J., Harrenstien K., *Time Protocol*, RFC 868, May 1983

StJohns M., *Authentication Server*, RFC 931, January 1985

XINETD(1L)

AUTHOR

Panos Tsirigotis, CS Dept, University of Colorado, Boulder

NOTES

When the attributes *only_from* and *no_access* are not specified for a service (either directly or via *defaults*) the address check is considered successful (i.e. access will not be denied).

If the USERID log option is specified and the remote RFC 931 server sends back an ERROR reply, access will not be denied.

If the USERID log option is specified and the remote host does not run a RFC 931 server, there will be no indication in the log of that fact (other than the missing USERID log entry).

BUGS

Supplementary group ids are not supported.

If the INTERCEPT flag is not used, access control on the address of the remote host is not performed when *wait* is *yes* and *socket_type* is *stream*.

If the INTERCEPT flag is not used, access control on the address of the remote host for services where *wait* is *yes* and *socket_type* is *dgram* is performed only on the first packet. The server may then accept packets from hosts not in the access control list. This can happen with RPC services.

Unlisted RPC services are not supported, i.e. all RPC services must be registered in */etc/rpc*. Specifying an RPC service by its RPC program number is not (yet) possible.

There is no way to put a SPACE in an environment variable.

When *wait* is *yes* and *socket_type* is *stream*, the socket passed to the server can only accept connections.

The INTERCEPT flag is not supported for internal services or multi-threaded services.

Interception works by forking a process which acts as a filter between the remote host(s) and the local server. This obviously has a performance impact which depends on the volume of information exchanged. It is up to you to make the compromise between security and performance for each service.

PRONUNCIATION

zy-net-d

NAME

xinit – X Window System initializer

SYNOPSIS

xinit [[*client*] *options*] [— [*server*] [*display*] *options*]

DESCRIPTION

The *xinit* program is used to start the X Window System server and a first client program on systems that cannot start X directly from */etc/init* or in environments that use multiple window systems. When this first client exits, *xinit* will kill the X server and then terminate.

If no specific client program is given on the command line, *xinit* will look for a file in the user's home directory called *.xinitrc* to run as a shell script to start up client programs. If no such file exists, *xinit* will use the following as a default:

xterm –geometry +1+1 –n login –display :0

If no specific server program is given on the command line, *xinit* will look for a file in the user's home directory called *.xserverrc* to run as a shell script to start up the server. If no such file exists, *xinit* will use the following as a default:

X :0

Note that this assumes that there is a program named *X* in the current search path. However, servers are usually named *Xdisplaytype* where *displaytype* is the type of graphics display which is driven by this server. The site administrator should, therefore, make a link to the appropriate type of server on the machine, or create a shell script that runs *xinit* with the appropriate server.

Note, when using a *.xserverrc* script be sure to "exec" the real X server. Failing to do this can make the X server slow to start and exit. For example:

exec Xdisplaytype

An important point is that programs which are run by *xinitrc* should be run in the background if they do not exit right away, so that they don't prevent other programs from starting up. However, the last long-lived program started (usually a window manager or terminal emulator) should be left in the foreground so that the script won't exit (which indicates that the user is done and that *xinit* should exit).

An alternate client and/or server may be specified on the command line. The desired client program and its arguments should be given as the first command line arguments to *xinit*. To specify a particular server command line, append a double dash (—) to the *xinit* command line (after any client and arguments) followed by the desired server command.

Both the client program name and the server program name must begin with a slash (/) or a period (.). Otherwise, they are treated as an arguments to be appended to their respective startup lines. This makes it possible to add arguments (for example, foreground and background colors) without having to retype the whole command line.

If an explicit server name is not given and the first argument following the double dash (—) is a colon followed by a digit, *xinit* will use that number as the display number instead of zero. All remaining arguments are appended to the server command line.

EXAMPLES

Below are several examples of how command line arguments in *xinit* are used.

    xinit   This will start up a server named *X* and run the user's *xinitrc*, if it exists, or else start an *xterm*.

    xinit — /usr/X11R6/bin/Xqdss :1   This is how one could start a specific type of server on an alternate display.

    xinit –geometry =80x65+10+10 –fn 8x13 –j –fg white –bg navy   This will start up a server named *X*, and will append the given arguments to the default *xterm* command. It will ignore *xinitrc*.

XINIT(1)   XINIT(1)

      xinit −e widgets — ./Xsun −l −c   This will use the command *Xsun −l −c* to start the server and will append the arguments *−e widgets* to the default *xterm* command.

      xinit /usr/ucb/rsh fasthost cpupig −display ws:1 — :1 −a 2 −t 5   This will start a server named *X* on display 1 with the arguments *−a 2 −t 5*. It will then start a remote shell on the machine **fasthost** in which it will run the command *cpupig*, telling it to display back on the local workstation.

Below is a sample *xinitrc* that starts a clock, several terminals, and leaves the window manager running as the "last" application. Assuming that the window manager has been configured properly, the user then chooses the "Exit" menu item to shut down X.

```
xrdb −load $HOME/.Xresources
xsetroot −solid gray &
xclock −g 50x50−0+0 −bw 0 &
xload −g 50x50−50+0 −bw 0 &
xterm −g 80x24+0+0 &
xterm −g 80x24+0−0 &
twm
```

Sites that want to create a common startup environment could simply create a default *xinitrc* that references a site-wide startup file:

```
#!/bin/sh
. /usr/local/lib/site.xinitrc
```

Another approach is to write a script that starts *xinit* with a specific shell script. Such scripts are usually named *x11*, *xstart*, or *startx* and are a convenient way to provide a simple interface for novice users:

```
#!/bin/sh
xinit /usr/local/lib/site.xinitrc — /usr/X11R6/bin/X bc
```

ENVIRONMENT VARIABLES

      DISPLAY   This variable gets set to the name of the display to which clients should connect.

      XINITRC   This variable specifies an init file containing shell commands to start up the initial windows. By default, *xinitrc* in the home directory will be used.

FILES

    .xinitrc   default client script
    xterm   client to run if *.xinitrc* does not exist
    .xserverrc default server script
    X   server to run if *.xserverrc* does not exist

SEE ALSO

X(1), *startx*(1), *Xserver*(1), *xterm*(1)

AUTHOR

Bob Scheifler, MIT Laboratory for Computer Science

XLSATOMS(1)

NAME

xlsatoms - list interned atoms defined on server

SYNOPSIS

xlsatoms [-options ...]

DESCRIPTION

Xlsatoms lists the interned atoms. By default, all atoms starting from 1 (the lowest atom value defined by the protocol) are listed until unknown atom is found. If an explicit range is given, *xlsatoms* will try all atoms in the range, regardless of whether or not any are undefined.

OPTIONS

−display *dpy* This option specifies the X server to which to connect.

−format *string* This option specifies a *printf*-style string used to list each atom <*value,name*> pair, printed in that order (*value* is an *unsigned long* and *name* is a *char **). *Xlsatoms* will supply a newline at the end of each line. The default is *%ld\t%s*.

−range *[low]-[high]* This option specifies the range of atom values to check. If *low* is not given, a value of 1 assumed. If *high* is not given, *xlsatoms* will stop at the first undefined atom at or above *low*.

−name *string* This option specifies the name of an atom to list. If the atom does not exist, a message will be printed on the standard error.

SEE ALSO

X(1), Xserver(1), xprop(1)

ENVIRONMENT

DISPLAY   to get the default host and display to use.

AUTHOR

Jim Fulton, MIT X Consortium

NAME

xlsclients - list client applications running on a display

SYNOPSIS

xlsclients [-display *displayname*] [-a] [-l] [-m maxcmdlen]

DESCRIPTION

Xlsclients is a utility for listing information about the client applications running on a display. It may be used to generate scripts representing a snapshot of the user's current session.

OPTIONS

–display *displayname* This option specifies the X server to contact.

–a This option indicates that clients on all screens should be listed. By default, only those clients on the default screen are listed.

–l List in long format, giving the window name, icon name, and class hints in addition to the machine name and command string shown in the default format.

–m *maxcmdlen* This option specifies the maximum number of characters in a command to print out. The default is 10000.

ENVIRONMENT

DISPLAY To get the default host, display number, and screen.

SEE ALSO

X(1), xwininfo(1), xprop(1)

AUTHOR

Jim Fulton, MIT X Consortium

NAME

xlsfonts – server font list displayer for X

SYNOPSIS

xlsfonts [–options ...] [–fn pattern]

DESCRIPTION

Xlsfonts lists the fonts that match the given *pattern*. The wildcard character "*" may be used to match any sequence of characters (including none), and "?" to match any single character. If no pattern is given, "*" is assumed.

The "*" and "?" characters must be quoted to prevent them from being expanded by the shell.

OPTIONS

–display *host*:*dpy*   This option specifies the X server to contact.

–l   Lists some attributes of the font on one line in addition to its name.

–ll   Lists font properties in addition to **–l** output.

–lll   Lists character metrics in addition to **–ll** output.

–m   This option indicates that long listings should also print the minimum and maximum bounds of each font.

–C   This option indicates that listings should use multiple columns. This is the same as **–n 0**.

–1   This option indicates that listings should use a single column. This is the same as **–n 1**.

–w *width*   This option specifies the width in characters that should be used in figuring out how many columns to print. The default is 79.

–n *columns*   This option specifies the number of columns to use in displaying the output. By default, it will attempt to fit as many columns of font names into the number of character specified by **–w** *width*.

–u   This option indicates that the output should be left unsorted.

–o   This option indicates that *xlsfonts* should do an **OpenFont** (and **QueryFont**, if appropriate) rather than a **ListFonts**. This is useful if **ListFonts** or **ListFontsWithInfo** fail to list a known font (as is the case with some scaled font systems).

–fn *pattern*   This option specifies the font name pattern to match.

SEE ALSO

X(1), Xserver(1), xset(1), xfd(1), *X Logical Font Description Conventions*

ENVIRONMENT

DISPLAY   to get the default host and display to use.

BUGS

Doing "xlsfonts -l" can tie up your server for a very long time. This is really a bug with single-threaded non-preemptable servers, not with this program.

AUTHOR

Mark Lillibridge, MIT Project Athena; Jim Fulton, MIT X Consortium; Phil Karlton, SGI

XMKMF(1)

NAME

xmkmf – create a Makefile from an Imakefile

SYNOPSIS

xmkmf [-a] [*topdir* [*curdir*]]

DESCRIPTION

The *xmkmf* command is the normal way to create a *Makefile* from an *Imakefile* shipped with third-party software.

When invoked with no arguments in a directory containing an *Imakefile,* the *imake* program is run with arguments appropriate for your system (configured into *xmkmf* when X was built) and generates a *Makefile.*

When invoked with the *–a* option, *xmkmf* builds the *Makefile* in the current directory, and then automatically executes "make Makefiles" (in case there are subdirectories), "make includes", and "make depend" for you. This is the normal way to configure software that is outside the X Consortium build tree.

If working inside the X Consortium build tree (unlikely unless you are an X developer, and even then this option is never really used), the *topdir* argument should be specified as the relative pathname from the current directory to the top of the build tree. Optionally, *curdir* may be specified as a relative pathname from the top of the build tree to the current directory. It is necessary to supply *curdir* if the current directory has subdirectories, or the *Makefile* will not be able to build the subdirectories. If a *topdir* is given, *xmkmf* assumes nothing is installed on your system and looks for files in the build tree instead of using the installed versions.

SEE ALSO

imake(1)

XMODMAP(1)

NAME

xmodmap - utility for modifying keymaps in X

SYNOPSIS

xmodmap [-options ...] [filename]

DESCRIPTION

The *xmodmap* program is used to edit and display the keyboard *modifier map* and *keymap table* that are used by client applications to convert event keycodes into keysyms. It is usually run from the user's session startup script to configure the keyboard according to personal tastes.

OPTIONS

The following options may be used with *xmodmap*:

–display *display*   This option specifies the host and display to use.

–help   This option indicates that a brief description of the command line arguments should be printed on the standard error channel. This will be done whenever an unhandled argument is given to *xmodmap*.

–grammar   This option indicates that a help message describing the expression grammar used in files and with –e expressions should be printed on the standard error.

–verbose   This option indicates that *xmodmap* should print logging information as it parses its input.

–quiet   This option turns off the verbose logging. This is the default.

–n   This option indicates that *xmodmap* should not change the mappings, but should display what it would do, like *make(1)* does when given this option.

–e *expression*   This option specifies an expression to be executed. Any number of expressions may be specified from the command line.

–pm   This option indicates that the current modifier map should be printed on the standard output.

–pk   This option indicates that the current keymap table should be printed on the standard output.

–pke   This option indicates that the current keymap table should be printed on the standard output in the form of expressions that can be fed back to *xmodmap*.

–pp   This option indicates that the current pointer map should be printed on the standard output.

–   A lone dash means that the standard input should be used as the input file.

The *filename* specifies a file containing *xmodmap* expressions to be executed. This file is usually kept in the user's home directory with a name like *.xmodmaprc*.

EXPRESSION GRAMMAR

The *xmodmap* program reads a list of expressions and parses them all before attempting to execute any of them. This makes it possible to refer to keysyms that are being redefined in a natural way without having to worry as much about name conflicts.

keycode *NUMBER = KEYSYMNAME ...*   The list of keysyms is assigned to the indicated keycode (which may be specified in decimal, hex or octal and can be determined by running the *xev* program.

keycode any = *KEYSYMNAME* ... If no existing key has the specified list of keysyms assigned to it, a spare key on the keyboard is selected and the keysyms are assigned to it. The list of keysyms may be specified in decimal, hex or octal.

keysym *KEYSYMNAME* = *KEYSYMNAME* ... The *KEYSYMNAME* on the left hand side is translated into matching keycodes used to perform the corresponding set of **keycode** expressions. The list of keysym names may be found in the header file *<X11/keysymdef.h>* (without the *XK_* prefix) or the keysym database *<XRoot>/lib/X11/XKeysymDB* where <XRoot> refers to the root of the X11 install tree. Note that if the same keysym is bound to multiple keys, the expression is executed for each matching keycode.

clear *MODIFIERNAME* This removes all entries in the modifier map for the given modifier, where valid name are: **Shift**, **Lock**, **Control**, **Mod1**, **Mod2**, **Mod3**, **Mod4**, and **Mod5** (case does not matter in modifier names, although it does matter for all other names). For example, "clear Lock" will remove all any keys that were bound to the shift lock modifier.

add *MODIFIERNAME* = *KEYSYMNAME* ... This adds all keys containing the given keysyms to the indicated modifier map. The keysym names are evaluated after all input expressions are read to make it easy to write expressions to swap keys (see the EXAMPLES section).

remove *MODIFIERNAME* = *KEYSYMNAME* ... This removes all keys containing the given keysyms from the indicated modifier map. Unlike **add,** the keysym names are evaluated as the line is read in. This allows you to remove keys from a modifier without having to worry about whether or not they have been reassigned.

pointer = default This sets the pointer map back to its default settings (button 1 generates a code of 1, button 2 generates a 2, etc.).

pointer = *NUMBER* ... This sets to pointer map to contain the indicated button codes. The list always starts with the first physical button.

Lines that begin with an exclamation point (!) are taken as comments.

If you want to change the binding of a modifier key, you must also remove it from the appropriate modifier map.

EXAMPLES

Many pointers are designed such that the first button is pressed using the index finger of the right hand. People who are left-handed frequently find that it is more comfortable to reverse the button codes that get generated so that the primary button is pressed using the index finger of the left hand. This could be done on a 3 button pointer as follows: % xmodmap -e "pointer = 3 2 1"

Many applications support the notion of Meta keys (similar to Control keys except that Meta is held down instead of Control). However, some servers do not have a Meta keysym in the default keymap table, so one needs to be added by hand. The following command will attach Meta to the Multi-language key (sometimes labeled Compose Character). It also takes advantage of the fact that applications that need a Meta key simply need to get the keycode and don't require the keysym to be in the first column of the keymap table. This means that applications that are looking for a Multi_key (including the default modifier map) won't notice any change. % xmodmap -e "keysym Multi_key = Multi_key Meta_L"

Similarly, some keyboards have an Alt key but no Meta key. In that case the following may be useful: % xmodmap -e "keysym Alt_L = Meta_L Alt_L"

One of the more simple, yet convenient, uses of *xmodmap* is to set the keyboard's "rubout" key to generate an alternate keysym. This frequently involves exchanging Backspace with Delete to be more comfortable to the user. If the *ttyModes* resource in *xterm* is set as well, all terminal emulator windows will use the same key for erasing characters: % xmodmap -e "keysym BackSpace = Delete"
% echo "XTerm*ttyModes: erase ^?" | xrdb -merge

Some keyboards do not automatically generate less than and greater than characters when the comma and period keys are shifted. This can be remedied with *xmodmap* by resetting the bindings for the comma and period with the following scripts:

```
!
! make shift-, be $<$ and shift-. be $>$
!
keysym comma = comma less
keysym period = period greater
```

One of the more irritating differences between keyboards is the location of the Control and Shift Lock keys. A common use of *xmodmap* is to swap these two keys as follows:

```
!
! Swap Caps_Lock and Control_L
!
remove Lock = Caps_Lock
remove Control = Control_L
keysym Control_L = Caps_Lock
keysym Caps_Lock = Control_L
add Lock = Caps_Lock
add Control = Control_L
```

The *keycode* command is useful for assigning the same keysym to multiple keycodes. Although unportable, it also makes it possible to write scripts that can reset the keyboard to a known state. The following script sets the backspace key to generate Delete (as shown above), flushes all existing caps lock bindings, makes the CapsLock key be a control key, make F5 generate Escape, and makes Break/Reset be a shift lock.

```
!
! On the HP, the following keycodes have key caps as listed:
!
!       101     Backspace
!       55      Caps
!       14      Ctrl
!       15      Break/Reset
```

XMODMAP(1)   XMODMAP(1)

```
!       86      Stop
!       89      F5
!
keycode 101 = Delete
keycode 55 = Control_R
clear Lock
add Control = Control_R
keycode 89 = Escape
keycode 15 = Caps_Lock
add Lock = Caps_Lock
```

ENVIRONMENT

   DISPLAY   to get default host and display number.

SEE ALSO

X(1), xev(1), *Xlib* documentation on key and pointer events

BUGS

Every time a **keycode** expression is evaluated, the server generates a *MappingNotify* event on every client. This can cause some thrashing. All of the changes should be batched together and done at once. Clients that receive keyboard input and ignore *MappingNotify* events will not notice any changes made to keyboard mappings.

Xmodmap should generate "add" and "remove" expressions automatically whenever a keycode that is already bound to a modifier is changed.

There should be a way to have the *remove* expression accept keycodes as well as keysyms for those times when you really mess up your mappings.

AUTHOR

Jim Fulton, MIT X Consortium, rewritten from an earlier version by David Rosenthal of Sun Microsystems.

XON(1)

NAME

xon – start an X program on a remote machine

SYNOPSIS

xon remote-host [-access] [-debug] [-name window-name] [-nols] [-screen screen-no] [-user user-name] [command ...]

DESCRIPTION

Xon runs the specified command (default xterm -ls) on the remote machine using rsh, remsh, or rcmd. Xon passes the DISPLAY, XAUTHORITY and XUSERFILESEARCHPATH environment variables to the remote command.

When no command is specified, xon runs 'xterm -ls'. It additionally specifies the application name to be 'xterm-*remote-host*' and the window title to be '-flremote-host'.

Xon can only work when the remote host will allow you to log in without a password, by having an entry in the .rhosts file permitting access.

OPTIONS

Note that the options follow the remote host name (as they do with rlogin).

- **-access**   Runs xhost locally to add the remote host to the host access list in the X server. This won't work unless xhost is given permission to modify the access list.

- **-debug**   Normally, xon disconnects the remote process from stdin, stdout and stderr to eliminate the daemon processes which usually connect them across the network. Specifying the **-debug** option leaves them connected so that error messages from the remote execution are sent back to the originating host.

- **-name window-name**   This specifies a different application name and window title for the default command (xterm).

- **-nols**   Normally xon passes the -ls option to the remote xterm; this option suspends that behaviour.

- **-screen screen-no**   This changes the screen number of the DISPLAY variable passed to the remote command.

- **-user user-name**   By default, xon simply uses rsh/remsh/rcmd to connect to the remote machine using the same user name as on the local machine. This option cause xon to specify an alternative user name. This will not work unless you have authorization to access the remote account, by placing an appropriate entry in the remote users .rhosts file.

BUGS

Xon can get easily confused when the remote-host, user-name or various environment variable values contain white space.

Xon has no way to send the appropriate X authorization information to the remote host.

XPROP(1)

NAME

xprop - property displayer for X

SYNOPSIS

xprop [-help] [-grammar] [-id *id*] [-root] [-name *name*] [-frame] [-font *font*] [-display *display*] [-len *n*] [-notype] [-fs *file*] [-remove *property-name*] [-spy] [-f *atom format* [*dformat*]]* [*format* [*dformat*] *atom*]*

SUMMARY

The *xprop* utility is for displaying window and font properties in an X server. One window or font is selected using the command line arguments or possibly in the case of a window, by clicking on the desired window. A list of properties is then given, possibly with formatting information.

OPTIONS

- **-help**   Print out a summary of command line options.

- **-grammar**   Print out a detailed grammar for all command line options.

- **-id** *id*   This argument allows the user to select window *id* on the command line rather than using the pointer to select the target window. This is very useful in debugging X applications where the target window is not mapped to the screen or where the use of the pointer might be impossible or interfere with the application.

- **-name** *name*   This argument allows the user to specify that the window named *name* is the target window on the command line rather than using the pointer to select the target window.

- **-font** *font*   This argument allows the user to specify that the properties of font *font* should be displayed.

- **-root**   This argument specifies that X's root window is the target window. This is useful in situations where the root window is completely obscured.

- **-display** *display*   This argument allows you to specify the server to connect to; see *X(1)*.

- **-len** *n*   Specifies that at most *n* bytes of any property should be read or displayed.

- **-notype**   Specifies that the type of each property should not be displayed.

- **-fs** *file*   Specifies that file *file* should be used as a source of more formats for properties.

- **-frame**   Specifies that when selecting a window by hand (i.e. if none of **-name**, **-root**, or **-id** are given), look at the window manager frame (if any) instead of looking for the client window.

- **-remove** *property-name*   Specifies the name of a property to be removed from the indicated window.

- **-spy**   Examine window properties forever, looking for property change events.

- **-f** *name format* [*dformat*]   Specifies that the *format* for *name* should be *format* and that the *dformat* for *name* should be *dformat*. If *dformat* is missing, " = $0+\n" is assumed.

DESCRIPTION

For each of these properties, its value on the selected window or font is printed using the supplied formatting information if any. If no formatting information is supplied, internal defaults are used. If a property is not defined on the selected window or font, "not defined" is printed as the value for that property. If no property list is given, all the properties possessed by the selected window or font are printed.

A window may be selected in one of four ways. First, if the desired window is the root window, the -root argument may be used. If the desired window is not the root window, it may be selected in two ways on the command line, either by id number such as might be obtained from *xwininfo*, or by name if the window possesses a name. The -id argument selects a window by id number in either decimal or hex (must start with 0x) while the -name argument selects a window by name.

The last way to select a window does not involve the command line at all. If none of -font, -id, -name, and -root are specified, a crosshairs cursor is displayed and the user is allowed to choose any visible window by pressing any pointer button in the desired window. If it is desired to display properties of a font as opposed to a window, the -font argument must be used.

Other than the above four arguments and the -help argument for obtaining help, and the -grammar argument for listing the full grammar for the command line, all the other command line arguments are used in specifying both the format of the properties to be displayed and how to display them. The -len *n*

argument specifies that at most *n* bytes of any given property will be read and displayed. This is useful for example when displaying the cut buffer on the root window which could run to several pages if displayed in full.

Normally each property name is displayed by printing first the property name then its type (if it has one) in parentheses followed by its value. The -notype argument specifies that property types should not be displayed. The -fs argument is used to specify a file containing a list of formats for properties while the -f argument is used to specify the format for one property.

The formatting information for a property actually consists of two parts, a *format* and a *dformat*. The *format* specifies the actual formatting of the property (i.e., is it made up of words, bytes, or longs?, etc.) while the *dformat* specifies how the property should be displayed.

The following paragraphs describe how to construct *format*s and *dformat*s. However, for the vast majority of users and uses, this should not be necessary as the built in defaults contain the *format*s and *dformat*s necessary to display all the standard properties. It should only be necessary to specify *format*s and *dformat*s if a new property is being dealt with or the user dislikes the standard display format. New users especially are encouraged to skip this part.

A *format* consists of one of 0, 8, 16, or 32 followed by a sequence of one or more format characters. The 0, 8, 16, or 32 specifies how many bits per field there are in the property. Zero is a special case meaning use the field size information associated with the property itself. (This is only needed for special cases like type INTEGER which is actually three different types depending on the size of the fields of the property)

A value of 8 means that the property is a sequence of bytes while a value of 16 would mean that the property is a sequence of words. The difference between these two lies in the fact that the sequence of words will be byte swapped while the sequence of bytes will not be when read by a machine of the opposite byte order of the machine that originally wrote the property. For more information on how properties are formatted and stored, consult the Xlib manual.

Once the size of the fields has been specified, it is necessary to specify the type of each field (i.e., is it an integer, a string, an atom, or what?) This is done using one format character per field. If there are more fields in the property than format characters supplied, the last character will be repeated as many times as necessary for the extra fields. The format characters and their meaning are as follows:

	a	The field holds an atom number. A field of this type should be of size 32.
	b	The field is an boolean. A 0 means false while anything else means true.
	c	The field is an unsigned number, a cardinal.
	i	The field is a signed integer.
	m	The field is a set of bit flags, 1 meaning on.
	s	This field and the next ones until either a 0 or the end of the property represent a sequence of bytes. This format character is only usable with a field size of 8 and is most often used to represent a string.
	x	The field is a hex number (like 'c' but displayed in hex - most useful for displaying window ids and the like)

An example *format* is 32ica which is the format for a property of three fields of 32 bits each, the first holding a signed integer, the second an unsigned integer, and the third an atom.

The format of a *dformat* unlike that of a *format* is not so rigid. The only limitations on a *dformat* is that one may not start with a letter or a dash. This is so that it can be distinguished from a property name or an argument. A *dformat* is a text string containing special characters instructing that various fields be printed at various points in a manner similar to the formatting string used by printf. For example, the *dformat* " is ($0, $1 \)\n" would render the POINT 3, -4 which has a *format* of 32ii as " is (3, -4)\n".

Any character other than a $, ?, \, or a (in a *dformat* prints as itself. To print out one of $, ?, \, or (precede it by a \. For example, to print out a $, use \$. Several special backslash sequences are provided as shortcuts. \n will cause a newline to be displayed while \t will cause a tab to be displayed. \o where o is an octal number will display character number o.

A $ followed by a number *n* causes field number *n* to be displayed. The format of the displayed field depends on the formatting character used to describe it in the corresponding *format*. I.e., if a cardinal is described by 'c' it will print in decimal while if it is described by a 'x' it is displayed in hex.

If the field is not present in the property (this is possible with some properties), <field not available> is displayed instead. $n+ will display field number *n* then a comma then field number *n*+1 then another comma then ... until the last field defined. If field *n* is not defined, nothing is displayed. This is useful for a property that is a list of values.

A ? is used to start a conditional expression, a kind of if-then statement. ?*exp*(*text*) will display *text* if and only if *exp* evaluates to non-zero. This is useful for two things. First, it allows fields to be displayed if and only if a flag is set. And second, it allows a value such as a state number to be displayed as a name rather than as just a number. The syntax of *exp* is as follows:

exp ::= *term* | *term*=*exp* | !*exp*
term ::= *n* | $*n* | m*n*

The ! operator is a logical "not", changing 0 to 1 and any non-zero value to 0. = is an equality operator. Note that internally all expressions are evaluated as 32 bit numbers so -1 is not equal to 65535. = returns 1 if the two values are equal and 0 if not. *n* represents the constant value *n* while $*n* represents the value of field number *n*. m*n* is 1 if flag number *n* in the first field having format character 'm' in the corresponding *format* is 1, 0 otherwise.

Examples: ?m3(count: $3\n) displays field 3 with a label of count if and only if flag number 3 (count starts at 0!) is on. ?$2=0(True)?!$2=0(False) displays the inverted value of field 2 as a boolean.

In order to display a property, *xprop* needs both a *format* and a *dformat*. Before *xprop* uses its default values of a *format* of 32x and a *dformat* of " = { $0+ }\n", it searches several places in an attempt to find more specific formats. First, a search is made using the name of the property. If this fails, a search is made using the type of the property. This allows type STRING to be defined with one set of formats while allowing property WM_NAME which is of type STRING to be defined with a different format. In this way, the display formats for a given type can be overridden for specific properties.

XPROP(1)   XPROP(1)

The locations searched are in order: the format if any specified with the property name (as in 8x WM_NAME), the formats defined by -f options in last to first order, the contents of the file specified by the -fs option if any, the contents of the file specified by the environmental variable XPROPFORMATS if any, and finally *xprop*'s built in file of formats.

The format of the files referred to by the -fs argument and the XPROPFORMATS variable is one or more lines of the following form:

name format [dformat]

Where *name* is either the name of a property or the name of a type, *format* is the *format* to be used with *name* and *dformat* is the *dformat* to be used with *name*. If *dformat* is not present, " = $0+\n" is assumed.

EXAMPLES

To display the name of the root window: *xprop* -root WM_NAME

To display the window manager hints for the clock: *xprop* -name xclock WM_HINTS

To display the start of the cut buffer: *xprop* -root -len 100 CUT_BUFFER0

To display the point size of the fixed font: *xprop* -font fixed POINT_SIZE

To display all the properties of window # 0x200007: *xprop* -id 0x200007

ENVIRONMENT

    DISPLAY   To get default display.

    XPROPFORMATS Specifies the name of a file from which additional formats are to be obtained.

SEE ALSO

X(1), xwininfo(1)

AUTHOR

Mark Lillibridge, MIT Project Athena

XRDB(1)

NAME
xrdb - X server resource database utility

SYNOPSIS
xrdb [-option ...] [*filename*]

DESCRIPTION

Xrdb is used to get or set the contents of the RESOURCE_MANAGER property on the root window of screen 0, or the SCREEN_RESOURCES property on the root window of any or all screens, or everything combined. You would normally run this program from your X startup file.

Most X clients use the RESOURCE_MANAGER and SCREEN_RESOURCES properties to get user preferences about color, fonts, and so on for applications. Having this information in the server (where it is available to all clients) instead of on disk, solves the problem in previous versions of X that required you to maintain *defaults* files on every machine that you might use. It also allows for dynamic changing of defaults without editing files.

The RESOURCE_MANAGER property is used for resources that apply to all screens of the display. The SCREEN_RESOURCES property on each screen specifies additional (or overriding) resources to be used for that screen. (When there is only one screen, SCREEN_RESOURCES is normally not used, all resources are just placed in the RESOURCE_MANAGER property.)

The file specified by *filename* (or the contents from standard input if - or no filename is given) is optionally passed through the C preprocessor with the following symbols defined, based on the capabilities of the server being used:

SERVERHOST=*hostname*	the hostname portion of the display to which you are connected.
SRVR_*name*	the SERVERHOST hostname string turned into a legal identifier. For example, "my-dpy.lcs.mit.edu" becomes SRVR_my_dpy_lcs_mit_edu.
HOST=*hostname*	the same as **SERVERHOST**.
DISPLAY_NUM=*num*	the number of the display on the server host.
CLIENTHOST=*hostname*	the name of the host on which *xrdb* is running.
CLNT_*name*	the CLIENTHOST hostname string turned into a legal identifier. For example, "expo.lcs.mit.edu" becomes CLNT_expo_lcs_mit_edu.
RELEASE=*num*	the vendor release number for the server. The interpretation of this number will vary depending on VENDOR.
REVISION=*num*	the X protocol minor version supported by this server (currently 0).
VERSION=*num*	the X protocol major version supported by this server (should always be 11).
VENDOR="*vendor*"	a string literal specifying the vendor of the server.
VNDR_*name*	the VENDOR name string turned into a legal identifier. For example, "MIT X Consortium" becomes VNDR_MIT_X_Consortium.
EXT_*name*	A symbol is defined for each protocol extension supported by the server. Each extension string name is turned into a legal identifier. For example, "X3D-PEX" becomes EXT_X3D_PEX.
NUM_SCREENS=*num*	the total number of screens.

XRDB(1)

SCREEN_NUM=*num*   the number of the current screen (from zero).

BITS_PER_RGB=*num*   the number of significant bits in an RGB color specification. This is the log base 2 of the number of distinct shades of each primary that the hardware can generate. Note that it usually is not related to PLANES.

CLASS=*visualclass*   one of StaticGray, GrayScale, StaticColor, PseudoColor, TrueColor, DirectColor. This is the visual class of the root window.

CLASS_*visualclass*=*visualid*   the visual class of the root window in a form you can *#ifdef* on. The value is the numeric id of the visual.

COLOR   defined only if CLASS is one of StaticColor, PseudoColor, TrueColor, or DirectColor.

CLASS_*visualclass_depth*=*num*   A symbol is defined for each visual supported for the screen. The symbol includes the class of the visual and its depth; the value is the numeric id of the visual. (If more than one visual has the same class and depth, the numeric id of the first one reported by the server is used.)

HEIGHT=*num*   the height of the root window in pixels.

WIDTH=*num*   the width of the root window in pixels.

PLANES=*num*   the number of bit planes (the depth) of the root window.

X_RESOLUTION=*num*   the x resolution of the screen in pixels per meter.

Y_RESOLUTION=*num*   the y resolution of the screen in pixels per meter.

SRVR_*name*, CLNT_*name*, VNDR_*name*, and EXT_*name* identifiers are formed by changing all characters other than letters and digits into underscores (_).

Lines that begin with an exclamation mark (!) are ignored and may be used as comments.

Note that since *xrdb* can read from standard input, it can be used to the change the contents of properties directly from a terminal or from a shell script.

OPTIONS

xrdb program accepts the following options:

     –help   This option (or any unsupported option) will cause a brief description of the allowable options and parameters to be printed.

     –display *display*   This option specifies the X server to be used; see *X(1)*. It also specifies the screen to use for the *-screen* option, and it specifies the screen from which preprocessor symbols are derived for the *-global* option.

     –all   This option indicates that operation should be performed on the screen-independent resource property (RESOURCE_MANAGER), as well as the screen-specific property (SCREEN_RESOURCES) on every screen of the display. For example, when used in conjunction with *-query*, the contents of all properties are output. For *-load*, *-override* and *-merge*, the input file is processed once for each screen. The resources which occur in common in the output for every screen are collected, and these are applied as the screen-independent resources. The remaining resources are applied for each individual per-screen property. This the default mode of operation.

     –global   This option indicates that the operation should only be performed on the screen-independent RESOURCE_MANAGER property.

–screen This option indicates that the operation should only be performed on the SCREEN_RESOURCES property of the default screen of the display.

–screens This option indicates that the operation should be performed on the SCREEN_RESOURCES property of each screen of the display. For *-load*, *-override* and *-merge*, the input file is processed for each screen.

–n This option indicates that changes to the specified properties (when used with *-load*, *-override* or *-merge*) or to the resource file (when used with *-edit*) should be shown on the standard output, but should not be performed.

–quiet This option indicates that warning about duplicate entries should not be displayed.

-cpp *filename* This option specifies the pathname of the C preprocessor program to be used. Although *xrdb* was designed to use CPP, any program that acts as a filter and accepts the -D, -I, and -U options may be used.

-nocpp This option indicates that *xrdb* should not run the input file through a preprocessor before loading it into properties.

–symbols This option indicates that the symbols that are defined for the preprocessor should be printed onto the standard output.

–query This option indicates that the current contents of the specified properties should be printed onto the standard output. Note that since preprocessor commands in the input resource file are part of the input file, not part of the property, they won't appear in the output from this option. The –edit option can be used to merge the contents of properties back into the input resource file without damaging preprocessor commands.

–load This option indicates that the input should be loaded as the new value of the specified properties, replacing whatever was there (i.e. the old contents are removed). This is the default action.

–override This option indicates that the input should be added to, instead of replacing, the current contents of the specified properties. New entries override previous entries.

–merge This option indicates that the input should be merged and lexicographically sorted with, instead of replacing, the current contents of the specified properties.

–remove This option indicates that the specified properties should be removed from the server.

–retain This option indicates that the server should be instructed not to reset if *xrdb* is the first client. This never be necessary under normal conditions, since *xdm* and *xinit* always act as the first clients.

–edit *filename* This option indicates that the contents of the specified properties should be edited into the given file, replacing any values already listed there. This allows you to put changes that you have made to your defaults back into your resource file, preserving any comments or preprocessor lines.

–backup *string* This option specifies a suffix to be appended to the filename used with **–edit** to generate a backup file.

–D*name[=value]* This option is passed through to the preprocessor and is used to define symbols for use with conditionals such as # ifdef.

–U*name* This option is passed through to the preprocessor and is used to remove any definitions of this symbol.

–I*directory* This option is passed through to the preprocessor and is used to specify a directory to search for files that are referenced with *#include*.

FILES

Generalizes ~/.Xdefaults files.

XRDB(1)

SEE ALSO
X(1), Xlib Resource Manager documentation, Xt resource documentation

ENVIRONMENT
DISPLAY   to figure out which display to use.

BUGS
The default for no arguments should be to query, not to overwrite, so that it is consistent with other programs.

AUTHORS
Bob Scheifler, Phil Karlton, rewritten from the original by Jim Gettys

XSERVER(1)

NAME

Xserver – X Window System display server

SYNOPSIS

X [option ...]

DESCRIPTION

X is the generic name for the X Window System display server. It is frequently a link or a copy of the appropriate server binary for driving the most frequently used server on a given machine.

STARTING THE SERVER

The X server is usually started from the X Display Manager program *xdm(1)*. This utility is run from the system boot files and takes care of keeping the server running, prompting for usernames and passwords, and starting up the user sessions.

Installations that run more than one window system may need to use the *xinit(1)* utility instead of *xdm*. However, *xinit* is to be considered a tool for building startup scripts and is not intended for use by end users. Site administrators are **strongly** urged to use *xdm*, or build other interfaces for novice users.

The X server may also be started directly by the user, though this method is usually reserved for testing and is not recommended for normal operation. On some platforms, the user must have special permission to start the X server, often because access to certain devices (e.g. /dev/mouse) is restricted.

When the X server starts up, it typically takes over the display. If you are running on a workstation whose console is the display, you may not be able to log into the console while the server is running.

OPTIONS

All of the X servers accept the following command line options:

:*displaynumber*
: the X server runs as the given *displaynumber*, which by default is 0. If multiple X servers are to run simultaneously on a host, each must have a unique display number. See the DISPLAY NAMES section of the *X(1)* manual page to learn how to specify which display number clients should try to use.

–a *number*
: sets pointer acceleration (i.e. the ratio of how much is reported to how much the user actually moved the pointer).

–ac
: disables host-based access control mechanisms. Enables access by any host, and permits any host to modify the access control list. Use with extreme caution. This option exists primarily for running test suites remotely.

–audit *level*
: Sets the audit trail level. The default level is 1, meaning only connection rejections are reported. Level 2 additionally reports all successful connections and disconnects. Level 0 turns off the audit trail. Audit lines are sent as standard error output.

–auth *authorization-file*
: Specifies a file which contains a collection of authorization records used to authenticate access. See also the *xdm* and *Xsecurity* manual pages.

bc
: disables certain kinds of error checking, for bug compatibility with previous releases (e.g., to work around bugs in R2 and R3 xterms and toolkits). Deprecated.

–bs
: disables backing store support on all screens.

–c
: turns off key-click.

c *volume*
: sets key-click volume (allowable range: 0-100).

XSERVER(1)　　　　　　　　　　　　　　　　　　　　　　　　　　　XSERVER(1)

–cc *class*　　　　sets the visual class for the root window of color screens. The class numbers are as specified in the X protocol. Not obeyed by all servers.

–co *filename*　　sets name of RGB color database. The default is <XRoot>/lib/X11/rgb, where <XRoot> refers to the root of the X11 install tree.

–config *filename*　　reads more options from the given file. Options in the file may be separated by newlines if desired. If a '#' character appears on a line, all characters between it and the next newline are ignored, providing a simple commenting facility. The **–config** option itself may appear in the file.

–core　　causes the server to generate a core dump on fatal errors.

–dpi *resolution*　　sets the resolution of the screen, in dots per inch. To be used when the server cannot determine the screen size from the hardware.

–deferglyphs *whichfonts*　　specifies the types of fonts for which the server should attempt to use deferred glyph loading. *whichfonts* can be all (all fonts), none (no fonts), or 16 (16 bit fonts only).

–f *volume*　　sets feep (bell) volume (allowable range: 0-100).

–fc *cursorFont*　　sets default cursor font.

–fn *font*　　sets the default font.

–fp *fontPath*　　sets the search path for fonts. This path is a comma separated list of directories which the X server searches for font databases.

–help　　prints a usage message.

–I　　causes all remaining command line arguments to be ignored.

–kb　　disables the XKEYBOARD extension if present.

–p *minutes*　　sets screen-saver pattern cycle time in minutes.

–pn　　permits the server to continue running if it fails to establish all of its well-known sockets (connection points for clients), but establishes at least one.

–r　　turns off auto-repeat.

r　　turns on auto-repeat.

–s *minutes*　　sets screen-saver timeout time in minutes.

–su　　disables save under support on all screens.

–t *number*　　sets pointer acceleration threshold in pixels (i.e. after how many pixels pointer acceleration should take effect).

–terminate　　causes the server to terminate at server reset, instead of continuing to run.

–to *seconds*　　sets default connection timeout in seconds.

–tst　　disables all testing extensions (e.g., XTEST, XTrap, XTestExtension1).

tty*xx*　　ignored, for servers started the ancient way (from init).

v　　sets video-off screen-saver preference.

–v　　sets video-on screen-saver preference.

–wm　　forces the default backing-store of all windows to be WhenMapped. This is a backdoor way of getting backing-store to apply to all windows. Although all mapped windows will have backing store, the backing store attribute value reported by the server for a window will be the last value established by a client. If it has never been set by a client, the server will report the default value, NotUseful. This behavior is required by the X protocol, which allows the server to exceed the client's backing store expectations but does not provide a way to tell the client that it is doing so.

–x *extension*   loads the specified extension at init. This is a no-op for most implementations.

SERVER DEPENDENT OPTIONS

Some X servers accept the following options:

–ld *kilobytes*   sets the data space limit of the server to the specified number of kilobytes. A value of zero makes the data size as large as possible. The default value of –1 leaves the data space limit unchanged.

–lf *files*   sets the number-of-open-files limit of the server to the specified number. A value is zero makes the limit as large as possible. The default value of –1 leaves the limit unchanged.

–ls *kilobytes*   sets the stack space limit of the server to the specified number of kilobytes. A value of zero makes the stack size as large as possible. The default value of –1 leaves the stack space limit unchanged.

–logo   turns on the X Window System logo display in the screen-saver. There is currently no way to change this from a client.

nologo   turns off the X Window System logo display in the screen-saver. There is currently no way to change this from a client.

XDMCP OPTIONS

X servers that support XDMCP have the following options. See the *X Display Manager Control Protocol* specification for more information.

–query *host-name*   Enable XDMCP and send Query packets to the specified host.

–broadcast   Enable XDMCP and broadcast BroadcastQuery packets to the network. The first responding display manager will be chosen for the session.

–indirect *host-name*   Enable XDMCP and send IndirectQuery packets to the specified host.

–port *port-num*   Use an alternate port number for XDMCP packets. Must be specified before any –query, –broadcast or –indirect options.

–class *display-class*   XDMCP has an additional display qualifier used in resource lookup for display-specific options. This option sets that value, by default it is "MIT-Unspecified" (not a very useful value).

–cookie *xdm-auth-bits*   When testing XDM-AUTHENTICATION-1, a private key is shared between the server and the manager. This option sets the value of that private data (not that it is very private, being on the command line!).

–displayID *display-id*   Yet another XDMCP specific value, this one allows the display manager to identify each display so that it can locate the shared key.

XKEYBOARD OPTIONS

X servers that support the XKEYBOARD extension accept the following options:

	–xkbdir *directory*	base directory for keyboard layout files
	–xkbmap *filename*	keyboard description to load on startup
	[+-]accessx	enable(+) or disable(-) AccessX key sequences
	–ar1 *milliseconds*	sets the length of time in milliseconds that a key must be depressed before autorepeat starts
	–ar2 *milliseconds*	sets the length of time in milliseconds that should elapse between autorepeat-generated keystrokes

Many servers also have device-specific command line options. See the manual pages for the individual servers for more details.

NETWORK CONNECTIONS

The X server supports client connections via a platform-dependent subset of the following transport types: TCPIP, Unix Domain sockets, DECnet, and several varieties of SVR4 local connections. See the DISPLAY NAMES section of the *X(1)* manual page to learn how to specify which transport type clients should try to use.

SECURITY

The X server implements a platform-dependent subset of the following authorization protocols: MIT-MAGIC-COOKIE-1, XDM-AUTHORIZATION-1, SUN-DES-1, and MIT-KERBEROS-5. See the *Xsecurity(1)* manual page for information on the operation of these protocols.

Authorization data required by the above protocols is passed to the server in a private file named with the **–auth** command line option. Each time the server is about to accept the first connection after a reset (or when the server is starting), it reads this file. If this file contains any authorization records, the local host is not automatically allowed access to the server, and only clients which send one of the authorization records contained in the file in the connection setup information will be allowed access. See the *Xau* manual page for a description of the binary format of this file. See *xauth(1)* for maintenance of this file, and distribution of its contents to remote hosts.

The X server also uses a host-based access control list for deciding whether or not to accept connections from clients on a particular machine. If no other authorization mechanism is being used, this list initially consists of the host on which the server is running as well as any machines listed in the file */etc/X*n*.hosts*, where **n** is the display number of the server. Each line of the file should contain either an Internet hostname (e.g. expo.lcs.mit.edu) or a DECnet hostname in double colon format (e.g. hydra::). There should be no leading or trailing spaces on any lines. For example:

    joesworkstation
    corporate.company.com
    star::
    bigcpu::

Users can add or remove hosts from this list and enable or disable access control using the *xhost* command from the same machine as the server.

The X protocol intrinsically does not have any notion of window operation permissions or place any restrictions on what a client can do; if a program can connect to a display, it has full run of the screen. Sites that have better authentication and authorization systems might wish to make use of the hooks in the libraries and the server to provide additional security models.

SIGNALS

The X server attaches special meaning to the following signals:

	SIGHUP	This signal causes the server to close all existing connections, free all resources, and restore all defaults. It is sent by the display manager whenever the main user's main application (usually an *xterm* or window manager) exits to force the server to clean up and prepare for the next user.

SIGTERM   This signal causes the server to exit cleanly.

SIGUSR1   This signal is used quite differently from either of the above. When the server starts, it checks to see if it has inherited SIGUSR1 as SIG_IGN instead of the usual SIG_DFL. In this case, the server sends a SIGUSR1 to its parent process after it has set up the various connection schemes. *Xdm* uses this feature to recognize when connecting to the server is possible.

FONTS

The X server can obtain fonts from directories and/or from font servers. The list of directories and font servers the X server uses when trying to open a font is controlled by the *font path*.

The default font path is
<XRoot>/lib/X11/fonts/misc/,
<XRoot>/lib/X11/fonts/Speedo/,
<XRoot>/lib/X11/fonts/Type1/,
<XRoot>/lib/X11/fonts/75dpi/,
<XRoot>/lib/X11/fonts/100dpi/where <XRoot> refers to the root of the X11 install tree.

The font path can be set with the **–fp** option or by *xset(1)* after the server has started.

FILES

/etc/X**n**.hosts   Initial access control list for display number **n**

<XRoot>/lib/X11/fonts/misc, <XRoot>/lib/X11/fonts/75dpi,
  <XRoot>/lib/X11/fonts/100dpi Bitmap font directories

<XRoot>/lib/X11/fonts/Speedo, <XRoot>/lib/X11/fonts/Type1   Outline font directories

<XRoot>/lib/X11/fonts/PEX   PEX font directories

<XRoot>/lib/X11/rgb.txt   Color database

/tmp/.X11-unix/X**n**   Unix domain socket for display number **n**

/tmp/rcX**n**   Kerberos 5 replay cache for display number **n**

/usr/adm/X**n**msgs   Error log file for display number **n** if run from *init(8)*

<XRoot>/lib/X11/xdm/xdm-errors   Default error log file if the server is run from *xdm(1)*

Note: <XRoot> refers to the root of the X11 install tree.

SEE ALSO

General information: X(1)

Protocols: *X Window System Protocol, The X Font Service Protocol, X Display Manager Control Protocol*

Fonts: bdftopcf(1), mkfontdir(1), xfs(1), xlsfonts(1), xfontsel(1), xfd(1), *X Logical Font Description Conventions*

Security: Xsecurity(1), xauth(1), Xau(1), xdm(1), xhost(1)

Starting the server: xdm(1), xinit(1)

Controlling the server once started: xset(1), xsetroot(1), xhost(1)

Server-specific man pages: Xdec(1), XmacII(1), Xsun(1), Xnest(1), Xvfb(1), XF86_Accel(1), XF86_Mono(1), XF86_SVGA(1), XF86_VGA16(1), XFree86(1)

Server internal documentation: *Definition of the Porting Layer for the X v11 Sample Server, Strategies for Porting the X v11 Sample Server, Godzilla's Guide to Porting the X V11 Sample Server*

XSERVER(1)

AUTHORS

The sample server was originally written by Susan Angebranndt, Raymond Drewry, Philip Karlton, and Todd Newman, from Digital Equipment Corporation, with support from a large cast. It has since been extensively rewritten by Keith Packard and Bob Scheifler, from MIT.

XSET(1)

NAME

xset - user preference utility for X

SYNOPSIS

xset [-display *display*] [-b] [b on/off] [b [*volume* [*pitch* [*duration*]]] [[-]bc] [-c] [c on/off] [c [*volume*]] [[-+]fp[-+=] *path*[,*path*[,...]]] [fp default] [fp rehash] [[-]led [*integer*]] [led on/off] [m[ouse] [*accel_mult*[/*accel_div*] [*threshold*]]] [m[ouse] default] [p *pixel color*] [[-]r [keycode]] [r on/off] [s [*length* [*period*]]] [s blank/noblank] [s expose/noexpose] [s on/off] [s default] [s activate] [s reset] [q]

DESCRIPTION

This program is used to set various user preference options of the display.

OPTIONS

–display *display*   This option specifies the server to use; see *X(1)*.

b   The **b** option controls bell volume, pitch and duration. This option accepts up to three numerical parameters, a preceding dash(-), or a 'on/off' flag. If no parameters are given, or the 'on' flag is used, the system defaults will be used. If the dash or 'off' are given, the bell will be turned off. If only one numerical parameter is given, the bell volume will be set to that value, as a percentage of its maximum. Likewise, the second numerical parameter specifies the bell pitch, in hertz, and the third numerical parameter specifies the duration in milliseconds. Note that not all hardware can vary the bell characteristics. The X server will set the characteristics of the bell as closely as it can to the user's specifications.

bc   The **bc** option controls *bug compatibility* mode in the server, if possible; a preceding dash(-) disables the mode, otherwise the mode is enabled. Various pre-R4 clients pass illegal values in some protocol requests, and pre-R4 servers did not correctly generate errors in these cases. Such clients, when run against an R4 server, will terminate abnormally or otherwise fail to operate correctly. Bug compatibility mode explicitly reintroduces certain bugs into the X server, so that many such clients can still be run. This mode should be used with care; new application development should be done with this mode disabled. The server must support the MIT-SUNDRY-NONSTANDARD protocol extension in order for this option to work.

c   The **c** option controls key click. This option can take an optional value, a preceding dash(-), or an 'on/off' flag. If no parameter or the 'on' flag is given, the system defaults will be used. If the dash or 'off' flag is used, keyclick will be disabled. If a value from 0 to 100 is given, it is used to indicate volume, as a percentage of the maximum. The X server will set the volume to the nearest value that the hardware can support.

fp= *path*,...   The **fp=** sets the font path to the entries given in the path argument. The entries are interpreted by the server, not by the client. Typically they are directory names or font server names, but the interpretation is server-dependent.

fp default   The **default** argument causes the font path to be reset to the server's default.

fp rehash   The **rehash** argument resets the font path to its current value, causing the server to reread the font databases in the current font path. This is generally only used when adding new fonts to a font directory (after running *mkfontdir* to recreate the font database).

–fp or fp–   The **–fp** and **fp–** options remove elements from the current font path. They must be followed by a comma-separated list of entries.

XSET(1)   XSET(1)

fp or fp
: This **fp** and **fp** options prepend and append elements to the current font path, respectively. They must be followed by a comma-separated list of entries.

led
: The **led** option controls the keyboard LEDs. This controls the turning on or off of one or all of the LEDs. It accepts an optional integer, a preceding dash(-) or an 'on/off' flag. If no parameter or the 'on' flag is given, all LEDs are turned on. If a preceding dash or the flag 'off' is given, all LEDs are turned off. If a value between 1 and 32 is given, that LED will be turned on or off depending on the existence of a preceding dash. A common LED which can be controlled is the "Caps Lock" LED. "xset led 3" would turn led #3 on. "xset -led 3" would turn it off. The particular LED values may refer to different LEDs on different hardware.

m
: The **m** option controls the mouse parameters. The parameters for the mouse are 'acceleration' and 'threshold'. The acceleration can be specified as an integer, or as a simple fraction. The mouse, or whatever pointer the machine is connected to, will go 'acceleration' times as fast when it travels more than 'threshold' pixels in a short time. This way, the mouse can be used for precise alignment when it is moved slowly, yet it can be set to travel across the screen in a flick of the wrist when desired. One or both parameters for the **m** option can be omitted, but if only one is given, it will be interpreted as the acceleration. If no parameters or the flag 'default' is used, the system defaults will be set.

p
: The **p** option controls pixel color values. The parameters are the color map entry number in decimal, and a color specification. The root background colors may be changed on some servers by altering the entries for BlackPixel and WhitePixel. Although these are often 0 and 1, they need not be. Also, a server may choose to allocate those colors privately, in which case an error will be generated. The map entry must not be a read-only color, or an error will result.

r
: The **r** option controls the autorepeat. If a preceding dash or the 'off' flag is used, autorepeat will be disabled. If no parameters or the 'on' flag is used, autorepeat will be enabled. If a specific keycode is specified as a parameter, autorepeat for that keycode is enabled or disabled.

s
: The **s** option lets you set the screen saver parameters. This option accepts up to two numerical parameters, a 'blank/noblank' flag, an 'expose/noexpose' flag, an 'on/off' flag, an 'activate/reset' flag, or the 'default' flag. If no parameters or the 'default' flag is used, the system will be set to its default screen saver characteristics. The 'on/off' flags simply turn the screen saver functions on or off. The 'activate' flag forces activation of screen saver even if the screen saver had been turned off. The 'reset' flag forces deactivation of screen saver if it is active. The 'blank' flag sets the preference to blank the video (if the hardware can do so) rather than display a background pattern, while 'noblank' sets the preference to display a pattern rather than blank the video. The 'expose' flag sets the preference to allow window exposures (the server can freely discard window contents), while 'noexpose' sets the preference to disable screen saver unless the server can regenerate the screens without causing exposure events. The length and period parameters for the screen saver function determines how long the server must be inactive for screen saving to activate, and the period to change the background pattern to avoid burn in. The arguments are specified in seconds. If only one numerical parameter is given, it will be used for the length.

q
: The **q** option gives you information on the current settings.

These settings will be reset to default values when you log out.

Note that not all X implementations are guaranteed to honor all of these options.

SEE ALSO
X(1), Xserver(1), xmodmap(1), xrdb(1), xsetroot(1)

AUTHOR
Bob Scheifler, MIT Laboratory for Computer Science
David Krikorian, MIT Project Athena (X11 version)

XSTDCMAP(1)

NAME

xstdcmap - X standard colormap utility

SYNOPSIS

xstdcmap [-all] [-best] [-blue] [-default] [-delete *map*] [-display *display*] [-gray] [-green] [-help] [-red] [-verbose]

DESCRIPTION

The *xstdcmap* utility can be used to selectively define standard colormap properties. It is intended to be run from a user's X startup script to create standard colormap definitions in order to facilitate sharing of scarce colormap resources among clients. Where at all possible, colormaps are created with read-only allocations.

OPTIONS

The following options may be used with *xstdcmap*:

- **–all** This option indicates that all six standard colormap properties should be defined on each screen of the display. Not all screens will support visuals under which all six standard colormap properties are meaningful. *xstdcmap* will determine the best allocations and visuals for the colormap properties of a screen. Any previously existing standard colormap properties will be replaced.
- **–best** This option indicates that the RGB_BEST_MAP should be defined.
- **–blue** This option indicates that the RGB_BLUE_MAP should be defined.
- **–default** This option indicates that the RGB_DEFAULT_MAP should be defined.
- **–delete** *map* This option specifies that a specific standard colormap property, or all such properties, should be removed. *map may be one of:* default, best, red, green, blue, gray, or all.
- **–display** *display* This option specifies the host and display to use; see X(1).
- **–gray** *This option indicates that the RGB_GRAY_MAP should be defined.*
- **–green** *This option indicates that the RGB_GREEN_MAP should be defined.*
- **–help** *This option indicates that a brief description of the command line arguments should be printed on the standard error. This will be done whenever an unhandled argument is given to xstdcmap.*
- **–red** *This option indicates that the RGB_RED_MAP should be defined.*
- **–verbose** *This option indicates that xstdcmap should print logging information as it parses its input and defines the standard colormap properties.*

ENVIRONMENT

DISPLAY   to get default host and display number.

SEE ALSO

X(1)

AUTHOR

Donna Converse, MIT X Consortium

XTERM(1)

NAME

xterm – terminal emulator for X

SYNOPSIS

xterm [*–toolkitoption* ...] [*–*option ...]

DESCRIPTION

The *xterm* program is a terminal emulator for the X Window System. It provides DEC VT102 and Tektronix 4014 compatible terminals for programs that can't use the window system directly. If the underlying operating system supports terminal resizing capabilities (for example, the SIGWINCH signal in systems derived from 4.3bsd), *xterm* will use the facilities to notify programs running in the window whenever it is resized.

The VT102 and Tektronix 4014 terminals each have their own window so that you can edit text in one and look at graphics in the other at the same time. To maintain the correct aspect ratio (height/width), Tektronix graphics will be restricted to the largest box with a 4014's aspect ratio that will fit in the window. This box is located in the upper left area of the window.

Although both windows may be displayed at the same time, one of them is considered the "active" window for receiving keyboard input and terminal output. This is the window that contains the text cursor. The active window can be chosen through escape sequences, the "VT Options" menu in the VT102 window, and the "Tek Options" menu in the 4014 window.

EMULATIONS

The VT102 emulation is fairly complete, but does not support smooth scrolling, VT52 mode, the blinking character attribute nor the double-wide and double-size character sets. *Termcap*(5) entries that work with *xterm* include "xterm," "vt102," "vt100" and "ansi," and *xterm* automatically searches the termcap file in this order for these entries and then sets the "TERM" and the "TERMCAP" environment variables.

Many of the special *xterm* features may be modified under program control through a set of escape sequences different from the standard VT102 escape sequences. (See the *Xterm Control Sequences* document.)

The Tektronix 4014 emulation is also fairly good. It supports 12-bit graphics addressing, scaled to the window size. Four different font sizes and five different lines types are supported. There is no write-through or defocused mode support. The Tektronix text and graphics commands are recorded internally by *xterm* and may be written to a file by sending the COPY escape sequence (or through the **Tektronix** menu; see below). The name of the file will be "**COPY***yy–MM–dd.hh*:*mm*:*ss*", where *yy*, *MM*, *dd*, *hh*, *mm* and *ss* are the year, month, day, hour, minute and second when the COPY was performed (the file is created in the directory *xterm* is started in, or the home directory for a login *xterm*).

OTHER FEATURES

Xterm automatically highlights the text cursor when the pointer enters the window (selected) and unhighlights it when the pointer leaves the window (unselected). If the window is the focus window, then the text cursor is highlighted no matter where the pointer is.

In VT102 mode, there are escape sequences to activate and deactivate an alternate screen buffer, which is the same size as the display area of the window. When activated, the current screen is saved and replaced with the alternate screen. Saving of lines scrolled off the top of the window is disabled until the normal screen is restored. The *termcap*(5) entry for *xterm* allows the visual editor *vi*(1) to switch to the alternate screen for editing and to restore the screen on exit.

In either VT102 or Tektronix mode, there are escape sequences to change the name of the windows. See *Xterm Control Sequences* for details.

OPTIONS

The *xterm* terminal emulator accepts all of the standard X Toolkit command line options as well as the following (if the option begins with a '+' instead of a '–', the option is restored to its default value):

–help   This causes *xterm* to print out a verbose message describing its options.

–132   Normally, the VT102 DECCOLM escape sequence that switches between 80 and 132 column mode is ignored. This option causes the DECCOLM escape sequence to be recognized, and the *xterm* window will resize appropriately.

–ah   This option indicates that *xterm* should always highlight the text cursor. By default, *xterm* will display a hollow text cursor whenever the focus is lost or the pointer leaves the window.

ah   This option indicates that *xterm* should do text cursor highlighting based on focus.

–b *number*   This option specifies the size of the inner border (the distance between the outer edge of the characters and the window border) in pixels. The default is 2.

–cb   Set the *vt100* resource **cutToBeginningOfLine** to FALSE.

cb   Set the *vt100* resource **cutToBeginningOfLine** to TRUE.

–cc *characterclassrange:value*[,...]   This sets classes indicated by the given ranges for using in selecting by words. See the section specifying character classes.

–cn   This option indicates that newlines should not be cut in line-mode selections.

cn   This option indicates that newlines should be cut in line-mode selections.

–cr *color*   This option specifies the color to use for text cursor. The default is to use the same foreground color that is used for text.

–cu   This option indicates that *xterm* should work around a bug in the *more*(1) program that causes it to incorrectly display lines that are exactly the width of the window and are followed by a line beginning with a tab (the leading tabs are not displayed). This option is so named because it was originally thought to be a bug in the *curses*(3x) cursor motion package.

cu   This option indicates that *xterm* should not work around the *more*(3x) bug mentioned above.

–e *program* [*arguments ...*]   This option specifies the program (and its command line arguments) to be run in the *xterm* window. It also sets the window title and icon name to be the basename of the program being executed if neither *–T* nor *–n* are given on the command line. **This must be the last option on the command line.**

–fb *font*   This option specifies a font to be used when displaying bold text. This font must be the same height and width as the normal font. If only one of the normal or bold fonts is specified, it will be used as the normal font and the bold font will be produced by overstriking this font. The default is to do overstriking of the normal font.

–im   Turn on the **useInsertMode** resource.

+im   Turn off the **useInsertMode** resource.

–j   This option indicates that *xterm* should do jump scrolling. Normally, text is scrolled one line at a time; this option allows *xterm* to move multiple lines at a time so that it doesn't fall as far behind. Its use is strongly recommended since it make *xterm* much faster when scanning through large amounts of text. The VT100 escape sequences for enabling and disabling smooth scroll as well as the "VT Options" menu can be used to turn this feature on or off.

XTERM(1)

j This option indicates that *xterm* should not do jump scrolling.

−ls This option indicates that the shell that is started in the *xterm* window will be a login shell (i.e., the first character of argv[0] will be a dash, indicating to the shell that it should read the user's .login or .profile).

ls This option indicates that the shell that is started should not be a login shell (i.e. it will be a normal "subshell").

−mb This option indicates that *xterm* should ring a margin bell when the user types near the right end of a line. This option can be turned on and off from the "VT Options" menu.

mb This option indicates that margin bell should not be rung.

−mc milliseconds This option specifies the maximum time between multi-click selections.

−ms *color* This option specifies the color to be used for the pointer cursor. The default is to use the foreground color.

−nb *number* This option specifies the number of characters from the right end of a line at which the margin bell, if enabled, will ring. The default is 10.

−rw This option indicates that reverse-wraparound should be allowed. This allows the cursor to back up from the leftmost column of one line to the rightmost column of the previous line. This is very useful for editing long shell command lines and is encouraged. This option can be turned on and off from the "VT Options" menu.

rw This option indicates that reverse-wraparound should not be allowed.

−aw This option indicates that auto-wraparound should be allowed. This allows the cursor to automatically wrap to the beginning of the next line when when it is at the rightmost position of a line and text is output.

aw This option indicates that auto-wraparound should not be allowed.

−s This option indicates that *xterm* may scroll asynchronously, meaning that the screen does not have to be kept completely up to date while scrolling. This allows *xterm* to run faster when network latencies are very high and is typically useful when running across a very large internet or many gateways.

s This option indicates that *xterm* should scroll synchronously.

−sb This option indicates that some number of lines that are scrolled off the top of the window should be saved and that a scrollbar should be displayed so that those lines can be viewed. This option may be turned on and off from the "VT Options" menu.

sb This option indicates that a scrollbar should not be displayed.

−sf This option indicates that Sun Function Key escape codes should be generated for function keys.

sf This option indicates that the standard escape codes should be generated for function keys.

−si This option indicates that output to a window should not automatically reposition the screen to the bottom of the scrolling region. This option can be turned on and off from the "VT Options" menu.

si This option indicates that output to a window should cause it to scroll to the bottom.

−sk This option indicates that pressing a key while using the scrollbar to review previous lines of text should cause the window to be repositioned automatically in the normal position at the bottom of the scroll region.

sk This option indicates that pressing a key while using the scrollbar should not cause the window to be repositioned.

−sl *number* This option specifies the number of lines to save that have been scrolled off the top of the screen. The default is 64.

XTERM(1)   XTERM(1)

−t   This option indicates that *xterm* should start in Tektronix mode, rather than in VT102 mode. Switching between the two windows is done using the "Options" menus.

t   This option indicates that *xterm* should start in VT102 mode.

−tm *string*   This option specifies a series of terminal setting keywords followed by the characters that should be bound to those functions, similar to the *stty* program. Allowable keywords include: intr, quit, erase, kill, eof, eol, swtch, start, stop, brk, susp, dsusp, rprnt, flush, weras, and lnext. Control characters may be specified as ^char (e.g. ^c or ^u) and ^? may be used to indicate delete.

−tn *name*   This option specifies the name of the terminal type to be set in the TERM environment variable. This terminal type must exist in the *termcap(5)* database and should have *li#* and *co#* entries.

−ut   This option indicates that *xterm* shouldn't write a record into the the system log file */etc/utmp*.

ut   This option indicates that *xterm* should write a record into the system log file */etc/utmp*.

−vb   This option indicates that a visual bell is preferred over an audible one. Instead of ringing the terminal bell whenever a Control-G is received, the window will be flashed.

vb   This option indicates that a visual bell should not be used.

−wf   This option indicates that *xterm* should wait for the window to be mapped the first time before starting the subprocess so that the initial terminal size settings and environment variables are correct. It is the application's responsibility to catch subsequent terminal size changes.

wf   This option indicates that *xterm* show not wait before starting the subprocess.

−C   This option indicates that this window should receive console output. This is not supported on all systems. To obtain console output, you must be the owner of the console device, and you must have read and write permission for it. If you are running X under *xdm* on the console screen you may need to have the session startup and reset programs explicitly change the ownership of the console device in order to get this option to work.

−S*ccn*   This option specifies the last two letters of the name of a pseudoterminal to use in slave mode, plus the number of the inherited file descriptor. The option is parsed "%c%c%d". This allows *xterm* to be used as an input and output channel for an existing program and is sometimes used in specialized applications.

The following command line arguments are provided for compatibility with older versions. They may not be supported in the next release as the X Toolkit provides standard options that accomplish the same task.

%geom   This option specifies the preferred size and position of the Tektronix window. It is shorthand for specifying the "*tekGeometry*" resource.

geom   This option specifies the preferred position of the icon window. It is shorthand for specifying the "*iconGeometry*" resource.

−T *string*   This option specifies the title for *xterm*'s windows. It is equivalent to **−title**.

−n *string*   This option specifies the icon name for *xterm*'s windows. It is shorthand for specifying the "*iconName*" resource. Note that this is not the same as the toolkit option **−name** (see below). The default icon name is the application name.

−r   This option indicates that reverse video should be simulated by swapping the foreground and background colors. It is equivalent to **−rv**.

–w *number*   This option specifies the width in pixels of the border surrounding the window. It is equivalent to **–borderwidth** or **–bw**.

The following standard X Toolkit command line arguments are commonly used with *xterm*:

–bg *color*   This option specifies the color to use for the background of the window. The default is "white."

–bd *color*   This option specifies the color to use for the border of the window. The default is "black."

–bw *number*   This option specifies the width in pixels of the border surrounding the window.

–fg *color*   This option specifies the color to use for displaying text. The default is "black."

–fn *font*   This option specifies the font to be used for displaying normal text. The default is *fixed*.

–name *name*   This option specifies the application name under which resources are to be obtained, rather than the default executable file name. *Name* should not contain "." or "*" characters.

–title *string* This option specifies the window title string, which may be displayed by window managers if the user so chooses. The default title is the command line specified after the **–e** option, if any, otherwise the application name.

–rv   This option indicates that reverse video should be simulated by swapping the foreground and background colors.

–geometry *geometry*   This option specifies the preferred size and position of the VT102 window; see *X(1)*.

–display *display*   This option specifies the X server to contact; see *X(1)*.

–xrm *resourcestring*   This option specifies a resource string to be used. This is especially useful for setting resources that do not have separate command line options.

–iconic   This option indicates that *xterm* should ask the window manager to start it as an icon rather than as the normal window.

RESOURCES

The program understands all of the core X Toolkit resource names and classes as well as:

iconGeometry (class **IconGeometry**)   Specifies the preferred size and position of the application when iconified. It is not necessarily obeyed by all window managers.

iconName (class **IconName**)   Specifies the icon name. The default is the application name.

termName (class **TermName**)   Specifies the terminal type name to be set in the TERM environment variable.

title (class **Title**)   Specifies a string that may be used by the window manager when displaying this application.

ttyModes (class **TtyModes**)   Specifies a string containing terminal setting keywords and the characters to which they may be bound. Allowable keywords include: intr, quit, erase, kill, eof, eol, swtch, start, stop, brk, susp, dsusp, rprnt, flush, weras, and lnext. Control characters may be specified as ^char (e.g. ^c or ^u) and ^? may be used to indicate Delete. This is very useful for overriding the default terminal settings without having to do an *stty* every time an *xterm* is started.

useInsertMode (class **UseInsertMode**)]" Force use of insert mode by adding appropriate entries to the TERMCAP environment variable. This is useful if the system termcap is broken. The default is "false."

utmpInhibit (class **UtmpInhibit**) Specifies whether or not *xterm* should try to record the user's terminal in */etc/utmp*.

sunFunctionKeys (class **SunFunctionKeys**) Specifies whether or not Sun Function Key escape codes should be generated for function keys instead of standard escape sequences.

waitForMap (class **WaitForMap**) Specifies whether or not *xterm* should wait for the initial window map before starting the subprocess. The default is "false."

The following resources are specified as part of the *vt100* widget (class *VT100*):

allowSendEvents (class **AllowSendEvents**) Specifies whether or not synthetic key and button events (generated using the X protocol SendEvent request) should be interpreted or discarded. The default is "false" meaning they are discarded. Note that allowing such events creates a very large security hole.

alwaysHighlight (class **AlwaysHighlight**) Specifies whether or not *xterm* should always display a highlighted text cursor. By default, a hollow text cursor is displayed whenever the pointer moves out of the window or the window loses the input focus.

appcursorDefault (class **AppcursorDefault**) If "true," the cursor keys are initially in application mode. The default is "false."

appkeypadDefault (class **AppkeypadDefault**) If "true," the keypad keys are initially in application mode. The default is "false."

autoWrap (class **AutoWrap**) Specifies whether or not auto-wraparound should be enabled. The default is "true."

bellSuppressTime (class **BellSuppressTime**) Number of milliseconds after a bell command is sent during which additional bells will be suppressed. Default is 200. If set non-zero, additional bells will also be suppressed until the server reports that processing of the first bell has been completed; this feature is most useful with the visible bell.

boldFont (class **BoldFont**) Specifies the name of the bold font to use instead of overstriking.

c132 (class **C132**) Specifies whether or not the VT102 DECCOLM escape sequence should be honored. The default is "false."

cutNewline (class **CutNewline**) If false, triple clicking to select a line does not include the Newline at the end of the line. If true, the Newline is selected. The default is "true."

cutToBeginningOfLine (class **CutToBeginningOfLine**) If false, triple clicking to select a line selects only from the current word forward. If true, the entire line is selected. The default is "true."

charClass (class **CharClass**) Specifies comma-separated lists of character class bindings of the form [*low*–]*high*:*value*. These are used in determining which sets of characters should be treated the same when doing cut and paste. See the section on specifying character classes.

curses (class **Curses**) Specifies whether or not the last column bug in *more*(1) should be worked around. See the **–cu** option for details. The default is "false."

background (class **Background**) Specifies the color to use for the background of the window. The default is "white."

foreground (class **Foreground**) Specifies the color to use for displaying text in the window. Setting the class name instead of the instance name is an easy way to have everything that would normally appear in the text color change color. The default is "black."

cursorColor (class **Foreground**) Specifies the color to use for the text cursor. The default is "black."

eightBitInput (class **EightBitInput**) If true, Meta characters input from the keyboard are presented as a single character with the eighth bit turned on. If false, Meta characters are converted into a two-character sequence with the character itself preceded by ESC. The default is "true."

eightBitOutput (class **EightBitOutput**) Specifies whether or not eight-bit characters sent from the host should be accepted as is or stripped when printed. The default is "true."

font (class **Font**) Specifies the name of the normal font. The default is "fixed."

font1 (class **Font1**) Specifies the name of the first alternative font.

font2 (class **Font2**) Specifies the name of the second alternative font.

font3 (class **Font3**) Specifies the name of the third alternative font.

font4 (class **Font4**) Specifies the name of the fourth alternative font.

font5 (class **Font5**) Specifies the name of the fifth alternative font.

font6 (class **Font6**) Specifies the name of the sixth alternative font.

geometry (class **Geometry**) Specifies the preferred size and position of the VT102 window.

hpLowerleftBugCompat (class **HpLowerleftBugCompat**) Specifies whether to work around a bug in HP's *xdb*, which ignores termcap and always sends ESC F to move to the lower left corner. "true" causes xterm to interpret ESC F as a request to move to the lower left corner of the screen. The default is "false."

internalBorder (class **BorderWidth**) Specifies the number of pixels between the characters and the window border. The default is 2.

jumpScroll (class **JumpScroll**) Specifies whether or not jump scroll should be used. The default is "true."

loginShell (class **LoginShell**) Specifies whether or not the shell to be run in the window should be started as a login shell. The default is "false."

marginBell (class **MarginBell**) Specifies whether or not the bell should be run when the user types near the right margin. The default is "false."

multiClickTime (class **MultiClickTime**) Specifies the maximum time in milliseconds between multi-click select events. The default is 250 milliseconds.

multiScroll (class **MultiScroll**) Specifies whether or not scrolling should be done asynchronously. The default is "false."

nMarginBell (class **Column**) Specifies the number of characters from the right margin at which the margin bell should be rung, when enabled.

pointerColor (class **Foreground**) Specifies the foreground color of the pointer. The default is "XtDefaultForeground."

pointerColorBackground (class **Background**) Specifies the background color of the pointer. The default is "XtDefaultBackground."

pointerShape (class **Cursor**) Specifies the name of the shape of the pointer. The default is "xterm."

resizeGravity (class **ResizeGravity**) Affects the behavior when the window is resized to be taller or shorter. **NorthWest** specifies that the top line of text on the screen stay fixed. If the window is made shorter, lines are dropped from the bottom; if the window is made taller, blank lines are added at the bottom. This is compatible with the behavior in R4. **SouthWest** (the default) specifies that the bottom line of text on the screen stay fixed. If the window is made taller, additional saved lines will be scrolled down onto the screen; if the window is made shorter, lines will be scrolled off the top of the screen, and the top saved lines will be dropped.

reverseVideo (class **ReverseVideo**) Specifies whether or not reverse video should be simulated. The default is "false."

reverseWrap (class **ReverseWrap**) Specifies whether or not reverse-wraparound should be enabled. The default is "false."

saveLines (class **SaveLines**) Specifies the number of lines to save beyond the top of the screen when a scrollbar is turned on. The default is 64.

scrollBar (class **ScrollBar**) Specifies whether or not the scrollbar should be displayed. The default is "false."

scrollTtyOutput (class **ScrollCond**) Specifies whether or not output to the terminal should automatically cause the scrollbar to go to the bottom of the scrolling region. The default is "true."

scrollKey (class **ScrollCond**) Specifies whether or not pressing a key should automatically cause the scrollbar to go to the bottom of the scrolling region. The default is "false."

scrollLines (class **ScrollLines**) Specifies the number of lines that the *scroll-back* and *scroll-forw* actions should use as a default. The default value is 1.

signalInhibit (class **SignalInhibit**) Specifies whether or not the entries in the "Main Options" menu for sending signals to *xterm* should be disallowed. The default is "false."

tekGeometry (class **Geometry**) Specifies the preferred size and position of the Tektronix window.

tekInhibit (class **TekInhibit**) Specifies whether or not the escape sequence to enter Tektronix mode should be ignored. The default is "false."

tekSmall (class **TekSmall**) Specifies whether or not the Tektronix mode window should start in its smallest size if no explicit geometry is given. This is useful when running *xterm* on displays with small screens. The default is "false."

tekStartup (class **TekStartup**) Specifies whether or not *xterm* should start up in Tektronix mode. The default is "false."

titeInhibit (class **TiteInhibit**) Specifies whether or not *xterm* should remove remove *ti* and *te* termcap entries (used to switch between alternate screens on startup of many screen-oriented programs) from the TERMCAP string. If set, *xterm* also ignores the escape sequence to switch to the alternate screen.

translations (class **Translations**) Specifies the key and button bindings for menus, selections, "programmed strings," etc. See **ACTIONS** below.

visualBell (class **VisualBell**) Specifies whether or not a visible bell (i.e. flashing) should be used instead of an audible bell when Control-G is received. The default is "false."

The following resources are specified as part of the *tek4014* widget (class *Tek4014*):

width (class **Width**) Specifies the width of the Tektronix window in pixels.

height (class **Height**) Specifies the height of the Tektronix window in pixels.

fontLarge (class **Font**) Specifies the large font to use in the Tektronix window.

font2 (class **Font**) Specifies font number 2 to use in the Tektronix window.

font3 (class **Font**) Specifies font number 3 to use in the Tektronix window.

XTERM(1) XTERM(1)

fontSmall (class **Font**)   Specifies the small font to use in the Tektronix window.

initialFont (class **InitialFont**)   Specifies which of the four Tektronix fonts to use initially. Values are the same as for the *set-tek-text* action. The default is "large."

ginTerminator (class **GinTerminator**)   Specifies what character(s) should follow a GIN report or status report. The possibilities are "none," which sends no terminating characters, "CRonly," which sends CR, and "CR&EOT," which sends both CR and EOT. The default is "none."

The resources that may be specified for the various menus are described in the documentation for the Athena **SimpleMenu** widget. The name and classes of the entries in each of the menus are listed below.

The *mainMenu* has the following entries:

 securekbd (class **SmeBSB**)   This entry invokes the **secure()** action.

 allowsends (class **SmeBSB**)   This entry invokes the **allow-send-events(toggle)** action.

 redraw (class **SmeBSB**)   This entry invokes the **redraw()** action.

 line1 (class **SmeLine**)   This is a separator.

 suspend (class **SmeBSB**)   This entry invokes the **send-signal(tstp)** action on systems that support job control.

 continue (class **SmeBSB**)   This entry invokes the **send-signal(cont)** action on systems that support job control.

 interrupt (class **SmeBSB**)   This entry invokes the **send-signal(int)** action.

 hangup (class **SmeBSB**)   This entry invokes the **send-signal(hup)** action.

 terminate (class **SmeBSB**)   This entry invokes the **send-signal(term)** action.

 kill (class **SmeBSB**)   This entry invokes the **send-signal(kill)** action.

 line2 (class **SmeLine**)   This is a separator.

 quit (class **SmeBSB**)   This entry invokes the **quit()** action.

The *vtMenu* has the following entries:

 scrollbar (class **SmeBSB**)   This entry invokes the **set-scrollbar(toggle)** action.

 jumpscroll (class **SmeBSB**)   This entry invokes the **set-jumpscroll(toggle)** action.

 reversevideo (class **SmeBSB**)   This entry invokes the **set-reverse-video(toggle)** action.

 autowrap (class **SmeBSB**)   This entry invokes the **set-autowrap(toggle)** action.

 reversewrap (class **SmeBSB**)   This entry invokes the **set-reversewrap(toggle)** action.

 autolinefeed (class **SmeBSB**)   This entry invokes the **set-autolinefeed(toggle)** action.

 appcursor (class **SmeBSB**)   This entry invokes the **set-appcursor(toggle)** action.

 appkeypad (class **SmeBSB**)   This entry invokes the **set-appkeypad(toggle)** action.

 scrollkey (class **SmeBSB**)   This entry invokes the **set-scroll-on-key(toggle)** action.

 scrollttyoutput (class **SmeBSB**)   This entry invokes the **set-scroll-on-tty-output(toggle)** action.

 allow132 (class **SmeBSB**)   This entry invokes the **set-allow132(toggle)** action.

 cursesemul (class **SmeBSB**)   This entry invokes the **set-cursesemul(toggle)** action.

 visualbell (class **SmeBSB**)   This entry invokes the **set-visualbell(toggle)** action.

marginbell (class **SmeBSB**)   This entry invokes the **set-marginbell(toggle)** action.

altscreen (class **SmeBSB**)   This entry is currently disabled.

line1 (class **SmeLine**)   This is a separator.

softreset (class **SmeBSB**)   This entry invokes the **soft-reset()** action.

hardreset (class **SmeBSB**)   This entry invokes the **hard-reset()** action.

clearsavedlines (class **SmeBSB**)"   This entry invokes the **clear-saved-lines()** action.

line2 (class **SmeLine**)   This is a separator.

tekshow (class **SmeBSB**)   This entry invokes the **set-visibility(tek,toggle)** action.

tekmode (class **SmeBSB**)   This entry invokes the **set-terminal-type(tek)** action.

vthide (class **SmeBSB**)   This entry invokes the **set-visibility(vt,off)** action.

The *fontMenu* has the following entries:

fontdefault (class **SmeBSB**)   This entry invokes the **set-vt-font(d)** action.

font1 (class **SmeBSB**)   This entry invokes the **set-vt-font(1)** action.

font2 (class **SmeBSB**)   This entry invokes the **set-vt-font(2)** action.

font3 (class **SmeBSB**)   This entry invokes the **set-vt-font(3)** action.

font4 (class **SmeBSB**)   This entry invokes the **set-vt-font(4)** action.

font5 (class **SmeBSB**)   This entry invokes the **set-vt-font(5)** action.

font6 (class **SmeBSB**)   This entry invokes the **set-vt-font(6)** action.

fontescape (class **SmeBSB**)   This entry invokes the **set-vt-font(e)** action.

fontsel (class **SmeBSB**)   This entry invokes the **set-vt-font(s)** action.

The *tekMenu* has the following entries:

tektextlarge (class **SmeBSB**)   This entry invokes the **set-tek-text(l)** action.

tektext2 (class **SmeBSB**)   This entry invokes the **set-tek-text(2)** action.

tektext3 (class **SmeBSB**)   This entry invokes the **set-tek-text(3)** action.

tektextsmall (class **SmeBSB**)   This entry invokes the **set-tek-text(s)** action.

line1 (class **SmeLine**)   This is a separator.

tekpage (class **SmeBSB**)   This entry invokes the **tek-page()** action.

tekreset (class **SmeBSB**)   This entry invokes the **tek-reset()** action.

tekcopy (class **SmeBSB**)   This entry invokes the **tek-copy()** action.

line2 (class **SmeLine**)   This is a separator.

vtshow (class **SmeBSB**)   This entry invokes the **set-visibility(vt,toggle)** action.

vtmode (class **SmeBSB**)   This entry invokes the **set-terminal-type(vt)** action.

tekhide (class **SmeBSB**)   This entry invokes the **set-visibility(tek,toggle)** action.

The following resources are useful when specified for the Athena Scrollbar widget:

thickness (class **Thickness**)   Specifies the width in pixels of the scrollbar.

background (class **Background**)   Specifies the color to use for the background of the scrollbar.

foreground (class **Foreground**)   Specifies the color to use for the foreground of the scrollbar. The "thumb" of the scrollbar is a simple checkerboard pattern alternating pixels for foreground and background color.

POINTER USAGE

Once the VT102 window is created, *xterm* allows you to select text and copy it within the same or other windows.

The selection functions are invoked when the pointer buttons are used with no modifiers, and when they are used with the "shift" key. The assignment of the functions described below to keys and buttons may be changed through the resource database; see **ACTIONS** below.

Pointer button one (usually left) is used to save text into the cut buffer. Move the cursor to beginning of the text, and then hold the button down while moving the cursor to the end of the region and releasing the button. The selected text is highlighted and is saved in the global cut buffer and made the PRIMARY selection when the button is released. Double-clicking selects by words. Triple-clicking selects by lines. Quadruple-clicking goes back to characters, etc. Multiple-click is determined by the time from button up to button down, so you can change the selection unit in the middle of a selection. If the key/button bindings specify that an X selection is to be made, *xterm* will leave the selected text highlighted for as long as it is the selection owner.

Pointer button two (usually middle) 'types' (pastes) the text from the PRIMARY selection, if any, otherwise from the cut buffer, inserting it as keyboard input.

Pointer button three (usually right) extends the current selection. (Without loss of generality, you can swap "right" and "left" everywhere in the rest of this paragraph.) If pressed while closer to the right edge of the selection than the left, it extends/contracts the right edge of the selection. If you contract the selection past the left edge of the selection, *xterm* assumes you really meant the left edge, restores the original selection, then extends/contracts the left edge of the selection. Extension starts in the selection unit mode that the last selection or extension was performed in; you can multiple-click to cycle through them.

By cutting and pasting pieces of text without trailing new lines, you can take text from several places in different windows and form a command to the shell, for example, or take output from a program and insert it into your favorite editor. Since the cut buffer is globally shared among different applications, you should regard it as a 'file' whose contents you know. The terminal emulator and other text programs should be treating it as if it were a text file, i.e., the text is delimited by new lines.

The scroll region displays the position and amount of text currently showing in the window (highlighted) relative to the amount of text actually saved. As more text is saved (up to the maximum), the size of the highlighted area decreases.

Clicking button one with the pointer in the scroll region moves the adjacent line to the top of the display window.

Clicking button three moves the top line of the display window down to the pointer position.

Clicking button two moves the display to a position in the saved text that corresponds to the pointer's position in the scrollbar.

Unlike the VT102 window, the Tektronix window dows not allow the copying of text. It does allow Tektronix GIN mode, and in this mode the cursor will change from an arrow to a cross. Pressing any key will send that key and the current coordinate of the cross cursor. Pressing button one, two, or three will return the letters 'l', 'm', and 'r', respectively. If the 'shift' key is pressed when a pointer button is pressed, the corresponding upper case letter is sent. To distinguish a pointer button from a key, the high bit of the character is set (but this is bit is normally stripped unless the terminal mode is RAW; see *tty*(4) for details).

MENUS

Xterm has four menus, named *mainMenu*, *vtMenu*, *fontMenu*, and *tekMenu*. Each menu pops up under the correct combinations of key and button presses. Most menus are divided into two section, separated by a horizontal line. The top portion contains various modes that can be altered. A check mark appears next to a mode that is currently active. Selecting one of these modes toggles its state. The bottom portion of the menu are command entries; selecting one of these performs the indicated function.

The **xterm** menu pops up when the "control" key and pointer button one are pressed in a window. The *mainMenu* contains items that apply to both the VT102 and Tektronix windows. The **Secure** Keyboard mode is be used when typing in passwords or other sensitive data in an unsecure environment; see **SECURITY** below. Notable entries in the command section of the menu are the **Continue**, **Suspend**, **Interrupt**, **Hangup**, **Terminate** and **Kill** which sends the SIGCONT, SIGTSTP, SIGINT, SIGHUP, SIGTERM and SIGKILL signals, respectively, to the process group of the process running under *xterm* (usually the shell). The **Continue** function is especially useful if the user has accidentally typed CTRL-Z, suspending the process.

The *vtMenu* sets various modes in the VT102 emulation, and is popped up when the "control" key and pointer button two are pressed in the VT102 window. In the command section of this menu, the soft reset entry will reset scroll regions. This can be convenient when some program has left the scroll regions set incorrectly (often a problem when using VMS or TOPS-20). The full reset entry will clear the screen, reset tabs to every eight columns, and reset the terminal modes (such as wrap and smooth scroll) to their initial states just after *xterm* has finished processing the command line options.

The *fontMenu* sets the font used in the VT102 window. In addition to the default font and a number of alternatives that are set with resources, the menu offers the font last specified by the Set Font escape sequence (see the document *Xterm Control Sequences*) and the current selection as a font name (if the PRIMARY selection is owned).

The *tekMenu* sets various modes in the Tektronix emulation, and is popped up when the "control" key and pointer button two are pressed in the Tektronix window. The current font size is checked in the modes section of the menu. The **PAGE** entry in the command section clears the Tektronix window.

SECURITY

X environments differ in their security consciousness. Most servers, run under *xdm*, are capable of using a "magic cookie" authorization scheme that can provide a reasonable level of security for many people. If your server is only using a host-based mechanism to control access to the server (see *xhost(1)*), then if you enable access for a host and other users are also permitted to run clients on that same host, there is every possibility that someone can run an application that will use the basic services of the X protocol to snoop on your activities, potentially capturing a transcript of everything you type at the keyboard. This is of particular concern when you want to type in a password or other sensitive data. The best solution to this problem is to use a better authorization mechanism that host-based control, but a simple mechanism exists for protecting keyboard input in *xterm*.

The **xterm** menu (see **MENUS** above) contains a **Secure Keyboard** entry which, when enabled, ensures that all keyboard input is directed *only* to *xterm* (using the GrabKeyboard protocol request). When an application prompts you for a password (or other sensitive data), you can enable **Secure Keyboard** using the menu, type in the data, and then disable **Secure Keyboard** using the menu again. Only one X client at a time can secure the keyboard, so when you attempt to enable **Secure Keyboard** it may fail. In this case, the bell will sound. If the **Secure Keyboard** succeeds, the foreground and background colors will be exchanged (as if you selected the **Reverse Video** entry in the **Modes** menu); they will be exchanged again when you exit secure mode. If the colors do *not* switch, then you should be *very* suspicious that you are being spoofed. If the application you are running displays a prompt before asking for the password, it is safest to enter secure mode *before* the prompt gets displayed, and to make sure that the prompt gets displayed correctly (in the new colors), to minimize the probability of spoofing. You can also bring up the menu again and make sure that a check mark appears next to the entry.

Secure Keyboard mode will be disabled automatically if your xterm window becomes iconified (or otherwise unmapped), or if you start up a reparenting window manager (that places a title bar or other decoration around the window) while in **Secure Keyboard** mode. (This is a feature of the X protocol not easily overcome.) When this happens, the foreground and background colors will be switched back and the bell will sound in warning.

CHARACTER CLASSES

Clicking the middle mouse button twice in rapid succession will cause all characters of the same class (e.g. letters, white space, punctuation) to be selected. Since different people have different preferences for what should be selected (for example, should filenames be selected as a whole or only the separate subnames), the default mapping can be overridden through the use of the *charClass* (class *CharClass*) resource.

This resource is a series of comma-separated of *range:value* pairs. The *range* is either a single number or *low-high* in the range of 0 to 127, corresponding to the ASCII code for the character or characters to be set. The *value* is arbitrary, although the default table uses the character number of the first character occurring in the set.

The default table is

```
static int charClass[128] = {
/* NUL SOH STX ETX EOT ENQ ACK BEL */
    32, 1, 1, 1, 1, 1, 1, 1,
/* BS HT NL VT NP CR SO SI */
    1, 32, 1, 1, 1, 1, 1, 1,
/* DLE DC1 DC2 DC3 DC4 NAK SYN ETB */
    1, 1, 1, 1, 1, 1, 1, 1,
/* CAN EM SUB ESC FS GS RS US */
    1, 1, 1, 1, 1, 1, 1, 1,
/* SP ! " # $ % & ' */
    32, 33, 34, 35, 36, 37, 38, 39,
/* ( ) * + , - . / */
    40, 41, 42, 43, 44, 45, 46, 47,
/* 0 1 2 3 4 5 6 7 */
    48, 48, 48, 48, 48, 48, 48, 48,
/* 8 9 : ; < = > ? */
    48, 48, 58, 59, 60, 61, 62, 63,
/* @ A B C D E F G */
    64, 48, 48, 48, 48, 48, 48, 48,
/* H I J K L M N O */
    48, 48, 48, 48, 48, 48, 48, 48,
/* P Q R S T U V W */
    48, 48, 48, 48, 48, 48, 48, 48,
/* X Y Z [ \ ] ^ _ */
    48, 48, 48, 91, 92, 93, 94, 48,
/* ` a b c d e f g */
    96, 48, 48, 48, 48, 48, 48, 48,
/* h i j k l m n o */
    48, 48, 48, 48, 48, 48, 48, 48,
/* p q r s t u v w */
    48, 48, 48, 48, 48, 48, 48, 48,
/* x y z { | } ~ DEL */
    48, 48, 48, 123, 124, 125, 126, 1};
```

For example, the string "33:48,37:48,45-47:48,64:48" indicates that the exclamation mark, percent sign, dash, period, slash, and ampersand characters should be treated the same way as characters and numbers. This is useful for cutting and pasting electronic mailing addresses and filenames.

ACTIONS

It is possible to rebind keys (or sequences of keys) to arbitrary strings for input, by changing the translations for the vt100 or tek4014 widgets. Changing the translations for events other than key and button events is not expected, and will cause unpredictable behavior. The following actions are provided for using within the *vt100* or *tek4014* **translations** resources:

bell([*percent*])   This action rings the keyboard bell at the specified percentage above or below the base volume.

ignore() This action ignores the event but checks for special pointer position escape sequences.

insert() This action inserts the character or string associated with the key that was pressed.

insert-seven-bit() This action is a synonym for **insert()**

insert-eight-bit() This action inserts an eight-bit (Meta) version of the character or string associated with the key that was pressed. The exact action depends on the value of the **eightBitInput** resource.

insert-selection(*sourcename* [, ...]) This action inserts the string found in the selection or cutbuffer indicated by *sourcename*. Sources are checked in the order given (case is significant) until one is found. Commonly-used selections include: *PRIMARY*, *SECONDARY*, and *CLIPBOARD*. Cut buffers are typically named *CUT_BUFFER0* through *CUT_BUFFER7*.

keymap(*name*) This action dynamically defines a new translation table whose resource name is *name* with the suffix *Keymap* (case is significant). The name *None* restores the original translation table.

popup-menu(*menuname*) This action displays the specified popup menu. Valid names (case is significant) include: *mainMenu*, *vtMenu*, *fontMenu*, and *tekMenu*.

secure() This action toggles the *Secure Keyboard* mode described in the section named **SECURITY**, and is invoked from the **securekbd** entry in *mainMenu*.

select-start() This action begins text selection at the current pointer location. See the section on **POINTER USAGE** for information on making selections.

select-extend() This action tracks the pointer and extends the selection. It should only be bound to Motion events.

select-end(*destname* [, ...]) This action puts the currently selected text into all of the selections or cutbuffers specified by *destname*.

select-cursor-start() This action is similar to **select-start** except that it begins the selection at the current text cursor position.

select-cursor-end(*destname* [, ...]) This action is similar to **select-end** except that it should be used with **select-cursor-start**.

set-vt-font(*d/1/2/3/4/5/6/e/s* [,*normalfont* [, *boldfont*]]) This action sets the font or fonts currently being used in the VT102 window. The first argument is a single character that specifies the font to be used: *d* or *D* indicate the default font (the font initially used when *xterm* was started), *1* through *6* indicate the fonts specified by the *font1* through *font6* resources, *e* or *E* indicate the normal and bold fonts that have been set through escape codes (or specified as the second and third action arguments, respectively), and *s* or *S* indicate the font selection (as made by programs such as *xfontsel(1)*) indicated by the second action argument.

start-extend() This action is similar to **select-start** except that the selection is extended to the current pointer location.

start-cursor-extend() This action is similar to **select-extend** except that the selection is extended to the current text cursor position.

string(*string*) This action inserts the specified text string as if it had been typed. Quotation is necessary if the string contains whitespace or non-alphanumeric characters. If the string argument begins with the characters "0x", it is interpreted as a hex character constant.

scroll-back(*count* [,*units*]) This action scrolls the text window backward so that text that had previously scrolled off the top of the screen is now visible. The *count* argument indicates the number of *units* (which may be *page*, *halfpage*, *pixel*, or *line*) by which to scroll.

scroll-forw(*count* [,*units*])   This action scrolls is similar to **scroll-back** except that it scrolls the other direction.

allow-send-events(*on/off/toggle*)   This action set or toggles the **allowSendEvents** resource and is also invoked by the **allowsends** entry in *mainMenu*.

redraw()   This action redraws the window and is also invoked by the *redraw* entry in *mainMenu*.

send-signal(*signame*)   This action sends the signal named by *signame* to the *xterm* subprocess (the shell or program specified with the –*e* command line option) and is also invoked by the **suspend**, **continue**, **interrupt**, **hangup**, **terminate**, and **kill** entries in *mainMenu*. Allowable signal names are (case is not significant): *tstp* (if supported by the operating system), *suspend* (same as *tstp*), *cont* (if supported by the operating system), *int*, *hup*, *term*, *quit*, *alrm*, *alarm* (same as *alrm*) and *kill*.

quit()   This action sends a SIGHUP to the subprogram and exits. It is also invoked by the **quit** entry in *mainMenu*.

set-scrollbar(*on/off/toggle*)   This action toggles the **scrollbar** resource and is also invoked by the **scrollbar** entry in *vtMenu*.

set-jumpscroll(*on/off/toggle*)   This action toggles the **jumpscroll** resource and is also invoked by the **jumpscroll** entry in *vtMenu*.

set-reverse-video(*on/off/toggle*)   This action toggles the *reverseVideo* resource and is also invoked by the **reversevideo** entry in *vtMenu*.

set-autowrap(*on/off/toggle*)   This action toggles automatic wrapping of long lines and is also invoked by the **autowrap** entry in *vtMenu*.

set-reversewrap(*on/off/toggle*)   This action toggles the **reverseWrap** resource and is also invoked by the **reversewrap** entry in *vtMenu*.

set-autolinefeed(*on/off/toggle*)   This action toggles automatic insertion of linefeeds and is also invoked by the **autolinefeed** entry in *vtMenu*.

set-appcursor(*on/off/toggle*)   This action toggles the handling Application Cursor Key mode and is also invoked by the **appcursor** entry in *vtMenu*.

set-appkeypad(*on/off/toggle*)   This action toggles the handling of Application Keypad mode and is also invoked by the **appkeypad** entry in *vtMenu*.

set-scroll-on-key(*on/off/toggle*)   This action toggles the **scrollKey** resource and is also invoked from the **scrollkey** entry in *vtMenu*.

set-scroll-on-tty-output(*on/off/toggle*)   This action toggles the **scrollTtyOutput** resource and is also invoked from the **scrollttyoutput** entry in *vtMenu*.

set-allow132(*on/off/toggle*)   This action toggles the **c132** resource and is also invoked from the **allow132** entry in *vtMenu*.

set-cursesemul(*on/off/toggle*)   This action toggles the **curses** resource and is also invoked from the **cursesemul** entry in *vtMenu*.

set-visual-bell(*on/off/toggle*)   This action toggles the **visualBell** resource and is also invoked by the **visualbell** entry in *vtMenu*.

set-marginbell(*on/off/toggle*)   This action toggles the **marginBell** resource and is also invoked from the **marginbell** entry in *vtMenu*.

set-altscreen(*on/off/toggle*)   This action toggles between the alternate and current screens.

soft-reset()   This action resets the scrolling region and is also invoked from the **softreset** entry in *vtMenu*.

hard-reset()   This action resets the scrolling region, tabs, window size, and cursor keys and clears the screen. It is also invoked from the **hardreset** entry in *vtMenu*.

XTERM(1)   XTERM(1)

  clear-saved-lines()   This action does **hard-reset**() (see above) and also clears the history of lines saved off the top of the screen. It is also invoked from the **clearsavedlines** entry in *vtMenu*.

  set-terminal-type(*type*)   This action directs output to either the *vt* or *tek* windows, according to the *type* string. It is also invoked by the **tekmode** entry in *vtMenu* and the **vtmode** entry in *tekMenu*.

  set-visibility(*vt/tek,on/off/toggle*)   This action controls whether or not the *vt* or *tek* windows are visible. It is also invoked from the **tekshow** and **vthide** entries in *vtMenu* and the **vtshow** and **tekhide** entries in *tekMenu*.

  set-tek-text(*large/2/3/small*)   This action sets font used in the Tektronix window to the value of the resources **tektextlarge**, **tektext2**, **tektext3**, and **tektextsmall** according to the argument. It is also by the entries of the same names as the resources in *tekMenu*.

  tek-page()   This action clears the Tektronix window and is also invoked by the **tekpage** entry in *tekMenu*.

  tek-reset()   This action resets the Tektronix window and is also invoked by the *tekreset* entry in *tekMenu*.

  tek-copy()   This action copies the escape codes used to generate the current window contents to a file in the current directory beginning with the name COPY. It is also invoked from the *tekcopy* entry in *tekMenu*.

  visual-bell()   This action flashes the window quickly.

The Tektronix window also has the following action:

  gin-press(*l/L/m/M/r/R*)   This action sends the indicated graphics input code.

The default bindings in the VT102 window are:

Shift <KeyPress> Prior: scroll-back(1,halfpage) \n\
Shift <KeyPress> Next: scroll-forw(1,halfpage) \n\
Shift <KeyPress> Select: select-cursor-start() \
select-cursor-end(PRIMARY, CUT_BUFFER0) \n\
Shift <KeyPress> Insert: insert-selection(PRIMARY, CUT_BUFFER0) \n\
~Meta<KeyPress>: insert-seven-bit() \n\
Meta<KeyPress>: insert-eight-bit() \n\
!Ctrl <Btn1Down>: popup-menu(mainMenu) \n\
!Lock Ctrl <Btn1Down>: popup-menu(mainMenu) \n\
!Mod2 Ctrl <Btn1Down>: popup-menu(mainMenu) \n\
!Mod2 Lock Ctrl <Btn1Down>: popup-menu(mainMenu) \n\
~Meta <Btn1Down>: select-start() \n\
~Meta <Btn1Motion>: select-extend() \n\
!Ctrl <Btn2Down>: popup-menu(vtMenu) \n\
!Lock Ctrl <Btn2Down>: popup-m

The default bindings in the Tektronix window are:

~Meta<KeyPress>: insert-seven-bit() \n\
Meta<KeyPress>: insert-eight-bit() \n\
!Ctrl <Btn1Down>: popup-menu(mainMenu) \n\
!Lock Ctrl <Btn1Down>: popup-menu(mainMenu) \n\
!Mod2 Ctrl <Btn1Down>: popup-menu(mainMenu) \n\
!Mod2 Lock Ctrl <Btn1Down>: popup-menu(mainMenu) \n\
!Ctrl <Btn2Down>: popup-menu(tekMenu) \n\
!Lock Ctrl <Btn2Down>: popup-menu(tekMenu) \n\
!Mod2 Ctrl <Btn2Down>: popup-menu(tekMenu) \n\
!Mod2 Lock Ctrl <Btn2Down>: popup-menu(tekMenu) \n\
Shift ~Meta<Btn1Down>: gin-press(L) \n\
~Meta<Btn1Down>: gin-press(l) \n\
Shift ~Meta<Btn2Down>: gin-press(M) \n\
~Meta<Btn2Down>: gin-press(m) \n\

Shift ~Meta<Btn3Down>: gin-press(R) \n\
~Meta<Btn3Down>: gin-press(r)

Below is a sample how of the **keymap()** action is used to add special keys for entering commonly-typed works:

*VT100.Translations: #override <Key>F13: keymap(dbx)
VT100.dbxKeymap.translations: \
<Key>F14: keymap(None) \n\
<Key>F17: string("next") string(0x0d) \n\
<Key>F18: string("step") string(0x0d) \n\
<Key>F19: string("continue") string(0x0d) \n\
<Key>F20: string("print ") insert-selection(PRIMARY, CUT_BUFFER0)

ENVIRONMENT

Xterm sets the environment variables "TERM" and "TERMCAP" properly for the size window you have created. It also uses and sets the environment variable "DISPLAY" to specify which bit map display terminal to use. The environment variable "WINDOWID" is set to the X window id number of the *xterm* window.

SEE ALSO

resize(1), X(1), pty(4), tty(4)
Xterm Control Sequences

BUGS

Large pastes do not work on some systems. This is not a bug in *xterm*; it is a bug in the pseudo terminal driver of those systems. *xterm* feeds large pastes to the pty only as fast as the pty will accept data, but some pty drivers do not return enough information to know if the write has succeeded.

Many of the options are not resettable after *xterm* starts.

Only fixed-width, character-cell fonts are supported.

This program still needs to be rewritten. It should be split into very modular sections, with the various emulators being completely separate widgets that don't know about each other. Ideally, you'd like to be able to pick and choose emulator widgets and stick them into a single control widget.

There needs to be a dialog box to allow entry of the Tek COPY file name.

AUTHORS

Far too many people, including:

Loretta Guarino Reid (DEC-UEG-WSL), Joel McCormack (DEC-UEG-WSL), Terry Weissman (DEC-UEG-WSL), Edward Moy (Berkeley), Ralph R. Swick (MIT-Athena), Mark Vandevoorde (MIT-Athena), Bob McNamara (DEC-MAD), Jim Gettys (MIT-Athena), Bob Scheifler (MIT X Consortium), Doug Mink (SAO), Steve Pitschke (Stellar), Ron Newman (MIT-Athena), Jim Fulton (MIT X Consortium), Dave Serisky (HP), Jonathan Kamens (MIT-Athena)

xvidtune(1)   xvidtune(1)

NAME
xvidtune – video mode tuner for XFree86

SYNOPSIS
xvidtune [**-prev** | **-next** | **-unlock** | **-query** | **-saver** *suspendtime* [*offtime*]] [*–toolkitoption* ...]

DESCRIPTION
Xvidtune is a client interface to the XFree86 X server video mode extension (XFree86-VidModeExtension).

When given one of the non-toolkit options, xvidtune provides a command line interface to either switch the video mode or get/set monitor power saver timeouts.

Without any options (or with only toolkit options) it presents the user with various buttons and sliders that can be used to interactively adjust existing video modes. It will also print the settings in a format suitable for inclusion in an XF86Config file.

Note: The original mode settings can be restored by pressing the 'R' key, and this can be used to restore a stable screen in situations where the screen becomes unreadable.

The available buttons are:

Left
Right
Up
Down

10 Adjust the video mode so that the display will be moved in the appropriate direction.

Wider
Narrower
Shorter
Taller

10 Adjust the video mode so that the display size is altered appropriately.

Quit	Exit the program.
Apply	Adjust the current video mode to match the selected settings.
Auto	Cause the Up/Down/Right/Left, Wider/Narrower/Shorter/Taller, Restore, and the special S3 buttons to be applied immediately. This button can be toggled.
Test	Temporarily switch to the selected settings.
Restore	Return the settings to their original values.
Fetch	Query the server for its current settings.
Show	Print the currently selected settings to stdout in XF86Config "Modeline" format. The primary selection is similarly set.
Next	Switch the Xserver to the next video mode.
Prev	Switch the Xserver to the previous video mode.

For some S3-based cards (964 and 968) the following are also available:

InvertVCLK	Change the VCLK invert/non-invert state.
EarlySC	Change the Early SC state. This affects screen wrapping.

BlankDelay1
BlankDelay2

10 Set the blank delay values. This affects screen wrapping. Acceptable values are in the range 0–7. The values may be incremented or decremented with the '+' and '-' buttons, or by pressing the '+' or '-' keys in the text field.

For S3-864/868 based cards *InvertVCLK* and *BlankDelay1* may be useful. For S3 Trio32/Trio64 cards only *InvertVCLK* is available. At the moment there are no default settings available for these chips in the video mode extension and thus this feature is disabled in xvidtune. It can be enabled by setting any of the optional S3 commands in the screen section of XF86Config, e.g. using

10 **blank_delay** "" 0

OPTIONS

xvidtune accepts the standard X Toolkit command line options as well as the following:

- **–prev** Switch the Xserver to the previous video mode.
- **–next** Switch the Xserver to the next video mode.
- **–unlock** Normally, *xvidtune* will disable the switching of video modes via hot-keys while it is running. If for some reason the program did not exit cleanly and they are still disabled, the program can be re-run with this option to re-enable the mode switching key combinations.
- **–saver** *suspendtime* [*offtime*] Set the "suspend" and "off" screensaver inactivity timeouts. The values are in seconds.
- **–query** Display the monitor parameters and extended screensaver timeouts.

SEE ALSO

XF86Config(4/5)

AUTHORS

Kaleb S. Keithley, X Consortium.
Additions and modifications by Jon Tombs, David Dawes, and Joe Moss.

XWININFO(1)

NAME
xwininfo – window information utility for X

SYNOPSIS
xwininfo [–help] [–id *id*] [–root] [–name *name*] [–int] [–children] [–tree] [–stats] [–bits] [–events] [–size] [–wm] [–shape] [–frame] [–all] [–english] [–metric] [–display *display*]

DESCRIPTION
Xwininfo is a utility for displaying information about windows. Various information is displayed depending on which options are selected. If no options are chosen, **–stats** is assumed.

The user has the option of selecting the target window with the mouse (by clicking any mouse button in the desired window) or by specifying its window id on the command line with the **–id** option. Or instead of specifying the window by its id number, the **–name** option may be used to specify which window is desired by name. There is also a special **–root** option to quickly obtain information on the screen's root window.

OPTIONS

- **–help**   Print out the 'Usage:' command syntax summary.

- **–id** *id*   This option allows the user to specify a target window *id* on the command line rather than using the mouse to select the target window. This is very useful in debugging X applications where the target window is not mapped to the screen or where the use of the mouse might be impossible or interfere with the application.

- **–name** *name*   This option allows the user to specify that the window named *name* is the target window on the command line rather than using the mouse to select the target window.

- **–root**   This option specifies that X's root window is the target window. This is useful in situations where the root window is completely obscured.

- **–int**   This option specifies that all X window ids should be displayed as integer values. The default is to display them as hexadecimal values.

- **–children**   This option causes the root, parent, and children windows' ids and names of the selected window to be displayed.

- **–tree**   This option is like **–children** but displays all children recursively.

- **–stats**   This option causes the display of various attributes pertaining to the location and appearance of the selected window. Information displayed includes the location of the window, its width and height, its depth, border width, class, colormap id if any, map state, backing-store hint, and location of the corners.

- **–bits**   This option causes the display of various attributes pertaining to the selected window's raw bits and how the selected window is to be stored. Displayed information includes the selected window's bit gravity, window gravity, backing-store hint, backing-planes value, backing pixel, and whether or not the window has save-under set.

- **–events**   This option causes the selected window's event masks to be displayed. Both the event mask of events wanted by some client and the event mask of events not to propagate are displayed.

- **–size**   This option causes the selected window's sizing hints to be displayed. Displayed information includes: for both the normal size hints and the zoom size hints, the user supplied location if any; the program supplied location if any; the user supplied size if any; the program supplied size if any; the minimum size if any; the maximum size if any; the resize increments if any; and the minimum and maximum aspect ratios if any.

−wm This option causes the selected window's window manager hints to be displayed. Information displayed may include whether or not the application accepts input, what the window's icon window # and name is, where the window's icon should go, and what the window's initial state should be.

−shape This option causes the selected window's window and border shape extents to be displayed.

−frame This option causes window manager frames to be considered when manually selecting windows.

−metric This option causes all individual height, width, and x and y positions to be displayed in millimeters as well as number of pixels, based on what the server thinks the resolution is. Geometry specifications that are in **+x+y** form are not changed.

−english This option causes all individual height, width, and x and y positions to be displayed in inches (and feet, yards, and miles if necessary) as well as number of pixels. **−metric** and **−english** may both be enabled at the same time.

−all This option is a quick way to ask for all information possible.

−display *display* This option allows you to specify the server to connect to; see *X(1)*.

EXAMPLE

The following is a sample summary taken with no options specified:

xwininfo: Window id: 0x60000f "xterm"

Absolute upper-left X: 2 Absolute upper-left Y: 85 Relative upper-left X: 0 Relative upper-left Y: 25 Width: 579 Height: 316 Depth: 8 Visual Class: PseudoColor Border width: 0 Class: InputOutput Colormap: 0x27 (installed) Bit Gravity State: NorthWestGravity Window Gravity State: NorthWestGravity Backing Store State: NotUseful Save Under State: no Map State: IsViewable Override Redirect State: no Corners: +2+85 -699+85 -699-623 +2-623 -geometry 80x24+0+58

ENVIRONMENT

DISPLAY To get the default host and display number.

SEE ALSO

X(1), xprop(1)

BUGS

Using **−stats −bits** shows some redundant information.

The -geometry string displayed must make assumptions about the window's border width and the behavior of the application and the window manager. As a result, the location given is not always correct.

AUTHOR

Mark Lillibridge, MIT Project Athena

NAME

ytalk - A multi-user chat program.

SYNOPSIS

ytalk [-x] username...

DESCRIPTION

YTalk V3.0 Patch Level 1

YTalk is in essence a multi-user chat program. It works almost exactly like the UNIX talk program and even communicates with the same talk daemon(s), but YTalk allows for multiple connections.

The *username* field may be formatted in several different ways:

name - some user on your machine

name@host - some user on a different machine

name#tty - some user on a particular terminal

name#tty@host - some user on a particular tty on a different machine

name@host#tty - same as "name#tty@host"

You can specify multiple user names on the command line, ie:

ytalk george fred@hissun.edu marc@grumpy.cc

The -x option disables the X11 interface (described below).

For each user on the command line, YTalk will attempt to connect to the talk daemon on the specified user's host and determine if that user has left an invitation for you to call. If not, YTalk leaves an invitation for him and tells his talk daemon to send an announcement to his screen. There is not yet a dedicated YTalk daemon, but there will be. Right now, YTalk is able to communicate with BOTH existing versions of UNIX talk daemons. For any particular host, YTalk will attempt to communicate with a talk daemon the caller's host also supports. If the two hosts have no daemon in common, then UNIX talk will not function at all, but a connection is possible through (and only through) YTalk.

Once a connection has been established between two users, they can chat back and forth to their hearts' content. The connection is terminated when one of them hits control-C or selects quit off the main menu.

YTalk is perfectly compatible with UNIX talk and they can even converse with each other without any problems. However, many of the features of YTalk can only operate when you are connected to a user who is also using YTalk. For the rest of this document, it will be assumed that all connected users are using YTalk, unless otherwise stated.

If you specified more than one user on the YTalk command line, then YTalk will process and add each user to the conversation as they respond to your invitation. As each new user enters the conversation, the screen is further subdivided into smaller and smaller windows, one for each connected user. Right now, the number of connected users is limited by the number of lines on your terminal (or window), for each connected user needs at least three lines.

YTalk does implement primitive support of the X11 Windowing System. If the environment variable DISPLAY is set, then YTalk attempts to connect to that X server. Further details about the X11 interface (and how to turn it off) are given below.

As each new user is added to the conversation, YTalk will transmit information about that user to all other connected YTalk users so that their screens will also subdivide and incorporate the new user. If the new user is using UNIX talk, then information about him will NOT be transmitted, for his screen would be unable to accept multiple connections. I have given brief thought to allowing at least the output of UNIX talk users to be transmitted to all connected YTalk users, but I have not written any code to do so. Note that even though UNIX talk cannot handle multiple connections, it is still possible for YTalk to handle multiple UNIX "talk" connections. For example, george (using YTalk) could communicate with fred and joe (both using UNIX talk), but fred and joe would be unaware of each other. The best way to understand the limitations that UNIX "talk" places on YTalk is to test various connections between the two and see how things work.

ESCAPE MENU

Whenever you are using YTalk, you can hit the *ESCAPE* key to bring up a menu which at this moment has these options:

a: add a user

d: delete a user

o: options

s: shell

u: user list

w: output user to file

q: quit

By choosing option "a", you are given the opportunity to type the name of any user you wish to include into the conversation. Again, YTalk will accept an invitation from that user if an invitation exists, or will leave an invitation and ring the given user.

By choosing option "d", you can select the name of a connection to terminate.

By choosing option "o", you can view and/or modify any of the YTalk options. See the OPTIONS section below for a list of YTalk options.

By choosing option "s", you can invoke a shell in your YTalk window. All other users will see what happens in your shell. YTalk will automatically resize your window down to the size of the smallest window you are connected to, in order to ensure that all users always see the same thing.

The "u" option displays a list of connected and unconnected users, as well as their window sizes and what version of talk software they are running.

By choosing option "w", you can select any connected user and type the name of a file, and all further output from that user will be dumped to the specified file. The file, if it exists, will be OVERWRITTEN. By choosing "w" and the same user again, further output to the file will be terminated.

Oh, one other thing: when user A attempts to ytalk to user B, but user B is already ytalking with user C, user A's YTalk program will realize that user B is already using YTalk, and will communicate with user B's YTalk program directly in order to initialize the conversation. User B will see a nice windowed message like:

Do you wish to talk with user A?

and he will be prompted for a yes/no answer. This, in my opinion, is much preferable to blitting the announcement message and messing up user B's screen.

RUNTIME OPTIONS

When you select Options off of the main menu, you are given the opportunity to edit the YTalk options. The current options are:

s: turn scrolling [off/on]

w: turn word-wrap [off/on]

i: turn auto-import [off/on]

v: turn auto-invite [off/on]

r: turn auto-rering [off/on]

a: turn asides [off/on]

If *scrolling* is turned on, then a user's window will scroll when he reaches the bottom, instead of wrapping back around to the top.

If *word-wrap* is turned on, then any word which would overextend the right margin will be automatically moved to the next line on your screen.

If *auto-import* is turned on, then YTalk will assume that you wish to talk to any users which connect to other YTalk users which are connected to you. That last sentence does make sense; try again. YTalk will add these users to your session automatically, without asking you for verification.

If *auto-invite* is turned on, then YTalk will automatically accept any connection requested by another user and add them to your session. You will not be asked for verification.

If *auto-rering* is turned on, then YTalk will automatically re-ring any user who does not respond to your invitation within 30 seconds. You will not be asked for verification.

If *asides* is turned on (it may not be available), then keyboard input received while the input focus is in a specific users' window will only be sent to that user. See the X11 interface description below.

Any of these options can be set to your preference in your .ytalkrc file, as described below.

YTALK STARTUP FILE

If your home directory contains a file named ".ytalkrc" then YTalk will read this file while starting up. All YTalk runtime options, as well as some startup options, can be set in this file.

SETTING BOOLEAN OPTIONS

Boolean options can be pre-set with the following syntax:

turn *option* [off | on]

where *option* is one of *scrolling*, *word-wrap*, *auto-import*, *auto-invite*, *auto-rering*, *asides*, or *X*. Setting these options works just like described above. Turning *X* on or off will enable or disable the X11 Interface described below. For example, one could enable word-wrap with the line:

turn word-wrap on

SETTING RE-ADDRESS MODES

The purpose of readdressing is to allow Ytalk connections across point-to-point network gateways where the local machines know themselves by a different address (and typically hostname) than the remote machines. The basic syntax of a readdress command is this:

readdress *from-address to-address domain*

The *readdress* statement simply makes a claim that the machine(s) in *domain* communicate with the machine(s) at *from-address* by sending a packet to *to-address*. Since most users have no use for this whatsoever, I'll describe it only briefly.

THIS IS NOT ROUTING. For example, my machine at home is connected via PPP to the network at my office. My machine at home thinks its ethernet address is 192.188.253.1 and its hostname is "talisman.com". The network at my office has the address 192.67.141.0. When I'm connected via PPP, my home machine is placed into the office network as address 192.67.141.9 with hostname "talisman.austin.eds.com".

YTalk needs to know that if it is running on domain 192.67.141.0 and receives packets from 192.188.253.1 that it should respond to 192.67.141.9, not 192.188.253.1. right? right. okay, okay, okay. I put this line into my .ytalkrc on both ends:

readdress talisman talisman.austin.eds.com 192.67.141.0

On my home end, this translates to:

readdress 192.188.253.1 192.67.141.9 192.67.141.0

which tells my home machine to advertise itself as "192.67.141.9" instead of "192.188.253.1" when YTalk-ing to machines on the network "192.67.141.0". On the office end, the readdress command translates to:

readdress 192.67.141.9 192.67.141.9 192.67.141.0

which the office machines basically ignore.

Enough. For more information on how to use this, consult the source code or send me a letter. :-)

X11 INTERFACE

If the DISPLAY environment variable is defined when YTalk starts up, then YTalk will attempt to communicate with that X server. A window will be created for you and each user you are connected to. The X11 Interface can be disabled either by specifying -x on the command line or by putting this line into your .ytalkrc file:

turn X off

A window is created for each individual user in the conversation. If the input focus is in the main window (ie: the one with "ytalk" in the title bar) then anything typed will be sent to all connected users. If the input focus is in one of the users' windows, then anything typed will be sent as an aside to only that user. If the "aside" option is turned off (see above) then ytalk will beep and not accept anything typed when the input focus is not in the main window.

YTalk consults the X11 Resource Database for these user-definable configuration options:

YTalk.display: X server to connect to, defaulting to the DISPLAY environment variable.

YTalk.reverse: reverse black/white pixels.

YTalk.font: font to use, defaulting to "9x15".

YTalk.geometry: window size, defaulting to "80x24".

FUTURE WORK

Work is being done on the following ideas:

1) private conversations which do not get interrupted or transmitted to all YTalk connections,

2) a dedicated YTalk daemon.

FILES

/usr/local/etc/ytalkrc System-wide defaults file.

$HOME/.ytalkrc User's local configuration file. This file overrides options set in the system ytalkrc file.

AUTHOR

Britt Yenne yenne@austin.eds.com

CONTRIBUTORS

Special thanks to Carl Edman for numerous code patches, beta testing, and comments. I think this guy spends as much time on ytalk as I do. Special thanks to Tobias Hahn and Geoff W. for beta testing and suggestions. Thanks to Sitaram Ramaswamy for the original YTalk manpage. Thanks to Magnus Hammerin for Solaris 2.* support. Thanks to Jonas Yngvesson for aside messages in X. Thanks to Andreas Stolcke for fixing the X resource database calls. Thanks to John Vanderpool, Shih-Chen Huang, Andrew Myers, Duncan Sinclair, Evan McLean, and Larry Schwimmer for comments and ideas. The README file shipped with ytalk gives detailed attributions.

BUGS

If you have any ideas, comments, or questions, I'd be happy to hear from you at: ytalk@austin.eds.com

ZDIFF(1)   ZDIFF(1)

NAME

zcmp, zdiff – compare compressed files

SYNOPSIS

zcmp [cmp_options] file1 [file2]
zdiff [diff_options] file1 [file2]

DESCRIPTION

Zcmp and *zdiff* are used to invoke the *cmp* or the *diff* program on compressed files. All options specified are passed directly to *cmp* or *diff*. If only 1 file is specified, then the files compared are *file1* and an uncompressed *file1*.gz. If two files are specified, then they are uncompressed if necessary and fed to *cmp* or *diff*. The exit status from *cmp* or *diff* is preserved.

SEE ALSO

cmp(1), diff(1), zmore(1), zgrep(1), znew(1), zforce(1), gzip(1), gzexe(1)

BUGS

Messages from the *cmp* or *diff* programs refer to temporary filenames instead of those specified.

503

ZFORCE(1)

NAME

zforce – force a '.gz' extension on all gzip files

SYNOPSIS

zforce [name ...]

DESCRIPTION

zforce forces a .gz extension on all *gzip* files so that *gzip* will not compress them twice. This can be useful for files with names truncated after a file transfer. On systems with a 14 char limitation on file names, the original name is truncated to make room for the .gz suffix. For example, 12345678901234 is renamed to 12345678901.gz. A file name such as foo.tgz is left intact.

SEE ALSO

gzip(1), znew(1), zmore(1), zgrep(1), zdiff(1), gzexe(1)

ZGREP(1)

NAME

zgrep – search possibly compressed files for a regular expression

SYNOPSIS

zgrep [grep_options] [*-e*] *pattern filename*...

DESCRIPTION

Zgrep is used to invoke the *grep* on compress'ed or gzip'ed files. All options specified are passed directly to *grep*. If no file is specified, then the standard input is decompressed if necessary and fed to grep. Otherwise the given files are uncompressed if necessary and fed to *grep*.

If *zgrep* is invoked as *zegrep* or *zfgrep* then *egrep* or *fgrep* is used instead of *grep*. If the GREP environment variable is set, *zgrep* uses it as the *grep* program to be invoked. For example:

for sh: GREP=fgrep zgrep string files for csh: (setenv GREP fgrep; zgrep string files)

AUTHOR

Charles Levert (charles@comm.polymtl.ca)

SEE ALSO

grep(1), egrep(1), fgrep(1), zdiff(1), zmore(1), znew(1), zforce(1), gzip(1), gzexe(1)

ZMORE(1)

NAME

zmore – file perusal filter for crt viewing of compressed text

SYNOPSIS

zmore [name ...]

DESCRIPTION

Zmore is a filter which allows examination of compressed or plain text files one screenful at a time on a soft-copy terminal. *zmore* works on files compressed with *compress,* pack or *gzip,* and also on uncompressed files. If a file does not exist, *zmore* looks for a file of the same name with the addition of a .gz, .z or .Z suffix.

Zmore normally pauses after each screenful, printing –More– at the bottom of the screen. If the user then types a carriage return, one more line is displayed. If the user hits a space, another screenful is displayed. Other possibilities are enumerated later.

Zmore looks in the file */etc/termcap* to determine terminal characteristics, and to determine the default window size. On a terminal capable of displaying 24 lines, the default window size is 22 lines. To use a pager other than the default *more,* set environment variable PAGER to the name of the desired program, such as *less.*

Other sequences which may be typed when *zmore* pauses, and their effects, are as follows (*i* is an optional integer argument, defaulting to 1) :

i <space> display *i* more lines, (or another screenful if no argument is given)

^D   display 11 more lines (a "scroll"). If *i* is given, then the scroll size is set to *i* .

d   same as ^D (control-D)

i z   same as typing a space except that *i* , if present, becomes the new window size. Note that the window size reverts back to the default at the end of the current file.

i s   skip *i* lines and print a screenful of lines

i f   skip *i* screenfuls and print a screenful of lines

q or Q   quit reading the current file; go on to the next (if any)

e or q   When the prompt –More–(Next file: *file*) is printed, this command causes zmore to exit.

s   When the prompt –More–(Next file: *file*) is printed, this command causes zmore to skip the next file and continue.

=   Display the current line number.

i /expr   search for the *i* -th occurrence of the regular expression *expr.* If the pattern is not found, *zmore* goes on to the next file (if any). Otherwise, a screenful is displayed, starting two lines before the place where the expression was found. The user's erase and kill characters may be used to edit the regular expression. Erasing back past the first column cancels the search command.

i n   search for the *i* -th occurrence of the last regular expression entered.

!command   invoke a shell with *command* . The character '!' in "command" are replaced with the previous shell command. The sequence "\!" is replaced by "!".

:q or :Q   quit reading the current file; go on to the next (if any) (same as q or Q).

. (dot) repeat the previous command.

The commands take effect immediately, i.e., it is not necessary to type a carriage return. Up to the time when the command character itself is given, the user may hit the line kill character to cancel the numerical argument being formed. In addition, the user may hit the erase character to redisplay the –More– message.

At any time when output is being sent to the terminal, the user can hit the quit key (normally control–\). *Zmore* will stop sending output, and will display the usual –More– prompt. The user may then enter one of the above commands in the normal manner. Unfortunately, some output is lost when this is done, due to the fact that any characters waiting in the terminal's output queue are flushed when the quit signal occurs.

The terminal is set to *noecho* mode by this program so that the output can be continuous. What you type will thus not show on your terminal, except for the / and ! commands.

If the standard output is not a teletype, then *zmore* acts just like *zcat,* except that a header is printed before each file.

FILES

/etc/termcap Terminal data base

SEE ALSO

more(1), gzip(1), zdiff(1), zgrep(1), znew(1), zforce(1), gzexe(1)

Section II
System Calls

INTRO(2) Linux Programmer's Manual INTRO(2)

NAME

intro – Introduction to system calls

DESCRIPTION

This chapter describes the Linux system calls.

Calling Directly

Calling Directly
In most cases, it is unnecessary to invoke a system call directly, but there are times with the Standard C library does not implement a nice function call for you.

Synopsis

Synopsis
#include <linux/unistd.h>

A _syscall macro

desired system call

Setup

Setup
The important thing to know about a system call is its prototype. You need to know how many arguments, their types, and the function return type. There are six macros that make the actual call into the system easier. They have the form:

_syscall$X$(*type,name,type1,arg1,type2,arg2,*...)

> where X is 0..5, which is the number of arguments taken by the system call
>
> *type* is the return type of the system call
>
> *name* is the name of the system call
>
> *typeN* is the Nth argument's type
>
> *argN* is the name of the Nth argument

These macros create a function called *name* with the arguments you specify. Once you include the _syscall() in your source file, you call the system call by *name*.

EXAMPLE

```
#include <stdio.h>
#include <linux/unistd.h> /* for _syscallX macros/related stuff */
#include <linux/kernel.h> /* for struct sysinfo */

_syscall1(int, sysinfo, struct sysinfo *, info);

/* Note: if you copy directly from the nroff source, remember to
REMOVE the extra backslashes in the printf statement. */

int main(void)
{
struct sysinfo s_info;
int error;

error = sysinfo(&s_info);
printf("code error = %d\n", error);
printf("Uptime = %ds\nLoad: 1 min %d / 5 min %d / 15 min %d\n"
"RAM: total %d / free %d / shared %d\n"
"Memory in buffers = %d\nSwap: total %d / free %d\n"
"Number of processes = %d\n",
s_info.uptime, s_info.loads[0],
s_info.loads[1], s_info.loads[2],
```

INTRO(2)

```
   s_info.totalram, s_info.freeram,
   s_info.sharedram, s_info.bufferram,
   s_info.totalswap, s_info.freeswap,
   s_info.procs);
   return(0);
}
```

Sample Output

```
code error = 0
uptime = 502034s
Load: 1 min 13376 / 5 min 5504 / 15 min 1152
RAM: total 15343616 / free 827392 / shared 8237056
Memory in buffers = 5066752
Swap: total 27881472 / free 24698880
Number of processes = 40
```

NOTES

The _syscall() macros DO NOT produce a prototype. You may have to create one, especially for C++ users.

System calls are not required to return only positive or negative error codes. You need to read the source to be sure how it will return errors. Usually, it is the negative of a standard error code, e.g., –**EPERM**. The _syscall() macros will return the result *r* of the system call when *r* is nonnegative, but will return –1 and set the variable *errno* to –*r* when *r* is negative.

Some system calls, such as **mmap**, require more than five arguments. These are handled by pushing the arguments on the stack and passing a pointer to the block of arguments.

When defining a system call, the argument types MUST be passed by-value or by-pointer (for aggregates like structs).

FILES

/usr/include/linux/unistd.h

AUTHORS

Look at the header of the manual page for the author(s) and copyright conditions. Note that these can be different from page to page!

_EXIT(2) Linux Programmer's Manual _EXIT(2)

NAME

_exit – terminate the current process

SYNOPSIS

#include <unistd.h>

void _exit(int *status***);**

DESCRIPTION

_exit terminates the calling process immediately. Any open file descriptors belonging to the process are closed; any children of the process are inherited by process 1, init, and the process's parent is sent a **SIGCHLD** signal.

status is returned to the parent process as the process's exit status, and can be collected using one of the **wait** family of calls.

RETURN VALUE

_exit never returns.

CONFORMING TO

SVID, AT&T, POSIX, X/OPEN, BSD 4.3

NOTES

_exit does not call any functions registered with the ANSI C **atexit** function and does not flush standard I/O buffers. To do these things, use **exit**(3).

SEE ALSO

fork(2), **execve**(2), **waitpid**(2), **wait4**(2), **kill**(2), **wait**(3), **exit**(3)

ACCEPT(2) Linux Programmer's Manual ACCEPT(2)

NAME

accept – accept a connection on a socket

SYNOPSIS

#include <sys/types.h>
#include <sys/socket.h>
int accept(int *s*, struct sockaddr **addr*, int **addrlen*);

DESCRIPTION

The argument *s* is a socket that has been created with **socket**(2), bound to an address with **bind**(2), and is listening for connections after a **listen**(2). The **accept** argument extracts the first connection request on the queue of pending connections, creates a new socket with the same properties of *s* and allocates a new file descriptor for the socket. If no pending connections are present on the queue, and the socket is not marked as non-blocking, **accept** blocks the caller until a connection is present. If the socket is marked non-blocking and no pending connections are present on the queue, **accept** returns an error as described below. The accepted socket may not be used to accept more connections. The original socket *s* remains open.

The argument *addr* is a result parameter that is filled in with the address of the connecting entity, as known to the communications layer. The exact format of the *addr* parameter is determined by the domain in which the communication is occurring. The *addrlen* is a value-result parameter; it should initially contain the amount of space pointed to by *addr*; on return it will contain the actual length (in bytes) of the address returned. This call is used with connection-based socket types, currently with **SOCK_STREAM**.

It is possible to **select**(2) a socket for the purposes of doing an **accept** by selecting it for read.

For certain protocols which require an explicit confirmation, such as **ISO** or **DATAKIT**, **accept** can be thought of as merely dequeuing the next connection request and not implying confirmation. Confirmation can be implied by a normal read or write on the new file descriptor, and rejection can be implied by closing the new socket.

One can obtain user connection request data without confirming the connection by issuing a **recvmsg**(2) call with an *msg_iovlen* of 0 and a non-zero *msg_controllen*, or by issuing a **getsockopt**(2) request. Similarly, one can provide user connection rejection information by issuing a **sendmsg**(2) call with providing only the control information, or by calling **setsockopt**(2).

RETURN VALUES

The call returns –1 on error. If it succeeds, it returns a non-negative integer that is a descriptor for the accepted socket.

ERRORS

EBADF   The descriptor is invalid.

ENOTSOCK The descriptor references a file, not a socket.

EOPNOTSUPP The referenced socket is not of type **SOCK_STREAM**.

EFAULT   The *addr* parameter is not in a writable part of the user address space.

EWOULDBLOCK The socket is marked non-blocking and no connections are present to be accepted.

HISTORY

The **accept** function appeared in BSD 4.2.

SEE ALSO

bind(2), **connect**(2), **listen**(2), **select**(2), **socket**(2)

BSD Man Page   24 July 1993   513

ACCESS(2) Linux Programmer's Manual ACCESS(2)

NAME

access – check user's permissions for a file

SYNOPSIS

#include <unistd.h>
int access(const char *pathname*, **int** *mode*);

DESCRIPTION

access checks whether the process would be allowed to read, write or test for existence of the file (or other file system object) whose name is *pathname*.

mode is a mask consisting of one or more of **R_OK**, **W_OK**, **X_OK** and **F_OK**.

R_OK, **W_OK** and **X_OK** request testing for reading, writing and executing the file, respectively. **F_OK** requests checking whether merely testing for the existence of the file would be allowed (this depends on the permissions of the directories in the path to the file, as given in *pathname*.)

The check is done with the process's *real* uid and gid, rather than with the effective ids as is done when actually attempting an operation. This is to allow set-UID programs to easily determine the invoking user's authority.

Only access bits are checked, not the file type or contents. Therefore, if a directory is found to be "writable," it probably means that files can be created in the directory, and not that the directory can be written as a file. Similarly, a DOS file may be found to be "executable," but the **execve**(2) call will still fail.

RETURN VALUE

On success, zero is returned. On error, −1 is returned, and *errno* is set appropriately.

ERRORS

EACCES The requested access would be denied, either to the file itself or one of the directories in *pathname*.

EFAULT *pathname* points outside your accessible address space.

EINVAL *mode* was incorrectly specified.

ENAMETOOLONG *pathname* is too long.

ENOENT A directory component in *pathname* would have been accessible but does not exist or was a dangling symbolic link.

ENOTDIR A component used as a directory in *pathname* is not, in fact, a directory.

ENOMEM Insufficient kernel memory was available.

ELOOP *pathname* contains a reference to a circular symbolic link, i.e., a symbolic link containing a reference to itself.

CONFORMING TO

SVID, AT&T, POSIX, X/OPEN, BSD 4.3

SEE ALSO

stat(2), **open**(2), **chmod**(2), **chown**(2), **setuid**(2), **setgid**(2).

NAME

acct – switch process accounting on or off

SYNOPSIS

#include <unistd.h>
int acct(const char **filename***);**

DESCRIPTION

WARNING: Since this function is not implemented as of Linux 0.99.11, it will always return −1 and set *errno* to **ENOSYS**. If acctkit is installed the function performs 'as advertised'.

When called with the name of an existing file as argument, accounting is turned on, records for each terminating process are appended to *filename* as it terminates. An argument of **NULL** causes accounting to be turned off.

RETURN VALUE

On success, zero is returned. On error, −1 is returned, and *errno* is set appropriately.

NOTES

No accounting is produced for programs running when a crash occurs. In particular, nonterminating processes are never accounted for.

SEE ALSO

acct(5)

ADJTIMEX(2)

NAME

adjtimex – tune kernel clock

SYNOPSIS

#include <sys/timex.h>

int adjtimex(struct timex *buf***);**

DESCRIPTION

Linux uses David Mill's clock adjustment algorithm. **adjtimex** reads and optionally sets adjustment parameters for this algorithm.

adjtimex takes a pointer to a *timex* structure, updates kernel parameters from field values, and returns the same structure with current kernel values. This structure is declared as follows:

```
struct timex
{
int mode; /* mode selector */
long offset; /* time offset (usec) */
long frequency; /* frequency offset (scaled ppm) */
long maxerror; /* maximum error (usec) */
long esterror; /* estimated error (usec) */
int status; /* clock command/status */
long time_constant; /* pll time constant */
long precision; /* clock precision (usec) (read only) */
long tolerance; /* clock frequency tolerance (ppm)
(read only) */
struct timeval time; /* (read only) */
long tick; /* usecs between clock ticks */
};
```

The *mode* field determines which parameters, if any, to set. It may contain a bitwise-*or* combination of zero or more of the following bits:

```
#define ADJ_OFFSET 0x0001 /* time offset */
#define ADJ_FREQUENCY 0x0002 /* frequency offset */
#define ADJ_MAXERROR 0x0004 /* maximum time error */
#define ADJ_ESTERROR 0x0008 /* estimated time error */
#define ADJ_STATUS 0x0010 /* clock status */
#define ADJ_TIMECONST 0x0020 /* pll time constant */
#define ADJ_TICK 0x4000 /* tick value */
#define ADJ_OFFSET_SINGLESHOT 0x8001 /* old-fashioned adjtime */
```

Ordinary users are restricted to a zero value for *mode*. Only the superuser may set any parameters.

RETURN VALUE

On success, **adjtimex** returns the value of *buf.status*:

```
#define TIME_OK 0 /* clock synchronized */
#define TIME_INS 1 /* insert leap second */
#define TIME_DEL 2 /* delete leap second */
#define TIME_OOP 3 /* leap second in progress */
#define TIME_BAD 4 /* clock not synchronized */
```

On failure, **adjtimex** returns –1 and sets *errno*.

ERRORS

	EFAULT	*buf* does not point to writeable memory.
	EPERM	*buf.mode* is non-zero and the user is not super-user.

EINVAL An attempt is made to set *buf.offset* to a value outside the range −131071 to +131071, or to set *buf.status* to a value other than those listed above, or to set *buf.tick* to a value outside the range 900000/**HZ** to 1100000/**HZ**, where **HZ** is the system timer interrupt frequency.

SEE ALSO
settimeofday(2).

ALARM(2)

NAME

alarm – set an alarm clock for delivery of a signal

SYNOPSIS

#include <unistd.h>
long alarm(long *seconds***);**

DESCRIPTION

alarm arranges for a **SIGALRM** signal to be delivered to the process in *seconds* seconds.

If *seconds* is zero, no new **alarm** is scheduled.

In any event any previously set **alarm** is cancelled.

RETURN VALUE

alarm returns the number of seconds remaining until any previously scheduled alarm was due to be delivered, or zero if there was no previously scheduled alarm.

NOTES

alarm and **setitimer** share the same timer; calls to one will interfere with use of the other.

Scheduling delays can, as ever, cause the execution of the process to be delayed by an arbitrary amount of time.

CONFORMING TO

SVID, AT&T, POSIX, X/OPEN, BSD 4.3

SEE ALSO

setitimer(2), **signal**(2), **sigaction**(2), **gettimeofday**(2), **select**(2), **pause**(2), **sleep**(3)

NAME

bdflush – start, flush, or tune buffer-dirty-flush daemon

SYNOPSIS

int bdflush(int *func,* **long** **address);*
int bdflush(int *func,* **long** *data);*

DESCRIPTION

bdflush starts, flushes, or tunes the buffer-dirty-flush daemon. Only the super-user may call **bdflush**.

If *func* is negative or 0, and no daemon has been started, then **bdflush** enters the daemon code and never returns.

If *func* is 1, some dirty buffers are written to disk.

If *func* is 2 or more and is even (low bit is 0), then *address* is the address of a long word, and the tuning parameter numbered (*func*–2)/2 is returned to the caller in that address.

If *func* is 3 or more and is odd (low bit is 1), then *data* is a long word, and the kernel sets tuning parameter numbered (*func*–3)/2 to that value.

The set of parameters, their values, and their legal ranges are defined in the kernel source file *fs/buffer.c*.

RETURN VALUE

If *func* is negative or 0 and the daemon successfully starts, **bdflush** never returns. Otherwise, the return value is 0 on success and –1 on failure, with *errno* set to indicate the error.

ERRORS

EPERM   Caller is not super-user.

EFAULT *address* points outside your accessible address space.

EBUSY   An attempt was made to enter the daemon code after another process has already entered.

EINVAL An attempt was made to read or write an invalid parameter number, or to write an invalid value to a parameter.

SEE ALSO

fsync(2), sync(2), update(8), sync(8)

BIND(2)

NAME

bind – bind a name to a socket

SYNOPSIS

#include <sys/types.h>
#include <sys/socket.h>

int bind(int *sockfd*, **struct sockaddr** **my_addr*, **int** *addrlen*);

DESCRIPTION

bind gives the socket, *sockfd*, the local address *my_addr*. *my_addr* is *addrlen* bytes long. Traditionally, this is called "assigning a name to a socket" (when a socket is created with **socket**(2), it exists in a name space (address family) but has no name assigned.)

NOTES

Binding a name in the UNIX domain creates a socket in the file system that must be deleted by the caller when it is no longer needed (using **unlink**(2)).

The rules used in name binding vary between communication domains. Consult the manual entries in section 4 for detailed information.

RETURN VALUE

On success, zero is returned. On error, −1 is returned, and *errno* is set appropriately.

ERRORS

EBADF   *sockfd* is not a valid descriptor.

EINVAL   The socket is already bound to an address. This may change in the future: see *linux/unix/sock.c* for details.

EACCES   The address is protected, and the user is not the super-user.

The following errors are specific to UNIX domain (AF_UNIX) sockets:

EINVAL   The *addr_len* was wrong, or the socket was not in the **AF_UNIX** family.

EROFS   The socket inode would reside on a read-only file system.

EFAULT   *my_addr* points outside your accessible address space.

ENAMETOOLONG   *my_addr* is too long.

ENOENT   The file does not exist.

ENOMEM   Insufficient kernel memory was available.

ENOTDIR   A component of the path prefix is not a directory.

EACCES   Search permission is denied on a component of the path prefix.

ELOOP   *my_addr* contains a circular reference (i.e., via a symbolic link)

HISTORY

The **bind** function call appeared in BSD 4.2.

SEE ALSO

accept(2), **connect**(2), **listen**(2), **socket**(2), **getsockname**(2)

BRK(2)

NAME

brk, sbrk – change data segment size

SYNOPSIS

#include <unistd.h>

int brk(void **end_data_segment***);**
void *sbrk(ptrdiff_t*increment***);**

DESCRIPTION

brk sets the end of the data segment to the value specified by *end_data_segment*. *end_datasegment* must be greater than end of the text segment and it must be 16kB before the end of the stack.

sbrk increments the program's data space by *increment* bytes. **sbrk** isn't a system call, it is just a C library wrapper.

RETURN VALUE

On success, **brk** returns zero, and **sbrk** returns a pointer to the start of the new area. On error, −1 is returned, and *errno* is set to **ENOMEM**.

CONFORMING TO

BSD 4.3

brk and **sbrk** are not defined in the C Standard and are deliberately excluded from the POSIX.1 standard (see paragraphs B.1.1.1.3 and B.8.3.3).

SEE ALSO

execve(2), **getrlimit**(2), **malloc**(3), **end**(3)

CHDIR(2)   Linux Programmer's Manual   CHDIR(2)

NAME

chdir, fchdir – change working directory

SYNOPSIS

#include <unistd.h>

int chdir(const char **path***);**
int fchdir(int *fd***);**

DESCRIPTION

chdir changes the current directory to that specified in *path*.

fchdir is identical to **chdir**, only that the directory is given as an open file descriptor.

RETURN VALUE

On success, zero is returned. On error, −1 is returned, and *errno* is set appropriately.

ERRORS

Depending on the file system, other errors can be returned. The more general errors are listed below:

EPERM   The process does not have execute permission on the directory.

EFAULT   *path* points outside your accessible address space.

ENAMETOOLONG   *path* is too long.

EBADF   The *fd* is not a valid file descriptor.

ENOENT   The file does not exist.

ENOMEM   Insufficient kernel memory was available.

ENOTDIR   A component of the path prefix is not a directory.

EACCES   Search permission is denied on a component of the path prefix.

ELOOP   *path* contains a circular reference (i.e., via a symbolic link)

SEE ALSO

getcwd(3), **chroot**(2)

CHMOD(2)

NAME

chmod, fchmod – change permissions of a file

SYNOPSIS

#include <sys/types.h>
#include <sys/stat.h>

int chmod(const char **path*, **mode_t** *mode***);**
int fchmod(int *fildes*, **mode_t** *mode***);**

DESCRIPTION

The mode of the file given by *path* or referenced by *filedes* is changed.

Modes are specified by *or'ing* the following:

S_ISUID	04000	set user ID on execution
S_ISGID	02000	set group ID on execution
S_ISVTX	01000	sticky bit
S_IRUSR (S_IREAD)	00400	read by owner
S_IWUSR (S_IWRITE)	00200	write by owner
S_IXUSR (S_IEXEC)	00100	execute/search by owner
S_IRGRP	00040	read by group
S_IWGRP	00020	write by group
S_IXGRP	00010	execute/search by group
S_IROTH	00004	read by others
S_IWOTH	00002	write by others
S_IXOTH	00001	execute/search by others

The effective UID of the process must be zero or must match the owner of the file.

The effective UID or GID must be appropriate for setting execution bits.

Depending on the file system, set user ID and set group ID execution bits may be turned off if a file is written. On some file systems, only the super-user can set the sticky bit, which may have a special meaning (i.e., for directories, a file can only be deleted by the owner or the super-user).

RETURN VALUE

On success, zero is returned. On error, −1 is returned, and *errno* is set appropriately.

ERRORS

Depending on the file system, other errors can be returned. The more general errors for **chmod** are listed below:

EPERM   The effective UID does not match the owner of the file, and is not zero.

EROFS   The named file resides on a read-only file system.

EFAULT   *path* points outside your accessible address space.

ENAMETOOLONG   *path* is too long.

ENOENT   The file does not exist.

ENOMEM   Insufficient kernel memory was available.

ENOTDIR   A component of the path prefix is not a directory.

EACCES	Search permission is denied on a component of the path prefix.
ELOOP	*path* contains a circular reference (i.e., via a symbolic link)

The general errors for **fchmod** are listed below:

EBADF	The descriptor is not value.
ENOENT	See above.
EPERM	See above.
EROFS	See above.

SEE ALSO
open(2), chown(2), stat(2)

CHOWN(2)

NAME

chown, fchown – change ownership of a file

SYNOPSIS

#include <sys/types.h>
#include <unistd.h>

int chown(const char **path*, **uid_t** *owner*, **gid_t** *group*)**;**
int fchown(int *fd*, **uid_t** *owner*, **gid_t** *group*)**;**

DESCRIPTION

The owner of the file specified by *path* or by *fd* is changed. Only the super-user may change the owner of a file. The owner of a file may change the group of the file to any group of which that owner is a member. The super-user may change the group arbitrarily.

If the *owner* or *group* is specified as −1, then that ID is not changed.

RETURN VALUE

On success, zero is returned. On error, −1 is returned, and *errno* is set appropriately.

ERRORS

Depending on the file system, other errors can be returned. The more general errors for **chown** are listed below:

EPERM	The effective UID does not match the owner of the file, and is not zero; or the *owner* or *group* were specified incorrectly.
EROFS	The named file resides on a read-only file system.
EFAULT	*path* points outside your accessible address space.
ENAMETOOLONG	*path* is too long.
ENOENT	The file does not exist.
ENOMEM	Insufficient kernel memory was available.
ENOTDIR	A component of the path prefix is not a directory.
EACCES	Search permission is denied on a component of the path prefix.
ELOOP	*path* contains a circular reference (i.e., via a symbolic link)

The general errors for **fchown** are listed below:

EBADF	The descriptor is not value.
ENOENT	See above.
EPERM	See above.
EROFS	See above.

NOTES

The prototype for **fchown** is only available if __USE_BSD is defined.

SEE ALSO

chmod(2), **flock**(2)

CHROOT(2)

NAME

chroot – change root directory

SYNOPSIS

#include <unistd.h>

int chroot(const char **path***);**

DESCRIPTION

chroot changes the root directory to that specified in *path*. This directory will be used for path name beginning with /. The root directory is inherited by all children of the current process.

Only the super-user may change the root directory.

RETURN VALUE

On success, zero is returned. On error, –1 is returned, and *errno* is set appropriately.

ERRORS

Depending on the file system, other errors can be returned. The more general errors are listed below:

EPERM The effective UID does not match the owner of the file, and is not zero; or the *owner* or *group* were specified incorrectly.

EROFS The named file resides on a read-only file system.

EFAULT *path* points outside your accessible address space.

ENAMETOOLONG *path* is too long.

ENOENT The file does not exist.

ENOMEM Insufficient kernel memory was available.

ENOTDIR A component of the path prefix is not a directory.

EACCES Search permission is denied on a component of the path prefix.

ELOOP *path* contains a circular reference (i.e., via a symbolic link)

SEE ALSO

chdir(2)

CLONE(2) Linux Programmer's Manual CLONE(2)

NAME

clone – create a child process

SYNOPSIS

#include <linux/sched.h>
#include <linux/unistd.h>

pid_t clone(void **sp***, unsigned long** *flags***)**

DESCRIPTION

clone is an alternate interface to **fork**, with more options. **fork** is equivalent to **clone(0, SIGCLD|COPYVM)**.

If *sp* is non-zero, the child process uses *sp* as its initial stack pointer.

The low byte of *flags* contains the signal sent to the parent when the child dies. *flags* may also be bitwise-or'ed with either or both of **COPYVM** or **COPYFD**.

If **COPYVM** is set, child pages are copy-on-write images of the parent pages. If **COPYVM** is not set, the child process shares the same pages as the parent, and both parent and child may write on the same data.

If **COPYFD** is set, the child's file descriptors are copies of the parent's file descriptors. If **COPYFD** is not set, the child's file descriptors are shared with the parent.

RETURN VALUE

On success, the PID of the child process is returned in the parent's thread of execution, and a 0 is returned in the child's thread of execution. On failure, a –1 will be returned in the parent's context, no child process will be created, and *errno* will be set appropriately.

ERRORS

ENOSYS **clone** will always return this error, unless your kernel was compiled with **CLONE_ACTUALLY_WORKS_OK** defined.

EAGAIN **fork** cannot allocate sufficient memory to copy the parent's page tables and allocate a task structure for the child.

BUGS

By default, **CLONE_ACTUALLY_WORKS_OK** is not defined.
There is no entry for **clone** in **/lib/libc.so.4.5.26**.
Comments in the kernel as of 1.1.46 indicate that it mis-handles the case where **COPYVM** is not set.

SEE ALSO

fork(2)

CLOSE(2)

NAME

close – close a file descriptor

SYNOPSIS

#include <unistd.h>
int close(int *fd***);**

DESCRIPTION

close closes a file descriptor, so that it no longer refers to any file and may be reused.

If *fd* is the last copy of a particular file descriptor the resources associated with it are freed; for example any locks held are removed and if the descriptor was the last reference to a file which has been removed using **unlink** the file is deleted.

RETURN VALUE

close returns zero on success, or −1 if an error occurred.

ERRORS

EBADF   *fd* isn't a valid open file descriptor.

CONFORMING TO

SVID, AT&T, POSIX, X/OPEN, BSD 4.3

NOTES

Not checking the return value of close is a common but nevertheless serious programming error. File system implementations which use techniques as "write-behind" to increase performance may lead to *write*(2) succeeding, although the data has not been written yet. The error status may be reported at a later write operation, but it is guaranteed to be reported on closing the file. Not checking the return value when closing the file may lead to silent loss of data. This can especially be observed with NFS and disk quotas.

SEE ALSO

open(2), **fcntl**(2), **shutdown**(2), **unlink**(2), **fclose**(3).

CONNECT(2)

NAME

connect – initiate a connection on a socket

SYNOPSIS

#include <sys/types.h>
#include <sys/socket.h>

int connect(int *sockfd*, **struct sockaddr** *****serv_addr*, **int** *addrlen*)**;**

DESCRIPTION

The parameter *sockfd* is a socket. If it is of type **SOCK_DGRAM**, this call specifies the peer with which the socket is to be associated; this address is that to which datagrams are to be sent, and the only address from which datagrams are to be received. If the socket is of type **SOCK_STREAM** , this call attempts to make a connection to another socket. The other socket is specified by **serv_addr**, which is an address in the communications space of the socket. Each communications space interprets the **serv_addr**, parameter in its own way. Generally, stream sockets may successfully **connect** only once; datagram sockets may use **connect** multiple times to change their association. Datagram sockets may dissolve the association by connecting to an invalid address, such as a null address.

RETURN VALUE

If the connection or binding succeeds, zero is returned. On error, –1 is returned, and *errno* is set appropriately.

ERRORS

See the Linux kernel source code for details.

HISTORY

The **connect** function call first appeared in BSD 4.2.

SEE ALSO

accept(2), **bind**(2), **listen**(2), **socket**(2), **getsockname**(2)

DUP(2)

NAME

dup, dup2 – duplicate a file descriptor

SYNOPSIS

#include <unistd.h>
int dup(int *oldfd***);**
int dup2(int *oldfd***, int** *newfd***);**

DESCRIPTION

dup and **dup2** create a copy of the file descriptor *oldfd*.

The old and new descriptors may be used interchangeably. They share locks, file position pointers and flags; for example, if the file position is modified by using **lseek** on one of the descriptors, the position is also changed for the other.

The two descriptors do not share the close-on-exec flag, however.

dup uses the lowest-numbered unused descriptor for the new descriptor.

dup2 makes *newfd* be the copy of *oldfd*, closing *newfd* first if necessary.

RETURN VALUE

dup and **dup2** return the new descriptor, or −1 if an error occurred (in which case, *errno* is set appropriately).

ERRORS

EBADF   *oldfd* isn't an open file descriptor, or *newfd* is out of the allowed range for file descriptors.

EMFILE The process already has the maximum number of file descriptors open and tried to open a new one.

WARNING

The error returned by **dup2** is different to that returned by **fcntl**(...,**F_DUPFD**,...) when *newfd* is out of range. On some systems **dup2** also sometimes returns **EINVAL** like **F_DUPFD**.

CONFORMING TO

SVID, AT&T, POSIX, X/OPEN, BSD 4.3

SEE ALSO

fcntl (2), **open** (2), **close** (2).

NAME

execve – execute program

SYNOPSIS

#include <unistd.h>

int execve (const char *filename***, const char** *argv* **[], const char** *envp***[]);**

DESCRIPTION

execve() executes the program pointed to by *filename*. *filename* must be either a binary executable, or a shell script starting with a line of the form "*#! interpreter* [arg]".

execve() does not return on success, and the text, data, bss, and stack of the calling process are overwritten by that of the program loaded. The program invoked inherits the calling process's PID, and any open file descriptors that are not set to close on exec. Signals pending on the parent process are cleared.

If the current program is being ptraced, a **SIGTRAP** is sent to it after a successful **execve()**.

RETURN VALUE

On success, **execve()** does not return, on error −1 is returned, and *errno* is set appropriately.

ERRORS

EACCES	The file is not a regular file.
EACCES	Execute permission is denied for the file.
EPERM	The file system is mounted *noexec*.
EPERM	The file system is mounted *nosuid* and the file has an SUID or SGID bit set.
E2BIG	The argument list is too big.
ENOEXEC	The magic number in the file is incorrect.
EFAULT	*filename* points outside your accessible address space.
ENAMETOOLONG	*filename* is too long.
ENOENT	The file does not exist.
ENOMEM	Insufficient kernel memory was available.
ENOTDIR	A component of the path prefix is not a directory.
EACCES	Search permission is denied on a component of the path prefix.
ELOOP	*filename* contains a circular reference (i.e., via a symbolic link)

CONFORMING TO

SVID, AT&T, POSIX, X/OPEN, BSD 4.3

NOTES

SUID and SGID processes can not be **ptrace()**'d SUID or SGID.

A maximum line length of 127 characters is allowed for the first line in a #! executable shell script. This may be circumvented by changing the max size of buf, in which case you will become bound by the 1024 byte size of a buffer, which is not easily worked around.

SEE ALSO

execl(3), **fork**(2)

FCNTL(2)

NAME
fcntl – manipulate file descriptor

SYNOPSIS
#include <unistd.h>
#include <fcntl.h>
int fcntl(int *fd*, **int** *cmd***);**
int fcntl(int *fd*, **int** *cmd*, **long** *arg***);**

DESCRIPTION
fcntl performs one of various miscellaneous operations on *fd*. The operation in question is determined by *cmd*:

F_DUPFD   Makes *arg* be a copy of *fd*, closing *fd* first if necessary.
           The same functionality can be more easily achieved by using **dup2**.
           The old and new descriptors may be used interchangeably. They share locks, file position pointers and flags; for example, if the file position is modified by using **lseek** on one of the descriptors, the position is also changed for the other.
           The two descriptors do not share the close-on-exec flag, however.
           On success, the new descriptor is returned.

F_GETFD   Read the close-on-exec flag. If the low-order bit is 0, the file will remain open across **exec**, otherwise it will be closed.

F_SETFD   Set the close-on-exec flag to the value specified by *arg* (only the least significant bit is used).

F_GETFL   Read the descriptor's flags (all flags (as set by **open**(2)) are returned).

F_SETFL   Set the descriptor's flags to the value specified by *arg*. Only **O_APPEND** and **O_NONBLOCK** may be set.
           The flags are shared between copies (made with **dup** etc.) of the same file descriptor. The flags are shared between copies (made with **dup** etc.) of the same file descriptor.
           The flags and their semantics are described in **open**(2).

F_GETLK, F_SETLK, and F_SETLKW   Manage discretionary file locks.

F_GETOWN   Get the process ID (or process group) of the owner of a socket.
           Process groups are returned as negative values.

F_SETOWN   Set the process or process group that owns a socket.
           For these commands, ownership means receiving **SIGIO** or **SIGURG** signals.
           Process groups are specified using negative values.

RETURN VALUE
The return value depends on the operation:

F_DUPFD   The new descriptor.
F_GETFD   Value of flag.
F_GETFL   Value of flags.
F_GETOWN   Value of descriptor owner.

On error, −1 is returned, and *errno* is set appropriately.

ERRORS

EBADF   *fs* is not an open file descriptor.

EINVAL   For **F_DUPFD**, *arg* is negative or is greater than the maximum allowable value.

EINVAL   For **F_DUPFD**, the process already has the maximum number of file descriptors open.

NOTES

The errors returned by **dup2** are different from those returned by **F_DUPFD**.

CONFORMING TO

SVID, AT&T, POSIX, X/OPEN, BSD 4.3

SEE ALSO

open(2), F_DUPFD(2), F_GETFD(2), F_GETFL(2), F_GETLK(2), socket(2).

FLOCK(2)

NAME

flock – apply or remove an advisory lock on an open file

SYNOPSIS

#include <sys/file.h>

int flock(int fd**, int** operation**)**

DESCRIPTION

Apply or remove an advisory lock on an open file. The file is specified by *fd*. Valid operations are given below:

- **LOCK_SH** Shared lock. More than one process may hold a shared lock for a given file at a given time.
- **LOCK_EX** Exclusive lock. Only one process may hold an exclusive lock for a given file at a given time.
- **LOCK_UN** Unlock.
- **LOCK_NB** Don't block when locking. May be specified (by *or*'ing) along with one of the other operations.

  A single file may not simultaneously have both shared and exclusive locks.

  A file is locked (i.e., the inode), *not* the file descriptor. So, **dup**(2) and **fork**(2) do not create multiple instances of a lock.

RETURN VALUE

On success, zero is returned. On error, –1 is returned, and *errno* is set appropriately.

ERRORS

EWOULDBLOCK   The file is locked an the **LOCK_NB** flag was selected.

NOTES

Under Linux, **flock** is implemented as a call to **fcntl**. Please see **fcntl**(2) for more details on errors.

SEE ALSO

open(2), **close**(2), **dup**(2), **execve**(2), **fcntl**(2), **fork**(2),

FORK(2)

NAME

fork, vfork – create a child process

SYNOPSIS

#include <unistd.h>

pid_t fork(void);
pid_t vfork(void);

DESCRIPTION

fork creates a child process that differs from the parent process only in its PID and PPID, and in the fact that resource utilizations are set to 0. File locks and pending signals are not inherited.

Under Linux, **fork** is implemented using copy-on-write pages, so the only penalty incurred by fork is the time and memory required to duplicate the parent's page tables, and to create a unique task structure for the child.

RETURN VALUE

On success, the PID of the child process is returned in the parent's thread of execution, and a 0 is returned in the child's thread of execution. On failure, a –1 will be returned in the parent's context, no child process will be created, and *errno* will be set appropriately.

ERRORS

EAGAIN   **fork** cannot allocate sufficient memory to copy the parent's page tables and allocate a task structure for the child.

BUGS

Under Linux, **vfork** is merely an alias for **fork**.
fork does never return the error **ENOMEM**.

CONFORMING TO

SVID, AT&T, POSIX, X/OPEN, BSD 4.3

SEE ALSO

clone(2), **execve**(2), **wait**(2)

NAME

fsync – synchronize a file's in-core state with that on disk

SYNOPSIS

#include <unistd.h>

int fsync(int *fd***);**

DESCRIPTION

fsync copies all in-core parts of a file to disk.

RETURN VALUE

On success, zero is returned. On error, −1 is returned, and *errno* is set appropriately.

ERRORS

EBADF   fd is not a valid open file descriptor.

EROFS   **EINVAL fd** is bound to a special file which doesn't support synchronization.

EIO   An error occurred during synchronization.

SEE ALSO

bdflush(2), **fsync**(2), **update**(8), **sync**(8)

GETDENTS(2)

NAME
getdents – get directory entries

SYNOPSIS
#include <unistd.h>
#include <linux/dirent.h>
#include <linux/unistd.h>
_syscall3(int, getdents, uint, fd, struct dirent *, dirp, uint, count);
int getdents(unsigned int *fd***, struct dirent *** *dirp***, unsigned int** *count***);**

DESCRIPTION
getdents reads several *dirent* structures from the directory pointed at by *fd* into the memory area pointed to by *dirp*. The parameter *count* is the size of the memory area.

The *dirent* structure is declared as follows:

struct dirent
{
long d_ino; /* inode number */
off_t d_off; /* offset to next *dirent* */
unsigned short d_reclen; /* length of this *dirent* */
char d_name [NAME_MAX+1]; /* file name (null-terminated) */
}

d_ino is an inode number. *d_off* is the distance from the start of the directory to the start of the next *dirent*. *d_reclen* is the size of this entire *dirent*. *d_name* is a null-terminated file name.

This call supersedes **readdir**(2).

RETURN VALUE
On success, the number of bytes read is returned. On end of directory, 0 is returned. On error, −1 is returned, and *errno* is set appropriately.

ERRORS
> **EBADF** Invalid file descriptor *fd*.
>
> **ENOTDIR** File descriptor does not refer to a directory.

SEE ALSO
readdir(2), **readdir**(3)

GETDOMAINNAME(2) Linux Programmer's Manual GETDOMAINNAME(2)

NAME
getdomainname, setdomainname – get/set domain name

SYNOPSIS
#include <unistd.h>

int getdomainname(char **name***, size_t** *len***);**
int setdomainname(const char **name***, size_t** *len***);**

DESCRIPTION
These functions are used to access or to change the domain name of the current processor.

RETURN VALUE
On success, zero is returned. On error, −1 is returned, and *errno* is set appropriately.

ERRORS
    EINVAL   For **getdomainname**, *name* points to **NULL** or *name* is longer than *len*.

    EPERM   For **setdomainname**, the caller was not the superuser.

    EINVAL   For **setdomainname**, *len* was too long.

CONFORMING TO
POSIX does not specify these calls.

BUGS
getdomainname is not compliant with other implementations, since they always return *len* bytes, even if *name* is longer. Linux, however, returns **EINVAL** in this case (as of DLL 4.4.1 libraries).

NOTES
Under Linux, **getdomainname** is implemented at the library level by calling **uname**(2).

SEE ALSO
gethostname(2), **sethostname**(2), **uname**(2)

GETDTABLESIZE(2)   Linux Programmer's Manual   GETDTABLESIZE(2)

NAME
getdtablesize – get descriptor table size

SYNOPSIS
#include <unistd.h>

int getdtablesize(void);

DESCRIPTION
getdtablesize returns the maximum number of files a process can have open.

NOTES
getdtablesize is implemented as a library function in DLL 4.4.1. This function returns **OPEN_MAX** (set to 256 in Linux 0.99.11) if **OPEN_MAX** was defined when the library was compiled. Otherwise, −1 is returned, and *errno* is set to **ENOSYS**.

SEE ALSO
close(2), **dup**(2), **open**(2)

NAME

getgid, getegid – get group identity

SYNOPSIS

#include <unistd.h>

gid_t getgid(void);
gid_t getegid(void);

DESCRIPTION

getgid returns the real group ID of the current process.

getegid returns the effective group ID of the current process.

The real ID corresponds to the ID of the calling process. The effective ID corresponds to the set ID bit on the file being executed.

ERRORS

These functions are always successful.

CONFORMS TO

POSIX, BSD 4.3

SEE ALSO

setregid(2), **setgid**(2)

NAME

getgroups, setgroups – get/set group access list

SYNOPSIS

#include <unistd.h>

int getgroups(int *size*, **gid_t** *list*[]**);**

#define _USE_BSD
#include <grp.h>

int setgroups(size_t *size*, **const gid_t** **list***);**

DESCRIPTION

getgroups	Up to *size* supplemental groups are returned in *list*. If *size* is zero, *list* is not modified, but the total number of supplemental groups for the process is returned.
setgroups	Sets the supplemental groups for the process. Only the super-user may use this function.

RETURN VALUE

getgroups	On success, the number of groups stored in *list* is returned (if *size* is zero, however, the number of supplemental group IDs associated with the process is returned). On error, –1 is returned, and *errno* is set appropriately.
setgroups	On success, zero is returned. On error, –1 is returned, and *errno* is set appropriately.

ERRORS

EFAULT	*list* has an invalid address.
EPERM	For **setgroups**, the user is not the super-user.
EINVAL	For **setgroups**, *gidsetsize* is greater than **NGROUPS** (32 for Linux 0.99.11).

CONFORMING TO

getgroups conforms to POSIX.1 (and is present in BSD 4.3). Since **setgroups** requires privilege, it is not covered under POSIX.1.

BUGS

The _USE_BSD flag probably shouldn't be required for **setgroups**.

SEE ALSO

initgroups(3),

NAME

gethostid, sethostid – get or set the unique identifier of the current host

SYNOPSIS

#include <unistd.h>

long int gethostid(void);
int sethostid(long int hostid);

DESCRIPTION

Get or set a unique 32-bit identifier for the current machine. The 32-bit identifier is intended to be unique among all UNIX systems in existence. This normally resembles the Internet address for the local machine, as returned by **gethostbyname**(3), and thus usually never needs to be set.

The **sethostid** call is restricted to the superuser.

The *hostid* argument is stored in the file */etc/hostid*.

RETURN VALUES

gethostid returns the 32-bit identifier for the current host as set by **sethostid**(2).

CONFORMING TO

POSIX.1 does not define these functions, but ISO/IEC 9945-1:1990 mentions them in B.4.4.1.

FILES

/etc/hostid

SEE ALSO

hostid(1), **gethostbyname**(3)

NAME

gethostname, sethostname – get/set host name

SYNOPSIS

#include <unistd.h>

int gethostname(char *name*, **size_t** *len*);
int sethostname(const char *name*, **size_t** *len*);

DESCRIPTION

These functions are used to access or to change the host name of the current processor.

RETURN VALUE

On success, zero is returned. On error, –1 is returned, and *errno* is set appropriately.

ERRORS

EINVAL   *len* is negative or, for **sethostname**, *len* is larger than the maximum allowed size, or, for **gethostname** on Linux/i386, *len* is smaller than the actual size.

EPERM   For **sethostname**, the caller was not the superuser.

EFAULT   *name* is an invalid address.

CONFORMING TO

POSIX.1 does not define these functions, but ISO/IEC 9945-1:1990 mentions them in B.4.4.1.

BUGS

Some other implementations of **gethostname** successfully return *len* bytes even if *name* is longer. Linux/Alpha complies with this behaviour. Linux/i386, however, returns **EINVAL** in this case (as of DLL 4.6.27 libraries).

NOTES

Under Linux/Alpha, **gethostname** is a system call. Under Linux/i386, **gethostname** is implemented at the library level by calling **uname**(2).

SEE ALSO

getdomainname(2), setdomainname(2), uname(2)

NAME

getitimer, setitimer – get or set value of an interval timer

SYNOPSIS

#include <sys/time.h>

int getitimer(int *which*, struct itimerval **value*); int setitimer(int *which*, const struct itimerval **value*, struct itimerval **ovalue*);

DESCRIPTION

The system provides each process with three interval timers, each decrementing in a distinct time domain. When any timer expires, a signal is sent to the process, and the timer (potentially) restarts.

> ITIMER_REAL   decrements in real time, and delivers **SIGALRM** upon expiration.
>
> ITIMER_VIRTUAL decrements only when the process is executing, and delivers **SIGVTALRM** upon expiration.
>
> ITIMER_PROF   decrements both when the process executes and when the system is executing on behalf of the process. Coupled with **ITIMER_VIRTUAL**, this timer is usually used to profile the time spent by the application in user and kernel space. **SIGPROF** is delivered upon expiration.

Timer values are defined by the following structures:

```
struct itimerval {
struct timeval it_interval; /* next value */
struct timeval it_value; /* current value */
};
struct timeval {
long tv_sec; /* seconds */
long tv_usec; /* microseconds */
};
```

Getitimer(2) fills the structure indicated by *value* with the current setting for the timer indicated by *which* (one of **ITIMER_REAL**, **ITIMER_VIRTUAL**, or **ITIMER_PROF**). The element **it_value** is set to the amount of time remaining on the timer, or zero if the timer is disabled. Similarly, **it_interval** is set to the reset value. **Setitimer**(2) sets the indicated timer to the value in *value*. If *ovalue* is nonzero, the old value of the timer is stored there.

Timers decrement from *it_value* to zero, generate a signal, and reset to *it_interval*. A timer which is set to zero (*it_value* is zero or the timer expires and *it_interval* is zero) stops.

Both *tv_sec* and *tv_usec* are significant in determining the duration of a timer.

Timers will never expire before the requested time, instead expiring some short, constant time afterwards, dependent on the system timer resolution (currently 10ms). Upon expiration, a signal will be generated and the timer reset. If the timer expires while the process is active (always true for **ITIMER_VIRT**) the signal will be delivered immediately when generated. Otherwise the delivery will be offset by a small time dependent on the system loading.

RETURN VALUE

On success, zero is returned. On error, –1 is returned, and *errno* is set appropriately.

ERRORS

> EFAULT   *value* or *ovalue* are not valid pointers.
>
> EINVAL   *which* is not one of **ITIMER_REAL**, **ITIMER_VIRT**, or **ITIMER_PROF**.

SEE ALSO

gettimeofday(2), **sigaction**(2), **signal**(2).

BUGS

Under Linux, the generation and delivery of a signal are distinct, and there each signal is permitted only one outstanding event. It's therefore conceivable that under pathologically heavy loading, **ITIMER_REAL** will expire before the signal from a previous expiration has been delivered. The second signal in such an event will be lost.

NAME

getpagesize – get system page size

SYNOPSIS

#include <unistd.h>

size_t getpagesize(void);

DESCRIPTION

Return the number of bytes in a page. This is the system's page size, which is not necessarily the same as the hardware page size.

NOTES

getpagesize is implemented as a library function in DLL 4.4.1. Depending on what is defined when the library is compiled, this function returns **EXEC_PAGESIZE** (set to 4096 in Linux 0.99.11), **NBPG** (set to 4096 in Linux 0.99.11), or **NBPC** (not defined in Linux 0.99.11 or DLL 4.4.1 libraries).

SEE ALSO

sbrk(2)

NAME

getpeername – get name of connected peer

SYNOPSIS

int getpeername(int *s***, struct sockaddr ****name***, int ****namelen***);**

DESCRIPTION

Getpeername returns the name of the peer connected to socket *s*. The *namelen* parameter should be initialized to indicate the amount of space pointed to by *name*. On return it contains the actual size of the name returned (in bytes). The name is truncated if the buffer provided is too small.

RETURN VALUE

On success, zero is returned. On error, –1 is returned, and *errno* is set appropriately.

ERRORS

EBADF   The argument *s* is not a valid descriptor.

ENOTSOCK   The argument *s* is a file, not a socket.

ENOTCONN   The socket is not connected.

ENOBUFS   Insufficient resources were available in the system to perform the operation.

EFAULT   The *name* parameter points to memory not in a valid part of the process address space.

HISTORY

The **getpeername** function call appeared in BSD 4.2.

SEE ALSO

accept(2), **bind**(2), **getsockname**(2)

NAME

getpid, getppid – get process identification

SYNOPSIS

#include <unistd.h>

pid_t getpid(void);
pid_t getppid(void);

DESCRIPTION

getpid returns the process ID of the current process. (This is often used by routines that generate unique temporary file names.)

getppid returns the process ID of the parent of the current process.

CONFORMING TO

POSIX, BSD 4.3, SVID

SEE ALSO

exec(2), **fork**(2), **kill**(2), **mkstemp**(3), **tmpnam**(3), **tempnam**(3), **tmpfile**(3)

GETPRIORITY(2)

NAME

getpriority, setpriority – get/set program scheduling priority

SYNOPSIS

#include <sys/time.h>
#include <sys/resource.h>

int getpriority(int *which*, **int** *who*);
int setpriority(int *which*, **int** *who*, **int** *prio*);

DESCRIPTION

The scheduling priority of the process, process group, or user, as indicated by *which* and *who* is obtained with the **getpriority** call and set with the **setpriority** call. *Which* is one of **PRIO_PROCESS**, **PRIO_PGRP**, or **PRIO_USER**, and *who* is interpreted relative to *which* (a process identifier for **PRIO_PROCESS**, process group identifier for **PRIO_PGRP**, and a user ID for **PRIO_USER**). A zero value of *who* denotes the current process, process group, or user. *Prio* is a value in the range –20 to 20. The default priority is 0; lower priorities cause more favorable scheduling.

The **getpriority** call returns the highest priority (lowest numerical value) enjoyed by any of the specified processes. The **setpriority** call sets the priorities of all of the specified processes to the specified value. Only the super-user may lower priorities.

RETURN VALUES

Since **getpriority** can legitimately return the value –1, it is necessary to clear the external variable prior to the call, then check it afterward to determine if a –1 is an error or a legitimate value. The **setpriority** call returns 0 if there is no error, or –1 if there is.

ERRORS

    ESRCH   No process was located using the *which* and *who* values specified.

    EINVAL   *Which* was not one of **PRIO_PROCESS**, **PRIO_PGRP**, or **PRIO_USER**.

In addition to the errors indicated above, **setpriority** will fail if:

    EPERM   A process was located, but neither its effective nor real user ID matched the effective user ID of the caller.

    EACCES   A non super-user attempted to lower a process priority.

HISTORY

These function calls appeared in BSD 4.2.

SEE ALSO

nice(1), **fork**(2), **renice**(8)

GETRLIMIT(2)

NAME

getrlimit, getrusage, setrlimit – get/set resource limits and usage

SYNOPSIS

#include <sys/time.h>
#include <sys/resource.h>
#include <unistd.h>

int getrlimit (int *resource*, **struct rlimit** **rlim*);
int getrusage (int *who*, **struct rusage** **usage*);
int setrlimit (int *resource*, **const struct rlimit** **rlim*);

DESCRIPTION

getrlimit and **setrlimit** get and set resource limits respectively. *resource* should be one of:

RLIMIT_CPU /* CPU time in ms */
RLIMIT_FSIZE /* Maximum filesize */
RLIMIT_DATA /* max data size */
RLIMIT_STACK /* max stack size */
RLIMIT_CORE /* max core file size */
RLIMIT_RSS /* max resident set size */

The following are not yet implemented [Documenter's note: as of when?]:

RLIMIT_MEMLOCK /* max locked-in-memory address space*/
RLIMIT_NPROC /* max number of processes */
RLIMIT_OFILE /* max number of open files */

A resource may unlimited if you set the limit to **RLIM_INFINITY**.

The **rlimit** structure is defined as follows :

>   struct rlimit
>   {
>   int rlim_cur;
>   int rlim_max;
>   };

getrusage returns the current resource usages, for a *who* of either **RUSAGE_SELF** or **RUSAGE_CHILDREN**.

>   struct rusage
>   {
>   struct timeval ru_utime; /* user time used */
>   struct timeval ru_stime; /* system time used */
>   long ru_maxrss; /* maximum resident set size */
>   long ru_ixrss; /* integral shared memory size */
>   long ru_idrss; /* integral unshared data size */
>   long ru_isrss; /* integral unshared stack size */
>   long ru_minflt; /* page reclaims */
>   long ru_majflt; /* page faults */
>   long ru_nswap; /* swaps */
>   long ru_inblock; /* block input operations */
>   long ru_oublock; /* block output operations */
>   long ru_msgsnd; /* messages sent */
>   long ru_msgrcv; /* messages received */
>   long ru_nsignals; /* signals received */
>   long ru_nvcsw; /* voluntary context switches */
>   long ru_nivcsw; /* involuntary context switches */
>   };

RETURN VALUE

On success, zero is returned. On error, –1 is returned, and *errno* is set appropriately.

GETRLIMIT(2) Linux Programmer's Manual GETRLIMIT(2)

ERRORS

EINVAL **getrlimit** or **setrlimit** is called with a bad *resource*, or **getrusage** is called with a bad *who*.

EPERM A non-superuser tries to call **setrlimit**().

CONFORMING TO
BSD 4.3

SEE ALSO
ulimit(2), **quota**(2)

NAME

getsockname – get socket name

SYNOPSIS

int getsockname(int s ", struct sockaddr *" name ", int *" namelen)

DESCRIPTION

Getsockname returns the current *name* for the specified socket. The *namelen* parameter should be initialized to indicate the amount of space pointed to by *name*. On return it contains the actual size of the name returned (in bytes).

RETURN VALUE

On success, zero is returned. On error, –1 is returned, and *errno* is set appropriately. A 0 is returned if the call succeeds, –1 if it fails.

ERRORS

EBADF The argument *s* is not a valid descriptor.

ENOTSOCK The argument *s* is a file, not a socket.

ENOBUFS Insufficient resources were available in the system to perform the operation.

EFAULT The *name* parameter points to memory not in a valid part of the process address space.

HISTORY

The **getsockname** function call appeared in BSD 4.2.

BUGS

Names bound to sockets in the UNIX domain are inaccessible; **getsockname** returns a zero length name.

SEE ALSO

bind(2), **socket**(2)

GETSOCKOPT(2) — Linux Programmer's Manual

NAME

getsockopt, setsockopt – get and set options on sockets

SYNOPSIS

#include <sys/types.h>
#include <sys/socket.h>

int getsockopt(int *s*, **int** *level*, **int** *optname*, **void** **optval*, **int** **optlen*);

int setsockopt(int *s*, **int** *level*, **int** *optname*, **const void** **optval*, **int** *optlen*);

DESCRIPTION

Getsockopt and **setsockopt** manipulate the *options* associated with a socket. Options may exist at multiple protocol levels; they are always present at the uppermost **socket** level.

When manipulating socket options the level at which the option resides and the name of the option must be specified. To manipulate options at the socket level, *level* is specified as **SOL_SOCKET** . To manipulate options at any other level the protocol number of the appropriate protocol controlling the option is supplied. For example, to indicate that an option is to be interpreted by the **TCP** protocol, *level* should be set to the protocol number of **TCP**; see **getprotoent**(3).

The parameters *optval* and *optlen* are used to access option values for **setsockopt**. For **getsockopt** they identify a buffer in which the value for the requested option(s) are to be returned. For **getsockopt**, *optlen* is a value-result parameter, initially containing the size of the buffer pointed to by *optval*, and modified on return to indicate the actual size of the value returned. If no option value is to be supplied or returned, *optval* may be NULL.

Optname and any specified options are passed uninterpreted to the appropriate protocol module for interpretation. The include file *sys/socket.h* contains definitions for socket level options, described below. Options at other protocol levels vary in format and name; consult the appropriate entries in section 4 of the manual.

Most socket-level options utilize an *int* parameter for *optval*. For **setsockopt**, the parameter should be non-zero to enable a boolean option, or zero if the option is to be disabled. **SO_LINGER** uses a *struct* linger parameter, defined in *sys/socket.h*, which specifies the desired state of the option and the linger interval (see below). **SO_SNDTIMEO** and **SO_RCVTIMEO** use a *struct* timeval parameter, defined in *sys/time.h*.

The following options are recognized at the socket level. Except as noted, each may be examined with **getsockopt** and set with **setsockopt** .

SO_DEBUG	enables recording of debugging information
SO_REUSEADDR	enables local address reuse
SO_KEEPALIVE	enables keep connections alive
SO_DONTROUTE	enables routing bypass for outgoing messages
SO_LINGER	linger on close if data present
SO_BROADCAST	enables permission to transmit broadcast messages
SO_OOBINLINE	enables reception of out-of-band data in band
SO_SNDBUF	set buffer size for output
SO_RCVBUF	set buffer size for input
SO_SNDLOWAT	set minimum count for output
SO_RCVLOWAT	set minimum count for input
SO_SNDTIMEO	set timeout value for output
SO_RCVTIMEO	set timeout value for input
SO_TYPE	get the type of the socket (get only)
SO_ERROR	get and clear error on the socket (get only)

BSD Man Page 24 July 1993

SO_DEBUG enables debugging in the underlying protocol modules.

SO_REUSEADDR indicates that the rules used in validating addresses supplied in a **bind**(2) call should allow reuse of local addresses.

SO_KEEPALIVE enables the periodic transmission of messages on a connected socket. Should the connected party fail to respond to these messages, the connection is considered broken and processes using the socket are notified via a

SIGPIPE signal when attempting to send data.

SO_DONTROUTE indicates that outgoing messages should bypass the standard routing facilities. Instead, messages are directed to the appropriate network interface according to the network portion of the destination address.

SO_LINGER controls the action taken when unsent messages are queued on socket and a **close**(2) is performed. If the socket promises reliable delivery of data and **SO_LINGER** is set, the system will block the process on the **close** attempt until it is able to transmit the data or until it decides it is unable to deliver the information (a timeout period, termed the linger interval, is specified in the **setsockopt** call when **SO_LINGER** is requested). If **SO_LINGER** is disabled and a **close** is issued, the system will process the close in a manner that allows the process to continue as quickly as possible.

The option **SO_BROADCAST** requests permission to send broadcast datagrams on the socket. Broadcast was a privileged operation in earlier versions of the system. With protocols that support out-of-band data, the **SO_OOBINLINE** option requests that out-of-band data be placed in the normal data input queue as received; it will then be accessible with **recv** or **read** calls without the **MSG_OOB** flag. Some protocols always behave as if this option is set. **SO_SNDBUF** and **SO_RCVBUF** are options to adjust the normal buffer sizes allocated for output and input buffers, respectively. The buffer size may be increased for high-volume connections, or may be decreased to limit the possible backlog of incoming data. The system places an absolute limit on these values.

SO_SNDLOWAT is an option to set the minimum count for output operations. Most output operations process all of the data supplied by the call, delivering data to the protocol for transmission and blocking as necessary for flow control. Nonblocking output operations will process as much data as permitted subject to flow control without blocking, but will process no data if flow control does not allow the smaller of the low water mark value or the entire request to be processed. A **select**(2) operation testing the ability to write to a socket will return true only if the low water mark amount could be processed. The default value for **SO_SNDLOWAT** is set to a convenient size for network efficiency, often 1024. **SO_RCVLOWAT** is an option to set the minimum count for input operations. In general, receive calls will block until any (non-zero) amount of data is received, then return with smaller of the amount available or the amount requested. The default value for **SO_SNDLOWAT** is 1. If **SO_SNDLOWAT** is set to a larger value, blocking receive calls normally wait until they have received the smaller of the low water mark value or the requested amount. Receive calls may still return less than the low water mark if an error occurs, a signal is caught, or the type of data next in the receive queue is different than that returned.

SO_SNDTIMEO is an option to set a timeout value for output operations. It accepts a *struct* timeval parameter with the number of seconds and microseconds used to limit waits for output operations to complete. If a send operation has blocked for this much time, it returns with a partial count or with the error **EWOULDBLOCK** if no data were sent. In the current implementation, this timer is restarted each time additional data are delivered to the protocol, implying that the limit applies to output portions ranging in size from the low water mark to the high water mark for output. **SO_RCVTIMEO** is an option to set a timeout value for input operations. It accepts a *struct* timeval parameter with the number of seconds and microseconds used to limit waits for input operations to complete. In the current implementation, this timer is restarted each time additional data are received by the protocol, and thus the limit is in effect an inactivity timer. If a receive operation has been blocked for this much time without receiving additional data, it returns with a short count or with the error **EWOULDBLOCK** if no data were received.

Finally, **SO_TYPE** and **SO_ERROR** are options used only with *setsockopt*. **SO_TYPE** returns the type of the socket, such as **SOCK_STREAM**; it is useful for servers that inherit

GETSOCKOPT(2)   Linux Programmer's Manual   GETSOCKOPT(2)

sockets on startup. **SO_ERROR** returns any pending error on the socket and clears the error status. It may be used to check for asynchronous errors on connected datagram sockets or for other asynchronous errors.

RETURN VALUE

On success, zero is returned. On error, −1 is returned, and *errno* is set appropriately.

ERRORS

EBADF   The argument *s* is not a valid descriptor.

ENOTSOCK The argument *s* is a file, not a socket.

ENOPROTOOPT The option is unknown at the level indicated.

EFAULT   The address pointed to by *optval* is not in a valid part of the process address space. For **getsockopt**, this error may also be returned if *optlen* is not in a valid part of the process address space.

HISTORY

These system calls appeared in BSD 4.2.

BUGS

Several of the socket options should be handled at lower levels of the system.

SEE ALSO

ioctl(2), **socket**(2), **getprotoent**(3), **protocols**(5)

NAME

gettimeofday, settimeofday – get / set time

SYNOPSIS

#include <sys/time.h>
#include <unistd.h>

int gettimeofday(struct timeval *tv*, **struct timezone** *tz*);
int settimeofday(const struct timeval *tv* , **const struct timezone** *tz*);

DESCRIPTION

gettimeofday and **settimeofday** can set the time as well as a timezone. *tv* is a **timeval** struct, as specified in /usr/include/sys/time.h:

struct timeval {
long tv_sec; /* seconds */
long tv_usec; /* microseconds */
};

and *tz* is a **timezone** :

struct timezone {
int tz_minuteswest;
/* minutes west of Greenwich */
int tz_dsttime;
/* type of dst correction */
};

With daylight savings times defined as follows :

DST_NONE /* not on dst */
DST_USA /* USA style dst */
DST_AUST /* Australian style dst */
DST_WET /* Western European dst */
DST_MET /* Middle European dst */
DST_EET /* Eastern European dst */
DST_CAN /* Canada */
DST_GB /* Great Britain and Eire */
DST_RUM /* Rumania */
DST_TUR /* Turkey */
DST_AUSTALT /* Australian style with shift in 1986 */

And the following macros are defined to operate on this :
#define timerisset(tvp)\
((tvp)->tv_sec || (tvp)->tv_usec)
#define timercmp(tvp, uvp, cmp)\
((tvp)->tv_sec cmp (uvp)->tv_sec ||\
(tvp)->tv_sec == (uvp)->tv_sec &&\
(tvp)->tv_usec cmp (uvp)->tv_usec)
#define timerclear(tvp)
((tvp)->tv_sec = (tvp)->tv_usec = 0)

If either *tv* or *tz* is null, the corresponding structure is not set or returned.

Only the super user may use **settimeofday**.

ERRORS

  EPERM **settimeofday** is called by someone other than the superuser.

  EINVAL Timezone (or something else) is invalid.

CONFORMING TO

BSD 4.3

GETTIMEOFDAY(2)

SEE ALSO
date(1), adjtimex(2), time(2), ctime(3), ftime(3)

GETUID(2)

NAME

getuid, geteuid – get user identity

SYNOPSIS

#include <unistd.h>

uid_t getuid(void);
uid_t geteuid(void);

DESCRIPTION

getuid returns the real user ID of the current process.

geteuid returns the effective user ID of the current process.

The real ID corresponds to the ID of the calling process. The effective ID corresponds to the set ID bit on the file being executed.

ERRORS

These functions are always successful.

CONFORMS TO

POSIX, BSD 4.3

SEE ALSO

setreuid(2), **setuid**(2)

IDLE(2) Linux Programmer's Manual IDLE(2)

NAME

idle – make process 0 idle

SYNOPSIS

#include <unistd.h>

void idle(void);

DESCRIPTION

idle is an internal system call used during bootstrap. It marks the process's pages as swappable, lowers its priority, and enters the main scheduling loop. **idle** never returns.

Only process 0 may call **idle**. Any user process, even a process with super-user permission, will receive **EPERM**.

RETURN VALUE

idle never returns for process 0, and always returns –1 for a user process.

ERRORS

    EPERM   Always, for a user process.

Linux 1.1.46 21 August 1994 559

IOCTL(2)　　　　　　　　Linux Programmer's Manual　　　　　　　　IOCTL(2)

NAME

ioctl – control device

SYNOPSIS

#include <sys/ioctl.h>

int ioctl(int *d*, **int** *request*, **...)**

[The "third" argument is traditionally **char** *argp, and will be so named for this discussion.]

DESCRIPTION

The **ioctl** function manipulates the underlying device parameters of special files. In particular, many operating characteristics of character special files (e.g. terminals) may be controlled with **ioctl** requests. The argument *d* must be an open file descriptor.

An ioctl *request* has encoded in it whether the argument is an *in* parameter or *out* parameter, and the size of the argument *argp* in bytes. Macros and defines used in specifying an ioctl *request* are located in the file *sys/ioctl.h*.

RETURN VALUE

On success, zero is returned. On error, −1 is returned, and *errno* is set appropriately.

ERRORS

EBADF　　*d* is not a valid descriptor.

ENOTTY　*d* is not associated with a character special device.

ENOTTY　The specified request does not apply to the kind of object that the descriptor *d* references.

EINVAL　*Request* or *argp* is not valid.

HISTORY

An **ioctl** function call appeared in Version 7 AT&T UNIX.

SEE ALSO

execve(2), **fcntl**(2), **mt**(4), **sd**(4), **tty**(4)

IOPERM(2)

NAME

ioperm – set port input/output permissions

SYNOPSIS

#include <unistd.h>

int ioperm(unsigned long *from***, unsigned long** *num***, int** *turn_on***);**

DESCRIPTION

Ioperm sets the port access permission bits for the process for *num* bytes starting from port address **from** to the value **turn_on**. The use of **ioperm** require root privileges.

Only the first 0x3ff I/O ports can be specified in this manner. For more ports, the **iopl** function must be used.

RETURN VALUE

On success, zero is returned. On error, −1 is returned, and *errno* is set appropriately.

CONFORMING TO

ioperm is Linux specific.

SEE ALSO

iopl(2)

IOPL(2)

NAME

iopl – change I/O privilege level

SYNOPSIS

#include <unistd.h>

int iopl(int *level***);**

DESCRIPTION

iopl changes the I/O privilege level of the current process, as specified in *level*.

This call is necessary to allow 8514-compatible X servers to run under Linux. Since these X servers require access to all 65536 I/O ports, the **ioperm** call is not sufficient.

In addition to granting unrestricted I/O port access, running at a higher I/O privilege level also allows the process to disable interrupts. This will probably crash the system, and is not recommended.

The I/O privilege level for a normal process is 0.

RETURN VALUE

On success, zero is returned. On error, −1 is returned, and *errno* is set appropriately.

ERRORS

EINVAL   *level* is greater than 3.

EPERM   The current user is not the super-user.

NOTES FROM THE KERNEL SOURCE

iopl has to be used when you want to access the I/O ports beyond the 0x3ff range: to get the full 65536 ports bitmapped you'd need 8kB of bitmaps/process, which is a bit excessive.

SEE ALSO

ioperm(2)

IPC(2) Linux Programmer's Manual IPC(2)

NAME

ipc – System V IPC system calls

SYNOPSIS

int ipc(unsigned int *call,* **int** *first,* **int** *second,* **int** *third,* **void** **ptr,* **long** *fifth);*

DESCRIPTION

ipc is a common kernel entry point for the System V IPC calls for messages, semaphores, and shared memory. *call* determines which IPC function to invoke; the other arguments are passed through to the appropriate call.

User programs should call the appropriate functions by their usual names. Only standard library implementors and kernel hackers need to know about **ipc**.

SEE ALSO

msgctl(2), **msgget**(2), **msgrcv**(2), **msgsnd**(2), **semctl**(2), **semget**(2), **semop**(2), **shmat**(2), **shmctl**(2), **shmdt**(2), **shmget**(2)

KILL(2)

NAME

kill – send signal to a process

SYNOPSIS

#include <signal.h>
int kill(pid_t *pid*, **int** *sig*);

DESCRIPTION

kill() can be used to send any signal to any process group or process.

If *pid* is positive, then signal *sig* is sent to *pid*. In this case, 0 is returned on success, or a negative value on error.

If *pid* equals –1, then *sig* is sent to every process except for the first one, from higher numbers in the proc table to lower. In this case, 0 is returned on success, or the last error condition from **send_sig()** is returned.

If *pid* is less than –1, then *sig* is sent to every process in the process group *–pid*. In this case, the number of processes the signal was sent to is returned, or a negative value for failure.

RETURN VALUE

On success, zero is returned. On error, –1 is returned, and *errno* is set appropriately.

ERRORS

EINVAL   An invalid signal is sent.

ESRCH   The pid or process group does not exist.

EPERM   The effective userid of the process calling **kill()** is not equal to the effective userid of *pid*, unless the superuser called **kill()**.

BUGS

It is impossible to send a signal to task number one, the init process, for which it has not installed a signal handler. This is done to assure the system is not brought down accidentally.

CONFORMING TO

SVID, AT&T, POSIX.1, X/OPEN, BSD 4.3

SEE ALSO

_exit(2), **exit**(2), **signal**(2), **signal**(7)

KILLPG(2) Linux Programmer's Manual KILLPG(2)

NAME
killpg – send signal to a process group

SYNOPSIS
#include <signal.h>

int killpg(int *pgrp*, **int** *sig*);

DESCRIPTION
Killpg sends the signal *sig* to the process group *pgrp*. See **sigaction**(2) for a list of signals. If *pgrp* is 0, **killpg** sends the signal to the sending process's process group.

The sending process and members of the process group must have the same effective user ID, or the sender must be the super-user. As a single special case the continue signal **SIGCONT** may be sent to any process that is a descendant of the current process.

RETURN VALUE
On success, zero is returned. On error, –1 is returned, and *errno* is set appropriately.

ERRORS

EINVAL	*Sig* is not a valid signal number.
ESRCH	No process can be found in the process group specified by *pgrp*.
ESRCH	The process group was given as 0 but the sending process does not have a process group.
EPERM	The sending process is not the super-user and one or more of the target processes has an effective user ID different from that of the sending process.

HISTORY
The **killpg** function call appeared in BSD4.0.

SEE ALSO
kill(2), **getpgrp**(2), **signal**(2)

LINK(2)

NAME

link – make a new name for a file

SYNOPSIS

#include <unistd.h>

int link(const char **oldpath***, const char ****newpath***);**

DESCRIPTION

link creates a new link (also known as a hard link) to an existing file.

If *newpath* exists it will *not* be overwritten.

This new name may be used exactly as the old one for any operation; both names refer to the same file (and so have the same permissions and ownership) and it is impossible to tell which name was the 'original'.

RETURN VALUE

On success, zero is returned. On error, –1 is returned, and *errno* is set appropriately.

ERRORS

EXDEV *oldpath* and *newpath* are not on the same filesystem.

EPERM The filesystem containing *oldpath* and *newpath* does not support the creation of hard links.

EFAULT *oldpath* or *newpath* points outside your accessible address space.

EACCES Write access to the directory containing *newpath* is not allowed for the process's effective uid, or one of the directories in *oldpath* or *newpath* did not allow search (execute) permission.

ENAMETOOLONG *oldpath* or *newpath* was too long.

ENOENT A directory component in *oldpath* " or " newpath does not exist or is a dangling symbolic link.

ENOTDIR A component used as a directory in *oldpath* or *newpath* is not, in fact, a directory.

ENOMEM Insufficient kernel memory was available.

EROFS The file is on a read-only filesystem.

EEXIST *newpath* already exists.

EMLINK The file referred to by *oldpath* already has the maximum number of links to it.

ELOOP *oldpath* or *newpath* contains a reference to a circular symbolic link, ie a symbolic link whose expansion contains a reference to itself.

ENOSPC The device containing the file has no room for the new directory entry.

EPERM *oldpath* is the **.** " or " .. entry of a directory.

NOTES

Hard links, as created by **link**, cannot span filesystems. Use **symlink** if this is required.

CONFORMING TO

SVID, AT&T, POSIX, BSD 4.3

BUGS

On NFS file systems, the return code may be wrong in case the NFS server performs the link creation and dies before it can say so. Use *stat(2)* to find out if the link got created.

SEE ALSO

symlink(2), **unlink**(2), **rename**(2), **open**(2), **stat**(2), **ln**(1), **link**(8).

LISTEN(2)

NAME

listen – listen for connections on a socket

SYNOPSIS

#include <sys/socket.h>

int listen(int *s*, **int** *backlog***);**

DESCRIPTION

To accept connections, a socket is first created with **socket**(2), a willingness to accept incoming connections and a queue limit for incoming connections are specified with **listen**, and then the connections are accepted with **accept**(2). The **listen** call applies only to sockets of type **SOCK_STREAM** or **SOCK_SEQPACKET**.

The *backlog* parameter defines the maximum length the queue of pending connections may grow to. If a connection request arrives with the queue full the client may receive an error with an indication of **ECONNREFUSED**, or, if the underlying protocol supports retransmission, the request may be ignored so that retries may succeed.

RETURN VALUE

On success, zero is returned. On error, –1 is returned, and *errno* is set appropriately.

ERRORS

EBADF   The argument *s* is not a valid descriptor.

ENOTSOCK The argument *s* is not a socket.

EOPNOTSUPP The socket is not of a type that supports the operation **listen**.

HISTORY

The **listen** function call appeared in BSD 4.2.

BUGS

The *backlog* is currently limited (silently) to 5. [Documenter's note: is this true for Linux?]

SEE ALSO

accept(2), **connect**(2), **socket**(2)

LLSEEK(2)

NAME

_llseek – reposition read/write file offset

SYNOPSIS

#include <unistd.h>

#include <linux/unistd.h>

_syscall5(int, _llseek, uint, fd, ulong, hi, ulong, lo, loff_t *, res, uint, wh);

int _llseek(unsigned int *fd*, **unsigned long** *offset_high*, **unsigned long** *offset_low*, **loff_t ***result*, **unsigned int** *whence*);

DESCRIPTION

The _llseek function repositions the offset of the file descriptor *fd* to *(offset_high<<32)* | offset_low bytes relative to the beginning of the file, the current position in the file, or the end of the file, depending on whether *whence* is **SEEK_SET**, **SEEK_CUR**, or **SEEK_END**, respectively. It returns the resulting file position in the argument *result*.

RETURN VALUES

Upon successful completion, _llseek returns 0. Otherwise, a value of −1 is returned and *errno* is set to indicate the error.

ERRORS

EBADF   *fd* is not an open file descriptor.

EINVAL   *whence* is invalid.

CONFORMS TO

This function is Linux-specific.

BUGS

There is no support for files with a size of 4GB or more.

SEE ALSO

lseek(2)

LSEEK(2)

NAME

lseek – reposition read/write file offset

SYNOPSIS

#include <unistd.h>

off_t lseek(int *fildes*, **off_t** *offset*, **int** *whence*);

DESCRIPTION

The **lseek** function repositions the offset of the file descriptor *fildes* to the argument *offset* according to the directive *whence*. The argument *fildes* must be an open file descriptor. **Lseek** repositions the file pointer *fildes* as follows:

If *whence* is **SEEK_SET**, the offset is set to *offset* bytes.

If *whence* is **SEEK_CUR**, the offset is set to its current location plus *offset* bytes.

If *whence* is **SEEK_END**, the offset is set to the size of the file plus *offset* bytes.

The **lseek** function allows the file offset to be set beyond the end of the existing end-of-file of the file. If data is later written at this point, subsequent reads of the data in the gap return bytes of zeros (until data is actually written into the gap).

Some devices are incapable of seeking. The value of the pointer associated with such a device is undefined.

RETURN VALUES

Upon successful completion, **lseek** returns the resulting offset location as measured in bytes from the beginning of the file. Otherwise, a value of –1 is returned and *errno* is set to indicate the error.

ERRORS

EBADF   *Fildes* is not an open file descriptor.

ESPIPE *Fildes* is associated with a pipe, socket, or FIFO.

EINVAL *Whence* is not a proper value.

CONFORMS TO

POSIX, BSD 4.3

BUGS

This document's use of *whence* is incorrect English, but maintained for historical reasons.

SEE ALSO

dup(2), **open**(2), **fseek**(3)

MKDIR(2)

Linux Programmer's Manual

NAME

mkdir – create a directory

SYNOPSIS

#include <sys/types.h>
#include <fcntl.h>
#include <unistd.h>
int mkdir(const char *pathname*, mode_t *mode*);

DESCRIPTION

mkdir attempts to create a directory named *pathname*.

mode specifies the permissions to use. It is modified by the process's **umask** in the usual way: the permissions of the created file are (**mode & ~umask**).

The newly created directory will be owned by the effective uid of the process. If the directory containing the file has the set group id bit set, or if the filesystem is mounted with BSD group semantics, the new directory will inherit the group ownership from its parent; otherwise it will be owned by the effective gid of the process.

If the parent directory has the set group id bit set then so will the newly created directory.

RETURN VALUE

mkdir returns zero on success, or -1 if an error occurred (in which case, *errno* is set appropriately).

ERRORS

EEXIST *pathname* already exists (not necessarily as a directory).

EFAULT *pathname* points outside your accessible address space.

EACCES The parent directory does not allow write permission to the process, or one of the directories in *pathname* did not allow search (execute) permission.

ENAMETOOLONG *pathname* was too long.

ENOENT A directory component in *pathname* does not exist or is a dangling symbolic link.

ENOTDIR A component used as a directory in *pathname* is not, in fact, a directory.

ENOMEM Insufficient kernel memory was available.

EROFS *pathname* refers to a file on a read-only filesystem and write access was requested.

ELOOP *pathname* contains a reference to a circular symbolic link, ie a symbolic link whose expansion contains a reference to itself.

ENOSPC The device containing *pathname* has no room for the new directory.
ENOSPC The new directory cannot be created because the user's disk quota is exhausted.

CONFORMING TO

BUGS

In some older versions of Linux (for example, 0.99pl7) all the normal filesystems sometime allow the creation of two files in the same directory with the same name. This occurs only rarely and only on a heavily loaded system. It is believed that this bug was fixed in the Minix filesystem in Linux 0.99pl8 pre-release; and it is hoped that it was fixed in the other filesystems shortly afterwards.

There are many infelicities in the protocol underlying NFS.

SEE ALSO

read(2), write(2), fcntl(2), close(2), unlink(2), open(2), mknod(2), stat(2), umask(2), mount(2), socket(2), socket(2), fopen(3).

MKNOD(2)

NAME

mknod – create a directory

SYNOPSIS

#include <sys/types.h>
#include <sys/stat.h>
#include <fcntl.h>
#include <unistd.h>

int mknod(const char **pathname*, **mode_t** *mode*, **dev_t** *dev*);

DESCRIPTION

mknod attempts to create a filesystem node (file, device special file or named pipe) named *pathname*, specified by *mode* and *dev*.

mode specifies both the permissions to use and the type of node to be created.

It should be a combination (using bitwise OR) of one of the file types listed below and the permissions for the new node.

The permissions are modified by the process's **umask** in the usual way: the permissions of the created node are **(mode & ~umask)**.

The file type should be one of **S_IFREG**, **S_IFCHR**, **S_IFBLK** and **S_IFIFO** to specify a normal file (which will be created empty), character special file, block special file or FIFO (named pipe), respectively, or zero, which will create a normal file.

If the file type is **S_IFCHR** or **S_IFBLK** then *dev* specifies the major and minor numbers of the newly created device special file; otherwise it is ignored.

The newly created node will be owned by the effective uid of the process. If the directory containing the node has the set group id bit set, or if the filesystem is mounted with BSD group semantics, the new node will inherit the group ownership from its parent directory; otherwise it will be owned by the effective gid of the process.

RETURN VALUE

mknod returns zero on success, or -1 if an error occurred (in which case, *errno* is set appropriately).

ERRORS

EPERM *mode* requested creation of something other than a FIFO (named pipe), and the caller is not the superuser; also returned if the filesystem containing *pathname* does not support the type of node requested. **EINVAL** *mode* requested creation of something other than a normal file, device special file or FIFO. **EEXIST** *pathname* already exists.

EFAULT *pathname* points outside your accessible address space.

EACCES The parent directory does not allow write permission to the process, or one of the directories in *pathname* did not allow search (execute) permission.

ENAMETOOLONG *pathname* was too long.

ENOENT A directory component in *pathname* does not exist or is a dangling symbolic link.

ENOTDIR A component used as a directory in *pathname* is not, in fact, a directory.

ENOMEM Insufficient kernel memory was available.

EROFS *pathname* refers to a file on a read-only filesystem and write access was requested.

ELOOP *pathname* contains a reference to a circular symbolic link, ie a symbolic link whose expansion contains a reference to itself.

ENOSPC The device containing *pathname* has no room for the new node.

CONFORMING TO
BUGS

In some older versions of Linux (for example, 0.99pl7) all the normal filesystems sometime allow the creation of two files in the same directory with the same name. This occurs only rarely and only on a heavily loaded system. It is believed that this bug was fixed in the Minix filesystem in Linux 0.99pl8 pre-release; and it is hoped that it was fixed in the other filesystems shortly afterwards.

mknod cannot be used to create directories or socket files, and cannot be used to create normal files by users other than the superuser.

There are many infelicities in the protocol underlying NFS.

SEE ALSO

read(2), **write**(2), **fcntl**(2), **close**(2), **unlink**(2), **open**(2), **mkdir**(2), stat(2), **umask**(2), **mount**(2), **socket**(2), **socket**(2), **fopen**(3).

MMAP(2)

Linux Programmer's Manual

MMAP(2)

NAME

mmap, munmap – map or unmap files or devices into memory

SYNOPSIS

#include <sys/types.h>
#include <sys/mman.h>

caddr_t mmap(caddr_t *addr*, **size_t** *len*, **int** *prot* , **int** *flags*, **int** *fd*, **off_t offset**);
int munmap(caddr_t *addr*, **size_t** *len*);

DESCRIPTION

WARNING: This is a BSD man page. Linux 0.99.11 can't map files, and can't do other things documented here.

The **mmap** function causes the pages starting at *addr* and continuing for at most *len* bytes to be mapped from the object described by *fd*, starting at byte offset *offset*. If *offset* or *len* is not a multiple of the pagesize, the mapped region may extend past the specified range.

If *addr* is non-zero, it is used as a hint to the system. (As a convenience to the system, the actual address of the region may differ from the address supplied.) If *addr* is zero, an address will be selected by the system. The actual starting address of the region is returned. A successful **mmap** deletes any previous mapping in the allocated address range.

The protections (region accessibility) are specified in the *prot* argument by *or*'ing the following values:

- PROT_EXEC   Pages may be executed.
- PROT_READ   Pages may be read.
- PROT_WRITE   Pages may be written.

The *flags* parameter specifies the type of the mapped object, mapping options and whether modifications made to the mapped copy of the page are private to the process or are to be shared with other references. Sharing, mapping type and options are specified in the *flags* argument by *or*;ing the following values:

- MAP_ANON   Map anonymous memory not associated with any specific file. The file descriptor used for creating MAP_ANON regions is used only for naming, and may be specified as –1 if no name is associated with the region.
- MAP_FILE   Mapped from a regular file or character-special device memory.
- MAP_FIXED   Do not permit the system to select a different address than the one specified. If the specified address cannot be used, **mmap** will fail. If MAP_FIXED is specified, *addr* must be a multiple of the pagesize. Use of this option is discouraged.
- MAP_HASSEMAPHORE   Notify the kernel that the region may contain semaphores and that special handling may be necessary.
- MAP_INHERIT   Permit regions to be inherited across **exec**(2) system calls.
- MAP_PRIVATE   Modifications are private.
- MAP_SHARED   Modifications are shared.

The **munmap** system call deletes the mappings for the specified address range, and causes further references to addresses within the range to generate invalid memory references.

The current design does not allow a process to specify the location of swap space. In the future we may define an additional mapping type, **MAP_SWAP**, in which the file descriptor argument specifies a file or device to which swapping should be done.

RETURN VALUES

Upon successful completion, **mmap** returns a pointer to the mapped region. Otherwise, a value of −1 is returned and *errno* is set to indicate the error.

ERRORS

For **mmap**:

EACCES	The flag PROT_READ was specified as part of the *prot* parameter and *fd* was not open for reading. The flags **PROT_WRITE**, **MAP_SHARED** and **MAP_WRITE** were specified as part of the *flags* and *prot* parameters and *fd* was not open for writing.
EBADF	*Fd* is not a valid open file descriptor.
EINVAL	One of **MAP_ANON** or **MAP_FILE** was not specified as part of the *flags* parameter. **MAP_FIXED** was specified and the *addr* parameter was not page aligned. did not reference a regular or character special file.
ENOMEM	**MAP_FIXED** was specified and the *addr* parameter wasn't available. **MAP_ANON** was specified an insufficient memory was available.

BUGS

This is a BSD man page. Many of the details explained here are *not* implemented under Linux. Please consult the Linux kernel source code for complete details on the current implementation of the **mmap** function.

SEE ALSO

getpagesize(2), **phys**(2)

NAME

modify_ldt – get or set ldt

SYNOPSIS

#include <linux/ldt.h> **#include** <linux/unistd.h>

_syscall3(int, modify_ldt, int, func, void *, ptr, unsigned long, bytecount)

int modify_ldt(int *func*, **void** **ptr*, **unsigned long** *bytecount*);

DESCRIPTION

modify_ldt reads or writes the local descriptor table (ldt) for a process. The ldt is a per-process memory management table used by the i386 processor. For more information on this table, see an Intel 386 processor handbook.

When *func* is 0, **modify_ldt** reads the ldt into the memory pointed to by *ptr*. The number of bytes read is the smaller of *bytecount* and the actual size of the ldt.

When *func* is 1, **modify_ldt** modifies one ldt entry. *ptr* points to a *modify_ldt_ldt_s* structure and *bytecount* must equal the size of this structure.

RETURN VALUE

On success, **modify_ldt** returns either the actual number of bytes read (for reading) or 0 (for writing). On failure, **modify_ldt** returns –1 and sets *errno*.

ERRORS

ENOSYS   *func* is neither 0 nor 1.

EINVAL   *ptr* is 0, or *func* is 1 and *bytecount* is not equal to the size of the structure *modify_ldt_ldt_s*, or *func* is 1 and the new ldt entry has illegal values.

EFAULT   *ptr* points outside the address space.

SEE ALSO

vm86(2)

NAME

get_kernel_syms, create_module, init_module, delete_module – loadable module support

SYNOPSIS

#include <linux/module.h>
int get_kernel_syms(struct kernel_sym *table);
int create_module(char *module_name, unsigned long size);
int init_module(char *module_name, char *code, unsigned codesize,
struct mod_routines *routines, struct symbol_table *symtab);
int delete_module(char *module_name);

struct kernel_sym {
unsigned long value;
char name[SYM_MAX_NAME];
};

struct mod_routines {
int (*init)(void);
void (*cleanup)(void);
};

struct module_ref {
struct module *module;
struct module_ref *next;
};

struct internal_symbol {
void *addr;
char *name;
};

struct symbol_table {
int size; /* total, including string table!!! */
int n_symbols;
int n_refs;
struct internal_symbol symbol[0];
struct module_ref ref[0];
};

DESCRIPTION

These system calls have not yet been included in any library, which means that they have to be called by the **syscall(_NR_function)** mechanism. -tag -width flag *Nm* get_kernel_syms(table); has two uses: first, if **table** is NULL, this call will only return the number of symbols, including module names, that are available. This number should be used to reserve memory for that many items of **struct** kernel_sym.

If **table** is not NULL, this call will copy all kernel symbols and module names (and version info) from the kernel to the space pointed to by **table**. The entries are ordered in module LIFO order. For each module an entry that decribes the module will be followed by entries describing the symbols exported by this module.

Note that for symbols that describe a module, the **value** part of the structure will contain the **kernel** address of the structure that describes the module.

The **name** part of the structure is the module name prepended with **#**, as in **#my_module**. The symbol that describes a module will appear before the symbols defined by this module. Ahead of the kernel resident symbols, a module name symbol with the "dummy" name **#** will appear. This information can be used to build a table of module references when modules are stacked (or layered). **create_module(module_name,** size); will allocate **size** bytes of kernel space for a module, and also create the necessary kernel structures for the new module called **name.** The module will now exist in kernel space, with the status **MOD_UNINITIALIZED. init_module(module_name,** code, codesize, routines, symtab);

This is the actual "module loader", that will load the module named **name** into the kernel. The parameters **code** and **codesize** refer to the relocated binary object module that is **codesize** bytes long. Note that the first 4 bytes will be used as a reference counter in kernel space, updated by the MOD_INC_USE_COUNT and MOD_DEC_USE_COUNT macros.
The functions described in **routines** will be used to start and stop the module. These pointers should therefore contain the adresses of the **init_module()** and **cleanup_module()** functions that have to be defined for all loadable modules.
If a module wants to export symbols for use by other modules, or if the module makes references to symbols defined by other modules, the parameter **symtab** has to point to a structure that describes these. A NULL value for **symtab** means that no symbols are exported and no references to other modules are made.
The **symtab** that will be copied into the kernel consist of a **symbol_table** structure immediately followed by a string table, containing the names of the symbols defined by the module. The **size** element has to include the size of this string table as well. Special considerations: The **n_symbols** and **n_refs** elements tells how many symbols and how many module references are included in the **symbol_table** structure. Immediately after these integers, the array of symbol definitions follow. The **name** element in each **struct** internal_symbol should actually not be an ordinary pointer, but instead the **offset** of the corresponding string table entry relative to the start of the symbol_table structure.

When all defined symbols have been listed, the symbol_table structure continues with the array of module references, as described by the **struct** module_ref elements. Only the **module** field of these structures have to be initialized. The module adresses that were obtained from a previous **get_kernel_syms** call, for elements with names starting with **#** should be copied to this field.

If the module could be successfully loaded, and if the call to the module function **init_module()** also succeeds, the status of the module will be changed to MOD_RUNNING. Otherwise, the kernel memory occupied by module will be freed. **delete_module(module_name);** should be used to unload a module. If the module reference count shows that the module is not active, and if there are no references to this module from other modules, the module function **cleanup_module()** will be called. If all these steps succeed, the kernel memory occupied by the module and its structures will be freed.

DIAGNOSTICS
If there are any errors, these functions will return the value -1, and the global variable **errno** will contain the error number. A descriptive text will also be written on the console device.

SEE ALSO
insmod 1 , **rmmod** 1 , **lsmod** 1 , **ksyms** 1

HISTORY
The module support was first concieved by Anonymous (as far as I know...).
Linux version by Bas Laarhoven <bas@vimec.nl>,
0.99.14 version by Jon Tombs <jon@gtex02.us.es>,
extended by Bjorn Ekwall <bj0rn@blox.se>.

BUGS
Naah...

MOUNT(2)

NAME

mount, umount – mount and unmount filesystems.

SYNOPSIS

#include <sys/mount.h>
#include <linux/fs.h>

int mount(const char *specialfile*, **const char** * *dir* , **const char** * *filesystemtype*, **unsigned long** *rwflag* , **const void** * *data*);

int umount(const char *specialfile*);

int umount(const char *dir*);

DESCRIPTION

mount attaches the filesystem specified by *specialfile* (which is often a device name) to the directory specified by *dir*.

umount removes the attachment of the filesystem specified by *specialfile* or *dir*.

Only the super-user may mount and unmount filesystems.

The *filesystemtype* argument may take one of the values listed in /proc/filesystems (like "minix", "ext2", "msdos", "proc", "nfs", "iso9660" etc.).

The *rwflag* argument has the magic number 0xC0ED in the top 16 bits, and various mount flags (as defined in <linux/fs.h>) in the low order 16 bits:

#define MS_RDONLY 1 /* mount read-only */
#define MS_NOSUID 2 /* ignore suid and sgid bits */
#define MS_NODEV 4 /* disallow access to device special files */
#define MS_NOEXEC 8 /* disallow program execution */
#define MS_SYNC 16 /* writes are synced at once */
#define MS_REMOUNT 32 /* alter flags of a mounted FS */
#define MS_MGC_VAL 0xC0ED0000

If the magic number is absent, then the last two arguments are not used.

The *data* argument is interpreted by the different file systems.

RETURN VALUE

On success, zero is returned. On error, –1 is returned, and *errno* is set appropriately.

ERRORS

The error values given below result from filesystem type independent errors. Each filesystem type may have its own special errors and its own special behavior. See the kernel source code for details.

EPERM   The user is not the super-user.

ENODEV   *Filesystemtype* not configured in the kernel.

ENOTBLK   *Specialfile* is not a block device (if a device was required).

EBUSY   *Specialfile* is already mounted. Or, it cannot be remounted read-only, because it still holds files open for writing. Or, it cannot be mounted on *dir* because *dir* is still busy (it is the working directory of some task, the mount point of another device, has open files, etc.).

EINVAL   *Specialfile* had an invalid superblock. Or, a remount was attempted, while *specialfile* was not already mounted on *dir*. Or, an umount was attempted, while *dir* was not a mount point.

EFAULT   One of the pointer arguments points outside the user address space.

ENOMEM   The kernel could not allocate a free page to copy filenames or data into.

ENAMETOOLONG	A pathname was longer than MAXPATHLEN.
ENOENT	A pathname was empty or had a nonexistent component.
ENOTDIR	The second argument, or a prefix of the first argument, is not a directory.
EACCES	A component of a path was not searchable. Or, mounting a read-only filesystem was attempted without giving the MS_RDONLY flag. Or, the block device *Specialfile* is located on a filesystem mounted with the MS_NODEV option.
ENXIO	The major number of the block device *specialfile* is out of range.
EMFILE	(In case no block device is required:) Table of dummy devices is full.

CONFORMING TO
These functions are rather Linux-specific.

SEE ALSO
mount(8), umount(8)

MPROTECT(2)

NAME
mprotect – control allowable accesses to a region of memory

SYNOPSIS
#include <sys/mman.h>
int mprotect(caddr_t *addr*, **size_t** **len*, **int** *prot*);

DESCRIPTION
mprotect controls how a section of memory may be accessed. If an access is disallowed by the protection given it, the program receives a SIGSEGV.

prot **is a bitwise-or of the following values:**

PROT_NONE	The memory cannot be accessed at all.
PROT_READ	The memory can be read.
PROT_WRITE	The memory can be written to.
PROT_EXEC	The memory can contain executing code.

The new protection replaces any existing protection. For example, if the memory had previously been marked PROT_READ, and mprotect is then called with *prot* **PROT_WRITE, it will no longer be readable.**

RETURN VALUE
On success, **mprotect** returns zero. On error, –1 is returned, and *errno* is set appropriately.

ERRORS

EINVAL	*addr* is not a valid pointer.
EFAULT	The memory cannot be accessed.
EACCES	The memory cannot be given the specified access. This can happen, for example, if you **mmap**(2) a file to which you have read-only access, then ask **mprotect** to mark it **PROT_WRITE**.
ENOMEM	Internal kernel structures could not be allocated.

EXAMPLE

```
#include <stdio.h>
#include <stdlib.h>
#include <errno.h>
#include <sys/mman.h>

int
main(void)
{
char *p;
char c;

/* Allocate a buffer; it will have the default
protection of PROT_READ|PROT_WRITE. */
p = malloc(1024);
if (!p) {
perror("Couldn't malloc(1024)");
exit(errno);
}

c = p[666]; /* Read; ok */
p[666] = 42; /* Write; ok */

/* Mark the buffer read-only. */
```

Linux 1.2   1995-06-23

MPROTECT(2) Linux Programmer's Manual MPROTECT(2)

```
if (mprotect(p, 1024, PROT_READ)) {
    perror("Couldn't mprotect");
    exit(errno);
}

c = p[666]; /* Read; ok */
p[666] = 42; /* Write; program dies on SIGSEGV */

exit(0);
}
```

SEE ALSO
mmap(2)

MSGCTL(2)

NAME

msgctl – message control operations

SYNOPSIS

\# include <sys/types.h>
\# include <sys/ipc.h>
\# include <sys/msg.h>

int msgctl (int *msqid***, .BI** *int* **cmd , .BI** *struct***msqid_ds*** ″**buf** *)* **int** *cmd***, struct msqid_ds** ******buf* **)**

DESCRIPTION

The function performs the control operation specified by *cmd* on the message queue with identifier *msqid*. Legal values for *cmd* are:

IPC_STAT   Copy info from the message queue data structure into the structure pointed to by *buf*. The user must have read access privileges on the message queue.

IPC_SET   Write the values of some members of the **msqid_ds** structure pointed to by *buf* to the message queue data structure, updating also its **msg_ctime** member. Considered members from the user supplied **struct msqid_ds** pointed to by *buf* are msg_perm.uid msg_perm.gid msg_perm.mode /* only lowest 9-bits */ msg_qbytes The calling process effective user–ID must be one among super–user, creator or owner of the message queue. Only the super–user can raise the **msg_qbytes** value beyond the system parameter **MSGMNB**.

IPC_RMID   Remove immediately the message queue and its data structures awakening all waiting reader and writer processes (with an error return and **errno** set to **EIDRM**). The calling process effective user–ID must be one among super–user, creator or owner of the message queue.

RETURN VALUE

If successful, the return value will be **0**, otherwise **–1** with **errno** indicating the error.

ERRORS

For a failing return, **errno** will be set to one among the following values:

EACCESS   The argument *cmd* is equal to **IPC_STAT** but the calling process has no read access permissions on the message queue *msqid*.

EFAULT   The argument *cmd* has value **IPC_SET** or **IPC_STAT** but the address pointed to by *buf* isn't accessible.

EIDRM   The message queue was removed.

EINVAL   Invalid value for *cmd* or *msqid*.

EPERM   The argument *cmd* has value **IPC_SET** or **IPC_RMID** but the calling process effective user–ID has insufficient privileges to execute the command. Note this is also the case of a non super–user process trying to increase the **msg_qbytes** value beyond the value specified by the system parameter **MSGMNB**.

NOTES

The **IPC_INFO**, **MSG_STAT** and **MSG_INFO** control calls are used by the **ipcs**(1) program to provide information on allocated resources. In the future these can be modified as needed or moved to a proc file system interface.

SEE ALSO
ipc(5), **msgget**(2), **msgsnd**(2), **msgrcv**(2).

NAME

msgget – get a message queue identifier

SYNOPSIS

\# include <sys/types.h>
\# include <sys/ipc.h>
\# include <sys/msg.h>

int msgget (key_t *key***, int** *msgflg* **)**

DESCRIPTION

The function returns the message queue identifier associated to the value of the *key* argument. A new message queue is created if *key* has value **IPC_PRIVATE** or *key* isn't **IPC_PRIVATE**, no existing message queue is associated to *key*, and **IPC_CREAT** is asserted in *msgflg* (i.e. *msgflg* &IPC_CREAT isn't zero). The presence in *msgflg* of the fields **IPC_CREAT** and **IPC_EXCL** plays the same role, with respect to the existence of the message queue, as the presence of **O_CREAT** and **O_EXCL** in the mode argument of the **open**(2) system call: i.e. the **msgget** function fails if *msgflg* asserts both **IPC_CREAT** and **IPC_EXCL** and a message queue already exists for *key*.

Upon creation, the lower 9 bits of the argument *msgflg* define the access permissions (for owner, group and others) to the message queue in the same format, and with the same meaning, as for the access permissions parameter in the **open**(2) or **creat**(2) system calls (though the execute permissions are not used by the system).

Furthermore, while creating, the system call initializes the system message queue data structure **msqid_ds** as follows:

> **msg_perm.cuid** and **msg_perm.uid** are set to the effective user–ID of the calling process.
>
> **msg_perm.cgid** and **msg_perm.gid** are set to the effective group–ID of the calling process.
>
> The lowest order 9 bits of **msg_perm.mode** are set to the lowest order 9 bit of *msgflg*.
>
> **msg_qnum**, **msg_lspid**, **msg_lrpid**, **msg_stime** and **msg_rtime** are set to 0.
>
> **msg_ctime** is set to the current time.
>
> **msg_qbytes** is set to the system limit **MSGMNB**.

If the message queue already exists, the access permissions are verified, and a check is made to see if it is marked for destruction.

RETURN VALUE

If successful, the return value will be the message queue identifier (a positive integer), otherwise –1 with **errno** indicating the error.

ERRORS

For a failing return, **errno** will be set to one among the following values:

> **EACCES** A message queue exists for *key*, but the calling process has no access permissions to the queue.
>
> **EEXIST** A message queue exists for **key** and *msgflg* was asserting both **IPC_CREAT** and **IPC_EXCL**.
>
> **EIDRM** The message queue is marked as to be removed.
>
> **ENOENT** No message queue exists for *key* and *msgflg* wasn't asserting **IPC_CREAT**.
>
> **ENOMEM** A message queue has to be created but the system has not enough memory for the new data structure.
>
> **ENOSPC** A message queue has to be created but the system limit for the maximum number of message queues (**MSGMNI**) would be exceeded.

NOTES

IPC_PRIVATE isn't a flag field but a **key_t** type. If this special value is used for *key*, the system call ignores everything but the lowest order 9 bits of *msgflg* and creates a new message queue (on success).

The following is a system limit on message queue resources affecting a **msgget** call:

> **MSGMNI**   System wide maximum number of message queues: policy dependent.

BUGS

Use of **IPC_PRIVATE** don't inhibits to other processes the access to the allocated message queue.

As for the files, there is currently no intrinsic way for a process to ensure exclusive access to a message queue. Asserting both **IPC_CREAT** and **IPC_EXCL** in *msgflg* only ensures (on success) that a new message queue will be created, it doesn't imply exclusive access to the message queue.

SEE ALSO

ftok(3), **ipc**(5), **msgctl**(2), **msgsnd**(2), **msgrcv**(2).

MSGOP(2) Linux Programmer's Manual MSGOP(2)

NAME

msgop – message operations

SYNOPSIS

\# include <sys/types.h>
\# include <sys/ipc.h>
\# include <sys/msg.h>

int msgsnd (int *msqid*, **struct msgbuf** **msgp"*, **int** *msgsz*, **int** *msgflg* **)**

int msgrcv (int *msqid*, **struct msgbuf** **msgp*, **int** *msgsz*, **long** *msgtyp*, **int** *msgflg* **)**

DESCRIPTION

To send or receive a message the calling process allocates a structure that looks like the following

struct msgbuf {
long mtype; /* message type, must be > 0 */
char mtext[1]; /* message data */
};

but with an array **mtext** of size *msgsz*, a non-negative integer value. The structure member **mtype** must have a strictly positive integer value that can be used by the receiving process for message selection (see the section about **msgrcv**).

The calling process must have write access permissions to send and read access permissions to receive a message on the queue.

The **msgsnd** system call enqueue a copy of the message pointed to by the *msgp* argument on the message queue whose identifier is specified by the value of the *msqid* argument.

The argument *msgflg* specifies the system call behaviour if enqueuing the new message will require more than **msg_qbytes** in the queue. Asserting **IPC_NOWAIT** the message will not be sent and the system call fails returning with **errno** set to **EAGAIN**. Otherwise the process is suspended until the condition for the suspension no longer exists (in which case the message is sent and the system call succeeds), or the queue is removed (in which case the system call fails with **errno** set to **EIDRM**), or the process receives a signal that has to be caught (in which case the system call fails with **errno** set to **EINTR**).

Upon successful completion the message queue data structure is updated as follows:

msg_lspid is set to the process-D of the calling process.

msg_qnum is incremented by 1.

msg_stime is set to the current time.

The system call **msgrcv** reads a message from the message queue specified by *msqid* into the **msgbuf** pointed to by the *msgp* argument removing from the queue, on success, the read message.

The argument *msgsz* specifies the maximum size in bytes for the member **mtext** of the structure pointed to by the *msgp* argument. If the message text has length greater than *msgsz*, then if the *msgflg* argument asserts **MSG_NOERROR**, the message text will be truncated (and the truncated part will be lost), otherwise the message isn't removed from the queue and the system call fails returning with **errno** set to **E2BIG**.

The argument *msgtyp* specifies the type of message requested as follows:

If *msgtyp* is **0**, then the message on the queue's front is read.

If *msgtyp* is greater than **0**, then the first message on the queue of type *msgtyp* is read if **MSG_EXCEPT** isn't asserted by the *msgflg* argument, otherwise the first message on the queue of type not equal to *msgtyp* will be read.

If *msgtyp* is less than **0**, then the first message on the queue with the lowest type less than or equal to the absolute value of *msgtyp* will be read.

The *msgflg* argument asserts none, one or more (or–ing them) among the following flags:

> **IPC_NOWAIT** For immediate return if no message of the requested type is on the queue. The system call fails with errno set to **ENOMSG**.
>
> **MSG_EXCEPT** Used with *msgtyp* greater than **0** to read the first message on the queue with message type that differs from *msgtyp*.
>
> **MSG_NOERROR** To truncate the message text if longer than *msgsz* bytes.

If no message of the requested type is available and **IPC_NOWAIT** isn't asserted in *msgflg*, the calling process is blocked until one of the following conditions occurs:

> A message of the desired type is placed on the queue.
>
> The message queue is removed from the system. In such a case the system call fails with **errno** set to **EIDRM**.
>
> The calling process receives a signal that has to be caught. In such a case the system call fails with **errno** set to **EINTR**.

Upon successful completion the message queue data structure is updated as follows:

> **msg_lrpid** is set to the process-D of the calling process.
>
> **msg_qnum** is decremented by 1.
>
> **msg_rtime** is set to the current time.

RETURN VALUE

On a failure both functions return **−1** with **errno** indicating the error, otherwise **msgsnd** returns **0** and **msgrvc** returns the number of bytes actually copied into the **mtext** array.

ERRORS

When **msgsnd** fails, at return **errno** will be set to one among the following values:

EAGAIN	The message can't be sent due to the **msg_qbytes** limit for the queue and **IPC_NOWAIT** was asserted in *mgsflg*.
EACCES	The calling process has no write access permissions on the message queue.
EFAULT	The address pointed to by *msgp* isn't accessible.
EIDRM	The message queue was removed.
EINTR	Sleeping on a full message queue condition, the process received a signal that had to be caught.
EINVAL	Invalid *msqid* value, or nonpositive *mtype* value, or invalid *msgsz* value (less than 0 or greater than the system value **MSGMAX**).
ENOMEM	The system has not enough memory to make a copy of the supplied **msgbuf**.

When **msgrcv** fails, at return **errno** will be set to one among the following values:

E2BIG	The message text length is greater than *msgsz* and **MSG_NOERROR** isn't asserted in *msgflg*.
EACCES	The calling process has no read access permissions on the message queue.
EFAULT	The address pointed to by *msgp* isn't accessible.
EIDRM	While the process was sleeping to receive a message, the message queue was removed.
EINTR	While the process was sleeping to receive a message, the process received a signal that had to be caught.
EINVAL	Illegal *msgqid* value, or *msgsz* less than **0**.
ENOMSG	**IPC_NOWAIT** was asserted in *msgflg* and no message of the requested type existed on the message queue.

NOTES

The followings are system limits affecting a **msgsnd** system call:

MSGMAX   Maximum size for a message text: the implementation set this value to 4080 bytes.

MSGMNB   Default maximum size in bytes of a message queue: policy dependent. The super–user can increase the size of a message queue beyond **MSGMNB** by a **msgctl** system call.

The implementation has no intrinsic limits for the system wide maximum number of message headers (**MSGTQL**) and for the system wide maximum size in bytes of the message pool (**MSGPOOL**).

SEE ALSO

ipc(5), **msgctl**(2), **msgget**(2), **msgrcv**(2), **msgsnd**(2).

NICE(2)

NAME

nice – change process priority

SYNOPSIS

#include <unistd.h>

int nice(int *inc*);

DESCRIPTION

nice adds *inc* to the priority for the calling pid. Note that only the superuser may specify a negative increment, or priority increase. Note that internally, a higher number is a higher priority. Do not confuse this with the priority scheme as used by the **nice** interface.

RETURN VALUE

On success, zero is returned. On error, –1 is returned, and *errno* is set appropriately.

ERRORS

EPERM A non-super user attempts to do a priority increase, a numerical decrease, by supplying a negative *inc*.

CONFORMING TO

SVID EXT, AT&T, X/OPEN, BSD 4.3

SEE ALSO

nice(1), **setpriority**(2), **fork**(2), **renice**(8)

OBSOLETE(2)　　　　Linux Programmer's Manual　　　　OBSOLETE(2)

NAME

oldfstat, oldlstat, oldstat, oldolduname, olduname – obsolete system calls

SYNOPSIS

Obsolete system calls.

DESCRIPTION

The Linux 1.3.6 kernel implements these calls to support old executables. These calls return structures which have grown since their first implementation, but old executables must continue to receive old smaller structures.

Current executables should be linked with current libraries and never use these calls.

SEE ALSO

fstat(2), **lstat**(2), **stat**(2), **uname**(2), **undocumented**(2), **unimplemented**(2)

OPEN(2)

NAME

open, creat – open and possibly create a file or device

SYNOPSIS

#include <sys/types.h>
#include <sys/stat.h>
#include <fcntl.h>
int open(const char **pathname*, **int** *flags***);**
int open(const char **pathname*, **int** *flags*, **mode_t** *mode***);**
int creat(const char **pathname*, **mode_t** *mode***);**

DESCRIPTION

open attempts to open a file and return a file descriptor (a small, non-negative integer for use in **read**, **write**, etc.)

flags is one of **O_RDONLY**, **O_WRONLY** or **O_RDWR** which request opening the file read-only, write-only or read/write, respectively.

flags may also be bitwise-*or*'d with one or more of the following:

O_CREAT	If the file does not exist it will be created.
O_EXCL	When used with **O_CREAT**, if the file already exists it is an error and the **open** will fail. *See* BUGS below, though.
O_NOCTTY	If *pathname* refers to a terminal device — see **tty**(4) — it will not become the process's controlling terminal even if the process does not have one.
O_TRUNC	If the file already exists it will be truncated.
O_APPEND	The file is opened in append mode. Initially, and before each **write**, the file pointer is positioned at the end of the file, as if with **lseek**.
O_NONBLOCK or **O_NDELAY**	The file is opened in non-blocking mode. Neither the **open** nor any subsequent operations on the file descriptor which is returned will cause the calling process to wait.
O_SYNC	The file is opened for synchronous I/O. Any **write**s on the resulting file descriptor will block the calling process until the data has been physically written to the underlying hardware. *See* BUGS below, though.

Some of these optional flags can be altered using **fcntl** after the file has been opened.

mode specifies the permissions to use if a new file is created. It is modified by the process's **umask** in the usual way: the permissions of the created file are **(mode & ~umask)**.

mode should always be specified when **O_CREAT** is in the *flags*, and is ignored otherwise.

creat is equivalent to **open** with *flags* equal to **O_CREAT|O_WRONLY|O_TRUNC**.

RETURN VALUE

open and **creat** return the new file descriptor, or –1 if an error occurred (in which case, *errno* is set appropriately).

ERRORS

EEXIST	*pathname* already exists and **O_CREAT** and **O_EXCL** were used.
EISDIR	*pathname* refers to a directory and the access requested involved writing.
ETXTBSY	*pathname* refers to an executable image which is currently being executed and write access was requested..
EFAULT	*pathname* points outside your accessible address space.

EACCES	The requested access to the file is not allowed, or one of the directories in *pathname* did not allow search (execute) permission.
ENAMETOOLONG	*pathname* was too long.
ENOENT	A directory component in *pathname* does not exist or is a dangling symbolic link.
ENOTDIR	A component used as a directory in *pathname* is not, in fact, a directory.
EMFILE	The process already has the maximum number of files open.
ENFILE	The limit on the total number of files open on the system has been reached.
ENOMEM	Insufficient kernel memory was available.
EROFS	*pathname* refers to a file on a read-only filesystem and write access was requested.
ELOOP	*pathname* contains a reference to a circular symbolic link, ie a symbolic link whose expansion contains a reference to itself.
ENOSPC	*pathname* was to be created but the device containing *pathname* has no room for the new file.

CONFORMING TO

SVID, AT&T, POSIX, X/OPEN, BSD 4.3

BUGS

O_SYNC is not currently implemented (as of Linux 0.99pl7).

There are many infelicities in the protocol underlying NFS, affecting amongst others **O_SYNC**, **O_NDELAY**, and **O_APPEND**.

O_EXCL is broken on NFS file systems, programs which rely on it for performing locking tasks will contain a race condition. The solution for performing atomic file locking using a lockfile is to create a unique file on the same fs (e.g., incorporating hostname and pid), use **link**(2) to make a link to the lockfile and use **stat**(2) on the unique file to check if its link count has increased to 2. Do not use the return value of the **link()** call.

SEE ALSO

read(2), **write**(2), **fcntl**(2), **close**(2), **unlink**(2), **mknod**(2), **stat**(2), **umask**(2), **mount**(2), **socket**(2), **socket**(2), **fopen**(3), **link**(2).

NAME

pause – wait for signal

SYNOPSIS

#include <unistd.h>

int pause(void);

DESCRIPTION

pause causes the process to sleep until a signal is received.

RETURN VALUE

pause always returns −1, and *errno* is set to **ERESTARTNOHAND**.

ERRORS

    EINTR   signal was received.

CONFORMING TO

SVID, AT&T, POSIX, X/OPEN, BSD 4.3

SEE ALSO

kill(2), **select**(2), **signal**(2)

NAME

phys – allow a process to access physical addresses [NOT IMPLEMENTED]

SYNOPSIS

int phys(int *physnum*, **char** **virtaddr*, **long** *size*,
char **physaddr*);

DESCRIPTION

WARNING: Since this function is not implemented as of Linux 0.99.11, it will always return −1 and set *errno* to **ENOSYS**.

phys maps arbitrary physical memory into a process's virtual address space. *physnum* is number (0‥3) that specifies which of the 4 physical spaces to set up. Up to 4 **phys** calls can be active at any one time. *virtaddr* is the process's virtual address. *size* is the number of bytes to map in. *physaddr* is the physical address to map in.

Valid *virtaddr* and *physaddr* values are constrained by hardware and must be at an address multiple of the resolution of the CPU's memory management scheme. If *size* is non zero, *size* is rounded up to the next MMU resolution boundary. If *size* is zero, any previous **phys**(2) mapping for that *physnum* is nullified.

RETURN VALUE

On success, zero is returned. On error, −1 is returned, and *errno* is set appropriately.

CONFORMING TO

v7

BUGS

phys is very machine dependent.

SEE ALSO

mmap(2), **munmap**(2)

PIPE(2) Linux Programmer's Manual PIPE(2)

NAME

pipe – create pipe

SYNOPSIS

#include <unistd.h>

int pipe(int *filedes***[2]);**

DESCRIPTION

pipe creates a pair of file descriptors, pointing to a pipe inode, and places them in the array pointed to by *filedes*. *filedes[0]* is for reading, *filedes[1]* is for writing.

RETURN VALUE

On success, zero is returned. On error, –1 is returned, and *errno* is set appropriately.

ERRORS

- **EMFILE** Too many file descriptors are in use by the process.
- **ENFILE** The system file table is full.
- **EFAULT** *filedes* is not valid.

SEE ALSO

read(2), **write**(2), **fork**(2), **socketpair**(2)

PROFIL(2)

NAME
profil – execution time profile

SYNOPSIS
#include <unistd.h>

int profil(char *buf*, **int** *bufsiz*, **int** *offset*, **int** *scale*);

DESCRIPTION
Under Linux 0.99.11, *profil* is not implemented in the kernel. Instead, the DLL 4.4.1 libraries provide a user-space implementation.

Buf points to *bufsiz* bytes of core. Every virtual 10 milliseconds, the user's program counter (PC) is examined: *offset* is subtracted and the result is multiplied by *scale*. If this address is in *buf*, then the word pointed to is incremented.

If *scale* is less than 2 or *bufsiz* is zero, profiling is disabled.

RETURN VALUE
Zero is always returned.

BUGS
profil cannot be used on a program that also uses **ITIMER_PROF** itimers.

Calling **profil** with an invalid *buf* will result in a core dump.

True kernel profiling provides more accurate results.

SEE ALSO
gprof(1), **setitimer**(2), **signal**(2), **sigaction**(2)

PTRACE(2)

NAME

ptrace – process trace

SYNOPSIS

#include <sys/ptrace.h>

int ptrace(int *request***, int** *pid***, int** *addr***, int** *data***);**

DESCRIPTION

Ptrace provides a means by which a parent process may control the execution of a child process, and examine and change its core image. Its primary use is for the implementation of breakpoint debugging. A traced process runs until a signal occurs. Then it stops and the parent will be notified with **wait**(2). When the process is in the stopped state, its memory can be read and written. The parent can also cause the child to continue execution, with optional ignoring the signal which caused stopping.

The value of the *request* argument determines the precise action of the system call:

PTRACE_TRACEME	This process is to be traced by its parent. The parent should be expecting to trace the child.
PTRACE_PEEKTEXT, PTRACE_PEEKDATA	Read word at location *addr*.
PTRACE_PEEKUSR	Read word at location *addr* in the **USER** area.
PTRACE_POKETEXT, PTRACE_POKEDATA	Write word at location *addr*.
PTRACE_POKEUSR	Write word at location *addr* in the **USER** area.
PTRACE_SYSCALL, PTRACE_CONT	Restart after signal.
PTRACE_KILL	Send the child a **SIGKILL** to make it exit.
PTRACE_SINGLESTEP	Set the trap flag for single stepping.
PTRACE_ATTACH	Attach to the process specified in *pid*.
PTRACE_DETACH	Detach a process that was previously attached.

NOTES

init, the process with process ID 1, may not use this function.

RETURN VALUE

On success, zero is returned. On error, –1 is returned, and *errno* is set appropriately.

ERRORS

EPERM	The specified process (i.e., **init**), cannot be traced, or is already being traced.
ESRCH	The specified process does not exist.
EIO	*Request* is not valid.

CONFORMING TO

SVID EXT, AT&T, X/OPEN, BSD 4.3

SEE ALSO

gdb(1), **exec**(2), **signal**(2), **wait**(2)

READ(2)

Linux Programmer's Manual

NAME

read – read from a file descriptor

SYNOPSIS

#include <sys/types.h>
#include <unistd.h>
int read(int *fd***, char ****buf***, size_t** *count***);**

DESCRIPTION

read reads up to *count* bytes from file descriptor *fd* into the buffer starting at *buf*.

RETURN VALUE

On success, the number of bytes read are returned (zero indicates end of file). On error, –1 is returned, and *errno* is set appropriately.

ERRORS

EINTR   The call was interrupted by a signal before any data was read.

EAGAIN   Non-blocking I/O has been selected using **O_NONBLOCK** and no data was immediately available for reading.

EISDIR   *fd* refers to a directory.

EBADF   *fd* is not a valid file descriptor or is not open for reading.

EINVAL   *fd* is attached to an object which is unsuitable for reading.

EFAULT   *buf* is outside your accessible address space.

Other errors may occur, depending on the object connected to *fd*.

CONFORMING TO

SVID, AT&T, POSIX, X/OPEN, BSD 4.3

SEE ALSO

readdir(2), **write**(2), **write**(2), **fcntl**(2), **close**(2), **lseek**(2), **select**(2), **readlink**(2), **ioctl**(2), **fread**(3).

READDIR(2)

NAME

readdir – read directory entry

SYNOPSIS

#include <unistd.h>
#include <linux/dirent.h>
#include <linux/unistd.h>
_syscall3(int, readdir, uint, fd, struct dirent *, dirp, uint, count);
int readdir(unsigned int *fd***, struct dirent ****dirp***, unsigned int** *count***);**

DESCRIPTION

This is not the function you are interested in. Look at **readdir**(3) for the POSIX conforming C library interface. This page documents the bare kernel system call interface, which can change, and which is superseded by **getdents**(2).

readdir reads one *dirent* structure from the directory pointed at by *fd* into the memory area pointed to by *dirp*. The parameter *count* is ignored; at most one dirent structure is read.

The *dirent* structure is declared as follows:

```
struct dirent
{
long d_ino; /* inode number */
off_t d_off; /* offset to this dirent */
unsigned short d_reclen; /* length of this d_name */
char d_name [NAME_MAX+1]; /* file name (null-terminated) */
}
```

d_ino is an inode number. *d_off* is the distance from the start of the directory to this *dirent*. *d_reclen* is the size of *d_name*, not counting the null terminator. *d_name* is a null-terminated file name.

RETURN VALUE

On success, 1 is returned. On end of directory, 0 is returned. On error, –1 is returned, and *errno* is set appropriately.

ERRORS

EBADF   Invalid file descriptor *fd*.

ENOTDIR File descriptor does not refer to a directory.

CONFORMING TO

This system call is Linux specific.

SEE ALSO

getdents(2), **readdir**(3)

NAME

readlink – read value of a symbolic link

SYNOPSIS

#include <unistd.h>

int readlink(const char *path***, char** *buf***, size_t** *bufsiz***);**

DESCRIPTION

Readlink places the contents of the symbolic link *path* in the buffer *buf*, which has size *bufsiz*. **Readlink** does not append a **NUL** character to *buf*.

RETURN VALUES

The call returns the count of characters placed in the buffer if it succeeds, or a –1 if an error occurs, placing the error code in the global variable *errno*.

ERRORS

- **ENOTDIR**   A component of the path prefix is not a directory.
- **EINVAL**   The pathname contains a character with the high-order bit set.
- **ENAMETOOLONG**   A component of a pathname exceeded 255 characters, or an entire path name exceeded 1023 characters.
- **ENOENT**   The named file does not exist. **EACCES** Search permission is denied for a component of the path prefix.
- **ELOOP**   Too many symbolic links were encountered in translating the pathname.
- **EINVAL**   The named file is not a symbolic link.
- **EIO**   An I/O error occurred while reading from the file system.
- **EFAULT**   *Buf* extends outside the process's allocated address space.

HISTORY

The **readlink** function call appeared in BSD 4.2.

SEE ALSO

stat(2), lstat(2), symlink(2)

REBOOT(2)

Linux Programmer's Manual

NAME
reboot – reboot or disable Cntrl-Alt-Del

SYNOPSIS
#include <unistd.h>

int reboot (int *magic*, **int** *magic_too*, **int** *flag*);

DESCRIPTION
reboot reboots the system, or enables/disables CAD.

If *magic* == 0xfee1dead && *magictoo* == 672274793, then the action performed will be based on *flag*.

If *flag* = 0x1234567, then a hard reset is performed.
If *flag* = 0x89abcdef, then CAD is enabled.
If *flag* = 0, then CAD is disabled and a signal is sent to process ID 1.

Note that **reboot**() does *not* **sync**()!

Only the super-user may use this function.

RETURN VALUE
On success, zero is returned. On error, −1 is returned, and *errno* is set appropriately.

ERRORS
    EINVAL   Bad *magic* numbers or *flag*.

    EPERM   A non-root user attempts to call **reboot**.

CONFORMING TO
reboot is Linux specific.

SEE ALSO
sync(2), **ctrlaltdel**(8), **halt**(8), **reboot**(8)

RECV(2)

NAME

recv, recvfrom, recvmsg – receive a message from a socket

SYNOPSIS

#include <sys/types.h>
#include <sys/socket.h>

int recv(int *s*, **void** **buf*, **int** *len*, **unsigned int** *flags*);

int recvfrom(int *s*, **void** **buf*, **int** *len*, **unsigned int** *flags* **struct sockaddr** **from*, **int** **fromlen*);

int recvmsg(int *s*, **struct msghdr** **msg*, **unsigned int** *flags*);

DESCRIPTION

WARNING: This is a BSD man page. As of Linux 0.99.11, **recvmsg** was not implemented.

Recvfrom and **recvmsg** are used to receive messages from a socket, and may be used to receive data on a socket whether or not it is connection-oriented.

If *from* is non-nil, and the socket is not connection-oriented, the source address of the message is filled in. *Fromlen* is a value-result parameter, initialized to the size of the buffer associated with *from*, and modified on return to indicate the actual size of the address stored there.

The **recv** call is normally used only on a *connected* socket (see **connect**(2)) and is identical to **recvfrom** with a nil *from* parameter. As it is redundant, it may not be supported in future releases.

All three routines return the length of the message on successful completion. If a message is too long to fit in the supplied buffer, excess bytes may be discarded depending on the type of socket the message is received from (see **socket**(2)).

If no messages are available at the socket, the receive call waits for a message to arrive, unless the socket is nonblocking (see **fcntl**(2)) in which case the value −1 is returned and the external variable *errno* set to **EWOULDBLOCK**. The receive calls normally return any data available, up to the requested amount, rather than waiting for receipt of the full amount requested; this behavior is affected by the socket-level options **SO_RCVLOWAT** and **SO_RCVTIMEO** described in **getsockopt**(2).

The **select**(2) call may be used to determine when more data arrive.

The *flags* argument to a recv call is formed by *or*'ing one or more of the values:

    MSG_OOB   process out-of-band data
    MSG_PEEK   peek at incoming message
    MSG_WAITALL wait for full request or error

The **MSG_OOB** flag requests receipt of out-of-band data that would not be received in the normal data stream. Some protocols place expedited data at the head of the normal data queue, and thus this flag cannot be used with such protocols. The **MSG_PEEK** flag causes the receive operation to return data from the beginning of the receive queue without removing that data from the queue. Thus, a subsequent receive call will return the same data. The **MSG_WAITALL** flag requests that the operation block until the full request is satisfied. However, the call may still return less data than requested if a signal is caught, an error or disconnect occurs, or the next data to be received is of a different type than that returned.

The **recvmsg** call uses a *msghdr* structure to minimize the number of directly supplied parameters. This structure has the following form, as defined in *sys/socket.h*:

```
struct msghdr {
caddr_t msg_name; /* optional address */
u_int msg_namelen; /* size of address */
struct iovec *msg_iov; /* scatter/gather array */
u_int msg_iovlen; /* # elements in msg_iov */
```

```
caddr_t msg_control; /* ancillary data, see below */
u_int msg_controllen; /* ancillary data buffer len */
int msg_flags; /* flags on received message */
};
```

Here *msg_name* and *msg_namelen* specify the destination address if the socket is unconnected; *msg_name* may be given as a null pointer if no names are desired or required. *Msg_iov* and *msg_iovlen* describe scatter gather locations, as discussed in **read**(2). *Msg_control*, which has length *msg_controllen*, points to a buffer for other protocol control related messages or other miscellaneous ancillary data. The messages are of the form:

```
struct cmsghdr {
u_int cmsg_len; /* data byte count, including hdr */
int cmsg_level; /* originating protocol */
int cmsg_type; /* protocol-specific type */
/* followed by
u_char cmsg_data[]; */
};
```

As an example, one could use this to learn of changes in the data-stream in XNS/SPP, or in ISO, to obtain user-connection-request data by requesting a recvmsg with no data buffer provided immediately after an **accept** call.

Open file descriptors are now passed as ancillary data for **AF_UNIX** domain sockets, with *cmsg_level* set to **SOL_SOCKET** and *cmsg_type* set to **SCM_RIGHTS**.

The *msg_flags* field is set on return according to the message received. **MSG_EOR** indicates end-of-record; the data returned completed a record (generally used with sockets of type **SOCK_SEQPACKET**). **MSG_TRUNC** indicates that the trailing portion of a datagram was discarded because the datagram was larger than the buffer supplied. **MSG_CTRUNC** indicates that some control data were discarded due to lack of space in the buffer for ancillary data. **MSG_OOB** is returned to indicate that expedited or out-of-band data were received.

RETURN VALUES

These calls return the number of bytes received, or −1 if an error occurred.

ERRORS

> **EBADF**   The argument *s* is an invalid descriptor.
>
> **ENOTCONN**   The socket is associated with a connection-oriented protocol and has not been connected (see **connect**(2) and **accept**(2)).
>
> **ENOTSOCK**   The argument *s* does not refer to a socket.
>
> **EWOULDBLOCK**   The socket is marked non-blocking, and the receive operation would block, or a receive timeout had been set, and the timeout expired before data were received.
>
> **EINTR**   The receive was interrupted by delivery of a signal before any data were available.
>
> **EFAULT**   The receive buffer pointer(s) point outside the process's address space.

HISTORY

These function calls appeared in BSD 4.2.

SEE ALSO

fcntl(2), **read**(2), **select**(2), **getsockopt**(2), **socket**(2)

RENAME(2)

NAME

rename – change the name or location of a file

SYNOPSIS

#include <unistd.h>

int rename(const char *oldpath, const char *newpath);

DESCRIPTION

rename renames a file, moving it between directories if required.

Any other hard links to the file (as created using **link**) are unaffected.

If *newpath* already exists it will be atomically overwritten (subject to a few conditions - see ERRORS below), so that there is no point at which another process attempting to access *newpath* will find it missing.

If *newpath* exists but the operation fails for some reason or the system crashes **rename** guarantees to leave an instance of *newpath* in place.

However, when overwriting there will probably be a window in which both *oldpath* and *newpath* refer to the file being renamed.

If *oldpath* refers to a symbolic link the link is renamed; if *newpath* refers to a symbolic link the link will be overwritten.

RETURN VALUE

On success, zero is returned. On error, –1 is returned, and *errno* is set appropriately.

ERRORS

EISDIR *newpath* is an existing directory, but *oldpath* is not a directory.

EXDEV *oldpath* and *newpath* are not on the same filesystem.

ENOTEMPTY *newpath* is a non-empty directory.

EBUSY *newpath* exists and is the current working directory or root directory of some process.

EINVAL An attempt was made to make a directory a subdirectory of itself.

EMLINK *oldpath* already has the maximum number of links to it, or it was a directory and the directory containing *newpath* has the maximum number of links.

ENOTDIR A component used as a directory in *oldpath* or *newpath* is not, in fact, a directory.

EFAULT *oldpath* or *newpath* points outside your accessible address space.

EACCES Write access to the directory containing *oldpath* or *newpath* is not allowed for the process's effective uid, or one of the directories in *oldpath* or *newpath* did not allow search (execute) permission, or *oldpath* was a directory and did not allow write permission (needed to update the .. entry).

EPERM The directory containing *oldpath* has the sticky bit set and the process's effective uid is neither the uid of the file to be deleted nor that of the directory containing it, or the filesystem containing *pathname* does not support renaming of the type requested.

ENAMETOOLONG *oldpath* or *newpath* was too long.

ENOENT A directory component in *oldpath* " or " *newpath* does not exist or is a dangling symbolic link.

ENOMEM Insufficient kernel memory was available.

EROFS The file is on a read-only filesystem.

ELOOP *oldpath* or *newpath* contains a reference to a circular symbolic link, ie a symbolic link whose expansion contains a reference to itself.

ENOSPC The device containing the file has no room for the new directory entry.

CONFORMING TO

POSIX, BSD 4.3, ANSI C

BUGS

Currently (Linux 0.99pl7) most of the filesystems except Minix will not allow any overwriting **rename**s involving directories. You get **EEXIST** if you try.

On NFS filesystems, you can not assume that only because the operation failed, the file was not renamed. If the server does the rename operation and then crashes, the retransmitted RPC which will be processed when the server is up again causes a failure. The application is expected to deal with this. See *link*(2) for a similar problem.

SEE ALSO

link(2), unlink(2), symlink(2), mv(1), link(8).

RMDIR(2)

NAME

rmdir – delete a directory

SYNOPSIS

#include <unistd.h>

int rmdir(const char **pathname***);**

DESCRIPTION

rmdir deletes a directory, which must be empty.

RETURN VALUE

On success, zero is returned. On error, –1 is returned, and *errno* is set appropriately.

ERRORS

EPERM The filesystem containing *pathname* does not support the removal of directories.

EFAULT *pathname* points outside your accessible address space.

EACCES Write access to the directory containing *pathname* was not allowed for the process's effective uid, or one of the directories in *pathname* did not allow search (execute) permission.

EPERM The directory containing *pathname* has the sticky-bit (**S_ISVTX**) set and the process's effective uid is neither the uid of the file to be deleted nor that of the directory containing it.

ENAMETOOLONG *pathname* was too long.

ENOENT A directory component in *pathname* does not exist or is a dangling symbolic link.

ENOTDIR *pathname*, or a component used as a directory in *pathname*, is not, in fact, a directory.

ENOTEMPTY *pathname* contains entries other than . and .. .

EBUSY *pathname* is the current working directory or root directory of some process.

ENOMEM Insufficient kernel memory was available.

EROFS *pathname* refers to a file on a read-only filesystem.

ELOOP *pathname* contains a reference to a circular symbolic link, ie a symbolic link containing a reference to itself.

CONFORMING TO

SVID, AT&T, POSIX, BSD 4.3

BUGS

Infelicities in the protocol underlying NFS can cause the unexpected disappearance of directories which are still being used.

SEE ALSO

rename(2), **mkdir**(2), **chdir**(2), **unlink**(2), **rmdir**(1), **rm**(1)

SELECT(2)

Linux Programmer's Manual

NAME

select – synchronous I/O multiplexing

SYNOPSIS

#include <sys/time.h>
#include <sys/types.h>
#include <unistd.h>

int select(int *n*, **fd_set** *readfds, **fd_set** *writefds, **fd_set** *exceptfds, **struct timeval** *timeout);

FD_CLR(int *fd*, **fd_set** *set);
FD_ISSET(int *fd*, **fd_set** *set);
FD_SET(int *fd*, **fd_set** *set);
FD_ZERO(fd_set *set);

DESCRIPTION

select waits for a number of file descriptors to change status.

Three independent sets of descriptors are watched. Those listed in *readfds* will be watched to see if characters become available for reading, those in *writefds* will be watched to see if it is ok to immediately write on them, and those in *exceptfds* will be watched for exceptions. On exit, the sets are modified in place to indicate which descriptors actually changed status.

Four macros are provided to manipulate the sets. **FD_ZERO** will clear a set. **FD_SET** and **FD_CLR** add or remove a given descriptor from a set. **FD_ISSET** tests to see if a descriptor is part of the set; this is useful after **select** returns.

n is the highest-numbered descriptor in any of the three sets, plus 1.

timeout is an upper bound on the amount of time elapsed before **select** returns. It may be zero, causing select to return immediately. If the timeout is NULL (no timeout), **select** can block indefinitely.

RETURN VALUE

On success, **select** returns the number of descriptors contained in the descriptor sets, which may be zero if the timeout expires before anything interesting happens. On error, –1 is returned, and *errno* is set appropriately; the sets and timeout become undefined, so do not rely on their contents after an error.

ERRORS

EBADF An invalid file descriptor was given in one of the sets.
EINTR A non blocked signal was caught.
EINVAL *n* is negative.
ENOMEM select was unable to allocate memory for internal tables.

NOTES

Some code calls **select** with all three sets empty, **n** zero, and a non-null timeout as a fairly portable way to sleep with subsecond precision.

On Linux, *timeout* is modified to reflect the amount of time not slept; most other implementations do not do this. This causes problems both when Linux code which reads *timeout* is ported to other operating systems, and when code is ported to Linux that reuses a struct timeval for multiple **select**s in a loop without reinitializing it. Consider *timeout* to be undefined after **select** returns.

EXAMPLE

#include <stdio.h>
#include <sys/time.h>
#include <sys/types.h>
#include <unistd.h>

```
int
main(void)
{
    fd_set rfds;
    struct timeval tv;
    int retval;

    /* Watch stdin (fd 0) to see when it has input. */
    FD_ZERO(&rfds);
    FD_SET(0, &rfds);
    /* Wait up to five seconds. */
    tv.tv_sec = 5;
    tv.tv_usec = 0;

    retval = select(1, &rfds, NULL, NULL, &tv);
    /* Don't rely on the value of tv now! */

    if (retval)
        printf("Data is available now.\n");
        /* FD_ISSET(0, &rfds) will be true */
    else
        printf("No data within five seconds.\n");

    exit(0);
}
```

SEE ALSO

accept(2), **connect**(2), **read**(2), **recv**(2), **send**(2), **write**(2)

SEMCTL(2)

NAME

semctl – semaphore control operations

SYNOPSIS

include <sys/types.h>
include <sys/ipc.h>
include <sys/sem.h>

int semctl (int *semid***, int** *semnun***, int** *cmd***, union semun** *arg* **)**

DESCRIPTION

The function performs the control operation specified by *cmd* on the semaphore set (or on the *sumun*-nth semaphore of the set) identified by *semid*. The first semaphore of the set is indicated by a value **0** for *semun*.

The type of *arg* is the union

union semun {
int val; /* used for SETVAL only */
struct semid_ds *buf; /* for IPC_STAT and IPC_SET */
ushort *array; /* used for GETALL and SETALL */
};

Legal values for *cmd* are

IPC_STAT Copy info from the semaphore set data structure into the structure pointed to by *arg*.**buf**. The argument *semnum* is ignored. The calling process must have read access privileges on the semaphore set.

IPC_SET Write the values of some members of the **semid_ds** structure pointed to by *arg*.**buf** to the semaphore set data structure, updating also its **sem_ctime** member. Considered members from the user supplied **struct semid_ds** pointed to by *arg*.**buf** are sem_perm.uid sem_perm.gid
sem_perm.mode /* only lowest 9-bits */
The calling process effective user–ID must be one among super–user, creator or owner of the semaphore set. The argument *semnum* is ignored.

IPC_RMID Remove immediately the semaphore set and its data structures awakening all waiting processes (with an error return and **errno** set to **EIDRM**). The calling process effective user–ID must be one among super–user, creator or owner of the semaphore set. The argument *semnum* is ignored.

GETALL Return **semval** for all semaphores of the set into *arg*.**array**. The argument *semnum* is ignored. The calling process must have read access privileges on the semaphore set.

GETNCNT The system call returns the value of **semncnt** for the *semno*–th semaphore of the set (i.e. the number of processes waiting for an increase of **semval** for the *semno*–th semaphore of the set). The calling process must have read access privileges on the semaphore set.

GETPID The system call returns the value of **sempid** for the *semno*–th semaphore of the set (i.e. the pid of the process that executed the last **semop** call for the *semno*–th semaphore of the set). The calling process must have read access privileges on the semaphore set.

GETVAL The system call returns the value of **semval** for the *semno*–th semaphore of the set. The calling process must have read access privileges on the semaphore set.

GETZCNT The system call returns the value of **semzcnt** for the *semno*–th semaphore of the set (i.e. the number of processes waiting for **semval**

SEMCTL(2) Linux Programmer's Manual SEMCTL(2)

of the *semno*–th semaphore of the set to become 0). The calling process must have read access privileges on the semaphore set.

SETALL Set **semval** for all semaphores of the set using *arg*.**array**, updating also the **sem_ctime** member of the **semid_ds** structure associated to the set. Undo entries are cleared for altered semaphores in all processes. Processes sleeping on the wait queue are awakened if some **semval** becomes 0 or increases. The argument *semnum* is ignored. The calling process must have alter access privileges on the semaphore set.

SETVAL Set the value of **semval** to *arg*.**val** for the *semnum*–th semaphore of the set, updating also the **sem_ctime** member of the **semid_ds** structure associated to the set. Undo entry is cleared for altered semaphore in all processes. Processes sleeping on the wait queue are awakened if **semval** becomes 0 or increases. The calling process must have alter access privileges on the semaphore set.

RETURN VALUE

On fail the system call returns −1 with **errno** indicating the error. Otherwise the system call returns a nonnegative value depending on *cmd* as follows:

GETNCNT the value of **semncnt**.
GETPID   the value of **sempid**.
GETVAL   the value of **semval**.
GETZCNT the value of **semzcnt**.

ERRORS

For a failing return, **errno** will be set to one among the following values:

EACCESS The calling process has no access permissions needed to execute *cmd*.
EFAULT   The address pointed to by *arg*.**buf** or *arg*.**array** isn't accessible.
EIDRM   The semaphore set was removed.
EINVAL   Invalid value for *cmd* or *semid*.
EPERM   The argument *cmd* has value **IPC_SET** or **IPC_RMID** but the calling process effective user–ID has insufficient privileges to execute the command.
ERANGE   The argument *cmd* has value **SETALL** or **SETVAL** and the value to which **semval** has to be set (for some semaphore of the set) is less than 0 or greater than the implementation value **SEMVMX**.

NOTES

The **IPC_INFO**, **SEM_STAT** and **SEM_INFO** control calls are used by the **ipcs**(1) program to provide information on allocated resources. In the future these can be modified as needed or moved to a proc file system interface.

The following system limit on semaphore sets affects a **semctl** call:

SEMVMX Maximum value for **semval**: implementation dependent (32767).

SEE ALSO

ipc(5), **shmget**(2), **shmat**(2), **shmdt**(2).

SEMGET(2)　　　　　　　Linux Programmer's Manual　　　　　　　SEMGET(2)

NAME

semget – get a semaphore set identifier

SYNOPSIS

#include <sys/types.h>
#include <sys/ipc.h>
#include <sys/sem.h>

int semget (key_t *key***, int** *nsems***, int** *semflg* **)**

DESCRIPTION

The function returns the semaphore set identifier associated to the value of the argument *key*. A new set of *nsems* semaphores is created if *key* has value **IPC_PRIVATE** or *key* isn't **IPC_PRIVATE**, no existing message queue is associated to *key*, and **IPC_CREAT** is asserted in *semflg* (i.e. *semflg*&**IPC_CREAT** isn't zero). The presence in *semflg* of the fields **IPC_CREAT** and **IPC_EXCL** plays the same role, with respect to the existence of the semaphore set, as the presence of **O_CREAT** and **O_EXCL** in the mode argument of the **open**(2) system call: i.e. the **msgget** function fails if *semflg* asserts both **IPC_CREAT** and **IPC_EXCL** and a semaphore set already exists for *key*.

Upon creation, the lower 9 bits of the argument *semflg* define the access permissions (for owner, group and others) to the semaphore set in the same format, and with the same meaning, as for the access permissions parameter in the **open**(2) or **creat**(2) system calls (though the execute permissions are not used by the system, and write permissions, for a semaphore set, effectively means alter permissions).

Furthermore, while creating, the system call initializes the system semaphore set data structure **semid_ds** as follows:

> **sem_perm.cuid** and **sem_perm.uid** are set to the effective user–ID of the calling process.
>
> **sem_perm.cgid** and **sem_perm.gid** are set to the effective group–ID of the calling process.
>
> The lowest order 9 bits of **sem_perm.mode** are set to the lowest order 9 bit of *semflg*.
>
> **sem_nsems** is set to the value of *nsems*.
>
> **sem_otime** is set to 0.
>
> **sem_ctime** is set to the current time.

The argument *nsems* can be **0** (a don't care) when the system call isn't a create one. Otherwise *nsems* must be greater than **0** and less or equal to the maximum number of semaphores per semid, (**SEMMSL**).

If the semaphore set already exists, the access permissions are verified, and a check is made to see if it is marked for destruction.

RETURN VALUE

If successful, the return value will be the semaphore set identifier (a positive integer), otherwise **–1** with **errno** indicating the error.

ERRORS

For a failing return, **errno** will be set to one among the following values:

> **EACCES**　　A semaphore set exists for *key*, but the calling process has no access permissions to the set.
>
> **EEXIST**　　A semaphore set exists for **key** and *semflg* was asserting both **IPC_CREAT** and **IPC_EXCL**.
>
> **EIDRM**　　The semaphore set is marked as to be deleted.
>
> **ENOENT**　　No semaphore set exists for *key* and *semflg* wasn't asserting **IPC_CREAT**.

ENOMEM A semaphore set has to be created but the system has not enough memory for the new data structure.

ENOSPC A semaphore set has to be created but the system limit for the maximum number of semaphore sets (**SEMMNI**), or the system wide maximum number of semaphores (**SEMMNS**), would be exceeded.

NOTES

IPC_PRIVATE isn't a flag field but a **key_t** type. If this special value is used for *key*, the system call ignores everything but the lowest order 9 bits of *semflg* and creates a new semaphore set (on success).

The followings are limits on semaphore set resources affecting a **semget** call:

SEMMNI System wide maximum number of semaphore sets: policy dependent.

SEMMSL Maximum number of semaphores per semid: implementation dependent (500 currently).

SEMMNS System wide maximum number of semaphores: policy dependent. Values greater than **SEMMSL** * SEMMNI makes it irrelevant.

BUGS

Use of **IPC_PRIVATE** don't inhibits to other processes the access to the allocated semaphore set.

As for the files, there is currently no intrinsic way for a process to ensure exclusive access to a semaphore set. Asserting both **IPC_CREAT** and **IPC_EXCL** in *semflg* only ensures (on success) that a new semaphore set will be created, it doesn't imply exclusive access to the semaphore set.

The data structure associated with each semaphore in the set isn't initialized by the system call. In order to initialize those data structures, one has to execute a subsequent call to semctl(2) to perform a **SETVAL** or a **SETALL** command on the semaphore set.

SEE ALSO

ftok(3), ipc(5), semctl(2), semop(2).

SEMOP(2)

Linux Programmer's Manual

SEMOP(2)

NAME
semop – semaphore operations

SYNOPSIS
include <sys/types.h>
include <sys/ipc.h>
include <sys/sem.h>

int semop (int *semid*, **struct sembuf** **sops*, **unsigned** *nsops* **)**

DESCRIPTION
The function performs operations on selected members of the semaphore set indicated by *semid*. Each of the *nsops* elements in the array pointed to by *sops* specify an operation to be performed on a semaphore by a **struct sembuf** including the following members:

short sem_num; /* semaphore number: 0 = first */
short sem_op; /* semaphore operation */
short sem_flg; /* operation flags */

Flags recognized in **sem_flg** are **IPC_NOWAIT** and **SEM_UNDO**. If an operation asserts **SEM_UNDO**, it will be undone when the process exits.

The system call semantic assures that the operations will be performed if and only if all of them will succeed. Each operation is performed on the **sem_num**–th semaphore of the semaphore set – where the first semaphore of the set is semaphore **0** – and is one among the following three.

If **sem_op** is a positive integer, the operation adds this value to **semval**. Furthermore, if **SEM_UNDO** is asserted for this operation, the system updates the process undo count for this semaphore. The operation always goes through, so no process sleeping can happen. The calling process must have alter permissions on the semaphore set.

If **sem_op** is zero, the process must have read access permissions on the semaphore set. If **semval** is zero, the operation goes through. Otherwise, if **IPC_NOWAIT** is asserted in **sem_flg**, the system call fails (undoing all previous actions performed) with **errno** set to **EAGAIN**. Otherwise **semzcnt** is incremented by one and the process sleeps until one of the following occurs:

> **semval** becomes 0, at which time the value of **semzcnt** is decremented.
>
> The semaphore set is removed: the system call fails with **errno** set to **EIDRM**.
>
> The calling process receives a signal that has to be caught: the value of **semzcnt** is decremented and the system call fails with **errno** set to **EINTR**.

If **sem_op** is less than zero, the process must have alter permissions on the semaphore set. If **semval** is greater than or equal to the absolute value of **sem_op**, the absolute value of **sem_op** is subtracted by **semval**. Furthermore, if **SEM_UNDO** is asserted for this operation, the system updates the process undo count for this semaphore. Then the operation goes through. Otherwise, if **IPC_NOWAIT** is asserted in **sem_flg**, the system call fails (undoing all previous actions performed) with **errno** set to **EAGAIN**. Otherwise **semncnt** is incremented by one and the process sleeps until one of the following occurs:

> **semval** becomes greater or equal to the absolute value of **sem_op**, at which time the value of **semncnt** is decremented, the absolute value of **sem_op** is subtracted from **semval** and, if **SEM_UNDO** is asserted for this operation, the system updates the process undo count for this semaphore.
>
> The semaphore set is removed from the system: the system call fails with **errno** set to **EIDRM**.
>
> The calling process receives a signal that has to be caught: the value of **semncnt** is decremented and the system call fails with **errno** set to **EINTR**.

In case of success, the **sempid** member of the structure **sem** for each semaphore specified in the array pointed to by *sops* is set to the process–ID of the calling process. Furthermore both **sem_otime** and **sem_ctime** are set to the current time.

SEMOP(2) Linux Programmer's Manual SEMOP(2)

RETURN VALUE

If successful the system call returns **0**, otherwise it returns **−1** with **errno** indicating the error.

ERRORS

For a failing return, **errno** will be set to one among the following values:

E2BIG The argument *nsops* is greater than **SEMOPM**, the maximum number of operations allowed per system call.

EACCES The calling process has no access permissions on the semaphore set as required by one of the specified operations.

EAGAIN An operation could not go through and **IPC_NOWAIT** was asserted in its *sem_flg*.

EFAULT The address pointed to by *sops* isn't accessible.

EFBIG For some operation the value of **sem_num** is less than 0 or greater than or equal to the number of semaphores in the set.

EIDRM The semaphore set was removed.

EINTR Sleeping on a wait queue, the process received a signal that had to be caught.

EINVAL The semaphore set doesn't exist, or *semid* is less than zero, or *nsops* has a non-positive value.

ENOMEM The **sem_flg** of some operation asserted **SEM_UNDO** and the system has not enough memory to allocate the undo structure.

ERANGE For some operation **semop+semval** is greater than **SEMVMX**, the implementation dependent maximum value for **semval**.

NOTES

The **sem_undo** structures of a process aren't inherited by its child on execution of a **fork**(2) system call. They are instead inherited by the substituting process resulting by the execution of the **exec**(2) system call.

The followings are limits on semaphore set resources affecting a **semop** call:

SEMOPM Maximum number of operations allowed for one **semop** call: policy dependent.

SEMVMX Maximum allowable value for **semval**: implementation dependent (32767).

The implementation has no intrinsic limits for the adjust on exit maximum value (**SEMAEM**), the system wide maximum number of undo structures (**SEMMNU**) and the per process maximum number of undo entries system parameters.

BUGS

The system maintains a per process **sem_undo** structure for each semaphore altered by the process with undo requests. Those structures are free at process exit. One major cause for unhappiness with the undo mechanism is that it does not fit in with the notion of having an atomic set of operations an array of semaphores. The undo requests for an array and each semaphore therein may have been accumulated over many **semopt** calls. Should the process sleep when exiting, or should all undo operations be applied with the **IPC_NOWAIT** flag in effect? Currently those undo operations which go through immediately are applied, and those that require a wait are ignored silently. Thus harmless undo usage is guaranteed with private semaphores only.

SEE ALSO

ipc(5), **semctl**(2), **semget**(2).

Linux 0.99.13 November 1, 1993

SEND(2)

NAME
send, sendto, sendmsg – send a message from a socket

SYNOPSIS
#include <sys/types.h>
#include <sys/socket.h>

int send(int *s*, const void **msg*, int *len* , unsigned int *flags*);

int sendto(int *s*, const void **msg*, int *len* unsigned int *flags*, const struct sockaddr **to*, int *tolen*);

int sendmsg(int *s*, const struct msghdr **msg* , unsigned int *flags*);

DESCRIPTION
WARNING: This is a BSD man page. As of Linux 0.99.11, **sendmsg** was not implemented.

Send, **sendto**, and **sendmsg** are used to transmit a message to another socket. **Send** may be used only when the socket is in a *connected* state, while **sendto** and **sendmsg** may be used at any time.

The address of the target is given by *to* with *tolen* specifying its size. The length of the message is given by *len*. If the message is too long to pass atomically through the underlying protocol, the error **EMSGSIZE** is returned, and the message is not transmitted.

No indication of failure to deliver is implicit in a **send**. Locally detected errors are indicated by a return value of –1.

If no messages space is available at the socket to hold the message to be transmitted, then **send** normally blocks, unless the socket has been placed in non-blocking I/O mode. The **select**(2) call may be used to determine when it is possible to send more data.

The *flags* parameter may include one or more of the following:

#define MSG_OOB 0x1 /* process out-of-band data */
#define MSG_DONTROUTE 0x4 /* bypass routing, use direct interface */

The flag **MSG_OOB** is used to send *out-of-band* data on sockets that support this notion (e.g. **SOCK_STREAM**); the underlying protocol must also support *out-of-band* data. **MSG_DONTROUTE** is usually used only by diagnostic or routing programs.

See **recv**(2) for a description of the *msghdr* structure.

RETURN VALUES
The call returns the number of characters sent, or –1 if an error occurred.

ERRORS
- **EBADF** An invalid descriptor was specified.
- **ENOTSOCK** The argument *s* is not a socket.
- **EFAULT** An invalid user space address was specified for a parameter.
- **EMSGSIZE** The socket requires that message be sent atomically, and the size of the message to be sent made this impossible.
- **EWOULDBLOCK** The socket is marked non-blocking and the requested operation would block.
- **ENOBUFS** The system was unable to allocate an internal buffer. The operation may succeed when buffers become available.
- **ENOBUFS** The output queue for a network interface was full. This generally indicates that the interface has stopped sending, but may be caused by transient congestion.

HISTORY
These function calls appeared in BSD 4.2.

BSD Man Page   24 July 1993

SEND(2) Linux Programmer's Manual SEND(2)

SEE ALSO
fcntl(2), **recv**(2), **select**(2), **getsockopt**(2), **socket**(2), **write**(2)

SETGID(2)

NAME

setgid – set group identity

SYNOPSIS

#include <unistd.h>

int setgid(gid_t *gid*)

DESCRIPTION

setgid sets the effective group ID of the current process. If the caller is the superuser, the real and saved group ID's are also set.

Under Linux, **setgid** is implemented like SYSV with SAVED_IDS. This allows a setgid (other than root) program to drop all of it's group privileges, do some un-privileged work, and then re-engage the original effective group ID in a secure manner.

If the user is root or the program is setgid root, special care must be taken. The **setgid** function checks the effective gid of the caller and if it is the superuser, all process related group ID's are set to *gid*. After this has occurred, it is impossible for the program to regain root privileges.

RETURN VALUE

On success, zero is returned. On error, –1 is returned, and *errno* is set appropriately.

ERRORS

EPERM   The user is not the super-user, and *gid* does not match the effective or saved group ID of the calling process.

CONFORMING TO

System V

SEE ALSO

getgid(2), **setregid**(2), **setegid**(2)

SETPGID(2)

NAME
setpgid, getpgid, setpgrp, getpgrp – set/get process group

SYNOPSIS
#include <unistd.h>

int setpgid(pid_t *pid*, **pid_t** *pgid*);
pid_t getpgid(pid_t *pid*);
int setpgrp(void);
pid_t getpgrp(void);

DESCRIPTION
setpgid sets the process group ID of the process specified by *pid* to *pgid*. If *pid* is zero, the process ID of the current process is used. If *pgid* is zero, the process ID of the process specified by *pid* is used.

getpgid returns the process group ID of the process specified by *pid*. If *pid* is zero, the process ID of the current process is used.

In the Linux DLL 4.4.1 library, **setpgrp** simply calls **setpgid(0,0)**.

getpgrp is equivalent to **getpgid(0)**.

Process groups are used for distribution of signals, and by terminals to arbitrate requests for their input: processes that have the same process group as the terminal are foreground and may read, while others will block with a signal if they attempt to read.

These calls are thus used by programs such as **csh**(1) to create process groups in implementing job control. The **TIOCGPGRP** and **TIOCSPGRP** calls described in **termios**(4) are used to get/set the process group of the control terminal.

RETURN VALUE
On success, **setpgid** and **setpgrp** return zero. On error, –1 is returned, and *errno* is set appropriately.

getpgid returns a process group on success. On error, –1 is returned, and *errno* is set appropriately.

getpgrp always returns the current process group.

ERRORS
    EINVAL   *pgid* is less than 0.
    EPERM   Various permission violations.
    ESRCH   *pid* does not match any process.

SEE ALSO
getuid(2), **setsid**(2), **tcsetpgrp**(3), **termios**(4)

SETREGID(2)

NAME
setregid, setegid – set real and / or effective group ID

SYNOPSIS
#include <unistd.h>

int setregid(gid_t *rgid*, **gid_t** *egid*);
int setegid(gid_t *egid*);

DESCRIPTION
setregid sets real and effective group ID's of the current process. Un-privileged users may change the real group ID to the effective group ID and vice-versa.

Prior to Linux 1.1.38, the saved ID paradigm, when used with **setregid** or **setegid** was broken. Starting at 1.1.38, it is also possible to set the effective group ID from the saved user ID.

Only the super-user may make other changes.

Supplying a value of −1 for either the real or effective group ID forces the system to leave that ID unchanged.

Currently (libc-4.x.x), **setegid**(*egid*) is functionally equivalent to **setregid**(*-1*, *egid*).

If the real group ID is changed or the effective group ID is set to a value not equal to the previous real group ID, the saved group ID will be set to the new effective group ID.

RETURN VALUE
On success, zero is returned. On error, −1 is returned, and *errno* is set appropriately.

ERRORS
EPERM   The current process is not the super-user and changes other than (i) swapping the effective group ID with the real group ID or (ii) setting one to the value of the other or (iii) setting the effective group ID to the value of the saved group ID was specified.

HISTORY
The **setregid** function call appeared in BSD 4.2.

CONFORMING TO
BSD 4.3

SEE ALSO
getgid(2), **setgid**(2)

NAME

setreuid, seteuid – set real and / or effective user ID

SYNOPSIS

#include <unistd.h>

int setreuid(uid_t *ruid***, uid_t** *euid***);**
int seteuid(uid_t *euid***);**

DESCRIPTION

setreuid sets real and effective user ID's of the current process. Un-privileged users may change the real user ID to the effective user ID and vice-versa.

Prior to Linux 1.1.37, the saved ID paradigm, when used with **setreuid** or **seteuid** was broken.

Starting at 1.1.37, it is also possible to set the effective user ID from the saved user ID.

Only the super-user may make other changes.

Supplying a value of −1 for either the real or effective user ID forces the system to leave that ID unchanged.

Currently (libc-4.x.x), **seteuid**(*euid*) is functionally equivalent to **setreuid**(*-1*, *euid*).

If the real user ID is changed or the effective user ID is set to a value not equal to the previous real user ID, the saved user ID will be set to the new effective user ID.

RETURN VALUE

On success, zero is returned. On error, −1 is returned, and *errno* is set appropriately.

ERRORS

EPERM The current process is not the super-user and changes other than (i) swapping the effective user ID with the real user ID or (ii) setting one to the value of the other or (iii) setting the effective user ID to the value of the saved user ID was specified.

HISTORY

The **setreuid** function call appeared in BSD 4.2.

CONFORMING TO

BSD 4.3

SEE ALSO

getuid(2), **setuid**(2)

SETSID(2) System calls SETSID(2)

NAME

setsid – creates a session and sets the process group ID

SYNOPSIS

#include <unistd.h>

pid_t setsid(void);

DESCRIPTION

setsid() creates a new session if the calling process is not a process group leader. The calling process is the leader of the new session, the process group leader if the new process group, and has no controlling tty. The process group ID of the calling process is set to the PID of the calling process. The calling process will be the only process in this new process group and in this new session.

RETURN VALUE

The process group ID of the calling process.

ERRORS

On error, –1 will be returned. The only error which can happen is EPERM.

CONFORMING TO

POSIX

SEE ALSO

setpgid(2)

SETUID(2)

NAME
setuid – set user identity

SYNOPSIS
#include <unistd.h>

int setuid(uid_t *uid***)**

DESCRIPTION
setuid sets the effective user ID of the current process. If the caller is the superuser, the real and saved user ID's are also set.

Under Linux, **setuid** is implemented like SYSV with SAVED_IDS. This allows a setuid (other than root) program to drop all of it's user privileges, do some un-privileged work, and then re-engage the original effective user ID in a secure manner.

If the user is root or the program is setuid root, special care must be taken. The **setuid** function checks the effective uid of the caller and if it is the superuser, all process related user ID's are set to *uid*. After this has occurred, it is impossible for the program to regain root privileges.

RETURN VALUE
On success, zero is returned. On error, −1 is returned, and *errno* is set appropriately.

ERRORS
EPERM The user is not the super-user, and *uid* does not match the effective or saved user ID of the calling process.

CONFORMING TO
System V

SEE ALSO
getuid(2), **setreuid**(2), **seteuid**(2)

NAME

setup – setup devices and file systems, mount root file system

SYNOPSIS

#include <unistd.h>

_syscall0(int, setup);

int setup(void);

DESCRIPTION

setup is called once from within *linux/init/main.c*. It calls initialization functions for devices and file systems configured into the kernel and then mounts the root file system.

No user process may call **setup**. Any user process, even a process with super-user permission, will receive **EPERM**.

CONFORMING TO

This function is Linux specific.

RETURN VALUE

setup always returns –1 for a user process.

ERRORS

    EPERM   Always, for a user process.

SHMCTL(2)

NAME

shmctl – shared memory control

SYNOPSIS

#include <sys/ipc.h>

#include <sys/shm.h>

int shmctl(int *shmid*, **int** *cmd*, **struct shmid_ds** **buf*);

DESCRIPTION

shmctl() allows the user to receive information on a shared memory segment, set the owner, group, and permissions of a shared memory segment, or destroy a segment. The information about the segment identified by *shmid* is returned in a *shmid_ds* structure:

```
struct shmid_ds {
  struct ipc_perm shm_perm; /* operation perms */
  int shm_segsz; /* size of segment (bytes) */
  time_t shm_atime; /* last attach time */
  time_t shm_dtime; /* last detach time */
  time_t shm_ctime; /* last change time */
  unsigned short shm_cpid; /* pid of creator */
  unsigned short shm_lpid; /* pid of last operator */
  short shm_nattch; /* no. of current attaches */
  /* the following are private */
  unsigned short shm_npages; /* size of segment (pages) */
  unsigned long *shm_pages;
  struct shm_desc *attaches; /* descriptors for attaches */
};
```

The fields in the member *shm_perm* can be set:

```
struct ipc_perm
{
  key_t key;
  ushort uid; /* owner euid and egid */
  ushort gid;
  ushort cuid; /* creator euid and egid */
  ushort cgid;
  ushort mode; /* lower 9 bits of access modes */
  ushort seq; /* sequence number */
};
```

The following *cmds* are available:

IPC_STAT is used to copy the information about the shared memory segment into the buffer *buf*. The user must have **read** access to the shared memory segment.

IPC_SET is used to apply the changes the user has made to the *uid*, *gid*, or *mode* members of the *shm_perms* field. Only the lowest 9 bits of *mode* are used. The *shm_ctime* member is also updated. The user must be the owner, creator, or the super-user.

IPC_RMID is used to mark the segment as destroyed. It will actually be destroyed after the last detach. (I.e., when the *shm_nattch* member of the associated structure *shmid_ds* is zero.) The user must be the owner, creator, or the super-user.

The user *must* ensure that a segment is eventually destroyed; otherwise its pages that were faulted in will remain in memory or swap.

In addition, the **super-user** can prevent or allow swapping of a shared memory segment with the following *cmds*: (Linux only)

SHMCTL(2) Linux Programmer's Manual SHMCTL(2)

SHM_LOCK   prevents swapping of a shared memory segment. The user must fault in any pages that are required to be present after locking is enabled.

SHM_UNLOCK   allows the shared memory segment to be swapped out.

The **IPC_INFO**, **SHM_STAT** and **SHM_INFO** control calls are used by the **ipcs**(1) program to provide information on allocated resources. In the future, these man be modified as needed or moved to a proc file system interface.

SYSTEM CALLS

fork()   After a **fork()** the child inherits the attached shared memory segments.

exec()   After an **exec()** all attached shared memory segments are detached (not destroyed).

exit()   Upon **exit()** all attached shared memory segments are detached (not destroyed).

RETURN VALUE

0 is returned on success, −1 on error.

ERRORS

On error, **errno** will be set to one of the following:

EACCESS   is returned if **IPC_STAT** is requested and *shm_perm.modes* does not allow read access for *msqid*.

EFAULT   The argument *cmd* has value **IPC_SET** or **IPC_STAT** but the address pointed to by *buf* isn't accessible.

EINVAL   is returned if *shmid* is not a valid identifier, or *cmd* is not a valid command.

EIDRM   is returned if *shmid* points to a removed identifier.

EPERM   is returned if **IPC_SET** or **IPC_RMID** is attempted, and the user is not the creator, the owner, or the super-user, and the user does not have permission granted to their group or to the world.

SEE ALSO

shmget(2), **shmop**(2)

SHMGET(2)

NAME

shmget – allocates a shared memory segment

SYNOPSIS

#include <sys/ipc.h>

#include <sys/shm.h>

int shmget(key_t *key*, **int** *size*, **int** *shmflg***);**

DESCRIPTION

shmget() returns the identifier of the shared memory segment associated to the value of the argument *key*. A new shared memory segment, with size equal to the round up of *size* to a multiple of **PAGE_SIZE**, is created if *key* has value **IPC_PRIVATE** or *key* isn't **IPC_PRIVATE**, no shared memory segment is associated to *key*, and **IPC_CREAT** is asserted in *shmflg* (i.e. *shmflg***&IPC_CREAT** isn't zero). The presence in

shmflg is composed of:

    IPC_CREAT   to create a new segment. If this flag is not used, then **shmget()** will find the segment associated with *key*, check to see if the user has permission to receive the *shmid* associated with the segment, and ensure the segment is not marked for destruction.

    IPC_EXCL   used with **IPC_CREAT** to ensure failure if the segment exists.

    mode_flags (lowest 9 bits)   specifying the permissions granted to the owner, group, and world. Presently, the execute permissions are not used by the system.

If a new segment is created, the access permissions from *shmflg* are copied into the *shm_perm* member of the *shmid_ds* structure that defines the segment. The *shmid_ds* structure:

```
struct shmid_ds {
    struct ipc_perm shm_perm; /* operation perms */
    int shm_segsz; /* size of segment (bytes) */
    time_t shm_atime; /* last attach time */
    time_t shm_dtime; /* last detach time */
    time_t shm_ctime; /* last change time */
    unsigned short shm_cpid; /* pid of creator */
    unsigned short shm_lpid; /* pid of last operator */
    short shm_nattch; /* no. of current attaches */
};

struct ipc_perm
{
    key_t key;
    ushort uid; /* owner euid and egid */
    ushort gid;
    ushort cuid; /* creator euid and egid */
    ushort cgid;
    ushort mode; /* lower 9 bits of shmflg */
    ushort seq; /* sequence number */
};
```

Furthermore, while creating, the system call initializes the system shared memory segment data structure **shmid_ds** as follows:

shm_perm.cuid and **shm_perm.uid** are set to the effective user–ID of the calling process.

shm_perm.cgid and **shm_perm.gid** are set to the effective group–ID of the calling process.

The lowest order 9 bits of **shm_perm.mode** are set to the lowest order 9 bit of *shmflg*.

SHMGET(2)   Linux Programmer's Manual   SHMGET(2)

shm_segsz is set to the value of *size*.

shm_lpid, **shm_nattch**, **shm_atime** and **shm_dtime** are set to **0**.

shm_ctime is set to the current time.

If the shared memory segment already exists, the access permissions are verified, and a check is made to see if it is marked for destruction.

SYSTEM CALLS

fork()   After a **fork()** the child inherits the attached shared memory segments.

exec()   After an **exec()** all attached shared memory segments are detached (not destroyed).

exit()   Upon **exit()** all attached shared memory segments are detached (not destroyed).

RETURN VALUE

A valid segment identifier, *shmid*, is returned on success, −1 on error.

ERRORS

On failure, **errno** is set to one of the following:

EINVAL   is returned if **SHMMIN** > *size* or *size* > **SHMMAX**, or *size* is greater than size of segment.

EEXIST   is returned if **IPC_CREAT** | IPC_EXCL was specified and the segment exists.

EIDRM   is returned if the segment is marked as destroyed, or was removed.

ENOSPC   is returned if all possible shared memory id's have been taken (**SHMMNI**) or if allocating a segment of the requested *size* would cause the system to exceed the system-wide limit on shared memory (**SHMALL**).

ENOENT   is returned if no segment exists for the given *key*, and **IPC_CREAT** was not specified.

EACCES   is returned if the user does not have permission to access the shared memory segment.

ENOMEM   is returned if no memory could be allocated for segment overhead.

NOTES

IPC_PRIVATE isn't a flag field but a **key_t** type. If this special value is used for *key*, the system call ignores everything but the lowest order 9 bits of *shmflg* and creates a new shared memory segment (on success).

The followings are limits on shared memory segment resources affecting a **shmget** call:

SHMALL   System wide maximum of shared memory pages: policy dependent.

SHMMAX   Maximum size in bytes for a shared memory segment: implementation dependent (currently 4M).

SHMMIN   Minimum size in bytes for a shared memory segment: implementation dependent (currently 1 byte, though **PAGE_SIZE** is the effective minimum size).

SHMMNI   System wide maximum number of shared memory segments: implementation dependent (currently 4096).

The implementation has no specific limits for the per process maximum number of shared memory segments (**SHMSEG**).

BUGS

Use of **IPC_PRIVATE** don't inhibits to other processes the access to the allocated shared memory segment.

As for the files, there is currently no intrinsic way for a process to ensure exclusive access to a shared memory segment. Asserting both **IPC_CREAT** and **IPC_EXCL** in *shmflg* only ensures (on success) that a new shared memory segment will be created, it doesn't imply exclusive access to the segment.

SEE ALSO

ftok(3), ipc(5), shmctl(2), shmat(2), shmdt(2).

SHMOP(2)

NAME

shmop – shared memory operations

SYNOPSIS

#include <sys/types.h>
#include <sys/ipc.h>
#include <sys/shm.h>

char *shmat (int *shmid,* **char ****shmaddr,* **int** *shmflg* **)**

int shmdt (char **shmaddr)*

DESCRIPTION

The function **shmat** attaches the shared memory segment identified by **shmid** to the data segment of the calling process. The attaching address is specified by *shmaddr* with one of the following criteria:

> If *shmaddr* is **0**, the system tries to find an unmapped region in the range 1 – 1.5G starting from the upper value and coming down from there.
>
> If *shmaddr* isn't **0** and **SHM_RND** is asserted in *shmflg*, the attach occurs at address equal to the rounding down of *shmaddr* to a multiple of **SHMLBA**. Otherwise *shmaddr* must be a page aligned address at which the attach occurs.

If **SHM_RDONLY** is asserted in *shmflg*, the segment is attached for reading and the process must have read access permissions to the segment. Otherwise the segment is attached for read and write and the process must have read and write access permissions to the segment. There is no notion of write-only shared memory segment.

The **brk** value of the calling process is not altered by the attach. The segment will automatically detached at process exit. The same segment may be attached as a read and as a read-write one, and more than once, in the process's address space.

On a successful **shmat** call the system updates the members of the structure **shmid_ds** associated to the shared memory segment as follows:

> **shm_atime** is set to the current time.
>
> **shm_lpid** is set to the process-ID of the calling process.
>
> **shm_nattch** is incremented by one.

Note that the attach succeeds also if the shared memory segment is marked as to be deleted.

The function **shmdt** detaches from the calling process's data segment the shared memory segment located at the address specified by *shmaddr*. The detaching shared memory segment must be one among the currently attached ones (to the process's address space) with *shmaddr* equal to the value returned by the its attaching **shat** call.

On a successful **shmdt** call the system updates the members of the structure **shmid_ds** associated to the shared memory segment as follows:

> **shm_dtime** is set to the current time.
>
> **shm_lpid** is set to the process-ID of the calling process.
>
> **shm_nattch** is decremented by one. If it becomes 0 and the segment is marked for deletion, the segment is deleted.

The occupied region in the user space of the calling process is unmapped.

SYSTEM CALLS

> **fork()**   After a **fork()** the child inherits the attached shared memory segments.
>
> **exec()**   After an **exec()** all attached shared memory segments are detached (not destroyed).
>
> **exit()**   Upon **exit()** all attached shared memory segments are detached (not destroyed).

SHMOP(2) Linux Programmer's Manual SHMOP(2)

RETURN VALUE

On a failure both functions return **−1** with **errno** indicating the error, otherwise **shmat** returns the address of the attached shared memory segment, and **shmdt** returns **0**.

ERRORS

When **shmat** fails, at return **errno** will be set to one among the following values:

EACCES   The calling process has no access permissions for the requested attach type.

EINVAL   Invalid *shmid* value, unaligned (i.e., not page-aligned and **SHM_RND** was not specified) or invalid *shmaddr* value, or failing attach at **brk**.

ENOMEM   Could not allocate memory for the descriptor or for the page tables.

The function **shmdt** can fails only if there is no shared memory segment attached at *shmaddr*, in such a case at return **errno** will be set to **EINVAL**.

NOTES

On executing a **fork**(2) system call, the child inherits all the attached shared memory segments.

The shared memory segments attached to a process executing an **exec**(2) system call will not be attached to the resulting process.

The following is a system parameter affecting a **shmat** system call:

SHMLBA   Segment low boundary address multiple. Must be page aligned. For the current implementation the **SHMBLA** value is **PAGE_SIZE**.

The implementation has no intrinsic limit to the per process maximum number of shared memory segments (**SHMSEG**).

SEE ALSO

ipc(5), **shmctl**(2), **shmget**(2).

Linux 0.99.13 November 28, 1993 631

SHUTDOWN(2)

NAME

shutdown – shut down part of a full-duplex connection

SYNOPSIS

#include <sys/socket.h>

int shutdown(int *s*, **int** *how*);

DESCRIPTION

The *shutdown* call causes all or part of a full-duplex connection on the socket associated with *s* to be shut down. If *how* is 0, further receives will be disallowed. If *how* is 1, further sends will be disallowed. If *how* is 2, further sends and receives will be disallowed.

RETURN VALUE

On success, zero is returned. On error, −1 is returned, and *errno* is set appropriately.

ERRORS

EBADF   *S* is not a valid descriptor.

ENOTSOCK   *S* is a file, not a socket.

ENOTCONN   The specified socket is not connected.

HISTORY

The **shutdown** function call appeared in BSD 4.2.

SEE ALSO

connect(2), **socket**(2)

SIGACTION(2)

NAME
sigaction, sigprocmask, sigpending, sigsuspend – POSIX signal handling functions.

SYNOPSIS
#include <signal.h>

int sigaction(int *signum*, **const struct sigaction ****act*, **struct sigaction ****oldact*);

int sigprocmask(int *how*, **const sigset_t ****set*, **sigset_t ****oldset*);

int sigpending(sigset_t *set);

int sigsuspend(const sigset_t *mask);

DESCRIPTION
The **sigaction** system call is used to change the action for a signal. If *act* is non–null, the new action for signal *signum* is installed from *act*. If *oldact* is non–null, the previous action is saved in *oldact*.

The **sigaction** structure is defined as

struct sigaction {
void (*sa_handler)();
sigset_t sa_mask;
int sa_flags;
void (*sa_restorer)(void);
}

sa_handler may be **SIG_DFL** for the default action, **SIG_IGN** to ignore this signal, or a pointer to a signal handling function.

sa_mask gives a mask of signals which should be blocked during execution of the signal handler.

sa_flags is the bitwise OR of zero or more of the following flags

SA_NOCLDSTOP	Do not generate SIGCHLD signals when child processes terminate.
SA_ONESHOT	Restore the signal action to the default state once the signal handler has been called. This is the default behavior.
SA_RESTART	The opposite to **SA_ONESHOT**, do not restore the signal action. This provides behavior compatible with BSD signal semantics.
SA_NOMASK	Do not prevent the signal from being received from within its own signal handler.

The *sa_restorer* element is obsolete and should not be used.

The **sigprocmask** call is used to change the list of currently blocked signals. The behavior of the call is dependent on the value of *how*, as follows.

SIG_BLOCK	The set of blocked signals is the union of the current set and the *set* argument.
SIG_UNBLOCK	The signals in *set* are removed from the current set of blocked signals. It is legal to attempt to unblock a signal which is not blocked.
SIG_SETMASK	The set of blocked signals is set to the argument *set*.

If *oldset* is non–null, the previous value of the signal mask is stored in *oldset*.

The **sigpending** call allows the examination of pending signals (ones which have been raised while blocked). The signal mask of pending signals is stored in *set*.

The **sigsuspend** call temporarily replaces the signal mask for the process with that given by *mask* and then suspends the process until a signal is received.

RETURN VALUES

sigaction, **sigprocmask**, **sigpending** and **sigsuspend** return 0 on success and -1 on error.

ERRORS

EINVAL An invalid signal was specified. This will also be generated if an attempt is made to change the action for SIGKILL or SIGSTOP, which cannot be caught.

EFAULT *act*, *oldact* or the signal handler point to memory which is not a valid part of the process address space.

EINTR System call was interrupted.

NOTES

It is not possible to block SIGKILL or SIGSTOP with the sigprocmask call. Attempts to do so will be silently ignored.

The POSIX spec only defines **SA_NOCLDSTOP**. Use of **SA_ONESHOT** and **SA_RESTART** is non-portable.

sigaction can be called with a null second argument to query the current signal handler. It can also be used to check whether a given signal is valid for the current machine by calling it with null second and third arguments.

See **sigsetops**(3) for details on manipulating signal sets.

CONFORMING TO

POSIX

SEE ALSO

kill(1), **kill**(2), **killpg**(2), **pause**(2), **raise**(3), **siginterrupt**(3), **signal**(2), **signal**(7), **sigsetops**(3), **sigvec**(2)

SIGACTION(2) Linux Programmer's Manual SIGACTION(2)

NAME

signal – ANSI C signal handling.

SYNOPSIS

#include <signal.h>
void (*signal(int *signum*, **void (****handler***)(int)))(int);**

DESCRIPTION

The **signal** system call installs a new signal handler for signal *signum*. The signal handler is set to *handler* which may be a user specified function, or one of the following:

    SIG_IGN   Ignore the signal.
    SIG_DFL   Reset the signal to its default behavior.

RETURN VALUE

signal returns the previous value of the signal handler, or **SIG_ERR** on error.

NOTES

Signal handlers cannot be set for **SIGKILL** or **SIGSTOP**.

Unlike BSD systems, signals under Linux are reset to their default behavior when raised.

If you're confused by the prototype at the top of this manpage, it may help to see it separated out thus:

typedef void (*sighandler_t)(int);
sighandler_t signal(int *signum*, **sighandler_t** *handler***);**

CONFORMING TO

ANSI C

SEE ALSO

kill(1), **kill**(2), **killpg**(2), **pause**(2), **raise**(3), **sigaction**(2), **signal**(7), **sigsetops**(3), **sigvec**(2)

Linux 1.0 24 September 1994 635

SIGBLOCK(2)

NAME

sigblock, sigmask – block signals

SYNOPSIS

#include <signal.h>

int sigblock(int *mask***); int sigmask(** *signum***);**

DESCRIPTION

This interface is made obsolete by: **sigprocmask**(2).

Sigblock adds the signals specified in *mask* to the set of signals currently being blocked from delivery. Signals are blocked if the corresponding bit in *mask* is a 1; the macro **sigmask** is provided to construct the mask for a given *signum*.

It is not possible to block **SIGKILL** or **SIGSTOP** ; this restriction is silently imposed by the system.

RETURN VALUES

The previous set of masked signals is returned.

HISTORY

These function calls appeared in BSD 4.3 and have been deprecated.

SEE ALSO

kill(2), **sigprocmask**(2), **sigsetmask**(2), **siggetops**(3)

NAME

sigpause – atomically release blocked signals and wait for interrupt

SYNOPSIS

#include <signal.h>

int sigpause(int *sigmask***);**

DESCRIPTION

This interface is made obsolete by **sigsuspend**(2).

Sigpause assigns *sigmask* to the set of masked signals and then waits for a signal to arrive; on return the set of masked signals is restored. *Sigmask* is usually 0 to indicate that no signals are to be blocked. **Sigpause** always terminates by being interrupted, returning −1 with *errno* set to **EINTR**

HISTORY

The **sigpause** function call appeared in BSD 4.3 and has been deprecated.

SEE ALSO

sigsuspend(2), **kill**(2), **sigaction**(2), **sigprocmask**(2), **sigblock**(2), **sigvec**(2)

SIGVEC(2)

NAME
sigvec – software signal facilities

SYNOPSIS
#include <bsd/signal.h>

int sigvec(int *sig*, **struct sigvec ****vec*, **struct sigvec ****ovec***)**;

DESCRIPTION
WARNING: Under Linux DLL 4.4.1, **sigvec** is #defined'd to be **sigaction**.

This interface is made obsolete by **sigaction**(2).

SEE ALSO
sigaction(2), **signal**(2)

SOCKET(2)

NAME

socket – create an endpoint for communication

SYNOPSIS

#include <sys/types.h>
#include <sys/socket.h>

int socket(int *domain*, **int** *type*, **int** *protocol*);

DESCRIPTION

Socket creates an endpoint for communication and returns a descriptor.

The *domain* parameter specifies a communications domain within which communication will take place; this selects the protocol family which should be used. These families are defined in the include file *sys/socket.h*. The currently understood formats are

AF_UNIX	(UNIX internal protocols)
AF_INET	(ARPA Internet protocols)
AF_ISO	(ISO protocols)
AF_NS	(Xerox Network Systems protocols)
AF_IMPLINK	(IMP host at IMP link layer)

The socket has the indicated *type*, which specifies the semantics of communication. Currently defined types are:

SOCK_STREAM
SOCK_DGRAM
SOCK_RAW
SOCK_SEQPACKET
SOCK_RDM

A **SOCK_STREAM** type provides sequenced, reliable, two-way connection based byte streams. An out-of-band data transmission mechanism may be supported. A **SOCK_DGRAM** socket supports datagrams (connectionless, unreliable messages of a fixed (typically small) maximum length). A **SOCK_SEQPACKET** socket may provide a sequenced, reliable, two-way connection-based data transmission path for datagrams of fixed maximum length; a consumer may be required to read an entire packet with each read system call. This facility is protocol specific, and presently implemented only for **PF_NS**. **SOCK_RAW** sockets provide access to internal network protocols and interfaces. The types **SOCK_RAW**, which is available only to the super-user, and **SOCK_RDM**, which is planned, but not yet implemented, are not described here.

The *protocol* specifies a particular protocol to be used with the socket. Normally only a single protocol exists to support a particular socket type within a given protocol family. However, it is possible that many protocols may exist, in which case a particular protocol must be specified in this manner. The protocol number to use is particular to the communication domain in which communication is to take place; see **protocols**(5).

Sockets of type **SOCK_STREAM** are full-duplex byte streams, similar to pipes. A stream socket must be in a *connected* state before any data may be sent or received on it. A connection to another socket is created with a **connect**(2) call. Once connected, data may be transferred using **read**(2) and **write**(2) calls or some variant of the **send**(2) and **recv**(2) calls. When a session has been completed a **close**(2) may be performed. Out-of-band data may also be transmitted as described in **send**(2) and received as described in **recv**(2).

The communications protocols used to implement a **SOCK_STREAM** insure that data is not lost or duplicated. If a piece of data for which the peer protocol has buffer space cannot be successfully transmitted within a reasonable length of time, then the connection is considered broken and calls will indicate an error with –1 returns and with **ETIMEDOUT** as the specific code in the global variable *errno*. The protocols optionally keep sockets *warm* by forcing transmissions roughly every minute in the absence of other activity. An error is then indicated if no response can be elicited on an otherwise idle connection for a extended

SOCKET(2)   Linux Programmer's Manual   SOCKET(2)

period (e.g. 5 minutes). A **SIGPIPE** signal is raised if a process sends on a broken stream; this causes naive processes, which do not handle the signal, to exit.

SOCK_SEQPACKET sockets employ the same system calls as **SOCK_STREAM** sockets. The only difference is that **read**(2) calls will return only the amount of data requested, and any remaining in the arriving packet will be discarded.

SOCK_DGRAM and **SOCK_RAW** sockets allow sending of datagrams to correspondents named in **send**(2) calls. Datagrams are generally received with **recvfrom**(2), which returns the next datagram with its return address.

An **fcntl**(2) call can be used to specify a process group to receive a **SIGURG** signal when the out-of-band data arrives. It may also enable non-blocking I/O and asynchronous notification of I/O events via **SIGIO**.

The operation of sockets is controlled by socket level *options*. These options are defined in the file *sys/socket.h*. **Setsockopt**(2) and **getsockopt**(2) are used to set and get options, respectively.

RETURN VALUES

A −1 is returned if an error occurs, otherwise the return value is a descriptor referencing the socket.

ERRORS

EPROTONOSUPPORT	The protocol type or the specified protocol is not supported within this domain.
EMFILE	The per-process descriptor table is full.
ENFILE	The system file table is full.
EACCESS	Permission to create a socket of the specified type and/or protocol is denied.
ENOBUFS	Insufficient buffer space is available. The socket cannot be created until sufficient resources are freed.

HISTORY

The **socket** function call appeared in BSD 4.2.

SEE ALSO

accept(2), **bind**(2), **connect**(2), **getprotoent**(3), **getsockname**(2), **getsockopt**(2), **ioctl**(2), **listen**(2), **read**(2), **recv**(2), **select**(2), **send**(2), **shutdown**(2), **socketpair**(2), **write**(2)

"An Introductory 4.3 BSD Interprocess Communication Tutorial" is reprinted in *UNIX* Programmer's Supplementary Documents Volume 1

"BSD Interprocess Communication Tutorial" is reprinted in *UNIX* Programmer's Supplementary Documents Volume 1

SOCKETCALL(2)

NAME

socketcall – socket system calls

SYNOPSIS

int socketcall(int *call,* **unsigned long** **args);*

DESCRIPTION

socketcall is a common kernel entry point for the socket system calls. *call* determines which socket function to invoke. *args* points to a block containing the actual arguments, which are passed through to the appropriate call.

User programs should call the appropriate functions by their usual names. Only standard library implementors and kernel hackers need to know about **socketcall**.

SEE ALSO

accept(2), **bind**(2), **connect**(2), **getpeername**(2), **getsockname**(2), **getsockopt**(2), **listen**(2), **recv**(2), **recvfrom**(2), **send**(2), **sendto**(2), **setsockopt**(2), **shutdown**(2), **socket**(2), **socketpair**(2)

SOCKETPAIR(2)

NAME

socketpair – create a pair of connected sockets

SYNOPSIS

#include <sys/types.h>
#include <sys/socket.h>

int socketpair(int *d*, int *type*, int *protocol*, int *sv*[2]);

DESCRIPTION

The call creates an unnamed pair of connected sockets in the specified domain *d*, of the specified *type*, and using the optionally specified *protocol*. The descriptors used in referencing the new sockets are returned in *sv*[0] and *sv*[1]. The two sockets are indistinguishable.

RETURN VALUE

On success, zero is returned. On error, −1 is returned, and *errno* is set appropriately.

ERRORS

EMFILE   Too many descriptors are in use by this process.

EAFNOSUPPORT   The specified address family is not supported on this machine.

EPROTONOSUPPORT   The specified protocol is not supported on this machine.

EOPNOSUPPORT   The specified protocol does not support creation of socket pairs.

EFAULT   The address *sv* does not specify a valid part of the process address space.

HISTORY

The **socketpair** function call appeared in BSD 4.2.

BUGS

This call is currently implemented only for the **UNIX** domain. [Documenter's note: is this true for Linux?]

SEE ALSO

read(2), write(2), pipe(2)

STAT(2)   Linux Programmer's Manual   STAT(2)

NAME

stat, fstat, lstat – get file status

SYNOPSIS

#include <sys/stat.h>
#include <unistd.h>

int stat(const char **file_name,* **struct stat** **buf***);**
int fstat(int *filedes,* **struct stat** **buf***);**
int lstat(const char **file_name,* **struct stat** **buf***);**

DESCRIPTION

These functions return information about the specified file. You do not need any access rights to the file to get this information but you need search rights to all directories named in the path leading to the file.

stat stats the file pointed to by *file_name* and fills in *buf*.

lstat is identical to **stat**, only the link itself is stated, not the file that is obtained by tracing the links.

fstat is identical to stat, only the open file pointed to by *filedes* (as returned by *fopen(3)*) is stated in place of *file_name*.

They all return a *stat* structure, which is declared as follows:

```
struct stat
{
    dev_t st_dev; /* device */
    ino_t st_ino; /* inode */
    umode_t st_mode; /* protection */
    nlink_t st_nlink; /* number of hard links */
    uid_t st_uid; /* user ID of owner */
    gid_t st_gid; /* group ID of owner */
    dev_t st_rdev; /* device type (if inode device) */
    off_t st_size; /* total size, in bytes */
    unsigned long st_blksize; /* blocksize for filesystem I/O */
    unsigned long st_blocks; /* number of blocks allocated */
    time_t st_atime; /* time of last access */
    time_t st_mtime; /* time of last modification */
    time_t st_ctime; /* time of last change */
};
```

Note that *st_blocks* may not always be in terms of blocks of size *st_blksize*, and that *st_blksize* may instead provide a notion of the "preferred" blocksize for efficient file system I/O.

Not all of the Linux filesystems implement all of the time fields. Traditionally, *st_atime* is changed by **mknod**(2), **utime**(2), **read**(2), **write**(2), and **truncate**(2).

Traditionally, *st_mtime* is changed by **mknod**(2), **utime**(2), and **write**(2). The *st_mtime* is *not* changed for changes in owner, group, hard link count, or mode.

Traditionally, *st_ctime* is changed by writing or by setting inode information (i.e., owner, group, link count, mode, etc.).

The following macros are defined to check the file type:

S_ISLNK(m)	is it a symbolic link?
S_ISREG(m)	regular file?
S_ISDIR(m)	directory?
S_ISCHR(m)	character device?
S_ISBLK(m)	block device?
S_ISFIFO(m)	fifo?

S_ISSOCK(m)   socket?

The following flags are defined for the *st_mode* field:

S_IFMT	0017 0000	bitmask for the file type bitfields
S_IFSOCK	0140000	socket
S_IFLNK	0120000	symbolic link
S_IFREG	0100000	regular file
S_IFBLK	0060000	block device
S_IFDIR	0040000	directory
S_IFCHR	0020000	character device
S_IFIFO	0010000	fifo
S_ISUID	0004000	set UID bit
S_ISGID	0002000	set GID bit
S_ISVTX	0001000	sticky bit
S_IRWXU	00700	user (file owner) has read, write and execute permission
S_IRUSR (S_IREAD)	00400	user has read permission
S_IWUSR (S_IWRITE)	00200	user has write permission
S_IXUSR (S_IEXEC)	00100	user has execute permission
S_IRWXG	00070	group has read, write and execute permission
S_IRGRP	00040	group has read permission
S_IWGRP	00020	group has write permission
S_IXGRP	00010	group has execute permission
S_IRWXO	00007	others have read, write and execute permission
S_IROTH	00004	others have read permission
S_IWOTH	00002	others have write permisson
S_IXOTH	00001	others have execute permission

RETURN VALUE

On success, zero is returned. On error, −1 is returned, and *errno* is set appropriately.

ERRORS

EBADF   *filedes* is bad.
ENOENT   File does not exist.

CONFORMING TO

SVID (not **lstat**()), AT&T (not **lstat**()), POSIX (not **lstat**()), X/OPEN (not **lstat**()), BSD 4.3

SEE ALSO

chmod(2), **chown**(2), **readlink**(2), **utime**(2)

STATFS(2)

NAME
statfs, fstatfs – get file system statistics

SYNOPSIS
#include <sys/vfs.h>

int statfs(const char *path*, **struct statfs** *buf*);
int fstatfs(int *fd*, **struct statfs** *buf*);

DESCRIPTION
returns information about a mounted file system. *Path* is the path name of any file within the mounted filesystem. *Buf* is a pointer to a *statfs* structure defined as follows:

```
struct statfs {
long f_type; /* type of filesystem (see below) */
long f_bsize; /* optimal transfer block size */
long f_blocks; /* total data blocks in file system */
long f_bfree; /* free blocks in fs */
long f_bavail; /* free blocks avail to non-superuser */
long f_files; /* total file nodes in file system */
long f_ffree; /* free file nodes in fs */
fsid_t f_fsid; /* file system id */
long f_namelen; /* maximum length of filenames */
long f_spare[6]; /* spare for later */
};
```

File system types:

linux/ext2_fs.h: EXT2_OLD_SUPER_MAGIC 0xEF51
linux/ext2_fs.h: EXT2_SUPER_MAGIC 0xEF53
linux/ext_fs.h: EXT_SUPER_MAGIC 0x137D
linux/iso_fs.h: ISOFS_SUPER_MAGIC 0x9660
linux/minix_fs.h: MINIX_SUPER_MAGIC 0x137F /* orig. minix */
linux/minix_fs.h: MINIX_SUPER_MAGIC2 0x138F /* 30 char minix */
linux/minix_fs.h: NEW_MINIX_SUPER_MAGIC 0x2468 /* minix V2 */
linux/msdos_fs.h: MSDOS_SUPER_MAGIC 0x4d44
linux/nfs_fs.h: NFS_SUPER_MAGIC 0x6969
linux/proc_fs.h: PROC_SUPER_MAGIC 0x9fa0
linux/xia_fs.h: _XIAFS_SUPER_MAGIC 0x012FD16D

Fields that are undefined for a particular file system are set to –1. **Fstatfs** returns the same information about an open file referenced by descriptor *fd*.

RETURN VALUE
On success, zero is returned. On error, –1 is returned, and *errno* is set appropriately.

ERRORS
For **statfs**:

ENOTDIR A component of the path prefix of *Path* is not a directory.
EINVAL *path* contains a character with the high-order bit set.
ENAMETOOLONG The length of a component of *path* exceeds 255 characters, or the length of *path* exceeds 1023 characters. [Documenter's note: are these values correct for Linux?]
ENOENT The file referred to by *path* does not exist.
EACCES Search permission is denied for a component of the path prefix of *path*.
ELOOP Too many symbolic links were encountered in translating *path*.
EFAULT *Buf* or *path* points to an invalid address.

	EIO	An I/O error occurred while reading from or writing to the file system.

For **fstatfs**:

	EBADF	*Fd* is not a valid open file descriptor.
	EFAULT	*Buf* points to an invalid address.
	EIO	An I/O error occurred while reading from or writing to the file system.

# SEE ALSO
stat(2)

STIME(2)

NAME
stime – set time

SYNOPSIS
#include <time.h>

int stime(time_t *t*);

DESCRIPTION
stime sets the system's idea of the time and date. Time, pointed to by *t*, is measured in seconds from 00:00:00 GMT January 1, 1970. **stime()** may only be executed by the super user.

RETURN VALUE
On success, zero is returned. On error, −1 is returned, and *errno* is set appropriately.

ERRORS
EPERM   The caller is not the super-user.

CONFORMING TO
SVID, AT&T, X/OPEN

SEE ALSO
date(1)

SWAPON(2)

NAME

swapon, swapoff – start/stop swapping to file/device

SYNOPSIS

#include <unistd.h>
#include <linux/swap.h>

int swapon(const char **path*, **int** *swapflags*);
int swapoff(const char **path*);

DESCRIPTION

swapon sets the swap area to the file or block device specified by *path*. **swapoff** stops swapping to the file or block device specified by *path*.

swapon takes a *swapflags* argument. If *swapflags* has the *SWAP_FLAG_PREFER* bit turned on, the new swap area will have a higher priority than default. The priority is encoded as:
(prio << SWAP_FLAG_PRIO_SHIFT) & SWAP_FLAG_PRIO_MASK
These functions may only be used by the super-user.

PRIORITY

Each swap area has a priority, either high or low. The default priority is low. Within the low-priority areas, newer areas are even lower priority than older areas.

All priorities set with *swapflags* are high-priority, higher than default. They may have any non-negative value chosen by the caller. Higher numbers mean higher priority.

Swap pages are allocated from areas in priority order, highest priority first. For areas with different priorities, a higher-priority area is exhausted before using a lower-priority area. If two or more areas have the same priority, and it is the highest priority available, pages are allocated on a round-robin basis between them.

As of Linux 1.3.6, the kernel usually follows these rules, but there are exceptions.

RETURN VALUE

On success, zero is returned. On error, −1 is returned, and *errno* is set appropriately.

ERRORS

Many other errors can occur if *path* is not valid.

EPERM	The user is not the super-user, or more than **MAX_SWAPFILES** (defined to be 8 in Linux 1.3.6) are in use.
EINVAL	is returned if *path* exists, but is neither a regular path nor a block device.
ENOENT	is returned if *path* does not exist.
ENOMEM	is returned if there is insufficient memory to start swapping.

CONFORMING TO

These functions are Linux specific.

NOTES

The partition or path must be prepared with **mkswap**(8).

HISTORY

The second 'swapflags' argument was introduced in Linux 1.3.2.

SEE ALSO

mkswap(8), **swapon**(8), **swapoff**(8)

SYMLINK(2)

NAME
symlink – make a new name for a file

SYNOPSIS
#include <unistd.h>

int symlink(const char **oldpath***, const char** **newpath***);**

DESCRIPTION
symlink creates a symbolic link named *oldpath* which contains *newpath*.

Symbolic links are interpreted at run-time, as if the contents of the link were substituted into the path being followed to find a file or directory.

Symbolic links may contain .. path components, which (if used at the start of the link) refer to the parent directories of that in which the link resides.

A symbolic link (also known as a soft link) may point to an existing file or to a nonexistent one; the latter case is known as a dangling link.

The permissions of a symbolic link are irrelevant; the ownership is ignored when following the link, but is checked when removal or renaming of the link is requested and the link is in a directory with the sticky bit set.

If *newpath* exists it will *not* be overwritten.

RETURN VALUE
On success, zero is returned. On error, –1 is returned, and *errno* is set appropriately.

ERRORS
EPERM The filesystem containing *pathname* does not support the creation of symbolic links.

EFAULT *oldpath* or *newpath* points outside your accessible address space.

EACCES Write access to the directory containing *newpath* is not allowed for the process's effective uid, or one of the directories in *newpath* did not allow search (execute) permission.

ENAMETOOLONG *oldpath* or *newpath* was too long.

ENOENT A directory component in *newpath* does not exist or is a dangling symbolic link, or *oldpath* is the empty string.

ENOTDIR A component used as a directory in *newpath* is not, in fact, a directory.

ENOMEM Insufficient kernel memory was available.

EROFS The file is on a read-only filesystem.

EEXIST *newpath* already exists.

ELOOP *newpath* contains a reference to a circular symbolic link, ie a symbolic link whose expansion contains a reference to itself.

ENOSPC The device containing the file has no room for the new directory entry.

NOTES
No checking of *oldpath* is done.

Deleting the name referred to by a symlink will actually delete the file (unless it also has other hard links). If this behaviour is not desired, use **link**.

CONFORMING TO
SVID, AT&T, POSIX, BSD 4.3

BUGS

See **open**(2) re multiple files with the same name, and NFS.

SEE ALSO

link(2), **unlink**(2), **rename**(2), **open**(2), **lstat**(2), **ln**(1), **link**(8).

SYNC(2)

NAME
sync – commit buffer cache to disk.

SYNOPSIS
#include <unistd.h>

int sync(void);

DESCRIPTION
sync first commits inodes to buffers, and then buffers to disk.

RETURN VALUE
sync always returns 0.

CONFORMING TO
SVID, AT&T, X/OPEN, BSD 4.3

BUGS
sync() only schedules the writes, so it may return before the actual writing is done.

SEE ALSO
bdflush(2), **fsync**(2), **update**(8), **sync**(8)

SYSINFO(2)

NAME

sysinfo – returns information on overall system statistics

SYNOPSIS

As of Linux 0.99.10 and image release 4.4 **#include** <linux/kernel.h>
#include <linux/sys.h>

int sysinfo(struct sysinfo **info***);**

DESCRIPTION

sysinfo returns information in the following structure:

struct sysinfo {
long uptime; /* Seconds since boot */
unsigned long loads[3]; /* 1, 5, and 15 minute load averages */
unsigned long totalram; /* Total usable main memory size */
unsigned long freeram; /* Available memory size */
unsigned long sharedram; /* Amount of shared memory */
unsigned long bufferram; /* Memory used by buffers */
unsigned long totalswap; /* Total swap space size */
unsigned long freeswap; /* swap space still available */
unsigned short procs; /* Number of current processes */
char _f[22]; /* Pads structure to 64 bytes */
};

sysinfo provides a simple way of getting overall system statistics. This is more portable than reading */dev/kmem*.

RETURN VALUE

On success, zero is returned. On error, –1 is returned, and *errno* is set appropriately.

ERRORS

EFAULT   pointer to *struct sysinfo* is invalid

CONFORMING TO

This function is Linux-specific.

BUGS

The Linux DLL 4.4.1 libraries do not contain a proper prototype for this function.

NAME

syslog – read and/or clear kernel message ring buffer; set console_loglevel

SYNOPSIS

#include <unistd.h>
#include <linux/unistd.h>
_syscall3(int, syslog, int, type, char *, bufp, int, len);
int syslog(int *type***, char ****bufp***, int** *len***);**

DESCRIPTION

This is probably not the function you are interested in. Look at **syslog**(3) for the C library interface. This page only documents the bare kernel system call interface.

The *type* argument determines the action taken by **syslog**.

Quoting from *kernel/printk.c*: /*
Commands to sys_syslog:

0 – Close the log. Currently a NOP.
1 – Open the log. Currently a NOP.
2 – Read from the log.
3 – Read up to the last 4k of messages in the ring buffer.
4 – Read and clear last 4k of messages in the ring buffer
5 – Clear ring buffer.
6 – Disable printk's to console
7 – Enable printk's to console
8 – Set level of messages printed to console
/

Only function 3 is allowed to non-root processes.

The kernel log buffer
The kernel has a cyclic buffer of length LOG_BUF_LEN (4096) in which messages given as argument to the kernel function *printk()* are stored (regardless of their loglevel).

The call **syslog** (2,*buf,len*) waits until this kernel log buffer is nonempty, and then reads at most *len* bytes into the buffer *buf*. It returns the number of bytes read. Bytes read from the log disappear from the log buffer: the information can only be read once. This is the function executed by the kernel when a user program reads */proc/kmsg*.

The call **syslog** (3,*buf,len*) will read the last *len* bytes from the log buffer (nondestructively), but will not read more than was written into the buffer since the last 'clear ring buffer' command (which does not clear the buffer at all). It returns the number of bytes read.

The call **syslog** (4,*buf,len*) does precisely the same, but also executes the 'clear ring buffer' command.

The call **syslog** (5,*dummy,idummy*) only executes the 'clear ring buffer' command.

The loglevel
The kernel routine *printk()* will only print a message on the console, if it has a loglevel less than the value of the variable *console_loglevel*
(initially DEFAULT_CONSOLE_LOGLEVEL (7), but set to 10 if the kernel commandline contains the word 'debug', and to 15 in case of a kernel fault - the 10 and 15 are just silly, and equivalent to 8). This variable is set (to a value in the range 1-8) by the call **syslog** (8,*dummy,value*). The calls **syslog** (*type,dummy,idummy*) with *type* equal to 6 or 7, set it to 1 (kernel panics only) or 7 (all except debugging messages), respectively.

Every text line in a message has its own loglevel. This level is
DEFAULT_MESSAGE_LOGLEVEL - 1 (6) unless the line starts with <d> where *d* is a digit in the range 1-7, in which case the level is *d*. The conventional meaning of the loglevel is defined in <*linux/kernel.h*> as follows:

#define KERN_EMERG "<0>" /* system is unusable */
#define KERN_ALERT "<1>" /* action must be taken immediately */

```
#define KERN_CRIT    "<2>"  /* critical conditions */
#define KERN_ERR     "<3>"  /* error conditions */
#define KERN_WARNING "<4>"  /* warning conditions */
#define KERN_NOTICE  "<5>"  /* normal but significant condition */
#define KERN_INFO    "<6>"  /* informational */
#define KERN_DEBUG   "<7>"  /* debug-level messages */
```

RETURN VALUE

In case of error, -1 is returned, and *errno* is set. Otherwise, for *type* equal to 2, 3 or 4, **syslog**() returns the number of bytes read, and otherwise 0.

ERRORS

EPERM An attempt was made to change console_loglevel or clear the kernel message ring buffer by a process without root permissions.

EINVAL Bad parameters.

ERESTARTSYS System call was interrupted by a signal - nothing was read.

CONFORMING TO

This system call is Linux specific.

SEE ALSO

syslog(3)

TERMIOS(2)

NAME

termios, tcgetattr, tcsetattr, tcsendbreak, tcdrain, tcflush, tcflow, cfgetospeed, cfgetispeed, cfsetispeed, cfsetospeed, tcgetpgrp, tcsetpgrp – get and set terminal attributes, line control, get and set baud rate, get and set terminal foreground process group ID

SYNOPSIS

#include <termios.h>
#include <unistd.h>

int tcgetattr (int *fd***, struct termios ****termios_p* **);**

int tcsetattr (int *fd***, int** *optional_actions***, struct termios ****termios_p* **);**

int tcsendbreak (int *fd***, int** *duration* **);**

int tcdrain (int *fd* **);**

int tcflush (int *fd***, int** *queue_selector* **);**

int tcflow (int *fd***, int** *action* **);**

speed_t cfgetospeed (struct termios *termios_p **);**

int cfsetospeed (struct termios **termios_p***, speed_t** *speed* **);**

speed_t cfgetispeed (struct termios *termios_p **);**

int cfsetispeed (struct termios **termios_p***, speed_t** *speed* **);**

pid_t tcgetpgrp (int *fd* **);**

int tcsetpgrp (int *fd***, pid_t** *pgrpid* **);**

DESCRIPTION

The termios functions describe a general terminal interface that is provided to control asynchronous communications ports.

Many of the functions described here have a *termios_p* argument that is a pointer to a **termios** structure. This structure contains the following members:

tcflag_t *c_iflag*; /* input modes */
tcflag_t *c_oflag*; /* output modes */
tcflag_t *c_cflag*; /* control modes */
tcflag_t *c_lflag*; /* local modes */
cc_t *c_cc*[**NCCS**]; /* control chars */

c_iflag flag constants:

> **IGNBRK** ignore BREAK condition on input
>
> **BRKINT** If **IGNBRK** is not set, generate **SIGINT** on BREAK condition, else read BREAK as character \0.
>
> **IGNPAR** ignore framing errors and parity errors.
>
> **PARMRK** if **IGNPAR** is not set, prefix a character with a parity error or framing error with \377 \0. If neither **IGNPAR** nor **PARMRK** is set, read a character with a parity error or framing error as \0.
>
> **INPCK** enable input parity checking
>
> **ISTRIP** strip off eighth bit
>
> **INLCR** translate NL to CR on input
>
> **IGNCR** ignore carriage return on input
>
> **ICRNL** translate carriage return to newline on input (unless **IGNCR** is set)
>
> **IUCLC** map uppercase characters to lowercase on input
>
> **IXON** enable XON/XOFF flow control on output
>
> **IXANY** enable any character to restart output

IXOFF enable XON/XOFF flow control on input

IMAXBEL ring bell when input queue is full

c_oflag flag constants:

OPOST enable implementation-defined output processing

OLCUC map lowercase characters to uppercase on output

ONLCR map NL to CR-NL on output

OCRNL map CR to NL on output

ONOCR don't output CR at column 0

ONLRET don't output CR

OFILL send fill characters for a delay, rather than using a timed delay

OFDEL fill character is ASCII DEL. If unset, fill character is ASCII NUL

NLDLY newline delay mask. Values are NL0 and NL1.

CRDLY carriage return delay mask. Values are CR0, CR1, CR2, or CR3.

TABDLY horizontal tab delay mask. Values are TAB0, TAB1, TAB2, TAB3, or XTABS. A value of XTABS expands tabs to spaces (with tab stops every eight columns).

BSDLY backspace delay mask. Values are BS0 or BS1.

VTDLY vertical tab delay mask. Values are VT0 or VT1.

FFDLY form feed delay mask. Values are FF0 or FF1.

c_cflag flag constants:

CSIZE character size mask. Values are CS5, CS6, CS7, or CS8.

CSTOPB set two stop bits, rather than one.

CREAD enable receiver.

PARENB enable parity generation on output and parity checking for input.

PARODD parity for input and output is odd.

HUPCL lower modem control lines after last process closes the device (hang up).

CLOCAL ignore modem control lines

CIBAUD mask for input speeds (not used).

CRTSCTS flow control.

c_lflag flag constants:

ISIG when any of the characters INTR, QUIT, SUSP, or DSUSP are received, generate the corresponding signal.

ICANON enable canonical mode. This enables the special characters EOF, EOL, EOL2, ERASE, KILL, REPRINT, STATUS, and WERASE, and buffers by lines.

XCASE if ICANON is also set, terminal is uppercase only. Input is converted to lowercase, except for characters preceded by \. On output, uppercase characters are preceded by \ and lowercase characters are converted to uppercase.

ECHO echo input characters.

ECHOE if ICANON is also set, the ERASE character erases the preceding input character, and WERASE erases the preceding word.

ECHOK if ICANON is also set, the KILL character erases the current line.

ECHONL if ICANON is also set, echo the NL character even if ECHO is not set.

ECHOCTL if ECHO is also set, ASCII control signals other than TAB, NL, START, and STOP are echoed as ^X, where X is the character with ASCII code 0x10 greater than the control signal. For example, character 0x28 (BS) is echoed as ^H.

ECHOPRT if **ICANON** and **IECHO** are also set, characters are printed as they are being erased.

ECHOKE if **ICANON** is also set, KILL is echoed by erasing each character on the line, as specified by **ECHOE** and **ECHOPRT**.

FLUSHO output is being flushed. This flag is toggled by typing the DISCARD character.

NOFLSH disable flushing the input and output queues when generating the SIGINT and SIGQUIT signals, and flushing the input queue when generating the SIGSUSP signal.

TOSTOP send the SIGTTOU signal to the process group of a background process which tries to write to its controlling terminal.

PENDIN all characters in the input queue are reprinted when the next character is read. (**bash** handles typeahead this way.)

IEXTEN enable implementation-defined input processing.

tcgetattr() gets the parameters associated with the object referred by *fd* and stores them in the **termios** structure referenced by *termios_p*. This function may be invoked from a background process; however, the terminal attributes may be subsequently changed by a foreground process.

tcsetattr() sets the parameters associated with the terminal (unless support is required from the underlying hardware that is not available) from the **termios** structure referred to by *termios_p*. *optional_actions* specifies when the changes take effect:

TCSANOW the change occurs immediately.

TCSADRAIN the change occurs after all output written to *fd* has been transmitted. This function should be used when changing parameters that affect output.

TCSAFLUSH the change occurs after all output written to the object referred by *fd* has been transmitted, and all input that has been received but not read will be discarded before the change is made.

tcsendbreak() transmits a continuous stream of zero-valued bits for a specific duration, if the terminal is using asynchronous serial data transmission. If *duration* is zero, it transmits zero-valued bits for at least 0.25 seconds, and not more that 0.5 seconds. If *duration* is not zero, it sends zero-valued bits for *duration**N seconds, where N is at least 0.25, and not more than 0.5.

If the terminal is not using asynchronous serial data transmission, **tcsendbreak()** returns without taking any action.

tcdrain() waits until all output written to the object referred to by *fd* has been transmitted.

tcflush() discards data written to the object referred to by *fd* but not transmitted, or data received but not read, depending on the value of *queue_selector*:

TCIFLUSH flushes data received but not read.

TCOFLUSH flushes data written but not transmitted.

TCIOFLUSH flushes both data received but not read, and data written but not transmitted.

tcflow() suspends transmission or reception of data on the object referred to by *fd*, depending on the value of *action*:

TCOOFF suspends output.

TCOON restarts suspended output.

TCIOFF transmits a STOP character, which stops the terminal device from transmitting data to the system.

TCION transmits a START character, which starts the terminal device transmitting data to the system.

TERMIOS(2) Linux Programmer's Manual TERMIOS(2)

The default on open of a terminal file is that neither its input nor its output is suspended.

The baud rate functions are provided for getting and setting the values of the input and output baud rates in the **termios** structure. The new values do not take effect until **tcsetattr()** is successfully called.

Setting the speed to **B0** instructs the modem to "hang up". The actual bit rate corresponding to **B38400** may be altered with **setserial**(8).

The input and output baud rates are stored in the **termios** structure.

cfgetospeed() returns the output baud rate stored in the **termios** structure pointed to by *termios_p*.

cfsetospeed() sets the output baud rate stored in the **termios** structure pointed to by *termios_p* to *speed*, which must be one of these constants: B0
B50
B75
B110
B134
B150
B200
B300
B600
B1200
B1800
B2400
B4800
B9600
B19200
B38400
B57600
B115200
B230400

The zero baud rate, **B0**, is used to terminate the connection. If B0 is specified, the modem control lines shall no longer be asserted. Normally, this will disconnect the line. **CBAUDEX** is a mask for the speeds beyond those defined in POSIX.1 (57600 and above). Thus, **B57600** & **CBAUDEX** is nonzero.

cfgetispeed() returns the input baud rate stored in the **termios** structure.

cfsetispeed() sets the input baud rate stored in the **termios** structure to *speed*. If the input baud rate is set to zero, the input baud rate will be equal to the output baud rate.

tcgetpgrp() returns process group ID of foreground processing group, or -1 on error.

tcsetpgrp() sets process group ID to *pgrpid*. *pgrpid* must be the ID of a process group in the same session.

RETURN VALUES

cfgetispeed() returns the input baud rate stored in the **termios** structure.

cfgetospeed() returns the output baud rate stored in the **termios** structure.

tcgetpgrp() returns process group ID of foreground processing group, or -1 on error.

All other functions return:

    0 on success.

    -1 on failure and set *errno* to indicate the error.

SEE ALSO

setserial(8)

TIME(2)

NAME

time – get time in seconds

SYNOPSIS

#include <time.h>

time_t time(time_t *****t***);**

DESCRIPTION

time returns the time since 00:00:00 GMT, January 1, 1970, measured in seconds.

If *t* is non null, the return value is also stored in the memory pointed to by *t*.

CONFORMING TO

SVID, AT&T, POSIX, X/OPEN, BSD 4.3
Under BSD 4.3, this call is obsoleted by **gettimeofday**(2).

SEE ALSO

ctime(3), **date**(1), **ftime**(3), **gettimeofday**(2)

NAME

times – get process times

SYNOPSIS

#include <sys/times.h>

clock_t times(struct tms **buf*);

DESCRIPTION

times stores the current process times in *buf*.

struct tms is as defined in */usr/include/sys/times.h*:

```
struct tms {
time_t tms_utime; /* user time */
time_t tms_stime; /* system time */
time_t tms_cutime; /* user time of children */
time_t tms_cstime; /* system time of children */
};
```

times returns the number of clock ticks that have elapsed since the system has been up.

CONFORMING TO

SVID, AT&T, POSIX, X/OPEN, BSD 4.3

SEE ALSO

time(1), **getrusage**(2), **wait**(2)

TRUNCATE(2)

NAME

truncate, ftruncate – truncate a file to a specified length

SYNOPSIS

#include <unistd.h>

int truncate(const char **path,* **size_t** *length***);**
int ftruncate(int *fd,* **size_t** *length***);**

DESCRIPTION

Truncate causes the file named by *path* or referenced by *fd* to be truncated to at most *length* bytes in size. If the file previously was larger than this size, the extra data is lost. With **ftruncate**, the file must be open for writing.

RETURN VALUE

On success, zero is returned. On error, −1 is returned, and *errno* is set appropriately.

ERRORS

For **truncate**:

ENOTDIR	A component of the path prefix is not a directory.
EINVAL	The pathname contains a character with the high-order bit set.
ENAMETOOLONG	A component of a pathname exceeded 255 characters, or an entire path name exceeded 1023 characters.
ENOENT	The named file does not exist.
EACCES	Search permission is denied for a component of the path prefix.
EACCES	The named file is not writable by the user.
ELOOP	Too many symbolic links were encountered in translating the pathname.
EISDIR	The named file is a directory.
EROFS	The named file resides on a read-only file system.
ETXTBSY	The file is a pure procedure (shared text) file that is being executed.
EIO	An I/O error occurred updating the inode.
EFAULT	*Path* points outside the process's allocated address space.

For **Ftruncate**:

EBADF	The *fd* is not a valid descriptor.
EINVAL	The *fd* references a socket, not a file.
EINVAL	The *fd* is not open for writing.

HISTORY

These function calls appeared in BSD 4.2.

BUGS

These calls should be generalized to allow ranges of bytes in a file to be discarded.

SEE ALSO

open(2)

UMASK(2)

NAME
umask – set file creation mask

SYNOPSIS
#include <sys/stat.h>

int umask(int *mask***);**

DESCRIPTION
umask sets the umask to *mask* & 0777.

RETURN VALUE
The previous value of the mask is returned.

CONFORMING TO
SVID, AT&T, POSIX, X/OPEN, BSD 4.3

SEE ALSO
creat(2), **open**(2)

NAME

uname – get name and information about current kernel

SYNOPSIS

#include <sys/utsname.h>

int uname(struct utsname *buf*);

DESCRIPTION

uname returns system information in *buf*. The *utsname* struct is as defined in /usr/include/sys/utsname.h :

```
struct utsname {
    char sysname[65];
    char nodename[65];
    char release[65];
    char version[65];
    char machine[65];
    char domainname[65];
};
```

RETURN VALUE

On success, zero is returned. On error, −1 is returned, and *errno* is set appropriately.

ERRORS

EFAULT   *buf* is not valid.

CONFORMING TO

SVID, AT&T, POSIX, X/OPEN

SEE ALSO

uname(1), **getdomainname**(2), **gethostname**(2)

UNDOCUMENTED(2)   Linux Programmer's Manual   UNDOCUMENTED(2)

NAME

personality, setfsgid, setfsuid, siggetmask, sigreturn, sigsetmask, sysfs – undocumented system calls

SYNOPSIS

Undocumented system calls.

DESCRIPTION

As of Linux 1.3.6, there are 144 system calls listed in */usr/include/linux/unistd.h*. This man page mentions those calls which are implemented in the kernel but not yet documented in man pages. Some of these calls do not have prototypes in the DLL 4.6.27 include files.

SOLICITATION

If you have information about these system calls, please look in the kernel source code, write a man page (using a style similar to that of the other Linux section 2 man pages), and send it to **aeb@cwi.nl** for inclusion in the next man page release from the Linux Documentation Project.

SEE ALSO

obsolete(2), **unimplemented**(2)

UNIMPLEMENTED(2)   Linux Programmer's Manual   UNIMPLEMENTED(2)

NAME

afs_syscall, break, gtty, lock, mpx, prof, quotactl, stty, ustat – unimplemented system calls

SYNOPSIS

Unimplemented system calls.

DESCRIPTION

These system calls are not implemented in the Linux 1.2.4 kernel.

RETURN VALUE

These system calls always return −1 and set *errno* to **ENOSYS**.

SEE ALSO

obsolete(2), **undocumented**(2)

UNLINK(2)

NAME

unlink – delete a name and possibly the file it refers to

SYNOPSIS

#include <unistd.h>

int unlink(const char **pathname***);**

DESCRIPTION

unlink deletes a name from the filesystem. If that name was the last link to a file and no processes have the file open the file is deleted and the space it was using is made available for reuse.

If the name was the last link to a file but any processes still have the file open the file will remain in existence until the last file descriptor referring to it is closed.

If the name referred to a symbolic link the link is removed.

If the name referred to a socket, fifo or device the name for it is removed but processes which have the object open may continue to use it.

RETURN VALUE

On success, zero is returned. On error, –1 is returned, and *errno* is set appropriately.

ERRORS

EFAULT   *pathname* points outside your accessible address space.

EACCES   Write access to the directory containing *pathname* is not allowed for the process's effective uid, or one of the directories in *pathname* did not allow search (execute) permission.

EPERM   The directory containing *pathname* has the sticky-bit (S_ISVTX) set and the process's effective uid is neither the uid of the file to be deleted nor that of the directory containing it.

ENAMETOOLONG   *pathname* was too long.

ENOENT   A directory component in *pathname* does not exist or is a dangling symbolic link.

ENOTDIR   A component used as a directory in *pathname* is not, in fact, a directory.

EISDIR   *pathname* refers to a directory.

ENOMEM   Insufficient kernel memory was available.

EROFS   *pathname* refers to a file on a read-only filesystem.

CONFORMING TO

SVID, AT&T, POSIX, X/OPEN, BSD 4.3

BUGS

Infelicities in the protocol underlying NFS can cause the unexpected disappearance of files which are still being used.

SEE ALSO

link(2), **rename**(2), **open**(2), **rmdir**(2), **mknod** (2), **mkfifo** (3),**remove**(3), **rm**(1), **unlink**(8).

NAME

uselib – select shared library

SYNOPSIS

#include <unistd.h>

int uselib(const char *</i>library</i>);

DESCRIPTION

uselib selects the shared library binary that will be used by this processes.

RETURN VALUE

On success, zero is returned. On error, −1 is returned, and *errno* is set appropriately.

ERRORS

In addition to all of the error codes returned by **open**(2) and **mmap**(2), the following may also be returned:

ENOEXEC   The file specified by *library* is not executable, or does not have the correct magic numbers.

EACCES   The library specified by *library* is not readable.

CONFORMING TO

uselib() is Linux specific.

SEE ALSO

open(2), **mmap**(2), **ldd**(1), **gcc**(1), **ar**(1), **ld**(1)

UTIME(2)　　　　　　　Linux Programmer's Manual　　　　　　　UTIME(2)

NAME

utime, utimes – change access and/or modification times of an inode

SYNOPSIS

#include <sys/types.h>
#include <utime.h>

int utime(const char **filename***, struct utimbuf ****buf***);**

#include <sys/time.h>

int utimes(char **filename***, struct timeval ****tvp***);**

DESCRIPTION

utime changes the access and modification times of the inode specified by *filename* to the *actime* and *modtime* fields of *buf* respectively. If *buf* is **NULL**, then the access and modification times of the file are set to the current time. The *utimbuf* structure is:

struct utimbuf {
time_t actime; /* access time */
time_t modtime; /* modification time */
};

In the Linux DLL 4.4.1 libraries, **utimes** is just a wrapper for **utime**: *tvp*[0].*tv_sec* is *actime*, and *tvp*[1].*tv_sec* is *modtime*. The *timeval* structure is:

struct timeval {
long tv_sec; /* seconds */
long tv_usec; /* microseconds */
};

RETURN VALUE

On success, zero is returned. On error, −1 is returned, and *errno* is set appropriately.

ERRORS

Other errors may occur.

    EACCESS　　Permission to write the file is denied.
    ENOENT　　*filename* does not exist.

CONFORMING TO

utime: SVID, POSIX
utimes: BSD 4.3

SEE ALSO

stat(2)

VHANGUP(2)

NAME
vhangup – virtually hangup the current tty

SYNOPSIS
#include <unistd.h>

int vhangup(void);

DESCRIPTION
vhangup simulates a hangup on the current terminal. This call arranges for other users to have a clean tty at login time.

RETURN VALUE
On success, zero is returned. On error, −1 is returned, and *errno* is set appropriately.

ERRORS
EPERM   The user is not the super-user.

SEE ALSO
init(8)

NAME

vm86 – enter virtual 8086 mode

SYNOPSIS

#include <sys/vm86.h>

int vm86(struct vm86_struct * *info*);

DESCRIPTION

Enter VM86 mode with information as specified in *info*:

```
struct vm86_struct {
struct vm86_regs regs;
unsigned long flags;
unsigned long screen_bitmap;
};

struct vm86_regs {
/*
normal regs, with special meaning for the segment descriptors..
/
long ebx;
long ecx;
long edx;
long esi;
long edi;
long ebp;
long eax;
long __null_ds;
long __null_es;
long __null_fs;
long __null_gs;
long orig_eax;
long eip;
long cs;
long eflags;
long esp;
long ss;
/*
these are specific to v86 mode:
/
long es;
long ds;
long fs;
long gs;
};
```

RETURN VALUE

On success, zero is returned. On error, −1 is returned, and *errno* is set appropriately.

ERRORS

    EPERM   Saved kernel stack exists. [Documenter's note: what does this imply?]

WAIT(2) Linux Programmer's Manual WAIT(2)

NAME

wait, waitpid – wait for process termination

SYNOPSIS

#include <sys/types.h>
#include <sys/wait.h>

pid_t wait(int *status***)**
pid_t waitpid(pid_t *pid***, int** *status***, int** *options***);**

DESCRIPTION

The **wait** function suspends execution of the current process until a child has exited, or until a signal is delivered whose action is to terminate the current process or to call a signal handling function. If a child has already exited by the time of the call (a so–called "zombie" process), the function returns immediately. Any system resources used by the child are freed.

The **waitpid** function suspends execution of the current process until a child as specified by the *pid* argument has exited, or until a signal is delivered whose action is to terminate the current process or to call a signal handling function. If a child as requested by *pid* has already exited by the time of the call (a so–called "zombie" process), the function returns immediately. Any system resources used by the child are freed.

The value of *pid* can be one of:

< –1 which means to wait for any child process whose process group ID is equal to the absolute value of

  –1 which means to wait for any child process whose process group ID is equal to the absolute value of *pid*.

  –1 which means to wait for any child process; this is the same behaviour which **wait** exhibits.

   0 which means to wait for any child process whose process group ID is equal to that of the calling process.

 > 0 which means to wait for the child whose process ID is equal to the value of *pid*.

The value of *options* is an exclusive OR of zero or more of the following constants:

> **WNOHANG**   which means to return immediately if no child has exited.
>
> **WUNTRACED** which means to also return for children which are stopped, and whose status has not been reported.

If *status* is not **NULL**, **wait** or **waitpid** store status information in the location pointed to by *statloc*.

This status can be evaluated with the following macros (these macros take the stat buffer as an argument — not a pointer to the buffer!):

> **WIFEXITED**(*status*)   is non –zero if the child exited normally.
>
> **WEXITSTATUS**(*status*) evaluates to the least significant eight bits of the return code of the child which terminated, which may have been set as the argument to a call to **exit()** or as the argument for a **return** statement in the main program. This macro can only be evaluated if **WIFEXITED** returned non–zero.
>
> **WIFSIGNALED**(*status*) returns true if the child process exited because of a signal which was not caught.
>
> **WTERMSIG**(*status*)   returns the number of the signal that caused the child process to terminate. This macro can only be evaluated if **WIFSIGNALED** returned non–zero.

Linux   24 July 1993   671

WAIT(2)　　　　　　　　Linux Programmer's Manual　　　　　　　　WAIT(2)

WIFSTOPPED(*status*)　　returns true if the child process which caused the return is currently stopped; this is only possible if the call was done using **WUNTRACED**.

WSTOPSIG(*status*)　　returns the number of the signal which caused the child to stop. This macro can only be evaluated if **WIFSTOPPED** returned non–zero.

RETURN VALUE

The process ID of the child which exited, –1 on error or zero if **WNOHANG** was used and no child was available (in which case, *errno* is set to an appropriate value).

ERRORS

ECHILD　　if the child process specified in *pid* does not exist.

EPERM　　if the effective userid of the calling process does not match that of the process being waited for, and the effective userid of the calling process it not that of the superuser.

ERESTARTSYS　if **WNOHANG** was not set and an unblocked signal or a **SIGCHLD** was caught; this is an extension to the POSIX.1 standard.

CONFORMS TO

POSIX.1

SEE ALSO

signal(2), **wait4**(2), **signal**(7)

NAME

wait3, wait4 – wait for process termination, BSD style

SYNOPSIS

#define _USE_BSD
#include <sys/types.h>
#include <sys/resource.h>
#include <sys/wait.h>
pid_t wait3(int *status*, **int** *options*,
struct rusage **rusage*)
pid_t wait4(pid_t *pid*, **int** **status*, **int** *options*,
struct rusage **rusage*)

DESCRIPTION

The **wait3** function suspends execution of the current process until a child has exited, or until a signal is delivered whose action is to terminate the current process or to call a signal handling function. If a child has already exited by the time of the call (a so–called "zombie" process), the function returns immediately. Any system resources used by the child are freed.

The **wait4** function suspends execution of the current process until a child as specified by the *pid* argument has exited, or until a signal is delivered whose action is to terminate the current process or to call a signal handling function. If a child as requested by *pid* has already exited by the time of the call (a so–called "zombie" process), the function returns immediately. Any system resources used by the child are freed.

The value of *pid* can be one of:

< −1   which means to wait for any child process whose process group ID is equal to the absolute value of *pid*.

−1   which means to wait for any child process; this is equivalent to calling **wait3**.

0   which means to wait for any child process whose process group ID is equal to that of the calling process.

> 0   which means to wait for the child whose process ID is equal to the value of *pid*.

The value of *options* is an exclusive OR of zero or more of the following constants:

        WNOHANG   which means to return immediately if no child is there to be waited for.

        WUNTRACED   which means to also return for children which are stopped, and whose status has not been reported.

If *status* is not **NULL**, **wait3** or **wait4** store status information in the location pointed to by *statloc*.

This status can be evaluated with the following macros:

        WIFEXITED(**status*)   is non –zero if the child exited normally.

        WEXITSTATUS(**status*)   evaluates to the least significant eight bits of the return code of the child which terminated, which may have been set as the argument to a call to **exit** or as the argument for a **return** statement in the main program. This macro can only be evaluated if **WIFEXITED** returned non–zero.

        WIFSIGNALED(**status*)   returns true if the child process exited because of a signal which was not caught.

        WTERMSIG(**status*)   returns the number of the signal that caused the child process to terminate. This macro can only be evaluated if **WIFSIGNALED** returned non–zero.

WIFSTOPPED(*status*)	returns true if the child process which caused the return is currently stopped; this is only possible if the call was done using **WUNTRACED**.
WSTOPSIG(*status*)	returns the number of the signal which caused the child to stop. This macro can only be evaluated if **WIFSTOPPED** returned non–zero.

If *rusage* is not **NULL**, the **struct** rusage as defined in <**sys/resource.h**> it points to will be filled with accounting information. See **getrusage**(2) for details.

RETURN VALUE

The process ID of the child which exited, –1 on error or zero if **WNOHANG** was used and no child was available (in which case, *errno* will be set appropriately).

ERRORS

ECHILD	if the child process specified in *pid* does not exist.
EPERM	if the effective userid of the calling process does not match that of the process being waited for, and the effective userid of the calling process it not that of the superuser.
ERESTARTSYS	if **WNOHANG** was not set and an unblocked signal or a **SIGCHLD** was caught; this is an extension to the POSIX.1 standard.

CONFORMS TO

POSIX.1

SEE ALSO

signal(2), **getrusage**(2), **wait**(2), **signal**(7)

WRITE(2)

NAME

write – write to a file descriptor

SYNOPSIS

#include <sys/types.h>
#include <unistd.h>

size_t write(int *fd***, const char** **buf***, size_t** *count***);**

DESCRIPTION

write writes up to *count* bytes from file descriptor *fd* from the buffer starting at *buf*.

RETURN VALUE

On success, the number of bytes written are returned (zero indicates nothing was written). On error, –1 (or MAXINT, as size_t is unsigned) is returned, and *errno* is set appropriately.

ERRORS

EBADF *fd* is not a valid file descriptor or is not open for writing.

EINVAL *fd* is attached to an object which is unsuitable for writing.

EFAULT *buf* is outside your accessible address space.

EPIPE *fd* is connected to a pipe or socket whose reading end is closed. When this happens the writing process will receive a **SIGPIPE** signal; if it catches, blocks or ignores this the error **EPIPE** is returned.

EAGAIN Non-blocking I/O has been selected using **O_NONBLOCK** and there was no room in the pipe or socket connected to *fd* to write the data immediately.

EINTR The call was interrupted by a signal before any data was written.

ENOSPC The device containing the file referred to by *fd* has no room for the data.

Other errors may occur, depending on the object connected to *fd*.

CONFORMING TO

SVID, AT&T, POSIX, X/OPEN, BSD 4.3

SEE ALSO

open(2), **read**(2), **fcntl**(2), **close**(2), **lseek**(2), **select**(2), **ioctl**(2), **fwrite**(3).

Section III
Library Functions

NAME

intro – Introduction to library functions

DESCRIPTION

This chapter describes all library functions excluding the library functions described in chapter 2, which implement system calls. There are various function groups which can be identified by a letter which is appended to the chapter number:

- (3C) These functions, the functions from chapter 2 and from chapter 3S are contained in the C standard library libc, which will be used by *cc*(1) by default.
- (3S) These functions are parts of the *stdio*(3S) library. They are contained in the standard C library libc.
- (3M) These functions are contained in the arithmetic library libm. They are used by *f77*(1) FORTRAN compiler by default, but not by the

  cc (1) C compiler, which needs the option **–lm**.
- (3F) These functions are part of the FORTRAN library libF77. There are no special compiler flags needed to use these functions.
- (3X) Various special libraries. The manual pages documenting their functions specify the library names.

AUTHORS

Look at the header of the manual page for the author(s) and copyright conditions. Note that these can be different from page to page!

NAME

abort – cause abnormal program termination

SYNOPSIS

#include <stdlib.h>
void abort(void);

DESCRIPTION

The **abort()** function causes abnormal program termination unless the signal SIGABORT is caught and the signal handler does not return. If the **abort()** function causes program termination, all open streams are closed and flushed.

If the SIGABORT function is blocked or ignored, the **abort()** function will still override it.

RETURN VALUE

The **abort()** function never returns.

CONFORMING TO

SVID 3, POSIX, BSD 4.3, ISO 9899

SEE ALSO

sigaction(2), **exit**(3)

NAME

abs – computes the absolute value of an integer.

SYNOPSIS

#include <stdlib.h>
int abs(int *j***);**

DESCRIPTION

The **abs()** function computes the absolute value of the integer argument *j*.

RETURN VALUE

Returns the absolute value of the integer argument.

CONFORMING TO

SVID 3, POSIX, BSD 4.3, ISO 9899

NOTES

Trying to take the absolute value of the most negative integer is not defined.

SEE ALSO

ceil(3), **floor**(3), **fabs**(3), **labs**(3), **rint**(3)

NAME

acos – arc cosine function

SYNOPSIS

#include <math.h>
double acos(double *x*);

DESCRIPTION

The **acos()** function calculates the arc cosine of *x*; that is the value whose cosine is *x*. If *x* falls outside the range −1 to 1, **acos()** fails and *errno* is set.

RETURN VALUE

The **acos()** function returns the arc cosine in radians and the value is mathematically defined to be between 0 and PI (inclusive).

ERRORS

  EDOM *x* is out of range.

CONFORMING TO

SVID 3, POSIX, BSD 4.3, ISO 9899

SEE ALSO

asin(3), **atan**(3), **atan2**(3), **cos**(3), **sin**(3), **tan**(3)

NAME

acosh – inverse hyperbolic cosine function

SYNOPSIS

#include <math.h>
double acosh(double x**);**

DESCRIPTION

The **acosh()** function calculates the inverse hyperbolic cosine of x; that is the value whose hyperbolic cosine is x. If x

is less than 1.0, **acosh()** returns not-a-number (NaN) and *errno*

is set.

ERRORS

    EDOM x is out of range.

CONFORMING TO

SVID 3, POSIX, BSD 4.3, ISO 9899

SEE ALSO

asinh(3), **atanh**(3), **cosh**(3), **sinh**(3), **tanh**(3)

NAME

alloca – memory allocator

SYNOPSIS

#include <stdlib.h>

void *alloca(size_t *size***);**

DESCRIPTION

The **alloca** function allocates *size* bytes of space in the stack frame of the caller. This temporary space is automatically freed on return.

RETURN VALUES

The **alloca** function returns a pointer to the beginning of the allocated space. If the allocation failed, a **NULL** pointer is returned.

HISTORY

There is evidence that the **alloca** function appears in 32v, pwb, pwb.2, 3bsd, and 4bsd. There is a man page for it in BSD 4.3. Linux uses the GNU version.

BUGS

The **alloca** function is machine dependent.

SEE ALSO

brk(2), **pagesize**(2), **calloc**(3), **malloc**(3), **realloc**(3)

NAME

asin – arc sine function

SYNOPSIS

#include <math.h>
double asin(double *x***);**

DESCRIPTION

The **asin()** function calculates the arc sine of x; that is the value whose sine is x. If x falls outside the range −1 to 1, **asin()** fails and *errno* is set.

RETURN VALUE

The **asin()** function returns the arc sine in radians and the value is mathematically defined to be between -PI/2 and PI/2 (inclusive).

ERRORS

    EDOM x is out of range.

CONFORMING TO

SVID 3, POSIX, BSD 4.3, ISO 9899

SEE ALSO

acos(3), **atan**(3), **atan2**(3), **cos**(3), **sin**(3), **tan**(3)

NAME

asinh – inverse hyperbolic sine function

SYNOPSIS

#include <math.h>
double asinh(double *x***);**

DESCRIPTION

The **asinh()** function calculates the inverse hyperbolic sine of *x*; that is the value whose hyperbolic sine is *x*.

CONFORMING TO

SVID 3, POSIX, BSD 4.3, ISO 9899

SEE ALSO

acosh(3), **atanh**(3), **cosh**(3), **sinh**(3), **tanh**(3)

ASSERT(3)

NAME

assert – Abort the program if assertion is false.

SYNOPSIS

#include <assert.h>
void assert (int *expression***);**

DESCRIPTION

assert() prints an error message to standard output and terminates the program by calling **abort()** if **expression** is false (i.e., compares equal to zero). This only happens when the macro **NDEBUG** is undefined.

RETURN VALUE

No value is returned.

CONFORMS TO

ANSI - C

BUGS

assert() is implemented as a macro; if the expression tested has side - effects, program behaviour will be different depending on whether **NDEBUG** is defined. This may create Heisenbugs which go away when debugging is turned on.

SEE ALSO

exit(3), **abort**(3)

ATAN(3)

NAME

atan – arc tangent function

SYNOPSIS

#include <math.h>
double atan(double *x***);**

DESCRIPTION

The **atan()** function calculates the arc tangent of x; that is the value whose tangent is x.

RETURN VALUE

The **atan()** function returns the arc tangent in radians and the value is mathematically defined to be between -PI/2 and PI/2 (inclusive).

CONFORMING TO

SVID 3, POSIX, BSD 4.3, ISO 9899

SEE ALSO

acos(3), **asin**(3), **atan2**(3), **cos**(3), **sin**(3), **tan**(3)

NAME

atan2 – arc tangent function of two variables

SYNOPSIS

#include <math.h>
double atan2(double *y*, **double** *x*);

DESCRIPTION

The **atan2()** function calculates the arc tangent of the two variables *x* and *y*. It is similar to calculating the arc tangent of *y* / *x*, except that the signs of both arguments are used to determine the quadrant of the result.

RETURN VALUE

The **atan2()** function returns the result in radians, which is between -PI and PI (inclusive).

CONFORMING TO

SVID 3, POSIX, BSD 4.3, ISO 9899

SEE ALSO

acos(3), **asin**(3), **atan**(3), **cos**(3), **sin**(3), **tan**(3)

NAME

atanh – inverse hyperbolic tangent function

SYNOPSIS

#include <math.h>
double atanh(double x**);**

DESCRIPTION

The **atanh()** function calculates the inverse hyperbolic tangent of x; that is the value whose hyperbolic tangent is x. If the absolute value of x is greater than 1.0, **acosh()** returns not-a-number (NaN) and *errno* is set.

ERRORS

EDOM x is out of range.

CONFORMING TO

SVID 3, POSIX, BSD 4.3, ISO 9899

SEE ALSO

asinh(3), **acosh**(3), **cosh**(3), **sinh**(3), **tanh**(3)

NAME

atexit – register a function to be called at normal program termination

SYNOPSIS

#include <stdlib.h>
int atexit(void (**function*)(void));

DESCRIPTION

The **atexit**() function registers the given *function* to be called at normal program termination, whether via **exit**(2) or via return from the program's **main**. Functions so registered are called in the reverse order of their registration; no arguments are passed.

RETURN VALUE

The **atexit**() function returns the value 0 if successful; otherwise the value −1 is returned and the global variable *errno* is set to indicate the error.

ERRORS

    ENOMEM   Insufficient memory available to add the function.

CONFORMING TO

SVID 3, BSD 4.3, ISO 9899

SEE ALSO

exit(3), **on_exit**(3)

NAME

atof – convert a string to a double.

SYNOPSIS

#include <stdlib.h>
double atof(const char **nptr***);**

DESCRIPTION

The **atof()** function converts the initial portion of the string pointed to by *nptr* to double. The behaviour is the same as

strtod(nptr, (char **)NULL);

except that **atof()** does not detect errors.

RETURN VALUE

The converted value.

CONFORMING TO

SVID 3, POSIX, BSD 4.3, ISO 9899

SEE ALSO

atoi(3), **atol**(3), **strtod**(3), **strtol**(3), **strtoul**(3)

NAME

atoi – convert a string to an integer.

SYNOPSIS

#include <stdlib.h>
int atoi(const char *_nptr_);

DESCRIPTION

The **atoi()** function converts the initial portion of the string pointed to by _nptr_ to int. The behaviour is the same as

strtol(nptr, (char **)NULL, 10);

except that **atoi()** does not detect errors.

RETURN VALUE

The converted value.

CONFORMING TO

SVID 3, POSIX, BSD 4.3, ISO 9899

SEE ALSO

atof(3), **atol**(3), **strtod**(3), **strtol**(3), **strtoul**(3)

NAME

atol – convert a string to a long integer.

SYNOPSIS

#include <stdlib.h>
long atol(const char *****nptr***);**

DESCRIPTION

The **atol()** function converts the initial portion of the string pointed to by *nptr* to long. The behaviour is the same as

strtol(nptr, (char **)NULL, 10);

except that **atol()** does not detect errors.

RETURN VALUE

The converted value.

CONFORMING TO

SVID 3, POSIX, BSD 4.3, ISO 9899

SEE ALSO

atof(3), **atoi**(3), **strtod**(3), **strtol**(3), **strtoul**(3)

NAME

bcmp – compare byte strings

SYNOPSIS

#include <string.h>
int bcmp(const void *$s1$*, **const void** *$s2$*, **int** n**);**

DESCRIPTION

The **bcmp()** function compares the first n bytes of the strings $s1$ and $s2$. If the two strings are equal, **bcmp()** returns 0, otherwise it returns a non-zero result. If n is zero, the two strings are assumed to be equal.

RETURN VALUE

The **bcmp()** function returns 0 if the strings are equal, otherwise a non-zero result is returned.

CONFORMING TO

BSD 4.3

SEE ALSO

memcmp(3), **strcasecmp**(3), **strcmp**(3), **strcoll**(3), **strncmp**(3), **strncasecmp**(3)

NAME

bcopy – copy byte strings

SYNOPSIS

#include <string.h>
void bcopy (const void *src***, void** *dest***, int** *n***);**

DESCRIPTION

The **bcopy()** function copies the first *n* bytes of the source string *src* to the destination string *dest*. If *n* is zero, no bytes are copied.

RETURN VALUE

The **bcopy()** function returns no value.

CONFORMING TO

BSD 4.3

SEE ALSO

memccpy(3), **memcpy**(3), **memmove**(3), **strcpy**(3), **strncpy**(3)

BSEARCH(3)

NAME

bsearch – binary search of a sorted array.

SYNOPSIS

#include <stdlib.h>
void *bsearch(const void *key***, const void** *base***, size_t** *nmemb***,
size_t** *size***, int (*** *compar* **)(const void *, const void *));**

DESCRIPTION

The **bsearch()** function searches an array of *nmemb* objects, the initial member of which is pointed to by *base*, for a member that matches the object pointed to by *key*. The size of each member of the array is specified by *size*.

The contents of the array should be in ascending sorted order according to the comparison function referenced by *compar*. The *compar* routine is expected to have two arguments which point to the *key* object and to an array member, in that order, and should return an integer less than, equal to, or greater than zero if the *key* object is found, respectively, to be less than, to match, or be greater than the array member.

RETURN VALUE

The **bsearch()** function returns a pointer to a matching member of the array, or NULL if no match is found. If there are multiple elements that match the key, the element returned is unspecified.

CONFORMING TO

SVID 3, BSD 4.3, ISO 9899

SEE ALSO

qsort(3)

NAME

bcmp, bcopy, bzero, memccpy, memchr, memcmp, memcpy, memfrob, memmem, memmove, memset – byte string operations

SYNOPSIS

#include <string.h>
int bcmp(const void *s1, const void *s2, int n);
void bcopy(const void *src, void *dest, int n);
void bzero(void *s, int n);
void *memccpy(void *dest, const void *src, int c, size_t n);
void *memchr(const void *s, int c, size_t n);
int memcmp(const void *s1, const void *s2, size_t n);
void *memcpy(void *dest, const void *src, size_t n);
void *memfrob(void *s, size_t n);
void *memmem(const void *needle, size_t needlelen,
const void *haystack, size_t haystacklen);
void *memmove(void *dest, const void *src, size_t n);
void *memset(void *s, int c, size_t n);

DESCRIPTION

The byte string functions perform operations on strings that are not NULL-terminated. See the individual man pages for descriptions of each function.

SEE ALSO

bcmp(3), **bcopy**(3), **bzero**(3), **memccpy**(3), **memchr**(3), **memcmp**(3), **memcpy**(3), **memfrob**(3), **memmem**(3), **memmove**(3), **memset**(3)

NAME

htonl, htons, ntohl, ntohs – convert values between host and network byte order

SYNOPSIS

#include <netinet/in.h>
unsigned long int htonl(unsigned long int *hostlong***);**
unsigned short int htons(unsigned short int *hostshort***);**
unsigned long int ntohl(unsigned long int *netlong***);**
unsigned short int ntohs(unsigned short int *netshort***);**

DESCRIPTION

The **htonl()** function converts the long integer *hostlong* from host byte order to network byte order.

The **htons()** function converts the short integer *hostshort* from host byte order to network byte order.

The **ntohl()** function converts the long integer *netlong* from network byte order to host byte order.

The **ntohs()** function converts the short integer *netshort* from network byte order to host byte order.

On the i80x86 the host byte order is Least Significant Byte first, whereas the network byte order, as used on the Internet, is Most Significant Byte first.

CONFORMING TO

BSD 4.3

SEE ALSO

gethostbyname(3), **getservent**(3)

BZERO(3)

NAME

bzero – write zeros to a byte string

SYNOPSIS

#include <string.h>
void bzero(void *s*, **int** *n*);

DESCRIPTION

The **bzero()** function sets the first *n* bytes of the byte string *s* to zero.

RETURN VALUE

The **bzero()** function returns no value.

CONFORMING TO

BSD 4.3

SEE ALSO

memset(3), **swab**(3)

CATGETS(3)

NAME
catgets – get message from a message catalog

SYNOPSIS
#include <features.h>
#include <nl_types.h>
char *catgets(nl_catd catalog, int set_number, int message_number, char *message);

DESCRIPTION
catgets( ) reads the message *message_number*, in set *set_number*, from the message catalog identified by *catalog*. *catalog* is a catalog descriptor returned from an earlier call to **catopen**(3). The fourth argument *message* points to a default message string which will be returned by **catgets( )** if the identified message catalog is not currently open, or damaged. The message-text is contained in an internal buffer area and should be copied by the application if it is to be saved or modified. The return string is always terminated with a null byte.

RETURN VALUES
On success, **catgets( )** returns a pointer to an internal buffer area containing the null-terminated message string. **catgets( )** returns a pointer to *message* if it fails because the message catalog specified by *catalog* is not currently open. Otherwise, **catgets( )** returns a pointer to an empty string if the message catalog is available but does not contain the specified message.

NOTES
These functions are only available in libc.so.4.4.4c and above.

SEE ALSO
catopen(3), **setlocale**(3)

CATOPEN(3)

NAME

catopen, catclose – open/close a message catalog

SYNOPSIS

#include <features.h>
#include <nl_types.h>
nl_catd catopen(char *name, int flag)
void catclose(nl_catd catalog);

DESCRIPTION

catopen( ) opens a message catalog and returns a catalog descriptor. *name* specifies the name of the message catalog to be opened. If *name* specifies and absolute path, (i.e. contains a '/') then *name* specifies a pathname for the message catalog. Otherwise, the environment variable **NLSPATH** is used with *name* substituted for **%N** (see **locale**(5)). If NLSPATH does not exist in the environment, or if a message catalog cannot be opened in any of the paths specified by **NLSPATH**, then the following paths are searched in order

/etc/locale/LC_MESSAGES
/usr/lib/locale/LC_MESSAGES
/usr/lib/locale/name/LC_MESSAGES

In all cases *LC_MESSAGES* stands for the current setting of the **LC_MESSAGES** category of locale from a previous call to **setlocale**() and defaults to the "C" locale. In the last search path *name* refers to the catalog name.

The *flag* argument to catopen is used to indicate the type of loading desired. This should be either **MCLoadBySet** or **MCLoadAll**. The former value indicates that only the required set from the catalog is loaded into memory when needed, whereas the latter causes the initial call to **catopen**() to load the entire catalog into memory.

catclose( ) closes the message catalog identified by *catalog*. It invalidates any subsequent references to the message catalog defined by *catalog*.

RETURN VALUES

catopen( ) returns a message catalog descriptor of type *nl_catd* on success. On failure, it returns –1.

catclose( ) returns 0 on success, or -1 on failure.

NOTES

These functions are only available in libc.so.4.4.4c and above. In the case of linux, the catalog descriptor *nl_catd* is actually a mmap()'ed area of memory and not a file descriptor, thus allowing catalogs to be shared.

SEE ALSO

catgets(3), **setlocale**(3)

CEIL(3)

NAME

ceil – smallest integral value not less than x

SYNOPSIS

#include <math.h>
double ceil (double *x***);**

DESCRIPTION

The **ceil()** function rounds *x* upwards to the nearest integer, returning that value as a double.

CONFORMING TO

SVID 3, POSIX, BSD 4.3, ISO 9899

SEE ALSO

abs(3), **fabs**(3), **floor**(3), **labs**(3), **rint**(3)

NAME

clock – Determine processor time

SYNOPSIS

#include <time.h>
clock_t clock(void);

DESCRIPTION

The **clock()** function returns an approximation of processor time used by the program.

RETURN VALUE

The value returned is the CPU time used so far as a **clock_t**; to get the number of seconds used, divide by **CLOCKS_PER_SEC**.

CONFORMS TO

ANSI C

BUGS

The C standard allows for arbitrary values at the start of the program; take the difference between the value returned from a call to **clock()** at the start of the program and the end to get maximum portability.

The **times()** function call returns more information.

SEE ALSO

times(2)

CLOSEDIR(3)

NAME

closedir – close a directory

SYNOPSIS

#include <sys/types.h>
#include <dirent.h>
int closedir(DIR *dir);

DESCRIPTION

The **closedir()** function closes the directory stream associated with *dir*. The directory stream descriptor *dir* is not available after this call.

RETURN VALUE

The **closedir()** function returns 0 on success or –1 on failure.

ERRORS

EBADF   Invalid directory stream descriptor *dir*.

CONFORMING TO

SVID 3, POSIX, BSD 4.3

SEE ALSO

close(2), **opendir**(3), **readdir**(3), **rewinddir**(3), **seekdir**(3), **telldir**(3), **scandir**(3)

NAME

confstr – get configuration dependent string variables

SYNOPSIS

#define _USE_POSIX_2
#include <unistd.h>
size_t confstr(int *name***, char** **buf***, size_t** *len***);**

DESCRIPTION

confstr() gets the value of configuration – dependent string variables.

The *name* argument is the system variable to be queried. The following variables are supported:

> **_CS_PATH**   A value for the **PATH** variable which indicates where all the POSIX.2 standard utilities can be found.

If *buf* is not **NULL**, and *len* is not zero, **confstr()** copies the value of the string to *buf* truncated to *len* – 1 characters if necessary, with a null character as termination. This can be detected by comparing the return value of **confstr()** against *len*.

If *len* is zero and *buf* is **NULL**, **confstr()** just returns the value as defined below.

RETURN VALUE

If *name* does not correspond to a valid configuration variable, **confstr()** returns 0.

EXAMPLES

The following code fragment determines the path where to find the POSIX.2 system utilities:
char *pathbuf; size_t n;
n = confstr(_CS_PATH,NULL,(size_t)0);
if ((pathbuf = malloc(n)) == NULL) abort();
confstr(_CS_PATH, pathbuf, n);

ERRORS

If the value of *name* is invalid, *errno* is set to **EINVAL**.

CONFORMS TO

proposed POSIX.2

BUGS

POSIX.2 is not yet an approved standard; the information in this manpage is subject to change.

SEE ALSO

sh(1), **exec**(2), **system**(3)

NAME

copysign – copy sign of a number

SYNOPSIS

#include <math.h>
double copysign(double *x*, **double** *y*);

DESCRIPTION

The **copysign()** function returns a value whose absolute value matches *x*, but whose sign matches that of *y*.

CONFORMING TO

BSD 4.3

NAME

cos – cosine function

SYNOPSIS

#include <math.h>
double cos(double *x***);**

DESCRIPTION

The **cos**() function returns the cosine of *x*, where *x* is given in radians.

RETURN VALUE

The **cos**() function returns a value between −1 and 1.

CONFORMING TO

SVID 3, POSIX, BSD 4.3, ISO 9899

SEE ALSO

acos(3), **asin**(3), **atan**(3), **atan2**(3), **sin**(3), **tan**(3)

NAME

cosh – hyperbolic cosine function

SYNOPSIS

#include <math.h>
double cosh(double *x*);

DESCRIPTION

The **cosh()** function returns the hyperbolic cosine of *x*, which is defined mathematically as exp(x) + exp(-x) / 2.

CONFORMING TO

SVID 3, POSIX, BSD 4.3, ISO 9899

SEE ALSO

acosh(3), **asinh**(3), **atanh**(3), **sinh**(3), **tanh**(3)

NAME

crypt – password and data encryption

SYNOPSIS

#include <unistd.h>

char *crypt(const char ***key, const char ***salt**);**

DESCRIPTION

crypt is the password encryption function. It is based on the Data Encryption Standard algorithm with variations intended (among other things) to discourage use of hardware implementations of a key search.

key is a user's typed password.

salt is a two-character string chosen from the set [**azAZ09./**]. This string is used to perturb the algorithm in one of 4096 different ways.

By taking the lowest 7 bit of each character of the *key*, a 56-bit key is obtained. This 56-bit key is used to encrypt repeatedly a constant string (usually a string consisting of all zeros). The returned value points to the encrypted password, a series of 13 printable ASCII characters (the first two characters represent the salt itself). The return value points to static data whose content is overwritten by each call.

Warning: The key space consists of equal $7.2e16$ possible values. Exhaustive searches of this key space are possible using massively parallel computers. Software, such as **crack**(1), is available which will search the portion of this key space that is generally used by humans for passwords. Hence, password selection should, at minimum, avoid common words and names. The use of a **passwd**(1) program that checks for crackable passwords during the selection process is recommended.

The DES algorithm itself has a few quirks which make the use of the **crypt**(3) interface a very poor choice for anything other than password authentication. If you are planning on using the **crypt**(3) interface for a cryptography project, don't do it: get a good book on encryption and one of the widely available DES libraries.

CONFORMING TO

SVID, X/OPEN, BSD 4.3

SEE ALSO

login(1), **passwd**(1), **encrypt**(3), **getpass**(3), **passwd**(5)

NAME

ctermid – get controlling terminal name

SYNOPSIS

#include <stdio.h>
char *ctermid(char *s);

DESCRIPTION

ctermid() returns a string which is the pathname for the current controlling terminal for this process. If *s* is **NULL**, a static buffer is used, otherwise *s* points to a buffer used to hold the terminal pathname. The symbolic constant **L_ctermid** is the maximum number of characters in the returned pathname.

RETURN VALUE

The pointer to the pathname.

CONFORMS TO

POSIX.1

BUGS

The path returned may not uniquely identify the controlling terminal; it may, for example, be **/dev/tty**.

It is not assured that the program can open the terminal.

SEE ALSO

ttyname(3)

NAME

asctime, ctime, gmtime, localtime, mktime – transform binary date and time to ASCII

SYNOPSIS

#include <time.h>
char *asctime(const struct tm *`timeptr`);
char *ctime(const time_t *`timep`);
struct tm *gmtime(const time_t *`timep`);
struct tm *localtime(const time_t *`timep`);
time_t mktime(struct tm *`timeptr`);
extern char *`tzname`[2];
long int `timezone`;
extern int `daylight`;

DESCRIPTION

The **ctime()**, **gmtime()** and **localtime()** functions all take an argument of data type *time_t* which represents calendar time. When interpreted as an absolute time value, it represents the number of seconds elapsed since 00:00:00 on January 1, 1970, Coordinated Universal Time (UTC).

The **asctime()** and **mktime()** functions both take an argument representing broken-down time which is a binary representation separated into year, month, day, etc. Broken-down time is stored in the structure *tm* which is defined in <*time.h*> as follows:

```
struct tm
{
int tm_sec; /* seconds */
int tm_min; /* minutes */
int tm_hour; /* hours */
int tm_mday; /* day of the month */
int tm_mon; /* month */
int tm_year; /* year */
int tm_wday; /* day of the week */
int tm_yday; /* day in the year */
int tm_isdst; /* daylight saving time */
};
```

The members of the *tm* structure are:

tm_sec	The number of seconds after the minute, normally in the range 0 to 59, but can be up to 61 to allow for leap seconds.
tm_min	The number of minutes after the hour, in the range 0 to 59.
tm_hour	The number of hours past midnight, in the range 0 to 23.
tm_mday	The day of the month, in the range 1 to 31.
tm_mon	The number of months since January, in the range 0 to 11.
tm_year	The number of years since 1900.
tm_wday	The number of days since Sunday, in the range 0 to 6.
tm_yday	The number of days since January 1, in the range 0 to 365.
tm_isdst	A flag that indicates whether daylight saving time is in effect at the time described. The value is positive if daylight saving time is in effect, zero if it is not, and negative if the information is not available.

The **ctime()** function converts the calendar time *timep* into a string of the form

"Wed Jun 30 21:49:08 1993\n".

The abbreviations for the days of the week are 'Sun', 'Mon', 'Tue', 'Wed', 'Thu', 'Fri', and 'Sat'. The abbreviations for the months are 'Jan', 'Feb', 'Mar', 'Apr', 'May', 'Jun', 'Jul',

'Aug', 'Sep', 'Oct', 'Nov', and 'Dec'. The return value points to a statically allocated string which might be overwritten by subsequent calls to any of the date and time functions. The function also sets the external variable *tzname* with information about the current time zone.

The **gmtime()** function converts the calendar time *timep* to broken-down time representation, expressed in Coordinated Universal Time (UTC).

The **localtime()** function converts the calendar time *timep* to broken-time representation, expressed relative to the user's specified time zone. The function sets the external variables *tzname* with information about the current time zone, *timezone* with the difference between Coordinated Universal Time (UTC) and local standard time in seconds, and *daylight* to a non-zero value if standard US daylight savings time rules apply.

The **asctime()** function converts the broken-down time value *timeptr* into a string with the same format as **ctime()**. The return value points to a statically allocated string which might be overwritten by subsequent calls to any of the date and time functions.

The **mktime()** function converts a broken-down time structure to calendar time representation. The function ignores the specified contents of the structure members *tm_wday* and *tm_yday* and recomputes them from the other information in the broken-down time structure. Calling **mktime()** also sets the external variable *tzname* with information about the current time zone. If the specified broken-down time cannot be represented as calendar time, **mktime()** returns a value of (time_t)(−1) and does not alter the *tm_wday* and *tm_yday* members of the broken-down time structure.

CONFORMING TO

SVID 3, POSIX, BSD 4.3, ISO 9899

SEE ALSO

date(1), **gettimeofday**(2), **time**(2), **tzset**(3), **difftime**(3), **strftime**(3)

NAME

difftime – calculate time difference

SYNOPSIS

#include <time.h>
double difftime(time_t *time1*, **time_t** *time0*);

DESCRIPTION

The **difftime()** function returns the number of seconds elapsed between time *time1* and time *time0*. The two times are specified in calendar time, which represents the time elapsed since 00:00:00 on January 1, 1970, Coordinated Universal Time (UTC).

CONFORMING TO

SVID 3, BSD 4.3, ISO 9899

SEE ALSO

date(1), **gettimeofday**(2), **time**(2), **ctime**(3), **gmtime**(3), **localtime**(3)

NAME

div – computes the quotient and remainder of integer division

SYNOPSIS

#include <stdlib.h>
div_t div(int *numer***, int** *denom***);**

DESCRIPTION

The **div**() function computes the value *numer/denom* and returns the quotient and remainder in a structure named *div_t* that contains two integer members named *quot* and *rem*.

RETURN VALUE

The *div_t* structure.

CONFORMING TO

SVID 3, BSD 4.3, ISO 9899

SEE ALSO

ldiv(3)

NAME

drand48, erand48, lrand48, nrand48, mrand48, jrand48, srand48, seed48, lcong48 – generate uniformly distributed pseudo-random numbers

SYNOPSIS

#include <stdlib.h>
double drand48(void);
double erand48(unsigned short int *xsubi*[3]);
long int lrand48(void);
long int nrand48(unsigned short int *xsubi*[3]);
long int mrand48(void);
long int jrand48(unsigned short int *xsubi*[3]);
void srand48(long int *seedval*);
unsigned short int * seed48(unsigned *short* **int** *seed16v [3]*);
void lcong48(unsigned short int *param*[7]);

DESCRIPTION

These functions generate pseudo-random numbers using the linear congruential algorithm and 48-bit integer arithmetic.

The **drand48()** and **erand48()** functions return non-negative double-precision floating-point values uniformly distributed between [0.0, 1.0).

The **lrand48()** and **nrand48()** functions return non-negative long integers uniformly distributed between 0 and 2^{31}.

The **mrand48()** and **jrand48()** functions return signed long integers uniformly distributed between -2^{31} and 2^{31}.

The **srand48()**, **seed48()** and **lcong48()** functions are initialization functions, one of which should be called before using **drand48()**, **lrand48()** or **mrand49()**. The functions **erand48()**, **nrand48()** and **jrand48()** do not require an initialization function to be called first.

All the functions work by generating a sequence of 48-bit integers, Xi, according to the linear congruential formula:

Xn+1 = (aXn + c) mod m, where n >= 0

The parameter $m = 2^{48}$, hence 48-bit integer arithmetic is performed. Unless **lcong48()** is called, *a* and *c* are given by:

a = 0x5DEECE66D
c = 0xB

The value returned by any of the functions **drand48()**, **erand48()**, **lrand48()**, **nrand48()**, **mrand48()** or **jrand48()** is computed by first generating the next 48-bit Xi in the sequence. Then the appropriate number of bits, according to the type of data item to be returned, is copied from the high-order bits of Xi and transformed into the returned value.

The functions **drand48()**, **lrand48()** and **mrand48()** store the last 48-bit Xi generated in an internal buffer. The functions **erand48()**, **nrand48()** and **jrand48()** require the calling program to provide storage for the successive Xi values in the array argument *xsubi*. The functions are initialized by placing the initial value of Xi into the array before calling the function for the first time.

The initializer function **srand48()** sets the high order 32-bits of Xi to the argument *seedval*. The low order 16-bits are set to the arbitrary value 0x330E.

The initializer function **seed48()** sets the value of Xi to the 48-bit value specified in the array argument *seed16v*. The previous value of Xi is copied into an internal buffer and a pointer to this buffer is returned by **seed48()**.

The initialization function **lcong48()** allows the user to specify initial values for Xi, *a* and *c*. Array argument elements *param[0-2]* specify Xi, *param[3-5]* specify *a*, and *param[6]* specifies *c*. After **lcong48()** has been called, a subsequent call to either **srand48()** or **seed48()** will restore the standard values of *a* and *c*.

CONFORMING TO

SVID 3

NOTES

These functions are declared obsolete by SVID 3, which states that rand(3) should be used instead.

SEE ALSO

rand(3), random(3)

NAME

drem – floating-point remainder function

SYNOPSIS

#include <math.h>
double drem(double *x,* **double** *y***);**

DESCRIPTION

The **drem()** function computes the remainder of dividing *x* by *y*. The return value is $x - n * y$, where *n* is the quotient of x / y, rounded to the nearest integer. If the quotient is 1/2, it is rounded to the even number.

RETURN VALUE

The **drem()** function returns the remainder, unless *y* is zero, when the function fails and *errno* is set.

ERRORS

    EDOM   The denominator *y* is zero.

CONFORMING TO

BSD 4.3

SEE ALSO

fmod(3)

ECVT(3)

NAME

ecvt, fcvt – convert a floating-point number to a string.

SYNOPSIS

#include <stdlib.h>

char *ecvt(double *number*, size_t *ndigits*, int **decpt*, int **sign*);

char *fcvt(double *number*, size_t *ndigits*, int **decpt*, int **sign*);

DESCRIPTION

The **ecvt()** function converts *number* to a NULL terminated string of *ndigits* digits, and returns a pointer to the string. The string itself does not contain a decimal point; however, the position of the decimal point relative to the start of the string is stored in *decpt*. A negative value for *decpt* means that the decimal point is to the left of the start of the string. If the sign of *number* is negative, *sign* is set to a non-zero value, otherwise it's set to 0.

The **fcvt()** function is identical to **ecvt()**, except that *ndigits* specifies the number of digits after the decimal point.

RETURN VALUE

Both the **ecvt()** and **fcvt()** functions return a pointer to a static string containing the ASCII representation of *number*. The static string is overwritten by each call to **ecvt()** or **fcvt()**.

SEE ALSO

gcvt(3), **sprintf**(3)

ERF(3)　　　　　　　　Linux Programmer's Manual　　　　　　　　ERF(3)

NAME

erf, erfc – error function and complementary error function

SYNOPSIS

#include <math.h>
double erf(double *x***);**
double erfc (double *x***);**

DESCRIPTION

The **erf()** function returns the error function of *x*; defined as

erf(x) = 2/sqrt(pi)* integral from 0 to x of exp(-t*t) dt

The **erfc()** function returns the complementary error function of *x*, that is 1.0 - erf(x).

CONFORMING TO

SVID 3, BSD 4.3

SEE ALSO

exp(3)

BSD　　　　　　　　　　　　　June 25, 1993

EXEC(3)

NAME

execl, execlp, execle, exect, execv, execvp – execute a file

SYNOPSIS

#include <unistd.h>

extern char **environ;

int execl(const char *path, const char *arg, ...); .br .BI int execlp(const char *file, const char *arg, ...); .br .BI int execle(const char *path, const char *arg
int execlp(const char *file, const char *arg, ...);

int execle(const char *path, const char *arg
int execle(const char *path, const char *arg , ..., char * const envp[]);
int exect(const char *path, char *const argv[]);
int execv(const char *path, char *const argv[]);
int execvp(const char *file, char *const argv[]);

DESCRIPTION

The **exec** family of functions replaces the current process image with a new process image. The functions described in this manual page are front-ends for the function **execve**(2). (See the manual page for **execve** for detailed information about the replacement of the current process.)

The initial argument for these functions is the pathname of a file which is to be executed.

The *const char *arg* and subsequent ellipses in the **execl**, **execlp**, and **execle** functions can be thought of as *arg0, arg1, ..., argn*. Together they describe a list of one or more pointers to null-terminated strings that represent the argument list available to the executed program. The first argument, by convention, should point to the file name associated with the file being executed. The list of arguments *must* be terminated by a **NULL** pointer.

The **exect**, **execv**, and **execvp** functions provide an array of pointers to null-terminated strings that represent the argument list available to the new program. The first argument, by convention, should point to the file name associated with the file begin executed. The array of pointers *must* be terminated by a **NULL** pointer.

The **execle** and **exect** functions also specify the environment of the executed process by following the **NULL** pointer that terminates the list of arguments in the parameter list or the pointer to the argv array with an additional parameter. This additional parameter is an array of pointers to null-terminated strings and *must* be terminated by a **NULL** pointer. The other functions take the environment for the new process image from the external variable *environ* in the current process.

Some of these functions have special semantics.

The functions **execlp** and **execvp** will duplicate the actions of the shell in searching for an executable file if the specified file name does not contain a slash (/) character. The search path is the path specified in the environment by the **PATH** variable. If this variable isn't specified, the default path "/bin:/usr/bin:" is used (is this true for Linux?). In addition, certain errors are treated specially.

If permission is denied for a file (the attempted **execve** returned **EACCES**), these functions will continue searching the rest of the search path. If no other file is found, however, they will return with the global variable *errno* set to **EACCES**.

If the header of a file isn't recognized (the attempted **execve** returned **ENOEXEC**), these functions will execute the shell with the path of the file as its first argument. (If this attempt fails, no further searching is done.)

If the file is currently busy (the attempted **execve** returned **ETXTBUSY**), these functions will sleep for several seconds, periodically re-attempting to execute the file. (Is this true for Linux?).

The function **exect** executes a file with the program tracing facilities enabled (see **ptrace**(2).

RETURN VALUES

If any of the **exec** functions returns, an error will have occurred. The return value is −1, and the global variable *errno* will be set to indicate the error.

FILES

/bin/sh

ERRORS

Execl, **execle**, **execlp** and **execvp** may fail and set *errno* for any of the errors specified for the library functions **execve**(2) and **malloc**(3).

Exect and **execv** may fail and set *errno* for any of the errors specified for the library function **execve**(2).

SEE ALSO

sh(1), **execve**(2), **fork**(2), **trace**(2), **environ**(7), **ptrace**(2)

COMPATIBILITY

Historically, the default path for the **execlp** and **execvp** functions was ":/bin:/usr/bin". This was changed to place the current directory last to enhance system security.

The behavior of **execlp** and **execvp** when errors occur while attempting to execute the file is historic practice, but has not traditionally been documented and is not specified by the POSIX standard.

Traditionally, the functions **execlp** and **execvp** ignored all errors except for the ones described above and **ENOMEM** and **E2BIG**, upon which they returned. They now return if any error other than the ones described above occurs.

STANDARDS

Execl, **execv**, **execle**, **execlp** and **execvp** conform to IEEE Std1003.1-88 ("POSIX").

EXIT(3)

NAME

exit – cause normal program termination

SYNOPSIS

#include <stdlib.h>
void exit(int *status***);**

DESCRIPTION

The **exit()** function causes normal program termination and the value of *status* is returned to the parent. All functions registered with **atexit()** and **on_exit()** are called in the reverse order of their registration, and all open streams are flushed and closed.

RETURN VALUE

The **exit()** function does not return.

CONFORMING TO

SVID 3, POSIX, BSD 4.3, ISO 9899

SEE ALSO

_exit(2), **atexit**(3), **on_exit**(3)

NAME

exp, log, log10, pow – exponential, logarithmic and power functions

SYNOPSIS

#include <math.h>
double exp(double *x***);**
double log(double *x***);**
double log10(double *x***);**
double pow(double *x***, double** *y* **);**

DESCRIPTION

The **exp**() function returns the value of e (the base of natural logarithms) raised to the power of x.

The **log**() function returns the natural logarithm of x.

The **log10**() function returns the base-10 logarithm of x.

The **pow**() function returns the value of x raised to the power of y.

ERRORS

The **log**() function can return the following errors:

    EDOM   The argument x is negative.

    ERANGE   The argument x is zero. The log of zero is not defined.

The **pow**() function can return the following error:

    EDOM   The argument x is negative and y is not an integral value. This would result in a complex number.

CONFORMING TO

SVID 3, POSIX, BSD 4.3, ISO 9899

SEE ALSO

sqrt(3), **cbrt**(3)

NAME

fabs – absolute value of floating-point number

SYNOPSIS

#include <math.h>
double fabs(double *x***);**

DESCRIPTION

The **fabs()** function returns the absolute value of the floating-point number *x*.

CONFORMING TO

SVID 3, POSIX, BSD 4.3, ISO 9899

SEE ALSO

abs(3), **ceil**(3), **floor**(3), **labs**(3), **rint**(3)

FCLOSE(3)

NAME
fclose – close a stream

SYNOPSIS
#include <stdio.h>

int fclose(FILE **stream***);**

DESCRIPTION
The **fclose** function dissociates the named *stream* from its underlying file or set of functions. If the stream was being used for output, any buffered data is written first, using **fflush**(3).

RETURN VALUES
Upon successful completion 0 is returned. Otherwise, **EOF** is returned and the global variable *errno* is set to indicate the error. In either case no further access to the stream is possible.

ERRORS
    EBADF   The argument *stream* is not an open stream.

The **fclose** function may also fail and set *errno* for any of the errors specified for the routines **close**(2) or **fflush**(3).

SEE ALSO
close(2), **fflush**(3), **fopen**(3), **setbuf**(3)

STANDARDS
The **fclose** function conforms to ANSI C3.159-1989 ("ANSI C").

FERROR(3)

NAME

clearerr, feof, ferror, fileno – check and reset stream status

SYNOPSIS

#include <stdio.h>

void clearerr(FILE **stream***);**
int feof(FILE **stream***);**
int ferror(FILE **stream***);**
int fileno(FILE **stream***);**

DESCRIPTION

The function **clearerr** clears the end-of-file and error indicators for the stream pointed to by *stream*.

The function **feof** tests the end-of-file indicator for the stream pointed to by *stream*, returning non-zero if it is set. The end-of-file indicator can only be cleared by the function **clearerr**.

The function **ferror** tests the error indicator for the stream pointed to by *stream*, returning non-zero if it is set. The error indicator can only be reset by the **clearerr** function.

The function **fileno** examines the argument *stream* and returns its integer descriptor.

ERRORS

These functions should not fail and do not set the external variable *errno*.

SEE ALSO

open(2), **stdio**(3)

STANDARDS

The functions **clearerr**, **feof**, and **ferror** conform to C3.159-1989 ("ANSI C").

NAME

fflush, fpurge – flush a stream

SYNOPSIS

#include <stdio.h>

**int fflush(FILE **stream*);
**int fpurge(FILE **stream*);

DESCRIPTION

The function **fflush** forces a write of all buffered data for the given output or update *stream* via the stream's underlying write function. The open status of the stream is unaffected.

If the *stream* argument is **NULL**, **fflush** flushes *all* open output streams. (Does this happen under Linux?)

The function **fpurge** erases any input or output buffered in the given *stream*. For output streams this discards any unwritten output. For input streams this discards any input read from the underlying object but not yet obtained via **getc**(3); this includes any text pushed back via **ungetc**.

RETURN VALUES

Upon successful completion 0 is returned. Otherwise, **EOF** is returned and the global variable *errno* is set to indicate the error.

ERRORS

> **EBADF**   *Stream* is not an open stream, or, in the case of **fflush**, not a stream open for writing.

The function **fflush** may also fail and set *errno* for any of the errors specified for the routine **write**(2).

BUGS

Linux may not support **fpurge**.

SEE ALSO

write(2), **fopen**(3), **fclose**(3), **setbuf**(3)

STANDARDS

The **fflush** function conforms to ANSI C3.159-1989 ("ANSI C").

NAME

ffs – find first bit set in a word

SYNOPSIS

#include <string.h>
int **ffs**(int *i*);

DESCRIPTION

The **ffs**() function returns the position of the first bit set in the word *i*. The least significant bit is position 1 and the most significant position 32.

RETURN VALUE

The **ffs**() function returns the position of the first bit set, or NULL if no bits are set.

CONFORMING TO

BSD 4.3

NAME

fgetgrent – get group file entry

SYNOPSIS

#include <grp.h>
#include <stdio.h>
#include <sys/types.h>
struct group *fgetgrent(FILE *stream);

DESCRIPTION

The **fgetgrent()** function returns a pointer to a structure containing the group information from the file *stream*. The first time it is called it returns the first entry; thereafter, it returns successive entries. The file *stream* must have the same format as */etc/group*.

The *group* structure is defined in <*grp.h*> as follows:

struct group {
char *gr_name; /* group name */
char *gr_passwd; /* group password */
gid_t gr_gid; /* group id */
char **gr_mem; /* group members */
};

RETURN VALUE

The **fgetgrent()** function returns the group information structure, or NULL if there are no more entries or an error occurs.

ERRORS

ENOMEM   Insufficient memory to allocate group information structure.

CONFORMING TO

SVID 3

SEE ALSO

getgrnam(3), **getgrgid**(3), **getgrent**(3), **setgrent**(3), **endgrent**(3)

NAME

fgetpwent – get password file entry

SYNOPSIS

#include <pwd.h>
#include <stdio.h>
#include <sys/types.h>
struct passwd *fgetpwent(FILE *stream);

DESCRIPTION

The **fgetpwent()** function returns a pointer to a structure containing the broken out fields of a line in the file *stream*. The first time it is called it returns the first entry; thereafter, it returns successive entries. The file *stream* must have the same format as */etc/passwd*.

The *passwd* structure is defined in *<pwd.h>* as follows:

struct passwd {
char *pw_name; /* user name */
char *pw_passwd; /* user password */
uid_t pw_uid; /* user id */
gid_t pw_gid; /* group id */
char *pw_gecos; /* real name */
char *pw_dir; /* home directory */
char *pw_shell; /* shell program */
};

RETURN VALUE

The **fgetpwent()** function returns the passwd structure, or NULL if there are no more entries or an error occurs.

ERRORS

    ENOMEM   Insufficient memory to allocate passwd structure.

CONFORMING TO

SVID 3

SEE ALSO

getpwnam(3), **getpwuid**(3), **getpwent**(3), **setpwent**(3), **endpwent**(3), **getpw**(3), **putpwent**(3)

FLOOR(3)

NAME

floor – largest integral value not greater than x

SYNOPSIS

#include <math.h>
double floor(double *x***);**

DESCRIPTION

The **floor()** function rounds *x* downwards to the nearest integer, returning that value as a double.

CONFORMING TO

SVID 3, POSIX, BSD 4.3, ISO 9899

SEE ALSO

abs(3), **fabs**(3), **ceil**(3), **rint**(3)

FMOD(3)

NAME

fmod – floating-point remainder function

SYNOPSIS

#include <math.h>
double fmod(double *x*, **double** *y*);

DESCRIPTION

The **modf()** function computes the remainder of dividing *x* by *y*. The return value is $x - n * y$, where n is the quotient of x / y, rounded towards zero to an integer.

RETURN VALUE

The **fmod()** function returns the remainder, unless *y* is zero, when the function fails and *errno* is set.

ERRORS

EDOM   The denominator *y* is zero.

CONFORMING TO

SVID 3, POSIX, BSD 4.3, ISO 9899

SEE ALSO

drem(3)

FNMATCH(3)

NAME

fnmatch – match filename or pathname

SYNOPSIS

#include <fnmatch.h>
int fnmatch(const char **pattern*, **const char** **strings*, **int** *flags*);

DESCRIPTION

The **fnmatch()** checks the *strings* argument and checks if it matches *pattern* argument, which is a shell wildcard pattern.

The *flags* argument modifies the behaviour; it is the bitwise OR of zero or more of the following flags:

FNM_NOESCAPE If this flag is set, treat backslash as an ordinary character, instead of an escape character.

FNM_PATHNAME If this flag is set, match a slash in *string* only with a slash in *pattern* and not, for example, with a [] – sequence containing a slash.

FNM_PERIOD If flag this is set, a leading period in *string* has to be matched exactly by a period in *pattern*. A period is considered to be leading if it is the first character in *string*, or if both **FNM_PATHNAME** is set and the period immediately follows a slash.

RETURN VALUE

Zero if *string* matches *pattern*, **FNM_NOMATCH** if there is no match or another value if there is an error.

CONFORMS TO

proposed POSIX.2

BUGS

POSIX.2 is not yet an approved standard; the information in this manpage is subject to change.

SEE ALSO

sh(1), **glob**(3), **glob**(7)

NAME

fopen, fdopen, freopen – stream open functions

SYNOPSIS

#include <stdio.h>

FILE *fopen(char **path***, char ****mode***);**
FILE *fdopen(int *fildes***, char ****mode***);**
FILE *freopen(char **path***, char ****mode***, FILE ****stream***);**

DESCRIPTION

The **fopen** function opens the file whose name is the string pointed to by *path* and associates a stream with it.

The argument *mode* points to a string beginning with one of the following sequences (Additional characters may follow these sequences.):

- **r**   Open text file for reading. The stream is positioned at the beginning of the file.
- **r+**   Open for reading and writing. The stream is positioned at the beginning of the file.
- **w**   Truncate file to zero length or create text file for writing. The stream is positioned at the beginning of the file.
- **w+**   Open for reading and writing. The file is created if it does not exist, otherwise it is truncated. The stream is positioned at the beginning of the file.
- **a**   Open for writing. The file is created if it does not exist. The stream is positioned at the end of the file.
- **a+**   Open for reading and writing. The file is created if it does not exist. The stream is positioned at the end of the file.

The *mode* string can also include the letter "b" either as a third character or as a character between the characters in any of the two-character strings described above. This is strictly for compatibility with ANSI C3.159-1989 ("ANSI C") and has no effect; the "b" is ignored. Linux may not behave this way.

Any created files will have mode
S_IRUSR|S_IWUSR|S_IRGRP|S_IWGRP|S_IROTH|S_IWOTH
(0666), as modified by the process' umask value (see **umask**(2).

Reads and writes may be intermixed on read/write streams in any order, and do not require an intermediate seek as in previous versions of *stdio*. This is not portable to other systems, however, and may not work under Linux (someone should find out and fix this manpage); ANSI C requires that a file positioning function intervene between output and input, unless an input operation encounters end-of-file.

The **fdopen** function associates a stream with the existing file descriptor, *fildes*. The *mode* of the stream must be compatible with the mode of the file descriptor.

The **freopen** function opens the file whose name is the string pointed to by *path* and associates the stream pointed to by *stream* with it. The original stream (if it exists) is closed. The *mode* argument is used just as in the **fopen** function. The primary use of the **freopen** function is to change the file associated with a standard text stream (*stderr*, *stdin*, or *stdout*).

RETURN VALUES

Upon successful completion **fopen**, **fdopen** and **freopen** return a **FILE** pointer. Otherwise, **NULL** is returned and the global variable *errno* is set to indicate the error.

ERRORS

    EINVAL   The *mode* provided to **fopen**, **fdopen**, or **freopen** was invalid.

The **fopen**, **fdopen** and **freopen** functions may also fail and set *errno* for any of the errors specified for the routine **malloc**(3).

The **fopen** function may also fail and set *errno* for any of the errors specified for the routine **open**(2).

The **fdopen** function may also fail and set *errno* for any of the errors specified for the routine **fcntl**(2).

The **freopen** function may also fail and set *errno* for any of the errors specified for the routines **open**(2), **fclose**(3) and **fflush**(3).

SEE ALSO

open(2), **fclose**(3)

STANDARDS

The **fopen** and **freopen** functions conform to ANSI C3.159-1989 ("ANSI C"). The **fdopen** function conforms to IEEE Std1003.1-1988 ("POSIX").

FPATHCONF(3)

NAME
fpathconf, pathconf – get configuration values for files

SYNOPSIS
#include <unistd.h>
long fpathconf(int *filedes*, **int** *name*);
long pathconf(char **path*, **int** *name*);

DESCRIPTION
fpathconf() gets a value for the configuration option *name* for the open file descriptor *filedes*.

pathconf() gets a value for configuration option *name* for the file name *path*.

The corresponding macros defined in <**unistd.h**> minimum values; if an application wants to take advantage of values which may change, a call to **fpathconf()** or **pathconf()** can be made, which may yield more liberal results.

Setting *name* equal to one of the following constants returns the following configuration options:

- **_PC_LINK_MAX** — returns the maximum number of links to the file. If *filedes* or *path* refer to a directory, then the value applies to the whole directory. The corresponding macro is **_POSIX_LINK_MAX**.

- **_PC_MAX_CANON** — returns the maximum length of a formatted input line, where *filedes* or *path* must refer to a terminal. The corresponding macro is **_POSIX_MAX_CANON**.

- **_PC_MAX_INPUT** — returns the maximum length of an input line, where *filedes* or *path* must refer to a terminal. The corresponding macro is **_POSIX_MAX_INPUT**.

- **_PC_NAME_MAX** — returns the maximum length of a filename in the directory *path* or *filedes*. the process is allowed to create. **_POSIX_MAX_**.

- **_PC_PATH_MAX** — returns the maximum length of a relative pathname when *path* or *filedes* is the current working directory. The corresponding macro is **_POSIX_PATH_MAX**.

- **_PC_PIPE_BUF** — returns the size of the pipe buffer, where *filedes* must refer to a pipe or FIFO and *path* must refer to a FIFO. The corresponding macro is **_POSIX_PIPE_BUF**.

- **_PC_CHOWN_RESTRICTED** — returns nonzero if the **chown**(2) call may not be used on this file. If *filedes* or *path* refer to a directory, then this applies to all files in that directory. The corresponding macro is **_POSIX_CHOWN_RESTRICTED**.

- **_PC_NO_TRUNC** — returns nonzero if accessing filenames longer than **_POSIX_NAME_MAX** generates an error. The corresponding macro is **_POSIX_NO_TRUNC**.

- **_PC_VDISABLE** — returns nonzero if special character processing can be disabled, where *filedes* or *path* must refer to a terminal.

RETURN VALUE
The limit is returned, if one exists. If the system does not have a limit for the requested resource, −1 is returned, and *errno* is unchanged. If there is an error, −1 is returned, and *errno* is set to reflect the nature of the error.

CONFORMS TO

POSIX.1 Files with name lengths longer than the value returned for *name* equal to _PC_NAME_MAX may exist in the given directory.

Some returned values may be huge; they are not suitable for allocating memory.

SEE ALSO

getconf(1), **statfs**(2), **open**(2), **sysconf**(3)

NAME

fread, fwrite – binary stream input/output

SYNOPSIS

#include <stdio.h>

int fread(void **ptr*, **size_t** *size*, **size_t** *nmemb*, **FILE** **stream*);

int fwrite(void **ptr*, **size_t** *size*, **size_t** *nmemb*, **FILE** **stream*);

DESCRIPTION

The function **fread** reads *nmemb* elements of data, each *size* bytes long, from the stream pointed to by *stream*, storing them at the location given by *ptr*.

The function **fwrite** writes *nmemb* elements of data, each *size* bytes long, to the stream pointed to by *stream*, obtaining them from the location given by *ptr*.

RETURN VALUES

fread and **fwrite** return the number of items successfully read or written (i.e., not the number of characters). If an error occurs, or the end-of-file is reached, the return value is a short item count (or zero).

fread does not distinguish between end-of-file and error, and callers must use **feof**(3) and **ferror**(3) to determine which occurred.

SEE ALSO

feof(3), **ferror**(3), **read**(2), **write**(2)

STANDARDS

The functions **fread** and **fwrite** conform to ANSI C3.159-1989 ("ANSI C").

NAME

frexp – convert floating-point number to fractional and integral components

SYNOPSIS

#include <math.h>
double frexp(double *x***, int ****exp***);**

DESCRIPTION

The **frexp()** function is used to split the number *x* into a normalized fraction and an exponent which is stored in *exp*.

RETURN VALUE

The **frexp()** function returns the normalized fraction. If the argument *x* is not zero, the normalized fraction is *x* times a power of two, and is always in the range 1/2 (inclusive) to 1 (exclusive). If *x* is zero, then the normalized fraction is zero and zero is stored in *exp*.

CONFORMING TO

SVID 3, POSIX, BSD 4.3, ISO 9899

SEE ALSO

ldexp(3), **modf**(3)

FSEEK(3)

NAME

fgetpos, fseek, fsetpos, ftell, rewind – reposition a stream

SYNOPSIS

#include <stdio.h>

int fseek(FILE *stream, long offset, int whence);
long ftell(FILE *stream);
void rewind(FILE *stream);
int fgetpos(FILE *stream, fpos_t *pos);
int fsetpos(FILE *stream, fpos_t *pos);

DESCRIPTION

The **fseek** function sets the file position indicator for the stream pointed to by *stream*. The new position, measured in bytes, is obtained by adding *offset* bytes to the position specified by *whence*. If *whence* is set to **SEEK_SET**, **SEEK_CUR**, or **SEEK_END**, the offset is relative to the start of the file, the current position indicator, or end-of-file, respectively. A successful call to the **fseek** function clears the end-of-file indicator for the stream and undoes any effects of the **ungetc**(3) function on the same stream.

The **ftell** function obtains the current value of the file position indicator for the stream pointed to by *stream*.

The **rewind** function sets the file position indicator for the stream pointed to by *stream* to the beginning of the file. It is equivalent to:

(void)fseek(stream, 0L, SEEK_SET)

except that the error indicator for the stream is also cleared (see **clearerr**(3).

The **fgetpos** and **fsetpos** functions are alternate interfaces equivalent to **ftell** and **fseek** (with whence set to **SEEK_SET**), setting and storing the current value of the file offset into or from the object referenced by *pos*. On some non-UNIX systems an **fpos_t** object may be a complex object and these routines may be the only way to portably reposition a text stream.

RETURN VALUES

The **rewind** function returns no value. Upon successful completion, **fgetpos**, **fseek**, **fsetpos** return 0, and **ftell** returns the current offset. Otherwise, –1 is returned and the global variable errno is set to indicate the error.

ERRORS

    EBADF   The *stream* specified is not a seekable stream.

    EINVAL   The *whence* argument to **fseek** was not **SEEK_SET**, **SEEK_END**, or **SEEK_CUR**.

The function **fgetpos**, **fseek**, **fsetpos**, and **ftell** may also fail and set *errno* for any of the errors specified for the routines **fflush**(3), **fstat**(2), **lseek**(2), and **malloc**(3).

SEE ALSO

lseek(2)

STANDARDS

The **fgetpos**, **fsetpos**, **fseek**, **ftell**, and **rewind** functions conform to ANSI C3.159-1989 ("ANSI C").

NAME

ftime – return date and time

SYNOPSIS

#include <sys/timeb.h>

int ftime(struct timeb *tp);

DESCRIPTION

Return current date and time in *tp*, which is declared as following:

```
struct timeb {
    time_t time;
    unsigned short millitm;
    short timezone;
    short dstflag;
};
```

RETURN VALUE

This function always returns 0.

NOTES

Under Linux, this function is not implemented in a compatibility library instead of in the kernel.

CONFORMING TO

V7, BSD 4.3
Under BSD 4.3, this call is obsoleted by **gettimeofday**(2).

SEE ALSO

time(2)

FTOK(3)

NAME

ftok – convert a pathname and a project identifier to a System V IPC key

SYNOPSIS

#include <sys/types.h>
#include <sys/ipc.h>

key_t ftok (char *pathname,* **char** *proj* **)**

DESCRIPTION

The function converts the pathname of an existing accessible file and a project identifier into a **key_t** type System V IPC key.

RETURN VALUE

On success the return value will be the converted **key_t** value, otherwise **–1** with **errno** indicating the error as for the **stat**(2) system call.

BUGS

The generated **key_t** value is obtained **stat**-ing the disk file corresponding to *pathname* in order to get its i–node number and the minor device number of the filesystem on which the disk file resides, then by combining the 8 bit *proj* value along with the lower 16 bits of the i–node number, along with the 8 bits of the minor device number. The algorithm does not guarantee a unique key value. In fact

> Two different names linking to the same file produce same key values.
>
> Using the lower 16 bits of the i–node number, gives some chance (also usually small) to have same key values for file names referring to different i–nodes.
>
> Not discriminating among major device numbers, gives some chance of collision (also usually small) for systems with multiple disk controllers.

SEE ALSO

ipc(5), **msgget**(2), **semget**(2), **shmget**(2), **stat**(2).

FTW(3)

NAME

ftw – file tree walk

SYNOPSIS

#include <ftw.h>

int ftw(const char **directory,* **int** *(*funcptr* **)(const char** **file,* **struct stat** **sb,* **int** *flag),* **int** *depth***);**

DESCRIPTION

ftw() walks through the directory tree starting from the indicated *directory*. For each found entry in the tree, it calls *funcptr* with the full pathname of the entry relative to *directory*, a pointer to a the second argument is a pointer to the **stat**(2) structure for the entry and an int, which value will be one of the following:

FTW_F Item is a normal file
FTW_D Item is a directory
FTW_NS The stat failed on the item
FTW_DNR Item is a directory which can't be read

Warning: Anything other than directories, like symbolic links, gets the **FTW_F** tag.

ftw() recursively calls itself for traversing found directories. To avoid using up all a program's file descriptors, the *depth* specifies the number of simultaneous open directories. When the depth is exceeded, **ftw()** will become slower because directories have to be closed and reopened.

To stop the tree walk, *funcptr* returns a non-zero value; this value will become the return value of **ftp()**. Otherwise, **ftw()** will continue until it has traversed the entire tree, in which case it will return zero, or until it hits an error such as a **malloc**(3) failure, in which case it will return –1.

Because **ftp()** uses dynamic data structures, the only safe way to exit out of a tree walk is to return a non-zero value. To handle interrupts, for example, mark that the interrupt occurred and return a non-zero value—don't use **longjmp**(3) unless the program is going to terminate.

SEE ALSO

stat(2)

GCVT(3)

NAME

gcvt – convert a floating-point number to a string.

SYNOPSIS

#include <stdlib.h>
char *gcvt(double *number***, size_t** *ndigit***, char ****buf***);**

DESCRIPTION

The **gcvt()** function converts *number* to a minimal length NULL terminated ASCII string and stores the result in *buf*. It produces *ndigit* significant digits in either printf() F format or E format.

RETURN VALUE

The **gcvt()** function returns the address of the string pointed to by *buf*.

SEE ALSO

ecvt(3), **fcvt**(3), **sprintf**(3)

NAME

getcwd, get_current_dir_name, getwd – Get current working directory

SYNOPSIS

#include <unistd.h>
char *getcwd(char **buf*, size_t *size*);
char *get_current_working_dir_name(void);
char *getwd(char **buf*);

DESCRIPTION

The **getcwd()** function copies the absolute pathname of the current working directory to the array pointed to by *buf*, which is of length *size*.

If the current absolute path name would require a buffer longer than *size* elements, **NULL** is returned, and *errno* is set to **ERANGE**; an application should check for this error, and allocate a larger buffer if necessary.

As an extension to the POSIX.1 standard, **getcwd()** allocates the buffer dynamically using **malloc()** if *buf* is **NULL** on call. In this case, the allocated buffer has the length *size* unless *size* is less than zero, when *buf* is allocated as big as necessary. It is possible (and, indeed, advisable) to **free()** the buffers if they have been obtained this way.

get_current_dir_name, which is only prototyped if **__USE_GNU** is defined, will **malloc**(3) an array big enough to hold the current directory name. If the environment variable **PWD** is set, and its value is correct, then that value will be returned.

getwd, which is only prototyped if **__USE_BSD** is defined, will **malloc**(3) an array big enough to hold the absolute pathname of the current working directory.

RETURN VALUE

NULL on failure (for example, if the current directory is not readable), with *errno* set accordingly, and *buf* on success.

CONFORMS TO

POSIX.1

SEE ALSO

chdir(2), ,**free**(3), **malloc**(3)

GETDIRENTRIES(3)

NAME
getdirentries – get directory entries in a filesystem independent format

SYNOPSIS
#define _USE_BSD or **#define** _USE_MISC
#include <dirent.h>

ssize_t getdirentries(int *fd***, char ****buf***, size_t** *nbytes* **, off_t ****basep***);**

DESCRIPTION
Read directory entries from the directory specified by *fd* into *buf*. At most *nbytes* are read. Reading starts at offset **basep*, and **basep* is updated with the new position after reading.

RETURN VALUE
getdirentries returns the number of bytes read or zero when at the end of the directory. If an error occurs, −1 is returned, and *errno* is set appropriately.

ERRORS
See the Linux library source code for details.

SEE ALSO
open(2), **lseek**(2)

NAME

getenv – get an environment variable

SYNOPSIS

#include <stdlib.h>
char *getenv(const char *****name***);**

DESCRIPTION

The **getenv()** function searches the environment list for a string that matches the string pointed to by *name*. The strings are of the form *name = value*.

RETURN VALUE

The **getenv()** function returns a pointer to the value in the environment, or NULL if there is no match.

CONFORMING TO

SVID 3, POSIX, BSD 4.3, ISO 9899

SEE ALSO

putenv(3), **setenv**(3), **unsetenv**(3)

NAME

getgrent, setgrent, endgrent – get group file entry

SYNOPSIS

#include <grp.h>
#include <sys/types.h>
struct group *getgrent(void);
void setgrent(void);
void endgrent(void);

DESCRIPTION

The **getgrent()** function returns a pointer to a structure containing the group information from */etc/group*. The first time it is called it returns the first entry; thereafter, it returns successive entries.

The **setgrent()** function rewinds the file pointer to the beginning of the */etc/group* file.

The **endgrent()** function closes the */etc/group* file.

The *group* structure is defined in <*grp.h*> as follows:

struct group {
char *gr_name; /* group name */
char *gr_passwd; /* group password */
gid_t gr_gid; /* group id */
char **gr_mem; /* group members */
};

RETURN VALUE

The **getgrent()** function returns the group information structure, or NULL if there are no more entries or an error occurs.

ERRORS

    ENOMEM   Insufficient memory to allocate group information structure.

FILES

/etc/group group database file

CONFORMING TO

SVID 3, BSD 4.3

SEE ALSO

fgetgrent(3), **getgrnam**(3), **getgrgid**(3)

NAME

j0, j1, jn, y0, y1, yn – Bessel functions

SYNOPSIS

#include <math.h>
double j0(double x**);**
double j1(double x**);**
double jn(int n**, double** x**);**
double y0(double x**);**
double y1(double x**);**
double yn(int n**, double** x**);**

DESCRIPTION

The **j0()** and **j1()** functions return Bessel functions of x of the first kind of orders 0 and 1, respectively. The **jn()** function returns the Bessel function of x of the first kind of order n.

The **y0()** and **y1()** functions return Bessel functions of x of the second kind of orders 0 and 1, respectively. The **yn()** function returns the Bessel function of x of the second kind of order n.

For the functions **y0()**, **y1()** and **yn()**, the value of x must be positive. For negative values of x, these functions return –HUGE_VAL.

CONFORMING TO

SVID 3, BSD 4.3

BUGS

There are errors of up to 2e–16 in the values returned by **j0()**, **j1()** and **jn()** for values of x between –8 and 8.

NAME

getgrnam, getgrgid – get group file entry

SYNOPSIS

#include <grp.h>
#include <sys/types.h>
struct group *getgrnam(const char **name***);**
struct group *getgrgid(gid_t *gid***);**

DESCRIPTION

The **getgrnam()** function returns a pointer to a structure containing the group information from */etc/group* for the entry that matches the group name *name*.

The **getgrgid()** function returns a pointer to a structure containing the group information from */etc/group* for the entry that matches the group gid *gid*.

The *group* structure is defined in *<grp.h>* as follows:

```
struct group {
char *gr_name; /* group name */
char *gr_passwd; /* group password */
gid_t gr_gid; /* group id */
char **gr_mem; /* group members */
};
```

RETURN VALUE

The **getgrnam()** and **getgrgid()** functions return the group information structure, or NULL if the matching entry is not found or an error occurs.

ERRORS

ENOMEM Insufficient memory to allocate group information structure.

FILES

/etc/group group database file

CONFORMING TO

SVID 3, POSIX, BSD 4.3

SEE ALSO

fgetgrent(3), **getgrent**(3), **setgrent**(3), **endgrent**(3)

GETHOSTBYNAME(3) Linux Programmer's Manual GETHOSTBYNAME(3)

NAME

gethostbyname, gethostbyaddr, sethostent, endhostent, herror – get network host entry

SYNOPSIS

#include <netdb.h>
extern int h_errno;
struct hostent *gethostbyname(const char *name**);**
struct hostent *gethostbyaddr(const char *addr**, int** len**, int** type**);**
void sethostent(int stayopen**);**
void endhostent(void);
void herror(const char *s**);**

DESCRIPTION

The **gethostbyname()** function returns a structure of type *hostent* for the given host *name*. The current domain and its parents are searched unless *name* ends in a dot. If *name* doesn't end in a dot and the environment variable **HOSTALIASES** is set, the alias file pointed to by **HOSTALIASES** will first be searched for *name*.

The **gethostbyaddr()** function returns a structure of type *hostent* for the given host address *addr* of length *len* and address type *type*. The only valid address type is currently AF_INET.

The **sethostent()** function specifies, if *stayopen* is true (1), that a connected TCP socket should be used for the name server queries and that the connection should remain open during successive queries. Otherwise, name server queries will use UDP datagrams.

The **endhostent()** function ends the use of a TCP connection for name server queries.

The **herror()** function prints the error message associated with the current value of *h_errno* on stderr.

The domain name queries carried out by **gethostbyname()** and **gethostbyaddr()** use a combination of any or all of the name server **named**(8), a broken out line from */etc/hosts*, and the Network Information Service (NIS or YP), depending upon the contents of the *order* line in */etc/host.conf*. (See **resolv+**(8)). The default action is to query **named**(8), followed by */etc/hosts*.

The *hostent* structure is defined in <*netdb.h*> as follows:

```
struct hostent {
char *h_name; /* official name of host */
char **h_aliases; /* alias list */
int h_addrtype; /* host address type */
int h_length; /* length of address */
char **h_addr_list; /* list of addresses */
}
#define h_addr h_addr_list[0] /* for backward compatibility */
```

The members of the *hostent* structure are:

h_name	The official name of the host.
h_aliases	A zero-terminated array of alternative names for the host.
h_addrtype	The type of address; always AF_INET at present.
h_length	The length of the address in bytes.
h_addr_list	A zero-terminated array of network addresses for the host in network byte order.
h_addr	The first address in *h_addr_list* for backward compatibility.

RETURN VALUE

The **gethostbyname()** and **gethostbyaddr()** functions return the *hostent* structure or a NULL pointer if an error occurs. On error, the *h_errno* variable holds an error number.

GETHOSTBYNAME(3) Linux Programmer's Manual GETHOSTBYNAME(3)

ERRORS

The variable *h_errno* can have the following values:

> **HOST_NOT_FOUND**   The specified host is unknown.
>
> **NO_ADDRESS**   The requested name is valid but does not have an IP address.
>
> **NO_RECOVERY**   A non-recoverable name server error occurred.
>
> **TRY_AGAIN**   A temporary error occurred on an authoritative name server. Try again later.

FILES

/etc/host.conf resolver configuration file
/etc/hosts host database file

CONFORMING TO

BSD 4.3

SEE ALSO

resolver(3), **hosts**(5), **hostname**(7), **resolv+** (8), **named**(8)

BSD   April 19, 1993   752

NAME

getmntent, setmntent, addmntent, endmntent, hasmntopt – get file system descriptor file entry

SYNOPSIS

#include <stdio.h>
#include <mntent.h>
FILE *setmntent(const char *****filep, **const char *****type**);
struct mntent *getmntent(FILE *****filep);
int addmntent(FILE *****filep, **const struct mntent *****mnt**);
int endmntent(FILE *****filep);
char *hasmntopt(const struct mntent *****mnt, **const char *****opt**);

DESCRIPTION

These routines are used to access the file system description file */etc/fstab* and the mounted file system description file */etc/mstab*.

The **setmntent()** function opens the file system description file *filep* and returns a file pointer which can be used by **getmntent()**. The argument *type* is the type of access required and can take the same values as the *mode* argument of fopen(3).

The **getmntent()** function reads the next line from the file system description file *filep* and returns a pointer to a structure containing the broken out fields from a line in the file. The pointer points to a static area of memory which is overwritten by subsequent calls to **getmntent()**.

The **addmntent()** function adds the mntent structure *mnt* to the end of the open file *filep*.

The **endmntent()** function closes the file system description file *filep*.

The **hasmntopt()** function scans the *mnt_opts* field (see below) of the mntent structure *mnt* for a substring that matches *opt*. See <*mntent.h*> for valid mount options.

The *mntent* structure is defined in <*mntent.h*> as follows:

```
struct mntent {
char *mnt_fsname; /* name of mounted file system */
char *mnt_dir; /* file system path prefix */
char *mnt_type; /* mount type (see mntent.h) */
char *mnt_opts; /* mount options (see mntent.h) */
int mnt_freq; /* dump frequency in days */
int mnt_passno; /* pass number on parallel fsck */
};
```

RETURN VALUE

The **getmntent()** function returns a pointer to the mntent structure or NULL on failure.

The **addmntent()** function returns 0 on success and 1 on failure.

The **endmntent()** functions always returns 1.

The **hasmntopt()** function returns the address of the substring if a match is found and NULL otherwise.

FILES

/etc/fstab file system description file
/etc/mtab mounted file system description file

CONFORMING TO

BSD 4.3

SEE ALSO

fopen(3), **fstab**(5)

GETNETENT(3)

NAME

getnetent, getnetbyname, getnetbyaddr, setnetent, endnetent – get network entry

SYNOPSIS

#include <netdb.h>
struct netent *getnetent(void);
struct netent *getnetbyname(const char *name);
struct netent *getnetbyaddr(long net, int type);
void setnetent(int stayopen);
void endnetent(void);

DESCRIPTION

The **getnetent()** function reads the next line from the file /etc/networks and returns a structure netent containing the broken out fields from the line. The /etc/networks file is opened if necessary.

The **getnetbyname()** function returns a netent structure for the line from /etc/networks that matches the network name.

The **getnetbyaddr()** function returns a netent structure for the line that matches the network number net of type type.

The **setnetent()** function opens and rewinds the /etc/networks file. If stayopen is true (1), then the file will not be closed between calls to **getnetbyname()** and **getnetbyaddr()**.

The **endservent()** function closes /etc/networks.

The netent structure is defined in <netdb.h> as follows:

```
struct netent {
char *n_name; /* official network name */
char **n_aliases; /* alias list */
int n_addrtype; /* net address type */
unsigned long int n_net; /* network number */
}
```

The members of the netent structure are:

n_name	The official name of the network.
n_aliases	A zero terminated list of alternative names for the network.
n_addrtype	The type of the network number; always AF_INET.
n_net	The network number in host byte order.

RETURN VALUE

The **getnetent()**, **getnetbyname()** and **getnetbyaddr()** functions return the netent structure, or a NULL pointer if an error occurs or the end of the file is reached.

FILES

/etc/networks networks database file

CONFORMING TO

BSD 4.3

SEE ALSO

getprotoent(3), **getservent**(3), **networks**(5)

GETOPT(3)

NAME

getopt – Read command line options

SYNOPSIS

#include <unistd.h>
int getopt(int *argc***, char * const** *argv[ ]***, const char *** *optstring***);**
extern char * *optarg***;**
extern int *optind***,** *opterr***,** *optopt***;**
#include <getopt.h>
int getopt_long(int *argc***, char * const** *argv[ ]***, const char *** *shortopts***, const struct option**
longopts, int** *longind***);**

DESCRIPTION

The **getopt()** function parses the command line arguments. Its arguments *argc* and *argv* are the argument count and array as passed to the **main()** function on program invocation. *optstring* is a list of available option characters. If such a character is followed by a colon, the option takes an argument, which is placed in *optarg*.

The external variable *optind* is the index of the next array element of *argv[ ]* to be processed; it communicates from one call of **getopt()** to the next which element to process.

The **getopt_long()** function works like **getopt()** except that it also accepts long options, started out by two dashes. If these take values, it is either in the form **–arg=value** or **–arg value**. It takes the additional arguments *longopts* which is a pointer to the first element of an array of
struct option declared in <**getopt.h**> as

struct option {
const char *name;
int has_arg;
int *flag;
int val;
};

The meaning of the different fields are:

- *name*   is the name of the long option.
- *has_arg*   is a boolean value which should be set to nonzero if the long option takes a value.
- *flag*   determines the return value if **getopt_long()** returns a value for a long option; if it is non-zero, zero is returned as a function value, otherwise *val*.
- *val*   determines the value to return if *flag* is zero.

The last element of the array has to be filled with zeroes.

The *option_index* points to the index of the long option relative to *longopts*.

RETURN VALUE

The **getopt()** function returns the option character if the option was found successfully, ':' if there was a missing parameter for one of the options, '?' for an unknown option character and −1 for the end of the option list.

EXAMPLE

The following example program, from the source code, illustrates the use of **getopt_long()** with most of its features.

```
#include <stdio.h>

int
```

```
main (argc, argv)
    int argc;
    char **argv;
{
  int c;
  int digit_optind = 0;
  while (1)
  {
   int this_option_optind = optind ? optind : 1;
   int option_index = 0;
   static struct option long_options[] =
   {
    {"add", 1, 0, 0},
    {"append", 0, 0, 0},
    {"delete", 1, 0, 0},
    {"verbose", 0, 0, 0},
    {"create", 1, 0, 'c'},
    {"file", 1, 0, 0},
    {0, 0, 0, 0}
   };
   c = getopt_long (argc, argv, "abc:d:012",
                    long_options, &option_index);
   if (c == -1)
     break;
   switch (c)
     {
     case 0:
       printf ("option %s", long_options[option_index].name);
       if (optarg)
         printf (" with arg %s", optarg);
       printf ("");
       break;
     case '0':
     case '1':
     case '2':
       if (digit_optind != 0 && digit_optind != this_option_optind)
         printf ("digits occur in two different argv-elements.");
       digit_optind = this_option_optind;
       printf ("option %c", c);
       break;
     case 'a':
       printf ("option a");
       break;
     case 'b':
       printf ("option b");
       break;
     case 'c':
       printf ("option c with value '%s'", optarg);
       break;
     case 'd':
       printf ("option d with value '%s'", optarg);
       break;
     case '?':
       break;
     default:
       printf ("?? getopt returned character code 0%o ??", c);
     }
  }
  if (optind $<$ argc)
  {
   printf ("non-option ARGV-elements: ");
```

```
        while (optind $<$ argc)
            printf ("%s ", argv[optind++]);
        printf ("");
    }
    exit (0);
}
```

BUGS

This manpage is confusing.

CONFORMS TO

    getopt() :   POSIX.1

NAME

getpass – get a password

SYNOPSIS

#include <pwd.h>
#include <unistd.h>

char *getpass(const char * prompt **);**

DESCRIPTION

The **getpass** function displays a prompt to, and reads in a password from, */dev/tty*. If this file is not accessible, **getpass** displays the prompt on the standard error output and reads from the standard input.

The password may be up to _PASSWORD_LEN (currently 128) characters in length. Any additional characters and the terminating newline character are discarded. (This may be different in Linux.)

Getpass turns off character echoing while reading the password.

RETURN VALUES

Getpass returns a pointer to the null terminated password.

FILES

/dev/tty

SEE ALSO

crypt(3)

HISTORY

A **getpass** function appeared in Version 7 AT&T UNIX.

BUGS

The **getpass** function leaves its result in an internal static object and returns a pointer to that object. Subsequent calls to **getpass** will modify the same object.

The calling process should zero the password as soon as possible to avoid leaving the cleartext password visible in the process's address space.

GETPROTOENT(3)

NAME

getprotoent, getprotobyname, getprotobynumber, setprotoent, endprotoent – get protocol entry

SYNOPSIS

#include <netdb.h>
struct protoent *getprotoent(void);
struct protoent *getprotobyname(const char *name***);**
struct protoent *getprotobynumber(int *proto***);**
void setprotoent(int *stayopen***);**
void endprotoent(void);

DESCRIPTION

The **getprotoent()** function reads the next line from the file */etc/protocols* and returns a structure *protoent* containing the broken out fields from the line. The */etc/protocols* file is opened if necessary.

The **getprotobyname()** function returns a *protoent* structure for the line from */etc/protocols* that matches the protocol name *name*.

The **getprotobynumber()** function returns a *protoent* structure for the line that matches the protocol number *number*.

The **setprotoent()** function opens and rewinds the */etc/protocols* file. If *stayopen* is true (1), then the file will not be closed between calls to **getprotobyname()** or **getprotobynumber()**.

The **endprotoent()** function closes */etc/protocols*.

The *protoent* structure is defined in *<netdb.h>* as follows:

```
struct protoent {
char *p_name; /* official protocol name */
char **p_aliases; /* alias list */
int p_proto; /* protocol number */
}
```

The members of the *protoent* structure are:

    p_name   The official name of the protocol.

    p_aliases   A zero terminated list of alternative names for the protocol.

    p_proto   The protocol number.

RETURN VALUE

The **getprotoent()**, **getprotobyname()** and **getprotobynumber()** functions return the *protoent* structure, or a NULL pointer if an error occurs or the end of the file is reached.

FILES

/etc/protocols protocol database file

CONFORMING TO

BSD 4.3

SEE ALSO

getservent(3), **getnetent**(3), **protocols**(5)

GETPW(3)

Linux Programmer's Manual

GETPW(3)

NAME

getpw – Re-construct password line entry

SYNOPSIS

#include <pwd.h>
#include <sys/types.h>
int getpw(uid_t *uid*, **char** **buf*);

DESCRIPTION

The **getpw()** function re-constructs the password line entry for the given user uid *uid* in the buffer *buf*. The returned buffer contains a line of format

name:passwd:uid:gid:gecos:dir:shell

The *passwd* structure is defined in <*pwd.h*> as follows:

```
struct passwd {
char *pw_name; /* user name */
char *pw_passwd; /* user password */
uid_t pw_uid; /* user id */
gid_t pw_gid; /* group id */
char *pw_gecos; /* real name */
char *pw_dir; /* home directory */
char *pw_shell; /* shell program */
};
```

RETURN VALUE

The **getpw()** function returns 0 on success, or −1 if an error occurs.

ERRORS

ENOMEM   Insufficient memory to allocate passwd structure.

FILES

/etc/passwd password database file

SEE ALSO

fgetpwent(3), **getpwent**(3), **setpwent**(3), **endpwent**(3), **getpwnam**(3), **getpwuid**(3), **putpwent**(3)

GNU   April 9, 1993   760

NAME

getpwent, setpwent, endpwent – get password file entry

SYNOPSIS

#include <pwd.h>
#include <sys/types.h>
struct passwd *getpwent(void);
void setpwent(void);
void endpwent(void);

DESCRIPTION

The **getpwent()** function returns a pointer to a structure containing the broken out fields of a line from */etc/passwd*. The first time it is called it returns the first entry; thereafter, it returns successive entries.

The **setpwent()** function rewinds the file pointer to the beginning of the */etc/passwd* file.

The **endpwent()** function closes the */etc/passwd* file.

The *passwd* structure is defined in *<pwd.h>* as follows:

struct passwd {
char *pw_name; /* user name */
char *pw_passwd; /* user password */
uid_t pw_uid; /* user id */
gid_t pw_gid; /* group id */
char *pw_gecos; /* real name */
char *pw_dir; /* home directory */
char *pw_shell; /* shell program */
};

RETURN VALUE

The **getpwent()** function returns the passwd structure, or NULL if there are no more entries or an error occurs.

ERRORS

ENOMEM   Insufficient memory to allocate passwd structure.

FILES

/etc/passwd password database file

CONFORMING TO

SVID 3, BSD 4.3

SEE ALSO

fgetpwent(3), **getpwnam**(3), **getpwuid**(3), **getpw**(3), **putpwent**(3)

GETPWNAM(3)

NAME

getpwnam, getpwuid – get password file entry

SYNOPSIS

#include <pwd.h>
#include <sys/types.h>
struct passwd *getpwnam(const char * *name***);**
struct passwd *getpwuid(uid_t *uid***);**

DESCRIPTION

The **getpwnam()** function returns a pointer to a structure containing the broken out fields of a line from */etc/passwd* for the entry that matches the user name *name*.

The **getpwuid()** function returns a pointer to a structure containing the broken out fields of a line from */etc/passwd* for the entry that matches the user uid *uid*.

The *passwd* structure is defined in *<pwd.h>* as follows:

```
struct passwd {
char *pw_name; /* user name */
char *pw_passwd; /* user password */
uid_t pw_uid; /* user id */
gid_t pw_gid; /* group id */
char *pw_gecos; /* real name */
char *pw_dir; /* home directory */
char *pw_shell; /* shell program */
};
```

RETURN VALUE

The **getpwnam()** and **getpwuid()** functions return the passwd structure, or NULL if the matching entry is not found or an error occurs.

ERRORS

    ENOMEM   Insufficient memory to allocate passwd structure.

FILES

/etc/passwd password database file

CONFORMING TO

SVID 3, POSIX, BSD 4.3

SEE ALSO

fgetpwent(3), **getpwent**(3), **setpwent**(3), **endpwent**(3), **getpw**(3), **putpwent**(3)

NAME

fgetc, fgets, getc, getchar, gets, ungetc – input of characters and strings

SYNOPSIS

#include <stdio.h>
int fgetc(FILE *stream);
char *fgets(char *s, int size, FILE *stream);
int getc(FILE *stream);
int getchar(void);
char *gets(char *s);
int ungetc(int c, FILE *stream);

DESCRIPTION

fgetc() reads the next character from *stream* and returns it as an **unsigned** char cast to an **int**, or **EOF** on end of file or error.

getc() is equivalent to **fgetc()** except that it may be implemented as a macro which evaluates *stream* more than once.

getchar() is equivalent to **getc(***stdin***)**.

gets() reads a line from *stdin* into the buffer pointed to by *s* until either a terminating newline or **EOF**, which it replaces with '\0'. No check for buffer overrun is performed (see **BUGS** below).

fgets() reads in at most one less than *n* characters from *stream* and stores them into the buffer pointed to by *s*. Reading stops after an **EOF** or a newline. If a newline is read, it is stored into the buffer. A '\0' is stored after the last character in the buffer.

ungetc() pushes *c* back to *stream*, cast to **unsigned char**, where it is available for subsequent read operations. Pushed - back characters will be returned in reverse order; only one push-back is guaranteed.

Calls to the functions described here can be mixed with each other and with calls to other input functions from the **stdio** library for the same input stream.

RETURN VALUES

fgetc(), **getc()** and **getchar()** return the character read as an **unsigned** char cast to an **int** or **EOF** on end of file or error.

gets() and **fgets()** return *s* on success, and **NULL** on end of file or error.

ungetc() returns *c* on success, or **EOF** on error.

CONFORMS TO

ANSI - C, POSIX.1

BUGS

Because it is impossible to tell without knowing the data in advance how many characters **gets()** will read, and because **gets()** will continue to store characters past the end of the buffer, it is extremely dangerous to use. It has been used to break computer security. Use **fgets()** instead.

It is not advisable to mix calls to input functions from the **stdio** library with low - level calls to **read()** for the file descriptor associated with the input stream; the results will be undefined and very probably not what you want.

SEE ALSO

read(2), **write**(2), **fopen**(3), **fread**(3), **scanf**(3), **puts**(3), **fseek**(3), **ferror**(3)

GETSERVENT(3)

NAME

getservent, getservbyname, getservbyport, setservent, endservent – get service entry

SYNOPSIS

#include <netdb.h>
struct servent *getservent(void);
struct servent *getservbyname(const char * name **, const char *** proto **);**
struct servent *getservbyport(int port **, const char *** proto **);**
void setservent(int stayopen **);**
void endservent(void);

DESCRIPTION

The **getservent()** function reads the next line from the file /etc/services and returns a structure servent containing the broken out fields from the line. The /etc/services file is opened if necessary.

The **getservbyname()** function returns a servent structure for the line from /etc/services that matches the service name using protocol proto.

The **getservbyport()** function returns a servent structure for the line that matches the port port using protocol proto.

The **setservent()** function opens and rewinds the /etc/services file. If stayopen is true (1), then the file will not be closed between calls to **getservbyname()** and **getservbyport()**.

The **endservent()** function closes /etc/services.

The servent structure is defined in <netdb.h> as follows:

struct servent {
char *s_name; /* official service name */
char **s_aliases; /* alias list */
int s_port; /* port number */
char *s_proto; /* protocol to use */
}

The members of the servent structure are:

> s_name   The official name of the service.
>
> s_aliases   A zero terminated list of alternative names for the service.
>
> s_port   The port number for the service given in network byte order.
>
> s_proto   The name of the protocol to use with this service.

RETURN VALUE

The **getservent()**, **getservbyname()** and **getservbyport()** functions return the servent structure, or a NULL pointer if an error occurs or the end of the file is reached.

FILES

/etc/services services database file

CONFORMING TO

BSD 4.3

SEE ALSO

getprotoent(3), **getnetent**(3), **services**(5)

GETUSERSHELL(3)

NAME

getusershell, setusershell, endusershell – get legal user shells

SYNOPSIS

#include <unistd.h>
char *getusershell(void);
void setusershell(void);
void endusershell(void);

DESCRIPTION

The **getusershell()** function returns the next line from the file */etc/shells*, opening the file if necessary. The line should contain the pathname of a valid user shell. If */etc/shells* does not exist or is unreadable, **getusershell()** behaves as if */bin/sh* and */bin/csh* were listed in the file.

The **setusershell()** function rewinds */etc/shells*.

The **endusershell()** function closes */etc/shells*.

RETURN VALUE

The **getusershell()** function returns a NULL pointer on end-of-file.

FILES

/etc/shells

CONFORMING TO

BSD 4.3

SEE ALSO

shells(5)

NAME

getutent, getutid, getutline, pututline, setutent, endutent, utmpname – access utmp file entries

SYNOPSIS

#include <utmp.h>

struct utmp *getutent(void);
struct utmp *getutid(struct utmp **ut***);**
struct utmp *getutline(struct utmp **ut***);**

void pututline(struct utmp **ut***);**

void setutent(void);
void endutent(void);

void utmpname(const char **file***);**

DESCRIPTION

utmpname() sets the name of the utmp-format file for the other utmp functions to access. If utmpname() is not used to set the filename before the other functions are used, they assume **_PATH_UTMP**, as defined in <*paths.h*>.

setutent() rewinds the file pointer to the beginning of the utmp file. It is generally a Good Idea to call it before any of the other functions.

endutent() closes the utmp file. It should be called when the user code is done accessing the file with the other functions.

getutent() reads a line from the current file position in the utmp file. It returns a pointer to a structure containing the fields of the line.

getutid() searches forward from the current file position in the utmp file based upon *ut*. If *ut*->ut_type is **RUN_LVL, BOOT_TIME, NEW_TIME,** or **OLD_TIME**, getutid() will find the first entry whose ut_type field matches *ut*->ut_type. If *ut*->ut_type is **INIT_PROCESS, LOGIN_PROCESS, USER_PROCESS,** or **DEAD_PROCESS**, getutid() will find the first entry whose ut_id field matches *ut*->ut_id.

getutline() searches forward from the current file position in the utmp file. It scans entries whose ut_type is **USER_PROCESS** or **LOGIN_PROCESS** and returns the first one whose ut_line field matches *ut*->ut_line.

pututline() writes the utmp structure *ut* into the utmp file. It uses getutid() to search for the proper place in the file to insert the new entry. If it cannot find an appropriate slot for *ut*, pututline() will append the new entry to the end of the file.

RETURN VALUE

getutent(), getutid(), and getutline() return a pointer to a **struct utmp**, which is defined in <*utmp.h*>.

FILES

/var/run/utmp – database of currently logged-in users
/var/log/wtmp – database of past user logins

CONFORMING TO

XPG 2, SVID 2, Linux FSSTND 1.2

SEE ALSO

utmp(5)

GLOB(3)

Linux Programmer's Manual

GLOB(3)

NAME

glob, globfree – find pathnames matching a pattern, free memory from glob()

SYNOPSIS

#include <**glob.h**>

int glob(const char **pattern*, **int** *flags*, **int** *errfunc*(**const char** * *epath*, **int** *eerrno*),"*glob_t *pglob*");

void globfree(glob_t **pglob*);

DESCRIPTION

The **glob()** function searches for all the pathnames matching *pattern* according to the rules used by the shell (see **glob**(7)). No tilde expansion or parameter substitution is done.

The **globfree()** function frees the dynamically allocated storage from an earlier call to **glob()**.

The results of a **glob()** call are stored in the structure pointed to by *pglob*, which is a **glob_t** which is declared in <**glob.h**> as

typedef struct {
int gl_pathc; /* Count of paths matched so far */
char **gl_pathv; /* List of matched pathnames. */
int gl_offs; /* Slots to be reserved in 'gl_pathv'. */
int gl_flags; /* Flags for globbing */
} glob_t;

Results are stored in dynamically allocated storage.

The parameter *flags* is made up of bitwise OR of zero or more the following symbolic constants, which modify the of behaviour of **glob()**:

> **GLOB_ERR** which means to return upon read error (because a directory does not have read permission, for example).
>
> **GLOB_MARK** which means to append a slash to each path which corresponds to a directory,
>
> **GLOB_NOSORT** which means don't sort the returned pathnames (they are by default),
>
> **GLOB_DOOFS** which means that **pglob->gl_offs** slots will be reserved at the beginning of the list of strings in **pglob->pathv**,
>
> **GLOB_NOCHECK** which means that, if no pattern matches, to return the original pattern,
>
> **GLOB_APPEND** which means to append to the results of a previous call. Do not set this flag on the first invocation of **glob()**.
>
> **GLOB_NOESCAPE** which means that meta characters cannot be quoted by backspaces, and
>
> **GLOB_PERIOD** which means that a leading period can be matched by meta characters.

If *errfunc* is not **NULL**, it will be called in case of an error with the arguments *epath* a pointer to the path which failed and *eerrno* the value of *errno* as returned from one of the calls to **opendir()**, **readdir()**, or **stat()**. If *errfunc* returns non – zero, or if **GLOB_ERR** is set, **glob()** will terminate after the call to *errfunc*.

Upon successful return, *pglob->gl_pathc* contains the number of matched pathnames and *pglob->gl_pathv* a pointer to the list of matched pathnames. The first pointer after the last pathname is **NULL**.

It is possible to call **glob()** several times. In that case, the **GLOB_APPEND** flag has to be set in *flags* on the second and later invocations.

RETURN VALUES

On successful completion, **glob()** returns zero. Other possible returns are:

GLOB_NOSPACE	for running out of memory,
GLOB_ABEND	for a read error, and
GLOB_NOMATCH	for no found matches.

EXAMPLES

One example of use is the following code, which simulates typing
ls -l *.c ../*.c
in the shell. glob_t globbuf;
globbuf.gl_offs = 2;
glob("*.c", GLOB_DOOFS, NULL, &globbuf);
glob("../*.c", GLOB_DOOFS | GLOB_APPEND, NULL, &globbuf);
globbuf.gl_pathv[0] = "ls";
globbuf.gl_pathv[1] = "-l";
execvp("ls", &globbuf.gl_pathv[0]);

CONFORMS TO

proposed POSIX.2

BUGS

The **glob()** function may fail due to failure of underlying function calls, such as **malloc()** or **opendir()**. These will store their error code in *errno*.

POSIX.2 is not yet an approved standard; the information in this manpage is subject to change.

SEE ALSO

ls(1), **sh**(1), **exec**(2), **stat**(2), **malloc**(3), **opendir**(3), **readdir**(3), **wordexp**(3), **glob**(7)

HOSTS_ACCESS(3)

NAME

hosts_access, hosts_ctl – access control library

SYNOPSIS

#include "log_tcp.h"
extern int allow_severity;
extern int deny_severity;
int hosts_access(daemon, client)
char *daemon;
struct client_info *client;
int hosts_ctl(daemon, client_name, client_addr, client_user)
char *daemon;
char *client_name;
char *client_addr;
char *client_user;

DESCRIPTION

The routines described in this document are part of the *libwrap.a* library. They implement a pattern-based access control language with optional shell commands that are executed when a pattern fires.

In all cases, the daemon argument should specify a daemon process name (argv[0] value). The client host address should be a valid address, or FROM_UNKNOWN if address lookup failed. The client host name and user name should be empty strings if no information is available, FROM_UNKNOWN if lookup failed, or an actual host or user name.

hosts_access() consults the access control tables described in the *hosts_access(5)* manual page. hosts_access() returns zero if access should be denied.

hosts_ctl() is a wrapper around the hosts_access() routine with a perhaps more convenient interface (though it does not pass on enough information to support automated remote user-name lookups). hosts_ctl() returns zero if access should be denied.

The *allow_severity* and *deny_severity* variables determine how accepted and rejected requests may be logged. They must be provided by the caller and may be modified by rules in the access control tables.

DIAGNOSTICS

Problems are reported via the syslog daemon.

SEE ALSO

hosts_access(5), format of the access control tables. hosts_options(5), optional extensions to the base language.

FILES

/etc/hosts.access, /etc/hosts.deny, access control tables.

BUGS

The functions described here do not make copies of their string-valued arguments. Beware of data from functions that overwrite their results upon each call.

hosts_access() uses the strtok() library function. This may interfere with other code that relies on strtok().

AUTHOR

Wietse Venema (wietse@wzv.win.tue.nl)
Department of Mathematics and Computing Science
Eindhoven University of Technology
Den Dolech 2, P.O. Box 513, 5600 MB Eindhoven, The Netherlands

NAME

hcreate, hdestroy, hsearch – hash table management

SYNOPSIS

#include <search.h>
ENTRY *hsearch(ENTRY *item*, **ACTION** *action*);

DESCRIPTION

This three functions allow the user to create a hash table of type *ENTRY* (defined in <**search.h**>) which associates a key with any data. The implementation uses **malloc(3)**.

First the table must be created with the function **hcreate()**. *nel* is an estimation of the table size which will suffice the needs. For better algorithms this value can be corrected upwards.

The corresponding function *hdestroy()* frees the memory occupied by the hash table for that a new table can be constructed.

hsearch() is the function for searching and inserting. Which action is done is controlled by the parameter *action*. It is of the type *ACTION* (also defined in <search.h>) and can have the values *ENTER* or *FIND*. *ENTER* means to insert the given *item* and *FIND* means to only search. Unsuccesful actions result in a return value *NULL*.

RETURN VALUE

hcreate() return zero if the hash table cannot be succesfully installed.

hsearch() return *NULL* if either action is *ENTER* and the hash table is full or action is *FIND* and the *item* cannot be find in the hash table.

BUGS

The implementation can manage only one hash table at a time.

SEE ALSO

bsearch(3),**lsearch**(3),**malloc**(3)

NAME

hypot – Euclidean distance function

SYNOPSIS

#include <math.h>
double hypot(double *x*, **double** *y*);

DESCRIPTION

The **hypot()** function returns the sqrt(x*x + y*y). This is the length of the hypotenuse of a right-angle triangle with sides of length *x* and *y*, or the distance of the point (x, y) from the origin.

CONFORMING TO

SVID 3, BSD 4.3

SEE ALSO

sqrt(3)

NAME

index, rindex – locate character in string

SYNOPSIS

#include <string.h>
char *index(const char *s, int c);
char *rindex(const char *s, int c);

DESCRIPTION

The **index()** function returns a pointer to the first occurrence of the character c in the string s.

The **rindex()** function returns a pointer to the last occurrence of the character c in the string s.

The terminating NULL character is considered to be a part of the strings.

RETURN VALUE

The **index()** and **rindex()** functions return a pointer to the matched character or NULL if the character is not found.

CONFORMING TO

BSD 4.3

SEE ALSO

memchr(3), **strchr**(3), **strpbrk**(3), **strrchr**(3), **strsep**(3), **strspn**(3), **strstr**(3), **strtok**(3)

INET(3)

NAME

inet_addr, inet_network, inet_ntoa, inet_makeaddr, inet_lnaof, inet_netof – Internet address manipulation routines

SYNOPSIS

#include <sys/socket.h>
#include <netinet/in.h>
#include <arpa/inet.h>
unsigned long int inet_addr(const char *`cp`);
unsigned long int inet_network(const char *`cp`);
char *inet_ntoa(struct in_addr `in`**);**
struct in_addr inet_makeaddr(int `net`**, int** `host`**);**
unsigned long int inet_lnaof(struct in_addr `in`**);**
unsigned long int inet_netof(struct in_addr `in`**);**

DESCRIPTION

The **inet_addr()** function converts the Internet host address `cp` from numbers-and-dots notation into binary data in network byte order. If the input is invalid, −1 is returned.

The **inet_network()** function extracts the network number in network byte order from the address `cp` in numbers-and-dots notation. If the input is invalid, −1 is returned.

The **inet_ntoa()** function converts the Internet host address `in` given in network byte order to a string in standard numbers-and-dots notation. The string is returned in a statically allocated buffer, which subsequent calls will overwrite.

The **inet_makeaddr()** function makes an Internet host address in network byte order by combining the network number `net` with the local address `host` in network `net`, both in local host byte order.

The **inet_lnaof()** function returns the local host address part of the Internet address `in`. The local host address is returned in local host byte order.

The **inet_netof()** function returns the network number part of the Internet Address `in`. The network number is returned in local host byte order.

The structure `in_addr` as used in **inet_ntoa()**, **inet_makeaddr()**, **inet_lnaof()** and **inet_netof()** is defined in `netinet/in.h` as:

```
struct in_addr {
unsigned long int s_addr;
}
```

Note that on the i80x86 the host byte order is Least Significant Byte first, whereas the network byte order, as used on the Internet, is Most Significant Byte first.

CONFORMING TO

BSD 4.3

SEE ALSO

gethostbyname(3), **getnetent**(3), **hosts**(5), **networks**(5)

INFNAN(3)

NAME

infnan – deal with infinite or not-a-number (NaN) result

SYNOPSIS

#include <math.h>
double infnan(int *error***);**

DESCRIPTION

The **infnan()** function returns a suitable value for infinity and "not-a-number" (NaN) results. The value of *error* can be ERANGE to represent infinity or anything else to represent NaN. *errno* is also set.

RETURN VALUE

If *error* is ERANGE (Infinity), HUGE_VAL is returned.

If *error* is -ERANGE (-Infinity), -HUGE_VAL is returned.

If *error* is anything else, NAN is returned.

ERRORS

    ERANGE   The value of *error* is positive or negative infinity.

    EDOM   The value of *error* is "not-a-number" (NaN).

CONFORMING TO

BSD 4.3

NAME

initgroups – initialize the supplementary group access list

SYNOPSIS

#include <grp.h>
#include <sys/types.h>
int initgroups(const char **user***, gid_t** *group***);**

DESCRIPTION

The **initgroups()** function initializes the group access list by reading the group database */etc/group* and using all groups of which *user* is a member. The additional group *group* is also added to the list.

RETURN VALUE

The **initgroups()** function returns 0 on success, or −1 if an error occurs.

ERRORS

EPERM   The calling process does not have sufficient privileges.

ENOMEM   Insufficient memory to allocate group information structure.

FILES

/etc/group   group database file

CONFORMING TO

SVID 3, BSD 4.3

SEE ALSO

getgroups(2), **setgroups**(2)

NAME

isalnum, isalpha, iscntrl, isdigit, isgraph, islower, isprint, ispunct, isspace, isupper, isxdigit – character classification routines

SYNOPSIS

#include <ctype.h>
int isalnum (int c);
int isalpha (int c);
int iscntrl (int c);
int isdigit (int c);
int isgraph (int c);
int islower (int c);
int isprint (int c);
int ispunct (int c);
int isspace (int c);
int isupper (int c);
int isxdigit (int c);

DESCRIPTION

These functions check whether c, which must have the value of an **unsigned** char or **EOF**, falls into a certain character class according to the current locale.

isalnum()	checks for an alphanumeric character; it is equivalent to (isalpha(c) || isdigit(c)).
isalpha()	checks for an alphabetic character; it is equivalent to (isupper(c) || islower(c)).
iscntrl()	checks for a control character.
isdigit()	checks for a digit.
isgraph()	checks for any printable character except space.
islower()	checks for a lower - case character.
isprint()	checks for any printable character including space.
ispunct()	checks for any printable character which is not a space or an alphanumeric character.
isspace()	checks for white - space characters. In the and locales, these are: space, form-feed ('\f'), newline ('\n'), carriage return ('\r'), horizontal tab ('\t'), and vertical tab ('\v').
isupper()	checks for an uppercase letter.
isxdigit()	checks for a hexadecimal digits, i.e. one of 0 1 2 3 4 5 6 7 8 9 0 a b c d e f A B C D E F

RETURN VALUE

The values returned are nonzero if the character c falls into the tested class, and a zero value if not.

CONFORMS TO

ANSI - C, BSD 4.3

BUGS

The details of what characters belong into which class depend on the current locale. For example, **isupper()** will not recognize an A - umlaut as an uppercase letter in the default **C** locale.

SEE ALSO

toupper(3), **setlocale**(3), **ascii**(7), **locale**(7)

ISATTY(3)

NAME

isatty – does this descriptor refer to a terminal

SYNOPSIS

#include <unistd.h>
int isatty (int *desc* **);**

DESCRIPTION

returns 1 if *desc* is an open descriptor connected to a terminal and 0 else.

CONFORMING TO

SVID, AT&T, X/OPEN, BSD 4.3

SEE ALSO

fstat(2), **ttyname**(3)

NAME

isinf, isnan, finite – test for infinity or not-a-number (NaN)

SYNOPSIS

#include <math.h>
int isinf(double *value***);**
int isnan(double *value***);**
int finite(double *value***);**

DESCRIPTION

The **isinf()** function returns −1 if *value* represents negative infinity, 1 if *value* represents positive infinity, and 0 otherwise.

The **isnan()** function returns a non-zero value if *value* is "not-a-number" (NaN), and 0 otherwise.

The **finite()** function returns a non-zero value if *value* is finite or is not a "not-a-number" (NaN) value, and 0 otherwise.

CONFORMING TO

BSD 4.3

NAME

killpg – send signal to all members of a process group.

SYNOPSIS

#include <signal.h>
int killpg(pid_t *pidgrp*, **int** *signal*);

DESCRIPTION

The **killpg()** function causes signal *signal* to be sent to all the processes in the process group *pidgrp* or to the processes' own process group if *pidgrp* is equal to zero.

It is equivalent to **kill(-***pidgrp***,***signal***);**

RETURN VALUE

The value returned is −1 on error, or 0 for success.

ERRORS

Errors are returned in *errno* and can be one of the following:

EINVAL	for an invalid signal,
ESRCH	for a process group which does not exist, and
EPERM	if the userid of the calling process is not equal to that of the process the signal is sent to, and the userid is not that of the superuser.

CONFORMS TO

???

SEE ALSO

kill(2), **signal**(2), **signal**(7)

NAME

labs – computes the absolute value of a long integer.

SYNOPSIS

#include <stdlib.h>
long int labs(long int *j***);**

DESCRIPTION

The **labs()** function computes the absolute value of the long integer argument *j*.

RETURN VALUE

Returns the absolute value of the long integer argument.

CONFORMING TO

SVID 3, BSD 4.3, ISO 9899

NOTES

Trying to take the absolute value of the most negative integer is not defined.

SEE ALSO

abs(3), **ceil**(3), **floor**(3), **fabs**(3), **rint**(3)

NAME

ldexp – multiply floating-point number by integral power of 2

SYNOPSIS

#include <math.h>
double ldexp(double *x*, **int** *exp***);**

DESCRIPTION

The **ldexp()** function returns the result of multiplying the floating-point number *x* by 2 raised to the power *exp*.

CONFORMING TO

SVID 3, POSIX, BSD 4.3, ISO 9899

SEE ALSO

frexp(3), **modf**(3)

NAME

ldiv – computes the quotient and remainder of long integer division.

SYNOPSIS

#include <stdlib.h>
ldiv_t ldiv(long int *numer*, **long int** *denom*);

DESCRIPTION

The **ldiv()** function computes the value *numer/denom* and returns the quotient and remainder in a structure named *ldiv_t* that contains two long integer members named *quot* and *rem*.

RETURN VALUE

The *ldiv_t* structure.

CONFORMING TO

SVID 3, BSD 4.3, ISO 9899

SEE ALSO

div(3)

LGAMMA(3)

NAME

lgamma – log gamma function

SYNOPSIS

#include <math.h>
double lgamma(double *x***);**

DESCRIPTION

The **lgamma()** function returns the log of the absolute value of the Gamma function. The sign of the Gamma function is returned in the external integer *signgam*.

For negative integer values of *x*, **lgamma()** returns HUGE_VAL and *errno* is set to ERANGE.

ERRORS

      ERANGE   Invalid argument - negative integer value of *x*.

CONFORMING TO

SVID 3, BSD 4.3

SEE ALSO

infnan(3)

LOCALECONV(3) Linux Programmer's Manual LOCALECONV(3)

NAME

localeconv – get numeric formatting information

SYNOPSIS

#include <locale.h>
struct lconv *localeconf(void);

DESCRIPTION

The **localeconf()** function returns a string to a **struct** lconv for the current locale.

CONFORMS TO

ANSI C, POSIX.1

Linux supports the portable locales **C** and **POSIX** and also the European Latin-1 **ISO-8859-1**, and Russian **KOI-8** locales.

The **printf()** family of functions may or may not honor the current locale.

SEE ALSO

locale(1), **localedef**(1), **strcoll**(3), **isalpha**(3), **setlocale**(3), **strftime**(3), **locale**(7)

LONGJMP(3)

NAME
longjmp – non-local jump to a saved stack context

SYNOPSIS
#include <setjmp.h>

void longjmp(jmp_buf *env,* **int** *val);*

DESCRIPTION
longjmp() and **setjmp**(3) are useful for dealing with errors and interrupts encountered in a low-level subroutine of a program. **longjmp()** restores the environment saved by the last call of **setjmp()** with the corresponding *env* argument. After **longjmp()** is completed, program execution continues as if the corresponding call of **setjmp()** had just returned the value *val.* **longjmp()** cannot cause 0 to be returned. If longjmp is invoked with a second argument of 0, 1 will be returned instead.

RETURN VALUE
This function never returns.

CONFORMING TO
POSIX

NOTES
POSIX does not specify if the signal context will be restored or not. If you want to save restore signal masks, use *siglongjmp*(3) **longjmp()** makes programs hard to understand and maintain. If possible an alternative should be used.

SEE ALSO
setjmp(3), sigsetjmp(2), siglongjmp(2)

NAME

calloc, malloc, free, realloc – Allocate and free dynamic memory

SYNOPSIS

#include <stdlib.h>
void *calloc(size_t *nmemb*, **size_t** *size*);
void *malloc(size_t *size*);
void free(void *ptr);
void *realloc(void *ptr, **size_t** *size*);

DESCRIPTION

calloc() allocates memory for an array of *nmemb* elements of *size* bytes each and returns a pointer to the allocated memory. The memory is set to zero.

malloc() allocates *size* bytes and returns a pointer to the allocated memory. The memory is not cleared.

free() frees the memory space pointed to by *ptr*, which must have been returned by a previous call to **malloc()**, **calloc()** or **realloc()**. If *ptr* is **NULL**, no operation is performed.

realloc() changes the size of the memory block pointed to by *ptr* to *size* bytes. The contents will be unchanged to the minimum of the old an new sizes; newly allocated memory will be uninitialized. If *ptr* is **NULL**, the call is equivalent to **malloc(size)**; if size is equal to zero, the call is equivalent to **free**(*ptr*). Unless *ptr* is **NULL**, it must have been returned by an earlier call to **malloc()**, **calloc()** or **realloc()**.

RETURN VALUES

For **calloc()** and **malloc()**, the value returned is a pointer to the allocated memory, which is suitably aligned for any kind of variable, or **NULL** if the request fails.

free() returns no value.

realloc() returns a pointer to the newly allocated memory, which is suitably aligned for any kind of variable and may be different from *ptr*, or **NULL** if the request fails or if size was equal to 0. If **realloc()** fails the original block is left untouched - it is not freed or moved.

CONFORMS TO

ANSI - C

SEE ALSO

brk(2)

MBLEN(3)

NAME

mblen – determine the number of bytes in a character

SYNOPSIS

#include <stdlib.h>
int mblen(const char *s***, size_t** *n***);**

DESCRIPTION

The **mblen()** function scans the first *n* bytes of the string *s* and returns the number of bytes in a character. The **mblen()**

function is equivalent to

mbtowc((wchat_t *)0, s, n);

except that the shift state of the **mbtowc()** function is not affected.

RETURN VALUE

The **mblen()** returns the number of bytes in a character or −1 if the character is invalid or 0 if *s* is a NULL string.

CONFORMING TO

SVID 3, ISO 9899

SEE ALSO

mbstowcs(3), **mbtowc**(3), **wcstombs**(3), **wctomb**(3)

NAME

mbstowcs – convert a multibyte string to a wide character string.

SYNOPSIS

#include <stdlib.h>
size_t mbstowcs(wchar_t *pwcs*, **const char** *s*, **size_t** *n***);**

DESCRIPTION

The **mbstowcs()** function converts a sequence of multibyte characters from the array *s* into a sequence of wide characters and stores up to *n* wide characters in the array *pwcs*.

RETURN VALUE

mbstowcs() returns the number of wide characters stored or −1 if *s* contains an invalid multibyte character.

CONFORMING TO

SVID 3, ISO 9899

SEE ALSO

mblen(3), **mbtowc**(3), **wcstombs**(3), **wctomb**(3)

NAME

mbtowc – convert a multibyte character to a wide character.

SYNOPSIS

#include <stdlib.h>
int mbtowc(wchar_t *pwc*, **const char** *s*, **size_t** *n*);

DESCRIPTION

The **mbtowc**() function converts a multibyte character *s*, which is no longer than *n* bytes, into a wide character and, if *pwc* is not NULL, stores the wide character in *pwc*.

RETURN VALUE

mbtowc() returns the number of bytes in the multibyte character or −1 if the multibyte character is not valid.

CONFORMING TO

SVID 3, ISO 9899

SEE ALSO

mblen(3), **mbstowcs**(3), **wcstombs**(3), **wctomb**(3)

NAME

memccpy – copy memory area

SYNOPSIS

#include <string.h>
void *memccpy(void **dest***, const void ****src***, int** *c***, size_t** *n***);**

DESCRIPTION

The **memccpy()** function copies no more than *n* bytes from memory area *src* to memory area *dest*, stopping when the character *c* is found.

RETURN VALUE

The **memccpy()** function returns a pointer to the next character in *dest* after *c*, or NULL if *c* was not found in the first *n* characters of *src*.

CONFORMING TO

SVID 3, BSD 4.3

SEE ALSO

bcopy(3), **memcpy**(3), **memmove**(3), **strcpy**(3), **strncpy**(3)

NAME

memchr – scan memory for a character

SYNOPSIS

#include <string.h>
void *memchr(const void *s, int c, size_t n);

DESCRIPTION

The **memchr()** function scans the first *n* bytes of the memory area pointed to by *s* for the character *c*. The first byte to match *c* (interpreted as an unsigned character) stops the operation.

RETURN VALUE

The **memchr()** function returns a pointer to the matching byte or NULL if the character does not occur in the given memory area.

CONFORMING TO

SVID 3, BSD 4.3, ISO 9899

SEE ALSO

index(3), **rindex**(3), **strchr**(3), **strpbrk**(3), **strrchr**(3), **strsep**(3), **strspn**(3), **strstr**(3)

NAME

memcmp – compare memory areas

SYNOPSIS

#include <string.h>
int memcmp(const void *s1*, **const void** *s2*, **size_t** *n*);

DESCRIPTION

The **memcmp()** function compares the first *n* bytes of the memory areas *s1* and *s2*. It returns an integer less than, equal to, or greater than zero if *s1* is found, respectively, to be less than, to match, or be greater than *s2*.

RETURN VALUE

The **memcmp()** function returns an integer less than, equal to, or greater than zero if the first *n* bytes of *s1* is found, respectively, to be less than, to match, or be greater than the first *n* bytes of *s2*.

CONFORMING TO

SVID 3, BSD 4.3, ISO 9899

SEE ALSO

bcmp(3), **strcasecmp**(3), **strcmp**(3), **strcoll**(3), **strncmp**(3), **strncasecmp**(3)

NAME

memcpy – copy memory area

SYNOPSIS

#include <string.h>
void *memcpy(void **dest***, const void ****src***, size_t** *n***);**

DESCRIPTION

The **memcpy()** function copies *n* bytes from memory area *src* to memory area *dest*. The memory areas may not overlap. Use **memmove**(3) if the memory areas do overlap.

RETURN VALUE

The **memcpy()** function returns a pointer to *dest*.

CONFORMING TO

SVID 3, BSD 4.3, ISO 9899

SEE ALSO

bcopy(3), **memccpy**(3), **memmove**(3), **strcpy**(3), **strncpy**(3)

NAME

memfrob – frobnicate (encrypt) a memory area

SYNOPSIS

#include <string.h>
void *memfrob(void *s, size_t n);

DESCRIPTION

The **memfrob()** function encrypts the first n bytes of the memory area s by exclusive-ORing each character with the number 42. The effect can be reversed by using **memfrob()** on the encrypted memory area.

Note that this function is not a proper encryption routine as the XOR constant is fixed, and is only suitable for hiding strings.

RETURN VALUE

The **memfrob()** function returns a pointer to the encrypted memory area.

CONFORMING TO

The **memfrob()** function is unique to the Linux C Library and GNU C Library.

SEE ALSO

strfry(3)

NAME

memmem – locate a substring

SYNOPSIS

#include <string.h>
void *memmem(const void *needle***, size_t** *needlelen***,
const void** *haystack***, size_t** *haystacklen"***);"**

DESCRIPTION

The **memmem()** function finds the first occurrence of the substring *needle* of length *needlelen* in the memory area *haystack* of length *haystacklen*.

RETURN VALUE

The **memmem()** function returns a pointer to the beginning of the substring, or NULL if the substring is not found.

SEE ALSO

strstr(3)

NAME

memmove – copy memory area

SYNOPSIS

#include <string.h>
void *memmove(void **dest***, const void ****src***, size_t** *n***);**

DESCRIPTION

The **memmove()** function copies *n* bytes from memory area *src* to memory area *dest*. The memory areas may overlap.

RETURN VALUE

The **memmove()** function returns a pointer to *dest*.

CONFORMING TO

SVID 3, BSD 4.3, ISO 9899

SEE ALSO

bcopy(3), **memccpy**(3), **memcpy**(3), **strcpy**(3), **strncpy**(3)

MEMSET(3)

NAME

memset – fill memory with a constant byte

SYNOPSIS

#include <string.h>
void *memset(void *s,* **int** *c,* **size_t** *n***);**

DESCRIPTION

The **memset()** function fills the first *n* bytes of the memory area pointed to be *s* with the constant byte *c*.

RETURN VALUE

The **memset()** function returns a pointer to the memory area *s*.

CONFORMING TO

SVID 3, BSD 4.3, ISO 9899

SEE ALSO

bzero(3), **swab**(3)

NAME

mkstemp – create a unique temporary file

SYNOPSIS

#include <unistd.h>
int *mkstemp(char **template***);**

DESCRIPTION

The **mkstemp()** function generates a unique temporary file name from *template*. The last six characters of *template* must be XXXXXX and these are replaced with a string that makes the filename unique. The file is then created with mode read/write and permissions 0666.

RETURN VALUE

The **mkstemp()** function returns the file descriptor fd of the temporary file.

ERRORS

  EINVAL The last six characters of *template* were not XXXXXX.
  EEXIST The temporary file is not unique.

CONFORMING TO

BSD 4.3

SEE ALSO

mktemp(3), **tmpnam**(3), **tempnam**(3), **tmpfile**(3)

NAME

mktemp – make a unique temporary file name

SYNOPSIS

#include <unistd.h>
char *mktemp(char **template***);**

DESCRIPTION

The **mktemp()** function generates a unique temporary file name from *template*. The last six characters of *template* must be XXXXXX and these are replaced with a string that makes the filename unique.

RETURN VALUE

The **mktemp()** function returns a pointer to *template* on success, and NULL on failure.

ERRORS

EINVAL The last six characters of *template* were not XXXXXX.

CONFORMING TO

BSD 4.3. POSIX dictates tmpnam().

SEE ALSO

mkstemp(3), **tmpnam**(3), **tempnam**(3), **tmpfile**(3)

MODF(3)

NAME

modf – extract signed integral and fractional values from floating-point number

SYNOPSIS

#include <math.h>
double modf(double *x*, **double** **iptr*);

DESCRIPTION

The **modf()** function breaks the argument *x* into an integral part and a fractional part, each of which has the same sign as *x*. The integral part is stored in *iptr*.

RETURN VALUE

The **modf()** function returns the fractional part of *x*.

CONFORMING TO

SVID 3, POSIX, BSD 4.3, ISO 9899

SEE ALSO

frexp(3), **ldexp**(3)

NEWCTIME(3)

NAME
asctime, ctime, difftime, gmtime, localtime, mktime – convert date and time to ASCII

SYNOPSIS
extern char *tzname[2];

void tzset()

#include <sys/types.h>

char *ctime(clock)
const time_t *clock;

double difftime(time1, time0)
time_t time1;
time_t time0;

#include <time.h>

char *asctime(tm)
const struct tm *tm;

struct tm *localtime(clock)
const time_t *clock;

struct tm *gmtime(clock)
const time_t *clock;

time_t mktime(tm)
struct tm *tm;

cc ... -lz

DESCRIPTION

Ctime converts a long integer, pointed to by *clock*, representing the time in seconds since 00:00:00 UTC, January 1, 1970, and returns a pointer to a 26-character string of the form
Thu Nov 24 18:22:48 1986
All the fields have constant width.

Localtime and *gmtime* return pointers to "tm" structures, described below. *Localtime* corrects for the time zone and any time zone adjustments (such as Daylight Saving Time in the U.S.A.). Before doing so, *localtime* calls *tzset* (if *tzset* has not been called in the current process). After filling in the "tm" structure, *localtime* sets the **tm_isdst**'th element of **tzname** to a pointer to an ASCII string that's the time zone abbreviation to be used with *localtime*'s return value.

Gmtime converts to Coordinated Universal Time.

Asctime converts a time value contained in a "tm" structure to a 26-character string, as shown in the above example, and returns a pointer to the string.

Mktime converts the broken-down time, expressed as local time, in the structure pointed to by *tm* into a calendar time value with the same encoding as that of the values returned by the *time* function. The original values of the **tm_wday** and **tm_yday** components of the structure are ignored, and the original values of the other components are not restricted to their normal ranges. (A positive or zero value for **tm_isdst** causes *mktime* to presume initially

801

that summer time (for example, Daylight Saving Time in the U.S.A.) respectively, is or is not in effect for the specified time. A negative value for **tm_isdst** causes the *mktime* function to attempt to divine whether summer time is in effect for the specified time.) On successful completion, the values of the **tm_wday** and **tm_yday** components of the structure are set appropriately, and the other components are set to represent the specified calendar time, but with their values forced to their normal ranges; the final value of **tm_mday** is not set until **tm_mon** and **tm_year** are determined. *Mktime* returns the specified calendar time; If the calendar time cannot be represented, it returns **-1**.

Difftime returns the difference between two calendar times, (*time1* - *time0*), expressed in seconds.

Declarations of all the functions and externals, and the "tm" structure, are in the <**time.h**> header file. The structure (of type) **struct** tm includes the following fields:

int tm_sec; / seconds (0 - 60) /
int tm_min; / minutes (0 - 59) /
int tm_hour; / hours (0 - 23) /
int tm_mday; / day of month (1 - 31) /
int tm_mon; / month of year (0 - 11) /
int tm_year; / year − 1900 /
int tm_wday; / day of week (Sunday = 0) /
int tm_yday; / day of year (0 - 365) /
int tm_isdst; / is summer time in effect? /
char tm_zone; / abbreviation of timezone name /
long tm_gmtoff; / offset from UTC in seconds /

The *tm_zone* and *tm_gmtoff* fields exist, and are filled in, only if arrangements to do so were made when the library containing these functions was created. There is no guarantee that these fields will continue to exist in this form in future releases of this code.

Tm_isdst is non-zero if summer time is in effect.

Tm_gmtoff is the offset (in seconds) of the time represented from UTC, with positive values indicating east of the Prime Meridian.

FILES

/usr/local/etc/zoneinfo time zone information directory
/usr/local/etc/zoneinfo/localtime local time zone file
/usr/local/etc/zoneinfo/posixrules used with POSIX-style TZ's
/usr/local/etc/zoneinfo/GMT for UTC leap seconds

If **/usr/local/etc/zoneinfo/GMT** is absent, UTC leap seconds are loaded from **/usr/local/etc/zoneinfo/posixrules**.

SEE ALSO

getenv(3), newtzset(3), time(2), tzfile(5)

NOTES

The return values point to static data; the data is overwritten by each call. The **tm_zone** field of a returned **struct tm** points to a static array of characters, which will also be overwritten at the next call (and by calls to *tzset*).

Avoid using out-of-range values with *mktime* when setting up lunch with promptness sticklers in Riyadh.

NEWTZSET(3)

NAME
tzset – initialize time conversion information

SYNOPSIS
void tzset()

cc ... -lz

DESCRIPTION
Tzset uses the value of the environment variable **TZ** to set time conversion information used by *localtime*. If **TZ** does not appear in the environment, the best available approximation to local wall clock time, as specified by the *tzfile*(5)-format file **localtime** in the system time conversion information directory, is used by *localtime*. If **TZ** appears in the environment but its value is a null string, Coordinated Universal Time (UTC) is used (without leap second correction). If **TZ** appears in the environment and its value is not a null string:

> if the value begins with a colon, it is used as a pathname of a file from which to read the time conversion information;
>
> if the value does not begin with a colon, it is first used as the pathname of a file from which to read the time conversion information, and, if that file cannot be read, is used directly as a specification of the time conversion information.

When **TZ** is used as a pathname, if it begins with a slash, it is used as an absolute pathname; otherwise, it is used as a pathname relative to a system time conversion information directory. The file must be in the format specified in *tzfile*(5).

When **TZ** is used directly as a specification of the time conversion information, it must have the following syntax (spaces inserted for clarity):

> *std offset*[*dst*[*offset*][,*rule*]]

Where:

> *std* and *dst*   Three or more bytes that are the designation for the standard (*std*) or summer (*dst*) time zone. Only *std* is required; if *dst* is missing, then summer time does not apply in this locale. Upper- and lowercase letters are explicitly allowed. Any characters except a leading colon (:), digits, comma (,), minus (), plus (), and ASCII NUL are allowed.
>
> *offset*   Indicates the value one must add to the local time to arrive at Coordinated Universal Time. The *offset* has the form:
>
>> *hh*[:*mm*[:*ss*]]
>>
>> The minutes (*mm*) and seconds (*ss*) are optional. The hour (*hh*) is required and may be a single digit. The *offset* following *std* is required. If no *offset* follows *dst*, summer time is assumed to be one hour ahead of standard time. One or more digits may be used; the value is always interpreted as a decimal number. The hour must be between zero and 24, and the minutes (and seconds) — if present — between zero and 59. If preceded by a "", the time zone shall be east of the Prime Meridian; otherwise it shall be west (which may be indicated by an optional preceding "").
>
> *rule*   Indicates when to change to and back from summer time. The *rule* has the form:
>
>> *date*/*time*,*date*/*time*

where the first *date* describes when the change from standard to summer time occurs and the second *date* describes when the change back happens. Each *time* field describes when, in current local time, the change to the other time is made.

The format of *date* is one of the following:

J*n* The Julian day *n* (1*n*\\365). Leap days are not counted; that is, in all years — including leap years — February 28 is day 59 and March 1 is day 60. It is impossible to explicitly refer to the occasional February 29. .TP .I Leap days are not counted; that is, in all years — including leap years — February 28 is day 59 and March 1 is day 60. It is impossible to explicitly refer to the occasional February 29.

n The zero-based Julian day (0*n*\\365). Leap days are counted, and it is possible to refer to February 29. .TP .BI M m . n . d The .IR d' th day .RI *(0"**d*\\6) of week .I n of month .I m of the year .RI *(1"**n*\\5, .RI *1"**m*\\12, where week 5 means "the last .I d day in month .IR m " which may occur in either the fourth or the fifth week). Week 1 is the first week in which the .IR d' th day occurs. Day zero is Sunday. .RE .I15 Leap days are counted, and it is possible to refer to February 29.

M*m***.***n***.***d* The *d*'th day (0*d*\\6) of week .I n of month .I m of the year .RI *(1"**n*\\5, .RI *1"**m*\\12, where week 5 means "the last .I d day in month .IR m " which may occur in either the fourth or the fifth week). Week 1 is the first week in which the .IR d' th day occurs. Day zero is Sunday. .RE .I15 of week *n* of month *m* of the year (1*n*\\5, .RI *1"**m*\\12, where week 5 means "the last .I d day in month .IR m " which may occur in either the fourth or the fifth week). Week 1 is the first week in which the .IR d' th day occurs. Day zero is Sunday. .RE .I15 1*m*\\12, where week 5 means "the last .I d day in month .IR m " which may occur in either the fourth or the fifth week). Week 1 is the first week in which the .IR d' th day occurs. Day zero is Sunday. .RE .I15 where week 5 means "the last *d* day in month *m*" which may occur in either the fourth or the fifth week). Week 1 is the first week in which the *d*'th day occurs. Day zero is Sunday.

The *time* has the same format as *offset* except that no leading sign ("" or "") is allowed. The default, if *time* is not given, is **02:00:00**.

If no *rule* is present in **TZ**, the rules specified by the *tzfile*(5)-format file **posixrules** in the system time conversion information directory are used, with the standard and summer time offsets from UTC replaced by those specified by the *offset* values in **TZ**.

For compatibility with System V Release 3.1, a semicolon (;) may be used to separate the *rule* from the rest of the specification.

If the **TZ** environment variable does not specify a *tzfile*(5)-format and cannot be interpreted as a direct specification, UTC is used.

FILES

/usr/local/etc/zoneinfo time zone information directory
/usr/local/etc/zoneinfo/localtime local time zone file
/usr/local/etc/zoneinfo/posixrules used with POSIX-style TZ's
/usr/local/etc/zoneinfo/GMT for UTC leap seconds

If **/usr/local/etc/zoneinfo/GMT** is absent, UTC leap seconds are loaded from **/usr/local/etc/zoneinfo/posixrules**.

SEE ALSO
getenv(3), newctime(3), time(2), tzfile(5)

NAME

on_exit – register a function to be called at normal program termination.

SYNOPSIS

#include <stdlib.h>
int on_exit(void (**function***)(int , void *), void ****arg***);**

DESCRIPTION

The **on_exit()** function registers the given *function* to be called at normal program termination, whether via **exit**(2) or via return from the program's **main**. The *function* is passed the argument to **exit**(3) and the *arg* argument from **on_exit()**.

RETURN VALUE

The **on_exit()** function returns the value 0 if successful; otherwise the value −1 is returned.

SEE ALSO

exit(3), **atexit**(3)

NAME

opendir – open a directory

SYNOPSIS

#include <sys/types.h>
#include <dirent.h>
DIR *opendir(const char **name***);**

DESCRIPTION

The **opendir()** function opens a directory stream corresponding to the directory *name*, and returns a pointer to the directory stream. The stream is positioned at the first entry in the directory.

RETURN VALUE

The **opendir()** function returns a pointer to the directory stream or NULL if an error occurred.

ERRORS

EACESS	Permission denied.
EMFILE	Too many file descriptors in use by process.
ENFILE	Too many files are currently open in the system.
ENOENT	Directory does not exist, or *name* is an empty string.
ENOMEM	Insufficient memory to complete the operation.
ENOTDIR	*name* is not a directory.

CONFORMING TO

SVID 3, POSIX, BSD 4.3

SEE ALSO

open(2), **readdir**(3), **closedir**(3), **rewinddir**(3), **seekdir**(3), **telldir**(3), **scandir**(3)

NAME

perror – print a system error message

SYNOPSIS

#include <stdio.h>

void perror(const char *s);

DESCRIPTION

perror produces a message on the standard error output, describing the last error encountered during a call to a system or library function. The argument string s is printed first, then a colon and a blank, then the message and a new-line. To be of most use, the argument string should include the name of the program that incurred the error. The error number is taken from the external variable errno, which is set when errors occur but not cleared when non-erroneous calls are made.

CONFORMING TO

ANSI C, POSIX

SEE ALSO

errno(2), **strerror**(3)

NAME

popen, pclose – process I/O

SYNOPSIS

#include <stdio.h>
FILE *popen(const char *command, const char *type);
int pclose(FILE *stream);

DESCRIPTION

The **popen** function opens a process by creating a pipe, forking, and invoking the shell. Since a pipe is by definition unidirectional, the *type* argument may specify only reading or writing, not both; the resulting stream is correspondingly read-only or write-only.

The *command* argument is a pointer to a null-terminated string containing a shell command line. This command is passed to */bin/sh* using the **–c** flag; interpretation, if any, is performed by the shell. The *mode* argument is a pointer to a null-terminated string which must be either 'r' for reading or 'w' for writing.

The return value from **popen** is a normal standard I/O stream in all respects save that it must be closed with **pclose** rather than **fclose**. Writing to such a stream writes to the standard input of the command; the command's standard output is the same as that of the process that called **popen**, unless this is altered by the command itself. Conversely, reading from a "popened" stream reads the command's standard output, and the command's standard input is the same as that of the process that called **popen**.

Note that output **popen** streams are fully buffered by default.

The **pclose** function waits for the associated process to terminate and returns the exit status of the command as returned by **wait4**.

RETURN VALUE

The **popen** function returns **NULL** if the **fork**(2) or **pipe**(2) calls fail, or if it cannot allocate memory.

The **pclose** function returns –1 if *stream* is not associated with a "popened" command, if *stream* already "pclosed", or if **wait4** returns an error.

ERRORS

The **popen** function does not reliably set *errno*. (Is this true for Linux?)

SEE ALSO

fork(2), **sh**(1), **pipe**(2), **wait4**(2), **fflush**(3), **fclose**(3), **fopen**(3), **stdio**(3), **system**(3)

BUGS

Since the standard input of a command opened for reading shares its seek offset with the process that called **popen**, if the original process has done a buffered read, the command's input position may not be as expected. Similarly, the output from a command opened for writing may become intermingled with that of the original process. The latter can be avoided by calling **fflush**(3) before **popen**.

Failure to execute the shell is indistinguishable from the shell's failure to execute command, or an immediate exit of the command. The only hint is an exit status of 127. (Is this true under Linux?)

The **popen** argument always calls **sh**, never calls **csh**.

HISTORY

A **popen** and a **pclose** function appeared in Version 7 AT&T UNIX.

PRINTF(3)

NAME

printf, fprintf, sprintf, vprintf, vfprintf, vsprintf – formatted output conversion

SYNOPSIS

#include <stdio.h>

int printf(const char **format*, **...);**
int fprintf(FILE **stream*, **const char** **format*, **...);**
int sprintf(char **str*, **const char** **format*, **...);**

#include <stdarg.h>

int vprintf(const char **format*, **va_list** *ap*);
int vfprintf(FILE **stream*, **const char** **format*, **va_list** *ap*);
int vsprintf(char **str*, **char** **format*, **va_list** *ap*);

DESCRIPTION

The **printf** family of functions produces output according to a *format* as described below. **Printf** and **vprintf** write output to *stdout*, the standard output stream; **fprintf** and **vfprintf** write output to the given output *stream*; **sprintf**, and **vsprintf** write to the character string *str*. These functions write the output under the control of a *format* string that specifies how subsequent arguments (or arguments accessed via the variable-length argument facilities of **stdarg**(3) are converted for output. These functions return the number of characters printed (not including the trailing '\0' used to end output to strings).

The format string is composed of zero or more directives: ordinary characters (not %), which are copied unchanged to the output stream; and conversion specifications, each of which results in fetching zero or more subsequent arguments. Each conversion specification is introduced by the character %. The arguments must correspond properly (after type promotion) with the conversion specifier. After the %, the following appear in sequence:

% Zero or more of the following flags:

\# specifying that the value should be converted to an "alternate form". For **c**, **d**, **i**, **n**, **p**, **s**, and **u** conversions, this option has no effect. For **o** conversions, the precision of the number is increased to force the first character of the output string to a zero (except if a zero value is printed with an explicit precision of zero). For **x** and **X** conversions, a non-zero result has the string '0x' (or '0X' for **X** conversions) prepended to it. For **e**, **E**, **f**, **g**, and **G** conversions, the result will always contain a decimal point, even if no digits follow it (normally, a decimal point appears in the results of those conversions only if a digit follows). For **g** and **G** conversions, trailing zeros are not removed from the result as they would otherwise be.

0 specifying zero padding. For all conversions except **n**, the converted value is padded on the left with zeros rather than blanks. If a precision is given with a numeric conversion (**d**, **i**, **o**, **u**, **i**, **x**, and **X**), the **0** flag is ignored.

– (a negative field width flag) indicates the converted value is to be left adjusted on the field boundary. Except for **n** conversions, the converted value is padded on the right with blanks, rather than on the left with blanks or zeros. A – overrides a **0** if both are given.

% (a space) specifying that a blank should be left before a positive number produced by a signed conversion (**d**, **e**, **E**, **f**, **g**, **G**, or **i**).

+ specifying that a sign always be placed before a number produced by a signed conversion. A + overrides a space if both are used.

% An optional decimal digit string specifying a minimum field width. If the converted value has fewer characters than the field width, it will be padded with spaces on the left (or right, if the left-adjustment flag has been given) to fill out the field width.

% An optional precision, in the form of a period ('.') followed by an optional digit string. If the digit string is omitted, the precision is taken as zero. This gives the minimum number of digits to appear for **d, i, o, u, x,** and **X** conversions, the number of digits to appear after the decimal-point for **e, E,** and **f** conversions, the maximum number of significant digits for **g** and **G** conversions, or the maximum number of characters to be printed from a string for **s** conversions.

% The optional character **h**, specifying that a following **d, i, o, u, x,** or **X** conversion corresponds to a *short* int or *unsigned* short int argument, or that a following **n** conversion corresponds to a pointer to a *short* int argument.

% The optional character **l** (ell) specifying that a following **d, i, o, u, x,** or **X** conversion applies to a pointer to a *long* int or *unsigned* long int argument, or that a following **n** conversion corresponds to a pointer to a *long* int argument.

% The character **L** specifying that a following **e, E, f, g,** or **G** conversion corresponds to a *long* double argument.

% A character that specifies the type of conversion to be applied.

A field width or precision, or both, may be indicated by an asterisk '*' instead of a digit string. In this case, an *int* argument supplies the field width or precision. A negative field width is treated as a left adjustment flag followed by a positive field width; a negative precision is treated as though it were missing.

The conversion specifiers and their meanings are:

diouxX The *int* (or appropriate variant) argument is converted to signed decimal (**d** and **i**), unsigned octal (**o**, unsigned decimal (**u**, or unsigned hexadecimal (**x** and **X**) notation. The letters **abcdef** are used for **x** conversions; the letters **ABCDEF** are used for **X** conversions. The precision, if any, gives the minimum number of digits that must appear; if the converted value requires fewer digits, it is padded on the left with zeros.

DOU The *long* int argument is converted to signed decimal, unsigned octal, or unsigned decimal, as if the format had been **ld, lo,** or **lu** respectively. These conversion characters are deprecated, and will eventually disappear.

eE The *double* argument is rounded and converted in the style [−]d.ddde*(Pmdd where there is one digit before the decimal-point character and the number of digits after it is equal to the precision; if the precision is missing, it is taken as 6; if the precision is zero, no decimal-point character appears. An **E** conversion uses the letter **E** (rather than **e**) to introduce the exponent. The exponent always contains at least two digits; if the value is zero, the exponent is 00.

f The *double* argument is rounded and converted to decimal notation in the style [-]ddd.ddd, where the number of digits after the decimal-point character is equal to the precision specification. If the precision is missing, it is taken as 6; if the precision is explicitly zero, no decimal-point character appears. If a decimal point appears, at least one digit appears before it.

g The *double* argument is converted in style **f** or **e** (or **E** for **G** conversions). The precision specifies the number of significant digits. If the precision is missing, 6 digits are given; if the precision is zero, it is treated as 1. Style **e** is used if the exponent from its conversion is less than −4 or greater than or equal to the precision. Trailing zeros are removed from the fractional part of the result; a decimal point appears only if it is followed by at least one digit.

c The *int* argument is converted to an *unsigned char*, and the resulting character is written.

s The *"char*"* argument is expected to be a pointer to an array of character type (pointer to a string). Characters from the array are written up to (but not including) a terminating **NUL** character; if a precision is specified, no more than the number specified are written. If a precision is given, no null character need be present; if the precision is not specified, or is greater than the size of the array, the array must contain a terminating **NUL** character.

p The "*void **" pointer argument is printed in hexadecimal (as if by **%#x** or **%#lx**).

n The number of characters written so far is stored into the integer indicated by the "*int **" (or variant) pointer argument. No argument is converted.

% A '%' is written. No argument is converted. The complete conversion specification is '%%'.

In no case does a non-existent or small field width cause truncation of a field; if the result of a conversion is wider than the field width, the field is expanded to contain the conversion result.

EXAMPLES

To print a date and time in the form 'Sunday, July 3, 10:02', where *weekday* and *month* are pointers to strings:

#include <stdio.h>
fprintf(stdout, "%s, %s %d, %.2d:%.2d\n",
weekday, month, day, hour, min);

To print to five decimal places:

#include <math.h>
#include <stdio.h>
fprintf(stdout, "pi = %.5f\n", 4 * atan(1.0));

To allocate a 128 byte string and print into it:

```
#include <stdio.h>
#include <stdlib.h>
#include <stdarg.h>
char *newfmt(const char *fmt, ...)
{
            char *p;
            va_list ap;
            if ((p = malloc(128)) == NULL)
                    return (NULL);
            va_start(ap, fmt);
            (void) vsnprintf(p, 128, fmt, ap);
            va_end(ap);
            return (p);
}
```

SEE ALSO

printf(1), **scanf**(3)

STANDARDS

The **fprintf, printf, sprintf, vprintf, vfprintf**, and **vsprintf** functions conform to ANSI C3.159-1989 ("ANSI C").

BUGS

Some floating point conversions under Linux cause memory leaks.

The conversion formats **%D**, **%O**, and **%U** are not standard and are provided only for backward compatibility. These may not be provided under Linux.

PRINTF(3)   Linux Programmer's Manual   PRINTF(3)

The effect of padding the **%p** format with zeros (either by the **0** flag or by specifying a precision), and the benign effect (i.e., none) of the **#** flag on **%n** and **%p** conversions, as well as other nonsensical combinations such as **%Ld**, are not standard; such combinations should be avoided.

Because **sprintf** and **vsprintf** assume an infinitely long string, callers must be careful not to overflow the actual space; this is often impossible to assure.

NAME

psignal – print signal message

SYNOPSIS

#include <signal.h>
void psignal(int *sig*, const char **s);
extern const char *const *sys_siglist*[]

DESCRIPTION

The **psignal()** function displays a message on *stderr* consisting of the string *s*, a colon, a space, and a string describing the signal number *sig*. If *sig* is invalid, the message displayed will indicate an unknown signal.

The array *sys_siglist* holds the signal description strings indexed by signal number.

RETURN VALUE

The **psignal()** function returns no value.

CONFORMING TO

BSD 4.3

SEE ALSO

perror(3), **strsignal**(3)

NAME

putenv – change or add an environment variable

SYNOPSIS

#include <stdlib.h>
int putenv(const char *string***);**

DESCRIPTION

The **putenv()** function adds or changes the value of environment variables. The argument *string* is of the form *name = value*. If *name* does not already exist in the environment, then *string* is added to the environment. If *name* does exist, then the value of *name* in the environment is changed to *value*.

RETURN VALUE

The **putenv()** function returns zero on success, or −1 if an error occurs.

ERRORS

ENOMEM   Insufficient space to allocate new environment.

CONFORMING TO

SVID 3, POSIX, BSD 4.3

SEE ALSO

getenv(3), **setenv**(3), **unsetenv**(3)

PUTPWENT(3)

NAME

putpwent – write a password file entry

SYNOPSIS

#include <pwd.h>
#include <stdio.h>
#include <sys/types.h>
int putpwent(const struct passwd *p*, **FILE** **stream*);

DESCRIPTION

The **putpwent()** function writes a password entry from the structure *p* in the file associated with *stream*.

The *passwd* structure is defined in *<pwd.h>* as follows:

```
struct passwd {
char *pw_name; /* user name */
char *pw_passwd; /* user password */
uid_t pw_uid; /* user id */
gid_t pw_gid; /* group id */
char *pw_gecos; /* real name */
char *pw_dir; /* home directory */
char *pw_shell; /* shell program */
};
```

RETURN VALUE

The **putpwent()** function returns 0 on success, or −1 if an error occurs.

ERRORS

    EINVAL   Invalid (NULL) argument given.

CONFORMING TO

SVID 3

SEE ALSO

fgetpwent(3), **getpwent**(3), **setpwent**(3), **endpwent**(3), **getpwnam**(3), **getpwuid**(3), **getpw**(3)

PUTS(3)

NAME

fputc, fputs, putc, putchar, puts – output of characters and strings

SYNOPSIS

#include <stdio.h>
int fputc(int *c*, **FILE ****stream***);**
int fputs(const char *s, **FILE ****stream***);**
int putc(int *c*, **FILE ****stream***);**
int putchar(int *c***);**
int puts(char **s***);**
int ungetc(int *c*, **FILE ****stream***);**

DESCRIPTION

fputc() writes the character *c*, cast to an **unsigned char**, to *stream*.

fputs() writes the string *s* to *stream*, without its trailing '**\0**'.

putc() is equivalent to **fputc()** except that it may be implemented as a macro which evaluates *stream* more than once.

putchar(*c***);** is equivalent to **putc(***c*,*stdout***)**.

puts() writes the string *s* and a trailing newline to *stdout*.

Calls to the functions described here can be mixed with each other and with calls to other output functions from the **stdio** library for the same output stream.

RETURN VALUES

fputc(), **putc()** and **putchar()** return the character written as an **unsigned** char cast to an **int** or **EOF** on error.

puts() and **fputs()** return a non - negative number on success, or **EOF** on error.

CONFORMS TO

ANSI - C, POSIX.1

BUGS

It is not advisable to mix calls to output functions from the **stdio** library with low - level calls to **write()** for the file descriptor associated with the same output stream; the results will be undefined and very probably not what you want.

SEE ALSO

write(2), **fopen**(3), **fwrite**(3), **scanf**(3), **gets**(3), **fseek**(3), **ferror**(3)

QSORT(3)

NAME

qsort − sorts an array

SYNOPSIS

#include <stdlib.h>

void qsort(void **base***, size_t** *nmemb***, size_t** *size***, int (****compar***)(const void *, const void *));**

DESCRIPTION

The **qsort()** function sorts an array with *nmemb* elements of size *size*. The *base* argument points to the start of the array.

The contents of the array are sorted in ascending order according to a comparison function pointed to by *compar*, which is called with two arguments that point to the objects being compared.

The comparison function must return an integer less than, equal to, or greater than zero if the first argument is considered to be respectively less than, equal to, or greater than the second. If two members compare as equal, their order in the sorted array is undefined.

RETURN VALUE

The **qsort()** function returns no value.

CONFORMING TO

SVID 3, POSIX, BSD 4.3, ISO 9899

SEE ALSO

sort(1)

RAISE(3)

NAME
raise – send a signal.

SYNOPSIS
#include <signal.h>
int raise (int *sig***);**

DESCRIPTION
raise() sends a signal to the current process. It is equivalent to **kill(getpid(),***sig***)**

RETURN VALUE
Zero for success, nonzero for failure.

CONFORMS TO
ANSI - C

SEE ALSO
kill(2), **signal**(2), **getpid**(2)

NAME

rand, srand – random number generator.

SYNOPSIS

#include <stdlib.h>
int rand(void);
void srand(unsigned int *seed*);

DESCRIPTION

The **rand()** function returns a pseudo-random integer between 0 and RAND_MAX.

The **srand()** function sets its argument as the seed for a new sequence of pseudo-random integers to be returned by **rand()**. These sequences are repeatable by calling **srand()** with the same seed value.

If no seed value is provided, the **rand()** function is automatically seeded with a value of 1.

RETURN VALUE

The **rand()** function returns a value between 0 and RAND_MAX. The **srand()** returns no value.

NOTES

The versions of **rand()** and **srand()** in the Linux C Library use the same random number generator as **random()** and **srandom()**, so the lower-order bits should be as random as the higher-order bits. However, on older **rand()** implementations, the lower-order bits are much less random than the higher-order bits.

In *Numerical* Recipes in C: The Art of Scientific Computing (William H. Press, Brian P. Flannery, Saul A. Teukolsky, William T. Vetterling; New York: Cambridge University Press, 1990 (1st ed, p. 207)), the following comments are made:

"If you want to generate a random integer between 1 and 10, you should always do it by

j=1+(int) (10.0*rand()/(RAND_MAX+1.0));

and never by anything resembling

j=1+((int) (1000000.0*rand()) % 10);

(which uses lower-order bits)."

Random-number generation is a complex topic. The *Numerical* Recipes in C book (see reference above) provides an excellent discussion of practical random-number generation issues in Chapter 7 (Random Numbers).

For a more theoretical discussion which also covers many practical issues in depth, please see Chapter 3 (Random Numbers) in Donald E. Knuth's *The Art of Computer Programming*, volume 2 (Seminumerical Algorithms), 2nd ed.; Reading, Massachusetts: Addison-Wesley Publishing Company, 1981.

CONFORMING TO

SVID 3, BSD 4.3, ISO 9899

SEE ALSO

random(3), **srandom**(3), **initstate**(3), **setstate**(3)

NAME

random, srandom, initstate, setstate – random number generator.

SYNOPSIS

#include <stdlib.h>
long int random(void);
void srandom(unsigned int *seed***);**
char *initstate(unsigned int *seed***, char ****state***, int** *n***);**
char *setstate(char **state***);**

DESCRIPTION

The **random()** function uses a non-linear additive feedback random number generator employing a default table of size 31 long integers to return successive pseudo-random numbers in the range from 0 to RAND_MAX. The period of this random number generator is very large, approximately $16*((2**31)-1)$.

The **srandom()** function sets its argument as the seed for a new sequence of pseudo-random integers to be returned by **random()**. These sequences are repeatable by calling **srandom()** with the same seed value. If no seed value is provided, the **random()** function is automatically seeded with a value of 1.

The **initstate()** function allows a state array *state* to be initialized for use by **random()**. The size of the state array *n* is used by **initstate()** to decide how sophisticated a random number generator it should use — the larger the state array, the better the random numbers will be. *seed* is the seed for the initialization, which specifies a starting point for the random number sequence, and provides for restarting at the same point.

The **setstate()** function changes the state array used by the **random()** function. The state array *state* is used for random number generation until the next call to **initstate()** or **setstate()**. *state* must first have been initialized using **initstate()**.

RETURN VALUE

The **random()** function returns a value between 0 and RAND_MAX. The **srandom()** function returns no value. The **initstate()**

and **setstate()** functions return a pointer to the previous state array.

ERRORS

    EINVAL   A state array of less than 8 bytes was specified to **initstate()**.

NOTES

Current "optimal" values for the size of the state array *n* are 8, 32, 64, 128, and 256 bytes; other amounts will be rounded down to the nearest known amount. Using less than 8 bytes will cause an error.

CONFORMING TO

BSD 4.3

SEE ALSO

rand(3), **srand**(3)

READDIR(3)

NAME
readdir – read a directory

SYNOPSIS
#include <sys/types.h>
#include <dirent.h>
struct dirent *readdir(DIR **dir***);**

DESCRIPTION
The **readdir()** function returns a pointer to a dirent structure representing the next directory entry in the directory stream pointed to be *dir*. It returns NULL on reaching the end-of-file or if an error occurred.

The data returned by **readdir()** is overwritten by subsequent calls to **readdir()** for the same directory stream.

RETURN VALUE
The **readdir()** function returns a pointer to a dirent structure, or NULL if an error occurs or end-of-file is reached.

ERRORS
    EBADF   Invalid directory stream descriptor *dir*.

CONFORMING TO
SVID 3, POSIX, BSD 4.3

SEE ALSO
read(2), **opendir**(3), **closedir**(3), **rewinddir**(3), **seekdir**(3), **telldir**(3), **scandir**(3)

READV(3) Linux Programmer's Manual READV(3)

NAME

readv, writev – read or write data into multiple buffers

SYNOPSIS

#include <sys/uio.h>

int readv(int *filedes*, **const struct iovec** **vector*, **size_t** *count*);

int writev(int *filedes*, **const struct iovec** **vector*, **size_t** *count*);

DESCRIPTION

The **readv()** function reads *count* blocks from the file associated with the file descriptor *filedes* into the multiple buffers described by *vector*.

The **writev()** function writes at most *count* blocks described by

vector to the file associated with the file descriptor *vector*.

The pointer vector points to a **struct** iovec defined in <**sys/uio.h**> as

```
struct iovect
{
void *iovbase; /* Starting address */
size_t iov_len; /* Number of bytes */
};
```

Buffers are processed in the order *vector[0]*, *vector[1]*, ... *vector[count]*.

The **readv()** function works just like **read**(2) except that multiple buffers are filled.

The **writev()** function works just like **write**(2) except that multiple buffers are written out.

RETURN VALUES

The **readv()** function returns the number of bytes or –1 on error; the **writev()** function returns the number of bytes written.

ERRORS

The **readv()** and **writev()** functions can fail and set *errno* to the following values:

EBADF	*fd* is not a valid file descriptor.
EINVAL	*fd* is unsuitable for reading (for **readv()** or writing **writev()**.
EFAULT	*buf* is outside the processes' address space.
EAGAIN	Non-blocking I/O had been selected in the **open()** call, and reading or writing could not be done immediately.
EINTR	Reading or writing was interrupted before any data was transferred.

CONFORMS TO

unknown

BUGS

It is not advisable to mix calls to functions like **readv()** or **writev()**, which operate on file descriptors, with the functions from the stdio library; the results will be undefined and probably not what you want.

SEE ALSO

read(2), **write**(2)

REALPATH(3)

NAME

realpath – returns the canonicalized absolute pathname.

SYNOPSIS

#include <sys/param.h>
#include <unistd.h>
char *realpath(char *path***, char** *resolved_path[ ]***);**

DESCRIPTION

realpath expands all symbolic links and resolves references to '/./', '/../' and extra '/' characters in the null terminated string named by *path* and stores the canonicalized absolute pathname in the buffer of size **MAXPATHLEN** named by *resolved_path*. The resulting path will have no symbolic link, '/./' or '/../' components.

RETURN VALUE

If there is no error, it returns a pointer to the *resolved_path*.

Otherwise it returns a NULL pointer and places in *resolved_path* the absolute pathname of the *path* component which could not be resolved. The global variable *errno* is set to indicate the error.

ERRORS

  ENOTDIR A component of the path prefix is not a directory.

  EINVAL The pathname contains a character with the high-order bit set.

  ENAMETOOLONG A component of a pathname exceeded **MAXNAMLEN** characters, or an entire path name exceeded **MAXPATHLEN** characters.

  ENOENT The named file does not exist. **EACCES** Search permission is denied for a component of the path prefix.

  ELOOP Too many symbolic links were encountered in translating the pathname.

  EIO An I/O error occurred while reading from the file system.

SEE ALSO

readlink(2), getcwd(3)

REMOVE(3)

NAME

remove – delete a name and possibly the file it refers to

SYNOPSIS

#include <stdio.h>

int remove(const char **pathname***);**

DESCRIPTION

remove deletes a name from the filesystem. If that name was the last link to a file and no processes have the file open the file is deleted and the space it was using is made available for reuse.

If the name was the last link to a file but any processes still have the file open the file will remain in existence until the last file descriptor referring to it is closed.

If the name referred to a symbolic link the link is removed.

If the name referred to a socket, fifo or device the name for it is removed but processes which have the object open may continue to use it.

RETURN VALUE

On success, zero is returned. On error, –1 is returned, and *errno* is set appropriately.

ERRORS

EFAULT   *pathname* points outside your accessible address space.

EACCES   Write access to the directory containing *pathname* is not allowed for the process's effective uid, or one of the directories in *pathname* did not allow search (execute) permission.

EPERM   The directory containing *pathname* has the sticky-bit (S_ISVTX) set and the process's effective uid is neither the uid of the file to be deleted nor that of the directory containing it.

ENAMETOOLONG   *pathname* was too long.

ENOENT   A directory component in *pathname* does not exist or is a dangling symbolic link.

ENOTDIR   A component used as a directory in *pathname* is not, in fact, a directory.

EISDIR   *pathname* refers to a directory.

ENOMEM   Insufficient kernel memory was available.

EROFS   *pathname* refers to a file on a read-only filesystem.

CONFORMING TO

SVID, AT&T, POSIX, X/OPEN, BSD 4.3

BUGS

In-felicities in the protocol underlying NFS can cause the unexpected disappearance of files which are still being used.

SEE ALSO

unlink(2), **rename**(2), **open**(2), **rmdir**(2), **mknod**(2), **mkfifo**(3), **link**(2), **rm**(1), **unlink**(8).

RESOLVER(3)

NAME

res_init, res_query, res_search, res_querydomain, res_mkquery, res_send, dn_comp, dn_expand – resolver routines

SYNOPSIS

#include <netinet/in.h>

#include <arpa/nameser.h>

#include <resolv.h>

extern struct state _res;

int res_init(void);

int res_query(const char *dname*, **int** *class*, **int** *type*, **unsigned** char *answer*, **int** *anslen*);

int res_search(const char *dname*, **int** *class*, **int** *type*, **unsigned**char *answer*, **int** *anslen*);

int res_querydomain(const char *name*, **const char** *domain*, **int** *class*, **int** *type*, **unsigned char** *answer*, **int** *anslen*);

int res_mkquery(int *op*, **const char** *dname*, **int** *class*, **int** *type*, char *data*, *int* **datalen**, **struct rrec** *newrr*, **char** *buf*, **int** *buflen*);

int res_send(const char *msg*, **int** *msglen*, **char** *answer*, **int** *anslen*);

int dn_comp(unsigned char *exp_dn*, **unsigned char** *comp_dn*, *int* **length**, **unsigned char** **dnptrs**, *unsigned char* *exp_dn*, **unsigned char** **lastdnptr*);

int dn_expand(unsigned char *msg*, **unsigned char** *eomorig*, **unsigned char** *comp_dn*, **unsigned char** *exp_dn*, **int** *length*);

DESCRIPTION

These functions make queries to and interpret the responses from Internet domain name servers.

The **res_init()** function reads the configuration files (see resolv+(8)) to get the default domain name, search order and name server address(es). If no server is given, the local host is tried. If no domain is given, that associated with the local host is used. It can be overridden with the environment variable LOCALDOMAIN. **res_init()** is normally executed by the first call to one of the other functions.

The **res_query()** function queries the name server for the fully-qualified domain name *name* of specified *type* and *class*. The reply is left in the buffer *answer* of length *anslen* supplied by the caller.

The **res_search()** function makes a query and waits for the response like **res_query()**, but in addition implements the default and search rules controlled by RES_DEFNAMES and RES_DNSRCH (see description of *_res* options below).

The **res_querydomain()** function makes a query using **res_query()** on the concatenation of *name* and *domain*.

The following functions are lower-level routines used by **res_query()**.

The **res_mkquery()** function constructs a query message in *buf* of length *buflen* for the domain name *dname*. The query type *op* is usually QUERY, but can be any of the types defined in <*arpa/nameser.h*>. *newrr* is currently unused.

The **res_send()** function sends a pre-formatted query given in *msg* of length *msglen* and returns the answer in *answer* which is of length *anslen*. It will call **res_init()**, if it has not already been called.

The **dn_comp()** function compresses the domain name *exp_dn* and stores it in the buffer *comp_dn* of length *length*. The compression uses an array of pointers *dnptrs* to previously compressed names in the current message. The first pointer points to the beginning of the message and the list ends with NULL. The limit of the array is specified by *lastdnptr*. if *dnptr* is NULL, domain names are not compressed. If *lastdnptr* is NULL, the list of labels is not updated.

The dn_expand() function expands the compressed domain name *comp_dn* to a full domain name, which is placed in the buffer *exp_dn* of size *length*. The compressed name is contained in a query or reply message, and *msg* points to the beginning of the message.

The resolver routines use global configuration and state information contained in the structure *_res*, which is defined in <*resolv.h*>. The only field that is normally manipulated by the user is *_res.options*. This field can contain the bitwise "or" of the following options:

RES_INIT True if **res_init()** has been called.

RES_DEBUG Print debugging messages.

RES_AAONLY Accept authoritative answers only. **res_send()** continues until it fins an authoritative answer or returns an error. [Not currently implemented].

RES_USEVC Use TCP connections for queries rather than UDP datagrams.

RES_PRIMARY Query primary domain name server only.

RES_IGNTC Ignore truncation errors. Don't retry with TCP. [Not currently implemented].

RES_RECURSE Set the recursion desired bit in queries. Recursion is carried out by the domain name server, not by **res_send()**. [Enabled by default].

RES_DEFNAMES If set, **res_search()** will append the default domain name to single component names, ie. those that do not contain a dot. [Enabled by default].

RES_STAYOPEN Used with RES_USEVC to keep the TCP connection open between queries.

RES_DNSRCH If set, **res_search()** will search for host names in the current domain and in parent domains. This option is used by **gethostbyname**(3). [Enabled by default].

RETURN VALUE

The **res_init()** function returns 0 on success, or −1 if an error occurs.

The **res_query()**, **res_search()**, **res_querydomain()**, **res_mkquery()** and **res_send()** functions return the length of the response, or −1 if an error occurs.

The **dn_comp()** and **dn_expand()** functions return the length of the compressed name, or −1 if an error occurs.

FILES

/etc/resolv.conf resolver configuration file
/etc/host.conf resolver configuration file

CONFORMING TO

BSD 4.3

SEE ALSO

gethostbyname(3), **hostname**(7), **named**(8), **resolv+**(8)

NAME

rewinddir – reset directory stream

SYNOPSIS

#include <sys/types.h>
#include <dirent.h>
void rewinddir(DIR *dir);

DESCRIPTION

The **rewinddir()** function resets the position of the directory stream *dir* to the beginning of the directory.

RETURN VALUE

The **readdir()** function returns no value.

CONFORMING TO

SVID 3, POSIX, BSD 4.3

SEE ALSO

opendir(3), **readdir**(3), **closedir**(3), **seekdir**(3), **telldir**(3), **scandir**(3)

NAME

rint – round to closest integer

SYNOPSIS

#include <math.h>
double rint(double *x***);**

DESCRIPTION

The **rint()** function rounds *x* to an integer value according to the prevalent rounding mode. The default rounding mode is to round to the nearest integer.

RETURN VALUE

The **rint()** function returns the integer value as a floating-point number.

CONFORMING TO

BSD 4.3

SEE ALSO

abs(3), **ceil**(3), **fabs**(3), **floor**(3), **labs**(3)

NAME

scandir, alphasort – scan a directory for matching entries

SYNOPSIS

#include <dirent.h>

int scandir(const char **dir***, struct dirent ******namelist***, int (****select***)(const struct dirent *), int (****compar***)(const void *, const void *));**

int alphasort(const struct dirent **a***, const struct dirent ****b***);**

DESCRIPTION

The **scandir()** function scans the directory *dir*, calling **select()** on each directory entry. Entries for which **select()** returns non-zero are stored in strings allocated via **malloc()**, sorted using **qsort()** with the comparison function **compar()**, and collected in array *namelist* which is allocated via **malloc()**.

The **alphasort()** function can be used as the comparison function for the **scandir()** function to sort the directory entries into alphabetical order. Its parameters are the two directory entries, *a* and *b*, to compare.

RETURN VALUE

The **scandir()** function returns the number of directory entries selected or –1 if an error occurs.

The **alphasort()** function returns an integer less than, equal to, or greater than zero if the first argument is considered to be respectively less than, equal to, or greater than the second.

ERRORS

    ENOMEM   Insufficient memory to complete the operation.

CONFORMING TO

BSD 4.3

SEE ALSO

opendir(3), **readdir**(3), **closedir**(3), **rewinddir**(3), **telldir**(3), **seekdir**(3)

SCANF(3) Linux Programmer's Manual SCANF(3)

NAME
scanf, fscanf, sscanf, vscanf, vsscanf, vfscanf – input format conversion

SYNOPSIS
#include <stdio.h>
int scanf(const char **format, ...***);**
int fscanf(FILE **stream,* **const char** **format, ...***);**
int sscanf(const char **str,* **const char** **format, ...***);**
#include <stdarg.h>
int vscanf(const char **format,* **va_list** *ap***);**
int vsscanf(const char **str,* **const char** **format,* **va_list** *ap***);**
int vfscanf(FILE **stream,* **const char** **format,* **va_list** *ap***);**

DESCRIPTION
The **scanf** family of functions scans input according to a *format* as described below. This format may contain *conversion specifiers*; the results from such conversions, if any, are stored through the *pointer* arguments. The **scanf** function reads input from the standard input stream *stdin,* **fscanf** reads input from the stream pointer *stream,* and **sscanf** reads its input from the character string pointed to by *str.*

The **vfscanf** function is analogous to **vfprintf**(3) and reads input from the stream pointer *stream* using a variable argument list of pointers (see **stdarg**(3). The **vscanf** function scans a variable argument list from the standard input and the **vsscanf** function scans it from a string; these are analogous to the **vprintf** and **vsprintf** functions respectively.

Each successive *pointer* argument must correspond properly with each successive conversion specifier (but see 'suppression' below). All conversions are introduced by the % (percent sign) character. The *format* string may also contain other characters. White space (such as blanks, tabs, or newlines) in the *format* string match any amount of white space, including none, in the input. Everything else matches only itself. Scanning stops when an input character does not match such a format character. Scanning also stops when an input conversion cannot be made (see below).

CONVERSIONS
Following the % character introducing a conversion there may be a number of *flag* characters, as follows:

* *   Suppresses assignment. The conversion that follows occurs as usual, but no pointer is used; the result of the conversion is simply discarded.
* **h**   Indicates that the conversion will be one of **dioux** or **n** and the next pointer is a pointer to a *short* int (rather than *int*).
* **l**   Indicates either that the conversion will be one of **dioux** or **n** and the next pointer is a pointer to a *long* int (rather than *int*), or that the conversion will be one of **efg** and the next pointer is a pointer to *double* (rather than *float*).
* **L**   Indicates that the conversion will be **efg** and the next pointer is a pointer to *long double.* (This type is not implemented; the **L** flag is currently ignored—this may not be true for Linux.)

In addition to these flags, there may be an optional maximum field width, expressed as a decimal integer, between the % and the conversion. If no width is given, a default of 'infinity' is used (with one exception, below); otherwise at most this many characters are scanned in processing the conversion. Before conversion begins, most conversions skip white space; this white space is not counted against the field width.

The following conversions are available:

* **%**   Matches a literal '%'. That is, '%%' in the format string matches a single input '%' character. No conversion is done, and assignment does not occur.
* **d**   Matches an optionally signed decimal integer; the next pointer must be a pointer to *int.*

D Equivalent to **ld**; this exists only for backwards compatibility.

i Matches an optionally signed integer; the next pointer must be a pointer to *int*. The integer is read in base 16 if it begins with '0x' or '0X', in base 8 if it begins with '0', and in base 10 otherwise. Only characters that correspond to the base are used.

o Matches an octal integer; the next pointer must be a pointer to *unsigned int*.

O Equivalent to **lo**; this exists for backwards compatibility.

u Matches an optionally signed decimal integer; the next pointer must be a pointer to *unsigned int*.

x Matches an optionally a signed hexadecimal integer; the next pointer must be a pointer to *unsigned int*.

X Equivalent to **lx**; this violates the ANSI C3.159-1989 ("ANSI C") but is backwards compatible with previous UNIX systems—I don't know what Linux does with this.

f Matches an optionally signed floating-point number; the next pointer must be a pointer to *float*.

e Equivalent to **f**.

g Equivalent to **f**.

E Equivalent to **lf**; this violates the ANSI C3.159-1989 ("ANSI C") but is backwards compatible with previous UNIX systems—I don't know what Linux does with this.

F Equivalent to **lf**; this exists only for backwards compatibility.

s Matches a sequence of non-white-space characters; the next pointer must be a pointer to *char*, and the array must be large enough to accept all the sequence and the terminating **NUL** character. The input string stops at white space or at the maximum field width, whichever occurs first.

c Matches a sequence of *width* count characters (default 1); the next pointer must be a pointer to *char*, and there must be enough room for all the characters (no terminating **NUL** is added). The usual skip of leading white space is suppressed. To skip white space first, use an explicit space in the format.

[Matches a nonempty sequence of characters from the specified set of accepted characters; the next pointer must be a pointer to *char*, and there must be enough room for all the characters in the string, plus a terminating **NUL** character. The usual skip of leading white space is suppressed. The string is to be made up of characters in (or not in) a particular set; the set is defined by the characters between the open bracket [character and a close bracket] character. The set *excludes* those characters if the first character after the open bracket is a circumflex ˆ. To include a close bracket in the set, make it the first character after the open bracket or the circumflex; any other position will end the set. The hyphen character - is also special; when placed between two other characters, it adds all intervening characters to the set. To include a hyphen, make it the last character before the final close bracket. For instance, '[ˆ]0-9-]' means the set 'everything except close bracket, zero through nine, and hyphen'. The string ends with the appearance of a character not in the (or, with a circumflex, in) set or when the field width runs out.

p Matches a pointer value (as printed by '%p' in **printf**(3); the next pointer must be a pointer to *void*.

n Nothing is expected; instead, the number of characters consumed thus far from the input is stored through the next pointer, which must be a pointer to *int*. This is *not* a conversion, although it can be suppressed with the * flag.

For backwards compatibility, other conversion characters (except '\0') are taken as if they were '%d' or, if uppercase, '%ld', and a 'conversion' of '%\0' causes an immediate return of **EOF**. The **F** and **X** conversions will be changed in the future to conform to the ANSI C standard, after which they will act like and respectively. The behavior of Linux on the non-standard points is not known by this documenter.

RETURN VALUES

These functions return the number of input items assigned, which can be fewer than provided for, or even zero, in the event of a matching failure. Zero indicates that, while there was input available, no conversions were assigned; typically this is due to an invalid input character, such as an alphabetic character for a '%d' conversion. The value **EOF** is returned if an input failure occurs before any conversion such as an end-of-file occurs. If an error or end-of-file occurs after conversion has begun, the number of conversions which were successfully completed is returned.

SEE ALSO

strtol(3), **strtoul**(3), **strtod**(3), **getc**(3), **printf**(3)

STANDARDS

The functions **fscanf**, **scanf**, and **sscanf** conform to ANSI C3.159-1989 ("ANSI C").

BUGS

Differences for Linux are not known at this time. The following is for the BSD version:

The current situation with **%F** and **%X** conversions is unfortunate.

All of the backwards compatibility formats will be removed in the future.

Numerical strings are truncated to 512 characters; for example, **%f** and **%d** are implicitly **%512f** and **%512d**.

NAME

seekdir – set the position of the next readdir() call in the directory stream.

SYNOPSIS

#include <dirent.h>
void seekdir(DIR *dir, off_t offset);

DESCRIPTION

The **seekdir**() function sets the location in the directory stream from which the next **readdir**() call will start. **seekdir**() should be used with an offset returned by **telldir**().

RETURN VALUE

The **seekdir**() function returns no value.

CONFORMING TO

BSD 4.3

SEE ALSO

lseek(2), **opendir**(3), **readdir**(3), **closedir**(3), **rewinddir**(3), telldir **(3),** scandir (3)

NAME

setbuf, setbuffer, setlinebuf, setvbuf – stream buffering operations

SYNOPSIS

#include <stdio.h>

int setbuf(FILE **stream*, **char** **buf***);**
int setbuffer(FILE **stream*, **char** **buf*, **size_t** *size***);**
int setlinebuf(FILE **stream***);**
int setvbuf(FILE **stream*, **char** **buf*, **int** *mode* , **size_t** *size***);**

DESCRIPTION

The three types of buffering available are unbuffered, block buffered, and line buffered. When an output stream is unbuffered, information appears on the destination file or terminal as soon as written; when it is block buffered many characters are saved up and written as a block; when it is line buffered characters are saved up until a newline is output or input is read from any stream attached to a terminal device (typically stdin). The function **fflush**(3) may be used to force the block out early. (See **fclose**(3).) Normally all files are block buffered. When the first I/O operation occurs on a file, **malloc**(3) is called, and a buffer is obtained. If a stream refers to a terminal (as *stdout* normally does) it is line buffered. The standard error stream *stderr* is always unbuffered.

The **setvbuf** function may be used at any time on any open stream to change its buffer. The *mode* parameter must be one of the following three macros:

    _IONBF   unbuffered
    _IOLBF   line buffered
    _IOFBF   fully buffered

Except for unbuffered files, the *buf* argument should point to a buffer at least *size* bytes long; this buffer will be used instead of the current buffer. If the argument *buf* is **NULL**, only the mode is affected; a new buffer will be allocated on the next read or write operation. The *setvbuf* function may be used at any time, but can only change the mode of a stream when it is not "active": that is, before any I/O, or immediately after a call to **fflush**.

The other three calls are, in effect, simply aliases for calls to **setvbuf**. The **setbuf** function is exactly equivalent to the call

setvbuf(stream, buf, buf ? _IOFBF : _IONBF, BUFSIZ);

The **setbuffer** function is the same, except that the size of the buffer is up to the caller, rather than being determined by the default **BUFSIZ**. The **setlinebuf** function is exactly equivalent to the call:

setvbuf(stream, (char *)NULL, _IOLBF, 0);

SEE ALSO

fopen(3), **fclose**(3), **fread**(3), **malloc**(3), **puts**(3), **printf**(3)

STANDARDS

The **setbuf** and **setvbuf** functions conform to ANSI C3.159-1989 ("ANSI C").

BUGS

The **setbuffer** and **setlinebuf** functions are not portable to versions of BSD before 4.2BSD, and may not be available under Linux. On 4.2BSD and 4.3BSD systems, **setbuf** always uses a suboptimal buffer size and should be avoided. You must make sure that both *buf* and the space it points to still exist by the time *stream* is closed, which also happens at program termination. For example, the following is illegal:

```
#include <stdio.h>
int main()
{
```

```
    char buf[BUFSIZ];
    setbuf(stdin, buf);
    printf("Hello, world!\n");
    return 0;
}
```

NAME

setenv – change or add an environment variable

SYNOPSIS

#include <stdlib.h>
int setenv(const char **name***, const char** **value***, int** *overwrite***);**
void unsetenv(const char **name***);**

DESCRIPTION

The **setenv()** function adds the variable *name* to the environment with the value *value*, if *name* does not already exist. If *name* does exist in the environment, then its value is changed to *value* if *overwrite* is non-zero; if *overwrite* is zero, then the value of *name* is not changed.

The **unsetenv()** function deletes the variable *name* from the environment.

RETURN VALUE

The **setenv()** function returns zero on success, or –1 if there was insufficient space in the environment.

CONFORMING TO

BSD 4.3

SEE ALSO

getenv(3), **putenv**(3)

NAME

setjmp – save stack context for non-local goto

SYNOPSIS

#include <setjmp.h>

int setjmp(jmp_buf *env* **);**

DESCRIPTION

setjmp and **longjmp**(3) are useful for dealing with errors and interrupts encountered in a low-level subroutine of a program. **setjmp()** saves the stack context/environment in *env* for later use by **longjmp()**. The stack context will be invalidated if the function which called **setjmp()** returns.

RETURN VALUE

It returns the value 0 if returning directly and non-zero when returning from **longjmp()** using the saved context.

CONFORMING TO

POSIX

NOTES

POSIX does not specify if the signal context will be saved or not. If you want to save signal masks, use **sigsetjmp**(3). **setjmp()** makes programs hard to understand and maintain. If possible an alternative should be used.

SEE ALSO

longjmp(3), **sigsetjmp**(2), **siglongjmp**(2)

NAME

setlocale – set the current locale.

SYNOPSIS

#include <locale.h>
char *setlocale(int *category*, **const char** * *locale***);**

DESCRIPTION

The **setlocale()** function is used to set or query the program's current locale. If *locale* is C or POSIX, the current locale is set to the portable locale.

If *locale* is , the locale is set to the default locale which is selected from the environment variable **LANG**.

On startup of the main program, the portable locale is selected as default.

The argument *category* determines which functions are influenced by the new locale:

- **LC_ALL** for all of the locale.
- **LC_COLLATE** for the functions **strcoll()** and **strxfrm()**.
- **LC_CTYPE** for the character classification and conversion routines.
- **LC_MONETARY** for **localeconv()**.
- **LC_NUMERIC** for the decimal character.
- **LC_TIME** for **strftime()**. **NULL** if the request cannot not be honored. This string may be allocated in static storage.

A program may be made portable to all locales by calling **setlocale(LC_ALL,** """"""""") after program initialization, by using the values returned from a **localeconv()** call for locale – dependent information and by using **strcoll()** or **strxfrm()** to compare strings.

CONFORMS TO

ANSI C, POSIX.1

Linux supports the portable locales C and POSIX and also the European Latin-1 , and Russian locales.

The **printf()** family of functions may or may not honor the current locale.

SEE ALSO

locale(1), **localedef**(1), **strcoll**(3), **isalpha**(3), **localeconv**(3), **strftime**(3), **locale**(7)

NAME

siginterrupt – allow signals to interrupt system calls

SYNOPSIS

#include <signal.h>
int siginterrupt(int *sig*, **int** *flag*);

DESCRIPTION

The **siginterrupt()** function changes the restart behaviour when a system call is interrupted by the signal *sig*. If the *flag* argument is false (0), then systems calls will be restarted if interrupted by the specified signal *sig*. This is the default behaviour in Linux. However, when a new signal handler is specified with the **signal**(2) function, the system call is interrupted by default.

If the *flags* argument is true (1) and no data has been transferred, then a system call interrupted by the signal *sig* will return −1 and the global variable *errno* will be set to *EINTR*.

If the *flags* argument is true (1) and data transfer has started, then the system call will be interrupted and will return the actual amount of data transferred.

RETURN VALUE

The **siginterrupt()** function returns 0 on success, or −1 if the signal number *sig* is invalid.

ERRORS

  EINVAL The specified signal number is invalid.

CONFORMING TO

BSD 4.3

SEE ALSO

signal(2)

NAME

sigemptyset, sigfillset, sigaddset, sigdelset, sigismember – POSIX signal set operations.

SYNOPSIS

#include <signal.h>

int sigemptyset(sigset_t *set*);

int sigfillset(sigset_t *set*);

int sigaddset(sigset_t *set*, const int *signum*);

int sigdelset(sigset_t *set*, const int *signum*);

int sigismember(const sigset_t *set*, const int *signum*);

DESCRIPTION

The **sigsetops**(3) functions allow the manipulation of POSIX signal sets.

sigemptyset initializes the signal set given by *set* to empty, with all signals excluded from the set.

sigfillset initializes *set* to full, including all signals.

sigaddset and **sigdelset** add and delete respectively signal *signum* from *set*.

sigismember tests whether *signum* is a member of *set*.

RETURN VALUES

sigemptyset, **sigfullset**, **sigaddset** and **sigdelset** return 0 on success and -1 on error.

sigismember returns 1 if *signum* is a member of *set*, 0 if *signum* is not a member, and -1 on error.

ERRORS

    EINVAL   *sig* is not a valid signal.

CONFORMING TO

POSIX

SEE ALSO

sigaction(2), **sigpending**(2), **sigprocmask**(2), **sigsuspend**(2)

NAME

sin – sine function

SYNOPSIS

#include <math.h>
double sin(double *x***);**

DESCRIPTION

The **sin()** function returns the sine of *x*, where *x* is given in radians.

RETURN VALUE

The **sin()** function returns a value between –1 and 1.

CONFORMING TO

SVID 3, POSIX, BSD 4.3, ISO 9899

SEE ALSO

acos(3), **asin**(3), **atan**(3), **atan2**(3), **cos**(3), **tan**(3)

NAME

sinh – hyperbolic sine function

SYNOPSIS

#include <math.h>
double sinh(double *x***);**

DESCRIPTION

The **sinh()** function returns the hyperbolic sine of *x*, which is defined mathematically as exp(x) - exp(-x) / 2.

CONFORMING TO

SVID 3, POSIX, BSD 4.3, ISO 9899

SEE ALSO

acosh(3), **asinh**(3), **atanh**(3), **cosh**(3), **tanh**(3)

SLEEP(3)　　　　　　　Linux Programmer's Manual　　　　　　　SLEEP(3)

NAME

sleep – Sleep for the specified number of seconds

SYNOPSIS

#include <unistd.h>
unsigned int sleep(unsigned int *seconds***);**

DESCRIPTION

sleep() makes the current process sleep until *seconds* seconds have elapsed or a signal arrives which is not ignored.

RETURN VALUE

Zero if the requested time has elapsed, or the number of seconds left to sleep.

CONFORMS TO

POSIX.1

BUGS

sleep() may be implemented using **SIGALRM**; mixing calls to **alarm()** and **sleep()** is a bad idea.

Using **longjmp()** from a signal handler or modifying the handling of **SIGALRM** while sleeping will cause undefined results.

SEE ALSO

signal(2), **alarm**(2)

SQRT(3)

NAME

sqrt – square root function

SYNOPSIS

#include <math.h>
double sqrt(double *x***);**

DESCRIPTION

The **sqrt()** function returns the non-negative square root of *x*. It fails and sets *errno* to EDOM, if *x* is negative.

ERRORS

EDOM   *x* is negative.

CONFORMING TO

SVID 3, POSIX, BSD 4.3, ISO 9899

SEE ALSO

hypot(3)

NAME

stdarg – variable argument lists

SYNOPSIS

#include <stdarg.h>

void va_start(va_list *ap*, *last*);
type va_arg(va_list *ap*, *type*);
void va_end(va_list *ap*);

DESCRIPTION

A function may be called with a varying number of arguments of varying types. The include file *stdarg.h* declares a type **va_list** and defines three macros for stepping through a list of arguments whose number and types are not known to the called function.

The called function must declare an object of type **va_list** which is used by the macros **va_start**, **va_arg**, and **va_end**.

The **va_start** macro initializes *ap* for subsequent use by **va_arg** and **va_end**, and must be called first.

The parameter *last* is the name of the last parameter before the variable argument list, i.e., the last parameter of which the calling function knows the type.

Because the address of this parameter is used in the **va_start** macro, it should not be declared as a register variable, or as a function or an array type.

The **va_start** macro returns no value.

The **va_arg** macro expands to an expression that has the type and value of the next argument in the call. The parameter *ap* is the **va_list ap** initialized by **va_start**. Each call to **va_arg** modifies *ap* so that the next call returns the next argument. The parameter *type* is a type name specified so that the type of a pointer to an object that has the specified type can be obtained simply by adding a * to *type*.

If there is no next argument, or if *type* is not compatible with the type of the actual next argument (as promoted according to the default argument promotions), random errors will occur.

The first use of the **va_arg** macro after that of the **va_start** macro returns the argument after *last*. Successive invocations return the values of the remaining arguments.

The **va_end** macro handles a normal return from the function whose variable argument list was initialized by **va_start**.

The **va_end** macro returns no value.

EXAMPLES

The function *foo* takes a string of format characters and prints out the argument associated with each format character based on the type.

```
void foo(char *fmt, ...)
{
va_list ap;
int d;
char c, *p, *s;
va_start(ap, fmt);
while (*fmt)
switch(*fmt++) {
case 's': /* string */
s = va_arg(ap, char *);
printf("string %s\n", s);
break;
case 'd': /* int */
d = va_arg(ap, int);
```

```
printf("int %d\n", d);
break;
case 'c': /* char */
c = va_arg(ap, char);
printf("char %c\n", c);
break;
}
va_end(ap);
}
```

STANDARDS

The **va_start**, **va_arg**, and **va_end** macros conform to ANSI C3.159-1989 ("ANSI C").

COMPATIBILITY

These macros are *not* compatible with the historic macros they replace. A backward compatible version can be found in the include file *varargs.h*.

BUGS

Unlike the **varargs** macros, the **stdarg** macros do not permit programmers to code a function with no fixed arguments. This problem generates work mainly when converting **varargs** code to **stdarg** code, but it also creates difficulties for variadic functions that wish to pass all of their arguments on to a function that takes a **va_list** argument, such as **vfprintf**(3).

STDIO(3) Linux Programmer's Manual STDIO(3)

NAME
stdio – standard input/output library functions

SYNOPSIS
#include <stdio.h>

FILE *stdin;
FILE *stdout;
FILE *stderr;

DESCRIPTION
The standard I/O library provides a simple and efficient buffered stream I/O interface. Input and output is mapped into logical data streams and the physical I/O characteristics are concealed. The functions and macros are listed below; more information is available from the individual man pages.

A stream is associated with an external file (which may be a physical device) by *opening* a file, which may involve creating a new file. Creating an existing file causes its former contents to be discarded. If a file can support positioning requests (such as a disk file, as opposed to a terminal) then a *file* position indicator associated with the stream is positioned at the start of the file (byte zero), unless the file is opened with append mode. If append mode is used, the position indicator will be placed the end-of-file. The position indicator is maintained by subsequent reads, writes and positioning requests. All input occurs as if the characters were read by successive calls to the **fgetc**(3) function; all output takes place as if all characters were read by successive calls to the **fputc**(3) function.

A file is disassociated from a stream by *closing* the file. Output streams are flushed (any unwritten buffer contents are transferred to the host environment) before the stream is disassociated from the file. The value of a pointer to a **FILE** object is indeterminate after a file is closed (garbage).

A file may be subsequently reopened, by the same or another program execution, and its contents reclaimed or modified (if it can be repositioned at the start). If the main function returns to its original caller, or the **exit**(3) function is called, all open files are closed (hence all output streams are flushed) before program termination. Other methods of program termination, such as **abort**(3) do not bother about closing files properly.

At program startup, three text streams are predefined and need not be opened explicitly — *standard* input (for reading conventional input), — *standard* output (for writing conventional input), and *standard* error (for writing diagnostic output). These streams are abbreviated *stdin*,*stdout* and *stderr*. When opened, the standard error stream is not fully buffered; the standard input and output streams are fully buffered if and only if the streams do not to refer to an interactive device.

Output streams that refer to terminal devices are always line buffered by default; pending output to such streams is written automatically whenever an input stream that refers to a terminal device is read. In cases where a large amount of computation is done after printing part of a line on an output terminal, it is necessary to **fflush**(3) the standard output before going off and computing so that the output will appear.

The **stdio** library is a part of the library **libc** and routines are automatically loaded as needed by the compilers **cc**(1) and **pc**(1). The **SYNOPSIS** sections of the following manual pages indicate which include files are to be used, what the compiler declaration for the function looks like and which external variables are of interest.

The following are defined as macros; these names may not be re-used without first removing their current definitions with **#undef**: **BUFSIZ**, **EOF**, **FILENAME_MAX**, **FOPEN_MAX**, **L_cuserid**, **L_ctermid**, **L_tmpnam**, **NULL**, **SEEK_END**, **SEEK_SET**, **SEE_CUR**, **TMP_MAX**, **clearerr**, **feof**, **ferror**, **fileno**, **fropen**, **fwopen**, **getc**, **getchar**, **putc**, **putchar**, **stderr**, **stdin**, **stdout**. Function versions of the macro functions **feof**, **ferror**, **clearerr**, **fileno**, **getc**, **getchar**, **putc**, and **putchar** exist and will be used if the macros definitions are explicitly removed.

STDIO(3)

SEE ALSO
open(2), **close**(2), **read**(2), **write**(2)

BUGS
The standard buffered functions do not interact well with certain other library and system functions, especially **vfork** and **abort**. This may not be the case under Linux.

STANDARDS
The **stdio** library conforms to ANSI C3.159-1989 ("ANSI C").

LIST OF FUNCTIONS

Function	Description
clearerr	check and reset stream status
fclose	close a stream
fdopen	stream open functions
feof	check and reset stream status
ferror	check and reset stream status
fflush	flush a stream
fgetc	get next character or word from input stream
fgetline	get a line from a stream
fgetpos	reposition a stream
fgets	get a line from a stream
fileno	check and reset stream status
fopen	stream open functions
fprintf	formatted output conversion
fpurge	flush a stream
fputc	output a character or word to a stream
fputs	output a line to a stream
fread	binary stream input/output
freopen	stream open functions
fropen	open a stream
fscanf	input format conversion
fseek	reposition a stream
fsetpos	reposition a stream
ftell	reposition a stream
fwrite	binary stream input/output
getc	get next character or word from input stream
getchar	get next character or word from input stream
gets	get a line from a stream
getw	get next character or word from input stream
mktemp	make temporary file name (unique)
perror	system error messages
printf	formatted output conversion
putc	output a character or word to a stream
putchar	output a character or word to a stream
puts	output a line to a stream

putw	output a character or word to a stream	
remove	remove directory entry	
rewind	reposition a stream	
scanf	input format conversion	
setbuf	stream buffering operations	
setbuffer	stream buffering operations	
setlinebuf	stream buffering operations	
setvbuf	stream buffering operations	
sprintf	formatted output conversion	
sscanf	input format conversion	
strerror	system error messages	
sys_errlist	system error messages	
sys_nerr	system error messages	
tempnam	temporary file routines	
tmpfile	temporary file routines	
tmpnam	temporary file routines	
ungetc	un-get character from input stream	
vfprintf	formatted output conversion	
vfscanf	input format conversion	
vprintf	formatted output conversion	
vscanf	input format conversion	
vsprintf	formatted output conversion	
vsscanf	input format conversion	

NAME

strcasecmp, strncasecmp – compare two strings ignoring case

SYNOPSIS

#include <string.h>
int strcasecmp(const char *s1*, **const char** *s2*);
int strncasecmp(const char *s1*, **const char** *s2*, **size_t** *n*);

DESCRIPTION

The **strcasecmp()** function compares the two strings *s1* and *s2*, ignoring the case of the characters. It returns an integer less than, equal to, or greater than zero if *s1* is found, respectively, to be less than, to match, or be greater than *s2*.

The **strncasecmp()** function is similar, except it only compares the first *n* characters of *s1*.

RETURN VALUE

The **strcasecmp()** and **strncasecmp()** functions return an integer less than, equal to, or greater than zero if *s1*

(or the first *n* bytes thereof) is found, respectively, to be less than, to match, or be greater than *s2*.

CONFORMING TO

BSD 4.3

SEE ALSO

bcmp(3), **memcmp**(3), **strcmp**(3), **strcoll**(3), **strncmp**(3)

NAME

strcat, strncat – concatenate two strings

SYNOPSIS

#include <string.h>
char *strcat(char **dest***, const char ****src***);**
char *strncat(char **dest***, const char ****src***, size_t** *n***);**

DESCRIPTION

The **strcat()** function appends the *src* string to the *dest* string overwriting the '\0' character at the end of *dest*, and then adds a terminating '\0' character. The strings may not overlap, and the *dest* string must have enough space for the result.

The **strncat()** function is similar, except that only the first *n* characters of *src* are appended to *dest*.

RETURN VALUE

The **strcat()** and **strncat()** functions return a pointer to the resulting string *dest*.

CONFORMING TO

SVID 3, POSIX, BSD 4.3, ISO 9899

SEE ALSO

bcopy(3), **memccpy**(3), **memcpy**(3), **strcpy**(3), **strncpy**(3)

STRCHR(3)

NAME

strchr, strrchr – locate character in string

SYNOPSIS

#include <string.h>
char *strchr(const char **s***, int** *c***);**
char *strrchr(const char **s***, int** *c***);**

DESCRIPTION

The **strchr()** function returns a pointer to the first occurrence of the character *c* in the string *s*.

The **strrchr()** function returns a pointer to the last occurrence of the character *c* in the string *s*.

RETURN VALUE

The **strchr()** and **strrchr()** functions return a pointer to the matched character or NULL if the character is not found.

CONFORMING TO

SVID 3, POSIX, BSD 4.3, ISO 9899

SEE ALSO

index(3), **memchr**(3), **rindex**(3), **strpbrk**(3), **strsep**(3), **strspn**(3), **strstr**(3), **strtok**(3)

NAME

strcmp, strncmp – compare two strings

SYNOPSIS

#include <string.h>
int strcmp(const char *s1*, **const char** *s2*);
int strncmp(const char *s1*, **const char** *s2*, **size_t** *n*);

DESCRIPTION

The **strcmp()** function compares the two strings *s1* and *s2*. It returns an integer less than, equal to, or greater than zero if *s1* is found, respectively, to be less than, to match, or be greater than *s2*.

The **strncmp()** function is similar, except it only compares the first *n* characters of *s1*.

RETURN VALUE

The **strcmp()** and **strncmp()** functions return an integer less than, equal to, or greater than zero if *s1* (or the first *n* bytes thereof) is found, respectively, to be less than, to match, or be greater than *s2*.

CONFORMING TO

SVID 3, POSIX, BSD 4.3, ISO 9899

SEE ALSO

bcmp(3), **memcmp**(3), **strcasecmp**(3), **strncasecmp**(3), **strcoll**(3)

NAME

strcoll – compare two strings using the current locale

SYNOPSIS

#include <string.h>
int strcoll(const char *s1*, **const char** *s2*);

DESCRIPTION

The **strcoll()** function compares the two strings *s1* and *s2*. It returns an integer less than, equal to, or greater than zero if *s1* is found, respectively, to be less than, to match, or be greater than *s2*. The comparison is based on strings interpreted as appropriate for the program's current locale for category *LC_COLLATE*. (See **setlocale**(3)).

RETURN VALUE

The **strcoll()** function returns an integer less than, equal to, or greater than zero if *s1* is found, respectively, to be less than, to match, or be greater than *s2*, when both are interpreted as appropriate for the current locale.

CONFORMING TO

SVID 3, BSD 4.3, ISO 9899

NOTES

The Linux C Library currently hasn't implemented the complete POSIX-collating.

In the *"POSIX"* or *"C"* locales **strcoll()** is equivalent to **strcmp()**.

SEE ALSO

bcmp(3), **memcmp**(3), **strcasecmp**(3), **strcmp**(3), **strxfrm**(3), **setlocale**(3)

NAME

strcpy, strncpy – copy a string

SYNOPSIS

#include <string.h>
char *strcpy(char **dest***, const char ****src***);**
char *strncpy(char **dest***, const char ****src***, size_t** *n***);**

DESCRIPTION

The **strcpy()** function copies the string pointed to be *src* (including the terminating '\0' character) to the array pointed to by *dest*. The strings may not overlap, and the destination string *dest* must be large enough to receive the copy.

The **strncpy()** function is similar, except that only the first *n* bytes of *src* are copied.

In the case where the length of *src* is less than that of *n*, the remainder of *dest* will be padded with nulls.

RETURN VALUE

The **strcpy()** and **strncpy()** functions return a pointer to the destination string *dest*.

CONFORMING TO

SVID 3, POSIX, BSD 4.3, ISO 9899

SEE ALSO

bcopy(3), **memccpy**(3), **memcpy**(3), **memmove**(3)

STRDUP(3) Linux Programmer's Manual STRDUP(3)

NAME

strdup – duplicate a string

SYNOPSIS

#include <string.h>

char *strdup(const char **s***);**

DESCRIPTION

The **strdup()** function returns a pointer to a new string which is a duplicate of the string *s*. Memory for the new string is obtained with **malloc**(3), and can be freed with **free**(3).

RETURN VALUE

The **strdup()** function returns a pointer to the duplicated string, or NULL if insufficient memory was available.

ERRORS

ENOMEM   Insufficient memory available to allocate duplicate string.

CONFORMING TO

SVID 3, BSD 4.3

SEE ALSO

calloc(3), **malloc**(3), **realloc**(3), **free**(3)

NAME

strerror – return string describing error code

SYNOPSIS

#include <string.h>
char *strerror(int *errnum***);**

DESCRIPTION

The **strerror()** function returns a string describing the error code passed in the argument *errno*. The string can only be used until the next call to **strerror()**.

RETURN VALUE

The **strerror()** function returns the appropriate description string, or an unknown error message if the error code is unknown.

CONFORMING TO

SVID 3, POSIX, BSD 4.3, ISO 9899

SEE ALSO

errno(2), **perror**(3), **strsignal**(3)

NAME

strfry – randomize a string

SYNOPSIS

#include <string.h>
char *strfry(char *****string***);**

DESCRIPTION

The **strfry()** function randomizes the contents of *string* by using **rand**(3) to randomly swap characters in the string. The result is an anagram of *string*.

RETURN VALUE

The **strfry()** functions returns a pointer to the randomized string.

CONFORMING TO

The **strfry()** function is unique to the Linux C Library and GNU C Library.

SEE ALSO

memfrob(3)

STRFTIME(3) — Linux Programmer's Manual

NAME
strftime – format date and time

SYNOPSIS
#include <time.h>

size_t strftime(char *s,* **size_t** *max,* **const char** **format,* **const struct tm** **tm*);

DESCRIPTION
The **strftime()** function formats the broken-down time *tm* according to the format specification *format* and places the result in the character array *s* of size *max*.

Ordinary characters placed in the format string are copied to *s* without conversion. Conversion specifiers are introduced by a '%' character, and are replaced in *s* as follows:

%a	The abbreviated weekday name according to the current locale.
%A	The full weekday name according to the current locale.
%b	The abbreviated month name according to the current locale.
%B	The full month name according to the current locale.
%c	The preferred date and time representation for the current locale.
%d	The day of the month as a decimal number (range 0 to 31).
%H	The hour as a decimal number using a 24-hour clock (range 00 to 23).
%I	The hour as a decimal number using a 12-hour clock (range 01 to 12).
%j	The day of the year as a decimal number (range 001 to 366).
%m	The month as a decimal number (range 10 to 12).
%M	The minute as a decimal number.
%p	Either 'am' or 'pm' according to the given time value, or the corresponding strings for the current locale.
%S	The second as a decimal number.
%U	The week number of the current year as a decimal number, starting with the first Sunday as the first day of the first week.
%W	The week number of the current year as a decimal number, starting with the first Monday as the first day of the first week.
%w	The day of the week as a decimal, Sunday being 0.
%x	The preferred date representation for the current locale without the time.
%X	The preferred time representation for the current locale without the date.
%y	The year as a decimal number without a century (range 00 to 99).
%Y	The year as a decimal number including the century.
%Z	The time zone or name or abbreviation.
%%	A literal '%' character.

The broken-down time structure *tm* is defined in <*time.h*> as follows:

```
struct tm
{
int tm_sec; /* seconds */
int tm_min; /* minutes */
int tm_hour; /* hours */
int tm_mday; /* day of the month */
int tm_mon; /* month */
int tm_year; /* year */
int tm_wday; /* day of the week */
int tm_yday; /* day in the year */
```

```
int tm_isdst; /* daylight saving time */
};
```

The members of the *tm* structure are:

tm_sec   The number of seconds after the minute, normally in the range 0 to 59, but can be up to 61 to allow for leap seconds.

tm_min   The number of minutes after the hour, in the range 0 to 59.

tm_hour   The number of hours past midnight, in the range 0 to 23.

tm_mday   The day of the month, in the range 1 to 31.

tm_mon   The number of months since January, in the range 0 to 11.

tm_year   The number of years since 1900.

tm_wday   The number of days since Sunday, in the range 0 to 6.

tm_yday   The number of days since January 1, in the range 0 to 365.

tm_isdst   A flag that indicates whether daylight saving time is in effect at the time described. The value is positive if daylight saving time is in effect, zero if it is not, and negative if the information is not available.

RETURN VALUE

The **strftime()** function returns the number of characters placed in the array *s*, not including the terminating NULL character. If the value equals *max*, it means that the array was too small.

CONFORMING TO

SVID 3, POSIX, BSD 4.3, ISO 9899

SEE ALSO

date(1), **time**(2), **ctime**(3), **setlocale**(3), **sprintf**(3)

NOTES

The function supports only those locales specified in **locale**(7)

STRING(3) Linux Programmer's Manual STRING(3)

NAME

strcasecmp, strcat, strchr, strcmp, strcoll, strcpy, strcspn, strdup, strfry, strlen, strncat, strncmp, strncpy, strncasecmp, strpbrk, strrchr, strsep, strspn, strstr, strtok, strxfrm, index, rindex – string operations

SYNOPSIS

#include <string.h>
int strcasecmp(const char *s1*, **const char** *s2*);
char *strcat(char *dest*, **const char** *src*);
char *strchr(const char *s*, **int** *c*);
int strcmp(const char *s1*, **const char** *s2*);
int strcoll(const char *s1*, **const char** *s2*);
char *strcpy(char *dest*, **const char** *src*);
size_t strcspn(const char *s*, **const char** *reject*);
char *strdup(const char *s*);
char *strfry(char *string*);
size_t strlen(const char *s*);
char *strncat(char *dest*, **const char** *src*, **size_t** *n*);
int strncmp(const char *s1*, **const char** *s2*, **size_t** *n*);
char *strncpy(char *dest*, **const char** *src*, **size_t** *n*);
int strncasecmp(const char *s1*, **const char** *s2*, **size_t** *n*);
char *strpbrk(const char *s*, **const char** *accept*);
char *strrchr(const char *s*, **int** *c*);
char *strsep(char **stringp*, **const char** *delim*);
size_t strspn(const char *s*, **const char** *accept*);
char *strstr(const char *haystack*, **const char** *needle*);
char *strtok(char *s*, **const char** *delim*);
size_t strxfrm(char *dest*, **const char** *src*, **size_t** *n*);
char ***index(const*char *s, int* **c**);
char *rindex(const char *s*, **int** *c*);

DESCRIPTION

The string functions perform string operations on NULL-terminated strings. See the individual man pages for descriptions of each function.

SEE ALSO

index(3), **rindex**(3), **strcasecmp**(3), **strcat**(3), **strchr**(3), **strcmp**(3), **strcoll**(3), **strcpy**(3), **strcspn**(3), **strdup**(3), **strfry**(3), **strlen**(3), **strncat**(3), **strncmp**(3), **strncpy**(3), **strncasecmp**(3), **strpbrk**(3), **strrchr**(3), **strsep**(3), **strspn**(3), **strstr**(3), **strtok**(3), **strxfrm**(3)

STRLEN(3)

NAME

strlen – calculate the length of a string

SYNOPSIS

#include <string.h>
size_t strlen(const char *s);

DESCRIPTION

The **strlen()** function calculates the length of the string *s*, not including the terminating '\0' character.

RETURN VALUE

The **strlen()** function returns the number of characters in *s*.

CONFORMING TO

SVID 3, POSIX, BSD 4.3, ISO 9899

SEE ALSO

string(3)

STRPBRK(3)

NAME
strpbrk – search a string for any of a set of characters

SYNOPSIS
#include <string.h>
char *strpbrk(const char ***s, const char ***accept**);**

DESCRIPTION
The **strpbrk()** function locates the first occurrence in the string *s* of any of the characters in the string *accept*.

RETURN VALUE
The **strpbrk()** function returns a pointer to the character in *s* that matches one of the characters in *accept*.

CONFORMING TO
SVID 3, POSIX, BSD 4.3, ISO 9899

SEE ALSO
index(3), **memchr**(3), **rindex**(3), **strchr**(3), **strsep**(3), **strspn**(3), **strstr**(3), **strtok**(3)

STRPTIME(3)

NAME

strptime – convert a string representation of time to a time tm structure

SYNOPSIS

#include <time.h>

char *strptime(char **buf***, const char ****format***, const struct tm ****tm***);**

DESCRIPTION

strptime( ) is the complementary function to **strftime( )** and converts the character string pointed to by *buf* to a time value, which is stored in the **tm** structure pointed to by *tm*, using the format specified by *format*. *format* is a character string that consists of field descriptors and text characters, reminiscent of **scanf**(3). Each field descriptor consists of a % character followd by another character that specifies the replacement for the field descriptor. All other characters are copied from *format* into the result. The following field descriptors are supported:

%%	same as %
%a	
%A	day of week, using locale's weekday names; either the abbreviated or full name may be specified
%b	
%B	
%h	month, using locale's month names; either the abbreviated or full name may be specified
%c	date and time as %x %X
%C	date and time, in locale's long-format date and time representation
%d	
%e	day of month (1-31; leading zeroes are permitted but not required)
%D	date as %m/%d/%y
%H	
%k	hour (0-23; leading zeroes are permitted but not required)
%I	
%l	hour (0-12; leading zeroes are permitted but not required)
%j	day number of year (001-366)
%m	month number (1-12; leading zeroes are permitted but not required)
%M	minute (0-59; leading zeroes are permitted but not required)
%p	locale's equivalent of AM or PM
%r	time as %I:%M:%S %p
%R	time as %H:%M
%S	seconds (0-61; leading zeroes are permitted but not required. Extra second allowed for leap years)
%T	time as %H:%M:%S
%w	weekday number (0-6) with Sunday as the first day of the week
%x	date, using locale's date format
%X	time, using locale's time format
%y	year within century (0-99; leading zeroes are permitted but not required. Unfortunately this makes the assumption that we are stuck in the 20th century as 1900 is automatically added onto this number for the tm_year field)

%Y   year, including century (for example, 1988)

Case is ignored when matching items such as month or weekday names.

The broken-down time structure *tm* is defined in <*time.h*> as follows:

```
struct tm
{
int tm_sec; /* seconds */
int tm_min; /* minutes */
int tm_hour; /* hours */
int tm_mday; /* day of the month */
int tm_mon; /* month */
int tm_year; /* year */
int tm_wday; /* day of the week */
int tm_yday; /* day in the year */
int tm_isdst; /* daylight saving time */
};
```

RETURN VALUE

The **strptime()** function returns a pointer to the character following the last character in the string pointed to by *buf*

SEE ALSO

strftime(3), **time**(2), **setlocale**(3), **scanf**(3)

BUGS

The return values point to static data, whose contents are overwritten by each call.

NOTES

This function is only available in libraries newer than version 4.6.5

The function supports only those locales specified in **locale**(7)

NAME

strsep – extract token from string

SYNOPSIS

#include <string.h>

char *strsep(char ***stringp***, const char ****delim***);**

DESCRIPTION

The **strsep()** function returns the next token from the string *stringp* which is delimited by *delim*. The token is terminated with a '\0' character and *stringp* is updated to point past the token.

RETURN VALUE

The **strsep()** function returns a pointer to the token, or NULL if *delim* is not found in *stringp*.

CONFORMING TO

BSD 4.3

SEE ALSO

index(3), **memchr**(3), **rindex**(3), **strchr**(3), **strpbrk**(3), **strspn**(3), **strstr**(3), **strtok**(3)

NAME

strsignal – return string describing signal

SYNOPSIS

#include <string.h>
char *strsignal(int *sig***);**
extern const char * const *sys_siglist***[]**

DESCRIPTION

The **strsignal()** function returns a string describing the signal number passed in the argument *sig*. The string can only be used until the next call to **strsignal()**.

The array *sys_siglist* holds the signal description strings indexed by signal number.

RETURN VALUE

The **strsignal()** function returns the appropriate description string, or an unknown signal message if the signal number is invalid.

SEE ALSO

psignal(3), **strerror**(3)

NAME

strspn, strcspn – search a string for a set of characters

SYNOPSIS

#include <string.h>
size_t strspn(const char *s, const char *accept);
size_t strcspn(const char *s, const char *reject);

DESCRIPTION

The **strspn()** function calculates the length of the initial segment of *s* which consists entirely of characters in *accept*.

The **strcspn()** function calculates the length of the initial segment of *s* which consists entirely of characters not in *reject*.

RETURN VALUE

The **strspn()** function returns the number of characters in the initial segment of *s* which consist only of characters from *accept*.

The **strcspn()** function returns the number of characters in the initial segment of *s* which are not in the string *reject*.

CONFORMING TO

SVID 3, POSIX, BSD 4.3, ISO 9899

SEE ALSO

index(3), **memchr**(3), **rindex**(3), **strchr**(3), **strpbrk**(3), **strsep**(3), **strstr**(3), **strtok**(3)

STRSTR(3)

NAME

strstr – locate a substring

SYNOPSIS

#include <string.h>
char *strstr(const char **haystack***, const char ****needle***);**

DESCRIPTION

The **strstr()** function finds the first occurrence of the substring *needle* in the string *haystack*. The terminating '\0' characters are not compared.

RETURN VALUE

The **strstr()** function returns a pointer to the beginning of the substring, or NULL if the substring is not found.

SEE ALSO

index(3), **memchr**(3), **rindex**(3), **strchr**(3), **strpbrk**(3), **strsep**(3), **strspn**(3), **strtok**(3)

STRTOD(3)

NAME

strtod – convert ASCII string to double

SYNOPSIS

#include <stdlib.h>

double strtod(const char **nptr***, char** ***endptr***);**

DESCRIPTION

The **strtod** function converts the initial portion of the string pointed to by *nptr* to **double** representation.

The expected form of the string is an optional plus ("+") or minus sign ("-") followed by a sequence of digits optionally containing a decimal-point character, optionally followed by an exponent. An exponent consists of an "E" or "e", followed by an optional plus or minus sign, followed by a sequence of digits.

Leading white-space characters in the string (as defined by the **isspace**(3) function) are skipped.

RETURN VALUES

The **strtod** function returns the converted value, if any.

If *endptr* is not **NULL**, a pointer to the character after the last character used in the conversion is stored in the location referenced by *endptr*.

If no conversion is performed, zero is returned and the value of *nptr* is stored in the location referenced by *endptr*.

If the correct value would cause overflow, plus or minus **HUGE_VAL** is returned (according to the sign of the value), and **ERANGE** is stored in *errno*. If the correct value would cause underflow, zero is returned and **ERANGE** is stored in *errno*.

ERRORS

    ERANGE   Overflow or underflow occurred.

SEE ALSO

atof(3), **atoi**(3), **atol**(3), **strtol**(3), **strtoul**(3)

STANDARDS

The **strtod** function conforms to ANSI-C.

BUGS

This is a BSD manual page and may not reflect the current Linux implementation.

STRTOK(3)

NAME

strtok – extract token from string

SYNOPSIS

#include <string.h>
char *strtok(char **s***, const char ****delim***);**

DESCRIPTION

The **strtok()** function breaks the string *s* into a series of tokens delimited by *delim*. The first call to **strtok()** should have *s* as the first argument. Subsequent calls should have the first argument set to NULL. The separator string *delim* may be different for each call.

The first call to **strtok()** returns the first token in *s* or NULL if *delim* is not found in *s*. A pointer to the next character is saved for the next call to **strtok**. Subsequent calls return subsequent tokens until delim is no longer found, when NULL is returned.

RETURN VALUE

The **strtok()** function returns a pointer to the next token, or NULL if there are no more tokens.

CONFORMING TO

SVID 3, POSIX, BSD 4.3, ISO 9899

SEE ALSO

index(3), **memchr**(3), **rindex**(3), **strchr**(3), **strpbrk**(3), **strsep**(3), **strspn**(3), **strstr**(3)

STRTOL(3) Linux Programmer's Manual STRTOL(3)

NAME

strtol – convert a string to a long integer.

SYNOPSIS

#include <stdlib.h>
long int strtol(const char *nptr, **char** **endptr, **int** base**);**

DESCRIPTION

The **strtol()** function converts the string in *nptr* to a long integer value according to the given *base*, which must be between 2 and 36 inclusive, or be the special value 0.

The string must begin with an arbitrary amount of white space (as determined by **isspace**(3)) followed by a single optional '+' or '-' sign. If *base* is zero or 16, the string may then include a '0x' prefix, and the number will be read in base 16; otherwise, a zero *base* is taken as 10 (decimal) unless the next character is '0', in which case it is taken as 8 (octal).

The remainder of the string is converted to a long int value in the obvious manner, stopping at the first character which is not a valid digit in the given base. (In bases above 10, the letter 'A' in either upper or lower case represents 10, 'B' represents 11, and so forth, with 'Z' representing 35.)

If *endptr* is not NULL, **strtol()** stores the address of the first invalid character in *endptr*. If there were no digits at all, **strtol()** stores the original value of *nptr* in *endptr*. (Thus, if *nptr* is not '\0' but **endptr is '\0' on return, the entire string is valid.)

RETURN VALUE

The **strtol()** function returns the result of the conversion, unless the value would underflow or overflow. If an underflow occurs, **strtol()** returns LONG_MIN. If an overflow occurs, **strtol()** returns LONG_MAX. In both cases, *errno* is set to ERANGE.

ERRORS

    ERANGE   The given string was out of range; the value converted has been clamped.

CONFORMING TO

SVID 3, BSD 4.3, ISO 9899

SEE ALSO

atof(3), **atoi**(3), **atol**(3), **strtod**(3), **strtoul**(3)

BUGS

Ignores the current locale.

STRTOUL(3)

NAME

strtoul – convert a string to an unsigned long integer.

SYNOPSIS

#include <stdlib.h>
unsigned long int strtol(const char *nptr*, **char** **endptr*, **int** *base*);

DESCRIPTION

The **strtoul()** function converts the string in *nptr* to an unsigned long integer value according to the given *base*, which must be between 2 and 36 inclusive, or be the special value 0.

The string must begin with an arbitrary amount of white space (as determined by **isspace**(3)) followed by a single optional '+' or '-' sign. If *base* is zero or 16, the string may then include a '0x' prefix, and the number will be read in base 16; otherwise, a zero *base* is taken as 10 (decimal) unless the next character is '0', in which case it is taken as 8 (octal).

The remainder of the string is converted to an unsigned long int value in the obvious manner, stopping at the first character which is not a valid digit in the given base. (In bases above 10, the letter 'A' in either upper or lower case represents 10, 'B' represents 11, and so forth, with 'Z' representing 35.)

If *endptr* is not NULL, **strtoul()** stores the address of the first invalid character in **endptr*. If there were no digits at all, **strtoul()** stores the original value of *nptr* in **endptr*. (Thus, if **nptr* is not '\0' but ***endptr* is '\0' on return, the entire string is invalid.)

RETURN VALUE

The **strtoul()** function returns either the result of the conversion or, if there was a leading minus sign, the negation of the result of the conversion, unless the original (non-negated) value would overflow; in the latter case, **strtoul()** returns ULONG_MAX and sets the global variable *errno* to ERANGE.

ERRORS

    ERANGE   The given string was out of range; the value converted has been clamped.

CONFORMING TO

SVID 3, BSD 4.3, ISO 9899

SEE ALSO

atof(3), **atoi**(3), **atol**(3), **strtod**(3), **strtol**(3)

BUGS

Ignores the current locale.

NAME

strxfrm – string transformation

SYNOPSIS

#include <string.h>
size_t strxfrm(char *dest***, const char** *src***, size_t** *n***);**

DESCRIPTION

The **strxfrm()** function transforms the *src* string into a form such that the result of **strcmp()** on two strings that have been transformed with **strxfrm()** is the same as the result of **strcoll()** on the two strings before their transformation. The first *n* characters of the transformed string are placed in *dest*. The transformation is based on the program's current locale for category *LC_COLLATE*. (See **setlocale**(3)).

RETURN VALUE

The **strxfrm()** function returns the number of bytes required to store the transformed string in *dest* excluding the terminating '\0' character. If the value returned is *n* or more, the contents of *dest* are indeterminate.

CONFORMING TO

SVID 3, BSD 4.3, ISO 9899

NOTES

The Linux C Library currently hasn't implemented the complete POSIX-collating.

In the *"POSIX"* or *"C"* locales **strxfrm()** is equivalent to copying the string with **strncpy()**.

SEE ALSO

bcmp(3), **memcmp**(3), **strcasecmp**(3), **strcmp**(3), **strcoll**(3), **setlocale**(3)

NAME

swab – swap adjacent bytes

SYNOPSIS

#include <string.h>
void swab(const void *from*, **void** *to*, **size_t** *n*);

DESCRIPTION

The **swab()** function copies *n* bytes from the array pointed to by *from* to the array pointed to by *to*, exchanging adjacent even and odd bytes. This function is used to exchange data between machines that have different low/high byte ordering.

RETURN VALUE

The **swab()** function returns no value.

CONFORMING TO

SVID 3, BSD 4.3

SEE ALSO

bstring(3)

SYSCONF(3)

NAME

sysconf – Get configuration information at runtime

SYNOPSIS

#include <unistd.h>
long sysconf(int *name***);**

DESCRIPTION

sysconf() provides a way for the application to determine values for system limits or options at runtime.

The equivalent macros defined in <**unistd.h**> can only give conservative values; if an application wants to take advantage of values which may change, a call to **sysconf()** can be made, which may yield more liberal results.

For getting information about a particular file, see **fpathconf()** or **pathconf()**.

The following values are supported for *name*. First, the POSIX.1 compatible values:

    _SC_ARG_MAX   The maximum length of the arguments to the **exec()** family of functions; the corresponding macro is **ARG_MAX**.

    _SC_CHILD_MAX   The number of simultaneous processes per user id, the corresponding macro is **_POSIX_CHILD_MAX**.

    _SC_CLK_TCK   The number of clock ticks per second; the corresponding macro is **CLK_TCK**.

    _SC_STREAM_MAX   The maximum number of streams that a process can have open at any time. The corresponding POSIX macro is **STREAM_MAX**, the corresponding standard C macro is **FOPEN_MAX**.

    _SC_TZNAME_MAX   The maximum number of bytes in a timezone name, the corresponding macro is **TZNAME_MAX**.

    _SC_OPEN_MAX   The maximum number of files that a process can have open at any time, the corresponding macro is **_POSIX_OPEN_MAX**.

    _SC_JOB_CONTROL   This indicates whether POSIX – style job control is supported, the corresponding macro is **_POSIX_JOB_CONTROL**.

    _SC_SAVED_IDS   This indicates whether a process has a saved set-user-ID and a saved set-group-ID; the corresponding macro is **_POSIX_SAVED_IDS**.

    _SC_VERSION   indicates the year and month the POSIX.1 standard was approved in the format **YYYYMML;the** value **199009L** indicates the most recent revision, 1990.

Next, the POSIX.2 values:

    _SC_BC_BASE_MAX   indicates the maximum *obase* value accepted by the **bc**(1) utility; the corresponding macro is **BC_BASE_MAX**.

    _SC_BC_DIM_MAX   indicates the maximum value of elements permitted in an array by **bc**(1); the corresponding macro is **BC_DIM_MAX**.

    _SC_BC_SCALE_MAX   indicates the maximum *scale* value allowed by **bc**(1); the corresponding macro is **BC_SCALE_MAX**.

    _SC_BC_STRING_MAX   indicates the maximum length of a string accepted by **bc**(1); the corresponding macro is **BC_STRING_MAX**.

    _SC_COLL_WEIGHTS_MAX   indicates the maximum numbers of weights that can be assigned to an entry of the **LC_COLLATE** order keyword in the locale definition

	file; the corresponding macro is **COLL_WEIGHTS_MAX**.
_SC_EXPR_NEST_MAX	is the maximum number of expressions which can be nested within parentheses by **expr**(1). The corresponding macro is **EXPR_NEST_MAX**.
_SC_LINE_MAX	The maximum length of a utility's input line length, either from standard input or from a file. This includes length for a trailing newline. The corresponding macro is **LINE_MAX**.
_SC_RE_DUP_MAX	The maximum number of repeated occurrences of a regular expression when the interval notation \{m,n\} is used. The value of the corresponding macro is **RE_DUP_MAX**.
_SC_2_VERSION	indicates the version of the POSIX.2 standard in the format of YYYYMML. The corresponding macro is **POSIX2_VERSION**.
_SC_2_DEV	indicates whether the POSIX.2 C language development facilities are supported. The corresponding macro is **POSIX2_C_DEV**.
_SC_2_FORT_DEV	indicates whether the POSIX.2 FORTRAN development utilities are supported. The corresponding macro is **POSIX2_FORT_RUN**.
_SC_2_FORT_RUN	indicates whether the POSIX.2 FORTRAN runtime utilities are supported. The corresponding macro is **POSIX2_FORT_RUN**.
POSIX2_LOCALEDEF	indicates whether the POSIX.2 creation of locates via **locale**(1) is supported. The corresponding macro is **POSIX2_LOCALEDEF**.
_SC_2_SW_DEV	indicates whether the POSIX.2 software development utilities option is supported. The corresponding macro is **POSIX2_SW_DEV**.

RETURN VALUE

The value returned is the value of the system resource, 1 if a queried option is available, 0 if it is not, or −1 on error. The variable *errno* is not set.

CONFORMS TO

POSIX.1, proposed POSIX.2

BUGS

It is difficult use **ARG_MAX** because it is not specified how much of the argument space for **exec**() is consumed by the user's environment variables.

Some returned values may be huge; they are not suitable for allocating memory.

POSIX.2 is not yet an approved standard; the information in this manpage is subject to change.

SEE ALSO

bc(1), **expr**(1), **locale**(1), **fpathconf**(3), **pathconf**(3)

SYSLOG(3)

NAME
closelog, openlog, syslog – send messages to the system logger

SYNOPSIS
#include <syslog.h>

void openlog(char *ident, **int** option, **int** facility**)**

void syslog(int priority, **char** *format, ...**)**

void closelog(void **)**

DESCRIPTION

closelog() closes the descriptor being used to write to the system logger. The use of **closelog()** is optional.

openlog() opens a connection to the system logger for a program. The string pointed to by ident is added to each message, and is typically set to the program name. Values for option and facility are given in the next section. The use of **openlog()** is optional; It will automatically be called by **syslog()** if necessary, in which case ident will default to NULL.

syslog() generates a log message, which will be distributed by **syslogd**(8). priority is a combination of the facility and the level, values for which are given in the next section. The remaining arguments are a format , as in **printf**(3) and any arguments required by the format, except that the two character %m will be replaced by the error message string (strerror) corresponding to the present value of errno.

PARAMETERS

This section list the parameters used to set the values of option, facility, and priority.

option

The option argument to **openlog()** is an OR of any of these:

LOG_CONS	write directly to system console if there is an error while sending to system logger
LOG_NDELAY	open the connection immediately (normally, the connection is opened when the first message is logged)
LOG_PERROR	print to stderr as well
LOG_PID	include PID with each message

facility

The facility argument is used to specify what type of program is logging the message. This lets the configuration file specify that messages from different facilities will be handled differently.

LOG_AUTH	security/authorization messages (DEPRECATED Use **LOG_AUTHPRIV** instead)
LOG_AUTHPRIV	security/authorization messages (private)
LOG_CRON	clock daemon (**cron** and **at**)
LOG_DAEMON	other system daemons
LOG_KERN	kernel messages
LOG_LOCAL0 through **LOG_LOCAL7**	reserved for local use
LOG_LPR	line printer subsystem
LOG_MAIL	mail subsystem
LOG_NEWS	USENET news subsystem
LOG_SYSLOG	messages generated internally by **syslogd**
LOG_USER(default)	generic user-level messages
LOG_UUCP	UUCP subsystem

level
This determines the importance of the message. The levels are, in order of decreasing importance:

LOG_EMERG   system is unusable
LOG_ALERT   action must be taken immediately
LOG_CRIT   critical conditions
LOG_ERR   error conditions
LOG_WARNING warning conditions
LOG_NOTICE normal, but significant, condition
LOG_INFO   informational message
LOG_DEBUG   debug-level message

HISTORY
A **syslog** function call appeared in BSD 4.2.

SEE ALSO
logger(1), **syslog.conf**(5), **syslogd**(8)

NAME

system – execute a shell command

SYNOPSIS

#include <stdlib.h>
int system (const char * *string***);**

DESCRIPTION

system() executes a command specified in *string* by calling **/bin/sh -c** *string*, and returns after the command has been completed. During execution of the command, **SIGCHLD** will be blocked, and **SIGINT** and **SIGQUIT** will be ignored.

RETURN VALUE

The value returned is 127 if the **execve()** call for **/bin/sh** fails, −1 if there was another error and the return code of the command otherwise.

If the value of *string* is **NULL**, **system()** returns nonzero if the shell is available, and zero if not.

system() does not affect the wait status of any other children.

CONFORMS TO

ANSI C, POSIX.1, proposed POSIX.2, BSD 4.3

BUGS

Do not use **system()** from a program with suid or sgid privileges, because strange values for some environment variables might be used to subvert system integrity. Use the **exec**(2) family of functions instead, but not **execlp**(2) or **execvp**(2).

The check for the availability of **/bin/sh** is not actually performed; it is always assumed to be available.

It is possible for the shell command to return 127, so that code is not a sure indication that the **execve()** call failed; check *errno* to make sure.

SEE ALSO

sh(1), **exec**(2), **signal**(2)

TAN(3)

NAME

tan – tangent function

SYNOPSIS

#include <math.h>
double tan(double *x***);**

DESCRIPTION

The **tan()** function returns the tangent of *x*, where *x* is given in radians.

CONFORMING TO

SVID 3, POSIX, BSD 4.3, ISO 9899

SEE ALSO

acos(3), **asin**(3), **atan**(3), **atan2**(3), **cos**(3), **sin**(3)

NAME

tanh – hyperbolic tangent function

SYNOPSIS

#include <math.h>
double tanh(double x**);**

DESCRIPTION

The **tanh()** function returns the hyperbolic tangent of x, which is defined mathematically as sinh(x) / cosh(x).

CONFORMING TO

SVID 3, POSIX, BSD 4.3, ISO 9899

SEE ALSO

acosh(3), **asinh**(3), **atanh**(3), **cosh**(3), **sinh**(3)

NAME

telldir – return current location in directory stream.

SYNOPSIS

#include <dirent.h>
off_t telldir(DIR **dir***);**

DESCRIPTION

The **telldir()** function returns the current location associated with the directory stream *dir*.

RETURN VALUE

The **telldir()** function returns the current location in the directory stream or −1 if an error occurs.

ERRORS

EBADF   Invalid directory stream descriptor *dir*.

CONFORMING TO

BSD 4.3

SEE ALSO

opendir(3), **readdir**(3), **closedir**(3), **rewinddir**(3), **seekdir**(3), **scandir**(3)

NAME

tempnam – create a name for a temporary file

SYNOPSIS

#include <stdio.h>

char *tempnam(const char **dir***, const char ****pfx***);**

DESCRIPTION

The **tempnam()** function generates a unique temporary filename using up to five characters of *pfx*, if it is not NULL. The directory to place the file is searched for in the following order:-

a) The directory specified by the environment variable *TMPDIR*, if it is writable.

b) The directory specified by the argument *dir*, if it is not NULL.

c) The directory specified by *P_tmpdir*.

d) The directory *tmp*.
   The storage for the filename is allocated by **malloc()**, and so can be free'd by the function **free()**.

RETURN VALUE

The **tempnam()** function returns a pointer to the unique temporary filename, or NULL if a unique filename cannot be generated.

ERRORS

    EEXIST   Unable to generate a unique filename.

CONFORMING TO

SVID 3, BSD 4.3

SEE ALSO

mktemp(3), **mkstemp**(3), **tmpnam**(3), **tmpfile**(3)

NAME

tmpfile – create a temporary file

SYNOPSIS

#include <stdio.h>
FILE *tmpfile (void);

DESCRIPTION

The **tmpfile()** function generates a unique temporary filename using the path prefix *P_tmpdir* defined in <*stdio.h*>. The temporary file is then opened in binary read/write (w+b) mode. The file will be automatically deleted when it is closed or the program terminates.

RETURN VALUE

The **tmpfile()** function returns a stream descriptor, or NULL if a unique filename cannot be generated or the unique file cannot be opened.

ERRORS

EACCES	Search permission denied for directory in file's path prefix.
EEXIST	Unable to generate a unique filename.
EMFILE	Too many file descriptors in use by process.
ENFILE	Too many files open in system.
EROFS	Read-only filesystem.

CONFORMING TO

SVID 3, POSIX, BSD 4.3, ISO 9899

SEE ALSO

mktemp(3), **mkstemp**(3), **tmpnam**(3), **tempnam**(3)

NAME

tmpnam – create a name for a temporary file

SYNOPSIS

#include <stdio.h>
char *tmpnam(char *s);

DESCRIPTION

The **tmpnam()** function generates a unique temporary filename using the path prefix *P_tmpdir* defined in <*stdio.h*>. If the argument *s* is NULL, **tmpnam()** returns the address of an internal static area which holds the filename, which is overwritten by subsequent calls to **tmpnam()**. If *s* is not NULL, the filename is returned in *s*.

RETURN VALUE

The **tmpnam()** function returns a pointer to the unique temporary filename, or NULL if a unique name cannot be generated.

ERRORS

EEXIST   Unable to generate a unique filename.

CONFORMING TO

SVID 3, POSIX, BSD 4.3, ISO 9899

SEE ALSO

mktemp(3), **mkstemp**(3), **tempnam**(3), **tmpfile**(3)

NAME

toupper, tolower – convert letter to upper or lower case

SYNOPSIS

#include <ctype.h>
int toupper (int c);
int tolower (int c);

DESCRIPTION

toupper() converts the letter c to upper case, if possible.

tolower() converts the letter c to lower case, if possible.

RETURN VALUE

The value returned is that of the converted letter, or c if the conversion was not possible.

CONFORMS TO

ANSI - C, BSD 4.3

BUGS

The details of what constitutes an uppercase or lowercase letter depend on the current locale. For example, the default locale does not know about umlauts, so no conversion is done for them.

In some non - English locales, there are lowercase letters with no corresponding uppercase equivalent; the German sharp s is one example.

SEE ALSO

isalpha(3), **setlocale**(3), **locale**(7)

TTYNAME(3)

NAME

ttyname – return name of a terminal

SYNOPSIS

#include <unistd.h>
char *ttyname (int *desc* **);**

DESCRIPTION

Returns a pointer to the pathname of the terminal device that is open on the file descriptor *desc*, or **NULL** on error (for example, if *desc* is not connected to a terminal).

CONFORMING TO

POSIX.1

SEE ALSO

isatty(3), **fstat**(3)

TZSET(3)

NAME

tzset – initialize time conversion information

SYNOPSIS

#include <time.h>
void tzset (void);
extern char **tzname*[2]

DESCRIPTION

The **tzset()** function initializes the *tzname* variable from the TZ environment variable. This function is automatically called by the other time conversion functions that depend on the time zone.

If the TZ variable does not appear in the environment, the *tzname* variable is initialized with the best approximation of local wall clock time, as specified by the **tzfile**(5)-format file */usr/lib/zoneinfo/localtime*.

If the TZ variable does appear in the environment but its value is NULL or its value cannot be interpreted using any of the formats specified below, Coordinated Universal Time (UTC) is used.

The value of TZ can be one of three formats. The first format is used when there is no daylight saving time in the local time zone:

std offset

The *std* string specifies the name of the time zone and must be three or more alphabetic characters. The *offset* string immediately follows *std* and specifies the time value to be added to the local time to get Coordinated Universal Time (UTC). The *offset* is positive if the local time zone is west of the Prime Meridian and negative if it is east. The hour must be between 0 and 24, and the minutes and seconds 0 and 59.

The second format is used when there is daylight saving time:

std offset dst [offset],start[/time],end[/time]

There are no spaces in the specification. The initial *std* and *offset* specify the standard time zone, as described above. The *dst* string and *offset* specify the name and offset for the corresponding daylight savings time zone. If the offset is omitted, it defaults to one hour ahead of standard time.

The *start* field specifies when daylight savings time goes into effect and the *end* field specifies when the change is made back to standard time. These fields may have the following formats:

> J*n*   This specifies the Julian day with *n* between 1 and 365. February 29 is never counted even in leap years.
>
> *n*   This specifies the Julian day with *n* between 1 and 365. February 29 is counted in leap years.
>
> M*m.w.d*   This specifies day *d* (0 <= *d* <= 6) of week *w* (1 <= *w* <= 5) of month *m* (1 <= *m* <= 12). Week 1 is the first week in which day *d* occurs and week 5 is the last week in which day *d* occurs. Day 0 is a Sunday.

The *time* fields specify when, in the local time currently in effect, the change to the other time occurs. If omitted, the default is 02:00:00.

The third format specifies that the time zone information should be read from a file:

:[filespec]

If the file specification *filespec* is omitted, the time zone information is read from */usr/lib/zoneinfo/localtime* which is in tzfile(5) format. If *filespec* is given, it specifies another tzfile(5)-format file to read the time zone information from. If *filespec* does not begin with a '/', the file specification is relative to the system time conversion information directory */usr/lib/zoneinfo*.

FILES

/usr/lib/zoneinfo system time zone directory
/usr/lib/zoneinfo/localtime local time zone file
/usr/lib/zoneinfo/posixrules rules for POSIX-style TZ's

CONFORMING TO

SVID 3, POSIX, BSD 4.3

SEE ALSO

date(1), **gettimeofday**(2), **time**(2), **ctime**(3), **getenv**(3), **tzfile**(5)

NAME

usleep – suspend execution for interval of microseconds

SYNOPSIS

#include <unistd.h>
void usleep(unsigned long *usec***);**

DESCRIPTION

The **usleep()** function suspends execution of the calling process for *usec* microseconds. The sleep may be lengthened slightly by any system activity or by the time spent processing the call.

CONFORMING TO

BSD 4.3

SEE ALSO

setitimer(2), **getitimer**(2), **sleep**(3), **alarm**(3), **select**(3)

NAME

wcstombs – convert a wide character string to a multibyte character string.

SYNOPSIS

#include <stdlib.h>
size_t wcstombs(char **s,* **const wchar_t** **pwcs,* **size_t** *n***);**

DESCRIPTION

The **wcstombs()** function converts a sequence of wide characters from the array *pwcs* into a sequence of multibyte characters and stores up to *n* bytes of multibyte characters in the array *s*.

RETURN VALUE

wcstombs() returns the number of bytes stored in *s* or −1 if *s* contains an invalid wide character.

CONFORMING TO

SVID 3, ISO 9899

SEE ALSO

mblen(3), **mbtowc**(3), **mbstowcs**(3), **wctomb**(3)

NAME

wctomb – convert a wide character to a multibyte character.

SYNOPSIS

#include <stdlib.h>
int wctomb(char *s***, wchar_t** *wchar***);**

DESCRIPTION

The **wctomb()** function converts a wide character *wchar* into a multibyte character and, if *s* is not NULL, stores the multibyte character representation in *s*.

RETURN VALUE

wctomb() returns the number of bytes in the multibyte character or –1 if the wide character is not valid.

CONFORMING TO

SVID 3, ISO 9899

SEE ALSO

mblen(3), **mbstowcs**(3), **mbtowc**(3), **wcstombs**(3)

Section IV

Special files

NAME

intro – Introduction to special files

DESCRIPTION

This chapter describes special files.

FILES

/dev/* — device files

AUTHORS

Look at the header of the manual page for the author(s) and copyright conditions. Note that these can be different from page to page!

NAME

console – console terminal and virtual consoles

DESCRIPTION

A Linux system has up to 63 *virtual consoles* (character devices with major number 4 and minor number 1 to 63), usually called **/dev/tty**n with 1 n 63. The current console is also addressed by **/dev/console** or **/dev/tty0**, the character device with major number 4 and minor number 0. The device files /dev/* are usually created using the script MAKEDEV, or using mknod(1), usually with mode 0622 and owner root.tty.

Before kernel version 1.1.54 the number of virtual consoles was compiled into the kernel (in tty.h: #define NR_CONSOLES 8) and could be changed by editing and recompiling. Since version 1.1.54 virtual consoles are created on the fly, as soon as they are needed.

Common ways to start a process on a console are: (a) tell init(8) (in inittab(5)) to start a getty(8) on the console; (b) ask open(1) to start a process on the console; (c) start X - it will find the first unused console, and display its output there. (There is also the ancient doshell(8).)

Common ways to switch consoles are: (a) use Alt+Fn or Ctrl+Alt+Fn to switch to console n; AltGr+Fn might bring you to console n+12 [here Alt and AltGr refer to the left and right Alt keys, respectively]; (b) use Alt+RightArrow or Alt+LeftArrow to cycle through the presently allocated consoles; (c) use the program chvt(1). (The key mapping is user settable, see loadkeys(1); the above mentioned key combinations are according to the default settings.)

The command **disalloc**(8) will free the memory taken by the screen buffers for consoles that no longer have any associated process.

PROPERTIES

Consoles carry a lot of state. I hope to document that some other time. The most important fact is that the consoles simulate vt100 terminals. In particular, a console is reset to the initial state by printing the two characters ESC c.

FILES

/dev/console
*/dev/tty**

SEE ALSO

console_ioctl(4), **chvt**(1), **loadkeys**(1), **mknod**(1), **open**(1), **tty**(4), **ttys**(4), **disalloc**(8), **getty**(8), **init**(8), **resizecons**(8), **setfont**(8), **mapscrn**(8)

NAME

console ioctl's – ioctl's for console terminal and virtual consoles

DESCRIPTION

WARNING: If you use the following information you are going to burn yourself.

WARNING: ioctl's are undocumented Linux internals, liable to be changed without warning. Use POSIX functions.

The following Linux-peculiar **ioctl()** requests are supported. Each requires a third argument, assumed here to be *argp*.

KDGETLED Get state of LEDs. *argp* points to a long int. The lower three bits of *argp are set to the state of the LEDs, as follows:
LED_CAP 0x04 caps lock led LEC_NUM 0x02 num lock led LED_SCR 0x01 scroll lock led

KDSETLED Set the LEDs. The LEDs are set to correspond to the lower three bits of *argp*. However, if a higher order bit is set, the LEDs revert to normal: displaying the state of the keyboard functions of caps lock, num lock, and scroll lock.

Before 1.1.54, the leds just reflected the state of the corresponding keyboard flags, and KDGETLED/KDSETLED would also change the keyboard flags. Since 1.1.54 the leds can be made to display arbitrary information, but by default they display the keyboard flags. The following two ioctl's are used to access the keyboard flags.

KDGKBLED Get keyboard flags CapsLock, NumLock, ScrollLock (not lights). *argp* points to a char which is set to the flag state. The low order three bits (mask 0x7) get the current flag state, and the low order bits of the next nibble (mask 0x70) get the default flag state. (Since 1.1.54)

KDSKBLED Set keyboard flags CapsLock, NumLock, ScrollLock (not lights). *argp* has the desired flag state. The low order three bits (mask 0x7) have the flag state, and the low order bits of the next nibble (mask 0x70) have the default flag state. (Since 1.1.54)

KDGKBTYPE Get keyboard type. This returns the value KB_101, defined as 0x02.

KDADDIO Add I/O port as valid. Equivalent to ioperm(arg,1,1).

KDDELIO Delete I/O port as valid. Equivalent to ioperm(arg,1,0).

KDENABIO Enable I/O to video board. Equivalent to ioperm(0x3b4, 0x3df-0x3b4+1, 1).

KDDISABIO Disable I/O to video board. Equivalent to ioperm(0x3b4, 0x3df-0x3b4+1, 0).

KDSETMODE Set text/graphics mode. *argp* is one of these:
KD_TEXT 0x00 KD_GRAPHICS 0x01

KDGETMODE Get text/graphics mode. *argp* points to a long which is set to one of the above values.

KDMKTONE Generate tone of specified length. The lower 16 bits of *argp* specify the period in clock cycles, and the upper 16 bits give the duration in msec. If the duration is zero, the sound is turned off. Control returns immediately. For example, *argp* = (125<<16) + 0x637 would specify the beep normally associated with a ctrl-G.

KIOCSOUND Start or stop sound generation. The lower 16 bits of *argp* specify the period in clock cycles (that is, *argp* = 1193180/frequency). *argp* = 0 turns sound off. In either case, control returns immediately.

GIO_FONT Gets screen font in expanded form. *argp* points to an 8192 byte array.

PIO_FONT Sets screen font. Load font into the EGA/VGA character generator. *argp* points to a 8192 byte map, with 32 bytes per character. Only first N of them are used for an 8xN font ($0 < N <= 32$).

GIO_SCRNMAP Get screen mapping from kernel. *argp* points to an area of size E_TABSZ.

PIO_SCRNMAP Loads the "user definable" (fourth) table in the kernel which maps bytes into console screen symbols. *argp* points to an area of size E_TABSZ.

GIO_UNIMAP Get unicode-to-font mapping from kernel. *argp* points to a
struct unimapdesc {
u_short *entry_ct*;
struct unipair **entries*;
};
where *entries* points to an array of
struct unipair {
u_short *unicode*;
u_short *fontpos*;
};
(Since 1.1.92.)

PIO_UNIMAP Put unicode-to-font mapping in kernel. *argp* points to a struct unimapdesc. (Since 1.1.92)

PIO_UNIMAPCLR Clear table, possibly advise hash algorithm. *argp* points to a
struct unimapinit {
u_short *advised_hashsize*; /* 0 if no opinion */
u_short *advised_hashstep*; /* 0 if no opinion */
u_short *advised_hashlevel*; /* 0 if no opinion */
};
(Since 1.1.92.)

KDGKBMODE Gets current keyboard mode. *argp* points to a long which is set to one of these:
K_RAW 0x00 K_XLATE 0x01 K_MEDIUMRAW 0x02 K_UNICODE 0x03

KDSKBMODE Sets current keyboard mode. *argp* is a long equal to one of the above values.

KDGKBMETA Gets meta key handling mode. *argp* points to a long which is set to one of these:
K_METABIT 0x03 set high order bit K_ESCPREFIX 0x04 escape prefix

KDSKBMETA Sets meta key handling mode. *argp* is a long equal to one of the above values.

KDGKBENT Gets one entry in key translation table (keycode to action code). *argp* points to a
struct kbentry {
u_char *kb_table*;
u_char *kb_index*;
u_short *kb_value*;
};
with the first two members filled in: *kb_table* selects the key table (0 <= *kb_table* < MAX_NR_KEYMAPS), and *kb_index* is the keycode (0 <= *kb_index* < NR_KEYS). *kb_value* is set to the corresponding action code, or K_HOLE if there is no such key, or K_NOSUCHMAP if *kb_table* is invalid.

KDSKBENT Sets one entry in translation table. *argp* points to a struct kbentry.

KDGKBSENT Gets one function key string. *argp* points to a
struct kbsentry {
u_char *kb_func*;
u_char *kb_string*[512];
};
kb_string is set to the (NULL terminated) string corresponding to the *kb_func*th function key action code.

KDSKBSENT Sets one function key string entry. *argp* points to a struct kbsentry.

KDGKBDIACR Read kernel accent table. *argp* points to a

```
struct kbdiacrs {
unsigned int kb_cnt;
struct kbdiacr kbdiacr[256];
};
```

where *kb_cnt* is the number of entries in the array, each of which is a
struct kbdiacr { u_char *diacr, base, result*; };

KDGETKEYCODE Read kernel keycode table entry (scan code to keycode). *argp* points to a

struct kbkeycode { unsigned int *scancode, keycode*; };

keycode is set to correspond to the given *scancode*. (89 <= *scancode* <= 255 only. For 1 <= *scancode* <= 88, *keycode*==*scancode*.) (Since 1.1.63.)

KDSETKEYCODE Write kernel keycode table entry. *argp* points to struct kbkeycode. (Since 1.1.63.)

KDSIGACCEPT The calling process indicates its willingness to accept the signal *argp* when it is generated by pressing an appropriate key combination. (1 <= *argp* <= NSIG).
(See spawn_console() in linux/drivers/char/keyboard.c.)

VT_OPENQRY Returns the first available (non-opened) console. *argp* points to an int which is set to the number of the vt (1 <= *argp* <= MAX_NR_CONSOLES).

VT_GETMODE Get mode of active vt. *argp* points to a

```
struct vt_mode {
char mode; /* vt mode */
char waitv; /* if set, hang on writes if not active */
short relsig; /* signal to raise on release req */
short acqsig; /* signal to raise on acquisition */
short frsig; /* unused (set to 0) */
};
```

...which is set to the mode of the active vt. *mode* is set to one of these values:
VT_AUTO auto vt switching VT_PROCESS process controls switching VT_ACKACQ acknowledge switch

VT_SETMODE Set mode of active vt. *argp* points to a struct vt_mode.

VT_GETSTATE Get global vt state info. *argp* points to a

```
struct vt_stat {
ushort v_active; /* active vt */
ushort v_signal; /* signal to send */
ushort v_state; /* vt bitmask */
};
```

For each vt in use, the corresponding bit in the *v_state* member is set. (Kernels 1.0 through 1.1.92.)

VT_RELDISP Release a display.

VT_ACTIVATE Switch to vt *argp* (1 <= *argp* <= MAX_NR_CONSOLES).

VT_WAITACTIVE Wait until vt *argp* has been activated.

VT_DISALLOCATE Deallocate the memory associated with vt *argp*. (Since 1.1.54.)

VT_RESIZE Set kernel's idea of screensize. *argp* points to a

```
struct vt_sizes {
ushort v_rows; /* # rows */
ushort v_cols; /* # columns */
ushort v_scrollsize; /* no longer used */
};
```

(Since 1.1.54.) Note that this does not change the videomode. See resizecons(8).

The action of the following ioctls depends on the first byte in the struct pointed to by *argp*, referred to here as the *subcode*. These are legal only for the superuser or the owner of the current tty.

"TIOCLINUX, subcode=0" Dump the screen. Disappeared in 1.1.92. (With kernel 1.1.92 or later, read from /dev/vcsN or /dev/vcsaN instead.)

"TIOCLINUX, subcode=1" Get task information. Disappeared in 1.1.92.

"TIOCLINUX, subcode=2" Set selection. *argp* points to a
struct {char *subcode*; short *xs, ys, xe, ye*; short *sel_mode*; }
xs and *ys* are the starting column and row. *xe* and *ye* are the ending column and row. (Upper left corner is row=column=1.) *sel_mode* is 0 for character-by-character selection, 1 for word-by-word selection, or 2 for line-by-line selection. The indicated screen characters are highlighted and saved in the static array sel_buffer in devices/char/console.c.

"TIOCLINUX, subcode=3" Paste selection. The characters in the selection buffer are written to *fd*.

"TIOCLINUX, subcode=4" Unblank the screen.

"TIOCLINUX, subcode=5" Sets contents of a 256-bit look up table defining characters in a "word", for word-by-word selection. (Since 1.1.32.)

"TIOCLINUX, subcode=6" *argp* points to a char which is set to the value of the kernel variable *shift_state*. (Since 1.1.32.)

"TIOCLINUX, subcode=7" *argp* points to a char which is set to the value of the kernel variable *report_mouse*. (Since 1.1.33.)

"TIOCLINUX, subcode=8" Dump screen width and height, cursor position, and all the character-attribute pairs. (Kernels 1.1.67 through 1.1.91 only. With kernel 1.1.92 or later, read from /dev/vcsa* instead.)

"TIOCLINUX, subcode=9" Restore screen width and height, cursor position, and all the character-attribute pairs. (Kernels 1.1.67 through 1.1.91 only. With kernel 1.1.92 or later, write to /dev/vcsa* instead.)

"TIOCLINUX, subcode=10" Handles the Power Saving feature of the new generation of monitors. VESA screen blanking mode is set to *argp*[1], which governs what screen blanking does:

0: Screen blanking is disabled.

1: The current video adapter register settings are saved, then the controller is programmed to turn off the vertical synchronization pulses. This puts the monitor into "standby" mode. If your monitor has an Off_Mode timer, then it will eventually power down by itself.

2: The current settings are saved, then both the vertical and horizontal synchronization pulses are turned off. This puts the monitor into "off" mode. If your monitor has no Off_Mode timer, or if you want your monitor to power down immediately when the blank_timer times out, then you choose this option. (*Caution:* Powering down frequently will damage the monitor.)

(Since 1.1.76.)

RETURN VALUES

-1 for error, and *errno* is set.

ERRORS

errno may take on these values:

EBADF	file descriptor is invalid.
%	ENOTTY file descriptor is not associated with a character special device, or the specified request does not apply to it.
EINVAL	file descriptor or *argp* is invalid.
EPERM	permission violation.

CONSOLE_IOCTLS(4)   Linux Programmer's Manual   CONSOLE_IOCTLS(4)

WARNING

Do not regard this man page as documentation of the Linux console ioctl's. This is provided for the curious only, as an alternative to reading the source. Ioctl's are undocumented Linux internals, liable to be changed without warning. (And indeed, this page more or less describes the situation as of kernel version 1.1.94; there are many minor and not-so-minor differences with earlier versions.)

Very often, ioctl's are introduced for communication between the kernel and one particular well-known program (fdisk, hdparm, setserial, tunelp, loadkeys, selection, setfont, etc.), and their behavior will be changed when required by this particular program.

Programs using these ioctl's will not be portable to other versions of Unix, will not work on older versions of Linux, and will not work on future versions of Linux.

Use POSIX functions.

SEE ALSO

kbd_mode(1), loadkeys(1), dumpkeys(1), mknod(1), setleds(1), setmetamode(1), ioperm(2), termios(2), execve(2), fcntl(2), mt(4), sd(4), tty(4), ttys(4), vcs(4), vcsa(4), mapscrn(8), setfont(8), resizecons(8), */usr/include/linux/kd.h*, */usr/include/linux/vt.h*

Linux   April 20, 1995   902

NAME

fd – floppy disk device

CONFIGURATION

Floppy drives are block devices with major number 2. Typically they are owned by root.floppy and have either mode 0660 (access checking via group membership) or mode 0666 (everybody has access). For the following devices, *n* is the drive number. It is 0 for the first drive, 1 for the second etc. To get a minor number for a specific drive connected to the first controller, add *n* to the minor base number. If it is connected to the second controller, add *n*+128 to the minor base number. **Warning: If you use formats with more tracks than supported by your drive, you may damage it mechanically.** Trying once if more tracks than the usual 40/80 are supported should not damage it, but no warranty is given for that. Don't create device entries for those formats to prevent their usage if you are not sure.

Drive independent device files which automatically detect the media format and capacity:

Name	Base minor #
fd*n*	0

5.25 inch double density device files:

Name	Capac.	Cyl.	Sect.	Heads	Base minor #
fd*n*d360	360K	40	9	2	4

5.25 inch high density device files:

Name	Capac.	Cyl.	Sect.	Heads	Base minor #
fd*n*h360	360K	40	9	2	20
fd*n*h410	410K	41	10	2	48
fd*n*h420	420K	42	10	2	64
fd*n*h720	720K	80	9	2	24
fd*n*h880	880K	80	11	2	80
fd*n*h1200	1200K	80	15	2	8
fd*n*h1440	1440K	80	18	2	40
fd*n*h1476	1476K	82	18	2	56
fd*n*h1494	1494K	83	18	2	72
fd*n*h1600	1600K	80	20	2	92

3.5 inch double density device files:

Name	Capac.	Cyl.	Sect.	Heads	Base minor #
fd*n*D360	360K	80	9	1	12
fd*n*D720	720K	80	9	2	16
fd*n*D800	800K	80	10	2	120
fd*n*D1040	1040K	80	13	2	84
fd*n*D1120	1120K	80	14	2	88

3.5 inch high density device files:

Name	Capac.	Cyl.	Sect.	Heads	Base minor #
fd*n*H360	360K	40	9	2	12
fd*n*H720	720K	80	9	2	16
fd*n*H820	820K	82	10	2	52
fd*n*H830	830K	83	10	2	68
fd*n*H1440	1440K	80	18	2	28
fd*n*H1600	1600K	80	20	2	124
fd*n*H1680	1680K	80	21	2	44
fd*n*H1722	1722K	82	21	2	60
fd*n*H1743	1743K	83	21	2	76
fd*n*H1760	1760K	80	22	2	96
fd*n*H1840	1840K	80	23	2	116
fd*n*H1920	1920K	80	24	2	100

3.5 inch extra density device files:

Name	Capac.	Cyl.	Sect.	Heads	Base minor #
fdnE2880	2880K	80	36	2	32
fdnCompaQ	2880K	80	36	2	36
fdnE3200	3200K	80	40	2	104
fdnE3520	3520K	80	44	2	108
fdnE3840	3840K	80	48	2	112

DESCRIPTION

fd special files access the floppy disk drives in raw mode. The following **ioctl**(2) calls are supported by **fd** devices:

FDCLRPRM clears the media information of a drive (geometry of disk in drive).

FDSETPRM sets the media information of a drive. The media information will be lost when the media is changed.

FDDEFPRM sets the media information of a drive (geometry of disk in drive). The media information will not be lost when the media is changed. This will disable auto-detection. In order to re-enable autodetection, you have to issue an **FDCLRPRM** .

FDGETDRVTYP displays the type of a drive (name parameter). For formats which work in several drive types, **FDGETDRVTYP** returns a name which is appropriate for the oldest drive type which supports this format.

FDFLUSH invalidates the buffer cache for the given drive.

FDFLUSH invalidates the buffer cache for the given drive.

FDSETMAXERRS sets the error thresholds for reporting errors, aborting the operation, recalibrating, resetting, and reading sector by sector.

FDSETMAXERRS gets the current error tresholds.

FDGETDRVTYP gets the internal name of the drive.

FDWERRORCLR clears the write error statistics.

FDWERRORGET reads the write error statistics. These include the total number of write errors, the location and disk of the first write error, and the location and disk of the last write error. Disks are identified by a generation number which is incremented at (almost) each disk change.

FDTWADDLE Switch the drive motor off for a few microseconds. This might be needed in order to access a disk whose sectors are too close together.

FDSETDRVPRM sets various drive parameters.

FDGETDRVPRM reads these parameters back.

FDGETDRVSTAT gets the cached drive state (disk changed, write protected et al.)

FDPOLLDRVSTAT polls the drive and return its state.

FDGETFDCSTAT gets the floppy controller state.

FDRESET resets the floppy controller under certain conditions.

FDRAWCMD sends a raw command to the floppy controller.

For more precise information, consult also the <linux/fd.h> and <linux/fdreg.h> include files, as well as the manual page for floppycontrol.

NOTES

The various formats allow to read and write many types of disks. However, if a floppy is formatted with a too small inter sector gap, performance may drop, up to needing a few seconds to access an entire track. To prevent this, use interleaved formats. It is not possible to read floppies which are formatted using GCR (group code recording), which is used by Apple II and Macintosh computers (800k disks). Reading floppies which are hard sectored (one hole per sector, with the index hole being a little skewed) is not supported. This used to be common with older 8 inch floppies.

FILES
/dev/fd*

AUTHORS
Alain Knaff (Alain.Knaff@imag.fr), David Niemi (niemidc@clark.net), Bill Broadhurst (bbroad@netcom.com).

SEE ALSO
floppycontrol(1), **mknod**(1), **chown**(1), **getfdprm**(1), **superformat**(1), **mount**(8), **setfdprm**(8)

NAME

hd – MFM/IDE hard disk device

DESCRIPTION

Hd* are block devices to access the MFM/IDE hard disk drives in raw mode.

They are typically created by:

mknod -m 660 /dev/hda b 3 0
mknod -m 660 /dev/hda1 b 3 1
mknod -m 660 /dev/hda2 b 3 2
...
mknod -m 660 /dev/hda8 b 3 8
mknod -m 660 /dev/hdb b 3 64
mknod -m 660 /dev/hdb1 b 3 65
mknod -m 660 /dev/hdb2 b 3 66
...
mknod -m 660 /dev/hdb8 b 3 72
chown root.disk /dev/hd*

FILES

/dev/hd*

SEE ALSO

mknod(1), **chown**(1), **mount**(8)

NAME

lp – line printer devices

SYNOPSIS

#include <linux/lp.h>

CONFIGURATION

lp[02] are character devices for the parallel line printers; they have major number 6 and minor number 02. The minor numbers correspond to the printer port base addresses 0x03bc, 0x0378 and 0x0278. Usually they have mode 220 and are owned by root and group lp. You can use printer ports either with polling or with interrupts. Interrupts are recommended when high traffic is expected, e.g. for laser printers. For usual dot matrix printers polling will usually be enough. The default is polling.

DESCRIPTION

The following *ioctl*(2) calls are supported:

int ioctl(int *fd*, **LPTIME, int** *arg*) Sets the amount of time that the driver sleeps before rechecking the printer when the printer's buffer appears to be filled to *arg*. If you have a fast printer, decrease this number; if you have a slow printer then increase it. This is in hundredths of a second, the default 2 being 0.05 seconds. It only influences the polling driver.

int ioctl(int *fd*, **LPCHAR, int** *arg*) Sets the maximum number of busy-wait iterations which the polling driver does while waiting for the printer to get ready for receiving a character to *arg*. If printing is too slow, increase this number; if the system gets too slow, decrease this number. The default is 1000. It only influences the polling driver.

int ioctl(int *fd*, **LPABORT, int** *arg*) If *arg* is 0, the printer driver will retry on errors, otherwise it will abort. The default is 0.

int ioctl(int *fd*, **LPABORTOPEN, int** *arg*) If *arg* is 0, *open*(2) will be aborted on error, otherwise error will be ignored. The default is to ignore it.

int ioctl(int *fd*, **LPCAREFUL, int** *arg*) If *arg* is 0, then the out-of-paper, offline and error signals are required to be false on all writes, otherwise they are ignored. The default is to ignore them.

int ioctl(int *fd*, **LPWAIT, int** *arg*) Sets the number of busy waiting iterations to wait before strobing the printer to accept a just-written character, and the number of iterations to wait before turning the strobe off again, to *arg*. The specification says this time should be 0.5 microseconds, but experience has shown the delay caused by the code is already enough. For that reason, the default value is 0. This is used for both the polling and the interrupt driver.

int ioctl(int *fd*, **LPSETIRQ, int** *arg*) This ioctl() requires superuser privileges. It takes an int containing the new IRQ as argument. As a side effect, the printer will be reset. When *arg* is 0, the polling driver will be used, which is also default.

int ioctl(int *fd*, **LPGETIRQ, int** *arg) Stores the currently used IRQ in *arg*.

int ioctl(int *fd*, **LPGETSTATUS, int** *arg) Stores the value of the status port in *arg*. The bits have the following meaning:

LP_PBUSY	inverted busy input, active high
LP_PACK	unchanged acknowledge input, active low
LP_POUTPA	unchanged out-of-paper input, active high
LP_PSELECD	unchanged selected input, active high
LP_PERRORP	unchanged error input, active low

Refer to your printer manual for the meaning of the signals. Note that undocumented bits may also be set, depending on your printer.

int ioctl(int *fd*, **LPRESET**)Resets the printer. No argument is used.

FILES
/dev/lp*

AUTHORS
The printer driver was originally written by Jim Weigand and Linus Torvalds. It was further improved by Michael K. Johnson. The interrupt code was written by Nigel Gamble. Alan Cox modularised it. LPCAREFUL, LPABORT, LPGETSTATUS were added by Chris Metcalf.

SEE ALSO
mknod(1), **chown**(1), **chmod**(1), **tunelp**(8), **lpcntl**(8)

NAME

mem, kmem, port – system memory, kernel memory and system ports

DESCRIPTION

Mem is a character device file that is an image of the main memory of the computer. It may be used, for example, to examine (and even patch) the system.

Byte addresses in mem are interpreted as physical memory addresses. References to non-existent locations cause errors to be returned.

Examining and patching is likely to lead to unexpected results when read-only or write-only bits are present.

It is typically created by:

mknod -m 660 /dev/mem c 1 1
chown root.mem /dev/mem

The file kmem is the same as mem, except that the kernel virtual memory rather than physical memory is accessed.

It is typically created by:

mknod -m 640 /dev/kmem c 1 2
chown root.mem /dev/kmem

Port is similar to mem, but the IO ports are accessed.

It is typically created by:

mknod -m 660 /dev/port c 1 4
chown root.mem /dev/port

FILES

/dev/mem
/dev/kmem
/dev/port

SEE ALSO

mknod(1), **chown**(1), **ioperm**(2)

NAME

null, zero – data sink

DESCRIPTION

Data written on a **null** or **zero** special file is discarded.

Reads from the **null** special file always return end of file, whereas reads from **zero** always return \0 characters.

null and **zero** are typically created by:

mknod -m 666 /dev/null c 1 3
mknod -m 666 /dev/zero c 1 5
chown root.mem /dev/null /dev/zero

NOTES

If these devices are not writable and readable for all users, many programs will act strange.

FILES

/dev/null
/dev/zero

SEE ALSO

mknod(1), **chown**(1)

RAM(4)

NAME

ram – ram disk device

DESCRIPTION

Ram is a block device to access the ram disk in raw mode.

It is typically created by:

mknod -m 660 /dev/ram b 1 1
chown root.disk /dev/ram

FILES

/dev/ram

SEE ALSO

mknod(1), **chown**(1), **mount**(8)

SD(4)

NAME
sd – Driver for SCSI Disk Drives

SYNOPSIS
#include <linux/hdreg.h>

CONFIG
The block device name has the following form: **sd**/p, where *l* is a letter denoting the physical drive, and *p* is a number denoting the partition on that physical drive. Often, the partition number, *p*, will be left off when the device corresponds to the whole drive.

SCSI disks have a major device number of 8, and a minor device number of the form (16 * *drive_number*) + *partition_number*, where *drive_number* is the number of the physical drive in order of detection, and *partition_number* is as follows:

partition 0 is the whole drive
partitions 1-4 are the DOS "primary" partitions
partitions 5-8 are the DOS "extended" (or "logical") partitions

For example, **/dev/sda** will have major 8, minor 0, and will refer to all of the first SCSI drive in the system; and **/dev/sdb3** will have major 8, minor 19, and will refer to the third DOS "primary" partition on the second SCSI drive in the system.

At this time, only block devices are provided. Raw devices have not yet been implemented.

DESCRIPTION
The following ioctl's are provided:

    HDIO_REQ   Returns the BIOS disk parameters in the following structure:
```
struct hd_geometry {
unsigned char heads;
unsigned char sectors;
unsigned short cylinders;
unsigned long start;
};
```
A pointer to this structure is passed as the **ioctl**(2) parameter.

The information returned in the parameter is the disk geometry of the drive *as understood by DOS!* This geometry is *not* the physical geometry of the drive. It is used when constructing the drive's partition table, however, and is needed for convenient operation of **fdisk**(1),**efdisk**(1), and **lilo**(1). If the geometry information is not available, zero will be returned for all of the parameters.

    BLKGETSIZE   Returns the device size in sectors. The **ioctl**(2) parameter should be a pointer to a **long**.

    BLKRRPART   Forces a re-read of the SCSI disk partition tables. No parameter is needed.

The **scsi**(4) ioctl's are also supported. If the **ioctl**(2) parameter is required, and it is NULL, then **ioctl**(2) will return -EINVAL.

FILES
/dev/sd[a-h]: the whole device
/dev/sd[a-h][0-8]: individual block partitions

SEE ALSO
scsi(4)

NAME

st – SCSI tape device

SYNOPSIS

#include <sys/mtio.h>
int ioctl(int *fd***, int** *request* **[, (void *)***arg3***])**
int ioctl(int *fd***, MTIOCTOP, (struct mtop *)***mt_cmd***)**
int ioctl(int *fd***, MTIOCGET, (struct mtget *)***mt_status***)**
int ioctl(int *fd***, MTIOCPOS, (struct mtpos *)***mt_pos***)**

DESCRIPTION

The **st** driver provides the interface to a variety of SCSI tape devices. Currently, the driver takes control of all detected devices of type sequential-access. The **st** driver uses major device number 9.

Each device uses two minor device numbers: a principal minor device number, *n*, assigned sequentially in order of detection, and a no-rewind device number, (*n*+ 128). Devices opened using the principal device number will be sent a REWIND command when they are closed. Devices opened using the no-rewind device number will not. Options such as density or block size are not coded in the minor device number. These options must be set by explicit **ioctl**() calls and remain in effect when the device is closed and reopened.

Devices are typically created by:

mknod -m 660 /dev/st0 c 9 0
mknod -m 660 /dev/st1 c 9 1
mknod -m 660 /dev/nst0 c 9 128
mknod -m 660 /dev/nst1 c 9 129

There is no corresponding block device. The character device provides buffering and read-ahead by default and supports reads and writes of arbitrary size (limited by the driver's internal buffer size, which defaults to 32768 bytes, but can be changed either by using a kernel startup option or by changing a compile-time constant).

Device **/dev/tape** is usually created as a hard or soft link to the default tape device on the system.

IOCTLS

The driver supports three ioctl requests. Requests not recognized by the **st** driver are passed to the **scsi** driver. The definitions below are from
/usr/include/linux/mtio.h:

MTIOCTOP Perform a tape operation

This request takes an argument of type **(struct mtop *)**. Not all drives support all operations. The driver returns an EIO error if the drive rejects an operation.

/* Structure for MTIOCTOP – mag tape op command: */
struct mtop {
short mt_op; /* operations defined below */
int mt_count; /* how many of them */
};

Magnetic Tape operations:

> MTBSF Backward space over **mt_count** filemarks.
>
> MTBSFM Backward space over **mt_count** filemarks. Reposition the tape to the EOT side of the last filemark.
>
> MTBSR Backward space over **mt_count** records (tape blocks).
>
> MTBSS Backward space over **mt_count** setmarks.
>
> MTEOM Go to the end of the recorded media (for appending files).

MTERASE Erase tape.

MTFSF Forward space over **mt_count** filemarks.

MTFSFM Forward space over **mt_count** filemarks. Reposition the tape to the BOT side of the last filemark.

MTFSR Forward space over **mt_count** records (tape blocks).

MTFSS Forward space over **mt_count** setmarks.

MTNOP No op – flushes the driver's buffer as a side effect. Should be used before reading status with MTIOCGET.

MTOFFL Rewind and put the drive off line.

MTRESET Reset drive.

MTRETEN Retension tape.

MTREW Rewind.

MTSEEK Seek to the tape block number specified in **mt_count**. This operation requires either a SCSI-2 drive that supports the LOCATE command (device-specific address) or a Tandberg-compatible SCSI-1 drive (Tandberg, Archive Viper, Wangtek, ...). The block number should be one that was previously returned by MTIOCPOS because the number is device-specific.

MTSETBLK Set the drive's block length to the value specified in **mt_count**. A block length of zero sets the drive to variable block size mode.

MTSETDENSITY Set the tape density to the code in **mt_count**. Some useful density codes are:

18 0x00 Implicit 0x11 QIC-525
0x04 QIC-11 0x12 QIC-1350
0x05 QIC-24 0x13 DDS
0x0F QIC-120 0x14 Exabyte EXB-8200
0x10 QIC-150 0x15 Exabyte EXB-8500

MTWEOF Write **mt_count** filemarks.

MTWSM Write **mt_count** setmarks.

MTSETDRVBUFFER Set various drive and driver options according to bits encoded in **mt_count**. These consist of the drive's buffering mode, 6 Boolean driver options and the buffer write threshold. These parameters are initialized only when the device is first detected. The settings persist when the device is closed and reopened. A single operation can affect (a) just the buffering mode, (b) just the Boolean options, or (c) just the write threshold.

A value having zeros in the high-order 4 bits will be used to set the drive's buffering mode. The buffering modes are:

12

0 The drive will not report GOOD status on write commands until the data blocks are actually written to the medium.

1 The drive may report GOOD status on write commands as soon as all the data has been transferred to the drive's internal buffer.

2 The drive may report GOOD status on write commands as soon as (a) all the data has been transferred to the drive's internal buffer, and (b) all buffered data from different initiators has been successfully written to the medium.

To control the write threshold the value in **mt_count** must include the constant MT_ST_WRITE_THRESHOLD logically ORed with a block count in the low 28 bits. The block count refers to 1024-byte blocks, not the physical block size on the tape. The threshold cannot exceed the driver's internal buffer size (see **DESCRIPTION**, above).

To set and clear the Boolean options the value in **mt_count** must include the constant MT_ST_BOOLEANS logically ORed with whatever combination of the following options is desired. Any options not specified will be set false. The Boolean options are:

MT_ST_BUFFER_WRITES (Default: true) Buffer all write operations. If this option is false and the drive uses a fixed block size, then all write operations must be for a multiple of the block size. This option must be set false to write reliable multi-volume archives.

MT_ST_ASYNC_WRITES (Default: true) When this options is true write operations return immediately without waiting for the data to be transferred to the drive if the data fits into the driver's buffer. The write threshold determines how full the buffer must be before a new SCSI write command is issued. Any errors reported by the drive will be held until the next operation. This option must be set false to write reliable multi-volume archives.

MT_ST_READ_AHEAD (Default: true) This option causes the driver to provide read buffering and read-ahead. If this option is false and the drive uses a fixed block size, then all read operations must be for a multiple of the block size.

MT_ST_TWO_FM (Default: false) This option modifies the driver behavior when a file is closed. The normal action is to write a single filemark. If the option is true the driver will write two filemarks and backspace over the second one.

Note: This option should not be set true for QIC tape drives since they are unable to overwrite a filemark. These drives detect the end of recorded data by testing for blank tape rather than two consecutive filemarks.

MT_ST_DEBUGGING (Default: false) This option turns on various debugging messages from the driver (effective only if the driver was compiled with DEBUG defined).

MT_ST_FAST_EOM (Default: false) This option causes the MTEOM operation to be sent directly to the drive, potentially speeding up the operation but causing the driver to lose track of the current file number normally returned by the MTIOCGET request. If MT_ST_FAST_EOM is false the driver will respond to an MTEOM request by forward spacing over files.

EXAMPLE **struct mtop** *mt_cmd*;
mt_cmd.mt_op = **MTSETDRVBUFFER**;
mt_cmd.mt_count = **MT_ST_BOOLEANS** |
MT_ST_BUFFER_WRITES |
MT_ST_ASYNC_WRITES;
ioctl(*fd*, **MTIOCTOP**, &*mt_cmd*);

MTIOCGET Get status
This request takes an argument of type (**struct mtget ***). The driver returns an EIO error if the drive rejects an operation.

```
/* structure for MTIOCGET - mag tape get status command */
struct mtget {
long mt_type;
long mt_resid;
/* the following registers are device dependent */
long mt_dsreg;
long mt_gstat;
long mt_erreg;
/* The next two fields are not always used */
daddr_t mt_fileno;
daddr_t mt_blkno;
};
```

mt_type 11 The header file defines many values for **mt_type**, but the current driver reports only the generic types MT_ISSCSI1 (Generic SCSI-1 tape) and MT_ISSCSI2 (Generic SCSI-2 tape).

mt_resid is always zero. (Not implemented for SCSI tape drives.)

mt_dsreg reports the drive's current settings for block size (in the low 24 bits) and density (in the high 8 bits). These fields are defined by MT_ST_BLKSIZE_SHIFT, MT_ST_BLKSIZE_MASK, MT_ST_DENSITY_SHIFT, and MT_ST_DENSITY_MASK.

mt_gstat reports generic (device independent) status information. The header file defines macros for testing these status bits:

GMT_EOF(x): The tape is positioned just after a filemark (always false after an MT-SEEK operation).

GMT_BOT(x): The tape is positioned at the beginning of the first file (always false after an MTSEEK operation).

GMT_EOT(x): A tape operation has reached the physical End Of Tape.

GMT_SM(x): The tape is currently positioned at a setmark (always false after an MT-SEEK operation).

GMT_EOD(x): The tape is positioned at the end of recorded data.

GMT_WR_PROT(x): The drive is write-protected. For some drives this can also mean that the drive does not support writing on the current medium type.

GMT_ONLINE(x): The last **open()** found the drive with a tape in place and ready for operation.

GMT_D_6250(x), GMT_D_1600(x), GMT_D_800(x): This generic status information reports the current density setting for 9-track " tape drives only.

GMT_DR_OPEN(x): The drive does not have a tape in place.

GMT_IM_REP_EN(x): Immediate report mode (not supported).

mt_erreg The only field defined in **mt_erreg** is the recovered error count in the low 16 bits (as defined by MT_ST_SOFTERR_SHIFT and MT_ST_SOFTERR_MASK). Due to inconsistencies in the way drives report recovered errors, this count is often not maintained.

mt_fileno reports the current file number (zero-based). This value is set to -1 when the file number is unknown (e.g., after MTBSS or MTSEEK).

mt_blkno reports the block number (zero-based) within the current file. This value is set to -1 when the block number is unknown (e.g., after MTBSF, MTBSS, or MT-SEEK).

MTIOCPOS Get tape position
This request takes an argument of type **(struct mtpos *)** and reports the drive's notion of the current tape block number, which is not the same as **mt_blkno** returned by MTIOC-GET. This drive must be a SCSI-2 drive that supports the READ POSITION command (device-specific address) or a Tandberg-compatible SCSI-1 drive (Tandberg, Archive Viper, Wangtek, ...).

/* structure for MTIOCPOS - mag tape get position command */
struct mtpos {
long mt_blkno; /* current block number */
};

RETURN VALUE

EIO The requested operation could not be completed.

ENOSPC A write operation could not be completed because the tape reached end-of-medium.

EACCES An attempt was made to write or erase a write-protected tape. (This error is not detected during **open()**.)

ENXIO During opening, the tape device does not exist.

EBUSY The device is already in use or the driver was unable to allocate a buffer.

EOVERFLOW An attempt was made to read or write a variable-length block that is larger than the driver's internal buffer.

EINVAL An **ioctl()** had an illegal argument, or a requested block size was illegal.

ENOSYS Unknown **ioctl()**.

COPYRIGHT

Copyright 1995 Robert K. Nichols.

Permission is granted to make and distribute verbatim copies of this manual provided the copyright notice and this permission notice are preserved on all copies. Additional permissions are contained in the header of the source file.

SEE ALSO

mt(1)

TTY(4)

NAME
tty – controlling terminal

DESCRIPTION
The file **/dev/tty** is a character file with major number 5 and minor number 0, usually of mode 0666 and owner root.tty. It is a synonym for the controlling terminal of a process, if any.

In addition to the **ioctl()** requests supported by the device that **tty** refers to, the following **ioctl()** request is supported:

> **TIOCNOTTY** Detach the current process from its controlling terminal, and remove it from its current process group, without attaching it to a new process group (that is, set its process group ID to zero). This **ioctl()** call only works on file descriptors connected to **/dev/tty**; this is used by daemon processes when they are invoked by a user at a terminal. The process attempts to open **/dev/tty**; if the open succeeds, it detaches itself from the terminal by using **TIOCNOTTY**, while if the open fails, it is obviously not attached to a terminal and does not need to detach itself.

FILES
/dev/tty

SEE ALSO
mknod(1), **chown**(1), **getty**(1), **termios**(2), **console**(4), **ttys**(4)

NAME

ttys – serial terminal lines /indexterminal!serial terminal lines

DESCRIPTION

ttyS[0-3] are character devices for the serial terminal lines.

They are typically created by:

mknod -m 660 /dev/ttyS0 c 4 64 # base address 0x03f8
mknod -m 660 /dev/ttyS1 c 4 65 # base address 0x02f8
mknod -m 660 /dev/ttyS2 c 4 66 # base address 0x03e8
mknod -m 660 /dev/ttyS3 c 4 67 # base address 0x02e8
chown root.tty /dev/ttyS[0-3]

FILES

/dev/ttyS[0-3]

SEE ALSO

mknod(1), **chown**(1), **getty**(1), **tty**(4)

VCS(4)

NAME

vcs, vcsa – virtual console memory

DESCRIPTION

/dev/vcs0 is a character device with major number 7 and minor number 0, usually of mode 0644 and owner root.tty. It refers to the memory of the currently displayed virtual console terminal.

/dev/vcs[1-63] are character devices for virtual console terminals, they have major number 7 and minor number 1 to 63, usually mode 0644 and owner root.tty. **/dev/vcsa[0-63]** are the same, but including attributes, and prefixed with four bytes giving the screen dimensions and cursor position: *lines, columns, x, y*. ($x = y = 0$ at the top left corner of the screen.)

These replace the screendump ioctls of **console**(4), so the system administrator can control access using file system permissions.

The devices for the first eight virtual consoles may be created by:

for x in 0 1 2 3 4 5 6 7 8; do
mknod -m 644 /dev/vcs$x c 7 $x;
mknod -m 644 /dev/vcsa$x c 7 $[$x+128];
done
chown root.tty /dev/vcs*

No **ioctl()** requests are supported.

EXAMPLES

You may do a screendump on vt3 by switching to vt1 and typing *cat /dev/vcs3 >foo*.

This program displays the character and screen attributes under the cursor of the second virtual console, then changes the background color there:

```
#include <unistd.h>
#include <stdio.h>
#include <fcntl.h>
void main()
{ int fd;
struct {char lines, cols, x, y;} scrn;
char ch, attrib;
fd = open("/dev/vcsa2", O_RDWR);
(void)read(fd, &scrn, 4);
(void)lseek(fd, 4 + 2*(scrn.y*scrn.cols + scrn.x), 0);
(void)read(fd, &ch, 1);
(void)read(fd, &attrib, 1);
printf("ch='%c' attrib=0x%02x\n", ch, attrib);
attrib ^= 0x10;
(void)lseek(fd, -1, 1);
(void)write(fd, &attrib, 1);
}
```

FILES

/dev/vcs[0-63]
/dev/vcsa[0-63]

AUTHOR

Andries Brouwer <aeb@cwi.nl>

HISTORY

Introduced with version 1.1.92 of the Linux kernel.

SEE ALSO

console(4), **tty**(4), **ttys**(4), **selection**(1)

Section V

File Formats

NAME

intro – Introduction to file formats

DESCRIPTION

This chapter describes various file formats and the used C structures, if any.

AUTHORS

Look at the header of the manual page for the author(s) and copyright conditions. Note that these can be different from page to page!

adduser.conf(5)

NAME

adduser.conf – configuration file for **adduser(8)** and **addgroup(8)**.

SYNOPSIS

/etc/adduser.conf

DESCRIPTION

The file *adduser.conf* contains defaults for the programs **adduser(8)** and **addgroup(8)**. Each option takes the form *option= value*.

The valid configuration options are:

DSHELL The login shell to be used for all new users. Defaults to */bin/bash*.

DHOME The directory in which new home directories should be created. Defaults to */home*.

SKEL The directory from which skeletal user configuration files should be copied. Defaults to */etc/skel*.

FIRST_UID specifies the lowest valid UID for normal users on your system. IDs below **FIRST_UID** are reserved for administrative and system accounts. Defaults to 1000.

USERGROUPS The USERGROUPS variable can be either **yes** or **no**. If **yes**, each created user will be given their own group to use as a default, and their setup will arrange to have them create files group-writeable by default, thus allowing them to effectively use group-writeable filespace areas (such as /usr/local). If **no**, each created user will be placed in the group whose GID is **USERS_GID** (see below), and they will create files not group-writeable by default.

USERS_GID If **USERGROUPS** is **no**, then **USERS_GID** is the GID given to all newly-created users. The default value is 100.

FILES

/etc/adduser.conf

SEE ALSO

adduser(8)

ALIASES(5)

NAME
aliases – aliases file for sendmail

SYNOPSIS
aliases

DESCRIPTION
This file describes user ID aliases used by The file resides in and is formatted as a series of lines of the form
name: name_1, name2, name_3, . . .

The name is the name to alias, and the name_n are the aliases for that name. Lines beginning with white space are continuation lines. Lines beginning with # are comments.

Aliasing occurs only on local names. Loops can not occur, since no message will be sent to any person more than once.

After aliasing has been done, local and valid recipients who have a .forward file in their home directory have messages forwarded to the list of users defined in that file.

This is only the raw data file; the actual aliasing information is placed into a binary format in the files and using the program newaliases 1 . A newaliases command should be executed each time the aliases file is changed for the change to take effect.

SEE ALSO
newaliases 1 , dbm 3 , sendmail 8

"SENDMAIL Installation and Operation Guide"

"SENDMAIL An Internetwork Mail Router"

BUGS
Because of restrictions in dbm 3 a single alias cannot contain more than about 1000 bytes of information. You can get longer aliases by "chaining"; that is, make the last name in the alias be a dummy name which is a continuation alias.

HISTORY
The aliases file format appeared in BSD 4.0 .

NAME

DEVINFO – device entry database

DESCRIPTION

DEVINFO is a text file that describes all the possible devices for a system. It is used by **MAKEDEV**(8) to create special file entries in **/dev**. It may be named either **/dev/DEVINFO** or **/etc/devinfo**. Information about custom local devices, if any, should be placed in **DEVINFO.local** or **/etc/devinfo.local**, which has the same syntax.

The file format is free-form. Both C, C++, and shell comments are understood. There are basically four statements:

> ignore { *proc-device...* }   This causes the specified names to be ignored if found in **/proc/devices**.
>
> batch { *device...* }   This creates a "batch" – a collection of devices which will all be created when the batch is invoked. For example, in the standard **DEVINFO**, "generic" is a batch.
>
> block *device-spec*   This defines one or more block devices.
>
> char *device-spec*   This defines one or more character devices.

Here is a sample *device-spec*:

```
(std, 1) {
mem (kmem) : 1
null (public) : 3
core -> "/proc/kcore"
}
```

This example defines a group of devices called "std", with major number 1. Running will create all the devices in the group; running, for example, would make just the one device "null".

It is possible to specify, instead of just "std", something like "std=foo". In this case, the stuff on the right-hand side of the equals sign specifies a name from **/proc/devices**, and the major number will be retrieved from there if present. If an entry from **/proc/devices** is specified, the explicit major number may be omitted. In this case, if the number is not found in /proc/devices, attempts to create the device will be rejected.

Inside the braces is a list of specific devices. The name in parenthesis is the "class" - this is something specified in **MAKEDEV.cfg** (q.v.) that determines the ownership and permissions of the special file created. In the above example, the device "mem" was set to have the class "kmem", but "null" was set to be "public". Ordinarily you'd define "public" to be mode 666, but "kmem" to be mode 660 and owned by group kmem. The number after the colon is the minor number for this particular device – for instance, 3 for "null".

You may also specify a symbolic link with "->". For instance, above, "core" was made a link to **/proc/kcore**. Note that names may contain any characters, but names that contain things other than alphanumerics, dash, and underscore should be put in double quotes.

An entire range of devices can be created: you may specify a range of numbers in brackets, like this:

tty[1-8] (tty) : 1

This creates tty1–tty8 with minor device numbers starting with 1. If you specify the range in hex (prefixed by 0x) the device names will be created numbered in hex, as is normal for ptys. The range may appear inside the name string, but there may only be one range.

There is a special syntax for creating the entire banks of devices for a hard drive:

hd[a-d] 8/64

DEVINFO(5)

What this means is as follows: create hda, and 8 partitions on hda (hda1 through hda8), starting with minor number 0. Then create hdb, and 8 partitions, starting with minor number 64. Then hdc, etc., with minor number 64*2 = 128. And so forth. These are automatically placed in the class "disk". The necessary groups and batches are created so you can ask **MAKEDEV** to create "hd" or "hda" or "hda1" and expect it to do the correct thing.

Note that simple arithmetic is permitted for specifying the minor device number, as this often makes things much clearer and less likely to be accidentally broken.

SEE ALSO
MAKEDEV(8), **MAKEDEV.cfg**(5)

NAME

environ – user environment

SYNOPSIS

extern char **environ;

DESCRIPTION

An array of strings called the 'environment' is made available by **exec**(2) when a process begins. By conventions these strings have the form '*name=value*'. The following names are used by various commands:

>   **PATH** The sequence of directory prefixes that **sh**(1) and many other programs apply in searching for a file known by an incomplete path name. The prefixes are separated by ':'.
>
>   **HOME** A user's login directory, set by **login**(1) from the password file **passwd**(5).
>
>   **SHELL** The file name of the users login shell.

Further names may be placed in the environment by the **export** command and 'name=value' in **sh**(1), or by the **setenv** command if you use **csh**(1). Arguments may also be placed in the environment at the point of an **exec**(2). You should check not to conflict with certain shell variables, like: **MAIL**, **PS1**, **PS2**, **IFS** etc.

SEE ALSO

login(1), sh(1), bash (1), csh (1), tcsh (1),.BR exec (2), system (3) **exec**(2), **system**(3)

EXPORTS(5)

NAME

exports – NFS file systems being exported

SYNOPSIS

/etc/exports

DESCRIPTION

The file */etc/exports* serves as the access control list for file systems which may be exported to NFS clients. It it used by both the NFS mount daemon, *mountd*(8) and the NFS file server daemon *nfsd*(8).

The file format is similar to the SunOS *exports* file, except that netgroup names are not permitted, and several additional options are permitted. Each line contains a mount point and a list of machine names allowed to mount the file system at that point. An optional parenthesized list of mount parameters may follow each machine name. Blank lines are ignored, and a # introduces a comment to the end of the line.

These are the parameters that are currently recognized. * and +.

	insecure	Permit non-authenticated access from this machine.
	unix-rpc*	Require UNIX-domain RPC authentication from this machine. This simply requires that requests originate on an internet port IPPORT_RESERVED.
	secure-rpc+	Require secure RPC authentication from this machine. See the Sun documentation on Secure RPC.
	kerberos+	Require Kerberos authentication on accesses from this machine. See the MIT documentation on the Kerberos third-party authentication system.
	root_squash	Map requests from uid 0 on the client to uid NOBODY_UID (a compile-time option) on the server.
	no_root_squash*	Don't map requests from uid 0.
	root_squash*	Mount file hierarchy read-only.
	rw	Mount file hierarchy read-write.
	link_relative*	Convert absolute symbolic links (where the link contents start with a slash) into relative links by prepending the necessary number of ../'s to get from the directory containing the link to the root on the server. This has subtle, perhaps questionable, semantics when the file hierarchy is not mounted at its root.
	link_absolute	Leave all symbolic link as they are (the normal behavior for Sun-supplied NFS servers).
	map_identity*	Assume the client and server share the same uid/gid space.
	map_daemon	Map local and remote names and numeric ids using a lname/uid map daemon on the client from which the NFS request originated, to map between the client and server uid spaces (see ugidd(8)). This only works if nfsd(8) is compiled with Mark Shand's ugidd code.

(* indicates defaults) (+ indicates not implemented)

EXAMPLE

```
# sample /etc/exports file
/ master(rw) trusty(rw)
/projects proj*.local.domain(rw)
/usr *.local.domain(ro)
/pub (ro,insecure,root_quash)
```

FILES

/etc/exports

EXPORTS(5)

DIAGNOSTICS

An error parsing the file is reported using syslogd(8) as level NOTICE from a DAEMON whenever nfsd(8) or mountd(8) is started up. Any unknown host is reported at that time, but often not all hosts are not yet known to named(8) at boot time, thus as hosts are found they are reported with the same syslogd(8) parameters.

SEE ALSO

mountd(8), nfsd(8)

FSTAB(5)

NAME
fstab – static information about the filesystems

SYNOPSIS
#include <fstab.h>

DESCRIPTION
The file **fstab** contains descriptive information about the various file systems. **fstab** is only read by programs, and not written; it is the duty of the system administrator to properly create and maintain this file. Each filesystem is described on a separate line; fields on each line are separated by tabs or spaces. The order of records in **fstab** is important because **fsck**(8), **mount**(8), and **umount**(8) sequentially iterate through .B fstab doing their thing.

The first field, .RI (fs_spec), describes the block special device or remote filesystem to be mounted.

The second field, .RI (fs_file), describes the mount **oint** for**the** filesystem.**For** swap**partitions,** this sequentially iterate through **fstab** doing their thing.

The first field, (*fs_spec*), describes the block special device or remote filesystem to be mounted.

The second field, (*fs_file*), describes the mount point for the filesystem. For swap partitions, this field should be specified as "none".

The third field, (*fs_vfstype*), describes the type of the filesystem. The system currently supports three types of filesystems:

minix	a local filesystem, supporting filenames of length 14 or 30 characters.
ext	a local filesystem with longer filenames and larger inodes. This filesystem has been replaced by the *ext2* file system, and should no longer be used.
ext2	a local filesystem with longer filenames, larger inodes, and lots of other features.
xiafs	a local filesystem with longer filenames, larger inodes, and lots of other features.
msdos	a local filesystem for MS-DOS partitions.
hpfs	a local filesystem for HPFS partitions.
iso9660	a local filesystem used for CD-ROM drives.
nfs	a filesystem for mounting partitions from remote systems.
swap	a disk partition to be used for swapping.

If *vfs_fstype* is specified as "ignore" the entry is ignored. This is useful to show disk partitions which are currently unused.

The fourth field, (*fs_mntops*), describes the mount options associated with the filesystem.

It is formatted as a comma separated list of options. It contains at least the type of mount plus any additional options appropriate to the filesystem type. For documentation on all of the available options, see **mount**(8).

The fifth field, (*fs_freq*), is used for these filesystems by the **dump**(8) command to determine which filesystems need to be dumped. If the fifth field is not present, a value of zero is returned and **dump** will assume that the filesystem does not need to be dumped.

The sixth field, (*fs_passno*), is used by the **fsck**(8) program to determine the order in which filesystem checks are done at reboot time. The root filesystem should be specified with a *fs_passno* of 1, and other filesystems should have a *fs_passno* of 2. Filesystems within a drive will be checked sequentially, but filesystems on different drives will be checked at the same time to utilize parallelism available in the hardware. If the sixth field is not present or zero, a value of zero is returned and **fsck** will assume that the filesystem does not need to be checked.

The proper way to read records from **fstab** is to use the routines **getmntent**(3).

FILES
/etc/fstab The file **fstab** resides in */etc*.

BUGS
Linux does not, currently, support the special fields for **dump** and **fsck**.

The documentation in **mount**(8) is often more up-to-date.

SEE ALSO
getmntent(3), **mount**(8), **swapon**(8)

HISTORY
The **fstab** file format appeared in 4.0BSD.

GROFF_FONT(5)

NAME

groff_font – format of groff device and font description files

DESCRIPTION

The groff font format is roughly a superset of the ditroff font format. Unlike the ditroff font format, there is no associated binary format. The font files for device *name* are stored in a directory **dev***name*. There are two types of file: a device description file called **DESC** and for each font *F* a font file called *F*. These are text files; there is no associated binary format.

DESC file format

The DESC file can contain the following types of line:

- **res***n* There are *n* machine units per inch.
- **hor***n* The horizontal resolution is *n* machine units.
- **vert***n* The vertical resolution is *n* machine units.
- **sizescale***n* The scale factor for pointsizes. By default this has a value of 1. One scaled point is equal to one point/*n*. The arguments to the **unitwidth** and **sizes** commands are given in scaled points.
- **unitwidth***n* Quantities in the font files are given in machine units for fonts whose point size is *n* scaled points.
- **tcommand** This means that the postprocessor can handle the **t** and **u** output commands.
- **sizes***s1***s2...s***n***0** This means that the device has fonts at *s1, s2, ... sn* scaled points. The list of sizes must be terminated by a **0**. Each s*i* can also be a range of sizes *m–n*. The list can extend over more than one line.
- **styles***S1***S2...S***m* The first *m* font positions will be associated with styles *S1 ... Sm*.
- **fonts***n***F1***F2***F3...F***n* Fonts *F1 ... Fn* will be mounted in the font positions *m*+1, ...,*m*+*n* where *m* is the number of styles. This command may extend over more than one line. A font name of **0** will cause no font to be mounted on the corresponding font position.
- **family***fam* The default font family is *fam*.
- **charset** This line and everything following in the file are ignored. It is allowed for the sake of backwards compatibility.

The res, unitwidth, fonts and sizes lines are compulsory. Other commands are ignored by **troff** but may be used by postprocessors to store arbitrary information about the device in the DESC file.

Font file format

A font file has two sections. The first section is a sequence of lines each containing a sequence of blank delimited words; the first word in the line is a key, and subsequent words give a value for that key.

- **name***F* The name of the font is *F*.
- **spacewidth***n* The normal width of a space is *n*.
- **slant***n* The characters of the font have a slant of *n* degrees. (Positive means forward.)
- **ligatures***lig1***lig2...lign**[**0**] Characters *lig1, lig2,...,lign* are ligatures; possible ligatures are **ff**, **fi**, **fl** and **ffl**. For backwards compatibility, the list of ligatures may be terminated with a **0**. The list of ligatures may not extend over more than one line.
- **special** The font is *special*; this means that when a character is requested that is not present in the current font, it will be searched for in any special fonts that are mounted.

Groff Version 1.09 14 February 1994

Other commands are ignored by **troff** but may be used by postprocessors to store arbitrary information about the font in the font file.

The first section can contain comments which start with the **#** character and extend to the end of a line.

The second section contains one or two subsections. It must contain a *charset* subsection and it may also contain a *kernpairs* subsection. These subsections can appear in any order. Each subsection starts with a word on a line by itself.

The word **charset** starts the charset subsection. The **charset** line is followed by a sequence of lines. Each line gives information for one character. A line comprises a number of fields separated by blanks or tabs. The format is

> name metrics type code comment

name identifies the character: if *name* is a single character *c* then it corresponds to the groff input character *c*; if it is of the form *c* where c is a single character, then it corresponds to the groff input character *c*; otherwise it corresponds to the groff input character \[*name*] (if it is exactly two characters *xx* it can be entered as \(*xx*.) Groff supports eight bit characters; however some utilities have difficulties with eight bit characters. For this reason, there is a convention that the name **char***n* is equivalent to the single character whose code is *n* . For example, **char163** would be equivalent to the character with code 163 which is the pounds sterling sign in ISO Latin-1. The name —— is special and indicates that the character is unnamed; such characters can only be used by means of the \N escape sequence in **troff**.

The *type* field gives the character type:

1   means the character has an descender, for example, p;
2   means the character has an ascender, for example, b;
3   means the character has both an ascender and a descender, for example, (.

The *code* field gives the code which the postprocessor uses to print the character. The character can also be input to groff using this code by means of the \N escape sequence. The code can be any integer. If it starts with a **0** it will be interpreted as octal; if it starts with **0x** or **0X** it will be intepreted as hexadecimal.

Anything on the line after the code field will be ignored.

The *metrics* field has the form:
width[,*height*[,*depth*[,*italic_correction*[, left_italic_correction [, **subscript_correction**]]]]]

There must not be any spaces between these subfields. Missing subfields are assumed to be 0. The subfields are all decimal integers. Since there is no associated binary format, these values are not required to fit into a variable of type char as they are in ditroff. The *width* **subfields gives the width of the character. The** *height* **subfield gives the height of the character (upwards is positive); if a character does not extend above the baseline, it should be given a zero height, rather than a negative height. The** *depth* **subfield gives the depth of the character, that is, the distance below the lowest point below the baseline to which the character extends (downwards is positive); if a character does not extend below above the baseline, it should be given a zero depth, rather than a negative depth. The** *italic_correction* **subfield gives the amount of space that should be added after the character when it is immediately to be followed by a character from a roman font. The** *left_italic_correction* **subfield gives the amount of space that should be added before the character when it is immediately to be preceded by a character from a roman font. The** *subscript_correction* **gives the amount of space that should be added after a character before adding a subscript. This should be less than the italic correction.**

A line in the charset section can also have the format

> name "

This indicates that *name* **is just another name for the character mentioned in the preceding line.**

GROFF_FONT(5)

The word kernpairs starts the kernpairs section. This contains a sequence of lines of the form:

    c1 c2 n

This means that when character *c1* appears next to character *c2* the space between them should be increased by *n*. Most entries in kernpairs section will have a negative value for *n*.

FILES

/usr/lib/groff/font/dev*name*/DESC   Device description file for device *name*.

    /usr/lib/groff/font/dev*name*/*F*   Font file for font *F* of device *name*.

SEE ALSO

groff_out(5), **gtroff**(1).

GROFF_OUT(5)

NAME

groff_out – groff intermediate output format

DESCRIPTION

This manual page describes the format output by GNU troff. The output format used by GNU troff is very similar to that used by Unix device-independent troff. Only the differences are documented here.

The argument to the s command is in scaled points (units of *points*/n, where *n* is the argument to the sizescale command in the DESC file.) The argument to the x Height command is also in scaled points.

The first three output commands are guaranteed to be:

    x*T*device
    x*res*n*h*v
    x init

If the tcommand line is present in the DESC file, troff will use the following two commands

    t*xxx*   *xxx* is any sequence of characters terminated by a space or a newline; the first character should be printed at the current position, the the current horizontal position should be increased by the width of the first character, and so on for each character. The width of the character is that given in the font file, appropriately scaled for the current point size, and rounded so that it is a multiple of the horizontal resolution. Special characters cannot be printed using this command.

    u*n*xxx   This is same as the t command except that after printing each character, the current horizontal position is increased by the sum of the width of that character and *n*.

Note that single characters can have the eighth bit set, as can the names of fonts and special characters.

The names of characters and fonts an be of arbitrary length; drivers should not assume that they will be only two characters long.

When a character is to be printed, that character will always be in the current font. Unlike device-independent troff, it is not necessary for drivers to search special fonts to find a character.

The D drawing command has been extended. These extensions will not be used by GNU pic if the –n option is given.

    D*f n*\n   Set the shade of gray to be used for filling solid objects to *n*; *n* must be an integer between 0 and 1000, where 0 corresponds solid white and 1000 to solid black, and values in between correspond to intermediate shades of gray. This applies only to solid circles, solid ellipses and solid polygons. By default, a level of 1000 will be used. Whatever color a solid object has, it should completely obscure everything beneath it. A value greater than 1000 or less than 0 can also be used: this means fill with the shade of gray that is currently being used for lines and text. Normally this will be black, but some drivers may provide a way of changing this.

    D*C d*\n   Draw a solid circle with a diameter of *d* with the leftmost point at the current position.

    D*E dx dy*\n   Draw a solid ellipse with a horizontal diameter of *dx* and a vertical diameter of *dy* with the leftmost point at the current position.

Dp dx_1 dy_1 dx_2 dy_2 ... dx_n dy_n\n Draw a polygon with, for $i = 1, ..., n+1$, the i-th vertex at the current position $+ \sum_{j=1}^{i-1}(dx_j, dy_j)$. At the moment, GNU pic only uses this command to generate triangles and rectangles.

DP dx_1 dy_1 dx_2 dy_2 ... dx_n dy_n\n Like Dp but draw a solid rather than outlined polygon.

Dt n\n Set the current line thickness to n machine units. Traditionally Unix troff drivers use a line thickness proportional to the current point size; drivers should continue to do this if no Dt command has been given, or if a Dt command has been given with a negative value of n. A zero value of n selects the smallest available line thickness.

A difficulty arises in how the current position should be changed after the execution of these commands. This is not of great importance since the code generated by GNU pic does not depend on this. Given a drawing command of the form

\D$c$ x_1 y_1 x_2 y_2 ... x_n y_n

where c is not one of c, e, l, a or ~, Unix troff will treat each of the x_i as a horizontal quantity, and each of the y_i as a vertical quantity and will assume that the width of the drawn object is $\sum_{i=1}^{n} x_i$, and that the height is $\sum_{i=1}^{n} y_i$. (The assumption about the height can be seen by examining the st and sb registers after using such a D command in a \w escape sequence.) This rule also holds for all the original drawing commands with the exception of De. For the sake of compatibility GNU troff also follows this rule, even though it produces an ugly result in the case of the Df, Dt, and, to a lesser extent, DE commands. Thus after executing a D command of the form

Dc x_1 y_1 x_2 y_2 ... x_n y_n\n

the current position should be increased by $(\sum_{i=1}^{n} x_i, \sum_{i=1}^{n} y_i)$.

There is a continuation convention which permits the argument to the x X command to contain newlines: when outputting the argument to the x X command, GNU troff will follow each newline in the argument with a + character (as usual, it will terminate the entire argument with a newline); thus if the line after the line containing the x X command starts with +, then the newline ending the line containing the x X command should be treated as part of the argument to the x X command, the + should be ignored, and the part of the line following the + should be treated like the part of the line following the x X command.

SEE ALSO

groff_font(5)

GROUP(5)

NAME

group – user group file

DESCRIPTION

/etc/group is an ASCII file which defines the groups to which users belong. There is one entry per line, and each line has the format:

group_name:passwd:GID:user_list

The field descriptions are:

group_name   the name of the group.

password   the (encrypted) group password. If this field is empty, no password is needed.

GID   the numerical group ID.

user_list   all the group member's user names, separated by commas.

FILES

/etc/group

SEE ALSO

login(1), **newgrp**(1), **passwd**(5)

HOSTS_ACCESS(5)

NAME

hosts_access – format of host access control files

DESCRIPTION

This manual page describes a simple access control language that is based on client (host name/address, user name) and server (process name) patterns. Examples are given at the end. The impatient reader can skip to the EXAMPLES section for a quick introduction.

In the following text, *daemon* is the the process name of a network daemon process, and *client* is the name and/or address of a host requesting service. Network daemon process names are specified in the inetd configuration file.

ACCESS CONTROL FILES

The access control software consults two files. The search stops at the first match:

> Access will be granted when a (daemon,client) pair matches an entry in the */etc/hosts.allow* file.
>
> Otherwise, access will be denied when a (daemon,client) pair matches an entry in the */etc/hosts.deny* file.
>
> Otherwise, access will be granted.

A non-existing access control file is treated as if it were an empty file. Thus, access control can be turned off by providing no access control files.

ACCESS CONTROL RULES

Each access control file consists of zero or more lines of text. These lines are processed in order of appearance. The search terminates when a match is found.

> A newline character is ignored when it is preceded by a backslash character.
>
> Blank lines or lines that begin with a '#' character are ignored.
>
> All other lines should satisfy the following format, things between [] being optional:
>
> > daemon_list : client_list [: shell_command]

daemon_list is a list of one or more daemon process names (argv[0] values) or wildcards (see below).

client_list is a list of one or more host names, host addresses, patterns or wildcards (see below) that will be matched against the remote host name or address.

List elements should be separated by blanks and/or commas.

With the exception of NIS (YP) netgroup lookups, all access control checks are case insensitive.

PATTERNS

The access control language implements the following patterns:

> A string that begins with a '.' character. A client name or address is matched if its last components match the specified pattern. For example, the pattern '.tue.nl' matches the host name 'wzv.win.tue.nl'.
>
> A string that ends with a '.' character. A client name or address is matched if its first fields match the given string. For example, the pattern '131.155.' matches the address of (almost) every host on the Eindhoven University network (131.155.x.x).
>
> A string that begins with a '@' character is treated as a netgroup name. Netgroups are usually supported on systems with NIS (formerly YP) data bases. A client host name is matched if it is a (host) member of the specified netgroup.
>
> An expression of the form 'n.n.n.n/m.m.m.m' is interpreted as a 'net/mask' pair. A client address is matched if 'net' is equal to the bitwise AND of the address and the 'mask'. For example, the net/mask pattern '131.155.72.0/255.255.254.0' matches every address in the range '131.155.72.0' through '131.155.73.255'.

WILDCARDS

The access control language supports explicit wildcards:

    ALL   If this token appears in a daemon_list, it matches all network daemon process names. If the ALL token appears in a client_list, it matches all client names and addresses.

    LOCAL   Matches any string that does not contain a dot character. Typical use is in client_lists.

    UNKNOWN   Matches any host whose name *or* address are unknown. Should be used with care: host names may be unavailable due to temporary name server problems. A network address will be unavailable when the software cannot figure out what type of network it is talking to.

    KNOWN   Matches any host whose name *and* address are known. Should be used with care: host names may be unavailable due to temporary name server problems. A network address will be unavailable when the software cannot figure out what type of network it is talking to.

    FAIL   Like the ALL wildcard, but causes the software to pretend that the scan of the current access control table fails. FAIL is being phased out; it will become an undocumented feature. The EXCEPT operator (see below) is a much cleaner alternative.

OPERATORS

    EXCEPT   Intended use is of the form: 'list_1 EXCEPT list_2'; this construct matches anything that matches *list_1* unless it matches *list_2*. This construct can be used in daemon_lists and in client_lists. The EXCEPT operator can be nested: if the control language would permit the use of parentheses, 'a EXCEPT b EXCEPT c' would parse as '(a EXCEPT (b EXCEPT c))'.

SHELL COMMANDS

If the first-matched access control rule contains a shell command, that command is subjected to the following substitutions:

  %a expands to the remote host address.

  %c expands to client information: user@host, user@address, a host name, or just an address, depending on how much information is available.

  %h expands to the remote host name (or address, if the host name is unavailable).

  %d expands to the daemon process name (argv[0] value).

  %p expands to the daemon process id.

  %u expands to the remote user name (or "unknown").

  %% expands to a single '%' character.

Characters in % expansions that may confuse the shell are replaced by underscores. The result is executed by a */bin/sh* child process with standard input, output and error connected to */dev/null*. Specify an '&' at the end of the command if you do not want to wait until it has completed.

Shell commands should not rely on the PATH setting of the inetd. Instead, they should use absolute path names, or they should begin with an explicit PATH=whatever statement.

REMOTE USERNAME LOOKUP

When the client host supports the RFC 931 protocol or one of its descendants (TAP, IDENT) the wrapper programs can retrieve additional information about the owner of a connection. Remote username information, when available, is logged together with the client host name, and can be used to match patterns like:

HOSTS_ACCESS(5)

    daemon_list : ... user_pattern@host_pattern ...

The daemon wrappers can be configured at compile time to perform rule-driven username lookups (default) or to always interrogate the client host. In the case of rule-driven username lookups, the above rule would cause username lookup only when both the *daemon_list* and the *host_pattern* match.

A user pattern has the same syntax as a daemon process name, host name or host address pattern, so the same wildcards etc. apply (but netgroup membership of users is not supported). One should not get carried away with username lookups, though.

> The remote username information cannot be trusted when it is needed most, i.e. when the remote system has been compromised. In general, ALL and (UN)KNOWN are the only user name patterns that make sense.

> Username lookups are possible only with TCP-based services, and only when the client host runs a suitable daemon; in all other cases the result is "unknown".

> A well-known UNIX kernel bug may cause loss of service when username lookups are blocked by a firewall. The wrapper README document describes a procedure to find out if your kernel has this bug.

> Username lookups cause noticeable delays for PC users. The default timeout for username lookups is 10 seconds: too short to cope with slow networks, but long enough to irritate PC users.

Selective username lookups can alleviate the last problem. For example, a rule like:

    daemon_list : @pcnetgroup ALL@ALL

would match members of the pc netgroup without doing username lookups, but would perform username lookups with all other systems.

EXAMPLES

The language is flexible enough that different types of access control policy can be expressed with a minimum of fuss. Although the language uses two access control tables, the most common policies can be implemented with one of the tables being trivial or even empty.

When reading the examples below it is important to realize that the allow table is scanned before the deny table, that the search terminates when a match is found, and that access is granted when no match is found at all.

The examples use host and domain names. They can be improved by including address and/or network/netmask information, to reduce the impact of temporary name server lookup failures.

MOSTLY CLOSED

In this case, access is denied by default. Only explicitly authorized hosts are permitted access.

The default policy (no access) is implemented with a trivial deny file:

/etc/hosts.deny:

    ALL: ALL

> This denies all service to all hosts, unless they are permitted access by entries in the allow file.

> The explicitly authorized hosts are listed in the allow file. For example:

/etc/hosts.allow:

    ALL: LOCAL @some_netgroup
    ALL: .foobar.edu EXCEPT terminalserver.foobar.edu

> The first rule permits access to all services from hosts in the local domain (no '.' in the host name) and from members of the *some_netgroup* netgroup. The second rule permits access to all services from all hosts in the *.foobar.edu*

domain, with the exception of *terminalserver.foobar.edu*.

MOSTLY OPEN

Here, access is granted by default; only explicitly specified hosts are refused service.

The default policy (access granted) makes the allow file redundant so that it can be omitted. The explicitly non-authorized hosts are listed in the deny file. For example:

/etc/hosts.deny:

> ALL: some.host.name, .some.domain
> ALL EXCEPT in.fingerd: other.host.name, .other.domain
>
> The first rule denies some hosts all services; the second rule still permits finger requests from other hosts.

BOOBY TRAPS

The next example permits tftp requests from hosts in the local domain. Requests from any other hosts are denied. Instead of the requested file, a finger probe is sent to the offending host. The result is mailed to the superuser.

/etc/hosts.allow:

> in.tftpd: LOCAL, .my.domain
> /etc/hosts.deny:
> in.tftpd: ALL: (/some/where/safe_finger -l @%h | \
> /usr/ucb/mail -s %d-%h root) &
>
> The safe_finger command comes with the tcpd wrapper and should be installed in a suitable place. It limits possible damage from data sent by the remote finger server. It gives better protection than the standard finger command.
>
> The expansion of the %h (remote host) and %d (service name) sequences is described in the section on shell commands.
>
> Warning: do not booby-trap your finger daemon, unless you are prepared for infinite finger loops.
>
> On network firewall systems this trick can be carried even further. The typical network firewall only provides a limited set of services to the outer world. All other services can be "bugged" just like the above tftp example. The result is an excellent early-warning system.

DIAGNOSTICS

An error is reported when a syntax error is found in a host access control rule; when the length of an access control rule exceeds the capacity of an internal buffer; when an access control rule is not terminated by a newline character; when the result of %<character> expansion would overflow an internal buffer; when a system call fails that shouldn't. All problems are reported via the syslog daemon.

FILES

/etc/hosts.allow, (daemon,client) pairs that are granted access.
/etc/hosts.deny, (daemon,client) pairs that are denied access.

SEE ALSO

tcpd(8) tcp/ip daemon wrapper program.

BUGS

If a name server lookup times out, the host name will not be available to the access control software, even though the host is registered.

Domain name server lookups are case insensitive; NIS (formerly YP) netgroup lookups are case sensitive.

AUTHOR
Wietse Venema (wietse@wzv.win.tue.nl)
Department of Mathematics and Computing Science
Eindhoven University of Technology
Den Dolech 2, P.O. Box 513, 5600 MB Eindhoven, The Netherlands

HOSTS_OPTIONS(5) HOSTS_OPTIONS(5)

NAME

hosts_options – host access control language extensions

DESCRIPTION

This document describes optional extensions to the language described in the hosts_access(5) document. The extensions are enabled at program build time by editing the Makefile.

The extensible language uses the following format:

> daemon_list : client_list : option : option ...

The first two fields are described in the hosts_access(5) manual page. The remainder of the rules is a list of zero or more options. Any ":" characters within options should be protected with a backslash.

An option is of the form "keyword" or "keyword = value". Options are processed in the specified order. With some options, the value is subjected to %<character> substitutions.

OPTIONS

> severity = mail.info   Change the severity level at which the event will be logged. Facility names (such as mail) are optional, and are not supported on systems with older syslog implementations. The severity option can be used to emphasize or to completely ignore specific events.
>
> allow (deny)   Grant (deny) service, even when the matched rule was found in the *hosts.deny (hosts.allow)* file. These options must appear at the end of a rule.

With the *allow* and *deny* keywords it is possible to keep all access control rules within a single file, for example in the *hosts.allow* file. For example,

> ALL: .friendly.domain: allow
>
> ALL: ALL: deny

permits access from specific hosts only. On the other hand,

> ALL: .trouble.makers: deny
>
> ALL: ALL: allow

permits access from all hosts except a few trouble makers.

> twist = shell_command   Replace the current process by an instance of the specified shell command, after performing the %<character> expansions described in the hosts_access(5) manual page. Stdin, stdout and stderr are connected to the remote client process. This option must appear at the end of a rule.
> Examples:
>
> in.ftpd : ... : twist = /bin/echo 421 Some bounce message
>
> sends a customized bounce message to the remote client instead of running the real ftp daemon.
>
> in.telnetd : ... : twist = PATH=/some/other; exec in.telnetd
>
> would run /some/other/in.telnetd without polluting its command-line array or its process environment.
>
> Warning: in case of UDP services, do not twist into commands that use the standard I/O or the read(2)/write(2) routines to communicate with the client process; UDP requires other I/O primitives.
>
> spawn = shell_command   Execute the shell command in a child process, after performing the %<character> expansions described in the hosts_access(5) manual page. The command is executed with stdin, stdout and stderr

943

connected to the null device, so that it won't mess up the conversation with the remote host. Example:

spawn = (/some/where/safe_finger -l @%h | /usr/ucb/mail root) &

executes, in a background child process, the shell command "safe_finger -l @%h | mail root" after replacing %h by the name or address of the remote host.

The example uses the "safe_finger" command instead of the regular "finger" command, to limit possible damage from data sent by the finger server. The "safe_finger" command is part of the daemon wrapper package; it is a wrapper around the regular finger command that filters the data sent by the remote host.

umask = 022 Like the umask command that is built into the shell. An umask of 022 prevents the creation of files with group and world write permission. The umask argument should be an octal number.

keepalive Causes the server to periodically send a message to the client. The connection is considered broken when the client does not respond. The keepalive option can be useful when users turn off their machine while it is still connected to a server. The keepalive option is not useful for datagram (UDP) services.

linger = number_of_seconds Specifies how long the kernel will try to deliver not-yet delivered data after the server process closes a connection.

nice = niceval

nice (no argument) Change the nice value of the process (default 10). Specify a positive value to spend more CPU resources on other processes.

user = nobody Assume the privileges of the "nobody" account. This is useful with inetd implementations that run all services with root privilege. It is good practice to run services such as "finger" at a reduced privilege level.

group = tty Assume the privileges of the "tty" group. This is useful mostly in combination with the "user" option. In order to switch both user and group ids, switch group id before switching user id.

setenv = name value Place a (name, value) pair into the process environment. The value is subjected to %<character> expansions and may contain whitespace (but leading and trailing blanks are stripped off).

Warning: many network daemons reset their environment before spawning a login or shell process.

rfc931 = timeout_in_seconds

rfc931 (no argument) Look up the remote user name with the RFC 931 (IDENT, etc.) protocol. This option is silently ignored in case of services based on transports other than TCP. It requires that the client system runs an RFC 931 (IDENT, etc.) -compliant daemon, and may cause noticeable delays with connections from non-UNIX hosts. The timeout period is optional. If no timeout is specified a default value is taken.

DIAGNOSTICS

When a syntax error is found in an access control rule, the error is reported to the syslog daemon; further options will be ignored, and service is denied.

SEE ALSO

hosts_access(5), the default access control language

AUTHOR

Wietse Venema (wietse@wzv.win.tue.nl)
Department of Mathematics and Computing Science

Eindhoven University of Technology
Den Dolech 2, P.O. Box 513, 5600 MB Eindhoven, The Netherlands

NAME

inittab – format of the inittab file used by the SysV-compatible init process

DESCRIPTION

The inittab file describes which processes are started at bootup and during normal operation (e.g. /etc/rc, gettys...). Init distinguishes multiple *runlevels*, of which each can have its own set of processes that are started. Valid runlevels are **0–6** and **A**, **B** and **C** for **ondemand** entries. An entry in the inittab file has the following format:

id:runlevels:action:process

Lines beginning with '#' are ignored.

id
: is a unique two-character-sequence which identifies an entry in inittab.

    Note: For gettys or other login processes, the *id* field should be the tty suffix of the corresponding tty, e.g. **1** for **tty1**. Otherwise, the login accounting will not work correctly. This is a bug in login and will be fixed.

runlevels
: describes in which runlevels the specified action should be taken.

action
: describes which action should be taken.

process
: specifies the process to be executed. If the process field starts with a '+' character, init will not do utmp and wtmp accounting for that process. This is needed for gettys that insist on doing their own utmp/wtmp housekeeping. This is also a historic bug.

Valid actions are:

respawn
: The process will be restarted whenever it terminates (e.g. getty).

wait
: The process will be started once when the specified runlevel is entered and init will wait for its termination.

once
: The process will be executed once when the specified runlevel is entered.

boot
: The process will be executed during system boot. The *runlevel* field is ignored.

bootwait
: The process will be executed during system boot, while init waits for its termination (e.g. /etc/rc). The *runlevel* field is ignored.

off
: This does nothing.

ondemand
: A process marked with an **ondemand** runlevel will be executed whenever the specified ondemand runlevel is called. However, no runlevel change will occur.

initdefault
: An **initdefault**-entry specifies the runlevel which should be entered after system boot. If none exists, init will ask for a runlevel on the console.

sysinit
: The process will be executed during system boot. It will be executed before any **boot** or **bootwait** entries.

powerwait
: The process will be executed when **init** receives the SIGPWR signal, indicating that there is something wrong with the power. **Init** will wait for the process to finish before continuing.

powerfail
: As **powerwait**, but init will not wait for the processes completion.

powerokwait
: The process will be executed when **init** receives the SIGPWR signal, provided there is a file called **/etc/powerstatus** containing the word **OK**. This means that the power has come back again.

ctrlaltdel
: The process will be executed when **init** receives the SIGINT signal. This means that someone on the system console has pressed the **CTRL–ALT–DEL** key combination. Typically one wants to execute some

sort of **shutdown** either to get into single–user level or to reboot the machine.

The *runlevel*-field may contain multiple characters for different runlevels, e.g. **123** if the process should be started in runlevels 1, 2 and 3. **ondemand**-entries may contain an **A, B** or **C**. The *runlevel*-field of **sysinit, boot** and **bootwait** entries are ignored.

When the runlevel is changed, any running processes that are not specified for the new runlevel are killed, first with SIGTERM then with SIGKILL

EXAMPLES

This is an example of a inittab which resembles the old Linux inittab:

```
# inittab for linux
id:1:initdefault:
rc::bootwait:/etc/rc
1:1:respawn:/etc/getty 9600 tty1
2:1:respawn:/etc/getty 9600 tty2
3:1:respawn:/etc/getty 9600 tty3
4:1:respawn:/etc/getty 9600 tty4
```

This inittab file executes **/etc/rc** during boot and starts gettys on tty1–tty4.

A more elaborate inittab with different runlevels (see the comments inside):

```
# Level to run in
id:4:initdefault:
ud::boot:/etc/update
rc::bootwait:/etc/rc
cr::boot:/etc/crond
#
# level 1: getty on tty1
# level 2: getty on tty1-4
# level 3: tty1-4, dialin via modem(ttys2)
# level 4: tty1-4, ttyb
#
mr:126:once:/usr/bin/nodialin
mi:345:once:/usr/bin/dialin
1:1234:respawn:/etc/getty 9600 tty1
2:234:respawn:/etc/getty 9600 tty2
3:234:respawn:/etc/getty 9600 tty3
4:234:respawn:/etc/getty 9600 tty4
s2:3:respawn:/etc/mgetty ttys2 19200
b:4:respawn:/etc/getty 19200L ttyb
ca::ctrlaltdel:/etc/shutdown -t3 -rf now
```

FILES

/etc/inittab

AUTHOR

Init was written by Miquel van Smoorenburg (miquels@drinkel.nl.mugnet.org), the manual page was written by Sebastian Lederer (lederer@francium.informatik.uni-bonn.de) and modified by Michael Haardt (u31b3hs@pool.informatik.rwth-aachen.de).

SEE ALSO

init(8), telinit(8)

IPC(5)

NAME
ipc – System V interprocess communication mechanisms

SYNOPSIS
\# include <sys/types.h>
\# include <sys/ipc.h>
\# include <sys/msg.h>
\# include <sys/sem.h>
\# include <sys/shm.h>

DESCRIPTION
The manual page refers to the Linux implementation of the System V interprocess communication mechanisms: message queues, semaphore sets and shared memory segments. In the following, the word **resource** means an instantiation of one among such mechanisms.

Resource Access Permissions
For each resource the system uses a common structure of type **struct ipc_perm** to store information needed in determining permissions to perform an ipc operation. The **ipc_perm** structure, defined by the <*sys/ipc.h*> system header file, includes the following members:

ushort cuid; /* creator user id */
ushort cgid; /* creator group id */
ushort uid; /* owner user id */
ushort gid; /* owner group id */
ushort mode; /* r/w permissions */

The **mode** member of the **ipc_perm** structure defines, with its lower 9 bits, the access permissions to the resource for a process executing an ipc system call. The permissions are interpreted as follows:

0400 Read by user.
0200 Write by user.
0040 Read by group.
0020 Write by group.
0004 Read by others.
0002 Write by others.

Bits 0100, 0010 and 0001 (the execute bits) are unused by the system. Furthermore "write" effectively means "alter" for a semaphore set.

The same system header file defines also the following symbolic constants:

IPC_CREAT	Create entry if key doesn't exists.
IPC_EXCL	Fail if key exists.
IPC_NOWAIT	Error if request must wait.
IPC_PRIVATE	Private key.
IPC_RMID	Remove resource.
IPC_SET	Set resource options.
IPC_STAT	Get resource options.

Note that **IPC_PRIVATE** is a **key_t** type, while all the others symbolic constants are flag fields or-able into an **int** type variable.

Message Queues
A message queue is uniquely identified by a positive integer (its *msqid*) and has an associated data structure of type **struct msquid_ds**, defined in <*sys/msg.h*>, containing the following members:

struct ipc_perm msg_perm;
ushort msg_qnum; /* no of messages on queue */
ushort msg_qbytes; /* bytes max on a queue */

```
ushort msg_lspid; /* pid of last msgsnd call */
ushort msg_lrpid; /* pid of last msgrcv call */
time_t msg_stime; /* last msgsnd time */
time_t msg_rtime; /* last msgrcv time */
time_t msg_ctime; /* last change time */
```

    msg_perm   **ipc_perm** structure that specifies the access permissions on the message queue.

    msg_qnum   Number of messages currently on the message queue.

    msg_qbytes   Maximum number of bytes of message text allowed on the message queue.

    msg_lspid   ID of the process that performed the last **msgsnd** system call.

    msg_lrpid   ID of the process that performed the last **msgrcv** system call.

    msg_stime   Time of the last **msgsnd** system call.

    msg_rtime   Time of the last **msgcv** system call.

    msg_ctime   Time of the last system call that changed a member of the **msqid_ds** structure.

Semaphore Sets

A semaphore set is uniquely identified by a positive integer (its *semid*) and has an associated data structure of type **struct semid_ds**, defined in <*sys/sem.h*>, containing the following members:

```
struct ipc_perm sem_perm;
time_t sem_otime; /* last operation time */
time_t sem_ctime; /* last change time */
ushort sem_nsems; /* count of sems in set */
```

    sem_perm   **ipc_perm** structure that specifies the access permissions on the semaphore set.

    sem_otime   Time of last **semop** system call.

    sem_ctime   Time of last **semctl** system call that changed a member of the above structure or of one semaphore belonging to the set.

    sem_nsems   Number of semaphores in the set. Each semaphore of the set is referenced by a non-negative integer ranging from **0** to **sem_nsems–1**.

A semaphore is a data structure of type **struct sem** containing the following members:

```
ushort semval; /* semaphore value */
short sempid; /* pid for last operation */
ushort semncnt; /* no. of awaiting semval to increase */
ushort semzcnt; /* no. of awaiting semval = 0 */
```

    semval   Semaphore value: a non-negative integer.

    sempid   ID of the last process that performed a semaphore operation on this semaphore.

    semncnt   Number of processes suspended awaiting for **semval** to increase.

    semznt   Number of processes suspended awaiting for **semval** to become zero.

Shared Memory Segments

A shared memory segment is uniquely identified by a positive integer (its *shmid*) and has an associated data structure of type **struct shmid_ds**, defined in <*sys/shm.h*>, containing the following members:

```
struct ipc_perm shm_perm;
int shm_segsz; /* size of segment */
ushort shm_cpid; /* pid of creator */
ushort shm_lpid; /* pid, last operation */
short shm_nattch; /* no. of current attaches */
time_t shm_atime; /* time of last attach */
time_t shm_dtime; /* time of last detach */
time_t shm_ctime; /* time of last change */
```

	shm_perm	ipc_perm structure that specifies the access permissions on the shared memory segment.
	shm_segsz	Size in bytes of the shared memory segment.
	shm_cpid	ID of the process that created the shared memory segment.
	shm_lpid	ID of the last process that executed a **shmat** or **shmdt** system call.
	shm_nattch	Number of current alive attaches for this shared memory segment.
	shm_atime	Time of the last **shmat** system call.
	shm_dtime	Time of the last **shmdt** system call.
	shm_ctime	Time of the last **shmctl** system call that changed **shmid_ds**.

SEE ALSO

ftok(3), msgctl(2), msgget(2), msgrcv(2), msgsnd(2), semctl(2), semget(2), semop(2), shmat(2), shmctl(2), shmget(2), shmdt (2).

NAME

issue – issue identification file

DESCRIPTION

The file **/etc/issue** is an text file which contains a message or system identification to be printed before the login prompt. It may contain various *@char* and *\char* sequences, if supported by **getty**(1).

FILES

/etc/issue

SEE ALSO

getty(1)

MAKEDEV.cfg(5)

NAME

MAKEDEV.cfg – configuration for MAKEDEV(8)

DESCRIPTION

MAKEDEV.cfg is a text file that tells **MAKEDEV**(8) what to do (and, equally importantly, what not to do.) Unlike **DEVINFO**(5), which is meant to be centrally maintained, it contains all local configuration for a particular site and all customization. There are basically two kinds of declaration in this file: a "class" declaration and an "omit" declaration.

A class declaration has the form

class *name* : *owner group-owner permissions*

This says that any devices placed in the specified class by **DEVINFO** should be created with this ownership and these permissions. A sample entry might be

class public: root system 0666

This says that devices marked "public" should be owned by root.system and have mode 666.

An omit declaration has the form

omit { *device...* }

This causes the specified devices to never be created, **EVEN IF EXPLICITLY SPECIFIED**. Use caution when setting this up. The intent is to be able to run MAKEDEV update and not have it create all sorts of useless devices you'd never use.

SEE ALSO

MAKEDEV(8), **DEVINFO**(5)

MODULES(5)

NAME

/etc/modules - kernel modules to load at boot time

DESCRIPTION

The **/etc/modules** file contains the names of kernel modules that are to be loaded at boot time, one per line. Comments begin with a '#', and everything on the line after them are ignored.

NAME

motd – message of the day

DESCRIPTION

/etc/motd is an ASCII file which contents are showed by login(1) before it executes the login shell.

FILES

/etc/motd

SEE ALSO

login(1)

NAME

nfs – nfs fstab format and options

SYNOPSIS

/etc/fstab

DESCRIPTION

The *fstab* file contains information about which filesystems to mount where and with what options. For NFS mounts, it contains the server name and exported server directory to mount from, the local directory that is the mount point, and the NFS specific options that control the way the filesystem is mounted. Here is an example from an */etc/fstab* file from an NFS mount.

server:/usr/local/pub /pub nfs timeo=14,intr

Options

- *rsize=n* The number of bytes NFS uses when reading files from an NFS server. The default value is dependent on the kernel, currently 1024 bytes.

- *wsize=n* The number of bytes NFS uses when writing files to an NFS server. The default value is dependent on the kernel, currently 1024 bytes.

- *timeo=n* The value in tenths of a second before sending the first retransmission after an RPC timeout. The default value is 7 tenths of a second. After the first timeout, the timeout is doubled after each successive timeout until a maximum timeout of 60 seconds is reached or the enough retransmissions have occured to cause a major timeout. Then, if the filesystem is hard mounted, each new timeout cascade restarts at twice the initial value of the previous cascade, again doubling at each retransmission. The maximum timeout is always 60 seconds. Better overall performance may be achieved by increasing the timeout when mounting on a busy network, to a slow server, or through several routers or gateways.

- *retrans=n* The number of minor timeouts and retransmissions that must occur before a major timeout occurs. The default is 3 timeouts. When a major timeout occurs, the file operation is either aborted or a "server not responding" message is printed on the console.

- *acregmin=n* The minimum time in seconds that attributes of a regular file should be cached before requesting fresh information from a server. The default is 3 seconds.

- *acregmax=n* The maximum time in seconds that attributes of a regular file can be cached before requesting fresh information from a server. The default is 60 seconds.

- *acdirmin=n* The minimum time in seconds that attributes of a directory should be cached before requesting fresh information from a server. The default is 30 seconds.

- *acdirmax=n* The maximum time in seconds that attributes of a directory can be cached before requesting fresh information from a server. The default is 60 seconds.

- *actimeo=n* Using actimeo sets all of *acregmin, acregmax, acdirmin,* and *acdirmax* to the same value. There is no default value.

- *retry=n* The number of times to retry a backgrounded NFS mount operation before giving up. The default value is 10000 times.

- *namlen=n* When an NFS server does not support version two of the RPC mount protocol, this option can be used to specify the maximum length of a filename that is supported on the remote filesystem. This is used to support the POSIX pathconf functions. The default is 255 characters.

port=n The numeric value of the port to connect to the NFS server on. If the port number is 0 (the default) then query the remote host's portmapper for the port number to use. If the remote host's NFS daemon is not registered with its portmapper, the standard NFS port number 2049 is used instead.

mountport=n The numeric value of the **mountd** port.

mounthost=name The name of the host running **mountd**.

mountprog=n Use an alternate RPC program number to contact the mount daemon on the remote host. This option is useful for hosts that can run multiple NFS servers. The default value is 100005 which is the standard RPC mount daemon program number.

mountvers=n Use an alternate RPC version number to contact the mount daemon on the remote host. This option is useful for hosts that can run multiple NFS servers. The default value is version 1.

nfsprog=n Use an alternate RPC program number to contact the NFS daemon on the remote host. This option is useful for hosts that can run multiple NFS servers. The default value is 100003 which is the standard RPC NFS daemon program number.

nfsvers=n Use an alternate RPC version number to contact the NFS daemon on the remote host. This option is useful for hosts that can run multiple NFS servers. The default value is version 2.

bg If the first NFS mount attempt times out, continue trying the mount in the background. The default is to not to background the mount on timeout but fail.

fg If the first NFS mount attempt times out, fail immediately. This is the default.

soft If an NFS file operation has a major timeout then report an I/O error to the calling program. The default is to continue retrying NFS file operations indefinitely.

hard If an NFS file operation has a major timeout then report "server not responding" on the console and continue retrying indefinitely. This is the default.

intr If an NFS file operation has a major timeout and it is hard mounted, then allow signals to interupt the file operation and cause it to return EINTR to the calling program. The default is to not allow file operations to be interrupted.

posix Mount the NFS filesystem using POSIX semantics. This allows an NFS filesystem to properly support the POSIX pathconf command by querying the mount server for the maximum length of a filename. To do this, the remote host must support version two of the RPC mount protocol. Many NFS servers support only version one.

nocto Supress the retrieval of new attributes when creating a file.

noac Disable all forms of attribute caching entirely. This extracts a server performance penalty but it allows two different NFS clients to get reasonable good results when both clients are actively writing to common filesystem on the server.

tcp Mount the NFS filesystem using the TCP protocol instead of the default UDP protocol. Many NFS severs only support UDP.

udp Mount the NFS filesystem using the UDP protocol. This is the default. All of the non-value options have corresponding nooption forms. For example, nointr means don't allow file operations to be interrupted.

FILES

/etc/fstab

SEE ALSO

fstab(5), **mount**(8), **umount**(8)

AUTHOR

"Rick Sladkey" <jrs@world.std.com>

BUGS

The bg, fg, retry, posix, and nocto options are parsed by mount but currently are silently ignored. The tcp and namlen options are implemented but are not currently supported by the Linux kernel. The umount command should notify the server when an NFS filesystem is unmounted.

NAME

nologin – prevent usual users from log into the system

DESCRIPTION

/etc/nologin is used by **login**(1); if this file exists, login will allow access only to root; other users are given a "System going down" message.

FILES

/etc/nologin

SEE ALSO

login(1), **shutdown**(8)

NAME

passwd – password file

DESCRIPTION

Passwd is an ASCII file which contains a list of the system's users and the passwords they must use for access. The password file should have read access for everyone, which is ok because of the encryption, but write access only for the superuser. If you create a new login, leave the password field empty and use **passwd**(2) to fill it. A star or something like that in the password field means, that this user can not login via **login**(1). If your root file system is on /dev/ram, you must save a changed password file to your root file system floppy, before you shutdown the system and check the access rights. If you want to create user groups, their GID's must be equal and there must be an entry in */etc/group*, or no group will exist.

There is one entry per line, and each line has the format:

login_name:passwd:UID:GID:user_name:directory:shell

The field descriptions are:

login_name	the name of the user on the system.
password	the encrypted optional user password.
UID	the numerical user ID.
GID	the numerical group ID for this user.
user_name	the (optional) comment field (often a full user name).
directory	the user's $HOME directory.
shell	the program to run at login (if empty, use /bin/sh).

FILES

/etc/passwd

SEE ALSO

passwd(1), **login**(1), **group**(5)

PROC(5)

NAME

/proc – process information pseudo-filesystem

DESCRIPTION

/proc is a pseudo-filesystem which is used as an interface to kernel data structures rather than reading and interpreting /dev/kmem.

The following outline gives a quick tour through the /proc hierarchy.

[number]
There is a numerical subdirectory for each running process; the subdirectory is named by the process ID. Each contains the following pseudo-files and directories.

cmdline
This holds the complete command line for the process, unless the whole process has been swapped out, or unless the process is a zombie. In either of these later cases, there is nothing in this file: i.e. a read on this file will return as having read 0 characters. This file is null-terminated, but not newline-terminated.

cwd
This is a link current working directory of the process. To find out the cwd of process 20, for instance, you can do this:
cd /proc/20/cwd; pwd

environ
This file contains the environment for the process. There are no newlines in this file: the entries are separated by null characters, and there is a null character at the end. Thus, to print out the environment of process 10, you would do:
cat /proc/10/environ | tr "\000" "\n"
This file is also null-terminated and not newline terminated.

exe
a pointer to the binary which was executed, and appears as a symbolic link. *readlink(2)* on the exe special file returns a string in the format:
[device]:inode
For example, [0301]:1502 would be inode 1502 on device major 03 (IDE, MFM, etc. drives) minor 01 (first partition on the first drive).
Also, the symbolic link can be dereferenced normally - attempting to open "exe" will open the executable. You can even type */proc/[number]/exe* to run another copy of the same process as [number].
find(1) with the -inum option can be used to locate the file.

fd
This is a subdirectory containing one entry for each file which the process has open, named by its file descriptor, and which is a symbolic link to the actual file (as the exe entry does). Thus, 0 is standard input, 1 standard output, 2 standard error, etc.
Programs that will take a filename, but will not take the standard input, and which write to a file, but will not send their output to standard output, can be effectively foiled this way, assuming that -i is the flag designating an input file and -o is the flag designating an output file:
foobar -i /proc/self/fd/0 -o /proc/self/fd/1 ...
and you have a working filter. Note that this will not work for programs that seek on their files, as the files in the fd directory are not seekable.
/proc/self/fd/N is approximately the same as /dev/fd/N in some UNIX and UNIX-like systems. Most Linux MAKEDEV scripts symbolically link /dev/fd to /proc/self/fd, in fact.

maps
A file containing the currently mapped memory regions and their access permissions.

25 Dec 1994

The format is:
address perms offset dev inode
```
00000000-0002f000 r-x- 00000400 03:03 1401
0002f000-00032000 rwx-p 0002f400 03:03 1401
00032000-0005b000 rwx-p 00000000 00:00 0
60000000-60098000 rwx-p 00000400 03:03 215
60098000-600c7000 rwx-p 00000000 00:00 0
bfffa000-c0000000 rwx-p 00000000 00:00 0
```
Where address is the address space in the process that it occupies, perms is a set of permissions: r = read
w = write
x = execute
s = shared
p = private (copy on write)
offset is the offset into the file/whatever, dev is the device (major:minor), and inode is the inode on that device. 0 indicates that no inode is associated with the memory region, as the case would be with bss.

mem
This is not the same as the mem (1,1) device, despite the fact that it has the same device numbers. The /dev/mem device is the physical memory before any address translation is done, but the mem file here is the memory of the process that accesses it. This cannot be *mmap(2)* '-1"ed currently, and will not be until a general *mmap(2)* is added to the kernel. (This might have happened by the time you read this.)

mmap
Directory of maps by *mmap(2)* which are symbolic links like exe, fd/*, etc. Note that maps includes a superset of this information, so /proc/*/mmap should be considered obsolete.
"0" is usually libc.so.4.
/proc/*/mmap was removed in Linux kernel version 1.1.40. (It really **was** obsolete!)

root
Unix and linux support the idea of a per-process root of the filesystem, set by the *chroot(2)* system call. Root points to the file system root, and behaves as exe, fd/*, etc. do.

stat
Status information about the process. This is used by *ps(1)* '-1'.
The fields, in order, with their proper *scanf(3)* format specifiers, are:

pid %d The process id.

comm %s The filename of the executable, in parentheses. This is visible whether or not the executable is swapped out.

state %c One character from the string "RSDZT" where R is running, S is sleeping in an interruptible wait, D is sleeping in an uninterruptible wait or swapping, Z is zombie, and T is traced or stopped (on a signal).

ppid %d The PID of the parent.

pgrp %d The process group ID of the process.

session %d The session ID of the process.

tty %d The tty the process uses.

tpgid %d The process group ID of the process which currently owns the tty that the process is connected to.

flags %u The flags of the process. Currently, every flag has the math bit set, because crt0.s checks for math emulation, so this is not included in the output. This is probably a bug, as not every process is a compiled C program. The math bit should be a decimal 4, and the traced bit is decimal 10.

minflt %u The number of minor faults the process has made, those which have not required loading a memory page from disk.

cminflt %u	The number of minor faults that the process and its children have made.
majflt %u	The number of major faults the process has made, those which have required loading a memory page from disk.
cmajflt %u	The number of major faults that the process and its children have made.
utime %d	The number of jiffies that this process has been scheduled in user mode.
stime %d	The number of jiffies that this process has been scheduled in kernel mode.
cutime %d	The number of jiffies that this process and its children have been scheduled in user mode.
cstime %d	The number of jiffies that this process and its children have been scheduled in kernel mode.
counter %d	The current maximum size in jiffies of the process's next timeslice, of what is currently left of its current timeslice, if it is the currently running process.
priority %d	The standard nice value, plus fifteen. The value is never negative in the kernel.
timeout %u	The time in jiffies of the process's next timeout.
itrealvalue %u	The time (in jiffies) before the next SIGALRM is sent to the process due to an interval timer.
starttime %d	Time the process started in jiffies after system boot.
vsize %u	Virtual memory size
rss %u	Resident Set Size: number of pages the process has in real memory, minus 3 for administrative purposes. This is just the pages which count towards text, data, or stack space. This does not include pages which have not been demand-loaded in, or which are swapped out.
rlim %u	Current limit in bytes on the rss of the process (usually 2,147,483,647).
startcode %u	The address above which program text can run.
endcode %u	The address below which program text can run.
startstack %u	The address of the start of the stack.
kstkesp %u	The current value of esp (32-bit stack pointer), as found in the kernel stack page for the process.
kstkeip %u	The current EIP (32-bit instruction pointer).
signal %d	The bitmap of pending signals (usually 0).
blocked %d	The bitmap of blocked signals (usually 0, 2 for shells).
sigignore %d	The bitmap of ignored signals.
sigcatch %d	The bitmap of catched signals.
wchan %u	This is the "channel" in which the process is waiting. This is the address of a system call, and can be looked up in a namelist if you need a textual name. (If you have an up-to-date /etc/psdatabase, then try *ps -l* to see the WCHAN field in action)
cpuinfo	No information.
devices	Text listing of major numbers and device groups. This can be used by MAKEDEV scripts for consistency with the kernel.
dma	No information. It is probably the DMA (direct memory access) channels in use.
filesystems	A text listing of the filesystems which were compiled into the kernel. Incidentally, this is used by *mount(1)* to cycle through different filesystems when none is specified.

interrupts	This is used to record the number of interrupts per each IRQ on (at least) the i386 architechure. Very easy to read formatting, done in ASCII.
ioports	No information. It is probably Input-Output port regions that are in use.
kcore	This file represents the physical memory of the system and is stored in the core file format. With this pseudo-file, and an unstripped kernel (/usr/src/linux/tools/zSystem) binary, GDB can be used to examine the current state of any kernel data structures. The total length of the file is the size of physical memory (RAM) plus 4KB.
kmsg	This file can be used instead of the *syslog(2)* system call to log kernel messages. A process must have superuser privileges to read this file, and only one process should read this file. This file should not be read if a syslog process is running which uses the *syslog(2)* system call facility to log kernel messages. Information in this file is retrieved with the *dmesg(8)* program).
ksyms	This holds the kernel exported symbol definitions used by the *modules(X)* tools to dynamically link and bind loadable modules.
loadavg	The load average numbers give the number of jobs in the run queue averaged over 1, 5 and 15 minutes. They are the same as the load average numbers given by *uptime(1)* and other programs.
malloc	This file is only present if CONFIGDEBUGMALLOC was defined during compilation.
meminfo	This is used by *free(1)* to report the amount of free and used memory (both physical and swap) on the system as well as the shared memory and buffers used by the kernel. It is in the same format as *free(1)* '-1', except in bytes rather than KB.
modules	A text list of the modules that have been loaded by the system.
net	various net pseudo-files, all of which give the status of some part of the networking layer. These files contain ASCII structures, and are therefore readable with cat. However, the standard *netstat(8)* suite provides much cleaner access to these files.
arp	This holds an ASCII readable dump of the kernel ARP table used for address resolutions. It will show both dynamically learned and pre-programmed ARP entries. The format is: IP address HW type Flags HW address 10.11.100.129 0x1 0x6 00:20:8A:00:0C:5A 10.11.100.5 0x1 0x2 00:C0:EA:00:00:4E 44.131.10.6 0x3 0x2 GW4PTS Where 'IP address' is the IPv4 address of the machine, the 'HW type' is the hardware type of the address from RFC 826. The flags are the internal flags of the ARP structure (as defined in /usr/include/linux/if_arp.h) and the 'HW address' is the physical layer mapping for that IP address if it is known.
dev	The dev pseudo-file contains network device status information. This gives the number of received and sent packets, the number of errors and collisions and other basic statistics. These are used by the *ifconfig(8)* program to report device status. The format is: Inter-| Receive | Transmit face |packets errs drop fifo frame|packets errs drop fifo colls carrier lo: 0 0 0 0 0 2353 0 0 0 0 0 eth0: 644324 1 0 0 1 563770 0 0 0 581 0
ipx	No information.

ipx_route	No information.
rarp	This file uses the same format as the *arp* file and contains the current reverse mapping database used to provide *rarp(8)* reverse address lookup services. If RARP is not configured into the kernel this file will not be present.
raw	Holds a dump of the RAW socket table. Much of the information is not of use apart from debugging. The 'sl' value is the kernel hash slot for the socket, the 'local address' is the local address and protocol number pair."St" is the internal status of the socket. The "tx_queue" and "rx_queue" are the outgoing and incoming data queue in terms of kernel memory usage. The "tr", "tm->when" and "rexmits" fields are not used by RAW. The uid field holds the creator euid of the socket.
route	No information, but looks similar to *route(8)*
snmp	This file holds the ASCII data needed for the IP, ICMP, TCP and UDP management information bases for an snmp agent. As of writing the TCP mib is incomplete. It is hoped to have it completed by 1.2.0.
tcp	Holds a dump of the TCP socket table. Much of the information is not of use apart from debugging. The "sl" value is the kernel hash slot for the socket, the "local address" is the local address and port number pair. The "remote address" is the remote address and port number pair (if connected). 'St' is the internal status of the socket. The 'tx_queue' and 'rx_queue' are the outgoing and incoming data queue in terms of kernel memory usage. The "tr", "tm->when" and "rexmits" fields hold internal information of the kernel socket state and are only useful for debugging. The uid field holds the creator euid of the socket.
udp	Holds a dump of the UDP socket table. Much of the information is not of use apart from debugging. The "sl" value is the kernel hash slot for the socket, the "local address" is the local address and port number pair. The "remote address" is the remote address and port number pair (if connected). "St" is the internal status of the socket. The "tx_queue" and "rx_queue" are the outgoing and incoming data queue in terms of kernel memory usage. The "tr", "tm->when" and "rexmits" fields are not used by UDP. The uid field holds the creator euid of the socket. The format is: sl local_address rem_address st tx_queue rx_queue tr rexmits tm->when uid 1: 01642C89:0201 0C642C89:03FF 01 00000000:00000001 01:000071BA 00000000 0 1: 00000000:0801 00000000:0000 0A 00000000:00000000 00:00000000 6F000100 0 1: 00000000:0201 00000000:0000 0A 00000000:00000000 00:00000000 00000000 0
unix	Lists the UNIX domain sockets present within the system and their status. The format is: Num RefCount Protocol Flags Type St Path 0: 00000002 00000000 00000000 0001 03 1: 00000001 00000000 00010000 0001 01 /dev/printer Where 'Num' is the kernel table slot number, 'RefCount' is the number of users of the socket, 'Protocol' is currently always 0, 'Flags' represent the internal kernel flags holding the status of the socket. Type is always '1' currently (Unix domain datagram sockets are not yet supported in the kernel). 'St' is the internal state of the socket and Path is the bound path (if any) of the socket.
pci	No information. Looks like PCI chipset values on various slots.

self	This directory refers to the process accessing the /proc filesystem, and is identical to the /proc directory named by the process ID of the same process.
stat	kernel/system statistics
cpu 3357 0 4313 1362393	The number of jiffies (1/100ths of a second) that the system spent in user mode, user mode with low priority (nice), system mode, and the idle task, respectively. The last value should be 100 times the second entry in the uptime pseudo-file.
disk 0 0 0 0	The four disk entries are not implemented at this time. I'm not even sure what this should be, since kernel statistics on other machines usually track both transfer rate and I/Os per second and this only allows for one field per drive.
page 5741 1808	The number of pages the system paged in and the number that were paged out (from disk).
swap 1 0	The number of swap pages that have been brought in and out.
intr 1462898	The number of interrupts received from the system boot.
ctxt 115315	The number of context switches that the system underwent.
btime 769041601	boot time, in seconds since the epoch (January 1, 1970).
uptime	This file contains two numbers: the uptime of the system (seconds), and the amount of time spent in idle process (seconds).
version	This strings identifies the kernel version that is currently running. For instance: Linux version 1.0.9 (quinlan@phaze) #1 Sat May 14 01:51:54 EDT 1994

SEE ALSO

cat(1), find(1), free(1), mount(1), ps(1), tr(1), uptime(1), readlink(2), mmap(2), chroot(2), syslog(2), hier(7), arp(8), dmesg(8), netstat(8), route(8), ifconfig(8), procinfo(8) and much more

CONFORMS TO

This roughly conforms to a Linux 1.1 kernel. Please update this as necessary!

Last updated for Linux 1.1.81.

CAVEATS

Note that many strings (i.e., the environment and command line) are in the internal format, with sub-fields terminated by NUL bytes, so you may find that things are more readable if you use *od -c* or *tr "\000" "\n"* to read them.

This manual page is incomplete, possibly inaccurate, and is the kind of thing that needs to be updated very often.

BUGS

The */proc* file system may introduce security holes into processes running with **chroot**(2). For example, if */proc* is mounted in the **chroot** hierarchy, a **chdir**(2) to */proc/1/root* will return to the original root of the file system. This may be considered a feature instead of a bug, since Linux does not yet support the **fchroot**(2) call.

RESOLVER(5)

NAME

resolver – resolver configuration file

SYNOPSIS

/etc/resolv.conf

DESCRIPTION

The *resolver* is a set of routines in the C library (*resolv*(3)) that provide access to the Internet Domain Name System. The resolver configuration file contains information that is read by the resolver routines the first time they are invoked by a process. The file is designed to be human readable and contains a list of keywords with values that provide various types of resolver information.

On a normally configured system this file should not be necessary. The only name server to be queried will be on the local machine, the domain name is determined from the host name, and the domain search path is constructed from the domain name.

The different configuration options are:

> **nameserver** Internet address (in dot notation) of a name server that the resolver should query. Up to MAXNS (currently 3) name servers may be listed, one per keyword. If there are multiple servers, the resolver library queries them in the order listed. If no **nameserver** entries are present, the default is to use the name server on the local machine. (The algorithm used is to try a name server, and if the query times out, try the next, until out of name servers, then repeat trying all the name servers until a maximum number of retries are made).
>
> **domain** Local domain name. Most queries for names within this domain can use short names relative to the local domain. If no **domain** entry is present, the domain is determined from the local host name returned by *gethostname* (2); the domain part is taken to be everything after the first '.'. Finally, if the host name does not contain a domain part, the root domain is assumed.
>
> **search** Search list for host-name lookup. The search list is normally determined from the local domain name; by default, it begins with the local domain name, then successive parent domains that have at least two components in their names. This may be changed by listing the desired domain search path following the *search* keyword with spaces or tabs separating the names. Most resolver queries will be attempted using each component of the search path in turn until a match is found. Note that this process may be slow and will generate a lot of network traffic if the servers for the listed domains are not local, and that queries will time out if no server is available for one of the domains.
>
> The search list is currently limited to six domains with a total of 256 characters.

The *domain* and *search* keywords are mutually exclusive. If more than one instance of these keywords is present, the last instance will override.

The keyword and value must appear on a single line, and the keyword (e.g. **nameserver**) must start the line. The value follows the keyword, separated by white space.

FILES

/etc/resolv.conf

SEE ALSO

gethostbyname(3N), resolver(3), hostname(7), named(8)
Name Server Operations Guide for BIND

NAME

securetty – file which lists ttys from which root can log in

DESCRIPTION

/etc/securetty is used by **login(1);** the file contains tty lines (without leading /dev/) on which root is allowed to login.

FILES

/etc/securetty

SEE ALSO

login(1)

NAME

shells – pathnames of valid login shells

DESCRIPTION

/etc/shells is a text file which contains the full pathnames of valid login shells.

EXAMPLES

/etc/shells may contain the following paths:

/bin/sh
/bin/csh

FILES

/etc/shells

SEE ALSO

chsh(1)

SYSLOG.CONF(5)

NAME

syslog.conf – syslogd(8) configuration file

DESCRIPTION

The syslog.conf file is the configuration file for the syslogd(8) program. It consists of lines with two fields: the *selector* field which specifies the types of messages and priorities to which the line applies, and an *action* field which specifies the action to be taken if a message syslogd received matches the selection criteria. There may not be *any* spaces in the action field. The *selector* field is separated from the *action* field by one or more tab or space characters (this is a departure from the standard BSD way of doing things: both tabs and spaces may be used to separate the selector from the action).

The *Selector* functions are encoded as a *facility*, a period ("."), and a *level*, with no intervening white-space. Both the *facility* and the *level* are case insensitive.

The *facility* describes the part of the system generating the message, and is one of the following keywords: auth, authpriv, cron, daemon, kern, lpr, mail, mark, news, syslog, user, uucp and local0 through local7. These keywords (with the exception of mark) correspond to the similar Dv LOG_ values specified to the openlog(3) and syslog(3) library routines.

The *level* describes the severity of the message, and is a keyword, optionally preceded by an equals ("="), from the following ordered list (higher to lower): emerg, alert, crit, err, warning, notice, info, and debug. These keywords correspond to the similar Dv LOG_ values specified to the syslog library routine.

See syslog(3) for a further descriptions of both the *facility* and *level* keywords and their significance.

If a received message matches the specified facility and is of the specified level (or a higher level if level was specified without "="), the action specified in the action field will be taken.

Multiple selectors may be specified for a single action by separating them with semicolon (";") characters. It is important to note, however, that each selector can modify the ones preceding it.

Multiple facilities may be specified for a single level by separating them with comma (",") characters.

An asterisk ("*") can be used to specify all facilities or all levels.

The special facility "mark" receives a message at priority "info" every 20 minutes (see syslogd(8)). This is not enabled by a facility field containing an asterisk.

The special level "none" disables a particular facility.

The action field of each line specifies the action to be taken when the selector field selects a message. There are four forms:

- A pathname (beginning with a leading slash). Selected messages are appended to the file.
- A hostname (preceded by an at ("@") sign). Selected messages are forwarded to the syslogd program on the named host.
- A comma separated list of users. Selected messages are written to those users if they are logged in.
- An asterisk. Selected messages are written to all logged-in users.

Blank lines and lines whose first non-blank character is a hash ("#") character are ignored.

EXAMPLES

A configuration file might appear as follows:

```
# Log all kernel messages, authentication messages of
# level notice or higher and anything of level err or
# higher to the console.
```

SYSLOG.CONF(5)

```
# Don't log private authentication messages!
*.err;kern.*;auth.notice;authpriv.none    /dev/console

# Log anything (except mail) of level info or higher.
# Don't log private authentication messages!
*.info;mail.none;authpriv.none            /var/log/messages

# Log debug messages only
*.=debug                                  /var/log/debug

# The authpriv file has restricted access.
authpriv.*                                /var/log/secure

# Log all the mail messages in one place.
mail.*                                    /var/log/maillog

# Everybody gets emergency messages, plus log them on another
# machine.
*.emerg                                   *
*.emerg                                   @arpa.berkeley.edu

# Root and Eric get alert and higher messages.
*.alert                                   root,eric

# Save mail and news errors of level err and higher in a
# special file.
uucp,news.crit                            /var/log/spoolerr
```

FILES

- /etc/syslog.conf The syslogd(8) configuration file.

BUGS

The effects of multiple selectors are sometimes not intuitive. For example "mail.crit,*.err" will select "mail" facility messages at the level of "err" or higher, not at the level of "crit" or higher.

SEE ALSO

syslog(3), syslogd(8)

TERMCAP(5)

NAME

termcap – terminal capability database

DESCRIPTION

/etc/termcap is an ASCII file that lists the capabilities of many different types of terminal. Programs can read termcap to find the particular escape codes needed to control the visual attributes of the terminal actually in use. (Other aspects of the terminal are handled by stty.) The termcap database is indexed on the TERM environment variable.

Termcap entries must be defined on a single logical line, with '\' used to suppress the newline. Fields are separated by ':'. The first field of each entry starts at the left-hand margin, and contain a list of names for the terminal, separated by '|'. The first subfield contains a short name consisting of two characters. It is a relict of system V6, where a system wide database of 16 bit (equals these two characters) per terminal existed. This name can consist of capital or small letters. The second subfield contains the name used by the environment variable TERM. It should be spelled in lowercase letters. Selectable hardware capabilities should be marked by appending a hyphen and a suffix to this name. See below for an example. Usual suffixes are w (more than 80 characters), am (automatic margins), nam (no automatic margins) and rv (reverse video display). The third subfield contains a long and descriptive name for this termcap entry.

Subsequent fields contain the terminal capabilities; any continued capability lines must be indented one tab from the left margin.

Although there is no defined order, it is suggested to write first boolean, then numeric and at last string capabilities, each sorted alphabetically without looking at lower or upper spelling. Capabilities of similar functions can be written in one line.

Example for:

Head line: vt|vt101|DEC VT 101 terminal in 80 character mode:\Head line: Vt|vt101-w|DEC VT 101 terminal in (wide) 132 character mode:\Boolean: :bs:\Numeric: :co#80:\String: :sr=\E[H:\

Boolean Capabilities

	5i	Printer will not echo on screen
	am	Automatic margins which means automatic line wrap
	bs	Control-H (8 dec.) performs a backspace
	bw	Backspace on left margin wraps to previous line and right margin
	da	Display retained above screen
	db	Display retained below screen
	eo	A space erases all characters at cursor position
	es	Escape sequences and special characters work in status line
	gn	Generic device
	hc	This is a hardcopy terminal
	HC	The cursor is hard to see when not on bottom line
	hs	Has a status line
	hz	Hazeltine bug, the terminal can not print tilde characters
	in	Terminal inserts nulls, not spaces, to fill whitespace
	km	Terminal has a meta key
	mi	Cursor movement works in insert mode
	ms	Cursor movement works in standout/underline mode
	NP	No pad character
	NR	ti does not reverse te

	nx	No padding, must use XON/XOFF
	os	Terminal can overstrike
	ul	Terminal underlines although it can not overstrike
	xb	Beehive glitch, f1 sends ESCAPE, f2 sends ^C
	xn	Newline/wraparound glitch
	xo	Terminal uses xon/xoff protocol
	xs	Text typed over standout text will be displayed in standout
	xt	Teleray glitch, destructive tabs and odd standout mode

Numeric Capabilities

	co	Number of columns
	dB	Delay in milliseconds for backspace on hardcopy terminals
	dC	Delay in milliseconds for carriage return on hardcopy terminals
	dF	Delay in milliseconds for form feed on hardcopy terminals
	dN	Delay in milliseconds for new line on hardcopy terminals
	dT	Delay in milliseconds for tabulator stop on hardcopy terminals
	dV	Delay in milliseconds for vertical tabulator stop on hardcopy terminals
	it	Difference between tab positions
	lh	Height of soft labels
	lm	Lines of memory
	lw	Width of soft labels
	li	Number of lines
	Nl	Number of soft labels
	pb	Lowest baud rate which needs padding
	sg	Standout glitch
	ug	Underline glitch
	vt	virtual terminal number
	ws	Width of status line if different from screen width

String Capabilities

	!1	shifted save key
	!2	shifted suspend key
	!3	shifted undo key
	#1	shifted help key
	#2	shifted home key
	#3	shifted input key
	#4	shifted cursor left key
	%0	redo key
	%1	help key
	%2	mark key
	%3	message key
	%4	move key
	%5	next-object key
	%6	open key

%7	options key	
%8	previous-object key	
%9	print key	
%a	shifted message key	
%b	shifted move key	
%c	shifted next key	
%d	shifted options key	
%e	shifted previous key	
%f	shifted print key	
%g	shifted redo key	
%h	shifted replace key	
%i	shifted cusor right key	
%j	shifted resume key	
&0	shifted cancel key	
&1	reference key	
&2	refresh key	
&3	replace key	
&4	restart key	
&5	resume key	
&6	save key	
&7	suspend key	
&8	undo key	
&9	shifted begin key	
*0	shifted find key	
*1	shifted command key	
*2	shifted copy key	
*3	shifted create key	
*4	shifted delete character	
*5	shifted delete line	
*6	select key	
*7	shifted end key	
*8	shifted clear line key	
*9	shifted exit key	
@0	find key	
@1	begin key	
@2	cancel key	
@3	close key	
@4	command key	
@5	copy key	
@6	create key	
@7	end key	
@8	enter/send key	
@9	exit key	

al	Insert one line	
AL	Indert %1 lines	
ac	Pairs of block graphic characters to map alternate character set	
ae	End alternative character set	
as	Start alternative character set for block graphic characters	
bc	Backspace, if not ^H	
bl	Audio bell	
bt	Move to previous tab stop	
cb	Clear from beginning of line to cursor	
cc	Dummy command character	
cd	Clear to end of screen	
ce	Clear to end of line	
ch	Move cursor horizontally only to column %1	
cl	Clear screen and cursor home	
cm	Cursor move to row %1 and column %2 (on screen)	
CM	Move cursor to row %1 and column %2 (in memory)	
cr	Carriage return	
cs	Scroll region from line %1 to %2	
ct	Clear tabs	
cv	Move cursor vertically only to line %1	
dc	Delete one character	
DC	Delete %1 characters	
dl	Delete one line	
DL	Delete %1 lines	
dm	Begin delete mode	
do	Cursor down one line	
DO	Cursor down #1 lines	
ds	Disable status line	
eA	Enable alternate character set	
ec	Erase %1 characters starting at cursor	
ed	End delete mode	
ei	End insert mode	
ff	Formfeed character on hardcopy terminals	
fs	Return character to its position before going to status line	
F1	The string sent by function key f11	
F2	The string sent by function key f12	
F3	The string sent by function key f13	
...	...	
F9	The string sent by function key f19	
FA	The string sent by function key f20	
FB	The string sent by function key f21	
...	...	
FZ	The string sent by function key f45	

Fa	The string sent by function key f46	
Fb	The string sent by function key f47	
...	...	
Fr	The string sent by function key f63	
hd	Move cursor a half line down	
ho	Cursor home	
hu	Move cursor a half line up	
i1	Initialization string 1 at login	
i3	Initialization string 3 at login	
is	Initialization string 2 at login	
ic	Insert one character	
IC	Insert %1 characters	
if	Initialization file	
im	Begin insert mode	
ip	Insert pad time and needed special characters after insert	
iP	Initialization program	
K1	upper left key on keypad	
K2	center key on keypad	
K3	upper right key on keypad	
K4	bottom left key on keypad	
K5	bottom right key on keypad	
k0	Function key 0	
k1	Function key 1	
k2	Function key 2	
k3	Function key 3	
k4	Function key 4	
k5	Function key 5	
k6	Function key 6	
k7	Function key 7	
k8	Function key 8	
k9	Function key 9	
k;	Function key 10	
ka	Clear all tabs key	
kA	Insert line key	
kb	Backspace key	
kB	Back tab stop	
kC	Clear screen key	
kd	Cursor down key	
kD	Key for delete character under cursor	
ke	turn keypad off	
kE	Key for clear to end of line	
kF	Key for scolling forward/down	
kh	Cursor home key	

kH	Cursor hown down key	
kI	Insert character/Insert mode key	
kl	Cursor left key	
kL	Key for delete line	
kM	Key for exit insert mode	
kN	Key for next page	
kP	Key for previous page	
kr	Cursor right key	
kR	Key for scolling backward/up	
ks	Turn keypad on	
kS	Clear to end of screen key	
kt	Clear this tab key	
kT	Set tab here key	
ku	Cursor up key	
l0	Label of zeroth function key, if not f0	
l1	Label of first function key, if not f1	
l2	Label of first function key, if not f2	
...	...	
la	Label of tenth function key, if not f10	
le	Cursor left one character	
ll	Move cursor to lower left corner	
LE	Cursor left %1 characters	
LF	Turn soft labels off	
LO	Turn soft labels on	
mb	Start blinking	
MC	Clear soft margins	
md	Start bold mode	
me	End all mode like so, us, mb, md and mr	
mh	Start half bright mode	
mk	Dark mode (Characters invisible)	
ML	Set left soft margin	
mm	Put terminal in meta mode	
mo	Put terminal out of meta mode	
mp	Turn on protected attribute	
mr	Start reverse mode	
MR	Set right soft margin	
nd	Cursor right one character	
nw	Carriage return command	
pc	Padding character	
pf	Turn printer off	
pk	Program key %1 to send string %2 as if typed by user	
pl	Program key %1 to execute string %2 in local mode	
pn	Program soft label %1 to to show string %2	

po	Turn the printer on
pO	Turn the printer on for %1 (<256) bytes
ps	Print screen contents on printer
px	Program key %1 to send string %2 to computer
r1	Reset string 1 to set terminal to sane modes
r2	Reset string 2 to set terminal to sane modes
r3	Reset string 3 to set terminal to sane modes
RA	disable automatic margins
rc	Restore saved cursor position
rf	Reset string file name
RF	Request for input from terminal
RI	Cursor right %1 characters
rp	Repeat character %1 for %2 times
rP	Padding after character sent in replace mode
rs	Reset string
RX	Turn off XON/XOFF flow control
sa	Set %1 %2 %3 %4 %5 %6 %7 %8 %9 attributes
SA	enable automatic margins
sc	Save cursor position
se	End standout mode
sf	Normal scroll one line
SF	Normal scroll %1 lines
so	Start standout mode
sr	Reverse scroll
SR	scroll back %1 lines
st	Set tabulator stop in all rows at current column
SX	Turn on XON/XOFF flow control
ta	move to next hardware tab
tc	Read in terminal description from another entry
te	End program that uses cursor motion
ti	Begin program that uses cursor motion
ts	Move cursor to column %1 of status line
uc	Underline character under cursor and move cursor right
ue	End underlining
up	Cursor up one line
UP	Cursor up %1 lines
us	Start underlining
vb	Visible bell
ve	Normal cursor visible
vi	Cursor unvisible
vs	Standout cursor
wi	Set window from line %1 to %2 and column %3 to %4
XF	XOFF character if not ^S

There are several ways of defining the control codes for string capabilities: Normal characters except '^',',','\' and '%' represent themselves. A '^x' means Control-x. Control-A equals 1 decimal. \x means a special code. x can be one of the following charaters:

E	Escape (27)
n	Linefeed (10)
r	Carriage return (13)
t	Tabulation (9)
b	Backspace (8)
f	Form feed (12)
0	Null character. A \xxx specifies the octal character xxx.
i	Increments paramters by one.
r	Single parameter capability
+	Add value of next character to this parameter and do binary output
2	Do ASCII output of this parameter with a field with of 2
d	Do ASCII output of this parameter with a field with of 3
%	Print a '%'

If you use binary output, then you should avoid the null character because it terminates the string. You should reset tabulator expansion if a tabulator can be the binary output of a parameter.

Warning: The above metacharacters for parameters may be wrong, they document Minix termcap which may not be compatible with Linux termcap.

The block graphic characters can be specified by three string capabilities:

as start the alternative charset
ae end it
ac pairs of characters. The first character is the name of the block graphic
symbol and the second characters is its definition.

The following names are available:

+	right arrow (>)
,	left arrow (<)
.	down arrow (v)
0	full square (#)
I	latern (#)
-	upper arrow (^)
'	rhombus (+)
a	chess board (:)
f	degree (')
g	plus-minus (#)
h	square (#)
j	right bottom corner (+)
k	right upper corner (+)
l	left upper corner (+)
m	left bottom corner (+)
n	cross (+)
o	upper horizontal line (-)

q	middle horizontal line (-)
s	bottom horizontal line (_)
t	left tee (+)
u	right tee (+)
v	bottom tee (+)
w	normal tee (+)
x	vertical line (|)
~	paragraph (???)

The values in parentheses are suggested defaults which are used by curses, if the capabilities are missing.

SEE ALSO
termcap(3)

TTYTYPE(5)

NAME

ttytype – terminal name and device list

DESCRIPTION

Ttytype is an ASCII file that lists the names of terminals, as used in termcap, in association with the names of the ttys (minus /dev/) to which they are attached. It is used by the program tset to set the environment variable TERM to the correct terminal name for the user's current tty.

EXAMPLE

A typical /etc/ttytype is:

con80x25 tty1
vt320 ttys0

FILES

/etc/ttytype

SEE ALSO

getty(1), **termcap**(5)

TZFILE(5)   TZFILE(5)

NAME

tzfile – time zone information

SYNOPSIS

#include <tzfile.h>

DESCRIPTION

The time zone information files used by *tzset*(3) begin with bytes reserved for future use, followed by six four-byte values of type **long**, written in a "standard" byte order (the high-order byte of the value is written first). These values are, in order:

tzh_ttisgmtcnt	The number of GMT/local indicators stored in the file.
tzh_ttisstdcnt	The number of standard/wall indicators stored in the file.
tzh_leapcnt	The number of leap seconds for which data is stored in the file.
tzh_timecnt	The number of "transition times" for which data is stored in the file.
tzh_typecnt	The number of "local time types" for which data is stored in the file (must not be zero).
tzh_charcnt	The number of characters of "time zone abbreviation strings" stored in the file.

The above header is followed by *tzh_timecnt* four-byte values of type **long**, sorted in ascending order. These values are written in "standard" byte order. Each is used as a transition time (as returned by *time*(2)) at which the rules for computing local time change. Next come *tzh_timecnt* one-byte values of type **unsigned char**; each one tells which of the different types of "local time" types described in the file is associated with the same-indexed transition time. These values serve as indices into an array of *ttinfo* structures that appears next in the file; these structures are defined as follows:

```
struct ttinfo {
long tt_gmtoff;
int tt_isdst;
unsigned int tt_abbrind;
};
```

Each structure is written as a four-byte value for *tt_gmtoff* of type **long**, in a standard byte order, followed by a one-byte value for *tt_isdst* and a one-byte value for *tt_abbrind*. In each structure, *tt_gmtoff* gives the number of seconds to be added to GMT, *tt_isdst* tells whether *tm_isdst* should be set by *localtime* (3) and *tt_abbrind* serves as an index into the array of time zone abbreviation characters that follow the *ttinfo* structure(s) in the file.

Then there are *tzh_leapcnt* pairs of four-byte values, written in standard byte order; the first value of each pair gives the time (as returned by *time(2)*) at which a leap second occurs; the second gives the *total* number of leap seconds to be applied after the given time. The pairs of values are sorted in ascending order by time.

Then there are *tzh_ttisstdcnt* standard/wall indicators, each stored as a one-byte value; they tell whether the transition times associated with local time types were specified as standard time or wall clock time, and are used when a time zone file is used in handling POSIX-style time zone environment variables.

Finally there are *tzh_ttisgmtcnt* GMT/local indicators, each stored as a one-byte value; they tell whether the transition times associated with local time types were specified as GMT or local time, and are used when a time zone file is used in handling POSIX-style time zone environment variables.

Localtime uses the first standard-time *ttinfo* structure in the file (or simply the first *ttinfo* structure in the absence of a standard-time structure) if either *tzh_timecnt* is zero or the time argument is less than the first transition time recorded in the file.

SEE ALSO
newctime(3)

UTMP(5)   Linux Programmer's Manual   UTMP(5)

NAME

utmp, wtmp – login records

SYNOPSIS

#include <utmp.h>

DESCRIPTION

The **utmp** file allows one to discover information about who is currently using the system. There may be more users currently using the system, because not all programs use utmp logging. **Warning: utmp** must not be writable, because many system programs depend on its integrity. You risk faked system logfiles and modifications of system files if you leave **utmp** writable to any user. The file is a sequence of entries with the following structure declared in the include file:

```
#define UT_UNKNOWN 0
#define RUN_LVL 1
#define BOOT_TIME 2
#define NEW_TIME 3
#define OLD_TIME 4
#define INIT_PROCESS 5
#define LOGIN_PROCESS 6
#define USER_PROCESS 7
#define DEAD_PROCESS 8
#define UT_LINESIZE 12
#define UT_NAMESIZE 8
#define UT_HOSTSIZE 16
struct utmp {
short ut_type; /* type of login */
pid_t ut_pid; /* pid of process */
char ut_line[UT_LINESIZE]; /* device name of tty – "/dev/" */
char ut_id[2]; /* init id or abbrev. ttyname */
time_t ut_time; /* login time */
char ut_user[UT_NAMESIZE]; /* user name */
char ut_host[UT_HOSTSIZE]; /* host name for remote login */
long ut_addr; /* IP addr of remote host */
};
```

This structure gives the name of the special file associated with the user's terminal, the user's login name, and the time of login in the form of *time*(2). String fields are terminated by '\0' if they are shorter than the size of the field.

The **wtmp** file records all logins and logouts. Its format is exactly like **utmp** except that a null user name indicates a logout on the associated terminal. Furthermore, the terminal name **"~"** with user name **"shutdown"** or **"reboot"** indicates a system shutdown or reboot and the pair of terminal names **"|"/"}"** logs the old/new system time when *date*(1) changes it. **wtmp** is maintained by *login*(1), and *init*(1) and some very of *getty*(1). Neither of these programs creates the file, so if it is removed record-keeping is turned off.

FILES

/var/adm/utmp
/var/adm/wtmp

CONFORMING TO

Linux utmp entries neither conform to v7/BSD nor to SYSV: They are a mix of the two. v7/BSD has less fields, most importantly it lacks **ut_type**, which causes native v7/BSD-like programs to display for example dead or login entries. SYSV has one more field to log the exit status of dead processes. Linux uses the BSD conventions for line contents, as documented above. SYSV only uses the type field to mark them and logs informative messages such as e.g. **"new time"** in the line field. **UT_UNKNOWN** seems to be a Linux invention. There is no type **ACCOUNTING** in Linux. SYSV has no **ut_host** or **ut_addr** fields.

RESTRICTIONS

The file format is machine dependent, so it is recommended that it is processed only on the machine architecture where it got created.

SEE ALSO

ac(1), **date**(1), **last**(1), **login**(1), **who**(1), **getutent**(3), **init**(8)

XF86Config(4/5)　　　　　　　　　　　　　　　　　　　　　　　XF86Config(4/5)

NAME

XF86Config - Configuration File for XFree86

DESCRIPTION

XFree86 uses a configuration file called **XF86Config** for its initial setup. This configuration file is searched for in the following places:

>   /etc/XF86Config
>   <XRoot>/lib/X11/XF86Config.*hostname*
>   <XRoot>/lib/X11/XF86Config

where <XRoot> refers to the root of the X11 install tree.

This file is composed of a number of sections. Each section has the form:

>   Section "*SectionName*"
>   *SectionEntry* ...
>   EndSection

The section names are:

>   **Files** (File pathnames)
>   **ServerFlags** (Server flags)
>   **Keyboard** (Keyboard configuration)
>   **Pointer** (Pointer configuration)
>   **Monitor** (Monitor description)
>   **Device** (Graphics device description)
>   **Screen** (Screen configuration)

The **Files** section is used to specify the default font path and the path to the RGB database. These paths can also be set from the command line (see *Xserver(1)*). The entries available for this section are:

FontPath *"path"*　sets the search path for fonts. This path is a comma separated list of directories which the X server searches for font databases. Multiple **FontPath** entries may be specified, and they will be concatenated to build up the fontpath used by the server.

>   X11R6 allows the X server to request fonts from a font server. A font server is specified by placing a
>
>   "<trans>/<hostname>:<port_number>"
>
>   entry into the fontpath. For example, the fontpath
>
>   "/usr/X11R6/lib/X11/fonts/misc/,tcp/zok:7100"
>
>   tells the X server to first try to locate the font in the local directory /usr/X11R6/lib/X11/fonts/misc. If that fails, then request the font from the *font server* running on machine zok listening for connections on TCP port number 7100.

RGBPath *"path"*　sets the path name for the RGB color database.

The **ServerFlags** section is used to specify some miscellaneous X server options. The entries available for this section are:

NoTrapSignals　　This prevents the X server from trapping a range of unexpected fatal signals and exiting cleanly. Instead, the X server will die and drop core where the fault occurred. The default behaviour is for the X server exit cleanly, but still drop a core file. In general you never want to use this option unless you are debugging an X server problem.

DontZap　　This disallows the use of the **Ctrl+Alt+Backspace** sequence. This sequence allows you to terminate the X server. Setting **DontZap** allows this key sequence to be passed to clients.

DontZoom　　This disallows the use of the **Ctrl+Alt+Keypad-Plus** and **Ctrl+Alt+Keypad-Minus** sequences.

XFree86　　　　　　　　　　　　Version 3.1.2　　　　　　　　　　　　985

These sequences allows you to switch between video modes. Setting **DontZoom** allows these key sequences to be passed to clients.

The **Keyboard** section is used to specify the keyboard input device, parameters and some default keyboard mapping options. The entries available for this section are:

Protocol *"kbd-protocol"*
kbd-protocol may be either **Standard** or **Xqueue**. **Xqueue** is specified when using the event queue driver on SVR3 or SVR4.

AutoRepeat *delay rate*
changes the behavior of the autorepeat of the keyboard. This does not work on all platforms.

ServerNumLock
forces the X server to handle the numlock key internally. The X server sends a different set of keycodes for the numpad when the numlock key is active. This enables applications to make use of the numpad.

LeftAlt *mapping* **RightAlt** *mapping* **AltGr** *mapping* **ScrollLock** *mapping* **RightCtl** *mapping*

*Allows a default mapping to be set for the above keys (note that **AltGr** is a synonym for **RightAlt**). The values that may be specified for mapping are:*

> Meta
> Compose
> ModeShift
> ModeLock
> ScrollLock
> Control

> The default mapping when none of these options are specified is:

> LeftAlt Meta
> RightAlt Meta
> ScrollLock Compose
> RightCtl Control

XLeds *led ...*
makes *led* available for clients instead of using the traditional function (Scroll Lock, Caps Lock & Num Lock). *led* is a list of numbers in the range 1 to 3.

VTSysReq
enables the SYSV-style VT switch sequence for non-SYSV systems which support VT switching. This sequence is Alt-SysRq followed by a function key (Fn). This prevents the X server trapping the keys used for the default VT switch sequence.

VTInit *"command"*
Runs *command* after the VT used by the server has been opened. The command string is passed to "/bin/sh -c", and is run with the real user's id with stdin and stdout set to the VT. The purpose of this option is to allow system dependent VT initialisation commands to be run. One example is a command to disable the 2-key VT switching sequence which is the default on some systems.

The **Pointer** section is used to specify the pointer device and parameters. The entries available for this section are:

Protocol *"protocol-type"*
specifies the pointer device protocol type. The protocol types available are:

> **BusMouse**
> **Logitech**
> **Microsoft**
> **MMSeries**

XF86Config(4/5)   XF86Config(4/5)

        Mouseman
        MouseSystems
        PS/2
        MMHitTab
        Xqueue
        OSMouse

One should specify **BusMouse** for the Logitech bus mouse. Also, many newer Logitech serial mice use either the **Microsoft** or **MouseMan** protocol. **Xqueue** should be specified here if it was used in the **Keyboard** section. **OSMouse** refers to the event-driver mouse interface available on SCO's SVR3. This may optionally be followed by a number specifying the number of buttons the mouse has.

        Device *"pointer-dev"*   specifies the device the server should open for pointer input (eg, **/dev/tty00** or **/dev/mouse**). A device should not be specified when using the **Xqueue** or **OSMouse** protocols.

        BaudRate *rate*   sets the baudrate of the serial mouse to *rate*. For mice that allow dynamic speed adjustments (like Logitech) the baudrate is changed in the mouse. Otherwise the rate is simply set on the computer's side to allow mice with non-standard rates (the standard rate is 1200).

        Emulate3Buttons   enables the emulation of the third mouse button for mice which only have two physical buttons. The third button is emulated by pressing both buttons simultaneously.

        Emulate3Timeout *timeout*   sets the time (in milliseconds) that the server waits before deciding if two buttons were pressed "simultaneously" when 3 button emulation is enabled. The default timeout is 50ms.

        ChordMiddle   handles mice which send left+right events when the middle button is used (like some Logitech Mouseman mice).

        SampleRate *rate*   sets the number of motion/button-events the mouse sends per second. This is currently only supported for some Logitech mice.

        ClearDTR   This option clears the DTR line on the serial port used by the mouse. This option is only valid for a mouse using the **MouseSystems** protocol. Some dual-protocol mice require DTR to be cleared to operate in MouseSystems mode. Note, in versions of XFree86 prior to 2.1, this option also cleared the RTS line. A separate **ClearRTS** option has since been added for mice which require this.

        ClearRTS   This option clears the RTS line on the serial port used by the mouse. This option is only valid for a mouse using the **MouseSystems** protocol. Some dual-protocol mice require both DTR and RTS to be cleared to operate in MouseSystems mode. Both the **ClearDTR** and **ClearRTS** options should be used for such mice.

The **Monitor** sections are used to define the specifications of a monitor and a list of video modes suitable for use with a monitor. More than one **Monitor** section may be present in an XF86Config file. The entries available for this section are:

        Identifier *"ID string"*   This specifies a string by which the monitor can be referred to in a later **Screen** section. Each **Monitor** section should have a unique ID string.

        VendorName *"vendor"*   This optional entry specifies the monitor's manufacturer.

        ModelName *"model"*   This optional entry specifies the monitor's model.

XFree86   Version 3.1.2   987

HorizSync *horizsync-range* gives the range(s) of horizontal sync frequencies supported by the monitor. *horizsync-range* may be a comma separated list of either discrete values or ranges of values. A range of values is two values separated by a dash. By default the values are in units of kHz. They may be specified in MHz or Hz if **MHz** or **Hz** is added to the end of the line. The data given here is used by the X server to determine if video modes are within the specifications of the monitor. This information should be available in the monitor's handbook.

VertRefresh *vertrefresh-range* gives the range(s) of vertical refresh frequencies supported by the monitor. *vertrefresh-range* may be a comma separated list of either discrete values or ranges of values. A range of values is two values separated by a dash. By default the values are in units of Hz. They may be specified in MHz or kHz if **MHz** or **kHz** is added to the end of the line. The data given here is used by the X server to determine if video modes are within the specifications of the monitor. This information should be available in the monitor's handbook.

Gamma *gamma-value(s)* This is an optional entry that can be used to specify the gamma correction for the monitor. It may be specified as either a single value or as three separate RGB values. Not all X servers are capable of using this information.

Mode *"name"* indicates the start of a multi-line video mode description. The mode description is terminated with an **EndMode** line. The mode description consists of the following entries:

DotClock *clock* is the dot clock rate to be used for the mode.

HTimings *hdisp hsyncstart hsyncend htotal* specifies the horizontal timings for the mode.

VTimings *vdisp vsyncstart vsyncend vtotal* specifies the vertical timings for the mode.

Flags *"flag"* ... specifies an optional set of mode flags. **"Interlace"** indicates that the mode is interlaced. **"DoubleScan"** indicates a mode where each scanline is doubled. **"+HSync"** and **"-HSync"** can be used to select the polarity of the HSync signal. **"+VSync"** and **"-VSync"** can be used to select the polarity of the VSync signal. **"Composite"**, can be used to specify composite sync on hardware where this is supported. Additionally, on some hardware, **"+CSync"** and **"-CSync"** may be used to select the composite sync polarity.

Modeline *"name" mode-description* is a single line format for specifying video modes. The *mode-description* is in four sections, the first three of which are mandatory. The first is the pixel clock. This is a single number specifying the pixel clock rate for the mode. The second section is a list of four numbers specifying the horizontal timings. These numbers are the *hdisp, hsyncstart, hsyncend, htotal*. The third section is a list of four numbers specifying the vertical timings. These numbers are *vdisp, vsyncstart, vsyncend, vtotal*. The final section is a list of flags specifying other characteristics of the mode. **Interlace** indicates that the mode is interlaced. **"DoubleScan"** indicates a mode where each scanline is doubled. **+HSync** and **–HSync** can be used to select the polarity of the

HSync signal. **+VSync** and **−VSync** can be used to select the polarity of the VSync signal. **Composite** can be used to specify composite sync on hardware where this is supported. Additionally, on some hardware, **"+CSync"** and **"−CSync"** may be used to select the composite sync polarity.

The **Device** sections are used to define a graphics device (video board). More than one **Device** section may be present in an XF86Config file. The entries available for this section are:

Identifier *"ID string"* — This specifies a string by which the graphics device can be referred to in a later **Screen** section. Each **Device** section should have a unique ID string.

VendorName *"vendor"* — This optional entry specifies the graphics device's manufacturer.

BoardName *"model"* — This optional entry specifies the name of the graphics device.

Chipset *"chipset-type"* — This optional entry specifies the chipset used on the graphics board. In most cases this entry is not required because the X servers will probe the hardware to determine the chipset type.

Ramdac *"ramdac-type"* — This optional entry specifies the type of RAMDAC used on the graphics board. This is only used by a few of the X servers, and in most cases it is not required because the X servers will probe the hardware to determine the RAMDAC type where possible.

DacSpeed *speed* — This optional entry specifies the RAMDAC speed rating (which is usually printed on the RAMDAC chip). The speed is in MHz. This is only used by a few of the X servers, and only needs to be specified when the speed rating of the RAMDAC is different from the default built in to the X server.

Clocks *clock ...* — specifies the dotclocks that are on your graphics board. The clocks are in MHz, and may be specified as a floating point number. The value is stored internally to the nearest kHz. The ordering of the clocks is important. It must match the order in which they are selected on the graphics board. Multiple **Clocks** lines may be specified. For boards with programmable clock chips, the **ClockChip** entry should be used instead of this. A **Clocks** entry is not mandatory for boards with non-programmable clock chips, but is highly recommended because it prevents the clock probing phase during server startup. This clock probing phase can cause problems for some monitors.

ClockChip *"clockchip-type"* — This optional entry is used to specify the clock chip type on graphics boards which have a programmable clock generator. Only a few X servers support programmable clock chips. For details, see the appropriate X server manual page.

ClockProg *"command"* [*textclock*] — This optional entry runs *command* to set the clock on the graphics board instead of using the internal code. The command string must consist of the full pathname (and no flags). When using this option, a **Clocks** entry is required to specify which clock values are to be made available to the server (up to 128 clocks may be specified). The optional *textclock* value is used to tell the server that *command* must be run to restore the textmode clock at server exit (or when VT switching). *textclock* must match one of the values in the **Clocks** entry. This parameter is required when the clock used for text mode is a programmable clock.

The command is run with the real user's id with stdin and stdout set to the graphics console device. Two arguments are passed to the command. The first is the clock frequency in MHz as a floating point number and the second is the index of the clock in the **Clocks** entry. The command should return an exit status of 0 when successful, and something in the range 1–254 otherwise.

The command is run when the initial graphics mode is set and when changing screen resolution with the hotkey sequences. If the program fails at initialisation the server exits. If it fails during a mode switch, the mode switch is aborted but the server keeps running. It is assumed that if the command fails the clock has not been changed.

Option *"optionstring"*   This optional entry allows the user to select certain options provided by the drivers. Multiple **Option** entries may be given. The supported values for *optionstring* are given in the appropriate X server manual pages.

VideoRam *mem*   This optional entry specifies the amount of videoram that is installed on the graphics board. This is measured in kBytes. In most cases this is not required because the X server probes the graphics board to determine this quantity.

BIOSBase *baseaddress*   This optional entry specifies the base address of the video BIOS for the VGA board. This address is normally 0xC0000, which is the default the X servers will use. Some systems, particularly those with on-board VGA hardware, have the BIOS located at an alternate address, usually 0xE0000. If your video BIOS is at an address other than 0xC0000, you must specify the base address in the XF86Config file. Note that some X servers don't access the BIOS at all, and those which do only use the BIOS when searching for information during the hardware probe phase.

MemBase *baseaddress*   This optional entry specifies the memory base address of a graphics board's linear frame buffer. This entry is only used by a few X servers, and the interpretation of this base address may be different for different X servers. Refer to the appropriate X server manual page for details.

IOBase *baseaddress*   This optional entry specifies the IO base address. This entry is only used for a few X servers. Refer to the appropriate X server manual page for details.

DACBase *baseaddress*   This optional entry specifies the DAC base address. This entry is only used for a few X servers. Refer to the appropriate X server manual page for details.

POSBase *baseaddress*   This optional entry specifies the POS base address. This entry is only used for a few X servers. Refer to the appropriate X server manual page for details.

COPBase *baseaddress*   This optional entry specifies the coprocessor base address. This entry is only used for a few X servers. Refer to the appropriate X server manual page for details.

VGABase *baseaddress*   This optional entry specifies the VGA memory base address. This entry is only used for a few X servers. Refer to the appropriate X server manual page for details.

Instance *number*   This optional entry specifies the instance (which indicates if the chip is integrated on the motherboard or on an expansion card). This entry is only used for a few X servers. Refer to the appropriate X server manual page for details.

Speedup *"selection"*   This optional entry specifies the selection of speedups to be enabled. This entry is only used for a few X servers. Refer to the appropriate X server manual page for details.

S3MNAdjust *M N*   This optional entry is specific to the S3 X server. For details, refer to the *XF86_S3(1)* manual page.

S3MClk *clock*   This optional entry is specific to the S3 X server. For details, refer to the *XF86_S3(1)* manual page.

S3RefClock *clock*   This optional entry is specific to the S3 X server. For details, refer to the *XF86_S3(1)* manual page.

The **Screen** sections are used to specify which graphics boards and monitors will be used with a particular X server, and the configuration in which they are to be used. The entries available for this section are:

Driver *"driver-name"*   Each **Screen** section must begin with a **Driver** entry, and the *driver-name* given in each **Screen** section must be unique. The driver name determines which X server (or driver type within an X server when an X server supports more than one head) reads and uses a particular **Screen** section. The driver names available are:

Accel
Mono
SVGA
VGA2
VGA16

Accel is used by all the accelerated X servers (see *XF86_Accel(1)*). **Mono** is used by the non-VGA mono drivers in the 2-bit and 4-bit X servers (see *XF86_Mono(1)* and *XF86_VGA16(1)*). **VGA2** and **VGA16** are used by the VGA drivers in the 2-bit and 4-bit X servers respectively. **SVGA** is used by the XF86_SVGA X server.

Device *"device-id"*   specifies which graphics device description is to be used.

Monitor *"monitor-id"*   specifies which monitor description is to be used.

ScreenNo *scrnum*   This optional entry overrides the default screen numbering in a multi-headed configuration. The default numbering is determined by the ordering of the **Screen** sections in the *XF86Config* file. To override this, all relevant **Screen** sections must have this entry specified.

BlankTime *time*   sets the inactivity timeout for the blanking phase of the screensaver. *time* is in minutes, and the default is 10. This is equivalent to the Xserver's '-s' flag, and the value can be changed at run-time with *xset(1)*.

SuspendTime *time*   sets the inactivity timeout for the "suspend" phase of the screensaver. *time* is in minutes, the default is 15, and it can be changed at run-time with *xvidtune(1)*. This is only suitable for VESA DPMS compatible monitors, and is only supported currently by some Xservers. The "power_saver" Option must be set for this to be enabled.

XF86Config(4/5)   XF86Config(4/5)

OffTime *time* — sets the inactivity timeout for the "off" phase of the screensaver. *time* is in minutes, the default is 30, and it can be changed at run-time with *xvidtune(1)*. This is only suitable for VESA DPMS compatible monitors, and is only supported currently by some Xservers. The "power_saver" Option must be set for this to be enabled.

SubSection "Display" — This entry is a subsection which is used to specify some display specific parameters. This subsection is terminated by an **EndSubSection** entry. For some X servers and drivers (those requiring a list of video modes) this subsection is mandatory. For X servers which support multiple display depths, more than one **Display** subsection may be present. When multiple **Display** subsections are present, each must have a unique **Depth** entry. The entries available for the **Display** subsection are:

Depth *bpp* — This entry is mandatory when more than one **Display** subsection is present in a **Screen** section. When only one **Display** subsection is present, it specifies the default depth that the X server will run at. When more than one **Display** subsection is present, the depth determines which gets used by the X server. The subsection used is the one matching the depth at which the X server is run at. Not all X servers (or drivers) support more than one depth. Permitted values for *bpp* are 8, 15, 16, 24 and 32. Not all X servers (or drivers) support all of these values. *bpp* values of 24 and 32 are treated equivalently by those X servers which support them.

Weight *RGB* — This optional entry specifies the relative RGB weighting to be used for an X server running at 16bpp. This may also be specified from the command line (see *XFree86(1)*). Values supported by most 16bpp X servers are **555** and **565**. For further details, refer to the appropriate X server manual page.

Virtual *xdim ydim* — This optional entry specifies the virtual screen resolution to be used. *xdim* must be a multiple of either 8 or 16 for most colour X servers, and a multiple of 32 for the monochrome X server. The given value will be rounded down if this is not the case. For most X servers, video modes which are too large for the specified virtual size will be rejected. If this entry is not present, the virtual screen resolution will be set to accommodate all the valid video modes given in the **Modes** entry. Some X servers do not support this entry. Refer to the appropriate X server manual pages for details.

ViewPort *x0 y0* — This optional entry sets the upper left corner of the initial display. This is only relevant when the virtual screen resolution is different from the resolution of the initial video mode. If this entry is not given, then the initial display will be centered in the virtual display area.

Modes *"modename"* ... — This entry is mandatory for most X servers, and it specifies the list of video modes to use. The video mode names must correspond to those specified in the appropriate **Monitor** section. Most X servers will delete modes from this list which don't satisfy various requirements. The first valid mode in this list will be the default display mode for startup. The list of valid modes is converted internally into a circular list. It is possible to switch to the next mode with **Ctrl+Alt+Keypad-Plus** and to the previous mode with **Ctrl+Alt+Keypad-Minus**.

XFree86   Version 3.1.2   992

InvertVCLK *"modename"* 0|1 This optional entry is specific to the S3 server only. It may be used to change the default VCLK invert/non-invert state for individual modes. If *"modename"* is "" the setting applies to all modes unless unless overridden by later entries.

EarlySC *"modename"* 0|1 This optional entry is specific to the S3 server only. It may be used to change the default EarlySC setting for individual modes. This setting can affect screen wrapping. If *"modename"* is "" the setting applies to all modes unless unless overridden by later entries.

BlankDelay *"modename" value1 value2* This optional entry is specific to the S3 server only. It may be used to change the default blank delay settings for individual modes. This can affect screen wrapping. *value1* and *value2* must be integers in the range 0–7. If *"modename"* is "" the setting applies to all modes unless unless overridden by later entries.

Visual *"visual-name"* This optional entry sets the default root visual type. This may also be specified from the command line (see *Xserver(1)*). The visual types available for 8bpp X servers are (default is **PseudoColor**):

StaticGray
GrayScale
StaticColor
PseudoColor
TrueColor
DirectColor

The visual type available for the 16bpp and 32bpp X servers is **TrueColor**.

The visual type available for the 1bpp X server is **StaticGray**.

The visual types available for the 4bpp X server are (default is **PseudoColor**):

StaticGray
GrayScale
StaticColor
PseudoColor

Option *"optionstring"* This optional entry allows the user to select certain options provided by the drivers. Multiple **Option** entries may be given. The supported values for *optionstring* are given in the appropriate X server manual pages.

Black *red green blue* This optional entry allows the "black" colour to be specified. This is only supported with the VGA2 driver in the XF86_Mono server (for details see *XF86_Mono(1)*).

White *red green blue* This optional entry allows the "white" colour to be specified. This is only supported with the VGA2 driver in the XF86_Mono server (for details see *XF86_Mono(1)*).

For an example of an XF86Config file, see the file installed as <XRoot>/lib/X11/XF86Config.eg.

FILES

/etc/XF86Config
<XRoot>/lib/X11/XF86Config.*hostname* <XRoot>/lib/X11/XF86Config
Note: <XRoot> refers to the root of the X11 install tree.

SEE ALSO

X(1), Xserver(1), XFree86(1), XF86_SVGA(1), XF86_VGA16(1), XF86_Mono(1), XF86_S3(1), XF86_8514(1), XF86_Mach8(1), XF86_Mach32(1), XF86_P9000(1), XF86_AGX(1), XF86_W32(1).

AUTHORS

Refer to the *XFree86(1)* manual page.

Section VI

Games

NAME

intro – Introduction to games

DESCRIPTION

This chapter describes all the games and funny little programs available on the system.

AUTHORS

Look at the header of the manual page for the author(s) and copyright conditions. Note that these can be different from page to page!

BANNER(6)

NAME

banner – print large banner on printer

SYNOPSIS

/usr/games/banner [**–w***n*] message ...

DESCRIPTION

Banner prints a large, high quality banner on the standard output. If the message is omitted, it prompts for and reads one line of its standard input. If **–w** is given, the output is scrunched down from a width of 132 to *n* , suitable for a narrow terminal. If *n* is omitted, it defaults to 80.

The output should be printed on a hard-copy device, up to 132 columns wide, with no breaks between the pages. The volume is great enough that you may want a printer or a fast hardcopy terminal, but if you are patient, a decwriter or other 300 baud terminal will do.

BUGS

Several ASCII characters are not defined, notably <, >, [,], \, ˆ, ⌐, {, }, |, and ˜. Also, the characters ", ', and & are funny looking (but in a useful way).

The **–w** option is implemented by skipping some rows and columns. The smaller it gets, the grainier the output. Sometimes it runs letters together.

AUTHOR

Mark Horton

DDATE(6)

NAME

ddate – converts boring normal dates to fun Discordian Dates

SYNOPSIS

ddate

DESCRIPTION

ddate prints the date in Discordian Date format.

AUTHOR

Druel the Chaotic aka Jeremy Johnson (mpython@gnu.ai.mit.edu)
Modifications for Unix by Lee Harvey Oswald Smith, K.S.C.
Five tons of flax.

Section VII

Miscellaneous

INTRO(7)

NAME

intro – Introduction to miscellany section

DESCRIPTION

This chapter describes miscellaneous things such as nroff macro packages, tables, C header files, the file hierarchy, general concepts, and other things which don't fit anywhere else.

AUTHORS

Look at the header of the manual page for the author(s) and copyright conditions. Note that these can be different from page to page!

ASCII(7) Linux Programmer's Manual ASCII(7)

NAME

ascii – the ASCII character set encoded in octal, decimal, and hexadecimal

DESCRIPTION

The following table contains the 128 ASCII characters.

C program '\X' escapes are noted.

Oct	Dec	Hex	Char	Oct	Dec	Hex	Char
000	0	00	NUL '\0'	100	64	40	@
001	1	01	SOH	101	65	41	A
002	2	02	STX	102	66	42	B
003	3	03	ETX	103	67	43	C
004	4	04	EOT	104	68	44	D
005	5	05	ENQ	105	69	45	E
006	6	06	ACK	106	70	46	F
007	7	07	BEL '\a'	107	71	47	G
010	8	08	BS '\b'	110	72	48	H
011	9	09	HT '\t'	111	73	49	I
012	10	0A	LF '\n'	112	74	4A	J
013	11	0B	VT '\v'	113	75	4B	K
014	12	0C	FF '\f'	114	76	4C	L
015	13	0D	CR '\r'	115	77	4D	M
016	14	0E	SO	116	78	4E	N
017	15	0F	SI	117	79	4F	O
020	16	10	DLE	120	80	50	P
021	17	11	DC1	121	81	51	Q
022	18	12	DC2	122	82	52	R
023	19	13	DC3	123	83	53	S
024	20	14	DC4	124	84	54	T
025	21	15	NAK	125	85	55	U
026	22	16	SYN	126	86	56	V
027	23	17	ETB	127	87	57	W
030	24	18	CAN	130	88	58	X
031	25	19	EM	131	89	59	Y
032	26	1A	SUB	132	90	5A	Z
033	27	1B	ESC	133	91	5B	[
034	28	1C	FS	134	92	5C	\'\\'
035	29	1D	GS	135	93	5D	]
036	30	1E	RS	136	94	5E	^
037	31	1F	US	137	95	5F	_
040	32	20	SPACE	140	96	60	`
041	33	21	!	141	97	61	a
042	34	22	"	142	98	62	b
043	35	23	#	143	99	63	c
044	36	24	$	144	100	64	d

Miscellaneous

Oct	Dec	Hex	Char	Oct	Dec	Hex	Char
045	37	25	%	145	101	65	e
046	38	26	&	146	102	66	f
047	39	27	'	147	103	67	g
050	40	28	(	150	104	68	h
051	41	29	)	151	105	69	i
052	42	2A	*	152	106	6A	j
053	43	2B	+	153	107	6B	k
054	44	2C	,	154	108	6C	l
055	45	2D	−	155	109	6D	m
056	46	2E	.	156	110	6E	n
057	47	2F	/	157	111	6F	o
060	48	30	0	160	112	70	p
061	49	31	1	161	113	71	q
062	50	32	2	162	114	72	r
063	51	33	3	163	115	73	s
064	52	34	4	164	116	74	t
065	53	35	5	165	117	75	u
066	54	36	6	166	118	76	v
067	55	37	7	167	119	77	w
070	56	38	8	170	120	78	x
071	57	39	9	171	121	79	y
072	58	3A	:	172	122	7A	z
073	59	3B	;	173	123	7B	{
074	60	3C	<	174	124	7C	|
075	61	3D	=	175	125	7D	}
076	62	3E	>	176	126	7E	~
077	63	3F	?	177	127	7F	DEL

HISTORY

An **ascii** manual page appeared in Version 7 AT&T UNIX.

SEE ALSO

iso_8859_1(7)

GROFF_ME(7)

NAME
groff_me – troff macros for formatting papers

SYNOPSIS
groff –me [options] file ...
troff –me [options] file ...

DESCRIPTION
This manual page describes the GNU version of the –me macros, which is part of the groff document formatting system. This version can be used with both GNU troff and Unix troff. This package of *troff* macro definitions provides a canned formatting facility for tech%nical papers in various formats.

The macro requests are defined below. Many *troff* requests are unsafe in conjunction with this package, however, these requests may be used with impunity after the first .pp:

.bp begin new page
.br break output line here
.sp n insert n spacing lines
.ls n (line spacing) n=1 single, n=2 double space
.na no alignment of right margin
.ce n center next n lines
.ul n underline next n lines

Output of the *pic, eqn, refer,* and *tbl* preprocessors is acceptable as input.

FILES
/usr/lib/groff/tmac/tmac.e

SEE ALSO
groff(1), **gtroff**(1)
–me Reference Manual, Eric P. Allman
Writing Papers with Groff Using –me

REQUESTS
This list is incomplete; see *The –me Reference Manual* for interesting details.

a

Request Initial Cause Explanation

Value Break

.(c - yes Begin centered block

.(d - no Begin delayed text

.(f - no Begin footnote

.(l - yes Begin list

.(q - yes Begin major quote

.(x x - no Begin indexed item in index *x*

.(z - no Begin floating keep

.)c - yes End centered block

.)d - yes End delayed text

.)f - yes End footnote

.)l - yes End list

.)q - yes End major quote

.)x - yes End index item

.)z - yes End floating keep

.++ *m H* - no Define paper section. *m* defines the part of the paper, and can be **C** (chapter), **A** (appendix), **P** (preliminary, e.g., abstract, table of contents, etc.), **B** (bibliography), **RC** (chapters renumbered from page one each chapter), or **RA** (appendix renumbered from page one).

.+c *T* - yes Begin chapter (or appendix, etc., as set by .++). *T* is the chapter title.

.1c 1 yes One column format on a new page.

.2c 1 yes Two column format.

.EN - yes Space after equation produced by *eqn* or *neqn*.

.EQ *x y* - yes Precede equation; break out and add space. Equation number is *y*. The optional argument *x* may be *I* to indent equation (default), *L* to left-adjust the equation, or *C* to center the equation.

.GE - yes End *gremlin* picture.

.GS - yes Begin *gremlin* picture.

.PE - yes End *pic* picture.

.PS - yes Begin *pic* picture.

.TE - yes End table.

.TH - yes End heading section of table.

.TS *x* - yes Begin table; if *x* is *H* table has repeated heading.

.b *x* no no Print *x* in boldface; if no argument switch to boldface.

.ba +*n* 0 yes Augments the base indent by *n*. This indent is used to set the indent on regular text (like paragraphs).

.bc no yes Begin new column

.bi *x* no no Print *x* in bold italics (nofill only)

.bu - yes Begin bulleted paragraph

.bx *x* no no Print *x* in a box (nofill only).

.ef '*x*'*y*'*z*' "" no Set even footer to x y z

.eh '*x*'*y*'*z*' "" no Set even header to x y z

.fo '*x*'*y*'*z*' "" no Set footer to x y z

.hx - no Suppress headers and footers on next page.

.he '*x*'*y*'*z*' "" no Set header to x y z

.hl - yes Draw a horizontal line

.i *x* no no Italicize *x*; if *x* missing, italic text follows.

.ip *x y* no yes Start indented paragraph, with hanging tag *x*. Indentation is *y* ens (default 5).

.lp yes yes Start left-blocked paragraph.

.np 1 yes Start numbered paragraph.

.of '*x*'*y*'*z*' "" no Set odd footer to x y z

.oh '*x*'*y*'*z*' "" no Set odd header to x y z

.pd - yes Print delayed text.

.pp no yes Begin paragraph. First line indented.

.r yes no Roman text follows.

.re - no Reset tabs to default values.

.sh n x - yes Section head follows, font automatically bold. n is level of section, x is title of section.

.sk no no Leave the next page blank. Only one page is remembered ahead.

.sm x - no Set x in a smaller pointsize.

.sz +n 10p no Augment the point size by n points.

.tp no yes Begin title page.

.u x - no Underline argument (even in *troff*). (Nofill only).

.uh - yes Like .sh but unnumbered.

.xp x - no Print index x.

NAME

groff_mm – groff mm macros

SYNOPSIS

groff –mgm [*options...*] [*files...*]

DESCRIPTION

The groff mm macros are intended to be compatible with the DWB mm macros with the following limitations:

- o no letter macros implemented (yet).
- o no Bell Labs localisms implemented.
- o the macros OK and PM is not implemented.
- o groff mm does not support cut marks

mgm is intended to be international. Therefore it is possible to write short national macrofiles which change all english text to the preferred language. Use **mgmse** as an example.

Groff mm has several extensions:

1C [1] Begin one column processing. An **1** as argmunet disabled the pagebreak.

APP name text Begin an appendix with name *name*. Automatic naming occurs if *name* is ''''. The appendixes starts with **A** if auto is used. An new page is ejected, and a header is also produced if the number variable **Aph** is non-zero. This is the default. The appendix always appear in the 'List of contents' with correct pagenumber. The name *APPENDIX* can be changed by setting the string **App** to the desired text.

APPSK name pages text Same as **.APP**, but the pagenr is incremented with *pages*. This is used when diagrams or other non-formatted documents are included as appendixes.

B1 Begin box (as the ms macro) Draws a box around the text.

B2 End box. Finish the box.

BVL Start of broken variable-item list. As VL but text begins always at the next line

COVER [arg] COVER begins a coversheet definition. It is important that **.COVER** appears before any normal text. **.COVER** uses *arg* to build the filename /usr/lib/groff/tmac/mm/*arg*.cov. Therefore it is possible to create unlimited types of coversheets. *ms.cov* is supposed to look like the **ms** coversheet. **.COVER** requires a **.COVEND** at the end of the cover-definition. Always use this order of the covermacros: .COVER
.TL
.AF
.AU
.AT
.AS
.AE
.COVEND However, only **.TL** and **.AU** are required.

COVEND This finish the cover description and prints the cover-page. It is defined in the cover file.

GETHN refname [varname] Includes the headernumber where the corresponding **SETR** *refname* was placed. Will be X.X.X. in pass 1. See **INITR**. If varname is used, **GETHN** sets the stringvariable *varname* to the headernumber.

GETPN refname [varname] Includes the pagenumber where the corresponding **SETR** *refname* was placed. Will be 9999 in pass 1. See **INITR**. If varname is used, **GETPN** sets the stringvariable *varname* to the pagenumber.

GETR refname Combines **GETHN** and **GETPN** with the text 'chapter' and ', page'. The string *Qrf* contains the text for reference:
.ds Qrf See chapter *[Qrfh], page *[Qrfp].
Qrf may be changed to support other languages. Strings *Qrfh* and *Qrfp* are set by **GETR** and contains the page and headernumber.

GETST refname [varname] Includes the string saved with the second argument to **.SETR**. Will be dummystring in pass 1. If varname is used, **GETST** sets the stringvariable *varname* to the saved string. See **INITR**.

INITR filename Initialize the refencemacros. References will be written to *filename.tmp* and *filename.qrf*. Requires two passes with groff. The first looks for references and the second includes them. **INITR** can be used several times, but it is only the first occurrence of **INITR** that is active. See also **SETR, GETPN** and **GETHN**.

MC column-size [column-separation] Begin multiple columns. Return to normal with 1C.

MT [arg [addressee]] Memorandum type. The *arg* is part of a filename in */usr/lib/groff/tmac/mm/*.MT*. Memorandum type 0 thru 5 are supported, including *"string"*. *Addressee* just sets a variable, used in the AT&T macros.

MOVE y-pos [x-pos [line-length]] Move to a position, pageoffset set to *x-pos*. If *line-length* is not given, the difference between current and new pageoffset is used. Use **PGFORM** without arguments to return to normal.

MULB cw1 space1 [cw2 space2 [cw3 ...]] Begin a special multi-column mode. Every columns width must be specified. Also the space between the columns must be specified. The last column does not need any space-definition. MULB starts a diversion and MULE ends the diversion and prints the columns. The unit for width and space is 'n', but MULB accepts all normal unitspecifications like 'c' and 'i'. MULB operates in a separate environment.

MULN Begin the next column. This is the only way to switch column.

MULE End the multi-column mode and print the columns.

PGFORM [linelength [pagelength [pageoffset [1]]]] Sets linelength, pagelength and/or pageoffset. This macro can be used for special formatting, like letterheads and other. **PGFORM** can be used without arguments to reset everything after a **MOVE**. A line-break is done unless the fourth argument is given. This can be used to avoid the pagenumber on the first page while setting new width and length.

PGNH No header is printed on the next page. Used to get rid off the header in letters or other special texts This macro must be used before any text to inhibit the pageheader on the first page.

SETR refname [string] Remember the current header and page-number as refname. Saves *string* if *string* is defined. *string* is retrieved with **.GETST**. See **INITR**.

TAB reset tabs to every 5n. Normally used to reset any previous tabpositions.

VERBON [flag [pointsize [font]]] Begin verbatim output using courier font. Usually for printing programs. All character has equal width. The pointsize can be changed with the second argument. By specifying the font-argument it is possible to use another font instead of courier. *flag* control several special features. It contains the sum of all wanted features.
Value

Description
1
Disable the escape-character (\). This is normally turned on during verbose output.
2
Add en empty line before the verbose text.
4
Add en empty line after the verbose text.
8
Print the verbose text with numbered lines. This adds four digitsized spaces in the beginning of each line. Finer control is available with the string-variable **Verbnm**. It contains all arguments to the **troff**-command **.nm**, normally '1'.
16
Indent the verbose text with five 'n':s. This is controlled by the number-variable **Verbin** (in units).

VERBOFF End verbatim output.

New variables in mgm:

App A string containing the word "APPENDIX".

Aph Print an appendix-page for every new appendix if this numbervariable is non-zero. No output will occur if **Aph** is zero, but there will always be an appendix-entry in the 'List of contents'.

Hps Numbervariable with the heading pre-space level. If the heading-level is less than or equal to **Hps**, then two lines will precede the section heading instead of one. Default is first level only. The real amount of lines is controlled by the variables **Hps1** and **Hps2**.

Hps1 This is the number of lines preceding **.H** when the heading-level is greater than **Hps**. Value is in units, normally 0.5v.

Hps2 This is the number of lines preceding **.H** when the heading-level is less than or equal to **Hps**. Value is in units, normally 1v.

Lifg String containing *Figure*.

Litb String containing *TABLE*.

Liex String containing *Exhibit*.

Liec String containing *Equation*.

Licon String containing *CONTENTS*.

Lsp

The size of an empty line. Normally 0.5v, but it is 1v if **n** is set (**.nroff**). **MO1 - MO12** Strings containing *January to December*.

Qrf *String containing "See chapter *[Qrfh], page \\n[Qrfp].".*

Pgps *Controls whether header and footer pointsize should follow the current setting or just change when the header and footer is defined.*
Value
Description
0
Pointsize will only change to the current setting when **.PH**, **.PF**, **.OH**, **.EH**, **.OF** *or* **.OE** *is executed.*
1
Pointsize will change after every **.S**. *This is the default.*

Sectf Flag controlling "section-figures". A non-zero value enables this. Se also register N.

Sectp Flag controlling "section-page-numbers". A non-zero value enables this. Se also register N.

.mgm Always 1.

A file called **locale** or **lang_locale** is read after the initiation of the global variables. It is therefore possible to localize the macros with companyname and so on.

The following standard macros are implemented:

2C Begin two column processing

AE Abstract end

AF [name of firm] Authors firm

AL [type [text-indent [1]]]] Start autoincrement list

AS [arg [indent]] Abstract start. Indent is specified in 'ens', but scaling is allowed.

AST [title] Abstract title. Default is 'ABSTRACT'.

AT title1 [title2 ...] Authors title

AU name [initials [loc [dept [ext [room [arg [arg [arg]]]]]]]] Author information

B [bold-text [prev-font-tex [...]]] Begin boldface No limit on the number of arguments.

BE End bottom block

BI [bold-text [italic-text [bold-text [...]]] Bold-italic. No limit on the number of arguments.

BL [text-indent [1]] Start bullet list

BR [bold-text [roman-text [bold-text [...]]] Bold-roman. No limit on the number of arguments.

BS Bottom block start

DE Display end

DF [format [fill [rindent]]] Begin floating display (no nesting allowed)

DL [text-indent [1]] Dash list start

DS [format [fill [rindent]]] Static display start. Can now have unlimited nesting. Also right adjusted text and block may be used (R or RB as format).

EC [title [override [flag [refname]]]] Equation title. If refname is used, then the equationnumber is saved with **.SETR**, and can be retrieved with **.GETST** refname.

EF [arg] Even-page footer.

EH [arg] Even-page header.

EN Equation end.

EQ [label] Equation start.

EX [title [override [flag [refname]]]] Exhibit title. If refname is used, then the exhibitnumber is saved with **.SETR**, and can be retrieved with **.GETST** refname.

FD [arg [1]] Footnote default format.

FE Footnote end.

FG [title [override [flag [refname]]]] Figure title. If refname is used, then the figurenumber is saved with **.SETR**, and can be retrieved with **.GETST** refname.

FS Footnote start. Footnotes in displays is now possible.

H level [heading-text [heading-suffix]] *Numbered heading.*

HC [hyphenation-character] *Set hyphenation character.*

HM [arg1 [arg2 [... [arg7]]]] *Heading mark style.*

HU heading-text *Unnumbered header.*

HX dlevel rlevel heading-text *Userdefined heading exit. Called just before printing the header.*

HY dlevel rlevel heading-text *Userdefined heading exit. Called just before printing the header.*

HZ dlevel rlevel heading-text *Userdefined heading exit. Called just after printing the header.*

I [italic-text [prev-font-text [italic-text [...]]]] *Italic.*

IB [italic-text [bold-text [italic-text [...]]]] *Italic-bold*

IR [italic-text [roman-text [italic-text [...]]]] *Italic-roman*

LB text-indent mark-indent pad type [mark [LI-space [LB-space]]] *List begin macro.*

LC [list level] *List-status clear*

LE   *List end.*

LI [mark [1]] *List item*

ML mark [text-indent] *Marked list start*

MT [arg [addressee]] *Memorandum type. See above note about MT.*

ND new-date *New date.*

OF [arg] *Odd-page footer*

OH [arg] *Odd-page header*

OP   *Skip to odd page.*

P [type] *Begin new paragraph.*

PE   *Picture end.*

PF [arg] *Page footer*

PH [arg] *Page header*

PS   *Picture start (from pic)*

PX   *Page-header user-defined exit.*

R   *Roman.*

RB [roman-text [bold-text [roman-text [...]]]] *Roman-bold.*

RD [prompt [diversion [string]]] *Read to diversion and/or string.*

RF   *Reference end*

RI [roman-text [italic-text [roman-text [...]]]] *Roman-italic.*

RL [text-indent [1]] *Reference list start*

RP [arg [arg]] *Produce reference page.*

RS [string-name] *Reference start.*

S [size [spacing]] *Set point size and vertical spacing. If any argument is equal 'P', then the previous value is used. A 'C' means current value, and 'D' default value. If '+' or '-' is used before the value, then increment or decrement of the current value will be done.*

SA [arg] *Set adjustment.*

SK [pages] *Skip pages.*

SM string1 [string2 [string3]] *Make a string smaller.*

SP [lines] Space vertically. lines can have any scalingfactor, like 3i or 8v.

TB [title [override [flag [refname]]]] Table title. If refname is used, then the tablenumber is saved with **.SETR**, and can be retrieved with **.GETST** refname.

TC [slevel [spacing [tlevel [tab [h1 [h2 [h3 [h4 [h5]]]]]]]]] Table of contents. All texts can be redefined, new stringvariables Lifg, Litb, Liex, Liec and Licon contains "Figure", "TABLE", "Exhibit", "Equation" and "CONTENTS". These can be redefined to other languages.

TE Table end.

TH [N] Table header.

TL Begin title of memorandum.

TM [num1 [num2 [...]]] Technical memorandum numbers used in **.MT**. Unlimited number of arguments may be given.

TP Top of page user-defined macro. Note that header and footer is printed in a separate environment. Linelength is preserved though.

TS [H] Table start

TX Userdefined table of contents exit.

TY Userdefined tbale of contents exit (no "CONTENTS").

VL [text-indent [mark-indent [1]]] Variable-item list start

VM [top [bottom]] Vertical margin.

WC [format] Footnote and display width control.

Strings used in mgm:

EM Em dash string

HF Fontlist for headings, normally "2 2 2 2 2 2 2". Nonnumeric fontnames may also be used.

HP Pointsize list for headings. Normally "0 0 0 0 0 0 0" which is the same as "10 10 10 10 10 10 10".

Lf Contains "LIST OF FIGURES".

Lt Contains "LIST OF TABLES".

Lx Contains "LIST OF EXHIBITS".

Le Contains "LIST OF EQUATIONS".

Rp Contains "REFERENCES".

Tm Contains \(tm, trade mark.

Number variables used in mgm:

Cl=2 Contents level [0:7], contents saved if heading level <= Cl

Cp=0 Eject page between LIST OF XXXX if Cp == 0

D=0 Debugflag, values >0 produces varying degree of debug. A value of 1 gives information about the progress of formatting.

De=0 Eject after floating display is output [0:1]

Df=5 Floating keep output [0:5]

Ds=1 space before and after display if == 1 [0:1]

Ej=0 Eject page

Eq=0 Equation lable adjust 0=left, 1=right

Fs=1 Footnote spacing

H1-H7 Heading counters

Hb=2 Heading break level [0:7]

Hc=0	Heading centering level, [0:7]	
Hi=1	Heading temporary indent [0:2] 0 -> 0 indent, left margin 1 -> indent to right, like .P 1 2 -> indent to line up with text part of preceding heading	
Hs=2	Heading space level [0:7]	
Ht=0	Heading numbering type 0 -> multiple (1.1.1 ...) 1 -> single	
Hu=2	Unnumbered heading level	
Hy=1	Hyphenation in body 0 -> no hyphenation 1 -> hyphenation 14 on	
Lf=1, **Lt**=1, **Lx**=1, **Le**=0	Enables (1) or disables (0) the printing of List of figures, List of tables, List of exhibits and List of equations.	
Li=6	List indent, used by .AL	
Ls=99	List space, if current listlevel > Ls then no spacing will occur around lists.	
N=0	Numbering style [0:5] 0 == (default) normal header for all pages. 1 == header replaces footer on first page, header is empty. 2 == page header is removed on the first page. 3 == "section-page" numbering enabled. 4 == page header is removed on the first page. 5 == "section-page" and "section-figure" numbering enabled. Se also the number-register Sectf and Sectp.	
Np=0	Numbered paragraphs. 0 == not numbered 1 == numbered in first level headings.	
Of=0	Format of figure,table,exhibit,equation titles. 0= ". " 1= " - "	
P	Current page-number, normally the same as % unless "section-page" numbering is enabled.	
Pi=5	paragraph indent	
Ps=1	paragraph spacing	
Pt=0	Paragraph type. 0 == left-justified 1 == indented .P 2 == indented .P except after .H, .DE or .LE.	
Si=5	Display indent.	

AUTHOR

Jörgen Hägg, Lund Institute of Technology, Sweden <jh@efd.lth.se>

FILES

/usr/lib/groff/tmac/tmac.gm

/usr/lib/groff/tmac/mm/*.cov

/usr/lib/groff/tmac/mm/*.MT

/usr/lib/groff/tmac/mm/locale

SEE ALSO

groff(1), **gtroff**(1), **gtbl**(1), **gpic**(1), **geqn**(1)
mm(7) **mgmse**(7)

NAME

groff_ms – groff ms macros

SYNOPSIS

groff –mgs [options...] [files...]

DESCRIPTION

This manual page describes the GNU version of the ms macros, which is part of the groff document formatting system. The groff ms macros are intended to be compatible with the documented behaviour of the 4.3 BSD Unix ms macros subject to the following limitations:

- the internals of groff ms are not similar to the internals of Unix ms and so documents that depend upon implementation details of Unix ms may well not work with groff ms;
- there is no support for typewriter-like devices;
- Berkeley localisms, in particular the **TM** and **CT** macros, are not implemented;
- groff ms does not provide cut marks;
- multiple line spacing is not allowed (use a larger vertical spacing instead);
- groff ms does not work in compatibility mode (eg with the **–C** option);
- the error-handling policy of groff ms is to detect and report errors, rather than silently to ignore them.

The groff ms macros make use of many features of GNU troff and therefore cannot be used with any other troff.

Bell Labs localisms are not implemented in either the BSD ms macros or in the groff ms macros.

Some Unix ms documentation says that the **CW** and **GW** number registers can be used to control the column width and gutter width respectively. This is not the case. These number registers are not used in groff ms.

Macros that cause a reset set the indent. Macros that change the indent do not increment or decrement the indent, but rather set it absolutely. This can cause problems for documents that define additional macros of their own. The solution is to use not the **in** request but instead the **RS** and **RE** macros.

The number register **GS** is set to 1 by the groff ms macros, but is not used by the Unix ms macros. It is intended that documents that need to determine whether they are being formatted with Unix ms or groff ms make use of this number register.

Footnotes are implemented so that they can safely be used within keeps and displays. Automatically numbered footnotes within floating keeps are not recommended. It is safe to have another ** between a ** and the corresponding **.FS**; it is required only that each **.FS** occur after the corresponding ** and that the occurrences of **.FS** are in the same order as the corresponding occurrences of **.

The strings *{ and *} can be used to begin and end a superscript.

Some Unix V10 ms features are implemented. The **B**, **I** and **BI** macros can have an optional third argument which will be printed in the current font before the first argument. There is a macro **CW** like **B** that changes to a constant-width font.

The following strings can be redefined to adapt the groff ms macros to languages other than English:

String Default Value
REFERENCES References
ABSTRACT ABSTRACT
TOC Table of Contents
MONTH1 January
MONTH2 February
MONTH3 March

Groff Version 1.09   9 January 1994

MONTH4 April
MONTH5 May
MONTH6 June
MONTH7 July
MONTH8 August
MONTH9 September
MONTH10 October
MONTH11 November
MONTH12 December

The font family is reset from the string **FAM**; at initialization if this string is undefined it is set to the current font family. The point size, vertical spacing, and inter-paragraph spacing for footnotes are taken from the number registers **FPS**, **FVS**, and **FPD**; at initialization these are set to \n(**PS**-2, \n[**FPS**]+2, and \n(**PD**/2 respectively; however, if any of these registers has been defined before initialization, it will not be set. The hyphenation flags (as set by the **.hy** request) are set from the **HY** register; if this has not been defined at initialization, it will be set to 14.

Right-aligned displays are available with **.DS R** and **.RD**.

The following conventions are used for names of macros, strings and number registers. External names available to documents that use the groff ms macros contain only uppercase letters and digits. Internally the macros are divided into modules. Names used only within one module are of the form module*name. Names used outside the module in which they are defined are of the form module@name. Names associated with a particular environment are of the form environment:name; these are used only within the **par** module, and name does not have a module prefix. Constructed names used to implement arrays are of the form array!index. Thus the groff ms macros reserve the following names:

> names containing *;
>
> names containing @;
>
> names containing :;
>
> names containing only uppercase letters and digits.

FILES
/usr/lib/groff/tmac/tmac.gs

SEE ALSO
groff(1), **gtroff**(1), **gtbl**(1), **gpic**(1), **geqn**(1)
ms(7)

HIER(7)

NAME

hier – Description of the file system hierarchy

DESCRIPTION

A typical Linux system has, among others, the following directories:

/ This is the root directory. This is where the whole tree starts.

/bin This directory contains executable programs which are executed often, are needed to bring the system up or repair it.

/dev Special or device files, which refer to physical devices. See mknod(1).

/dos If both MS–DOS and Linux are run on one computer, this is a typical place to mount a DOS file system.

/etc contains programs and other files necessary to system administration; normal users don't need any of this. Usually, this directory is not in their £PATH

/etc/skel When a new user account is created, files from this directory are usually copied into the user's home directory.

/etc/lilo The Linux Loader for booting the system goes here.

/install This is used by some installations scripts to keep track of which packages have been installed.

/lib Frequently–used object code libraries, including dynamic libraries, which are linked at the time an executable starts up, plus some executables which usually are not called directly.

/proc This is the directory where information about running processes can be obtained.

/proc/[0-9]+ This directory contains information about the process associated with its number; it has such files as the command line, the environment, the memory contents, or statistics about the process.

/proc/[0-9]+/fd A directory containing the file descriptors associated with the process.

/proc/[0-9]+/lib A directory containing the dynamic libraries associated with a process.

/proc/self This is a link to the directory associated with the calling process.

/tmp This directory contains temporary files which may be deleted with no notice, such as by a regular job or at system boot up.

/user This often is an empty directory, which can be used as a mount point for floppy disks.

/usr Less–frequently used commands and other things; this is often a mount point for a separate partition or volume.

/usr/TeX The TeX typesetting system.

/usr/TeX/bin Binary commands for the TeX system. /usr/TeX/lib This contains data files connected with TeX, and may contain further subdirectories.

/usr/TeX/man Manual pages with the TeX system.

/usr/TeX/src Sources associates with TeX.

/usr/X386 The X-indows system.

/usr/X386/bin Binaries which belong to the X–Windows system; often, there is a symbolic link from the more traditional /usr/bin/X11 to here.

/usr/X386/lib Data files associated with the X–Windows system.

/usr/X386/lib/X11 These contain miscellaneous files needed to run X; among them configuration files. Often, there is a symbolic link from /usr/lib/X11 to this directory.

/usr/adm   This often contains various log files.

/usr/bin   This contains binaries which are not needed so often, or are not needed for bringing the system up or repairing it. The decision whether to put something in /bin or /usr/bin should be guided by the simple consideration: "If I put it in /usr/bin and /usr is not available on boot, do I still get the system up?"

/usr/bin/X11   is the traditional place to look for X11 executables; on Linux, it usually is a symbolic link to /usr/X386/bin.

/usr/g++-include   Include files to use with the GNU C++ compiler.

/usr/homes   This contains the home directories for normal users.

/usr/include   Include files for the C compiler.

/usr/include/X11   Include files for the C compiler and the X–Windows system.

/usr/include/asm   Include files which declare some assembler functions. This should be a symbolic link to /usr/src/linux/include/asm.

/usr/include/linux   This contains information which may change from system release to system release and should be a symbolic link to /usr/src/linux/include/linux to get at operating system specific information.

/usr/lib   Less - frequently used object libraries, including dynamic libraries, plus some executables which usually are not invoked directly. More complicated programs may have whole subdirectories there.

/usr/lib/X11   The usual place for data files associated with X programs, and configuration files for the X system itself. On Linux, it usually is a symbolic link to /usr/X386/lib/X11.

/usr/lib/X11/app-defaults   X applications store their default resource (in other words, application defaults) here. If you want to change the way a certain program looks, this is the place to look.

/usr/lib/X11/config   This directory is used for the **imake**(1) utility which incorporates information about the system into Makefiles.

/usr/lib/X11/twm   Files for the **twm**(1) window manager.

/usr/lib/X11/xinit   Files for starting up the X Windows system.

/usr/lib/gcc-lib   contains configuration files for the system's C compiler, **gcc**(1).

/usr/lib/groff   Files for the groff document formatting system.

/usr/lib/uucp   Files for **uucp**(1).

/usr/lib/zoneinfo   Files for timezone information.

/usr/local   This is where programs which are local to the site typically go in. Some program packages, such as EMACS, may have their own subdirectories there.

/usr/local/bin   Binaries for programs local to the site go there.

/usr/local/lib   Files associated with locally installed programs go there.

/usr/local/man   Manpages associated with locally installed programs go there.

/usr/man   Manpages go in there, into their subdirectories.

/usr/man/cat[1-9]   These directories contain preformatted manual pages according to their manpage section.

/usr/man/man[1-9]   These directories contain manual pages which are in source code form.

/usr/openwin   Files associated with the Open Windows Window manager for X go there.

/usr/preserve   This is where **vi**(1) saves edit sessions so they can be restored later.

/usr/spool   Spooled (or queued) files for various programs.

/usr/spool/atjobs   Spooled jobs for **at**(1).

/usr/spool/cron   Spooled jobs for **cron**(1).

HIER(7) Linux Programmer's Manual HIER(7)

/usr/spool/lp1 Spooled files for a printer.

/usr/spool/mail User's mailboxes.

/usr/spool/smail Spooled files for the **smail**(1) mail delivery program.

/usr/spool/uucp Spooled files for **uucp**(1).

/usr/src Source files for different parts of the system.

/usr/src/libc-linux Sources for the C library.

/usr/src/linux This contains the sources for the operating system itself.

/usr/tmp An alternative place to store temporary files; often used if the files will be huge.

/var On some systems with more of a BSD flavour to them, this directory contains all the files which may change in size, such as spool and log files, and /usr only contains static files. Often, /var is just a symbolic link to /usr.

CONFORMS TO

The layout of this file system generally follows System V conventions.

BUGS

This list is not exhaustive; different systems may be configured differently.

SEE ALSO

find(1),**ln**(1),**mount**(1)

Linux April 24, 1993 1017

NAME

iso_8859_1 – the ISO 8859-1 character set encoded in octal, decimal, and hexadecimal

DESCRIPTION

The ISO 8859 standard includes several 8-bit extensions to the ASCII character set (also known as ISO 646-IRV). Especially important is ISO 8859-1, the "Latin Alphabet No. 1", which has become widely implemented and may already be seen as the de-facto standard ASCII replacement. ISO 8859-1 supports the following languages: Afrikaans, Basque, Catalan, Danish, Dutch, English, Faeroese, Finnish, French, Galician, German, Icelandic, Irish, Italian, Norwegian, Portuguese, Scottish, Spanish, and Swedish. Note that the ISO 8859-1 characters are also the first 256 characters of ISO 10646 (Unicode).

ISO 8859 Alphabets The full set of ISO 8859 alphabets includes:

ISO 8859-1	west European languages (Latin-1)
ISO 8859-2	east European languages (Latin-2)
ISO 8859-3	southeast European and miscellaneous languages (Latin-3)
ISO 8859-4	Scandinavian/Baltic languages (Latin-4)
ISO 8859-5	Latin/Cyrillic
ISO 8859-6	Latin/Arabic
ISO 8859-7	Latin/Greek
ISO 8859-8	Latin/Hebrew
ISO 8859-9	Latin-1 modification for Turkish (Latin-5)
ISO 8859-10	Lappish/Nordic/Eskimo languages (Latin-6)

ISO 8859-1 Characters
The following table displays the characters in ISO 8859 Latin-1, which are printable and unlisted in the **ascii**(7) manual page.

Oct	Dec	Hex	Char	Description
240	160	A0	?	NO-BREAK SPACE
241	161	A1	¡	INVERTED EXCLAMATION MARK
242	162	A2	?	CENT SIGN
243	163	A3	£	POUND SIGN
244	164	A4	?	CURRENCY SIGN
245	165	A5	?	YEN SIGN
246	166	A6	|	BROKEN BAR
247	167	A7	§	SECTION SIGN
250	168	A8	¨	DIAERESIS
251	169	A9	©	COPYRIGHT SIGN
252	170	AA	?	FEMININE ORDINAL INDICATOR
253	171	AB	<<	LEFT-POINTING DOUBLE ANGLE QUOTATION MARK
254	172	AC	?	NOT SIGN
255	173	AD	?	SOFT HYPHEN
256	174	AE	?	REGISTERED SIGN
257	175	AF	?	MACRON

Oct	Dec	Hex	Char	Description
260	176	B0	°	DEGREE SIGN
261	177	B1	±	PLUS-MINUS SIGN
262	178	B2	²	SUPERSCRIPT TWO
263	179	B3	³	SUPERSCRIPT THREE
264	180	B4	´	ACUTE ACCENT
265	181	B5	µ	MICRO SIGN
266	182	B6	¶	PILCROW SIGN
267	183	B7	·	MIDDLE DOT
270	184	B8	¸	CEDILLA
271	185	B9	¹	SUPERSCRIPT ONE
272	186	BA	º	MASCULINE ORDINAL INDICATOR
273	187	BB	>>	RIGHT-POINTING DOUBLE ANGLE QUOTATION MARK
274	188	BC	¼	VULGAR FRACTION ONE QUARTER
275	189	BD	½	VULGAR FRACTION ONE HALF
276	190	BE	¾	VULGAR FRACTION THREE QUARTERS
277	191	BF	¿	INVERTED QUESTION MARK
300	192	C0	À	LATIN CAPITAL LETTER A WITH GRAVE
301	193	C1	Á	LATIN CAPITAL LETTER A WITH ACUTE
302	194	C2	Â	LATIN CAPITAL LETTER A WITH CIRCUMFLEX
303	195	C3	Ã	LATIN CAPITAL LETTER A WITH TILDE
304	196	C4	Ä	LATIN CAPITAL LETTER A WITH DIAERESIS
305	197	C5	Å	LATIN CAPITAL LETTER A WITH RING ABOVE
306	198	C6	Æ	LATIN CAPITAL LIGATURE AE
307	199	C7	Ç	LATIN CAPITAL LETTER C WITH CEDILLA
310	200	C8	È	LATIN CAPITAL LETTER E WITH GRAVE
311	201	C9	É	LATIN CAPITAL LETTER E WITH ACUTE
312	202	CA	Ê	LATIN CAPITAL LETTER E WITH CIRCUMFLEX
313	203	CB	Ë	LATIN CAPITAL LETTER E WITH DIAERESIS
314	204	CC	Ì	LATIN CAPITAL LETTER I WITH GRAVE
315	205	CD	Í	LATIN CAPITAL LETTER I WITH ACUTE
316	206	CE	Î	LATIN CAPITAL LETTER I WITH CIRCUMFLEX
317	207	CF	Ï	LATIN CAPITAL LETTER I WITH DIAERESIS
320	208	D0	Ð	LATIN CAPITAL LETTER ETH
321	209	D1	Ñ	LATIN CAPITAL LETTER N WITH TILDE
322	210	D2	Ò	LATIN CAPITAL LETTER O WITH GRAVE
323	211	D3	Ó	LATIN CAPITAL LETTER O WITH ACUTE
324	212	D4	Ô	LATIN CAPITAL LETTER O WITH CIRCUMFLEX
325	213	D5	Õ	LATIN CAPITAL LETTER O WITH TILDE
326	214	D6	Ö	LATIN CAPITAL LETTER O WITH DIAERESIS
327	215	D7	×	MULTIPLICATION SIGN

Oct	Dec	Hex	Char	Description
330	216	D8	Ø	LATIN CAPITAL LETTER O WITH STROKE
331	217	D9	Ù	LATIN CAPITAL LETTER U WITH GRAVE
332	218	DA	Ú	LATIN CAPITAL LETTER U WITH ACUTE
333	219	DB	Û	LATIN CAPITAL LETTER U WITH CIRCUMFLEX
334	220	DC	Ü	LATIN CAPITAL LETTER U WITH DIAERESIS
335	221	DD	Ý	LATIN CAPITAL LETTER Y WITH ACUTE
336	222	DE	Þ	LATIN CAPITAL LETTER THORN
337	223	DF	ß	LATIN SMALL LETTER SHARP S
340	224	E0	à	LATIN SMALL LETTER A WITH GRAVE
341	225	E1	á	LATIN SMALL LETTER A WITH ACUTE
342	226	E2	â	LATIN SMALL LETTER A WITH CIRCUMFLEX
343	227	E3	ã	LATIN SMALL LETTER A WITH TILDE
344	228	E4	ä	LATIN SMALL LETTER A WITH DIAERESIS
345	229	E5	å	LATIN SMALL LETTER A WITH RING ABOVE
346	230	E6	æ	LATIN SMALL LIGATURE AE
347	231	E7	ç	LATIN SMALL LETTER C WITH CEDILLA
350	232	E8	è	LATIN SMALL LETTER E WITH GRAVE
351	233	E9	é	LATIN SMALL LETTER E WITH ACUTE
352	234	EA	ê	LATIN SMALL LETTER E WITH CIRCUMFLEX
353	235	EB	ë	LATIN SMALL LETTER E WITH DIAERESIS
354	236	EC	ì	LATIN SMALL LETTER I WITH GRAVE
355	237	ED	í	LATIN SMALL LETTER I WITH ACUTE
356	238	EE	î	LATIN SMALL LETTER I WITH CIRCUMFLEX
357	239	EF	ï	LATIN SMALL LETTER I WITH DIAERESIS
360	240	F0	ð	LATIN SMALL LETTER ETH
361	241	F1	ñ	LATIN SMALL LETTER N WITH TILDE
362	242	F2	ò	LATIN SMALL LETTER O WITH GRAVE
363	243	F3	ó	LATIN SMALL LETTER O WITH ACUTE
364	244	F4	ô	LATIN SMALL LETTER O WITH CIRCUMFLEX
365	245	F5	õ	LATIN SMALL LETTER O WITH TILDE
366	246	F6	ö	LATIN SMALL LETTER O WITH DIAERESIS
367	247	F7	÷	DIVISION SIGN
370	248	F8	ø	LATIN SMALL LETTER O WITH STROKE
371	249	F9	ù	LATIN SMALL LETTER U WITH GRAVE
372	250	FA	ú	LATIN SMALL LETTER U WITH ACUTE
373	251	FB	û	LATIN SMALL LETTER U WITH CIRCUMFLEX
374	252	FC	ü	LATIN SMALL LETTER U WITH DIAERESIS
375	253	FD	ý	LATIN SMALL LETTER Y WITH ACUTE
376	254	FE	þ	LATIN SMALL LETTER THORN
377	255	FF	ÿ	LATIN SMALL LETTER Y WITH DIAERESIS

SEE ALSO

ascii(7)

LOCALE(7) Linux Programmer's Manual LOCALE(7)

NAME

locale – Description of multi-language support

SYNOPSIS

#include <locale.h>

DESCRIPTION

A locale is a set of language and cultural rules. These cover aspects such as language for messages, different character sets, lexigraphic conventions, etc. A program needs to be able to determine its locale and act accordingly to be portable to different cultures.

The header <**locale.h**> declares data types, functions and macros which are useful in this task.

The functions it declares are **setlocale()** to set the current locale, and **localeconv()** to get information about number formatting.

There are different categories for local information a program might need; they are declared as macros. Using them as the first argument to the **setlocale()** function, it is possible to set one of these to the desired locale:

LC_COLLATE	This is used to change the behaviour of the functions **strcoll()** and **strxfrm()**, which are used to compare strings in the local alphabet. For example, the German sharp s is sorted as "ss".
LC_CTYPE	This changes the behaviour of the character handling and classification functions, such as **isupper()** and **toupper()**, and the multi–byte character functions such as **mblen()** or **wctomb()**.
LC_MONETARY	changes the behaviour of the information returned by **localeconv()** which describes the way numbers are usually printed, with details such as decimal point versus decimal comma.
LC_MESSAGES	changes the language messages are displayed in.
LC_TIME	changes the behaviour of the **strftime()** function to display the current time in a locally acceptable form; for example, most of Europe uses a 24–hour clock vs. the US' 12–hour clock.
LC_ALL	All of the above.

If the second argument to **setlocale()** is empty string, , for the default locale, it is determined using the following steps:

1. If there is a non-null environment variable **LC_ALL**, the value of **LC_ALL** is used.
2. If an environment variable with the same name as one of the categories above exists and is non-null, its value is used for that category.
3. If there is a non-null environment variable **LANG**, the value of **LANG** is used.

Values about local numeric formatting is made available in a **struct** lconv returned by the **localeconv()** function, which has the following declaration:

```
struct lconv
{
/* Numeric (non-monetary) information. */
char *decimal_point; /* Decimal point character. */
char *thousands_sep; /* Thousands separator. */
/* Each element is the number of digits in each group;
   elements with higher indices are farther left.
   An element with value CHAR_MAX means that no further grouping is done.
   An element with value 0 means that the previous element is used
   for all groups farther left. */
char *grouping;
```

Linux April 24, 1993 1021

```
/* Monetary information. */
/* First three chars are a currency symbol from ISO 4217.
   Fourth char is the separator. Fifth char is ' '. */
char *int_curr_symbol;
char *currency_symbol; /* Local currency symbol. */
char *mon_decimal_point; /* Decimal point character. */
char *mon_thousands_sep; /* Thousands separator. */
char *mon_grouping; /* Like 'grouping' element (above). */
char *positive_sign; /* Sign for positive values. */
char *negative_sign; /* Sign for negative values. */
char int_frac_digits; /* Int'l fractional digits. */
char frac_digits; /* Local fractional digits. */
/* 1 if currency_symbol precedes a positive value, 0 if succeeds. */
char p_cs_precedes;
/* 1 if a space separates currency_symbol from a positive value. */
char p_sep_by_space;
/* 1 if currency_symbol precedes a negative value, 0 if succeeds. */
char n_cs_precedes;
/* 1 if a space separates currency_symbol from a negative value. */
char n_sep_by_space;
/* Positive and negative sign positions:
   0 Parentheses surround the quantity and currency_symbol.
   1 The sign string precedes the quantity and currency_symbol.
   2 The sign string succeeds the quantity and currency_symbol.
   3 The sign string immediately precedes the currency_symbol.
   4 The sign string immediately succeeds the currency_symbol. */
char p_sign_posn;
char n_sign_posn;
};
```

CONFORMS TO

POSIX.1

At the moment, the only locales supported by Linux are the portable **C**, **POSIX** (identical to the "C" locale), **ISO-8859-1** (european latin-1) and **KOI-8** (russian) locales.

SEE ALSO

setlocale(3), **localeconf**(3), **locale**(1), **localedef**(1)

MAILADDR(7)

NAME

mailaddr – mail addressing description

DESCRIPTION

This manual page gives a brief introduction to SMTP mail addresses, as used on the Internet. These addresses are in the general format

user@domain

where a domain is a hierarchical dot separated list of subdomains. For example, the addresses

eric@monet.berkeley.edu
Eric Allman <eric@monet.berkeley.edu>
eric@monet.berkeley.edu (Eric Allman)

are valid forms of the same address.

The domain part ("monet.berkeley.edu") may be the name of an internet host, or it may be a logical mail address. The domain part is not case sensitive.

The local part ("eric") is often a user name, but its meaning is defined by the local software. It can be case sensitive, but usually isn't. If you see a local-part that looks like garbage, it is usually because of a gateway between an internal e-mail system and the net, here are some examples:

"surname/admd=telemail/c=us/o=hp/prmd=hp"@some.where
USER%SOMETHING@some.where
machine!machine!name@some.where
I2461572@some.where

(These are, respectively, an X.400 gateway, a gateway to an arbitrary inernal mail system that lacks proper internet support, an UUCP gateway, and the last one is just boring user-name policy.)

The real-name part ("Eric Allman") can either be placed first, outside <>, or last, inside (). (Strictly speaking the two aren't the same, but the difference is outside the scope of this page.) The name may have to be quoted using "" if it contains certain characters, most commonly ".":

"Eric P. Allman" <eric@monet.berkeley.edu>

Abbreviation

Many mail systems let users abbreviate the domain name. For instance, users at berkeley.edu may get away with "eric@monet" to send mail to Eric Allman. *This behavior is deprecated.*

Route-addrs

Under some circumstances it may be necessary to route a message through several hosts to get it to the final destination. Normally this happens automatically and invisibly, but sometimes not, particularly with old and broken software. Addresses which show these relays are termed "route-addrs." These use the syntax:

<@hosta,@hostb:user@hostc>

This specifies that the message should be sent to hosta, from there to hostb, and finally to hostc. Some hosts disregard route-addrs and send directly to hostc.

Route-addrs occur frequently on return addresses, since these are generally augmented by the software at each host. It is generally possible to ignore all but the "user@hostc" part of the address to determine the actual sender.

Postmaster.

Every site is required to have a user or user alias designated "postmaster" to which problems with the mail system may be addressed. The "postmaster" address is not case sensitive.

FREQUENTLY ASKED QUESTIONS

rtfm.mit.edu and many mirrors store a collection of FAQs. Please find and use a nearby FAQ archive; there are dozens or hundreds around the world. *mail/inter-network-guide* explains how to send mail between many different networks. *mail/country-codes* lists the top level domains (e.g. "no" is Norway and "ea" is Eritrea). *mail/college-email/part** gives some useful tips on how to locate e-mail addresses.

FILES

/etc/aliases
~/.forward

SEE ALSO

binmail(1), **mail**(1), **mconnect**(1), **forward**(5), **aliases**(5), **sendmail**(8), **vrfy**(8), RFC822 (Standard for the Format of Arpa Internet Text Messages).

NAME

man – macros to format man pages

SYNOPSIS

groff –Tacsii –man *file* ...

groff –Tps –man *file* ...

man [*section*] *title*

DESCRIPTION

This manual page explains the **groff tmac.an** macro package. This macro package should be used by developers when writing or porting man pages for Linux. It is fairly compatible with other versions of this macro package, so porting man pages should not be a major problem (exceptions include the NET-2 BSD release, which uses a totally different macro package).

Note that NET-2 BSD man pages can be used with **groff** simply by specifying the **–mdoc** option instead of the **–man** option. Using the **–mandoc** option is, however, recommended, since this will automatically detect which macro package is in use.

PREAMBLE

The first command in a man page should be

.TH *title section date source manual*,

where:

title	The title of the man page (e.g., *MAN*).	
section	The section number the man page should be placed in (e.g., 7).	
date	The date of the last revision—remember to change this every time a change is made to the man page, since this is the most general way of doing version control.	
source	The source of the command.	
	For binaries, use something like: *GNU, NET-2, SLS Distribution, MCC Distribution*.	
	For system calls, use the version of the kernel that you are currently looking at: *Linux 0.99.11*.	
	For library calls, use the source of the function: *GNU, BSD 4.3, Linux DLL 4.4.1*.	
manual	The title of the manual (e.g., *Linux Programmer's Manual*).	

The manual sections are traditionally defined as follows:

- **1** Commands — Those commands that can be executed by the user from within a shell.
- **2** System calls — Those functions which must be performed by the kernel.
- **3** Library calls — Most of the *libc* functions, such as **sort**(3).
- **4** Special files — Files found in */dev*.
- **5** File formats and conventions — The format for */etc/passwd* and other human-readable files.
- **6** Games
- **7** Macro packages and conventions — A description of the standard file system layout, this man page, and other things.
- **8** System management commands — Commands like **mount**(8), which only *root* can execute.

9 Kernel routines This is a non-standard manual section and is included because the source code to the Linux kernel is freely available under the GNU Public License and many people are working on changes to the kernel)

FONTS

Although there are many arbitrary conventions for man pages in the UNIX world, the existence of several hundred Linux-specific man pages defines our standards:

For functions, the arguments are always specified using italics, *even in the SYNOPSIS section*, where the rest of the function is specified in bold:

int myfunction(int *argc*, **char *****argv***);**

Filenames are always in italics (e.g., */usr/include/stdio.h*), except in the SYNOPSIS section, where included files are in bold (e.g., **#include** <**stdio.h**>).

Special macros, which are usually in upper case, are in bold (e.g., **MAXINT**).

When enumerating a list of error codes, the codes are in bold (this list usually uses the **.TP** macro).

Any reference to another man page (or to the subject of the current man page) is in bold. If the manual section number is given, it is given in roman, without any spaces (e.g., **man**(7)).

The commands to select the type face are given below:

.B	Bold
.BI	Bold alternating with italics
.BR	Bold alternating with Roman
.I	Italics
.IB	Italics alternating with bold
.IR	Italics alternating with Roman
.RB	Roman alternating with bold
.RI	Roman alternating with italics
.SB	Small alternating with bold
.SM	Small

Traditionally, each command can have up to six arguments, but the GNU version seems to remove this limitation. Arguments are delimited by spaces. Double quotes can be used to specify an argument which contains spaces. All of the arguments will be printed next to each other without intervening spaces, so that the **.BR** command can be used to specify a word in bold followed by a mark of punctuation in Roman.

SECTIONS

Sections are started with **.SH** followed by the heading name. If the name contains spaces and appears on the same line as **.SH**, then place the heading in double quotes. Traditional headings include: NAME, SYNOPSIS, DESCRIPTION, OPTIONS, FILES, SEE ALSO, DIAGNOSTICS, BUGS, and AUTHOR. The only required heading is *NAME*, which should be followed on the next line by a one line description of the program:

.SH NAME
chess \- the game of chess

It is extremely important that this format is followed, and that there is a backslash before the single dash which follows the command name. This syntax is used by the **makewhatis**(8) program to create a database of short command descriptions for the **whatis**(1) and **apropos**(1) commands.

OTHER MACROS

Other macros include the following:

.DT	Default tabs
.HP	Begin hanging indent
.IP	Begin paragraph with hanging tag. This is the same as **.TP**, except the tag is given on the same line, not on the following line.
.LP	Same as **.PP**
.PD	Set interparagraph distance to argument
.PP	Begin a new paragraph
.RE	End relative indent (indented paragraph)
.RS	Start relative indent (indented paragraph)
.SS	Subheading (like **.SH**, but used for a subsection)
.TP	Begin paragraph with hanging tag. The tag is given on the next line. This command is similar to **.IP**

FILES

/usr/local/lib/groff/tmac/tmac.an
/usr/man/whatis

SEE ALSO

groff(1), **man**(1), **whatis**(1), **apropos**(1), **makewhatis**(8)

SIGNAL(7)

NAME

signal – list of available signals

DESCRIPTION

Linux supports the following signals:

Signal name	Value	Action	Comment
SIGHUP	1	A	Hangup detected
SIGINT	2	A	Interrupt from keyboard
SIGQUIT	3	A	Quit from keyboard
SIGILL	4	A	Illegal Instruction
SIGTRAP	5	CG	Trace/breakpoint trap
SIGABRT	6	C	Abort
SIGUNUSED	7	AG	Unused signal
SIGFPE	8	C	Floating point exception
SIGKILL	9	AEF	Termination signal
SIGUSR1	10	A	User–defined signal 1
SIGSEGV	11	C	Invalid memory reference
SIGUSR2	12	A	User–defined signal 2
SIGPIPE	13	A	Write to pipe with no readers
SIGALRM	14	A	Timer signal from alarm(1).
SIGTERM	15	A	Termination signal
SIGSTKFLT	16	AG	Stack fault on coprocessor
SIGCHLD	17	B	Child terminated
SIGCONT	18		Continue if stopped
SIGTSTOP	19	DEF	Stop process
SIGTSTP	20	D	Stop typed at tty
SIGTTIN	21	D	tty input for background process
SIGTTOU	22	D	tty output for background process
SIGIO	23	AG	I/O error
SIGXCPU	24	AG	CPU time limit exceeded
SIGXFSZ	25	AG	File size limit exceeded
SIGVTALRM	26	AG	Virtual time alarm (???)
SIGPROF	27	AG	Profile signal
SIGWINCH	29	BG	Window resize signal

The letters in the "Action" column have the following meanings:

- A Default action is to terminate the process.
- B Default action is to ignore the signal.
- C Default action is to dump core.
- D Default action is to stop the process.
- E Signal cannot be caught.
- F Signal cannot be ignored.
- G Not a POSIX.1 conformant signal.

CONFORMS TO

POSIX.1

BUGS

A **SIGBUS** is missing; this is because the 386 hardware does not generate such a signal, but makes porting from other architectures unnecessarily difficult.

SUFFIXES(7)

NAME

suffixes – list of file suffixes

DESCRIPTION

It is customary to mark the contents of a file with the file suffix, which consists of a period, followed by one or more letters. Many standard utilities such as compilers use this to recognize the type of file they are dealing with, and the make(1) utility contains many rules for dealing with files based on suffix type.

Following is a list of suffixes which are likely to be found on a Linux system.

Suffix	File type
,v	Files for RCS (Revision Control System)
-	backup file
.C	C++ source code
.F	FORTRAN source with cpp(1) directives
.S	Assembler source with cpp(1) directives
.Z	File compressed using compress(1)
.[0-9]+pk	TeX font files
.[1-9]	Manual page for the corresponding section
.[1-9][a-z]	Manual page for section plus subsection
.a	static object code library
.afm	PostScript font metrics
.arc	ARC archive
.awk	AWK language program
.bak	Backup file
.bm	Bitmap source
.c	C source
.cat	Message catalog files
.cf	configuration file
.conf	configuration file
.config	configuration file
.cweb	Donald Knuth's WEB for C
.dat	data file
.def	Modula-2 source for definition modules
.def	other definition files
.diff	ASCII File differences
.doc	documentation file
.dvi	TeX device independent output
.el	EMACS lisp source
.elc	compiled EMACS lisp
.eps	encapsulated postscript
.f	FORTRAN source
.fas	pre-compiled common Lisp
.fi	FORTRAN include files
.gif	Graphics Interchange Format
.gsf	Ghostscript fonts
.gz	File compressed using gzip(1)
.h	C or C++ header files

.hlp	Help file
.i	C source after preprocessing
.icon	Bitmap source
.image	Bitmap source
.in	Input file for some utility
.info	Files for the EMACS info browser
.jpg	JPEG compressed picture format
.l	lex(1) or flex(1) files
.lib	Common Lisp library
.ln	Files for use with lint(1)
.lsp	Common Lisp source
.man	Manual page
.mf	Metafont (font generator for TeX) source
.mm	Sources for groff(1) in mm - format
.mod	Modula-2 source for implementation modules
.o	object file
.old	old or backup file
.out	Output file, often executable program (a.out)
.p	Pascal source
.patch	File differences from patch(1)
.pcf	X11 font files (???)
.pfa	Postscript font definition files
.pid	File to store daemon pid (e.g. crond.pid)
.pl	Perl script
.pr	Bitmap source
.ps	Postscript file
.r	RATFOR source
.rules	Rules for something
.s	Assembler source
.sa	Something to do with shared libraries (???)
.sc	sc(1) spreadsheed commands
.sh	sh(1) scripts
.shar	archive created by the shar(1) utility
.so	DLL dynamic library
.sty	LaTeX style files
.sym	Modula-2 compiled definition modules
.tar	archive created by the tar(1) utility
.tar.Z	tar archive compressed with compress(1)
.tar.gz	tar archive compressed with gzip(1)
.taz	Tar archive compressed with compress(1)

.tex	TeX or LaTeX source	
.texi	equivalent to *.texinfo*	
.texinfo	TeXinfo documentation source	
.tfm	TeX font metrics	
.tmpl	Template files	
.tpz	Tar archive compressed with gzip(1)	
.txt	Text file	
.uue	Binary file encoded with uuencode(1)	
.web	Donald Knuth's WEB	
.y	yacc(1) or bison(1) (parser generator) files	
.z	File compressed using pack(1) (or an old gzip(1))	
.zoo	ZOO archive	
~	EMACS or patch backup file	
rc	Startup file, e.g. .newsrc	

CONFORMS TO

General UNIX conventions

BUGS

This list is not exhaustive.

SEE ALSO

file(1), **make**(1)

TR2TEX(7) TR2TEX(7)

NAME

tr2tex – convert a document from troff to LaTeX

SYNOPSIS

tr2tex [**-m**] *filename*

DESCRIPTION

Tr2tex converts a document typeset in **troff** to a **LaTeX** format. It is intended to do the first pass of the conversion. The user should then finish up the rest of the conversion and customize the converted manuscript to his/her liking. It can also serve as a tutor for those who want to convert from troff to LaTeX.

Most of the converted document will be in LaTeX but some of it may be in plain **TeX**. It will also use some macros in **troffms.sty** or **troffman.sty** which are included in the package and must be available to the document when processed with LaTeX.

If there is more than one input file, they will all be converted into one LaTeX document.

Tr2tex understands most of the **-ms** and **-man** macros and **eqn** preprocessor symbols. It also understands several plain **troff** commands. Few **tbl** preprocessor commands are understood to help convert very simple tables.

When converting manuals, use the **-m** flag.

If a troff command cannot be converted, the line that contain that command will be commented out.

NOTE: if you have **eqn** symbols, you must have the in-line mathematics delimiter defined by **delim** in the file you are converting. If it is defined in another setup file, that setup file has to be concatenated with the file to be converted, otherwise **tr2tex** will regard the in-line math as ordinary text.

BUGS

Many of these bugs are harmless. Most of them cause local errors that can be fixed in the converted manuscript.

– Some macros and macro arguments are not recognized.

– Commands that are not separated from their argument by a space are not properly parsed (e.g .sp3i).

– When some operators (notably over, sub and sup) are renamed (via define), then they are encountered in the text, **tr2tex** will treat them as ordinary macros and will not apply their rules.

– rpile, lpile and cpile are treated the same as cpile.

– rcol, lcol are treated the same as ccol.

– Math-mode size, gsize, fat, and gfont are ignored.

– lineup and mark are ignored. The rules are so different.

– Some troff commands are translated to commands that require delimiters that have to be explicitly put. Since they are sometimes not put in troff, they can create problems. Example: .nf not closed by .fi.

– When local motions are converted to \raise or \lower, an \hbox is needed, which has to be put manually after the conversion.

– 'a sub i sub j' is converted to 'a_i_j' which TeX parses as 'a_i{}_j' with a complaint that it is vague. 'a sub {i sub j}' is parsed correctly and converted to 'a_{i_j}'.

– Line spacing is not changed within a paragraph in TeX (which is a bad practice anyway). TeX uses the last line spacing in effect in that paragraph.

TODO

Access registers via **.nr** command.

SEE ALSO

texmatch(9), trmatch(9).

AUTHOR

Kamal Al-Yahya, Stanford University

Section VIII

Administration and Privileged Commands

NAME

intro – Introduction to administration and privileged commands

DESCRIPTION

This chapter describes commands which either can be or are only used by the superuser, like daemons and machine or hardware related commands.

AUTHORS

Look at the header of the manual page for the author(s) and copyright conditions. Note that these can be different from page to page!

ADDUSER(8)

NAME

adduser, addgroup – add a user or group to the system

SYNOPSIS

adduser [––system [––home directory] [––group]] [––quiet] [––force-badname] [––help] [––version] [––debug] username

adduser [––quiet] [––force-badname] [––help] [––version] [––debug] username group

adduser [––group] [––quiet] [––force-badname] [––help] [––version] [––debug] group

DESCRIPTION

adduser and **addgroup** add users and groups to the system according to information provided in the configuration file */etc/adduser.conf*. **adduser** and **addgroup** automatically determine the UID or GID and places the entity in the password or group file, as appropriate.

If necessary, **adduser** creates a home directory for the new user, copies "skeletal" user files to it from */etc/skel* and allows the system administrator to set an initial password and finger information for the user.

Because it needs to be able to write to such files as */etc/passwd* **adduser** can only be run as root.

Generally, there are two types of users and groups on a system: those users that log into the system and those "non-user" accounts and groups which exist for various system tasks and projects. Henceforth, **user** will refer to the login type and **system** user or **group** will refer to the type used for system maintenance and projects.

By default, each user in Debian GNU/Linux is given a corresponding group with the same name and ID, allowing people easily to give access to their home directories to others. This option can be turned off in the configuration file, in which case each user is, by default, added to a group called **users**.

Under Debian GNU/Linux, IDs less than or equal to 100 are allocated by the base system maintainer for various purposes. IDs from 101 to the value specified in the configuration file (1000, by default) are used for system users and groups. IDs greater than 1000 are reserved for users and their corresponding groups.

When invoked with a single name, **adduser** creates a user with that name. When given two names, **adduser** assumes that the first name represents an existing user and that the second name represents an existing group. In this case, the user is added to the group.

OPTIONS

––system Create a system user. This user will be assigned the shell */bin/false* and have an asterisk in the password field. Unless otherwise specified, the user will be placed in the group *nogroup*. Skeletal configuration files will not be copied into the user's home directory.

––home *directory* when used with ––**system** , uses **directory** as the user's home directory, rather than the default specified in the configuration file. If the directory does not exist, it is created.

––group When combined with ––**system**, a group with the same name and ID as the system user is created. If not combined with ––**system**, a group with the given name is created. This is the default action if the program is invoked as **addgroup**.

––quiet Suppress progress messages.

––force–badname By default, user and group names are required to consist of a lowercase letter followed by one or more lowercase letters or numbers. This option forces **adduser** or **addgroup** to be more lenient.

––help Display brief instructions.

––version Display version and copyright information.

––debug Display a large quantity of debugging information.

ADDUSER(8)　　　　　　　　　　　　　　　　　　ADDUSER(8)

SEE ALSO
adduser.conf(5)

COPYRIGHT
Copyright (C) 1995 Ted Hajek, with a great deal borrowed from the original Debian **adduser** Copyright (C) 1994 Ian Murdock. **adduser** is free software; see the GNU General Public Licence version 2 or later for copying conditions. There is *no* warranty.

Debian GNU/Linux　　　　　　　Version 1.94　　　　　　　　　1038

AGETTY(8)   AGETTY(8)

NAME

agetty – alternative Linux getty

SYNOPSIS

agetty [-ihL] [-l login_program] [-m] [-t timeout] port baud_rate,... [term]
agetty [-ihL] [-l login_program] [-m] [-t timeout] baud_rate,... port [term]

DESCRIPTION

agetty opens a tty port, prompts for a login name and invokes the /bin/login command. It is normally invoked by *init(8)*.

agetty has several *non-standard* features that are useful for hard-wired and for dial-in lines:

- o Adapts the tty settings to parity bits and to erase, kill, end-of-line and uppercase characters when it reads a login name. The program can handle 7-bit characters with even, odd, none or space parity, and 8-bit characters with no parity. The following special characters are recognized: @ and Control-U (kill); #, DEL and back space (erase); carriage return and line feed (end of line).

- o Optionally deduces the baud rate from the CONNECT messages produced by Hayes(tm)-compatible modems.

- o Optionally does not hang up when it is given an already opened line (useful for call-back applications).

- o Optionally does not display the contents of the */etc/issue* file (System V only).

- o Optionally invokes a non-standard login program instead of */bin/login*.

- o Optionally turns on hard-ware flow control

- o Optionally forces the line to be local with no need for carrier detect.

This program does not use the */etc/gettydefs* (System V) or */etc/gettytab* (SunOS 4) files.

ARGUMENTS

port   A path name relative to the */dev* directory. If a "-" is specified, *agetty* assumes that its standard input is already connected to a tty port and that a connection to a remote user has already been established.

Under System V, a "-" port argument should be preceded by a "--".

baud_rate,...   A comma-separated list of one or more baud rates. Each time *agetty* receives a BREAK character it advances through the list, which is treated as if it were circular.

Baud rates should be specified in descending order, so that the null character (Ctrl-@) can also be used for baud rate switching.

term   The value to be used for the TERM environment variable. This overrides whatever init(8) may have set, and is inherited by login and the shell.

OPTIONS

-h   Enable hardware (RTS/CTS) flow control. It is left up to the application to disable software (XON/XOFF) flow protocol where appropriate.

-i   Do not display the contents of */etc/issue* before writing the login prompt. Terminals or communications hardware may become confused when receiving lots of text at the wrong baud rate; dial-up scripts may fail if the login prompt is preceded by too much text.

-l login_program   Invoke the specified *login_program* instead of /bin/login. This allows the use of a non-standard login program (for example, one that asks for a dial-up password or that uses a different password file).

-m   Try to extract the baud rate the *connect* status message produced by some Hayes(tm)-compatible modems. These status messages are of the form: "<junk><speed><junk>". *agetty* assumes that the modem emits its status

1039

AGETTY(8)   AGETTY(8)

message at the same speed as specified with (the first) *baud_rate* value on the command line.

Since the *-m* feature may fail on heavily-loaded systems, you still should enable BREAK processing by enumerating all expected baud rates on the command line.

-t timeout   Terminate if no user name could be read within *timeout* seconds. This option should probably not be used with hard-wired lines.

-L   Force the line to be local line with no need for carrier detect. This can be useful when you have locally attached terminal where the serial line does not set the carrier detect signal.

EXAMPLES

This section shows sample entries for the */etc/inittab* file.

For a hard-wired line:

   tty1:con80x60:/sbin/agetty 9600 tty1

For a dial-in line with a 9600/2400/1200 baud modem:

   ttyS1:dumb:/sbin/agetty -mt60 ttyS1 9600,2400,1200

These examples assume you use the simpleinit(8) init program for Linux. If you use a SysV like init (does /etc/inittab mention "respawn"?), refer to the appropriate manual page.

ISSUE ESCAPES

The */etc/issue* file may contain certain escape codes to display the system name, date and time etc. All escape codes consist of a backslash (\) immediately followed by one of the letters explained below.

b	Insert the baudrate of the current line.
d	Insert the current date.
s	Insert the system name, the name of the operating system.
l	Insert the name of the current tty line.
m	Insert the architecture identifier of the machine, eg. i486
n	Insert the nodename of the machine, also known as the hostname.
o	Insert the domainname of the machine.
r	Insert the release number of the OS, eg. 1.1.9.
t	Insert the current time.
u	Insert the number of current users logged in.
U	Insert the string "1 user" or "<n> users" where <n> is the number of current users logged in.
v	Insert the version of the OS, eg. the build-date etc.

Example: On my system, the following */etc/issue* file: This is \n.\o (\s \m \r) \t

displays as   This is thingol.orcan.dk (Linux i386 1.1.9) 18:29:30

FILES

/var/run/utmp, the system status file. /etc/issue, printed before the login prompt (System V only). /dev/console, problem reports (if syslog(3) is not used). /etc/inittab (Linux simpleinit(8) configuration file).

BUGS

The baud-rate detection feature (the *-m* option) requires that *agetty* be scheduled soon enough after completion of a dial-in call (within 30 ms with modems that talk at 2400 baud). For robustness, always use the *-m* option in combination with a multiple baud rate command-line argument, so that BREAK processing is enabled.

The text in the /etc/issue file and the login prompt are always output with 7-bit characters and space parity.

The baud-rate detection feature (the *-m* option) requires that the modem emits its status message *after* raising the DCD line.

DIAGNOSTICS

Depending on how the program was configured, all diagnostics are written to the console device or reported via the syslog(3) facility. Error messages are produced if the *port* argument does not specify a terminal device; if there is no utmp entry for the current process (System V only); and so on.

AUTHOR(S)

W.Z. Venema <wietse@wzv.win.tue.nl> Eindhoven University of Technology Department of Mathematics and Computer Science Den Dolech 2, P.O. Box 513, 5600 MB Eindhoven, The Netherlands

Peter Orbaek <poe@daimi.aau.dk> Linux port.

CREATION DATE

Sat Nov 25 22:51:05 MET 1989

LAST MODIFICATION

91/09/01 23:22:00

VERSION/RELEASE

1.29

ARP(8)

NAME

arp – manipulate the system ARP cache

SYNOPSIS

arp [-v] [-t type] -a [hostname]
arp [-v] -d hostname ...
arp [-v] [-t type] -s hostname hw_addr
arp [-v] -f filename

DESCRIPTION

Arp manipulates the kernel's ARP cache in various ways. The primary options are clearing an address mapping entry and manually setting up one. For debugging purposes, the **arp** program also allows a complete dump of the ARP cache.

OPTIONS

- **-v**   Tell the user what is going on by being verbose.

- **-t type**   When setting or reading the ARP cache, this optional parameter tells **arp** which class of entries it should check for. The default value of this parameter is **ether** (i.e. hardware code **0x01** for **IEEE 802.3 10Mbps Ethernet** . Other values might include network technologies such as **ARCnet** (arcnet) , **PROnet** (pronet) and **AX.25** (ax25) .

- **-a [hostname]**   Shows the entries of the specified hosts. If the **hostname** parameter is not used, **all** entries will be displayed.

- **-d hostname**   Remove the entrie(s) of the specified host. This can be used if the indicated host is brought down, for example.

- **-s hostname hw_addr**   Manually create an ARP address mapping entry for host **hostname** with hardware address set to **hw_addr** . The format of the hardware address is dependent on the hardware class, but for most classes one can assume that the usual presentation can be used. For the Ethernet class, this is 6 bytes in hexadecimal, separated by colons.

- **-f filename**   Similar to the **-s** option, only this time the address info is taken from file **filename** . This can be used if ARP entries for a lot of hosts have to be set up. The name of the data file is very often **/etc/ethers** , but this is not official.

    The format of the file is simple; it only contains ASCII text lines with a hostname, and a hardware address separated by whitespace.

In all places where a **hostname** is expected, one can also enter an **IP address** in dotted-decimal notation.

FILES

/proc/net/arp,
/etc/ethers

AUTHOR

Fred N. van Kempen, <waltje@uwalt.nl.mugnet.org>

BADBLOCKS(8)

NAME

badblocks – search a device for bad blocks

SYNOPSIS

badblocks [**–b** block-size] [**–o** output_file] [**–v**] [**–w**] device blocks-count

DESCRIPTION

badblocks is used to search for bad blocks on a device (usually a disk partition). *device* is the special file corresponding to the device (e.g /dev/hdXX). *blocks-count* is the number of blocks on the device.

OPTIONS

-b block-size		Specify the size of blocks in bytes.
-o output_file		Write the list of bad blocks to the specified file. Without this option, **badblocks** displays the list on its standard output.
-v		Verbose mode.
-w		Use write-mode test. With this option, **badblocks** scans for bad blocks by writing some patterns (0xaa, 0x55, 0xff, 0x00) on every block of the device, reading every block and comparing the contents.

WARNING

Never use the '-w' option on an device containing an existing file system. This option erases data!

AUTHOR

badblocks has been written by Remy Card <card@masi.ibp.fr>, the developer and maintainer of the ext2 fs.

BUGS

I had no chance to make reals tests of this program since I use IDE drives which remap bad blocks. I only made some tests on floppies.

AVAILABILITY

badblocks is available for anonymous ftp from ftp.ibp.fr and tsx-11.mit.edu in /pub/linux/packages/ext2fs.

SEE ALSO

e2fsck(8), mke2fs(8)

CFDISK(8)

NAME

cfdisk – Curses based disk partition table manipulator for Linux

SYNOPSIS

cfdisk [**–avz**] [**–c** *cylinders*] [**–h** *heads*] [**–s** *sectors-per-track*] [**-P** *opt*] [*device*]

DESCRIPTION

cfdisk is a curses based program for partitioning a hard disk drive. The *device* can be any one of the following:

/dev/hda [default]
/dev/hdb
/dev/sda
/dev/sdb
/dev/sdc
/dev/sdd

cfdisk first tries to read the geometry of the hard disk. If it fails, an error message is displayed and **cfdisk** exits. This should only happen when partitioning a SCSI drive on an adapter without a BIOS. To correct this problem, you can set the *cylinders*, *heads* and *sectors-per-track* on the command line. Next, **cfdisk** tries to read the current partition table from the disk drive. If it is unable to figure out the partition table, an error is displayed and the program will exit. This might also be caused by incorrect geometry information, and can be overridden on the command line. Another way around this problem is with the –z option. This will ignore the partition table on the disk.

The main display is composed of four sections, from top to bottom: the header, the partitions, the command line and a warning line. The header contains the program name and version number followed by the disk drive and its geometry. The partitions section always displays the current partition table. The command line is the place where commands and text are entered. The available commands are usually displayed in brackets. The warning line is usually empty except when there is important information to be displayed. The current partition is highlighted with reverse video (or an arrow if the –a option is given). All partition specific commands apply to the current partition.

The format of the partition table in the partitions section is, from left to right: Name, Flags, Partition Type, Filesystem Type and Size. The name is the partition device name. The flags can be *Boot*, which designates a bootable partition or *NC*, which stands for "Not Compatible with DOS or OS/2". DOS, OS/2 and possibly other operating systems require the first sector of the first partition on the disk and all logical partitions to begin on the second head. This wastes the second through the last sector of the first track of the first head (the first sector is taken by the partition table itself). **cfdisk** allows you to recover these "lost" sectors with the maximize command (**m**). *Note:* **fdisk**(8) and some early versions of DOS create all partitions with the number of sectors already maximized. For more information, see the maximize command below. The partition type can be one of *Primary* or *Logical*. For unallocated space on the drive, the partition type can also be *Pri/Log*, or empty (if the space is unusable). The filesystem type section displays the name of the filesystem used on the partition, if known. If it is unknown, then *Unknown* and the hex value of the filesystem type are displayed. A special case occurs when there are sections of the disk drive that cannot be used (because all of the primary partitions are used). When this is detected, the filesystem type is displayed as *Unusable*. The size field displays the size of the partition in megabytes (by default). It can also display the size in sectors and cylinders (see the change units command below). If an asterisks (*) appears after the size, this means that the partition is not aligned on cylinder boundaries.

DOS 6.x WARNING

The DOS 6.x FORMAT command looks for some information in the first sector of the data area of the partition, and treats this information as more reliable than the information in the partition table. DOS FORMAT expects DOS FDISK to clear the first 512 bytes of the data area of a partition whenever a size change occurs. DOS FORMAT will look at this extra

CFDISK(8)   Linux Programmer's Manual   CFDISK(8)

information even if the /U flag is given – we consider this a bug in DOS FORMAT and DOS FDISK.

The bottom line is that if you use cfdisk or fdisk to change the size of a DOS partition table entry, then you must also use **dd** to zero the first 512 bytes of that partition before using DOS FORMAT to format the partition. For example, if you were using cfdisk to make a DOS partition table entry for /dev/hda1, then (after exiting fdisk or cfdisk and rebooting Linux so that the partition table information is valid) you would use the command "dd if=/dev/zero of=/dev/hda1 bs=512 count=1" to zero the first 512 bytes of the partition. **BE EXTREMELY CAREFUL** if you use the **dd** command, since a small typo can make all of the data on your disk useless.

BE EXTREMELY CAREFUL if you use the **dd** command, since a small typo can make all of the data on your disk useless.

For best resutls, you should always use an OS-specific partition table program. For example, you should make DOS partitions with the DOS FDISK program and Linux partitions with the Linux fdisk or Linux cfdisk program.

COMMANDS

cfdisk commands can be entered by pressing the desired key (pressing *Enter* after the command is not necessary). Here is a list of the available commands:

    b   Toggle bootable flag of the current partition. This allows you to select which primary partition is bootable on the drive.

    d   Delete the current partition. This will convert the current partition into free space and merge it with any free space immediately surrounding the current partition. A partition already marked as free space or marked as unusable cannot be deleted.

    g   Change the disk geometry (cylinders, heads, or sectors-per-track). **WARNING:** This option should only be used by people who know what they are doing. A command line option is also available to change the disk geometry. While at the change disk geometry command line, you can choose to change cylinders (**c**), heads (**h**), and sectors per track (**s**). The default value will be printed at the prompt which you can accept by simply pressing the *Enter* key, or you can exit without changes by pressing the *ESC* key. If you want to change the default value, simply enter the desired value and press *Enter*. The altered disk parameter values do not take effect until you return the main menu (by pressing *Enter* or *ESC* at the change disk geometry command line. If you change the geometry such that the disk appears larger, the extra sectors are added at the end of the disk as free space. If the disk appears smaller, the partitions that are beyond the new last sector are deleted and the last partition on the drive (or the free space at the end of the drive) is made to end at the new last sector.

    h   Print the help screen.

    m   Maximize disk usage of the current partition. This command will recover the the unused space between the partition table and the beginning of the partition, but at the cost of making the partition incompatible with DOS, OS/2 and possibly other operating systems. This option will toggle between maximal disk usage and DOS, OS/2, etc. compatible disk usage. The default when creating a partition is to create DOS, OS/2, etc. compatible partitions.

    n   Create new partition from free space. If the partition type is *Primary* or *Logical*, a partition of that type will be created, but if the partition type is *Pri/Log*, you will be prompted for the type you want to create. Be aware that (1) there are only four slots available for primary partitions and (2) since there can be only one extended partition, which contains all of the logical drives, all of the logical drives must be contiguous (with no intervening primary partition). **cfdisk** next prompts you for the size of the partition you want to create. The default size, equal to the entire free space of the current partition, is display in megabytes. You can either press the *Enter* key to accept the default size or

CFDISK(8)   Linux Programmer's Manual   CFDISK(8)

enter a different size at the prompt. **cfdisk** accepts size entries in megabytes (**M**) [default], kilobytes (**K**), cylinders (**C**) and sectors (**S**) by entering the number immediately followed by one of (**M**, **K**, **C** or **S**). If the partition fills the free space available, the partition is created and you are returned to the main command line. Otherwise, the partition can be created at the beginning or the end of the free space, and **cfdisk** will ask you to choose where to place the partition. After the partition is created, **cfdisk** automatically adjusts the other partition's partition types if all of the primary partitions are used.

p   Print the partition table to the screen or to a file. There are several different formats for the partition that you can choose from:

r   Raw data format (exactly what would be written to disk)

s   Partition table in sector order format

t   Partition table in raw format

The *raw* data format will print the sectors that would be written to disk if a **write** command is selected. First, the primary partition table is printed, followed by the partition tables associated with each logical partition. The data is printed in hex byte by byte with 16 bytes per line.

The *partition* table in sector order format will print the partition table ordered by sector number. The fields, from left to right, are the number of the partition, the partition type, the first sector, the last sector, the offset from the first sector of the partition to the start of the data, the length of the partition, the filesystem type (with the hex value in parenthesis), and the flags (with the hex value in parenthesis). In addition to the primary and logical partitions, free and unusable space is printed and the extended partition is printed before the first logical partition.

If a partition does not start or end on a cylinder boundary or if the partition length is not divisible by the cylinder size, an asterisks (*) is printed after the non-aligned sector number/count. This usually indicates that a partition was created by an operating system that either does not align partitions to cylinder boundaries or that used different disk geometry information. If you know the disk geometry of the other operating system, you could enter the geometry information with the change geometry command (**g**).

For the first partition on the disk and for all logical partitions, if the offset from the beginning of the partition is not equal to the number of sectors per track (i.e., the data does not start on the first head), a number sign (#) is printed after the offset. For the remaining partitions, if the offset is not zero, a number sign will be printed after the offset. This corresponds to the *NC* flag in the partitions section of the main display.

The *partition* table in raw format will print the partition table ordered by partition number. It will leave out all free and unusable space. The fields, from left to right, are the number of the partition, the flags (in hex), the starting head, sector and cylinder, the filesystem ID (in hex), the ending head, sector and cylinder, the starting sector in the partition and the number of sectors in the partition. The information in this table can be directly translated to the *raw data format*.

The partition table entries only have 10 bits available to represent the starting and ending cylinders. Thus, when the absolute starting (ending) sector number is on a cylinder greater than 1023, the maximal values for starting (ending) head, sector and cylinder are printed. This is the method used by OS/2, and thus fixes the problems associated with OS/2's fdisk rewriting the partition table when it is not in this format. Since Linux and OS/2 use absolute sector counts, the values in the starting and ending head, sector and cylinder are not used.

q   Quit program. This will exit the program without writing any data to disk.

t   Change the filesystem type. By default, new partitions are created as *Linux* partitions, but since **cfdisk** can create partitions for other operating systems, change partition type allows you to enter the hex value of the filesystem you desire. A list of the know filesystem types is displayed. You can type in the filesystem type at the prompt or accept the default filesystem type [*Linux*].

u Change units of the partition size display. It will rotate through megabytes, sectors and cylinders.

W Write partition table to disk (must enter an upper case W). Since this might destroy data on the disk, you must either confirm or deny the write by entering 'yes' or 'no'. If you enter 'yes', **cfdisk** will write the partition table to disk and the tell the kernel to re-read the partition table from the disk. The re-reading of the partition table works is most cases, but I have seen it fail. Don't panic. It will be correct after you reboot the system. In all cases, I still recommend rebooting the system–just to be safe.

Up Arrow

Down Arrow Move cursor to the previous or next partition. If there are more partitions than can be displayed on a screen, you can display the next (previous) set of partitions by moving down (up) at the last (first) partition displayed on the screen.

CTRL-L Redraws the screen. In case something goes wrong and you cannot read anything, you can refresh the screen from the main command line.

? Print the help screen.

All of the commands can be entered with either upper or lower case letters (except for **Writes**). When in a sub-menu or at a prompt to enter a filename, you can hit the *ESC* key to return to the main command line.

OPTIONS

–a Use an arrow cursor instead of reverse video for highlighting the current partition.

–v Print the version number and copyright.

–z Start with zeroed partition table. This option is useful when you want to repartition your entire disk. *Note:* this option does not zero the partition table on the disk; rather, it simply starts the program without reading the existing partition table.

–c *cylinders*

–h *heads*

–s *sectors-per-track* Override the number of cylinders, heads and sectors per track read from the BIOS. If your BIOS or adapter does not supply this information or if it supplies incorrect information, use these options to set the disk geometry values.

–P *opt* Prints the partition table in specified formats. *opt* can be one or more of "r", "s" or "t". See the print command (above) for more information on the print formats.

SEE ALSO

fdisk(8)

BUGS

The current version does not support multiple disks (future addition).

AUTHOR

Kevin E. Martin (martin@cs.unc.edu)

NAME

chroot – change root directory and execute a program there

SYNOPSIS

chroot *directory program* [*arg* ...]

DESCRIPTION

chroot changes the root directory for a process to a new directory executes a program there.

SEE ALSO

chroot(2)

AUTHOR

Rick Sladkey <jrs@world.std.com>

CLOCK(8)

Linux Programmer's Manual

NAME

clock – manipulate the CMOS clock

SYNOPSIS

/sbin/clock [-u] -r
/sbin/clock [-u] -w
/sbin/clock [-u] -s
/sbin/clock [-u] -a

DESCRIPTION

clock manipulates the CMOS clock in variaous ways, allowing it to be read or written, and allowing synchronization between the CMOS clock and the kernel's version of the system time.

OPTIONS

- **–u** Indicates that the CMOS clock is set to Universal Time.
- **–r** Read CMOS clock and print the result to stdout.
- **–w** Write the system time into the CMOS clock.
- **–s** Set the system time from the CMOS clock.
- **–a** Set the system time from the CMOS clock, adjusting the time to correct for systematic error, and writting it back into the CMOS clock.

    This option uses the file */etc/adjtime* to determine how the clock changes. It contains three numbers:

    The first number is the correction in seconds per day (for example, if your clock runs 5 seconds fast each day, the first number should read -5.0).

The second number tells when **clock** was last used, in seconds since 1/1/1970.

The third number is the remaining part of a second that was left over after the last adjustment.

The following instructions are from the source code:

- a) create a file */etc/adjtime* containing as the first and only line: '0.0 0 0.0'
- b) run *clock -au* or *clock -a*, depending on whether your CMOS is in Universal or Local Time. This updates the second number.
- c) set your system time using the *date* command.
- d) update your CMOS time using *clock -wu* or *clock -w*
- e) replace the first number in */etc/adjtime* by your correction.
- f) put the command *clock -au* or *clock -a* in your */etc/rc.local*, or let **cron**(8) start it regularly.

FILES

/etc/adjtime
/etc/rc.local

AUTHORS

- **V1.0** Charles Hedrick, hedrick@cs.rutgers.edu, Apr 1992
- **V1.1** Modified for clock adjustments, Rob Hooft, hooft@chem.ruu.nl, Nov 1992
- **V1.2** Patches by Harald Koenig, koenig@nova.tat.physik.uni-tuebingen.de, applied by Rob Hooft, hooft@EMBL-Heidelberg.DE, Oct 1993

COMSAT(8)

NAME

comsat – biff server

SYNOPSIS

comsat

DESCRIPTION

Comsat is the server process which receives reports of incoming mail and notifies users if they have requested this service. Comsat receives messages on a datagram port associated with the biff service specification (see services 5 and inetd 8). The one line messages are of the form:

user@mailbox-offset

If the user specified is logged in to the system and the associated terminal has the owner execute bit turned on (by a biff y), the offset is used as a seek offset into the appropriate mailbox file and the first 7 lines or 560 characters of the message are printed on the user's terminal. Lines which appear to be part of the message header other than the From , &To , Date , or Subject lines are not included in the displayed message.

FILES

/var/run/utmp to find out who's logged on and on what terminals

SEE ALSO

biff 1 , inetd 8

BUGS

The message header filtering is prone to error. The density of the information presented is near the theoretical minimum.

Users should be notified of mail which arrives on other machines than the one to which they are currently logged in.

The notification should appear in a separate window so it does not mess up the screen.

HISTORY

The
command appeared in BSD 4.2 .

CROND(8)

NAME

crond – cron daemon (Dillon's Cron)

SYNOPSIS

crond [-l#] [-d[#]] [-f] [-b] [-c directory]

OPTIONS

crond is a background daemon that parses individual crontab files and executes commands on behalf of the users in question.

-**l**<**loglevel**> set logging level, default is 8.

-**d**[<**debuglevel**>] set debugging level, default is 0, if no level specified with -d option default is 1. This option also sets the logging level to 0 and causes crond to run in the foreground.

-**f** run crond in the foreground.

-**b** run crond in the background (default unless -d specified).

-**c directory** specify directory containing crontab files.

DESCRIPTION

crond is responsible for scanning the crontab files and running their commands at the appropriate time. The **crontab** program communicates with crond through the "cron.update" file which resides in crontabs directory, usually /var/spool/cron/crontabs. This is accomplished by appending the filename of the modified or deleted crontab file to "cron.update" which crond then picks up to resynchronize or remove its internal representation of the file.

Crond has a number of built in limitations to reduce the chance of it being ill-used. Potentially infinite loops during parsing are dealt with via a failsafe counter, and user crontabs are generally limited to 256 crontab entries. crontab lines may not be longer than 1024 characters, including the newline.

Whenever crond must run a job, it first creates a daemon-owned temporary file O_EXCL and O_APPEND to store any output, then fork()s and changes its user and group permissions to match that of the user the job is being run for, then exec's /bin/sh -c to run the job. The temporary file remains under the ownership of the daemon to prevent the user from tampering with it. Upon job completion, crond verifies the secureness of the mail file and, if it has been appended to, mails to the file to user. The **sendmail** program is run under the user's uid to prevent mail related security holes. Unlike **crontab**, the crond program does not leave an open descriptor to the file for the duration of the job's execution as this might cause crond to run out of descriptors. When **crontab** program allows a user to edit his crontab, it copies the crontab to a user owned file before running the user's prefered editor. The suid crontab programs keeps an open descriptor to the file which it later uses to copy the file back, thereby ensuring the user has not tampered with the file type.

Crond always synchronizes to the top of the minute, checking the current time against the list of possible jobs. The list is stored such that the scan goes very quickly, and crond can deal with several thousand entries without taking any noticable amount of cpu.

AUTHOR

Matthew Dillon (dillon@apollo.west.oic.com)

NAME

ctrlaltdel – set the function of the Ctrl-Alt-Del combination

SYNOPSIS

ctrlaltdel hard|soft

DESCRIPTION

Based on examination of the *linux/kernel/sys.c* code, it is clear that there are two supported functions that the Ctrl-Alt-Del sequence can perform: a *hard* reset, which immediately reboots the computer without calling **sync** (2) and without any other preparation; and a *soft* reset, which sends the SIGINT (interrupt) signal to the **init** process (this is always the process with PID 1). If this option is used, the **init** (8) program must support this feature. Since there are now several **init** (8) programs in the Linux community, please consult the documentation for the version that you are currently using.

ctrlaltdel is usually used in the */etc/rc.local* file.

FILES

/etc/rc.local

SEE ALSO

simpleinit(8), **init**(8)

AUTHOR

Peter Orbaek (poe@daimi.aau.dk)

CYTUNE(8)

NAME

cytune – Tune Cyclades driver parameters

SYNOPSIS

cytune [-q [-i *interval*]] ([-s *value*]|[-S *value*]) [-g|G] ([-t *timeout*]|[-T *timeout*]) *tty* [*tty* ...]

DESCRIPTION

cytune queries and modifies the interruption threshold for the Cyclades driver. Each serial line on a Cyclades card has a 12-byte FIFO for input (and another 12-byte FIFO for output). The "threshold" specifies how many input characters must be present in the FIFO before an interruption is raised. When a Cyclades tty is opened, this threshold is set to a default value based on baud rate:

Baud Threshold

50-4800 10
9600 8
19200 4
38400 2
57600-150000 1

If the threshold is set too low, the large number of interruptions can load the machine and decrease overall system throughput. If the threshold is set too high, the FIFO buffer can overflow, and characters will be lost. Slower machines, however, may not be able to deal with the interrupt load, and will require that the threshold be adjusted upwards.

If the cyclades driver was compiled with **ENABLE_MONITORING** defined, the cytune command can be used with the −q option to report interrupts over the monitoring interval and characters transferred over the monitoring interval. It will also report the state of the FIFO. The maximum number of characters in the FIFO when an interrupt occurred, the instantaneous count of characters in the FIFO, and how many characters are now in the FIFO are reported. This output might look like this:

/dev/cubC0: 830 ints, 9130 chars; fifo: 11 threshold, 11 max, 11 now
166.259866 interrupts/second, 1828.858521 characters/second

This output indicates that for this monitoring period, the interrupts were always being handled within one character time, because **max** never rose above **threshold**. This is good, and you can probably run this way, provided that a large number of samples come out this way. You will lose characters if you overrun the FIFO, as the Cyclades hardware does not seem to support the RTS RS-232 signal line for hardware flow control from the DCE to the DTE.

cytune will in query mode produce a summary report when ended with a SIGINT or when the threshold or timeout is changed.

There may be a responsiveness vs. throughput tradeoff. The Cyclades card, at the higher speeds, is capable of putting a very high interrupt load on the system. This will reduce the amount of CPU time available for other tasks on your system. However, the time it takes to respond to a single character may be increased if you increase the threshold. This might be noticed by monitoring **ping**(8) times on a SLIP link controlled by a Cyclades card. If your SLIP link is generally used for interactive work such as **telnet**(1), you may want to leave the threshold low, so that characters are responded to as quickly as possible. If your SLIP link is generally used for file transfer, WWW, and the like, setting the FIFO to a high value is likely to reduce the load on your system while not significantly affecting throughput. Alternatively, see the −t or −T options to adjust the time that the cyclades waits before flushing its buffer. Units are 5ms.

If you are running a mouse on a Cyclades port, it is likely that you would want to maintain the threshold and timeout at a low value.

OPTIONS

−s *value*   Set the current threshold to *value* characters. Note that if the *tty* is not being held open by another process, the threshold will be reset on the next open. Only values between 1 and 12, inclusive, are permitted.

−t *value*	Set the current flush timeout to *value* units. Note that if the *tty* is not being held open by another process, the threshold will be reset on the next open. Only values between 0 and 255, inclusive, are permitted. Setting *value* to zero forces the default, currently 0x20 (160ms), but soon to be 0x02 (10ms). Units are 5 ms.
−g	Get the current threshold and timeout.
−T *value*	Set the default flush timeout to *value* units. When the *tty* is next opened, this value will be used instead of the default. If *value* is zero, then the the value will default to 0x20 (160ms), soon to be 0x02 (10ms).
−G	Get the default threshold and flush timeout values.
−q	Gather statistics about the *tty*. The results are only valid if the Cyclades driver has been compiled with **ENABLE_MONITORING** defined. This is probably not the default.
−i *interval*	Statistics will be gathered every *interval* seconds.

BUGS

If you run two copies of cytune at the same time to report statistics about the same port, the 'ints', 'chars', and 'max' value will be reset and not reported correctly. **cytune**(8) should prevent this, but does not.

AUTHOR

Nick Simicich (njs@scifi.emi.net), with modifications by Rik Faith (faith@cs.unc.edu)

FILES

/dev/ttyC[0-8]
/dev/cubC[0-8]

SEE ALSO

setserial(8)

DEBUGFS(8)

NAME

debugfs – ext2 file system debugger

SYNOPSIS

debugfs [[**–w**] device]

DESCRIPTION

debugfs is a file system debugger. It can be used to examine and change the state of an ext2 file system.
device is the special file corresponding to the device containing the ext2 file system (e.g /dev/hdXX).

OPTIONS

-w   Specify that the file system should be open in read-write mode. Without this option, the file system is open in read-only mode.

COMMANDS

debugfs is an interactive debugger. It understands a number of commands.

    cd file

    chroot file

    close   Close the currently open file system.

    clri file   Clear the contents of the inode corresponding to *file*

    expand_dir, file   Expand a directory.

    find_free_block [goal]   Find the first free block, starting from *goal* and allocates it.

    find_free_inode [dir [mode]]   Find a free inode and allocates it.

    freeb block   Mark the block as not allocated.

    freei file   Free the inode corresponding to *file*

    help

    iname inode   Print the file name corresponding to *inode* (currently not implemented).

    initialize device blocksize   Create an ext2 file system on *device*

    kill_file file   Remove a file and deallocates its blocks.

    ln source_file dest_file   Create a link.

    ls [pathname]   Emulate the **ls**(1) command.

    modify_inode file   Modify the contents of the inode corresponding to *file*

    mkdir file   Make a directory.

    open [-w] device   Open a file system.

    pwd

    quit   Quit **debugfs**

    rm file   Remove a file.

    rmdir file   Remove a directory.

    setb block   Mark the block as allocated.

    seti file   Mark in use the inode corresponding to *file*

    show_super_stats   List the contents of the super block.

    stat file   Dump the contents of the inode corresponding to *file*

    testb block   Test if the block is marked as allocated.

    testi file   Test if the inode correponding to *file* is marked as allocated.

    unlink file   Remove a link.

AUTHOR

debugfs has been written by Theodore T'so <tytso@mit.edu>.

SEE ALSO

dumpe2fs(8), **e2fsck**(8), **mke2fs**(8)

NAME

dip - dialup IP connection handler.

SYNOPSIS

dip [-t]

dip [-ktv] [-m mtu] scriptfile

dip [-iv] [user_name]

DESCRIPTION

Dip handles the connections needed for dialup IP links, like SLIP or PPP. It can handle both incoming and outgoing connections, using password security for incoming connections. The outgoing connections use the system's dial(3) library if available.

COMMAND MODE

The first possible use of **dip** is as a standalone program to set up an outgoing IP connection. This can be done by invoking **dip** with the **-t** option, which means **enter TEST mode** and, more precisely, dumps you in the **COMMAND-MODE** of the dip program. You are reminded of this by the **DIP>** prompt, or, if you also specified the **-v** debugging flag, the **DIP [NNNN]>** prompt. The latter prompt also displays the current value of the global **errlvl** variable, which is used mostly when dip runs in **script** mode. For the interactive mode, it can be used to determine if the result of the previous command was OK or not.

The following is a sample taken from a live session:

$ dip -t
DIP: Dialup IP Protocol Driver version 3.3.7 (12/13/93)
Written by Fred N. van Kempen, MicroWalt Corporation.

DIP> _

The most helpful command in this mode is, of course, the **help** command, which should produce an output similar to this:

DIP> help
DIP knows about the following commands:

databits default dial echo flush
get goto help if init
mode modem parity print port
reset send sleep speed stopbits
term wait

DIP> _

All commands display how they should be used when invoking them with no or invalid arguments. Just experiment a little to get the feel of it, and have a look at the sample script files, which also use this command language.

DIALIN MODE

The second possible way of using **dip** is as a login shell for incoming IP connections, as in dialup SLIP and PPP connections. To make integration into the existing UNIX system as easy as possible, **dip** can be installed as simply as using it as a login shell in the system's password file. A sample entry looks like:

suunet:ij/SMxiTlGVCo:1004:10:UUNET:/tmp:/usr/bin/dip -i

When user **suunet** logs in, the **login(1)** program sets the home directory to **/tmp**, and executes the **dip** program with the **-i** option, which means that **dip** must run in **input** mode. **Dip** then tries to locate the name of the logged in user (i.e. the name corresponding to its current user id, as returned by the **getuid(2)** system call) in its database file. An optional single argument to the **dip** program in this mode can be the username that must be used in this lookup, regardless the current user id.

Dip now scans the **/etc/net/diphosts** file for an entry for the given user name. This file contains lines of text (much like the standard password file). The format looks like:

```
#
# diphosts This file describes a number of name to
# address mappings for the DIP program. It
# is used to determine which IP address to
# use for in incoming call of some user.
#
# Version: @(#)diphosts 1.00 12/10/92 FvK
#
# Author: Fred N. van Kempen,
# <waltje@uwalt.nl.mugnet.org>
#
suunet::uunet.uu.net:UUNET SLIP:SLIP,296

# End of diphosts.
```

The first field of a line identifies the user name, which we must match. The second field can contain an encrypted password. If this field is non-null, the **dip** program asks for an **External security password:** , which must match the password in this field. The third field contains the name (or raw IP address) of the host that is connecting to the system with this link. If a host name is given, the usual address resolving process is started, using either a name server or a local hosts file.

The fourth field may contain any text, it is not (yet) used by the **dip** program. In future releases, this info may be used in the system log files. Finally, the fifth field of a line contains a mixture of comma-separated flags. Possible flags are:

SLIP to indicate we must use the SLIP protocol.

PPP to indicate we must use the PPP protocol.

number which gives the MTU parameter of this connection.

After finding the correct line, **dip** puts the terminal line into **RAW** mode, and asks the system networking layer to allocate a channel of the desired protocol. Finally, if the channel is activated, it adds an entry to the system's **routing** table to make the connection work.

Dip now goes into an endless loop of sleeping, which continues until the conenction is physically aborted (i.e. the line is dropped). At that time, **dip** removes the entry it made in the system's routing table, and releases the protocol channel for re-use. It then exists, making room for another session.

DIALOUT MODE

The last way of using **dip** is as a program that initiates outgoing connections. To make life easier for the people who have to manage links of this type, **dip** uses a **chat script** to set up a link to a remote system. This gives the user an enourmous amount of flexibility when making the connection, which otherwise could require **many** command-line options. The path name of the script to be run is then given as the single argument to **dip** ; the program will automatically check if the file has a file name ending in a **.dip** part. This is not mandatory, just a tool to group scripts together in a single directory. A script should look something like this:

```
#
# sample.dip Dialup IP connection support program.
# This file (should show) shows how to use the DIP
# scripting commands to establish a link to a host.
# This host runs the 386bsd operating system, and
# thus can only be used for the "static" addresses.
#
# NOTE: We also need an examnple of a script used to
# connect to a "dynamic" SLIP server, like an Annex
# terminal server...
#
```

Version 3.3.7   12/13/93   1058

```
# Version: @(#)sample.dip 1.30 07/05/93
#
# Author: Fred N. van Kempen, <waltje@uWalt.NL.Mugnet.ORG>
#
main:
# First of all, set up our name for this connection.
# I am called "uwalt.hacktic.nl" (== 193.78.33.238)
get $local uwalt.hacktic.nl
# Next, set up the other side's name and address.
# My dialin machine is called 'xs4all.hacktic.nl' (== 193.78.33.42)
get $remote xs4all.hacktic.nl
# Set the desired serial port and speed.
port cua0
speed 38400
# Reset the modem and terminal line.
# This seems to cause trouble for some people!
reset
# Prepare for dialing.
send ATQ0V1E1X1
wait OK 2
if $errlvl != 0 goto error
dial 555-1234567
if $errlvl != 0 goto error
wait CONNECT 60
if $errlvl != 0 goto error
# We are connected. Login to the system.
login:
sleep 3
send \r\n\r\n
wait ogin: 10
if $errlvl != 0 goto error
send NO-WAY\n
wait ord: 5
if $errlvl != 0 goto error
send HA-HA\n
wait $ 30
if $errlvl != 0 goto error
loggedin:
# We are now logged in. Start the 'sliplogin' program,
# as this is not automatically done for me.
send sliplogin\n
wait SOME-STRING 15
# Set up the SLIP operating parameters.
get $mtu 1500
# Set Destination net/address as type 'default' (vice an address).
# This is used by the 'route' command to set the kernel routing table.
# Some machines seem to require this be done for SLIP to work properly.
default
# Say hello and fire up!
done:
print CONNECTED to $remote with address $rmtip
mode SLIP
goto exit
error:
print SLIP to $remote failed.
exit:
```

This script causes **dip** to dial up a host, log in, and get a **SLIP** interface channel going (in the same manner as with incoming connections). When all is set up, it simply goes into the background and waits for a hangup (or just a lethal signal), at which it hangs up and exists.

FILES
/etc/passwd, /etc/diphosts

AUTHORS
Fred N. van Kempen, waltje@uwalt.nl.mugnet.org,
Paul Mossip, <mossip@vizlab.rutgers.edu>,
Jeff Uphoff, <juphoff@aoc.nrao.edu>,
Jim Seagrave, <jes@grendel.demon.co.uk>
Olaf Kirch, <okir@monad.sub.de>

DMESG(8) Linux Programmer's Manual DMESG(8)

NAME

dmesg – print or control the kernel ring buffer

SYNOPSIS

dmesg [**−c**] [**−n** *level*]

DESCRIPTION

dmesg is used to examine or control the kernel ring buffer.

The program helps users to print out their bootup messages. Instead of copying the messages by hand, the user need only:

dmesg > boot.messages

and mail the *boot.messages* file to whoever can debug their problem.

OPTIONS

−c clear the ring buffer contents after printing.

−n*level* set the *level* at which logging of messages is done to the console. For example, **−n** 1 prevents all messages, expect panic messages, from appearing on the console. All levels of messages are still written to */proc/kmsg*, so **syslogd**(8) can still be used to control exactly where kernel messages appear. When the **−n** option is used, **dmesg** will *not* print or clear the kernel ring buffer.

When both options are used, only the last option on the command line will have an effect.

SEE ALSO

syslogd(8)

AUTHOR

Theodore Ts'o (tytso@athena.mit.edu)

DUMPE2FS(8)

NAME
dumpe2fs – dump filesystem information

SYNOPSIS
dumpe2fs device

DESCRIPTION
dumpe2fs prints the super block and blocks group information for the filesystem present on *device*.

dumpe2fs is similar to Berkeley's **dumpfs** program for the BSD Fast File System.

BUGS
You need to know the physical filesystem structure to understand the output.

AUTHOR
dumpe2fs has been written by Remy Card <card@masi.ibp.fr>, the developer and maintainer of the ext2 fs.

AVAILABILITY
dumpe2fs is available for anonymous ftp from ftp.ibp.fr and tsx-11.mit.edu in /pub/linux/packages/ext2fs.

SEE ALSO
e2fsck(8), **mke2fs**(8), **tune2fs**(8)

Version 0.5b   November 1994

E2FSCK(8)

NAME

e2fsck – check a Linux second extended file system

SYNOPSIS

e2fsck [**–panyrdfvtFV**] [**–b** *superblock*] [**–B** *blocksize*] [**–l**|**-L** *bad_blocks_file*] *device*

DESCRIPTION

e2fsck is used to check a Linux second extended file system.

    device   is the special file corresponding to the device (e.g /dev/hdXX).

OPTIONS

-a   This option does the same thing as the *-p* option. It is provided for backwards compatibility only; it is suggested that people use *-p* option whever possible.

-b *superblock*   Instead of using the normal superblock, use the alternative superblock specified by *superblock*.

-B *blocksize*   Normally, e2fsck will search for the superblock at various different block sizes in an attempt to find the appropriate block size. This search can be fooled in some cases. This option forces e2fsck to only try locating the superblock at a particular blocksize. If the superblock is not found, e2fsck will terminate with a fatal error.

-d   Print debugging output (useless unless you are debugging **e2fsck**).

-f   Force checking even if the file system seems clean.

-F   Flush the filesystem device's buffer caches before beginning. Only really useful for doing e2fsck time trials.

-l *filename*   Add the blocks listed in the file specified by *filename* to the list of bad blocks.

-L *filename*   Set the bad blocks list to be the list of blocks specified by *filename*. (This option is the same as the *-l* option, except the bad blocks list is cleared before the blocks listed in the file are added to the bad blocks list.)

-n   Open the filesystem read-only, and assume an answer of "no" to all questions. Allows **e2fsck** to be used non-interactively. (Note: if the *-l* or *-L* options are specified in addition to the *-n* option, then the filesystem will be opened read-write, to permit the bad-blocks list to be updated. However, no other changes will be made to the filesystem.)

-p   Automatically repair ("preen") the file system without any questions.

-r   This option does nothing at all; it is provided only for backwards compatibility.

-t   Print timing statistics for **e2fsck**. If this option is used twice, additional timing statistics are printed on a pass by pass basis.

-v   Verbose mode.

-V   Print version information and exit.

-y   Assume an answer of "yes" to all questions; allows **e2fsck** to be used non-interactively.

EXIT CODE

The exit code returned by **e2fsck** is the sum of the following conditions:
0 – No errors
1 – File system errors corrected
2 – File system errors corrected, system should
be rebooted if file system was mounted
4 – File system errors left uncorrected

8 – Operational error
16 – Usage or syntax error
128 – Shared library error

BUGS

Almost any piece of software will have bugs. If you manage to find a filesystem which causes **e2fsck** to crash, or which **e2fsck** is unable to repair, please report it to the author.

Please include as much information as possible in your bug report. Ideally, include a complete transcript of the **e2fsck** run, so I can see exactly what error messages are displayed. If you have a writeable filesystem where the transcript can be stored, the **script**(1) program is a handy way to save the output of e2fsck to a file.

It is also useful to send the output of **dumpe2fs**(8). If a specific inode or inodes seems to be giving **e2fsck** trouble, try running the **debugfs**(8) command and send the output of the *stat* command run on the relevant inode(s). If the inode is a directory, the debugfs *dump* command will allow you to extract the contents of the directory inode, which can sent to me after being first run through **uuencode**(1).

Always include the full version string which **e2fsck** displays when it is run, so I know which version you are running.

AUTHOR

This version of **e2fsck** is written by Theodore Ts'o <tytso@mit.edu>.

SEE ALSO

mke2fs(8), **tune2fs**(8), **dumpe2fs**(8), **debugfs**(8)

FDFORMAT(8)

NAME

fdformat – Low-level formats a floppy disk

SYNOPSIS

fdformat [**−n**] device

DESCRIPTION

fdformat does a low level format on a floppy disk. *device* is usually one of the following (for floppy devices, the major = 2, and the minor is shown for informational purposes only):

/dev/fd0d360 (minor = 4)
/dev/fd0h1200 (minor = 8)
/dev/fd0D360 (minor = 12)
/dev/fd0H360 (minor = 12)
/dev/fd0D720 (minor = 16)
/dev/fd0H720 (minor = 16)
/dev/fd0h360 (minor = 20)
/dev/fd0h720 (minor = 24)
/dev/fd0H1440 (minor = 28)
/dev/fd1d360 (minor = 5)
/dev/fd1h1200 (minor = 9)
/dev/fd1D360 (minor = 13)
/dev/fd1H360 (minor = 13)
/dev/fd1D720 (minor = 17)
/dev/fd1H720 (minor = 17)
/dev/fd1h360 (minor = 21)
/dev/fd1h720 (minor = 25)
/dev/fd1H1440 (minor = 29)

The generic floppy devices, /dev/fd0 and /dev/fd1, will fail to work with **fdformat** when a non-standard format is being used, or if the format has not been autodetected earlier. In this case, use **setfdprm**(8) to load the disk parameters.

OPTIONS

−n   No verify. This option will disable the verification that is performed after the format.

SEE ALSO

fd(4), **setfdprm**(8), **mkfs**(8), **emkfs**(8)

AUTHOR

Werner Almesberger (almesber@nessie.cs.id.ethz.ch)

NAME

fdisk – Partition table manipulator for Linux

SYNOPSIS

fdisk [**–l**] [**–v**] [**–s partition**] [device]

DESCRIPTION

fdisk is a menu driven program for manipulation of the hard disk partition table. The *device* is usually one of the following:

/dev/hda
/dev/hdb
/dev/sda
/dev/sdb

The *partition* is a *device* name followed by a partition number. For example, **/dev/hda1** is the first partition on the first hard disk in the system.

If possible, **fdisk** will obtain the disk geometry automatically. This is *not* necessarily the *physical* disk geometry, but is the disk geometry that MS-DOS uses for the partition table. If **fdisk** warns you that you need to set the disk geometry, please believe this statement, and set the geometry. This should only be necessary with certain SCSI host adapters (the drivers for which are rapidly being modified to provide geometry information automatically).

Whenever a partition table is printed out, a consistency check is performed on the partition table entries. This check verifies that the physical and logical start and end points are identical, and that the partition starts and ends on a cylinder boundary (except for the first partition).

Old versions of fdisk (all versions prior to 1.1r [including 0.93]) incorrectly mapped the cylinder/head/sector specification onto absolute sectors. This may result in the first partition on a drive failing the consistency check. If you use LILO to boot, this situation can be ignored. However, there are reports that the OS/2 boot manager will not boot a partition with inconsistent data.

Some versions of MS-DOS create a first partition which does not begin on a cylinder boundary, but on sector 2 of the first cylinder. Partitions beginning in cylinder 1 cannot begin on a cylinder boundary, but this is unlikely to cause difficulty unless you have OS/2 on your machine.

In version 1.1r, a BLKRRPART ioctl() is performed before exiting when the partition table is updated. This is primarily to ensure that removable SCSI disks have their partition table information updated. If the kernel does not update its partition table information, fdisk warns you to reboot. If you do not reboot your system after receiving such a warning, you may lose or corrupt the data on the disk. Sometimes BLKRRPART fails silently, when installing Linux, you should *always* reboot after editing the partition table.

DOS 6.x WARNING

The DOS 6.x FORMAT command looks for some information in the first sector of the data area of the partition, and treats this information as more reliable than the information in the partition table. DOS FORMAT expects DOS FDISK to clear the first 512 bytes of the data area of a partition whenever a size change occurs. DOS FORMAT will look at this extra information even if the /U flag is given – we consider this a bug in DOS FORMAT and DOS FDISK.

The bottom line is that if you use cfdisk or fdisk to change the size of a DOS partition table entry, then you must also use **dd** to zero the first 512 bytes of that partition before using DOS FORMAT to format the partition. For example, if you were using cfdisk to make a DOS partition table entry for /dev/hda1, then (after exiting fdisk or cfdisk and rebooting Linux so that the partition table information is valid) you would use the command "dd if=/dev/zero of=/dev/hda1 bs=512 count=1" to zero the first 512 bytes of the partition. **BE EXTREMELY CAREFUL** if you use the **dd** command, since a small typo can make all of the data on your disk useless.

FDISK(8) Linux Programmer's Manual FDISK(8)

BE EXTREMELY CAREFUL if you use the **dd** command, since a small typo can make all of the data on your disk useless.

For best resutls, you should always use an OS-specific partition table program. For example, you should make DOS partitions with the DOS FDISK program and Linux partitions with the Linux fdisk or Linux cfdisk program.

OPTIONS

−v   Prints version number of **fdisk** program.

−l   Lists the partition tables for **/dev/hda**, **/dev/hdb**, **/dev/sda**, **/dev/sdb**, **/dev/sdc**, **/dev/sdd**, **/dev/sde**, **/dev/sdf**, **/dev/sdg**, **/dev/sdh**, and then exits.

−s*partition*   If the *partition* is not a DOS partition (i.e., the partition id is greater than 10), then the *size* of that partition is printed on the standard output. This value is normally used as an argument to the **mkfs**(8) program to specify the size of the partition which will be formatted.

BUGS

Although this man page (written by faith@cs.unc.edu) is poor, there is *excellent* documentation in the README.fdisk file (written by LeBlanc@mcc.ac.uk) that should always be with the fdisk distribution. If you cannot find this file in the *util-linux-** directory or with the *fdisk.c* source file, then you should write to the distributor of your version of **fdisk** and complain that you do not have all of the available documentation.

AUTHOR

A. V. Le Blanc (LeBlanc@mcc.ac.uk)
v1.0r: SCSI and extfs support added by Rik Faith (faith@cs.unc.edu)
v1.1r: Bug fixes and enhancements by Rik Faith (faith@cs.unc.edu), with special thanks to Michael Bischoff (i1041905@ws.rz.tu-bs.de or mbi@mo.math.nat.tu-bs.de).
v1.3: Latest enhancements and bug fixes by A. V. Le Blanc, including the addition of the −s option. v2.0: Disks larger than 2GB are now fully supported, thanks to Remy Card's llseek support.

FSCK(8) FSCK(8)

NAME

fsck – check and repair a Linux file system

SYNOPSIS

fsck [**–AVRTN**] [**–s**] [**–t** *fstype*] [**fs-options**] *filesys* [...]

DESCRIPTION

fsck is used to check and optionally repair a Linux file system. *filesys* is either the device name (e.g. /dev/hda1, /dev/sdb2) or the mount point (e.g. /, /usr, /home) for the file system. If this fsck has several filesystems on different physical disk drives to check, this fsck will try to run them in parallel. This reduces the total amount time it takes to check all of the filesystems, since fsck takes advantage of the parallelism of multiple disk spindles.

The exit code returned by **fsck** is the sum of the following conditions:
0 – No errors
1 – File system errors corrected
2 – System should be rebooted
4 – File system errors left uncorrected
8 – Operational error
16 – Usage or syntax error
128 – Shared library error
The exit code returned when all file systems are checked using the **-A** option is the bit-wise OR of the exit codes for each file system that is checked.

In actuality, **fsck** is simply a front-end for the various file system checkers (**fsck**.*fstype*) available under Linux. The file system-specific checker is searched for in /sbin first, then in /etc/fs and /etc, and finally in the directories listed in the PATH environment variable. Please see the file system-specific checker manual pages for further details.

OPTIONS

- **-A** Walk through the */etc/fstab* file and try to check all file systems in one run. This option is typically used from the */etc/rc* system initalization file, instead of multiple commands for checking a single file system.

- **-R** When checking all file systems with the **–A** flag, skip the root file system (in case it's already mounted read-write).

- **-T** Don't show the title on startup.

- **-N** Don't execute, just show what would be done.

- **-s** Serialize fsck operations. This is a good idea if you checking multiple filesystems in and the checkers are in an interactive mode. (Note: **e2fsck** runs in an interactive mode by default. To make **e2fsck** run in a non-interactive mode, you must either specify the **-p** or **-a** option, if you wish for errors to be corrected automatically, or the **-n** option if you do not.)

- **-V** Produce verbose output, including all file system-specific commands that are executed.

- **-t***fstype* Specifies the type of file system to be checked. When the **–A** flag is specified, only filesystems that match *fstype* are checked. If *fstype* is prefixed with **no** only filesystems whose filesystem do not match *fstype* are checked.

  Normally, the filesystem type is deduced by searching for *filesys* in the */etc/fstab* file and using the corresponding entry. If the type can not be deduced, **fsck** will use the type specified by the **–t** option if it specifies a unique filesystem type. If this type is not available, the the default file system type (currently ext2) is used.

- **fs-options** Any options which are not understood by **fsck**, or which follow the – option are treated as file system-specific options to be passed to the file system-specific checker.

Currently, standardized file system-specific options are somewhat in flux. Although not guaranteed, the following options are supported by most file system checkers.

Version 0.5b   November 1994   1068

FSCK(8)

-a Automatically repair the file system without any questions (use this option with caution). Note that **e2fsck** supports **-a** for backwards compatibility only. This option is mapped to e2fsck's **-p** option which is safe to use, unlike the **-a** option that most file system checkers support.

-r Interactively repair the filesystem (ask for confirmations). Note: It is generally a bad idea to use this option if multiple fsck's are being run in parallel. Also note that this is **e2fsck** default behavior; it supports this option for backwards compatibility reasons only.

AUTHOR

Theodore Ts'o (tytso@mit.edu)

The manual page was shamelessly adapted from David Engel and Fred van Kempen's generic fsck front end program, which was in turn shamelessly adapted from Remy Card's version for the ext2 file system.

FILES

/etc/fstab.

SEE ALSO

fstab(5), **mkfs**(8), **fsck.minix**(8), **fsck.ext2**(8) or **e2fsck**(8), **fsck.xiafs**(8).

Version 0.5b November 1994 1069

NAME

fsck.minix – a file system consistency checker for Linux

SYNOPSIS

fsck.minix [**–larvsmf**] device

DESCRIPTION

fsck.minix performs a consistency check for the Linux MINIX filesystem. The current version supports the 14 character and 30 character filename options.

The program assumes the file system is quiescent. **fsck.minix** should not be used on a mounted device unless you can be sure nobody is writing to it (and remember that the kernel can write to it when it searches for files).

The device will usually have the following form: /dev/hda[1-8]
/dev/hdb[1-8]
/dev/sda[1-8]
/dev/sdb[1-8]

If the file system was changed (i.e., repaired), then **fsck.minix** will print "FILE SYSTEM HAS CHANGED" and will **sync**(2) three times before exiting. Since Linux does not currently have raw devices, there is *no* need to reboot at this time (versus a system which *does* have raw devices).

WARNING

fsck.minix should **not** be used on a mounted filesystem. Using **fsck.minix** on a mounted filesystem is very dangerous, due to the possibility that deleted files are still in use, and can seriously damage a perfectly good filesystem! If you absolutely have to run **fsck.minix** on a mounted filesystem (i.e., the root filesystem), make sure nothing is writing to the disk, and that no files are "zombies" waiting for deletion.

OPTIONS

- **–l** Lists all filenames
- **–r** Performs interactive repairs
- **–a** Performs automatic repairs (this option implies **–r**), and serves to answer all of the questions asked with the default. Note that this can be extremely dangerous in the case of extensive file system damage.
- **–v** Verbose
- **–s** Outputs super-block information
- **–m** Activates MINIX-like "mode not cleared" warnings
- **–f** Force file system check even if the file system was marked as valid (this marking is done by the kernel when the file system is unmounted).

SEE ALSO

fsck(8), **fsck.ext**(8), **fsck.ext2**(8), **fsck.xiafs**(8), **mkfs**(8), **mkfs.minix**(8), **mkfs.ext**(8), **mkfs.ext2**(8), **mkfs.xiafs**(8). **reboot**(8)

DIAGNOSTICS

There are numerous diagnostic messages. The ones mentioned here are the most commonly seen in normal usage.

If the device does not exist, **fsck.minix** will print "unable to read super block". If the device exists, but is not a MINIX file system, **fsck.minix** will print "bad magic number in super-block".

EXIT CODES

The exit code returned by **fsck.minix** is the sum of the following:

```
0  No errors
3  File system errors corrected, system should be rebooted if file system was mounted
4  File system errors left uncorrected
8  Operational error
16 Usage or syntax error
```

In point of fact, only 0, 3, 4, 7, 8, and 16 can ever be returned.

AUTHOR

Linus Torvalds (torvalds@cs.helsinki.fi)
Error code values by Rik Faith (faith@cs.unc.edu)
Added support for file system valid flag: Dr. Wettstein (greg%wind.uucp@plains.nodak.edu)
Check to prevent fsck of mounted filesystem added by Daniel Quinlan (quinlan@yggdrasil.com)

FTPD(8)   FTPD(8)

NAME

ftpd – DARPA Internet File Transfer Protocol server

SYNOPSIS

ftpd [-d] [-l] [-t timeout] [-T maxtimeout]

DESCRIPTION

Ftpd is the DARPA Internet File Transfer Protocol server process. The server uses the TCP protocol and listens at the port specified in the ftp service specification; see services 5 .

Available options:

    -d Debugging information is written to the syslog.

    -l Each ftp 1 session is logged in the syslog.

    -t The inactivity timeout period is set to timeout seconds (the default is 15 minutes).

    -T A client may also request a different timeout period; the maximum period allowed may be set to timeout seconds with the -T option. The default limit is 2 hours.

The ftp server currently supports the following ftp requests; case is not distinguished.

    Request "Description"
    ABOR "abort previous command"
    ACCT "specify account (ignored)"
    ALLO "allocate storage (vacuously)"
    APPE "append to a file"
    CDUP "change to parent of current working directory"
    CWD "change working directory"
    DELE "delete a file"
    HELP "give help information"
    LIST "give list files in a directory" Pq Dq Li "ls -lgA"
    MKD "make a directory"
    MDTM "show last modification time of file"
    MODE "specify data transfer" Em mode
    NLST "give name list of files in directory"
    NOOP "do nothing"
    PASS "specify password"
    PASV "prepare for server-to-server transfer"
    PORT "specify data connection port"
    PWD "print the current working directory"
    QUIT "terminate session"
    REST "restart incomplete transfer"
    RETR "retrieve a file"
    RMD "remove a directory"
    RNFR "specify rename-from file name"
    RNTO "specify rename-to file name"
    SITE "non-standard commands (see next section)"
    SIZE "return size of file"
    STAT "return status of server"

    STOR "store a file"
    STOU "store a file with a unique name"
    STRU "specify data transfer" Em structure
    SYST "show operating system type of server system"
    TYPE "specify data transfer" Em type
    USER "specify user name"
    XCUP "change to parent of current working directory (deprecated)"
    XCWD "change working directory (deprecated)"
    XMKD "make a directory (deprecated)"
    XPWD "print the current working directory (deprecated)"
    XRMD "remove a directory (deprecated)"

The following non-standard or UNIX specific commands are supported by the SITE request.

    Sy Request Sy Description
    UMASK change umask. Em E.g. SITE UMASK 002
    IDLE set idle-timer. Em E.g. SITE IDLE 60
    CHMOD change mode of a file. Em E.g. SITE CHMOD 755 filename
    HELP give help information. Em E.g. SITE HELP

The remaining ftp requests specified in Internet "RFC 959" are recognized, but not implemented. MDTM and SIZE are not specified in "RFC 959", but will appear in the next updated FTP RFC.

The ftp server will abort an active file transfer only when the ABOR command is preceded by a Telnet "Interrupt Process" (IP) signal and a Telnet "Synch" signal in the command Telnet stream, as described in Internet "RFC 959". If a STAT command is received during a data transfer, preceded by a Telnet IP and Synch, transfer status will be returned.

Ftpd interprets file names according to the globbing conventions used by csh 1 . This allows users to utilize the metacharacters Li &*?[] .

Ftpd authenticates users according to three rules.

> The user name must be in the password data base, and not have a null password. In this case a password must be provided by the client before any file operations may be performed.
>
> The user name must not appear in the file (see ftpusers 5).
>
> The user must have a standard shell returned by getusershell 3 .
>
> If the user name is anonymous or ftp , an anonymous ftp account must be present in the password file (user ftp) . In this case the user is allowed to log in by specifying any password (by convention this is given as the client host's name).

In the last case, ftpd takes special measures to restrict the client's access privileges. The server performs a chroot 2 command to the home directory of the ftp user. In order that system security is not breached, it is recommended that the ftp subtree be constructed with care; the following rules are recommended.

> Pa ~ftp Make the home directory owned by root and unwritable by anyone.
>
> Pa ~ftp/bin Make this directory owned by root and unwritable by anyone. The program ls 1 must be present to support the list command. This program should have mode 111.
>
> Pa ~ftp/etc Make this directory owned by root and unwritable by anyone. The files passwd 5 and group 5 must be present for the ls command to be able to produce owner names rather than numbers. The password field in passwd is not used, and should not contain real encrypted passwords. These files should be mode 444 and owned by root . Don't use the system's /etc/passwd file as the password file or the system's /etc/group file as the group file in the ~ftp/etc directory.

FTPD(8)

Pa ~ftp/pub Make this directory mode 755 and owned by root. Create a subdirectory in ~ftp/pub with the appropriate mode (777 or 733) if you want to allow normal users to upload files.

SEE ALSO

ftp 1 , getusershell 3 , ftpusers 5 , syslogd 8

BUGS

The anonymous account is inherently dangerous and should avoided when possible.

The server must run as the super-user to create sockets with privileged port numbers. It maintains an effective user id of the logged in user, reverting to the super-user only when binding addresses to sockets. The possible security holes have been extensively scrutinized, but are possibly incomplete.

HISTORY

The

command appeared in BSD 4.2 .

IFCONFIG(8)

NAME
ifconfig – configure a network interface

SYNOPSIS
ifconfig [interface]
ifconfig interface [aftype] options | address ...

DESCRIPTION
Ifconfig is used to set up (and maintain thereafter) the kernel-resident network interfaces. It is used at boot time to configure most of them to a running state. After that, it is usually only needed when debugging or when system tuning is needed.

If no arguments are given, **ifconfig** just displays the status of the currently defined interfaces. If the single **interface** argument is given, it displays the status of the given interface only. Otherwise, it assumes that things have to be set up.

Address Families
If the first argument after the interface name is recognized as the name of a supported address family, that address family is used for decoding and displaying all protocol addresses. Currently supported address families include **inet** (TCP/IP, default) and **ax25** (AMPR Packet Radio.)

OPTIONS

interface The name of the NET interface. This usually is a name like **wd0**, **sl3** or something like that: a device driver name followed by a unit number.

up This flag causes the interface to be activated. It is implicitly specified if the interface is given a new address (see below).

down This flag causes the driver for this interface to be shut down, and is useful when things start going wrong.

[–]arp Enable or disable the use of the ARP protocol on this interface. If the minus (–)sign is present, the flag is turned OFF.

[–]trailers Enable or disable the use of trailers on Ethernet frames. This is not used in the current implementation of NET.

[–]allmulti Enable or disable the **promiscuous** mode of the interface. This means that all incoming frames get sent to the network layer of the system kernel, allowing for networking monitoring.

metric N This parameter sets the interface metric. It is not used at present, but we implement it for the future.

mtu N This parameter sets the Maximum Transfer Unit (MTU) of an interface. For Ethernet, this is a number in the range of 1000-2000 (default is 1500). For SLIP, use something between 200 and 4096. Note, that the current implementation does not handle IP fragmentation yet, so you'd better make the MTU large enough!

dstaddr addr Set the "other end"'s IP address in case of a Point-To-Point link, like PPP. This keywords is obsoleted by the new **pointopoint** keyword.

netmask addr Set the IP network mask for this interface. This value defaults to the usual class A, B or C network mask (as deducted from the interface IP address), but it can be set to any value for the use of subnetting.

[-]broadcast [addr] If the address argument is also given, set the protocol broadcast address for this interface. Otherwise, it only sets the **IFF_BROADCAST** flag of the interface. If the keyword was preceded by a minus (-) sign, then the flag is cleared instead.

[-]pointopoint [addr] This keyword enables the **point-to-point** mode of an interface, meaning that it is a direct link between two machines with

IFCONFIG(8)   IFCONFIG(8)

nobody else listening on it (or, at least we hope that this is the case, grin :-)
If the address argument is also given, set the protocol address of the other side of the link, just like the obsolete **dstaddr** keyword does. Otherwise, it only sets the **IFF_POINTOPOINT** flag of the interface. If the keyword was preceded by a minus (-) sign, then the flag is cleared instead.

hw   Set the hardware address of this interface, if the device driver supports this operation. The keyword must be followed by the name of the hardware class and the printable ASCII equivalent of the hardware address. Hardware classes currently supported include **ether** (Ethernet), **ax25** (AMPR AX.25), and **ppp** although the latter is not really supported yet.

address   The host name or IP address (a host name will be resolved into an IP address) of that interface. This parameter is required, although the syntax doesn't currently require it.

FILES

/dev/net/socket

BUGS

None so far, although the syntax checking could be better.

AUTHOR

Fred N. van Kempen, <waltje@uwalt.nl.mugnet.org>

INETD(8) INETD(8)

NAME
inetd – internet super-server

SYNOPSIS
inetd [-d] [configuration file]

DESCRIPTION

Inetd should be run at boot time by (see rc 8). It then listens for connections on certain internet sockets. When a connection is found on one of its sockets, it decides what service the socket corresponds to, and invokes a program to service the request. After the program is finished, it continues to listen on the socket (except in some cases which will be described below). Essentially, inetd allows running one daemon to invoke several others, reducing load on the system.

The option available for inetd:

    -d Turns on debugging.

Upon execution, inetd reads its configuration information from a configuration file which, by default, is There must be an entry for each field of the configuration file, with entries for each field separated by a tab or a space. Comments are denoted by a "#" at the beginning of a line. There must be an entry for each field. The fields of the configuration file are as follows:

service name
socket type
protocol
wait/nowait[.max]
user[.group]
server program
server program arguments

To specify an Sun-RPC based service, the entry would contain these fields.

service name/version
socket type
rpc/protocol
wait/nowait[.max]
user[.group]
server program
server program arguments

The service-name entry is the name of a valid service in the file For internal services (discussed below), the service name must be the official name of the service (that is, the first entry in When used to specify a Sun-RPC based service, this field is a valid RPC service name in the file The part on the right of the / is the RPC version number. This can simply be a single numeric argument or a range of versions. A range is bounded by the low version to the high version - rusers/1-3 .

The socket-type should be one of stream , dgram , raw , rdm , or seqpacket , depending on whether the socket is a stream, datagram, raw, reliably delivered message, or sequenced packet socket.

The protocol must be a valid protocol as given in Examples might be tcp or udp . Rpc based services are specified with the rpc/tcp or rpc/udp service type.

The wait/nowait entry is applicable to datagram sockets only (other sockets should have a nowait entry in this space). If a datagram server connects to its peer, freeing the socket so inetd can received further messages on the socket, it is said to be a multi-threaded server, and should use the nowait entry. For datagram servers which process all incoming datagrams on a socket and eventually time out, the server is said to be single-threaded and should use a wait entry. Comsat 8 biff 1 and talkd 8 are both examples of the latter type of datagram server. Tftpd 8 is an exception; it is a datagram server that establishes pseudo-connections. It must be listed as wait in order to avoid a race; the server reads the first packet, creates a new socket, and then forks and exits to allow inetd to check for new service requests to spawn new servers. The optional max suffix (separated from wait or nowait by a dot) specifies the maximum number of server instances that may be spawned from inetd within an interval of 60 seconds. When omitted, max defaults to 40.

The user entry should contain the user name of the user as whom the server should run. This allows for servers to be given less permission than root. An optional group name can be specified by appending a dot to the user name followed by the group name. This allows for servers to run with a different (primary) group id than specified in the password file. If a group is specified and user is not root, the supplementary groups associated with that user will still be set.

The server-program entry should contain the pathname of the program which is to be executed by inetd when a request is found on its socket. If inetd provides this service internally, this entry should be internal .

The server program arguments should be just as arguments normally are, starting with argv[0], which is the name of the program. If the service is provided internally, the word internal should take the place of this entry.

Inetd provides several trivial services internally by use of routines within itself. These services are echo , discard , chargen (character generator), daytime (human readable time), and time (machine readable time, in the form of the number of seconds since midnight, January 1, 1900). All of these services are tcp based. For details of these services, consult the appropriate RFC from the Network Information Center.

Inetd rereads its configuration file when it receives a hangup signal, SIGHUP . Services may be added, deleted or modified when the configuration file is reread. Inetd creates a file /etc/inetd.pid that contains its process identifier.

SEE ALSO

comsat 8 , fingerd 8 , ftpd 8 , rexecd 8 , rlogind 8 , rshd 8 , telnetd 8 , tftpd 8

HISTORY

The

command appeared in BSD 4.3 . Support for Sun-RPC based services is modelled after that provided by Sun-OS 4.1 .

INIT(8) Linux Programmer's Manual INIT(8)

NAME

init, telinit – process control initialization

SYNOPSIS

/sbin/init [**–t sec**] [**0123456SsQq**]
/sbin/telinit [**–t sec**] [**0123456sSQqabc**]

DESCRIPTION

Init

Init is the father of all processes. Its primary role is to create processes from a script stored in the file **/etc/inittab** (see *inittab*(5)). This file usually has entries which cause **init** to spawn **getty**s on each line that users can log in. It also controls autonomous processes required by any particular system.

A *run level* is a software configuration of the system which allows only a selected group of processes to exist. The processes spawned by **init** for each of these *run levels* are defined in the **/etc/inittab** file. **Init** can be in one of eight *run levels*, **06** and **S** or **s**. The *run level* is changed by having a privileged user run **/sbin/telinit**, which sends appropriate signals to **init**, telling it which run level to change to.

After **init** is invoked as the last step of the kernel booting, it looks for the file **/etc/inittab** to see if there is an entry of the type **initdefault** (see *inittab*(5)). **initdefault** determines the initial run level of the system. If there is no such entry or no **/etc/inittab** at all, a *run level* has to be entered at the system console.

Run level **S** or **s** bring the system to single user mode and do not require an **/etc/initttab** file. In single user mode, **/bin/sh** is invoked on **/dev/console**.

/dev/console need not nessecarily be the physical system console. When init is told to enter **single user mode** or **runlevel 1** (either directly, by init **S** or by telling **shutdown** to enter maintenance mode) it will link the terminal line the command was executed from to **/dev/console**. The device **/dev/systty** is called the **physical system console** and the device **/dev/console** is called the **logical system console**. If the logical system console is not the physical system console, pressing the combination **CTRL-ALT-DEL** on the physical system console will force a relink of **/dev/console** to **/dev/systty**. A terminal line can only become the logical console if it's listed in the file /etc/securetty. All this is in preparation of the day that the **Linux** kernel will support serial consoles.

Beware: if you want to run X, or anything else that is aware of Virtual Consoles, the logical system console (/dev/console) needs to be the same as the physical system console (/dev/systty).

When entering single user mode, **init** reads the console's *ioctl*(2) states from **/etc/ioctl.save**. If this file does not exist, **init** initializes the line at **9600 baud** and with **CLOCAL** settings. When **init** leaves single user mode, it stores the console's *ioctl* settings in this file so it can re-use them for the next single-user session. If the logical system console is changed to another terminal line, the settings of the line from which the **init** or **telinit** command was given are stored in **/etc/ioctl.save** too, so that the terminal line will be initialized correctly in single user mode.

When entering a multi user mode the first time, **init** performs the **boot** and **bootwait** entries to allow file systems to be mounted before users can log in. Then all entries matching the *run level* are processed.

Each time a child terminates, **init** records the fact and the reason it died in **/etc/utmp** and **/var/adm/wtmp** if these files exist.

After it has spawned all of the processes specified, **init** waits for one of its descendant processes to die, a powerfail signal, or until it is signaled by **/sbin/telinit** to change the system's *run level*. When one of the above three conditions occurs, it re-examines the **/etc/inittab** file. New entries can be added to this file at any time. However, **init** still waits for one of the above three conditions to occur. To provide for an instantaneous response, the **Q** or **q** command can wake up **init** to re-examine the **/etc/inittab** file.

INIT(8) Linux Programmer's Manual INIT(8)

If **init** is not in single user mode and receives a powerfail signal, special powerfail entries are invoked.

When **init** is requested to change the *run level*, it sends the warning signal **SIGTERM** to all processes that are undefined in the new *run level*. It then waits 20 seconds before forcibly terminating these processes via the kill signal **SIGKILL**

Note that **init** assumes that all these processes (and their descendants) remain in the same process group which **init** originally created for them. If any process changes its process group affiliation it will not receive these signals. Such processes need to be terminated separately.

telinit

/sbin/telinit is linked to **/sbin/init**. It takes a one-character argument and signals **init** to perform the appropriate action. The following arguments serve as directives to **/sbin/telinit**:

- 0,1,2,3,4,5 or 6   tell **/sbin/init** to switch to the specified run level.
- a,b,c   tell **/sbin/init** to process only those **/etc/inittab** file entries having *run level* **a**, **b** or **c**.
- Q or q   tells **/sbin/init** to re-examine the **/etc/inittab** file.
- S or s   tells **/sbin/init** to switch to single user mode.

/sbin/telinit can also tell init how much time it should wait between sending processes the TERM and the KILL signal; default this is 20 seconds, but it can be changed by the **-t sec** option.

/sbin/telinit can be invoked only by users with appropriate privileges.

RUNLEVELS

Run levels **0, 1 and 6** are reserved. Runlevel 0 is used to halt the system, runlevel 6 is used to reboot the system and runlevel 1 is used to get the system down into single user mode. Runlevel **S** is not really ment to use directly, but more for the scripts that are executed when entering runlevel **1**. For more information on this, see the manpages for **shutdown**(1) and **inittab**(5).

FILES

/etc/inittab
/dev/console
/dev/systty
/etc/ioctl.save
/etc/utmp
/var/adm/wtmp

CONFORMING TO

Init is compatible with the System V init. The scripts that are used with it, however, are mostly more modelled after the **BSD** startup scripts. There are startup scripts available that let **Linux** boot more like a System V system, but most people find them too complex.

WARNINGS

Init assumes that processes and descendants of processes remain in the same process group which was originally created for them. If the processes change their group, **init** can't kill them and you may end up with two processes reading from one terminal line.

DIAGNOSTICS

If **/sbin/init** finds that it is continuously respawning an entry more than 10 times in 2 minutes, it will assume that there is an error in the command string, generate an error message on the system console, and refuse to respawn this entry until either 5 minutes has elapsed or it receives a signal. This prevents it from eating up system resources when someone makes a typographical error in the **/etc/inittab** file or the program for the entry is removed.

AUTHOR

Miquel van Smoorenburg (miquels@drinkel.nl.mugnet.org), initial manual page by Michael Haardt (u31b3hs@pool.informatik.rwth-aachen.de).

SEE ALSO

getty(1), login(1), sh(1), who(1), shutdown(1), kill(2), inittab(5), utmp(5).

IPCRM(8)

NAME
ipcrm – remove ipc facilities

SYNOPSIS
ipcrm [shm | msg | sem] *id*

DESCRIPTION
ipcrm will remove the resource specified by *id*.

SEE ALSO
ipcs(8)

AUTHOR
krishna balasubramanian (balasub@cis.ohio-state.edu)

IPCS(8)

NAME

ipcs – provide information on ipc facilities

SYNOPSIS

ipcs [–asmq] [–tclup]
ipcs [–smq] –i *id*
ipcs –h

DESCRIPTION

ipcs provides information on the ipc facilities for which the calling process has read acccess.

The **–i** option allows a specific resource *id* to be specified. Only information on this *id* will be printed.

Resources may be specified as follows:

    –m   shared memory segments
    –q   message queues
    –s   semaphore arrays
    –a   all (this is the default)

The output format may be specified as follows:

    –t   time
    –p   pid
    –c   creator
    –l   limits
    –u   summary

SEE ALSO

ipcrm(8)

AUTHOR

krishna balasubramanian (balasub@cis.ohio-state.edu)

NAME

kbdrate – reset the keyboard repeat rate and delay time

SYNOPSIS

kbdrate [–s] [–r rate] [–d delay]

DESCRIPTION

kbdrate is used to change the IBM keyboard repeat rate and delay time. The delay is the amount of time that a key must be depressed before it will start to repeat.

Using **kbdrate** without any options will reset the rate to 10.9 characters per second (cps) and the delay to 250 milliseconds (mS). These are the IBM defaults.

OPTIONS

–s Silent. No messages are printed.

–r *rate* Change the keyboard repeat rate to *rate* cps. The allowable range is from 2.0 to 30.0 cps. Only certain, specific values are possible, and the program will select the nearest possible value to the one specified. The possible values are given, in characters per second, as follows: 2.0, 2.1, 2.3, 2.5, 2.7, 3.0, 3.3, 3.7, 4.0, 4.3, 4.6, 5.0, 5.5, 6.0, 6.7, 7.5, 8.0, 8.6, 9.2, 10.0, 10.9, 12.0, 13.3, 15.0, 16.0, 17.1, 18.5, 20.0, 21.8, 24.0, 26.7, 30.0.

–d *delay* Change the delay to *delay* milliseconds. The allowable range is from 250 to 1000 mS, but the only possible values (based on hardware restrictions) are: 250mS, 500mS, 750mS, and 1000mS.

BUGS

Not all keyboards support all rates.

Not all keyboards have the rates mapped in the same way.

Setting the repeat rate on the Gateway AnyKey keyboard does not work. If someone with a Gateway figures out how to program the keyboard, please send mail to faith@cs.unc.edu.

FILES

/etc/rc.local
/dev/port

AUTHOR

Rik Faith (faith@cs.unc.edu)

KLOGD(1) — Linux System Administration — KLOGD(1)

NAME
klogd — kernel log daemon.

SYNOPSIS
klogd –c [n] –d –f [fname] –os

DESCRIPTION
klogd is a system daemon which intercepts and logs Linux kernel messages.

OPTIONS

- **–c** Sets the default log level of console messages to **[n]**.
- **–d** Enable debugging mode. This will generate **LOTS** of output to stderr.
- **–f** Log messages to the specified filename rather than to the syslog facility.
- **–o** Execute in 'one–shot' mode. This causes **klogd** to read and log all the messages that are found in the kernel message buffers. After a single read and log cycle the daemon exits.
- **–s** Force **klogd** to use the system call interface to the kernel message buffers.

OVERVIEW

The functionality of klogd has been typically incorporated into other versions of syslogd but this seems to be a poor place for it. In the modern Linux kernel a number of kernel messaging issues such as sourcing and prioritization must be addressed. Incorporating kernel logging into a separate process would appear to offer a cleaner separation of services.

In Linux there are two potential sources of kernel log information: the /proc filesystem and the syscall (sys_syslog) interface, although ultimately they are one and the same. Klogd is designed to choose whichever source of information is the most appropriate. It does this by first checking for the presence of a mounted /proc filesystem. If this is found the /proc/kmsg file is used as the source of kernel log information. If the proc filesystem is not mounted klogd uses a system call to obtain kernel messages. The command line switch (–s) can be used to force klogd to use the system call interface as its messaging source.

If kernel messages are directed through the syslogd daemon the klogd daemon, as of version 1.1, has the ability to properly prioritize kernel messages. Prioritization of the kernel messages was added at approximately the pl13 level of the kernel. The raw kernel messages are of the form:

    [0–7]Something said by the kernel.

The priority of the kernel message is encoded as a single numeric digit enclosed inside the <> pair. The definitions of these values is given in the kernel include file kernel.h. When a message is received from the kernel the klogd daemon reads this priority level and assigns the appropriate priority level to the syslog message. If file output (–f) is used the prioritization sequence is left pre–pended to the kernel message.

The klogd daemon also allows the ability to alter the presentation of kernel messages to the system console. Consequent with the prioritization of kernel messages was the inclusion of default messaging levels for the kernel. In a stock kernel the the default console log level is set to 7. Any messages with a priority level numerically lower than 7 (higher priority) appear on the console.

Messages of priority level 7 are considered to be 'debug' messages and will thus not appear on the console. Many administrators, particularly in a multi–user environment, prefer that all kernel messages be handled by klogd and either directed to a file or to the syslogd daemon. This prevents 'nuisance' messages such as line printer out of paper or disk change detected from cluttering the console.

KLOGD(1) Linux System Administration KLOGD(1)

By default the klogd daemon executes a system call to inhibit all kernel messages (except for panics) from being displayed on the console. The –c switch can be used to alter this behavior. The arguement given to the –c switch specifies the priority level of messages which will be directed to the console. Note that messages of a priority value LOWER than the indicated number will be directed to the console.

> For example, to have the kernel display all messages with a priority level of 3 (KERN_ERR) or more severe the following command would be executed:
>
> klogd –c 4

The definitions of the numeric values for kernel messages are given in the file kernel.h which can be found in the /usr/include/linux directory if the kernel sources are installed. These values parallel the syslog priority values which are defined in the file syslog.h found in the /usr/include/sys sub-directory.

The klogd daemon can also be used in a 'one–shot' mode for reading the kernel message buffers. One shot mode is selected by specifying the –o switch on the command line. Output will be directed to either the syslogd daemon or to an alternate file specified by the -f switch.

> For example, to read all the kernel messages after a system boot and record them in a file called krnl.msg the following command would be given.
>
> klogd -o -f ./krnl.msg

SIGNAL HANDLING

The klogd daemon will respond to six signals: SIGHUP, SIGINT, SIGKILL, SIGTERM, SIGTSTP and SIGCONT. The SIGINT, SIGKILL, SIGTERM and SIGHUP signals will cause the daemon to close its kernel log sources and terminate gracefully.

The SIGTSTP and SIGCONT singals are used to start and stop kernel logging. Upon receipt of a SIGTSTP signal the daemon will close its log sources and spin in an idle loop. Subsequent receipt of a SIGCONT signal will cause the daemon to go through its initialization sequence and rechoose an input source. Using SIGSTOP and SIGCONT in combination the kernel log input can be rechosen without stopping and restarting the daemon. For example if the /proc file system is to be un-mounted the following command sequence should be used:

> # kill -TSTP pid
> # umount /proc
> # kill -CONT pid

Notations will be made in the system logs with LOG_INFO priority documenting the start/stop of logging.

FILES

/proc/kmsg

BUGS

Probably numerous. Well formed context diffs appreciated.

AUTHOR

> Dr. Greg Wettstein (greg%wind.uucp@plains.nodak.edu)
> Enjellic Systems Development
> Oncology Research Divsion Computing Facility
> Roger Maris Cancer Center
> Fargo, ND 58122

LPC(8)

NAME
lpc – line printer control program

SYNOPSIS
lpc [command [argument ...]]

DESCRIPTION
Lpc is used by the system administrator to control the operation of the line printer system. For each line printer configured in /etc/printcap, lpc may be used to:

- disable or enable a printer,
- disable or enable a printer's spooling queue,
- rearrange the order of jobs in a spooling queue,
- find the status of printers, and their associated spooling queues and printer dameons.

Without any arguments, lpc will prompt for commands from the standard input. If arguments are supplied, lpc interprets the first argument as a command and the remaining arguments as parameters to the command. The standard input may be redirected causing lpc to read commands from file. Commands may be abreviated; the following is the list of recognized commands.

? [command ...]

help [command ...]   Print a short description of each command specified in the argument list, or, if no arguments are given, a list of the recognized commands.

Ic abort No all — printer   Terminate an active spooling daemon on the local host immediately and then disable printing (preventing new daemons from being started by lpr) for the specified printers.

clean No all — printer   Remove any temporary files, data files, and control files that cannot be printed (i.e., do not form a complete printer job) from the specified printer queue(s) on the local machine.

disable No all — printer   Turn the specified printer queues off. This prevents new printer jobs from being entered into the queue by lpr.

Ic down No all — printer message ...   Turn the specified printer queue off, disable printing and put *message* in the printer status file. The message doesn't need to be quoted, the remaining arguments are treated like echo(1). This is normally used to take a printer down and let others know why lpq(1) will indicate the printer is down and print the status message).

enable No all — printer   Enable spooling on the local queue for the listed printers. This will allow lpr(1) to put new jobs in the spool queue.

exit

quit   Exit from lpc.

restart all — printer   Attempt to start a new printer daemon. This is useful when some abnormal condition causes the daemon to die unexpectedly leaving jobs in the queue. Lpq will report that there is no daemon present when this condition occurs. If the user is the super-user, try to abort the current daemon first (i.e., kill and restart a stuck daemon).

start all — printer   Enable printing and start a spooling daemon for the listed printers.

status No all — printer   Display the status of daemons and queues on the local machine.

LPC(8)   LPC(8)

      stop all — printer   Stop a spooling daemon after the current job completes and disable printing.

      topq printer [jobnum ...] [user ...]   Place the jobs in the order listed at the top of the printer queue.

      up all — printer   Enable everything and start a new printer daemon. Undoes the effects of

FILES

- /etc/printcap printer description file
- /var/spool/* spool directories
- /var/spool/*/lock lock file for queue control

SEE ALSO

lpd(8), lpr(1), lpq(1), lprm(1), printcap(5)

DIAGNOSTICS

- **?Ambiguous command** abreviation matches more than one command
- **?Invalid command** no match was found
- **?Privileged command** command can be executed by root only

HISTORY

The lpc command appeared in BSD 4.2 .

BSD 4.2   March 16, 1991   1088

LPD(8)

NAME

lpd – line printer spooler daemon

SYNOPSIS

lpd [-l] [port#]

DESCRIPTION

Lpd is the line printer daemon (spool area handler) and is normally invoked at boot time from the rc(8) file. It makes a single pass through the printcap(5) file to find out about the existing printers and prints any files left after a crash. It then uses the system calls listen(2) and accept(2) to receive requests to print files in the queue, transfer files to the spooling area, display the queue, or remove jobs from the queue. In each case, it forks a child to handle the request so the parent can continue to listen for more requests.

Available options:

- -l The -l flag causes lpd to log valid requests received from the network. This can be useful for debugging purposes.
- port# The Internet port number used to rendezvous with other processes is normally obtained with getservbyname(3) but can be changed with the port# argument.

Access control is provided by two means. First, all requests must come from one of the machines listed in the file /etc/hosts.equiv or /etc/hosts.lpd . Second, if the rs capability is specified in the printcap entry for the printer being accessed, *lpr* requests will only be honored for those users with accounts on the machine with the printer.

The file *minfree* in each spool directory contains the number of disk blocks to leave free so that the line printer queue won't completely fill the disk. The *minfree* file can be edited with your favorite text editor.

The daemon begins processing files after it has successfully set the lock for exclusive access (descibed a bit later), and scans the spool directory for files beginning with *cf*. Lines in each *cf* file specify files to be printed or non-printing actions to be performed. Each such line begins with a key character to specify what to do with the remainder of the line.

- J
  Job Name. String to be used for the job name on the burst page.
- C
  Classification. String to be used for the classification line on the burst page.
- L
  Literal. The line contains identification info from the password file and causes the banner page to be printed.
- T
  Title. String to be used as the title for pr(1).
- H
  Host Name. Name of the machine where lpr was invoked.
- P
  Person. Login name of the person who invoked lpr. This is used to verify ownership by lprm.
- M
  Send mail to the specified user when the current print job completes.
- f
  Formatted File. Name of a file to print which is already formatted.
- l
  Like "f" but passes control characters and does not make page breaks.
- p
  Name of a file to print using pr(1) as a filter.

- t
  Troff File. The file contains troff(1) output (cat phototypesetter commands).
- n
  Ditroff File. The file contains device independent troff output.
- r
  DVI File. The file contains Tex 1 output DVI format from Standford).
- g
  Graph File. The file contains data produced by plot(3).
- c
  Cifplot File. The file contains data produced by cifplot.
- v
  The file contains a raster image.
- r
  The file contains text data with FORTRAN carriage control characters.
- 1
  Troff Font R. Name of the font file to use instead of the default.
- 2
  Troff Font I. Name of the font file to use instead of the default.
- 3
  Troff Font B. Name of the font file to use instead of the default.
- 4
  Troff Font S. Name of the font file to use instead of the default.
- W
  Width. Changes the page width (in characters) used by pr(1) and the text filters.
- I
  Indent. The number of characters to indent the output by (in ascii).
- U
  Unlink. Name of file to remove upon completion of printing.
- N
  File name. The name of the file which is being printed, or a blank for the standard input (when lpr is invoked in a pipeline).

If a file can not be opened, a message will be logged via syslog(3) using the LOG_LPR facility. Lpd will try up to 20 times to reopen a file it expects to be there, after which it will skip the file to be printed.

Lpd uses flock(2) to provide exclusive access to the lock file and to prevent multiple deamons from becoming active simultaneously. If the daemon should be killed or die unexpectedly, the lock file need not be removed. The lock file is kept in a readable ASCII form and contains two lines. The first is the process id of the daemon and the second is the control file name of the current job being printed. The second line is updated to reflect the current status of lpd for the programs lpq(1) and lprm(1).

FILES

- /etc/printcap printer description file
- /var/spool/* spool directories
- /var/spool/*/minfree minimum free space to leave
- /dev/lp* line printer devices
- /dev/printer socket for local requests
- /etc/hosts.equiv lists machine names allowed printer access
- /etc/hosts.lpd lists machine names allowed printer access, but not under same administrative control.

LPD(8) LPD(8)

SEE ALSO

lpc(8), pac(1), lpr(1), lpq(1), lprm(1), syslog(3), printcap(5)

4.2 BSD Line Printer Spooler Manual

HISTORY

An lpd daemon appeared in Version 6 AT&T UNIX.

MAKEDEV(8)

NAME
MAKEDEV – create and maintain filesystem device entries

SYNOPSIS
MAKEDEV [*–vcdnhV*] device or device-group name(s)

DESCRIPTION
MAKEDEV is used to maintain the special filesystem entries found in /dev. It creates, or optionally removes, one or more device entries. The names and device numbers are defined in the **devinfo** file (q.v.); site-specific configuration is found in the file MAKEDEV.cfg. **MAKEDEV** itself has no knowledge of device information.

OPTIONS

- *-v* Verbose mode; print out exactly what's being done.
- *-c* Create; create the specified devices. [default]
- *-d* Delete; remove the specified devices instead of creating them.
- *-n* Do nothing; only print what would be done. Implies -v as well.
- *-h* Print a usage message.
- *-V* Print the version string.

The following targets are special:

- *update* Run MAKEDEV in update mode. This reads the list of devices currently available from /proc/devices, and updates all entries in /dev to match the device numbers found there.
- *local* Run MAKEDEV to create local devices. This option is obsolete and just prints a warning message. Use devinfo.local and makedev.cfg to achieve the same results.

FILES

- */etc/devinfo* Device information
- */usr/local/etc/devinfo.local* Local device information
- */etc/devinfo.local* Alternate localtion for local device information
- */etc/makedev.cfg* Configuration file
- *MAKEDEV.cache* Cached data for 'update'
- */proc/devices* The kernel's list of current devices

AUTHOR
David A. Holland (dholland@husc.harvard.edu)

Based on the older **MAKEDEV** shell script written by Nick Holloway. Additional ideas were contributed by Rik Faith.

NOTES
The LALR(1) parser generator used to build makedev.c from makedev.syn is a commercial product. You won't be able to do a complete rebuild unless you have it.

SEE ALSO
devinfo(5), **makedev.cfg**(5)

MAKEDEV(8)　　　　　　Linux Programmer's Manual　　　　　　MAKEDEV(8)

NAME

MAKEDEV – create devices

SYNOPSIS

cd dev; ./MAKEDEV -V
cd dev; ./MAKEDEV [-n] [-v] update
cd dev; ./MAKEDEV [-n] [-v] [-d] *device ...*

DESCRIPTION

MAKEDEV is a script that will create the devices in /dev used to interface with drivers in the kernel.

Note that programs giving the error "ENOENT: No such file or directory" normally means that the device file is missing, whereas "ENODEV: No such device" normally means the kernel does not have the driver configured or loaded.

OPTIONS

- **–V**　　Print out version (actually RCS version information) and exit.
- **–n**　　Do not actually update the devices, just print the actions that would be performed.
- **–d**　　Delete the devices. The main use for this flag is by **MAKEDEV** itself.
- **–v**　　Be verbose. Print out the actions as they are performed. This is the same output as produced by **–n**.

CUSTOMISATION

Since there is currently no standardisation in what names are used for system users and groups, it is possible that you may need to modify **MAKEDEV** to reflect your site's settings. Near the top of the file is a mapping from device type to user, group and permissions (e.g. all CD-ROM devices are set from the $cdrom variable). If you wish to change the defaults, this is the section to edit.

DEVICES

General Options

- **update**　　This only works on kernels which have /proc/interrupts (introduced during 1.1.x). This file is scanned to see what devices are currently configured into the kernel, and this is compared with the previous settings stored in the file called DEVICES. Devices which are new since then or have a different major number are created, and those which are no longer configured are deleted.

- **generic**　　Create a generic subset of devices. This is the standard devices, plus floppy drives, various hard drives, pseudo-terminals, console devices, basic serial devices, busmice, and printer ports.

- **%**　　std Standard devices. These are: **mem** – acess to physical memory; **kmem** – access to kernel virtual memory; **null** – null device (infinite sink); **port** – access to I/O ports; **zero** – null byte source (infinite source); **core** – symlink to /proc/kcore (for kernel debugging); **full** – always returns ENOSPACE on write; **ram** – ramdisk; **tty** – to access the controlling tty of a process.

- **local**　　This simply runs **MAKEDEV.local**. This is a script that can create any local devices.

Virtual Terminals

- *console*　　This creates the devices associated with the console. This is the virtual terminals ttyx, where x can be from 0 though 63. The device tty0 is the currently active vt, and is also known as console. For each vt, there are two devices vcs*x* and vcsa*x*, which are used to generate screen-dumps of the vt (the **vcs***x* is just the text, and **vcsa***x* includes the attributes).

Serial Devices

ttyS{0..63} Serial ports and corresponding dialout device. For device **ttyS***x*, there is also the device **cua***x* which is used to dial out with. This can avoid the need for cooperative locks in simple situations.

cyclades Dial-in and dial-out devices for the cyclades intelligent I/O serial card. The dial in device is **ttyC***x* and the corresponding dial-out device is **cub***x* By default devices for 7 lines are created, but this can be changed to 15 by removing the comment.

Pseudo Terminals

pty[p-s] Each possible argument will create a bank of 16 master and slave pairs. The current kernel (1.2) is limited to 64 such pairs. The master pseudo-terminals are **pty[p-s][0-9a-f]**, and the slaves are **tty[p-s][0-9a-f]**.

Parallel Ports

lp Standard parallel ports. The devices are created **lp0**, **lp1**, and **lp2**. These correspond to ports at 0x3bc, 0x378 and 0x278. Hence, on some machines, the first printer port may actually be **lp1**.

par Alternative to *lp*. Ports are named **par***x* instead of **lp***x*.

Bus Mice

busmice The various bus mice devices. This creates the following devices: **logimouse** (Logitech bus mouse), **psmouse** (PS/2-style mouse), **msmouse** (Microsoft Inport bus mouse) and **atimouse** (ATI XL bus mouse) and **jmouse** (J-mouse).

Joystick Devices

js Joystick. Creates **js0** and **js1**.

Disk Devices

fd[0-7] Floppy disk devices. The device **fd***x* is the device which auto-detects the format, and the additional devices are fixed format (whose size is indicated in the name). The other devices are named as **fd***xLn*. The single letter *L* identifies the type of floppy disk (d = 5.25" DD, h = 5.25" HD, D = 3.5" DD, H = 3.5" HD, E = 3.5" ED). The number *n* represents the capacity of that format in K. Thus the standard formats are **fd***x***d360**, **fd***x***h1200**, **fd***x***D720**, **fd***x***H1440**, and fd*x*E2880.

For more information see Alain Knaff's fdutils package.

Devices **fd0*** through **fd3*** are floppy disks on the first controller, and devices **fd4*** through **fd7*** are floppy disks on the second controller.

hd[a-d] AT hard disks. The device **hd***x* provides access to the whole disk, with the partitions being **hd***x***[0-20]**. The four primary partitions are **hd***x***1** through **hd***x***4,** with the logical partitions being numbered from **hd***x***5** though **hd***x***20**. (A primary partition can be made into an extended partition, which can hold 4 logical partitions). By default, only the devices for 4 logical partitions are made. The others can be made by uncommenting them.

	Drives hda and hdb are the two on the first controller. If using the new IDE driver (rather than the old HD driver), then hdc and hdd are the two drives on the secondary controller. These devices can also be used to acess IDE CDROMs if using the new IDE driver.
xd[a-d]	XT hard disks. Partitions are the same as IDE disks.
sd[a-h]	SCSI hard disks. The partitions are similar to the IDE disks, but there is a limit of 11 logical partitions (sd$x$5 through sd$x$15). This is to allow there to be 8 SCSI disks.
loop	Loopback disk devices. These allow you to use a regular file as a block device. This means that images of filesystems can be mounted, and used as normal. This creates 8 devices loop0 through loop7.

Tape Devices

st[0-7]	SCSI tapes. This creates the rewinding tape device **st**x and the non-rewinding tape device **nst**x.
qic	QIC-80 tapes. The devices created are **rmt8**, **rmt16**, **tape-d**, and **tape-reset**.
ftape	Floppy driver tapes (QIC-117). There are 4 methods of access depending on the floppy tape drive. For each of access methods 0, 1, 2 and 3, the devices **rft**x (rewinding) and **nrft**x (non-rewinding) are created. For compatability, devices **ftape** and **nftape** are symlinks to **rft0** and **nrft0** respectively.

CDROM Devices

scd[0-7]	SCSI CD players.
sonycd	Sony CDU-31A CD player.
mcd	Mitsumi CD player.
cdu535	Sony CDU-535 CD player.
lmscd	LMS/Philips CD player.
sbpcd{,1,2,3}	Sound Blaster CD player. The kernel is capable of supporting 16 CDROMs, each of which is accessed as **sbpcd[0-9a-f]**. These are assigned in groups of 4 to each controller. **sbpcd** is a symlink to **sbpcd0**.

Scanner

logiscan	Logitech ScanMan32 & ScanMan 256.
m105scan	Mustek M105 Handscanner.
ac4096	A4Tek Color Handscanner.

Audio

audio	This creates the audio devices used by the sound driver. These include **mixer**, **sequencer**, **dsp**, and **audio**.
pcaudio	Devices for the PC Speaker sound driver. These are **pcmixer**, **pxsp**, and **pcaudio**.

Miscellaneous

sg	Generic SCSI devices. The devices created are **sg0** through **sg7**. These allow arbitary commands to be sent to any SCSI device. This allows for querying information about the device, or controlling SCSI devices that are not one of disk, tape or CDROM (e.g. scanner, writeable CDROM).
fd	To allow an arbitary program to be fed input from file descriptor x, use **/dev/fd/**x as the file name. This also creates BR /dev/stdin , BR /dev/stdout , and BR /dev/stderr . (Note, these are just symlinks into /proc/self/fd).

ibcs2	Devices (and symlinks) needed by the IBCS2 emulation.
apm	Devices for power management.
dcf	Driver for DCF-77 radio clock.
helloworld	Kernel modules demonstration device. See the modules source.
Network Devices	Linux used to have devices in /dev for controlling network devices, but that is no longer the case. To see what network devices are known by the kernel, look at /proc/net/dev.

SEE ALSO
Linux Allocated Devices, maintained by H. Peter Anvin, <Peter.Anvin@linux.org>.

AUTHOR
Nick Holloway

MKE2FS(8)   MKE2FS(8)

NAME

mke2fs – create a Linux second extended file system

SYNOPSIS

mke2fs [**–c** | **–l** filename] [**–b** block-size] [**–f** fragment-size] [**–i** bytes-per-inode] [**–m** reserved-blocks-percentage] [**–q**] [**–v**] [**–S**] device [blocks-count]

DESCRIPTION

mke2fs is used to create a Linux second extended file system on a device (usually a disk partition).
device is the special file corresponding to the device (e.g /dev/hdXX).
blocks-count is the number of blocks on the device. If omitted, **mke2fs** automagically figures the file system size.

OPTIONS

	-b block-size	Specify the size of blocks in bytes.
	-c	Check the device for bad blocks before creating the file system, using a fast read-only test.
	-f fragment-size	Specify the size of fragments in bytes.
	-i bytes-per-inode	Specify the bytes/inode ratio. **mke2fs** creates an inode for every *bytes-per-inode* bytes of space on the disk. This value defaults to 4096 bytes. *bytes-per-inode* must be at least 1024.
	-l filename	Read the bad blocks list from *filename*
	-m reserved-blocks-percentage	Specify the percentage of reserved blocks for the super-user. This value defaults to 5%.
	-q	Quiet execution. Useful if mke2fs is run in a script.
	-v	Verbose execution.
	-S	Write superblock and group descriptors only. This is useful if all of the superblock and backup superblocks are corrupted, and a last-ditch recovery method is desired. It causes mke2fs to reinitialize the superblock and group descriptors, while not touching the inode table and the block and inode bitmaps. The **e2fsck** program should be run immediately after this option is used, and there is no gaurantee that any data will be salvageable.

AUTHOR

This version of **mke2fs** has been written by Theodore T'so <tytso@mit.edu>.

BUGS

mke2fs accepts the -f option but currently ignores it because the second extended file system does not support fragments yet.
There may be some other ones. Please, report them to the author.

AVAILABILITY

mke2fs is available for anonymous ftp from ftp.ibp.fr and tsx-11.mit.edu in /pub/linux/packages/ext2fs.

SEE ALSO

badblocks(8), **dumpe2fs**(8), **e2fsck**(8), **tune2fs**(8)

MKFS(8)

NAME

mkfs – build a Linux file system

SYNOPSIS

mkfs [**–V**] [**–t** *fstype*] [**fs-options**] *filesys* [*blocks*]

DESCRIPTION

mkfs is used to build a Linux file system on a device, usually a hard disk partition. *filesys* is either the device name (e.g. /dev/hda1, /dev/sdb2) or the mount point (e.g. /, /usr, /home) for the file system. *blocks* is the number of blocks to be used for the file system.

The exit code returned by **mkfs** is 0 on success and 1 on failure.

In actuality, **mkfs** is simply a front-end for the various file system builders (**mkfs**.*fstype*) available under Linux. The file system-specific builder is searched for in /etc/fs first, then in /etc and finally in the directories listed in the PATH enviroment variable. Please see the file system-specific builder manual pages for further details.

OPTIONS

-V   Produce verbose output, including all file system-specific commands that are executed. Specifying this option more than once inhibits execution of any file system-specific commands. This is really only useful for testing.

-t*fstype* Specifies the type of file system to be built. If not specified, the type is deduced by searching for *filesys* in */etc/fstab* and using the corresponding entry. If the type can not be deduced, the default file system type (currently minix) is used.

fs-options File system-specific options to be passed to the real file system builder. Although not guaranteed, the following options are supported by most file system builders.

-c   Check the device for bad blocks before building the file system.

-l*filename* Read the bad blocks list from *filename*

-v   Produce verbose output.

BUGS

All generic options must precede and not be combined with file system-specific options. Some file system-specific programs do not support the *-v* (verbose) option, nor return meaningful exit codes. Also, some file system-specific programs do not automatically detect the device size and require the *blocks* parameter to be specified.

AUTHORS

David Engel (david@ods.com)
Fred N. van Kempen (waltje@uwalt.nl.mugnet.org)
Ron Sommeling (sommel@sci.kun.nl)
The manual page was shamelessly adapted from Remy Card's version for the ext2 file system.

SEE ALSO

fsck(8), mkfs.minix(8), mkfs.ext(8), mkfs.ext2(8), mkfs.xiafs(8).

NAME

mkfs – make a Linux MINIX filesystem

SYNOPSIS

mkfs [**−c**] [**−n** namelength] [**−i** inodecount] device size-in-blocks
mkfs [**−l** filename] device size-in-blocks

DESCRIPTION

mkfs creates a Linux MINIX file-system on a device (usually a disk partition).

The *device* is usually of the following form:

/dev/hda[1-8]
/dev/hdb[1-8]
/dev/sda[1-8]
/dev/sdb[1-8]

The *size-in-blocks* parameter is the desired size of the file system, in blocks. This information can be determined from the **fdisk**(8) program. Only block counts strictly greater than 10 and strictly less than 65536 are allowed.

OPTIONS

−c   Check the device for bad blocks before creating the file system. If any are found, the count is printed.

−n *namelength*   Specify the maximum length of filenames. No space is allowed between the **−n** and the *namelength*. Currently, *the* only *allowable* values are 14 and 30. **30** is the default.

−i *inodecount*   Specify the number of inodes for the filesystem.

−l *filename*   Read the bad blocks list from *filename*. The file has one bad block number per line. The count of bad blocks read is printed.

EXIT CODES

The exit code returned by **mkfs.minix** is one of the following:

- 0   No errors
- 8   Operational error
- 16   Usage or syntax error

SEE ALSO

fsck(8), **mkefs**(8), **efsck**(8), **reboot**(8)

AUTHOR

Linus Torvalds (torvalds@cs.helsinki.fi)
Error code values by Rik Faith (faith@cs.unc.edu)
Inode request feature by Scott Heavner (sdh@po.cwru.edu)
Support for the file system valid flag by Dr. Wettstein (greg%wind.uucp@plains.nodak.edu)

Check to prevent mkfs of mounted filesystem and boot sector clearing by Daniel Quinlan (quinlan@yggdrasil.com)

MKLOST+FOUND(8)   MKLOST+FOUND(8)

NAME

mklost+found – create a lost+found directory on a mounted Linux second extended file system

SYNOPSIS

mklost+found

DESCRIPTION

mklost+found is used to create a lost+found directory in the current working directory on a Linux second extended file system.
mklost+found pre-allocates disk blocks to the directory to make it usable by **e2fsck**

OPTIONS

There are none.

AUTHOR

mklost+found has been written by Remy Card <card@masi.ibp.fr>, the developer and maintainer of the ext2 fs.

BUGS

There are none :-)

AVAILABILITY

mklost+found is available for anonymous ftp from ftp.ibp.fr and tsx-11.mit.edu in /pub/linux/packages/ext2fs.

SEE ALSO

e2fsck(8), mke2fs(8)

Version 0.5b   November 1994   1100

MKSWAP(8)

NAME

mkswap – set up a Linux swap area

SYNOPSIS

mkswap [**–c**] *device* [*size-in-blocks*]

DESCRIPTION

mkswap sets up a Linux swap area on a device or in a file.

The *device* is usually of the following form:

/dev/hda[1-8]
/dev/hdb[1-8]
/dev/sda[1-8]
/dev/sdb[1-8]

The *size-in-blocks* parameter is the desired size of the file system, in blocks. This information is determined automatically by **mkswap** if it is omitted. Block counts are rounded down so that the total size is an integer multiple of the machine's page size. Only block counts in the range MINCOUNT..MAXCOUNT are allowed. If the block count exceeds the MAXCOUNT, it is truncated to that value and a warning message is issued.

The MINCOUNT and MAXCOUNT values for a swap area are:

MINCOUNT = 10 * PAGE_SIZE / 1024
MAXCOUNT = (PAGE_SIZE - 10) * 8 * PAGE_SIZE / 1024

For example, on a machine with 4kB pages (e.g., x86), we get:

MINCOUNT = 10 * 4096 / 1024 = 40
MAXCOUNT = (4096 - 10) * 8 * 4096 / 1024 = 130752

As each block is 1kB large, the swap area in this example could have a size that is anywhere in the range from 40kB up to 127.6875MB.

If you don't know the page size that your machine uses, you may be able to look it up with "cat /proc/cpuinfo".

The reason for the limit on MAXCOUNT is that a single page is used to hold the swap bitmap at the start of the swap area, where each bit represents a single page. The reason for the -10, is that the signature is "SWAP-SPACE" – 10 characters.

To setup a swap file, it is necessary to create that file before running **mkswap** . A sequence of commands similar to the following is reasonable for this purpose:

dd if=/dev/zero of=swapfile bs=1024 count=8192
mkswap swapfile 8192
sync
swapon swapfile

Note that a swap file must not contain any holes (so, using **cp**(1) to create the file is not acceptable).

OPTIONS

–c Check the device for bad blocks before creating the file system. If any are found, the count is printed. This option is meant to be used for swap partitions **only**, and should **not** be used for regular files! To make sure that regular files do not contain bad blocks, the partition that contains the regular file should have been created with **mkfs -c**.

SEE ALSO

fsck(8), **mkfs**(8), **fdisk**(8)

AUTHOR
Linus Torvalds (torvalds@cs.helsinki.fi)

MOUNT(8)

NAME

mount, umount – mount and dismount file systems

SYNOPSIS

mount [–afrwuvn] [–t *vfstype*]
mount [–frwuvn] [–o *remount* [,...]] *special* | *node*
mount [–frwun] [–t *vfstype*] [–o *options*] *special node*
umount [–an] [–t *vfstype*]
umount *special* | *node*

DESCRIPTION

The **mount** command calls the **mount**(2) system call to prepare and graft a *special* device on to the file system tree at the point *node*. If either *special* or *node* are not provided, the appropriate information is taken from the **fstab**(5) file. The special keyword *none* can be used instead of a path or *node* specification. This is useful when mounting the *proc* file system.

The system maintains a list of currently mounted file systems. If no arguments are given to **mount**, this list is printed.

Options available for the **mount** command:

- **–f** Causes everything to be done except for the actual system call; if it's not obvious, this "fakes" mounting the file system. This option is useful in conjunction with the –v flag to determine what the **mount** command is trying to do.

- **–o** Options are specified with a –o flag followed by a comma separated string of options. **N.B.,** many of these options are only useful when they appear in the */etc/fstab* file. The following options apply to any file system that is being mounted:

  async All I/O to the file system should be done asynchronously.

  auto Can be mounted with the –a option.

  defaults Use default options: **rw**, **suid**, **dev**, **exec**, **auto**, **nouser**, and **async**.

  dev Interpret character or block special devices on the file system.

  exec Permit execution of binaries.

  noauto Can only be mounted explicitly (i.e., the –a option will not cause the file system to be mounted).

  nodev Do not interpret character or block special devices on the file system. This options is useful for a server that has file systems containing special devices for architectures other than its own.

  noexec Do not allow execution of any binaries on the mounted file system. This options is useful for a server that has file systems containing binaries for architectures other than its own.

  nosuid Do not allow set-user-identifier or set-group-identifier bits to take effect.

  nouser Forbid an ordinary (i.e., non-root) user to mount the file system.

  remount Attempt to remount an already-mounted file system. This is commonly used to change the mount flags for a file system, especially to make a readonly file system writeable.

  ro Mount the file system read-only.

  rw Mount the file system read-write.

  suid Allow set-user-identifier or set-group-identifier bits to take effect.

  sync All I/O to the file system should be done synchronously.

  user Allow an ordinary user to mount the file system. Ordinary users always have the following options activated: **noexec**, **nosuid**, and **nodev** (unless overridden by the superuser by using, for example, the following option line: **user,exec,dev,suid**.

The following options apply only to certain file systems:

case=*value*
: For the *hpfs* file system, specify case as *lower* or *asis*.

check=*value*
: Tells the *ext2* file sysem kernel code to do some more checks while the file system is mounted. Currently (0.99.15), the following values can be specified with this option:

none
: no extra check is performed by the kernel code

normal
: The inodes and blocks bitmaps are checked when the file system is mounted (this is the default)

strict
: In addition to the *normal* checks, block deallocation checks that the block to free is in the data zone.

check=*value*
: For the *msdos* file system, three different levels of pickyness can be chosen:

relaxed
: Upper and lower case are accepted and equivalent, long name parts are truncated (e.g. verlongname.foobar becomes verylong.foo), leading and embedded spaces are accepted in each name part (name and extension).

normal
: Like "relaxed", but many special characters (*, ?, <, spaces, etc.) are rejected. This is the default.

strict
: Like "normal", but names may not contain long parts and special characters that are sometimes used on Linux, but are not accepted by MS-DOS are rejected. (+, =, spaces, etc.)

conv=*value*
: For the *msdos*, *hpfs*, and *iso9660* file systems, specify file conversion as *binary*, *text*, or *auto*. The *iso9660* file system also allows *value* to be *mtext*.

    The *msdos* file system can perform CRLF<–>NL (MS-DOS text format to UNIX text format) conversion in the kernel. The following conversion modes are available:

binary
: no translation is performed. This is the default.

text
: CRLF<–>NL translation is performed on all files.

auto
: CRLF<–>NL translation is performed on all files that don't have a "well-known binary" extension. The list of known extensions can be found at the beginning of *fs/msdos/misc.c* (as of 09913r, the list is: exe, com, bin, app, sys, drv, ovl, ovr, obj, lib, dll, pif, arc, zip, lha, lzh, zoo, tar, z, arj, tz, taz, tpz, gif, bmp, tif, gl, jpg, pcx, tfm, vf, gf, pk, pxl, dvi).

Programs that do computed lseeks won't like in-kernel text conversion.

For file systems mounted in **binary** mode, a conversion tool (fromdos/todos) is available.

block=*value*
: For the *iso9660* file system, set the blocksize.

bsdgroups
: See **grpid**

cruft
: For the *iso9660* file system, set the *cruft* flag to 'y'. This option is available because there are buggy premastering programs out there that leave junk in the top byte of the file size. This option clears the top byte, but restricts files to 16Mb maximum in the process.

debug
: For the *msdos* file system, turn on the *debug* flag. A version string and a list of file system parameters will be printed (these data are also printed if the parameters appear to be inconsistent).

debug
: For the *ext2fs* file system, causes the kernel code to display the file system parameters when the file system is mounted.

errors=*value*	For the *ext2fs* file system, specifies the error behavior:
continue	No special action is taken on errors (except marking the file system as erroneous). This is the default.
remount	
ro	The file system is remounted read only, and subsequent writes are refused.
panic	When an error is detected, the system panics.
fat=*value*	For the *msdos* file system, specify either a 12 bit fat or a 16 bit fat. This overrides the automatic FAT type detection routine. Use with caution!
gid=*value*	For the *msdos* and *hpfs* file systems, give every file a gid equal to *value*.
B grpid	Causes the *ext2fs* to use the BSD behavior when creating files: file are created with the group id of their parent directory.
map=*value*	For the *iso9660* file system, specify mapping as *off* or *normal*. In general, non-Rock Ridge discs have all of the filenames in upper case, and all of the filenames have a ";1" appended. The map option strips the ";1" and makes the name lower case. C.f. **norock**.
nocheck	For the *ext2fs*, turns of checking (see **check=none**).
nogrpid	Causes the *ext2fs* to use the System V behaviour when creating files: files are created with the group id of the creating process, unless the setgid bit is set on the parent directory. This is the default for all Linux file systems.
norock	Normal *iso9600* filenames appear in a 8.3 format (i.e., DOS-like restrictions on filename length), and in addition all characters are in upper case. Also there is no field for file ownership, protection, number of links, provision for block/character devices, etc.
	Rock Ridge is an extension to iso9660 that provides all of these unix like features. Basically there are extensions to each directory record that supply all of the additional information, and when Rock Ridge is in use, the filesystem is indistinguishable from a normal UNIX file system (except that it is read-only, of course).
	The **norock** switch disables the use of Rock Ridge extensions, even if available. C.f. **map**.
quiet	For the *msdos* file system, turn on the *quiet* flag. Attempts to chown or chmod files do not yield errors, although they fail. Use with caution!
sb=*value*	For the *ext2* file system, use an alternate superblock located at block *value*. *value* is numbered in 1024 bytes blocks. An *ext2* file system usually has backups of the super block at blocks 1, 8193, 16385 and so on.
sysvgroups	See **nogrpid**
uid=*value*	For the *msdos* and *hpfs* file systems, give every file a uid equal to *value*.
umask=*value*	For the *msdos* and *hpfs* file systems, give every file a umask of *value*. The radix defaults to octal.

The full set of options applied is determined by first extracting the options for the file system from the **fstab** table, then applying any options specified by the **–o** argument, and finally applying the **–r** or **–w** option.

If the *msdos* file system detects an inconsistency, it reports an error and sets the file system read-only. The file system can be made writeable again by remounting it.

-r   The file system object is to be mounted read-only.

-t *vfstype*   The argument following the **-t** is used to indicate the file system type. The file system types which are currently supported are listed in *linux/fs/filesystems.c*: *minux, ext, ext2, xiafs, msdos, hpfs, proc, nfs, iso9660, sysv, xenix, coherent*. Note that that last three are equivalent and that "xenix" and "coherent" will be removed at some point in the future — use "sysv" instead.

The type *minix* is the default. If no **-t** option is given, or if the "auto" type is specified, the superblock is probed for the filesystem type (minix, ext, ext2, xia are supported). If this probe fails and */proc/filesystems* exists, then all of the filesystems listed will be tried, *except* for those that are labeled "nodev" (e.g., "proc" and "nfs").

Note that the "auto" type may be useful for user-mounted floppies.

For example, the **mount** command:

mount -a -t nomsdos,ext

mounts all file systems except those of type *msdos* and *ext*.

-v   Verbose mode.

-w   The file system object is to be read and write.

-n   Mount without writing in */etc/mtab*.

Umount removes the *special* device grafted at point *node* from file system tree.

Options for the **umount** command:

-a   All of the file systems described in */etc/mtab* are unmounted.

-t *vfstype*   Is used to indicate the actions should only be taken on file systems of the specified type. More than one type may be specified in a comma separated list. The list of file system types can be prefixed with "no" to specify the file system types on which no action should be taken. (See example above for the **mount** command.)

FILES

/etc/fstab file system table
/etc/mtab˜ lock file
/etc/mtab.tmp temporary file

SEE ALSO

mount(2), **umount**(2), **fstab**(5), **swapon**(8)

BUGS

It is possible for a corrupted file system to cause a crash.

Some Linux file systems don't support **-o** *synchronous* (the ext2fs *does* support synchronous updates (a la BSD) when mounted with the **sync** option).

The **-o** *remount* may not be able to change mount parameters (all *ext2fs* parameters, except **sb**, are changeable with a remount, for example, but you can't change **gid** or **umask** for the *dosfs*).

HISTORY

A **mount** command appeared in Version 6 AT&T UNIX.

AUTHORS AND CONTRIBUTORS

The Linux **mount** command has a long and continuing history. Major releases are noted below, with the name of the primary modifier noted:

0.97.3: Doug Quale (quale@saavik.cs.wisc.edu).
0.98.5: H. J. Lu (hlu@eecs.wsu.edu).
0.99.2: Rick Sladkey (jrs@world.std.com).

MOUNT(8)　　　　　　　Linux Programmer's Manual　　　　　　　MOUNT(8)

0.99.6: Rick Sladkey (jrs@world.std.com).
0.99.10: Stephen Tweedie (sct@dcs.ed.ac.uk).
0.99.14: Rick Sladkey (jrs@world.std.com).

(File-system specific information added to man page on 27 November 1993 by Rik Faith with lots of information *and* text from the following file system authors: Werner Almesberger, Eric Youngdale, and Remy Card.)

MOUNTD(8)

NAME

mountd – NFS mount daemon

SYNOPSIS

/usr/etc/rpc.mountd [\ –f\ exports–file\ ] [\ –dhnprv\ ] [\ —debug\ ] [\ —exports–file=file\ ]
[\ —help\ ] [\ —-allow–non–root\ ] [\ —re–export\ ] [\ —version\ ]

DESCRIPTION

The *mountd* program is an NFS mount daemon.

OPTIONS

–f or **—exports–file** This option specifies the exports file, listing the clients that this server is prepared to serve and parameters to apply to each such mount (see exports(5)). By default exports are read from */etc/exports*.

–d or **—debug** Log each transaction verbosely to the syslog.

–h or **—help** Provide a short help summary.

–n or **—allow–non–root** Allow incoming mount requests to be honored even if they do not originate from reserved IP ports. Some older NFS client implementations require this. Some newer NFS client implementations don't believe in reserved port checking.

–p or **—promiscuous** Put the server into promiscuous mode where it will serve any host on the network.

–r or **—re–export** Allow imported NFS file-systems to be exported. This can be used to turn a machine into an NFS multiplier. Caution should be used when re-exporting loopback NFS mounts because re-entering the mount point will result in deadlock between the NFS client and the NFS server.

–v or **—version** Report the current version number of the program.

SEE ALSO

exports(5), nfsd(8), ugidd(8C)

BUGS

The current implementation (still) does not keep track of remote mounts.

NAME

netstat – Display active network connections

SYNOPSIS

netstat [[-a | [-t | -u | -w]] [-n | -o] | -x | -c]

netstat -r [-c] [-n]

netstat -v

DESCRIPTION

netstat displays the status of network connections on either TCP, UDP or RAW sockets to the system. By default, **netstat** only displays status on those TCP sockets which are not in the LISTEN state (i.e. connections to active processes). To obtain information about the kernel routing table, **netstat** may be invoked with the option **-r**. A listing of internal UNIX connetions can be obtained by invoking **netstat** with the option **-x**,

Netstat's display includes the following information for each socket:

Proto

The protocol (either TCP or UDP) used by the socket.

Recv-Q

The count of bytes not copied by the user program connected to this socket.

Send-Q

The count of bytes not acknoledged by the remote host.

Local Address

The local address (local hostname) and port number of the socket. Unless the **-n** switch is given, the socket address is resolved to its canonical hostname, and the port number is translated into the corresponding service name.

Foreign Address

The remote address (remote hostname) and port number of he socket. As with the local address:port, the **-n** switch turns off hostname and service name resolution.

(State)

The state of the socket. Since there are no states in RAW and usually no states used in UDP, this row may be left blank. Normally this can be one of several values:

ESTABLISHED	The socket has an established connection.
SYN_SENT	The socket is actively attempting to establish a connection.
SYN_RECV	The connection is being initialized.
FIN_WAIT1	The socket is closed, and the connection is shutting down.
FIN_WAIT2	Connection is closed, and the socket is waiting for a shutdown from the remote end.
TIME_WAIT	The socket is waiting after close for remote shutdown retransmission.
CLOSED	The socket is not being used.
CLOSE_WAIT	The remote end has shut down, waiting for the socket to close.
LAST_ACK	The remote end shut down, and the socket is closed. Waiting for acknowledgement.
LISTEN	The socket is listening for incoming connections.
UNKNOWN	The state of the socket is unknown.

NETSTAT(8)   Linux Programmer's Manual   NETSTAT(8)

If **netstat** is invoked with the option **-o**, additional information will be displayed afterte the state info. These informations are shown like this: keyword (time/backoff) and an optional asterisk. The keyword shows the state of the timer belonging to the socket, the time (in seconds) displayed is how long it will take the timer to expire, the backoff value indicates the current retry count for data transmission and the asterisk indicates that this timer is in the expiration queue. The latter might be removed in future but is helpful for debugging the TCP-Code for now.

Being invoked with the option **-x**, **netstat** displys a list of all active UNIX internal communication sockets.

Netstat's display includes the following information for each socket:

Proto
The protocol (usually unix) used by the socket.

RefCnt
The reference count (i.e. attached processes via this socket).

Flags
The only known Flag to me is SO_ACCEPTON (displayed as ACC) otherwise left blank. SO_ACCECPTON is used on unconnected sockets if their corresponding processes are waiting for a connect request.

Type
There are several types of socket access:

SOCK_DGRAM	The socket is used in Datagram (connectionless) mode.
SOCK_STREAM	This is a stream (connection) socket.
SOCK_RAW	The socket is used as a raw socket.
SOCK_RDM	This one serves reliably-delivered messages.
SOCK_SEQPACKET	This is a sequential packet socket.
SOCK_PACKET	This socket type is used as a linux specific way to get packets at the dev- (kernel)-level. It is assumed to be used to write things like RARP (Reverse Address Resolution Protocol) and similar things on the user level.
UNKNOWN	Who ever knows, what future will bering up - just fill in here :-)

State
This field will contain one of the following Keywords:

FREE	The socket is not allocated
LISTENING	The socket is listening for a connection request.
UNCONNECTED	The socket is not connected to another one.
CONNECTING	The socket is about to establish a connection.
CONNECTED	The socket is connected.
DISCONNECTING	The socket is disconnecting.
UNKNOWN	This state should never happen.

Path
This displays the path name as which the corresponding processes attached to the socket.

The network routing table (invoked with **netstat -r**) shows up the following information:

NETSTAT(8) Linux Programmer's Manual NETSTAT(8)

Destination net/address

The destination adress of a resolved host or hand-entered network is displayed. Unless the option **-n** is given, the hosts or nets are resolved. An entry named "default" shows up the default route for the kernel.

Gateway address

If there is no Asterisk ('*') displayed - any data will be routed to the dedicated gateway.

Flags

Possible routeing flags are:

- U   This route is useable
- G   Destiantion is a gateway
- H   Destiantion is a Host entry
- N   Destiantion is a Net entry
- R   Route will be reinstated after time-out
- D   This one is created dynamically (by redirection)
- M   This one is modified dynamically (by redirection)

RefCnt

Reference count for this route

Use

How many times this route was used yet

Iface

This is the name of the Interface, where this route belongs to

Options

- **-a**   Display information about all internet sockets, i.e. TCP, UDP and RAW, including those sockets that are listening only.
- **-c**   Generate a continuous listing of network status: network status is displayed every second until the program is interrupted.
- **-n**   Causes netstat not to resolve hostnames and service names when displaying remote and local address and port information.
- **-o**   Display timer states, expiration times and backoff state.
- **-r**   Display kernel routing table.
- **-t**   Display information about TCP sockets only, including those that are listening.
- **-u**   Display information about UDP sockets only.
- **-v**   Print version information.
- **-w**   Display information about raw sockets.
- **-x**   Display information about UNIX domain sockets.

FILES

/proc/net/tcp – TCP socket information

/proc/net/udp – UDP socket information

/proc/net/raw – RAW socket information

/proc/net/unix – Unix domain socket information

/proc/net/route – Kernel routing information

/etc/services – The services translation

NETSTAT(8)   Linux Programmer's Manual   NETSTAT(8)

BUGS
None reported yet (05/20/1993).

AUTHORS
The netstat user interface was written by Fred Baumgarten <dc6iq@insu1.etec.uni-karlsruhe.de>
the man page basically by Matt Welsh <mdw@tc.cornell.edu>.

NFSD(8) NFSD(8)

NAME

nfsd – NFS service daemon

SYNOPSIS

/usr/etc/rpc.nfsd [\-f\exports-file\] [\-dhnprv\] [\—debug\] [\—exports–file=file\] [\—help\] [\—allow–non–root\] [\—re–export\] [\—version\]

DESCRIPTION

The *nfsd* program is an NFS service daemon that handles client filesystem requests. Unlike *nfsd* on some other systems, *nfsd* operates as a normal user-level process. The server also differs from other NFS server implementations in that it mounts an entire file hierarchy not limited by the boundaries of physical file-systems. The implementation allows the clients read-only or read-write access to the file hierarchy of the server machine.

The *mountd* program starts an ancillary user-level mount daemon.

OPTIONS

–f or —**exports–file**   This option specifies the exports file, listing the clients that this server is prepared to serve and parameters to apply to each such mount (see exports(5)). By default exports are read from */etc/exports*.

–d or —**debug**   Log each transaction verbosely to the syslog.

–h or —**help**   Provide a short help summary.

–n or —**allow–non–root**   Allow incoming NFS requests to be honored even if they do not originate from reserved IP ports. Some older NFS client implementations require this. Some newer NFS client implementations don't believe in reserved port checking.

–p or —**promiscuous**   Put the server into promiscuous mode where it will serve any host on the network.

–r or —**re–export**   Allow imported NFS file-systems to be exported. This can be used to turn a machine into an NFS multiplier. Caution should be used when re-exporting loopback NFS mounts because re-entering the mount point will result in deadlock between the NFS client and the NFS server.

–v or —**version**   Report the current version number of the program.

SEE ALSO

exports(5), mountd(8), ugidd(8C)

AUTHORS

Mark Shand wrote the orignal unfsd. Don Becker extended unfsd to support authentication and allow read-write access and called it hnfs. Rick Sladkey added host matching, showmount -e support, mountd authentication, inetd support, and all of the portability and configuration code.

NAME

pac – printer/plotter accounting information

SYNOPSIS

pac [-P printer] [-c] [-m] [-p price] [-s] [-r] [name ...]

DESCRIPTION

Pac reads the printer/plotter accounting files, accumulating the number of pages (the usual case) or feet (for raster devices) of paper consumed by each user, and printing out how much each user consumed in pages or feet and dollars.

Options and operands available:

- -P printer
  Accounting is done for the named printer. Normally, accounting is done for the default printer (site dependent) or the value of the environment variable PRINTER is used.

- -c
  flag causes the output to be sorted by cost; usually the output is sorted alphabetically by name.

- -m
  flag causes the host name to be ignored in the accounting file. This allows for a user on multiple machines to have all of his printing charges grouped together.

- -p price
  The value price is used for the cost in dollars instead of the default value of 0.02 or the price specified in /etc/printcap .

- -r
  Reverse the sorting order.

- -s
  Accounting information is summarized on the summary accounting file; this summarization is necessary since on a busy system, the accounting file can grow by several lines per day.

- names
  Statistics are only printed for user(s) name; usually, statistics are printed for every user who has used any paper.

FILES

- /var/account/?acct raw accounting files
- /var/account/?_sum summary accounting files
- /etc/printcap printer capability data base

SEE ALSO

printcap(5)

BUGS

The relationship between the computed price and reality is as yet unknown.

HISTORY

The pac command appeared in BSD 4.0 .

PLIPCONFIG(8)

NAME

plipconfig – fine tune PLIP device parameters

SYNOPSIS

plipconfig interface
plipconfig interface [nibble NN] [trigger NN] [unit NN]

DESCRIPTION

Plipconfig is used to (hopefuly) improve PLIP performance by changing the default timing parameters used by the PLIP protocol. Results are dependent on the parallel port hardware, cable, and the CPU speed of each machine on each end of the PLIP link.

If the single **interface** argument is given, **plipconfig** displays the status of the given interface only. Otherwise, it will try to set the options.

OPTIONS

> **nibble NN**   Sets the nibble wait value in microseconds. Default is 3000.
> **trigger NN** Sets the trigger wait value in microseconds. Default is 500.
> **unit NN**   Sets the number of units of delay. Default is 1.

PLIP speed can in some cases be improved by lowering the default values. Values which are too low may cause excess use of CPU, poor interrupt response time resulting in serial ports dropping characters, or in dropping of PLIP packets. Changing the plip MTU can also affect PLIP speed.

SEE ALSO

ifconfig(8)

BUGS

None so far.

AUTHOR

John Paul Morrison, <jmorriso@bogomips.ee.ubc.ca>, <ve7jpm@ve7jpm.ampr.org>

NAME

ping – send ICMP ECHO_REQUEST packets to network hosts

SYNOPSIS

/etc/ping [**–r**] [**–v**] *host* [*packetsize*] [*count*]

DESCRIPTION

The DARPA Internet is a large and complex aggregation of network hardware, connected together by gateways. Tracking a single-point hardware or software failure can often be difficult. *Ping* utilizes the ICMP protocol's mandatory ECHO_REQUEST datagram to elicit an ICMP ECHO_RESPONSE from a host or gateway.
ECHO_REQUEST datagrams ("pings") have an IP and ICMP header, followed by a **struct timeval**, and then an arbitrary number of "pad" bytes used to fill out the packet. Default datagram length is 64 bytes, but this may be changed using the command-line option. Other options are:

    –r   Bypass the normal routing tables and send directly to a host on an attached network. If the host is not on a directly-attached network, an error is returned. This option can be used to ping a local host through an interface that has no route through it (e.g., after the interface was dropped by *routed*(8C)).

    –v   Verbose output. ICMP packets other than ECHO RESPONSE that are received are listed.

When using *ping* for fault isolation, it should first be run on the local host, to verify that the local network interface is up and running. Then, hosts and gateways further and further away should be "pinged". *Ping* sends one datagram per second, and prints one line of output for every ECHO_RESPONSE returned. No output is produced if there is no response. If an optional *count* is given, only that number of requests is sent. Round-trip times and packet loss statistics are computed. When all responses have been received or the program times out (with a *count* specified), or if the program is terminated with a SIGINT, a brief summary is displayed.

This program is intended for use in network testing, measurement and management. It should be used primarily for manual fault isolation. Because of the load it could impose on the network, it is unwise to use *ping* during normal operations or from automated scripts.

AUTHOR

Mike Muuss

SEE ALSO

netstat(1), ifconfig(8)

PORTMAP(8)   PORTMAP(8)

NAME

portmap – DARPA port to RPC program number mapper

SYNOPSIS

portmap [-d]

DESCRIPTION

Portmap is a server that converts RPC program numbers into DARPA protocol port numbers. It must be running in order to make RPC calls.

When an RPC server is started, it will tell portmap what port number it is listening to, and what RPC program numbers it is prepared to serve. When a client wishes to make an RPC call to a given program number, it will first contact portmap on the server machine to determine the port number where RPC packets should be sent.

Portmap must be started before any RPC servers are invoked.

Normally portmap forks and dissociates itself from the terminal like any other daemon. Portmap then logs errors using syslog 3 .

Option available:

> -d (debug) prevents portmap from running as a daemon, and causes errors and debugging information to be printed to the standard error output.

SEE ALSO

inetd.conf 5 , rpcinfo 8 , inetd 8

BUGS

If portmap crashes, all servers must be restarted.

HISTORY

The portmap command appeared in BSD 4.3

POWERD(8)

NAME

powerd – monitor a serial line connected to an UPS.

SYNOPSIS

/etc/powerd serial-device

DESCRIPTION

Powerd is a daemon process that sits in the background and monitors the state of the DCD line of the serial device. It is meant that this line is connected to an UPS (Uninterruptible Power Supply) so that it knows about the state of the UPS. As soon as **powerd** senses that the power is failing (it sees that DCD goes low) it notifies **init**(8) and init will execute the **powerwait** and **powerfail** entries. If powerd senses that the power has been restored, it notifies **init** again and init will execute the **powerokwait** entries.

ARGUMENTS

    serial-device   Some serial port that is not being used by some other device, and does not share an interrupt with any other serial port.

DIAGNOSTICS

Powerd regulary checks the **DSR** line to see if it's high. **DSR** should be directly connected to **DTR** and **powerd** keeps that line high, so if **DSR** is low then something is wrong with the connection. **Powerd** will notify you about this fact every two minutes. When it sees that the connection has been restored it will say so.

HOWTO

It's pretty simple to connect your UPS to the Linux machine. The steps are easy:

1. Make sure you have an UPS with a simple relais output: it should close its connections (make) if the power is gone, and it should open its connections (break) if the power is good.
2. Buy a serial plug. Connect the DTR line to the DSR line directly. Connect the DTR line and the DCD line with a **10 kilo ohm** resistor. Now connect the relais-output of the UPS to GROUND and the DCD line. If you don't know what pins DSR, DTR, DCD and GROUND are you can always ask at the store where you bought the plug.
3. You're all set.

BUGS

Well, not a real bug but powerd should be able to do a broadcast or something on the ethernet in case more Linux-boxes are connected to the same UPS and only one of them is connected to the UPS status line.

SEE ALSO

shutdown(8), init(8), inittab(5).

AUTHOR

Miquel van Smoorenburg, miquels@drinkel.nl.mugnet.org

RARP(8)   RARP(8)

NAME

rarp – manipulate the system RARP table

SYNOPSIS

rarp [-v] [-t type] -a [hostname]
rarp [-v] -d hostname ...
rarp [-v] [-t type] -s hostname hw_addr

DESCRIPTION

Rarp manipulates the kernel's RARP table in various ways. The primary options are clearing an address mapping entry and manually setting up one. For debugging purposes, the **arp** program also allows a complete dump of the RARP table.

OPTIONS

-v   Tell the user what is going on by being verbose.

-t type   When setting or reading the RARP table, this optional parameter tells **rarp** which class of entries it should check for. The default value of this parameter is **ether** (i.e. hardware code **0x01** for **IEEE 802.3 10Mbps Ethernet**. Other values might include network technologies such as **AX.25** (ax25).

-a [hostname]   Shows the entries of the specified hosts. If the **hostname** parameter is not used, **all** entries will be displayed.

-d hostname   Remove the entrie(s) of the specified host. This can be used if the indicated host is brought down, for example.

-s hostname hw_addr   Create an RARP address mapping entry for host **hostname** with hardware address set to **hw_addr** class, but for most classes one can assume that the usual presentation can be used. For the Ethernet class, this is 6 bytes in hexadecimal, separated by colons.

FILES

/proc/net/rarp,

AUTHORS

Ross D. Martin, <martin@trcsun3.eas.asu.edu>
Fred N. van Kempen, <waltje@uwalt.nl.mugnet.org>

NAME

rdev – query/set image root device, swap device, RAM disk size, or video mode

SYNOPSIS

rdev [**–rsvh**] [**–o** offset] [image [value [offset]]]
rdev [**–o** offset] [image [root_device [offset]]]
swapdev [**–o** offset] [image [swap_device [offset]]]
ramsize [**–o** offset] [image [size [offset]]]
vidmode [**–o** offset] [image [mode [offset]]]
rootflags [**–o** offset] [image [flags [offset]]]

DESCRIPTION

With no arguments, **rdev** outputs an */etc/mtab* line for the current root file system. With no arguments, **swapdev**, **ramsize**, **vidmode**, and **rootflags** print usage information.

In a bootable image for the Linux kernel, there are several pairs of bytes which specify the root device, the video mode, the size of the RAM disk, and the swap device. These pairs of bytes, by default, begin at offset 504 (decimal) in the kernel image:

498 Root flags
(500 and 502 Reserved)
504 RAM Disk Size
506 VGA Mode
508 Root Device
(510 Boot Signature)

rdev will change these values.

Typical values for the *image* parameter, which is a bootable Linux kernel image, are as follows:

/vmlinux
/vmlinux.test
/vmunix
/vmunix.test
/dev/fd0
/dev/fd1

When using the **rdev**, or **swapdev** commands, the *root_device* or *swap_device* parameter are as follows:

/dev/hda[1-8]
/dev/hdb[1-8]
/dev/sda[1-8]
/dev/sdb[1-8]

For the **ramsize** command, the **size** parameter specifies the size of the RAM disk in kilobytes.

For the **rootflags** command, the **flags** parameter contains extra information used when mounting root. Currently the only effect of these flags is to force the kernel to mount the root filesystem in readonly mode if **flags** is non-zero.

For the **vidmode** command, the **mode** parameter specifies the video mode:

-3 = Prompt
-2 = Extended VGA
-1 = Normal VGA
0 = as if "0" was pressed at the prompt
1 = as if "1" was pressed at the prompt
2 = as if "2" was pressed at the prompt
n = as if "n" was pressed at the prompt

If the *value* is not specified, the *image* will be examined to determine the current settings.

OPTIONS

- **-s**   Causes **rdev** to act like **swapdev**.
- **-r**   Causes **rdev** to act like **ramsize**.
- **-R**   Causes **rdev** to act like **rootflags**.
- **-v**   Causes **rdev** to act like **vidmode**.
- **-h**   Provides help.

BUGS

For historical reasons, there are two methods for specifying alternative values for the offset.

The user interface is cumbersome, non-intuitive, and should probably be re-written from scratch, allowing multiple kernel image parameters to be changed or examined with a single command.

If LILO is used, **rdev** is no longer needed for setting the root device and the VGA mode, since these parameters that **rdev** modifies can be set from the LILO prompt during a boot. However, **rdev** is still needed at this time for setting the RAM disk size. Users are encouraged to find the LILO documentation for more information, and to use LILO when booting their systems.

AUTHORS

Originally by Werner Almesberger (almesber@nessie.cs.id.ethz.ch)
Modified by Peter MacDonald (pmacdona@sanjuan.UVic.CA)
rootflags support added by Stephen Tweedie (sct@dcs.ed.ac.uk)

RENIC(8)

RENIC(8)

NAME

renice – alter priority of running processes

SYNOPSIS

renice priority [[-p] pid ...] [[-g] pgrp ...] [[-u] user ...]

DESCRIPTION

Renice alters the scheduling priority of one or more running processes. The following who parameters are interpreted as process ID's, process group ID's, or user names. Renice Ns 'ing a process group causes all processes in the process group to have their scheduling priority altered. Renice Ns 'ing a user causes all processes owned by the user to have their scheduling priority altered. By default, the processes to be affected are specified by their process ID's.

Options supported by renice :

- -g Force who parameters to be interpreted as process group ID's.
- -u Force the who parameters to be interpreted as user names.
- -p Resets the who interpretation to be (the default) process ID's.

For example,

   renice +1 987 -u daemon root -p 32

would change the priority of process ID's 987 and 32, and all processes owned by users daemon and root.

Users other than the super-user may only alter the priority of processes they own, and can only monotonically increase their "nice value" within the range 0 to PRIO_MAX (20). (This prevents overriding administrative fiats.) The super-user may alter the priority of any process and set the priority to any value in the range PRIO_MIN (–20) to PRIO_MAX . Useful priorities are: 20 (the affected processes will run only when nothing else in the system wants to), 0 (the "base" scheduling priority), anything negative (to make things go very fast).

FILES

- /etc/passwd to map user names to user ID's

SEE ALSO

getpriority(2), setpriority(2)

BUGS

Non super-users can not increase scheduling priorities of their own processes, even if they were the ones that decreased the priorities in the first place.

HISTORY

The renice command appeared in BSD 4.0 .

REXECD(8)

NAME

rexecd – remote execution server

SYNOPSIS

rexecd

DESCRIPTION

Rexecd is the server for the rexec 3 routine. The server provides remote execution facilities with authentication based on user names and passwords.

Rexecd listens for service requests at the port indicated in the "exec" service specification; see services 5 . When a service request is received the following protocol is initiated:

> The server reads characters from the socket up to a NUL \0 byte. The resultant string is interpreted as an ASCII number, base 10.
>
> If the number received in step 1 is non-zero, it is interpreted as the port number of a secondary stream to be used for the stderr . A second connection is then created to the specified port on the client's machine.
>
> A NUL terminated user name of at most 16 characters is retrieved on the initial socket.
>
> A NUL terminated, unencrypted password of at most 16 characters is retrieved on the initial socket.
>
> A NUL terminated command to be passed to a shell is retrieved on the initial socket. The length of the command is limited by the upper bound on the size of the system's argument list.
>
> Rexecd then validates the user as is done at login time and, if the authentication was successful, changes to the user's home directory, and establishes the user and group protections of the user. If any of these steps fail the connection is aborted with a diagnostic message returned.
>
> A NUL byte is returned on the initial socket and the command line is passed to the normal login shell of the user. The shell inherits the network connections established by rexecd .

DIAGNOSTICS

Except for the last one listed below, all diagnostic messages are returned on the initial socket, after which any network connections are closed. An error is indicated by a leading byte with a value of 1 (0 is returned in step 7 above upon successful completion of all the steps prior to the command execution).

> username too long The name is longer than 16 characters.
>
> password too long The password is longer than 16 characters.
>
> command too long The command line passed exceeds the size of the argument list (as configured into the system).
>
> Login incorrect. No password file entry for the user name existed or the wrong password was supplied.
>
> No remote directory. The chdir command to the home directory failed.
>
> Try again. A fork by the server failed.
>
> <shellname>: ... The user's login shell could not be started. This message is returned on the connection associated with the stderr , and is not preceded by a flag byte.

SEE ALSO

rexec 3

BUGS

A facility to allow all data and password exchanges to be encrypted should be present.

BSD 4.2   March 16, 1991

REXECD(8)   REXECD(8)

HISTORY

The rexecd command appeared in BSD 4.2 .

RLOGIND(8)

NAME

rlogind – remote login server

SYNOPSIS

rlogind [-aln]

DESCRIPTION

Rlogind is the server for the rlogin 1 program. The server provides a remote login facility with authentication based on privileged port numbers from trusted hosts.

Options supported by rlogind :

-a Ask hostname for verification.

-l Prevent any authentication based on the user's .rhosts file, unless the user is logging in as the superuser.

-n Disable keep-alive messages.

Rlogind listens for service requests at the port indicated in the "login" service specification; see services 5 . When a service request is received the following protocol is initiated:

The server checks the client's source port. If the port is not in the range 512-1023, the server aborts the connection.

The server checks the client's source address and requests the corresponding host name (see gethostbyaddr 3 , hosts 5 and named 8) . If the hostname cannot be determined, the dot-notation representation of the host address is used. If the hostname is in the same domain as the server (according to the last two components of the domain name), or if the -a option is given, the addresses for the hostname are requested, verifying that the name and address correspond. Normal authentication is bypassed if the address verification fails.

Once the source port and address have been checked, rlogind proceeds with the authentication process described in rshd 8 . It then allocates a pseudo terminal (see pty 4) , and manipulates file descriptors so that the slave half of the pseudo terminal becomes the stdin , stdout , and stderr for a login process. The login process is an instance of the login 1 program, invoked with the -f option if authentication has succeeded. If automatic authentication fails, the user is prompted to log in as if on a standard terminal line.

The parent of the login process manipulates the master side of the pseudo terminal, operating as an intermediary between the login process and the client instance of the rlogin program. In normal operation, the packet protocol described in pty 4 is invoked to provide $\hat{S}/\hat{Q}$ type facilities and propagate interrupt signals to the remote programs. The login process propagates the client terminal's baud rate and terminal type, as found in the environment variable, TERM ; see environ 7 . The screen or window size of the terminal is requested from the client, and window size changes from the client are propagated to the pseudo terminal.

Transport-level keepalive messages are enabled unless the -n option is present. The use of keepalive messages allows sessions to be timed out if the client crashes or becomes unreachable.

DIAGNOSTICS

All initial diagnostic messages are indicated by a leading byte with a value of 1, after which any network connections are closed. If there are no errors before login is invoked, a null byte is returned as in indication of success.

Try again. A fork by the server failed.

SEE ALSO

login 1 , ruserok 3 , rshd 8

BUGS

The authentication procedure used here assumes the integrity of each client machine and the connecting medium. This is insecure, but is useful in an "open" environment.

A facility to allow all data exchanges to be encrypted should be present.

A more extensible protocol should be used.

HISTORY

The rlogind command appeared in BSD 4.2 .

ROUTE(8)   ROUTE(8)

NAME

route – show / manipulate the IP routing table

SYNOPSIS

route [-vn]
route [-v] **add** [-net | -host] XXXX [gw GGGG] [metric MMMM] [netmask NNNN]
[mss NNNN] [window NNNN] [dev DDDD]
route [-v] **del** XXXX

DESCRIPTION

Route manipulates the kernel's IP routing table. Its primary use is to set up static routes to specific hosts or networks via an interface after it has been configured with the **ifconfig(8)** program. This version of **route** is intended solely for use with kernel versions 0.99pl14n and newer kernels.

OPTIONS

(none)	prints out the kernel routing table, listing destination address, gateway, netmask for route ("Genmask"), flags (U = Up, H = Host, G = Gateway, D = dynamic, M = Modified), Metric (currently not supported), Ref, Use and Iface (i.e. which device the route maps to).
-n	same as previous, but shows numerical addresses instead of trying to determine symbolic host names.
-v	is a flag for **verbose** (not actually used).
del XXXX	deletes the route associated with the destination address XXXX.
add	[-net	-host] XXXX [gw GGGG] [metric MMMM] [netmask NNNN] [dev DDDD] adds a route to the IP address XXXX. The route is a network route if (a) the **-net** modifier is used or (b) XXXX is found in **/etc/networks** by the **getnetbyname()** library function and no **-host** modifier is used.

The **gw** GGGG argument means that any IP packets sent to this address will be routed through the specified gateway. **NOTE:** The specified gateway must be reachable first. This usually means that you have to set up a static route to the gateway beforehand.

The **metric** MMMM modifier is not yet implemented (and with the **-v** option will actually print a warning).

The **netmask** NNNN modifier specifies the netmask of the route to be added. This only makes sense for a network route, and when the address XXXX actually makes sense with the specified netmask. If no netmask is given, **route** guesses it instead, so for most normal setups you won't need to specify a netmask.

The **mss** NNNN modifier specifies the TCP mss for the route to be added. This is normally used only for fine optimisation of routing setups.

The **window** NNNN modifier specifies the TCP window for the route to be added. This is typically only used on AX.25 networks and with drivers unable to handle back to back frames - such as the 3c501 or DE600.

The **dev** DDDD modifier forces the route to be associated with the specified device, as the kernel will otherwise try to determine the device on its own (by checking already existing routes and device specifications, and where the route is added to). In most normal networks you won't need this.

If **dev** DDDD is the last option on the command line, the word **dev** may be omitted, as it's the default. Otherwise the order of the route modifiers (metric - netmask - gw - dev) doesn't matter.

EXAMPLES

route add -net 127.0.0.0   adds the normal loopback entry, using netmask 255.0.0.0 (Class A net, determined from the destination address) and associated with the **lo** device (assuming this device was prviously set up correctly with **ifconfig(8)**).

route add -net 192.56.76.0 netmask 255.255.255.0 dev eth0   adds a route to the network 192.56.76.x via **eth0**. The Class C netmask modifier is not really necessary here because 192.* is a Class C IP address. The word **dev** can be omitted here.

route add default gw mango-gw   adds a default route (which will be used if no other route matches). All packets using this route will be gatewayed through "mango-gw". The device which will actually be used for that route depends on how we can reach "mango-gw" - the static route to "mango-gw" will have to be set up before.

route add ipx4 sl0

route add -net 192.57.66.0 netmask 255.255.255.0 gw ipx4   This command sequence adds the route to the "ipx4" host via the SLIP interface (assuming that "ipx4" is the SLIP host), and then adds the net 192.57.66.0 to be gatewayed through that host.

FILES

/proc/net/route
/etc/networks
/etc/hosts

SEE ALSO

ifconfig(8)

HISTORY

Route for Linux was originally written by Fred N. van Kempen, <waltje@uwalt.nl.mugnet.org> and then modified by Johannes Stille and Linus Torvalds for pl15. Alan Cox added the mss and window options for Linux 1.1.22.

ROUTED(8)

NAME

routed – network routing daemon

SYNOPSIS

routed [-d] [-g] [-q] [-s] [-t] [logfile]

DESCRIPTION

Routed is invoked at boot time to manage the network routing tables. The routing daemon uses a variant of the Xerox NS Routing Information Protocol in maintaining up to date kernel routing table entries. It used a generalized protocol capable of use with multiple address types, but is currently used only for Internet routing within a cluster of networks.

In normal operation routed listens on the udp 4 socket for the route 8 service (see services 5) for routing information packets. If the host is an internetwork router, it periodically supplies copies of its routing tables to any directly connected hosts and networks.

When routed is started, it uses the SIOCGIFCONF ioctl 2 to find those directly connected interfaces configured into the system and marked "up" (the software loopback interface is ignored). If multiple interfaces are present, it is assumed that the host will forward packets between networks. Routed then transmits a request packet on each interface (using a broadcast packet if the interface supports it) and enters a loop, listening for request and response packets from other hosts.

When a request packet is received, routed formulates a reply based on the information maintained in its internal tables. The response packet generated contains a list of known routes, each marked with a "hop count" metric (a count of 16, or greater, is considered "infinite"). The metric associated with each route returned provides a metric relative to the sender .

Response packets received by routed are used to update the routing tables if one of the following conditions is satisfied:

> No routing table entry exists for the destination network or host, and the metric indicates the destination is "reachable" (i.e. the hop count is not infinite).

> The source host of the packet is the same as the router in the existing routing table entry. That is, updated information is being received from the very internetwork router through which packets for the destination are being routed.

> The existing entry in the routing table has not been updated for some time (defined to be 90 seconds) and the route is at least as cost effective as the current route.

> The new route describes a shorter route to the destination than the one currently stored in the routing tables; the metric of the new route is compared against the one stored in the table to decide this.

When an update is applied, routed records the change in its internal tables and updates the kernel routing table. The change is reflected in the next response packet sent.

In addition to processing incoming packets, routed also periodically checks the routing table entries. If an entry has not been updated for 3 minutes, the entry's metric is set to infinity and marked for deletion. Deletions are delayed an additional 60 seconds to insure the invalidation is propagated throughout the local internet.

Hosts acting as internetwork routers gratuitously supply their routing tables every 30 seconds to all directly connected hosts and networks. The response is sent to the broadcast address on nets capable of that function, to the destination address on point-to-point links, and to the router's own address on other networks. The normal routing tables are bypassed when sending gratuitous responses. The reception of responses on each network is used to determine that the network and interface are functioning correctly. If no response is received on an interface, another route may be chosen to route around the interface, or the route may be dropped if no alternative is available.

Options supported by routed :

> -d Enable additional debugging information to be logged, such as bad packets received.

-g This flag is used on internetwork routers to offer a route to the "default" destination. This is typically used on a gateway to the Internet, or on a gateway that uses another routing protocol whose routes are not reported to other local routers.

-s Supplying this option forces routed to supply routing information whether it is acting as an internetwork router or not. This is the default if multiple network interfaces are present, or if a point-to-point link is in use.

-q This is the opposite of the -s option.

-t If the -t option is specified, all packets sent or received are printed on the standard output. In addition, routed will not divorce itself from the controlling terminal so that interrupts from the keyboard will kill the process.

Any other argument supplied is interpreted as the name of file in which routed Ns 's actions should be logged. This log contains information about any changes to the routing tables and, if not tracing all packets, a history of recent messages sent and received which are related to the changed route.

In addition to the facilities described above, routed supports the notion of "distant" passive and active gateways. When routed is started up, it reads the file to find gateways which may not be located using only information from the SIOGIFCONF ioctl 2 . Gateways specified in this manner should be marked passive if they are not expected to exchange routing information, while gateways marked active should be willing to exchange routing information (i.e. they should have a routed process running on the machine). Routes through passive gateways are installed in the kernel's routing tables once upon startup. Such routes are not included in any routing information transmitted. Active gateways are treated equally to network interfaces. Routing information is distributed to the gateway and if no routing information is received for a period of the time, the associated route is deleted. Gateways marked external are also passive, but are not placed in the kernel routing table nor are they included in routing updates. The function of external entries is to inform routed that another routing process will install such a route, and that alternate routes to that destination should not be installed. Such entries are only required when both routers may learn of routes to the same destination.

The is comprised of a series of lines, each in the following format:

<net|host> name1 gateway name2 metric value <passive |active|external>

The net or host keyword indicates if the route is to a network or specific host.

Name1 is the name of the destination network or host. This may be a symbolic name located in or (or, if started after named 8 , known to the name server), or an Internet address specified in "dot" notation; see inet 3 .

Name2 is the name or address of the gateway to which messages should be forwarded.

Value is a metric indicating the hop count to the destination host or network.

One of the keywords passive , active or external indicates if the gateway should be treated as passive or active (as described above), or whether the gateway is external to the scope of the routed protocol.

Internetwork routers that are directly attached to the Arpanet or Milnet should use the Exterior Gateway Protocol EGP to gather routing information rather then using a static routing table of passive gateways. EGP is required in order to provide routes for local networks to the rest of the Internet system. Sites needing assistance with such configurations should contact the Computer Systems Research Group at Berkeley.

FILES

Pa /etc/gateways for distant gateways

SEE ALSO

udp 4 , icmp 4 , XNSrouted 8 , htable 8

Internet Transport Protocols
XSIS 028112

ROUTED(8)

Xerox System Integration Standard

BUGS

The kernel's routing tables may not correspond to those of routed when redirects change or add routes. Routed should note any redirects received by reading the ICMP packets received via a raw socket.

Routed should incorporate other routing protocols, such as Xerox NS, XNSrouted 8 and EGP . Using separate processes for each requires configuration options to avoid redundant or competing routes.

Routed should listen to intelligent interfaces, such as an IMP , to gather more information. It does not always detect unidirectional failures in network interfaces (e.g., when the output side fails).

HISTORY

The routed command appeared in BSD 4.2 .

RPC.RUSERSD(8)

NAME
rpc.rusersd – logged in users server

SYNOPSIS
/usr/libexec/rpc.rusersd

DESCRIPTION
rpc.rusersd is a server which returns information about users currently logged in to the system.

The currently logged in users are queried using the rusers 1 command. The rpc.rusersd daemon is normally invoked by inetd 8 .

rpc.rusersd uses an RPC protocol defined in

SEE ALSO
rusers 1 , who 1 , w 1 , inetd 8

RPC.RWALLD(8)

NAME

rpc.rwalld – write messages to users currently logged in server

SYNOPSIS

/usr/libexec/rpc.rwalld

DESCRIPTION

rpc.rwalld is a server which will send a message to users currently logged in to the system. This server invokes the wall 1 command to actually write the messages to the system.

Messages are sent to this server by the rwall 1 command. The rpc.rwalld daemon is normally invoked by inetd 8 .

rpc.rwalld uses an RPC protocol defined in

SEE ALSO

rwall 1 , wall 1 , inetd 8

RPCINFO(8)

NAME

rpcinfo – report RPC information

SYNOPSIS

rpcinfo -p [host] rpcinfo [-n portnum] -u host program [version] rpcinfo [-n portnum] -t host program [version] rpcinfo -b program version rpcinfo -d program version

DESCRIPTION

rpcinfo makes an RPC call to an RPC server and reports what it finds.

OPTIONS

-p Probe the portmapper on host , and print a list of all registered RPC programs. If host is not specified, it defaults to the value returned by hostname 1 .

-u Make an RPC call to procedure 0 of program on the specified host using UDP , and report whether a response was received.

-t Make an RPC call to procedure 0 of program on the specified host using TCP , and report whether a response was received.

-n Use portnum as the port number for the -t and -u options instead of the port number given by the portmapper.

-b Make an RPC broadcast to procedure 0 of the specified program and version using UDP and report all hosts that respond.

-d Delete registration for the RPC service of the specified program and version . This option can be exercised only by the super-user.

The program argument can be either a name or a number.

If a version is specified, rpcinfo attempts to call that version of the specified program . Otherwise, rpcinfo attempts to find all the registered version numbers for the specified program by calling version 0 (which is presumed not to exist; if it does exist, rpcinfo attempts to obtain this information by calling an extremely high version number instead) and attempts to call each registered version. Note: the version number is required for -b and -d options.

EXAMPLES

To show all of the RPC services registered on the local machine use:

rpcinfo -p

To show all of the RPC services registered on the machine named klaxon use:

rpcinfo -p klaxon

To show all machines on the local net that are running the Yellow Pages service use:

rpcinfo -b ypserv 'version' — uniq

where 'version' is the current Yellow Pages version obtained from the results of the -p switch above.

To delete the registration for version 1 of the walld service use:

rpcinfo -d walld 1

SEE ALSO

rpc 5 , portmap 8

"RPC Programming Guide"

BUGS

In releases prior to SunOS 3.0, the Network File System (NFS) did not register itself with the portmapper; rpcinfo cannot be used to make RPC calls to the NFS server on hosts running such releases.

NAME

rshd – remote shell server

SYNOPSIS

rshd [-alnL]

DESCRIPTION

The rshd server is the server for the rcmd 3 routine and, consequently, for the rsh 1 program. The server provides remote execution facilities with authentication based on privileged port numbers from trusted hosts.

The rshd server listens for service requests at the port indicated in the "cmd" service specification; see services 5 . When a service request is received the following protocol is initiated:

> The server checks the client's source port. If the port is not in the range 512-1023, the server aborts the connection.
>
> The server reads characters from the socket up to a null ('\0') byte. The resultant string is interpreted as an ASCII number, base 10.
>
> If the number received in step 2 is non-zero, it is interpreted as the port number of a secondary stream to be used for the stderr . A second connection is then created to the specified port on the client's machine. The source port of this second connection is also in the range 512-1023.
>
> The server checks the client's source address and requests the corresponding host name (see gethostbyaddr 3 , hosts 5 and named 8) . If the hostname cannot be determined, the dot-notation representation of the host address is used. If the hostname is in the same domain as the server (according to the last two components of the domain name), or if the -a option is given, the addresses for the hostname are requested, verifying that the name and address correspond. If address verification fails, the connection is aborted with the message, "Host address mismatch."
>
> A null terminated user name of at most 16 characters is retrieved on the initial socket. This user name is interpreted as the user identity on the client Ns 's machine.
>
> A null terminated user name of at most 16 characters is retrieved on the initial socket. This user name is interpreted as a user identity to use on the server Ns 's machine.
>
> A null terminated command to be passed to a shell is retrieved on the initial socket. The length of the command is limited by the upper bound on the size of the system's argument list.
>
> Rshd then validates the user using ruserok 3 , which uses the file and the file found in the user's home directory. The -l option prevents ruserok 3 from doing any validation based on the user's ".rhosts" file, unless the user is the superuser.
>
> A null byte is returned on the initial socket and the command line is passed to the normal login shell of the user. The shell inherits the network connections established by rshd .

Transport-level keepalive messages are enabled unless the -n option is present. The use of keepalive messages allows sessions to be timed out if the client crashes or becomes unreachable.

The -L option causes all successful accesses to be logged to syslogd 8 as auth.info messages and all failed accesses to be logged as auth.notice .

DIAGNOSTICS

Except for the last one listed below, all diagnostic messages are returned on the initial socket, after which any network connections are closed. An error is indicated by a leading byte with a value of 1 (0 is returned in step 9 above upon successful completion of all the steps prior to the execution of the login shell).

> Locuser too long. The name of the user on the client's machine is longer than 16 characters.

Ruser too long. The name of the user on the remote machine is longer than 16 characters.

Command too long . The command line passed exceeds the size of the argument list (as configured into the system).

Login incorrect. No password file entry for the user name existed.

Remote directory. The chdir command to the home directory failed.

Permission denied. The authentication procedure described above failed.

Can't make pipe. The pipe needed for the stderr , wasn't created.

Can't fork; try again. A fork by the server failed.

<shellname>: ... The user's login shell could not be started. This message is returned on the connection associated with the stderr , and is not preceded by a flag byte.

SEE ALSO

rsh 1 , rcmd 3 , ruserok 3

BUGS

The authentication procedure used here assumes the integrity of each client machine and the connecting medium. This is insecure, but is useful in an "open" environment.

A facility to allow all data exchanges to be encrypted should be present.

A more extensible protocol (such as Telnet) should be used.

RWHOD(8)

NAME

rwhod – system status server

SYNOPSIS

rwhod

DESCRIPTION

Rwhod is the server which maintains the database used by the rwho 1 and ruptime 1 programs. Its operation is predicated on the ability to broadcast messages on a network.

Rwhod operates as both a producer and consumer of status information. As a producer of information it periodically queries the state of the system and constructs status messages which are broadcast on a network. As a consumer of information, it listens for other rwhod servers' status messages, validating them, then recording them in a collection of files located in the directory

The server transmits and receives messages at the port indicated in the "rwho" service specification; see services 5 . The messages sent and received, are of the form:

```
struct outmp {
char out_line[8]; /* tty name */
char out_name[8]; /* user id */
long out_time; /* time on */
};

struct whod {
char wd_vers;
char wd_type;
char wd_fill[2];
int wd_sendtime;
int wd_recvtime;
char wd_hostname[32];
int wd_loadav[3];
int wd_boottime;
struct whoent {
struct outmp we_utmp;
int we_idle;
} wd_we[1024 / sizeof (struct whoent)];
};
```

All fields are converted to network byte order prior to transmission. The load averages are as calculated by the w 1 program, and represent load averages over the 5, 10, and 15 minute intervals prior to a server's transmission; they are multiplied by 100 for representation in an integer. The host name included is that returned by the gethostname 2 system call, with any trailing domain name omitted. The array at the end of the message contains information about the users logged in to the sending machine. This information includes the contents of the utmp 5 entry for each non-idle terminal line and a value indicating the time in seconds since a character was last received on the terminal line.

Messages received by the rwho server are discarded unless they originated at an rwho server's port. In addition, if the host's name, as specified in the message, contains any unprintable ASCII characters, the message is discarded. Valid messages received by rwhod are placed in files named in the directory These files contain only the most recent message, in the format described above.

Status messages are generated approximately once every 3 minutes. Rwhod performs an nlist 3 on every 30 minutes to guard against the possibility that this file is not the system image currently operating.

SEE ALSO

rwho 1 , ruptime 1

BUGS

There should be a way to relay status information between networks. Status information should be sent only upon request rather than continuously. People often interpret the server dying or network communtication failures as a machine going down.

HISTORY

The rwhod command appeared in BSD 4.2 .

SENDMAIL(8)

NAME

sendmail – send mail over the internet

SYNOPSIS

sendmail [flags] [address ...]
newaliases
mailq [-v]
smtpd
bsmtp
runq

DESCRIPTION

Sendmail sends a message to one or more recipients, routing the message over whatever networks are necessary. Sendmail does internetwork forwarding as necessary to deliver the message to the correct place.

Sendmail is not intended as a user interface routine; other programs provide user-friendly front ends; sendmail is used only to deliver pre-formatted messages.

With no flags, sendmail reads its standard input up to an end-of-file or a line consisting only of a single dot and sends a copy of the message found there to all of the addresses listed. It determines the network(s) to use based on the syntax and contents of the addresses.

Local addresses are looked up in a file and aliased appropriately. Aliasing can be prevented by preceding the address with a backslash. Normally the sender is not included in any alias expansions, e.g., if 'john' sends to 'group', and 'group' includes 'john' in the expansion, then the letter will not be delivered to 'john'.

Flags are:

-ba Go into ARPANET mode. All input lines must end with a CR-LF, and all messages will be generated with a CR-LF at the end. Also, the "From:" and "Sender:" fields are examined for the name of the sender.

-bd Run as a daemon. This requires Berkeley IPC. Sendmail will fork and run in background listening on socket 25 for incoming SMTP connections. This is normally run from

-bi Initialize the alias database.

-bm Deliver mail in the usual way (default).

-bp Print a listing of the queue.

-bs Use the SMTP protocol as described in RFC821 on standard input and output. This flag implies all the operations of the -ba flag that are compatible with SMTP.

-bb Read batched SMTP (BSMTP) commands from standard input.

-bt Run in address test mode. This mode reads addresses and shows the steps in parsing; it is used for debugging configuration tables.

-bv Verify names only – do not try to collect or deliver a message. Verify mode is normally used for validating users or mailing lists.

-bz Create the configuration freeze file.

-C file Use alternate configuration file. Sendmail refuses to run as root if an alternate configuration file is specified. The frozen configuration file is bypassed.

-d X Set debugging value to X.

-F fullname Set the full name of the sender.

-f name Sets the name of the "from" person (i.e., the sender of the mail). -f can only be used by "trusted" users (normally root, daemon, and network) or if the person you are trying to become is the same as the person you are.

SENDMAIL(8)

-h N Set the hop count to N . The hop count is incremented every time the mail is processed. When it reaches a limit, the mail is returned with an error message, the victim of an aliasing loop. If not specified, "Received:" lines in the message are counted.

-n Don't do aliasing.

-o x value Set option x to the specified value . Options are described below.

-q time Processed saved messages in the queue at given intervals. If time is omitted, process the queue once. Time is given as a tagged number, with s being seconds, m being minutes, h being hours, d being days, and w being weeks. For example, -q1h30m or -q90m would both set the timeout to one hour thirty minutes. If time is specified, sendmail will run in background. This option can be used safely with -bd .

-M ident Process the queued message with the queue id ident .

-R addr Process the queued messages that have the string addr in one of the recipient addresses.

-S addr Process the queued messages that have the string addr in the sender address.

-r name An alternate and obsolete form of the -f flag.

-t Read message for recipients. To:, Cc:, and Bcc: lines will be scanned for recipient addresses. The Bcc: line will be deleted before transmission. Any addresses in the argument list will be suppressed, that is, they will not receive copies even if listed in the message header.

-v Go into verbose mode. Alias expansions will be announced, etc.

There are also a number of processing options that may be set. Normally these will only be used by a system administrator. Options may be set either on the command line using the -o flag or in the configuration file. These are described in detail in the "Sendmail Installation and Operation Guide" . The options are:

A file Use alternate alias file.

c On mailers that are considered "expensive" to connect to, don't initiate immediate connection. This requires queueing.

d x Set the delivery mode to x . Delivery modes are i for interactive (synchronous) delivery, b for background (asynchronous) delivery, and q for queue only – i.e., actual delivery is done the next time the queue is run.

D Try to automatically rebuild the alias database if necessary.

e x Set error processing to mode x . Valid modes are m to mail back the error message, w to "write" back the error message (or mail it back if the sender is not logged in), p to print the errors on the terminal (default), q to throw away error messages (only exit status is returned), and e to do special processing for the BerkNet. If the text of the message is not mailed back by modes m or w and if the sender is local to this machine, a copy of the message is appended to the file in the sender's home directory.

F mode The mode to use when creating temporary files.

f Save UNIX–style From lines at the front of messages.

g N The default group id to use when calling mailers.

H file The SMTP help file.

i Do not take dots on a line by themselves as a message terminator.

k N Checkpoint the queue file after every N successful deliveries (default 10). This avoids excessive duplicate deliveries when sending to long mailing lists interrupted by system crashes.

L n The log level.

m Send to "me" (the sender) also if I am in an alias expansion.

o If set, this message may have old style headers. If not set, this message is guaranteed to have new style headers (i.e., commas instead of spaces between addresses). If set, an adaptive algorithm is used that will correctly determine the header format in most cases.

Q queuedir Select the directory in which to queue messages.

r timeout The timeout on reads; if none is set, sendmail will wait forever for a mailer. This option violates the word (if not the intent) of the SMTP specification, show the timeout should probably be fairly large.

S file Save statistics in the named file.

s Always instantiate the queue file, even under circumstances where it is not strictly necessary. This provides safety against system crashes during delivery.

T time Set the timeout on undelivered messages in the queue to the specified time. After delivery has failed (e.g., because of a host being down) for this amount of time, failed messages will be returned to the sender. The default is three days.

t stz , dtz Set the name of the time zone.

U userdatabase If set, a user database is consulted to get forwarding information. You can consider this an adjunct to the aliasing mechanism, except that the database is intended to be distributed; aliases are local to a particular host. This may not be available if your sendmail does not have the USERDB option compiled in.

u N Set the default user id for mailers.

w If not set, name server lookups will us a querytype of ANY to find types CNAME , A , and MX , and will cause all existing records to be cached by our local server. If there is (might be) a wildcard MX in the local domain or its parents that are searched, you must set this option, which will use a querytype of CNAME only; otherwise, it would cause all fully-qualified names to match as names in the local domain.

In aliases, the first character of a name may be a vertical bar to cause interpretation of the rest of the name as a command to pipe the mail to. It may be necessary to quote the name to keep sendmail from suppressing the blanks from between arguments. For example, a common alias is:

msgs: "|/usr/bin/msgs -s"

Aliases may also have the syntax to ask sendmail to read the named file for a list of recipients. For example, an alias such as:

poets: ":include:/usr/local/lib/poets.list"

would read for the list of addresses making up the group.

Sendmail returns an exit status describing what it did. The codes are defined in sysexits.h :

EX_OK Successful completion on all addresses.

EX_NOUSER User name not recognized.

EX_UNAVAILABLE Catchall meaning necessary resources were not available.

EX_SYNTAX Syntax error in address.

EX_SOFTWARE Internal software error, including bad arguments.

EX_OSERR Temporary operating system error, such as cannot fork .

EX_NOHOST Host name not recognized.

EX_TEMPFAIL Message could not be sent immediately, but was queued.

If invoked as newaliases , sendmail will rebuild the alias database. If invoked as mailq , sendmail will print the contents of the mail queue. If invoked as smtpd , sendmail will fork and run as a daemon. If invoked as bsmtp , sendmail will process batched SMTP on standard input. If invoked as runq , sendmail will run through the mail queue and make what deliveries are possible.

SENDMAIL(8)   SENDMAIL(8)

FILES

Except for the file itself, the following pathnames are all specified in Thus, these values are only approximations.

/etc/aliases raw data for alias names
/etc/aliases.pag
/etc/aliases.dir data base of alias names
/etc/sendmail.cf configuration file
/etc/sendmail.fc frozen configuration
/etc/sendmail.hf help file
/var/log/sendmail.st collected statistics
/var/spool/mqueue/* temp files

SEE ALSO

binmail 1 , mail 1 , rmail 1 , syslog 3 , aliases 5 , mailaddr 7 , rc 8 ;

DARPA Internet Request For Comments RFC819 , RFC821 , RFC822 . "Sendmail An Internetwork Mail Router" SMM &No. 16 "Sendmail Installation and Operation Guide" SMM &No. 7

HISTORY

The sendmail command appeared in BSD 4.2 .

BSD 4   August 5, 1991   1142

SETFDPRM(8) Linux Programmer's Manual SETFDPRM(8)

NAME

setfdprm – sets user-provided floppy disk parameters

SYNOPSIS

setfdprm [**–p**] device name
setfdprm [**–p**] device size sectors heads tracks stretch gap rate spec1 fmt_gap
setfdprm [**–c**] device
setfdprm [**–y**] device
setfdprm [**–n**] device

DESCRIPTION

setfdprm is a utility that can be used to load disk parameters into the auto-detecting floppy devices, to clear old parameter sets and to disable or enable diagnostic messages.

Without any options, **setfdprm** loads the *device* (usually */dev/fd0* or */dev/fd1*) with a new parameter set with the *name* entry found in */etc/fdprm* (usually named 360/360, etc.). These parameters stay in effect until the media is changed.

OPTIONS

–p *device name*   Permanently loads a new parameter set for the specified auto-configuring floppy device for the configuration with *name* in */etc/fdprm*. Alternatively, the parameters can be given directly from the command line.

–c *device*   Clears the parameter set of the specified auto-configuring floppy device.

-y *device*   Enables format detection messages for the specified auto-configuring floppy device.

-n *device*   Disables format detection messages for the specified auto-configuring floppy device.

BUGS

This documentation is grossly incomplete.

FILES

/etc/fdprm

AUTHOR

Werner Almesberger (almesber@nessie.cs.id.ethz.ch)

Linux 0.99   20 November 1993   1143

SETSERIAL(8)

NAME

setserial – get/set Linux serial port information

SYNOPSIS

setserial [**–abqvVW**] device [parameter1 [arg]] ...

setserial -g [**–abv**] device1 ...

DESCRIPTION

setserial is a program designed to set and/or report the configuration information associated with a serial port. This information includes what I/O port and IRQ a particular serial port is using, and whether or not the break key should be interpreted as the Secure Attention Key, and so on.

During the normal bootup process, only COM ports 1-4 are initialized, using the default I/O ports and IRQ values, as listed below. In order to initialize any additional serial ports, or to change the COM 1-4 ports to a nonstadard configuration, the **setserial** program should be used. Typically it is called from an *rc.serial* script, which is usually run out of */etc/rc.local*.

The *device* argument or arguments specifies the serial device which should be configured or interrogated. It will usually have the following form: **/dev/cua[0-3]**.

If no parameters are specified, **setserial** will print out the port type (i.e., 8250, 16450, 16550, 16550A), the hardware I/O port, the hardware IRQ line, its "baud base," and some of its operational flags.

If the **–g** option is given, the arguments to setserial are interpreted as a list of devices for which the characteristics of those devices should be printed.

Without the **–g** option, the first argument to setserial is interpreted as the device to be modified or characteristics to be printed, and any additional arguments are interpreted as parameters which should be assigned to that serial device.

For the most part, superuser privilege is required to set the configuration parameters of a serial port. A few serial port parameters can be set by normal users, however, and these will be noted as exceptions in this manual page.

OPTIONS

Setserial accepts the following options:

- **–a** When reporting the configuration of a serial device, print all available information.
- **–b** When reporting the configuration of a serial device, print a summary of the device's configuration, which might be suitable for printing during the bootup process, during the /etc/rc script.
- **–q** Be quiet. **Setserial** will print fewer lines of output.
- **–v** Be verbose. **Setserial** will print additional status output.
- **–V** Display version and exit.
- **–W** Do wild interrupt initialization and exit.

PARAMETERS

The following parameters can be assigned to a serial port.

All argument values are assumed to be in decimal unless preceeded by "0x".

- **port** port_number The **port** option sets the I/O port, as described above.
- **irq** irq_number The **irq** option sets the hardware IRQ, as described above.
- **uart** uart_type This option is used to set the UART type. The permitted types are **none**, 8250, 16450, 16550, and 16550A. Since the 8250 and 16450 UARTS do not have FIFO's, and since

SETSERIAL(8)   Linux Programmer's Manual   SETSERIAL(8)

                       the original 16550 have bugs which make the FIFO's unusable, the FIFO will only be used on chips identifiied as 16550A UARTs. Setting the UART type to 8250, 16450, or 16550 will enable the serial port without trying to use the FIFO. Using UART type **none** will disable the port.

                       Some internal modems are billed as having a "16550A UART with a 1k buffer". This is a lie. They do not have really have a 16550A compatible UART; instead what they have is a 16450 compatible UART with a 1k receive buffer to prevent receiver overruns. This is important, because they do not have a transmit FIFO. Hence, they are not compatible with a 16550A UART, and the autoconfiguration process will correctly identify them as 16450's. If you attempt to override this using the **uart** parameter, you will see dropped characters during file transmissions. These UART's usually have other problems: the **skip_test** parameter also often must be specified.

autoconfig   When this parameter is given, **setserial** will ask the kernel to attempt to automatically configure the serial port. The I/O port must be correctly set; the kernel will attempt to determine the UART type, and if the **auto_irq** parameter is set, Linux will attempt to automatically determine the IRQ. The **autoconfigure** parameter should be given after the **port, auto_irq,** and **skip_test** parameters have been specified.

auto_irq   During autoconfiguration, try to determine the IRQ. This feature is not guaranteed to always produce the correct result; some hardware configurations will fool the Linux kernel. It is generally safer not to use the **auto_irq** feature, but rather to specify the IRQ to be used explicitly, using the **irq** parameter.

^auto_irq   During autoconfiguration, do *not* try to determine the IRQ.

skip_test   During autoconfiguration, skip the UART test. Some internal modems do not have National Semiconductor compatible UART's, but have cheap imitations instead. Some of these cheasy imitations UART's do not fully support the loopback detection mode, which is used by the kernel to make sure there really is a UART at a particular address before attempting to configure it. So for certain internal modems you will need to specify this parameter so Linux can initialize the UART correctly.

^skip_test   During autoconfiguration, do *not* skip the UART test.

baud_base baud_base   This option sets the base baud rate, which is the clock frequency divided by 16. Normally this value is 115200, which is also the fastest baud rate which the UART can support.

spd_hi   Use 57.6kb when the application requests 38.4kb. This parameter may be specified by a non-privileged user.

spd_vhi   Use 115kb when the application requests 38.4kb. This parameter may be specified by a non-privileged user.

spd_cust   Use the custom divisor to set the speed when the application requests 38.4kb. In this case, the baud rate is the **baud_base** divided by the **divisor**. This parameter may be specified by a non-privileged user.

spd_normal   Use 38.4kb when the application requests 38.4kb. This parameter may be specified by a non-privileged user.

divisor divisor   This option sets the custom divison. This divisor will be used then the **spd_cust** option is selected and the serial port

SETSERIAL(8) Linux Programmer's Manual SETSERIAL(8)

	is set to 38.4kb by the application. This parameter may be specified by a non-privileged user.
sak	Set the break key at the Secure Attention Key.
^sak	disable the Secure Attention Key.
fourport	Configure the port as an AST Fourport card.
^fourport	Disable AST Fourport configuration.
close_delay delay	Specify the amount of time, in hundredths of a second, that DTR should remain low on a serial line after the callout device is closed, before the blocked dialin device raises DTR again. The default value of this option is 50, or a half-second delay.
session_lockout	Lock out callout port (/dev/cuaXX) accesses across different sessions. That is, once a process has opened a port, do not allow a process with a different session ID to open that port until the first process has closed it.
^session_lockout	Do not lock out callout port accesses across different sessions.
pgrp_lockout	Lock out callout port (/dev/cuaXX) accesses across different process groups. That is, once a process has opened a port, do not allow a process in a different process group to open that port until the first process has closed it.
^pgrp_lockout	Do not lock out callout port accesses across different process groups.
hup_notify	Notify a process blocked on opening a dial in line when a process has finished using a callout line (either by closing it or by the serial line being hung up) by returning EAGAIN to the open.

The application of this parameter is for getty's which are blocked on a serial port's dial in line. This allows the getty to reset the modem (which may have had its configuration modified by the application using the callout device) before blocking on the open again. |
^hup_notify	Do not notify a process blocked on opening a dial in line when the callout device is hung up.
split_termios	Treat the termios settings used by the callout device and the termios settings used by the dialin devices as separate.
^split_termios	Use the same termios structure to store both the dialin and callout ports. This is the default option.
callout_nohup	If this particular serial port is opened as a callout device, do not hangup the tty when carrier detect is dropped.
^callout_nohup	Do not skip hanging up the tty when a serial port is opened as a callout device. Of course, the HUPCL termios flag must be enabled if the hangup is to occur.

CONSIDERATIONS OF CONFIGURING SERIAL PORTS

It is important to note that setserial merely tells the Linux kernel where it should expect to find the I/O port and IRQ lines of a particular serial port. It does *not* configure the hardware, the actual serial board, to use a particular I/O port. In order to do that, you will need to physically program the serial board, usually by setting some jumpers or by switching some DIP switches.

This section will provide some pointers in helping you decide how you would like to configure your serial ports.

The "standard MS-DOS" port associations are given below:

Setserial 2.10   27 August 1994   1146

/dev/ttyS0 (COM1), port 0x3f8, irq 4
/dev/ttyS1 (COM2), port 0x2f8, irq 3
/dev/ttyS2 (COM3), port 0x3e8, irq 4
/dev/ttyS3 (COM4), port 0x2e8, irq 3

Due to the limitations in the design of the AT/ISA bus architecture, normally an IRQ line may not be shared between two or more serial ports. If you attempt to do this, one or both serial ports will become unreliable if you try to use both simultaneously. This limitation can be overcome by special multi-port serial port boards, which are designed to share multiple serial ports over a single IRQ line. Multi-port serial cards supported by Linux include the AST FourPort, the Accent Async board, the Usenet Serial II board, the Bocaboard BB-1004, BB-1008, and BB-2016 boards, and the HUB-6 serial board.

The selection of an alternative IRQ line is difficult, since most of them are already used. The following table lists the "standard MS-DOS" assignments of available IRQ lines:

IRQ 3: COM2
IRQ 4: COM1
IRQ 5: LPT2
IRQ 7: LPT1

Most people find that IRQ 5 is a good choice, assuming that there is only one parallel port active in the computer. Another good choice is IRQ 2 (aka IRQ 9); although this IRQ is sometimes used by network cards, and very rarely VGA cards will be configured to use IRQ 2 as a vertical retrace interrupt. If your VGA card is configured this way; try to disable it so you can reclaim that IRQ line for some other card. It's not necessary for Linux and most other Operating systems.

The only other available IRQ lines are 3, 4, and 7, and these are probably used by the other serial and parallel ports. (If your serial card has a 16bit card edge connector, and supports higher interrupt numbers, then IRQ 10, 11, 12, and 15 are also available.)

On AT class machines, IRQ 2 is seen as IRQ 9, and Linux will interpret it in this manner.

IRQ's other than 2 (9), 3, 4, 5, 7, 10, 11, 12, and 15, should *not* be used, since they are assigned to other hardware and cannot, in general, be changed. Here are the "standard" assignments:

IRQ 0 Timer channel 0
IRQ 1 Keyboard
IRQ 2 Cascade for controller 2
IRQ 3 Serial port 2
IRQ 4 Serial port 1
IRQ 5 Parallel port 2 (Reserved in PS/2)
IRQ 6 Floppy diskette
IRQ 7 Parallel port 1
IRQ 8 Real-time clock
IRQ 9 Redirected to IRQ2
IRQ 10 Reserved
IRQ 11 Reserved
IRQ 12 Reserved (Auxillary device in PS/2)
IRQ 13 Math coprocessor
IRQ 14 Hard disk controller
IRQ 15 Reserved

CAUTION

CAUTION: Using an invalid port can lock up your machine.

FILES
/etc/rc.local /etc/rc.serial

SEE ALSO

tty(4), ttys(4), kernel/chr_drv/serial.c

AUTHOR

The original version of setserial was written by Rick Sladkey (jrs@world.std.com), and was modified by Michael K. Johnson (johnsonm@stolaf.edu).

This version has since been rewritten from scratch by Theodore Ts'o (tytso@mit.edu) on 1/1/93. Any bugs or problems are solely his responsibility.

SETSID(8)

NAME

setsid – run a program in a new session

SYNOPSIS

setsid *program* [*arg* ...]

DESCRIPTION

setsid runs a program in a new session.

SEE ALSO

setsid(2)

AUTHOR

Rick Sladkey <jrs@world.std.com>

SHOWMOUNT(8)

NAME

showmount – show mount information for an NFS server

SYNOPSIS

/usr/etc/showmount [\-adehv\] [\—all\] [\—directories\] [\—exports\] [\—help\] [\—version\] [\host\]

DESCRIPTION

showmount queries the mount daemon on a remote host for information about the state of the NFS server on that machine. With no options **showmount** lists the set of clients who are mounting from that host. The output from **showmount** is designed to appear as though it were processesed through "sort -u".

OPTIONS

-a or —all   List both the client hostname and mounted directory in host:dir format.

-d or —directories   List only the directories mounted by some client.

-e or —exports   Show the NFS server's export list.

-h or —help   Provide a short help summary.

-v or —version   Report the current version number of the program.

—no–headers   Suppress the decriptive headings from the output.

SEE ALSO

rpc.mountd(8), **rpc.nfsd**(8)

BUGS

The completeness and accurary of the information that **showmount** displays varies according to the NFS server's implementation. Because **showmount** sorts and uniqs the output, it is impossible to determine from the output whether a client is mounting the same directory more than once.

AUTHOR

Rick Sladkey <jrs@world.std.com>

SHUTDOWN(8)

NAME

shutdown – close down the system

SYNOPSIS

shutdown [–h | –r] [–fqs] [now | hh:ss | +mins]
reboot [–h | –r] [–fqs] [now | hh:ss | +mins]
fastboot [–h | –r] [–fqs] [now | hh:ss | +mins]
halt [–h | –r] [–fqs] [now | hh:ss | +mins]
fasthalt [–h | –r] [–fqs] [now | hh:ss | +mins]

DESCRIPTION

In general, **shutdown** prepares the system for a power down or reboot. A absolute or delta time can be given, and periodic messages will be sent to all users warning of the shutdown.

halt is the same as **shutdown -h -q now**

fasthalt is the same as **shutdown -h -q -f now**

reboot is the same as **shutdown -r -q now**

fastboot is the same as **shutdown -r -q -f now**

The default delta time, if none is specified, is 2 minutes.

Five minutes before shutdown (or immediately, if shutdown is less than five minutes away), the */etc/nologin* file is created with a message stating that the system is going down and that logins are no longer permitted. The **login** (1) program will not allow non-superusers to login during this period. A message will be sent to all users at this time.

When the shutdown time arrives, **shutdown** notifies all users, tells **init**(8) not to spawn more **getty**(8)'s, writes the shutdown time into the */var/log/wtmp* file, kills all other processes on the system, **sync**(2)'s, unmounts all the disks, **sync**(2)'s again, waits for a second, and then either terminates or reboots the system.

OPTIONS

- **–h** Halt the system. Do not reboot. This option is used when powering down the system.
- **–r** Reboot the system.
- **–f** Fast. When the system is rebooted, the file systems will not be checked. This is arranged by creating */fastboot*, which */etc/rc* must detect (and delete).
- **–q** Quiet. This uses a default broadcast message, and does not prompt the user for one.
- **–s** Reboot in single user mode. This is arranged by creating */etc/singleboot*, which **simpleinit**(8) detects (and deletes).

FILES

/etc/rc
/fastboot
/etc/singleboot
/etc/nologin
/var/log/wtmp

SEE ALSO

umount(8), **login**(1), **reboot**(2), **simpleinit**(8), **init**(8)

BUGS

Unlike the BSD **shutdown**, users are notified of shutdown only once or twice, instead of many times, and at shorter and shorter intervals as "apocalypse approaches."

AUTHOR

poe@daimi.aau.dk
Modified by jrs@world.std.com

# SIMPLEINIT(8)	Linux Programmer's Manual	SIMPLEINIT(8)

NAME

simpleinit – process control initialization

SYNOPSIS

init [**single**]

DESCRIPTION

init is invoked as the last step in the Linux boot sequence. If the **single** option is used, or if the file */etc/singleboot* exists, then single user mode will be entered, by starting */bin/sh*. If the file */etc/securesingle* exists, then the root password will be required to start single user mode. If the root password does not exist, or if */etc/passwd* does not exist, the checking of the password will be skipped.

If the file */etc/TZ* exists, then the contents of that file will be read, and used to set the TZ environment variable for each process started by **simpleinit**. This "feature" is only available if it's configured at compile-time. It's not normally needed.

After single user mode is terminated, the */etc/rc* file is executed, and the information in */etc/inittab* will be used to start processes.

While **init** is running, several signals are trapped, with special action taken. Since **init** has PID 1, sending signals to the **init** process is easy with the **kill**(1) command.

If **init** catches a SIGHUP (hangup) signal, the */etc/inittab* will be read again.

If **init** catches a SIGTSTP (terminal stop) signal, no more processes will be spawned. This is a toggle, which is reset is **init** catches another SIGTSTP signal.

If **init** catches a SIGINT (interrupt) signal, **init** will sync a few times, and try to start *reboot*. Failing this, **init** will execute the system **reboot**(2) call. Under Linux, it is possible to configure the Ctrl-Alt-Del sequence to send a signal to **init** instead of rebooting the system.

THE INITTAB FILE

Because of the number of init programs which are appearing in the Linux community, the documentation for the */etc/inittab* file, which is usually found with the **inittab**(5) man page, is presented here:

The format is

ttyline:termcap-entry:getty-command

An example is as follows:

tty1:console:/sbin/getty 9600 tty1
tty2:console:/sbin/getty 9600 tty2
tty3:console:/sbin/getty 9600 tty3
tty4:console:/sbin/getty 9600 tty4
tty5:console:/sbin/getty 9600 tty5
ttyS1:dumb:/sbin/getty 9600 ttyS1
ttyS2:dumb:/sbin/getty -m -t60 2400 ttyS2

Lines beginning with the # character are treated as comments. Please see documentation for the **getty** (8) command that you are using, since there are several of these in the Linux community at this time.

FILES

/etc/inittab
/etc/singleboot
/etc/securesingle
/etc/TZ
/etc/passwd
/etc/rc

SEE ALSO

inittab(5), **ctrlaltdel**(8) **reboot**(8), **termcap**(5), **getty**(8), **agetty**(8), **shutdown**(8)

BUGS

This program is called **simpleinit** to distinguish it from the System V compatible versions of init which are starting to appear in the Linux community. **simpleinit** should be linked to, or made identical with, *init* for correct functionality.

AUTHOR

Peter Orbaek (poe@daimi.aau.dk)
Version 1.20, with patches for singleuser mode by Werner Almesberger

SLATTACH(8)

NAME

slattach – attach a network interface to a serial line

SYNOPSIS

slattach [-v] [-p proto] [-s speed] [tty]

DESCRIPTION

Slattach is a tiny little program that can be used to put a normal terminal ("serial") line into one of several "network" modes, thus allowing you to use it for point-to-point links to other computers.

OPTIONS

[-v] Enable debugging output. Useful when determining why a given setup doesn't work.

[-p proto] Set a specific kind of protocol to use on the line. The default is set to **cslip**, i.e. compressed SLIP. Other possible values are **slip** (normal SLIP), **ppp** (Point-to-Point Protocol) and **kiss** (AX.25 TNC protocol).

[-s speed] Set a specific line speed, other than the default.

If no arguments are given, the current terminal line (usually: the login device) is used. Otherwise, an attempt is made to claim the indicated terminal port, lock it, and open it.

FILES

/dev/cua*

BUGS

None so far.

AUTHOR

Fred N. van Kempen, <waltje@uwalt.nl.mugnet.org>

SLIPLOGIN(8)   SLIPLOGIN(8)

NAME
sliplogin – attach a serial line network interface

SYNOPSIS
sliplogin [loginname]

DESCRIPTION
Sliplogin is used to turn the terminal line on standard input into a Serial Line IP SLIP link to a remote host. To do this, the program searches the file for an entry matching loginname (which defaults to the current login name if omitted). If a matching entry is found, the line is configured appropriately for slip (8-bit transparent i/o) and converted to SLIP line discipline. Then a shell script is invoked to initialize the slip interface with the appropriate local and remote IP address, netmask, etc.

The usual initialization script is but, if particular hosts need special initialization, the file will be executed instead if it exists. The script is invoked with the parameters

> slipunit The unit number of the slip interface assigned to this line. E.g., 0 for sl0 .
>
> speed The speed of the line.
>
> args The arguments from the entry, in order starting with loginname .

Only the super-user may attach a network interface. The interface is automatically detached when the other end hangs up or the sliplogin process dies. If the kernel slip module has been configured for it, all routes through that interface will also disappear at the same time. If there is other processing a site would like done on hangup, the file or is executed if it exists. It is given the same arguments as the login script.

Format of /etc/slip.hosts
Comments (lines starting with a '#') and blank lines are ignored. Other lines must start with a loginname but the remaining arguments can be whatever is appropriate for the file that will be executed for that name. Arguments are separated by white space and follow normal sh 1 quoting conventions (however, loginname cannot be quoted). Usually, lines have the form loginname local-address remote-address netmask opt-args

where local-address and remote-address are the IP host names or addresses of the local and remote ends of the slip line and netmask is the appropriate IP netmask. These arguments are passed directly to ifconfig 8 . Opt-args are optional arguments used to configure the line.

EXAMPLE
The normal use of sliplogin is to create a entry for each legal, remote slip site with sliplogin as the shell for that entry. E.g., Sfoo:ikhuy6:2010:1:slip line to foo:/tmp:/usr/sbin/sliplogin

(Our convention is to name the account used by remote host hostname as Shostname .) Then an entry is added to that looks like:

Sfoo 'hostname' foo netmask

where 'hostname' will be evaluated by sh to the local host name and netmask is the local host IP netmask.

Note that sliplogin must be setuid to root and, while not a security hole, moral defectives can use it to place terminal lines in an unusable state and/or deny access to legitimate users of a remote slip line. To prevent this, a site can create a group, say slip , that only the slip login accounts are put in then make sure that is in group slip and mode 4550 (setuid root, only group slip can execute binary).

DIAGNOSTICS
Sliplogin logs various information to the system log daemon, syslogd 8 , with a facility code of daemon . The messages are listed here, grouped by severity level.

Error Severity

SLIPLOGIN(8) SLIPLOGIN(8)

ioctl (TCGETS): reason A TCGETS ioctl to get the line parameters failed.
ioctl (TCSETS): reason A TCSETS ioctl to set the line parameters failed.
/etc/slip.hosts: reason The file could not be opened.
access denied for user No entry for user was found in

Notice Severity

"attaching slip unit" unit for loginname SLIP unit unit was successfully attached.

SEE ALSO
slattach 8 , syslogd 8

HISTORY
The sliplogin command

NAME

swapon, swapoff – enable/disable devices and files for paging and swapping

SYNOPSIS

/sbin/swapon –a
/sbin/swapon *specialfile* ...
/sbin/swapoff –a
/sbin/swapoff *specialfile* ...

DESCRIPTION

Swapon is used to specify devices on which paging and swapping are to take place. Calls to **swapon** normally occur in the system multi-user initialization file */etc/rc* making all swap devices available, so that the paging and swapping activity is interleaved across several devices and files.

Normally, the first form is used:

>   –a   All devices marked as "sw" swap devices in */etc/fstab* are made available.

Swapoff disables swapping on the specified devices and files, or on all swap entries in */etc/fstab* when the –a flag is given.

SEE ALSO

swapon(2), swapoff(2), fstab(5), init(8), mkswap(8), rc(8), mount(8)

FILES

/dev/hd[ab]? standard paging devices
/dev/sd[ab]? standard (SCSI) paging devices
/etc/fstab ascii filesystem description table

HISTORY

The **swapon** command appeared in 4.0BSD.

AUTHORS

See the Linux **mount**(8) man page for a complete author list. Primary contributors include Doug Quale, H. J. Lu, Rick Sladkey, and Stephen Tweedie.

SYNC(8)

NAME

sync – flush Linux filesystem buffers

SYNOPSIS

sync

DESCRIPTION

sync executes **sync**(2), which flushes the filesystem buffers to disk. **sync** should be called before the processor is halted in an unusual manner (i.e., before causing a kernel panic when debugging new kernel code). In general, the processor should be halted using the **reboot**(8), or **halt**(8) commands, which will attempt to put the system in a quiescent state before calling **sync**(2).

From Linus: "Note that **sync** is only guaranteed to schedule the dirty blocks for writing: it can actually take a short time before all the blocks are finally written. If you are doing the **sync** with the expectation of killing the machine soon after, please take this into account and sleep for a few seconds. [The **reboot**(8) command takes these precautions.]

SEE ALSO

sync(2), **update**(8), **reboot**(8), **halt**(8)

AUTHOR

Linus Torvalds (torvalds@cs.helsinki.fi)

Linux 0.99   20 November 1993   1159

SYSKLOGD(1)

NAME

sysklogd — Linux system logging utilities.

DESCRIPTION

sysklogd provides two system utilities which provide support for system logging and kernel message trapping. Support of both inetd and unix domain sockets enables this utility package to support both local and remote logging.

System logging is provided by a version of syslogd derived from the stock BSD sources. Support for kernel logging is provided by the klogd utility which allows kernel logging to be conducted in either a standlaone fashion or as a client of syslogd.

While the syslogd sources have been heavily modified a couple of notes are in order. First of all there has been a systematic attempt to insure that syslogd follows as its default, standard BSD behavior. The second important concept to note is that this version of syslogd interacts transparently with the version of syslog found in the standard libraries. If a binary linked to the standard shared libraries fails to function correctly we would like an example of the anomalous behavior.

CONFIGURATION FILE SYNTAX DIFFERENCES

Syslogd uses a slightly different syntax for its configuration file than the original BSD sources. Originally all messages of a specific priority and above were forwarded to the log file.

> For example the following line caused ALL output from daemon the daemon facilities to go into /usr/adm/daemons:
>
> # Sample syslog.conf
> daemon.debug /usr/adm/daemons

Under the new scheme this behavior remains the same. The difference is the addition of two new wildcard specifiers the asterick (*) and the equals sign (=). The * specifies that all messages for the specified facility are to be directed to the destination. Note that this behavior is degenerate with specifying a priority level of debug. Users have indicated that the asterick notation is more intuitive.

The (=) wildcard is used to restrict logging to the specified priority class. This allows, for example, routing only debug messages to a particular logging source.

> For example the following line in syslog.conf would direct debug messages from all sources to the /usr/adm/debug file.
>
> # Sample syslog.conf
> daemon.=debug /usr/adm/debug

This may take some acclimization for those individuals used to the pure BSD behavior but testers have indicated that this syntax is somewhat more flexible than the BSD behavior. Note that these changes should not affect standard syslog.conf files. You must specifically modify the configuration files to obtain the enhanced behavior.

SUPPORT FOR REMOTE LOGGING

These modifications provide network support to the syslogd facility. Network support means that messages can be forwarded from one node running syslogd to another node running syslogd where they will be actually logged to a disk file.

The strategy is to have syslogd listen on a unix domain socket for locally generated log messages. This behavior will allow syslogd to interoperate with the syslog found in the standard C library. At the same time syslogd listens on the standard syslog port for messages forwarded from other hosts. To have this work correctly the services files (typically found in /usr/etc/inet) must have the following entry:

> syslog 514/udp

To cause messages to be forwarded to another host replace the normal file line in the syslog.conf file with the name of the host to which the messages is to be sent prepended with an @.

> For example, to forward **ALL** messages to a remote host use the following syslog.conf entry:
>
> \# Sample syslogd configuration file to
> \# messages to a remote host forward all.
> .* @hostname
>
> To forward all **kernel** messages to a remote host the configuration file would be as follows:
>
> \# Sample configuration file to forward all kernel
> \# messages to a remote host.
> kern.* @hostname

OUTPUT TO NAMED PIPES (FIFO's)

This version of syslogd has support for logging output to named pipes (fifo's). A fifo or named pipe can be used as a destination for log messages by prepending a | to the name of the file. This is handy for debugging. Note that the fifo must be created with the mkfifo command before syslogd is started.

> The following configuration file routes debug messages from the kernel to a fifo:
>
> \# Sample configuration to route kernel debugging
> \# messages ONLY to /usr/adm/debug which is a
> \# named pipe.
> kern.=debug |/usr/adm/debug

INSTALLATION CONCERNS

There is probably one important consideration when installing this version of syslogd. This version of syslogd is dependent on proper formatting of messages by the syslog function. The functioning of the syslog function in the shared libraries changed somewhere in the region of libc.so.4.[2-4].n. The specific change was to null-terminate the message before transmitting it to the /dev/log socket. Proper functioning of this version of syslogd is dependent on null-termination of the message.

This problem will typically manifest itself if old statically linked binaries are being used on the system. Binaries using old versions of the syslog function will cause empty lines to be logged followed by the message with the first character in the message removed. Relinking these binaries to newer versions of the shared libraries will correct this problem.

SECURITY THREATS

There is the potential for the syslogd daemon to be used as a conduit for a denial of service attack. Thanks go to John Morrison (jmorriso@rflab.ee.ubc.ca) for alerting me to this potential. A rogue program(mer) could very easily flood the syslogd daemon with syslog messages resulting in the log files consuming all the remaining space on the filesystem. Activating logging over the inet domain sockets will of course expose a system to risks outside of programs or individuals on the local machine.

Version 1.2 of the utility set will address this problem. In the meantime there are a number of methods of protecting a machine:

1. Logging can be directed to an isolated or non-root filesystem which, if filled, will not impair the machine.
2. The ext2 filesystem can be used which can be configured to limit a certain percentage of a filesystem to usage by root only. **NOTE** that this will require syslogd to be run as a non-root process. **ALSO NOTE** that this will prevent usage of remote logging since syslogd will be unable to bind to the 514/UDP socket.
3. Disabling inet domain sockets will limit risk to the local machine.

4. Use step 3 and if the problem persists and is not secondary to a rogue program/daemon get a 3.5 ft (approx. 1 meter) length of sucker rod* and have a chat with the user in question.

sucker rod def. — 3/4, 7/8 or 1in. hardened steel rod, male threaded on each end. Primary use in the oil industry in Western North Dakota and other locations to pump 'suck' oil from oil wells. Secondary uses are for the construction of cattle feed lots and for dealing with the occassional recalcitrant or belligerant individual.

FILES

/etc/syslog.conf

BUGS

Primarily security concerns to be addressed in Version 1.2

SEE ALSO

klogd(1)

COLLABORATORS

Dr. Greg Wettstein (greg%wind.uucp@plains.nodak.edu)

Enjellic Systems Development

Oncology Research Division Computing Facility

Roger Maris Cancer Center

Fargo, ND

greg%wind.uucp@plains.nodak.edu

Stephen Tweedie

Department of Computer Science

Edinburgh University, Scotland

Juha Virtanen

jiivee@hut.fi

Shane Alderton

shane@scs.apana.org.au

SYSLOGD(8)

NAME

syslogd – log systems messages

SYNOPSIS

syslogd [-f config_file] [-m mark_interval] [-p log_socket]

DESCRIPTION

Syslogd reads and logs messages to the system console, log files, other machines and/or users as specified by its configuration file. The options are as follows:

- -f Specify the pathname of an alternate configuration file; the default is /etc/syslog.conf

- -m Select the number of minutes between "mark" messages; the default is 20 minutes.

- -p Specify the pathname of an alternate log socket; the default is /dev/log .

Syslogd reads its configuration file when it starts up and whenever it receives a hangup signal. For information on the format of the configuration file, see syslog.conf(5).

Syslogd reads messages from the UNIX domain socket /dev/log , from an Internet domain socket specified in /etc/services , and from the special device /dev/klog (to read kernel messages).

Syslogd creates the file /var/run/syslog.pid, and stores its process id there. This can be used to kill or reconfigure syslogd .

The message sent to syslogd should consist of a single line. The message can contain a priority code, which should be a preceding decimal number in angle braces, for example, <5>. This priority code should map into the priorities defined in the include file <sys/syslog.h>.

FILES

- /etc/syslog.conf The configuration file.
- /var/run/syslog.pid The process id of current syslogd .
- /dev/log Name of the UNIX domain datagram log socket.
- /dev/klog The kernel log device.

SEE ALSO

logger(1), syslog(3), services(5), syslog.conf(5)

HISTORY

The syslogd command appeared in BSD 4.3 .

TALKD(8)

NAME

talkd – remote user communication server

SYNOPSIS

talkd

DESCRIPTION

Talkd is the server that notifies a user that someone else wants to initiate a conversation. It acts a repository of invitations, responding to requests by clients wishing to rendezvous to hold a conversation. In normal operation, a client, the caller, initiates a rendezvous by sending a CTL_MSG to the server of type LOOK_UP (see protocols/talkd.h) . This causes the server to search its invitation tables to check if an invitation currently exists for the caller (to speak to the callee specified in the message). If the lookup fails, the caller then sends an ANNOUNCE message causing the server to broadcast an announcement on the callee's login ports requesting contact. When the callee responds, the local server uses the recorded invitation to respond with the appropriate rendezvous address and the caller and callee client programs establish a stream connection through which the conversation takes place.

SEE ALSO

talk 1 , write 1

HISTORY

The talkd command appeared in BSD 4.3 .

TELNETD(8)

NAME

telnetd – DARPA TELNET protocol server

SYNOPSIS

/etc/telnetd [–debug [*port*]] [–l] [–D options] [–D report] [–D exercise] [–D netdata] [–D ptydata]

DESCRIPTION

Telnetd is a server which supports the DARPA standard **TELNET** virtual terminal protocol. *Telnetd* is invoked by the internet server (see *inetd*(8)), normally for requests to connect to the **TELNET** port as indicated by the */etc/services* file (see *services*(5)). If the **–debug** may be used, to start up **telnetd** manually, instead of through *inetd*(8). If started up this way, *port* may be specified to run *telnetd* on an alternate TCP port number.

The **–D** option may be used for debugging purposes. This allows *telnet* to print out debugging information to the connection, allowing the user to see what telnetd is doing. There are several modifiers: **options** prints information about the negotiation of **TELNET** options, **report** prints the **options** information, plus some additional information about what processing is going on, **netdata** displays the data stream received by *telnetd*, **ptydata** displays data written to the pty, and **exercise** has not been implemented yet.

Telnetd operates by allocating a pseudo-terminal device (see *pty*(4)) for a client, then creating a login process which has the slave side of the pseudo-terminal as **stdin**, **stdout**, and **stderr**. *Telnetd* manipulates the master side of the pseudo-terminal, implementing the **TELNET** protocol and passing characters between the remote client and the login process.

When a **TELNET** session is started up, *telnetd* sends **TELNET** options to the client side indicating a willingness to do *remote* echo of characters, to *suppress* go *ahead*, to do *remote* flow *control*, and to receive *terminal* type *information*, *terminal* speed *information*, and *window* size information from the remote client. If the remote client is willing, the remote terminal type is propagated in the environment of the created login process. The pseudo-terminal allocated to the client is configured to operate in cooked mode, and with XTABS and CRMOD enabled (see *tty*(4)).

Telnetd is willing to *do*: *echo*, *binary*, *suppress* go *ahead*, and *timing mark*. *Telnetd* is willing to have the remote client *do*: *linemode*, *binary*, *terminal type*, *terminal speed*, *window size*, *toggle* flow *control*, *environment*, *X* display *location*, and *suppress* go *ahead*.

If the file */etc/issue.net* is present, *telnetd* will show its contents before the login prompt of a telnet session (see *issue.net*(5)).

SEE ALSO

telnet(1), issue.net(5)

BUGS

Some **TELNET** commands are only partially implemented.

Because of bugs in the original 4.2 BSD *telnet*(1), *telnetd* performs some dubious protocol exchanges to try to discover if the remote client is, in fact, a 4.2 BSD *telnet*(1).

Binary mode has no common interpretation except between similar operating systems (Unix in this case).

The terminal type name received from the remote client is converted to lower case. *Telnetd* never sends **TELNET** *go* ahead commands.

TFTPD(8)

NAME

tftpd – DARPA Trivial File Transfer Protocol server

SYNOPSIS

tftpd [directory ...]

DESCRIPTION

Tftpd is a server which supports the DARPA Trivial File Transfer Protocol. The TFTP server operates at the port indicated in the tftp service description; see services 5 . The server is normally started by inetd 8 .

The use of tftp 1 does not require an account or password on the remote system. Due to the lack of authentication information, tftpd will allow only publicly readable files to be accessed. Files may be written only if they already exist and are publicly writable. Note that this extends the concept of public to include all users on all hosts that can be reached through the network; this may not be appropriate on all systems, and its implications should be considered before enabling tftp service. The server should have the user ID with the lowest possible privilege.

Access to files may be restricted by invoking tftpd with a list of directories by including pathnames as server program arguments in In this case access is restricted to files whose names are prefixed by the one of the given directories.

SEE ALSO

tftp 1 , inetd 8

HISTORY

The tftpd command appeared in BSD 4.2 .

NAME

timed – time server daemon

SYNOPSIS

timed [-M] [-t] [-d] [-i network] [-n network] [-F host1 host2 ...]

DESCRIPTION

This is a time server daemon and is normally invoked at boot time from the rc 8 file. It synchronizes the host's time with the time of other machines in a local area network running timed 8 . These time servers will slow down the clocks of some machines and speed up the clocks of others to bring them to the average network time. The average network time is computed from measurements of clock differences using the ICMP timestamp request message.

The service provided by timed is based on a master-slave scheme. When timed 8 is started on a machine, it asks the master for the network time and sets the host's clock to that time. After that, it accepts synchronization messages periodically sent by the master and calls adjtime 2 to perform the needed corrections on the host's clock.

It also communicates with date 1 in order to set the date globally, and with timedc 8 , a timed control program. If the machine running the master crashes, then the slaves will elect a new master from among slaves running with the -M flag. A timed running without the -M or -F flags will remain a slave. The -t flag enables timed to trace the messages it receives in the file Tracing can be turned on or off by the program timedc 8 . The -d flag is for debugging the daemon. It causes the program to not put itself into the background. Normally timed checks for a master time server on each network to which it is connected, except as modified by the options described below. It will request synchronization service from the first master server located. If permitted by the -M flag, it will provide synchronization service on any attached networks on which no current master server was detected. Such a server propagates the time computed by the top-level master. The -n flag, followed by the name of a network which the host is connected to (see networks 5) , overrides the default choice of the network addresses made by the program. Each time the -n flag appears, that network name is added to a list of valid networks. All other networks are ignored. The -i flag, followed by the name of a network to which the host is connected (see networks 5) , overrides the default choice of the network addresses made by the program. Each time the -i flag appears, that network name is added to a list of networks to ignore. All other networks are used by the time daemon. The -n and -i flags are meaningless if used together.

Timed checks for a master time server on each network to which it is connected, except as modified by the -n and -i options described above. If it finds masters on more than one network, it chooses one network on which to be a "slave," and then periodically checks the other networks to see if the masters there have disappeared.

One way to synchronize a group of machines is to use an NTP daemon to synchronize the clock of one machine to a distant standard or a radio receiver and -F Ar hostname to tell its timed daemon to trust only itself.

Messages printed by the kernel on the system console occur with interrupts disabled. This means that the clock stops while they are printing. A machine with many disk or network hardware problems and consequent messages cannot keep good time by itself. Each message typically causes the clock to lose a dozen milliseconds. A time daemon can correct the result.

Messages in the system log about machines that failed to respond usually indicate machines that crashed or were turned off. Complaints about machines that failed to respond to initial time settings are often associated with "multi-homed" machines that looked for time masters on more than one network and eventually chose to become a slave on the other network.

WARNING

If two or more time daemons, whether timed , NTP , try to adjust the same clock, temporal chaos will result. If both

and another time daemon are run on the same machine, ensure that the -F flag is used, so

TIMED(8)   TIMED(8)

that timed never attempts to adjust the local clock.

The protocol is based on UDP/IP broadcasts. All machines within the range of a broadcast that are using the TSP protocol must cooperate. There cannot be more than a single administrative domain using the -F flag among all machines reached by a broadcast packet. Failure to follow this rule is usually indicated by complaints concerning "untrusted" machines in the system log.

FILES

/var/log/timed.log tracing file for timed

/var/log/timed.masterlog log file for master timed

SEE ALSO

date 1 , adjtime 2 , gettimeofday 2 , icmp 4 , timedc 8 , "TSP: The Time Synchronization Protocol for UNIX 4.3BSD" R. Gusella, S. Zatti

HISTORY

The timed daemon appeared in BSD 4.3 .

TIMEDC(8) TIMEDC(8)

NAME
timedc – timed control program

SYNOPSIS
timedc [command] [argument ...]

DESCRIPTION
Timedc is used to control the operation of the timed 8 program. It may be used to:

    Measure the differences between machines' clocks,

    Find the location where the master time server is running,

    Enable or disable tracing of messages received by timed , and

    Perform various debugging actions.

Without any arguments, timedc will prompt for commands from the standard input. If arguments are supplied, timedc interprets the first argument as a command and the remaining arguments as parameters to the command. The standard input may be redirected causing timedc to read commands from a file. Commands may be abbreviated; recognized commands are:

    Ic ? Op Ar command ...

    Ic help Op Ar command ... Print a short description of each command specified in the argument list, or, if no arguments are given, a list of the recognized commands.

    Ic clockdiff Ar host ... Compute the differences between the clock of the host machine and the clocks of the machines given as arguments.

    msite [host ...] Show the master time server for specified host(s).

    trace {on | off} Enable or disable the tracing of incoming messages to timed in the file

    election host Asks the daemon on the target host to reset its "election" timers and to ensure that a time master has been elected.

    quit Exit from timedc.

Other commands may be included for use in testing and debugging timed ; the help command and the program source may be consulted for details.

FILES
    /var/log/timed.log tracing file for timed

    /var/log/timed.masterlog log file for master timed

SEE ALSO
date 1 , adjtime 2 , icmp 4 , timed 8 , "TSP: The Time Synchronization Protocol for UNIX 4.3BSD" R. Gusella, S. Zatti

DIAGNOSTICS
    ?Ambiguous command abbreviation matches more than one command

    ?Invalid command no match found

    ?Privileged command command can be executed by root only

HISTORY
The timedc command appeared in BSD 4.3 .

TIMEDC(8)   TIMEDC(8)

8June 6, 1993BSD 4.3

NAME

traceroute – print the route packets take to network host

SYNOPSIS

traceroute [-m max_ttl] [-n] [-p port] [-q nqueries] [-r] [-s src_addr] [-t tos] [-w waittime] host [packetsize]

DESCRIPTION

The Internet is a large and complex aggregation of network hardware, connected together by gateways. Tracking the route one's packets follow (or finding the miscreant gateway that's discarding your packets) can be difficult. Traceroute utilizes the IP protocol 'time to live' field and attempts to elicit an ICMP TIME_EXCEEDED response from each gateway along the path to some host.

The only mandatory parameter is the destination host name or IP number. The default probe datagram length is 38 bytes, but this may be increased by specifying a packet size (in bytes) after the destination host name.

Other options are:

    m max_ttl Set the max time-to-live (max number of hops) used in outgoing probe packets. The default is 30 hops (the same default used for TCP connections).

    n Print hop addresses numerically rather than symbolically and numerically (saves a nameserver address-to-name lookup for each gateway found on the path).

    p port Set the base UDP port number used in probes (default is 33434). Traceroute hopes that nothing is listening on UDP ports base to base+nhops-1 at the destination host (so an ICMP PORT_UNREACHABLE message will be returned to terminate the route tracing). If something is listening on a port in the default range, this option can be used to pick an unused port range.

    q nqueries Set the number of probes per "ttl" to nqueries (default is three probes).

    r Bypass the normal routing tables and send directly to a host on an attached network. If the host is not on a directly-attached network, an error is returned. This option can be used to ping a local host through an interface that has no route through it (e.g., after the interface was dropped by routed 8) .

    s src_addr Use the following IP address (which must be given as an IP number, not a hostname) as the source address in outgoing probe packets. On hosts with more than one IP address, this option can be used to force the source address to be something other than the IP address of the interface the probe packet is sent on. If the IP address is not one of this machine's interface addresses, an error is returned and nothing is sent.

    t tos Set the type-of-service in probe packets to the following value (default zero). The value must be a decimal integer in the range 0 to 255. This option can be used to see if different types-of-service result in different paths. (If you are not running a BSD 4.3 tahoe or later system, this may be academic since the normal network services like telnet and ftp don't let you control the TOS) . Not all values of TOS are legal or meaningful – see the IP spec for definitions. Useful values are probably (low delay) and (high throughput).

    v Verbose output. Received ICMP packets other than TIME_EXCEEDED and UN- REACHABLE Ns s are listed.

    w Set the time (in seconds) to wait for a response to a probe (default 3 sec.).

This program attempts to trace the route an IP packet would follow to some internet host by launching UDP probe packets with a small ttl (time to live) then listening for an ICMP "time exceeded" reply from a gateway. We start our probes with a ttl of one and increase by one until we get an ICMP "port unreachable" (which means we got to "host") or hit a max (which defaults to 30 hops & can be changed with the -m flag). Three probes (changed with

TIMEDC(8) TIMEDC(8)

-q flag) are sent at each ttl setting and a line is printed showing the ttl, address of the gateway and round trip time of each probe. If the probe answers come from different gateways, the address of each responding system will be printed. If there is no response within a 3 sec. timeout interval (changed with the -w flag), a "*" is printed for that probe.

We don't want the destination host to process the UDP probe packets so the destination port is set to an unlikely value (if some clod on the destination is using that value, it can be changed with the -p flag).

A sample use and output might be:

```
[yak 71]% traceroute nis.nsf.net.
traceroute to nis.nsf.net (35.1.1.48), 30 hops max, 56 byte packet
 1  helios.ee.lbl.gov (128.3.112.1)     19 ms    19 ms     0 ms
 2  lilac-dmc.Berkeley.EDU (128.32.216.1)    39 ms    39 ms    19 ms
 3  lilac-dmc.Berkeley.EDU (128.32.216.1)    39 ms    39 ms    19 ms
 4  ccngw-ner-cc.Berkeley.EDU (128.32.136.23)    39 ms    40 ms    39 ms
 5  ccn-nerif22.Berkeley.EDU (128.32.168.22)    39 ms    39 ms    39 ms
 6  128.32.197.4 (128.32.197.4)    40 ms    59 ms    59 ms
 7  131.119.2.5 (131.119.2.5)    59 ms    59 ms    59 ms
 8  129.140.70.13 (129.140.70.13)    99 ms    99 ms    80 ms
 9  129.140.71.6 (129.140.71.6)    139 ms    239 ms    319 ms
10  129.140.81.7 (129.140.81.7)    220 ms    199 ms    199 ms
11  nic.merit.edu (35.1.1.48)    239 ms    239 ms    239 ms
```

Note that lines 2 & 3 are the same. This is due to a buggy kernel on the 2nd hop system – lbl-csam.arpa – that forwards packets with a zero ttl (a bug in the distributed version of 4.3 BSD) . Note that you have to guess what path the packets are taking cross-country since the NSFNet (129.140) doesn't supply address-to-name translations for its NSS Ns es .

A more interesting example is:

```
[yak 72]% traceroute allspice.lcs.mit.edu.
traceroute to allspice.lcs.mit.edu (18.26.0.115), 30 hops max
 1  helios.ee.lbl.gov (128.3.112.1)     0 ms     0 ms     0 ms
 2  lilac-dmc.Berkeley.EDU (128.32.216.1)    19 ms    19 ms    19 ms
 3  lilac-dmc.Berkeley.EDU (128.32.216.1)    39 ms    19 ms    19 ms
 4  ccngw-ner-cc.Berkeley.EDU (128.32.136.23)    19 ms    39 ms    39 ms
 5  ccn-nerif22.Berkeley.EDU (128.32.168.22)    20 ms    39 ms    39 ms
 6  128.32.197.4 (128.32.197.4)    59 ms    119 ms    39 ms
 7  131.119.2.5 (131.119.2.5)    59 ms    59 ms    39 ms
 8  129.140.70.13 (129.140.70.13)    80 ms    79 ms    99 ms
 9  129.140.71.6 (129.140.71.6)    139 ms    139 ms    159 ms
10  129.140.81.7 (129.140.81.7)    199 ms    180 ms    300 ms
11  129.140.72.17 (129.140.72.17)    300 ms    239 ms    239 ms
12   * * *
13  128.121.54.72 (128.121.54.72)    259 ms    499 ms    279 ms
14   * * *
15   * * *
16   * * *
17   * * *
18  ALLSPICE.LCS.MIT.EDU (18.26.0.115)    339 ms    279 ms    279 ms
```

Note that the gateways 12, 14, 15, 16 & 17 hops away either don't send ICMP "time exceeded" messages or send them with a ttl too small to reach us. 14 – 17 are running the MIT C Gateway code that doesn't send "time exceeded"s. God only knows what's going on with 12.

The silent gateway 12 in the above may be the result of a bug in the 4.[23] BSD network code (and its derivatives): 4.x (x <= 3) sends an unreachable message using whatever ttl remains in the original datagram. Since, for gateways, the remaining ttl is zero, the ICMP "time exceeded" is guaranteed to not make it back to us. The behavior of this bug is slightly more interesting when it appears on the destination system:

```
1   helios.ee.lbl.gov (128.3.112.1)    0 ms    0 ms    0 ms
2   lilac-dmc.Berkeley.EDU (128.32.216.1)    39 ms   19 ms   39 ms
3   lilac-dmc.Berkeley.EDU (128.32.216.1)    19 ms   39 ms   19 ms
4   ccngw-ner-cc.Berkeley.EDU (128.32.136.23)    39 ms   40 ms   19 ms
5   ccn-nerif35.Berkeley.EDU (128.32.168.35)    39 ms   39 ms   39 ms
6   csgw.Berkeley.EDU (128.32.133.254)    39 ms   59 ms   39 ms
7   * * *
8   * * *
9   * * *
10  * * *
11  * * *
12  * * *
13  rip.Berkeley.EDU (128.32.131.22)    59 ms !  39 ms !  39 ms !
```

Notice that there are 12 "gateways" (13 is the final destination) and exactly the last half of them are "missing". What's really happening is that rip (a Sun-3 running Sun OS3.5) is using the ttl from our arriving datagram as the ttl in its ICMP reply. So, the reply will time out on the return path (with no notice sent to anyone since ICMP's aren't sent for ICMP's) until we probe with a ttl that's at least twice the path length. I.e., rip is really only 7 hops away. A reply that returns with a ttl of 1 is a clue this problem exists. Traceroute prints a "!" after the time if the ttl is <= 1. Since vendors ship a lot of obsolete (DEC Ultrix, Sun 3.x) or non-standard HPUX software, expect to see this problem frequently and/or take care picking the target host of your probes. Other possible annotations after the time are !H , !N , !P (got a host, network or protocol unreachable, respectively), !S or !F (source route failed or fragmentation needed – neither of these should ever occur and the associated gateway is busted if you see one). If almost all the probes result in some kind of unreachable, traceroute will give up and exit.

This program is intended for use in network testing, measurement and management. It should be used primarily for manual fault isolation. Because of the load it could impose on the network, it is unwise to use traceroute during normal operations or from automated scripts.

AUTHOR

Implemented by Van Jacobson from a suggestion by Steve Deering. Debugged by a cast of thousands with particularly cogent suggestions or fixes from C. Philip Wood, Tim Seaver and Ken Adelman.

SEE ALSO

netstat 1 , ping 8

TUNE2FS(8)   TUNE2FS(8)

NAME

tune2fs – adjust tunable filesystem parameters on second extended filesystems

SYNOPSIS

tune2fs [**-l**] [**-c** *max-mount-counts*] [**-e** *errors-behavior*] [**-i** *interval-between-checks*] [**-m** *reserved-blocks-percentage*] [**-r** *reserved-blocks-count*] [**-u** *user*] [**-g** *group*] device

DESCRIPTION

tune2fs adjusts tunable filesystem parameters on a Linux second extended filesystem.

Never use tune2fs on a read/write mounted filesystem to change parameters!

OPTIONS

- *-c* max-mount-counts — adjust the maximal mounts count between two filesystem checks.
- *-e* errors-behavior — change the behavior of the kernel code when errors are detected. *errors-behavior* can be one of the followings:
  continue Continue normal execution.
  remount-ro Remount the filesystem read-only.
  panic Causes a kernel panic.
- *-g* group — set the user group which can benefit from the reserved blocks.
  group can be a numerical gid or a group name.
- *-i* interval-between-checks[d|m|w] — adjust the maximal time between two filesystem checks. No postfix or 'd' result in days, 'm' in months, and 'w' in weeks. A value of zero will disable the timedependent checking.
- *-l* — list the contents of the filesystem superblock.
- *-m* reserved-blocks-percentage — adjust the reserved blocks percentage on the given device.
- *-r* reserved-blocks-count — adjust the reserved blocks count on the given device.
- *-u* user — set the user who can benefit from the reserved blocks.
  user can be a numerical uid or a user name.

BUGS

We didn't find any bugs yet. Perhaps there are bugs but it's unlikely.

WARNING

Use this utility on your own risk. You're modifying filesystems.

AUTHOR

tune2fs has been written by Remy Card <card@masi.ibp.fr>, the developer and maintainer of the ext2 fs.
tune2fs uses the ext2fs library written by Theodore T'so <tytso@mit.edu>.
This manual page was written by Christian Kuhtz <chk@data-hh.Hanse.DE>.
Timedependent checking was added by Uwe Ohse <uwe@tirka.gun.de>.

AVAILABILITY

tune2fs is available for anonymous ftp from ftp.ibp.fr and tsx-11.mit.edu in /pub/linux/packages/ext2fs.

SEE ALSO

dumpe2fs(8), **e2fsck**(8), **mke2fs**(8)

Version 0.5b   November 1994   1173

NAME

tunelp – set various parameters for the lp device

SYNOPSIS

tunelp <*device*> [-i <*IRQ*> | -t <*TIME*> | -c <*CHARS*> | -w <*WAIT*> | -a [on|off] | -o [on|off] | -C [on|off] | -r | -s | -q [on|off]]

DESCRIPTION

tunelp sets several parameters for the /dev/lp? devices, for better performance (or for any performance at all, if your printer won't work without it...) Without parameters, tells whether the device is using interrups, and if so, which one. With parameters, sets the device characteristics accordingly. The parameters are as follows:

-i <*IRQ*> is the IRQ to use for the parallel port in question. If this is set to something non-zero, -t and -c have no effect. If your port does not use interrupts, this option will make printing stop. **tunelp** -i 0 restores non-interrupt driven (polling) action, and your printer should work again. If your parallel port does support interrupts, interrupt-driven printing should be somewhat faster and efficient, and will probably be desireable.

-t <*TIME*> is the amount of time in jiffies that the driver waits if the printer doesn't take a character for the number of tries dictated by the -c parameter. 10 is the default value. If you want fastest possible printing, and don't care about system load, you may set this to 0. If you don't care how fast your printer goes, or are printing text on a slow printer with a buffer, then 500 (5 seconds) should be fine, and will give you very low system load. This value generally should be lower for printing graphics than text, by a factor of approximately 10, for best performance.

-c <*CHARS*> is the number of times to try to output a character to the printer before sleeping for -t <*TIME*>. It is the number of times around a loop that tries to send a character to the printer. 120 appears to be a good value for most printers. 250 is the default, because there are some printers that require a wait this long, but feel free to change this. If you have a very fast printer like an HP laserjet 4, a value of 10 might make more sense. If you have a *really* old printer, you can increase this farther.

Setting -t <*TIME*> to 0 is equivalent to setting -c <*CHARS*> to infinity.

-w <*WAIT*> is the a busy loop counter for the strobe signal. While most printers appear to be able to deal with an extremely short strobe, some printers demand a longer one. Increasing this from the default 0 may make it possible to print with those printers. This may also make it possible to use longer cables.

-a [on|off] This is whether to abort on printer error – the default is not to. If you are sitting at your computer, you probably want to be able to see an error and fix it, and have the printer go on printing. On the other hand, if you aren't, you might rather that your printer spooler find out that the printer isn't ready, quit trying, and send you mail about it. The choice is yours.

-o [on|off] This option is much like -a. It makes any open() of this device check to see that the device is on-line and not reporting any out of paper or other errors. This is the correct setting for most versions of lpd.

-C [on|off] This option adds extra ("careful") error checking. When this option is on, the printer driver will ensure that the printer is on-line and not reporting any out of paper or other errors before sending data. This is particularly useful for printers that normally appear to accept data when turned off.

-s This option returns the current printer status, both as a decimal number from 0..255, and as a list of active flags. When this option is specified, -q off, turning off the display of the current IRQ, is implied.

-o, -C, and -s all require a Linux kernel version of 1.1.76 or later.

-r This option resets the port. It requires a Linux kernel version of 1.1.80 or later.

-q [on|off] This option sets printing the display of the current IRQ setting.

UPDATE_STATE(8) Linux Programmer's Manual UPDATE_STATE(8)

NAME
update_state – update system state

SYNOPSIS
update_state

DESCRIPTION
update_state updates a bunch of system state. It takes a long time to execute, and would be suitable for execution in a cron job.

Currently, **update_state** performs the following functions: updates the locate database (in */usr/lib/locate*), updates the *whatis* database (in */usr/man*, */usr/local/man*, */usr/X386/man*, and */usr/interviews/man*), and updates the TeX ls-R cache file (in */usr/lib/texmf*).

BUGS
The script expects things to be where the FSSTND says they are. example, if you have **makewhatis**(8) in */usr/lib*, where it would be traditionally, then you lose, because it should be in */usr/bin*.

SEE ALSO
cron(8), find(1), locate(1),

AUTHOR
Rik Faith (faith@cs.unc.edu)

uucico(8)

NAME

uucico – UUCP file transfer daemon

SYNOPSIS

uucico [options]

DESCRIPTION

The *uucico* daemon processes file transfer requests queued by *uucp* (1) and *uux* (1). It is started when *uucp* or *uux* is run (unless they are given the **–r** option). It is also typically started periodically using entries in the *crontab* table(s).

When invoked with **–r1, ––master, –s, ––system,** or **–S,** the daemon will place a call to a remote system, running in master mode. Otherwise the daemon will start in slave mode, accepting a call from a remote system. Typically a special login name will be set up for UUCP which automatically invokes *uucico* when a call is made.

When *uucico* terminates, it invokes the *uuxqt* (8) daemon, unless the **–q** or **––nouuxqt** option is given; *uuxqt* (8) executes any work orders created by *uux* (1) on a remote system, and any work orders created locally which have received remote files for which they were waiting.

If a call fails, *uucico* will normally refuse to retry the call until a certain (configurable) amount of time has passed. This may be overriden by the **-f, –force,** or **-S** option.

The **–l, ––prompt, –e,** or **––loop** options may be used to force *uucico* to produce its own prompts of "login: " and "Password:". When another daemon calls in, it will see these prompts and log in as usual. The login name and password will normally be checked against a separate list kept specially for *uucico* rather than the */etc/passwd* file; it is possible on some systems to direct *uucico* to use the */etc/passwd* file. The **–l** or **––prompt** option will prompt once and then exit; in this mode the UUCP administrator or the superuser may use the **–u** or **––login** option to force a login name, in which case *uucico* will not prompt for one. The **–e** or **––loop** option will prompt again after the first session is over; in this mode *uucico* will permanently control a port.

If *uucico* receives a SIGQUIT, SIGTERM or SIGPIPE signal, it will cleanly abort any current conversation with a remote system and exit. If it receives a SIGHUP signal it will abort any current conversation, but will continue to place calls to (if invoked with **–r1** or **––master**) and accept calls from (if invoked with **–e** or **––loop**) other systems. If it receives a SIGINT signal it will finish the current conversation, but will not place or accept any more calls.

OPTIONS

The following options may be given to *uucico*.

–r1, ––master		Start in master mode (call out to a system); implied by **–s, ––system,** or **–S.** If no system is specified, call any system for which work is waiting to be done.
–r0, ––slave		Start in slave mode. This is the default.
–s system, **––system** system		Call the named system.
–S system		Call the named system, ignoring any required wait. This is equivalent to **–s** system **–f**.
–f, ––force		Ignore any required wait for any systems to be called.
–l, ––prompt		Prompt for login name and password using "login: " and "Password:". This allows *uucico* to be easily run from *inetd* (8). The login name and password are checked against the UUCP password file, which probably has no connection to the file */etc/passwd*. The **––login** option may be used to force a login name, in which cause *uucico* will only prompt for a password.
–p port, **––port** port		Specify a port to call out on or to listen to.

uucico(8)   uucico(8)

-e, --loop   Enter endless loop of login/password prompts and slave mode
                       daemon execution. The program will not stop by itself; you
                       must use *kill* (1) to shut it down.

-w, --wait   After calling out (to a particular system when **-s, --system,**
                       or **-S** is specifed, or to all systems which have work when just
                       -r1 or **--master** is specifed), begin an endless loop as with
                       --loop.

-q, --nouuxqt   Do not start the *uuxqt* (8) daemon when finished.

-c, --quiet   If no calls are permitted at this time, then don't make the call,
                       but also do not put an error message in the log file and do not
                       update the system status (as reported by *uustat* (1)). This can
                       be convenient for automated polling scripts, which may want
                       to simply attempt to call every system rather than worry about
                       which particular systems may be called at the moment. This
                       option also suppresses the log message indicating that there is
                       no work to be done.

-C, --ifwork   Only call the system named by **-s, --system** or **-S** if there is
                       work for that system.

-D, --nodetach   Do not detach from the controlling terminal. Normally *uucico*
                       detaches from the terminal before each call out to another sys-
                       tem and before invoking *uuxqt*. This option prevents this.

-u name, **--login** name Set the login name to use instead of that of the invok-
                       ing user. This option may only be used by the UUCP adminis-
                       trator or the superuser. If used with **--prompt,** this will cause
                       uucico to prompt only for the password, not the login name.

-z, --try-next   If a call fails after the remote system is reached, try the next
                       alternate rather than simply exiting.

-i type, **--stdin** type Set the type of port to use when using standard input. The
                       only support port type is TLI, and this is only available on ma-
                       chines which support the TLI networking interface. Specify-
                       ing **-iTLI** causes *uucico* to use TLI calls to perform I/O.

-x type, **-X** type, **--debug** type Turn on particular debugging types. The follow-
                       ing types are recognized: abnormal, chat, handshake, uucp-
                       proto, proto, port, config, spooldir, execute, incoming, outgo-
                       ing.

                       Multiple types may be given, separated by commas, and the
                       --debug option may appear multiple times. A number may
                       also be given, which will turn on that many types from the fore-
                       going list; for example, **--debug** 2 is equivalent to **--debug**
                       abnormal,chat.

                       The debugging output is sent to the debugging file, usually one
                       of /usr/spool/uucp/Debug,
                       /usr/spool/uucp/DEBUG, or /usr/spool/uucp/.Admin/audit.local.

-I file, **--config** file Set configuration file to use. This option may not be avail-
                       able, depending upon how *uucico* was compiled.

-v, --version   Report version information and exit.

--help   Print a help message and exit.

-u login   This option is ignored. It is only included because some ver-
                       sions of uucpd invoke *uucico* with it.

FILES

The file names may be changed at compilation time or by the configuration file, so these are only approximations.

/usr/lib/uucp/config - Configuration file.

/usr/lib/uucp/passwd - Default UUCP password file.
/usr/spool/uucp - UUCP spool directory.
/usr/spool/uucp/Log - UUCP log file.
/usr/spool/uucppublic - Default UUCP public directory.
/usr/spool/uucp/Debug - Debugging file.

SEE ALSO

kill(1), uucp(1), uux(1), uustat(1), uuxqt(8)

AUTHOR

Ian Lance Taylor <ian@airs.com>

NAME

vmstat – Report virtual memory statistics

SYNOPSIS

vmstat [-n] [delay [count]]

DESCRIPTION

vmstat reports information about processes, memory, paging, block IO, traps, and cpu activity.

The first report produced gives averages since the last reboot. Additional reports give information on a sampling period of length *delay*. The process and memory reports are instantaneous in either case.

Options

The *-n* switch causes the header to be displayed only once rather than periodically.

delay is the delay between updates in seconds. If no delay is specified, only one report is printed with the average values since boot.

count is the number of updates. If no count is specified and delay is defined, *count* defaults to infinity.

FIELD DESCRIPTIONS

Procs
r: The number of processes waiting for run time.
b: The number of processes in uninterruptable sleep.
w: The number of processes swapped out but otherwise runnable. This
field is calculated, but Linux never desperation swaps.

Memory
swpd: the amount of virtual memory used (kB).
free: the amount of idle memory (kB).
buff: the amount of memory used as buffers (kB).

Swap
si: Amount of memory swapped in from disk (kB/s).
so: Amount of memory swapped to disk (kB/s).

IO
bi: Blocks sent to a block device (blocks/s).
bo: Blocks received from a block device (blocks/s).

System
in: The number of interrupts per second, including the clock.
cs: The number of context switches per second.

CPU
These are percentages of total CPU time.
us: user time
sy: system time
id: idle time

NOTES

vmstat
does not require special permissions.

These reports are intended to help identify system bottlenecks. Linux **vmstat**
does not count itself as a running process.

All linux blocks are currently 1k, except for CD-ROM blocks which are 2k.

FILES
/proc/meminfo
/proc/stat
/proc/*/stat

SEE ALSO
ps(1), top(1), free(1)

BUGS
Does not tabulate the block io per device or count the number of system calls.

AUTHOR
Written by Henry Ware <al172@yfn.ysu.edu>.

NAME

vipw – edit the password file

SYNOPSIS

vipw

DESCRIPTION

Vipw edits the password file after setting the appropriate locks, and does any necessary processing after the password file is unlocked. If the password file is already locked for editing by another user, vipw will ask you to try again later. The default editor for vipw is vi(1).

ENVIRONMENT

If the following environment variable exists it will be utilized by vipw :

- EDITOR The editor specified by the string
- EDITOR will be invoked instead of the default editor vi(1).

SEE ALSO

passwd(1), vi(1), passwd(5)

HISTORY

The vipw command appeared in BSD 4.0 .

ZDUMP(8)   ZDUMP(8)

NAME

zdump – time zone dumper

SYNOPSIS

zdump [**–v**] [**–c** cutoffyear] [zonename ...]

DESCRIPTION

Zdump prints the current time in each *zonename* named on the command line.

These options are available:

    –v   For each *zonename* on the command line, print the current time, the time at the lowest possible time value, the time one day after the lowest possible time value, the times both one second before and exactly at each detected time discontinuity, the time at one day less than the highest possible time value, and the time at the highest possible time value, Each line ends with **isdst=1** if the given time is Daylight Saving Time or **isdst=0** otherwise.

    –c *cutoffyear*   Cut off the verbose output near the start of the given year.

SEE ALSO

newctime(3), tzfile(5), zic(8)

ZIC(8)

NAME

zic – time zone compiler

SYNOPSIS

zic [**–v**] [**–d** *directory*] [**–l** *localtime*] [**–p** *posixrules*] [**–L** *leapsecondfilename*] [**–s**] [**–y** *command*] [*filename ...*]

DESCRIPTION

Zic reads text from the file(s) named on the command line and creates the time conversion information files specified in this input. If a *filename* is –, the standard input is read.

These options are available:

–d *directory*   Create time conversion information files in the named directory rather than in the standard directory named below.

–l *timezone*   Use the given time zone as local time. *Zic* will act as if the input contained a link line of the form

        Link *timezone* localtime

–p *timezone*   Use the given time zone's rules when handling POSIX-format time zone environment variables. *Zic* will act as if the input contained a link line of the form

        Link *timezone* posixrules

–L *leapsecondfilename*   Read leap second information from the file with the given name. If this option is not used, no leap second information appears in output files.

–v   Complain if a year that appears in a data file is outside the range of years representable by *time*(2) values.

–s   Limit time values stored in output files to values that are the same whether they're taken to be signed or unsigned. You can use this option to generate SVVS-compatible files.

–y *command*   Use the given *command* rather than **yearistype** when checking year types (see below).

Input lines are made up of fields. Fields are separated from one another by any number of white space characters. Leading and trailing white space on input lines is ignored. An unquoted sharp character (#) in the input introduces a comment which extends to the end of the line the sharp character appears on. White space characters and sharp characters may be enclosed in double quotes (") if they're to be used as part of a field. Any line that is blank (after comment stripping) is ignored. Non-blank lines are expected to be of one of three types: rule lines, zone lines, and link lines.

A rule line has the form

Rule NAME FROM TO TYPE IN ON AT SAVE LETTER/S
For example:

Rule US 1967 1973 – Apr lastSun 2:00 1:00 D
The fields that make up a rule line are:

    NAME   Gives the (arbitrary) name of the set of rules this rule is part of.

    FROM   Gives the first year in which the rule applies. Any integer year can be supplied; the Gregorian calendar is assumed. The word **minimum** (or an abbreviation) means the minimum year representable as an integer. The word **maximum** (or an abbreviation) means the maximum year representable as an integer. Rules can describe times that are not representable as time values, with the unrepresentable times ignored;

this allows rules to be portable among hosts with differing time value types.

TO Gives the final year in which the rule applies. In addition to **minimum** and **maximum** (as above), the word **only** (or an abbreviation) may be used to repeat the value of the **FROM** field.

TYPE Gives the type of year in which the rule applies. If **TYPE** is – then the rule applies in all years between **FROM** and **TO** inclusive. If **TYPE** is something else, then *zic* executes the command

yearistype *year type*

to check the type of a year: an exit status of zero is taken to mean that the year is of the given type; an exit status of one is taken to mean that the year is not of the given type.

IN Names the month in which the rule takes effect. Month names may be abbreviated.

ON Gives the day on which the rule takes effect. Recognized forms include: 5 the fifth of the month
lastSun the last Sunday in the month
lastMon the last Monday in the month
Sun>=8 first Sunday on or after the eighth
Sun<=25 last Sunday on or before the 25th
Names of days of the week may be abbreviated or spelled out in full. Note that there must be no spaces within the **ON** field.

AT Gives the time of day at which the rule takes effect. Recognized forms include: 2 time in hours
2:00 time in hours and minutes
15:00 24-hour format time (for times after noon)
1:28:14 time in hours, minutes, and seconds
Any of these forms may be followed by the letter **w** if the given time is local wall clock time, **s** if the given time is local standard time, or **u** (or **g** or **z**) if the given time is universal time; in the absence of an indicator, wall clock time is assumed.

SAVE Gives the amount of time to be added to local standard time when the rule is in effect. This field has the same format as the **AT** field (although, of course, the **w** and **s** suffixes are not used).

LETTER/S Gives the variable part (for example, the S or D in EST or EDT) of time zone abbreviations to be used when this rule is in effect. If this field is –, the variable part is null.

A zone line has the form

Zone NAME GMTOFF RULES/SAVE FORMAT [UNTIL]
For example:

Zone Australia/Adelaide 9:30 Aus CST 1971 Oct 31 2:00
The fields that make up a zone line are:

NAME The name of the time zone. This is the name used in creating the time conversion information file for the zone.

GMTOFF The amount of time to add to GMT to get standard time in this zone. This field has the same format as the **AT** and **SAVE** fields of rule lines; begin the field with a minus sign if time must be subtracted from GMT.

RULES/SAVE The name of the rule(s) that apply in the time zone or, alternately, an amount of time to add to local standard time. If this field is – then standard time always applies in the time zone.

FORMAT The format for time zone abbreviations in this time zone. The pair of characters %s is used to show where the variable part of the time zone abbreviation goes. Alternately, a slash (/) separates standard and daylight abbreviations.

UNTIL The time at which the GMT offset or the rule(s) change for a location. It is specified as a year, a month, a day, and a time of day. If this is specified, the time zone information is generated from the given GMT offset and rule change until the time specified.

The next line must be a continuation line; this has the same form as a zone line except that the string Zone and the name are omitted, as the continuation line will place information starting at the time specified as the **UNTIL** field in the previous line in the file used by the previous line. Continuation lines may contain an **UNTIL** field, just as zone lines do, indicating that the next line is a further continuation.

A link line has the form

Link LINK-FROM LINK-TO
For example:

Link US/Eastern EST5EDT
The **LINK-FROM** field should appear as the **NAME** field in some zone line; the **LINK-TO** field is used as an alternate name for that zone.

Except for continuation lines, lines may appear in any order in the input.

Lines in the file that describes leap seconds have the following form:

Leap YEAR MONTH DAY HH:MM:SS CORR R/S
For example:
Leap 1974 Dec 31 23:59:60 + S
The **YEAR**, **MONTH**, **DAY**, and **HH:MM:SS** fields tell when the leap second happened. The **CORR** field should be + if a second was added or - if a second was skipped. The **R/S** field should be (an abbreviation of) Stationary if the leap second time given by the other fields should be interpreted as GMT or (an abbreviation of) Rolling if the leap second time given by the other fields should be interpreted as local wall clock time.

NOTE

For areas with more than two types of local time, you may need to use local standard time in the **AT** field of the earliest transition time's rule to ensure that the earliest transition time recorded in the compiled file is correct.

FILE

/usr/local/etc/zoneinfo standard directory used for created files

SEE ALSO

newctime(3), tzfile(5), zdump(8)

Section IX
Kernel Reference Guide

NAME

add_timer, del_timer, init_timer – manage event timers

SYNOPSIS

#include <asm/param.h>
#include <linux/timer.h>
extern void add_timer(struct timer_list * *timer*);
extern int del_timer(struct timer_list * *timer*);
extern inline void init_timer(struct timer_list * *timer*);

DESCRIPTION

add_timer schedules an event, adding it to a linked list of events maintained by the kernel.
del_timer deletes a scheduled event. *timer* points to a

struct timer_list {
struct timer_list **next*;
struct timer_list **prev*;
unsigned long *expires*;
unsigned long *data*;
void (**function*)(unsigned *long*);
};

init_timer sets *next* and *prev* to **NULL**. This is required for the argument of **add_timer**. *expires* is the desired duration of the timer in jiffies, where there are **HZ** (typically 100) jiffies per second. When the timer expires, *function* is called with *data* as its argument. It is the responsibility of *function* to delete the event. If the same function is managing several timers, the argument can be used to distinguish which one expired.

RETURN VALUE

del_timer returns zero on error - if *next* or *prev* are not **NULL**, but the timer was not found.
del_timer also sets *expires* to the time remaining before the timer expires, and sets *next* and *prev* to **NULL**. Thus, calling **del_timer** followed immediately by **add_timer** is a no-op provided a kernel tick does not occur between the two calls.

AUTHOR

Linus Torvalds

ADJUST_CLOCK(9)   Kernel Reference Guide   ADJUST_CLOCK(9)

NAME

adjust_clock – Adjusts startup time counter to tick in GMT

SYNOPSIS

linux/kernel/sys.c
void adjust_clock();

DESCRIPTION

This routine adjusts the startup time by adding the time zone information to it. The goal is to get the startup time ticking in GMT time.

NOTES

This routine is called from *settimeofday*(2) when the timezone information is **first** set.

AUTHOR

Ty's Tytso (?)

SEE ALSO

settimeofday(2)

CTRL_ALT_DEL(9)　　　Kernel Reference Guide　　　CTRL_ALT_DEL(9)

NAME

ctrl_alt_del – routes the keyboard interrupt ctrl-alt-del key sequence

SYNOPSIS

linux/kernel/sys.c

void ctrl_alt_del(void);

DESCRIPTION

This simple routine tests the variable C_A_D for a true/false condition. If it is true then a hard reset is done by the system. Otherwise, a signal SIGINT is sent to the process with the process ID 1, usually a program called **init**.

WARNINGS

This routine is in interrupt mode. It can not sync() your system. Data loss may occur. It is recommended that you configure your system to send a signal to **init**, where you can control the shutdown.

NOTES

The default of this function is to do hard resets immediately.

AUTHOR

Linus Torvalds

SEE ALSO

reboot(2), **reset_hard_now**(9), **sync**(2)

NAME

file_table – detailed description of the table and table entry

SYNOPSIS

From #include <linux/fs.h>

struct file {
mode_t f_mode;
dev_t f_rdev; /* needed for /dev/tty */
off_t f_pos;
unsigned short f_flags;
unsigned short f_count;
unsigned short f_reada;
struct file *f_next, *f_prev;
struct inode *f_inode;
struct file_operations *f_op;
}; From linux/fs/file_table.c

struct file *first_file;
int nr_files = 0;

DESCRIPTION

The **file table** is fundamentally important to any UNIX system. It is where all open files (Linux includes closed files as well) are stored and managed by the kernel. For Linux, you can hardly do anything without referencing it in some way.

Linux stores its file table as a *double circular linked list*. The root pointer to the "head" of this list is *first_file*. Also, a count of how many entries are in the file table is maintained, called *nr_files*. Under this scheme, the file table for Linux could be as large memory could hold. Unfortunately, this would be unmanageable in most cases. Your computer would be in the kernel most of the time when processes are more important. To keep this from happening, *nr_files* is tested against *NR_FILE* to limit the number of file table entries.

Understanding the Structure of the File Table

The file table is organized as a *double circular linked list*. Imagine, a circle of people with everyone facing the same direction. Each person is facing so that one arm is in the circle and the other arm is outside the circle. Now, if each person put his or her right hand on the shoulder of the person in front of him or her and if each person touched the person behind him or her with his or her left hand. You have formed two circles of arms, one inside and the other outside. The right arms represent pointers to the *next* entry (or person). The left arms represent pointers to the previous entry (or person).

The file structure, a file table entry

At first glance, a table entry looks quite simple. A entry contains how a file was opened, what tty device, a reference count, pointers to another entries, pointer to v-node (the vfs i-node) and filesystem specific i-node information, etc.

> *f_mode* After "and"ing with O_ACCMODE, this is what bits 0 and 1 mean.
> 00 = no permissions needed
> 01 = read-permission
> 10 = write-permission
> 11 = read-write
>
> *f_rdev* It is only used with tty lines. It contains the major and minor numbers of the tty device.
>
> *f_pos* The current position in a file, if meaningful.
>
> *f_flags* Storage for the flags from open() and fcntl()
>
> *f_count* Reference counter
>
> *f_reada* This is a boolean variable where true means that an actual read is needed.
>
> *f_next, f_prev* Pointers to other entries
>
> *f_inode* Pointer to v-node and fs specific i-node information

FILE_TABLE(9) Kernel Reference Guide FILE_TABLE(9)

f_op Pointer to a file's operations

AUTHOR
Linus Torvalds

SEE ALSO
insert_file_free(9), **remove_file_free**(9), **put_last_free**(9) **grow_files**(9), **file_table_init**(9), **get_empty_filp**(9)

FILE_TABLE_INIT(9)　　　Kernel Reference Guide　　　FILE_TABLE_INIT(9)

NAME

file_table_init – initializes the file table in the kernel

SYNOPSIS

linux/fs/file_table.c unsigned long file_table_init(unsigned long *start*, unsigned long *end*);

DESCRIPTION

This routine is called from *kernel_start*() in linux/init/main.c. It sets *first_file*, a **struct file** pointer, to NULL. This is the head of the linked list of open files maintained in the kernel, the infamous file table in all UNIXs.

RETURN VALUE

Returns *start*

NOTES

Since this is part of the kernel's startup routine, it has the option to allocate memory, in kernel space, for itself. It does not need to do this and returns the *new* start of memory for the next initializing section. In this case, *start* is returned unmodified.

AUTHOR

Linus Torvalds

FILESYSTEMS(9)

NAME

filesystems – details the table of configured file systems

SYNOPSIS

linux/fs/filesystems.c

From #include <linux/fs.h>

```
struct file_system_type {
struct super_block *(*read_super) (struct super_block *, void *, int);
char *name;
int requires_dev;
};
```

DESCRIPTION

This source code makes a data structure call *file_systems*[] which contain all the configured filesystems for the kernel. It is used primarily in linux/fs/super.c for many of the mounting of filesystems functions.

The meanings

This first member, in struct file_system_type, is a function pointer to a routine that will read in the super_block. A super_block generically means an i-node or special place on the device where information about the overall filesystem in stored.

The *name* is just the string representation of the name of a specific filesystem, e.g. "ext2" or "minix".

The final member, int *requires_dev*, is a boolean value. If it is true then the filesystem requires a block device (?). For false, it is unclear what happens but an unnamed device is used, e.g. proc and nfs is this way.

AUTHOR

Linus Torvalds

SEE ALSO

Fill in later.

NAME

get_empty_filp – fetches an unreferenced entry from the file table

SYNOPSIS

linux/fs/file_table.c

struct file *get_empty_filp(void);

DESCRIPTION

This routine will seek out an entry that is not being referenced by any processes. If none are found then it will add new entries to the file table, minimum of *NR_FILE* entries.

NOTES

Due to grow_files(), a whole page of entries is created at one time. This may make more than *NR_FILE* entries. Also when an unreferenced entry is found, it is moved to the "end" of the file table. This heuristic is used to hopefully speed up finding unreferenced entries.

RETURN VALUE

NULL No entries were found and the file table is full.

Returns a pointer to the entry in the file table.

AUTHOR

Linus Torvalds

SEE ALSO

grow_files(9)

NAME

grow_files – adds entries to the file table

SYNOPSIS

linux/fs/file_table.c

void grow_files(void);

DESCRIPTION

This function adds entries to the file table. First, it allocates a page of memory. It fills the entire page with entries, adding each to the file table.

AUTHOR

Linus Torvalds

SEE ALSO

insert_file_free(9), **remove_file_free**(9), **put_last_free**(9)

NAME

in_group_p – searches group IDs for a match

SYNOPSIS

linux/kernel/sys.c

int in_group_p(gid_t *grp*);

DESCRIPTION

Searches supplementary group IDs and the effective group ID for a match with *grp*.

RETURN VALUE

Returns true (1) if found; otherwise, false (0).

AUTHOR

Linus Torvalds

SEE ALSO

getgroups(2), **getgid**(2), **getegid**(2), **setgid**(2), **setregid**(2), **setgroups**(2)

NAME

insert_file_free – adds a file entry into the file table

SYNOPSIS

linux/fs/file_table.c

static void insert_file_free(struct file *file);

DESCRIPTION

This nightmare of pointers adds *file* into the file table with the root pointer at *file*. This is a building block of the file table management.

AUTHOR

Linus Torvalds

SEE ALSO

file_table_init(9), **remove_file_free**(9), **put_last_free**(9)

See **file_table**(9) for details on the file table structure.

NAME

kernel_mktime – convert startup struct mktime into the number of seconds since 00:00:00 January 1, 1970

SYNOPSIS

linux/kernel/mktime.c

long kernel_mktime(struct mktime * time);

DESCRIPTION

This routine is called from time_init(void), linux/init/main.c. kernel_mktime() converts *struct mktime* (initialized from CMOS) into an encoded long.

Conversion Method

First an array, *month[12]*, is created holding how many seconds has passed to reach a peculiar month, for a *leap* year. Next, it subtracts 70 from the current year, making 1970 the beginning year. It is math magic after this point, please look yourself. If you know why it does this, then send email (see nroff source).

RETURN VALUE

Returns the encoded time in a long

FILES

linux/kernel/mktime.c home of routine

NOTES

This routine is call only during startup of the kernel.

Historically, the value (encoded long) counts the number of seconds since the **Epoch**, which occurred at 00:00:00 January 1, 1970 and is called *Coordinated Universal Time (UTC)*. In older manuals, this event is called *Greenwich Mean Time (GMT)*.

WARNINGS

kernel_mktime() doesn't check to see if the year is greater than 1969. Be sure your CMOS is set correctly. It is customary to set on-board clocks to GMT and let processes who ask for the time to convert it to local time, if necessary.

RESTRICTIONS

For kernel use only.

AUTHOR

Linus Torvalds

NAME

proc_sel – select a process by a criteria

SYNOPSIS

linux/kernel/sys.c

#include <linux/resource.h>

static int proc_sel(struct task_struct *p, int *which*, int *who*);

DESCRIPTION

Compares a task *p* to supplied information or the current task in some aspect of priority. If *who* is zero then the comparison is task *p* and the current task. Otherwise, *who* and **p* are the supplied information for the comparison.

OPTIONS

Valid values of *which*:

> PRIO_PROCESS Compares process ID numbers
>
> There is an exception here. If *who* is not zero and task *p* is the current task then true is **always** returned.
>
> PRIO_PGRP Compares process group leader numbers
>
> PRIO_USER Compares user id numbers

RETURN VALUE

Returns truth values (0, 1)

AUTHOR

Linus Torvalds

ALSO SEE

sys_setpriority(2), **sys_getpriority**(2)

NAME

put_file_last – moves a file to the "end" of the file table

SYNOPSIS

linux/fs/file_table.c

static void put_last_free(struct file *file*);

DESCRIPTION

This function will remove *file* from the file table and insert it again at the "end". You can access by:

first_file->prev

AUTHOR

Linus Torvalds

SEE ALSO

insert_file_free(9), **remove_file_free**(9)

NAME

remove_file_free – remove a file table entry from the linked list

SYNOPSIS

linux/fs/file_table.c

static void remove_file_free(struct file **file*);

DESCRIPTION

This routine removes the *file* from the table. This is used mostly for moving a file to the "end" of the list.

AUTHOR

Linus Torvalds

SEE ALSO

insert_file_free(9), **put_file_last**(9)

Index

/dev/hd?, 906
/dev/null, 910
/dev/sd?, 912
/dev/st?, 913
/dev/tty?, 918
/dev/ttyS[0-3], 919
/etc/DEVINFO, 925
/etc/adduser.conf, 923
/etc/fstab, 955
/etc/group, 937
/etc/hosts, 213
/etc/inittab, 946
/etc/issue, 951
/etc/modules, 953
/etc/motd, 954
/etc/nologin, 958
/etc/resolv.conf, 966
/etc/securetty, 967
/etc/shells, 968
/etc/termcap, 971
/etc/utmp, 983
/etc/wtmp, 983
/etd/passwd, 959
/proc, 960
_exit, 512
_llseek, 568, 569

abort, 679
abs, 680
absolute pathname, 824
accept, 513
access, 514
access control
    file format, 938
    language extensions, 943
    library, 769
acct, 515
acos, 681
acosh, 682
add_timer, 1188
addftinfo, 9
addgroup, 1037
addmntent, 753
address resolution protocol, 1042
adduser, 1037
    configuration file, 923
adduser.conf, 923
adjtimex, 516
adjust_clock, 1189
afmtodit, 10
afs_syscall, 665
agetty, 1039
alarm, 518
aliases, 924
alloca, 683
alphasort, 830
appres, 12

ar, 13
arch, 16
archive manipulation, 13
arp, 1042
as, 17
ascii, 1001
asctime, 711, 801
asin, 684
asinh, 685
assert, 686
atan, 687
atan2, 688
atanh, 689
atexit, 690
atof, 691
atoi, 692
atol, 693
awk, 127

badblocks, 1043
banner, 997
bash, 19
bcmp, 694
bcopy, 695
bdflush, 519
bibliographic databases
    make index, 149
    search, 150, 231
biff, 58
biff server, 1050
binary search, 696
bind, 520
bit bucket, 910
break, 665
brk, 521
bsearch, 696
bstring, 697
buffer cache
    write to disk, 519, 651
buffer-dirty-flush daemon, 519
byte strings
    comparing, 694
    copying, 695
    operations on, 697
    writing zeros to, 699
byteorder, 698
bzero, 699

C
    preprocessor interface to make, 214
cal, 59
calendar, 59
calloc, 786
capture terminal session, 321
cat, 60
catclose, 701
catgets, 700

1203

INDEX()

catopen, 701
ceil, 702
cfdisk, 1044
cfgetispeed, 655
cfgetospeed, 655
cfsetispeed, 655
cfsetospeed, 655
character
    find number of bytes, 787
character classification, 776
character set
    ASCII, 1001
    ISO 8859-1, 1018
chattr, 61
chdir, 522
chfn, 62
chgrp, 63
chkdupexe, 64
chmod, 65, 523
chown, 66, 525
chroot, 526, 1048
chsh, 67
cksum, 70
clear, 71
clearerr, 726
clock, 703, 1049
    manipulate, 1049
clone, 527
close, 528
closedir, 704
closelog, 879
col, 72
colcrt, 73
colrm, 74
column, 75
comm, 76
command
    locate source, 403
command line, reading options, 147, 755
compare
    byte strings, 694
    memory areas, 792
    sorted files, 76
    strings, 851, 854
comparison
    compressed files, 503
computer infinity, 774
comsat, 1050
confstr, 705
connect, 529
console, 897
console ioctl's, 898
console terminal, 897, 898
conversion
    string to long integer, 873
    double to string, 718
    floating-point to integer plus fraction, 739
    floating-point to string, 744
    groff to TeX dvi, 170
    host to network byte order, 698
    lower to upper case, 888
    multibyte character wide character, 789
    multibyte string to wide character string, 788
    network to host byte order, 698
    object code to NLM, 270
    pathname to IPC key, 742
    string to double, 871
    string to double, 691
    string to integer, 692
    string to long integer, 693, 874
    time, 801, 803, 890
    time format, 711
    upper to lower case, 888
    wide character string to multibyte character string, 893
    wide character to multibyte character, 894
copy
    files, 77
copysign, 706
cos, 707
cosh, 708
cp, 77
creat, 592
create session, 622, 1149
create_module, 577
crond, 1051
crontab, 79
crypt, 709
csplit, 81
ctags, 68
ctermid, 710
ctime, 711, 801
ctrl-alt-del, 1190
ctrlaltdel, 1052
cu, 83
cut, 86
Cyclades driver tuner, 1053
cytune, 1053

daemon
    execute scheduled commands, 79, 1051
    ftp, 1072
    internet services, 439
    kernel logging, 1085
    logged in user info, 1132
    monitor UPS, 1118
    network routing, 1129
    NFS mount, 1108
    printer, 1089
    remote execution, 1123
    remote login, 1125
    remote shell, 1135
    remote user communication, 1164
    system status, 1137
    telnet, 1165
    time server, 1167
    trivial file transfer protocol, 1166

INDEX()

UUCP execution, 398
UUCP file transfer, 1176
write messages to users, 1133
data encryption, 709
data segment
  resizing, 521
data sink, 910
database
  find files, 234
date, 87
  conversion to Discordian, 998
dd, 89
ddate, 998
debug
  filesystem, 1055
  tag files, 68
debugfs, 1055
del_timer, 1188
delete_module, 577
depmod, 90
descriptor table size, 539
development tools
  assembler, 17
  convert object code to NLM, 270
  copy/translate object files, 273
  display info on object files, 275
  generate archive index, 292
  library archiver, 13
  link editor, 225
  list object file symbols, 271
  list object section size, 332
  make, 249
  print strings, 337
  strip symbols from object files, 338
device
  control, 560
  create, 592, 1092, 1093
  database, 925
  floppy disk, 903
  hard disk, 906
  line printer, 907
  memory, 909
  ramdisk, 911
  SCSI disk, 912
  SCSI tape, 913
  search for bad blocks, 1043
  setup, 624
  swap, 648, 1101
  terminal, 918
device file
  create, 572
DEVINFO, 925
df, 93
dialup IP, 1057
difftime, 713, 801
dip, 1057
dir, 245
directory
  change working, 522
  changing root, 526, 1048
  closing, 704

create, 258, 570, 572
create lost+found, 1100
delete, 607
get stream location, 884
get current working, 745
get entries, 537, 746
list contents, 245
open, 807
read, 822
read entry, 600
reposition stream pointer, 834
scan for matches, 830
shadow, 233
stream reset, 828
disk
  partition manipulator, 1044, 1066
div, 714
dmesg, 1061
dn_comp, 826
dnsdomainname, 213
domain name
  get, 538
  set, 538
domainname, 94
drand48, 715
drem, 717
dsplit, 95
du, 96
dumpe2fs, 1062
dup, 530
dup2, 530

e2fsck, 1063
ecvt, 718
editres, 97
egrep, 167
electronic mail, 1139
electronic mail addresses, 1023
elvis, 103
  crash protection, 105
  crash recovery, 106
elvprsv, 105
elvrec, 106
endgrent, 748
endhostent, 751
endmntent, 753
endnetent, 754
endprotoent, 759
endpwent, 761
endservent, 764
endusershell, 765
endutent, 766
environ, 927
environment
  change, 815, 837
erand48, 715
erf, 719
erfc, 719
event timer, 1188
ex, 103
execl, 720

1205

INDEX()

execle, 720
execlp, 720
exect, 720
executable file
  compression, 207
execute
  command lines, 406
execution profiling, 157
execution time profile, 597
execv, 720
execve, 531
execvp, 720
exit, 722
exp, 723
expand, 107
exports, 928

fabs, 724
fchdir, 522
fchmod, 523
fchown, 525
fclose, 725
fcntl, 532
fcvt, 718
fd, 903
fdformat, 1065
fdisk, 1044, 1066
fdopen, 734
feof, 726
ferror, 726
fflush, 727
ffs, 728
fgetc, 763
fgetgrent, 729
fgetpos, 740
fgetpwent, 730
fgets, 763
fgrep, 167
FIFO
  create, 260
file
  change name, 605
  change owner, 525
  checksum, 70
  close stream, 725
  closing, 528
  comparison, 76
  compression
    force .gz extension, 504
    search, 505
    view, 506
  compression/expansion, 202
  concatenation, 60
  copy, 77
  count bytes, 70
  create, 592
  create link, 566
  create temporary, 798, 799, 885–887
  creation mask, 662
  display selected lines, 238
  duplicate descriptor, 530

INDEX()

execution, 720
flush stream, 727
get configuration value, 736
issue identification, 951
list attributes, 247
locking, 534
manipulate descriptor, 532
match name, 733
navigation, 743
password, 959
permissions, 514, 523
print to screen, 60
read, 599
remote copy, 293
remote distribution, 294
remove link, 666, 825
reposition read/write offset, 568, 569
reverse lines, 301
splitter, 95
status, 643
stream error, 726
stream input/output, 738
stream open, 734
stream repositioning, 740
suffixes, 1029
swap, 648
symbolic link, 649
truncate, 661
underlining, 384
viewer, 262
write to, 675
file name database
  update, 387
file table, 1196
file transfer program, 118
  trivial, 354
file tree walk, 743
file utilities
  change access permissions, 65
  change group, 63
  change owner, 66
  change timestamp, 360
  convert and copy, 89
  copy, 77
  copy files, set attributes, 219
  disk summary, 93, 96
  find file, 108
  link files, 232
  list directory, 245
  make FIFOs, 260
  make special files, 261
  make directories, 258
  remove, 304
  remove directory, 305
  rename, 264
file_table, 1191, 1198
file_table_init, 1193
fileno, 726
filesystem
  change attributes, 61
  check, 1063

1206

check and repair, 1068
consistency check, 1070
create, 1097–1099
data, 1194
debugger, 1055
dump information, 1062
flush buffers, 1159
get statistics, 645
get/set descriptor file entry, 753
information, 930
mount and unmount, 579, 1103
process information, 960
setup, 624
tune, 1173
filter
    display files in dump format, 209, 278
find, 108
    character in string, 772
    duplicate executables, 64
    files to match pattern, 234
    pathnames matching pattern, 767
find first bit set, 728
finger
    change information, 62
finite, 778
flock, 534
floor, 731
floppy disk
    low level format, 1065
floppy disk drive, 903
fmod, 732
fmt, 114, 115
fnmatch, 733
fold, 116
follow a pathname, 265
fopen, 734
fork, 535
fpathconf, 736
fprintf, 810
fpurge, 727
fputc, 817
fputs, 817
fread, 738
free, 117, 786
freopen, 734
frexp, 739
fscanf, 831
fsck, 1068
fsck.minix, 1070
fseek, 740
fsetpos, 740
fstab, 930, 955
fstat, 643
fstatfs, 645
fsync, 536
ftell, 740
ftime, 741
ftok, 742
ftp, 118
ftpd, 1072

ftruncate, 661
ftw, 743
fuser, 126
fwrite, 738

gas, 17
gawk, 127
gcvt, 744
geqn, 141
get
    characters and strings, 763
    configuration info, 877
    date and time, 87, 741
    directory location, 884
    domain name, 94, 213
    file status, 643
    filesystem statistics, 645
    host id, 212
    host name, 213
    kernel information, 663
    local descriptor table, 576
    message queue identifier, 585
    numeric formatting information, 784
    process group, 619
    semaphore set identifier, 612
    serial port info, 1144
    service entry, 764
    shared memory segment, 627
    terminal attributes, 655
    terminal name, 889
    time, 659
    user identity, 558
    utmp file entries, 766
get environment variable, 747
get_current_dir_name, 745
get_empty_filp, 1195
get_kernel_syms, 577
getc, 763
getchar, 763
getcwd, 745
getdents, 537
getdirentries, 746
getdomainname, 538
getdtablesize, 539
getegid, 540
getenv, 747
geteuid, 558
getgid, 540
getgrent, 748
getgrgid, 750
getgrnam, 750
getgroups, 541
gethostbyaddr, 751
gethostbyname, 751
gethostid, 542
gethostname, 543
getitimer, 544
getmntent, 753
getnetbyaddr, 754
getnetbyname, 754
getnetent, 754

1207

getopt, 147, 755
getpagesize, 546
getpass, 758
getpeername, 547
getpgid, 619
getpgrp, 619
getpid, 548
getppid, 548
getpriority, 549
getprotobyname, 759
getprotobynumber, 759
getprotoent, 759
getpw, 760
getpwent, 761
getpwnam, 762
getpwuid, 762
getrlimit, 550
getrusage, 550
gets, 763
getservbyname, 764
getservbyport, 764
getservent, 764
getsockname, 552
getsockopt, 553
gettimeofday, 556
getty
    alternate, 1039
getuid, 558
getusershell, 765
getutent, 766
getutid, 766
getutline, 766
getwd, 745
gindxbib, 149
glob, 767
globfree, 767
glookbib, 150
gmake, 249
gmtime, 711, 801
gnroff, 151
GNU, 89
    archive indexer, 292
    archiver, 13
    assembler, 17
    Bourne–Again SHell, 19
    change file access, 65
    change file owner, 66
    change group, 63
    checksum, 70, 340
    date, 87
    directory lister, 245
    directory maker, 258
    directory remover, 305
    disk space summarizer, 93
    disk usage summarizer, 96
    duplicate line remover, 386
    FIFO maker, 260
    file comparison, 76
    file concatenater, 60
    file copier, 77
    file cutter, 86
    file dumper, 278
    file expander, 107
    file finder, 108
    file head display, 208
    file joiner, 220
    file linker, 232
    file mover, 264
    file paster, 282
    file remover, 304
    file sorter, 333
    file splitter, 81, 335
    file stripper, 338
    file tail display, 345
    inode maker, 261
    line numberer, 268
    linker, 225
    list object section size, 332
    object code to NLM converter, 270
    object file copier/translator, 273
    object file dumper, 275
    object symbol lister, 271
    profiler, 157
    reverse printer, 344
    string printer, 337
    text file printer, 284
    text folder, 116
    text formatter, 114
    touch, 360
    translator filter, 361
    unexpand, 385
    word counter, 402
gpic, 152
gprof, 157
grefer, 159
grep, 167
grodvi, 170
groff, 172
    add font info, 9
    create font files, 10, 353
    font description, 932
    format tables, 186
    front end, 172
    guess options, 176
    intermediate output format, 935
    interpret .so requests, 185
    mm macros, 1006
    ms macros, 1013
    PostScript driver, 177
    preprocess bibliographic references, 159
    tty driver, 183
groff_font, 932
groff_me, 1003
groff_mm, 1006
groff_ms, 1013
groff_out, 935
grog, 176
grops, 177
grotty, 183
group, 937
    change, 63

1208

INDEX()

        get file entry, 729, 748, 750
        get identity, 540
        get/set access list, 541
        initialize access list, 775
        login to, 267
        set ID in process, 620
        set identity, 618
grow_files, 1196
gsoelim, 185
gtbl, 186
gtroff, 188
gtty, 665
gunzip, 202
gzexe, 207
gzip, 202

hard drive, 906
hash table management, 770
hasmntopt, 753
hcreate, 770
hd, 906
hdestroy, 770
head, 208
herror, 751
hexdump, 209
host
        get network entry, 751
        get/set identifier, 542
        get/set name, 543
host name
        get or set, 213
hostid, 212
hostname, 213
hosts_access, 769, 938
hosts_ctl, 769
hosts_options, 943
hsearch, 770
htonl, 698
htons, 698
hypot, 771

I/O
        change privilege level, 562
        set port permissions, 561
idle, 559
ifconfig, 1075
imake, 214
in_group_p, 1197
index, 772
inet_addr, 773
inet_lnaof, 773
inet_makeaddr, 773
inet_netof, 773
inet_network, 773
inet_ntoa, 773
infnan, 774
init, 1079, 1153
init_module, 577
init_timer, 1188
initgroups, 775
initstate, 821

inittab, 946
inode
        change access time, 668
        create, 261
input, 103
insert_file_free, 1198
insmod, 217
install, 219
internet
        address manipulation, 773
        resolver, 826
        services daemon, 439
interprocess communication, 563, 948
interval timer, 544
intro
        administration(section 8), 1036
        file formats(section 5), 922
        games(section 6), 996
        library functions(section 3), 678
        miscellany(section 7), 1000
        special files(section 4), 896
        system calls(section 2), 510
        user commands(section 1), 8
ioctl, 560
ioperm, 561
iopl, 562
ipc, 563, 948
        provide information, 1083
        remove, 1082
ipcrm, 1082
ipcs, 1083
isalnum, 776
isalpha, 776
isatty, 777
iscntrl, 776
isdigit, 776
isgraph, 776
isinf, 778
islower, 776
isnan, 778
iso_8859_1, 1018
isprint, 776
ispunct, 776
isspace, 776
issue, 951
isupper, 776
isxdigit, 776

j0, 749
j1, 749
jn, 749
join, 220
jrand48, 715
jump to stack context, 785

kbdrate, 1084
kernel
        clock, 516, 1189
        get information, 663
        loadable module support, 577
        log daemon, 1085

modules, 953
print messages, 1061
read messages, 653
show exported symbols, 223
kernel_mktime, 1199
keyboard
reset rate, 1084
keyboard interrupt, 1190
kill, 221, 564
killall, 222
killpg, 565, 779
klogd, 1085
kmem, 909
ksyms, 223

labs, 780
language
pattern scanning and processing, 127
last, 224
lcong48, 715
ld, 225
ldexp, 781
ldiv, 782
lgamma, 783
link, 566
listen, 567
lkbib, 231
ln, 232
lndir, 233
locale, 1021
localeconv, 784
localtime, 711, 801
locate, 234
lock, 665
log, 723
log10, 723
logger, 235
login, 236
show last login, 224
login records, 983
login shell
change, 67
pathnames, 968
longjmp, 785
look, 238
lp, 907
lpc, 1087
lpd, 1089
lpq, 239
lpr, 240
lprm, 242
lptest, 244
ls, 245
lsattr, 247
lsmod, 248
lstat, 643

magic cookie, 255
mail
notification, 58
mail aliases

rebuild database, 266
mailaddr, 1023
make, 249
create dependencies, 252
directory hierarchy, 259
generate Makefile, 454
makedepend, 252
MAKEDEV, 1092, 1093
MAKEDEV.cfg, 952
malloc, 786
man, 1025
macros, 1025
math function
Bessel function, 749
arc cosine, 681
arc sine, 684
arc tangent, 687
copy sign, 706
cosine, 707
error function, 719
Euclidean distance, 771
exponential, 723
float times integral power of 2, 781
floating-point absolute value, 724
floating-point remainder, 717, 732, 800
hyperbolic cosine, 708
hyperbolic sine, 843
hyperbolic tangent, 883
integer absolute value, 680
integer division, 714
integer rounding, 829
inverse hyperbolic cosine, 682
inverse hyperbolic sine, 685
inverse hyperbolic tangent, 689
largest integer, 731
log gamma function, 783
logarithm, 723
long integer absolute value, 780
long integer division, 782
random number generator, 715, 820, 821
sine, 842
square root, 845
tangent, 882
test for infinity, 778
two variable arc tangent, 688
math functions
ceiling, 702
mblen, 787
mbstowcs, 788
mbtowc, 789
mcookie, 255
MD5 message digests
check, 256
generate, 256
md5sum, 256
mem, 909
memccpy, 790
memchr, 791
memcmp, 792

1210

INDEX()

memcpy, 793
memfrob, 794
memmem, 795
memmove, 796
memory
    access to physical, 595
    allocation, 683, 786
    compare, 792
    copy, 790, 793, 796
    display amount free, 117
    encryption, 794
    fill, 797
    kernel, 909
    locate substring, 795
    mapping files/devices, 574
    protect access, 581
    scan for a character, 791
    statistics, 1179
    system, 909
memset, 797
mesg, 257
message
    block, 257
    send to user, 405
message catalog
    closing, 701
    getting message from, 700
    opening, 701
message of the day, 954
message queue
    control operations, 583
    get identifier, 585
    operations, 587
mkdir, 258, 570
mkdirhier, 259
mkefs, 1097
mkfifo, 260
mkfs, 1098, 1099
mklost+found, 1100
mknod, 261, 572
mkstemp, 798
mkswap, 1101
mktemp, 799
mktime, 711, 801
mmap, 574
modf, 800
modify_ldt, 576
modprobe, 90
module
    handle automatically, 90
    install, 217
    show loaded, 248
    unload, 306
modules, 953
more, 262
motd, 954
mount, 579, 1103
mount root filesystem, 624
mountd, 1108
mprotect, 581
mpx, 665

INDEX()

msgctl, 583
msgget, 585
msgop, 587
multi-language support, 1021
multiple buffer I/O, 823
munmap, 574
mv, 264

namei, 265
NaN(not-a-number), 774, 778
netstat, 1109
Netware Locatable Module, 270
network
    display active connections, 1109
    get/set entry, 754
network file system, 955
network host entry, 751
network interface
    attach serial line, 1156
    attach to serial line, 1155
    configure, 1075
network packet
    trace route, 1170
newaliases, 266
newgrp, 267
newtzset, 803
NFS
    export filesystems, 928
    mount daemon, 1108
    show mount information, 1150
nfs, 955
nice, 590
nl, 268
nlmconv, 270
nm, 271
nologin, 958
nrand48, 715
nroff
    emulation, 151
ntohl, 698
ntohs, 698
null, 910

objcopy, 273
objdump, 275
object file
    list symbols, 271
obsolete system calls, 591
od, 278
on_exit, 806
open, 592
opendir, 807
openlog, 879

pac, 1114
packet internet groper, 1116
page
    get size, 546
passwd, 281, 959
password
    change, 281

1211

INDEX() INDEX()

    edit file, 1181
    encryption, 709
    file, 959
    get, 758
    get file entry, 730, 761, 762
    reconstruct entry, 760
    write entry, 816
paste, 282
pathconf, 736
pattern matching, 167
pause, 594
pclose, 809
peer, get name, 547
perror, 808
personality, 664
pfbtops, 283
phys, 595
ping, 1116
pipe, 596
    close, 809
    create, 596
    open, 809
PLIP
    fine tune device parameters, 1115
plipconfig, 1115
popen, 809
port, 909
PostScript
    extract bounding box, 289
pow, 723
powerd, 1118
pr, 284
print
    banner, 997
    characters and strings, 817
    formatted output, 810
    kernel ring buffer, 1061
    lines matching pattern, 167
    machine architecture, 16
    signal message, 814
    system error message, 808
printer, 907
    accounting, 1114
    control program, 1087
    daemon, 1089
    list queue, 239
    program, 240
    remove jobs from queue, 242
    set parameters, 1174
    test, 244
printf, 810
proc, 960
proc_sel, 1200
process
    accounting, 515
    change priority, 590, 1122
    creation, 527, 535
    debug, 598
    display, 357
    display tree, 290
    get identification, 548

    get times, 660
    I/O, 809
    identification, 126
    information filesystem, 960
    kill, 222
    select by criteria, 1200
    send signal, 564
    set group ID, 620–622
    set/get group, 619
    signal group, 565, 779
    suspend execution, 844, 892
    swapper, 559
    termination, 221, 512
    wait for termination, 671, 673
process control initialization, 1079, 1153
process status, 286
processor time determination, 703
prof, 665
profil, 597
program
    debug, 686
    execute, 531
    function called at termination, 690, 806
    get/set scheduling priority, 549
    termination, 722
protocol entry
    get/set, 759
ps, 286
ps database
    update, 291
psbb, 289
psignal, 814
pstree, 290
psupdate, 291
ptrace, 598
put_file_last, 1201
putc, 817
putchar, 817
putenv, 815
putpwent, 816
puts, 817
pututline, 766

qsort, 818
quicksort, 818
quotactl, 665

raise, 819
ram, 911
ram disk, 911
rand, 820
random, 821
ranlib, 292
rarp, 1119
RARP table
    maintenance, 1119
rcp, 293
rdev, 1120
rdist, 294
read, 599

1212

INDEX()

formatted input, 831
readdir, 600, 822
readlink, 601
readv, 823
realloc, 786
realpath, 824
reboot, 602, 1052
reconfig, 297
recv, 603
recvfrom, 603
recvmsg, 603
remote login, 302
remote procedure call, 307
remote shell, 310
remote start client, 311
remote start rsh helper, 313
remote status display, 317
remove, 825
remove_file_free, 1202
rename, 605
renice, 1122
res_init, 826
res_mkquery, 826
res_query, 826
res_querydomain, 826
res_search, 826
res_send, 826
reset, 300, 364
resolver, 966
resource
    get/set limits, 550
rev, 301
rewind, 740
rewinddir, 828
rexecd, 1123
rindex, 772
rint, 829
rlogin, 302
rlogind, 1125
rm, 304
rmdir, 305, 607
rmmod, 306
root
    login, 967
route, 1127
routed, 1129
routing table
    show/manipulate, 1127
RPC
    protocol compiler, 307
    report information, 1134
rpc.rusersd, 1132
rpc.rwalld, 1133
rpcgen, 307
rpcinfo, 1134
rsh, 310
rshd, 1135
rstart, 311
rstartd, 313
rup, 317
rusers, 318

INDEX()

rwall, 319
rwho, 320
rwhod, 1137

save stack context, 838
sbrk, 521
scandir, 830
scanf, 831
scheduled program execution, 79, 1051
script, 321
SCSI disk drive, 912
SCSI tape drive, 913
sd, 912
securetty, 967
sed, 322
seed48, 715
seekdir, 834
select, 608
semaphore
    control, 610
    get identifier, 612
    operations, 614
semctl, 610
semget, 612
semop, 614
send, 616
    mail over the internet, 1139
sendmail, 1139
    aliases, 924
sendmsg, 616
sendto, 616
serial port
    get/set information, 1144
service
    get/set entry, 764
set
    current locale, 839
    date and time, 87
    devices, 1120
    domain name, 94, 213
    environment variable, 837
    file creation mask, 662
    floppy disk parameters, 1143
    group ID, 620, 622
    host id, 212
    host name, 213
    I/O port permissions, 561
    local descriptor table, 576
    process group, 619
    serial port info, 1144
    service entry, 764
    terminal attributes, 329, 655
    time, 647
    user ID, 621, 623
    utmp file entries, 766
setbuf, 835
setbuffer, 835
setdomainname, 538
setegid, 620
setenv, 837
seteuid, 621

INDEX()

setfdprm, 1143
setfsgid, 664
setfsuid, 664
setgid, 618
setgrent, 748
setgroups, 541
sethostent, 751
sethostid, 542
sethostname, 543
setitimer, 544
setjmp, 838
setlinebuf, 835
setlocale, 839
setmntent, 753
setnetent, 754
setpgid, 619
setpgrp, 619
setpriority, 549
setprotoent, 759
setpwent, 761
setregid, 620
setreuid, 621
setrlimit, 550
setserial, 1144
setservent, 764
setsid, 622, 1149
setsockopt, 553
setstate, 821
setterm, 329
settimeofdaye, 556
setuid, 623
setup, 624
setusershell, 765
setutent, 766
setvbuf, 835
shared library
    select, 667
shared memory
    allocation, 627
    control, 625
    operations, 630
shell, 19
    set/get, 765
shell command
    execute, 881
shells, 968
shmctl, 625
shmget, 627
shmop, 630
showmount, 1150
showrgb, 331
shutdown, 632, 1151
sigaction, 633
sigaddset, 841
sigblock, 636
sigdelset, 841
sigemptyset, 841
sigfillset, 841
siggetmask, 664
siginterrupt, 840
sigismember, 841

INDEX()

sigmask, 636
signal, 635
    alarm, 518
    atomically release, 637
    block, 636
    handling, 633
    in string format, 868
    interrupt system call, 840
    list, 1028
    print message, 814
    process group, 565, 779
    send, 564, 819
    software facilities, 638
    wait for, 594
signal set
    operations, 841
sigpause, 637
sigpending, 633
sigprocmask, 633
sigreturn, 664
sigsetmask, 664
sigsuspend, 633
sigvec, 638
simpleinit, 1153
sin, 842
sinh, 843
size, 332
slattach, 1155
sleep, 844
sliplogin, 1156
socket, 639
    accepting connections on, 513
    binding names to, 520
    get name, 552
    get/set options, 553
    initiatiating connection to, 529
    listen for connections, 567
    receive message from, 603
    send message from, 616
    shut down, 632
    system calls, 641
socketcall, 641
socketpair, 642
sockets
    create pair, 642
sort, 333
split, 335
sprintf, 810
sqrt, 845
srand, 820
srand48, 715
srandom, 821
sscanf, 831
st, 913
standard input/output, 848
startx, 336
stat, 643
statfs, 645
stdarg, 846
stdio, 848
stime, 647

INDEX()

strcasecmp, 851
strcat, 852
strchr, 853
strcmp, 854
strcoll, 855
strcpy, 856
strcspn, 869
strdup, 857
stream buffering, 835
strerror, 858
strfry, 859
strftime, 860
string, 862
    calculate length, 863
    character search, 864, 869
    comparison, 851, 854, 855
    concatenate, 852
    convert to double, 871
    convert to long integer, 874
    convert to long integer, 873
    copy, 856, 857
    date and time, 860, 865
    error code, 858
    extract token, 867, 872
    find character, 772
    getting configuration dependent, 705
    locate character in, 853
    locate substring, 795
    operations, 862
    randomize, 859
    signal description, 868
    substring search, 870
    swap adjacent bytes, 876
    transformation, 875
    wide character to multibyte character, 893
strings, 337
strip, 338
strlen, 863
strncasecmp, 851
strncat, 852
strncmp, 854
strncpy, 856
strpbrk, 864
strptime, 865
strrchr, 853
strsep, 867
strsignal, 868
strspn, 869
strstr, 870
strtod, 871
strtok, 872
strtol, 873
strtoul, 874
strxfrm, 875
stty, 665
suffixes, 1029
sum, 340
SuperProbe, 341
swab, 876
swap area

setup, 1101
swapoff, 648, 1158
swapon, 648, 1158
swapping
    enable/disable, 1158
symbolic link
    read value, 601
symlink, 649
sync, 651, 1159
synchronize files in memory and on disk, 536
synchronous I/O multiplexing, 608
sysconf, 877
sysfs, 664
sysinfo, 652
sysklogd, 1160
syslog, 653, 879
syslog.conf, 969
syslogd, 969, 1163
system, 881
    add user, group, 1037
    ARP cache, 1042
    load average, 356
    log, 235
    logging, 653, 879, 969
    logging utilities, 1160, 1163
    ports, 909
    shutdown, 1151
    statistics, 652
    update state, 1175
    uptime, 388

tac, 344
tail, 345
talk, 346
talkd, 1164
tan, 882
tanh, 883
tcdrain, 655
tcflow, 655
tcflush, 655
tcgetattr, 655
tcgetpgrp, 655
tcsendbreak, 655
tcsetattr, 655
tcsetpgrp, 655
telinit, 1079
telldir, 884
telnet, 347
telnetd, 1165
tempnam, 885
termcap, 971
terminal
    capture session, 321
    clear screen, 71
    control operations, 655
    database of capabilities, 971
    descriptor, 777
    device, 918
    get name, 889
    getting name, 710

1215

INDEX()

hangup, 669
initialization, 364
name and device list, 980
reset, 300
set attributes, 329
termios, 655
TeX
    pictures, 152
text
    format, 115
    processing, 127
text filter
    columnate lists, 75
    nroff output, 73
    remove columns from a file, 74
    remove reverse line feeds, 72
text utiliites
    checksum, 340
text utilites
    context split, 81
    paste files, 282
    sort files, 333
    translate characters, 361
text utilities
    checksum, 70
    convert for printing, 284
    convert spaces to tabs, 385
    convert tabs to spaces, 107
    count words, 402
    cut files, 86
    dump files, 278
    file comparison, 76
    file concatenation, 60
    format, 114
    join file lines, 220
    number file lines, 268
    remove duplicate lines, 386
    reverse print, 344
    show file head, 208
    show file tail, 345
    split file, 335
    wrap text, 116
text utils
    stream-oriented editor, 322
tfmtodit, 353
tftp, 354
tftpd, 1166
time
    calculate difference, 713
    conversion, 890
    convert, 801, 803
    formatted, 860
    get, 659
    get/set, 556
    server, 1167
    set, 647
    show, 703, 741
time zone
    compiler, 1183
    dumper, 1182
time zone information, 981

timed, 1167
    control program, 1169
timedc, 1169
times, 660
tload, 356
tmpfile, 886
tmpnam, 887
tolower, 888
top, 357
topological sort, 367
touch, 360
toupper, 888
tr, 361
trace process, 598
TRACEROUTE, 1170
traceroute, 1170
translate
    Postscript font to ASCII, 283
troff
    equation formatting, 141
    macros for formatting papers, 1003
    pictures, 152
truncate, 661
tset, 364
tsort, 367
tty, 918
ttynam, 889
ttys, 919
ttytype, 980
tune2fs, 1173
tunelp, 1174
twm, 368
tzfile, 981
tzset, 803, 890

ul, 384
umask, 662
umount, 579, 1103
uname, 663
undocumented system calls, 664
unexpand, 385
ungetc, 763
Unicode, 1018
unimplemented system calls, 665
uniq, 386
Unix to Unix copy, 389
unlink, 666
update_state, 1175
updatedb, 387
UPS
    monitor, 1118
uptime, 388
uselib, 667
user environment, 927
user ID
    set, 621, 623
users
    communication, 346
    network chatting, 499
    send message to, 319
    spying on, 318, 320, 400

INDEX()

usleep, 892
ustat, 665
utime, 668
utimes, 668
utmp, 983
    access file entries, 766
utmpname, 766
uucico, 1176
UUCP, 389
    call unix system, 83
    execution daemon, 398
    file transfer daemon, 1176
    remote command execution, 395
    status inquiry and control, 391
uucp, 389
uustat, 391
uux, 395
uuxqt, 398

variable argument lists, 846
vcs, 920
vcsa, 920
vdir, 245
vfork, 535
vfprintf, 810
vfscanf, 831
vhangup, 669
vi, 103
video hardware
    probe and identify, 341
view, 103
vipw, 1181
virtual 8086 mode, 670
virtual console, 897, 898
    memory, 920
vm86, 670
vmstat, 1179
vprintf, 810
vscanf, 831
vsprintf, 810
vsscanf, 831

w, 400
wait, 671
wait3, 673
wait4, 673
waitpid, 671
wall, 401
wc, 402
wcstombs, 893
wctomb, 894
whereis, 403
write, 405, 675
    message to users, 401
writev, 823
wtmp, 983

X
    authority file utility, 408
    color management system, 411
    configuration

INDEX()

    generate, 428
    display font, 429
    display information utility, 427
    display manager, 413
    display server, 468
    initialize session, 336
    initializer, 449
    list application resource database, 12
    list atoms, 451
    list client applications, 452
    list fonts, 453
    modify keymap, 455
    property displayer, 460
    resource database utility, 464
    resource editor, 97
    server access control, 437
    set parameters, 474
    standard colormap utility, 477
    start program on remote machine, 459
    system console monitor, 412
    tab window manager, 368
    terminal emulator, 478
    uncompile rgb database, 331
    update configuration, 297
    window information utility, 497
X11R6, 432
    configuration, 985
xargs, 406
xauth, 255, 408
xcmsdb, 411
xconsole, 412
xdm, 413
xdpyinfo, 427
XF86Config, 985
xf86config, 428
xfd, 429
XFree86, 432
    configuration, 985
    video mode tuner, 495
    video probe, 341
xhost, 437
xinetd, 439
xinit, 449
xlsatoms, 451
xlsclients, 452
xlsfonts, 453
xmkmf, 454
xmodmap, 455
xon, 459
xprop, 460
xrdb, 464
Xserver, 468
xset, 474
xstdcmap, 477
xterm, 478
xvidtune, 495
xwininfo, 497

y0, 749
y1, 749

yn, 749
ytalk, 499

zcat, 202
zcmp, 503
zdiff, 503
zdump, 1182
zero, 910
zforce, 504
zgrep, 505
zic, 1183
zmore, 506